The Dancer Defects

The Dancer Defects

The Struggle for Cultural Supremacy During the Cold War

DAVID CAUTE

OXFORD
UNIVERSITY PRESS

OXFORD

UNIVERSITY PRESS

Great Clarendon Street, Oxford ox2 6DP

Oxford University Press is a department of the University of Oxford.
It furthers the University's objective of excellence in research, scholarship,
and education by publishing worldwide in

Oxford New York

Auckland Bangkok Buenos Aires Cape Town Chennai
Dar es Salaam Delhi Hong Kong Istanbul Karachi Kolkata
Kuala Lumpur Madrid Melbourne Mexico City Mumbai Nairobi
São Paulo Shanghai Taipei Tokyo Toronto

Oxford is a registered trade mark of Oxford University Press
in the UK and in certain other countries

Published in the United States
by Oxford University Press Inc., New York

British Library Cataloguing in Publication Data
Data available

Library of Congress Cataloging in Publication Data
Data available

ISBN 0–19–924908–3

10 9 8 7 6 5 4 3 2 1

Typeset by Kolam Informations Services Pvt, Ltd, Pondicherry, India
Printed in Great Britain
on acid-free paper by
T. J. International Ltd, Padstow, Cornwall.

For Martha

Preface

This book started out as a larger design, embracing literature and the key academic disciplines, as well as what is to be found in these pages: theatre, film, classical and popular music, ballet, painting and sculpture, and exhibition culture. However, the available material from the United States, the Soviet Union, and Europe is so vast that my findings in the fields of fiction, literary criticism, political theory, and historiography are now scheduled for a subsequent volume.

Meanwhile, I would like to thank colleagues to whom I am indebted for advice and assistance, particularly those who have checked and corrected my translations from foreign languages. Frank Althaus, Elena Smolina, and Vera Adian provided invaluable help with Russian texts. I thank Frank for his patience and encouragement as the years passed. Elena worked miracles on my behalf in Moscow as facilitator of archival access and interpreter during film screenings at Belye Stolby, the central state film archive an hour's dash from Moscow.

Professor Julian Graffy, of SSEES, University of London, has very kindly and beyond any call of duty supplied me with numerous videotapes of Stalin-era films, a contribution all the more generous and valuable since I ran afoul of the 1988 Copyright & Patents Act, which effectively denies freelance scholars access to video material held in educational libraries.

In Russia the following kindly offered me permission to access material, or valuable time, perspectives, and historical recall: Svetlana Dzhaforova, Naum Kleiman (director, Museum of Cinema), Vitaly Mishin (deputy director, Pushkin Museum), Alla Evgeniovna Osipenko, Lydia Romachkova (deputy director and curator of avant-garde art, Tretyakov Museum), Ekaterina Kyrilovna Simonovna (daughter of Konstantin (Kyril) Simonov), Ella and Ivan Zadorozhnyuk, and Mark Zak (deputy director of the State Institute for Film Research, NIIK).

For all manner of help, I am grateful to Sergei Bek, Nicole Boireau, Anna Caute, Colin Chambers, Michel Ciment, Jessica C. E. Gienow-Hecht, Cora Sol Goldstein, D. W. Ellwood, Ronald Hayman, J. L. Krabbendam, Marc Lazar, Alan Nadel, Nora Sayre, Giles Scott-Smith, Solomon Volkov, Peter Watson, and the late John Willett.

Not least of my debts is to my editor and copy-editor Jeff New, who subjected the text to the most expert, well informed, and scrupulous critique imaginable. I am grateful to Ruth Parr for commissioning the book, and to her colleagues at Oxford University Press, Anne Gelling and Kay Rogers, for much appreciated editorial support and guidance. I thank Dr. Michael C. Tombs for his excellent index. Debbie C. Hughes kindly gave me expert help with picture research.

My wife Martha Caute has been not only my primary editor, lucid critic, and internet wizard, but also the author's prime support through six sometimes difficult years of work. This book, like so many others previously, is dedicated in profound gratitude and love to her.

Note on Transliteration and Usage

I have broadly adhered to the Library of Congress Russian transliteration system, except in the many cases of well-known names familiar in other forms, e.g. Yevtushenko for Evtushenko, or the Tretyakov Gallery for Tret'iakov.

Where Russian authors have translated work listed in the Bibliography, I have used the name as published in English throughout: for example, Smelianskii is Smeliansky and Il'ia Erenburg is Ilya Ehrenburg. Where their published work cited in the Bibliography is exclusively in Russian, I have adhered to the Library of Congress system: for example, Gorodinskii. In the cases of authors with both translated and untranslated work listed, I have used the translated form in the main text—for example, Maya Turovskaya (Maia Turovskaia) and Dmitry (Dmitrii) Shostakovich.

In the case of German or French translations of Russian works, I have used the translated versions of the author's names in the References and the Bibliography but the normal English version in the main text: for example, Pudovkin (Pudowkin), Rabin (Rabine).

Titles of Russian newspapers and magazines follow the Library of Congress system (*Izvestiia*), if only because sometimes more familiar versions vary (*Izvestya* and *Izvestiya*).

When quoting from any non-Russian text I have stayed with the original.

Similar problems of consistency attend English–English and American–English (for example, labour/labor or defence/defense): here I have followed OUP custom and practice which, given my own branch of the language tree, means 'American Federation of Labor' but 'organized labour in the United States'.

Contents

Part V. Art Wars

List of Illustrations

Introduction:
The Culture War

The cold war between the Soviet Union and the West was simultaneously a traditional political-military confrontation between empires, between the *pax americana* and the *pax sovietica*,[1] and at the same time an ideological and cultural contest on a global scale and without historical precedent.[2] The cultural cold war was shaped by the new primacy of ideology; by the shared and bitterly contested heritage of the European Enlightenment; and, not least, by the astonishing global ascendancy of printing presses, of film, radio, and television, not overlooking the proliferation of theatres and concert halls open to the broad public, particularly in the USSR.

By the time John F. Kennedy occupied the White House in 1961, Russia's sputnik in the sky signalled to the West that the Soviet system was offering an unexpectedly formidable educational and scientific challenge: the team that got the first astronaut or cosmonaut on the moon and brought him back alive would not only be cock of the cosmic walk but would inherit the Earth. The Soviet Union faltered and failed in that endeavour; twenty years later, between 1989 and 1991, the Communist system itself collapsed throughout the Soviet constellation of satellites, culminating in the disintegration of the USSR itself. The curtain came down on the hammer and sickle after seventy years of Party hegemony; the city of Leningrad is now St Petersburg.

Leaving aside the role of God invoked by Kennedy and every other American president, was the defeat of the Soviet system primarily 'economic', a failure to keep pace with American cybernetics and computers in a world economy increasingly dependent on silicone chips and software? Or did the Soviet leviathan succumb to the heart-stopping weight of its own military armour?[3] These were certainly powerful factors, yet the mortal 'stroke' which finally buried Soviet Communism was arguably moral, intellectual, and cultural as well as economic and technological. Citizens of the USSR and the satellite People's Democracies had long since ceased to believe in the system's viability and pretensions; suddenly—the swiftness of the debacle astonished expert observers—they were no longer prepared to put up with its elephantine insistence on self-preservation and they were no longer to be intimidated. The policies of reform and renewal associated with Mikhail Gorbachev, *perestroika*, and *glasnost* located culture and information as key sites for urgent change, but reform became the harbinger of death. Microchips and glass fibres were pulling the USSR closer to the rest of the world—as indeed the Voice of America, Radio Liberty, the BBC, and Deutsche Welle had been doing for many years. As the veil of secrecy lifted on the regime's past and present abuses, 'the repressed awareness of the lie poured out into the open in a flood'.[4] It was too late for Orwell's Big Brother to adopt a more indulgent teleface, too late to proclaim himself a liberal of sorts; too late for Stalin's heirs to embrace the First Amendment of the American Constitution.

With the advantage of hindsight, we may now conclude that the moral, ideological, and cultural defeat of the Soviet system was set in motion as soon as the cold war began, post-1945. The Russians could produce books by the million, and reduce illiteracy by impressive percentages, and cultivate a fine scientific culture; they could subsidize ballet companies on a lavish scale; they could win international chess tournaments and send the first man into space; they could build impressive medical research laboratories, triumph on the athletics track, and win Nobel Prizes—yet they were losing the wider *Kulturkampf* from the outset because they were afraid of freedom and were seen to be afraid.

The contagion temporarily spread to their rivals but did not become endemic. A revived Red Scare, a Great Fear of Communism, descended on America in the era of Joseph McCarthy, imperilling the liberties which the Truman–Eisenhower Loyalty–Security Program was supposed to defend. 'Are you now or have you ever been a member of the Communist Party?' demanded the Congressional inquisitors. 'Have you ever belonged to any of the five hundred organizations listed by the attorney-general?' American cold war culture owed as much (some would say more) to domestic conflicts, to an anti-New Deal backlash, to racial tensions. 'Communism' became a synonym for even the mildest version of reformist socialism. The strident evangelism of apostate ex-Communists was regarded with fastidious distaste by West Europeans, whom American policy-makers regarded as 'soft on Communism'.

The State Department, the Central Intelligence Agency, and the Voice of America accordingly directed their initial cold war cultural offensive not so much at the virtually impenetrable USSR as at the wide-open cultures of Western Europe, where Communist parties were strong and pro-Soviet 'illusions' widespread. Where, also, America was commonly regarded as a vast PX store with Mickey Mouse on the labels and Joe McCarthy smashing the furniture. This is one reason why painting, sculpture, theatre, cinema, classical music, jazz, rock, ballet, national exhibitions, and chess even, were increasingly promoted to relevance alongside the more traditional (and expensive) weapons of the military-industrial complex, the orchestrators of a permanent one-minute-from-midnight crisis, the midnight of nuclear war.

But what form should America's cultural promotion take? To what extent did the resurgent anti-Communist campaign, the Republican Congressional victory of 1946, the Loyalty–Security Program, the emergence of the Subversive Activities Control Board, and the attorney-general's (notorious) list, contribute to a marked shift in cultural production? The answer cannot be quantified, but most of the indicators point in one direction: literature, theatre, and art fired up by the radical, burning convictions of the Roosevelt era—*Waiting for Lefty*, the Living Newspaper, the Mexican murals—was 'exiting right'. The universities were now offering prestigious annual lectures to the high modernists, and the colleges were back with curricula based on Proust, Joyce, Eliot, and Pound. Farewell to *The Grapes of Wrath*, to Dreiser and Sinclair Lewis, to Group Theatre and the radical radio drama of the war years. Why did Arthur Miller stand almost alone in the post-war decade? He knew the answer long before the House Un-American Activities Committee (HUAC) subpoenaed him.

The cultural contest between the capitalist democracies and the Communist states was a unique historical phenomenon which can be explored effectively only by comparing the narratives of both camps. No previous imperial contest had involved furious disputes in genetics, prize-fights between philosophers, literary brawls capable of inflicting grievous bodily harm, musical uproar, duels with paint-brushes, the sending of ballet companies home without a single pirouette performed, defecting cellists, absconding ballet dancers, the hurling of greasepaint between the theatres of divided Berlin, the theft of musical film scores, a great composer yelling hatred into a microphone, a national chess team refusing to travel if subject to fingerprinting on arrival, jammed jazz on the airwaves, the erection of iron curtains against the sound of rock, and the padlocking of painters (Pablo Picasso among them). Never before had empires felt so compelling a need to prove their virtue, to demonstrate their spiritual superiority, to claim the high ground of 'progress', to win public support and admiration by gaining ascendancy in each and every event of what might be styled the Cultural Olympics.[5]

Despite the exclusionary rhetoric of damnation's pulpit, and despite America's constant appeals to God, to 'Faith', each protagonist was laying prior claim to a common heritage, the European Enlightenment. The Communist debt to the Enlightenment and the passionate attachment of the Soviet leadership to 'culture' was partly mediated through Marxism and partly through the broader Westernizing movement reaching back at least to Peter the Great and constantly challenged by Slavophiles. Soviet Enlightenment values included faith in progress, modernization (but not 'modernity'), urbanization, science, technology, and rationality, harnessing nature to man's needs.[6] The USSR and the USA both strove, in this 'century of the masses', to out-educate, out-perform, out-write, out-produce, out-argue, outshine the other.

The contest was possible only because both sides were agreed on cultural values to an extent that may seem astonishing, given the huge divide between a 'totalitarian' system and a pluralistic democracy. Soviet Communism had inherited its professed humanistic values from the Western Enlightenment even though its actual behaviour seemed to fit a different tradition, that of oriental despotism. The 1936 Soviet Constitution, though violated to the point of farce by Stalinist practice, professed to guarantee freedom of conscience, of speech, of assembly, of demonstration, and the inviolability of the individual and his home, alongside the right to work, to leisure, to maintenance in old age and sickness, to education, to sexual and racial equality. There was also a remarkable consensus between the rival systems as to what constituted 'progress'. Both aspired to universal literacy and the highest possible standards of education from kindergarten to university. Both claimed to be opposed to racial discrimination. Both set a premium on public health-care, public hygiene, swimming pools, games fields, and increased life expectancy. Both boasted of providing the better public libraries—more books for more satisfied readers.[7] Neither would yield to the other regarding sexual equality and the advancement of women. Both capitalism and Communism promised superior provision in all such fields.

A tournament requires an agreed field of play. The struggle in the arts between classicism and modernism, realism and abstraction, amounted to a series of civil wars within agreed territory. The annual Tchaikovsky Competition in Moscow or the Cannes Film Festival depended on agreed values and skills; ballet companies in Moscow, Leningrad, Kiev, London, New York, and Paris shared a heritage and a choreographical language. A Nobel Prize awarded to the 'wrong' Russian writer caused apoplexy in the Kremlin; a Soviet dog orbiting in space caused all American dogs to howl. When Nikita Khrushchev famously declared, 'We will bury you!', he was predicting something akin to what happened in reverse thirty years later, in 1989–91—a moral and ideological collapse; our ballerinas will dance across your ruined stages, our paintings will hang from the peeling walls of your galleries, our books will occupy your library shelves, the Voice of America will broadcast Shostakovich, not Elvis Presley. In this context, the term 'cold war' can be understood not merely as a military conflict deferred, held in reserve, but also as the continuous pursuit of victory by other means. Every Soviet ballet company returning from America to triumphant acclaim and without suffering the defection of a prima ballerina, every Soviet *Palme d'or* at the Cannes Film Festival, every curtain call for the Berliner Ensemble in London, was worth a Red Army division on the Elbe. The Soviet press eagerly recorded every word of praise for Soviet cultural achievements uttered in the capitals of bourgeois decadence, New York, London, and Paris. This threw an unacknowledged strain on Marxian determinism: the 'bourgeois' press denigrated Soviet achievements until the sheer force of reality somehow imposed itself, silencing the sneers—at which moment the Western critic ceased to be a 'notorious bourgeois spokesman' and was reincarnated as 'the respected French/British theatre expert'. But not only praise from abroad was harvested; hostile voices were zealously collected and filed; as Dostoyevsky had noted, Russians tended 'to fall in love with the injuries done and insults offered to them'.

There is no precedent or parallel for the cultural cold war between the Soviet and American world-systems. Despite the intensity of religious and cultural animosity during the holy wars and *jihads* of earlier centuries, the Crusades, the Moorish invasions of Spain, the Thirty Years War, all of them were conducted by armed conquest. By contrast, in forty-five years of cold war, Americans and Russians brought down the occasional plane, little more. When the Catholic Counter-Reformation appeared off the coast of England in 1588, it took the form of the Spanish Armada, galleons of war; 400 years later the Soviet 'armada' came in the shape of films, choirs, ballet companies, and Radio Moscow. The 'total' physical war practised from 1939 to 1945 was followed by a 'total' ideological *and cultural* war between the victors. There was no precedent: Christians and Muslims, Catholics and Protestants, revolutionary France and conservative Britain, had not dispatched their best ballerinas, violinists, poets, actors, playwrights, painters, composers, comedians, and chess players into battle. Such a contest was not an available idea—and could not become one until the emergence of the mass media and an audience unique to the twentieth century and the decades immediately preceding it: 'the general public.'

This 'public' was the missing factor even during the first major international ideological conflict of the modern era following the French Revolution and Bonaparte's 'revolution for export'. The British sent Admiral Nelson to the battles of the Nile, Copenhagen, and Trafalgar, but they did not dispatch their champion athletes to better the Emperor's; neither London nor Paris paraded their most celebrated painters, actors, or orchestras in the other's capital to prove a political point. Although Bonapartism offered Europe a new, modernized, rationalized model of government, putting all *anciens régimes* in peril, neither Tory England nor Napoleonic France hurled housing statistics or claims concerning infant mortality at the other—indeed they had none to make. There was no shortage of government-inspired propaganda in newspapers, but only a small fraction of the populations read them. Radio had not come; the cottagers of the two nations heard only the lowing of cattle. By contrast, Hitler's Thousand Year Reich sustained its shrieking ideological imperative across the airwaves until the moment in May 1945 when the Red Army ran up the hammer and sickle over Radio Berlin. Only three months later an American play, Thornton Wilder's *Our Town*, was closed down in the Soviet sector of Berlin—the opening shot in a cultural contest between two Great Powers of broadly equal resources—and therefore not to be equated with the cultural, linguistic, and religious penetration of Africa and Asia previously practised by rival European nations in pursuit of colonial domination.

None of the Great Powers in earlier imperial confrontations had conceived of 'peaceful coexistence' as the pursuit of war by other means. The competitive element in East–West cultural intercourse during the cold war was often thinly masked as 'exchange' or 'diplomacy': an exchange of visits by academics, theatres, orchestras, galleries, apparently designed to foster goodwill and 'mutual understanding', could also be construed as a contest, a tournament, when the reviews were published. The handshake and the arm-wrestle merged into a single plaster cast of elusive contour. According to the sociologist David Riesman, writing in 1964, 'the Russians gear their system to show that they are as good or better than we are in those areas that we most prize—technology, sports and education'. He spoke of the 'American-like desires of the Soviet elite',[8] but equally relevant was their passion for culture and cultural achievement.

Kto kogo?, Lenin had asked—who will prevail over whom? Cold war cultural conflict had the effect of linking art to power, most obviously through censorship and repression but also by means of patronage and promotion, even when the art in question begged to be considered as an in-itself, an *en soi*, an ivory tower. When the State Department promoted art uncontaminated by politics or 'messages', the messenger became the message. On the other side of the 'iron curtain' *Pravda*, Radio Moscow, and the agit-prop cadres carried every Central Committee cultural resolution to factories and farms—an unprecedented mobilization of entire populations, the 'age of the masses'. Radio, film, newsreels, newspapers, subsidized printing presses, and later television were the guns, rockets, and smokescreens of this uniquely modern cultural warfare. The Ministry of Truth never closed. The massive jamming of Western radio broadcasts began in the year that George Orwell published *Nineteen Eighty-Four*. By 1949 the number of American newspapers able to obtain a visa for a permanent Moscow correspondent had been reduced to one. The Word was the Helen of this Trojan War.

The Bolshevik philosophy was of course centralized and authoritarian. The Russians did not believe—or no longer believed, yet could not publicly deny—Marx's doctrine that the working class generates proletarian consciousness. Quite the contrary! The Party resembled a common room of schoolmasters in permanent lament about the vulnerability of their pupils to wicked worldly pleasures, idleness, seductions, deviations. Left to themselves the Russian people, although nominally the rulers of the USSR, would go straight down the drain laid out for them by the artful capitalists. A. A. Zhdanov emerged as the schoolmaster of the schoolmasters. His edicts (in reality Stalin's), in the name of the Central Committee, on literature, music, art, theatre, and film did not attempt to conceal the authoritarian engineering of souls behind Soviet cultural policy. 'At the same time as we select Soviet man's finest feelings and qualities and reveal his future to him, we show our people what they should be like and castigate the survivals from yesterday that are hindering the Soviet people's progress.' Couldn't be plainer. Having led the defence of Leningrad during the Nazi siege, Andrey Aleksandrovich Zhdanov had returned to Moscow to resume central-government duties in 1944. The August–September 1946 decrees on Leningrad literary journals and writers, on theatre repertories, and on erring films, led on to subsequent campaigns in the fields of opera and symphonic music. Zhdanov used the drab newspaper *Kul'tura i zhizn'*, which appeared every ten days, to promote the campaign from its first issue; the shrill ideological crusades, violent purges, outbursts of Russian chauvinism, and strident cold-war rhetoric that marked the period from 1946 to 1949 have come to be known as the *Zhdanovshchina*.[9]

The Western Communist parties emerged from armed resistance to Nazi occupation alarmingly loyal, or servile, to the Moscow line, not least in the broad field of culture. Faithfully echoing Zhdanov's paternalism, the general secretary of the French Communist Party (PCF), Maurice Thorez, addressed the annual Congress at Strasbourg in 1947: 'To decadent works of bourgeois aesthetes, partisans of art for art's sake . . . we have opposed an art which would aid the working class in its struggle for liberation.' The word 'culture' appeared on the front pages of Soviet newspapers almost as insistently as 'heavy industry'. The tradition was strong: not only Marx but also his successors significantly tended to deride political opponents and reactionaries as 'philistine', suggesting an equation between the higher learning and culture, on the one hand, and progressive politics on the other. That the cultural values (*tsennost'*) propagated by the Soviet regime were on the whole 'conservative' is beyond doubt—the *New York Times* correspondent, James Reston, described the prevailing Soviet culture as 'conservative and almost Victorian'.[10]

For their part, Soviet cultural emissaries frequently reminded their French, German, British, and Italian colleagues of shared European cultural and educational values which supposedly set them apart from the brash Americans. In this respect Soviet conservatism dovetailed into nineteenth-century distrust of the populist frontier democracy described by de Tocqueville and Dickens. In *Culture and Anarchy* another eminent Victorian, Matthew Arnold, had warned of the pernicious cult of mediocrity prevailing in America. The philosopher Ernest Renan offered a similar disparaging verdict on America: popular education without higher education, vulgarity of manners, superficiality—a view elaborated by Oswald Spengler and updated by Karl Jaspers. A century after Renan, the Cambridge literary critic F. R. Leavis fulminated against 'the rootlessness, the vacuity, the inhuman scale, the failure of organic cultural life, the anti-human reductivism that favours the American neo-imperialism of the computer'.[11] Soviet ideologists, critics, and film-makers tended to depict America as uncultured, as a land of capitalist entrepreneurs selling low-level entertainment, ephemeral, narcotic trash, and Disneyland fantasies to a bemused populace.

From Marx, Engels, and not least Lenin, Stalinism inherited an inherently classical-realist aesthetic in literature and art, claiming to be the genuine heir to the Greek drama, the Renaissance, Shakespeare, Rembrandt, and Goethe. This claim went hand-in-glove with a sharp hostility towards the modernist avant-garde, damned as 'decadent', and its subversion of the 'timeless' rules of narrative in literature, of perspective in painting, of harmony in music. Lenin derided what he called 'the isms'—futurism, surrealism, impressionism, constructivism—which brashly subverted those timeless rules. It is an odd paradox that the cut-throat Bolshevik, the archetypal bearded nihilist with *le couteau entre les dents*, should have given birth to the reverential curator of 'heritage', the high priest of the very libraries, museums, and palaces that Mayakovsky had wanted to 'pepper' with bullets in his poem of December 1918, 'It's Too Early to Rejoice'. Gone were the days when a Mayakovsky could deride libraries and museums or liken Pushkin to a white general.[12]

For the Soviet population the vital term 'cultured'—*kul'turnyi*—carried, paradoxically, values normally associated with the bourgeoisie, not least 'correct' and 'respectable' comportment in public (for example, not entering a theatre auditorium with an overcoat). *Nyekul'turnyi* indicated someone who was coarse, uncouth. *Kul'tura* and *kul'turnost'* meant high culture, literature, scholarship, the arts. The mass migration of peasants to the towns in the era of the Five Year Plans only reinforced suspicion of 'low life', of the popular, vulgar, sardonic, and often criminal urban culture, which was condemned as *meshchanskii* or 'petty bourgeois'—the Marxist holdall for every sin and deviation. An upwardly mobile *nomenklatura* was darkly suspicious (as was A. A. Zhdanov's wife) of the siren songs from Berlin and Paris, where naked ladies enticed rich men in jazz bars and modelled for paintings that no Soviet worker could decently hang on his or her wall. The new Soviet intelligentsia, the guardians and teachers of 'lofty' (*vozvyshennyi*) values, were accorded benefits and status beyond the reach of all but a few Westerners. At every level of society Party functionaries behaved like stern, censorious schoolteachers determined to divert their children from bad habits and dangerous desires. Simultaneously, beyond the frontiers of the USSR the Party promoted Soviet writers, artists, and performers as an international weapon without rival, as Vladimir Kemenov, editor of the *VOKS Bulletin*, explained in the course of a polemic against decadent Western culture published in 1947:

This directing, mobilising role of Soviet culture was so powerful and important that its influence was felt far beyond the borders of the Soviet Union—in England, America, France and Latin America, in the Far and Near East, wherever Soviet films were shown, wherever books by Soviet writers, music by Soviet composers, paintings and posters by Soviet artists appeared . . .[13]

Kemenov was also writing in praise of the Zhdanov decrees from the Central Committee, bringing us to the question of whether the Party line in the arts applied mainly to content or to form—or, as one suspects, 'mainly to both'. Sheila Fitzpatrick, writing of the pre-war years, has remarked: 'Western and Soviet scholars alike have assumed that the party's primary interest in the cultural field was inculcation of Marxist and Communist values'. But, she continues,

In most situations, the orthodoxies of immediate practical relevance to the professions were not political. They were local professional orthodoxies . . . For a writer, conformity meant respect for Gorky, respect for the Russian classics, emulation of the style of Pushkin or Nekrasov in poetry, Tolstoy in the novel, and so on. In the theatre, conformity was emulation of Stanislavsky. For painters, the nineteenth-century 'wanderers' (*peredvizhniki*) provided the orthodox model; for composers,

Tchaikovsky and Rimsky-Korsakov...even writers were more likely to offend by flouting Gorky's principles of realism than by misrepresenting the process of socialist transformation in the countryside.[14]

Most of Fitzpatrick's supporting documentation concerns the late 1930s, and it is not clear to what extent her analysis is intended to apply to the post-war Stalinist period and the subsequent 'thaw', which is our time-frame here. Novelists, poets, and playwrights were constantly chided and censored for what they said, or failed to say, rather than for their style of writing. 'Formalism' was certainly a common charge against Soviet composers and artists, but in the fields of literature, theatre, and cinema it was usually directed against *foreign* writers and directors guilty of the various manifestations of 'bourgeois decadence', for example, the stream of consciousness, time-busting, narrative relativity, or 'the absurd'. Soviet novelists, scriptwriters, film directors, and playwrights were far more frequently strictured for the content of their work, as Western critics delighted to document. It was Eisenstein's historical verdict on Ivan the Terrible, not his expressionist montage, which brought down the shutters on Part 2 of *Ivan Grozny*. Boris Pasternak's famously banned novel, *Doctor Zhivago*, was quite orthodox in literary style and structure; it was his curse upon the Revolution that stuck in the Soviet throat. No one accused Aleksandr Solzhenitsyn of formalism; Yevgeni Yevtushenko angered conservatives by what he wrote about and by publishing his autobiography abroad without permission—not on account of his poetic style. The liberal literary magazine *Novy mir* and the conservative *Literaturnaia gazeta* were arguing less about poetics than about politics—the Stalinist legacy in Soviet life. Theatre directors increasingly parted company with the Stanislavsky method, allowing themselves Brechtian alienation effects, without incurring displeasure, but if a stage play 'got it wrong' about American subversion, Khrushchev's land reforms, or the new class of fat cats, the shutters came down. Sheila Fitzpatrick's emphasis on form rides more convincingly when one considers the field of music and that exotic hothouse plant, ballet; the Russians were far more protective of, and defensive about, their 'classical' tradition, their love of rhythm, harmony, melody, and dramatic storytelling, than they were concerned to produce ballets about collective farms or slave revolts in ancient Rome. Powdered princes and pastel princesses continued to float their fairy tales across the Bolshoi and Kirov stages.

The cultural taboos in force were the logical consequence of the Party line. Pessimism and angst were banned. In a country where one person out of twenty was incarcerated in the gulag, culture had to be hugely and wholly 'human', brimming with fraternity and optimism. Favoured terms of abuse tended to imply insanity and perversion: 'pathological, neuropathic, depths of indecency', etc. If fascists were 'animals', ordinary imperialists ran on three legs. Not only did hyenas abound, but news that Western chimpanzees had been set to emulate Rembrandt or Shakespeare was invariably greeted with an almost hysterical glee—*ergo!*—in the Soviet press. And hadn't the detested Igor Stravinsky dedicated a piece to a young elephant! Samuel Beckett's aphorism, that Man is as free as a slave crawling east across the deck of a ship sailing west was not known to the Soviet public, but was of course known to the censors; the less the Party trusted the people, the more earnestly Party culture lauded man.

But it is easy to miss the genuine virtues of Russian culture; with good reason the Soviet public enjoyed a cultural superiority complex. Isaiah Berlin commented of Soviet audiences:

These are perhaps not far removed from the kind of popular audiences for which Euripides and Shakespeare wrote...they still look on the world with the shrewd imagination and the unspoiled eye of intelligent children, the ideal public of the novelist, the dramatist and the poet...and it is probable that it is the absence of precisely this popular response that has made the art of England and France often seemed mannered, anaemic, and artificial.

The principal hope of a new flowering of the liberated Russian genius lies in the still unexhausted vitality, the omnivorous curiosity, the astonishingly undiminished moral and intellectual appetite of this most imaginative and least narrow of peoples...[15]

America, meanwhile, dressed its cold war shop window with avant-garde goods scarcely appreciated and rarely purchased by the large throng of shoppers within: full-blown modernism, abstract expressionism, colour-field canvases free from outside referents, buildings stripped of historical imagery, literary criticism focused on the inner life and stylistic innovation, an aesthetics resistant to social content and any programmatic element. Art for art's sake became art for America's sake. Quintessential to the Western case was the suppression of modernism in all fields under Stalin. The avant-garde became the talisman of political virtue—even though it was neither supported nor understood by the broad public in the Western countries themselves. James Burnham wrote to Nicolas Nabokov, on 16 June 1951, regarding the Congress for Cultural Freedom's projected Festival of the Twentieth Century in Paris: 'It seems to me that we should think of it as a kind of concentrated expression of "values" of our culture, a confident contrasting display of what they and we have to offer in the arts, music and literature, and an answer thereby to the question which side represents the future'. It must be done, Burnham added, 'on a really big scale. In terms of money, I think that it needs at least one and possibly as much as two million dollars'. Denis de Rougemont introduced the CCF's Paris Festival, known in France as 'L'Oeuvre du XX siècle', in the April 1952 issue of *Preuves*: 'Never before has one seen a similar freedom to investigate and postulate, never fewer doubts over expressiveness in the sciences, the arts, and literature; and never more so such a clumsy conformism eager to control the very sources of creation'.[16]

The philosopher Bertrand Russell had recently given offence to the Russians by insisting on BBC radio that it did not matter what kind of painting the artist painted, or what type of music the composer preferred; the only question was whether the artist or musician should be subject to external control. This went to the heart of the matter, but it introduces a problem of perspective for the historian: it is tempting to exaggerate the importance of the various schools of modernist music, art, or literature which the Soviet Party suppressed or carefully confined to small, private gatherings. One may forget that twelve-tone 'dodecaphonic music', abstract painting, and un-punctuated prose were not very popular in the West either; the critics and specialists who worked up a head of steam about Soviet suppression of cacophony or drip painting were noisy and influential, but even in Western cultural terms their enthusiasms and concerns existed on the outer margins of consensual taste. Yet we cannot consign such concerns to a short footnote; the creature which Bertrand Russell called 'external control' is a voracious rodent, never satisfied with minor pickings; it won't be content until it has bitten Meyerhold, Eisenstein, Akhmatova, Shostakovich, Prokofiev, Picasso, and Pasternak as well.

The prevailing Western perspective on Soviet culture, polished by repetition to the contours of an orthodoxy, was to regret the suppression of a brief golden age for the arts, post-Revolution, followed by the extinction of its living survivors during the ice age of socialist realism under Stalin. The *New York Times* correspondent Harrison E. Salisbury packaged the whole spectrum of Soviet cultural history into a prototypically Western view:

No theater was more dazzling than the Russian stage at the time of the revolution and in the years that followed. Those were the days when Konstantin Stanislavsky and Vladimir Nemirovich-Danchenko were still at the height of their powers . . . Vsevelod Meyerhold was bursting with new ideas, new techniques, which set the pace for the world. There were others: Aleksandr Tairov; Nikolai Okhlopov, with his revolutionary stage; Mayakovsky, creating new forms, breaking every ikon . . . Even before the revolution a fever had raced through the arts. Ballet was being transformed by Diaghilev, Bakst, Nijinsky, Stravinsky; art by Malevich, Kandinsky, Tatlin and Chagall . . . The film era of Eisenstein, Vsevelod Pudovkin and Aleksandr Dovzhenko was at hand . . . But all that was long past by 1967. Nowhere had the Stalinist police smashed down harder than on the world of tinsel and light, of poetry and imagination, of grease paint and mascara.[17]

Western cold war cultural criticism almost reversed Stalinist airbrushing: Bolshevik writers and artists of the Revolutionary avant-garde, feared or scorned in their lifetimes by Western commentators, were reinstated in the pantheon, restored to the canvas, only after they had died, preferably in the official disgrace which became a saving grace. In an early (1955) number of the CIA-funded magazine *Encounter*, T. R. Fyvel made this point with exemplary clarity:

Unlike the Nazis, the early Bolsheviks before Stalin were not committed to anti-intellectualism; quite the contrary. Still, the time is getting to be rather long ago when one could still square support for the Soviet experiment in politics with an *avant-garde* outlook in the arts—as at those cultural gatherings of the twenties and early thirties when one talked of Gorki and Shostakovich, of Mayakovsky, Pasternak, and Blok, of the Moscow Art Theatre, or perhaps best of all, of the superiority of the Soviet film and the breathtaking crowd scenes of Eisenstein and Pudovkin. It was the faith that not only a more egalitarian society but a greater culture, a truer 'people's art,' would emerge from the Soviet travail which helped many uneasy Left-wing waverers to accept the censorship and police, the 'kulaks' dying like sub-humans on railway stations, the killing off of political opponents, and all the rest.[18]

One cannot easily imagine what the contours of cold war cultural confrontation would have been had Lenin and Stalin adored and adopted the 'isms', the cultural avant-garde, while pursuing their crusade against capitalist imperialism. How would the West have coped if post-war Soviet culture had paraded under the banners of Mayakovsky, Meyerhold, Tatlin, Rodchenko, Malevich, Zoshchenko, and Stravinsky? Would the CIA have resorted to cultural road-shows featuring Andrew Wyeth, Norman Rockwell, Sinclair Lewis, and *The Grapes of Wrath*? But this did not and could not happen because a political dictatorship cannot tolerate genuinely free and innovative artistic activity. Fifty and sixty years after the Revolution the official Soviet position on this central issue, modernism and the fate of the avant-garde, was forced into a series of ragged retreats, interspersed with many fiesty counter-attacks. Such retreats were implicitly signalled in the strikingly different entries to be found in the second and third editions of the *Great Soviet Encyclopedia*. For example, the modernist movement in literature and the arts was crudely savaged and disposed of in a few dismal lines in the second edition (1954): 'decadent currents (impressionism, expressionism, construct-ivism) in bourgeois art and literature of the imperialist epoch...anti-national, cosmopolitan...'[19] By contrast, the third edition (1975), while continuing to define modernism as 'the principal trend in bourgeois art of the era of decadence', offered a long and elaborate essay by the veteran critic Mikhail Lifshits, displaying a taste for nuance unthinkable twenty years earlier. Modernism, according to Lifshits, could not be explained solely in terms of imperialist decline: 'Despite morbid features in their creative works, the nineteenth-century founders of Modernism [e.g. Baudelaire and Van Gogh] were highly talented as poets and artists...Modernist works provoked fury among cultural philistines, who considered them an encroachment on hearth and home'. By the mid-twentieth century (Lifshits continued), the penniless, anarchic 'outsiders' had become assimilated into 'the huge system of speculation and advertising' in the capitalist countries. Gambling on the emergence of new, fashionable schools had become a fever. But here Lifshits permitted himself yet another lapse into heresy:

Paradoxically, despite all this, the mutinous (*buntarskii*) character of modernism grows stronger, as, for example, in the 'anti-art' movement of the 1960s, which was linked to the 'new left'...The anti-bourgeois character of modernist currents is evidence of the crisis of this system, but, as theoreticians of the 'avant-garde' such as H. Marcuse concede, all rebelliousness in the arts is 'assimilated' by the ruling system without particular difficulties.

Herbert Marcuse, author of a derogatory study of Soviet Marxism, is here treated with respect. Modernists of the New Left are no longer disparaged as 'petty-bourgeois' but almost acclaimed as 'anti-bourgeois'. The shift of em-phasis is almost revolutionary, but the *Encyclopedia* was not in the business of capitulation and Lifshits went on to commiserate with honest artists who, constrained to work under 'late capitalism', suffered from:

a morbid dread of repeating what has already been done, and an abstract cult of contemporaneity unknown in the previous history of art. Modernism is a special psychological means by which an artist strives to surmount the ossification of culture by shutting himself within his own profession...So begins a series of formal experi-ments by means of which the artist hopes to subject to his will the flow of deformed 'contemporaneousness', or, where even this is impossible... [he produces] abstract art...pop art, op art, minimalist art, body art,[20] etc....Consciousness abdicates, striving to return to the world of things, of unconscious matter.[21]

In practice, it was the Soviet state which abdicated, not only pulling banned modernist works from museum cellars, but even sending them abroad, to Paris and America, with great fanfare and not a word about the years of suppression. The Soviet state had locked away decadent objets d'art and forbidden books without physically destroying them. The gilded icons of the Orthodox Church had for the most part survived the closure of churches and monasteries. In this regard the Soviet personality was a split personality, willing to kill poets but loath to burn their banned poems. The bourgeoisie was duly buried, but in shallow-earth graves, easily dug up; deeply reverential towards history and heritage, the regime shrank from the outright iconoclasm of the Nazis. Limbo was the preferred condition, and some of the best fine-arts graduates were specially trained as expert, dedicated guardian-curators of the cellars, of Limbo.

⌗ ⌗ ⌗

The Dancer Defects addresses the role of the display arts (including architecture and the staging of national achievement exhibitions), the performing arts (theatre, cinema, ballet), music (classical, jazz, and popular), and the fine arts (painting, sculpture, poster art). If words, rather than musical notes, *pas de deux*, or thespian gestures, are the building-bricks of politics, then theatre and cinema belong to the narrative arts, which can 'talk politics', whereas symphonies and ballets, dodecaphonic serialism, the saxophone and abstract expressionist painting, being wordless, carry their political implications through a contextual web of external factors. The same applied to the refrains of popular music—which is why, for example, the Beatles's 'Yeah yeah yeah' infuriated the leader of the East German Communist Party and the journal *Krokodil* into a *Nyet, nyet, nyet*.

Of course, not all of the cultural fields received equal prominence in the international media. A play staged in Moscow may remain inaccessible to Western audiences for linguistic reasons as much as geographical ones—whereas, by contrast, reels of film travel far and wide, reaching the screen helpfully subtitled. The banning of a symphony may not attract as much attention as the defection or forced exile of a cellist. Even a Soviet new-wave film awarded laurels at the Cannes Festival might not compete in its Western audience-reach with a translated novel of the Thaw. The printed book was still the most versatile traveller, and the big stories of the immediate post-Stalin era normally belonged to literature (Pasternak, Yevtushenko). Khrushchev's anger about the young Yevtushenko's decision to publish his auto-biography in the West sounded louder in the West than the Soviet leader's peasant diatribes against formalist artists whose works were known only to minuscule minorities. The world attention accorded in the 1960s and 1970s to the dissenting novelist Solzhenitsyn and the dissenting physicist Sakharov exceeded Western concern about the stifling of Eisenstein, Prokofiev, and Shostakovich immediately after the war.

PART I

Marking the Territory

Propaganda Wars and Cultural Treaties

In June 1945, one month after the defeat of Nazi Germany, Moscow laid on a lavish celebration to mark the 220th anniversary of the Russian Academy of Sciences. Among those invited to the grandiose gathering were eminent scientists and scholars from the United States and many European countries. Formal conferences and visits to laboratories during the day were followed by grand nights at the opera, the ballet, concerts, plays—the full panoply and embrace of Soviet state culture.[1] The Scientific Correspondent of the London *Times* (7 July) described in awed tones a banquet in 'the great white and gold hall of St George in the Kremlin, glittering with the lights of thousands of electric candles'. Alongside Stalin, the Soviet leaders and Academicians sat at the high table, with an abundance of music, singing, and dancing between the speeches and toasts.

A further token of Soviet–American friendship was the telegraphic chess match between the two countries which began on 1 September, when Mayor Fiorello La Guardia of New York sent greetings—and the first move—to Russia. A telegram sped from the Moscow Central Art Workers Club to the grand ballroom of the Henry Hudson Hotel, New York, bearing a mysterious message: second gego, fourth fefo, sixth kahi. A few minutes later the reply came: second gego seso, fourth fefo rero, sixth kahi vafi.[2] In Moscow most of the enthralled audience watched the match from the Railway Workers Club, where US Ambassador Averell Harriman paid a visit. The Soviet team won an impressive overall victory by $15\frac{1}{2} - 4\frac{1}{2}$ (1542–442 by the Russian system of scoring), a margin of victory which evidently surprised the Russians themselves; in keeping with the still extant spirit of friendship, their comments were modest and magnanimous.[3] *VOKS Bulletin* emphasized the scale on which chess was played in the USSR: 'Soviet grandmasters are selected from an army of players numbering millions'. The newspaper *Krasny sport* (*Red*

Sport) declared: 'What the chess players have achieved can and should be attained by athletes, footballers, swimmers and representatives of other sports'.[4]

At precisely that moment the footballers of Moscow Dinamo were arriving in London. There was nothing telegraphic about this encounter; the spirit of friendship was to be tested by sweat, mud, and fouls. Here was London in cold midwinter, with endemic, smoke-filled fogs covering the Thames, a bombed city in the grip of poverty. It was to be a good-will visit between victorious allies—in fact, 'meetings on the Elbe' had already taken place between service teams.[5] Soccer was then, as today, *the* most popular sport of all throughout Europe. The young Dmitri Shostakovich's ballet *The Golden Age* (1929–30, Op. 22) follows the adventures of a Soviet football team in a foreign city during the World Fair. The conflict between Soviet youth and the outside world is depicted in music-hall scenes which alternate with episodes on a sports ground; a naive exposure of urban temptations alternates with detective story intrigue.[6] Later, in the 1950s, the choreographer Igor Moiseyev parodied the sliding, tackling piles of human flesh that swarm over the hapless football in his popular show *Soccer*.

In that bleak November of 1945 the Moscow Dinamo ('Dynamo' in the English press) football squad arrived at Croydon airport in two lend-lease Dakotas. The Soviet party—thirty-seven men, eighteen of whom were players, one woman interpreter, and (according to the British press) several hundredweight of 'special diet' food—were sent to Wellington Barracks. They found mould on the walls, beds like stone, no hot water, no towels, no bed linen. Early newspaper reports of the Russians' behaviour around and about London emphasized their silence, their refusal to converse or answer questions, and their suspicion of the weight and hardness of the footballs on offer. The Soviet view was different: since its arrival, reported M. Kotov in *Pravda* (14 November), the Dinamo team had been a centre of attention and interest. Newsreels had shown the Soviet team on arrival and in training. Various players had already been dubbed with nicknames (*prozvishche*): centre-forward Konstantin Beskov, for example, was 'bomber' (*bombardir-ovshchik*), while the famous Dinamo goalkeeper, Aleksei Khomich, was 'the tiger'.

Dinamo duly produced fourteen points, or demands, like President Wilson at the 1919 Versailles Conference. They would play only against genuine club sides and they wanted an assurance that their opponents' teams would be chosen from a list submitted several days in advance. They demanded that the Soviet referee they had brought with them should be granted control of at least one game—a demand which offended the British. The Russians also had in mind the differing British and Continental interpretations of the rules: in particular, the British allowed vigorous shoulder-charging, not least of the goalkeeper. In Russia, as in the rest of Continental Europe, these were infringements.

The British, obsessed by food, were enormously interested in what the Russians were eating. They had supposedly brought a vast load of their own food, but soon after arrival their interpreter Elliseyeva was claiming that 'while they are in England they will eat good plain English food and nothing else', even when eating at the Embassy, as they usually did when in London. This included porridge, sausages, beef, cabbage, potatoes, white bread, beer, and—when it could be obtained in an ongoing era of ration cards—the incredible luxury of rump steak. The Russians were not averse to some fun: they not only trained at the White City Stadium but turned up there for greyhound racing, backing Wings for Victory at 5–1, which was pipped at the post by the Magic Eye photo. They visited the Cambridge Theatre to see *A Night in Venice*, the best musical in London; at the invitation of Jay Pomeroy, the show's Russian-born producer, who delivered a warm speech of welcome in Russian, they went backstage between acts, posed for photographs with the stars, and autographed programmes. The Russian-speaking reporter Olga Franklin of the right-wing *Daily Sketch* managed to spend time with the Dinamos in their hotel. She described them as gawping at magazines, poring over photographs of luxury kitchens and Hollywood belles, while eagerly studying the female fashion pictures. The team captain Semichastny stared at a picture of embracing Hollywood sweethearts.[7]

Thousands of Londoners were unable to gain entry to the first game against Chelsea at Stamford Bridge on 13 November, when 74,496 spectators used fair means or foul to squeeze into the ground. Before kick-off the visitors bemused their opponents by presenting them with red-and-white bouquets. One wag, unreported by *Pravda*, responded to this foreign custom by shouting: 'What's this, then, Chelsea's funeral?' (The Russians had been warned not to embrace and kiss British males on the cheek, a normal token of friendship at home, but they couldn't help shaking hands, which was only slightly less unacceptable.) *Pravda* (16 November) proudly relayed English press reactions to the Chelsea–Dinamo match, which ended in a 3–3 draw; the Soviet visitors' skills had confounded the experts (*znatoki*) and caused amazement.

Then to Wales. One party of Russians visited the docks, another drove out to Powell Duffryn Colliery at Abercynon. This was friendly political terrain; Communism and 'Bevanite' socialism were strong among the mining communities. At the main entrance to the stadium hung a large portrait of

Comrade Stalin, adorned with live flowers from the miners. A miners' band played the Soviet anthem. Under the headline 'Brilliant Victory of Soviet Footballers', Pravda reported the 10–1 victory over Cardiff City. Thousands of Muscovites who owned valve radios listened to the programme 'Latest News by Radio'.

Back in London, the match against Arsenal turned sour. The game was played in a fog so thick that it was hard to see from one side of the pitch to the other. Pleading that their own players were still on military duty abroad, Arsenal cheated by including famous players who did not belong to the club, including the magical winger Stanley Matthews (*Met'iuz* in the Soviet press). The Dinamo captain Mikhail Semichastny issued a press statement of protest, printed in full in *Pravda*. Moscow Radio referred to the home side as a 'combined English team'—*sbornoe angliiskikh komand*—the term normally used for a national team. The Soviet referee Latyshev made a number of decisions which angered the Arsenal players and brought out the worst in them. 'The referee has stopped the game', Vadim Sinyavsky told Moscow Radio listeners. 'He very rightly gives a free kick to the Russians for an attack on the goalkeeper, such a rough one and completely unnecessary. I should say the game is now very sharp'.[8] After the match referee Latyshev was accused by sections of the British press of bias: 'The Russians got all the breaks ... body-checks, elbow work, all went unpunished, but not so with the Arsenal'. The argument continued: Mikhail Semichastny, who sported (if that is the word) a black eye, cabled the Soviet Committee of Sports claiming that he had been struck twice in the face, and goalkeeper Khomich once.[9] With the score level at 3–3, reported *Pravda*, the 'match acquired a harsh (*rezkii*) character'. Dinamo won 4–3: *Eto bol'shaia pobeda sovetskogo sporta*— 'This is a big victory for Soviet sport'. The *Daily Worker* (7 December) pointed out the political moral of Dinamo's successful tour. In Britain working-class lads could kick a ball around the streets until turned off by adults, whereas the Soviet system provided 'proper physical training' for every citizen. 'Those who wish to play football are supplied, through their clubs, with the equipment, playing space, trainers, coaches, masseurs, doctors and referees necessary for them to engage in this very wholesome pursuit.'

On 14 December, a few months after the publication of his anti-Soviet satire *Animal Farm*, George Orwell offered a famous jeremiad in *Tribune*, 'The Sporting Spirit'. Orwell expressed amazement that people could still believe in sport as a source of good-will among nations: 'Even if one didn't know from concrete examples (the 1936 Olympic Games, for instance) that international sporting contests lead to orgies of hatred, one could deduce it from general principles ...' He closed with the hope that no British team would pay a return visit to the USSR. 'There are quite enough real causes of trouble already, and we need not add to them by encouraging young men to kick each other on the shins amid the roars of infuriated spectators'.[10]

The intellectuals were also beginning to kick each-others' shins. Ilya Ehrenburg's unflattering reports from the United States in the spring of 1946 were syndicated in such Communist publications as the Vienna *Volkstimme*, the Berlin *Tägliche Rundschau* (organ of the Soviet Military Government in Germany), and the Italian Communist daily *L'Unità*, but they were also widely quoted in the vilified American press.[11] Despite the common cause against Hitler, the Soviet press lost little time in painting a dire portrait of the life of the common people in the West. In December 1945, even as the Moscow Dinamo football team arrived in Britain, Reuters in Moscow reported a spate of stories condemning Britain as cold, hungry, beset by strikes, short of housing, and failing to restore war-damaged buildings. Writing in *Komsomol'skaia pravda*, Olga Chechitkina, a member of a recent Youth Delegation to London, indignantly described aristocrats on thoroughbred horses riding through Hyde Park while the common people lacked food, houses, and work.[12] Other Soviet writers reported seeing children held on leads like dogs (presumably the child-harness, much favoured by the nannies of upper-class toddlers), and veterans with barrel organs begging for bread. Yuri Zhukov depicted London as dominated by the black market, a sensationalistic monopoly press, and ruthless employers, with ordinary people short of a shilling for the gas meter. And—*nyekul'turnyi*—in cinemas you could smoke, chew oranges or gobble chips! Such reports brought derisive retorts from the British press: how could the Russians understand freedom?[13]

In September 1946 friendly contact was still possible: the Americans accepted an invitation from the Soviet Chess Federation to play a match in Moscow's Hall of Columns. 'The thousand strong crowd made a tremendous impression on our opponents, who were not spoiled by such attention at home', recalled Yuri Averbahk some thirty years later.[14] The atmosphere was again friendly; little or no political gloss was put on the inevitable Soviet victory.[15] A month later, in October, the first Soviet musical artists to visit the United States since the war ran into trouble. Two prominent Ukrainian singers from the Kiev State Opera, Zoya Haidai, soprano, and Ivan Patorzhinsky, basso, had arrived on 17 September after a tour of Canada as members of a delegation of five sent by the Ukrainian Society for Cultural Relations with Foreign Countries. The singers attended a meeting held by the Communist-front Slav Congress in New York, at which speeches were made hostile to the foreign policy of President Truman and Secretary of State

Byrnes. The President reacted angrily; on 30 September he cancelled the wartime rule exempting foreigners from the need to register as foreign agents unless diplomats or commercial agents. On 10 October the State Department required the entire Ukrainian concert party to register and be fingerprinted. Under instructions from the Soviet consul general, they left the United States rather than comply with the rule. The Soviet Embassy held a press conference to protest, and a number of American musical figures added their voices.[16]

This was to be the end, for many years, not only of Soviet sopranos and bassos in the United States, but virtually of any cultural exchange involving travelling artists (apart from political fellow-travellers like Paul Robeson). According to Joseph P. Lash, writing in the *New York Times* (26 March 1949), the Boston Symphony Orchestra offered to visit the USSR at its own expense, but the proposal was never taken up; a second proposal inviting the Leningrad Symphony Orchestra to perform in America as the BSO's guest again brought no result. The last years of Stalin, which coincided with the rise of McCarthyism, were a time of cultural deep freeze driven by a fierce propaganda war.

In June 1947 the Smith–Mundt Act (Public Law 402) was passed by the House of Representatives, 272–97. The impelling necessity of a 'culture, education and information war' against 'Soviet propaganda' had secured a remarkable bipartisan consensus despite traditional Republican isolationist reflexes. Supported by the American Legion and the Veterans of Foreign Wars, the Bill passed the Senate on 16 January 1948, and was signed into law by Truman as the United States Information and Educational Exchange Act,[17] which envisaged deploying every weapon of the media—print, radio, film, exhibitions—to foster a favourable image abroad of the United States. The $31.2 million appropriation for 1949 represented a doubling of the previous year's foreign information programme. The National Security Council ordered the State Department[18] to 'develop a vigorous and effective ideological campaign' to project American values, virtues, and interests on a global scale. The Korean War inevitably boosted expenditure on propaganda, the largest increases being targeted on the mass media: radio, press, and film, with television about to emerge as the forerunner.[19]

The media and culture war was at its most sharp and intimate in divided Germany. In the US zone four major radio stations were operating in Frankfurt, Bremen, Stuttgart, and Munich, each controlled by the military government but mainly staffed by Germans. Three times a day the stations offered a short-wave pickup of a fifteen-minute transmission from the Voice of America (*Stimme von Amerika* or *Stimme Amerikas*) broadcast in German from New

York. 'Amerika became in the German language (East Germany excepted) a sort of metaphor for a Disneyland territory lying outside history.'[20]

A massive propaganda campaign was directed at France, Italy, and the Marshall Plan countries. The United States inundated France with press releases, radio programmes, and documentary films, setting up information libraries, cultural exchange programmes, and pressure groups like the Association France–Etats-Unis. In 1949 some 15 per cent of the French population, according to the State Department, were listening to Voice of America programmes such as 'Ici New York'; during the last six months of 1950 an estimated 5 million French citizens viewed documentaries from the United States.[21] An American Embassy official explained:

We are providing maps of our country to school children and corn-husking demonstrations to farmers...We are making American music available to French radio listeners and showing French engineers how to reduce the costs of cutting and bending steel pipe. We are distributing films on American surgery and manuals of trade union organization.

The same official also noted that the American media were in any case flooding the country with commercially produced fiction, films, and magazines, concluding that as a contribution to Washington's political aims, the official cultural offensive was 'largely a waste of money when not actually harmful'.[22] A French historian, Marc Lazar, recalls the popularity, proven by attendance statistics, of American movies in general and Humphrey Bogart in particular in the Communist 'red belts' of industrial France, including northern Paris, Lorraine, and Marseilles. This held good at the height of the cold war.[23]

The Russians offered counter-propaganda no less vigorous. A Moscow Radio broadcast (20 June 1953), monitored in London, depicted Los Angeles as a place of misery, smelling of oil, and New York as a city where beggars visited Soviet ships in search of hot bortsch. A ship's captain, Valchuk, reported his shock at seeing emaciated children in Los Angeles, families living in shanties or even in old automobiles. Checking out this story, the *New York Times* (21 June) asked the Collector of Customs to search his files, but no record of the arrival of Captain Valchuk's ship, the *Suchan*, could be found. Veracity was always an issue.

By the mid-1950s, the apex of the 'McCarthy era', it was a case of one step forward, two steps back for America's declining prestige in Western Europe. Anti-Americanism now ran free far beyond the ranks of the Communists and their sympathizers. Congressional witch-hunters, feasting on publicity, were diverting European attention from revelations about Soviet forced labour and the show trials in Eastern Europe. The United States had erected its own Golden Curtain: scores of foreign scientists and scholars, writers and artists, many of them invited to attend international conferences at American universities, were prevented from entering the country. The US Post Office and US Customs denied citizens access to foreign mail and publications. By 1954 America's image and prestige in Western Europe had touched rock-bottom—not least because of the roughhouse approach to books, writers, intellectuals, and the arts—for example, the disastrous policy order No. 9, banning from the government's overseas libraries books written by Communists, fellow-travellers, and 'any controversial persons'—the latter phrase was soon expunged. Information Guide 272 to United States Information Service (USIS) libraries banned books, music, and paintings by the newly defined political lepers. It was McCarthy's eventual contention that 30,000 volumes by 418 authors were 'subversive' and should be purged from overseas libraries.[24]

In April 1953 the Wisconsin senator's aides Roy Cohn and David Schine, comic when not villainous, embarked on a highly publicized seventeen-day tour of twelve European cities, striking at one of the nation's major achievements, the cultural centres known as America House, established in small towns as well as capital cities; by 1949 they welcomed 23 million visitors annually. The Amerika Haus in Vienna, through which Cohn and Schine rampaged, hosted scientific lectures, concerts, Gospel performances, picture displays of 'American Super Highways', exhibits on 'Baseball', 'Mickey Mouse', and *Gone With the Wind*. Between January and March 1950, 4,200 short propaganda films had been shown throughout Austria.[25] In Vienna Cohn and Schine first called at the Soviet Information Center and pawed through the file-cards to discover which American authors were included: they found Mark Twain. Three blocks away, at Amerika Haus, they found Twain again. A major purge occurred in Berlin and throughout West Germany where the USIA had forty branch libraries, visited by an estimated 15 million people in the course of 1952. 'The burning of books is now progressing merrily in all American diplomatic missions abroad for all to see', reported the *Herald Tribune* (14 June 1953). West European Press coverage of the Cohn–Schine inquisition was the most hostile and derisive since the war. The humiliation of American liberalism was McCarthy's special purpose and joy. On 15 June he questioned James B. Conant, former president of Harvard and currently US high commissioner for Germany—an illustrious member of the Ivy League elite that McCarthy despised and loathed. Conant's squirming responses reflected the discomfort of American liberalism in the age of the great fear:

CONANT: I would not be in favor of having books by Communist authors on the
shelves [of overseas libraries]. If they are already there, I would be in favor of taking
them off.

MCCARTHY: You would not call that book burning if you took them off, would you? . . .

CONANT: I think in a case of this sort, if it can be done without publicity it would be
much better.[26]

The State Department wrote to all publishers inviting them to certify that
books purchased by USIS for its overseas libraries were not written by Communists or fellow-travellers.[27] The content of the book was usually less material than the fact that the author had taken the First or Fifth Amendment
when subpoenaed—but long-dead authors were not exempt: Franklin
L. Burdette, overseas library chief of the USIS, scratched Thoreau's *Walden*
from the approved list of paperbacks as the world celebrated the centenary of
its publication.[28] Foreign authors were no more immune than the dead: in
1954 all of Sartre's works, including the anti-Communist ones, were purged
from USIS libraries. Eisenhower, meanwhile, quoted from Milton's *Areopagi-
tica* when he congratulated USIA staff on their achievements:[29] 'Let Truth and
Falsehood Grapple; whoever knew Truth put to the worse in a free and open
encounter?'[30] Even in the 1960s Western governments were not invariably
keen on Milton's 'grappling': the spirit of the Attlee government's visa-ban on
foreign delegates to the Sheffield Peace Congress in 1950 was still going strong
in October 1963, when the Foreign Office refused visas to the writer Aleksandr
Korneichuk and his wife, both members of the Supreme Soviet wishing to
visit Britain on World Peace Council business. An editorial in *The Times*
(7 October) approved the Foreign Office's *nyet* in terms so illiberal that any
Pravda editorialist could have gone to bed with them: 'The fact is that the
British Government . . . are not prepared to throw the United Kingdom open
to Communist propaganda under the guise of a search for peace.'

⊞ ⊞ ⊞

No idea proved more attractive to the Western media than that of Churchill's
'Iron Curtain'[31] (predecessor to the 'Truman Doctrine')—the Soviet bloc as
garrison and gulag, holding by force vast captive populations behind barbed
wire, minefields, and (later) the Berlin Wall. The human stories belonging to
the bloodstained album—the 'Thirteen Who Fled' syndrome—were spread
across the stalls. The London *Observer* (20 February 1949) reported that '300
Russians Flee Country Every Month', heading for the Western zones of
Germany and assisted by two émigré organizations, one Ukrainian and one
Russian. Every defector like Victor Kravchenko, every asylum-seeker, every
Russian wife denied permission to join her American or British husband after

the war, every 'leap to freedom' by a Mrs Oskana Stepanova Kasenkina (an employee of the Soviet Consulate in New York who literally leapt from a window), was a potential headline and a victory for the West. The image of the Soviet citizen as a prisoner of the regime remained transcendent. The Kremlin did not 'dare' to expose its people to the brimming shop windows, the overflowing freedoms, of the West. Only a stone-hearted, Asiatic, totalitarian regime could clamp down on a tiny number of Soviet women who had married Westerners during the war. Mrs Perle Mesta, a former US ambassador to Luxembourg, declared her verdict after a VIP journey through the USSR in the year of Stalin's death: 'The greatest gift the Soviet Union can bestow on any man, woman or child is a permit to leave the country.'[32]

The performing arts and sports involving foreign tours, international competition, inescapably carried the risk of defection and loss of face. Paradoxically, the Soviet Union suffered its most humiliating losses among dancers, writers, chess players, film directors, and musicians only in the wake of the Thaw and partial de-Stalinization, when the frontier flags had been lowered to half-mast in a climate of hesitant domestic liberalization: not until the 1960s and 1970s did Nureyev, Kuznetsov, Makarova, Panov, Baryshnikov, Korchnoi, Tarkovsky, and Maxim Shostakovich defect, and only then did the Kremlin begin to forcibly expel dissident geniuses from their own country: Solzhenitsyn, Repin, Rostropovich, Vishnevskaya among them. When the Bolshoi or Kirov ballet companies visited Western capitals, or a soloist like Ashkenazy toured alone, they were accompanied by alert KGB minders monitoring every move, every unauthorized fraternization—in the young pianist's case, the fact that he picked up and read Pasternak's novel *Doctor Zhivago* while touring the United States was duly reported by the minder who shared his hotel rooms. The commissar may have welcomed a privileged posting to Paris or New York, but he did not trust his fellow-citizens to return home pure in spirit after such a trip—or to return home at all. The triumph on-stage of the Bolshoi or Kirov ballet companies, of a victorious athletics squad, and the cultural kudos they engendered, could be entirely negated by the loudly reported defection of a star performer.[33] If the boundaries of the cultural playing fields were broadly agreed, and both sides understood what a 'queen's gambit' or a 'Sicilian defence' meant, this consensus had its limits—and the limits, the points of divergence, lie at the heart of the cultural cold war. Long after the McCarthyite censor had fallen into disrepute and disuse, the Soviet censor kept emerging like Punch to wield his baton and call time. Fear of freedom—not least freedom of movement—continued to haunt not only the Central Committee and the *nomenklatura* but the whole fabric of Soviet society. Relatively few Soviet citizens were granted permission to travel to the West, and then mainly in KGB-monitored groups—and without their close relatives.

Soviet culture, like Soviet sport, was rich in talent, achievement, technical accomplishment, tradition, but it was fatally flawed by its fear of freedom (to adapt Erich Fromm's phrase). The system choked on the prospect of open traffic across frontiers. What more eloquent commentary on the psychosis of the Iron Curtain than the literature from Christian fundamentalists flown over the curtain by balloon? Harrison Salisbury and Hélène Lazareff were among scores of journalists and tourists who had their film, or their cameras, confiscated after innocently photographing colourful Soviet market-places. Even when travel and tourism within the USSR became officially encouraged after the Thaw, the Soviet press took care to maintain suspicion of all things foreign, *Komsomol'skaia pravda* warning that parcels of fruit, flowers, or clothes from the West might contain dangerous pests. If foreigners masquerading as bona-fide tourists might be up to no good, look out for visiting Western art critics, music critics, academics, journalists—'purveyors of spiritual poison'! In February 1965 *Trud* renewed the warning against foreign influences to cover exhibition guides abusing their welcome as guests by promoting abstract art. Such warnings were always designed, obviously, to freeze the outstretched hands of friendly or curious Soviet citizens. Luba Brezhneva has recalled a family encounter with her uncle, Leonid Brezhnev, tsar of the seventies: 'During one of our meetings . . . I asked him why I had to defend the right to read, why reading sounded like such a subversive idea to him. "Because," he said, "if everyone started doing what they feel like, there won't be any order in the country." '[34]

⊞ ⊞ ⊞

The organization vested with primary responsibility for sending the best Soviet talent abroad, and for receiving visiting foreign delegations, theatre companies, and sports teams, was the All-Union Society for Cultural Relations with Foreign Countries, known as VOKS.[35] Dating back to 1925, ostensibly an independent public society, VOKS was now responsible to the Council of Ministers for foreign exchanges in the fields of theatre, cinema, music, art, literature, ballet, the academic disciplines—and sport. Had VOKS simply operated as an intergovernmental 'travel agency', its activities would have prompted less aggravation in the West. VOKS, however, was also charged with supporting and subsidizing pro-Soviet foreign friendship societies keen to provide hospitality to Soviet delegations or performers, involving a degree of 'interference' in the domestic affairs of Western countries which the Russians themselves would not have accepted.[36]

By the late 1950s Khrushchev's government was set on negotiating through VOKS bilateral cultural exchange agreements with Western nations largely on Soviet terms—which in effect meant opening doors to ballerinas but not to radio waves; to orchestras but not to jazz groups; to selected scientists but not to critics of the bogus biologist Trofim Lysenko; to the *Daily Worker* but not to *The Times*; to the Royal Shakespeare Company but not to Beckett and Ionesco; to Reynolds and Hogarth but not to Van Gogh.

Following McCarthy's spectacular political eclipse, the American administration slowly recovered its nerve and prepared to engage in something approaching open cultural competition with the Soviet Union.[37] In October 1957 Congress removed the fingerprinting provision of the 1952 Immigration and Nationality Act, which the Russians detested. This was swiftly followed in January 1958 by the first bilateral, two-year, cultural agreement between the Soviet Union and the United States, covering exchanges not only of academics, students, teachers, doctors, and agronomists, but also of writers and performing artists, orchestras, musicians, theatre and ballet companies, as well as works of art. Was this agreement a landmark of huge significance? American and British theatre groups had already performed in Moscow and Leningrad without such diplomatic underpinning; on the other hand, was it a coincidence that an American pianist, Van Cliburn, won the Tchaikovsky Piano Competition in Moscow within weeks of this first cultural accord? The agreement certainly accelerated artistic exchanges, as well as the dual national exhibitions of 1959, but its practical impact was probably greatest in the field of scholarly exchanges.[38]

Meanwhile, Russians and British negotiators were making heavy weather of a parallel cultural treaty, which finally reached harbour a full year after the USA–USSR agreement, largely because the main British negotiator, Christopher Mayhew, chairman of the Soviet Relations Committee of the British Council, and his Soviet counterpart, A. Kuznetsov, acting chairman of VOKS, were fiercely at loggerheads over broadcast jamming and freedom of information.[39] The Anglo-Soviet cultural agreement was signed in Moscow on 29 March 1959, by Christopher Mayhew and Georgy Zhukov, chairman of VOKS. In a diplomatically turned burst of ironic humour, Zhukov remarked: 'With our American colleagues we worked for three months to reach agreement, with the West Germans two-and-a-half months, with the French a fortnight. With you we were successful after three days.'[40] Under the agreement the number of cultural exchanges would be doubled during 1959–60.

Tensions soon surfaced on the Soviet–American cultural front despite the formal agreement signed in January 1958. 'Sweetness and Lies', ran the headline of Roscoe Drummond's column in the *New York Herald Tribune*

(30 June 1958). Drummond argued that the 'cultural' (his derisive quote-marks) exchange had been 'thus far a very one-sided affair'. 'What Moscow wants is to shield the Soviet people from American views and to have Soviet officials free to spread sweetness and lies in the United States.' In April 1959 the Daughters of the American Revolution passed a resolution opposing cultural exchanges with the Communist bloc because the 'underlying purpose [is] the softening of Americans toward communism'. Mrs Julia C. Smith, of Alexandria, Virginia, quoted J. Edgar Hoover: 'I want no children in my country exposed to the culture of Russia.'[41] But Roscoe Drummond and the DAR did not represent mainstream American opinion, hesitant and confused as it was. Press cartoons tended to be friendly towards the cultural exchanges: for example, 'Toe in the Door' by the *Baltimore Evening Sun*'s Flannery showed a ballerina's foot delicately pushing through a gap in an iron door. In the *Philadelphia Evening Sun* the cartoonist Alexander showed two drawbridges carrying men in hats but not quite meeting across a span of water. The caption: 'Getting across to each other.' Drake of the *Christian Science Monitor* showed the sun smiling on a globe bonded by the 1959 Moscow and New York national exhibits over the caption, 'Fair Exchange.'

'As usual, the Soviet Union refused to let in jazz, American newspapers or free radio reception', complained the *Herald Tribune* after the third Soviet–American cultural agreement was signed on 26 February 1963. Proposed visits by Duke Ellington and Count Basie were turned down by the Russians, but the Moscow Puppets would visit America while the Baird Marionettes from Chicago toured the USSR. In January 1964, negotiating the fourth agreement, the United States was again pressing for the free circulation of American newspapers and periodicals, access for more newsmen, and the opening of a US Information Center in Moscow.[42]

By the fall of 1965 the war in Vietnam had virtually frozen Soviet–American relations. *Hello, Dolly!* would not after all be received in Moscow and Leningrad. An American do-it-yourself exhibition and a choral exchange were cancelled, as were tours by writers, artists, and educators. American guides at the 'Architecture USA' exhibition came under strong Soviet criticism. All future visits by Soviet artists to the United States were off. The Russians withdrew at the last minute from a scheduled Soviet–American track and basketball meeting, and cancelled a poetry reading at the Lincoln Center by Andrei Voznesensky. Washington warned that the Soviet cancellations put the entire cultural exchange agreement in jeopardy. In July 1967 the Soviet government postponed indefinitely a ten-week tour of America by more than 200 performers, including Bolshoi stars, which was due to open at the Metropolitan Opera House. Sol Hurok, the impresario of this 'Russian

Festival of Music and Drama,' had already sold tickets valued at $250,000 for the Metropolitan Opera House alone. This was the first time since the cultural exchanges formally began in 1958 that the Russians, shrewd *biznesmen* that they were, had actually torpedoed a major box-office investment.[43]

Pondering the ultimate fate of the Soviet Union, John Lewis Gaddis offers the metaphor of 'a troubled triceratops' whose demise went largely unanticipated, 'until the day the creature was found with all four feet in the air, still awesome but now bloated, stiff and quite dead'.[44] But Gaddis here refers to the USSR as a nuclear superpower, not as a cultural and ideological force; in the field of cultural competition the 'triceratops' had always carried symptoms of asthma and a visible limp. When it refused Prokofiev and Kapitsa permission to travel, persecuted Pasternak, imprisoned Sinyavsky, expelled Solzhenitsyn, shackled Valery Panov, internally exiled Sakharov, stripped Rostropovich and Vishnevskaya of citizenship, or confined Picasso's early canvases to a locked cellar of the Pushkin Museum—all examples of 'fear of freedom'—the huge creature's hobbled hooves slithered and sank in its own secretion of suspicion. By the mid-1980s the Soviet Union was seriously weakened by the drainage of talent among economists, medical experts, historians, philosophers, journalists, artists, musicians, literary critics, and top-flight professionals in other fields—not counting the departing Jews, a reservoir of talent that no nation could afford to lose.[45]

2

The Gladiatorial Exhibition

In the summer of 1959 two major national displays opened under the first cultural exchange treaty: the Soviet exhibition in New York, the American exhibition in Moscow. Tensions rose rapidly as the rivals prepared to put on show for the first time virtually everything they could claim to have achieved—economic, scientific, educational, and cultural—whether in reality, prototype, or dream. Rivalry was intense, competition ferocious: this was the era of Sputnik and Khrushchev's 'We will bury you'.

'On both sides', commented an editorial in the *Christian Science Monitor* (1 July 1959), 'competition by exhibition contains an important element of international strategy . . . "cultural exchange" is an item for cold war deployment very much as crimes or missiles are.' That, indeed, could be taken as our text for exegesis, genre by genre. A dress rehearsal had been staged the previous year at the Brussels World Fair, April–October 1958. The United States Information Service, announcing the forthcoming American exhibit in Belgium, promised: 'The US Pavilion will be approximately the size of the Roman Coliseum . . . one of the largest circular structures in the world . . . one of the lightest buildings ever constructed.'[1] In the event, the Czechoslovak pavilion won the architectural competition, while the American structure took fourth place.

Starting in 1851 with the Great Exhibition of the Works of Industry of All Nations, held at the Crystal Palace, London, world fairs had become 'temples of modernity' attracting vast interest.[2] Control and command of the 'modern'—with the largely agreed values implicit in that notion—was indeed what the capitalist and Communist systems were now fiercely contesting. The American tradition extended back through the New York World's Fair of 1939 to the World's Columbian Exhibition held in Chicago in 1893.[3]

Soviet civilization was no stranger to the prestige-yielding imperatives of exhibition culture. Under the management of David Shterenberg, a specialist in intense still-lifes, the USSR had set up a much admired pavilion at the 1925 Exposition internationale d'art et d'industrie in Paris, including a wide variety of modernistic trends. At the 1937 Paris International Exhibition of Arts and Technology, the Soviet and German pavilions had confronted each other on either side of the main avenue leading from the Eiffel Tower to the Tower of Peace—an ideal setting for laying claim to technological modernity (film, photography, wireless) while displaying state-sponsored painting and sculpture on the grand scale.

The permanent Exhibition of the Achievements of the People's Economy (VDNKh) occupied a 600-acre park site in a northern suburb of Moscow. Originally an agricultural exhibition when it opened in 1939, VDNKh became, in Jamey Gambrell's words, 'one of the wonders of the Soviet world, no less consecrated a site of pilgrimage than Lenin's mausoleum'. Following a shut-down during the war, in 1947 the Central Committee decided to rebuild and expand VDNKh; each new pavilion was, in Gambrell's phrase, 'a lavishly ornamented architectural folly'. Laid out with meticulous symmetry, graced by a round pond attended by gilded *devushky* in national costume from each Soviet republic, it still stands (2002) in defiance of a forgetful history, ice-cream architecture thick with plaster but surprisingly interrupted by an intricate stained-glass window here, a baroque façade there, visited half a century ago by over 8 million people a year. It was the motherland in miniature, the Disneyland of 'socialism in one country'. Today it's an emporium of free enterprise, large and small, dominated by kebabs and amplified rock music, but the old Soviet insiginia have not been mutilated and the usual stern Lenin still stands not far from an antiquated Aeroflot airliner and the space pavilion. Fifty years ago:

Viewers were inundated with statistics, graphs, and tables, all chronicling the amazing growth of socialist agriculture. Vivid three-dimensional dioramas and working model trains and tractors gave the pavilions the air of a toy store. In the Poultry Pavilion, for instance, a motor-driven procession of stuffed chicks and hens circled a pyramid of eggs above which a spinning placard touted the rise in Soviet egg consumption.[4]

The Americans, meanwhile, were displaying their own pyramids of eggs on the airwaves. The European Recovery Program (Marshall Plan) came with a heightened propaganda campaign, not only from the State Department but from private organizations like the American Federation of Labor (AFL) and the Congress of Industrial Organizations (CIO). Perhaps the most potent image projected abroad on film was that of American workers coming to work in their own cars—almost unimaginable at that time in Europe. The equation between prosperity and democracy was constantly hammered home.[5] The *New York Times* (14 November 1948) reported that 'Edward Adams, veteran Pennsylvania Railroad locomotive engineer, recorded yesterday his Voice of America broadcast to be heard in Germany this week in the bitter radio battle to win the German workers for Western democracy'. Adams, the driver of an electrically powered express from New York to Washington, talked about his salary, the buying power of the dollar, 'and what an American worker's salary... would get under the Soviet system'. (No mention was ever made of what an American worker's salary 'would get' in Britain or France, or of the destruction of Soviet industry and the decimation of Russia's male population by war.) The Voice of America was enlisting American workers and professional men to convince Germans that 'freedom of speech and a car in the garage are worth the entire collected works of Karl Marx...'. John Albert, who prepared these broadcasts on behalf of the German Section of the State Department, commented that after Hitler's propaganda Germans wanted 'facts'—not 'theories and slogans'.[6] The Voice never tired of comparative data on living standards. In the USSR it required four hours work to buy a cup of sugar, in America only one minute, nine seconds. The Voice's Czech service ran a series, 'America. A Classless Society', which explained that 'American capitalists raised the wages of their employees so that they could expand their enterprises'.[7] As for American women, the Voice told its overseas listeners that: 'The women like careers, but they are good mothers and wives, too, and work fairly hard around the house, although they have all manner of gadgets, frozen foods and husbands who help with the dishes.' *Time* (1 May 1950) observed sardonically that few American couples ever got divorced in the Voice's version. Meanwhile, domestic programmes like 'The Telephone Hour', 'The Hit Parade', 'University Theater', and 'Adventures in Science' became well known abroad via VoA.

Acute Soviet sensitivity about economic efficiency, technological advance, production statistics, and housing standards—in short, about 'performance'—had been in evidence since the 1930s, the era of the Five Year Plans, but most fiercely since 1945. What Western commentators called the Russian inferiority complex refused to depart, constantly sublimating itself in claims of superiority. Few of these commentators paused to glance sideways at—for example—rather desperate British claims, as power and empire declined, about the invention of mechanical looms, steam locomotives, jet engines, penicillin, and television tubes, which were not only heard in British school classrooms but put on public display in the Dome of Discovery at the 1951 Festival of Britain.[8] Nevertheless, it is clear that even in the age of the Soviet H-Bomb, the Sputnik, and the supersonic Ilyushin, the

Soviet State was for ever struggling against underdevelopment, both real and feared, reinforced by self-imposed insulation against the global market. The Western press relentlessly mocked hyperbolic Soviet claims to have invented the world and everything in it. Paul Ignotus recalled the jokes going around Budapest in 1946:

'Do you know who invented the wireless?'
'Popov, of course.'
'Who discovered the permanence of matter?'
'Lomonosov.'
'Who was the first man?'
'Adamov.'
'Who created him?'
'Jehov.'[9]

On 9 May 1947 the *New York Times* laughingly reported that Aleksandr Popov, not Marconi, had invented the radio. On 8 August the *Herald Tribune* ran a headline: 'Soviet Superiority in Science, Art, Literature and Industry Keynote of Campaign.' The magazine *Bolshevik* had accused the West of having stolen the discoveries of Russian science. The eighteenth-century advances achieved by Lomonsov—the law of the conservation of mass—had been wrongly attributed to Lavoisier, who pirated it. As for the electric light bulb, it belonged to Yablochkov, not Edison.[10] The following month a mocking article appeared in *Die Welt*, organ of the British military government in Hamburg, noting *Pravda*'s claim that the railway steam engine was the invention of Tscherepanov. *Die Welt* concluded that the USSR was attempting to immunize itself against Western achievements.[11]

Edmund Stevens, of the *Christian Science Monitor* (3 January 1950), derided *Literaturnaia gazeta*'s version of scientific history, by which the German Siemens literally stole the blueprints for the telegraph from Yakobi; the Wright brothers usurped the glory of Mozhaisky (more commonly rendered as Moschisky)—who was credited with flying near St Petersburg in 1882, twenty years before the lift-off at Kitty Hawk. Tsiolkovksy was the father of rocket propulsion, Polzunov built the steam locomotive ahead of Stephenson. A Russian beat Robert Fulton to the first steamboat, and the first submarine was built in Russia in the early nineteenth century. In the 1850s Blinov pioneered the first tractor. A Russian workman, Vasili Pyatov, invented the rolling process for the production of armour plate in the 1860s, 'but corrupt czarist officials who kowtowed to everything foreign callously transmitted this Russian invention to foreign concerns...'. The balloon was wrongly attributed to the French brothers Montgolfier, whereas in reality the first balloon flew near Nizhni-Novgorod much earlier. Other Russian firsts included the bicycle, the internal combustion engine, the tank, radar, television, synthetic rubber, and penicillin. (Nothing was said about the pencil.) Edmund Stevens warned that it would be wrong to discount all these claims as idle boasting, but the real purpose behind the 'inventions' campaign was the 'vital need of Russians to vindicate their self-respect and destroy the . . . old sense of inferiority'. On 2 April 1950 the *New York Times* reported a claim in *Literaturnaia gazeta* that Smera, court doctor to Grand Duke Vladimir of Kiev, invented printing a century before the Chinese and 400 years before Johann Gutenberg. A sardonic American editorial followed. On 8 May the London *Times* reported special Soviet broadcasts the previous day to celebrate the 55th anniversary of Aleksandr Popov's demonstration of his first radio set to the Russian Physics and Chemistry Society. A 'Special Correspondent' of the London *Financial Times* (25 August) commented that the Russian claim was 'made with some justification, it should in fairness be added'.

Although this campaign might be taken to reflect a strictly Russian pride in the nation's heritage, and therefore nothing to do with Communism, it did reflect the extremely powerful post-1945 doctrine that Soviet Communism, while of course multinational in content (the USSR) and international in aspiration (the Cominform), was the unique achievement of the uniquely gifted Russian people. A deluge of statistics poured forth to prove it.[12] In Soviet films of the late 1940s an official or army major would typically remark, with a gentle smile: 'We have no intention of imposing Communism on Germany, or anyone—Communism is something you have to deserve!'

The great contest of the national exhibitions still lay four years in the future when seven Soviet journalists, headed by Boris Polevoy of *Pravda*, set out on 7 October 1955 for a month's tour of the United States. Travelling as representatives of the Soviet government, they were granted exemption from the 'foreign agent' fingerprinting requirement.[13] 'Russians Learn of U.S. Comforts As Writers Tell of American Visit', reported the *New York Times* (26 December). The Soviet writers conceded that many Americans lived in comfortable homes with modern kitchens and bathrooms, and owned their own cars; indeed, *Izvestiia* accepted the existence of 58 million cars and trucks in the United States; a Chevrolet plant in Los Angeles turned out a new automobile every ninety seconds. 'Such statements', noted the *New York Times*'s Moscow correspondent, Welles Hangen, 'contrast sharply with the stories of armies of unemployed that have been repeated for years on end by the Soviet press.' The comment, as it turned out was premature. Writing in *Novoye vremya*, its chief editor, Valentin Berezhkov, contrasted the 'gleaming pots and pans' in one Cleveland housewife's 'spotless little kitchen' with figures from the *Labor Fact Book* published in 1950 by the Labor Research Association: 15 million American dwellings lacked flush toilets and 6 million were without running water. (The *New York Times* responded in McCarthyite mode, not by challenging the figures but by noting that the Labor Research Association was listed by the attorney-general, and that the book had been published by International Publishers, 'described by the Government as the official publishing house of the Communist Party'.)

The Russian visitors (like Ilya Ehrenburg before them, in 1946) were inclined to contrast American modernity with the more mature aesthetic values of old Europe. The playwright Anatoli Sofronov, writing in the magazine *Ogonek*, commented that for many Americans furniture covers held more interest 'than Rembrandt's canvases and the construction of a new garage more fascination than the architecture of the Louvre'. America might be modern but it was *nyekul'turnyi*. Soviet official culture thus deflected the pain of direct economic comparison by appealing to a vague, undefined, 'European' set of values which spurned crass materialism.[14]

⌗ ⌗ ⌗

By the time of the two great national exhibitions of 1959, each staged on the rival's terrain, Soviet scientific and educational prestige had soared aloft with the first Sputnik (4 October 1957), undermining America's hitherto sublime self-confidence. Under Stalin the Russians had been viewed from afar as brave fellows, coarse yet cultured, warm-hearted yet cruel, who would dispose of an enemy minefield by walking a thousand men across it, before the survivors settled by their camp fires to weep over verses by Pushkin, songs by Borodin. Quite suddenly they, 'the Reds', were 'better than us' not only at chess but at maths, physics, and space engineering; the 'space race' (as it almost immediately became) represented the quintessence of scientific and industrial competition in a form more congenial to the human imagination than the nuclear arms race—here was the questing, 'Jules Verne', face of man's unique species-ability to 'conquer nature'. To be 'first' became the obsessive target dominating public discussions and agency budgets: first into space, first to the moon, first to Venus. Weight, or 'payload', indicating the victory over gravity, soon became a metaphor for ideological superiority: Sputnik 1 weighed 83 kg; and Sputnik 2, which took the dog Laika into space, weighed 508 kg. What was the specific gravity of Communism?— the new puzzle beneath the philosopher's stone.

The broad laughter of a Soviet crowd was heard by Faubion Bowers when he attended the Moscow Circus the day after Sputnik was launched. One of the clowns was bouncing a rather deflated balloon. 'What are you doing?' his foil asked him. 'I am an American,' the clown replied, 'and I'm trying to launch *my* sputnik.'[15]

When the Americans responded to this laughter on 31 January 1958 with Explorer 1, it weighed a mere 13 kg. 'Khrushchev Jibes at American "Oranges" Circling the Earth', reported the despondent *New York Times* (16 May). The Soviet leader later claimed that Sputnik 3, which carried 1,327 kg of instruments, proved that the USSR had 'outstripped the United States in science and technology'. On 2 January 1959 the USSR successfully launched a rocket to the moon, carrying 796 pounds of instruments. 'Russia Again Ahead in Race Into Space', declared the *New York Times* (4 January). 'Soviet Success After U.S. Failures Jolts Hard-Won Confidence Here.' The USA had failed four times to send a rocket to the moon. The newspaper coverage was vast. 'Communism Pioneers Way to the Stars', declared the London *Daily Worker* (6 January). 'Soviets See This Generation Constructing Cities on the Moon', reported the *Herald Tribune* (2 February). The headline most amusingly conveying American gloom came on 5 June: 'Four Mice Lost in Space. U.S. Rocket Fails to Reach Orbit.' Soviet experts and sources were now quoted on everything: 'The Soviet Union plans to put the entire earth under surveillance with satellites equipped with optical and television instruments, a Soviet scientist has revealed' (*New York Times*, 26 April).

American educators hurried to the USSR in search of the grail. Returning from a month-long, 7,000-mile study of Soviet schools in June 1958, Dr Lawrence G. Derthick, United States commissioner of education, reported to the National Press Club on behalf of his delegation of ten. The Commissioner expressed 'astonishment' at the degree to which the USSR was 'committed to education as a means of national advancement'. Teachers and principals enjoyed

an abundance of staff assistance: curriculum experts, doctors, nurses, laboratory assistants. Teacher work loads and other working conditions are advantageous. Teacher prestige is high; salaries are at the levels of those of doctors and engineers...We saw scientific research establishments with trained staff running into thousands, and with excellent plants and equipment...The importance of science in Soviet education...is unquestioned. Biology, chemistry, physics and astronomy are required of every pupil regardless of his individual interests or aspirations.

About the implications for the United States, Commissioner Derthick was in no doubt:

Everywhere in Russia there is evidence not only of passionate love of country but a burning desire to surpass the United States in education, in production, in standard of living, in world trade—and in athletics. The slogan we saw most in posters, films and everywhere was 'reach and overreach America' ... They are convinced that time is on their side and they can win world supremacy through education and hard work.

At the 21st Party Congress in January 1959, Khrushchev claimed that enrolment in Soviet higher education was 'four times greater than in Britain, France, West Germany and Italy combined'.[16] But what about the silk stockings? On a hot May evening in Moscow's Theatre Square, shortly after the great chimes in the Kremlin's Spasky Tower had sounded midnight, the air fresh with the scent of flowering shrubs and trees that decorate the plaza, a large crowd had gathered, fascinated by half-a-dozen gleaming new foreign cars parked outside the Metropole Hotel. Along came Assistant Librarian Foster Palmer, of Harvard University, Mrs Palmer, and a friend. When it was learned that he was from Harvard, the visitors were plied with questions about whether there were really 3 million unemployed in America, what was the best school of metallurgy in the United States, whether Negroes could enter Harvard's library, about the 'Beat' writers Jack Kerouac and Allen Ginsburg, and about Willis Connover. Palmer professed he had never heard of Connover (a jazz commentator of the Voice of America, with fans throughout the Soviet Union).[17]

Each government, meanwhile, was jockeying for position and vetoing this or that exhibition proposal. Although the Soviet deputy minister of culture had invited the US Marine Band to play in Moscow and wear its uniforms on the streets as well as on-stage, the State Department turned down a Russian request that the Red Army Chorus be permitted to appear at the New York Coliseum.[18] The Soviet Union was said to be spending more than 10 million dollars in foreign exchange on its Exhibition of Science, Technology and Culture at the New York Coliseum. According to the *New York Times* (18 June 1959), this sum was 'well over half of the dollar revenue the Soviet Union earned all last year by exports to this country'. With almost one voice the American press decided to object to the Soviet exhibition's massive expenditure on prestige projects while living standards remained (comparatively) low. It's saucepans your people need, not spectaculars. Meanwhile, in an internal memorandum dated 13 February 1959, the Central Committee of the CPSU criticized the Ministry of Culture's proposals for the forthcoming exhibition as failing to show adequately the vast advances of Soviet public education and culture compared with Tsarist times.[19]

With street temperatures in the nineties, more than 40,000 visitors attended the Coliseum opening on 30 June. Eisenhower and Nixon made a flying visit, the president heading for the painting section, where he felt at home with the realism if not with the socialism. (The Soviet Central Committee was duly informed that crowds had gathered enthusiastically round Serov's *Visitors to Lenin*, Plastov's *Tractor Drivers' Supper*, and Yablonskaya's *Bread*.)[20]

The sceptical verdict of even-handed liberalism was eloquently conveyed by the *Manchester Guardian*'s Alistair Cooke,[21] impressed by the displays of Sputniks, new techniques of thoracic surgery, and free convalescent resorts for children, but cool-eyed in the face of Soviet display arts:

There are all the usual triumphant graphs showing literacy, cotton production, sheep breeding and electronic power rising like flashes of light from the black night of Czarism to the Soviet empyrean...this composite picture of the Soviet Union as a working-class heaven, a continent of inventive, free peoples living in the throb and glitter of atomic factories, taking their leisure in sparkling automobiles along splendid boulevards, exercising in sports stadiums...rescued from feudal poverty by vast housing projects, taking their ease in little, clean and commendably modern apartments; and, when old age comes on, stealing another healthy decade more by the grace of brilliant surgeons, glistening operating theatres and Black Sea sanitoria modelled after Jones Beach. We recognise the human scale only in the stuffy furnishings of the model flats, and in the appalling textiles the women are supposed to wear.[22]

Max Frankel, the *New York Times*'s hard-hitting Moscow correspondent, visited the Coliseum and wrote a report (30 June)—'Coliseum Exhibition Depicts Nation Not as It Is, but as It Wishes to Be'—which duly angered the Soviet press:

A visitor can see far more here in two hours than this correspondent saw in two years in the Soviet Union, far more especially of the stuff of Soviet wishful dreams...The Soviet exhibition strives for an image of abundance with an apartment that few Russians enjoy, with clothes and furs that are rarely seen on Moscow streets, and with endless variations of television, radio and recording equipment, cameras and binoculars that are not easily obtained in such quality or range in Soviet stores.

Frankel, however, did not challenge the authenticity of the three Sputniks that dominated the show or of the industrial exhibits and laboratory equipment: 'All the gleaming, blinking, buzzing and threshing equipment amassed at the Coliseum is testimony to costly but impressive Soviet strides.' Conceding that the displays of medical research and peaceful applications of atomic energy were overwhelmingly impressive, he nonetheless derided the exhibition's claims in such fields as agriculture, construction techniques, and transportation.[23] Frankel also anticipated the famous 'kitchen debate' between Khrushchev and Nixon in Moscow a few weeks later:

Few Russians enjoy built-in kitchen cabinets like those in the model apartment. A few similar sets caused a sensation last year when they were imported from Finland. The small refrigerator and old-fashioned gas range and sink, modest as they are, are the very best available to lucky Russians...A visit to the Soviet Union exposes glaring paradoxes of ugly slums and palatial subways, muddy roads and huge jet planes. These contrasts are glossed over at the Coliseum.

As for the Soviet clothes and models paraded[24]—'The alert viewer need do little more than look over the modestly modern-styled fashions on display and then note that virtually all the men and women employed as guides have been hastily dressed in American suits and dresses and shoes...'

At a recent Christian Dior show in Moscow, some 13,000 Muscovites had seen $1,500,000 worth of gowns and furs valued at $100,000 in the Wings of the Soviet Air Club, which was daily drenched in 'Diorama', 'Miss Dior', and other perfumes while a hi-fi system softly played the latest music from Paris and New York. Harrison E. Salisbury reported that Moscow women had literally fought for tickets to the Dior show, most of which went to women working in the clothing industry, young actresses, and girls who looked like the daughters of prominent Soviet officials: 'I saw girls who were starry-eyed. They sketched the first half-dozen models, and then forgot to sketch as the haze of Paris elegance wafted them into dreams that never could be fulfilled...I saw white-smocked ice-cream girls watch with bulging eyes, and mechanics whose jaws dropped.'[25]

A correspondent from the *Christian Science Monitor* (3 July), reporting typical exchanges between American visitors to the Coliseum and Soviet guides, heard the Americans pressing their hosts about overcrowded homes, the shortage of cars in the USSR, freedom of worship—and the ongoing crisis in Berlin:

[An] American youth persisted: 'Have you ever been to church?' The Russian admitted he had but added: 'Only old women go to churches and synagogues.' (Another guide admitted he gave his elderly mother money to put in her church.) Finally the American boy asked a straight-out question: 'Do you believe in God?' The Russian replied: 'I'm a scientist.'

The Russians were not always on the defensive. When someone asked the hydro-electric [expert] about the police state he replied: 'I've never seen so many police in the Soviet Union as were here with President Eisenhower at the opening of the exhibition. Our Mr Khrushchev goes about freely, or maybe with one or two men...'

'Answer me this,' piped in one man. 'Do you have a picture of Khrushchev in your home? Or Lenin? Or Stalin?'

'No,' replied the Russian, 'I have only art pictures in my home. Such pictures are for public buildings.'

Some of the most persistent American questions were about anti-Semitism. Questioners who remained unconvinced by the denials were invited to go and question Soviet Jewish guides in the biological section of the fair.

There were questions about the Berlin situation. 'Why don't you agree to free elections in both West and East Berlin and let the people do what they want?' asked one man. The Russians didn't seem to know too much about the situation, but they said over and over they want peace.

The Soviet view of these exchanges, as expressed in a classified Central Committee memorandum, was rather different. Anti-Soviet and disruptive elements who appeared at the Coliseum soon revealed themselves as being from the 'second wave of emigration' (i.e. 'the traitors of the Great Patriotic War'). Young Russian-speaking pickets at the entrance handed out leaflets and urged people not to go inside. The exhibition managers had to warn the police that if this was allowed to continue they could not guarantee the absence of reciprocal measures in Moscow—on the third day the demonstrations ceased. Provocative questions were asked about the plight of Jews in the USSR and the fate of Jewish writers and artists. Much 'processing' (*obrabotka*) of questions was apparent. Some attendants (fourteen of them being Soviet students currently studying in America) were asked if they worked for the secret service, how much they were paid, what their clothes cost. However, the provocateurs ended up looking miserable, as if 'driven into a corner' (*zatravlennye*). In general the public displayed 'more curiosity than animosity'. However, the space rocket which had launched the Sputniks did not command the attention expected, and 'some visitors demonstratively walked past it.'[26]

⌗ ⌗ ⌗

So to Moscow, where the devil had arrived with a licence to flaunt his wares. Buckminster Fuller's gold-anodized geodesic dome, 79 feet high, 200 feet in diameter, was the architectural focal point and information centre of the American National Exhibition in Moscow's Sokol'niki Park. A parsimonious Congress had authorized only $3.6 million, but Eisenhower and Harold McClellan, the general manager of the exposition, launched an appeal at a White House luncheon for leaders of industry, science, education, and the arts. The response of the capitalists was positive. Major manufacturers agreed to supply exhibits and pay the freight to Moscow. McClellan secured a complete underwriting of an automobile show, while RCA undertook half the costs for the operation of a colour television studio. Pepsi-Cola offered free soft drinks, installation and personnel, while Dixie Cup Co. came up with several million paper cups. IBM again contributed its RAMAC 'electronic brain' as it had done at the Brussels exhibition. In all some 450 companies contributed.[27] A nasty clash of civilizations worthy of the historian Arnold Toynbee occurred when the American Radiator and Standard Sanitary Corporation offered to provide free of charge 150 toilets, 50 urinals, and 50 wash-basins, but it might as well have offered to cover the Kremlin in whitewash; Soviet officials, perhaps fearing that every Soviet citizen who took such a comfort break might never say 'Lenin' again, rejected the offer and insisted on installing their own facilities in Sokol'niki Park. American proposals to give away free cosmetics and toy models of GM cars were also vetoed but, due to fierce campaigning by Chad McClellan, Pepsi narrowly survived an effort to veto its handout of free drinks, which was to become a successful effort to break permanently into the Soviet soft drinks market.[28]

Directly behind the dome stood the glass pavilion featuring displays of food, clothing, toys, sporting goods, travel information, art, books, newspapers, musical instruments, stereo equipment, and a colour television studio. The emphasis, McClellan explained, was on 'the great abundance of the goods and things which come to the American family and the American people as a result of our free society, our consumer-oriented society, this tremendous freedom of choice that exists in this country'.

Transported to Moscow after its favourable reception at the Brussels fair was the 360-degree Circlorama. Visitors could view the Walt Disney production 'Trip across the US', with a sound-track in Russian. Scattered around Sokol'niki Park were a model American home, the new 1959 automobiles, garden machinery, trucks and trailers, sports boats anchored in a specially constructed pond, camping gear, and a 'Jungle Jim' playground for children. McClellan reported that Soviet labour crews worked twenty-four hours at a stretch to meet the opening ceremony on 25 July. The American press had begun to complain bitterly about a local campaign denigrating the exhibit as a stunt designed to deceive the Soviet people about real living conditions in America.[29] According to an editorial in the *Herald Tribune* (14 April), 'Presenting America to Soviet Eyes', Tass was claiming that the model house wasn't typical at all: 'There is no more truth in showing this as a typical home of the American worker than, say, in showing the Taj Mahal as the typical home of the Bombay textile worker.' Subsequently Soviet Ambassador Menshikov's son, Stanislav, published an article suggesting that 85 per cent of the American population could not afford such a house.[30] Using Soviet documents from the Center for the Storage of Contemporary Documents (TSKhSD),[31] now restyled as RGANI, Walter L. Hixson has tracked the worried anticipatory response of the well-informed CPSU to what it accurately predicted the Americans would go for: electric kitchens, vacuum cleaners, refrigerators, air conditioners, books, magazines, newspapers, television and cinema—all dangerous. The Central Committee launched a counter-propaganda campaign to discourage a mass influx to the American exhibition and to prevent displays of 'inordinate admiration' incompatible with 'the dignity of Soviet man'. The Komsomol were to discuss measures 'to distract young people from displaying too much interest'. The second Central Committee decree directed newspaper editors and the State Committee for Radio and Television to mount a campaign exposing the 'bourgeois legend' of capitalist prosperity. *Pravda* duly launched the hostile propaganda campaign on 10 April. New Soviet and foreign films were to be shown on television to keep people away from Sokol'niki, a north Moscow park graced by a radial system of paths and concreted sites. The Exhibition of the Achievements of the People's Economy, the VDNKh, was to lay on additional mass events in July and August. Beginning the first week of June, lectures were delivered throughout Moscow emphasizing Soviet achievements. The Society for the Propagation of Political and Scientific Knowledge and a CPSU affiliate, the House of Political Enlightenment, arranged some 10,000 lectures.[32]

In short, the arrival of a brashly self-confident, free-wheeling, capitalist shop window in the heart of Moscow triggered the defence mechanisms available to the one-party state: diversionary attractions, dour ideological warnings, short assault courses in history, lectures to prove the non-existence of God—and an injunction to Komsomols to display a dignified indifference when face to face with the pulsing charms of American youth culture.

On 23 July the *Herald Tribune* was pleased to report that American mail-order catalogues were being stolen by Russian workers and staff who were helping to prepare the US pavilion. 'U.S. Cars and Models Distract Soviet Workmen at Fairgrounds', announced the *New York Times* over a story by Harrison E. Salisbury:

In the big, round tent-like building of the Circlorama a test run of the 360-degree film was being shown. Twenty or thirty Russian workmen and women stood in a darkened circle watching the stereoscopic picture in which they seemed to be at one moment riding a San Francisco cable car and at another whirling up to the very edge of the Grand Canyon. The Russians stood with eyes that could only be described as bulging. Their jaws dropped—as, to be honest, did those of the Americans who were watching . . . 'Look,' said a young American guide, 'they are smashed.'

'Moscow Women Line Up for U.S. Hairdo at Fair,' announced the *New York Times* (25 July). 'The blue plastic beauty parlor chairs in the Coiffures Americana pavilion did not remain empty for long.' The hair stylists, headed by Carl Pace of Bergdorf Goodman, found the Russian women 'most co-operative'. The American fashion show used skits: a formal wedding scene 'thrilled most of the women', while a rock 'n' roll skit demonstrating casual sport clothes 'was more carefully scrutinized for choreography'. The Russians thought some of the American models wore too much make-up.

Seventy-five American guides—twenty-seven women and forty-eight men—all fluent in Russian, had been chosen from more than one thousand applicants after taking language tests and interviews before a panel affiliated with the Foreign Service Institute.[33] Here the American machine moved from the confident panache of the gleaming free-enterprise exhibits to the worried frown of a socio-political system on trial. Just as in the New York Coliseum visitors might fire questions at the Soviet guides about God or Berlin or the Soviet Jews while their gaze appeared to rest on a model atomic energy plant, so here in Sokol'niki the American guides were thoroughly briefed on race relations, Little Rock, Arkansas, unemployment, the rich and the poor. One of the four black American guides was a graduate of the Russian Institute of Columbia University, another worked for the Russian section of the Library of Congress; both told the London *Sunday Times* (26 July) that Russians often asked them about Little Rock,[34] or the latest case of lynching, or how they got into a university. 'But what they find it most difficult to explain to a Russian is how it is possible that, if the American Government has ordered the desegregation of schools, this order is not obeyed.' Thereby hung a tale, or several.[35]

The US exhibition was opened by Richard M. Nixon with Nikita Khrushchev in attendance. Relations were not rendered more cordial by what Hixson calls 'an ill-timed and self-serving "Captive Nations" declaration issued only a week before Nixon's arrival in Moscow'. Congress passed a resolution calling for a week of prayer for the 'enslaved peoples' of Eastern Europe, which Eisenhower duly issued. Khrushchev was furious. The plan was to have Nixon show the Soviet leader how videotape, set up in the RCA-Ampex studio, worked. The chit-chat between the two men was to be played straight back to them—another American miracle. But Khrushchev launched into a vigorous campaign performance, and the famous debate in the kitchen of the model house, which occurred half an hour later, was (alas) not video-recorded. Strolling through the six-room, ranch-style house, the vice-president and the Soviet premier engaged in fierce argument, accompanied by about a hundred American photographers and reporters. Nixon asserted that the $14,000 house could be paid for over 25–30 years; many veterans bought such properties in the $10,000–$15,000 range, and 'most any steelworker could buy one'. Khrushchev retorted: 'You think the

Russians will be dumbfounded by this exhibition. But the fact is that nearly all newly built Russian houses have this equipment. You need dollars in the United States to get this house, but here all you need is to be born a citizen.' (Khrushchev's entire claim was hugely wide of the mark.) In the model kitchen, Nixon pointed to the freedom of consumer choice available to American housewives. Khrushchev countered that one kind of washing machine would be sufficient, if it worked (perhaps missing the point that machines manufactured under competition are more likely to work). That evening Nixon, in formally opening the exhibition, pointed out that 44 million American families owned 56 million cars, 50 million TV sets, and 143 million radios, while 31 million families owned their own homes. This, he said, came 'closest to the ideal of prosperity for all in a classless society'.[36] This classic cold war contest on the basis of agreed values did, of course, spill over into non-agreed values, hence the ongoing debate concerning the relationship of household technology to defence investment.[37]

Tens of thousands of Soviet citizens came to Sokol'niki Park to inspect and perhaps envy the devil. The crowds converging on Buckminster Fuller's gleaming geodesic dome, along handsomely landscaped walkways, to the music of a Soviet Army brass band, passed huge signs proclaiming peace to the world, glory to the Communist Party, and blessings to the Soviet people. But all planned patterns of movement, as Max Frankel reported following his return from New York, broke down as crowds far exceeding the anticipated 50,000 per day converged. 'The notion of having three shifts for viewing during the eleven-hour exhibit day was a fiction that was preserved only on the tickets and the pleading public address system.'

Radio Moscow interviewed Soviet engineers standing beside one of the twenty-two American cars on display. Their comments were not complimentary: 'Too luxurious and most likely very expensive.'[38] An *Izvestiia* headline (29 July) accused the United States of misleading the world about its own social conditions; the paper produced a photograph of piles of garbage and detritus, of washing lines and poverty, outside a traditional slum building (*dom trushchoba*) at the corner of 109th Street and Park Avenue, Manhattan. According to recent Congressional statistics (said *Izvestiia*), 13 million or one quarter of all houses in the United States consisted of such derelict buildings, inadequate for human needs. Thus the Soviet hosts abused their American guests: was this peaceful coexistence or war by other means? The Russians, having laid out a gracious, fountain-strewn plaza leading to American's front door, then staged a verbal massacre of the Odessa Steps as the Soviet crowds converged.[39] Covering the entire front page of *Izvestiia* (30 July), seven columns, was a report of Khrushchev's visit to an exhibition at the Dnepropetrovske machine-tool factory, under the heading ' "Our Strength is Colossal." ' Comparing Soviet and American achievements and standards of living, including butter production per head of population, Khrushchev thundered away (to applause, laughter, and helpful interjections): 'Golosa: *Pravil'no!* (Voices: *Very true!*) Golosa: *Ovoshchi est'! Mnogo ovoshchei!* (Voices: *There are vegetables! Plenty of vegetables!*)'

But the crowds continued to pour in to Sokol'niki Park, driven by the intensely know-all spirit of curiosity which was one of the paradoxical achievements of Soviet education. 'Russians Feel, Thump, Sit Upon And Above All Price U.S. Goods', ran a *New York Times* headline (1 August). Soviet visitors wanted to know how much everything cost—the vast majority of them were utterly innocent of the artificiality of the official 2.5 : 1 rouble-- dollar tourist exchange rate.

'How much do you earn?' Russians ask a Singer sewing machine demonstrator. 'How much does your suit cost?'

One woman smugly pronounced a genuine blue leather coat 'artificial', probably deceived by the softness of the leather.

The gadgetry at the demonstration kitchen excites the Russians. They look in awe at the electric can openers, the Pyrex dishes that do not break on the electric stoves, the paper cup-cake holders, the wall ovens. They wonder how the chocolate marbling gets into a marble cake and how an angel food cake can rise so high with only this powder and two eggs.

The *New York Times* (28 August) made play of the fact that the American library on wheels, a bright green Bookmobile, had been forced to close because so many books were stolen by Soviet visitors. It reopened after an emergency airlift of 2,000 books from the United States. The exhibition organizers turned the science of 'public opinion', familiar to all Americans but still outlawed in the USSR, to double advantage by inviting visitors to the exhibition to record their opinions, in secret, on an all-American voting machine.[40] Khrushchev himself had dismissively passed the machines by; guides were frequently asked why Americans needed such iron-clad secrecy when they voted. Max Frankel commented that Soviet voters received ballot papers listing an unopposed slate, which they dropped unmarked into a box. Booths were available for those who wished to strike out or write in names, but 'the booths are rarely used'.

A major source of attraction was the IBM RAMAC 305 electronic brain, which answered questions about American incomes, statistics, and material achievements. The IBM RAMAC 305 responded to 9,596 enquiries during the first ten days. Some examples:

* *What is the price of American cigarettes?*
* It varies from 20 to 30 cents. The average semi-skilled worker earns enough money in one hour to buy about eight packages.
* *What is meant by the American dream?*
* That all men shall be free to seek a better life, with free worship, thought, assembly, expression of belief and universal suffrage and education.
[The machine also invited questions about the Liberty Bell, the present direction in the development of American jazz, and rock 'n' roll.]
* *How many Negroes have been lynched in the United States since 1950?*
* Seven deaths—six Negroes and one white—have been classified as lynchings since 1950 by the Tuskegee Institute, a Negro college. Responsible Americans condemn lynching and the perpetrators are prosecuted.
* *What is the wardrobe of an average American woman in the middle-income group?*
* Winter coat, spring coat, raincoat, five house dresses, four afternoon 'dressy' dresses, three suits, three skirts, six blouses, two petticoats, five nightgowns, eight panties, five brassières, two corsets, two robes, six pairs of nylon stockings, two pairs of sports socks, three pairs of dress gloves, three pairs of play shorts, one pair of slacks, one play suit, and accessories.
* *What is the average income of the American family?*
* $6,100 in 1957.
* *How old is Louis Armstrong, popular American Negro musician?*
* He is 59. He was taught music in an orphanage and led his first band in 1917.[41]

The Soviet exhibition at the New York Coliseum closed after forty-two days, having received over 1 million visitors, compared to the 2.7 million who visited the American expo in Sokol'niki Park. In summation, the *New York Times* (11 August) commented that the USSR is 'a country in which the machine comes first and man second'. The American authorities had not demanded that the Soviet exhibition be purged of 'subversive' books— which was what happened in Moscow. When the TU-114 made its record and unprecedented flights from Moscow to New York and back, that fact had been fully reported by the American media, yet when the Boeing 720 broke the TU-114's record while carrying American correspondents to Moscow, not a word appeared in the Soviet newspapers. As for the 'concerted and vicious campaign of press depreciation to which our Moscow exhibition was subjected . . . one can hardly blame Khrushchev and company for shivering a bit about some mass exposure of Soviet citizens to a small slice of the truth about America.' After the Soviets fired a second lunar rocket on the eve of

Khrushchev's visit to America, the *New York Times* (13 September) called it 'a weapon of psychological warfare'—but discovered no psychological warfare at work when Vice-President Nixon claimed, without a glimmer of justification, that the USSR had failed three times during the previous two weeks to hit the moon.[42]

The 1959 US Exhibition in Moscow undoubtedly accelerated Soviet interest in consumer goods and design. The status of the decorative applied arts was raised and the concept of *dizain* came to stay, a foreign body under a foreign name, and not the same as decorative art and craft. Illustrated magazines like *Ogonek* carried photographs juxtaposing mass construction of apartment blocks with model interiors—'*Tvoi dom*—your house'—which marked a departure from the heavy, ornate furniture favoured in the late Stalin era. (The British architect Sir Hugh Casson reported his impressions of Moscow in 1954: 'At the hotel the atmosphere is friendly and again indescribably Victorian, with stuffed bears, bronze statuettes, brass spittoons, turkey carpets, high-capped parlour maids. More and more does Moscow in 1954 look like Manchester a century ago.')[43] But now, under Khrushchev in general and since the US Moscow exhibition in particular, the preference was for low, light, simple furniture, as reflected in a book published in 1962, *The Flat and its Furnishings*.[44] The 21st Party Congress of 1959 required artists to help the Party expunge 'petit bourgeois tastelessness', and in the years that followed much was published on aesthetic education and popular taste. The All-Union Research Institute for Technical Aesthetics was built in Moscow in 1960, with departments in many Soviet cities, one of its tasks being to apply rules of design to machines, refrigerators, and domestic equipment. This revived the heritage of the Russian avant-garde in the 1920s, and also of the hitherto disgraced cybernetics.[45] The Sovietologist Alain Besançon commented that since about 1958 Soviet architects:

had to adapt themselves to mass construction...assimilate a series of new techniques...which, in the West, have progressed hand-in-hand with an architectural aesthetic that owed a great deal to the new painting...Here again, the requirements of mass-production are getting the better of the heavy, curvilinear, last-century style that answered to the limited demand of a small minority which was in love—as Power in Russia traditionally is—with pomp and solemnity. But you cannot supply millions of people with carved armchairs, bronze electroliers in the Victorian style, or with huge sofas upholstered with red velvet. A fully elaborated international style emerged. Armchairs and chairs in moulded plastic, book-cases and cupboards in sections, geometrical shapes and vividly contrasted colours—all these today are to be found in the new Soviet flats...and restaurants.[46]

And yet the legacy of the 'heavy industry culture' died hard—to desert it was not unlike turning one's back on the Soviet war dead. The gigantic 1961 Soviet exhibition in Paris presented 'hero cities' and industrial progress rising from the devastation of war, smelters, refineries, hydroelectric stations, as well as the pursuit of peace. The emphasis was on progress running through past, present, and future, dominated by the cosmonaut Yuri Gagarin's achievement as the first man to orbit the Earth, large-scale models of atomic structures and planetary orbits.[47] The conquest of gravity now took pride of place. In 1966 the Space Pavilion of VDNKh was to become the centre-point of the exhibition grounds: a vast, 350-foot, curving monument, topped by a Vostok rocket, guarded at its base by Tsiolkovskii, 'founder of space exploration (*osnovopolozhnik kosmonavtiki*)', was erected where once had been a giant statue of Stalin. The old Republic 'confectionary' pavilions yielded to strictly functionalist ones devoted to Computer Technology, Metallurgy, and Radio Electronics—cool geometry seemed to promise political and cultural change. Close to VDNKh, the Soviet state unveiled the new television tower, 583 metres high, 'the highest self-supporting building in the world', while expelling Aleksandr Solzhenitsyn from the Union of Soviet Writers—before expelling him from his country.

PART II

Stage and Screen Wars:
Russia and America

PART 4

Stage and Screen Wars:
Russia and America

Broadway Dead, Says Soviet Critic

Aleksandr Herzen compared the theatre to the parliament which Romanov Russia did not have; a century later the Soviet theatre critic Anatoly Smeliansky added a further reflection: 'In Soviet Russia the theatre took the place of both the sham parliament and the half-strangled Church.'[1] The theatre, although less accessible to the rural population than the printed word, was regarded as a vital messenger of ideological imperatives, but by 1945 the Punch-and-Judy tradition of the itinerant agit-prop troupe, perhaps perched on a railway wagon, improvisatory, expressionist, and witty, had succumbed to the gilded grandeur of chandelier classicism—the theatre was now a place where you must leave your coat in the cloakroom before entering the auditorium.

The Soviet Central Committee's notorious cultural resolutions of 1946–8 brought terror and tears to every genre of cultural life—this was the *Zhdanovshchina*. Stalin's daughter, Svetlana Alliluyeva, whose second marriage was to Andrei Zhdanov's son, commented that Zhdanov viewed art from the bigoted and puritan points of view prevalent in the Party; his wife Zinaida, 'the ultimate embodiment of this mixture of Party bigotry and the complacency of the bourgeois woman', once remarked: 'Ilya Ehrenburg loves Paris so much because there are naked women there.'[2] The Central Committee resolution on theatre (26 August 1946), 'Concerning the Repertoire of the Playhouses and Measures for its Improvement', castigated Soviet theatres for their morbid preoccupation with performing 'bourgeois foreign dramatists'. English and American one-act plays recently published in Moscow were damned as 'cheap and trivial,' inculcating a view of life (*mirovozzrenie*) harmful to Soviet citizens. 'The grossest political mistake of the Arts Committee has been its wide circulation of such plays in the theatre world and their staging.' Soviet playwrights were enjoined to study the life and demands (*zaprosy*) of the people, and then compose works depicting 'the best character traits' of the Soviet people—optimism, devotion to the homeland, and faith in the 'victory of our cause'. This resolution, published in *Partiinaia zhizn'* (no. 1, 1946), complained that only three of the Moscow Art Theatre's current repertoire of twenty plays were contemporary in setting, and even these were 'feeble and ideologically empty'—a long list of failings followed, with a long list of Soviet theatres inculpated.[3] Zhdanovism threw Soviet theatre into crisis; the very defects imposed (solemnity, monotony, didact-cism, stereotypes) were precisely the faults castigated. 'The spectator finds on stage a scheme; instead of profound artistic thought, didactic discourse; instead of living Soviet people, conventionalized impersonations of virtues and vices', complained Vladimir Prokofiev in Zhdanov's *Kul'tura i zhizn'*.[4]

The maelstrom of recrimination in a climate of fear, bullying, and cold war crisis led on to the anti-cosmopolitan campaign: *Kul'tura i zhizn'* (30 January 1949) denounced 'rootless cosmopolitanism' among Soviet theatre critics, naming a number of Jews who were held to be lackeys of Western intrigue—this was the start of a pogrom in the theatre, music, architecture, poetry, cinema, and philosophy. The cosmopolitans were accused of 'aestheticism' and of belittling the artistic value of 'patriotic, purposeful' plays.[5] Then came 'confessions' of a group conspiracy, an 'anti-Soviet underground'.

The Western press not only publicized and derided each of the Party's cultural *diktats*—philosophy, literature, film, theatre, music, art—but was also quick to dispatch reports of current Soviet stage plays attacking Anglo-American treachery—an obsessional theme in the Soviet theatre from 1947 until the death of Stalin. In June 1947 the Kamerny Theatre staged *The Fate of Reginald Davis* (Sud'ba Redzhinal'da Devisa), by V. Kozkevnikov and I. Prut. The eponymous hero is an honest, pro-Roosevelt American, a captain in the US Army operating among partisans on the Italian–Yugoslav frontier, who becomes disillusioned by the sharp change in post-war American policy. The forces of international reaction are represented by Sir Albert Barding, ex-major, now working for the City, and by two American officers determined to establish commercial control of the area by securing protection for local fascists and by persecuting 'anti-fascists'—as *Moscow News* (22 June) explained. 'Six Anti-American Plays Now Running in Moscow', reported the London *Times* (14 April 1949), with more than a hint of exultancy: a seventh, *Behind Embassy Doors*, was coming soon. A satire on Hollywood with the inspired title *Under the Rustle of Your Eyelashes* set about exposing American film producers as crude mercenaries. The American press displayed a keen interest in *Eyelashes* and the 'new hit play', *Rokovoe nasledstvo* (*Fatal Inherit-ance*), performing at the Moscow Theatre of Satire, which evidently excited 'resounding laughter' among Muscovites. According to *Teatr*'s 'Chronicle of Theatrical Life' (April 1949), the play portrayed simple Soviet people taking a boat trip on the Volga who run into a party of American tourists, thus discovering the real morals of bourgeois society.[6] A succession of productions ridiculed American racism, Hollywood, HUAC, the Marshall Plan, the Voice of America, and American journalism,[7] among them Anatoli Surov's *The Mad Haberdasher* (1949), an attack on President Truman, and Lev Sheinin's *V seredine veka* (*At Mid-Century*, 1950) in the course of which American agents smuggle the physicist Berg out of Norway under the noses of the Germans and set him to work on the A-Bomb. But the good Berg is ruthlessly phased out after he begins to associate with a black dissident scientist, expresses disenchantment about the destruction of Hiroshima and Nagasaki, and becomes an active partisan of Peace. The German scientist Meier, a former Nazi, is brought to the United States to assist in the frame-up of Berg, who is falsely accused of passing secrets to Soviet agents. Convicted, the hero is taken in handcuffs to the docks and deported. At the end of the play he appears at a great International Peace Congress to deliver an impassioned condemnation of the warmongers.[8] A rush of Soviet plays surfaced to warn against unguarded co-operation with American scientists, notably Boris Stein's *Court of Honour*, later adapted as a motion picture, and Konstantin Simonov's *Alien Shadow*.[9]

Harrison Salisbury later recalled his visits to Moscow theatres in the company of his Russian language-teacher Nina (who does not seem to have suffered from the widespread fear of being seen with a foreigner). He saw

every single one of the anti-American plays which were showing in Moscow, from *Uncle Tom's Cabin* to *Another Part of the Forest*...it is only by re-reading the notes I made at the time that I am able to recapture the tawdriness of the Soviet theatre in the years 1949, 1950 and 1951. It was never possible at that time to convey through the Soviet censorship the full depth of slander and vituperation which was being spewed out against the United States and against Americans by the Kremlin's favored playwrights.[10]

Returning home, addressing the Drama Desk luncheon at Sardi's restaurant in New York, Salisbury explained that the twenty-three permanent Moscow repertory companies presented some 350 productions a year. Of these about one-third were pre-revolutionary classics, one-third were imported works, and one-third were new Soviet plays. 'From 1948 to 1952, the bulk of the new Soviet dramas consisted of propaganda pieces with plots from *Pravda*.'[11]

⌗ ⌗ ⌗

Soviet critics of the Stalin–Zhdanov era regarded with a jaundiced eye the non-political Western theatre spearheaded by leading contemporary writers such as Eugene O'Neill, Jean Anouilh, and T. S. Eliot. The canons of rejection in the Ministry of Culture's magazine *Teatr* extended to the so-called 'theatre of the absurd' (Beckett, Ionesco, Arrabal), sometimes known as 'anti-theatre,' which rapidly spread from Paris to New York and London in the 1950s; indeed, to anything owing a debt to surrealism or Kafka. Modernism in all its hideous masks was not only 'decadent' but a deliberate attempt to mystify audiences and divert their attention from current imperialist preparations for war. Aesthetic conservatism, the dogged subscription to 'realism', the conventions of the 'well-made play', and the teachings of Konstantin Stanislavsky remained paramount in Moscow.

The Soviet view of mainstream Broadway theatre was unrelentingly hostile. 'Broadway Dead, Says Soviet Critic', announced the *New York Times* (21 June 1949), reporting an article in *Teatr* by the critic I. Kulikova. In fact, Kulikova had already ridden into battle two years earlier, although clearly dependent for much of her information on the American magazine *Theatre Arts*, and providing no evidence of having herself ever set foot on Broadway. She cited *Theatre Arts* on the current state of Broadway: only thirty-seven so-called 'serious Broadway theatres' existed, but most of them were simply theatre buildings located in the vicinity and often empty. Kulikova explained that what Americans meant by the word 'theatre' was very different not only from the Soviet but also from the general European meaning. Inhabiting these thirty-seven theatres not a genuine theatre company (*truppa*) was to be found, nor a single theatre collective with a constant repertoire—merely tenant companies specially chosen for a particular production. Under the American system, the producer (Kulikova explained) acquires from the dramatist full rights (*sobstvennost'*), hires the director, and invites a 'star' or two to play the leading roles. The producer is tsar. When the writer and dramatist Konstantin Simonov returned from the United States he commented in *Kul'tur i zhizn'* that American contemporary theatre reminded him of a hotel—the occupants were often very famous but did not feel at home. Later Simonov wrote in *Masses and Mainstream* that he had never known more 'homeless' actors than on the American stage. Even the Americans (said Kulikova) have to admit the accuracy of this.[12] She then turned her fire on current productions,[13] comedies and dramas alike, her main target being Eugene O'Neill's *The Iceman Cometh*,[14] written in 1939 but first produced post-war, the main 'hit' (*gvozd'*) of the 1946–7 Broadway season:

The play is about tramps, drunks, and prostitutes. The action takes place in the lowest grade of bar (*kabachok*), a mud-stained psycho-pathological story in the spirit of the decadent 'philosopher' Sartre. This deeply decadent yet entertaining play by O'Neill serves the aim of reaction to the limit of frankness; hence the zealous promotion of it in the American reactionary press, keen to divert the people's attention and demonstrate the mindlessness and helplessness of the struggle for a better future [etc., etc.]¹⁵

The hero of *The Iceman Cometh* (said Kulikova) expresses the author's principal thought: 'The material the ideal free society must be constructed of is men themselves and you can't build a marble temple out of a mixture of mud and manure.' Indeed so; the sentiment quoted by Kulikova is expressed early in the play by Larry Slade, 'one-time Syndicalist-Anarchist', but now an inhabitant of Harry Hope's saloon and rooming house, a refuge for absolute no-hope alcoholics, a family of pipe-dreamers. Here 'tomorrow' is merely an eternal alibi, a shelter from the world, where men drink themselves into oblivion, escaping failed lives, retreating into alibis as familiar as the sound of a needle stuck in a groove. Kulikova was probably right; Larry speaks for the author when he tells young Parritt why he had quit the Movement after thirty years inside it.

LARRY: As history proves, to be a worldly success at anything, especially revolution, you have to wear blinders like a horse and see only straight in front of you. You have to see, too, that this is all black, and that is all white. As for my comrades in the Great Cause, I felt as Horace Walpole did about England, that he could love it if it weren't for the people in it.¹⁶

According to Kulikova, O'Neill's father had reacted to his son's *Beyond the Horizon* with the remark: 'So, you want all the spectators to return home and commit suicide, do you?' Like Kulikova and other Soviet critics, M. Morozov regarded Eugene O'Neill as America's leading dramatist:

It's with O'Neill that begins a tendency in American dramaturgy which could be defined as striving to put across any theme, even a serious and deep one, in the form of a sharp, spicy dish. O'Neill himself for a long time dreamed of hiding actors' faces under a mask... 'I don't like life,' writes O'Neill. Indeed from such quotations can be seen the real face of the current leading light (*korifei*) of the American theatre.¹⁷

In his 'Dve Kul'turi' (Two Cultures), published in *Teatr* (November 1947), Morozov began with an assertion of the influence and artistic supremacy of Russian theatre. 'Most English and American books on the history of theatre name the founder of the new drama as Ibsen. But in spite of that voices are already heard abroad: why Ibsen and not Ostrovsky? After all, Ibsen took the field significantly later, only in the 1870s!' With a pained longing Americans read about Soviet theatre, which not only talks about the people, and serves the people, but belongs to the people. Books in the English language about Soviet theatre rapidly sell out (*raskhodiatsia*); English and American readers learn from these books that theatre is an integral part (*uchastnik*) of the construction of life; that socialist realism not only interprets life but creates it. Currently or recently running in the United States were Konstantin Simonov's *The Russian People*, Leonid Leonov's *Invasion*, three plays by Aleksandr Afinogenov, as well as classics by Gogol, Ostrovsky, Tolstoy, Chekhov, and Gorky.[18]

In the meantime, Morozov reported, decadence prevailed on Broadway. An American journal had recently reproduced a picture by Marc Chagall showing a man with two faces, one *en face*, the other in profile, the left eye of the first face serving as the right eye of the second. This perverted image was reproduced with the aim of inspiring depressed (*priunyvshikh*) theatre workers to stage Sartre's *No Exit* (*Huis Clos*), now running on Broadway, in which the characters find themselves in hell, a room without windows or doors, three people detesting each other, condemned to eternal languor. All through this monstrous dramaturgy inundating American theatre in murky waves was found admiration for every manner of vile, cruel crime. It was no coincidence (said Morozov) that Sartre had promoted Jean Genet's book *The Thief's Journal*, which opens with the words: 'Treachery, theft and homosexuality—such will be my principle subjects.' (Genet's text actually begins: 'Convicts' garb is striped pink and white.')[19]

Morozov reported the sensational impact of Tennessee Williams's play *The Glass Menagerie*, which describes the tragic failure of a mother and her two grown-up children to understand one another in their intertwined love, the frustration they endure trying to escape their social and personal isolation.[20]

The play [reported Morozov] has four characters: mother, son, Tom, daughter, and the 'gentleman caller'. Tom works in a large shoeshop warehouse. The system mercilessly exploits him and turns him into a working automaton. Somewhere in his confused spirit living feeling stirs. Secretly he writes poetry...

Although Tennessee Williams's first steps in the region of dramaturgy were closely linked to Theater Guild [*sic*], one of America's progressive theatre organizations, yet since that time he has not touched on social problems. He says nothing in *The Glass Menagerie* about those forces which turned Tom into a robot, nor indicates any solution. No one in the play utters a word of genuine social protest.[21]

Morozov's version of the text is not ours. On the contrary, in his opening narrative, before the action begins, Tom talks of a 'dissolving economy' in the 1930s, when 'the huge middle class of America was matriculating in a school for the blind . . . In Spain there was Guernica. Here there were disturbances of labor, sometimes pretty violent . . . This is the social background of the play.'[22]

The play reminded Morozov of a heavy nightmare. 'In order to intensify this impression, the author in every possible way insists in the stage directions on the "unreality" of his play.'[23] Tom is full of hopeless despair. He says: 'I look around. The whole world is full of commonplace people. They all get born and they all die.' Afterwards news reaches us that Tom became a drunk in foreign parts and dies, perishes senselessly, thoughtlessly. (But again one wonders what version Morozov had been reading: there is in fact no sign of Tom's 'hopeless despair', of the words quoted, or the sentiments behind them in the text published in *Four Plays* (1956). Similarly there is no mention of Tom's drunkeness or death in foreign parts; the last words belong to him, as do the first words of the play, which indicate that he is telling a story set in the past, the mid-thirties.)

Returning to Broadway in 1949[24]—though evidence was still lacking that she had ever set foot in the New York she described—Kulikova began her 'American Theatre at the Service of Wall Street' with a long ideological rant about Wall Street (the demon's lair of post-war Soviet commentary, only later supplanted by the 'CIA'), adding to her vocabulary the 'Marshallization' of Europe and, of course, the evils of 'cosmopolitanism'; Kulikova used the word *del'tsy* (smart operators) more than once to describe the movers and shakers of Broadway theatre. The first casualty of American theatrical expansion occurred in England in 1947, according to Kulikova, citing (once again) *Theatre World*:

This happened with the help of English lackeys and a dollar-worshipper (*dollar-opoklonnik*) called 'Johns', who, choking with delight, showers compliments on American 'benefactors', who have deprived hundreds of English actors of their wages. The 'benefactors' imported various productions and reviews from Broadway and Hollywood to two leading London theatres, the Palladium and the Casino, which have the capacity to function all the year round.

But all was not well in the lair of the beast, Broadway itself, according to Kulikova's progressive sources, the English magazine *New Theatre* and the critic Rosamund Gilder. Of only sixty-one productions (compared to 350 in the 1928 season), 64 per cent had collapsed; only nineteen plays out of sixty-one had interested audiences, one of them being *Arsenic and Old Lace*.[25] Kulikova was also critical of the star system; Lynn Fontanne, for example, was still playing the roles of young girls at the age of 60. (A similar point was made in the West about the veteran Bolshoi ballerina Ulanova's attachment to such roles as Juliet.) Meanwhile, as Kulikova reported, it was open season for witch-hunters in the United States: on 1 February 1948 the Anti-American Activities Committee in California had investigated fifty-one local organizations, including the Actors' Laboratory Theatre. Chairman Senator Jack Tenney declared at one session: 'The investigators unmasked an irrefutable fact, that the Theatre Laboratories accomplished two productions of some Russian guy called Anton Chekhov.'[26] Kulikova, however, lapsed into an error equally sublime when she lamented that American college theatres depended heavily on detective and criminal plays like *Merry Gallows* and *Murder in the Cathedral*.[27]

Further evidence of the ongoing crisis of Broadway was brought to the readers of *Teatr* (April 1950) by I. Lapitsky, who began by citing Brooks Atkinson, renowned theatre critic of the *New York Times*. Broadway reminded him of a neurasthenic—not so much a provider of art but a form of behind-the-scenes trading organization (*torgashestvo*) lacking both stability of management and guarantee of work for artists and writers. All theatrical activity took place in an atmosphere of tension because of the high accident rate. Due to bankruptcies and a systematic reduction in the number of functioning theatres, up to 90 per cent of professional actors might be unemployed at any one time. Lapitsky added his own storm of statistics on thespian destitution in the United States, citing such progressive sources as *Masses and Mainstream* and the American Labor Party candidate for mayor of New York, Vito Marcantonio.[28] The Soviet critic then drew his readers' attention to a social stratum immune to unemployment, the one depicted in T. S. Eliot's commercially successful[29] *The Cocktail Party*, first performed at the Edinburgh Festival in 1949, on Broadway the same year, and in London the following spring. Lapitsky did not mention Edinburgh but evinced the New York–London sequence as further proof of American cultural domination, Eliot being a British citizen.

Aleksandr Fadeyev, first secretary of the Soviet Writers' Union until 1953, had earlier set the tone concerning Eliot in his harsh keynote address to the World Congress of Leaders of Culture for the Defence of Peace, which opened in Wroclaw (Vroslav), Poland, on 25 August 1948. In words widely circulated in the Western media, if only for their lamentable prejudice against jackals and hyenas, Fadeyev declared:

If jackals could learn to use the typewriter and hyenas could master the fountain pen, they no doubt would write just like Henry Miller, [T. S.] Eliot, [André] Malraux, and other Sartrists... The leader of the English decadents is the mystic and aesthete Eliot. Known for his pro-fascist sympathies, he recommends himself as follows: 'We are hollow people, people stuffed with rubbish.'[30]

I. Lapitsky's, 'Crisis of the American Theatre' carried on in the same vein concerning Eliot. Somewhat paraphrased, he reported as follows:

The Cocktail Party by the fascist poet T. S. Eliot is on at New York's Henry Miller Theater. The main characters are three English people, Edward and Lavinia Chamberlayne, a married couple, and the woman Edward loves, Celia Coplestone. The conflict brings them to a labyrinth of torment. In the last act, which is set two years later, another fashionable cocktail party takes places at the Chamberlaynes', and there we learn of the death of Celia in a colony called Kinkanja, where she was working as one of three white nurses in a plague hospital.

The play is on the level of a 'drawing room' comedy. Almost all the characters are guests of the Chamberlaynes, and the attitudes of the actors and the setting concentrates on conveying high society in the exquisite manner and 'refined' taste of the characters. But when the subject of the native uprising and the death of Celia comes up, the play adopts a mystical tone as if concerned with the redemption of sin. About the unsubmissive natives, characters speak with sharp hatred and malice. Eliot depicts the natives (tuzemtsy) as savages, members of a lower race, with the result that they, led by agitators or 'foreign agents'[31] (the expression Eliot uses), rise up against the English government. One of the victims of the 'unpleasant' rebels turns out to be Celia. But British forces, embodying justice, fair play, and civilization, suppress the uprising. The play has brought rapture (vostorg) to the American press. The strong promotion for The Cocktail Party is significant because the playwright, whom the New York Times calls 'the greatest poet', is closely linked to the Fascist Party of [Oswald] Mosley in England, and is well known for his racist, misanthropic outlook.[32]

Lapitsky had a point. Eliot's character Alex provides a grimly comic account, in the hyper-superior sang froid of the upper classes, of how the pagan natives ('the heathen') of Kinkanja regard monkeys as sacred animals, and therefore never to be killed, whereas the Christian converts kill, cook, and eat them encouraged by colonialists like Alex. Turning to the insurrection, Alex speaks of 'foreign agitators' who convince the heathen natives that the slaughter of monkeys by the Christians had put a curse on them which could only be expurgated by slaughtering the Christians and sometimes eating them— even though the Christians had eaten the sacred monkeys.[33] Eliot's dialogue establishes associations between natives and monkeys by repetition rather than assertion. By the time these natives have, and those natives have not, eaten monkeys, and then each other, all of them—ignorant, irrational, and hugely impressionable—seem to be leaping about in metaphorical trees. No Soviet critic of the Stalin era, or any era, could have resisted a few hundred words on this imperialist-fascist iniquity.

Was Eliot 'closely linked' to Oswald Mosley's British Union of Fascists, as Lapistky claimed? Oddly, it was his estranged and mentally unstable first wife, Vivienne, who joined Oswald Mosley's British Union of Fascists in 1932, but there is no sign of Eliot, a high Tory, moving in that direction,[34] despite his admiration for the writing of Charles Maurras and an early interest in Mussolini.[35] After the crudely anti-Semitic Ezra Pound was arrested in Italy in May 1945 for collaborating with America's enemies, Eliot cabled Archibald MacLeish, then assistant secretary of state, expressing an eager wish to help Pound.[36] All this was well known to Soviet observers of the Anglo-American literary scene. In the *Saturday Review* (11 June 1949) Eliot was accused of anti-Semitism, 'intellectual neo-fascism', and being a 'rootless expatriate' who should be dropped from the Bollingen Prize jury. The general uproar, which occurred three months before *The Cocktail Party* opened in New York at the Henry Miller Theater on 21 January 1950, no doubt inspired Lipitsky's polemic in *Teatr*. It was all part of the Marshall Plan: 'Under the Marshall Plan, the London stage is literally inundated by American plays, the heroes of which are gangsters, detectives and prostitutes.'

A major uproar was provoked in London at the end of last year by the production of Tennessee Williams's pornographic *A Streetcar Named Desire*. A question about imposing a ban (*zapreshchenie*) on it was asked in the English parliament. But the representatives of the Labour government hastened to take under its protection this boulevard production from Broadway. Strong protests again arose against the production of this play in Paris, where the idea of the superiority of 'American culture' has been forcibly implanted. Protests against vulgar American imports like *No Orchids for Miss Blandish*, at the Grand Guignol Theatre in Montmartre, had appeared in the French press; according to *Ce Soir*,[37] the play 'breaks records for the establishment of the 'Theatre of Horror'.

The ability to pass seamlessly from a major drama like *Streetcar* to slick entertainment like René Raymond's *Miss Blandish* was one of the inimitable skills of Soviet criticism. Lapitsky arrived at Rodgers and Hammerstein's musical *South Pacific* (1949). It was said (he said) to be based on a famous case of an American woman who refused to marry a rich plantation owner only because he had once been married to a Polynesian woman. Choking with pleasure (said Lipitsky), all American bourgeois critics had praised the show in concord, proving that the racist-fascist order prevails in their country. Lapitsky distorted the storyline of *South Pacific* in what had become an almost self-parodying Soviet style of commentary. In reality a young American lieutenant and a Polynesian girl sing a refrain about the artificiality of racial prejudice, which 'you've got to be carefully taught'; indeed, the show's defence of miscegenation upset some American audiences, particularly in the South, where theatres were picketed. Lapitsky found only racism everywhere: for example, in recent years Washington, DC had been without a single theatre for a single reason: the proprietor of the only theatre building did not wish to admit Negroes, even though they comprised one-third of the city's inhabitants.[38]

The Russians had developed two criteria for ranking a Western author or playwright as 'progressive' or 'degenerate'. Modernism (decadence) was to be condemned, regardless of the writer's political viewpoint; yet a 'realist' author like Upton Sinclair, Sinclair Lewis, or John Steinbeck, previously translated and lauded, fell into the abyss as soon as he publicly turned against the Soviet Union. But even as ageing angels grew horns, younger ones had to be found—notably Arthur Miller and Lillian Hellman, both of whom wrote in an accessible, realist mode; both attended the Waldorf Conference of March 1949; and both were to become targets for anti-Communist Congressional committees and blacklisting vigilantes. Hellman, a former correspondent in wartime Russia and an unrepentant fellow-traveller, was rewarded when her play *Another Part of the Forest* was presented by the Moscow Drama Theatre in 1949 under the title 'Ladies and Gentlemen', but it soon came under fire as lacking 'a merciless and scornful exposé of the awful capitalist reality', and for failing to show the true treatment of American Negroes. The *New York Times* (13 November 1949) was happy to pick up this story.

⊞ ⊞ ⊞

Soviet theatre of the late Stalin era suffered from a permanent crisis imposed by the conflict between dramatic standards and the Party line. More complex, the Party, like a dog biting its own tail, frequently savaged the results of its own diktats. 'Overcome the Lag in Dramaturgy'—*Preodolet' otstavanie dramaturgii*', declared *Literaturnaia gazeta* (26 March 1952). An editorial attacking the refusal by 'the dogmatic critics' to allow the portrayal of 'negative phenomena in our life' also blamed officials of the Arts Committee who 'have established a close, restrictive framework for playwrights' and who were responsible for 'the view *foisted on playwrights* that negative phenomena on the stage will necessarily be a distortion of reality'. The playwright Nikolai Virta explained that the mistaken theory of conflictless drama arose among playwrights like himself after sober reflection 'on the manner in which those of our plays which contain sharp life conflicts passed through the barbed-wire obstacles of the agencies in charge of repertory', where 'everything living, true to life, sharp, fresh, and unstereotyped was combed out'. He cited the history of his own play *Our Daily Bread*, which had come under fire from the Arts Committee, despite its initial support for the play, as 'a slander against the collective farms'.[39] It was as if motorists might wake up each day to a new, contradictory set of driving regulations, infringements, penalties: 'Our dramatists must expose and mercilessly scourge the survivals of capitalism, the manifesting of political unconcern, bureaucracy, stagnation, servility... [etc.]' But: 'One cannot tolerate plays in which the negative characters dominate everything and, moreover, are portrayed more vividly and expressively than the heroes.'[40] American government agencies and the press monitored these twists and howls with ill-disguised enthusiasm. For its first issue the USIA's *Problems of Communism* (no. 1, 1953) commissioned Paul Willen's 'The Crisis in Soviet Drama'. Eight years later, writing in the same journal, Jürgen Rühle—a recent defector from East Germany—commented: 'Of all the spheres of Soviet culture, theatre is perhaps the art which illustrates most glaringly the chasm between the hopes and achievements of the early, revolutionary period of Soviet history and the cultural bankruptcy of succeeding eras.'[41] Here again is visible the perennial, forked-tongue Western nostalgia for the early revolutionary years: 'In the years of revolutionary upheavals Bolshevism seemed to answer the basic demands and desires of the Russian people... Lenin, Trotsky, Lunacharsky, Bukharin, Radek were cultured and educated men for whom any forcible encroachment upon the creative processes of art was unthinkable...'[42] This was remarkable to read in an American government publication; if early Bolshevism had been so beneficent, why had US governments refused to accord diplomatic recognition to Soviet Russia from 1918 to 1933? Western cold war cultural criticism resembled Stalinist airbrushing in reverse: Bolsheviks came back into favour, and were restored to the canvas, only after they had died, preferably in disgrace.

Following Stalin's death, the call went out for some new Gogols.[43] The most outspoken attack on the higher bureaucracy was Leonid Zorin's drama *Gosti* (*The Guests*), which was performed a few times to public acclaim in the winter of 1953–4. The play's villain is Pyotr Kirpichev, head of a department in the Ministry of Justice. His father, Aleksei, an old Bolshevik idealist, and his high-minded sister Varvara, both condemn Pyotr's arrogant attitude towards the people. The acquisitive Pyotr—he enjoys a luxurious apartment, a summer house, a chauffeur-driven car—is willing to conceal a miscarriage of justice rather than risk the humiliation and loss of power that would result from exposure. The father denounces this as a tragic perversion and a betrayal. Pyotr's 19-year-old son Tema, a member of the Komsomol, enjoys access to a chauffeured car and a dacha, as well as an entrée to the maîtres d'hotel of the best restaurants—but finally rebels against his corrupt father.

The Guests was closely observed by American academic experts, including Harold Swayze and Harold Segel, who called the play 'one of the most powerful and unequivocal indictments of the Stalinist bureaucracy ever recorded in Soviet literature', adding: 'The Ministry of Culture lost little time in condemning the play as compounded of falsehoods and distortions and in calling for its suppression.'[44]

The German journalist Klaus Mehnert quoted a speech by Pyotr's principled sister Varvara, in which she uses 'the fatal word "class"':

VARVARA: Now where has this 'upper class' (*vysshii svet*) in our country come from?
TRUBIN: [a journalist]: Where did our 'upper class' come from? It is the spawn of meanness and greed, of inordinate ambition...

Varvara then concludes that it comes 'from power'.[45] A French visitor to Moscow, Hélène Lazareff, also discussed *The Guests* at some length. 'It revealed, in a dramatic fashion, the habits, indeed the very existence, of the new [Soviet] bourgeoisie.' Although published in February 1954 in the pages of the Ministry of Culture's official review *Teatr*, and although performed simultaneously at Moscow's Emalova Theatre, Leningrad's Gorky Theatre, and at numerous provincial theatres, the play was suddenly withdrawn by the Ministry of Culture when it had been playing to full houses for eight weeks in Moscow. At an extraordinary session of the Collegium of the Ministry of Culture of the USSR, *The Guests* was subject to scathing attack: 'The play was banned and Zorin fell into disgrace', reported Hélène Lazareff—even though the playwright had been introduced to her at the official reception for the visiting Comédie française by the minister of culture, Aleksandrov. She also reported that Zorin's condemnation by the jury of the Ministry of Culture was spread across five columns of *Sovetskaia kul'tura*:

The play misrepresents the very essence of the social order and the regime, and undermines its audience's faith in our society's unlimited power to make even and constant progress along the road to communism... No one is ignorant of the fact that the word 'power' has assumed in our country a clear and happy significance, and that everyone has an unshakeable faith, an ardent filial love for their own representatives in the State, who are the power of the people. Once again the Party points out that foreign ideologies are able to influence Soviet art and literature, as long as the forces of capitalism, imperial reaction and obscurantism are alive in the world.

Lazareff interpreted this: 'The unpardonable sin which Zorin committed was to have made evident the flaw in the system, which appears in the form of the emergence of a bourgeois class in the Soviet world.'[46] The Russian-speaking Hélène Lazareff and her husband Pierre (proprietor of the Paris evening paper *Le Soir*) were sharply critical of what they saw of Soviet theatre. Simonov's *Ivan the Terrible*, which they attended in Leningrad, 'in its closing scenes not merely excuses but actually glorifies the bloodiest reign in the history of the Tsars'. In Moscow they saw three new plays, including *In Love at Dawn* by Jaroslav Galanin, set in a Ukrainian village. The villainous Louka, once a Nazi collaborator, has returned to his native country as an American agent. Disguising his Machiavellian plans under a hearty manner, he tries to disorganize the kolkhoz and spread rumours of war while engaging in assassination plots. He is unmasked by his own father, wife, and family—good Communists. The Lazareffs were less than enthralled: 'All this is accompanied by violent speech-making on imperialist America, on the lack of vigilance among responsible people, on the dangers of being cosmopolitan, and the inevitable triumph of right.'

Plays like Aleksandr Korneichuk's *Kryl'ia* (*Wings*) and Aleksandr Shtein's *Personal'noe delo* (*A Personal Matter*)[47] were hastily presented to Soviet audiences in the mid-1950s; a strictly controlled dose of criticism of the cult of personality, offset by a glorification of Soviet ideology.[48] The lead item in the November 1954 issue of *Novy mir* was Korneichuk's *Wings* translated from the original Ukrainian. The play had been running in Kiev for some time, but no local critic had dared to write a review without a lead from Moscow, though the play is set in an agricultural region of the Ukraine during the second half of 1953, immediately after the arrest and execution of Beria. Finally transferred, *Wings* opened at the Mali Theatre in March 1955, attended by Bulganin, Khrushchev, Malenkov, and other leading members of the Party. 'I saw them applaud the most telling passages', reported the London *Daily Worker*'s Ralph Parker (1 March). 'Particularly effective is his revelation of the disastrous conditions in agriculture before Khrushchev took over responsibility...in 1953.' The negative hero of the play is chairman of a provincial executive council, an autocrat and tyrant who makes his gardener, an ex-soldier with many medals, spend hours digging for worms so that he can go fishing. He justifies whatever he does on the grounds that he is 'building communism'. Other members of the ruling class are also ridiculed as incompetent, lazy, or drunk. The director of the tractor station is less interested in his work than in duck-shooting and his dog. A supportive review by Simonov appeared in *Pravda* (17 May 1955).

Soviet popular theatre, meanwhile, continued to thrive in low profile, offering special delights and skills. Never short of a packed-in clientele was the Miniature Theatre on Zhelyabov Street in Leningrad, where audiences began laughing every evening at 8.30. Here the great Arkadi Raikin and thirteen other players directed withering satire at Soviet society without incurring official displeasure. Raikin, who carried the title Meritorious Artist of the RSFSR, conveyed the peculiarly Jewish humour which combines searing satire with sympathy for human weakness. Rakin's 'daughter' has fallen in love: 'How can you tell whether you love him until you know whether he has fulfilled his production norm?' the father yells at her. In another role, Raikin explains how he can always tell when summer has come—there are no soft drinks on sale and winter boots at last appear in the department stores. However, Clifton Daniel, reporting from Leningrad in the *New York Times* (30 January 1955), pointed out that neither Raikin nor anyone else 'pokes fun at the sacrosanct principles of Communism or the leaders of the Communist Party'. Another American visitor and Raikin-fan, Faubion Bowers, was told how, after the war, the actor-comedian had appeared in a command performance before Stalin. It was a biting winter and the fuel shortage was acute. In his skit, Raikin came on carrying a huge, empty sack and explained that he was on his way to get some wood from the relevant ministry. Later he reappeared with the sack bulging. ' "Amazing!" his friend exclaimed. "You really got your wood so quickly?" "Wood?" said Raikin. "These are just the forms I have to fill out." '

Writing in *Le Monde* (1 July 1955), André Pierre described a persistent crisis in Soviet theatre. Playhouses were recognizing a marked change in the taste of the theatre-going public, who now demanded entertainment and not, as André Pierre put it, 'the branch of a Marxist university and boring socialist realism burdened by conventional characters and didactic messages'. On 23 November *Le Monde* reported that Soviet theatres were conspicuously failing to sell tickets: the Pushkin Theatre was only 33 per cent full. Yet the new Party line and the emerging cult of Khrushchev demanded a custom-built didactic drama but, as Western commentators constantly pointed out, good playwrights are not tailors. Nikolai Pogodin's *We Three Went to the Virgin Lands*, first staged in November 1955, was the classic example of the Thaw, portraying the privations endured by young people who had patriotically responded to the call for volunteers to implement Khrushchev's virgin lands campaign. In the USIA's *Problems of Communism*, Jürgen Rühle offered a description of Pogodin's scenario (here paraphrased):

Letavin, the leading character of the play, decides to heed the government's call because 'here at home he is fed up with everything' and a girl has jilted him; Rakitkin, a hooligan, joins because he wants to elude the police . . . a seamstress speculates on the possibility of marrying an 'interesting person' en route . . . And so on. They encounter a dreary, crushing, barbaric existence: snow, wolves, blizzards. The pioneers also meet a deportee, a victim of forced labour—the forbidden subject.[49]

Despite early enthusiastic reviews, the play came under attack in an article 'Truth and Fabrication' in *Partinaia zhizn'* (no. 1, 1956). After Pogodin's play was condemned by *Pravda* as a 'serious failure', reprimanding the theatre and the producers of the television version, Pogodin undertook to rewrite it—a familiar sequence of events which proved predictably attractive to Western observers.[50]

The two sensations of the 1956 theatrical season were Nikolai Pogodin's *Sonet Petrarki* (*Petrarch's Sonnet*) and Samuil Alyoshin's *Odna* (*Alone*). In both plays a conventional, 'realistic' dramatic structure frames far-reaching questions about Soviet society. *Petrarch's Sonnet* portrays the love of a middle-aged married engineer for a young woman. Sukhodolov is burdened by an appalling wife, Kseniya, yet he is not unfaithful, meets the young woman he loves only twice, and does not touch her. The relationship, pursued almost wholly through correspondence, is romantic, idealistic, pristine, much in the spirit of Petrarch and the Laura of the sonnets. But others insist on reducing it to a tawdry extramarital affair, notably Klara, a lecturer on cultural topics and an ardent Communist, who reports the engineer to a Party official, insisting that Communist morality set limits to private behaviour. Pavel Mikhailovich, head of the Regional Committee, replies:

PAVEL: But a man can have certain intimate sides to his life which he will not reveal to anyone. He simply is not obliged to. There is no such rule.
[He also tells Klara:]
PAVEL: Thinking is one thing, but living off other people's thoughts is another. Try to think for yourself. You see, the Party's program allows great scope for independent thought . . . and how much Lenin offers . . . [Ellipses are the author's.]
KLARA: To think individually on each issue, individually to come to a decision—you would go mad, first of all. You can't live without guide-lines.

Finally Sukhodolov, a devoted Party member, and the young woman he loves part company, perhaps for ever, perhaps not, each ennobled by their experience of a pure love. Like other 'liberal' writers of the Thaw period, Nikolai Pogodin falls over himself to have his heroes profess the most utter devotion to the Party (and, it goes without saying, its absolute monopoly of power). A man can think for himself only if or because the Party 'allows great scope' for it.

SUKHODOLOV: I pledge my heart and soul to the Party; I'd lay down my life for it . . . But still a man can have a private side to his life . . .

Pavel Mikhailovich, head of the Regional Committee, also, engages in fulsome—some might say sickeningly saccharine—eulogies:

PAVEL:...but when I meet a man, a contemporary Soviet man in our country, endowed with great spiritual beauty...I see the future of the world, communism.

A further trick of Pogodin's, calculated to appease the Party, was to present the puritanical morality drilled into the Soviet people by the Party as 'middle-class'. Sukhodolov complains about his wife's 'middle-classness, her loud manners, her petty mind...'.

PAVEL: These petty middle-class people have to be fought. Why, they even want to see communism turned into a middle-class paradise. Comfort, satiety and empty-mindedness.[51]

The play was still playing to well-filled houses in 1959. As Harold Swayze saw it, '*Petrarch's Sonnet* is memorable above all for its vigorous defence of the view that an important part of man's inner life lies beyond the area in which the Party may legitimately exercise control.' Harold Segel calls the play 'an unvarnished indictment of the simplistic morality, suspicion and oppression of Stalinist Russia...'. In Segel's view, Pogodin is arguing for the right of the individual to the privacy of his emotions, for the complexity of emotional relations, and against a black-and-white view of the world embodied in 'guidelines'.[52] A Soviet critic, Viktor Komissarzhevsky, director of the Mali Theatre, writing for a Western audience while the play was still in performance, duly repeated the Party line of the moment, achieving the echo-chamber monotony which could render apparently liberal sentiments almost totalitarian in tone:

We still find people who regard with suspicion anything seemingly strange...Pogodin's play brands these indifferent and narrow-minded people. Their views, their tactics, are alien to the humane nature of our state. They run counter to Party ethics. The Party friends of Communist Sukhodolov help him to unravel the knot. When we leave our stage hero nothing stands in his and his sweetheart's way to follow the call of their hearts and be happy.[53]

The CIA-funded magazine *Encounter*'s 'From the Other Shore' (February 1958) was pleased to report that the Soviet Ministry of Culture, assessing the theatre season of 1956–7, had lamented the lack of a single Soviet play 'unmasking the intrigues of the enemies of peace, the instigators of a new war'. Theatre managers were censured for putting on frivolous bourgeois entertainments like *Dial 'M' for Murder*. The theatre scene—added *Encounter* with a smile—was even more decadent in Poland, where seventeen Western plays were in performance and not a single Soviet play had been seen for a year. *Kiss Me Kate* was the huge box-office success. Theatre managers duly came under attack from *Trybuna literacka*.[54]

What dulled the shine on *Encounter*'s derision was what might be called the reverse journey. Post-Hungary, post-Suez, a new generation of dissenting Western playwrights began to appear on Communist stages. The 'Angry Young Men' of the Royal Court Theatre in London, when discovered in translation on the far side of the Iron Curtain, did not appeal to Stephen Spender, an editor of *Encounter*. John Osborne's *Look Back in Anger* and *The Entertainer* reached Warsaw in 1958. Comparing Osborne's anger (and ashes) to the Polish director Wajda's newly released film *Ashes and Diamonds*, Spender concluded that the English playwright 'over-exploits the evils he attacks. So much is made of one Trafalgar Square meeting about Suez, of the feelings of a family over the death of a British officer in the fighting!' Spender's exclamation mark signals the triviality of such concerns, even though generated by the Anglo-French invasion of a sovereign Middle Eastern state, Egypt, in 1956. Poland, shaken to the core by the upheavals of the same year, was evidently the wrong place to be washing Britain's dirty linen. Spender derisively quoted the Polish critic Leszek Elecktorowicz, recommending *Look Back in Anger*: ' "The Crown unites this fragmentary, socially divided society... there is nothing an Englishman admires more than the splendour of the royal masquerade... the Empire is falling to pieces from old age and its old-type politicians are jostled around and commit follies." '

Spender rejoindered that the English catastrophe has not yet happened, whereas Poles, Hungarians, and Czechs were living within 'an all too palpable disaster'. He added, with classic cold war reasoning: 'Seeing *The Entertainer* in Warsaw is like seeing a play about characters who complain of headaches, performed in a hospital before an audience of inmates who have cancer.'[55]

Yet Soviet theatres in general preferred non-contentious Russian or Western classics.[56] 'The range of these plays is exceptional', wrote Faubion Bowers. 'They are not selected for their accord with Soviet ideology...' Yet Moscow's classical fare struck some visitors as lugubrious and long-winded. The actor Michael Redgrave, returning from a tour in the winter of 1958 with the Shakespeare Memorial Theatre,[57] declared himself bored stiff by stage adaptations of epic novels, including five hours of *The Idiot* in Leningrad and *Anna Karenina* at the Moscow Art Theatre. 'Both reminded me of what is called in America a "club sandwich": piquant delicacies interlarded between an intolerable deal of bread, and from the first bite indigestible.' On the other hand, Redgrave had been impressed at the Pushkin Theatre by a 'staggeringly detailed' production of Mikhail Bulgakov's *The Escape*, a story of the flight and degradation of White Russians during the Revolution. The acting was brilliant and the staging had a Brechtian element. He also adored the

Moscow Circus.[58] Returning from the same Shakespeare Memorial Theatre tour, the young director Peter Hall, in the words of the *Daily Telegraph* (31 December 1958), 'demolished the present Russian theatre . . . removed every trace of reputation from the Russian stage'. Lecturing to the fourth National Student Drama Festival at the University of London, Hall complained of museum-like stasis; Chekhov's *Three Sisters* still carried the same decor as in 1905. In every city theatre the play was performed within the established set because there was only one acceptable set. 'Everybody in the Russian theatre is at least ten years older than he should be for his part.' The speed and fluidity of the Stratford company's performances had been 'an extraordinary eye-opener' to Russians: a Russian performance of *The Winter's Tale* started at 7 p.m. and ended at 12.15 a.m. Hall quoted Stanislavsky: 'Art cannot tolerate frozen forms.' But the Russians had succeeded in freezing Stanislavsky. The influence of the Russian experimental theatre had been expunged. No actor in Leningrad, where the director Vsevelod Meyerhold, a victim of the pre-war purges, had worked, would talk about him. The newer plays Hall had attended were all 'unbelievably crude, sentimental and political'. He saw glimmers of hope: Bulgakov's plays were back on stage and the intelligent Russian just about knew of Arthur Miller—but not about Tennessee Williams, Jean Anouilh, or Samuel Beckett.[59]

⊞ ⊞ ⊞

A major issue among Western commentators[60] was the protracted disgrace, then partial rehabiliation, of the avant-garde director Vsevolod Meyerhold, a victim of the pre-war Stalin purges. The provocative Meyerhold, born in 1874, had advertised his low opinion of Stanislavsky and the 'imperialism' of the Moscow Art Theatre; closure of his own theatre, arrest, and death followed. Dmitri Shostakovich, a close but much younger admirer, recalled:

Stalin hated Meyerhold. It was hatred by default, you might say, because Stalin had never been present at a single production of Meyerhold's . . . Just before the Theatre of Meyerhold was shut down, Kaganovich came to a performance at the Theatre. He was very powerful. The Theatre's future depended on his opinion, as did Meyerhold's future . . . Kaganovich didn't like the play [and] left almost in the middle. Meyerhold, who was in his sixties then, ran out into the street after Kaganovich. Kaganovich and his retinue got into a car and drove off. Meyerhold ran after the car, he ran until he fell.[61]

Throughout Europe, extending to America during the Depression, politically radical theatre and cinema—Mayakovsky, Meyerhold, Tairov, Vakhtanghov, Brecht, Piscator, London's Unity Theatre, the Living Newspaper, the

Group Theatre—had achieved unprecedented levels of artistic innovation and brilliance in the twenties and thirties. Fusing naturalism with expressionism, the federally-subsidized Living Newspaper drew heavily on epic forms, alienation techniques, cinematic documentary, and the cabaret style of the Berlin and Paris cellars. A loudspeaker might serve as a raisonneur, inquiring, cajoling, pointing the moral of the action. Decor and montage were often blatantly symbolic—in *One Third of a Nation* slum congestion was conveyed by a large number of people crowding on to one small carpet. Indeed, the tired conventions of realism so dear to Stalin and Zhdanov were being subverted not only by expressionism—the dominant vanguard movement in the arts during the entirety of the twentieth century—but also by didacticism itself. Clifford Odets's *Waiting for Lefty* successfully employed an episodic structure, choral recitation, caricature, blatant stylization, slogans, and hot gospelling. A smash hit in America, the only known production of *Lefty* in the Soviet Union had been an obscure amateur affair performed in the mid-thirties by American expatriates, directed by Joseph Losey and possibly sponsored by VOKS.[62]

But Zhdanovism would not tolerate expressionism, with its implication of uncontrollable individuality, its challenge to authority. Not even Brecht had been performed in the Soviet Union at the time of his death. Gorky—it had to be a Russian—was canonized as the founder of socialist realism in drama after his final return from Italy in 1931 to occupy the splendid *art nouveau* merchant's villa in Moscow loaned to him by the Writers' Union. Gorky was canonized a 'classic' at the moment of death. But so-called realism offered a theatre of illusions; actors and spectators alike must believe unquestioningly that the action was 'real'; the fostering of uncritical, regimented belief was the key tenet of Stalinist aesthetics. Meyerhold would have none of it; an arresting portrait done in his heyday, 1925, by Pyotr Vilyams, shows a confident Meyerhold in profile, brandishing his unmistakable nose, with a modernistic stage set in the rear. But in Pyotr Konchalovsky's 'Portrait of Vsevelod Meyerhold 1937', the aquiline-nosed director is found in an elegant suit, stretched out on a chaise longue, affecting nonchalance to cover his despair, smoking a pipe, and with a dog draped across his legs, the violently coloured wall tapestry behind him unchanged from ten years earlier (1928), when Meyerhold posed for a photograph with the young Shostakovich. As the painter's grandson, the film director Andrei Mikhailov-Konchalovsky, comments, here is 'a man with an axe hanging over his head . . . shunned and spurned by everyone.'[63]

Central Committee archives show that among those who wrote to the military prosecutor's office in 1955 on behalf of Meyerhold's rehabilitation was the film director Grigorii Aleksandrov, who described him as an innovator, a combative revolutionary who 'got carried away by form' yet influenced Eisenstein and Vertov as well as producing Mayakovsky's plays. The three members of the celebrated Kukryniksy Brigade of painters, M. Kuprianov, P. Krylov, and N. Sokolov, wrote an undated (1955) letter to the military tribunal, describing themselves as proven opponents of formalism, and recalling how in 1929 they had been invited by Mayakovsky to design the sets for *The Bedbug*; each sketch had been approved by the playwright and Meyerhold, the director, who did not impose any formalistic requirements.

On 26 November 1955 the military council of the Supreme Court dropped charges and closed the file on the ground that 'Beria and his henchmen' had fabricated the case against Meyerhold. His Party membership was restored the same day. Even so, his creative development had been 'full of contradictions and ideological mistakes'. He had been guilty of formalism and 'pseudo-innovation'; of a nihilistic disregard for the 'classical heritage'.[64]

A special commission was set up to publish verbatim reports of Meyerhold's working practices during rehearsals and his polemics. The director Manfred Wekwerth, visiting Moscow with the Berliner Ensemble in 1957, reported that the grip of the Stanislavsky style and of the Moscow Art Theatre had recently been relaxed, allowing a renewed interest in the productions of Meyerhold, Aleksandr Tairov, and the young Eisenstein—in short, the suppressed expressionist heritage.[65] The revised Soviet Party line on Meyerhold was conveyed in *Teatr* (no. 3, 1957)—'He was nevertheless a complex personality, subject to decadent bourgeois influences'—and by the conformist critic Komissarzhevsky. All mention of Meyerhold's grim death was banned: the Soviet was still throttling itself on its own evasions, its vast fear of freedom of information. Meyerhold (according to Komissarzhevsky) had come to the Art Theatre at the turn of the century as a pupil of Stanislavsky's system, but later fell under the retrograde influence of symbolism and the 'vague abstractions of decadent art'. Despite his caustic satirical shows after the Revolution and his work with Mayakovsky, 'Meyerhold was guilty of many grave and dangerous errors', including exceedingly free interpretations of such classical masterpieces as Ostrovsky's *Forest* and Gogol's *The Inspector-General*. Komissarzhevsky did not mention Meyerhold's arrest or any political factor; he merely 'left the stage at a time of great emotional strain, when the audience cooled to this theatre, and he himself sought new, and possibly fruitful paths'.[66] No such mendacity could deceive the USIA's *Problems of Communism*, where Jürgen Rühle quoted Meyerhold at the First Congress of Soviet Theatrical Directors, Moscow, 1939, 'just a few days before his arrest':

...I prefer to be considered a formalist, I, for one, find the work in our theatres at present pitiful and terrifying...This pitiful and sterile something that aspires to the title of socialist realism has nothing in common with art...No longer can one identify the creative signature of the Mali Theatre, of the Vakhtangov Theater, of the Kamerni Theatre, or of the Moscow Art Theatre... In your effort to eradicate formalism, you have destroyed art.[67]

'This speech', added Rühle, 'cost Meyerhold his freedom and his life.' Meyerhold's fate became virtually the *cause célèbre* for Western critics sensing Moscow's growing vulnerability to the uncontrollable fallout from Khrushchev's revelations at the 20th Party Congress.[68]

And what of Vladimir Mayakovsky's subversive plays? The *enfant terrible* of Bolshevik poetry and dramaturgy had, famously, committed suicide in 1930 at the age of 37. Although a heroic-romantic statue was later erected in Mayakovsky Square, Moscow, the flamboyant poet was clearly an awkward customer for the stolid Stalinist literary bureaucracy to swallow; this being so, Western criticism, following the familiar pattern, embraced the iconoclastic, bourgeois-baiting Red poet, adoring *le couteau entre ses dents*.[69]

The first revival of Mayakovsky's plays in the USSR did not come until after Stalin's death, when the Pushkin Regional Dramatic Theatre made a move in the city of Pskov. *Literaturnaia gazeta* (24 December 1953) commented: 'The sharp, satirical sting of [Mayakovsky's] dramatic works was completely incompatible with these completely conflictless themes, those literally pre-digested plays, which at one time filled our repertoire.' Shortly thereafter the Moscow Theatre of Satire's production of *Bania* (*The Bathhouse*, 1930)[70] opened, using unexpected and startling stage effects, buffoonery, magic, pyrotechnic displays. Valentin Pluchek, who had acted under Meyerhold, directed revivals of *The Bathhouse* in 1953 and *The Bedbug* in 1955. When Brecht visited Moscow in that year he saw *The Bathhouse* at the Satire Theatre and was impressed by 'alienation effects everywhere'.[71] The principal satirized character of the earlier comedy *Klop* (*The Bedbug*, 1928) is Prisypkin, ex-factory worker and ex-Party member, who contracts a 'bourgeois-red marriage' with Elzevira Renaissance, the daughter of the owner of a private hairdressing salon. Part 1 of the comedy ends with a fire which breaks out during the wedding ceremony. Part 2 transports us fifty years into the future. The frozen body of Prisypkin is discovered and resuscitated by the Future Generation. All attempts to make a man of this philistine fail. After many mishaps, including an epidemic of kow-towing which affects even the dogs, so that 'they no longer bark or frisk, and only stand on their hind legs', he is locked up and exhibited at the zoo as *homo philistinis vulgis*.

Mayakovsky explained that he had called his next play *The Bathhouse* because it scrubbed and ironed out bureaucrats. The positive idea of innovation is represented by a group of worker-enthusiasts whose moving spirit is the inventor of the time-machine, Chudakov, and his devoted supporters, the Komsomol member Velocipedkin and three workers. Inertia and stagnation are represented by the philistine bureaucrats and their flunkeys. Whereas in *The Bedbug* the negative character is transported to 1979, in *The Bathhouse* a delegate of the future, the Phosphorescent Woman of 2030, appears in the present to applaud Chudakov and his comrades. According to the Soviet commentator Rostotsky, for Mayakovsky, unlike the petty-bourgeois H. G. Wells, the time machine was 'a concrete symbol of the all-conquering labour of those who are building a new life of the working class'. (Rostotsky did not mention the suppression of the plays after Mayakovsky's suicide, merely that they were 'not always well staged'.)

Moscow was now laying claim to the heritage of the expressionist avant-garde. In the Satire Theatre's deliberately anachronistic production of *The Bathhouse*, 'documentary' photography showed events long after Mayakovsky's death, including the first tractor produced in Stalingrad, the first Metro station, battles of the Great Patriotic War, and victory salutes.[72] A second stage enthroned the bureaucrat high above the ground where the inventor and his worker friends are trying in vain to push past the bureaucrat's secretary. Constructivist staircases joined the two levels. The time machine was represented by coloured lights and shadows projected on a transparent screen.[73] In short, this was 'Meyerhold without Meyerhold'.

The Mayakovsky revival in Moscow irritated some Western commentators. In *Problems of Communism*, Leo Laufer complained that a good part of Act 3 of *Bedbug* was missing from the revival, including satire on the banality, servility, and bureaucratic dictatorship in the Soviet theatre. 'Not one Soviet critic has dared to cut through the web of triteness and falsification, so carefully woven and rewoven in the course of two decades . . .'[74] The 1964 Anchor Books edition of *A History of Soviet Literature 1917–1964*, by Vera Alexandrova, a Russian émigré critic, gave a distorted impression of recent Soviet attitudes to Mayakovsky: 'All the textbooks on the history of Soviet literature . . . draw a line at *The Bedbug* and *The Bathhouse*.' The same assertion is repeated a page later, without a mention of the Mayakovsky productions post-Stalin.[75]

The memoirs of the veteran theatre director N. V. Petrov came out in 1960, three years before Alexandrova's book first appeared in America. At the Moscow Satire Theatre, and also in Leningrad, Petrov had recently directed a show called *Oni znali Maiakovskogo* (*They Knew Mayakovsky*), with designs by Tyshler and music by Rodion Shchedrin. Represented as a dramatic personality for the first time on the Soviet stage, Mayakovsky was played by the great actor Nikolai Cherkasov, famous for his portrayal of Alexander Nevsky and Ivan the Terrible in Eisenstein's films.[76] In Petrov's memoir Mayakovsky takes his place in a pantheon of Authorities or Guides, alongside Vladimir Nemirovich-Danchenko and Konstantin Stanislavsky, whose indispensable wisdom is anchored in quotations of resounding banality. All orthodoxies had to be synthesized, reconciled.[77] All three of Petrov's chosen Authorities are found grappling with the problems of reflecting daily life on stage while avoiding the naturalism denounced by Mayakovsky: 'the dead-mirror reflection of reality.'[78] The passage from Petrov below gives an idea of the extraordinary circularity and abstractness of Soviet cultural rhetoric:

And if we recall that the essence of 'spectacle-ness' (*zrelishchnost'*) and 'theatricality' (*teatral'nost'*) and 'particular-ness' (*osobennost'*), which are not to be found in life itself, carry within themselves not only aesthetic implications, but also profoundly philosophical ones, it becomes clear to us that all these questions above all affect our world-view.

Petrov quoted Mayakovsky's warning against verbosity but failed to heed it. Strident claims to superiority reflect the underlying anxiety: 'Our [theatre] art is the most advanced, deeply tendentious, fired by Marxist-Leninist ideology, leading humanity to the building of communism—and thereby making us, the Soviet artists, ceaselessly happy and proud.'[79]

❀ ❀ ❀

In 1954 the Comédie française had set foot on Russian soil for the first time since the Revolution. On 15 April Malenkov and other Soviet leaders visited the Vakhtangov Theatre to toast the French company after a performance of Molière's *Le Bourgeois Gentilhomme*.[80] The *New York Times* (16 April) counted twenty-two curtain calls. Fifteen thousand tickets were available for thirteen performances, but a ticket was almost impossible to obtain. Cinemas projected televised viewings of the performances to an estimated 5 million people. At Moscow's oldest theatre, the Mali, the company performed a short programme, 'Hommage à Molière'. 'There were queues for weeks at the Mali Theater box office', reported Harrison Salisbury. 'People gave up their jobs to queue for tickets . . . Taxi drivers who spoke no French and who had never heard of Molière discussed the Gallic visitors with enthusiasm.' All the papers reported ecstatic receptions. Robert Kemp, of *Le Monde*, described crowds outside the stage doors, offering greetings in simple French: '*Amour.*

Nous vous aimons...Aimez nos petits enfants...Revenez vite.' (Knowledge of the French language was, however, at a low ebb due to the post-war emphasis on English-language training.) Taking Kemp to be one of the actors, young girls waiting outside the hotel urged him to visit the school where they learned French. But when he passed this on to his official guides, the school-girls' initiative was rejected as out of order. '*Hélas*! I'm still sighing about it! The girls had such a happy air about them...They went away dancing, their little blond plaits bouncing on their frail necks.'[81]

Of Jean Yonnel's performance as Tartuffe, K. A. Zubov, chief stage director of the Mali, commented: 'He painted a graphic picture of a ruthless cynic and rascal masquerading as a model of piety. His Tartuffe is sinister rather than comic.' Noting that Molière used to be played in a grotesque style, with exaggeration and hyperbole, Zubov welcomed the more realistic emphasis. Louis Seigneur was brilliant in *Le Bourgeois Gentilhomme*, likewise André Falcon in Corneille's *Le Cid*, but here Zubov voiced polite reservations: despite superb technique, the production was 'a bit high-flown and declamatory'. By contrast, not the least bit theatrical, indeed highly realistic, rooted in the present-day provincial life of a petit-bourgeois family, was Jules Renard's modern play *Poil de carotte* (*Carrot Hair*), which fully absorbed the Soviet audience, every nuance and emotion.[82]

Meanwhile, on 30 April, the Soviet cargo ship *General Bagramian* put into Le Havre to unload 25 tons of scenery for the Bolshoi Ballet's imminent, but doomed, reciprocal visit to France (see pp. 471–2).

Peter Brook's production of *Hamlet* for the Shakespeare Memorial Theatre in December 1955 marked the first visit of a British theatre company since the Revolution—Paul Scofield played Hamlet, with Alec Clunes as Claudius. According to Smeliansky, the Brook–Scofield production 'stunned Moscow's theatre world...This was one of those productions that made an indelible impression on all who were to decide the course of Russian theatre for decades to come.'[83] Although Shakespeare was much translated, profoundly studied, and deeply revered in Russia, the bard's recent experiences in Stalin's 'Denmark' were more problematical than was generally understood in the West. In 1956 Boris Pasternak told Isaiah Berlin how the actor Livanov was to have performed in and produced Pasternak's adaptation of *Hamlet*. At a Kremlin reception the actor asked Stalin: 'Iosif Vissarionovich, how should one play *Hamlet*?' Stalin at first replied that he was no expert on theatrical matters, then added, '*Hamlet* is a decadent play and should not be performed at all'. Rehearsals were at once broken off and there was no performance of *Hamlet* until after Stalin's death.[84] With characteristic mordancy Dmitri Shostakovich later reflected:

The point is that in those days *Hamlet* was banned by the censors...In general our theatre has had trouble with Shakespeare, particularly with *Hamlet* and *Macbeth*. Stalin could stand neither of these plays...Shakespeare was a seer—man stalks power, walking knee-deep in blood. And he was so naïve, Shakespeare. Pangs of conscience and guilt and all that. *What* guilty conscience? Without issuing any formal directive, Stalin had let it be known that rehearsals of *Hamlet* at the Moscow Art Theatre were to discontinue...And *King Lear*? Everyone knows that our best Lear was Mikhoels in the Jewish Theatre and everyone his fate. A terrible fate. And what about the fate of our best translator of Shakespeare—Pasternak?...No, it's better not to become involved with Shakespeare. Only careless people would take on such a losing proposition. That Shakespeare is highly explosive.[85]

The Shakespeare Memorial Theatre returned in December 1958 with a wider repertoire: *Hamlet, Romeo and Juliet, Twelfth Night*.[86] Peter Hall, director-elect, reported that in Leningrad an audience of 2,500 gathered in the Palace of Culture of Co-operative Workers to see *Romeo and Juliet*. 'At the end they surged over the wooden seats to clap, wave, cheer and cry.' Praise came from professors and students of English for the fluidity and speed of Glen Byam Shaw's production, and the performances of Dorothy Tutin and Richard Johnson as the young lovers.[87] This is not say that the Soviet and English approaches to performing Shakespeare were in complete harmony. Faubion Bowers, critical of the Mayakovsky Theatre's current production of *Hamlet*, commented: 'The Russians are trying to maintain the grand classicism of turgid acting, the fashions and affectations of half a century ago. We [in the West] are trying to run away from them as fast as we can...It seems strange that the USSR, the country which extolled the word 'progressive', should continue to be so retrogressive in its attitude to its theatrical god, Shakespeare.'

The Soviet view, naturally, was rather different. Invited by the *Observer* to give his impressions of English theatre in 1958, Aleksandr Solodovnikov, director of the Moscow Art Theatre, was uncomplimentary: 'With us, Shakespeare is acted with all the actor's being, to the very tips of his fingers...In England those present remain majestically unmoved...The passionate and ardent Shakespeare drama suddenly turns into a set of wax figures.'[88] Certainly the Russians were prodigious Shakespeareans. A country-wide Shakespeare conference gathered annually in Moscow. '*Hamlet* (in two theatres), *Macbeth, Othello, King Lear, Romeo and Juliet, The Taming of the Shrew, Twelfth Night, The Merry Wives of Windsor*, and *The Winter's Tale* are currently featured on the Moscow stage', wrote Komissarzhevsky, referring to the years 1957–9.[89] Nor were Shakespeare productions necessarily 'conventional'. Komissarzhevsky described Yury Zavadsky's production of *The Merry Wives*

of Windsor at the Mossoviet Theatre: 'The merry atmosphere of the Elizabethan fairs continues also during the intermissions, when clowns appear in
radiant parodies of Falstaff . . . When we return to our seats we see a representative of the theatre, actor Konsovsky, in modern garb . . . a man of 1958,
[who] comments on the behaviour of the heroes of this ancient comedy. He
intervenes in the act and throws witty remarks at the characters. Sometimes
he channels the turbulent flow of the play into a lyrical or philosophical
vein . . .'[90]

It was during the Shakespeare Memorial Theatre tour in the cold winter of
1958[91] that an event occurred later immortalized in a play by Alan Bennett,
Secret Spies. The British diplomat, old Etonian, and Soviet agent Guy Burgess,
who had fled to Russia in 1951, turned up in Michael Redgrave's dressing
room, 'his eyes red with tears and his voice only just in control'. Redgrave
quoted him as saying: 'I suppose it's partly because I haven't heard this
glorious stuff in English for years but, believe me, this is the most wonderful
thing that could have happened.'

The Moscow Art Theatre, meanwhile, brought Chekhov's *The Cherry Orchard* to London in May 1958.[92] The *Manchester Guardian* (12 May) prefaced the
occasion with a remarkable editorial:

Here is a theatrical company, rigidly chained to the wheel of Communist orthodoxy,
whose every decision is subject to the dictation of party policy, triumphantly
interpreting the inspiration of classical drama . . . proving to the world that good
theatre can prosper in even the most tyrannical of states. Sputnik shattered our
illusions about science and Communism: clearly rigid political orthodoxy does not
stifle free inquiry in the laboratory. Apparently the same is also true in the theatre.[93]

But 'hatred and contempt for Communism' remained legitimate, added the
editorial. Very much in agreement was the émigré critic N. A. Gorchakov,
whose *The Theater in Soviet Russia* (1958) amounted to a passionate indictment of the whole Soviet theatrical scene since the eclipse of Meyerhold.[94]
Reviewing the book in her customary measured tone, Bertha Malnick
(Reader in Russian Studies at SSEES, University of London), contrasted
Gorchakov's 'indictment' and 'obituary' with the renaissance reported by a
recent (1957) publication from Iskusstvo in Moscow, *Spektakli etikh let (Plays
of These Years)*, 'these years' being 1953–6.

Gorchakov fitted the pattern of Western criticism in all cultural fields,
praising the innovatory experiments of the revolutionary years—Meyerhold's 'constructivism and biomechanics', Tairov's 'visible music', Vakhtangov's 'synthesis of the "romantic and the realistic"', in short, 'a great
period of innovation . . . unparalleled in the history of the international

stage'—then lamenting the philistine 'propagandist drivel' prevailing thereafter. Bertha Malnick justifiably asked of Gorchakov why he eulogized
productions by Meyerhold or Tairov of (say) Ostrovsky which were far from
what the playwright himself had in mind—'manhandling the classics'—and
which tended to abstract the drama from its social setting, while condemning Nemirovich-Danchenko, one of the lions of Soviet theatrical orthodoxy,
for turning Tolstoy 'from a philosopher to a vulgar sociologist'.

Malnick was a persuasive and well informed proponent of the 'internal-
ist' defence of Soviet culture. 'Is the power of the box-office greater or
less than that of a *Glaviskusstv* [arts boss]? Does money talk any less forcibly
than Marxism?' Did not the Western box office also produce standard-
izations and stereotypes? 'It is obviously just as easy to make a bad play
of *No Orchids for Miss B* as it is to write a hollow epic of *More Laurels
for Comrade S.*' Her classic fellow-travelling comment duly arrives: '... can
we comfort ourselves with a "freedom" which all too often takes the line
of least resistance to the lowest common denominators in human nature? ...
If the Soviet theatre and cinema has made its own mistakes in trying
to control content it has at least avoided deliberate smut and cultivated
"horror".'[95]

⊞ ⊞ ⊞

The challenge facing Soviet theatre in the 1960s had much to do with
Western theatre's headlong gallop into avant-garde meta-theatre, Brechtian
alienation, the theatre of the absurd, 'poor theatre', street theatre, happen-
ings, and improvisation—a large shift from playwrights' theatre (the text)
to directors' theatre. Jürgen Rühle, who had recently emigrated from East to
West Germany, offered a significant insight: 'The fact that the trend toward
the "theatrical theater" is now dominant in the whole Western world points
to the conclusion that this dramatic conception represents the legitimate
form of theatrical expression in contemporary democratic society.'[96]

Gradually a style developed in avant-garde Soviet theatres whose main
features are defined by Anatoly Smeliansky as rationalism, didacticism, clarity, and simplicity: 'By the late 1960s and 1970s, Soviet audiences were
coming to the theatre to hear "truths" unavailable in the press or other
media. The metaphoric *mise-en-scène*, Aesopic dialogue and actors' asides
were avidly sought and caught by an alert public.'[97] Yet this was also true
in Western capitals and university theatres. Young audiences were univer-
sally demanding and getting an anti-establishment theatre which jettisoned
the conventions of the realist tradition. Cold war culture was rapidly dissolving under the impact of a New Left and Soviet dissident attitudes. On

Mayakovsky Square were to be found the Theatre of Satire, the Moscow Council Theatre, the Sovremennik, Obraztsov's Puppet Theatre, and the Tchaikovsky Concert Hall. As the playwright Viktor Rozov reported, young Muscovites so ardently longed to see good theatre that they would beg for tickets to anything as one emerged from the Metro.[98]

Yet the established press, East and West, continued lifelong habits of treating iconoclasm and scathing satire from the far side of the Iron Curtain as symptoms of retreat, of defeat, of confirmation of the evils depicted—rather than as evidence of a living theatre. Either way, you couldn't win. 'New Moscow Play Spotlights Conflict with Bureaucracy. Call For Fresh Approach Applauded', announced *The Times* (20 January 1966) over a report from 'Monitor' in Moscow about *Shooting a Film* (*Snimatsia Kino*), a play by Aleksandr Radzinsky. This drama addressed 'the attitudes and reactions of a film director, a party official, a critic and the public to the decision to discontinue production work on a film thought to be socially and even politically risky'. The older generation in Radzinsky's play is represented by the head of the studio who, recalling that he began life as a historian under Stalin, delivers a deadpan indictment of the Party line:

My first work was about Shamil [a nineteenth-century Caucasian resistance leader]...But then attitudes changed...and at the end of the thirties he became an agent of imperialism. So I recognized my mistake. Then during the war he [Shamil] once again became the liberation movement. So I recognized that I was wrong in recognizing my mistake. Then in 1949 he once again became an agent and I recognized that I was wrong that I recognized I was wrong. I was wrong so often that it seemed to me that I was a mistake. But later, through habit, I recognized even this as a mistake and therefore I myself am not a mistake.

'Soviet producer has support of actors against faceless critics.' By now, at the start of the long Brezhnev era, even the West European Communist press was openly critical of neo-Stalinist rearguard actions. In the *Morning Star*[99] (28 June 1966), Peter Tempest reported: 'At an eight-hour trade union meeting, actors at Moscow's Satire Theatre have rebuffed an attempt to sack Valentin Pluchek, producer of Tvardovsky's anti-Stalinist play, *Tyorkin in the Hereafter.*' *The Times* reported (21 June 1968) that Ostrovsky's *A Lucrative Post* (1857) was drawing capacity audiences at Moscow's Satire Theatre 'because of its deliberately [*sic!*] topical message': 'A ripple of identification moves the audience when Yusov, the anti-intellectual chief clerk in a Tsarist office, talks about his pleasure in suppressing "those modern educated ones" and his preference for promoting drop-outs and nonentities because they always tend to remain grateful to him.'

Yuri Lyubimov had been re-establishing the radical expressionist tradition snuffed out in the Stalin purges, and drawing Soviet theatre back into the international culture.[100] In 1963 he staged Brecht's *The Good Person of Setzuan* with his third-year students at the Vakhtangov Institute, in a sharp, lively, ironic production, causing a furore. The audience went wild and the Institute's director cancelled further performances. From this student production sprang the Taganka Theatre Company, established in April 1964 in an old, dying theatre on Taganka Square. The building was duly renovated and portraits of Brecht, Vakhtangov, Meyerhold, and Stanislavsky (the latter on the insistence of the district Party committee) were hung in the foyer. Lyubimov, who initially insisted on bringing with him the actors he had trained at the Vakhtangov, was to remain precariously in charge for twenty years, reviving and developing the expressionist traditions of Tairov and Meyerhold. In *Ten Days that Shook the World* (1965), adapted from John Reed's celebrated account of the 1917 Revolution, Lyubimov used expressionistic alienation devices reminiscent of the American Federal Theater Project's Living Newspaper in the 1930s, Brecht,[101] and above all Meyerhold. The imprisonment of revolutionaries was represented by the prisoners holding their arms in the form of a rectangle round their faces, which were lit by a spot, creating the impression of heads behind bars.[102] Harrison Salisbury praised *Ten Days* and Lyubimov's collage production about Mayakovsky, *Poslushaite!* (*Listen!*)—portraying the conflict between 'the free, vital artist, and the sterile forces of banality and party bureaucracy. More and more it becomes apparent why its public première was long delayed.'[103] Oskar Rabin, a leading spirit among dissident artists, regarded the Taganka Theatre under Lyubimov as the most popular in Moscow. The two-hundredth performance at the Taganka of Voznesensky's poetic collection *Antimiry* (*Antiworlds*) took place on 2 July 1967. Returning from the United States, the poet had come under what Harrison Salisbury called 'something more than the usual cavilling by the party hacks. In part it reflected the courage and candor of the letter Voznesensky had sent to the Writers' Union supporting Solzhenitsyn in his plea for abolition of censorship.'[104] The massive artistic censorship exercised after 1968 inflicted a crushing blow on theatrical activity.

In March 1969 Minister of Culture Ekaterina Furtseva arrived with her retinue at the Taganka to inspect a preview of Boris Mozhayev's *The Man Alive*, a new play about a farmworker, Kuzhkin, who battles to scrape a living for his family against the corruption of the local party and the collective farm. In a happy ending his appeal to higher authority is heard and heeded. The critic John Elsom describes Furtseva's visit:

The theatre was cold and empty. Madame Furtseva sat at the back, wearing a fur coat, with her officials . . . When it was over Mme Furtseva turned to Boris Mozhayev and said, 'I suppose you think this is brave. It is not bravery. It is anti-Soviet. It is disgusting.' Mozhayev replied, 'I have written a comedy about our bad collective farms . . . ' 'Is this a comedy?' said Mme Furtseva. 'It is a tragedy. People will come out and ask, "Is this what we have built our revolution for?" The head of the collective farm is an alcoholic, the chief of the team is an alcoholic, the chairman of the executive is a rascal! And you, comrade Lyubimov, we can see in which direction you are taking your collective!' 'Don't frighten me,' said Lyubimov. 'I have been thrown out of this job many times and many respected people have defended me, many academicians!' 'I am the one in this country,' said Mme Furtseva, 'who is responsible for art in this country, not any academician. And nobody will support you.' A leading poet, Andrei Voznesensky, said quietly, 'I liked it. I have seen four rehearsals and it is deeply Russian and not anti-party, whatever party officials may think.' He was ruled out of order.[105] Vladekin from the Ministry's Commission of Acceptance summed up: 'Today's performance,' he said to Lyubimov, 'is an apotheosis of all your bad tendencies.'

The conversation then became uglier still, with mention of Solzhenitsyn's *One Day in the Life of Ivan Denisovich*, a recent *Pravda* attack on *Novy mir*, and Mme Furtseva's conclusion: 'From such things, the events in Prague began . . . ' According to another account, by Smeliansky, Furtseva clapped her bediamoned hands at the point where the poor angel was flying about, stopped the rehearsal, and shouted: 'Does this theatre have a Party cell in it, or doesn't it?' She called to individual actors and asked whether they weren't ashamed to be taking part in 'this disgraceful exhibition', then she bustled out, dropping her astrakhan coat, which one of her retinue picked up. The show was doomed.[106] Twenty-one years later Lyubimov revived *The Man Alive* when he returned from emigration—a major theatrical occasion full of emotion. But the Furtseva incident occurred in 1969, well before Yuri Lyubimov's long reign at the Taganka came to an end. Smeliansky recalls that the caustic songs of the widely adored Vladimir Vysotsky, a leading actor, bard, and iconoclast at Lyubimov's theatre, went unpublished and were officially non-existent, 'yet most of the populace knew them by heart, learning them from *magnitizdat*, bootleg tape recordings'.[107] (Lyubimov's show in honour of Vysotsky, who died of drug abuse at the age of 42 in 1980 during the Moscow Olympics, was banned.)

Lyubimov visited Paris in 1978, unveiling productions of Gorky's *The Mother*, *Hamlet*, and John Reed's *Ten Days*[108] at the Palais de Chaillot, but the Russians would not allow him to stage Tchaikovsky's *The Queen of Spades* (*La Dame de pique*) at the Paris Opéra. Two years later he was invited to direct Mussorgsky's *Boris Godunov* at the Opéra but was refused permission to leave the Soviet Union—ironically the job was taken by Joseph Losey, once an exile from American persecution. In 1983, now 65, Lyubimov visited England (with his Hungarian wife and 4-year–old son) to stage *Crime and Punishment* at the Lyric Theatre, Hammersmith, where he stressed Dostoyevsky's Christian message and his own complete repudiation of Raskolnikov's apology for murder which (he told *The Times*) had not gone down well with 'Russian schoolteachers'. This was said in the course of an inflammatory interview with Bryan Appleyard, deputy arts editor of *The Times* (5 September): 'His voice rises in anguish as he speaks of his humiliations at the hands of the *chinovniki*.' Lyubimov complained that three of his recent productions had been banned; thoroughly humiliated, he could no longer count on the personal support of General Secretary Yuri Andropov, now shackled to a kidney machine, leaving the hard-liner Konstantin Chernenko in charge, and giving full support to Minister of Culture Piotr Demichev. 'They never undertook a serious dialogue with me. They only lecture me', he told Appleyard. In one of the banned productions, Pushkin's *Boris Godunov*, Lyubimov had an actor out of costume address the audience with the same exasperated question that Godunov throws at the complacent masses: 'Why do you remain silent?'

The Times ran the story, day after day,[109] in the old cold war fashion, stressing Lyubimov's 'secret address' in London, and the dangers of kidnap or worse: 'His movements are being monitored by the British authorities.' When Pavel Filatov, an Embassy official, asked Lyubimov to step out on to the balcony of the Lyric Theatre for a private word, Lyubimov refused: 'I was not going to go out there. Anything might have happened.' 'Very well,' Filatov was said to have warned him, 'the crime has been committed, the punishment must follow. We have your telephone number and we will find you.' Lyubimov's little boy was terrified that his parents might be 'stolen'; Lyubimov's wife Katalin lost her job as 'a journalist in Budapest' as soon as the *Times* interview appeared; Appleyard himself had been mistaken by the Lyric cast for an armed MI5 minder; on and on *The Times* ran its hocus-pocus.

Andropov died and Lyubimov was dismissed as artistic director of the Taganka in March 1984, 'for neglecting his duties without good reason'. This was the reason given privately to the Taganka company by Vladim Shadrin, head of Moscow's cultural board, but no public announcement was made; as Dominique Dhombres, correspondent of *Le Monde* (13 March 1984) in Moscow put it, '*tout se passe en coulisse*—the action is in the wings'. She reckoned that the authorities had all along wanted to get rid of Lyubimov: why otherwise allow his wife and son to accompany him to England? Remaining loyal to Lyubimov, the actors of the Taganka protested, then accepted the inevitable: his productions remained prominent in the repertory. Hearing that Anatoly Efros, some fifteen years his junior, was to replace him as director of the Taganka, he described the news as 'incredible', since Efros himself had been dismissed as artistic director of the Komsomol Theatre in 1967, despite protests from the company, following a campaign in *Literaturnaia gazeta* against his 'taste for fashion'. Expelled from the Communist Party after thirty years, Lyubimov called down curses from abroad, described Minister of Culture Demichev as 'an ignorant fool', and Mikhail Zimianin, ideology secretary of the Central Committee, as 'our Goebbels'. It was one of the last histrionic performances of cold war culture, played up to the limit by the Western press, and equalling Lyubimov's own stormy production of *Rigoletto* at the Teatro Communale, Florence, where conductors, baritones, and sopranos flounced out and back again in the great tradition. In July 1984 Lyubimov was stripped of his Soviet citizenship. Working in France, Italy, and England, he went on to direct a remarkable *Hamlet* in London. Returning to Moscow in 1988, in the Gorbachev era, he resumed the directorship of the Taganka after Efros's death, but the company split into two theatres, the actor Gabenko leading the breakaway. The title of Yuri Lyubimov's recent memoirs, *Reminiscences of an Old Chatter-Box* (*Rasskazy starogo trepacha*, 2000), is disarmingly accurate.

The Russian Question:
A Russian Play

Among Soviet dramas of the early cold war, Konstantin Simonov's play *The Russian Question* (*Russkii vopros*) merits a chapter to itself. It was probably unique in confining its dramatis personae to American characters—not a Russian in sight. *The Russian Question* was the cold war play par excellence, promoted and disseminated with Stalin's approval in thirty Soviet theatres. In Germany the Soviet-zone première followed within a month of the opening night in Moscow, despite a storm of American protests, by which time German-language translations were already on sale at Berlin kiosks. Two weeks later the Soviet Embassy in London put out an English translation; news of a Stalin Prize soon followed. Production plans for Mikhail Romm's film of the play were announced almost immediately. At the end of the year, with the play still running, Stalin, Molotov, and Voroshilov appeared in the 'royal box' at the Moscow Art Theatre, the ultimate seal of approval.

The subject of *The Russian Question* was mounting American media hostility towards the USSR. Western 'slander' (*kleveta*) became as routine a component of the Soviet polemical vocabulary as the self-description of Soviet morality and Soviet man as 'lofty' (*vozvyshennyi*). Simonov's play was accompanied by a concerted campaign in the Soviet press against Western lies and distortions.

Only 30 years old when he visited the United States in February 1946, Konstantin Mikhailovich Simonov was already famous as a war reporter and novelist, like his more senior and cosmopolitan travelling companion Ilya Ehrenburg, friend of Picasso and acquaintance of the French surrealists. Simonov had achieved popularity during the war with his dispatches from the front, patriotic poems, and novel on the siege of Stalingrad, *Days and Nights* (1945). The Old Vic had presented his play *The Russians* in 1942, when he was only 26. His poem 'Wait for Me' (*Zhdi menia*) was recited like a prayer by millions during the war. The Russian-born British scholar Isaiah Berlin, visiting the USSR in the closing months of 1945, shortly before Simonov flew to America, noted that young Simonov 'has poured out a flood of work of inferior quality but impeccably orthodox sentiment, acclaiming the right type of Soviet hero, brave, puritanical, simple, noble, altruistic, entirely devoted to the service of his country'.[1]

Ehrenburg (representing *Izvestiia*), Simonov (*Krasnaia zvezda*), and Major-General Mikhail Galaktionov (military editor of *Pravda*), arrived in Washington as guests of the American Society of Newspaper Editors, travelling via Paris in the private plane of Lt.-Gen. Walter Bedell Smith, US ambassador to the USSR. Good-will, therefore, was the presiding spirit. On 19 April 300 of the host editors waited patiently for the Soviet guests to turn up. Ehrenburg was the first to speak (through an interpreter). Stressing that the struggle against fascism was not over, he complained of some 'malicious slanders' in the American press. Russia was a 'nice country' and the Russians liked it. Simonov told the gathering that his speech had been written on the back of a cigarette box. He didn't want his 7-year-old son to live through the horrors he had witnessed. It had taken Hitler 500 pages of *Mein Kampf* to describe the coming conquest of Russia, yet Soviet troops had responded with only two words, 'To Berlin'.[2]

The following day, at a forum meeting of the American editors, the three Russians were pressed on freer access for foreign correspondents wishing to visit the USSR. Ehrenburg, parrying and prevaricating, replied that he was not personally responsible for visa policy but would raise the matter when he got back to Moscow. If Simonov said anything it was not reported in the *New York Times*, but he certainly heard the full exchange—yet when his fictional newspaper tycoon MacPherson, in *The Russian Question*, decides to send the journalist Harry Smith to Russia, he says casually (and unrealistically), 'You'll fly in two weeks', assuming not only that a visa will be granted but that Smith will get it at once. According to an angry Harrison E. Salisbury, Ehrenburg and Simonov evaded all such questions as 'Why is it so difficult for American correspondents to be admitted to Russia?' Salisbury added that Simonov came away and wrote a play about an American correspondent who was able to tour the USSR without the visa issue even being raised.

Assistant Secretary of State William Benton now invited each of the visiting Soviet writers to travel around the United States and to choose his own itinerary. Simonov began by visiting West Virginia.

The presence of the three Russians raised American awareness of what was at stake. On 24 April a *New York Times* editorial pointed to an article in the monthly magazine *Smena*, published by *Pravda*, about the current strike-wave in America. The period of Ehrenburg's and Simonov's visit was one of massive labour unrest on the railways and in the mines, where 75,000 hard-coal miners went on strike.[3] For the *New York Times* this was a highly sensitive issue; the visiting Russians were observing at close quarters what might be termed their own dream scenario of capitalism in crisis; some drily sardonic editorial remarks followed about American workers who became 'unemployed by their own choice under the guidance of leaders whom they elected by democratic process'. But we find only the most fleeting of allusions to industrial unrest in *The Russian Question*.

At a luncheon given by the Overseas Press Club of America in the Lotos Club building, 110 West 57th Street, questions were fired about censorship of foreign correspondents' reports from Russia; Ehrenburg again promised to raise the matter, adding sharply that American journalists suffered from 'a feeling of superiority toward other people'. On 19 May the *New York Times* published a large, posed photograph of the three visitors, Simonov carrying a cane walking-stick and smiling across at Ehrenburg. Robert van Gelder described Simonov as inexhaustibly healthy, well built, ruddy features 'chunkily filled out'. Simonov told him that Hemingway and Steinbeck were among his favourite American authors, and promised that more translations of younger Americans would follow soon.[4]

On 29 May the visitors attended a rally of 20,000 people at Madison Square Garden, sponsored by the American Council of American–Soviet Friendship, and addressed by Andrei Gromyko, then Soviet representative to the UN, and by some of America's leading fellow-travellers.[5] Peace and friendship were the cardinal themes of the evening, and no doubt made an impression on Simonov. No echo of the venue is found in his play, but it provides a model (of sorts) for the final moments of Mikhail Romm's film version. The *New York Times* (31 May) reacted sharply to the Madison Square Garden rally, advising the three Russians to take note of a free press at work—particularly the widespread reporting of Gromyko's adverse comments and the fact that each of them, Ehrenburg, Simonov, and Galaktionov, had been allowed to see whatever interested him, 'including our worst as well as our best'. Did Ehrenburg convey 'our best as well as our worst' in his reports to Moscow? An intensely 'European' and cosmopolitan figure—he once tried to have Camembert cheese manufactured in a Moscow dairy according to the Norman recipe—he was clearly discomforted by the speed and newness of American civilization. 'There is much that is childish in Americans. An American likes everything new. . . He likes noise.' Ehrenburg complained of American press coverage of Soviet achievements: 'Russia is hidden from America by a smoke-screen of lies and this screen is the creation of many American newspapers.'

Writing in *Izvestiia* (9 July), he described the American press as: 'A gigantic lie, a swarming banality, a skyscraper of stupidity. Americans are proud of the right of their papers to sell themselves to Morgan and Coca Cola, to Standard Oil and Paramount.' Most of this was reported in the American press.

Simonov, by contrast, did not attract much American attention until the autumn, when he published a piece in *Pravda* (22 November) calling for an 'active and relentless ideological offensive' in the name of Communism, 'the only correct road for humanity'. Playwrights, producers, and actors, he announced, must be politicians; they must stress the superiority of Soviet people. Addressing the All-Union Conference of Playwrights and Theatre Workers, Simonov mixed platitude—'Am I in the ranks? Am I a fighter? Are my countrymen finding the struggle easier because of my help?'—with conformist abasement towards the Party. Like other leading intellectuals of the time, he knew that duty obliged him to echo Party criticisms of his colleagues (Korneichuk and Leonov) and of himself. Here he refers to himself with almost Chinese self-flagellation: 'Simonov is mentioned, for in his play *The Russians* he failed to elevate his concept of patriotism beyond a concept of mere Russian patriotism, to a concept of Soviet patriotism.' An ideological war on a world scale was now being waged, he continued, 'with unexampled ferocity'. It was a war that dramatists must fight without faltering, for Communism.[6] Clearly he was preparing the ground for his new play, written since his visit to the United States, *The Russian Question*.

That Simonov came away from America with personal grievances and grudges is evident from the early scenes of *The Russian Question*. The brash directness of the questioning by the American Society of Newspaper Editors which he had suffered—'What would happen to you gentlemen in case you wrote an editorial advocating the removal of Marshal Stalin?'—left all but the most case-hardened Soviet visitors seething. Where a correspondent of *Le Monde* or the London *Times* might shy away from asking such questions as almost indecent, Americans went straight for the obvious, even breaking the Russian social code by which you never take advantage of a guest who has your food in his mouth. In Act I, scene 1 of *The Russian Question*, MacPherson enters his private office and describes a luncheon for visiting Soviet journalists: 'At lunch they replied to a hundred impolite questions of ours with a hundred very very polite jabs.' MacPherson then cynically orders his servile hack, Hardy, to attend the following day's press conference and ask the Russians about rumours that they brought money with them to finance the current American coal strike. Late the following day, in the Press Bar, the paper's foreign editor Preston tells the hero, Harry Smith, what actually happened at the visiting Russians' final press conference:

PRESTON: [They] said they don't look on the greater part of our press as the voice of the American people . . .
SMITH: Not bad.
PRESTON: I rather liked it, too. I'll tear them to pieces for it today, though.

⊞   ⊞   ⊞

The setting[7] of the drama, which has ten characters, all American, is the newspaper empire of the tycoon MacPherson, a 60-year-old tyrant said to be 'owner and editor of a large New York paper and co-owner (*sovladelets*) of thirty-seven other papers'. If the 'owner and editor' sounds improbable, equally unreal is the description given to MacPherson's younger (40) partner in anti-Communist crime, Gould, 'editor and co-owner of a large paper in San Francisco and simultaneously one of the editors of MacPherson's newspaper [singular]'. Gould, we are told, has a slight limp, is coarse (*grubovat*), and 'likes to play the man of the people'. He had enjoyed a good war, rising to the rank of colonel in the US Air Force Intelligence, and took to the air only twice; his limp, which he mendaciously attributes to a Japanese sniper's bullet, was incurred in a car accident during a dirty weekend with Jessie. The good guys are progressive journalists struggling to make a living under the harsh tyranny of capitalism: Harry (*Garri*) Smith, currently down to $500 a month, and his friend Bob Murphy, too weak to refuse a job ($200 a week) from a tycoon he loathes, William Randolph Hearst.

In the first scene, Jessie, described as a pretty woman of 33, 'but looks younger', and who has had affairs, including one with Gould,[8] is discussing with him her intention to marry Harry Smith. 'I want to have my house, my children and some happiness of my own. I have had enough of playing the cuckoo.' She adds: 'He will go to Russia.' Here she refers to the central plot of the play, the stratagem by which the newspaper baron MacPherson, assisted by Gould, intends to exploit Smith's recent lack of productivity and financial difficulties (brought about by distress at the vanished prospects for a better world post-war) by offering him a huge sum to go to Russia and write a highly negative report—a report all the more dramatic by contrast to Smith's friendly book written in Russia in 1942. In short, the god that failed. This new report will be published as a book, preceded by serialization in one of MacPherson's newspapers.

The central dramatic thread of the play hinges on the question of literary rights, mainly book rights and newspaper serial rights in Harry Smith's 'The Russian Question', but Simonov makes a dog's dinner of it, failing to understand how these rights are contracted, the difference between primary and subsidiary (first serial) rights, and who provides the advance to the author, while contradicting his own 'rights' scenario(s) throughout the play. One of the play's several other improbabilities is that although Smith's glowing view of Russia shows no sign of having dimmed since the war, at no juncture of the play does MacPherson demand from Smith a guarantee that he will come back from the USSR with the damning indictment required.

Is Harry Smith a Communist or even a fellow-traveller? By no means! When MacPherson explains that he doesn't want Communism in America, Smith agrees: 'I also belong to the ranks of such people. Each to his own. The Russians have their system but we have ours'—*kazhdomu svoe: russkim—ikh stroi, a nam—nash*. What clearer declaration of the Stalinist doctrine of 'socialism in one country'?[9] Gould challenges Smith on whether he has read *The Communist Manifesto* and Lenin's *Imperialism, the Highest Stage of Capitalism*. Smith says he hasn't; no need; the Russians want peace.

As for the burning 'Russian question', Gould comments that the brave defenders of Stalingrad, so admired by Smith in 1942, have now penetrated the heart of Europe and have entered Korea (*vlezli v Korei*), while their pilots are flying over Vienna and Port Arthur. But Smith dismisses as nonsense—*kakaia chepukha*—the idea of the Russians conquering Europe, then America, then Australia, then Antarctica: 'I froze with them at the front near Gzhatsk. I drank vodka with them in the trenches. I saw Russian children who'd been hanged, and even if all you say is true, I can't write that book. Find someone else.'

MacPherson gives Smith three months to write the book for the (in 1946) huge sum of $30,000, more than double a journalist's annual salary, and six times what poor Smith is said to have recently come down to. A quarter is payable in advance on signature. Gould shows Smith an outline of the proposed book, including 'Ten reasons why the Russians want war'. When Smith scoffs, Gould retreats: they may not want war right now, but they will when they are strong enough, and in the meantime he favours a preventive war against world Communism. 'Communists are fanatics and the Russians are fanatics twice over.'[10] Given such clear evidence of what is expected of him, why does Smith accept the assignment and lose no time in marrying Jessie, buying a new house, and filling it with new furniture from the advance payment?

The newspaper's angry foreign editor, Preston, provides some interesting information about his boss MacPherson, while drinking whiskies with Smith:

PRESTON: During the war the boss got greedy, played up to the public, started going left . . . What he wants is extremes, because that's what his big bosses in Wall Street want . . .

SMITH: It's true, but it's nauseating.
PRESTON: Nauseating, but commonplace...

The main sub-plot concerns Smith's old friend Bob Murphy, who works for Hearst, writing whatever rubbish he is told to write. But he's philosophical about it: 'If I employed William Randolph Hearst, I too would make him write what I wanted him to write.'[11] To earn himself some extra money, $1,500, Murphy has agreed to fly on board a prototype of a new-model 'light sporting airplane without any special adaptations', manufactured by a new, 'still not solid', firm, 'Hutchison', the engine by 'Mekstrom', seeking commercial publicity by means of an altitude record with a passenger on board. Smith urges his friend not to take the risk, but Murphy has a sick mother and needs $600 quickly to send her to Rochester for medical treatment.[12] He confesses himself to be a beaten man with a 'mangy soul'.

Act II takes place four months later, in the summer of 1946. Smith is back from Russia, at his ease in his new country house graced by fine furniture, upholstery, and glassware. He is found pacing up and down, dictating to his faithful stenographer Meg Stanley. Russians are not lacking in humour, he is saying, but no one in the USSR smiles when they hear the word 'fascism'. Many Russians had asked him with hurt surprise how Americans could so quickly have forgotten about fascism.[13]

Enter Gould and MacPherson. The latter, the more interesting stage character, recalls how in his young days, although on the verge of bankruptcy, he put $5,000 on long-term deposit to mature on his sixtieth birthday, and how today he found a cheque for $14,230 waiting on his desk—reminding him that he is 60. He's going to throw a party on the proceeds and hopes that his old friend Winston Churchill will attend. He also hopes to get Harry Smith's anti-Soviet book (as he assumes it to be) out before the Congressional elections.

Resolute anti-Communist that he is, MacPherson appears to despise Gould's fanaticism. After all, the Russians destroyed capitalism 'at home,' in their own country (*u sebia doma*), whereas Gould aspires to destroy Communism in their country. When Gould sneers sarcastically, 'You're not intending to enrol in the Communist Party?' (an unlikely remark to MacPherson), the tycoon reminds him that he, Gould, is ruthless and merciless (*besposhchadnyi*) 'like all renegades'. Fifteen years earlier, it transpires, Gould had been a trade unionist leading a strike when he had abruptly reneged, offering MacPherson six articles unmasking the Red agitators. 'If the Communists ever took power in America, you'd be hanged', MacPherson growls—and if a Communist dictatorship were to descend on America:

'You would quickly paint yourself red again and hurry to betray your friends as you did fifteen years ago.'[14]

However improbable this may sound, Simonov is working along a line deeply etched into post-war Soviet consciousness: personal decency and honour and loyalty to the motherland count for as much as class consciousness. This line (by which villains display centuries-old, Shakespearean failings as well as a few specifically Marxist ones) reflected the vastly tutorial, schoolmasterly role of the Party inside the Soviet Union.

MacPherson is a pragmatist rather than a crusader. His aim is a 'minimum programme': keep the Russians under threat for five or six years, then demand three things: free access to their markets; an end to their state monopoly on external trade; and the leasing of important industrial concessions. But they can remain Communists, that's their affair.[15] One should add that numbers, ordinal and cardinal, litter Simonov's text to such an extent that one must conclude that the obsession is Simonov's rather than capitalism's.

At this halfway stage of the play the two proprietors, MacPherson and Gould, are still unaware that Smith is writing a favourable account of his trip to Russia, yet they show no inclination to ask him or he to tell them. They are still arguing about how big the question-mark should be at the end of the book's projected title, 'Do the Russians Want War?'. Harry Smith himself is not a persuasive or particularly attractive character, often terse, tight-lipped, scripted in what Simonov may have imagined to be the Hemingway style. When his friend Bob Murphy asks whether he was disappointed with the Russians, he replies:

SMITH: No.
MURPHY: And they were all splendid fellows, like they were during the war?
SMITH: Still the same. (*Vse takie zhe*).

Simonov particularly relishes the Hemingwayesque bonding of war and masculinity, frequently suggesting that wartime comradeship should remain paramount. Murphy wants to knock down the reptilian journalist Hardy for printing lies about the visiting Soviet journalists whom we heard about earlier: 'I ran into two of these Russian guys he [Hardy] wrote about when I was at the front, on the Elbe. I drank vodka with them. Damn it, they're newspapermen just like me ... Why does he have to finger them (*Zachem on ikh tronul*)? ... can't he find enough dirt without going after old friends, war correspondents? The bastard.'[16]

Conversely, anti-Communist Americans like Gould invariably turn out to be bogus wartime heroes, their medals a sham. Political virtue and bravery are inseparable. The Hemingway tone continues later when Murphy asks his friend Smith—on behalf of all of us seated in the auditorium—how he got involved in this 'hopeless affair' of the book, from which there is no exit.

SMITH: I don't know. Maybe. Maybe I couldn't do anything else. It was stronger than me. In Russia I became ashamed of myself, of you, of all of us, because we fill the whole of America with such poison to chew over breakfast every day. This so-called 'Russian Question' has for some time stopped being simply the Russian question. It's the touchstone on which the entire world now verifies people's honour and honesty. I remembered that I was a man. Yes, yes, a man, not simply an employee of MacPherson.[17]

Smith then talks about his honest old mother, proud to be an American woman in the tradition of Lincoln, not Hearst (and indeed, we later hear that Mother has sent a message of furious scorn when she hears, wrongly, that her Harry is writing an anti-Russian book): 'I decided to write this book even if I was damned for it. Even if only five of my friends read it . . . I've had enough of leaving a monopoly of honour to the Communists.[18] Even if they call me not left enough, to hell with them, they won't dare call me dishonest now.'[19] The key terms, then, are 'honest—man—honour—mother—American—Lincoln'. Nothing about class struggle. The play provides no report of where Smith travelled in Russia during his 1946 trip, whom he spoke to, what he found. Unlike most foreign correspondents, he tells few stories. His rare outbursts of eloquence are like flames erupting from dead embers.

Smith's book is now finished. His happy, domesticated wife Jessie, still in ignorance of its contents, throws a celebration party. Enter Smith in a navy-blue suit, bought for him by Jessie out of the modest $1,000 savings from her time in the army. Jessie twirls him around in front of Meg and Murphy.

Soon afterwards MacPherson, who has read four chapters of Smith's book, confronts him. Smith has written a book about Russia which MacPherson can neither stomach nor publish. The incensed proprietor then embarks upon a long and obsessive diatribe about how much money he has lost, is losing, and will lose as a result of Smith's delinquency, including the advance already paid to Smith, advance publicity costs, the $100,000 profit he had expected to make, plus a further $100,000 in quantifiable loss of prestige. 'And that's not all', he keeps saying. Even the 'political impact' that he had expected the book to make would have had its financial benefits.[20] Whether Simonov's relentless storm of figures and financial details are technically correct is doubtful. American financial culture does not categorize the failure to make an anticipated profit as a 'loss'. More seriously damaging to the play is Simonov's failure to understand the mentality of a wealthy newspaper magnate in the Hearst mould. Simonov insists that for a capitalist tycoon everything boils down to money, to dollars. But in reality a project such as this would not be conceived in financial terms; very wealthy men with monarchical mentalities—like the Hearst-figure in Orson Welles's film *Citizen Kane*—expect to spend their fortunes on their pet political causes. It's the power that Kane loves. For a rich man a newspaper is like a toybox full of firecrackers and man-traps. Even though Congressional elections were due to take place in November 1946—a major Republican victory, as it turned out—MacPherson never mentions the specifics of the mainstream politics he intends to influence, never discusses the use of red-baiting and anti-Soviet sentiment as a weapon against Truman's Democrats. The words 'Republican' and 'Democrat' do not appear. Indeed, they were almost taboo in early Soviet cold war literature; the real struggle was between '*Uoll Strit*' and the workers, the *rabochii klass*; electoral competition between the bourgeois parties was a diversionary charade. A Soviet writer could not describe President Truman (the unworthy successor to the great Roosevelt) as a target for reactionaries. Similarly, Simonov's America is a land where no one is heard to mention Stalin or 'Uncle Joe'; it's simply 'Russia' and 'the Russians'. There is, however, a mention of 'reds':

SMITH: By the way, Meg, have you noticed that more and more often the word 'red' is coming to mean the same thing as 'honest'?

Honest? By keeping silent about the pro-Soviet nature of the book he is writing, Smith has deceived not only MacPherson (and Gould) but also his own, increasingly loving and happy wife Jessie. This should be borne in mind when we come to Soviet critical reactions to the play.

Having threatened Smith with every kind of personal reprisal, MacPherson suggests bringing in a ghost writer to do the job rapidly. Smith will still keep $17,500 from the original promised advance payment of $30,000. MacPherson produces a new contract: 'Sign here.' Smith again refuses.

MACPHERSON: Very well! Things will go extremely badly for you. You will find yourself without work. You will be driven out of everywhere and will have nothing to eat.

But (he continues villainously) when Smith, destitute and desperate, finally crawls back to him on his knees, MacPherson will give him a job as a hack crime reporter. 'Two lines a month on fires and six on thefts', for a pitiful $25 a week, even though Smith is now 39 years old. 'Don't forget, I will help you in your darkest hour', MacPherson exits villainously.[21] Smith, as usual, is virtually silent throughout MacPherson's manic diatribe.

The sixth *kartina* or tableau opens in a bar, with Harry Smith sitting alone. He has the impression that everyone is in a hurry and no one wants to talk to him. Smith is waiting for the veteran publisher Kessler, who not only published his 1942 book about Russia but others as well. (Which makes it odd that Kessler addresses him as 'Mr Smith'.) On arrival, the old, asthmatic Kessler describes the entirely improbable arrangement by which MacPherson had fixed the publishing contract for Smith's book, indemnified Kessler against losses, undertaken to pay for the advertisements, and in return received 50 per cent of the revenue from the book. Yet legally all book rights remain (we are told) with Kessler. Clearly Simonov had got the contractual mechanics of American book publishing seriously wrong.

Harry Smith urges Kessler to go ahead and publish his book, regardless of its contents. 'It will earn you at least $100,000', he says, and Kessler does not dissent. 'What do you care about the contents of the book?' Smith says. 'You're a businessman.'[22] Kessler reveals that during the war he spent $2,000 on relief parcels (*posylki*) for Russia, that his parents were born in Mogilev, and that he therefore feels sympathy for the country. Kessler informs Smith that the previous night MacPherson had come to him and offered to buy all the rights to Smith's 'goddam book'.[23] Kessler refused. This very morning, curtly summoned by MacPherson, he found his own publishing catalogues and advertisements spread out on the tycoon's table. Mac-Pherson had threatened Kessler in specific terms: 'So you are planning to publish thirty-seven titles this year? I warn you, I will ensure that my thirty-eight newspapers give each of your titles the worst possible lousy review. Your losses will be exactly five times greater than your earnings on Smith's book.' MacPherson had promised to ruin Kessler just as he had threatened Smith, then 'smiled one of his twelve smiles' and wished Kessler good health and good luck in the same tone in which he'd promised to pick Harry Smith out of the gutter.[24] This is another example of MacPherson's inexorable and implausible precision—'exactly five times greater'—which characterizes the magnate throughout the play. Furthermore, even if his editors and literary editors were obsequiously to obey his instructions about killing off Kessler's publications, a fact of American literary life which escaped Simonov is that most titles are lucky to be reviewed anywhere. Any publicity is better than none. Kessler would be over the moon at the promise of every one of his thirty-seven titles getting a lousy review in all of MacPherson's thirty-eight newspapers.

The seventh and final tableau opens in the same domestic space as the fourth, which had reflected Smith's new-found prosperity after signing his book contract and returning from the USSR—but now the scene is one of

emblematic devastation. The writing-desk and the divan have been dismantled and two removal men are at work silently packing up furniture. Smith's
wife Jessie brings him a small basket of wild strawberries, but when he shows
no interest—*Zachem?*, he asks—she shrugs and empties them out of the
window. She wears a general air of resigned indifference; the stage direction
ravnodushno, 'indifferently', repeatedly prefaces what she says. But why
should she be 'indifferent' amid the debris of her home, the ruin of her
dream? The answer resides in Simonov's determination to denigrate Jessie,
and in his incompetence as a dramatist. 'I don't know anything any longer',
she says.

Fred Williams,[25] 50-year-old editor of a left-wing periodical, visits Harry
Smith, who explains the history of his new book about Russia; for two years
all book rights will belong to the publisher Kessler, but Kessler won't go
ahead in the face of MacPherson's veto, so Smith now proposes to extract
and rewrite ten episodes for Williams's paper. Williams shocks Smith by
declining the offer. He has suffered persecution for two months; the campaign against him has been orchestrated by ten different papers, including
ones belonging to Hearst, McCormick, and (the fictional) MacPherson.
Smear accusations that he is taking 'Moscow's money' have already lost
him 20,000 in circulation. The reason, Williams explains, is a series he sent
from Europe 'about the Popular Democracies Poland and Bulgaria, simply
honest and objective articles'. (In an alternative edition, also published in
1949,[26] it's 'Czechoslovakia and Bulgaria'! In Simonov's original text, as
performed in 1947, it was 'Yugoslavia and Bulgaria'; by the time of the
1949 editions Tito was 'objectively' a fascist. What neither Simonov nor
the Soviet commentators and theatre critics could do was mention the
specific complaints in the American press about Soviet conduct in Poland,
Bulgaria, Romania, and other parts of occupied Eastern Europe.)

Williams now feels obliged to keep silent about Russia and the Balkans.
When Smith urges him to show courage (the packer removes his chair as he
says it), the editor replies angrily that in the blink of an eye he could lose
everything. He intends to retreat, suffer, and wait. Williams confides now
that he ran into Gould 'in the club', where Gould took him into a corner and
cynically warned him that if he published Smith's articles he would be put
under 'judicial process': ten witnesses would swear for genuine US dollars to
have observed with their own eyes Williams receiving Russian money.[27]

A taxi appears—Jessie, it transpires, is leaving her ruined husband Smith
for good. She loves him and wanted to find the strength to stay with him, but
cannot face a life of poverty and unhappiness. The morning she had shouted
at him about money had been the turning-point.

Smith has been listening to radio transmissions of Bob Murphy's doomed test flight; Murphy reports that there is a lot of crackling at '13,100' (an American would say 40,000 feet), and soon afterwards the plane breaks up as Smith, now standing alone in the desolation of his empty house, listens in horrified silence, the radio being the only possession left to him.

The creepy journalist Hardy arrives to interview Smith and to earn, as Smith derisively puts it, 'your ten dollars a day'. 'Yours is no ordinary scandal', Hardy replies. Smith then dictates his rousing soliloquy of defiance, referring to himself as 'he', as if Hardy were composing the article. 'He was deprived of comforts, house, car, money, wife.' But 'he' (says Smith) has no intention of hanging himself, slitting his throat, or jumping from the twelfth floor. On the contrary, he is determined to begin again. Born an American, he intends to live and work in his native country.

SMITH: For a long time this man Smith naively imagined there was only one America. But he now knows there are two. And if fortunately for him, yes fortunately, there is no place for this man Smith in the America of Hearst, then he'll join the other America—the America of Abraham Lincoln, the America of Roosevelt![28]

This presidential name, normally in the genitive, *Ruzvel'ta*, is found time and again in Soviet cultural discourse—the America of Roosevelt, the anti-fascist army of Roosevelt. The president had died in April 1945 and so remained a partly mythological figure, sanctified by Russian discourse as uniquely progressive and pro-Soviet, although diplomatic documents show that Roosevelt had already engaged in sharp exchanges with Stalin regarding occupied Eastern Europe in the weeks before his death.

⌗ ⌗ ⌗

The opening production at the art-nouveau Lenin Komsomol Theatre, near Pushkin Square in Moscow, was directed by Serafima Birman, a Jewish actress and an ardent Communist, who had appeared in Eisenstein's *Ivan the Terrible*. Production notes in the RGALI archive reveal Birman to have been loquacious about contemporary world politics, uttering one banality after another. Simonov's own comments during rehearsals were often as politically crude and simplistic as the play itself: he talked of Gould as 'a Judas' to the labour movement and a man who 'gravitates towards Wall Street'. Imagine Germany in 1933, the playwright told the cast: Gould thinks that MacPherson will turn out to be an Alfred Hugenburg and that Gould himself will be Goebbels. In a note on the dress rehearsal (8 March 1947), Simonov warns, 'Don't hang Churchill's photograph next to Hitler's in the first scene'—*ne veshat' foto Cherchillia riadom s Gitlerom*; this must surely indicate that the producer was actively considering openly flaunting a photograph of Hitler in MacPherson's office.[29]

Simonov urged the actors to ignore American manners and habits: 'Comrades, You have to act neutrally without emphasizing the American-ness of the characters, and not emphasizing Russian qualities either, simply act people...no super-American tempo.'[30] Yet he fussed about the buttons of double-breasted suits, the size of tie knots, Smith's lacquered shoes, and how to drink whisky. He advised the cast that whisky is always drunk out of plain, not faceted, glasses; only 30 grams at a time; the barman adds the soda; the total liquid should not exceed three-fifths of a glass; and always sip it, never drink it in one gulp.

Reviewing the Moscow première, the *New York Times* (16 April 1947) offered an amorphous, almost contradictory comment: 'An interesting part of this play is not its attack on the American press, which is standard procedure for Soviet writers nowadays, but the fact that it leaves the audience with the idea that there is no effective opposition in America to the plans of the imperialist press lords it portrays.' The play was reviewed favourably—*une pièce vivante*—by the rather anti-American *Le Monde* (8 April), which likened Simonov's hero Harry Smith to Ibsen's Dr Stockmann, and noted that the première coincided with the presence in Moscow of an unusual number of Western journalists who had been granted visas for the Four-Power Foreign Ministers' Conference.[31]

What did serious Soviet theatre critics make of this hugely promoted but dramatically implausible play? Would political imperatives totally override their innately high theatrical standards? The text was obviously made available weeks in advance of the first night in Moscow. There was a distinct air of totalitarian co-ordination of reviews, many of which obediently mentioned Zhdanov's attack on the Leningrad magazine *Zvezda*; his guidelines applied to the whole of Soviet literature and drama. Huge reviews appeared all across the USSR: the file of cuttings in RGALI is unreadably thick. Criticisms were almost invariably aimed at performances rather than text, although, writing in *Trud* (3 April 1947), M. Charnyi did blame the playwright for the melodramatic quality of the final scene. In *Vechernaia Moskva*, (18 May), Al. Abramov commented that Simonov had written a 'political pamphlet', not a psychological drama.

The May 1947 issue of *Teatr* devoted two long pieces, by V. Aleksandrov and E. Surkov, to productions in Moscow and Leningrad. (The 'still-life' photographs of the actors, printed on paper of inferior quality, merely reinforce the atmosphere of 'dead-life', of a sterile, semi-documentary drama without genuine human animation.) Clearly the Party had handed out information packs to theatre critics and journalists. It was an operation of almost military precision—the same information, the same line, the same indignation, came up again and again. Both Aleksandrov and Surkov fully endorsed the politics and historical accuracy of the play, providing laborious documentation in support of its verisimilitude, including financial details—although Aleksandrov frequently introduced the phrase 'no exaggeration', suggesting defensiveness. As Surkov put it: 'There cannot be two truths in this world, only one. That is our truth. Remaining honest, Smith will inevitably understand this.'[32] Aleksandrov, reviewing the production at the Lenin Komsomol Theatre, Moscow, allowed himself a hint of heterodoxy: the 'Russian Question', though important, was not of the essence; if the conflict unfolding within the play had concerned information about the position of farmers or striking workers or racial inequality in the United States, we would also sympathize with Harry Smith.

According to Aleksandrov, whose piece was ironically entitled 'Amerikanskoe Schast'e' (American Happiness), the fate of Smith was by no means exceptional. 'We know how MacPherson's America treated radical journalists and radio commentators (like Steele and William Shirer), as well as government employees when they stand up for (*otstaivaiut*) their right to speak the truth.' Aleksandrov cited a report in George Seldes's book *Freedom of the Press*. John Swinton, a former editor of the *New York Tribune*, had addressed fellow-journalists: 'Not one of you can honestly speak his mind... I'm paid 150 dollars a week not to speak my mind in the pages of my newspaper... We are intellectual prostitutes.' Aleksandrov had no quarrel with that.[33]

As for the fictional magnate MacPherson's friendship with an off-stage Winston Churchill, Aleksandrov dutifully quoted Comrade Stalin's interview with *Pravda* (14 March 1946) following Churchill's 'Iron Curtain' speech at Fulton, Missouri: 'It remains to note that Mr Churchill and his friends startlingly (*porazitel'no*) recall in his respect Hitler and his friends', said Stalin.[34] And what about the first scene of the play, where MacPherson shows Gould a signed photograph of Mussolini?

MACPHERSON: One of the best of my collection.
GOULD: And the other gentleman remains in your safe for the time being?'
MACPHERSON: *Poka—da.* (For the time being, yes.)

'The other gentleman' being, of course, Hitler. Aleksandrov sought to justify this exchange (and allegation) in terms of a report by Ilya Ehrenburg in *Kul'tura i zhizn'*, published on 10 April 1947 in support of Simonov's play; according to Ehrenburg, he and Simonov had actually seen an autographed portrait of Mussolini in one of the New York newspapers during their visit to the United States.[35] (But in what context?)

Aleksandrov allowed himself a number of criticisms of the production at the Lenin Komsomol Theatre, in which he found too much theatrical convention; actors raised their voices excessively at the end of a question; a New York bar resembled the portico of a French tragedy in which plotters and tyrants meet. In the fourth scene Harry Smith appears in a new suit. Simonov's stage directions merely require Jessica to turn her husband around and solicit Meg Stanley's opinion of the suit. Smith says: 'That'll do, you're turning me round like a globe'—*dovol'no menia vertet', kak globus*.[36] But in the Moscow production (complained Aleksandrov) Smith marches back and forth in his new suit, ceremonially waving his hands, with a musical accompaniment.[37] That Aleksandrov was indirectly expressing criticism of the play itself was noted by M. Leonidov in *Sovetskoe iskusstvo* (18 July): 'He speaks about it evasively'—*On uklonchivo govorit ob etom*. Aleksandrov finished his review in *Teatr* by noting that the play was currently in production at five theatres in Moscow, three in Leningrad, and probably in almost all provincial theatres. 'This is a serious competition and difficult to predict who will win.'[38]

And the character Jessie? How was she to be played and interpreted? Aleksandrov agreed with David Zaslavsky, writing in *Kul'tura i zhizn'*, that the actress Valentina Serova, playing Jessie, sacrificed the weakness of the character—cynicism, ennui, calculation—by making her too attractive. (Serova was Simonov's muse, the inspiration of his poem *Zhdi menia i ia vernus'*—'Wait for me, and I will return'.) This is perplexing because, according to *Komsomol'skaia pravda* (3 April 1947), Serova played Jessie as a calculating materialist with no real love for Harry Smith.[39]

Aleksandrov clearly shared the prejudice of the majority of Soviet male critics, blaming Jessie for Harry Smith's acceptance of MacPherson's financial offer; after all, his current $500 a month, when the action begins, was twice the official poverty-line wage for a family of four—but his new wife wanted more, a big house, a Packard. (Simonov's 'notes on the play', dated 8 October 1946, reveal a significant cut, probably made during early rehearsals at the Lenin Komsomol Theatre. In the original version Jessie, about to abandon her husband, tells him something both true and moving: 'I'm glad I'm not pregnant. You cheated me.'[40] One may assume that this had to come out because Harry's shabby and chauvinistic treatment of his wife did not fit his political image.)

There were many actresses, many Jessies. At the Moscow Art Theatre Angelina Stepanova played her as a positive heroine, a woman capable of sacrifice.[41] Karpova's performance in Leningrad came under fire in *Vechernii Leningrad* (12 July) from a student of the philological department of Leningrad University: the actress showed Jessie as a self-loving sinner rather than a victim of capitalism. There were in fact three separate productions in Leningrad: at the Komedia Theatre the actress playing Jessie was said by *Sovetskoe iskusstvo* (18 July) to have stolen the show.

Reviewing the production at the Gorky Theatre, Leningrad, E. Surkov proved himself a bolder, livelier critic than Aleksandrov.[42] On taking his seat in the auditorium, he was disconcerted to find, sewn to the curtain, a confusedly piled-up montage of skyscrapers, one on the top of the other, by the designer V. Shestakov. 'The banality of this opening is obvious. The America depicted in Simonov's play is genuine, so why does the director, E. Agranenko, substitute cliché versions?'

It's clear that in order to bring about this production the director actually did not resist the temptation to indulge in cheap strivings for local colour. The characters in this play humorously exchange boxer's punches, leap up on to armchairs, slap one another, displaying by their 'eccentricities' the celebrated American colourfulness. They are thus depersonalized and standardized. The same goes for Shestakov's stage design.[43]

Surkov's strategy, not unlike Mark Antony's, was to say one thing while managing to convey the opposite. The play was a 'difficult' one because of its 'openness'. Simonov scorned the possibility of carrying on an intrigue with the spectator subjectively by cunning stratagems (*khitrospletenniia*). For example, we learn as early as the third scene what kind of book Smith is writing and what will follow from it. The play could have been written differently, more cunningly and with greater suspense.[44] Harry Smith himself was a 'difficult' role which had to be played on two levels, the psychological and the political—the declamatory side when he achieves political single-mindedness (*tselenapravlennost'*), even though his world outlook has not attained clarity and definition. The Leningrad actor playing Smith, B. Freimdlikh, underlined the dramatic character of Smith's fate, unlike A. Pelevin in Moscow, who only got across his objective thoughts. 'In tired fashion Pelevin propounds prepared theses which are inert and lacking in dynamism. By contrast Freimdlich carries the hero though severe experiences and carefully conveys his psychological suffering. Here and there he almost exaggerates Smith's reaction to what is going on.'

Turning to the sub-plot about Bob Murphy's fatal test-flight, Surkov commented that 'Bob Murphy is a character well known to every reader of Hemingway', but found no grounds to be moved by his 'paltry experience' and drunken, nihilistic pessimism: 'His death is not only his misfortune but also his own fault.' But opinions differed! Senior Lieutenant N. Popov, writing in *Krasnyi flot* (*Red Fleet*, 11 April), criticized A. Voroiskaia for her review in another naval newspaper, *Krasnyi Chernomorets* (*Black Sea Red*), in which she dared to suggest that Murphy was a victim of capitalism whose disreputable behaviour could be excused; Lieutenant Popov insisted that Murphy chose to work for Hearst's gang and his self-disgust was not enough. (The American scholar Harold Segel calls the story of Bob Murphy 'near absurdity'.)[45]

⊞ ⊞ ⊞

In April–May the Russians stoked the fires a whole lot hotter when they decided to put a German translation, *Die russische Frage*, into the Deutsches Theater in East Berlin. The impact of production in Berlin can be understood only in the context of the fierce media war between the victorious Allies. Reaching Berlin ahead of Western forces, the Red Army had seized Radio Berlin (Berliner Rundfunk) and refused to share its facilities with the other occupying forces when they arrived, although its studios were situated in what became the British sector of the city and its transmitter in the French sector. On 1 October 1945 the *New York Times* commented that the new staff of Radio Berlin, virtually in its entirety, had been recruited from the Free Germany Committee, founded in Moscow in 1943. Foreign Minister Molotov was invariably the quoted source of Radio Berlin's opinions; Marshal Zhukov was presented as the first Allied commander to import food into Germany to fend off starvation, the first to encourage the rebirth of the non-Nazi parties, and the first to redistribute the big estates to landless farmers.

What the Americans did have, for those Germans able to listen to English-language transmissions, was the Armed Forces Network (AFN); although the programmes were aimed at military personnel, local inhabitants comprised 90 per cent of the audience. Language, in any case, was not a barrier to jazz, dance music, and the latest hits. From 7 February 1946 the American Military Government (OMGUS) began broadcasting from its own Berlin station, Radio in the American Sector (RIAS).[46] Operating from the Schönberg telephone exchange, with eighty German technicians, editors, and artists working under the direction of Edmund Schechter, an official of the US Information Service, RIAS broadcast seven hours a day, including relays from the Voice of America, offering 64 per cent music, 26 per cent news and public affairs, 10 per cent miscellaneous.[47]

Western criticism of the Soviet-controlled Berliner Rundfunk intensified. The 'Goebbels theme', freely used in Communist propaganda, was now played back at the Communists. Complaints were pouring in against the one-sidedness and excessive political content of the programmes: 'Berliners declare that they can no more trust Radio Berlin now than when Goebbels was in charge of it. They demand that it should be placed under four-party and four-Power control, as is the city itself.'[48] The British zone newspaper, *Der Sozialdemokrat* (3 June), organ of the SDP faction opposed to fusion with the Communists, published a cartoon of a man holding a copy of the Communist daily paper *Neues Deutschland* under his left arm while standing at a microphone. Behind him is the shadow of Goebbels. The caption: *Berliner Rundfunk im Shatten des Meisters*—'Radio Berlin in the Shadow of the Master'. The *Christian Science Monitor* (11 September) complained that Radio Berlin gave the impression that there was only one democratic party in Germany, the Communist SED. Constant attacks on 'capitalism' and 'Fascism' covered anything incompatible with Soviet policy.

The print war ran parallel to the radio war. In the fall of 1945 OMGUS founded *Die Neue Zeitung* (*NZ*), published in Munich. By January 1946 circulation stood at 1.6 million, with 8–10 million readers, the aim being to inform Germans of American policies, views, way of life, business, sport— and also to present a model of American journalistic practice. The US Information Control Division (ICD) distributed the paper in all four zones including the Soviet, as well as Austria.[49] Charting the rapid evolution of *NZ*, Jessica C. E. Gienow-Hecht describes it as moving from 'a reminder of Soviet–American friendship' in 1946 to 'an anticommunist propaganda tool' a year later. 'Editors showcased the vast array of museums, art galleries, public libraries and newly published books in the United States. Many essays lauded American painters and literary figures as well as European film producers [working] in Hollywood and theater reviews from New York.' Particularly dangerous from the Soviet point of view was the strategy of the mainly Jewish editors of *NZ*: 'They packaged American culture and ideas in the context of German highbrow culture, *Bildung*, and gender conceptions, and emphasized hardcore democratic values, such as tolerance and individualism, by appealing to a very traditional German interpretation of *Kultur*, such as elitist art.'

By 1946 the *Neue Zeitung* was in effect banned by the Soviet Military Administration (SMAD) in the Soviet zone. Under protest from the ICD, Colonel Tiul'panov, a very military cultural commissar with a round, close-cropped skull, offered to lift the ban but never did. In August the Russians began confiscating copies. News-vendors who stocked the title were closed down and bundles were seized in transit after the Americans devised new strategies for shipment. In October 1947 the paper's print-run stood at 1,078,800. After research in the OMGUS archives, Gienow-Hecht reports that 'Soviet press officers threatened local distributors and salesmen with severe punishment, including years of imprisonment in forced labor camps, if they continued to sell *Neue Zeitung*.' (Not that the Soviet German-language press was without its successes. While banning *NZ* and virtually every other Western organ in the Soviet zone, they managed to sell 50,000 copies a day of *Tägliche Rundschau* in Munich (US zone) alone.)[50]

Simonov's play—an attack on America performed by German actors for the benefit of a German audience, was an unprecedented act of cultural aggression by one former ally against another. The Americans were incensed. In a letter of protest to Wolfgang Langhoff, *Intendant* of the Deutsches Theater, Frederic Mellinger, theater officer for the US Sector, angrily denounced Simonov's play as 'a malicious slander of American journalism and American intelligence'. Colonel Frank Howley, head of the US Military Government in Berlin, lodged a protest through the Cultural Affairs Committee of the Four-Power Kommandantura after protests by Frank N. Leonard, head of Berlin news control (USA), to his Soviet counterpart got nowhere.[51] *Die Neue Zeitung* (23 April 1947) published a protest by Brigadier-General Robert A. McClure, head of the information-control division of the Military Government, claiming that the forthcoming production amounted to a violation of the Potsdam Treaty. When the Deutsches Theater sent McClure's office 100 complimentary tickets, they were returned.

The Deutsches Theater pressed ahead to the première on 3 May. Langhoff went on radio to plead that at the beginning of the season he had staged an American play of Christian persuasion, *Eine Familie zur Diskussion*, as well as dramas by J. B. Priestley (*Gefährliche Kurven*) and Jean Anouilh (*Der Reisende ohne Gepäck*).[52] As for Simonov's play: 'The theme is not a specifically American one but primarily an international one.' By this Langhoff meant the problem of the powerful private group not answerable to anyone using propaganda to prepare the way for a third world war; but he then went on to describe Simonov's play in platitudinous terms, implicitly confirming that it was 'in erster Linie' all about the United States here and now. Asked whether such a play should be shown to German audiences, he replied that German spectators would understand that the play called for Soviet–American friendship on a democratic basis. Langhoff was merely repeating what the Russians had been telling the Americans in unofficial discussions: the play is anti-capitalist rather than anti-American.[53]

At this juncture, less than a week before the first night, the Soviet-zone *Tägliche Rundschau* (27 April) published an exceedingly long piece by 'G. W.', 'Der Mensch mit dem reinen Gewissen' (The Man with the Clean Conscience). The writer wanted to emphasize that Simonov's Harry Smith is not particularly interested in politics, is without clearly defined views, and is certainly no Communist: 'He believes before everything the evidence of his own eyes . . . He makes a mistake in accepting a commission to write an anti-Soviet book, about which one is more worried than inclined to condemn him unreservedly, since he is fundamentally only misled and wrongly informed'—*nur irregeführt und falsch unterrichtet*. (This last remark is incomprehensible; Smith is not 'wrongly informed'.)

Reporting from Berlin in *Tambovskaia pravda* (30 April 1947), Yuri Korolkov claimed to have sat in the stalls of the Deutsches Theater alongside New York correspondents dressed in check suits who left as soon as the curtain fell—the prototypes of the characters in the play. Following the 'two Americas' motif, Korol'kov also claimed to have seen in the gallery 'ordinary American soldiers' displaying appreciation. What made this reportage so remarkable was that the dispatch was sent and printed before the first performance took place.

The première went ahead. 'Berlin Lukewarm to Anti-US Play', reported the *New York Times* (4 May). The play 'fell with a soft flop on the stage of Max Reinhardt's Deutsches Theater this afternoon', wrote Delbert Clark. 'A curious incident at the end was the applause that broke in on [Harry Smith's] closing address to the audience and spoiled his peroration. He was forced to wait about thirty seconds before he could make his surefire references to Abraham Lincoln and Franklin D. Roosevelt.' (No mention of Hearst.) Clark found the play amateurish and its message naive, namely, that with the exception of the Chicago *Sun* and the *Daily Worker*, the American press was utterly corrupt, anti-Russian, and capable of printing falsehoods to drum up a war against Russia. 'I am sure that it could be shown to any random Communist audience in New York and be laughed off the stage, unless the audience was under orders not to laugh.' In the *Christian Science Monitor* (5 May), J. Emlyn Williams found the play 'very naïve', badly acted, and generally flat as a pancake. American journalists were depicted as drunks swallowing double whiskies every other minute. Williams pointed to Simonov's recent address to the Congress of Russian Actors and Dramatic Critics, insisting that 'in defence of Communism, most sacred of all things, all powers must be employed, including art'. Strolling through the corridors of the Deutsches Theater during the interval, Williams had heard conversations focusing on the likely impact on international relations.

'Anti-American Play in Berlin', announced the London *Times* (5 May): 'Politics have returned to the Berlin stage in as crude and crass a form as in the heyday of Hitler and Goebbels.' The play, already widely circulated in German translation, was lifeless, blatant propaganda. 'Groups of Communist sympathisers stayed on to recall the actors a dozen times as a demonstration of political faith.' Arno Scholz, chief editor of the social democratic *Telegraf* (4 May), licensed in the British sector of Berlin, felt that the actors did not believe in the lines they were forced to speak. 'Not a word is genuine, everything is mannered, ordered, overblown.' Writing in *Die Neue Zeitung* (6 and 9 May), Friedrich Luft ridiculed 'a play written in a crass, black-and-white, one-sided manner', 'shaming' for the Deutsches Theater and 'a retreat into amateurism (*Dilettantismus*) which really should have been avoided.' The leading actor was radically miscast—*Don Carlos mit dem Kaugummi*— 'Don Carlos with chewing-gum'—and, moreover, generally received no support from his female partner.

Successive reports in the *New York Times* (23 April, 4 May) described panic among the cast and frequent absences from rehearsals. Delbert Clark reported that Langhoff had difficulty in casting the play after protests from the actors' union and a spate of sudden, mysterious illnesses among actors. Lola Müthel and Karl-Heinz Schroth, due to perform the principal roles under the direction of Dr Harnack, had dropped out. On 10 May *Pravda*'s Berlin correspondent, Yuri Korolkov, claimed that actors living in the US or British sectors had been threatened with a blacklist. Lola Müthel, who was scheduled to play the female lead Jessie, had run into visa trouble and been faced with a choice between six months in prison or refusal to play the role. The official Soviet organ *Tägliche Rundschau* spoke of a witch hunt, 'a direct terrorizing of the theatre and actors'.

The play performed to thin houses despite a bombardment of laudatory reviews by Wolfgang Harich in *Tägliche Rundschau* (4 and 11 May, 29 June) describing *Die russische Frage* as a deep psychological drama: should a man compromise his honour and principles? Furthermore, Western-zone papers like *Sozialdemokrat* were in effect siding with Hearst and McCormick when urging the Berlin public to boycott the play. As for Arno Scholz, 'the British-licensed "socialist" ', he falsified the contents of the play even though the text was freely available at kiosks. Those who wanted the play banned or suppressed revealed how much their so-called 'democratic' principles were worth. Simonov had correctly detected in advance the current rabble-rousing (*überschreitenden Hetze*) against Communism and the Soviet Union.[54]

Crucial in the Soviet decision to outrage the Americans by performing the play under their noses was Major Aleksandr Dymshits, whose functions included editorial supervision of *Tägliche Rundschau*. When Simonov's travelling companion to the United States, Ilya Ehrenburg, had published largely derogatory reports which rapidly appeared in Soviet-sponsored

German translation, Dymshits had come out with a series of articles in *Tägliche Rundschau* defending Ehrenburg against his Western critics under such headings as 'Slanders (*Verleumungden*)—made in New York'. Dymshits denounced 'cultural totalitarianism' in the Western zones after the Americans and British banned the fellow-travelling Kulturbund. According to Dymshits, misconceptions about the Central Committee (Zhdanov) decrees on literature and theatre in the USSR were the result of malicious Western propaganda, 'slanders supplied by venal and arrogant journalists' who bemoaned 'the suppression of artistic freedom' and 'the imposition of pre-scribed ideological paradigms'. By November 1947 Simonov's play was to be found in six provincial theatres of the Soviet zone. Although Dymshits, writing to VOKS in Moscow, claimed that the play effectively demonstrated to Germans what 'the true America' was really like, he could not conceal that many Germans, interviewed on leaving the theatre, viewed it as little more than Soviet propaganda. One women in Dresden commented that the 'real Russian question' was shortage of potatoes and reparations (dismantling of German industrial plant).[55]

The Americans were determined to retaliate in this war of the theatres. Demanding no further productions of Clifford Odets's *Awake and Sing* in the Soviet sector, Mellinger also withdrew production rights to William Saroyan's *The Time of Your Life* (*Einmal im Leben*) and Paul Osborn's *Mornings at Seven* (*Spätsommer*), on the ground that the Russians had acquired the rights but not produced the plays. The Odets play, he said, 'would meet a completely different interpretation' if presented in repertory alongside Simonov's *The Russian Question*.[56] According to the Soviet critic I. Novodvorskaia, the Western reaction to *Die russische Frage*—which she hailed as 'an eye-opener'—reflected the obsequious slavishness to the Anglo-American newspaper proprietors stigmatized in the play itself.[57]

⌗ ⌗ ⌗

The publication of an English-language text in May 1947 coincided with a bombardment of Soviet polemics tending to echo Langhoff's protest-ation that American newspaper magnates were not alone in their infamy. R. Borisova complained that the 'great many' British newspapermen covering the recent Foreign Minister Conference in Moscow 'could see what they liked, talk to anyone they pleased, and send off their dispatches without censorship of any kind'. The Russians, evidently, had been poorly rewarded by 'slanders' about religion, architecture, building programmes, car production, and further slanders wilfully ignoring the scale of Nazi destruction which had contributed to housing shortages.[58]

In October 1947 *Russkii vopros*, recently *Die russische Frage*, became *The Russian Question* when it surfaced at the pro-Communist Unity Theatre in London, later earning a tribute in the Soviet magazine *Teatr* (July 1950), where E. Glukhareva praised such Unity productions as Clifford Odets's *Waiting for Lefty* (*V Ozhidanii Lefty*), Sean O'Casey's *The Star is Red* (*Zvezda stanovitsia krasnoi*), about the 'heroic struggle of the workers in Ireland', and plays by Ted Willis such as *Sabotage*. She concluded that Unity owed its success to its political direction and realistic style, 'adopted from Soviet theatre art'. Higher praise she knew not.[59]

By one account the Unity Theatre stumbled across *The Russian Question* in English translation when it was published in two supplements in the London Embassy's *Soviet Weekly* (15 and 22 May 1947), together with (distinctly uninspiring) photographs of the Moscow cast.[60] One doubts whether this was left to chance; in all probability the Soviet Embassy sent the English translation to Unity even before publication. The fact that diplomatic representatives of Russia, Yugoslavia, Bulgaria, and Romania attended the première speaks for itself. (Western input was not entirely lacking; a props credit in the Unity programme reads: 'American Type Cigarettes by Philip Morris and by Abdulla.') According to a report signed 'E.F.' in the *News Chronicle* (18 October), the play (produced[61] by Bill Rowbotham) lacked form and was poor theatre, although the Unity company did 'very well'. The magazine *Illustrated* (8 November) suffered an unexpected attack of seriousness, devoting a three-page spread of text and photographs to the Unity production. *Illustrated* was well informed, correctly reporting that the play was currently performing in Berlin and Dresden, in Budapest and Bucharest, but that this was the first production in the West. Although the Unity Theatre, sited in grim territory near Euston Station, seated only 332 spectators, a *Daily Worker* cutting in the archive (undated, but from about 7 November) celebrated the arrival of more than 6,000 spectators since *The Russian Question* opened on 17 October. There had been 125 block bookings by left-leaning trade unions, notably the Amalgamated Engineering Union and the Electrical Trades Union. The play was scheduled to run to 28 December.

Simonov won a Stalin Prize for *The Russian Question*, alongside Prokofiev for a concerto for violin and piano. 'Stalin, Molotov Applaud Play Lampooning American Press', declared the *Herald Tribune* (21 December 1947). Seven top Soviet leaders, headed by Stalin and Molotov, had taken a box near the stage of the Moscow Art Theatre on this winter night. Apparently applause was loudest at the end, when Harry Smith walks off declaring that there are two Americas. According to the *New York Times* (3 April 1948), the play had been shown in more than 600 theatres.[62]

Harry Smith remained a kind of ideal American for a few years. When *Izvestiia* attacked the previously lauded American novelist John Steinbeck for his critical observations in the *Herald Tribune* after a visit to Russia—yet another renegade—the Soviet paper adversely compared him to Simonov's noble character Harry Smith. Although Harrison Salisbury had done the disagreeable Simonov 'small favors' during his 1946 tour of America, when Salisbury arrived in Moscow three years later as correspondent of the *New York Times* and tried to contact both Ehrenburg and Simonov, he received no reply. 'Both gentlemen cut me dead on such rare occasions as I saw them.' As for *The Russian Question*, he dismissed it as 'obnoxious'.[63] Professor Harold Segel describes the play as 'more ludicrous than offensive'. Simonov himself, meanwhile, notably lacked the honour and truthfulness he demanded of American journalists. His notorious—indeed vile—article 'The Tasks Before Soviet Drama and Dramatic Criticism', published in *Pravda* (28 February, 1949), began by attacking 'the anti-patriots and the bourgeois cosmopolitans with their imitators who knowingly imitate them'. Well aware of the concurrent liquidation of Jewish/Yiddish intellectuals, he listed a number of critics by name, mainly Jews, castigating their 'criminal activities' in important editorial posts, etc.: 'Cosmopolitanism in art is the endeavour to cut away the national roots and national pride . . . to remove our culture and sell us into slavery to American imperialism. Cosmopolitanism in art is the endeavour to replace Gorky by Sartre, Tolstoy by the pornographer [Henry] Miller, to replace classical art, which ennobles mankind, by stupefying Hollywood concoctions.'[64] Simonov later admitted in *Novy mir* (December 1956) that he and other writers had lacked the courage to resist the anti-cosmopolitan campaign. In short, Simonov was no Harry Smith.[65]

⊞ ⊞ ⊞

Mikhail Romm made a series of films with foreign settings, although, according to his biographer Mark Zak, he never went abroad until the 1960s. His motion picture of *Russkii vopros* (Mosfilm, 1948) was shown all across the USSR and Eastern Europe, but there is no evidence of the film's distribution in the United States and the title does not appear in the *New York Times* index of films reviewed. An interview given by Romm indicates that he proudly 'crafted' the film script on conventional Hollywood principles—though 'Hollywood' is not the term he uses. Romm explains that the plot information conveyed at the beginning of the play through an extended conversation between Jessie and Gould had to be broken up in the film into separate episodes, what he called expository 'lumps' (*kuskom*) and 'little lumps' (*kusochek*), each with a strong visual interest for the spectator. A single conversation in MacPherson's office is divided up between a vestibule, an elevator, a barber's shop, a car travelling down Broadway in the evening, an airport, and a huge open-plan newspaper office packed like a 'news kitchen' with reporters.[66]

The film opened with newsreel shots of the Statue of Liberty and New York City, where American soldiers in period doughboy hats are shown ladling soup to the unemployed. Romm, whose credits included the screenplay as well as the production, also used newsreels from the era of the Depression showing slums, washing-lines, police on horseback, police baton-charging strikers, black rural poverty, the rich and glamorous alighting from huge cars, speeding printing-presses, blacks outside their poor hovels, the Empire State Building, chorus girls, manicured poodles, Times Square, vaudeveille, 'Ceasar and Cleopatra' in Broadway lights. This heavy-handed raid on the documentary archive is as subtle as a custard pie.

Taking up the live camerawork of Boris Volchek, the film—graced by Khachaturian's thumping soundtrack—cuts to the airport as Jessie waits for Harry Smith to fly in from Japan. Happy together, she gazing into his eyes in the back seat of a taxi, they drive into town, moving down Broadway past the garish neon advertisements. At the start of shooting Romm crassly instructed Elena Kuz'mina, against her inclinations: 'Play Jessie so that the spectator doesn't feel pity for her but, on the contrary, condemns her.' Romm's decision was made, Mark Zak says, in response to 'the far-reaching winds of the cold war'[67]—but Romm himself was that wind. On the role of the eternal Eve and the serpent, Romm had made no advance on the Book of Genesis.

Reaching the futuristically modern newspaper building, its lobby stream-lined and elegant, the smooth villain Gould—he has no limp in the film—makes a pass at Jessie in the elevator, and then accompanies her down a huge, open newsroom with staff and scores of reporters perching on desks wearing trilby hats or eyeshades. They reach MacPherson's luxurious office. The boss himself, wearing a bow tie, is the essence of affability—if he can get what he wants. Later, in the Press Bar, the long-nosed Gould shows Smith a press report about Russian journalists seen giving money to American strikers. '*Ne pravda*', retorts Smith indignantly. Well done is the frenetic downing of whiskies in the Press Bar, the alcoholic Bob Murphy in the lead. And, though they speak Russian, which creates its own atmosphere, one believes that these characters are American journalists. Romm and his cameraman catch the authentic body language and tempo; determined to say *Nyet* to MacPherson's vile book proposition, Harry Smith gets as far as thrusting a coin into a pay-phone, only to lose his nerve and replace the receiver.

The four-month transition to Smith's return from Russia is done in a split second; suddenly we see an idyllic, arboured, cottage in its cute garden in high summer, birds twittering. We explore the interior in the company of a beaming Jessie and an admiring Meg Stanley, Harry's loyal stenographer: slatted shades, ultra-modern kitchen, bookcases, the decor a blend of the modern and Disneyesque false-antique. The cost: $15,000, plus $5,000 for furniture.

After Smith, pipe in mouth, hands in pocket, pacing up and down, has been dictating pro-Russian sentiments to Meg for some time, he suddenly recalls the new Russia he had just seen: Red Square *cut* modern buildings *cut* petrol refineries *cut* car factories *cut* farms *cut* schools—all to Khachaturian's rousing music. Romm offers a parody of a parody, but in all seriousness. Romm was keen on back projections, a director's only resort when unable to film on location. One example is a remarkable long drive through New York in a huge, open car, Gould at the wheel, MacPherson the passenger, talking about Communism while passing beneath an overhead railway without slowing, and without encountering lights or crossroads for 1 minute 55 seconds—equivalent to a mile![68] MacPherson, in a double-breasted suit and carrying a cane, is on his way to Harry Smith's cottage garden to hector him about the Russians. Smith responds in a sequence so over-the-top as to be ridiculous. In a dozen quick cuts, to thunderous music, the normally mild-mannered journalist becomes a wild-eyed zealot as he frenziedly orates to Meg about the virtues of the Soviet Union and its defiance of the warmongers. This passage is not found in the play; evidently Romm felt that Smith was a character lacking in passion.

Now the book is finished, but the scene in which Jessica invites friends to celebrate, and parades Harry in the suit she has bought him, turning him 'like a globe', is not in the film, presumably because it cast her in too warm and sympathetic a light.

Smith's friend, the Hearst journalist Bob Murphy, of whom we have seen a great deal, turns up to show Smith and Jessie a full-page ad in MacPherson's Sunday edition: 'HARRY SMITH. RUSSIANS WANT WAR', we see in English. Jessie, beaming with delight (Kuz'mina tends to turn her features into a kind of headlamp, beaming on hold) reads the caption aloud for the benefit of her Soviet audience. Poor Jessie remains unaware of what her husband has really been writing. Cut to MacPherson, smoking through an ivory cigarette-holder (as villains do) while reading Smith's first chapters, his face clouding, darkening, flipping the pages with mounting fury until driven to yell down the phone to Gould. Cut to Gould driving in his open car through a city nightscape reminiscent of Fritz Lang's *Metropolis*. (Romm was clearly a keen student of Weimar cinema.) A furious Gould, in a dressy white scarf, drives Smith back into town, taking care to pass down Broadway, and leads him through the same vast newsroom, now empty—an effective contrast.

MacPherson rages and yells at Smith. Then, wearing black tie and dinner jacket, the tycoon drops his voice as his threats intensify, his hands calmly folded on his desk until they erupt in banging fury as he contemplates the race against time, the imminent Congressional elections—Smith has refused to sign the sheet of paper authorizing a ghosted rewrite.

Jessica is beginning to show her rising tension by lighting cigarettes before tossing them away; as a happy wife she had been running around in a pretty apron and definitely not smoking. Wearing yet another natty hat, she visits the suave Gould in his office. Her eyes flicker with calculation. He makes a proposition. She slaps his face. He shouts sneeringly about Harry; she slaps him some more. This scene is not in the play.

The long concluding episode in which the furniture is removed from the Smith home is accompanied by frenetically cheerful piano music, somewhat in the Scott Joplin mould, evidently coming from the radio, interrupted only when the Mercury Studio links up with Bob Murphy flying through the clouds in a toy plane and swigging from a flask.

Jessie is now drunk, bottle in hand, and possessed by so much fury that she almost strikes little Meg (as well she might, being the victim of Meg's complicity in Harry's long, deceitful silence about what he was really writing). Neither Simonov nor any Soviet commentator quite grasped how deeply Harry Smith's protracted and rather self-satisfied betrayal of his trusting wife must have affected Jessie. According to volume 3 of the semi-official *Istoria sovetskogo kino*, published twenty-five years later: 'You feel more sorry for her than condemnatory because she cannot bear the half-starving (*polugolodnyi*), destitute life awaiting her... Kuz'mina reveals the tragedy of the woman; corrupted but understanding her corruption, she lacks the strength and willpower to live differently.'[69]

Finally, Harry is seen from middle-range addressing a peace rally in a small version of what might be Madison Square Garden but might equally be Shakespeare's Globe Theatre filled with 1940s costumes. 'You are told that America's enemies are in the Soviet Union. It's a lie! America's enemies are in Washington! America's enemies are those who say that Russia is threatening us with a war!' Anything less like a real American audience is hard to imagine; Romm obviously cannot fathom how Americans express approval, which he conveys in short, staccato, and totally synchronized bursts of robotic clapping and whistling—rather Chinese—and equally synchronized booing whenever Smith mentions the devil's battalions (MacPherson, *Uoll Strit*, etc.). The camera does not dare to venture in close to investigate individual faces, idiosyncratic expressions. It's a one-party state, even in opposition. The crowd stands to hail a wild-eyed Harry Smith.

Reporting on the Moscow première, the *Herald Tribune* (7 March 1948) concluded that the film 'succeeds where the stage version failed in giving some touches of American life'—but had little else to say. The 100,000-rouble ($12,500 at the diplomatic rate of exchange) Stalin Prize was shared between the director, cameraman, and six actors.[70]

Romm's biographer, Mark Zak,[71] points out that there are only 313 cuts in *Russkii vopros* instead of the normal 800–900, Romm's theory being that it is more difficult to be untruthful in long, uncut takes. This film proves that the theory is fragile. Even so, Simonov's cartoon portrait of American journalism seems to have lodged in the accident-and-emergency department of the Soviet soul; Zak still contended, when interviewed in April 2002: 'It's a film about the two Americas. Jessie hesitates between the two Americas. It was a pamphlet film, an ideological film, an attempt to bring together journalism and imagery.' A pause. Did I not know, he asked me, that MacPherson's hero Churchill started the cold war with his speech in Fulton, Missouri, in March 1946, while Simonov was visiting America?

Soviet Cinema Under Stalin

Stalin's daughter Svetlana Alliluyeva, while still a schoolgirl, was frequently taken by her father to the Kremlin theatre to see films until two in the morning. 'How many wonderful films were shown for the first time on the little screen in the Kremlin! There was *Chapayev*, the Gorky trilogy, films about Peter the Great, *Circus* and *Volga-Volga*. All the best Soviet films were launched in that hall in the Kremlin.'[1] Svetlana Alliluyeva recalled that during her father's later years foreign films not released to the public were shown at weekends in government dachas. Most of them were American.[2] Dmitri Shostakovich recalled that 'Stalin loved films and he saw *The Great Waltz*, about Johann Strauss, many times, dozens of times . . . Stalin also liked Tarzan films, he saw all the episodes.'[3] Early in 1946 VOKS and the Soviet Information Bureau were still pressing the American Embassy for more films. Sunday-night screenings at Spaso House, the ambassador's residence, became regular events, attracting select Soviet intellectuals and guests from other countries. Then came the freeze. In February 1946 the Film Committee halted a screening of *Casablanca* (starring Humphrey Bogart and Ingrid Bergman) and confiscated the film. After protests from the Embassy it was eventually returned.[4] On 4 October *Vecherniaia Moskva* criticized Dom kino (House of Cinema), the clubhouse of film workers, which had shown sixty foreign films during the previous six months, including some with jazz and foxtrot. Soviet film production was fully committed to the cold war; American popular culture had to be fought at every level. On 8 January 1949 the *New York Times* happily reported that the display and production of photographs of Hollywood film stars had been banned the previous day. *Vecherniaia Moskva* had revealed that barber shops and beauty parlours were most prone to this sin—though Clark Gable was the only actor named. 'This unique advertising of American cinema trash has flowered for more than a year not only in Moscow, but also in Tashkent, Leningrad, Baku, and other cities.' The anti-foreign campaign picked up pace. The sheer charm, vivacity, and universal audience-appeal of Hollywood films posed a threat of atomic proportions. *Kul'tura i zhizn'* (30 May 1947) complained that audiences saw more foreign than Soviet films, and published letters of protest from outraged Soviet citizens. The foreign films were old ones, sometimes called 'trophy films', captured by the Red Army, including Tarzan films and non-political German comedies made during the war like *The Girl of my Dreams* (1944),[5] directed by Georg Jacoby, a musical featuring the Hungarian born Marika Rökk, a circus performer turned tap-dancer. A man who saw it in Tbilisi recalled years later, in 1986: 'Normal life stopped in the city. Everyone talked about the film, they ran to see it . . . whistled melodies from it . . . ' The German pictures in circulation were evidently huge moneyspinners at the box office.[6]

All of this amounted to a confirmation of the Western view that the Soviet film industry was unable, for ideological reasons, to provide the Soviet public with what it wanted. The *New York Times's* Moscow correspondent, Harrison E. Salisbury, reported with undisguised satisfaction that what captivated the Soviet public was an archive of 100 or 200 American films captured by the Red Army in Berlin: 'Each year a few of these oldies, Hollywood products of the thirties, were fed out to the Soviet houses with the original English sound-tracks and Russian subtitles. They were announced only as "new foreign pictures". But the public learned that this meant "Old American pictures" . . . ' The sensation of Moscow in the summer of 1954, for instance, was Greta Garbo in *Camille*. The record hit was Johnny Weismuller in *Tarzan*:

In the Red Army's captured film bag there were four old Weismuller *Tarzans*. They were fed out, one at a time, into the Soviet houses over a two-year period. People lined up for blocks to get in. Youngsters saw them again and again . . . Many a taxi-driver and even school children asked me whether Tarzan really lived. So great was the Tarzan fad that teenage boys took to wearing 'Tarzan haircuts'—a horrible kind of long bob.

In the early 1950s Salisbury heard boys promenading up Gorky Street on summer evenings calling to girls, '*Ekh . . . Dzhein*' ('Hey . . . Jane'). The fad became so widespread that the Party started a campaign against it, particularly the Tarzan haircuts and war-cries, 'which were said to be so piercing that they disturbed the cattle on collective farms and kept cows from giving milk'.[7] In an internal memorandum, the Central Committee's deputy head of science and culture reported (19 June 1954) that the American news agency AP had picked up an article in *Iskusstvo kino* suggesting that young Soviet people were impatiently looking forward (*s neterpeniem zhdali*) to a sequel to *Tarzan and the Royal Pirates*—AP had concluded that the Russians were failing to provide the films young people wanted. Summoned to the

Central Committee's Department of Science and Culture, the editor of *Iskusstvo kino* was warned not to repeat such mistakes.[8]

⊞   ⊞   ⊞

As with the parallel decrees on literature and (two years later) music, the real targets of the Central Committee's crude intervention of 4 September 1946 in the field of cinematography were great, free-spirited artists like Eisenstein, Shostakovich, and Prokofiev; but the real targets lay half-concealed behind the furious castigation poured on some mediocre film by Lukov,[9] or an indifferent opera by Muradeli.

Born in 1898, Sergei Eisenstein was one of the great masters and innovators of the silent screen. *Strike* (1924), *The Battleship Potemkin* (1925), and *October* (1928) won worldwide acclaim. The suppression of Eisenstein's films and the humiliating self-criticisms imposed on the world's greatest film director by the Stalinist system were grist to the mill of Western criticism. Isaiah Berlin was sat at the same Moscow table as a gloomy Eisenstein in November 1945: 'I asked him to what years of his life he looked back with the greatest pleasure. He replied that the early post-revolutionary period was far and away the best in his own life as a creative artist...a time when wild and marvellous things could be done with impunity. He spoke nostalgically of surrealists, futurists, formalists and Marxists all quarrelling and stimulating each other.'[10]

In Eisenstein's work montage is the dominant issue. Whereas classical Hollywood–Mosfilm montage is designed to deflect attention from the images as a consciously ordered series of discrete shots or frames, Eisenstein's 'collision montage' was aimed at intensifying this perception. Instead of creating an illusion of spatio-temporal unity, it underscores the shock caused by the juxtaposition of independent shots.[11] Despite the glories of the 1920s, the silent era, followed by his extended trip to Europe, Hollywood, and Mexico, Eisenstein's talents were 'called to order' and enlisted in the savage drama of collectivization; his project known as *Bezhin Meadow* took up the popular story of Pavlik Morozov, a boy who denounced his kulak family and paid for it with his life. Eisenstein viewed the subject through biblical lenses; the boy's murder by bearded, beast-like kulaks was presented as a tale of ritual sacrifice.[12] *Bezhin Meadow* was condemned and never shown; the director was forced to issue a statement of self-criticism accusing himself of a melo-dramatic treatment.[13]

Following the success of his *Aleksandr Nevsky* (1938), Eisenstein was re-stored to favour and appointed head of the Moscow Film School. In January 1941 Zhdanov informed him that he was expected to make a film about the sixteenth-century tsar Ivan the Terrible, a 'supertask' guaranteed especially favourable working conditions—indeed, this guarantee remained in force even after Eisenstein and other film-makers were evacuated to Alma-Ata on 14 October. The score was to be by Sergei Prokofiev. The project was no secret among those of Moscow's intelligentsia who had survived the purges; Boris Pasternak wrote to a friend on 4 February: 'The new passion, openly confessed, is for Ivan the Terrible, the *oprichnina*, and cruelty. This is the subject for new operas, plays, and film scripts. I am not joking.'[14]

For Eisenstein, hard at work on the screenplay, the key concepts were *velichstvo*, majesty, and *edinovlastie*, autocracy, set within the context of the sixteenth-century Russian renaissance. In January 1942 he sent his script to Moscow for approval; having read it, Stalin wrote to Ivan G. Bolshakov, chairman of the Committee for Cinema Affairs: 'The script has not turned out badly. Comrade Eisenstein had coped with the task. Ivan the Terrible as a progressive force of his time, and the *oprichniki* as his expedient instrument, have not turned out badly.' Shooting began at Alma-Ata in April 1943.[15] The first and second parts of the film were filmed simultaneously, but Eisenstein—who often wrote his caustic diary entries in German, referring to Ivan as Johannes der Schrecklich—abandoned the idea of releasing them at the same moment. The first part was to be the apologia, the second the tragedy; the actor Mikhail Kuznetsov, interviewed in 1967, recalled hearing Eisenstein say of Part 2, 'Stalin has killed more people [than Ivan] and he doesn't repent. Let him see this and perhaps he'll repent.'[16]

The decor, pace, strong chiaruscoro shadows, expressionist sets, constructivist influences, the surge and choreography of the mass scenes, all bear witness to the influence of the silent cinema. Eisenstein's style often overlaps with that of Pabst or Fritz Lang: eyes roll, eyebrows lift, figures skulk and lurk and slide into the warren of low tunnels which connect the chambers of the Moscow palaces like catacombs. The texture of clothes is magnificent, likewise the interiors of cathedrals and churches, the finger-rings, the naive and expressionist Christian paintings on the walls. Stylistically Eisenstein was irredeemably modernist. During an episode in Part 2—the wicked aunt of the Tsar sings a lament—Prokofiev's flat atonality echoes the music of Kurt Weill and Hanns Eisler.

Ideologically, however, Eisenstein strove to satisfy the cult of Stalin's personality by projecting Russia's need for a strong leader and ruthless reformer back into the sixteenth century. In Part 1 the commoners adore Ivan and urge him to take strong measures against the selfish, subversive, and unpatriotic boyars—who constantly defect to corrupt Poland or Livonia or the Hanseatic League—by setting up a kind of iron guard, or a

Party, called the *oprichniki*. It is the vigorous and patriotic *oprichniki* who lead the people out to the village of Alexandrov to summon the Tsar back to Moscow.

But in Part 2 Eisenstein's loyal subscription to the leader-cult is subverted by his sense of realism and artistic integrity. The Tsar—and the film itself— succumbs to a kind of hedonistic decadence. As life at Ivan's court becomes more Byzantine and luxurious, the leaders of the *oprichniki*, Ivan's faithful serviteurs who are sometimes more faithful to his principles than he, begin to roll their eyes with sadistic pleasure at the prospect of dispatching more boyars. They dance, dress up as monks, and give themselves over to mime-shows. A leader of the *oprichniki* is heard referring to the people at large as scum. At this juncture the black-and-white film suddenly lurches into violent colour. Now the supreme autocrat who loves power for power's sake, Ivan bullies and threatens his most loyal lieutenants when they contradict him. Eisenstein transforms a celebration into a tragedy. Instead of creating a historical parable of the apotheosis of Stalin, what he filmed in Part 2 was in effect a cryptogram of the internal state of the party in the 1930s and 1940s. Having made sure that the boyar candidate for the throne, Vladimir Staritsky, is intoxicated, Ivan crowns him the Fools' Tsar, and sends him off suitably costumed to a gloomy cathedral where he is murdered by the assassin lying in wait for Ivan. 'It was certainly this cryptogram, the parallels to the staged murder of Kirov, the circumstances surrounding the deaths of Frunze and Ordzhonikidze, the parallels to those who were made Stalin's fools in order to be later liquidated, which made the Grozny film unacceptable.'[17]

Part 1 was screened in the Kremlin on 25 December 1944, two weeks after the Artistic Council of the Committee on Cinema Affairs complained of its cold rationalism. At the end of March 1945 Bolshakov conveyed official permission for the two-part film to become a trilogy. On 26 January 1946 the radio announced the award of a Stalin Prize for Part 1—apparently at Stalin's personal insistence, though the Prize Committee had excluded it from consideration.

Part 2, almost completed, was shown privately at the Ministry of Cinematography to a group of film directors including Mikhail Romm, who later described the occasion:

But no one could bring themselves to say directly that in the character of Ivan the Terrible they keenly sensed an illusion to Stalin, in the figure of Malyuta Skuratov a reference to Beria, and in the *oprichniki* an allusion to their myrmidons . . . But from Eisenstein's impudence, from the gleam in his eyes, from his provocative and sceptical smile, we felt that he knew what he was doing and that he had decided to go for broke. It was dreadful.[18]

On 2 March Bolshakov decided to show Part 2 in the Kremlin. Stalin's reaction to the screening was deadly: 'This isn't a film—it's some kind of nightmare!' He and Beria conveyed acute irritation at the depiction of the *oprichniki*, Beria comparing the scene of the feast and dancing to a witches' sabbath while Stalin likened it to the Ku Klux Klan, adding: 'Ivan the Terrible is depicted as a weak-willed and spineless character—like Hamlet.' Finally Stalin told Bolshakov: 'During the war we didn't have time, but now we'll lick you [film directors] into shape.'[19] The Orgburo of the Central Committee met on 9 August under the chairmanship of Zhdanov, in the presence of Stalin. On 4 September the Central Committee published its notorious resolution criticizing Part 2 precisely in Stalin's terms. The film was held guilty of portraying 'the progressive army of the *oprichniki* as a band of degenerates, similar to the American Ku Klux Klan, and Ivan the Terrible, a man of strong will and character, as weak and spineless, something like Hamlet.'

On 20 October *Kul'tura i zhizn'*[20] published Eisenstein's abject repentance, 'On the Film *Ivan Groznyi*'. The RGALI archive contains his draft scribbled on very thin strips of paper, sometimes using foreign phrases like *qui s'excuse*. The archive also contains one typed version corrected by the secretary of the Writers' Union, Fadeyev, endorsed with the words *pravka A. A. Fadeeva* on the last page. Another version was vetted by P. Satukov.[21] Nothing was being left to chance with the ill-disciplined Eisenstein (who was no stranger to humiliating public self-criticism).[22] The film, he confessed, had centred too much on Ivan's doubts, portraying him as a weak-willed Hamlet, and too little on the strength of the man, his strong will and progressive historical role:

Some of us forget the incessant struggle against our Soviet ideals and ideology which goes on throughout the world . . . Like a bad sentry, we gaped at the unessential and secondary . . . The stern and timely warning of the Central Committee stops us, Soviet artists, from moving further along this dangerous and fatal path . . . In the second part of *Ivan the Terrible* we permitted a distortion of historical facts which made the film ideologically worthless and vicious . . . As a result in the film the progressive *oprichniki* were presented as a gang of degenerates something like the Ku Klux Klan . . . We must master the Lenin–Stalin method of perception of real life and history . . . and again create highly ideological artistic films worthy of the Stalin epoch.[23]

Many Western commentators, including Harvard's George Counts, were to reproduce this *mea culpa* as evidence of Stalinist censorship, the incompatibility of Soviet Communism with the higher arts. The American journal *New Leader* (7 December 1946) reprinted it in full. The bullying of Eisenstein became a jewel in the crown of Western cold war criticism, equal to the attacks on Prokofiev, Shostakovich, and, later, Pasternak.

More was to follow. On the night of 24–5 February 1947, Eisenstein and Nikolai Cherkasov, the illustrious stage and screen actor who had played Ivan, were received in the Kremlin by Stalin, Molotov, and Zhdanov at (typically) 11 p.m. Unknown to Western commentators for a further forty years, the discussion which followed grimly illustrates the Stalinist mentality at its apex—Stalin and his closest underlings. (At one point Zhdanov remarked: 'I have held power for six years myself, no problem.') Twenty-one typed pages of transcript can now be found in the RGALI archive,[24] set out like a script, the speaker's name on the left. Eisenstein, brave but naive, soon broke the golden rule: do not reply to a rhetorical question from Stalin. No answer was expected to the first question from the all-wise helmsman:[25]

STALIN: Have you studied history?

EISENSTEIN: More or less.

STALIN: More or less? I too have a little knowledge of history. Your portrayal of the *oprichnina* is wrong. The *oprichnina* was a royal army. As distinct from a feudal army...this was a standing army, a progressive army. You make the *oprichnina* look like the Ku-Klux-Klan.

EISENSTEIN: They wear white headgear; ours wore black.

MOLOTOV: That does not constitute a difference in principle.

STALIN: Your Tsar has turned out indecisive, like Hamlet. Everyone tells him what he ought to do, he does not take decisions himself. Tsar Ivan was a great and wise ruler...he dwarfs Louis XI. Ivan the Terrible's wisdom lay in his national perspective and his refusal to allow foreigners into his country...Peter I was also a great ruler, but he was too liberal in his dealings with foreigners...Catherine even more so....

ZHDANOV: Eisenstein's Ivan the Terrible comes out as a neurasthenic (*nevrastenik*).

MOLOTOV: There is a general reliance on psychologism...

STALIN: Ivan the Terrible was very cruel...you have to show why he *had* to be cruel. One of Ivan the Terrible's mistakes was to stop short of cutting up the five key feudal clans. Had he destroyed these five clans, there would have been no Time of Troubles.

Stalin shifted to a tone of encouragement when the actor Cherkasov (a member of the Supreme Soviet and a worldly individual) promised they would 'do better' in the proposed remake. Stalin replied to a question from the mainly silent Eisenstein: 'Will there be special instructions?' 'I am not giving you instructions, but the reactions of a spectator (*zritel'*).' He urged the director to take as long as he needed to remake Part 2, 'even three years', pointing out that the painter Il'ia Repin had worked on his canvas *Cossacks* (depicted writing a letter to the Sultan) for eleven years. The conversation ended with Stalin enquiring after Eisenstein's heart condition. This one-to-one blend of bullying and solicitude was reminiscent of Stalin's phone-call to Pasternak about Osip Mandelstam in 1934, but more sharply anticipated his call to Shostakovich—about Shostakovich—in 1949.[26]

Three weeks after this midnight discussion in the Kremlin, Part 1 opened in New York. Bosley Crowther of the *New York Times* (10 March 1947) eulogized 'a film of awesome and monumental impressiveness...', adding a murmured few words about 'the recently reported difficulties of this irrepressible man [Eisenstein] with the guardians of Soviet culture over the second part'. Four months later, on 31 July 1947, *Kul'tura i zhizn'* published a further required piece by Eisenstein, an overt contribution to the cold war, 'Dealers in Spiritual Poison' (*Postavshchiki dukhovnoi otravy*), in which he began by praising such progressive American films as *The Grapes of Wrath*, *Tobacco Road*, and (recently) Elia Kazan's *Boomerang* (1947), which showed how deprivation of sleep could reduce men to sign any confession. But the American cinema was in decline, said Eisenstein; blacklists were operating; clouds were gathering over Chaplin and other anti-fascist actors. Bing Crosby's *Going My Way* was guilty of insidious charm; film-makers set clever traps to capture viewers' hearts during 'two hours of indecency'. *Anna and the King of Siam* was impregnated with white racial superiority and the missionary role of American governesses teaching 'savages'. One of the most insidious features (*odna iz naibolee kovarnykh chert*) of American cinema was deployed to dull feelings of guilt about social inequality. Despite its technical advances, Hollywood's mentality was back in the Middle Ages, the time of the Crusades and even the Stone Age—Eisenstein used the word *mrak*, meaning 'darkness, gloom'.

The RGALI archive contains fragments of Eisenstein's subsequent speech at the Dom kino on 20 November, before a screening of Frank Capra's *Mr Smith Goes to Washington* (1939). Eisenstein began by likening the gathering in the Dom kino to a court about to 'condemn disgusting America' (*osudit' gnusnuiu Ameriku*)—'gnusnaia' was a word much in vogue in the Soviet press. The reason the film had not been banned in America, he said, was extremely sinister (*zloveshchii*)—the Americans were so cynical that they saw no cause to smother the film. He offered a passing tribute to Simonov's play *The Russian Question*, quoting its 'two Americas' thesis as true beyond doubt, then went on to remind his audience that Brecht had written a play about parents who make a disparaging remark about the Führer within earshot of their son, then worry whether the boy has gone to report on them or merely to buy sweets. 'We now gather that informing is the thing to do in the USA.' (Eisenstein, of course, had attempted in the ill-fated *Bezhin Meadow* to laud the legendary Russian boy who dutifully reported on his kulak parents.)

Referring to his trip to the United States in 1930, he read out an American document demanding his expulsion.[27]

American observers such as Arthur Schlesinger, Jr., Bertram D. Wolfe, and Frederick C. Barghoorn lamented—and in a certain sense celebrated—Eisenstein's humiliations.[28] Cinematography figured with increasing prominence in cold war scholarship and journalism. Addressing a gathering of artists and writers under the auspices of the American Committee for Cultural Freedom on 29 March 1952, Bertram Wolfe said of Eisenstein: 'He had a heart attack when the second part [of *Ivan*] was banned. Recovering a little, he wrote a curious and humiliating confession ... Eisenstein earned thereby a few more months of life, but in 1948, when he read the second attack on Shostakovich, he suffered a new heart attack and died the same evening.'[29] Dwight Macdonald described Eisenstein's self-criticism as, 'a macabre echo of his apology, ten years earlier, after *Bezhin Meadow* (*Bezhin lug*) was suppressed.'[30] But the dean of France's Communist film critics, Georges Sadoul, lauded Stalin's instructive meetings with Eisenstein and Pudovkin, in which he patiently explained their faults; Sadoul hoped that one day the stenographic records would be made public. He only regretted that Eisenstein had died too soon to achieve 'the Stalinist trilogy of which he dreamed: "The Caucasus", "Moscow", and "Victory".'[31]

The second part of *Ivan the Terrible* was declared missing or destroyed until 1958. The version which then became famous had been censored, with various scenes cut. The edition of the *Great Soviet Encyclopedia* published a year before the release of *Ivan* Part 2 mentioned only Part 1. Eisenstein was said to have successfully conveyed the atmosphere of Rus in the sixteenth century—'But the portraits of the central heroes of the films *Aleksandr Nevsky* and *Ivan the Terrible* were notable for elements of modernization and idealization.'[32] By contrast, the third edition, published in 1978, is laudatory: 'Eisenstein's last film ... dealt with the theme of power (*vlast*). With its profound historical subject matter and intensive use of the expressive devices of cinema, it became Eisenstein's second masterpiece'—no mention of any small problems that the film and its director had encountered along the way.[33] Volume 3 of the *Istoriia sovetskogo kino* offered a cloud of euphemisms and evasions on the subject of *Ivan the Terrible*. Stalin is never mentioned, either as a model for Eisenstein's tyrant or as the force behind the banning of Part 2. The damning Central Committee resolution of February 1946 likewise goes unmentioned: 'In February 1946 ratification and acceptance of this work was recognized (*priznano*) to be impossible. The second part of *Ivan Grozny* was released twelve years later. The passage of time had made possible a new evaluation.' New debates confirmed rather than refuted that *Ivan* was an 'immortal creation'.[34]

In December 1970 BBC's Omnibus screened two documentaries on Sergei Eisenstein in its 'Larger than Life' series, containing footage from Mosfilm and the Soviet State Archive, and interviews with such close Soviet collaborators of Eisenstein as his cameraman Eduard Tisse, his assistant director Grigorii Aleksandrov, and Mikhail Romm. Aleksandrov was co-producer of the documentaries, the result being that the BBC (and no doubt other Western networks) paid a high moral price for the archival treasures: fascinating clips from Eisenstein's sketchbooks, boy and man, his storyboarding of his films frame by frame, testimony about his childhood in Riga, his early work in the Moscow theatre, and his encyclopaedic knowledge of the film medium. The documentary described the director's use of actual participants in the October Revolution when filming *October* ten years later (he had quipped that there were more deaths during the filming than during the event itself).

Clearly this collaboration by the BBC, National Educational Television (USA), and the Novosti Press Agency carried its price in terms of censorship. The script attributed to Norman Swallow and narrated by Lindsay Anderson omitted any mention of Stalin, the Communist Party of the Soviet Union, the real reason for Eisenstein's non-productivity after his return to Russia from Mexico, the real reason for the suppression of *Bezhin Meadow*, the fact that *Aleksandr Nevsky* was withdrawn after the Nazi–Soviet Pact (an unmentionable event), the terms in which *Ivan the Terrible* was condemned, and Eisenstein's statement of self-abasement shortly before his death. His collaboration with Prokofiev on *Aleksandr Nevsky* and *Ivan* was celebrated—one sees Prokofiev at Eisenstein's funeral—without any mention of the composer's imminent disgrace. The documentary film otherwise relies on a succession of interviews with Communists and fellow-travellers (Joris Ivens and Ivor Montagu among them), without admitting a single voice ready to mention the oppressive conditions for film-making that prevailed under Stalin. The documentary was an example of corrupt cultural coexistence during the Brezhnev era at the very time when Solzhenitsyn, for example, was being expelled from the Soviet Writers' Union.[35]

⊞ ⊞ ⊞

A showpiece Soviet film, *Young Guard* (*Molodaia gvardiia*), reached America at the end of the year 1946. Written and directed by Sergei Gerasimov, based on the novel (later famously withdrawn and rewritten) by Aleksandr Fadeyev, secretary of the Soviet Writers' Union, with a score by Shostakovich, this was the film of all the talents and was generously reviewed by A. H. Weiler in the *New York Times* (26 December). The story tells of resistance by young workers to the German advance on the mining town of Krasnodon in July 1942. On the debit side, Weiler mentioned that 'this earnest and generally convincing tribute to the youth of the Soviets who gave their last full measure of devotion to an embattled homeland suffers from the blights of repetition, some primitive histrionics and rather obvious propaganda'. Even Soviet Russia's friends among American film critics were cooling by 1948. Bosley Crowther of the *New York Times* (26 November) damned Vsevolod Pudovkin's *Admiral Nakhimov* (Mosfilm) when it surfaced at the Stanley Theater.[36] Crowther (who had swallowed the Stalin purge trials in his review of *Mission to Moscow*) found it hard to believe that this 'plodding, dogmatic glorification of a Crimean naval hero, was the handiwork of the director of *Mother* and *the End of St Petersburg*'. Despite praise for the actor Alexei Diukki as the wily old sea dog, and for Pudovkin's 'magnificently staged bayonet charge across the Sevastopol trenches', the dialogue was 'textbook', the characters one-dimensional, and the pace 'lantern-slide'.[37]

In December 1948 the Soviet vice-minister of cinematography, Vassily Shcherbiny, urged Soviet film-makers to struggle against imperialists and warmongers, then named the forthcoming Soviet films which would do precisely that.[38] The Russians at this time coined the term 'artistic documentary' (*khudozestvenno dokumental'ny'*) to cover grandiose feature films which used war-documentary footage, but the 'Stalin cult' aspect depended entirely on non-documentary scenes shot in the studio. Peter Kenez calls Mikhail Chiaureli's *The Oath* (*Kliatva*—also known as *The Vow*, 1946) 'a turning point in the history of Soviet cinema . . . The characters have no functions in the development of a nonexistent story'.[39] Chiaureli was the cinematic maestro of the Stalin-cult:

In the simplicity of his [Stalin's] words there is the wisdom of the ages; in his eyes there is the brightness of genius . . . How to show in art the magnificence of this simplicity? Here in front of you is a person who comprehends with the profundity of a philosopher the complex organism of the universe, our world, the relationship of classes, societies and states . . . he does not seem to differ from any Soviet person, worker, peasant, scholar, artist. For all these people he is close, comprehensible, a family member.[40]

The title refers to Stalin's vow at Lenin's funeral that the Party would remain faithful to the dead leader's teachings. Chiaureli shows Stalin communing with the dead Lenin to the music of Tchaikovsky, vowing fidelity to his programme, then going on to organize the Five Year Plan despite the sabotage of American wreckers. In P. Pavlenko's script, the Stalin cult is fully in evidence and capitalized: STALIN'S OATH (KLIATVA) BECAME THE SYMBOL OF THE FAITH OF THE ENTIRE PEOPLE, THE PROGRAMME OF ITS LIFE.[41] The parallel story is of the Petrovs, a typical family whose head is murdered by kulaks and who are befriended by Stalin. In the middle of the war Stalin makes Varvara Petrovna feel at home in the Kremlin; while revering Stalin, this Mother Russia figure stands fearless in her shawl and tells him the truth about the life of the people while he listens, impressed. Stalin, played by the actor Gelovanni, is more often than not found in obsessive solitude communing with his pipe (no comrades, no Party), a bas-relief.

The once-great director Aleksandr Dovzhenko dutifully lauded this sombre, joyless portrait of Stalin, 'which brings us closer to the sublime era of Communism', yet Dovzhenko's own diary for 27 July 1945 contained an entirely conflicting entry: 'Comrade Stalin, even if you were God, I would not take your word that I am a nationalist who should be branded and dragged in the mud.'[42] Nothing excited such interest among Western commentators as the abasements of an Eisenstein, a Pudovkin, a Dovzhenko. At the Brussels World Exhibition in 1958 three films from the 'golden age' of Soviet cinema would be judged among the world's best twelve of all time: Eisenstein's *Battleship Potemkin* (*Bronenosets Potemkin*), Pudovkin's *Mother* (*Mat'*), and Dovzhenko's *Earth* (*Zemlia*)—though they were rarely screened in the USSR.[43] The long arm of fear[44] obliged Dovzhenko to parrot official, Stalin-inspired condemnations of colleagues' errors; for example, Pudovkin's feel for historical truth had 'deserted him' in the first version of *Admiral Nachimov*; in Part 2 of *Ivan* Eisenstein had 'lost his way and abandoned himself to palace intrigue with all kinds of horrors and dubious trivialities'.[45] Having struggled for four years to complete his film biography *Michurin*, Dovzhenko dutifully praised the entire genre as providing Soviet man with lofty examples of service and idealism leading to Communism.

The veteran Communist film critic Georges Sadoul described *The Oath* (*Le Serment* in France) as the first film which fitted the triumphant spirit of the era. It, like *The Battle of Stalingrad* and Chiaureli's *The Fall of Berlin*, 'quite naturally placed Stalin as the central figure and hero of the action'.[46] A somewhat coarser perspective came from the *News of the World* (5 January 1947), a best-selling London Sunday scandal-sheet known for its salacious contents, which dubbed *The Oath* the 'Film They Dare Not Show Paris', currently being shown 'in Prague and Stalin's other satellite capitals'. In a sequence of the film portraying the standard Soviet version of pre-war diplomacy, Georges Bonnet, France's foreign minister, was depicted as lying on a sofa in the Quai d'Orsay, listening to Negro spirituals and refusing to receive Stalin's emissary urgently sent to him to warn of the Nazi peril. The *News of the World* alleged that 'nude' Frenchwomen are seen lining the august staircase of the Foreign Ministry as the resolute Soviet envoy ascends to Bonnet's suite; and when the envoy tracks Bonnet to a nightclub, he finds the foreign minister dancing 'the Lambeth Walk' and humming 'Parlez-moi d'amour'. (Recommended, even without the nudes.)

Nudity being unheard of in the sexually prudish cinema of the Stalin era, not least in a film awarded a Stalin Prize First Class in 1947, it is not surprising to find that the naked French ladies lining the grand staircase are marble statues of antique goddesses. The Soviet ambassador, accompanied by the military attaché and the fictional hero Sergei, drive to the Quai d'Orsay for a scheduled meeting with Bonnet and a last, desperate attempt to forge a collective security military alliance against Hitler. The year is 1939:

AMBASSADOR: Interesting to find out what answer Bonnet has prepared to our proposal... Very likely it will be some more lies. Bonnet always lies.

Arriving at the French Foreign Ministry, the three Russians ascend the stairs, carefully ignoring the naked goddesses. Bonnet's secretary greets these Bolsheviks nervously, seats them in a waiting room, then hurries into his master's office where Bonnet is found listening not to Negro spirituals but to a hysterical rant on the radio by Adolf Hitler.

SECRETARY: Monsieur Ministre, the Russians are outside... Russians!

Bonnet waves him away, anxious not to miss a word of Hitler—until the British prime minister, Neville Chamberlain, telephones him in the middle of the speech. Bonnet is instantly all servility:

BONNET: Bonjour, sir, bonjour! Ah, you've been listening [to Hitler] too?

It's clear from Bonnet's responses that Chamberlain is expressing admiration for Hitler. The conversation over, Bonnet (and presumably Chamberlain) go back to listening to the Hitler-rant. The phone rings again, but this time it's pleasure calling; 'Celestina' wants to show Georges Bonnet her new dress. Addressing her as 'little one' (*kroshka*), Bonnet promises to join her later in a café, murmurs *sotto voce* to his secretary, 'Tell Monsieur President that I am going out', and instructs him to convey his regrets to the Russians waiting outside:

BONNET: Tell the Russians I'm very sorry.

SECRETARY: About what, Monsieur?

BONNET: You don't have to spell that out, my friend.

The Russians are politely sent packing. Descending the stairs, Sergei asks the Soviet ambassador:

SERGEI: Does this mean it's war?

AMBASSADOR: Yes, after Munich war became a reality.

SERGEI: Does it mean my journey to England and America is no longer necessary?

AMBASSADOR: England and America are not interested in us.

The next scene takes place in a high-society Parisian café. Sergei is greeted by a Negro doorman. Alerted that Monsieur Bonnet has arrived, the head-waiter scurries at breakneck speed to the entrance, bowing low as Bonnet enters with Celestina. Having seated his important guest, the head-waiter ventures to express hostility to Hitler:

HEAD-WAITER: There seem to be a lot of Hitler's friends with us tonight. Like flies before the rain. Something is definitely going to happen.

CELESTINA (*smiling*): Ah, Grégoire, I see you are a supporter of the anti-Hitler coalition.

HEAD-WAITER: Madame, how could it be otherwise?

Bonnet reminds him what war means—'Bombs!'—and the head-waiter hastily uncorks the champagne. Later Bonnet remarks to Celestina that he'd rather see France occupied by Hitler than make an alliance with the Bolsheviks. Celestina leads him on to the dance floor where the band is playing boogie-woogie (no mention of the 'Lambeth Walk', favoured by the *News of the World*).[47] Sergei and his appalled friends watch the foreign minister dancing, then depart in disgust.

SERGEI (*leaving*): And the fate of the world depends on this swine!

The film then changes into neo-documentary, agit-prop mode, an authoritative voice announcing a series of Hitlerian advances, interspersed with (a) shots of German tanks, etc. and (b) Bonnet dancing, dancing, and dancing. There is no hint of the Nazi–Soviet Pact of 22 August 1939.[48]

Between 1946 and 1953 Soviet studios produced seventeen film biographies, all of them glowing tributes to the talents and patriotism of leading Russian scientists, musicians, and military leaders. From a not untypical Western perspective, the heroes looked alike, the dialogues were virtually interchangable, and the characters never altered or developed. Peter Kenez writes: 'As geniuses they have great ideas and correct attitudes to everything from the first moment of our meeting them ... These films have more in common with the ancient lives of saints than with Marxism.' Glinka, Mussorgsky, and Rimsky-Korsakov get their inspiration from listening to folk music.[49]

In *Aleksandr Popov* the pioneering scientist explains electromagnetism to simple fishermen, who not only understand him but come up with brilliant suggestions for further work. Makarov, the progressive admiral, is attempting to persuade the conservative officers of the Ministry of the Navy to develop Popov's invention:

OFFICIAL: I already told you. We will find firms that will deliver what we need. Most likely an English firm.

MAKAROV: Why English?

OFFICIAL: Well, French.

MAKAROV: We should start something ourselves. But we will, by God, we will!

The same situations and almost the same words repeat themselves in other filmic biographies. In *Zhukovskii* the Russian inventor of the airplane says to the reactionary official: 'The military authorities should understand, colonel, that we ourselves can make airplanes. And you suggest that we should order them from abroad. Why? Why?'[50] V. Pudovkin's film ends with a gigantic picture of Stalin painted on a plane.[51]

In Soviet film biographies of the late Stalin era, foreigners, particularly Americans, are always desperate to steal or buy up Russian science. They steal Popov's invention of the radio after he refuses to allow himself to be bought: 'My work belongs to the fatherland. I am a Russian person . . .' Marconi is portrayed as no better than a common thief. The innocent scientific work of the great geographer Przhevalskii, beloved by the natives in Central Asia, arouses admiration, fear, and hostility in Disraeli and the British, but he prevails despite their intrigues.[52] The director Dovzhenko encountered a great deal of trouble making *Michurin*—it took four years and numerous changes. When a visiting American industrialist offers to ship the botanist's estate acre by acre to the United States for a huge dollar reward, Michurin replies: 'No. American dollars will never buy Russian land or Russian men!' Dovzhenko no doubt sincerely contrasted Soviet film biographies with the inevitable stress on private life in their bourgeois counterparts; even when the subject was Henry VIII, Edison, Lincoln, Chopin, Pasteur, Rembrandt, or Mozart, 'the forms [are] shallow and arid'. Dovzhenko insisted that 'private life should find its expression in public life'. In the West the artist had become a lackey of cliques mobilizing science for war and propagating racial discrimination: 'They reject Pasteur, all medicine, all health protection. So it's understandable if men like Beethoven, Pasteur, or Zola appear in these films as stupid, poorly cultivated, limited specialists, who do not emerge out of the narrow sphere of a "thrilling" plot and entertaining antics.'[53]

In the *Krokodil* issue of 30 September 1953 the satirist Yuri Blagov offered a number of humorous verses about typical genres of Soviet film, under the title 'A Timely Warning' (*Neobkhodimoe preduprezhdenie*). In a section on 'Historical-Biographical Films' Blagov made fun of well-known names uttering proven quotes, oblivious to everything except their own utterances as houses burned and meteors fell from the sky:

> Such well-known names as you'd expect,
> Appropriate quotes—all quite correct.
> The hero neither drinks nor walks,
> Nor eats, nor sleeps, but talks and talks.
>
> .   .   .   .
>
> He reels off speeches by the score,
> Enough to fill a book or more.
> His range of themes is wide and deep
> (The audience are all asleep.)[54]

Then there is *Love on the Kolhoz—Kolkhoznaia komediia*:

> He begs her soon to name the day,
> But this is what she has to say:
> 'Unless your prowess in the field
> Is much improved, I will not yield!'[55]

While scientific treachery—real or feared—haunted the American imagination, it was an equally obsessive theme in such Mosfilms as Abram Room's *Court of Honour (Sud chesti*, 1948).[56] Based on Boris Stein's long-running play about a venal Soviet scientist who passes secrets to an American drugs company, the film was directed, written, and photographed by Jews (A. Gal'perin was the cameraman) in what looked like a collective *sauve qui peut* at the height of the anti-cosmopolitan campaign. *Court of Honour* duly drew the hostile attention of the American press.[57] Two Soviet scientists, Dobrotvorskii and Losev, are on the verge of a major discovery (a wholly beneficent anaesthetic pain-killer). On the occasion of a trip to the United States they have talked to the foreign press, which declares hypocritically: 'Science Knows no Frontiers!' Losev turns out to be driven by vanity, craving the admiration of foreigners. The Americans make a return visit, headed by Professor Carter, who has lost control of his own research to a capitalist entrepreneur, and cleverly penetrate the beautifully equipped Soviet Research Institute's laboratory. At this juncture good Soviet citizens intervene—enough is enough. Vereiskii, a military surgeon and academician, who occupies a sumptuous dacha overlooking a river, makes sure that the visiting American predators are thwarted. Later he will turn public prosecutor before the Court of Honour, delivering a fulmination worthy of A. Vyshinsky.

The aim of the film was clearly to reinforce the all-pervasive xenophobia of the time, while simultaneously fulfilling the established cinematic task of turning reality on its head: it must be the Americans who crave to filch Soviet scientific secrets. The formula is simple: Soviet science is for peace, American science is for war. 'Our company has 200 million shareholders', a Soviet scientist tells Carter. But the two Soviet scientists who erred in divulging their work to Americans do not give up readily. They are stubborn, and one of them, the handsome Aleksandr Dobrotvorskii, is principled too, insisting that scientific knowledge must be shared across national frontiers, otherwise Churchill's slanders about the Iron Curtain would be justified. His wife, whose patriotic vigilance helps to foil the American spies, castigates her husband for his careless indiscretions when dealing with Americans: 'How was this possible?' she asks him. 'At an unofficial banquet you took a business card from a foreigner, which had his private number! Just like a child!' Stunned, Dobrotvorskii tears up the Yankee card and embraces her, but she later criticizes her husband for his conceit and folly before the Court of Honour set up by the Institute at the minister's command. Dobrotvorsksii's former teacher, who wears the black fez which old-school academicians invariably wear in films, thunders at him that Americans are thieves.

The Court of Honour was a Soviet institution, here very much resembling a film-set, with a raised platform confronting steeply raked seats under a statue of Lenin and a huge portrait of Stalin. Automated clapping in the short, staccato bursts which chill the blood, greets a nasty diatribe from our friend Surgeon-Academician-Prosecutor Vereiskii, upholding 'the banner of the primogeniture (*pervorodstvo*) of Russian science', and preserving the proud heritage of Pavlov, Lermontov, Mendelev, and Popov, all of whose discoveries had been shamelessly expropriated by foreigners, and now by 'the hired killers and overseas traders of death'. Vereiskii draws breath before attacking rootless cosmopolitans and 'passportless tramps'. 'We are the hope and conscience of humanity!' he screams. Abram Room's film reeks of elite privilege (special rations for academicians); American bacteriological experimentation is denounced at tables loaded with fruit, wine, and cigarettes. The symbols of Soviet virtue—Vereiskii, his daughter Olga, and her fiancé, a Marxist philosopher—hold a kind of *domashniaia partgruppa* cell meeting at home, even though Surgeon Vereiskii himself is not a Party member.

The vain culprit-scientist Losev, who refuses to repent—'I have nothing further to say'—cannot be saved from the terrible disease of 'kowtowing to the West', while the deputy health minister must suffer for his negligence in allowing Americans to visit the laboratory. Perhaps the most interesting character is Losev's wife Nina, a decorative, fashion-conscious woman (played by Lydia Sukharevskaia), but not excessively so, and perceptive.

Once a researcher, she is now 'just a housewife', too interested in hem-lines, invitations to premières, and ivory cigarette-holders. She realizes that her vain husband is too easily charmed by flattering American headlines, but she too basks in the glory: 'I am nothing without him.'

Not only characters in films, but film directors themselves were confronted by 'courts of honour'. Peter Kenez relates how in 1988 *Sovetskii ekran* published a memoir by Mikhail Romm, 'How I was handed over to a court of honour'. Once again the issue was anti-American xenophobia running wild in the *sauve qui peut* atmosphere of late Stalinism.[58]

The most vicious and destructive episode in cold war cultural conflict was the anti-cosmopolitan campaign, combining fear of American influence, xenophobia, and—above all—anti-Semitism. In an article entitled 'On the Aesthetic Cosmopolitan Group in the Cinema',[59] the deputy minister of the cinema, Vassily Shcherbin, declared: 'In the healthy milieu of the film industry the few people who still deny the merits of the Soviet cinema are contaminated with slavish kowtowing to foreign culture.' A number of well-known figures were denounced by the deputy minister as 'miserable tramps of humanity', 'homeless and nameless cosmopolitans', 'base spokesmen of reactionary aestheticism'.[60] Leonid Trauberg was berated for 'grovelling' to American cinema and for 'spreading and elaborating the false and un-Soviet myth that the American director [D. W.] Griffith was the father of world film art'.[61] Trauberg's thoroughly 'formalist' film, *Simple People* (*Prostye liudi*), had been sharply condemned by the Central Committee and banned: 'In this dirty, anti-patriotic activity his collaborators were M. Bleiman and N. Kovarskii...' In his book about Griffith, Mikhail Bleiman had dared to call this reactionary racist, ' "the father" of world cinematography'. Pudovkin was quoted: 'We must remove from our work all cosmopolitan and anti-patriotic little ideas. We must demand from all artists a moral-political cleanliness...' Konstantin Simonov spoke up to denigrate 'these little people [who] got on Hollywood's bandwagon'.[62]

No mention of the anti-Semitic 'anti-cosmopolitan' campaign is to be found in the Brezhnev-era *Istoriia sovetskogo kino*.

⊞   ⊞   ⊞

April 1949 brought the Moscow première of *The Meeting on the Elbe* (*Vstrecha na El'be*), written by the Tur brothers (as they were invariably described) and Lev Sheinin, and magnificently directed by one of Sergei Eisenstein's leading pupils, Grigorii Aleksandrov.[63] Based on the stage play *Gubernator provintsii* (*Governor of a Province*), by the same writers, now running in its second year at the Lenin Komsomol Theatre, Moscow, and many provincial theatres,[64] the thrust of the plot is how Americans sabotage friendly relations with the USSR.

The Tur brothers had served as war correspondents for *Izvestiia* during the final defeat and occupation of Germany. In the edition of 17 April 1945 they wrote: 'We have travelled through many German cities and have talked to many of these Hitlerites. What astounded us most was their complete lack of human dignity. Today they feign contrition or ignorance, assume Ash Wednesday faces, and display the humility of monks. But it is all play-acting.'[65] However, the exigences of Zhdanovism soon demanded of the Tur brothers a play in which German 'play-acting' was very thoroughly replaced by American villainy, the majority of Germans in the fictional 'Altenstadt' emerging as decent people innocent of Nazi crimes.

As panicked Germans clutching suitcases try to scramble aboard the last ferry to cross the Elbe, kicking each other into the water, Soviet tanks burst triumphantly through the several gates of an old Gothic arch and hurtle to the banks of the river, to a spirited film-score by Dmitri Shostakovich (whose serious music was currently banned in Soviet concert halls).[66] The agreed frontier between the American and Soviet armies, the Elbe, is journey's end for the Red Army. A haughty crowing cock is seen astride a swastika floating in midstream; steam gushes through the smashed fabric of a Teutonic statue. Moments later, American tanks appear on the far bank, to Shostakovich's adaptation of 'Yankee Doodle Dandy'—the theme song of American radio broadcasts to Russia—and hearty cheers from the assembled Ivans. Watching the Americans arrive on the opposite bank, a Soviet general remarks caustically: 'Yes, it's interesting that in the last days of the war a second front appeared.' American soldiers dive into the river and swim across, to be received by outstretched hands, brotherly embraces, and toasts in vodka which burn the throats of the Yanks. Observing this dangerously 'democratic' scene of fraternization with false affability, as a guest of honour on the Soviet side, a tubby American general, MacDermott (Vladimir Vladislavski), mutters to an aide: 'This is the most unfortunate consequence of the war.' Offered a pair of Soviet binoculars, and impressed by the superior optics, MacDermott assumes they are German, but the imprinted letters GPU are pointed out to him. He discreetly passes them to a subordinate.

Apart from the very occasional word in English—'Hullo'—all non-Russian characters in the film, Americans and Germans, speak and sound like cultivated Russians,[67] with the exception of Major Hill's chauffeur, who turns out to be of Ukrainian origin. By contrast, the Anglo-American film tradition demands thick accents of foreigners, particularly villains—as if speaking English badly is part of the crime. Full marks to the Russians.

Under our benevolent, tall, and handsome hero, Major Kuz'min (played by the popular Vladlen Davydov), the Soviet sector of Altenstadt benefits from food supplies and every kind of help. As a Soviet critic Gribachev, writing in *Kul'tura i zhizn'*, put it, 'Kuz'min gives the order for the seizure of the war factories and at the same time organizes the reconstruction of the town and opens the schools'. He is 'a man of crystal honesty and purity'[68]—an understatement. In this film, as in others, Russian characters are portrayed as being without blemish: no lapses, no black sheep, no 'contradictions'. When two (beautifully starched) German nuns turn up, short of oil for their convent lamps, a quick-witted Soviet sergeant manages to fix them up with machine-gun oil. Munitions factories are converted to the production of consumer goods. 'We must find a way to the heart of the German people!' declares a Red Army general. The official American attitude is in stark contrast: 'Why the hell do you bother with all that?' an American asks Major Kuz'min. 'Are you really interested in the fate of the Germans? I personally don't give a damn about them.'

Aleksandrov frequently resorts to the heroic, anthemic style found in Soviet statues and liberation ballets; when the Red Army throws open the gates of the town prison, the inmates storm out exultantly singing in Russian. The young 'democrat' Kurt Dietrich, joyful at his release, declares: 'We the German Communists and social democrats of the working class [etc. etc.] . . .'

The great drawbridge spanning the Elbe is masterfully worked and reworked by Aleksandrov throughout the film until, at the final shot, it parts the clasped hands of the two protagonists, Major Kuz'min and Major Hill (Mikhail Nazvanov). The mutual understanding between the two tank majors is strengthened by their common fate, to be appointed commandants, about which both are dissatisfied. Hill, a teacher in civilian life, dreams of creative and peaceful work but cannot explain why his government is 'actively preparing for war':

KUZ'MIN: Why have you immediately begun to restore the armaments factories in your zone, instead of destroying them in accordance with the Potsdam decisions?

HILL: It's a military secret (*voennaia taina*).

KUZ'MIN: I also think that it's a military secret, but a very dangerous one. Did you think about that? . . .

HILL: My general, MacDermott, says that a soldier isn't payed to think (*soldat dumat' ne polagaetsia*).

KUZ'MIN: Your general is not original in that assertion. He had a predecessor who asserted the same thing.

HILL: Who was that?

KUZ'MIN: Adolf Hitler.

On a later occasion Hill reminds the reactionary Senator Wood of this same 'fact' after the senator expresses the identical sentiment.

The elderly German liberal, Professor Dietrich, tells Kuz'min that he hates Nazis, 'though you won't believe me', but refuses to hand over his patents, which 'belong to Germany'. Dietrich hotly complains to Kuz'min that the Russians are taking away his laboratory to Russia, a laboratory belonging to a German firm one hundred years old. The Russian replies that it cannot atone for the destruction of one thousand years of Russian civilization wrought by Germany. Kuz'min frequently stresses that the Russians, unlike the Americans, do not blame the 'German people'. Dietrich nervously asks Kuz'min whether the Russians intend to impose the Soviet system on Germany. 'Not at all. Communism is something you have to deserve.' Kuz'min, although occupying commandant and master of all he surveys, always treats Dietrich with the respect due to a distinguished professor and father-figure.

Preparing for the municipal elections, Kuz'min receives Germans of all political parties then decides he wants a non-party Bürgermeister, Dietrich himself (Iu. Iurovski)—though 'non-party' turns out to be the KPD–SPD unity ticket forced through as a shotgun marriage in 1946. Ballot papers will hurtle into ballot boxes in a snowstorm of popular unanimity as Professor Dietrich is elected Bürgermeister. Soviet editing speeds up, with newsreel-style music, whenever reality poses an awkward complexity. By contrast, General MacDermott rapidly instructs a sinister German to set up various political parties, above all social democrats, to combat Communism.

A big row soon ensues between the newly installed Burgermeister and his son Kurt, placed in charge of the city's education by Kuz'min, when the father complains that Kurt has arrested two scientists whom the professor regards as colleagues.

'But they are Nazis, and you know it!' Kurt replies, banging the desk.

'They are good Germans!' replies the indignant professor.

Old Dietrich is duly duped by a neo-Nazi plot involving his daughter's husband, having been shown the empty safe in his laboratory and misled into believing the Russians have seized his patents. Unaware that his shifty son-in-law is involved in the American espionage network, he crosses over to the American zone, where he is received by a smiling General MacDermott who invites him to set up his laboratory-factory in the American zone, manufacture weapons, and foster and support anti-Communism, 'all paid for by the Marshall Plan'—although pedants might quibble here that the notorious plan did not emerge until two years after the war. The periodic screen caption *vremia shlo* ('later') does not clarify the intended historical time-span of the narrative.

The Americans are a mixed bunch. The ordinary ones admire the Russians, want peace—and well understand that it was the Russians who won the war. But American behaviour on the US bank of the Elbe becomes increasingly lamentable: GI's are shown rowdily carousing in a night-club (whose curved neon sign announces NIGHTCLUB), from which a Negro soldier is ejected by jeering whites. American officers are discovered drilling German civilians in the goose-step in front of the town-hall, and there are hints that the most decadent Americans, the ones with lopsided faces, suspicious moustaches, caps tilted rakishly, and cigarettes drooping from sneering lips, are abusing and exploiting German women.[69] The irony lies in the fact that the rigid decorum prevailing in Stalinist cinema rescues the Yanks from full exposure, just as it limits the scenes of American jazz-dancing to long shots involving none of the acrobatics and flashing thighs of contemporary boogie-woogie.

Venality is the presiding American sin. General MacDermott and his wife trade cigarettes to starving Germans in return for art treasures, gold, and furs, which are shipped home by plane. When chalking a white cross on requisitioned works of art, they apply the chalk to the canvas rather than the backing. Faina Ranevskaya plays the wife in a style later described by the *Istoriia sovetskogo kino*: 'She wears a broad, fixed smile fixed like false teeth and a greedy gleam in her eye; buy, grab, speculate while you can.'[70] Mrs MacDermott is having her portrait painted by an elderly German artist while talking to her husband; she keeps swinging her fixed smile back at the painter, whose version of it we see on his canvas. Laughingly she confides that she won't be paying the old German artist in cash, a tin of pork meat and a packet of cigarettes will do him. The phone rings during the portrait session; MacDermott is informed that there's a fuel crisis in England and wood fetches a high price there. His wife tells him to cut down the local forests and sell the wood to the English. 'Don't be a milksop in epaulettes. You don't put on your tight-fitting general's dress uniform in order to play nurse to the lousy Germans. All around are beautiful woodlands whose foliage rustles like dollars. Fell the darned wood and sell it to the English while it's not too late.'

Soviet male scriptwriters habitually portrayed the female of the American species as a symbol of greed, egging on her man to corruption in the capitalist Garden of Eden. Reviewing the film, the Soviet critic N. Gribachev eavesdrops on the general's wife and writes about her as if she belonged to reality rather than fiction.[71] The hero, Major Kuz'min, rejects the advances of the beautiful temptress-journalist-spy Jeanette Sherwood (played by the director's wife, Lyubov' Orlova),[72] who is sent to the Soviet zone to contact 'the old Hitlerite wolf' Herr Schrank, a Gestapo war criminal hiding under a false name, with a view to stealing Dietrich's secret military patents for weapons sights. The glamorous (*milovidnaia*) Sherwood, whose real name and identity will emerge at the end, when she drops her mask, as Miss Collins of the Federal Intelligence Service (*razvedka*), rolls her eyes and feigns tears in Kuz'min's presence, claiming that she was born in Germany and is searching for her poor, dear (sniff) anti-Nazi father in the Soviet zone. Due to Major Kuz'min's refusal to be bamboozled by a pretty woman whose cosmetic eyes roll like marbles, and the vigilance of an elderly German worker who pays for his patriotism with his life, Schrank will finally be caught with the stolen documents on the bridge over the Elbe, frustrated inches from the American line. Liubov' Orlova's performance is part-Garbo, part-Dietrich, and, no doubt, part-Orlova. The sideways-and-upwards glance of her eye-shadow at the handsome Major Kuz'min tells us all we need to know; indeed, if the Americans had spies like this, how could they lose? Orlova later recalled how she experienced much doubt and anxiety in casting herself in this new and unaccustomed role—although it was neither: in *The Error of Engineer Kochin* she had played a woman inveigled into a criminal conspiracy. 'I have observed such women abroad, well groomed, beautiful, well dressed, and simultaneously spiritually empty, without lofty strivings (*bez vysokikh stremlenii*) . . . fluctuating loyalties attached only to worship of the dollar.'[73] That such an outpouring of xenophobia should have been required for what is, after all, merely an amusing, larger-than-life, cartoon-caricature, must reflect the totally politicized condition of the Soviet mind in the Zhdanov era.

A blonde boy of about 13, who happens to be Professor Dietrich's daughter's son but is under his Nazi father's influence, recites a Nazi poem at the reopening ceremony of his school, and is responsible for distributing the Nazi leaflets which Kuz'min gently but firmly orders teachers, pupils (and visiting American friends) to tear up. The assembled male teachers, shifty and tight-jawed Nazi sympathizers, are arrayed in front of a vast Teutonic stone figure clasping a sword. The blond boy's short poem speaks passionately of a march across frontiers full of hatred and pride in blood. Later the boy will come to Kuz'min and explain that they were taught in class that Germany would extend to the Volga. Kuz'min answers that Russia does not wish to extend to the Elbe.

Having observed many horrors in the American zone, including the rapacious felling of a precious German woodland to serve the greed of the MacDermotts—needless to say, we never catch sight of whole factories rolling by train towards Russia—the honest Dietrich in his old-fashioned wing collar hurriedly returns to the Soviet zone, makes peace with his Communist son, and resumes his duties as Bürgermeister.

At a ball given by Hill in the American sector, Kuz'min, wearing his smart, white evening uniform, meets Senator Wood, a puppet of American million-aires, who is already calling erstwhile allies tomorrow's enemies. When Kuz'min tells him that anyone starting a future war will share Hitler's fate, the jovial senator comments that Hitler didn't have the atomic bomb. When Wood says, in effect, 'I don't like Russians and you don't like Americans, have another drink', Kuz'min replies with his usual sweet dignity that Russians do indeed love the America of Whitman, Mark Twain, Edison, Jack London, and Roosevelt. But the iconography of the film is a constant affirmation of Europe and its culture against the pillaging transatlantic philistine who defiles works of art, antiques, history itself. Russian characters invariably move with dignity and restraint; even the good Americans have a jack-in-the-box, neurotic tendency to fidget with their pockets, their little gadgets, their cigarettes. We hear Beethoven's 'Ode to Joy' as Mayor-Professor Dietrich unveils a new statue of Heinrich Heine in the town square. Unfortunately this has to be accompanied by polemical orations in the Zhdanov mode, with Dietrich's final declaration: 'Two worlds met on the two banks of the Elbe. Germany cannot remain between them . . . I have made my choice. I am remaining on your bank. On the bank where a new, peaceful, united, demo-cratic Germany is born.'

When Kuz'min reveals to Hill that the beautiful Jeanette Sherwood has been engaged in lying and espionage, the shocked American orders her to return to the United States immediately. Reaching the airfield (so obviously a studio set that it may be a directorial joke), he points her impatiently to the steps of her plane, only to discover that she is a powerful figure surrounded by yes-men, including General MacDermott, who smartly salutes her. On the steps of her plane, Sherwood-Collins throws off her cape, revealing a shapely and somewhat Ruritanian uniform, lights a cigarette, purringly expresses admiration for her opponent Major Kuz'min, 'a good diplomat', and dresses down Hill as a good-for-nothing too friendly with Kuz'min; she then flies off into the studio sky, her propellors blowing the cap from the head of the thoroughly disillusioned Major Hill. Aleksandrov was rightly proud of this scene.[74]

Poor Major Hill! When they meet for one last time on the bridge over the Elbe, he tells his friend Kuz'min that he is to be sent home to face the House Un-American Activities Committee. Kuz'min mutters *Tak.*—Ah. A farewell handshake follows, the two halves of the drawbridge rise, their hands are seen to hang in the air. But the Soviet theatre critic E. Severin, reviewing the original stage play, commented that Hill's apparent conversion was all very well and fine, but unfortunately difficult to believe, because in order to reach such a conclusion you would need to be a man more serious, thoughtful, and genuinely honest than Hill is: 'For the Soviet spectator Hill, while not lacking personal charm, is narrow-minded, carefree and conceited, and worthy of pity for his poverty of spirit and the baseness of his striving to "do honest business" while not understanding the political climate. He is pitiable because petty as he slides downhill into personal catastrophe.'[75]

Aleksandrov recalled that the film's prospects looked bleak when edited sections, shot in a remarkably short time, were shown to the artistic committee of the Ministry of Cinematography. At the ensuing conference in the Ministry much was said about an excessively respectful portrayal of yesterday's enemy, the Germans—although Aleksandrov objected that the film did not portray Germans in general, but representatives of different estates and classes, concealed Nazis, and the emergent supporters of a free democratic Germany. For this film, Aleksandrov remembered, the artistic committee of the Ministry was not the court of last instance; a day later *Vstrecha na El'be* was shown to the Central Committee. 'As usual, the deciding word belonged to Stalin. As the light was turned on in the viewing room, he rose and declared in a flat, low mutter: *"Fil'm sniat s bol'shim znaniem dela*—the film was shot with great knowledge of the facts." ' It was decided immediately to show it on the nation's screens. Aleksandrov claimed that it was warmly received in East Germany, 'evidence of its truthfulness'. On the day before an international conference of Communist newspaper editors opened in Bucharest, he was suddenly dispatched there with boxes of film. He flew on to Berlin, Prague, Warsaw, and back to Moscow, the whole journey accomplished within three days. Aleksandrov compared the life of this film to a kind of newspaper editorial. *Meeting on the Elbe* was awarded a Stalin Prize and a peace prize at the 1949 Karlovy Vary international film festival. Over a sardonic report by Harrison E. Salisbury, the *New York Times* ran one of its longer subheadings: 'Muscovites see Americans Portrayed as Mata Haris, Thieves of Russian Science and as Super-Knaves in Germany.' Salisbury reported long lines queuing outside Moscow cinemas to see (he said) the actress Orlova. Richard Stites comments: 'In moral message, casting, and *mise-en-scène* [such films] were the Soviet equivalents of the American anti-Communist pictures, *Red Menace* and *I Married a Communist.*'[76] But Aleksandrov's epic choreography, filmed by Eduard Tisse, along the banks of the Elbe as the two Allied armies greet each other, has no equivalent in the low-budget anti-Communist films produced by Hollywood. The Soviet cinema was producing history films, albeit a history distorted by top-down ideological directives, whereas Hollywood was producing anti-history films, in which the global canvas was replaced by pathology, by 'Communists' practising villainy, *le mal pour le mal*, for the hell of it. General MacDermott and his rapacious wife are caricatures, but their ideology and actions are closer to reality than those of the gangster 'Communists' in Hollywood's *Big Jim McLean* or *I Married a Communist*. Neither Billy Wilder nor Carol Reed would have been ashamed to have directed passages of *Meeting on the Elbe*, and Hollywood produced no soundtrack as good as Shostakovich's, not even the one Darryl Zanuck stole from him for *The Iron Curtain*. The film contains post-war fascist faces, tilted hats, and sly urban angles reminiscent of Reed's *The Third Man*—both films came out in 1949. On the evidence of the *New York Times* index of film reviews, *Meeting on the Elbe*, like many other prominent Soviet films of the era, did not reach New York.[77]

Writing a quarter of a century later, the director repeated the stock Soviet sentiments of the late 1940s in the standard phrases and clichés of that time. Although a major film-maker with a flair for comedy, Aleksandrov solemnly spoke of the film's valuable contribution to the struggle between two opposed principles in international politics, the peaceful and the aggressive.[78] This was typical of his generation: whatever their view of Stalin's internal repression, few of them later repudiated his foreign policy.

⊞　⊞　⊞

War films remained vehicles of ideological competition on both sides of the Iron Curtain—though American war movies did not suffer from the suffocating grip of an autocrat determined to 'paint' himself into eternity's gallery of immortals. Mosfilm's two-part *Battle of Stalingrad* (*Stalingradskaia bitva*), directed by Vladimir Petrov with a scenario by Nikolai Virta, was released in the West in 1950.[79] Alexander Werth, who had been a war correspondent during the battle, went to see the film in the Faubourg Montmartre. 'Remembering the empty houses of the Soviet film shows in the Charing Cross Road, I was astonished to find a very long queue outside.' Werth was disappointed: the whole story had become 'completely dehumanized... These were not the people I had known at Stalingrad—they were robots instead. The officers and the men [in the film] seemed to have only one full-time function: to carry out faithfully the orders of Comrade Stalin.' Stalin was ham-acted by the actor Alexei Diukki, while the Soviet commander Zhukov, semi-disgraced by a jealous Stalin since the war, was never mentioned.[80] When the archive-based second part of *The Battle of Stalingrad* reached America under title *The Victors and the Vanquished*, A. H. Weiler (A. W.) of the *New York Times* (1 May 1950) noted that once again Stalin was depicted as the guiding genius. The battle scenes were marvellous, a credit to Vladimir Petrov's direction, but 'the repetitious, static clips showing Stalin or his generals directing and planning the battle robs the film of much needed movement'.

The Korean War had brought international relations deeper into crisis when a major Soviet epic, Mikhail Chiaureli's *The Fall of Berlin* (*Padenie Berlina*, 1949), reached New York late in the day.[81] The film opens in the idyllic era of the Five Year Plans, the year 1941 (the Nazi–Soviet Pact is of course not mentioned), with children gaily singing a song by Shostakovich as they wend through a wide meadow bright with flowers, innocent of the war to come. The same uplifting song will be heard throughout and even woven into battle scenes. *The Fall of Berlin*—Mosfilm's seventieth-birthday present to Stalin, and justifiably regarded as the epitome of the personality cult—was shot in Agfacolor print-stock taken from Germany. Chiaureli, his camera operator L. Kosmatov, and the designer V. Kaplunovskii, called upon to create a work 'worthy of the great epoch of Stalin'—*dostoinye epochi velikogo Stalina*, strove to create a bright and consistent colour palette, whether for the scene in Stalin's garden, Aleksei (Alyosha) and Natasha in the sunlit field,[82] the children's excursion to the factory, or the battle scenes.[83]

The film begins in an idyllic peacetime setting; a model factory receives news of Stakhanovite awards for the hero Alyosha, a record-breaking steel-worker, and the schoolteacher heroine Natasha.[84] Everyone is brimming with health, everyone laughing and smiling, clapping and dancing. The workforce is thoroughly cultured, attending concerts and declaiming poetry: in Soviet culture love requires poetry, and sure enough hero and heroine quote Pushkin to one another. Portraits of Stalin hang from schoolrooms—indeed from everywhere. Natasha (played by Marina Kovaleva) delivers a speech to honour Aleksei, tears in her eyes as she gazes at a portrait of Stalin: 'Who gave us such a day? The greatest happiness would be ours if he could be with us. Long live Stalin!'

Her wish is fulfilled when Aloysha (B. Andreev) is summoned to meet his leader (Mikhail Gelovani). Wearing his white tunic, Stalin is found in an idyllic garden setting, carrying a hoe and serenely listening to the birds.[85] The sudden and treacherous German attack strikes as Alyosha and Natasha stroll in a field of poppies. The film now moves into its 'history' or 'artistic documentary' dimension: Stalin, Molotov, and the generals are seen conferring during the defence of Moscow. Hitler, the bloated Göring, and the limping Goebbels are found chatting with effusive diplomats from Japan and the Vatican. The Führer rants and raves (in Russian), on and on, gloating over maps. We see the blonde Eva Braun with her hats and cakes, and Göring's purloined paintings. Göring himself is found in conversation with what appears to be an American politician, toasting the imminent fall of

Stalingrad, but, backed by Shostakovich's music, the Russians triumph in that battle.

Returning to the personal story, soldier-in-arms Aloysha comes across Natasha's devastated home, where a loose drainpipe is still visible. Extreme theatricality prevails, in garish colour. The battlefront moves westward. The Red Army launches each attack with the primitive battle-cry: 'Stalin!' The fate of the civilian population is on the whole ignored by Chiaureli, with the exception of an excellent scene of Soviet civilian prisoners—Natasha among them—being beaten, shot, and driven from their stalag during an air-raid as Soviet tanks approach and burst through the gates.

At the Yalta Conference a bloated, oily, sly-eyed Churchill in a sky-blue uniform (a bad attempt at RAF blue) seems to be making dire and sceptical predictions while puffing at a cigar. Stalin, also a smoker, calmly unfolds his plans, with Roosevelt nodding in agreement.

Sagging under the shock of defeat, Hitler (played by V. Savelyev) stumbles about clutching a huge, tattered map, his hands trembling, observed by his faithful alsatian. The cameraman, L. Kosmatov, uses green shades with light blue and yellow spots to depict the Führer as a living corpse in a graveyard. As the director described it, the 'clowning' (*shutovskyi*) marriage of Hitler and Eva Braun is interrupted by shots of the flooding of the Berlin subway on Hitler's orders, drowning women, children, the wounded, and the old. Chiaureli later expressed pride in the incongruity of the joyous Mendelssohn wedding march in the background, but this crude juxtaposition, typical of his ponderous satire, merely buried the real soundscape, the thud of Russian shells above ground.[86]

A shot of Russians approaching the Brandenburg Gate is followed by Hitler in his bunker, still alive, whereas in fact his suicide occurred on 30 April. In a rare nice touch, Eva Braun first feeds the cyanide pill in a sandwich to the faithful dog: is she overcome by compassion or simply testing the poison?

Alyosha's Red Army unit is a microcosm of the Soviet Union. During every battle we have seen our hero with his faithful chums at his side, the noble but quick-tempered Uzbek Yussupov (a parallel role to Hollywood's token Indian), the Ukrainian Zaichenko, and the Georgian Kantaria. The first two fall (predictably) during the storming of the Reichstag. 'The name of Stalin is on all their lips', declared Chiaureli. These battle scenes, into which a small amount of documentary footage appears to be woven, are grandly done, and as the Soviet troops fight their way up to the Reichstag dome, yard by yard, they are resisted fiercely by fanatical Germans (all wearing officers's caps for some reason).

Victorious, the Red Army men gaze up at the sky as Stalin's fighter-escorted plane descends. Adulation here reaches religious proportions as Stalin walks slowly among banners of himself, to the sound of messianic choral music. Aloysha and Natasha are reunited, embrace, and are then led before Stalin; she half-touches him (or his hem) as if he were the living God. Yet Stalin did not in reality fly to Berlin until the Potsdam Conference three months later. The entire episode was fictitious. Writing in *VOKS Bulletin* for a foreign audience, Chiaureli offered a grave admission: 'In the final episode of the film we endeavoured to show that Stalin is the standard-bearer of peace... for all the peoples of the world... To bring out this great truth, we indulged in a bit of artistic fiction... Stalin arriving in Berlin upon its capture by the Soviet army. This did not take place in actual fact. But the artist can generalize fact and draw on fantasy.'[87] However, in the 1952 Russian-language version of Chiaureli's servile and mechanical reflections about 'the love of simple people of all countries for the leader and teacher of toiling mankind, the great creator of victory, the torch-bearer of freedom', the director referred to this final scene and the colour-palette richness of its depiction without mentioning that Stalin's appearance at the Berlin aerodrome was fictitious. Evidently he or the editors of the *VOKS Bulletin* had feared that foreign readers knew too much, whereas a Soviet audience's acceptance could be taken for granted.[88]

Svetlana Alliluyeva writes with moving simplicity of the four-year imprisonment of her half-brother Yakov Stalin, captured by the Nazis. 'My father told me that when the director Mikhail Chiaureli was making the film that turned out to be the lifeless spectacle *The Fall of Berlin*, he approached my father about an idea he'd had of showing Yakov as a war hero.' Stalin refused. 'Chiaureli was a hack who... would have made the same sort of false portrait out of Yakov that he did out of everybody else.' (These comments, 'lifeless spectacle', 'hack', 'false portrait', are presumably her own rather than Stalin's.)[89]

The film did not reach the United States for three years, following widespread distribution in Western Europe. Described in the *New York Times* (9 June 1952) by H.H.T. as a 'deafening blend of historical pageantry and wishful thinking', the storyline was dismissed with the worst insult known to American critics: 'Hollywood.' Chiaureli directed 'as though his life depended upon it'. Although H.H.T. found the film remarkable for its lifelike portrayals of Stalin, the Soviet generals, Churchill, and Roosevelt, as well as Hitler and Eva Braun, the reviewer dismissed as 'juvenile pulp fiction' the scene in which the shrieking Führer and a swooning Eva Braun carried out their marriage-suicide pact in the bunker beneath the Chancellery. Nor did

H.H.T. care for the Yalta conference scene where FDR meekly parrots the beneficent utterances of Stalin, who also 'expansively convinces a churlish and stubborn old Winston Churchill of the Soviet priority to strike Berlin while the iron is hot'. As for Stalin alighting by plane amid the Berlin victory celebrations, it was dismissed as 'a Gilbert and Sullivan frolic'. The American critics Babitsky and Rimberg were unforgiving: Chiarueli and his scenarist Pavlenko 'display almost unmatched cynicism in inventing episodes for the glorification of Stalin'— like the airport episode. 'It was common knowledge that Stalin was mortally afraid of showing himself among the people and was always carefully guarded from crowds.' Nevertheless, they conceded, this film and *the Battle of Stalingrad*, 'in respect of direction and camera work, were masterpieces of cinema art'.[90]

By contrast, the Communist screenwriter John Howard Lawson, one of the Hollywood Ten recently released from prison after their conviction for contempt of Congress, praised the Yalta sequence in *The Fall of Berlin*: 'the sympathetic portrait of Roosevelt, the emphasis on the growing understanding between him and Stalin, make the scene a masterpiece of historical interpretation.' Lawson also praised the film's cinematic technique, the use of contrasting images to heighten emotional impact, as in 'the intercutting of the wedding of Hitler and Eva Braun in a cellar under the ruined city, with scenes in the Berlin subway, showing men, women and children being drowned as a result of the Nazi decision to flood the subway'.[91]

After the death of Stalin *The Fall of Berlin* was to become a target for official Soviet criticism. Categorized as the third of the four 'artistic-documentaries', it was said to have lost touch with the 'majestic, cool restraint' of *The Vow* (*Kliatva*), falling into exaggerated passions and loud, crude colours. The film's hero, Aleksei Ivanov, is 'a symbolic image of Soviet man, a merely outward portrayal of strength, abstract' instead of 'psychologically developed'. The film was also castigated as 'sensational cinema in the worst sense of this word', as when the heroine Natasha is found leading her schoolchildren across a field full of poppies, singing a song to the happy life. The *Istoriia sovetskogo kino* condemns this as 'a badly rehearsed crowd scene' (*plokho srepetirovannuiu massovku*); furthermore, the declaration of love between Natasha and Aleksei is 'tasteless, theatrical, and false'. With gathering fury the *Istoriia* lambasted the film as 'extremely schematic, featureless, primitive, made up out of slogans, fine words, and dubious puns...'.[92] In the culminating storming of the Reichstag, Chiarueli is accused of 'carelessness' in dealing with the alternating frames, as Aleksei advances on Berlin and Hitler trembles below ground in his bunker. The mass scenes are imposing but 'badly done' and the hand-to-hand combats are 'extraordinarily non-naturalistic'. Remarkably, the Brezhnev-era *Istoriia* does not once mention the hagiographical portrayal of Stalin! Likewise, the appearances of Roosevelt and the cunning, drooling, double-chinned Churchill are passed over. Clearly the *Istoriia* employs 'Aesopian' codes of transference: an attack on the exaggerated virtues and achievements of the fictional hero Ivanov stands in for an attack on the cult of the unmentionable Stalin.

Shostakovich (for whom film-scores were bread-and-butter during the years when his symphonies and concertos were banned) remembered a time when Mosfilm, the country's major studio, was shooting 'only three films'.[93] As for Mikhail Edisherovich Chiaureli, he was 'one of the greatest scoundrels and bastards known to me. He was a great fan of my music, of which he understood absolutely nothing. Chiaureli couldn't tell a bassoon from a clarinet or a piano from a toilet bowl.' But it was Stalin who gripped Shostakovich's imagination: 'Stalin had his own projection room...he worked, like all criminals, at night. He didn't like to watch alone and he made all the members of the Politburo...join him. Stalin sat behind them all, in his own row; he didn't let anyone sit in his row.' On one occasion an unnamed director friend of Shostakovich was brought to the Kremlin. 'He was searched fifteen times on the way to the screening room, where he was seated in the first row, next to the Minister of Cinematography, Bolshakov. An industry that was producing three films a year still had its own minister.' The director sat petrified. 'He had turned into a giant receiver set: every squeak that came from Stalin seemed decisive, every cough seemed to toll his fate.' During the screening Stalin's secretary, Poskrebyshev, came in with a dispatch for Stalin. The director heard Stalin proclaim, 'What's this rubbish?' and believed he was passing judgement on his film. The director fainted, fell to the floor, was carried out by guards. 'And they didn't give him a new pair of pants for the ones he soiled, either.'[94]

Mosfilm's *Conspiracy of the Doomed* (*Zagovor obrechennykh*, 1950), directed by Mikhail Kalatozov' and written by N. Virta, was based on his successful play, awarded a Stalin Prize First Class when first staged in 1948.[95] The outstanding colour camerawork was by Mark Magidson, with music by V. Shebalin.

An American ambassador, MacHill (*Mak-Khill*)—the American villains in Soviet cold war films were almost invariably 'Macs'—tries to engineer a crop failure to force a nation resembling Czechoslovakia into the Marshall Plan, aided by social democrats, industrialists, and 'Titoists'—plus a treacherous church dignitary, Cardinal Birnch, probably modelled on the Hungarian primate Cardinal Mindzsenty, also accused of being an American agent.

The smooth MacHill, who inhabits a conveniently baroque embassy and specializes in anti-Soviet provocations, plots the assassination of the deputy premier, the Communist Hanna Likhita, with the connivance of corrupt clergy. M. Shtrauch plays MacHill, 'boorish and scheming behind his charming diplomatic manner' (as the *Istoriia* puts it). The square-shouldered Hanna is a heroine of the Spanish Civil War, an East Europeana Pasionaria, whom we first glimpse scuttling through woods pursued by Germans and their dogs; her megaphonic oratorical voice thunders throughout the film. She is well worth murdering,[96] not least whenever she eulogizes the Soviet Union and Stalin, 'the friend of the peasants'. 'When we talk to the Soviets, we feel like equals', she declares; whereas in Greece there are death camps, in Denmark suicides, blood terror in Italy, resistance fighters imprisoned in France, poverty and unemployment everywhere in the 'Marshallized countries'.

The crops have failed. Cardinal Birnch is found in his Harry Truman spectacles preaching to a huge crowd who keep crossing themselves: 'God is punishing us by drought', he thunders. A worker calls out: 'Two hundred million in the USSR abandoned God and they are not suffering drought.' As the *Istoriia sovetskogo kino* noted, A. Vertinskii plays Cardinal Birnch, an agent of the Vatican acting under American orders, with 'supple, rounded motions of his long, thin hands, his eyes empty and senile, a habitual expression of meekness suddenly giving way to blazing anger'. Cardinal Birnch directs a gang of murderers, spies, and saboteurs with the assistance of Cristina, a clever woman spy who heads the Christian Unity Party, occupies the agriculture portfolio in the coalition government, and finally brandishes a revolver when unmasked by Hanna. The food shortage, it turns out, has been artificially engineered by the Americans, their political lackeys, and grain-hoarding 'kulaks' (as Hanna roars during a Central Committee meeting, a huge portrait of Stalin behind her): 'It's a conspiracy of all the non-Communists,' she declares, 'to starve the people.'

In the broad-based coalition government the social democrats hold the key to the intended betrayal; although the young left socialists (like the character Mark) are honest men who desire an alliance with the Communists, the old right-wingers (like Mark's corrupt father) wear give-away handkerchiefs in their breast pockets and talk ingratiatingly of 'American aid' while slandering Soviet bread as 'poison and propaganda'. One of them is a millionaire who refuses to pay tax. Everyone wears his politics on his sleeve; the forces of reaction arrayed on the right-wing benches of parliament wear cunning, twisted, bitter, and, (invariably), elderly faces.

Enter here another of Mosfilm's American vamps, the nattily dressed Chicago journalist Kira Reichel (played by Valentina Serova), who will sport a succession of naughty outfits while handing out dollar bribes. Enter also the greasy, ingratiating ambassador of Tito's Yugoslavia. When the population respond to the Marshall Plan with a strike, Ambassador MacHill yells into the telephone: 'Put me through to the president of this lousy country!' When Reichel gets through to MacHill from a phone-box she keeps saying 'Yes, sir'.

Everyone in a Soviet film—strikers, peasants, railway workers—is sheathed in what might be described as Mosfilm-set cleanliness; even the buildings of a post-war European city show no trace of destruction, debris, dust, destitution. No patched clothes here, no ration cards, no queues. Soviet designers and costumes department were in desperate denial of reality—the drabness of life in the Soviet Union and Eastern Europe (which extended, of course, to Europe as a whole) had to be suppressed. This 'spring-clean' colouration set Soviet cinematography closer to Disney than to Italian neo-realism. When the good, anti-American mothers march on the parliament building pushing an armoured brigade of prams, they sparkle. 'We don't want to wear American dog collars'—*My ne khotim odevat' amerikanskii osheinik*. The classic Communist agit-prop aesthetics is nevertheless graced by spectacular compositions and framing of human beings in motion against gantries, cranes, and railway engines—all spotless.

The Americans arrive with a 'Peace Train' decorated with Lucky Strike ads and accompanied by the inevitable jazz. Their engine gushes thick black smoke, whereas progressive locomotives use only friendly white smoke. MacHill stages a grand ball with black ties and jazz, saxophones and trumpets, card games, whisky, and gleaming figurines amid the marble columns. Sinister figures smuggle in coffin-like crates labelled MILK on the Marshall Plan train—though guns are what spill out—while the cardinal preaches in the cathedral, the camera soaks up the vaults, crypts, and fine paintings, and Ambassador MacHill conspires in his futuristic private bar with its Mexican carvings, handing out the portfolios in the future, Marshallized government. 'I've overthrown so many governments with the help of social democrats', declares Ambassador MacHill.

Magidson's cameras revelled in the exotic and baroque potentialities of foreign intrigue, a spiral staircase, mutineers in black oilcloths running to seize the telegraph, post-office, and government buildings, the camera gliding before a detachment of workers in overalls, fists raised, pouring in from all the streets on the parliament building in the central square to demand the resignation of the reactionary government. As the *Istoriia sovetskogo kino* later commented, colour itself played a dramatic role here: the blood-red cloak of the cardinal-conspirator, the red calico banners held above the crowd at a mass meeting in honour of friendship with the Soviet Union.[97]

The 'workers' (People's Front) simply take over the parliament and country, arresting everyone in sight—no elections are required, only chants of 'Stalin! Stalin!' The new rulers emerge from a very high balcony to greet the vast throng of people below—the aesthetics of Stalinism to perfection. White doves are released. A cursing MacHill hastily burns his documents and leaves the country on virtually the same cardboard airplane that Orlova had mounted at the end of *Meeting on the Elbe*. Even so, Aleksandrov and Kalatozov had directed the best two cold war films of the late Stalin era in terms of vitality and cinematic values, although the *Istoriia* dismisses *Conspiracy of the Doomed* as a 'thoroughly conventional political lampoon' and Maya Turovskaya comments on the genre, 'These were not so much propagandist thrillers as pseudo-"foreign" films.'[98] The film did not reach America, and American critics were forced to castigate it on the basis of Soviet commentaries.[99]

The Vatican was again depicted as a centre of American-inspired espionage in a joint production of Lenfilm and Lithuanian Film Studios, *Nad Nemanom rassvet* (*Dawn over the Neman*, 1953), shot in colour by the Jewish director A. Faintsimmer. The cast was mainly Lithuanian—the Nemen river runs through Latvia and Lithuania.

The film opens with a joyful village homecoming—the son of the family, Taurus, now an agronomist, returns (in a taxi) after receiving his education from the 'Motherland'. Around a table groaning with food and wine, family, friends, and accordion celebrate. The scene is, as usual, a tribute to the wardrobe mistress, and even the happy geese and pigs are spotlessly turned out to welcome the agronomist. In a variant of the 'girl-meets-tractor' joke, a young man is told by his fiancée that she will marry him only when he persuades his father to join the collective farm.

Meanwhile the local priest (dark music) is discovered describing the collective farm as the devil's temptation. He imposes a penance on a woman who permitted herself even the thought of joining: 'You must be on your knees for as long as Christ walked the stations of the Cross.' In a nice juxtaposition, Faintsimmer shows a man kneeling in church and a man ploughing with an old horse—same thing.

The collective farm must win the drainage battle against the swamps: 'It's a matter of will not of money', a meeting is told, Stalin looming on the wall above. Even so the chairman of the collective is sceptical, fearing bank loans and debts, whereas his modern-minded son, the agronomist Taurus, gently seeks to persuade him that the Party and the State will support the venture, as will the scientists. But Taurus does his gentle persuasion in public, and when the meeting loudly applauds him the chairman-father finds himself humiliated. 'You are a viper, you must leave!' The legitimate generational challenge by Komsomols is in fact endemic to Stalin-era films, the fathers being depicted as kulaks at worst, unreconstructed at best. Ten years later, in the Khrushchev era, the young were increasingly distrusted by the authorities, on-screen and off.

The priest, meanwhile, instructs the virtuous maiden Birute not to marry Taurus because he doesn't attend church. The couple part company on the issue (but not for ever, as we might guess). Faintsimmer now transports us to the gaudy heart of darkness, St Peter's, Rome, for the big, baroque, supercolour Catholic mass, complete with cardinals, Swiss guards, ambassadors, statuary, ornate lamps—in short, the sumptuous decadence adored by Soviet film directors. (The prime location in reality was Vilnius Cathedral, on Soviet territory.)[100] The devil, as usual, has excellent taste and pots of money to fulfil it. In Rome we witness the arrival from Lithuania of 'certain circles' which will 'stop at nothing' to thwart Communism, landlord émigrés who spent the war years in Nazi Germany and now engaged in a deadly war against Communism under the cover of prayer. 'We must be masters of people's thoughts', a cardinal lectures the assembled bishops. 'We are soldiers of the cold war.' Predictably this leads on to American shades of khaki, the inevitable jazz scene in a bar, Lucky Strike cigarettes, and a Vatican agent wearing a trilby hat in cahoots with the Americans. The US ambassador is as usual up to his neck in intrigue—the plan on this occasion being to infiltrate poisoned seeds on the land reclaimed by the collective farm's drainage and irrigation scheme. (But Taurus in his laboratory will remain a step ahead of the saboteurs.)

Back home, the collective farmers celebrate the success of the irrigation scheme by folk-dancing in national costume and applauding Stalin's name. Units of the Soviet army move in, armed with maps. All ideological confusions resolved among the good people, weddings unite the happy couples. Taurus's repentant father makes a speech: 'Now there are no boundaries. It is the ordinary man who transforms the world and must be pure in heart.' The camerawork, by Andrei Moskvin (one of Eisenstein's two cameramen for *Ivan the Terrible*), is ravishing throughout.

'Slander of America and the American people filled Soviet literature, theater, films and press', retorted Babitsky and Rimberg after reading the screenplay of *Dawn over the Nemen* in *Iskusstvo kino*, their use of 'slander' and 'American people' closely echoing Soviet use.[101] Nevertheless, the term 'slander' seems impregnable when considering Faintsimmer's earliet film, *U nikh est' rodina* (*They Have a Native Land*, 1950), produced by Gorky Film Studios,[102] which took as its anguished theme the alleged treatment of Russian children captured in Germany by the British and Americans. The action takes place in 1949—in other words, the children have been held captive for four years.

In the first sequence the Nazis force a column of captive Soviet families on board ship to Germany; the children are seized and separated from the parents. In the final sequence, in the dead of night, the same children will be put aboard an American vessel bound for New York. 'They want to send them to be cannon fodder for a new war', explains the voice of a woman commentator.

In a Soviet textile factory mothers anxiously listen to the radio for news of their children living in the British zone of Germany. Cut to a stout British officer, Colonel Berkeley, poring over a map and plotting the secret transfer of the children. Obligingly he remarks that little dogs grow into big dogs. Soviet officers, led by Colonel Sorokin, race towards the orphanage in a car, alerted by the British intention of sending the children for adoption, only to be met by shameless British deceit and prevarication. 'Orphanage, you say? Sorry, can't help you.' And this despite our full-frontal view of Captain Scott lining up his orphanage children with a smug smile.[103] As is the convention in Soviet films, foreigners speak perfect Russian—no accents to emphasize villainy in the Anglo-American cinematic mode. A Soviet officer drily remarks: 'They all served in counter-intelligence.'

Kurt, a good German who once ran away from the Western front and can say 'Long live a united Germany' at any hour, is helping the good Red Cross nurse Smaida Langmann (played by the beautiful Lydia Smirnova), who begs him to pass lists of captive Russian children to Soviet officers. 'I can't do it', groans the frightened Kurt.

Cut back to the British officers. Along comes a gross German woman (Frau Wurst, 'Mrs Sausage', who owns a 'pub') looking for a domestic slave girl 'with blue eyes'. Captain Scott instantly obliges. 'I'm going to be your mummy', the German woman tells the little Russian girl Ira. 'She's very thin', Frau Wurst complains. 'I'm going to hurt my hands on her.' Ira becomes Irma. Another bad character, the American woman journalist beloved of Soviet film directors, on this occasion Miss Godford, takes photos of the handover: 'Smile girl, smile.'

Here comes Colonel Dobrynin with the Soviet repatriation mission bearing a letter from the mother of a little boy, Sasha, who is listed as Polish but is really Russian: 'His father died at Kharkov, his mother died in German captivity.' Nurse Langmann (a Latvian, it turns out) whispers to young Sasha that the Soviet motherland is the best, everyone is happy there. But the British, represented on this occasion by a 'noble lord', are unmoved. Soon afterwards Nurse Langmann is shot down in cold blood.

Frau Wurst is found in her Bierstube, with a Coca-Cola poster on the wall, raging at poor little Ira/Irma. 'My Führer cheated me, the British cheated me, and you're cheating me of tips!' Drunken American soldiers arrive to a hail of jazz and hurl themselves around disgracefully ('Drinks on the house!') They are bravely rebuked by a group of decent Germans who refuse American cigarettes and get into a fight with the crude, vulgar Yanks. In this genre of Soviet cold war film nationality is everything and class factors are nowhere to be found beyond the *Es lebe SED* ('Long Live the Socialist Unity Party') poster briefly glimpsed in the film outside the Soviet Military Mission. But the SED is merely an extension of Russian power.

Never quite made clear is what motive the British have for hanging on to the children, or having them adopted, but the film's message has to be understood in terms of the relentless Soviet cinematic reversal of the realities which haunted the Kremlin: in reality thousands of Soviet citizens attempted to evade repatriation to the USSR, and those who were returned faced Siberian internment. In *They Have a Native Land* the closing scene is one of happy reunion, with children flown home by airplane, flowers, smiling mothers, a hall graced by portraits of Lenin and Stalin, and a speech by a woman with medals pinned to her breast. Then comes the night scene already mentioned of other, less fortunate Soviet children being put aboard a ship bound for New York—yet another cinematic reversal of reality, in this case the century-old flow of willing Europeans through the increasingly resistant, fine-mesh barrier of Ellis Island and visa restrictions.

⌘ ⌘ ⌘

A well-informed critique of Soviet film culture and production by Joseph L. Anderson appeared in *Films in Review*, published by the National Board of Review of Motion Pictures, Inc., New York City.[104] The overall Soviet view of the politics of the Great Patriotic War as conveyed in major feature films was accurately summed up by Anderson as follows: (1) the Soviet Union defeated Germany and Japan without any help from the Allies; (2) it did so despite an Anglo-American conspiracy with the Axis; (3) the victory was the personal creation of Stalin.

The Anglo-American conspiracy with the Axis against the Soviet Union was a theme pursued long and hard in Soviet feature films—though Roosevelt was always held to be innocent. *Moscow News* and *Soviet News*

(9 May 1947) published extended extracts in English translation from Nikolai Virta's script of a famous film in production, *The Battle of Stalingrad*, which
were also read over Moscow Radio. The passages depicted Stalin and Molotov
urging a stubborn Churchill to embark on a second front in Europe (Roosevelt's role is sympathetic). 'Impossible this year', declares Churchill, who
proudly draws attention to North African and forthcoming Italian campaigns. 'No use to us', Molotov cuts in. Alone with Molotov, Stalin explains:
'They simply want to reach the Balkans first. They want us to be bled white so
they can dictate terms later. They want us to fight their battles for them.'
Such passages were widely reported—as the Russians intended—in the British and American press. In May 1947 Churchill, returning from Paris where
he had been awarded the Médaille militaire, waved away newsmen soliciting
a comment on the allegations against him in the script for *The Battle of
Stalingrad*.[105]

Mikhail Romm and the same cinematic team who made *The Russian
Question* went on to shoot Mosfilm's Stalin Prize-winning *Secret Mission*
(*Sekretnaia missiia,*) scripted by K. Isaev and M. Makliarskii, photography by
Boris Volchek, with music by A. Khachaturian. The film was first shown in
Moscow on 31 August 1950, bringing sharp diplomatic protests from Wash-
ington and London.

On the Western front the American armies are seen fleeing under the
impact of Von Rundstedt's January 1945 offensive in the Ardennes. Fear
and confusion prevail among Eisenhower's staff. A hatchet-faced Montgomery (wearing an exaggerated version of his famous black beret) is briefly
glimpsed ranting into a telephone: 'I have no intention of rescuing the
Americans! They can go to the devil! Let them run! I can't restrain runaways
(*begushchikh*).' Churchill appeals to Stalin for help. Stalin gallantly responds
by concentrating his forces at the banks of the Vistula and promising an
offensive on the central front during the second half of January.

Found chewing his habitual cigar at his country residence Chequers,
Churchill discloses to colleagues that the Americans are sending a special
mission to negotiate a separate peace with the Germans. The British premier
explains that he will make any sacrifice of special British commercial interests
in occupied Germany if only the Americans will now turn their fire on
Communist Russia. 'We made the mistake thirty years ago when we didn't
nip Bolshevism in the bud.' Romm tends to portray Churchill in profile, as if
shy of the actor's likeness: camera set-ups will accentuate Churchill's corpu-
lence as he sulks in harsh lighting at international conferences.

According to the American critic Joseph Anderson, Churchill hurries to
Moscow to beg for help in *Secret Mission*, but this is not the case. In both the

screenplay and the film there is simply an exchange of messages with Stalin on 6 and 7 January 1945. The fictional Senator Heywood, meanwhile, arrives in Berlin with the boast: 'We withheld the second front for two years to cheat the Russians.' Heinrich Himmler responds: 'We have left the Western front deserted.' In a shameless display of historical perjury, Romm shows German troops drawn up in good order surrendering to American forces in a ceremonial manner—though just how this fits in with the Ardennes offensive with which the film begins is not explained. Romm may be described as one of Soviet cinema's major forgers.

Anderson expressed outrage that in *Secret Mission* it is Roosevelt's vice-president, Harry S. Truman, who dispatches the wealthy Senator Heywood (he has shares in I.G. Farben) and the Army Intelligence agent Harvey under assumed names and Portuguese passports to divulge to Hitler the details of the forthcoming Soviet offensive and to plot the destruction of the USSR. Anderson commented that Truman, always the chief instigator of plots in Soviet films, is usually presented as a kind of Rasputin in modern dress.[106] But Truman does not appear in the film; the Nazi official Shellenberg, chief of the foreign political intelligence service, merely reminds Heywood in a Swiss air-raid shelter during an American bombing raid that Truman, the current vice-president, had once remarked early in the war, when still a senator, that if Nazi Germany was about to overwhelm Communist Russia, then the United States should assist Russia, and likewise should come to the rescue of Germany if Russia threatened to emerge supreme. 'Mr Senator,' Shellenberg tells Heywood, 'the time Truman was speaking about has now arrived.' Heywood replies dismissively that Truman is a 'big-mouth', adding: 'We have but one enemy, the Reds, and they are our enemies forever.'[107]

The great industrial magnate Krupp is seen hosting a secret meeting of American and German industrialists, introduced as they enter the lavish antechamber by the barking voice of a lackey. Seated at a round table symbolizing common interests, Krupp promises Heywood to preserve his war plants in West Germany while destroying his own factories before the Russians seize them in the East. The Nazi industrialists pay tribute to Heywood for constant support during the war: 'Thanks to your aid we received manganese, nickel, chromite, and rubber and were able to continue our work without disturbance.' Post-war American investment in a pseudo-conquered Germany will mean 'that we Germans lose some part of our independence, but better to lose part of your hair than to lose your head'. (All of this is overheard by our Soviet spy Masha Glukhova, played by Elena Kuz'mina, star of Romm's *The Russian Question*, hiding in the library with her ear to the wall.)

Heywood then goes on to the Balkans armed with a list of Nazi secret agents in the area, and seeks out Hitler sympathizers in Bulgaria, Yugoslavia, and Romania.[108] 'Move to Yugoslavia if you get into trouble', a leading Nazi advises the American—Mikhail Romm's tribute to the anti-Tito campaign of the late forties.

The *Istoriia sovteskogo kino* praised Romm's authentic portrayal of the Moabit district of Berlin, with its thick brick walls, the leaden waters of the Schree, an iron chain fence, the gloomy windows of office buildings. Keeping to severe black-and-white tones, Romm chose a style without sunlight, wet sidewalks, 'the gloomy colouring of the nasty German winter'.[109] But glamour was not lacking. Masha Glukhova, sent by the Soviet Party to break into Himmler's circle, wears a black raincoat and a forage cap pulled down over her eyes; her voice abrupt and muffled, her motions are automatic, and her performance of orders instantaneous. Glukhova releases a captured American pilot who, ordered to fly Senator Heywood to London for secret anti-Bolshevik talks, slugs the senator so hard that he wouldn't have kept a tooth in his head had he not been in a movie. 'Walk East', Glukhova says as she removes the handsome pilot's handcuffs.

Mikhail Romm issued an elaborate justification of the film's historical accuracy, its exposure of 'the heinous intrigues of those...for whom war is profitable': 'The Germans are to throw all their armies against the Eastern front and thwart the impending Soviet offensive...Once the Soviet forces are tied up in the East, the united armies of American-Anglo-German militarism can be hurled against the Soviet Union.'[110]

Neither he nor his film mentioned the Nazi–Soviet Pact of 22 August 1939, by which Hitler and Stalin agreed to carve up the whole of Poland between them—and then did so. This event was not justified, it was not denied, it had been airbrushed out of Soviet history. Romm insisted that the plot of *Secret Mission* was based on 'four historical facts', which he listed in detail, involving Allen Dulles, Max Aitken, son of Lord Beaverbrook, and Count Bernadotte (named by Romm as an intermediary between Eisenhower–Montgomery and Himmler). As a result the German armies surrendered in the West and left the Remagent Bridge intact so the Americans could cross the Rhine.[111] But Romm's history was as flawed and fallacious as his lifeless film.[112] Whatever the virtues of his famously long takes (as when Hitler rants to Himmler, without a cut or change of camera angle, that the German people who retreat deserve annihilation), Romm was essentially a documentary director who half-heartedly fell into step with the fictional elements of the Soviet 'artistic documentary' genre. Each conversation piece is contrived, static, dead.

On the day of the film's release in Moscow, 21 August 1950, State Department and Foreign Office condemnations of the calumny were relayed by the Voice of America and the BBC. The *Herald Tribune* (21 August) reported that 10,000 spectators had jammed an open-air theatre in Gorky Park to applaud the first screening, with co-ordinated reviews stressing the semi-documentary nature of the film. According to the brief London *Times* report (21 August)—'Allied Statesmen in Russian Film'—in the last scene of *Secret Mission* Churchill promises a new war, 'which may not be so hard to start but may cost the lives of half the world's population before it is ended'. *The Times* offered no comment.

America's running-sore and constant point of vulnerability, as Soviet cultural commandos well knew, was the Negro question. Screened some months after Stalin's death, Abram Room's *Serebryannaia pyl'* (*Silvery Dust*, 1953)[113] portrayed white racists as willing to sacrifice blacks in pursuit of military research of the 'deadly ray' variety. Two US chemical trusts, one from the North, one from the South, intent on conquering the world by chemical warfare, are abetted by a corrupt army general, a scientist called Steele, and an obvious former Nazi, 'Meester Schneider'. Most of the action takes place in a southern town, a studio stage-set called Fortskill. To obtain human guinea pigs for experimentation, Steele and other conspirators raid a peace meeting in the town square, assisted by a fascist clergyman of sinister pallor, routine vigilantes, and so on, seizing three black peace partisans. The plot involves false sexual allegations against a black Communist made under duress by a pretty white woman (who frequents bars and wears a pert little red hat throughout, but has a conscience). A bribed judge who hears the testimony of a corrupt, slouching sheriff, sentences all of the arrested Negroes to the electric chair. The Ku Klux Klan move in to do the job themselves, but the generals order the captives to be rescued from the fiery cross and put into a laboratory cage previously used for experimentation on monkeys. Just as they are about to die from exposure to the 'silvery dust', the girl who accused them admits that her testimony was false. The Negroes are saved by the peace partisans, who break into the laboratory and warn the cowed generals and businessmen that they will one day meet again in a people's court. The progressive whites are distinguished by their open, honest faces and the fact that they don't wear ties; the master race inhabit elegant modern mansions with high-tech interiors and treat the faithful Negro maid with curt indifference (the mistress of the house shows more affection for her dog), even when the maid pleads her imprisoned son's innocence on her knees. This colour film's provenance in a stage play is obvious—too much talk—but the inserted exterior shots are competently done by the celebrated cameraman Edvard Tisse, mainly by following American film models of cops, sheriffs, public confrontations, bar scenes, and the KKK. In any American version, however, there would be far more violence; even the brute heavies employed by the laboratory never get to swing a serious punch in *Silvery Dust.*

In the Political and Security Committee of the UN General Assembly, the US delegate, Dr Charles W. Mayo, complained that the film, showing in twenty-one Moscow cinemas, contained 'extravagant fictions in which the villains are all Americans. For many years the Soviet government has been busy at just this sort of thing...' Responding, Jacob A. Malik said that during his four-and-a-half years in America he had come across dozens of films packed with outrageous slanders against the Soviet Union.[114] James Reston expressed fury—'For Soviet Eyes Only'—in the *New York Times* (20 November 1953): it was 'probably the most venomous anti-American movie in the history of their film industry'—and in colour! And being shown all over Moscow! According to Reston, *Silvery Dust* had deliberately not been reviewed in the Soviet press, while censorship had prevented American correspondents in Moscow from filing reports.[115] Joseph L. Anderson expressed the general indictment:

The cold war and its avalanche of propaganda has extinguished what little art Soviet films retained during World War II... Current films reveal how completely the Soviets have substituted political harangue for cinematic technique. Actors, when not sermonizing, revert to the romanticism of the theatre of the turn of the century. Those who play villains from the Western world behave like feral children. The majority of these tirading films have indoor set-ups at front eye level angles and frequent one-minute takes. Outdoor action sequences, once the forte of Russian cameramen, are seldom seen. Despite a profusion of shots of actors in two planes, deep focus techniques have not been mastered, and the focus jumps back and forth with the action.[116]

In the USIA's new periodical, *Problems of Communism,*[117] Dwight Macdonald, trading heavily on information from Anderson, brought a first-class polemicist's gifts to the service of a crudely partisan demolition job. Recycling material he had originally published before the war in *Partisan Review,* Macdonald evoked the golden age of Soviet cinema in the 1920s—brilliant experimentation and creative artistry—before going on to describe the sequel, the 'banality...insipid triteness...saccharine optimism' of the 1930s followed by the September 1946 Central Committee decree. A distinguished essayist, Macdonald here fed himself on a second-hand diet of alleged Soviet 'admissions', for example: 'Out of the 260 scenarios recently submitted only 60 were ideologically acceptable (*Culture and Life,* 11 January

1949)...Most of the 200 young scenarists graduated by the Institute of Cinematography have left the movies (*Literary Gazette*, 4 September 1952).' He also quoted 'The Soviet Film Industry in 1946 and Today,' a highly selective compilation of Soviet press comments on the cinema put out by the US government (1 February 1952), and further 'mimeographed material from US Government, dated April 16, 1953', to the effect that in 1951 every Soviet film released had to be granted a Stalin Prize because there were so few of them.[118]

The Russians faced a huge problem in selling their films abroad, because distribution networks in the West were commercially owned and managed. Continental Concorde Cinema Co., Ltd., could distribute Soviet films in Britain only by selling them to dominant commercial chains like J. Arthur Rank. In 1952 the Russians were holding out for an agreement by which films like *Ballerina* and *The Fall of Berlin* would be shown in at least 300 British cinemas; J. Arthur Rank in turn was demanding a cash guarantee of £100,000 for each Soviet film he took. By the end of August a limited film deal had been signed with Rank, who took *The Big Top*.[119]

J. Bowen Evans, an anti-Communist commentator, warned of recent Soviet technical advances such as the introduction of stereophonic sound and Cinemascope-type screens. Their colour processing was 'excellent'. Films designed for foreign festivals and for gaining prestige abroad 'have some very strong features in their favor.' However: 'Audiences still complain about the slowness of the action, the garrulity of the heroes, and the stereotyped plots with their trivial conflicts.' This was to change; the international triumph of the Soviet New Wave was imminent. But the hard-boiled polemics of the late Stalin era were never officially regretted; indeed, they were defended deep into the Brezhnev years. Despite brief and ritualistic references to the cult of personality (*kul't lichnosti*), or 'the aggrandised role of a single individual', volume 3 of the *Istoriia sovetskogo kino 1919–1967*, published in Moscow in 1975, strongly endorsed the post-war, Zhdanovite, Central Committee decrees on the arts as 'fully preserving its relevance even today for the practice of Soviet art'.[120] Commenting on Russia's cold war feature films of the period 1945–50, the *Istoriia* came to the conclusion that, although the 'psychological portraits' were somewhat superficial, these motion pictures reflected the reality of the 'imperialist conspiracy'.[121]

Hollywood:
The Red Menace

Greta Garbo was not called to testify before the House Un-American Activities Committee, though she might have been when her delectable *Ninotchka* (1939) was rereleased in 1947. Reviewing Ernest Lubitsch's comedy in the *New York Times* (10 November 1939), Frank S. Nugent began gaily: 'Stalin won't like it. Molotoff may even recall his envoy from Metro-Goldwyn-Meyer...' Garbo's Ninotchka is a deadpan, sternly puritan, icily aloof, but stunningly beautiful Bolshevik emissary sent to Paris by her commissar to take over the duties of a comically floundering three-man mission entrusted with the sale of the former Duchess Swana's court jewels. The script (a collaborative effort) contains such lines as: 'The last mass trials were a great success. There are going to be fewer but better Russians.' Garbo–Ninotchka gets hugely drunk, succumbs to the charms of Melvyn Douglas and the American-in-Paris way of life, chooses a frivolous hat, and generally loses her Lenin. This was scarcely 'cold war' and could indeed have misled fans into believing that most Soviet commissars looked like Garbo, a big plus for Communism. *Ninotchka* reappeared—was it a coincidence?—one month after the House Un-American Activities Committee provoked headlines across the world by subpoenaing Hollywood actors, writers, composers, and directors to testify about their political affiliations, past and present.

The Russians who appeared in Hollywood's World War II movies were almost invariably brave and friendly Ivans and Natashas practising their own kind of patriotic 'democracy'. This went down well with Stalin; pro-Soviet Hollywood films shown in the USSR during the war or within a year of its ending included *The North Star* (1943), *Mission to Moscow* (1943), and *Song of Russia* (1944),[1] as well as some Disney and Deanna Durbin movies.

Directed by Michael Curtiz and written by the fellow-travelling writer Howard Koch, Warner Brothers' *Mission to Moscow* was loosely based on former Ambassador Joseph Davies's bestseller, which had been serialized in the *Reader's Digest*. The Moscow trials of 1937 and 1938 are garbled together so that Radek and Bukharin are defendants in the same trial alongside Marshal Tukhachevsky, who had been shot without a public hearing. The film insists on the guilt of the defendants in conspiring to overthrow the Soviet government in collusion with Germany and Japan. Vyshinsky appears as a humane prosecutor: an old Bolshevik confesses to being a paid German agent while Stalin beams with confidence and wisdom. As soon as the defendants are sentenced to death the film abruptly cuts to public parachute displays.[2] Bosley Crowther's review of *Mission to Moscow* in the *New York Times* (10 April 1943) is a remarkable document, not least because Crowther continued to review regularly for the paper for a further twenty years. Welcoming 'the most outspoken picture on a political subject that an American studio has ever made', Crowther entirely endorsed its point of view, namely that 'Russia's leaders saw, when the leaders of other nations dawdled, that the Nazis were a menace to the world'. As for its depiction of the Moscow trials, Crowther evidently agreed that the defendants were conspirators in a plot engineered by Trotsky with the Nazis and 'the Japs' [*sic*] 'to drain the strength of Russia and make it an easy victim for conquest'. Crowther (who did not mention the Nazi–Soviet Pact and the dismemberment of Poland) hoped that the picture would be 'a valuable influence to more clear-eyed and searching thought'.

Crowther's enthusiasm did not abate when he viewed Samuel Goldwyn's *The North Star* (*NYT*, 5 November 1943) after its release at two Broadway theatres, the New Victoria and the Palace, a rare honour. Directed by Lewis Milestone and based on a script by Lillian Hellman, this was a 'lyric and savage picture', a 'clamorous tribute' to Soviet resistance to 'the Fascist hordes'. Starting in the operetta mode, with music by Aaron Copland and lyrics by Ira Gershwin, the film swings into 'vehement reality' with the Nazi invasion. Crowther particularly praised—'a thrilling peak'—a melodramatic speech written by Hellman and given to Walter Huston as the village doctor, who kills a Nazi surgeon played by Erich von Stroheim.

Song of Russia, directed by Gregory Ratoff and written by Richard Collins[3] and Paul Jarrico, both Communists, featured the popular Robert Taylor as an American symphony orchestra conductor who goes to Russia on tour before the Nazi invasion (the film again does not mention the Nazi–Soviet Pact). Taylor falls for a Russian girl (Susan Peters) with whom he dines in a typically opulent Soviet night-club before visiting her parents' typically happy farm where (as the critic Nora Sayre comments), Susan Peters 'repairs ploughs and drives a tractor in a ruffled blouse and fresh lipstick'. No mention of collective farms is allowed. 'As in *The North Star*, the Russian farmers revel in the delusion that they own their own land . . . ' The lovers are married by a benevolent priest, but when the Germans invade they are separated. Retreating, the Russians burn their own towns. The natural exuberance of the Russian people in *Mission to Moscow* is exceeded only by their unbridled gaiety in *Song of Russia*. The dependable Bosley Crowther greeted *Song of Russia* (11 February 1944) as 'a honey of a topical musical film, full of rare good humor, rich vitality and a proper respect for the Russians' fight in this war'. By 1947, however, the euphoria was evaporating and these movies were coming under fire. Testifying before HUAC, the Russian émigré and right-wing publicist-novelist Ayn Rand complained about all the smiling faces in *Song of Russia* and the scores of radios owned by MGM's affluent Soviet peasants.

There was a brief period between the Allied victory and the creeping, engulfing cold war when many Americans still believed that wartime friendships and collaborations could continue. A comic reflection of this hope can be found in the headlines of the *Hollywood Reporter* through the summer of 1945:

22 June—RUSS SEEKING U.S. FILM STARS. Soviet Representative Due Here to Ink Bob Cummings For Role in Eisenstein Pic.

10 August—RUSSIA PLANS PRODUCTION HERE. Would Aim Films at World Market, Using Borrowed BO Names, Eisenstein [referred to as 'film czar in Moscow'] Expected.[4]

Two years later Hollywood was churning out anti-Communist films, mostly of B-movie quality and lacking even commercial 'carry'.

Soviet Russia was merely an incidental market for American cinematic penetration. Yet such was Russia's failure to produce more than a fraction of the feature-film output required by its large population that a deal was struck in October 1948, even though Berlin was blockaded and diplomatic relations frozen. Eric A. Johnston, president of the Association of Motion Picture Producers and a former head of the US Chamber of Commerce, arrived in Moscow during a European tour and persuaded the Russians not only to buy American films of their choice—but also to pay in the hardest of currencies, dollars. The agreement allowed the Soviet authorities to delete lines of dialogue and whole scenes, but not to add any.[5]

American cinematic imperialism was underpinned by the new Informational Media Guaranty Program. From 1948 to 1966 US film companies were to receive $16 million in government subsidies for exporting material reflecting 'the best of American life'. The head of Paramount Pictures declared: 'We, the industry, recognize the need for informing people in foreign lands about the things that have made America a great country and we think we know how to put across the message of our democracy. We want to do so on a commercial basis and we are prepared to face a loss in revenue if necessary.'[6]

It was French, not Soviet, film workers who vehemently protested against the new cinematic imperialism of Hollywood—and the French Communist press was not slow to add its own subtitles. The Blum–Byrnes Franco-American agreement ratified on 1 August 1946 contained a film clause by which French cinemas would be required for at least two years to show no more than four French films per quarter (rather than the nine per quarter previously insisted on). The Byrnes agreement was met by a storm of criticism in France. 'These accords jeopardize the very existence of dramatic art', protested the actor Louis Jouvet. 'The change in French taste may well be irremediable and fatal. Used to the wines of Burgundy and Bordeaux, our stomachs will now have to adjust to Coca-Cola.' Throughout 1947 the crisis in the French film industry deepened; employment fell from 2,132 in 1946 to 898. There were petitions, demonstrations, and even violence on the streets in 1948. Serge Guilbaut comments: 'The American film industry thus killed two birds with one stone. It got rid of French competition, and it knocked down the old quotas, thus allowing American films to take over the French market... Furthermore, Hollywood films were offered at unbeatable prices, since their production costs had already been recouped on the American market.'[7]

But the fact remains that audiences throughout Europe wanted to see American films. It was this preference rather than the arm-twisting accompanying the Marshall Plan which accounted for the fact that in 1951 61 per cent of the movies playing in Western Europe were American. (In Italy the figure was 65 per cent, in France 50 per cent.) The Fulbright scholar Herbert Kubly asked a cinema manager in San Gimignano, a Communist stronghold, why local audiences preferred American films; the manager explained that Russian films were 'too sober, not diverting [like] American films... When Linda Darnell and Jane Russell and Gary Cooper are the stars, then my house is filled and a line waits outside. These Russian films! One hardly hears any laughter during an entire evening.'[8]

⊞ ⊞ ⊞

The story of HUAC's protracted political witch hunt within the entertainment industry and the systematic blacklisting operation in film, television, and radio has been thoroughly documented[9]—and often naively recounted in magazine articles and television documentries, where the now-elderly victims sit beside swimming-pools, let drop a hall of fame of glamorous names, declare 'I love my country', present themselves as bastions of First-Amendment liberties, of 'dissent', of 'radicalism', of the New Deal, of blacks and unionized labour—while each new generation of indulgent interviewers omits to ask them why these admirable causes had to be fully dovetailed into a Party line dictated (as the most outrageous reactionaries correctly alleged) from Moscow, where one man, insisting on Byzantine ceremonial adulation, sent millions to forced labour and death while quite loudly and visibly (even from New York and California) imposing a different kind of gulag on literature, the arts, and scholarship. In short, was there no available route to socialism without Stalinism?

The 80th Congress, including HUAC, was dominated by a conservative coalition of Republicans and southern Democrats ('Dixiecrats') hostile to organized labour and to civil rights, in some cases anti-Semitic, and in all cases determined to reverse Roosevelt's New Deal by painting it Red. The central tactic during the post-war decade was naming names and 'guilt by association'. Film studios and television screens provided an ideal, high-profile theatre for this enterprise. In May 1947, for example, a HUAC sub-committee report alleged that 'some of the most flagrant Communist propaganda films [during the war] were produced as a result of White House pressure'. One of these was *Song of Russia*; its star, Robert Taylor, now 36 and a member of the Screen Actors Guild board of directors, emerged as one of HUAC's most bankable, friendly witnesses, adept at naming names. The Soviet film director Sergei Gerasimov[10] (who had eulogized the Stalin-worshipping Soviet film *The Oath*)[11] reacted rapidly with an article published by *Izvestiia* in May 1947. Robert Taylor had appeared before HUAC in executive session, accusing the Roosevelt administration of having prevented him from joining the navy until he agreed to star in *Song of Russia*, the film which, according to HUAC chairman J. Parnell Thomas, favoured the Soviet ideology and way of life over the American.[12] While it is unlikely that Taylor knew of or cared about the Soviet director's derisive comments, he for some reason came back before the Committee in open session on 22 October with an altered story. He still stressed that the US government had wanted *Song of Russia* to be made 'to strengthen the feeling of the American people toward the Russian people at that time'. Questioned as to whether he had met Mr Lowell Mellett, chief of the Bureau of Motion Pictures of the Office of War Information, Taylor said yes, but added hastily: 'If I ever gave the impression in anything that appeared previously that I was forced into making *Song of Russia*...I was not forced, because nobody can force you to make any picture.' This was not what HUAC wanted to hear, and Committee Counsel Robert Stripling immediately altered his line of questioning. The following day HUAC played host to Gary Cooper and the amenable Ronald Reagan, president of the Screen Actors Guild and future president of the USA.[13]

HUAC now subpoenaed forty-one witnesses from the film industry, nineteen of whom were expected to be 'unfriendly'; of these thirteen were Jews. The exchanges were acrimonious. Ten who refused to answer questions about Communist Party membership, pleading protection under the First Amendment, were later indicted for contempt of Congress, tried, and imprisoned.

Thrown into a panic, the studios hastened to purge their payrolls. Vigilante groups led by the American Legion (with its 2.5 million members and its million 'auxiliaries') picketed theatres showing any film written, directed, or performed by artistes deemed to have belonged to the CPUSA or the 'front' organizations listed by Truman's attorney-general—or any organization associated with 'progressive' causes. It was a continual process of smear and denunciation involving paid informers and publicity-hungry opportunists. The FBI, under its director J. Edgar Hoover, was fully committed to the purge, both overtly and covertly. Directors, writers, and actors became the subjects of vast FBI dossiers. By the time HUAC returned to the fertile pastures of Hollywood in 1951, resistant witnesses were relying primarily on the Fifth Amendment, which offers protection against self-incrimination.

In the capital of the film industry local papers like the *Hollywood Reporter* and *Hollywood Life* vied to capitalize on HUAC's return. *Hollywood Life* described Dore Schary, executive producer at MGM, as a 'Red Fellow Traveler' who had been 'connected . . . in a membership capacity of some sort' with American Youth for Democracy, the Hollywood Writers' Mobilization, and the NCCASP. *Hollywood Reporter's* Jimmie Tarantino revealed that the writer Dashiell Hammett was 'one of the red masterminds of the nation, with main headquarters in Hollywood and a sub-office in New York'. Tarantino could also reveal that Charlie Chaplin had been 'a card-carrying member of the Communist Party for many years'. As for Judy Holliday, '[she] only acts dumb. She's a smart cookie . . . The Commies got her a long time ago.'[14]

HUAC returned to Hollywood in 1953, 1955, 1956, and 1958, by which time seventy-two 'friendly' witnesses had named about 325 film people as past or present Communists. All studio work contracts now contained political disclaimer declarations. Leading stars abased themselves before the Committee, naming names and deeply regretting their own past errors as 'dupes' and 'stooges' of the Red Menace. 'I was duped and used. I was lied to', pleaded the actor Edward G. Robinson, gangster boss of the film *Little Ceasar*. The Committee's purpose was public humiliation and ritual purgation—not its avowed aim of gaining information. No 'friendly' or cowering witness ever revealed anything that the Committee did not already know from the FBI; indeed, hearings were regularly preceded by negotiations between Committee staff and lawyers. The director Edward Dmytryk, imprisoned for contempt as one of the 'Hollywood Ten', later made his peace with HUAC, consoling himself that 'not a single person I named hadn't been named at least half a dozen times'.

By the end of the post-war decade some 250 film artistes had been blacklisted and about 100 'graylisted'—the uncertain underworld of those who had been 'named' but never subpoenaed. Not a few hastened into exile before their passports were withdrawn, seeking work, often under pseudonyms, in England and elsewhere. In 1952 Charlie Chaplin, a resident of the United States for forty-one years but not a citizen, was planning a six-month visit to Europe, but his re-entry permit was indefinitely delayed while the Immigration Department sent teams of investigators to interview him:

'You say you've never been a Communist?'
'You made a speech in which you said "comrades"—what did you mean by that?'
'Have you ever committed adultery?'
'If this country were invaded, would you fight for it?'

Chaplin did not return to the United States until 1972, when he received a special Academy Award. The American Civil Liberties Union estimated that by 1953 the blacklist in radio extended to about 250 people. Some years later the *New York Times* calculated the total number affected in radio and television in 1954 as 1,500. Destitution, despair, and even suicide followed for the victims. The special factor attracting professional blacklisters to the radio and television industries was commercial sponsorship of programmes. In 1950 radio still commanded the lion's share of advertising revenue until the number of TV sets shot up from 9.8 million in 1950 to 40 million in 1956. Whatever the Soviet press alleged about profits dominating networks, sponsors, and advertising agencies was broadly correct. Private blacklisting companies prospered. The style of the magazine *Counterattack*, organ of 'American Business Consultants', 240 Madison Avenue, is illustrated in the issue of 29 February 1952:

WHAT DO YOU THINK OF THESE CELANESE STARS? . . . KIM HUNTER AND LLOYD GOUGH had leading roles . . . KIM HUNTER'S Communist front record was given in COUNTER-ATTACK . . . after she appeared on Johnson Wax program . . . GOUGH refused to say if he is now, or ever was . . . WHAT CAN YOU DO TO HELP DEFEAT THE COMMUNISTS? *Write to*: HAROLD BLANCKE, President, Celanese Corporation of America, 180 Madison Avenue, New York City, NY.

Three days after the outbreak of the Korean War, American Business Consultants published a book called *Red Channels*, subtitled 'The Report of Communist Influence in Radio and Television', listing 151 prominent performers, each name being followed by 'reported as' and then a list of damaging allegations which were known, in the parlance of the time, as 'citations'. Often former FBI men, the blacklisters enjoyed the full support of HUAC and other witch-hunting Congressional committees. The major networks capitulated. In December 1950 CBS announced that its 2,500 employees would be required to sign a loyalty oath statement based on the attorney-general's list; CBS hired American Business Consultants to investigate its employees. A spokesman for NBC referred to blacklisting as a necessary 'business safeguard'. In general, labour unions like the American Federation of Radio and Television Artists panicked and voted to bar anyone 'identified' as a Communist by the FBI, or anyone deemed 'unfriendly' by a Congressional committee.

⊞　⊞　⊞

Spy mania and patriotic paranoia rapidly infected Hollywood productions. The subject of *The Iron Curtain* (1948), produced by Darryl Zanuck and directed by William A. Wellman, was the attempts of Soviet espionage rings based in Canada to obtain America's atomic secrets during the war. Narrated by Lloyd C. Douglas in documentary style (a strategy common to anti-Communist movies), the Twentieth Century-Fox film, written by Milton Krims,[15] was based on the memoirs of the former code clerk in the Soviet Embassy in Ottawa, Igor Gouzenko, who defected in 1945, turning over to the Canadian government a mass of documentation concerning Soviet espionage.

At the outset Igor Gouzenko (played by Dana Andrews) flies to Canada, is drilled in false biographical details by a heavy-smoking Soviet Embassy official, and is then taken behind double doors punctured by spy-holes to the cipher section where Soviet classical music plays non-stop to prevent conversations being overheard. A beautiful Soviet secretary is immediately instructed to put Gouzenko through a standard induction test, luring him to an incredibly luxurious apartment normally used for seducing Canadians, but Igor sees through her, expresses his contempt by smashing a glass (old Russian habit)—and tells her he loves his wife.

We meet a smooth Canadian Communist leader with something of the appearance, charm, and feline manner of Orson Welles's character Harry Lime in *The Third Man*. Indeed, one keeps feeling this should all be set in Vienna rather than Ottawa, despite the snow. 'You must plant a few key people in the important departments', 'Harry Lime' tells the Soviet military attaché. A Canadian Air Force officer and an atomic scientist on secondment from England are among those recruited into espionage. It did, of course, all happen—though the viewer's credulity may wobble when the chief Communist tells one of his spies: 'We'll name a city after you, when we take over.'

Arriving from the USSR, Igor Gouzenko's nice wife Anna (Gene Tierney) is stunned by the comforts and mod-cons of their three-room apartment—though the bedroom contains two single beds with a Hays-code gap between them. She is going to have a baby. Happy couple. Long walks. Hearing singing from within a country church, they sense that there may be a higher Master than the one they have been indoctrinated to serve and whose portrait appears on all Soviet office walls in Canada:

ANNA: Before I came, I believed everything, now I can't understand.
IGOR: We must have faith in our leader. No more, Anna, you must not talk like that.

('Faith in our leader' was not an authentic Soviet way of expressing the Stalin cult.)

In the middle of the night Igor is summoned to take down in cipher an urgent message concerning uranium and American atomic science. The uranium project is now accorded absolute priority by Moscow. While preying on the elderly, fellow-travelling atomic scientist, the smooth Canadian Communist leader insolently plays Shostakovich on the phonograph: 'Let's be comfortable while we listen', he purrs. 'After all, this is the first flowering of proletarian culture.' Dr Norman hands over a uranium sample, which is flown to Moscow.

Disillusioned, Igor begins to smuggle out documents under the suspicious gaze of officials who keep asking, 'What are you doing?' He takes diaries and cables to the Canadian Justice Department building, bringing his wife and son with him, but he fails to obtain an interview with a government minister. Frustrated, fearful that the Russians will grab him and his family, he desperately tries a newspaper editor—again no luck. They treat him as a crackpot and send him away. When Soviet Embassy officials turn up at his apartment and threaten reprisals against his relatives in the USSR, the Royal Canadian Mounted Police (or two of them) burst in, summoned by a friendly neighbour, and the day is saved. In semi-documentary fashion we are told of the subsequent Royal Commission of Inquiry and the trials of the spies, including a Member of Parliament and an atomic scientist: 'Two pleaded guilty, eight were convicted.'

The film opened in 400 theatres—shortly before the Soviet Union exploded its first atomic weapon. In the *New York Times* (13 May 1948), Bosley

Crowther's outright hostility led him into some clumsy phrases: 'Hollywood fired its first shot in the "cold war" against Russia yesterday... It still seems extremely irresponsible to go all out with a wave of "hate the Red"... It still seems excessively sensational and dangerous to the dis-ease of our times to dramatize the myrmidons of Russia as so many sinister fiends.' (A 'myrmidon' turns out to mean 'hired ruffian' or 'base servant'.) Crowther complained that the Soviet boss-figures in the film were granite-faced gangster types who speak with heavy accents, while the good Russian, Dana Andrews, has no accent! But this was not true—most of the Russian characters speak normally. The Soviets, alleged Crowther, are depicted as hissers and Teutonic shouters; the secret head of the Canadian Communists is a 'fat, oily, sneering gent.' Nothing much had changed (wrote Crowther) since the same screen-writer, Milton Krims, had helped write *Confessions of a Nazi Spy*.

In April 1948 four composers, Shostakovich, Prokofiev, Khachaturian, and Nikolai Myaskovsky, wrote to *Izvestiia* (11 April) expressing their 'deep indignation' on learning—from the *New York Times* itself!—that their music has been stolen for the film *Iron Curtain* (*Zheleznyi zanaves*) made by the 'movie moguls' (*kinodel'tsy*) of Twentieth Century-Fox, which 'slanders our country' and 'kindles hatred' towards the Soviet people. The four Soviet creative artists angrily rejected the 'fraudulent trick' (*moshennicheskii priem*) and 'political blackmail' involved in violating the 'elementary rights of composers', indicative of the more general denial of the democratic rights which the USA boasts of and pays lip service to. The studio responded with a shabby explanation—works by Soviet composers lay in the public domain in the United States—but Fox had taken care to acquire the rights from Leeds Music Company and its subsidiary, AM RUSS, for $10,000.[16] The Soviet Embassy in Washington issued a diatribe against the film, written by Ilya Ehrenburg. 'The Communists Scream', was the *Herald Tribune*'s responding headline (13 May). On 5 June *Izvestiia* published 'The Fate of a Film Provocation' by 'R. Moran' (an American correspondent for Tass), reporting an action launched in the New York State Supreme Court against the theft of music by 'gangster methods'.

Following the spirit of *The Iron Curtain*, Hollywood's anti-Communist films on occasion ventured beyond the borders of the United States, exploring recent events in Eastern Europe. *The Red Danube* (1949), directed by George Sidney for MGM, centres around the efforts of Mother Superior Auxilia to shelter a pretty Volksdeutsche ballerina, who rightly fears the Russians will slap her into a concentration camp once they catch her. Thomas Pryor (T.M.P.) of the *New York Times* (9 Dec. 49), found *Red Danube* confusing and patronizing: 'Perhaps the film translators erred in not simply confining their drama to an exposition of the ruthlessness and duplicity of the Russians in professing humanitarian concerns over the repatriation of displaced Soviet subjects living in Vienna.' Reviewing another film with a Central European, cold war setting, *Guilty of Treason* (1949),[17] Pryor praised it for 'helping to bring into clearer focus the *modus vivendi* of Communistic imperialism . . . Cardinal Mindszenty stands as the symbol of hope and enlightenment . . . because he expounds a philosophy of human freedom and dignity which cannot be subverted . . . the Communists know that the man who puts God above the Kremlin can never be wholly enslaved.'[18] A Swiss production aimed largely at an English-language audience, *Four Men in a Jeep* (*Die Vier im Jeep*, 1951), directed by the Austrian émigré Leopold Lindtberg, starred the young Viveca Lindfors as a Viennese woman whose husband has escaped from a Soviet prisoner-of-war camp a few days before he would have been repatriated to the USSR. Set in neutral Vienna under Four Power rule, the film focuses on a hardboiled American military police sergeant who attempts to protect Lindfors and carries a grudge against his aloof Soviet counterpart Sergeant Voroschenko, despite the fact that the two had met conveniently at the Elbe five years previously. Although the Russian is the 'heavy' and walled into suspicion by the system he serves, he's not a bad fellow at heart.

Hollywood, declared the Soviet director S. Gerasimov, continued to distance itself from realism and the pressing problems of real people. Screenplays were becoming increasingly senseless and improbable, taking their material from the sphere of pathology (a favourite Soviet term), replacing reality with dreams or the feverish fantasies of drug addicts, and in so doing destroying the natural connections of time and space. As a tool of 'militant capitalism', Hollywood was propagating obscurantism, hatred of mankind, and dissipation, while excusing all the burdens of capitalist society, egoism, perjury, venality, greed, and hypocrisy. Not by chance did Hollywood produce so many films—yet not one of them was a true work of art, defined as a film with something real to say to the masses, and none had achieved genuine popularity.[19]

In Republic's *The Red Menace* (1949), directed by R. G. Springsteen, who had previously made twenty-five Roy Rogers movies, a discontented ex-GI, plied with liquor, women, and elaborate promises, joins the Communist Party in pursuit of social justice, only to find himself surrounded by dupes who want to get out, all of them disillusioned by the intolerance and brutality they are shocked to encounter. California Communists are revealed to be racists: 'We're wasting our time on these African ingrates.' An Italian who asks an irrelevant question is reviled as 'a Mussolini-spawned Dago'. A Party theorist goes off her head while being politely questioned by the Department of Justice: 'You're too late . . . !' she yells—'The legions—they're entering the city! In a few minutes they'll stand you up against the wall! You fools! Don't you hear them!' she laughs deliriously.[20] The *New York Times* (25 June 1949) condemned *The Red Menace* as inept and lurid.

Directed by Robert Stevenson for RKO Radio Pictures, *Woman on Pier 13* (1949), was originally scheduled as *I Married a Communist*.[21] The film portrays an innocent, all-American, and recently married wife, Mrs Bradley Collins (Laraine Day), who slowly discovers that her handsome, home-loving, husband (Robert Ryan) has a hidden past involving the sultry Communist Janis Carter. In short, Brad Collins, now vice-president of a shipping company, was once a Communist stevedore called Frank Johnson, a member of the Young Communist League, of the 'lost generation of the Depression' (as the film puts it)—and he had killed a shop steward during a strike in New Jersey. Now reformed, and working for a major shipping magnate, Collins has no intention of telling the truth to his wife—or anyone. 'You talk too much', he says before kissing her.

The role played by Janice Carter is that of Brad's former girlfriend, the extravagantly beautiful but wicked Christine Norman, typically found wearing furs off bare shoulders and a big black hat. She now works for the villain of the piece, Vanning (Thomas Gomez), a Communist union boss libellously and ludicrously 'modelled' on Harry Bridges, leader of the West Coast Longshoremen's and Warehousemen's Union (ILWU) and for years in notorious conflict with employers, the FBI, the Justice Department, and Congressional committees. Australian-born, Bridges was subjected to unending deportation proceedings. In 1949 he was prosecuted for perjuriously denying Communist Party membership, convicted, and sentenced to five years' imprisonment.[22] Yet Vanning, the fictional union boss in *I Married a Communist*, is given no specific biography and merely acts as a power-broking gangster.

We enter the Cornwall Shipping Company, where leaders of the stevedores' union are negotiating with Mr Cornwall (a very reasonable man, as employers tend to be). A sincere 'moderate' labour leader, Jim Travis, is explaining the need to reach a compromise and thus keep things out of the hands of 'hotheads and extremists'. Fine. But this does not suit the union boss, who sets Collins's old flame Christine to blackmail him into frustrating the negotiations with his employer, thus precipitating an all-out strike. The Communists' general motive is not clear; the Korean War had not begun, so sabotage of war materiel does not figure. Whatever the answer, (and probably there is none), we are in the familiar movie world of the gangster: dockside, night, garage, cars, men wearing nasty shoulders, the murder of a comrade accused of talking to the FBI: strapped, fettered, and dumped in the dock, his dying struggles are observed by the smiling killer.

The honest Brad Collins is so frightened of the union boss's threat to turn him over to the FBI for murder that he agrees to sabotage negotiations by recommending to Mr Cornwall a reduction in wages—'Go for a show-down'—and to lie to everyone, including his loving wife.

WATERFRONT PARLEYS START

STALEMATE LOOMS

UNION SPEAKERS FLAY OWNERS

NEGOTIATIONS CANCELLED BY BOTH SIDES

Meanwhile the Communist vamp Christine (who works for a magazine as a front) has been busy seducing Brad's innocent brother-in-law, Lowrie, as part of the Kremlin's master plan. But never depend on a woman. Love will have its way with them! She kisses young Lowrie with her eyes closed! She wants out from Satan's armpit! Meanwhile Brad Collins's good wife is not the dumb little thing she pretends to be. Her eyes are opening—they stay open even when Brad kisses her. Practically everyone is now about to get killed, including young Lowrie, who has been duped into believing the Party line on the strike, and Christine Norman, tossed from a Seattle hotel window as a fake suicide after she has told Brad's wife the whole truth.

We are heading for a full-scale waterfront shoot-out, with the union boss pumping away like James Cagney until he is hit and topples into the water. Brad Collins must also die, because his Communist past is a sin for which he has not sufficiently atoned.

The Woman on Pier 13 was one of the first of Hollywood's 'Red Menace' movies to be favourably received in the *New York Times* (16 June 1950). Thomas M. Pryor found it to be 'a right smart sampling of melodrama, fast paced and attractively padded with action and violence. It paints a fairly ugly picture of Communist machination in stirring up labour strife along the San Francisco waterfront and demonstrates that the party is quite ruthless when it comes to disciplining erring or backsliding members.' Pryor, who often signed himself T.M.P., described Janis Carter as 'quite an attractively subversive dish . . . '. As for equating Commies with gangsters, why not? 'After all outlaws are pretty much the same no matter what their objectives.' But Nora Sayre calls the film 'a savage smear' on Harry Bridges.[23]

Warner Brothers' *I Was a Communist for the FBI* (1951), directed by Gordon Douglas and based on the ghost-written *Saturday Evening Post* story of the alcoholic FBI informer and professional witness Matt Cvetic, was launched on 19 April 1951 at the Stanley Theater, Pittsburgh, attended by the city's mayor. In the film a leading Communist activist, Steve Nelson, is seen committing a fictitious murder.[24] The Party is portrayed as taking exultant credit for the Negro riots which brought havoc to Harlem and Detroit in 1943. Communists emerge as the true enemies of blacks, working people, and Jews. Incitement is the game. A Communist leader informs the comrades: 'To bring about Communism in America we must incite riots.' 'When blacks died', says an FBI agent, 'they never knew that their death warrants were signed in Moscow.' The Communists force a strike on the Pittsburgh steelworkers' union; those who refuse to join the picket line are beaten with steel bars wrapped in the *Jewish Daily Forward*, so that Jews will be blamed. Communists also arrange 'accidents' at the steel plant and replace badly injured workers with Party members. In reality almost 100 people lost their jobs following Cvetic's testimony, notably workers at three Pittsburgh steel companies.

Cvetic, played by Frank Lovejoy, becomes a martyr for the FBI and America, operating under deep cover and believed by everyone, his family included, to be a Communist, a 'slimy Red'. 'Never come near me again', his young son gasps. To maintain the deception, Cvetic even has to leave his mother's birthday party to attend a Communist reception for the notorious German Communist Gerhardt Eisler, in a fancy Pittsburgh hotel where champagne is swilled and caviar passed. 'This is how we're all going to live once we take over the country', a Party official smiles.

If the *New York Times* was owned, controlled, and callously manipulated by the monopoly capitalists (as Moscow held), these warmongers were clearly careless about their film critics: one day you got Thomas Pryor (the ruling class) and the next Bosley Crowther (spirit of Roosevelt)—whereas in *Pravda* you got the iron laws of history. Bosley Crowther (3 May 1951) consigned *I Was a Communist for the FBI* to the fires of infamy: 'this hissing and horrendous spy film', this 'erratic amalgam of journalism, melodrama, patriotic chest-thumping and reckless "red" smears...And all the way through, it drops suggestions—always from the villains' oily tongues—that people who embrace liberal causes...are Communist dupes.' (A sensitive subject: one of the 'liberal causes' embraced by Crowther himself, as we unkindly noted earlier, was the Moscow trials.)

Communist dupes were busier than usual in *My Son John* (1952), directed, produced, and co-authored (with Myles Connolly) by Leo McCarey.[25] Lucille (played by Helen Hayes) is a God-fearing, all-American mother, two of whose sons, clean-cut football players both, have eagerly enlisted for the Korean War, 'fighting on God's side'. Her third son, John, however, shocks his mother by ridiculing patriotic loyalty and by suggesting that the Bible should be understood symbolically rather than literally. Lucille forces John to swear on the Bible that he is not and never was a Communist; he duly perjures himself without compunction, then returns to his mysterious job in Washington. Enter the FBI, in the shape of Agent Stedman, who uses a car accident to infiltrate John's mother's home, eliciting information from her while concealing his real identity. Discovering that her son John is a Red, Lucille deduces that he must also be a spy and hands him over to the FBI with a long speech. 'Take him away! He has to be punished!' (One could not count the number of Western critics who expressed disgust at Soviet works of art encouraging children to report their disloyal parents. Yet some thirty Hollywood films made in the 1950s depicted informing as a vital civic response to the Red Menace.) The family as an institution becomes the locum of a struggle between good and evil. Nora Sayre wrote: 'In a period when sexual or political "deviation" were considered equally disgusting', John is 'sly, furtive, flirtatious with his mother and simmering with snide hostility toward his father...His overconfident smile hardly ever falls out of his face.' The Communist screenwriter John Howard Lawson remarked that the scene in which the mother renounces her son John 'hints at a sort of Freudian bond between the mother and the FBI agent. She talks to him about his [own] mother and how he must love her.'[26]

Recent critical evaluations of Hollywood's cold war output have tended to merge political explanations with neo-Freudian or feminist analysis. The trend, according to Michael Rogin, was to 'depoliticize politics by blaming subversion on personal influence. That influence, in cold war cinema, is female.' Enter mom and her insidious influence on the young male. As Rogin puts it: 'John has imbibed his mother's naïve humanitarianism and, to distance himself from her, taken it in a sinister direction.' On the other hand, in most of the Hollywood films under review in this chapter, there is no mom, literal or surrogate. Hollywood's recurrent gangster image of American Communism—Moscow's mob—is a mom-free zone. Clearly women are to be found among the enemy (as in *Woman on Pier 13*), but they were not normally portrayed as orchestrators of subversion, more as loving instruments of passion liable to 'turn good' on an act of conscience. Saving civilization remained on the whole a big male drama. One must agree with Rogin when, apparently switching his emphasis, he writes: 'Film makers were under pressures that may have reawakened infantile anxieties, but those pressures came from Moscow, Washington and Hollywood, not from mom. Soviet expansion on the one hand, American state invasion of the motion picture industry on the other, lay behind cold war cinema.'[27]

John's corruption is also linked to a suspect intellectualism: 'I was invited to homes where only superior minds communed', he confesses. 'It excited my freshman fancy to hear daring thoughts.' The father slams the family Bible on John's head and hurls him to his knees—indeed the movie opens with the whole family except the absent John going to church. Eventually John decides to confess but before he can do so the Party comrades slay him, gangland-style, on the steps of the Lincoln Memorial. Fortunately he has taped the speech he'd intended to deliver at the commencement ceremonies of his alma mater. His recorded voice addresses the stunned graduates: 'I am a living lie. I am a traitor, I am a native American. Communist. Spy. And may God have mercy on my soul.'

Once again Bosley Crowther (9 April 1952) fought back for liberalism against a film which 'seethes with the sort of emotionalism and illogic that is characteristic of so much thinking these days... Not only does it heroize the image of the ranting, song-singing patriot who distrusts and ridicules intellectuals', but it also pandered to guilt-by-association. John Howard Lawson lambasted the film's anti-intellectualism: 'When the Legionnaire hears the word culture, he reaches for his bottle... When men like the Legionnaire imitate Hitler's stormtroopers, as they did at Peekskill or Cicero, Illinois, they are generally intoxicated.'[28]

Stalin's obsessive desire for heroic portrayal in feature films was almost matched by J. Edgar Hoover's. The director of the FBI's self-promotion was now firmly focused on Communist-busting rather than crime-busting; his assistant, L. B. Nichols, was instructed to assist a number of anti-Communist film ventures which would extol the role of the FBI.[29] Hoover was on close terms with the New York agent-producer Louis de Rochemont, whose *Walk East on Beacon* (1952), directed by Alfred Werker, extols the FBI for 'protecting' us—and soon we see a shot of agents opening our mail. The film reveals a vast network of spies in Boston dedicated to purloining the results of an 'extraordinary scientific experiment' involving a brilliant 'new computer' devised by an eminent refugee mathematician (Finlay Currie), whose son is held hostage in East Berlin. Reviewing the film in the *New York Times* (29 May 52), A.W. (A. H. Weiler) praised it as a 'tribute to an arm of the law worthy of praise', but Nora Sayre, writing some years later, calls *Walk East on Beacon* 'another sham-documentary, "suggested by" J. Edgar Hoover's *Crime of the Century* and "produced with the cooperation of the FBI".'[30] She further comments:

However, in films that feature dauntless FBI agents, it's very difficult to tell them apart from the enemy, since both often lurk on street corners in raincoats and identical snap-brims while pretending to read newspapers, and also because many B-actors lack distinguishing features: they simply look alike. Just when you assume the miscreants are massing to plot, they turn out to be the heroes. You can sometimes spot a Communist because his shadow looms larger and blacker than his adversary's. Also, movie-Communists walk on a forward slant, revealing their dedication to the cause.[31]

As Sayre points out, stock screen Communists included the bad blonde (her straps showing through her blouse) who seduced young men on behalf of the Party; Communists who meet in the Boston Public Gardens amid the swan-boats, or carry a copy of *Reader's Digest* or a TWA flight-bag for identification. Mostly they exhale slowly before threatening someone's life or suggesting that 'harm' will come to his family. They hurl comrades in front of trains or out of windows, or hound them to suicide. The very few who are given a plausible reason for having joined the Party—they mistakenly believed they were fighting the Depression or fascism—are invariably the ones who decide to quit and get shoved under a train. The shovers are in it for the sheer joy of it.[32]

In *Big Jim McLain* (1952), directed by Edward Ludwig for Warner Brothers,[33] the vigilante actor John Wayne (like Ronald Reagan, a Hollywood super-patriot) plays Big Jim, a HUAC investigator pursuing—and whenever possible slugging—Communists operating on the Honolulu waterfront. This third-rate movie opens with a reverential view of the Un-American Activities Committee hearing room, and the Committee's name-plates, under Chairman Wood, are those of real politicians. The voice-over, which belongs to Wayne, immediately speaks of a campaign of slander against HUAC, and warns of 'slimy' agents of the Kremlin operating in American universities.

This is to be 'Operation Pineapple', featuring McLain and his younger assistant Baxter, 'a veteran of the Korean War'. Wearing trilby hats with ribbons, the two heroes are garlanded in flowers at Honolulu airport by scantily clad ladies—grass skirts and palm trees are going to be a feature of the anti-Communist decor throughout. The film soon introduces us to the villainous comrades under the command of the tall, suave Dr Neill, who leads a bourgeois existence in beautiful quarters. 'For security reasons, don't call me comrade', we hear. The comrades are white Americans; the local police are the Pacific islanders—no racism in this motion picture. It also transpires that a comrade guilty of defection must be rubbed out: 'Get rid of him. Don't bother me with the details but get rid of him.'

The heroine Nancy (Nancy Olson) works for the Communist doctor. Big Jim McLain, who is six feet four and 'a lot of man', takes her sailing and water-skiing to the accompaniment of zither music. It's time for flowered shorts then back to basics, interviewing an honest old couple who have written to the FBI because disillusioned by their son's tragic embrace of Communism. Here in Honolulu good American parents are applauded for informing on their children. Lest this be too heavy for us, we are shown Nancy's legs as she and Big Jim (a former Marine in the war) relax at the seaside. Nancy, of course, will not bother her pretty head with politics or think about anything beyond the safety and love of her man. Hollywood's anti-Communist movies invariably projected the standard, home-and-garden image of the ideal American woman-wife, ignorant of the wider world but wise enough to trust her man's judgement.

Jim's assistant Baxter, a father of two, gets murdered and dumped in the harbour after receiving a lethal injection from the Communist doctor. The plan is to paralyse the island's communications and stop the flow of materiel to 'the East' (Korea), and also to create a deadly epidemic in the harbour district. Big Jim goes in to have a punch-up with all of the lousy scum before their arrest. Continuing to confuse HUAC with the FBI, the film next displays the arrested conspirators, not before a court of law on indictment, but taking the Fifth Amendment before HUAC. Says Big Jim, voice-over: 'Sometimes I wonder why I stay on this job.' The film hit the sturdy reef of Bosley Crowther in the *New York Times* (13 September 1952), who castigated it as 'irresponsible and unforgivable'. Sayre's verdict is that in no other era have such dismal creations been launched as a form of public relations—self-protection, not box office, was Hollywood's motive.[34]

⊞ ⊞ ⊞

In the 1950s the biblical epic was the particularly privileged product of the American movie industry, including three of the five biggest grossing films of the decade: *Ben-Hur, The Robe*, and Cecil B. De Mille's *The Ten Command-ments*. Professor Alan Nadel describes the latter as 'a major product of American cold war ideology', a film which 'equates God's perspective with American global interests'.[35] Do we agree? As a general proposition, the acute hostility between Communism and God is unchallengeable: 'Our government makes no sense, unless it is founded in a deeply felt religious faith—and I don't care what it is.' Thus Dwight Eisenhower, running for president in 1952 and keen to trawl in every faith. A 'float for God' led the procession at Eisenhower's inauguration. In 1954 Congress created a Prayer Room for its members and the United States became, under a newly modified pledge of allegiance, a nation 'under God'.[36] When a national cross-section was asked in 1954 what Communists believed in, the most common answer was 'against religion'. Among the most successful of HUAC's publications was *100 Things You Should Know About Communism and Religion*, a booklet set out in the question-and-answer format of the catechism. A Gallup poll in 1955 indicated that 96.9 per cent of the population identified themselves as religious (70.8 per cent Protestant, 22.9 per cent Catholic, 3.1 per cent Jewish). The pagan gods servicing the great biblical epics of the 1950s carried names like CinemaScope, Vista Vision, and SuperScope, all popularly known as 'widescreen'.

Cecil B. DeMille's *The Ten Commandments* (1956) stood in its time second only to *Gone With The Wind* as a moneymaker. But did it, 'equate(s) God's perspective with American global interests'? The energetic DeMille (1881–1959), who had been making movies since 1913, had directed his original version of *The Ten Commandments* in 1923. Both director and producer of the new version, DeMille himself offers a personal prologue when he steps in front of a golden curtain to explain to his audience, that: 'The theme of this picture is whether men are to be ruled by God's law—or whether they are to be ruled by the whims of a dictator like Rameses. Are men the property of the state? Or are they free souls under God? This same battle continues throughout the world today.' (When a slave in the film asks, 'Is life in bondage better than death?' we may well catch a reverberation of 'Better dead than Red'.)[37]

The film melds an Old Testament storyline with New Testament figuration, thus embodying the 'Judeo-Christian' heritage. Condemned in Egypt, Moses (Charlton Heston) is punished in a loincloth, his arms chained to a crossbar in cruciform position. In the wilderness his wife Sephora washes his feet, anticipating the imagery of Mary Magdalen. Despite the Jewish setting and story, the film is essentially Christian, in Alan Nadel's view, because it renders Moses in the shape familiar as Jesus and as 'the forerunner of Christ'. He adds: 'Just as Christianity becomes the category that validates Judaism, DeMille's film validates the Jewish origins of its own production[38] by subsuming them under the rubric of cold war Christianity... In this scheme the "free World" is safe because true Jews are Christians and subversives are false Jews.'[39]

Yet DeMille demonstrates fidelity to two qualities of the Old Testament very far from—indeed antithetical to—the ethic of Christ or its 'Free World' update. The story told by DeMille is intensely tribalistic ('we' but not 'they' are God's people). Secondly, the emphasis on God as an agent of wrath and destruction is as clear in the film as in holy texts. The universality of Christianity as a message of love countervailing tyranny, and thus convertible into modern 'American freedom', is constantly undermined in the film by tribal-istic egoism and indiscriminate slaughter perpetrated by the Almighty.

Men must choose freedom against tyranny, but the Jews of the Old Testa-ment (and of *The Ten Commandments*) are different from the run of mortals, including Egyptians, only in one respect: they have been chosen by God, then left with that degree of existential choice that allows them, for example, to fall into punishable idolatory (worshipping the golden calf, etc.) The Egyptians, like all other nations and tribes who fell on the wrong side of God's gaze, simply get it in the neck. This cannot be interpreted as cold war ideology, which, like Christianity (or Islam), holds out the hand of salvation to everyone ('Only believe . . .'). What is more, DeMille's Moses, discovered in the bullrushes and brought up to believe himself an Egyptian prince, even a possible pharaoh, does not revert to Judaism as a doctrine, as a theology, an ideology; he simply identifies with the tribe of his birth as soon as he grasps that his true mother was indeed the Jewish woman who nursed him rather than the Egyptian princess who raised him. DeMille remains faithful to Old Testament tribalism: 'I tried to illustrate the angel of Death passing over Egypt, sparing the Hebrew families whose door-posts were marked with the blood of the lamb.'[40]

Nadel argues that the 'cold war's similarity to the conditions of DeMille's Egypt' endows the American doctrine of 'containment' with its 'religious mandate'.[41] But what 'similarity'? George Kennan's famous doctrine of 'con-tainment', semi-offically adopted by the State Department, was posited on the belief that the Soviet Union was set on military and ideological expan-sion. Nothing similar is said of Rameses's Egypt in *The Ten Commandments*; and the countervailing force, the God of the Jews, has no geographical programme of 'containment' beyond getting the captive Jews out of bond-age. Indeed, God lets them wander in the wilderness for forty years. Should we discover a 3,000–year-old version of atomic 'containment' in Moses's constant threats to Rameses—'You must obey!'—and his menacing miracles in the name of the Almighty, when staffs become snakes, blood pollutes water supplies, the sun is eclipsed, and all the first-born of Egypt die as their mothers wail?

In Alan Nadel's view the film reclaims the Middle East as part of the Judeo-Christian tradition, that is, the American sphere of influence, at the time of the rise of Gamal Nasser, tension over the Suez Canal, and Egyptian overtures to the USSR.[42] But the film does nothing of the sort. Such allusions are merely intrusive—indeed, filming had been completed on 13 August 1955, well before Nasser precipitated the Suez crisis and the Anglo-French-Israeli mili-tary invasion. De Mille had two meetings with Nasser: 'I was impressed. Some of Colonel Nasser's actions since then have raised serious questions in my mind, but in those still early days...I received a strong impression of its [Egypt's] leaders...sincerely dedicated to the welfare of their people...sensitive about their new-found independence, but by no means unfriendly to America, then at least.' Indeed Nasser and General Amer 'admitted to being confirmed fans of American movies'. In Egypt DeMille had 'dropped in unannounced at the USIA library' and 'found the large, well-lighted, well-stocked reading-room literally jammed with young Egyptians eagerly reading American books'.[43]

Nor can one agree with Nadel that 'DeMille contribute[s] to America's global economic policy by claiming the site of oil in the name of God.' This film does not claim any territory for anyone; at the end the Jews arrive at the River Jordan which, of course, is going the wrong way for oil. There is no hint or shadow of a hint, whether by parallel or indirection, that America or the 'West' is a surrogate force in the story. Moses's wide, panoramic gaze from the heights of Mount Sinai represents closeness to God, not to the Pentagon.[44]

Of course DeMille's fervent anti-Communism and his advocacy of the Hollywood purge are matters of record. According to Nora Sayre, he believed that there was 'a Red band encircling the earth', accused most of those who disagreed with him of being political deviants, and attributed criticism of his *Samson and Delilah* to Communist influence.[45] DeMille's *Autobiography* is not short of material to sustain the image of him as a cold warrior dedicated to the hegemony of 'Western' values. When *The Ten Commandments* opened in Europe in the autumn of 1957, DeMille received a blessing from Pius XII in Rome and a decoration from the president of Italy; in Germany he was received by President Theodore Heuss and had long talks with Chancellor Konrad Adenauer and West Berlin's mayor, Willy Brandt. In France he was awarded the Legion d'Honneur; in London Churchill, 'the greatest man of the twentieth century' according to DeMille, and now in final retirement, received him in bed.[46] In addition, DeMille extends the equation of anti-Communism with the 'Judeo-Christian' heritage by praising conservative Moslem leaders like Mohammed Ali, prime minister of Pakistan, 'who saw in the story of Moses, a prophet honoured equally by Moslems, Jews and Christians, a means of welding together adherents of all three faiths against the common enemy of all faiths, atheistic communism'. DeMille adds, not entirely convincingly, that the Koran 'was one of the primary sources for our production of *The Ten Commandments*'.[47] Which bit of the Koran, which sura, which verse?

But DeMille should not be confused with *The Ten Commandments*. The man was not the film. DeMille, the producer-director of the big-screen epic with a cast of thousands, is primarily a showman: whenever God speaks to Moses the most lurid visual effects, betokening astronomy, astrology, and zapp-bang pyrotechnics, accompany (for example) the dictation of the Ten Commandments on Sinai. This is not cold war aesthetics, and one should be wary of the recent tendency to discover the cold war in everything. Neither the Soviet menace nor the New Deal menace nor the Negro menace (triadic sources of America's version of the cold war) explains the sententious, 'neo-biblical' language DeMille employed as occasional narrator throughout the film, matched by a pretentious visual style in which Moses and Rameses are always found in statuesque poses, a succession of still-lifes interspersed with mass-spectaculars involving camels, oxen, and galloping geese whose gleaming white feathers, like the fair skins of the women, are never stained by desert sand. Statuesque poses were the standard Soviet images too; like-wise jutting jaws and blazing gaze and dazzling cleanliness. The picture, which cost $13 million, opened in New York in September 1956.

⊞ ⊞ ⊞

The ideology of American films was at its most interesting—and most contestable—when latent. The interpretative constructs most recently offered by film critics and media studies experts would most probably have been news to the screenwriters and directors themselves. For example, Robert Corber and Alan Nadel contend that cold war liberals attempted to contain the increasing heterogenity of American society by linking questions of gender and social identity to questions of national security. Discussing Hitchcock's film *Rear Window*, Corber argues that the hero Jeff (James Stewart), a photojournalist confined to his apartment by a broken leg, develops a voyeuristic interest in his backyard neighbours during a hot summer when all windows are open, in a manner which validates vigilante surveillance in defence of national security. Nadel adds that in this film, 'just as in the discourses surrounding the Soviets or atomic power itself, an invisible duality betrays appearances and confounds the powers of observation, upon which nevertheless rely the cold war's necessary bifurcations'.[48]

Commentators and critics hostile to the conformist or consensus political and sexual values of mainstream American culture insist that a film is 'really' in business to reinforce (or very occasionally, challenge) such values while apparently pursuing a storyline 'innocent' of ideology. It has been argued, for example, that Westerns and private-eye movies were used to 'promote' the simple moral virtues of the lone individual and thus reinforce the 'capitalist' ethic. This overlooks the fact that the moral virtues of the lone hero or heroine have been inseparable from storytelling since the time of Homer, and constitute an inherited cultural stock for writers and performers regardless of political context. Soviet socialist realism also promoted individual courage and even independence of spirit as prime values; the 'collective' could not flourish without hero and heroine. A Soviet novel, film, or play, no less than its American counterpart, is absorbed and interpreted by individuals, even if gathered together in a factory cinema at a management-set recreation hour, a Park of Culture, or a House of Pioneers. Inevitably individual heroes, heroines, villains, and parasites are the vectors of the Soviet message and the focus of audience empathy—though the earlier epic expressionism of Eisenstein, for example, achieved its power through collective choreography, the surging anti-ballet of mutinous sailors, soldiers, and workers. The 'hidden agenda' approach should be treated with reserve; too often the critic imposes his own obsession with reification and transference on film-makers who are merely pursuing standard codes of storytelling. (The critic and his laser thus achieve transcendence over the object of his gaze.)

⊞ ⊞ ⊞

According to John Cogley's scholarly *Report on Blacklisting* (1954), sponsored by the Fund for the Republic, the number of Hollywood movies focusing on serious social issues declined between 1947 and 1954, although more than fifty anti-Communist films were produced. The major exception, a film on its own, was *Salt of the Earth*, produced by the screenwriter Paul Jarrico.[49] With his fellow-Communist Herbert Biberman, Jarrico had founded an Independent Production Corporation to sustain blacklisted film-makers. More remarkable, *Salt of the Earth* employed—with the exception of the two lead roles—only amateur actors and was financed by the Communist-dominated Union of Mine, Mill and Smelter Workers, one of the most persecuted labour unions of the era following the Taft–Hartley Act. The key input was that of the scriptwriter Michael Wilson, likewise a Communist, who established the central storyline set in 1951 with its pre-eminent militant character, the miner's wife Esperanza. Certainly the film's feminism was as far ahead of its time as its portrayal of bitter class struggle in New Mexico between mill-owners and miners was unfashionable.

In May 1952 Roy Brewer, anti-Communist boss of Hollywood's most powerful union, the International Alliance of Theatrical Stage Employees (IATSE), and chairman of the American Federation of Labor (AFL) Film Council, not only refused Independent Productions Corporation a IATSE film crew but threatened to prevent the making of the movie. Jarrico, Biberman, Wilson, and others connected with the film were bitterly attacked from the floor of Congress by Rep. Donald L. Jackson (who called the movie 'a new weapon for Russia'), in the pages of the *Hollywood Reporter*, and by RKO studios (where Howard Hughes had fired Jarrico as a screenwriter). Local vigilante groups stormed the Silver City, New Mexico, locations, 'and one night a pitched gun battle took place at the ranch where the film crew was living'.[50] In July 1953 the press carried stories that Jarrico's attorney was preparing a damages suit against Brewer, Jackson, Hughes, and Pathé laboratories; Brewer responded by again urging his members to refuse to work on 'one of the most anti-American documentaries ever attempted'. But *Salt of the Earth* did get made. A rare classic of American socialist realism, luminously shot in the manner of Joseph Losey's *The Lawless*, the film opened at the Grande Theater, East 86th Street, New York, but scarcely anywhere outside a few major cities. Bosley Crowther's review in the *New York Times* (15 March 1954) displayed a detailed and sympathetic knowledge of the background, the blacklisting of Bibermann and Jarrico, the film's union sponsorship, the seizure of the actress Rosaura Revueltas as an illegal alien, and vigilante threats against the company in Silver City. As for the film's politics, Crowther found nothing to quarrel with, but he rightly identified the claims of the women to full participation in the strike as providing the 'raw emotion and power' in Michael Wilson's 'tautly muscled' script. For Crowther it was not so much 'the party line' as 'a calculated social document'. The Los Angeles *Daily News* commented indulgently: 'If there is propaganda in this picture it is not an alien one, but an assertion of principles...'

Infuriated not only by the film but by such favourable reviews, Pauline Kael launched a venomous attack on *Salt of the Earth* and its supporters, 'those liberals and progressives whose political thinking has never gone beyond the thirties'. The film was as 'clear a piece of Communist propaganda as we have had in many years'. *Salt* was 'extremely shrewd propaganda for the urgent business of the USSR; making colonial people believe they can expect no good from the United States...'. The film's dialogue resembled a pamphlet cut into parts, full of folksy lessons and pedagogical dialogue: 'This instalment plan, it's the curse of the working class.' Kael added various health warnings: 'If you have half an eye for this sort of thing, you'll know when you first see Esperanza's shiny radio that it will be taken away from her, just as you'll know when you see the photograph of Juarez that it wouldn't be framed except to be smashed' (by deputy sheriffs). Kael scoffed at Esperanza, 'the Madonna on the picket line'. Rosaura Revueltas, who totally identified with the role, was on record: 'In a way it seemed I had waited all my life to be in this picture. My own mother was a miner's daughter.' Kael derided the sentiment by (somewhat hysterically) imagining a film in which Greer

Garson 'had dreamed all her life of playing a noble Negro prostitute'. She scoffed at the collective endeavour of the strikers and the claimed documentary method of the producers: 'Although socially, economically and legally the United States has been expiating its sins against minorities in record time, it is still vulnerable. The Communists exploit this vulnerability: the message for export is that America is a fascist country which brutally oppresses the darker peoples.' Finally, replying to readers who accused her of McCarthyism, Kael asked: 'Is one not to call a spade a spade, because Senator McCarthy lumps together spades, shovels, and plain garden hoes?'[51] *Salt of the Earth* won the International Grand Prix for the best film shown in France during 1955, and a Karlovy Vary Festival award the same year, but it never achieved commercial distribution in the United States despite a protracted but futile legal action brought by the producers under the anti-trust laws, alleging conspiracy to blacklist.

Blacklisted dissidents—Michael Wilson, Sylvia Jarrico, Al Levitt, J. H. Lawson, Adrian Scott—belonging to the California Chapter of the Independent Citizens' Committee for the Arts, Sciences and Professions published nine issues of *Hollywood Review* between January 1953 and June 1956, each containing one major article which attempted to link trends in motion pictures with the cold war—violence, sadism, hatred, the glorification of brutality—or to offer criticism of Hollywood's depiction of minorities, women, and the foreign-born. The *Review* reached probably not more than 500 readers.

In two essays Michael Wilson sought to expose Hollywood's enlistment in the cold war and the Korean War through films exalting the killer instinct, blind obedience, and sacrificial death. A new breed of films expressed 'the doctrines of Manifest Destiny, the American Century, and white supremacy in gaudy technicolor'.[52] Not only Hollywood films of the Korean War but also those depicting World War II were now viewed by John Howard Lawson (the dean of Communist playwrights and screenwriters, recently imprisoned as one of the Hollywood Ten) as hymns to sadism, brutality, and mindless killing, because the war had retrospectively been drained of its progressive, pro-Soviet context. In the Hollywood studios Rommel was now a heroic gentleman[53] and honourable anti-Bolshevik—hence *Desert Fox*, in which Rommel and his friends 'have no objection to killing six million Jews, and break with Hitler only when they see that their class interests require an alliance with Wall Street'. The words are Lawson's, not Rommel's.

Lawson further embarked on a commendation of the motion pictures of the USSR, China, and the People's Democracies, 'films made in the lands where the people control production', with their 'complete absence of violence, brutality and pornography', their 'passionate affirmation of the life spirit':

> The Young Guard and other Soviet productions reflect the experience of a country in which the whole population was mobilized to meet an invading enemy... Hollywood dealt with soldiers fighting far from home, for a cause which they did not fully understand, in an army organized on the basis of caste and rigid discipline. Hollywood tended to stress the soldiers' cynicism, unreasoning courage, hatred of 'foreigners', contempt for women... Within a few years after the war, Soviet film-makers had completed the cycle of war films... But Hollywood moved to an increasingly direct glorification of militarism... as preparation for a third world holocaust.[54]

Lawson's attack extended to John Huston's beautifully framed movie about the life of Toulouse-Lautrec, *Moulin Rouge*, partly because it starred José Ferrer, who had repented past Communist associations for the benefit of HUAC, and to the same director's *The Red Badge of Courage* (1951). Writing in the prevailing idiom of the Soviet journal *Iskusstvo kino* (*Cinema Art*), Lawson contrasted the emphasis on moral degradation, sexual frustration, and drunkenness in *Moulin Rouge*, with *Mussorgsky*, an uplifting Soviet film about the composer who had also wrestled with the demon drink:

> The Soviet film-makers display no interest in the 'psychological' difficulties and personal frustrations of their protagonist. They assume that the historical reality of his career lies in his vast creative accomplishment... The Hollywood production sees life as sordid... and art as a sort of drug that enables exceptionally gifted persons to mock the destructive forces that surround the individual.[55]

⌗　⌗　⌗

The liberal revival in America emerged concurrently with the gradual demise of the blacklist. But films which set their face against witch-hunting almost invariably did so on limited terms: the persecuted hero or heroine had been *falsely* accused of Communism.

The script of Daniel Taradash's *Storm Center* (1956), written by Taradash and Elick Moll, took six years to reach the screen after Columbia's Harry Cohn finally agreed to finance it. The film depicts the fickle nature of small-town opinion when mobilized against someone who refuses to follow the conventional view. The mettlesome librarian (Bette Davis) is denounced not only for refusing to remove from the shelves a book called *The Communist Dream* after the city council demands that she do so, but also for her wartime membership of such groups as the 'Council for Better Relations with the Soviet Union'. Of course she had long ago resigned when she discovered that such groups were Communist fronts, but adults and children alike now refuse to speak to her. The library is set on fire. Evidently there could be no question of supporting the civil liberties of a Communist.[56] Bosley Crowther's review in the *New York Times* (22 October 1956) held that the lady was 'innocent of the charge' against her—and he did not pause to ask whether genuine Communists should be allowed to handle books. The film seemed to him too much like 'a hypothetical case put in a tract'. When the film reached France, the fact that the librarian was not a Communist, and therefore was portrayed as an 'innocent' victim of prejudice, provoked derision from Marcel Ranchal of the French film magazine, *Positif.*[57]

By the late fifties the tide was turning; a few Hollywood movies were emboldened to mock and parody cold war ideology, as witnessed in two successful films of the era, *Dr Strangelove* and *The Manchurian Candidate*. Stanley Kubrick came across a novel, *Red Alert* (1958), by Peter George, a retired RAF pilot, which imagined a psychotic American general unleashing a squadron of bombers against the USSR. This became the basis of Kubrick's film *Dr Strangelove; or, How I Learned to Stop Worrying and Love the Bomb*, which transformed a suspense thriller into a comedy of the absurd with assistance from the comic genius of the actor Peter Sellers. Equating cold war atomic madness with Americans' unresolved sexual neuroses, Kubrick had clearly taken note of the strange connection between bombs and sex to be found in the 1930s term 'bombshell' and, later, in the scanty bikini bathing costume so named by its designer soon after the Bikini Islands nuclear tests.[58] *Dr Strangelove* caused a storm but broke box-office records.

A second case is the adaptation of Richard Condon's novel *The Manchurian Candidate* into John Frankenheimer's film of the same name. Whereas Condon's novel represents middle-of-the-road liberalism, hostile in almost equal measure to McCarthyite witch-hunting and to the deeply hatched Communist plot to subvert the United States—indeed, Condon's storyline merges the two evils in the shape of the hero's wicked mother (played in the film by Angela Lansbury)—Frankenheimer is passionate in his indictment of a demagogic, opportunist, McCarthy-like politician, but only spoofingly annoyed with the Soviets and Chinese for brainwashing American POWs captured in Korea. Frankenheimer playfully parodies the scheming Russians, Chinese, and Koreans with tongue in cheek. Skipping Condon's brainwashing sequences, he contents himself with the surreal dream-recalls of Captain Ben Marco (Frank Sinatra). The Communists are thus dissolved into fantastical comic goons who set up a clinic in Manhattan staffed by film-set fake doctors and nurses. Guilt and fear are our key weapons, chortles the villainous Yen Lo: 'Your brain has not only been washed, as they say, it has also been dry-cleaned.'

The Army, the CIA, and the FBI (all hugely indebted to Frank Sinatra and his flair for solitaire) finally pool their patriotic resources to find the Red Queen and scotch the menace hanging over America: the nomination for president of a reactionary senator who is really the tool of the Soviet Union. Evidently the Kremlin had been plotting for years to get a 'fascist' elected president of the United States, an unlikely scenario that is not explained, beyond Richard Condon's analogous view that McCarthy was as much a threat to democracy as the Russians were. At the finale, as the hypnotized but now lucid hero Raymond (Laurence Harvey) climbs high on a gantry above the convention hall and assembles his rifle, one is reminded that the film was released a year before Lee Harvey Oswald chose a high depository window from which to assassinate President Kennedy. Had Oswald seen the film? Had he been 'hypnotized' while living in the USSR?[59]

Reports of the death of the old anti-Communism in the sixties have been exaggerated—witness *The Green Berets* (1968), a Warner Bros–Seven Arts film in Panavision Technicolor which grossed $8 million in the US market.[60] *The Green Berets* opens at the US Army John F. Kennedy Center, Fort Bragg, North Carolina, where we are inducted into a terrific celebration of the military ethos, everyone marchin' an' salutin', and a strikingly American version of it too: for example, the Special Forces combat units in training keep presenting themselves in a PR exercise to a panel of civilians, declaring themselves proficient in an unbelievable number of foreign languages (including those widely used in Indo-China, like German, Danish, etc.).

John Wayne—still sprightly at 61—is Colonel Mike Kirby. We gather that his passion in life is choreography—groups of soldiers, or girls in sarongs, walking and marching and walking back and forth, up and down—and Colonel Mike himself loves to be part of all the walking up and down. Helicopters fly in formation too, everyone and everything in step. The Vietcong die like aerobatic ballet-dancers.

Wayne hated liberal journalists yet contrived to blunt his own anger in the shape of Beckworth, a harmless, handsome-looking reporter tagging along with special forces in Vietnam. Never a hair out of place and with virtually nothing to say, Beckworth is never seen taking notes or dispatching a story, a dire case of an unscripted part—he doesn't send scandalous dispatches, he doesn't complain about napalm, chemical defoliation, and the uprooting of villagers into 'protected villages'; no, Beckworth of the 'Chronicle Herald' merely gazes into the middle-distance until gripped by the plight of an orphan boy adopted by American troops, whereupon he exchanges his invisible pen for a visible gun, his ever-spotless safari suit for combat fatigues.

The Green Berets, which runs for hours, on and on, is really a special-effects film for boys, with numerous massive explosions and bodies hurtling through the air. Indeed, high explosives and noise in general are almost a mark of moral virtue; the Cong, by contrast, lay lethal man-traps which grab and impale and strangle and garrotte the victim without a sound. Likewise, the Cong habit of trying to storm palisades by the use of simple ladders allows for images of sinister, writhing silhouettes against the glare of a good night's battle worthy of Hieronymus Bosch.

The capture of a top Communist general, snared by a beautiful Vietnamese woman whose father he had murdered, gives scope for some old colonial architecture dripping with foetid jungle vegetation, a quaintly old-fashioned Citroen car at the disposal of the Red general, plentiful servants, champagne on ice, and a tastefully evasive bedroom scene which suffers *coitus interruptus* as the free world pours in through the window. However, the raised Communist penis we don't see is as nothing compared to the spectacular hoisting of the trussed captive general into the air by balloon, and thence into an overflying US plane.[61] This shot alone wins the cold war for Hollywood.

⊞ ⊞ ⊞

Only eight years separates *The Green Berets* from the severe climate-change apparent in Martin Ritt's *The Front* (1976), set in the late forties, in which Woody Allen plays Howard Prince, a perky cashier working in a bar—an unsuccessful amateur bookmaker, a value-free lightweight with nothing on his mind except small schemes doomed to fail—as Vincent Canby put it in the *New York Times* (1 October 1976).

Improbably (but it doesn't matter), a successful TV writer, now blacklisted and describing himself as 'a Communist sympathizer', asks Howard Prince to 'front' for him by presenting his scripts under his own name. For a 10 per cent commission on $750–1,000 Howard blithely accepts.[62] It works wonderfully—Howard even wins the affections of a beautiful, classy, principled script editor, Florence (Andrea Marcovicci)—though she later ruins everything by resigning in protest against blacklisting and the general atmosphere of spying, informing, and intimidation. Soon Howard is asking for more blacklisted writers to represent; a rather unpleasant, proselytizing writer, describing himself very frankly as 'a Fifth Amendment Communist' opposed to the cold war, joins the stable, but Howard himself remains strictly apolitical and a cool liar, not least when suddenly famous and lionized; asked for his life story, he replies: 'I was a boxer and a seaman and all those things you gotta do to be a writer.' He tries to fit the role by buying classics in a bookstore, but balks at Dostoyevsky and forgets Melville when naming the giants of American literature. However, the film—apart from its collage opening sequence in the 'March of Time' mould, showing in rapid succession Frank Sinatra ('Young at Heart'), Truman, MacArthur's ticker-tape parade, Korean War veterans, Joe McCarthy's wedding, Joe diMaggio and Marilyn Monroe, civil-defence shelters, and women's fashions—does not attempt to rub home a philistine image of the era.

The close-up villains are the blacklisting agency, staffed by former FBI men calling themselves 'Freedom of Information' and fastening their hooks into panic-stricken television and film executives. This outfit is clearly modelled on the real blacklist agency American Business Consultants, which published the lethal periodical *Red Channels*. We see how 'Freedom of Information' tortures artists desperate for 'clearance' through the case of the comedian Hecky Brown (Brownstein), a $3,000-a-show actor now fired from the TV series that Howard Prince is supposedly writing, and grossly exploited when performing in smart hotels (he's given an envelope containing $250, which propels him into a fatal paroxysm of rage, a brilliant scene). What the blacklisting outfit wants, what the House Committee wants from witnesses, is not information but evidence of their 'sincere repentance' and 'full co-operation'—which in practice amounts to grovelling, praising the Committee's work, and, most important, forfeiting honour by naming friends and colleagues. The 'loyalty consultants' are the priests of the late-medieval ritual of expurgation which now governs the television studios and their commercial sponsors.

Played with magisterial pathos by Zero Mostel, Hecky Brown wriggles and squirms under questioning, sacrificing his dignity by pretending he'd only marched in a May Day parade because he was hot for a girl's ass, yet striving to preserve his honour by 'forgetting' her name and all the other names of those he marched with on the same parade. But in the end desperation leads Hecky to accept an invitation to spy on Howard Prince—the result being that Howard is exposed as a front for blacklisted writers. In self-disgust Hecky throws himself from the window of a luxury hotel after handing generous tips to staff. Freedom of Information secretly photographs mourners at the funeral. Howard Prince skulks in the shadows.

Howard is subpoenaed. And now his attitude passes through rapid mutations. First, why not collaborate on the friendly terms fixed up by the TV studio—why not name a few names they already know? Two out of three of his blacklisted writer-clients are appalled at the prospect. 'But what harm can it do you, fellas?' Howard keeps asking them. To this the script offers no pragmatic answer; it's simply not kosher, it's disgusting to collaborate with those skunks. 'Take the Fifth Amendment,' keeps yelling the unpleasant Communist writer, who had done precisely that. Howard then confesses to Florence that he is not and never was a writer. By now Howard is mutating towards winning her back after their mutual estrangement by somehow defying the Committee, by somehow playing the executive session his own way, by somehow... He doesn't know how. He still doesn't know when the session begins in an atmosphere of expectant cordiality. After a series of pathetic prevarications by Howard seated at the witness table, the Committee hands him a last chance to avoid a citation for contempt: had he ever known Hecky Brown? Hecky is dead, what does it matter?—but outrage finally grips Howard. He saunters insolently to the exit: 'Fellas, I don't recognize the right of this Committee to ask me these kinds of questions. And furthermore, you can go fuck yourselves.' Howard is last seen with one wrist in handcuffs and another around his proud girlfriend.

The Front reminds us how much rich Hollywood talent was buried by the blacklist.[63] The script broke new ground by not presenting the fictional blacklisted writers as 'innocents', victims of mistaken allegations, but rather as committed Communists who hold to their convictions.[64] A major factor guaranteeing a friendly reception for *The Front* was the dramatic change in attitude brought about by the Vietnam War, the rise of the New Left, and the revelations about J. Edgar Hoover's 'surveillance state'. But the neo-conservatives were alive and well alongside the New Left. Hilton Kramer's 'The Blacklist and the Cold War,' published in the *New York Times* (3 October 1976) when Kramer was the paper's chief art critic and art news editor, followed visits to *The Front* and the documentary *Hollywood on Trial*.[65] Kramer began by setting *The Front* in the current climate of revisionism among historians, film-makers, and producers. 'The point is, it seems, to acquit 1960s radicalism of all malevolent consequence, and to do so by portraying 1930s radicalism as similarly innocent... benign, altruistic, and admirable.' Later reconsidering (though not hugely) these events from the vantage point of the nineties, Kramer conceded: 'The investigations and the hearings were often conducted in an appalling manner. Their very nature created a situation in which informing became a career in itself, and innocent people *were* smeared and even destroyed by false accusations.' But! 'From which it does not follow, however, that all accusations *were* false.' And what about those other blacklists, 'the lists of anti-Communists who were denied work when Stalinist influence was at its height'?[66]

The secrecy maintained by unconverted Communist film people through the 1970s vexed even such radical film historians as Ceplair and Englund (who regarded the Rosenbergs as 'spies' rather than spies, and who believed that John Wexley's partisan *The Judgment of Julius and Ethel Rosenberg* had 'carefully and thoroughly destroyed the government's case').[67] They attended a Blacklist Retrospective in Los Angeles in May 1977, when *Salt of the Earth* was screened. Five of those instrumental in making this remarkable film sat on the stage answering questions from the audience. A man asked: 'What was the relation between the basic themes of the film—labour, ethnic, and female consciousness—and the Communist Party line?' The moment of truth. The audience held its breath. The panel members, all of whom had been Party members, were silent. Finally, Michael Wilson, who wrote the script, once again angrily dodged the question: 'We were *all* political—the film came out of our political beliefs.'[68]

The years passed, Soviet Communism expired, and—a curious footnote—Hollywood produced a film about the blacklist era which almost reverted, under no evident pressure, to the 'innocent victim' formula which had been eschewed in *The Front*. In *Guilty by Suspicion*,[69] the blacklisted hero David Merrill (Robert de Niro), now a successful film director and previously a decorated war hero dropped behind enemy lines, loses everything except his self-respect by refusing to name names to HUAC (whose blustering Congressmen are most realistically portrayed). The most dramatic dimension of this entirely accurate,[70] balanced, but uninspired film is its portrayal of a smooth, charming, but coolly ruthless Darryl Zanuck, production chief at Fox, who puts the fictional Merrill under exactly the same pressure to clear and purge himself as he did the real Elia Kazan, but with precisely the opposite result. Merrill, of course, never was a member of the Party (though one of his talented colleagues who leaves for England is a self-declared Communist); when testifying to HUAC, Merrill even borrows from Kazan the notion of having been 'thrown out' of pre-war meetings by the comrades because too independent-minded and argumentative. However, the comfortable and familiar politics of this is disrupted not only by a subpoenaed friend's abiding loyalty to the days of Stalingrad, but also by the revelation that even after the war Merrill had attended a rally of the Atomic Scientists' Association to 'ban the bomb', a view he still defends in February 1952. Reviewing the film in the *New York Times* (15 March 1991), Janet Maslin greeted a 'stirring and tragic evocation of terrible times' and pronounced David Merrill innocent because 'by no means any kind of political being'.

Witch Hunts:
Losey, Kazan, Miller

Despite some suicides, the American Inquisition did not as a rule break necks or even thumbs; it broke careers, it removed jobs, livelihood, the right to function. Surveillance, wire-tapping, mail-opening, men with long shadows positioned at street corners, the FBI. Joseph Losey, Elia Kazan, and Arthur Miller experienced the full force of the *pax americana* on home ground: Congressional committees, vigilante organizations like the Legion, private investigative agencies hired by studios and networks—all of whom aimed to render Soviet Russia's friends and admirers unemployable.

Miller wrote a play called *All My Sons*: Losey, Kazan, and Miller were all sons of thirties radicalism, all sons of the Five Year Plans and the light shining in the East. Losey and Kazan were directors, Miller a writer, but they were all men of the theatre and cinema whose best work can be counted among the century's finest.

Confronted by the persecution which we will chart in some detail, Losey finally escaped into exile and spent a decade in England trying to work under pseudonyms, before finally breaking out, post-hysteria, as creator of the films *The Servant, Accident, The Go-Between*, and *Don Giovanni*. By contrast Kazan, famous for his brilliant directing of plays by Miller and Tennessee Williams, and his way with actors like Brando, broke, reneged, named names, grovelled before HUAC, denounced Communism, and sought to justify informing. By contrast Arthur Miller, banished from the silver screen but supported by his worldwide success as the author of *All My Sons, Death of a Salesman, The Crucible*, and *A View from the Bridge*, stood his ground, refused to name others, and was taken to court for 'contempt of Congress'. Losey and Miller both condemned Kazan's role as renegade and informer, but Miller did so more cautiously and compassionately, Losey with a lasting rage fuelled, no doubt, by personal disappointment and professional envy. Fate granted him an unexpected revenge.

⊞ ⊞ ⊞

By an accident of timing, Joe Losey[1] was not targeted by the House Un-American Activities Committee during its first onslaught on Hollywood in 1947. This was no doubt because he had not yet turned in a feature film and had only recently moved to Hollywood from New York, where he was mainly involved in stage productions, then radio drama for NBC. In later years he, a classic casualty of the cold war, never bothered to apply under the Freedom of Information Act to be shown his own FBI file. He would probably have been surprised by the sheer scale of surveillance to which he was subjected from 1943 onward, and the number of regular FBI informers within the Hollywood studios. But he would have had to guess their identities from fragments of circumstantial evidence.[2]

Losey's file seems to have been activated by his friendship with Hanns Eisler, the most prominent Communist among German composers, with whom he stayed when he temporarily moved to Hollywood in December 1943. He had first met Eisler in 1935; subsequently Eisler wrote the scores for Losey's pre-war puppet film *Pete Roleum and his Cousins*, and for his documentary *A Child Went Forth*—and dedicated a movement of his *German Symphony* to Losey. In January 1940 Losey had written to the American consul in Havana, Cuba, on behalf of Eisler's application to be admitted as a resident of the United States. Eisler's home in Santa Monica was under heavy surveillance, his telephone tapped. In July 1944 the Bureau noted that Losey had been reported as an agent of the Soviet NKVD or OGPU. On 9 October a sixty-day mail cover was renewed.

'Obviously I got to know the left-wing people—Dalton Trumbo, Adrian Scott—I already knew John Howard Lawson, Sidney Buchman, Francis Faragoh.' According to Losey, he joined the CPUSA 'after the war', more specifically in 1946. On 14 January 1946 J. Edgar Hoover signed a memo to the attorney-general, describing Losey as a contact for various Soviet espionage agents and recommending a 'technical surveillance'. On 14 April the FBI, Los Angeles, reported that Losey and his wife were active in the Hollywood Independent Citizens Committee of the Arts, Sciences and Professions and in the 'Win the Peace' movement.

On 24 May 1946 Losey contacted an unidentified woman and discussed Truman's anti-stike legislation: 'fantastic, incredible, a step towards Fascism and would lead to revolution.' Two days later he telegrammed Senator

Downey, protesting the president's 'strike-breaking speech'. On 3 July the FBI, Los Angeles, reported: 'Subject is attempting to organise a mobile motion picture unit to fight the Ku Klux Klan activities locally. Contacts of Subject with Communists locally set out.' An FBI, Los Angeles, memo covering the year 1946 revealed obsessive interest in Losey's plan to direct 'Galleleo [sic] by Bertoldt [sic] Brecht', which might be 'a Communist propaganda medium'. Arriving in New York on 17 September, under close surveillance from the moment he reached La Guardia Airport, he was to become the first director to stage a Brecht play in English while working in collaboration with the playwright himself.[3] 'Es wird wohl Joe Losey', Brecht had told a colleague. And *wird* it was to be, even if not wholly *wohl*.

HUAC descended on Hollywood in 1947. On 15 October Losey staged a rally at the Los Angeles Shrine Auditorium, sponsored by Progressive Citizens of America, to raise money for the defence of the Hollywood Nineteen subpoenaed by the Committee. Following Brecht's appearance before HUAC on 30 October, the playwright took a train to New York accompanied by Losey and T. Edward Hambleton, flying on to England the following day, thence via Paris to Switzerland. Hellie Weigel, shortly to depart herself, gave Losey a present wrapped in tissue paper: 'You know Brecht, he can never do these things himself...' With the present—'an absolutely exquisite carved ivory opium pipe which he had picked up in China'—came a message from Brecht: 'You should relax.' Losey never saw him again.

Soon after the Committee adjourned its hearings, the big studios and producers in the Motion Picture Association (MPA) met at the Waldorf-Astoria, New York, on 24 November 1947. The upshot was an announcement that they intended to discharge or suspend without compensation those five of the Hollywood Ten still in their employ. Losey's head of production at RKO, Dore Schary, had boldly told HUAC that until it was proved that a Communist was a man dedicated to violent overthrow of the government, he would judge him by his personal capabilities alone. But now, after the MPA's Waldorf-Astora meeting, Schary too adopted the position that in order to protect the 'freedom' of the film industry it would be necessary to blacklist anyone thought to be a Communist. RKO fired Adrian Scott, one of the Hollywood Ten, as producer of *The Boy With Green Hair*,[4] which Losey was scheduled to direct—his first feature film for a major studio. Although Scott was a friend, Losey did not resign in protest; he directed the film, which was shot in Technicolor during the first months of 1948 for Schary on a large budget of $900,000.

'You want to send a message? Send it by Western Union.' This joke was often quoted by Ben Barzman, co-screenwriter on the project; Barzman and

Losey did indeed have a 'message' to send, and one not far removed from the priorities of the Party line: We Must Resist the Warmongers. The subsidiary message was directed against racism, though in a muddled fashion.[5] The basic problem with Losey's films from 1948 to 1960, the dawn of his 'Harold Pinter era,' can be summed up in two words: 'bad scripts.' Ten out of eleven of the pictures he directed during this period were written by left-wing Hollywood writers—or persecuted ex-Hollywood writers—cast in the Movie Mould and intent on smuggling messages into blatant melodrama. These writers were in general the friends of the Soviet Union but conditioned by Hollywood norms—their dialogue tended to be terse, tough, and sometimes crass. No exception, *The Boy With Green Hair* is structured on long narrative flashbacks—a distressed boy (Dean Stockwell) is telling his own story to a kindly doctor in a police station. Peter's memories begin with a candle-lit cake, a Christmas tree, the present of a dog, and his father's hands carving the roast: a series of comforting Christmas-card images of a good American home. This was what the carefully crafted culture of Hollywood's surviving Communists was about: the message was deep within the apple pie and the audience was assumed to inhabit a permanent Disneyland of fairy-tale typification: the boy is introduced to the small town's milkman, barber, doctor, and grocer in a rapid succession of typecastings. Several pat the boy on his nice mop of hair. Group psychology is indicated by repetition.

The boy's small-town school stages a war-orphan drive. The gymnasium walls are covered with posters of children hurt by war: 'Remember Greece', 'United Jewish Welfare Fund', 'United China Relief'. Later Peter, who is earning money as an errand boy for a grocery store, overhears ladies discussing war and peace, mainly in voice-over; disturbed, he drops a crate of milk. After his hair turns green in the bath—just why is never quite clear—he becomes the archetypal outsider: in the school playground the kids crowd round him, laughing, jeering—the stock confrontations. The angelic teacher Miss Brand gently chides her class in a passage later cut: 'The truth has never had an easy time—never—not even two thousand years ago . . .' (As in Losey's radio days at NBC early in World War II, Communist scriptwriters continued to pitch for Jesus alongside Lincoln.)

Howard Hughes took control of RKO before the film was released. Dore Schary, Losey's patron and protector, departed. The film was now the focus for an ideological struggle involving a highly placed RKO official, Peter Rathvon, 'a very nice man' with a 'vast, rather Mussolini office', according to Losey. At issue were four speeches in the grocery store, overheard by the boy Peter, a contrived dialogue between two town ladies representing the progressive (Mrs Fisher) and simple-minded (Mrs Clark) attitudes towards war:

MRS FISHER: The scientists say we'all be blown to bits in the next one. It might mean the end of the whole human race . . . It seems like it's human nature to want to kill.

MRS CLARK: Well, if it's human nature to kill, all the more reason we should be ready just in case the other fellow wants to start something.

Rathvon proposed the following revisions:

MRS A: Right now let's talk about being prepared and give the world time to talk about peace based on understanding. If we don't—

MRS B: If we don't we'll have another war just in time to get the next crop of youngsters.

Rathvon also scribbled on the script, in pencil: 'We were not ready for the fight . . . People must be ready to fight for what they believe in.'[6] The conflict here is not fundamental: in 1942 Barzman and Losey would have readily endorsed Rathvon's lines. Barzman's script reflected the shift in CPUSA policy as the 'patriotic war' of the anti-Nazi alliance yielded to the cold war. On 15 August 1948 the New York *Star* reported that the film's message would be doctored or removed by Hughes. Following a Hollywood preview, *Life* (6 December) devoted three pages, mainly pictures, to the film: 'Green Hair Trouble—Hollywood titans wage a battle over a modest little movie with a message. Howard Hughes hates messages . . . A crew of skilled technicians was turned loose with orders to blast the message out . . .' But failed. *Life* found two ideas in the film: that physical discrimination is bad; and that wars create suffering: 'These explosive ideas are so bathed in gentle humour and fantasy and pretty Technicolor and cloying music, and the story moves around so haphazardly that no one should be violently affected. Anyway, the whole family will probably have a good time at the show.'

The December 1948 issue of *Ebony*—supporting the film's condemnation of racial prejudice, for which green hair was a metaphor—claimed that Hughes spent $200,000 trying (and failing) to change the film's content. General release followed on 8 January 1949. In February *The Boy* received the National Screen Council's 'Blue Ribbon' Award for 'The Best Picture of the Month for the Whole Family'. Remarkably, at a time of cold war hysteria and purge within the film industry, the trade press was not inclined to attack the film's politics. Both *Variety* and the *Hollywood Reporter* (16 November 1948) were friendly, *Film Daily* was ecstatic.

When *The Boy* opened at the RKO Palace Theater, Bosley Crowther of the *New York Times* (13 January) praised this 'novel and noble endeavor to say something withering against war on behalf of the world's un-numbered children who are the most piteous victims thereof', but concluded that 'the gesture falls short of its aim'. *Time* magazine (10 January) complained that the film 'labors so clumsily to cram its ideas into the mold of "entertainment". As a result the message seems as contrived and insincere as a singing commercial, and just about as entertaining.' Yet no voice in the press condemned the film in explicitly cold war terms. Writing in the *Daily Worker* (13 January), Yose Yglesias liked the message but complained about 'its conventional picture of American small town life, its "cute" treatment of the boy, and its sentimental generalizations...' This review was clipped by the FBI and inserted in the Bureau's Losey File. In March 1949 Losey was listed among the sponsors of the Cultural and Scientific Conference for World Peace, held at the Waldorf-Astoria, New York (but he did not attend).[7] On 13 May he wrote to the Finnish writer Hella Wuolijoki: 'Fascism begins again. Unmistakably and faster. Also tougher and stronger. Little by little the liberals and honest democrats abdicate their prerogatives...Just now the prospects are horrifying.'

Within the Screen Directors' Guild a battle was heating up. In 1950 Joseph L. Mankiewicz was elected president of the SDG, having stated his opposition to a mandatory non-Communist oath for members. Cecil B. DeMille, a leading anti-Red vigilante, took advantage of Mankiewicz's absence in Europe to persuade the SDG's Board of Directors to pass a by-law imposing a mandatory oath. In October DeMille dispatched motorcycle couriers to all SDG members urging them to sign ballots to 'recall' (kick out) the recently elected president. Joe Mankiewicz himself now told his supporters: 'If we are going to oppose the loyalty oaths in principle then we have to make clear to everybody that none of us is Communist.' As Losey comments, this was entirely self-defeating: 'And I opposed it very strongly, as did Nick Ray, John Huston and Charles Walters.' But Mankiewicz brought along the lawyer Martin Gang, an expert in political 'clearance'. A hot debate raged. Gang, whose services Losey privately employed, 'leaned over me and said, "Go ahead and sign it. It's not perjury. It's not under oath." ' The rebel directors were persuaded to sign what Losey called a 'disgraceful statement':

I am not a member of the Communist Party, or affiliated with such party, and I do not believe in, and I am not a member nor do I support any organization that believes in or teaches the overthrow of the United States Government by force or by an illegal or unconstitutional method.

John Huston was number one on the list of signatories, Losey number seventeen, Billy Wilder number twenty-one. To resist a mandatory oath they had signed a 'voluntary' one.[8] In 1976 Losey was questioned by Michel Ciment, who suggested that what had happened in Russia had been 'much worse' than the trials and tribulations of the Hollywood Ten:

LOSEY: I doubt if it could have been—maybe worse but I doubt if it could have been.
CIMENT: People were killed.
LOSEY: Well, they weren't killed in court...
CIMENT: No—well they were killed in camps.
LOSEY: Yes, I know. I know now. They were also killed in a different way ['they' referring to Hollywood's victims].

Ciment also asked him whether American Communists had shut their eyes to what was happening in Russia. Losey replied: 'I don't think most of them knew it...I think the revelations of Khrushchev came as a profound shock.' Asked about the persecution of artists and intellectuals under Stalin, Losey replied: 'It was a horrible, disgusting period that all of us should be deeply and profoundly ashamed of...My attitude was closed...I at one point functioned on a Communist Cultural Committee that was grotesque.'[9]

In 1951 HUAC opened a new act in the Hollywood inquisition. The screenwriter Hugo Butler was subpoenaed as he began work on the screenplay of Losey's *The Big Night*; Butler's widow Jean recalls that he and Losey were 'driving around from one obscure little California motel to another, up and down the coast and inland...We were terribly paranoid; afraid to use phones...' The new HUAC hearings on Hollywood, the first since October 1947, were launched on 21 March 1951, three days after Harry Cohn, president of Columbia, announced a major collaboration with Stanley Kramer, whose team of directors would include Carl Foreman, Fred Zinnemann, and Joseph Losey. But, Losey later recalled: 'Sam Katz [chairman of the Stanley Kramer Company]...had heard that I was going to be involved in the Un-American hearings and he wanted me to sign an anti-Communist oath...' The lawyer Martin Gang suggested a formula: if Losey were subpoenaed by HUAC, Kramer could break the three-picture contract (worth about $200,000) for a payment of $10,000. Losey's files contain a letter drawn up by Martin Gang, to be sworn by Losey before a notary public:

I am not now, nor have I ever been, a member of the Communist Party. I feel that Communism is evil...that every decent American must oppose Communism and Communists in every possible manner...I feel that Soviet Russia is our country's greatest enemy...[And more in the same vein.]

I realize that you are employing me in reliance upon the statements I am making herein. I also realize that should any testimony be given before [HUAC], or any facts developed which contradict the statements herein...I give you the right to immediately cancel [the contract].

In that event Losey would keep the $10,000 advance. Although no evidence has been found that Losey actually signed this affidavit, it seems most unlikely that Kramer–Katz would have offered him the contract without it. Gang warned him that he was going to be named by two witnesses and advised him to testify in closed session: 'I simply said, "I'll have to think it over," and three days later I was on my way to Europe.'

Losey reached Paris on 17 July 1951. By the end of August he was staying at the Hotel Nettuno, Pisa, and was about to begin shooting a film eventually released as *Stranger on the Prowl*. His arrival in Italy was greeted by the Communist Party newspaper *L'Unità* with a two-page centre-spread, but news from home was bad. Martin Gang reported on 18 September: 'The inevitable happened today. You were named as a former member of the Communist Party. Fortunately, the witness who named you was a client of mine [Leo Townsend].' On 20 September Gang again urged Losey to testify in private to HUAC—what moral problem could there be in naming those already named? Why martyr yourself for a cause you no longer believe in? Losey would not do what Elia Kazan was soon to do. On 24 September Gang reported that the Stanley Kramer Company had indeed cancelled the agreement dated 1 July. The vigilantes had now received the green light; the *Los Angeles Times* (26 October) reported that the right-wing 'Wage Earners' Committee' was picketing five local picture theatres, including Paramount's, currently showing Losey's remake of Fritz Lang's film *M*. The FBI duly clipped the report. On 12 October 1952 Losey took a chance, risking arrest, when he made a clandestine visit to New York after fifteen months in Italy, England, and Franco's Spain (where he'd made a Shell demonstration film, mainly about the training of police dogs to attack demonstrators, which 'sickened' him). He ached for work in his native land, the America which remained wonderful despite the witch hunts. 'At one moment there was a really very strong possibility that I would do *The Crucible* of Arthur Miller, but Kermit Blumgarten . . . got cold feet . . . because of the political situation.' Losey left for permanent exile in England the day after Eisenhower's election in November, and did not return for fifteen years. In later times a widespread myth invaded the press in France, Britain, and even America—that Losey and most other Hollywood refugees had been hounded out of career and country by Senator Joseph McCarthy. McCarthy became a synonym for the entire blacklisting era and for the complex purge launched under the Truman administration. But McCarthy, as a senator, could not be a member of HUAC, which had jealously cornered the Hollywood market.[10]

Losey's British Certificate of Registration B 22181 (Aliens Order 1953) shows that on first arrival in London he stated his profession as 'Story Consultant and Script Writer' and was granted a four-month stay. The registration book was thereafter stamped by the Metropolitan Police, Piccadilly

Place, at irregular intervals. But for a foreign film-maker residing in Britain on sufferance, every employment had to be negotiated. Nor did the American Inquisition lose interest in the refugees abroad: Losey experienced systematic blacklisting, demands for further oaths of loyalty. Retaining and renewing his US passport became a nightmare after the FBI discovered that he had visited the Soviet Union in 1935 (when he directed Clifford Odets's play *Waiting for Lefty* in Moscow). On 31 December 1954 Walter M. Walsh, the US consul in London, requested him to hand over his passport on the ground that it was alleged by confidential informants that he was a Communist and a sponsor of the Cultural and Scientific Congress for Peace in 1949. In May 1955 Losey signed a legal deposition or affidavit stating that he had joined the CPUSA in 1946 and to the best of his recollection had left in 1947 or 1948—'I am not quite sure as to the exact date.' He added: 'I was baptised and confirmed in the High Anglican Church.' This evidently did the trick. On 28 May the State Department authorized the London Embassy to renew the passport. 'I must confess,' he told Hugo Butler in December 1956, 'that I am often desperately homesick and that I am tired to death fighting forever against losing odds.' Not until June 1968 was his lawyer Sidney Cohn able to inform him that the State Department would no longer ask: 'Are you now or were you ever..?'

⊞ ⊞ ⊞

Joe Losey and Elia Kazan had been co-founders (with Nicholas Ray) of 'the first attempt at a Communist collective theatre in New York'. Losey recalled: 'I directed Kazan in a thing called *Newsboy* some time around 1936, which was a highly left-wing agit-prop but very successful. I never liked him much.' Kazan quietly left the Communist Party in 1936—ten years before Losey, in less auspicious times, joined it,[11] but Kazan remained outwardly radical, supportive of the Hollywood Ten, keen on turning messages into art, friendly with the comrades. His *Viva Zapata!* came out in 1952, shortly before its brilliant ex-Communist director did his patriotic duty by naming names to HUAC. Scripted by John Steinbeck, the film starred Marlon Brando as Emiliano Zapata, a notable Mexican peasant leader of the second decade of the century.

Perhaps the most gifted director of his generation,[12] almost invariably bringing home the box office while harvesting the critical laurels, Kazan was closely associated with the work of Arthur Miller and Tennessee Williams. Closely linked to Lee Strasberg and the 'method' acting of the Actors Studio, Kazan cultivated such talents as Brando and James Dean.[13] Having directed a series of successful films for the production head of Fox, Darryl Zanuck,[14] a mogul in the classical Hollywood mode, Kazan had brought him the Zapata project with the added attraction of Marlon Brando. (Zanuck was sceptical about casting Brando, whose mumbled speech eluded him.)

The project was fraught with difficulties, political and national. Emiliano Zapata belonged to Mexico—yet who, what, and where did not also belong to Hollywood? Kazan wanted to shoot on location in Mexico, and that meant squaring not only the Mexican authorities but also the local film unions, where Communist influence was strong. Kazan and Steinbeck visited Cuernavaca to talk to the eminent cinematographer Gabriel Figueroa, *el presidente* of the Syndicate of Film Technicians and Workers. Kazan even told Figueroa he wanted him as cameraman, though he didn't, regarding his technique as romantic-sentimental Marxist. They showed Figueroa a script which he took away, his expression suggesting (according to Kazan) 'Gringo, keep off our soil!' How could a rebel like Zapata, committed to land reform, find acceptance in the movie theatres of an America in the grip of anti-socialist hysteria? When Figueroa met them again he explained that he didn't want the film made in Mexico unless there were changes in the script. Kazan bridled: 'I stopped listening to his words . . . but listened to the tone of his voice instead, and that was a familiar tone. I'd heard it years before on Twelfth Street in Comrade Jerome's office and from others in the Party. . .'[15] A member of Group Theatre's CP cell for two years from 1934, Kazan had developed an obsession about the experience:

I couldn't clean out of my mind the voice of V. J. Jerome and its tone of absolute authority as he passed on the Party's instructions for our Group Theatre cell and his expectation of unquestioning docility from me and the others. I heard again in my memory the voice, arrogant and absolute, of the Man from Detroit as he humiliated me before my 'comrades' in Lee Strasberg's apartment over Sutter's bakery.[16]

What Kazan now heard loudest, however, was Darryl Zanuck warning him to hide nothing either from himself or from HUAC. Years later Kazan was still wrestling with the remains of his conscience. Even since leaving the Party:

I'd thought what I was supposed to think. I'd forbidden myself doubt . . . why had I posed as a left-oriented liberal for so long? . . . It was only because, in that position I was 'in'. In what? Damn if I knew. But in . . . to stay in good with all sides, to be liked by everyone . . . just as I'd managed to have both Broadway and Hollywood, commercial success and artistic eminence.[17]

According to Kazan, Figueroa said: 'Suppose a Mexican company came up to Illinois to make a picture about Abraham Lincoln's life with a Mexican actor playing the lead, what would you think of that?' Kazan was not amused:

'I felt that the communists of Mexico were beginning to think of Zapata as useful, a figure they could glamorise in anti-gringo, pro-Mexican nationalist struggles... They didn't like our film because it showed him as being unclear.'[18] Then the Mexican national censorship board raised objections to the script of *Viva Zapata!*—though Kazan's autobiography does not detail what the objections were. Back in California, Kazan heard Zanuck's closest advisers at Fox urging him to give up on the project. Zanuck asked them, 'Do people round the lot think this picture Communistic?' Alarmed, Kazan offered to cut his salary from $162,000 to $100,000, which Zanuck accepted—with HUAC moving in he could probably have had the director for a banana. Eventually the film was shot in Texas; Kazan was instructed by Zanuck to 'go along our border with Mexico and find a location you can use', which Kazan interprets as heroic defiance, 'telling the Mexicans, their official state censor, and their Department of Defense, their generals and their politicos, to make their own films, he'd make his'.[19]

The story we wanted to tell was of a man who organized himself and his comrades, the people around him in his province, because of cruel and terrible injustices. [But]... once he got power, he didn't know how he wanted to exercise it. He was bewildered; and he began to find that power not only corrupted those around him, like his brother, but he had also begun to be corrupted by it himself. The third act was that he walked away from it, he walked away from the seat of power and so made himself vulnerable... he represented a Left position that was anti-authoritarian... in some way he was related to my life story.[20]

Stylistically, working from Steinbeck's material, Kazan found a way of 'jumping from crag to crag of the story... the first film I made that is structurally cinematic, where just a suggestion of an incident tells you more than the full playing out of it'.[21] He was helped and inspired by the discovery in Mexico of a photographic book, *Historia Gráfica de la Revolucion, 1900–1940*, full of pictures conveying what Henri Cartier-Bresson called 'the decisive moment'—for example, Pancho Villa and Zapata meeting in Mexico City, surrounded by their henchmen. Michel Ciment asked him why the film said not a word about American land seizures in Mexico. Kazan replied:

Zapata was in an isolated province. Where American imperialism was felt very strongly was in Pancho Villa's struggle; he was close to the US border. It was also felt very strongly on the east coast, where there was oil. But much less in Zapata's land, which was arid and stony and had no assets that anybody wanted.

All right: Time passed. Twenty years later the New Left, which is the students, the non-communist Left, the Left I've always felt an allegiance toward... loved *Viva Zapata!*

They used to ask me for a print and look at it again and again, just like they did *Battle of Algiers*,[22] because both made them understand what their problem was going to be.[23]

Kazan was bracing himself for the required purgation ritual of informing—of serving up names to HUAC.[24] He tells a garbled version of how, within the Screen Directors' Guild, Cecil B. DeMille had been

going for throats, including mine . . . Darryl Zanuck, in a burst of friendly candor, had told me there was a general suspicion—and I couldn't tell if he shared it—that I'd resigned from the Party only to throw people off the track, that I was still in fact a Communist. If I was cornered, I decided, I'd take a defiant position; I'd never bow to DeMille—or to the House Committee on Un-American Activities.[25]

But he didn't take it, and he did bow. He wasn't one of the twenty-five directors, including John Ford, William Wyler, and Fritz Lang, who signed a petition opposing DeMille's moves. Kazan asked his friend and collaborator Arthur Miller to call at his country home where he explained to 'Art' his decision to comply with HUAC: 'I said I'd hated the Communists for many years and didn't feel right about giving up my career to defend them. That I would give up my film career if it was in the interests of defending something I believed in but not this.' Miller listened. 'It was impossible not to feel his anguish, old friends that we were.' Kazan claims Miller put his arm round him and said: 'Don't worry about what I'll think. Whatever you do will be okay with me. Because I know your heart is in the right place.'[26] Miller himself indicates that it was this experience with Kazan that 'made the writing of *The Crucible* all but inevitable. Even if one could grant Kazan sincerity in his new-found anti-Communism, the concept of an America where such self-discoveries were pressed out of people was outrageous . . .' Miller expresses some sympathy for him. 'Yet this great director, left undefended by Twentieth Century-Fox executives, his longtime employers, was told that if he refused to name people he had known in the Party—actors, directors and writers—he would never be allowed to direct another picture in Hollywood, meaning the end of his career.'[27] Kazan's testimony produced a greater shock than anyone else's. 'It may be that Kazan had been loved more than any other . . .'—hence the betrayal. Even half a century later he could not shake off the onus of the era, as when in 1999 the Academy of Motion Picture Arts and Sciences awarded him an honorary Oscar, prompting protests from blacklistees and their descendants. Notices denouncing the award were placed in *Variety* and the *Hollywood Reporter*; the pavements outside the Dorothy Chandler Pavilion, Los Angeles, were blocked by angry pickets.[28]

Kazan appeared before HUAC in executive session on 14 January 1952, but the testimony was not made public. He came back on 10 April, again in executive session, no doubt to prevent heckling, this time to name the names he had withheld previously. He also tried to excuse a long list of collaborations with front organizations in the 1940s, claiming that he did not remember most of them: 'It is possible my name was used without my consent.' He admitted that his support for the Hollywood Ten in 1947 had 'represented my convictions at the beginning of the case', although he was later 'disgusted by the silence of the Ten and by their contemptuous attitude'.[29] He called his most recent film, *Viva Zapata!*, 'an anti-Communist picture'. As he had explained in detail in the *Saturday Review*[30] of 5 April, what fascinated Darryl Zanuck, Steinbeck, and himself was 'one nakedly dramatic act. In the moment of victory, he [Zapata] turned his back on power. In that moment, in the capital with his ragged troops, Zapata could have made himself president, dictator, caudillo. Instead, abruptly, and without explanation, he rode back to his village.' According to Kazan, Zapata 'must have felt, freshly and deeply, the impact of the ancient law: power corrupts. And he refused power.' This testimony was released to the press on 11 April, the day before the *New York Times* carried a paid advertisement by Kazan urging others to purge themselves as he had done.[31] He sought refuge (not unfashionably) in the mantle of Kafka's K: 'I was the accused in a gigantic public trial before unidentified judges, where the verdict, determined in advance, is known.'[32] Years later he was still denying the undeniable: '*The Nation* also slurred me, with the lie that I'd done it to preserve a fat Fox contract. The truth was that Darryl had called me into his office and explained that since I was now a controversial figure, he couldn't pay me my salary or anything like it on the last picture remaining on my contract.'[33]

In a book published in November 1953 by the Communist publishing house Masses and Mainstream, John Howard Lawson poured scorn on Kazan for everything he had recently done, even the film of *A Streetcar Named Desire*. Lawson posed two relevant questions about the moment when Zapata—*pace* Kazan's article in the *Saturday Review*—walked away from power. Was this historically accurate? And why was the incident, real or imaginary, treated by Kazan as 'the high point in our story'? Lawson dismissed with contempt the claim that Zapata had voluntarily renounced power; in reality he had found the forces arrayed again him, including a threatening United States, too strong. When Zapata rode out of the National Palace for the last time, rifle-fire and artillery were shaking Mexico City. Lawson concluded that Zanuck–Steinbeck–Kazan 'wanted a hero who surrenders' because cold war ideology was determined to demonstrate that power corrupts, not least revolutionary leaders—'whole regiments of scholars in the fields of sociology, political economy and history' had been mobilized to prove it. Furthermore:

The film presents Mexico as a land of corrupt generals and politicians, apparently acknowledging no obligation to a foreign power...The directional treatment, the lighting, setting, costumes and movement of the actors, are all designed to reinforce the impression that the people of Morelos are 'picturesque', artistically attractive, but totally incapable of effective organized action.

Under Kazan's direction, Brando played Zapata 'as a man who is not only culturally, but politically, illiterate. The actor employs the same tricks and mannerisms that he used a few months earlier to depict the brutally in-human "worker" in *A Streetcar Named Desire*.'[34] John Womack's scholarly biography of Zapata leaves no doubt that Lawson's Sovietistic view that Zapata was blocked by the Yankees is unfounded; more important, Kazan's claims for a power-shy Zapata also have no basis in history.[35]

⊞   ⊞   ⊞

Arthur Miller was effectively blacklisted in television, radio, and the movies until the late 1950s, but Broadway theatre remained relatively resistant to blacklisting. Miller recalled how the Catholic Church intervened when *All My Sons* was about to open at the Coronet Theater, Boston, before moving to Broadway; the issue was a single line, Joe Keller's final, despairing: 'A man can't be Jesus in this world.' Miller refused to cut it. Directed by Elia Kazan, *All My Sons* opened on 29 January at the Coronet Theater, New York, where it ran for 328 performances. The New York *Daily Worker* began by praising *Sons*, predicting that its very truthfulness would doom it to commercial failure, but when (as Miller himself recalled) the *New York Times* drama critic Brooks Atkinson turned the play in the direction of success, the *Worker* withdrew its support, finding it only a specious apology for capitalism. The play won the New York Drama Critics annual Circle Award despite competition from Eugene O'Neill's *The Iceman Cometh*. In May it reached Paris; the following year a movie appeared, with Edward G. Robinson as Joe Keller and Burt Lancaster as Chris.

Miller in his early years was much influenced by Ibsen and his device of the 'fatal secret'—used notably in *Pillars of Society*. Like Ibsen's *Ghosts*, *All My Sons* proceeds through a succession of revelatory conversations to expose a guilt-ridden past: the house built on a lie, the sins of the parents visited on the children. Miller's dramatic structure was, arguably, too mechanical and reliant on artificial plot devices, notably a slip of the tongue and the production of an improbable letter.[36]

Elia Kazan later recalled: 'Since the guilt was that of a businessman, ergo that of our business community, the play made a social statement.'[37] So did the 'real' fact that Wright Aeronautical Corporation of Ohio was revealed to have exchanged 'Condemned' tags on defective engines for 'Passed' tags, in cahoots with bribed army inspectors, shipping hundreds of failed machines to the armed forces. A number of officials went to jail.[38]

The most lethal anti-capitalist lines in *All My Sons* are Joe Keller's self-justifications to his son Chris when the truth is out. 'I'm in business, a man is in business . . . You lay forty years into a business and they knock you out in five minutes, what could I do . . . For you, a business for you!' To which his son replies in fury: 'Don't you have a country? Don't you live in the world?' The father finally shoots himself because his central (convenient) conviction, that the family is the ultimate, sacred entity, has disintegrated in the face of the fierce scorn of both his sons, the dead one and the live one. For them, all the young American pilots who died as a result of their father's crime were his 'sons'—hence the play's title. Raymond Williams calls Joe Keller's blinkered obsession classic Marxist alienation[39]—'Marxist', presumably, because Keller justifies his predictably murderous action in profit terms—though one can imagine a Soviet plant manager attempting to save his skin by similar means.

Although unfashionably social and prosaic in a period of metaphysical drama, often written in verse, *All My Sons* was soon in demand by German theatre *Intendants*, generating a crisis for the US Besatzungsbehörden, the occupation authorities, who came under pressure to ban the play from the National Commander of the Catholic War Veterans, Max Sorensen, the magazine *New Leader*, the National Association of Manufacturers, and the new blacklisting sheet *Counterattack*, set up in May 1947 at 240 Madison Avenue by three ex-FBI agents. The US Office of Military Government in Germany (OMGUS-Berlin) cabled the Civil Affairs Division of the State Department on 19 August 1947 and was instructed that *All My Sons* could only assist Moscow's propaganda line in Germany: 'Play's theme regarded as harmful to Reorientation Program. Request *no* further consideration be given its use.'[40] Miller later claimed that the play was removed from the US Army's repertoire in Europe along with virtually everything else he wrote—although *Death of a Salesman* occupied second place among American plays on the West German stage in 1949–50 as *Tod des Handlungsreisenden*. This may seem paradoxical, since the guilt of Willy Loman in *Salesman* is not caused by a single action, like Joe Keller's in *All My Sons*—it's the consciousness of a whole life.[41]

The suspicions of the witch-hunters were no doubt confirmed when *All My Sons* was staged at the Vakhtangov Theatre, Arbat Street, Moscow, in a translation by E. Golyshev and Iu. Semenov, with Yuri Lyubimov as Chris Keller.[42] Extracts quoted in reviews indicate that the translation was far from faithful; key passages clearly distort Miller's meaning by design rather than error. For example, Miller has his distraught hero Chris, when finally confronted by the truth about his father, declare: 'This is the land of the great big dogs, you don't love a man here, you eat him! That's the principle, the only one we live by—'. The Russian version (here retranslated) is significantly different: 'Here's America—America is the country of the frenzied hounds (*strana ostervenelykh psov*). Here people hate, here people devour. That's the code here; it's the only code by which America lives.'[43] But when Miller's Chris says 'here' and 'This is the land', does he mean the United States? Not really; he means his father's appalling version of American business ethics. When he says 'we' he does not mean 'we Americans', he is referring to his father's cynical philosophy of how everyone lives and survives in a business economy. Chris employs a sardonic idiom to register his passionate protest: in his view, to be an entrepreneur, to be in business, by no means requires a descent to Joe Keller's ethics. It doesn't mean putting profit before the lives of twenty-one young airmen. But what the Soviet audience at the Vakhtangov heard was an indictment of 'America'.

As in the case of Simonov's play *The Russian Question*, the reviews were in certain respects standardized, indicating a common briefing. All used the phrase 'in the country of the dollar' (*v strane dollara*). All began by praising two previous productions at the Vakhtangov, *The Russian Question* and *Deep Are the Roots* (*Glubokie korni*), a civil-rights drama by James Gowe and Armand d'Usseau also much favoured in the Soviet zone of Germany. All of the reviews referred to the US 'War Minister' (*Voennyi Ministr S Sh A*) as having banned Miller's *All My Sons* in 'the American zone of occupation of Europe' (i.e. not just in Germany). All regretted that Miller had resorted to the traditional 'family drama' (*semeinaia drama*). All praised the performances and A. I. Remizov's production.

V. Zhdanov (not to be confused with A. Zhdanov) was the most friendly of the critics. Writing in the trade union organ *Trud* (27 November 1948), he argued that the core of the play—'Is there nothing in your life except the business? Don't you have a country? Aren't you a man?'—exposes the financial interests of America's industrial magnates in preparing for a new war. (It doesn't.) Writing in *Izvestiia* (24 November), A. Borshchagovskii noted that despite the current reactionary climate, honourable artists like Howard Fast, Chaplin, and Miller were telling the world the truth about the 'country of the dollar'. *All My Sons* had 'suffered persecution' (*vyzvala goneniia i presledovanniia*), not only in the territories occupied by the US military but also in England.'[44] According to Borshchagovskii, Miller benefited from the influence of Gorky, but: 'We don't see the toilers of America, who have the moral right to appear in the role of denouncers of this rotten society.' *Izvestiia's* critic concluded (improbably): 'The strength and significance of this production is the unmasking of the criminal imperialist clique.'

Writing in *Moskovskii bol'shevik* (8 December), Ia. Grinvald regretted that the Vakhtangov had on this occasion made an unsuccessful choice which did not merit production on a Soviet stage. 'Miller's play does not show the America which is opposed to peace and democracy. In this play we do not see the America of Truman, Marshall, Baruch, the imperialist, fascist America striving for limitless expansion in the whole world.' Instead Miller depicted a limited, out-of-the-way, 'single-storey', provincial America absorbed in petty philistine concerns and irrelevant family conflicts. Miller could not transcend bourgeois liberalism. The damage done by wealth was far more clearly illustrated in the work of Balzac and Zola, 'not to speak of the great Russian classics Ostrovsky, Saltykov-Shchedrin, Tolstoy, Gorky'. To compare Miller's psychologically thin characters with Gorky was like comparing a lilliputian with the giants. (None of the Soviet critics mentioned Ibsen, the real influence on Miller.)

The harshest attack was delivered by Al. Abramov in *Vecherniaia Moskva* (1 December), who warned his readers that the play had won the drama critics' award in America—and who were the majority of these critics if not employees of the big capitalist papers, including the Hearst press? (So, comrades, think twice before you weep.)

It therefore seems that the leaders of the information services, acting in logical conformity with their class ideology, concluded a deal with Miller (*zakliuchivshie s Millerom dogovor*) for the production of his play in the US zones of occupation before the frightened bisons (*zubry*) of the War Ministry intervened. Strictly speaking, they had nothing to be frightened of: for all his progressive gestures, Miller does not challenge the capitalist system. For good reason the Communist press in America immediately exposed the play's ideological defects.

Abramov's attack was relentless: Miller's pathological portrait of a mother who refuses to believe that her dead son is dead was reminiscent of the reactionary authors O'Neill and Faulkner. So, concluded Abramov: 'Why was it necessary for a Soviet theatre to stage this idealized portrait of a mediocre (*zauriadnyi*) American bourgeois?' The Vakhtangov collective and the director of the play must now arrive at a decisive conclusion about its future repertoire.

Several months passed before the *Christian Science Monitor* (21 April 1949) announced that the play had been withdrawn, but this may have occurred sooner[45]—ironically, this was the time when the tall Miller was photographed, smilingly benignly, beside a tense Shostakovich and the even taller Fadeyev while attending the Waldorf Peace Conference in New York. Miller later reflected that 'Joe Keller is arraigned by his son for a wilfully unethical use of his economic position; and this, as the Russians said when they removed the play from their stages, bespeaks an assumption that the norm of capitalist behaviour is ethical, or at least can be, an assumption no Marxist can hold.'[46]

⊞ ⊞ ⊞

Kazan had directed Miller's play *All My Sons* and *Death of a Salesman*, but to offer him *The Crucible* was obviously out of the question after he had publicly named names. Thereby hangs a tale of witch hunts ancient and modern. Miller recalls: 'On a lucky afternoon I happened upon *The Devil in Massachusetts*, by Marion Starkey, a narrative of the Salem witch-hunt of 1692.' The central drama of *The Crucible* revolves around a succession of perjurious allegations made by frightened girls who have been discovered dancing naked and practising black magic in the forest. Searching through the transcripts in the Salem courthouse, Miller discovered that Abigail Williams, the prime mover of the hysteria among the children, 'cried out' her former mistress, Elizabeth Proctor, as a witch but was uniquely clear about John Proctor's innocence 'despite the urgings of the prosecutors'.[47] 'It was the fact that Abigail, their former servant, was their accuser, and her apparent desire to convict Elizabeth and save John that made the play conceivable for me.' As the chain of accusations lengthens, each accuser saves herself by confessing, informing, pointing the finger. Further deepening the parallel with the McCarthy era, the magistrate's court in *The Crucible* is so eager to record guilty verdicts that anyone bold enough to sign an affidavit for the defence is himself arrested for cross-examination.[48]

The Indian frontier—the Iron Curtain—lay close by, breeding a stifling unity until internal repression outstripped external dangers. In Salem, as in America under Truman and Eisenhower, witch hunts were also fired by old rivalries and hatreds, by a consuming property-lust which tempted each to cry 'witch' against his neighbour—hence the fierce, post-war assaults on the New Deal and the labour unions. Miller shows how the Salem court (in modern terms HUAC) develops a vested interest in a particular image of guilt. Says Deputy-Governor Danforth: 'a person is either with this court or he must be counted against it, there be no road between.' He adds, in tones familiar during the Red scares: 'there is a moving plot to topple Christ in this country!' Miller also accuses some of his characters of profiting commercially from the deaths of those they accuse: 'This man is killing his neighbours for their land!'

A signed confession to the court, or to Danforth, saves a man or woman from death, just as HUAC and the other committees of Congress demanded confession and purgation. But purgation arrives only with the incrimination of others. Miller uncannily anticipates his own behaviour when subpoenaed by HUAC in 1956, when he has his character John Proctor confess (falsely of course) on his own behalf but refuse to name anyone else: 'I speak of my own sins. I cannot judge another. *Crying out, with hatred*. I have no tongue for it.'[49] But when he learns that his confession is to be nailed in public display, he tears it up and is hanged.

Much of the interest and dramatic tension in *The Crucible* hinges on who can convince whom: will the court believe the hysterical girls or their sober and upstanding victims? Miller skilfully wrestles us through scene after scene of disputation as the protagonists struggle to convince Deputy-Governor Danforth of guilt or innocence. 'Is the accuser always holy now?' John Proctor asks. 'I'll tell you what's walking Salem—vengeance is walking Salem.' For all his sturdy-yeoman independence, his habit of ploughing on Sunday when necessity dictates, and his refusal to pay church dues when he chooses, John Proctor remains the prisoner of Christian certainties who cannot dispute the devil's existence,[50] or the need to extirpate his disciples; he can only shout aloud his own innocence and his wife's—whereas in Miller's time, at the onset of the cold war, the Devil had his own Party, overt as well as clandestine. For that reason alone, the historical parallel is tenuous, yet in a later edition of *The Crucible*, published in *Collected Plays* (1958), Miller inserted some discursive authorial interventions. The Reverend Hale, for example, is about to make his first entrance but is delayed by a Miller exegesis roaming across such subjects as Soviet fashions in female dress. As Hale waits in the wings, Miller tells us that:

At this writing, only England has held back from the temptations of contemporary diabolism. In the countries of the Communist ideology, all resistance of any import is linked to the totally malign capitalist succubi, and in America any man who is not reactionary in his views is open to the charge of alliance with the Red Hell . . . Once such an equation is effectively made, society becomes a congerie of plots and counter-plots, and the main role of government changes from that of the arbiter to that of the scourge of God.[51]

Anti-Communists were not slow to react. Robert Warshow, associate editor of *Commentary*, accused Miller of defending 'the astonishing phenomenon of Communist innocence'. In an interesting essay, Warshow complained that Miller had altered the facts surrounding the 1692 Salem trials; for example, the real Abigail Williams, one of the chief accusers and avid informers, had been 11 years old, but Miller turned her into a young woman and invented an adulterous relationship between her and John Proctor in order to motivate her denunciation of John and his wife.[52] According to Warshow, Miller had merely provided a facile theatrical motive, 'deliberately casting away the element of religious and psychological complexity which gives the Salem trials their dramatic interest in the first place'. But Warshow's main complaint was clearly political and contemporary: Miller invited the implication of a parallel with the 1950s but avoided spelling out 'how much like': witches were always a fantasy but Communist espionage was real, surely? 'Mr Miller is under no obligation to tell us whether he thinks the trial of Alger Hiss, let us say, was a "witch trial".' Likewise with the Rosenbergs. Warshow accused Miller of supporting the pose of American Communists, who passed themselves off as liberals and dissenters and who indignantly rejected the question 'Are you a Communist?' as a slur on proponents of peace and civil rights even when, as it happened, they were indeed Communists.[53] Warshow was far from alone among cold war liberals in attacking *The Crucible*. Irving Kristol called it 'a calamitous error to believe that because a vulgar demagogue [McCarthy] lashes out at both Communism and liberalism, as identical, it is necessary to protect Communism in order to defend liberalism.' Norman Thomas and Ernest Angell, chairman of the American Civil Liberties Union Board of Directors, agreed. So did the State Department, which denied Miller a passport; in 1954 he was unable to travel to Brussels to attend a production of *The Crucible*, but he did regain his passport the following year.[54]

Jean-Paul Sartre, at the height of his rapprochement with the Soviet Union, began work on a screen version of *The Crucible*, following the success of Marcel Aymé's translation for the stage, produced as *Les Sorcières de Salem* (*The Witches of Salem*) at the Sarah Bernhardt Theatre, Paris. Commenting on Aymé's version, before he himself was commissioned to write a screenplay, Sartre complained of being shown 'a man [John Proctor] who is pursued one doesn't know why', and of a 'disconcerting idealism' at the end. The death of Proctor:

seemed like a purely ethical attitude, not as the act of freedom he undertakes in order to reveal the scandal, to oppose his situation effectively, as the only action he can still take. Thus rendered insipid (*affadie*), emasculated (*châtrée*), Miller's play appears to me as a mystification, since each of us can see in it what he wants, and since each public will find in it only the confirmation of its own attitude. This is because the real political and social implications of the witch-hunting phenomenon don't appear in it clearly.[55]

Sartre's screen version made class conflict more explicit, building up the role of Deputy-Governor Danforth. The film of his 300-page screenplay, condensed and directed by Raymond Rouleau, was released in 1957, with music by Hanns Eisler, using the leading actors from the stage production, Yves Montand as John Proctor, Simone Signoret as Elizabeth, and Mylène Demongeot as Abigail.[56] Sartre enters into a general criticism of the Protestant ethic embracing sex, money, and power. The clerics link the devil with rebellion against the rich; a storekeeper remarks: 'There are no witches among the rich.' Proctor is hanged finally as a pre-revolutionary martyr; Sartre transforms his despairing suicide into hope for social change through the murder of a hero.[57] When the film was released at the Little Carnegie, New York, Bosley Crowther concluded that Sartre had achieved greater emotional depth than 'Mr Miller's somewhat cramped and peculiarly parochial account of the workings of vengeance, fear, suspicion, injustice and finally bravery'. The brilliant cast was French but the setting and costumes seemed authentic. 'It could be Brittany but it looks like New England . . .'

Reminiscing in 1967, Miller recalled that *The Crucible* was originally 'dismissed as a cold, anti-McCarthy tract, more an outburst than a play', but when it was staged again in March 1958, at the Martinique Theatre off-Broadway, it was more generously appraised by the critics and ran for 633 performances across fifteen months. 'It was simply that nobody was afraid anymore', Miller explained, whereas in McCarthy's heyday 'to have treated this fear as a tragic thing rather than as a necessary and realistic and highly moral sort of patriotism, was more than could be borne by liberals and conservatives alike'.

⊞ ⊞ ⊞

While Kazan did not direct *The Crucible*, Miller did not script Kazan's remarkable film *On the Waterfront*, though he had been scheduled to do so. Bicycling around Brooklyn in 1949, Miller had noticed graffiti chalked over pavements and walls and sides of trucks: DOVE PETE PANTO?—Where is Pete Panto? Everyone was afraid to discuss the fate of Panto, a local longshoreman who had tried to organize a protest in his local unit of the International Longshoremen's Association against the gangsters who controlled the harbour. Miller wrote a screenplay, *The Hook*, based on the event, the overt theme of which is gangsterism and mobster rule among longshoremen and their union officials. 'Pete Panto was sleeping in cement at the bottom of the river.' Miller and Kazan offered the script to the boss of Columbia Pictures, Harry Cohn, who showed it—with a caution typical of the time—to the most powerful, anti-Communist labour leader in Hollywood, Roy Brewer, who duly denounced Miller's script as 'a lie', adding that no loyal American could have written it, since such a movie would generate 'turmoil' in New York harbour, where military supplies for Korea were being loaded. Cohn and Brewer then handed the script to the Los Angeles office of the FBI, Cohn warning Miller that if the film were to be made despite Brewer's veto, union projectionists throughout the United States would refuse to show any movie from Columbia. When Brewer suggested that the script be reworked so that the docks were terrorized by Communists instead of gangsters, Miller refused to co-operate; in his view the real menace on the New York waterfront was the gangster Tony Anastasia, whose brother ran Murder, Inc. Cohn sent Miller a cable: 'IT'S INTERESTING HOW THE MINUTE WE TRY TO MAKE THE SCRIPT PRO-AMERICAN YOU PULL OUT.'

Kazan now turned from Miller's doomed script to one by Budd Shulberg, another former radical who had named fifteen names before HUAC in 1951, thus preceding Kazan into the ranks of prominent Hollywood informers. Schulberg's script was based on a series of Pulitzer Prize-winning articles by Malcolm Johnson of the *New York Sun*. Sam Spiegel finally took it on after many rejections. The moral necessity of informing became central to Schulberg's script. Although the villains remained, as with Miller, gangsters rather than Communists, the film was widely interpreted as an anti-Communist allegory.

Starring Marlon Brando and Eva Marie Saint, with music by Leonard Bernstein (his film debut) and a strong supporting cast headed by Karl Malden as the brave, snub-nosed, Irish-American priest Father Barry, Lee J. Cobb in a chilling performance as the waterfront gangster boss Johnny Friendly, and Rod Steiger, the film took as its locale the New York docks, described by A.W. of the *New York Times* (29 July 1954) as 'the brutal feudalism of the wharves'. But was it also an allegory about the necessity of informing against Communists, as later generations of commentators have generally held? If so, A.W. did not notice.

Terry Molloy (Brando), an ex-prizefighter, is the inarticulate tool of the ruthless labour leader Johnny Friendly, unregenerate monarch of the docks, who shakes down his own members as readily as the shipowners. Anyone foolish enough to squeal to the Crime Commission gets dispatched by Friendly's goons. Even when Father Barry gathers a few spirits in his bleak church to discuss the latest murder, the mobsters brazenly throw a brick through the church window and beat each fugitive as he hurries away into the night. This is where Terry Molloy's conversion begins—he is goaded into decency by the murder of a young port worker he knows and whose indignant sister he is about to love. The brave Father Barry and the girlfriend (Eva Marie Saint) act as his conscience, finally urging him to testify before the Crime Commission. The tall priest lashes out with a spontaneous uppercut when Terry Molloy refuses to hand over a gun and tells him to go to hell.

The film is a powerful study of conformity among a workforce cowed by gangster terror—yet also loyal to the ethic by which one does not betray the black sheep of the 'family' to outsiders. The gangsters arbitarily decide at the dock gates who shall be hired each day, in what jobs, at what rates of pay—and yet they are the union. The slouching, gum-chewing, delinquent Terry Molloy, evasive and cynical, believes in this ethic of loyalty implicitly but totally. You break it, you die. (Whenever Brando stops chewing gum it means he's thinking.) What, ironically, finally persuades him to testify is not so much his guilt about the murder of a friend, in which he had a part, or his feeling for the friend's sister, or his respect for Father Barry, but the fact that his own elder brother Charlie, a leading waterfront gangster and hitman for Johnny Friendly, cannot bring himself, when assigned to silence Terry, to do it; he lets him run free, hands him a gun as well—'You're going to need it'—and pays with his life for this brotherly love. Terry finds Charlie suspended by a hook after dark in the brutal streets. It is Terry's ultimate loyalty to the Molloy family which brings him to denounce the union.

When he does so his own adoring younger brother is so outraged that he tearfully kills all of Terry's pigeons in their rooftop coop (perhaps unlikely, since the murdered Charlie was elder brother to the boy as well). Worse is to come. The ex-boxer Terry bravely goes down to the waterfront after testifying, demanding work; all the men turn their backs on him; Terry has to win their loyalty by a primitive rite of physical courage and prowess, by fighting Johnny Friendly, which carries the action far from life and into the rituals of Hollywood.

The parallel proposed by Kazan and Schulberg does not stand up. In their film the personnel of the Crime Commission, briefly glimpsed, are not the crude, self-serving, and in some cases racist publicity hounds who in reality sat on HUAC and before whom Elia Kazan made his peace. The CPUSA did not enforce loyalty on its members—the 'D and D,' deaf-and-dumb, code of survival on the waterfront—by means of physical terror; nor did it, despite the worst efforts of Hollywood films like *The Woman on Pier 13*, murder recalcitrants.

But were they moral gangsters, America's Communists? 'I thought they were accessories to murder', Schulberg told Nora Sayre in the late 1970s, adding that Communists had been unable to admit that they 'were party to the worst oppression of the twentieth century'. Both the Mafia and the Watergate conspirators, he pointed out, would have remained inviolable if everyone had remained silent. In later years Kazan too has declined to apologize: 'The people who owe you an explanation (no apology expected) are those who, year after year, held the Soviets blameless for their crimes.'[58] His own radical years he describes as 'seventeen years of posturing'. The Kazan who finally informed was 'my true self'—even though his career happened to be on the line.

The New York Film Critics voted *On the Waterfront* the best film of 1954. The Academy of Motion Picture Arts and Sciences voted it the best picture, Kazan the best director, Brando the best actor. The film won eight Oscars. According to one commentator, the film 'vividly exemplifies the political ethos of the decade', further describing it 'as useful an entrée as any into the culture of the cold war'.[59] Yes and no: the ordinary, intelligent spectator would no more know that *On the Waterfront* carries a political allegory than the ordinary, intelligent child reader would know that *Animal Farm* is about Stalin.

Miller was dragged before HUAC four years after Kazan, but with very different results. America in the 1950s was a society riddled with informers, many of them whispering neighbours confiding suspicions to the FBI, others public and semi-professional, the ideal witnesses for the Congressional committees. Miller detested informing, returning to the theme in *A View from the Bridge* (1955), where the longshoreman Eddie's lust for his teenage niece so warps his good nature that he tips off immigration officers to the presence in his home of a pair of illegal aliens—his wife's Italian relatives. In 1956 HUAC subpoenaed the playwright on the pretext of an inquiry into the scandal of subversives being granted passports.[60]

After a notional discussion of passport regulations, the Committee soon turned to a general trawl through the playwright's life and work—had he opposed the Smith Act, and why had he been hostile to Ezra Pound, 'this anti-Communist writer'? The 'charges' against him included signing the *amici curiae* brief to the Supreme Court on behalf of the Hollywood Ten; signing Civil Rights Congress (a Communist front) statements against anti-Communist legislation and against HUAC itself; attending five or six meetings of Communist writers in 1947; and signing appeals on behalf of Gerhardt Eisler and Howard Fast.

Miller insisted that he had never applied to join the Party. Committee Counsel Richard Arens insisted that Miller had indeed applied, and 'the number of your application is 23345'. Miller flatly denied it—adding that he now regretted his 'great error' in not having come out in support of victims of post-war Communist persecution abroad. He also expressed regret for his past support of Communist-dominated organizations at home.

MR ARENS: Are you cognisant of the fact that your play, *The Crucible*, with respect to witch hunts in 1692, was the case history [*sic*] of a series of articles in the Communist press drawing parallels to the investigations of Communists and other subversives by Congressional committees?
MR MILLER: The comparison is inevitable, sir.

[At another juncture in the interrogation:]

MR ARENS: Was it likewise just a little farce, your play, *You're Next*, by Arthur Miller, attacking the House Committee on Un-American Activities?
MR MILLER: No, that would have been quite serious.
MR ARENS: Did you know that the play...was reproduced by the Communist Party?

Miller spoke freely about his own career and commitments but, like his hero John Proctor in *The Crucible*, adamantly drew the line at naming others: 'I will protect my sense of myself.' The Committee wanted him to name names, not because it needed or lacked those names but as an act of self-purgation. He refused and was cited for contempt of Congress by a vote of the House, 373–9. When the case came to trial in May 1957 Arens claimed that Miller had been a Party member from 1943 to 1947, but he declined to reveal his sources. Miller was convicted of contempt, but in August 1958 the ruling was reversed on a technicality.[61]

Miller staged a notable return to the Soviet stage in 1959, when *Death of a Salesman* was performed at the Pushkin Theatre, Leningrad, directed by Rafail Suslovich. No doubt the House Un-American Activities Committee had done Miller the service of reviving his prestige in the USSR. The Soviet critic Naum Berkovsky noted that Miller was 'far from rid of bourgeois thinking', although the play demonstrated that 'human life does not have the slightest value for [capitalism]'. The set-design by Aleksandr Tyshler reinforced the social point: the Lomans' modest, comfortable home 'is overshadowed by the windowed walls of skyscrapers and office buildings out of all proportion to human beings'. Particularly chilling, according to Berkovsky, was the final confrontation scene between the ageing salesman Willy Loman (played by Yuri Tolubeyev) and his boss, Howard Wagner, loath to kick Willy into the gutter but forced by the salesman's dismal failures to do so. In the Leningrad production Wagner's 'intonation is deliberately colourless and flowing; his words evaporate before he completes them'.[62]

Miller had told HUAC in 1956 that he might yet work with Kazan again—and it was indeed the chameleon Kazan who directed *After the Fall* for the Lincoln Center Repertory Company in January 1964. In this play the character Micky saves his career by informing on old friends. The character Lou confesses: 'When I returned from Russia and published my study of Soviet law—*Breaks off*. I left out many things I saw. I . . . lied. For a good cause, I thought, but all that lasts is the lie . . . And I lied for the Party. Over and over, year after year.' Even so, Lou insists that informing on colleagues and friends is no solution. 'Because if everyone broke faith there would be no civilization. That is why the Committee is the face of the philistine . . . that gang of cheap publicity hounds.'[63] But this leaves open the question: 'broke faith' with what? Recent legislation directed against racism and sexual discrimination may encourage witnesses to step forward and denounce guilty colleagues: no one objects. 'Whistle-blowing' within the medical profession or the police force is regarded as a public duty—'informers' become 'informants' performing a social duty with exemplary personal courage. Miller's position really rests on the premiss that he and his friends had made grave mistakes but, given the bad times, the war against Hitler, the climate of postwar reaction, they had been (almost) right to be wrong. It had been a shared experience, an idealistic comradeship, which ought not to be betrayed under odious pressure. But Miller warned against too much righteous fingerpointing: 'how many who knew by now that they had been supporting a paranoid and murderous Stalinist regime had really confronted their abetting it?'[64] More recently he has said that:

It was not long, perhaps four or five years, before the fraudulence of Soviet cultural claims was as clear to me as it should have been earlier. But I would never have found it believable, in the 50s or later, that with its thuggish self-righteousness and callous contempt for artists' freedoms, that the Soviet way of controlling culture could be successfully exported to America.

This is a tricky sentence, involving an agile and semi-disguised leap along the following lines: I thought they were good, but then I realized they were so bad that they were no threat here—so why persecute them?[65]

⌗   ⌗   ⌗

Losey never forgave Kazan for naming names before HUAC, though he was not among those named—indeed, Kazan never wished him any ill. As late as 1963, before the first showing of Losey's film *The Servant* in Paris, hearing that Kazan was in the audience Losey left the cinema, dragging Dirk Bogarde with him. Catharsis of a sort came at the 1972 Cannes Film Festival when Kazan was showing his latest film *The Visitors*, and Losey was president of the jury. The French press was already alert to Losey's enmity, *Paris Match* (May 1972) wrongly claiming that it was because of Kazan—*à cause de lui*— that Losey and others had been forced into exile. The magazine reported no handshake between Losey and Kazan when *The Visitors* was screened, the president of the jury having departed without a word. Kazan's film, shot in Super-8 and skilfully blown up, depicted the havoc wrought by returning Vietnam veterans on a comfortable and complacent group of American liberals. Losey's private notes, to be found on his *fiche de jury*, praised this aspect of the film as 'good and terrifying', but the main theme raised, as in *On the Waterfront*, was whether it was right to inform against a criminal comrade, in this case a rapist. Losey's *fiche* contains the following remarks: 'He is professional, skilful . . . Actors and all things relating brilliantly handled.' However, important political statements were 'mixed up with confused metaphor and personal whine. Kazan's problem has nothing to do with the peg on which he seeks to hang it. Enfin, a dirty, disgusting, meretricious film by a near master of everything but himself.' According to Kazan, another member of the jury, the actress Bibi Andersson, told him that Losey argued so vehemently against the film when the jury deliberated that its supporters, including herself, could get nowhere. Kazan's response—'I had to laugh . . . I didn't expect a left intellectual to forget in 1972 what had happened in 1952, because I hadn't forgotten either.'[66]

Soviet Cinema:
The New Wave

After Stalin's death the Soviet film industry was freer to produce films of high artistic quality aimed at Western festivals and audiences. Soviet papers began to publish lists of foreign films they would like to see and to make appreciative comments about Italian neo-realism.[1] The *New York Times* reported *Pravda*'s praise for Delbert Mann's *Marty*,[2] a great work of American neo-realism shown at the Cannes Festival. The *Pravda* review, by Sergei Yutkevich, the Soviet member of the Cannes jury, lauded the film as truly depicting the life of simple folk in America.[3] Four years later, when *Marty*, the story of a homely Bronx butcher's humdrum life until he begins to court a teacher, reached Moscow under the first Soviet–American cultural treaty, the audience in the Udarnik Theatre roared and applauded when Marty's girl tells her mother that she doesn't think in-laws should live with their married children. Intense interest was shown in the modest Bronx kitchen of Marty's home, the bar and lunchrooms he frequented, the elevated trains in the Bronx, the lively music at the dance-hall. The film moved into five large Moscow cinemas, with *Izvestiia* expressing pleasure at finding a film about ordinary Americans without violence, chase scenes, and Hollywood beauties. And Ernest Borgnine was a winner as the hero.[4]

The late 1950s and the 1960s witnessed a 'new wave' cultural renaissance, breaking out of the constrictive models of the collective-heroic and reaching a better-educated young audience hungry for films about personal experience and sentiment—like *Marty* or the work of Godard and Truffaut. The curse of Soviet cinema—indeed of Soviet culture—was the dominant and oppressive position occupied by war in general and the Great Patriotic War in particular. Virtually everything in human life was defined in adversarial terms; in art as in life, the Soviet citizen was relentlessly judged in terms of his or her war, his or her allegiance—the civil war against the Whites, the economic war against the kulaks, the anti-fascist struggle and resistance to Nazi invasion, and finally the new cold war against America. Where did you stand, comrade, and how did you behave? War had become a totalitarian project, equating Russian patriotism with love of the Communist Party, defining dissent as treason, and cultivating abject Stalin-worship as the only acceptable ethic. When the post-Stalin thaw removed the cult of personality from the film director's tapestry, it left intact the war ethic, the fixation with war as the yardstick of human behaviour. It haunts almost every film of the late 1950s, through to the most contentious of them, Marlen Khutsiev's *Ilich's Watchpost* (*Zastava Il'icha*, 1963), a truly 'civilian film' struggling to break free of the heavy legacy of the uniformed patriarchy. By this time the issue had converted itself into a generational conflict; every motion of independence, every blast from the saxophone, every abstract painting, amounted to a betrayal of the older generation's sacrifice and suffering during the war. 'We didn't need obscene paintings or boogie-woogie at Stalingrad! Those of us who survived the siege of Leningrad did so without any help from the theatre of the absurd!'

The first major attempt at a breakthrough in this regard was Grigorii Chukhrai's *The Forty-First* (*Sorok-pervyi*, 1956),[5] which won a jury prize award for its screenplay at the 1957 Cannes Festival. This film introduced and almost legitimated conflict between private emotion and public duty, proposing a tentative breakdown of the rigid moral divide between 'us' and 'them'. The notion of the enemy, endemic to Stalinist art—the Whites, the kulaks, the Trotsksyists, the traitors, the fascists, the warmongers—here suffers a serious complication. *The Forty-First* is also marked by impressive photography as Reds and Whites battle it out in the deserts of Kazakhstan, with the Kazakh tribespeople and camel-owners getting the raw end. The beautiful Mariutka (Izolda Izvitska), the only woman in the Red unit, is a crack marksman who is seen shooting her thirty-ninth and fortieth victims and cursing—'Missed, darn it!'—when the forty-first escapes.

The blond hero, a White Guard, Govoruch-Otrok (played by Oleg Strizhenov), is captured while carrying a message from Denikin to Kolchak, though the message remains in his head and the Reds are too noble to extract it by torture. With Hollywoodish improbability Mariutka, the only woman, is put in charge of the prisoner. She, unschooled and from Astrakhan, nevertheless has been writing naive-heroic poetry to which her prisoner, from St Petersburg, listens politely. The Reds are left in the desert without camels after a sentry falls asleep at night; following a desperate trek across the sands of the Kara Kum desert, remnants of the unit reach the Aral Sea and an encampment of Kazakhs. Seven continue overland but four set sail. Of these only

Mariutka and her White lieutenant survive a Crusoe-like storm and shipwreck.[6]

The two share a hut and their little food—she even sacrifices her poems to provide him with cigarette paper. She nurses him through fever and delirium, catches and cleans fish. 'What makes your eyes like that?' she asks. 'What will I tell the commissar if he dies? My handsome, blue-eyed gent.' Stars flash across the screen; a high chorus sings as waves break on the shore and the lovers enjoy their first kiss. He, the well educated White lieutenant, tells her the story of Robinson Crusoe and Friday. But their words of love are less persuasive and eloquent than their anger when they argue about the Revolution. They quarrel bitterly over his desire to lead a private life while others are fighting; she declares herself ashamed to have embraced him—though she still weeps with love. 'I longed for the revolution too,' he says, 'but soldiers spat in my face because I was an officer.'[7]

A sail appears on the horizon! The couple hesitate. Fishermen? Reds? No, Whites! Shouting and waving, the lieutenant runs into the waves. She shoots him in the back—dead, then runs to him crying 'Nyet! Nyet!' and cradles her dying 'blue-eyed gent' in the water. He is her forty-first victim, but a generation of Soviet filmgoers saw love triumph over class war for the first time.[8]

Soviet critics responded lukewarmly to Izolda Izvitska's performance as Mariutka, considering her too tender, too soft, too lyrical, too much the 'young lady' to fit Lavrenev's original character, a 'coarse, fiery, green-eyed proletarian woman.'[9] Writing in *Soviet Film* three years later, Stanislav Rostotsky gently accused Chukhrai of having sought out a subject which would arouse controversy. 'It owed its success more to professional skills than to genuine inspiration.'[10] But foreign readings of the final scene varied; reviewing the film in the *New York Times* (15 June 1957), H.H.T. regretted, rather simplistically, that the picture ends in 'a tragic endorsement of the lady's contention that Bolshevik might makes right'. He also expressed surprise at the Cannes 'writing laurel': 'Perhaps the jury was simply jolted by the very idea of a tender, idyllic and extended love interlude from the USSR, as penned by G. Koltunov.' What counted for H.H.T. was the marvellous photography by S. Urusevsky of the Kara Kum sands and the curling tides of the island. 'The eye is so smitten that the soundtrack hardly matters.'

A further dismantling of the patriotic imperative followed rapidly with the major triumph of the Soviet new wave, Mikhail Kalatozov's *The Cranes Are Flying* (*Letyat zhuravli*, 1957).[11] Here Eisenstein's heritage revives in updated form; the hand-held camera in perpetual motion, the sharply expressionist angles and short-focus optics, gave a sense of the vibrancy, immediacy, and uncertainty of real life, in contrast to the ponderous, neo-classical style of late Stalinism. International recognition came swiftly: *The Cranes Are Flying* won the 1958 Palme d'or at Cannes and was distributed by Warner Brothers under the first USA–USSR Cultural Exchange Agreement.

The time setting is once again the Great Patriotic War, and the young hero, Boris, displays heroism in the standard mould: he volunteers, he helps a wounded comrade under fire, he dies. But Boris (played by A. Balatov) merely marks out the terrain of his fiancée Veronika's passion and betrayal. Central to the film is the issue of sexual fidelity; the heroine's transgression is treated with ambivalent sympathy. For this reason Veronika (sensitively played by Tat'yana Samoilova, a product of the Mayakovsky Theatre, where her father was an actor) became as controversial a figure for critics and spectators as Mariutka in *The Forty-First*.

Although they are demonstrably in love—witness the early scene when the engaged couple are happily trying to put up blackout curtains—Boris does not fully disclose to her, as she chatters about wedding dresses, that he has volunteered for the front (even though his father and family decry such 'romanticism' and urge him to wait for conscription). Due to dramatic misunderstandings and an undiscovered love message left for Veronika by Boris inside a toy squirrel, both the young lovers believe that the other has neglected to say goodbye. In a brilliant scene, Veronika is hemmed in by crowds as Boris and the volunteers march away to the station. The actress herself later described Veronika's despair at that moment: 'She wants to cry out, to run, to knock her head against the wall. But she is motionless. Only her bitten lip reveals her despair.' It may be Veronika's self-restraint in the face of catastrophe which causes muted scandal.

Soon after Boris's departure and the loss of her own parents in a bombing raid, she moves in with Boris's family, the Borozdins, and is raped by her fiancé's cousin, Mark (A. Shvorin), a concert pianist who plays Scriabin to her while windowpanes shatter during an air-raid over Moscow.[12] But is it really rape in Kalatozov's film, or merely seduction? Veronika initially resists Mark's sexual advances with 'nyet, nyet' and with slaps. As Mark carries her limp body in his arms the film cuts to Boris's last minutes at the front. (Boris desperately carries a wounded comrade through a swamp before himself receiving the fatal bullet.)

Evacuated to the Caucasus together with Boris's father Dr Fyodor Ivanovich Borozdin and Boris's sister Irina, who is also a surgeon, Veronika lives in barracks and works in a hospital. Unaware of Boris's death, traumatized by his silence (no letter from him) and by her parents' death, reduced to a state not far from catatonic, she marries Mark, who promises to dedicate a concerto to her and claims to be too valuable for the army. 'But for the war, I'd play in Tchaikovsky Hall for you', he tells Veronika. He also passes off Veronika's toy squirrel, a present from Boris, as if it was a gift of his own to a young blonde at whose birthday party he has been invited to play the piano—this backfires when other guests discover Boris's letter of parting to Veronika stuffed inside the toy, and Veronika, seizing it, learns the truth. She also discovers that Mark is not only keeping company with other women, but had connived to have himself deferred from military service. Nikolai Chernov, business manager of the Philarmonic Society, who obtained a military deferment for Mark, borrows money from him and presses him to filch medicines from his uncle, Dr Fyodor Ivanovich.

Here the film introduces the other sector of wartime society, the black-marketeers, speculators, dropouts, and pleasure-seekers, but the fascinating character Antonia Nikolayevna Monstyrskaya plays a larger role in Viktor Rozov's original play, *Alive Forever*, than in the film. Bourgeois in spirit, loving her fine fashions and furniture, riding round in cars, she plans to marry Chernov even though he is already married. 'What can I do? Unfortunately, swindlers are frequently richer than honest men.'[13]

Soviet virtue is embodied in the figure of Boris's hard-working father, the surgeon Fyodor Ivanovich Borozdin. As Professor Josephine Woll has discovered in the RGALI archive, Borozdin's most politically contentious lines were deleted from the script. Looking up at the night sky, Fedor Ivanovich offers bitter reflections on the catastrophic defeats of 1941: 'The newspapers used to write that if and when the war started, it would be fought on foreign territory. But whose cities are burning, ours or the Germans'? Everybody sang songs (*vse pesenki peli*): We heard in all the songs, "We're peaceful people, but our armoured train waits in reserve" . . . What is it waiting for? Why doesn't it get moving?' His colleague Ivan Afanasevich offers the stock answer: 'The fascists invaded unexpectedly, treacherously.'

FYODOR IVANOVICH: Oh, those slippery fascists! Oh, those nasty men! They didn't even warn us! . . . What, we didn't know what they were like?

Ivan Afanasevich looks around anxiously. Jumps up. Dr B. continues to yell:

FYODOR IVANOVICH: Now we're publishing embarrassed reports from which it's not possible to understand anything. On the one hand, we're destroying them root and branch, on the other, we're retreating from one city after another.

IVAN AFANASEVICH: Quietly, Fedor Ivanovich, for God's sake softly. Of course I'm puzzled myself. (*Whispers.*) Do you think we can lose the war?[14]

As Woll comments, when the Artistic Council of Mosfilm[15] discussed and passed the script on 17 June 1956, this devastating exchange, presaging the revisionist attacks on Stalin's role in 1941, was not mentioned and presumably had already been cut. Kalatozov never filmed this scene.[16]

Veronika tells a woman friend that life has lost all point for her. She is redeemed when, running to kill herself by jumping from a railway bridge under the wheels of a train—to Russians an obvious literary reference—she rescues and adopts a lost child whom she names Boris after her fiancé.

The crucial development in *The Cranes Are Flying* is the film's subtle dissociation of private and public morality. Boris's severe and disapproving sister, Irina, an able scientist who early in the film sneers that her brother is still asleep at noon after a night out with Veronika, is later found wearing military uniform but unable to respond emotionally to Veronika's discovered orphan boy. Clearly a patriot and a good Communist, Irina represents emotional constipation.

In stylistic terms, *Cranes* may be viewed as a homage to the Soviet avant-garde of the 1920s. Even though Mikhail Kalatozov had been associated with Stalinist films—for example, *The Conspiracy of the Doomed* (1950)—*Cranes* reflects the influence of the early masters, Eisenstein, Pudovkin, and Vertov; indeed, the cameraman Sergei Urusevsky had been a pupil of Rodchenko. The emotive power of montage was used to describe aspects of history which had been banished from Soviet cinemas for years.[17]

First screened at Mosfilm in August 1957, when *Cranes* was first shown in Moscow there was a profound silence in the Udarnik Theatre. The film won the Palme d'or at the 11th Cannes Festival in May 1958, a major cultural triumph. Tat'yana Samoilova appeared in the glossy pages of *Soviet Film*,[18] wearing an off-the-shoulder gown to receive the congratulations of the director-general of the Centre nationale de la cinématographie, then again at the French Embassy in Moscow accepting the 'Victory' prize for best foreign actress.[19] Secretary of State Christian Herter and other dignitaries attended the Washington première in November 1959, the first picture shown under the new USA–USSR cultural exchange agreement.[20] Faubion Bowers greeted it warmly, while Bosley Crowther of the *New York Times* (22 March 1960) was astonished to find

a downright obsessive and overpowering revulsion to war and, in contrast, a beautifully tender, almost lyric, feeling for romantic love ... [and] a highly intimate, impressionistic style of cinematic narration ... popular in the days when Pudovkin and Dovzhenko were making heroic revolutionary films. It is a style used in silent pictures, full of angular shots and close-up views of running feet and anguished faces. But M. Kalatozov has brought it up to date ...[21]

Penelope Houston hailed Kalatozov and his cameraman Urusevsky's 're-morseless bravura emphasis, using all the camera tricks (hand-held camera; elaborate crane shot; helicopter shots) that the Soviet cinema had schooled itself to disregard'. On this Western and Soviet critics were unanimous. The *Istoriia sovetskogo kino* praises the magnificent 'brio' and 'sparkling frames' and 'perpetual movement' of the hand-held camerawork, the shortening of focus, the lighting effects, the imposing close-ups—a new, 'opened-up' cine-matography working through metaphor, composition, rhythm, and the poetic language of cinema. *Cranes* was an exemplar of 'genuinely contem-porary counterpoint', mobilizing all the resources of cinema for a massive indictment of war and influencing many later war films.[22] But the *Istoriia*—perhaps aware that the parade of 'weak' or decadent characters, seen after the family's evacuation to the Caucasus, held special interest for Western critics—was critical of the second half of the film with its 'half-hearted interpretation of the [emotional] conflict' and its search for 'elevated solu-tions' which 'concealed the root contradictions'. Whatever this may mean, it is certainly a pity that the film loses its nerve by ending with a 'Peace Movement' speech (delivered by a returning war hero from the platform of a railway engine), urging Russians to rebuild their country and never to allow war to wreak havoc again.[23]

Grigorii Chukhrai followed up the partial success of the *The Forty-First* with a major international triumph, *Ballad of a Soldier* (*Ballada o soldate*, 1959), written by Chukhrai and Valentin Ezhov. Starting out from a very modest impact on its release, this film about the sorrow and sacrifice of a generation won a Lenin Prize and a dozen international ones. But if Soviet cinema was to unveil a new view of man without the Party, of history without History,[24] *Ballad of a Soldier* made only hesitant steps in that direction. The war and its imperatives still sat in God's throne. Neither hero nor heroine, for all their charm, provided the faintest challenge to geriatric orthodoxy.

The prologue anticipates the epilogue: the widowed mother of the film's young hero, Alyosha (Alesh) Skvortsov, walks alone in her village. We learn from a male voice-over that this is the story of a young man, an ordinary Russian soldier, who will die. The action begins with a spectacular tank battle, the camera turning the world upside down with dizzying menace, the sky below, the earth up above; a German tank is crawling towards the defenceless figure of a Soviet soldier, Alesh, who is scampering across open ground with the tank in pursuit, before hurling himself behind an anti-tank gun and knocking out the fascist beast. This is the stuff of comic-strips and dreams, but Soviet culture still demanded the validating seal of service to the motherland before venturing into the minefields of private behaviour.

Cut to the command dugout. Alesh is to be rewarded for heroism. He mentions repairs to his mother's roof and is given two days to get home, two days to mend the roof, two days to return—it will be an almost allegorical pilgrim's progress, a good man threading himself through trials and tests which provided Soviet and Western audiences alike with an absorbing portrait of life in the rear. Fording a river on his way to the railway line, he is surrounded by comrades begging him to carry gifts and messages to relatives. He accepts two pieces of soap, one for a fellow-soldier's wife and one for his father. Thereby will hang a tale. He meets and befriends a despondent soldier who has lost a leg and believes his wife will no longer love him—another tale. 'Look after my case', the invalid tells Alesh. At the next station the disabled soldier's wife cannot be found, but when she appears and realizes what has happened to her husband, she greets him warmly (as every Soviet woman would!) Alesh slips away, embarrassed. (This scene was particularly dear to Chukhrai.)[25] Alesh is already behind time. Next he encounters a fat, indolent, and rapacious guard who won't let him on board into the horses' wagon without a bribe. Alesh gives him a precious tin of meat.

When the train halts, the beautiful young Shura slips aboard, having evaded the attention of the corrupt guard. Only after the train is under way does she spot Alesh, hidden in the straw. Terrified, she throws open the carriage door and tosses out her documents and food, as a prelude to jumping herself. The train stops again. A number of women want to board it but the guard scares them off. Discovering Shura, he threatens Alesh with a military tribunal. Alesh knocks him down. An officer arrives, bringing justice (as every Soviet officer would!). The 'villain' of the piece (yet no great villain) is this fat, hungry train-guard, Gavrilkin. In a fine display of curse-of-God Calvinism, the *Istoriia*[26] almost equates virtue with beauty when it contrasts Alesha's 'gentle, soft, Slavic face' with Gavrilkin's 'low-browed, pimply mug', and denounces his 'evil dullness and kulak greed'.[27]

The train travels on. Shura asks Alesh if he can believe in friendship between a man and a woman. He says yes. At the next stop Alesh runs to fetch water. Alone, Shura falls asleep, Hollywood-style lighting playing on her pretty face. Passing a first-aid station, Alesh comes across a loudspeaker with civilian workers gathered around, listening gravely. It is Levitan, the radio voice of Russia during the war, conveying the bad news that the Soviet army has evacuated Rostov and other key points. The elderly workers dutifully go back to their steady shovelling. Alesh misses the train—more time lost, but he is the blind pilgrim of human kindness, the building brick of Communism. Take, for example, the episode of 'the soap'. Suddenly he remembers the soap he is carrying as a gift to a comrade's wife and father in this very town. Off they run, Alesh and Shura, hand-in-hand. Finally they discover the wife's flat, but she is not living alone: a man's jacket hangs on the back of a chair. The wife asks Alesh not to tell her husband. 'Stop looking at me like that, you're too young to understand.' Disgusted, Alesh runs back up the stairs to retrieve the gift of soap. This time the wife instructs him to tell her husband the truth. Alesh and Shura hurry to a school gym where they find the father, a sick man, and give him the other bar of soap. 'Don't tell my son that his wife is cheating and don't tell him I'm sick.'

Alesh and Shura struggle aboard another crowded troop train, she disguised in his army coat. Their love affair is tenderly done and touchingly acted in an unmistakably Russian idiom, as the dogged engine with its rotating pistons slogs through birch groves and over rivers, sometimes under cruel enemy attack and always within the brilliantly photographed stark privations of the war in the East, and we long for the young couple not to be parted for ever; yet some of the lighting and framing suggests blatant 'Hollywood' romantics (in contrast to the stylistic integrity of the atonal, 'new wave', love scenes in *The Cranes are Flying*). In *Ballad* the hero is good, brave, kind, and cheerful, the ideal young Russian, and almost everyone else is good too, the heroine, the other soldiers, their officers, the mothers left behind, the citizens encountered on the long journey home, with the single exception of the guard Gavrilkin.

Now Alesh and Shura are together on a station platform saying goodbye. This is where her auntie lives and her journey ends. As the train pulls out she runs along the platform trying to keep pace. Alesh shouts the name of his village to her, but too late—she doesn't hear. Alone, her head is full of thoughts and images of him. More good deeds by Alesh follow. Now we see his mother running through the fields to greet him. They embrace. She cries. The other village women press him for news of their own relatives. He tells her heartbreaking news: he cannot stay; the roof will not be repaired this time; he must leave for the front at once. He realizes that she, the dearest person in his life, is the main victim of his naive philanthropy. 'Forgive me, mother.' She watches as his truck disappears across the plain. The voice-over concludes: 'So that is everything we wanted to tell you about our friend Alesh. He might have become a wonderful citizen, beautifying our land with gardens, and he will forever remain in our minds a Russian soldier.'

Time magazine hailed *Ballad of a Soldier* as 'the best Russian movie made since World War II'. When the film opened at the Murray Hill Theatre, New York, Bosley Crowther greeted it in the *New York Times* (27 December 1960) as 'one of the best Soviet films in years'. Praising the performances of Vladimir

Ivashov and Shanna Prokhorenko as the young lovers, Crowther finished
with a word for Antonina Maksimova as the mother:

her breath-taking racing from the fields to greet her boy, and her final statuesque
standing alone in the empty road after he has gone (as the text states, forever)...
[Chukhrai] has done such lovely things as use his camera to pace the tempo of his story
with the train, to catch the poetry of a girl's hair blowing wildly in the wind, to note
the irony of a child's soap bubbles floating down a stairwell as the hero descends from
his dismal discovery in the apartment where he went to deliver the soap.

Ballad of a Soldier was the first Soviet film entered in an American film
festival, winning the top prize at San Francisco in 1960. Chukhrai was
awarded the Order of Lenin. Crowther later professed disappointment with
Chukhrai's more overtly political *Clear Skies* (*Chistoe Nebo*, 1961), the first
Soviet film to show on-screen victims of unjust oppression. Initially suppressed, the film won First Prize at the 1961 Moscow Film Festival. Crowther
called it 'a piece of movie fiction that is as phony as a 13-ruble note . . . a style
of staging that fairly reeks of the studio . . . with all the falsities of artificial
lighting, flimsy stage sets and powdered-gypsum snow.' The colour photography was ghastly and the final 'splurge of propaganda' laughable.[28]

A more radical and depressing regression to the womb of all-embracing
war, to the re-erection of the bas-relief 'Soviet man', was Sergei Bondarchuk's
Fate of a Man (*Sud'ba cheloveka*, 1959). Based on a story by Sholokhov,[29] the
film describes one Russian's terrible sufferings: the hero loses his home, his
family, his health to the demon of war and fascism; grey with grief, he finally
adopts a war orphan. The film is narrated in voice-over by the hero, Andrei
Sokolov. Driving an ammunition truck under enemy air attack, he is taken
prisoner and herded into a ruined church where some prisoners pray and
others do not. The Nazis pull out and shoot 'Communists, Commissars,
Jews', including the good doctor who had slammed Andrei's dislocated
shoulder back into place. The music is terrible. Bondarchuk himself plays
the hero—who seems to owe a manly debt to Hemingway as well as Sholokhov—like the film star he is. The sadistic Kommandant who speaks 'perfect
Russian' and makes a habit of punching prisoners with a knuckle-duster,
summons the prisoner Andrei to the officers' mess and offers him death—but
first a large glass of vodka and the traditional slice of bread. Andrei swallows
the vodka at one gulp but declines the bread. The Nazi officers laugh appre-
ciatively; when he pulls it off with a second glass their laughter is admiring; a
third time and he earns a reprieve from death. But the voice-over refuses to
allow anything to speak for itself: 'Once again death had passed me by, only
touching me with its cold breath . . . ' Nothing is left to the imagination, and

the few opportunities to tell the truth about the war and Stalinism are flagrantly ignored in favour of a rosy orthodoxy.[30] When Andrei is liberated by the Red Army, instead of being interrogated by the NKVD or the military police then bundled off to a Soviet labour camp—the normal fate of Russian prisoners, not least those like Andrei discovered wearing a German uniform!—he is handsomely congratulated and sent straight home. Finding his village and family wiped out by bombs, he adopts an orphan boy. 'I'm your Dad', he says, bringing a shrieking outburst of emotion and gratitude from the boy: 'I knew you'd find me some day! I love you!'

⊞ ⊞ ⊞

What Western critics most preferred from Mosfilm or Lenfilm was Chekhov, Tolstoy, and long dresses. The secret at the box office was to set aside the entire Bolshevik period. The first Soviet film to win unstinting praise from Harrison Salisbury was *Anna on his Neck* (*Anna na shee*), based on a Chekhov short story. 'It was a beautiful picture, I thought . . . without a suspicion of ideology or politics . . . It was filled with the symbols of pre-revolutionary times. There was a beautiful Orthodox Church wedding. There were *troikas* racing through the snow streets of St Petersburg . . . court balls, officers, dancing.' And it was a box-office hit, too: queues of two and three blocks turned up around the twenty Moscow cinemas showing the films. 'I thought to myself that if I were a member of the new [post-Stalin] junta I would take a good long look at those queues and indulge in a little serious thought.'[31] The director Mikhail Romm also mentioned the film's success: 'Everyone saw *Anna na shee*.'[32]

Chekhov was a safe box-office investment. *Soviet Film* (November 1960) reported that in the French newspaper *Provençal* Josef Heifitz's *The Lady with the Little Dog* (which had received an award at the 13th Cannes Festival in May of that year) was welcomed as 'a charming, subtle, tender film'. Indeed it is, graced by fine acting, some deftly done comments on how the stinking rich treated the poor in Chekhov's day—for example, repeatedly throwing a spoon on the floor of a club restaurant to force the hovering lackey to absent himself while finding another—and beautifully photographed landscapes (although the over-bright, flat lighting imposed on the two lovers as they sit on a Black Sea hillside has nothing to do with the neighbouring cloud patterns and reeks of 'studio'); one could also fault Heifitz for some old-fashioned screen 'wipes'. Western audiences were delighted, after the long, dour years of ideology, to be sent an old-fashioned and very Russian story of adulterous passion in which the unhappy hero is allowed his humanity—though a wealthy banker. Penelope Houston adored the film, 'with its resonant melancholy and far-ranging sympathies'; the Soviet cinema's field of mastery, according to Houston, lay in its adaptations of literary classics: Tolstoy, Chekhov, Shakespeare, Cervantes. Yet despite the 'undertow of proud nostalgia' found in the new Chekhov films, with their 'frustrations and regrets', the Russians would 'jeer' at the same evocations in Antonioni's work. Soviet audiences 'are still carefully shielded from any infection by Western melancholy. It is a self-defensive morality.'[33] Houston quoted the director Sergei Youtkevich, 'most cosmopolitan of Soviet directors': when questioned by French journalists, he condemned the negative pessimism of Jean-Luc Godard's *A Bout de Souffle* and stressed the impossibility of showing Antonioni's *la Notte* in a Russian cinema: 'The audience wouldn't understand his innovations in screen language ... They would just laugh at it all. All that luxury, and those bored people, so lonely and so impotent. And their cars! And their comforts!'

Viktor Nekrasov, in a book for which he was later severely rebuked by Khrushchev, recalled a conversation in 1959 with an Italian film director who mentioned two Japanese directors unknown to him. Nekrasov had then confessed to the Italian that he had seen nothing by Bergman or Antonioni— not *La Dolce Vita* and not Chaplin's films *Limelight* and *A King in New York*. 'He couldn't believe his ears.' The Italian neo-realist directors were by now well known, and quite well exhibited, in the USSR: Rossellini, De Sica, Di Santis, Visconti, the early Fellini. But Nekrasov wanted to know why the USSR spent precious hard currency on two parts of *The Count of Monte Cristo* and on *Oklahoma!*—but not on Orson Welles's *Citizen Kane*, Alain Resnais's *Hiroshima mon Amour*, David Lean's *The Bridge On the River Kwai*—or on Andrzej Wajda's *Ashes and Diamonds*, 'all the films which have become milestones in the art of the film throughout the world'.[34]

Under the first Soviet–American cultural exchange agreement in 1958, the Russians agreed to distribute ten films, including *Roman Holiday*, *The Old Man and the Sea*, and *Oklahoma!*, while the American side contracted to distribute seven, including *The Idiot*, *Don Quixote*, and *Swan Lake*.[35] A new Anglo-Soviet cultural agreement was signed on 9 January 1961, but only days later the London *Observer* published a letter from G. Zhukov, chairman of VOKS, under the heading 'Culture and the Cold War', complaining that during 1960 only three Soviet films were shown in Britain: *The Fate of Man*, released in forty prints, *Ivan the Terrible* (two prints), and a newsreel of N. S. Khrushchev's visit to the United States (one print). By contrast, the Soviet public had seen eight British films running simultaneously in 400–600 cinemas.[36]

The problem of distributing Soviet films in the United States remained a running sore. American distributors complained to the State Department that Soviet films were a money-losing investment. Only a few had been successfully distributed—*Ballad of a Soldier*, *A Summer to Remember*, and *Fate of a Man*. 'Moscow to Halt U.S. Film Imports', warned the *New York Times* (28 March 1963). Sergei K. Romanovsky, chairman of VOKS, complained that the USSR had been forced to market its films through Art Kino Distributors, which reached far smaller audiences than large companies like United Artists.

⊞　⊞　⊞

During Khrushchev's general clampdown on the arts in 1962–3, a series of articles in *Oktyabr* and other conservative organs denounced recent films, including Marlen Khutsiev's *Ilich's Watchpost*. Khutsiev and his writer Gennadi Shpalikov (who was of the same generation as the young heroes of the film) had been at work on the project at the Gorky Studio[37] for two years, under the supervision of Sergei Gerasimov and with the initial support of the minister of culture, Ekaterina Furtseva.

Khutsiev had created a naturalistic, new-wave study of the everyday life of three young Muscovites in the Khrushchev era, one of them married and struggling to cope with his working wife's fatigued complaints, all searching for a moral key to life. Polikarpov, head of the Central Committee's cultural department, and Leonid Ilychev, chairman of the Ideological Commission created in November 1962, took a dim view of *Ilich's Watchpost*. At the March 1963 gathering of artists and intellectuals in the Kremlin, Khrushchev himself attacked the film during his main peroration as violating 'norms of public and private life that are entirely unacceptable to Soviet people . . . Even the best of the characters . . . are shown as not knowing how to live or what to live for . . . They are not fighters, nor remakers of the world . . . They are morally sick people . . . '. Like many of Khrushchev's cultural pronouncements, this was the far side of nonsense. Viktor Nekrasov's support for the film further incensed him. Writing in *Novy mir* (December 1962), Nekrasov had described *Ilich's Watchpost* as a major work of art; he had seen it in the company of the Polish director Andrzej Wajda, who declared himself stunned by Margarita Pilikhina's inspired photography. Nekrasov was reminded of *Marty*: 'Where shall we go, boys? What shall we do tonight?'[38] In *Both Sides of the Ocean*, a book which led Khrushchev to demand his expulsion from the Party, Nekrasov took his hat off to the screenplay by Khutsiev and Shpalikov,[39] congratulating them on 'not dragging in an old worker by his greying moustache, the one who understands everything and always has the right answer for anything you ask him'.[40] War between the generations had broken out, but the film was symptomatic of the deeper struggle to unshackle Soviet consciousness from its war psychosis. Khrushchev particularly objected to a dream sequence where the hero, Sergei, asks his father, killed in the war, for advice, only to discover that the father had been two years younger than he when he died. Khrushchev insisted that the father–son conflict depicted by Turgenev no longer applied.[41]

'New Soviet Film Awaits Scissors', announced the *New York Times* (15 March 1963). Khrushchev's outburst was discussed by Walter Laqueur, editor of *Soviet Survey*, and other Western commentators, who pointed out that starkly realistic British films such as *Saturday Night and Sunday Morning*, *Room at the Top*, and *A Taste of Honey* had been welcomed in Russia as exposures of capitalist inhumanity.

The problem of historical time, of the generations, is immediately sign-posted in *Ilich's Watchpost* by three young soldiers patrolling deserted streets in the uniform of the Civil War, with the *Internationale* heard, off; yet our 23-year-old hero Sergei (V. Popov) returns home to Moscow from military service in the early 1960s, taking up a job in a modern power station where technology has diminished the strain of labour. Sergei is required to be neither a war hero nor a Stakhanovite, and it is this new-found ease which presents him and his two pals, Kolia and Slava, with their puzzlement about giving life a meaning. As they stroll through Moscow on summer evenings— the city's students are on holiday—the three hear not only each other but the voices in their own heads. When Sergei joins the relaxed and genuinely celebratory May Day procession with its informal atmosphere, its floats and banners, brass band, sputniks, and portraits of Yuri Gagarin, what one critic called 'an unforced, joyful procession of free people', he is most interested in pursuing the unknown girl he has become infatuated with, Ania (M. Vertinskaia).

In Kolya's factory canteen we encounter two different models of the people who lead regular and more or less obligatory political discussions; the fat, middle-aged *rukovoditel' politzaniatiia*, or *politorganizator*, grumbles that you shouldn't let 'them' ask questions, they should just listen. But the older man says why not let them ask questions? The conflict here again follows the standard post-Stalin dramaturgical pattern: the grandfathers are presented as repositories of Leninist revolutionary virtue; the fathers are corrupt or gross; the young are in process of rejecting their fathers and seizing back the genuine idealism of the grandfathers. (Western pluralism is beyond the horizon.) In a later scene the fat one will try to suborn Kolia into writing a report claiming that the old man says dangerous and subversive things. Kolia calls him a *svoloch'* (scum or swine) and says he would beat him up if he was younger.

The pleasant, moody Sergei (who is forever smoking a cigarette but is no James Dean, no rebel, despite a physical resemblance and a habit of wandering through the empty Prospekts of Moscow at dawn) and his friends enjoy jazz, boogie-woogie, and dancing (though the style of dancing is strikingly sedate by Western standards). Sergei and Ania visit the Exhibition of Young Artists and find the paintings rather old-hat, *peredvizhniki*, and privately deride a man who is complaining he wants more realism: 'He wants to eat it', they laugh.

A long passage of quasi-documentary film is inserted, one of the celebrated poetry readings of the time at the Polytechnic Museum, featuring Yevtushenko, Voznesensky, Slutskii, Rozhdestvenskii, the beautiful Bella Akhmadulina, and the singing poet Bulat Okudzhava. We are among the *shestidesiatniki*, the liberals and dissidents of the sixties. This event was specifically organized for the benefit of the film crew but was otherwise authentic.[42] Members of the audience are invited to give their opinions; for example, an army officer urges the poets to write more about the Red Army, guarantor of peace. The wall behind the platform is decorated with the slogan *Eto molodost' mira*—Here is the youth of the world.

This leads on to a key scene, Sergei's chance meeting with Ania's father (L. Zolotukhin), a self-satisfied, cynical careerist who speaks slowly, solemnly, about having done a lot for the people, about the fecklessness and inactivity of Sergei and Anyia's generation, who regard people like himself as the *klassovyi vrag*—the class enemy. Ania calls her father a hypocrite and announces that she wants to leave home. 'I don't want to have to be grateful to you every minute of my life.' The father, who frequently refills Sergei's glass, tells them they are wasting their time with all this talking and moralizing: 'You should not trust people, just take care of yourself.'

Unlike a modern Western film set among the younger generation of the early 1960s, Khutsiev's *Ilich's Watchpost* typically takes care to pay tribute to those who fought and suffered in the Great Patriotic War (although this was not enough to mollify Khrushchev). Sergei lives with his mother (a doctor) and his sister; he himself sleeps in the living room. One day, rummaging through old books, they discover the wartime ration book or *kartochka*, which the mother had disastrously lost, forcing her to go to the countryside to dig up potatoes, despite winter nights and German troops. During the trip her husband, Sergei's father, had come home from the front on a two-hour visit and she had missed him, and then he was killed. Moved by this, Sergei speaks up in honour of potatoes (and folksongs) at a party for smart young people he attends with Ania, drawing cynical remarks about *kvasnoi patriotizm*—'jingoism'—from another guest. Then comes the dream sequence which so outraged Khrushchev. Returning home, and falling into a reverie, Sergei is visited by his dead father, a lieutenant in the uniform of 1941. They drink and smoke together and converse like pals, the father's rifle lying across the table. The following dialogue is paraphrased:

—You knew what you had to do. [Sergei]
—Is that not enough? [Father]
—I could do what you had to do but I don't know how to live my life now. I don't want to sound pretentious but I need to find something important in life....

—There are things you don't know. [Sergei]
—Yes, we didn't know. [Father]
—I envy you.
—No, I envy you. You are happier now.

Finally, after we have glimpsed his dead comrades, the father vanishes and Sergei cries out 'Papa!' Khrushchev was incensed: if a dog sees his pup drowning, he will always risk his own life to rescue it, insisted Russia's top dog. But equally unacceptable was the indifference of the young people in the film to the renovated pioneering idealism of Khrushchev's virgin lands initiative; the ebbing of Communist idealism in a climate of rising prosperity, high tech, and cultural thaw, symbolized by ever-present American jazz. There was criticism of Sergei's one-night stand with Ania, their candle-lit dance, their failure to condemn formalism when visiting the art exhibition, and so on. Mark Donskoi, a film director, is reported to have dismissed the heroes as 'some kind of Hamlets and bums (*shalopai*)'.[43] Writing in an *Encounter* booklet, *Khrushchev on Culture* (June 1963), Hugh Lunghi described the offending film as an allegory on the fate of Lenin's heritage in the hands of the younger Soviet generation, depicting them as perplexed at best, cynical wasters at worst. According to Lunghi, each of the Soviet 'new wave' directors had come under severe criticism for concentrating on private lives and individual psychology rather than the collective progress of society.

In July 1963 Aleksandr Dymshits, familiar to us in his post-war incarnation as the powerful cultural tsar of the Soviet zone of Germany, and now chief editor of the script division of the Gorky Film Studio, recommended what Tatiana Khlopliankina has discovered to be 'an array of revisions', including elimination from the film of the public poetry reading; shortening Sergei and Ania's visit to the art exhibit because insufficiently condemnatory of 'formalistic tendencies'; rewriting dialogue to avoid 'notes of scepticism'; and cutting the candle-lit dance ('people will copy it and start fires').[44] After Khrushchev's fall Khutsiev's film was retitled *I'm Twenty* (*Mne dvadtsat' let*), and re-edited; it made little impact on its release in 1965.[45] In 1987 it was restored to its original length and title.

Later, as head of the script and editorial committee (GSRK) of Goskino, discussing new scripts dealing with the cult of personality, Dymshits prefaced his remarks with the standard disclaimer about the cult: 'No one is trying to keep it in the dark'—similar to 'I'm no racist'. No one was trying to keep the cult in the dark, but:

> One must know when it belongs and when it doesn't. One must understand one's responsibility to educate the people...Some pictures show nothing but outrages and breaches of the law. As if there had been nothing else...Certainly there were difficulties. No one is trying to keep it in the dark. It was our Party that revealed the secret to mankind...But the Party is not interested in people—irresponsible, undemocratic people—exploiting this subject.

The refusal to exorcise past attitudes, the attachment and self-identification with the heroic Stalin era, was further apparent in Dymshits's intervention against a different film project, *Mountains in the Path* (*Gory v puti*), in June 1965: 'The film should not be about the era of the cult of personality because there was no such era. Rather there was an era of transition to Communism burdened by specific manifestations of the cult of personality...you [the scriptwriters] focus exclusively on the wounds in people's souls...An epoch of construction looks like an epoch of repression.'[46]

⌗　⌗　⌗

Moscow's third International Film Festival,[47] in July 1963, put Khrushchev's government and Minister of Culture Furtseva under exceptional stress. An unruly bunch of foreign egos and super-egos arrived in town. Many of them, particularly those from Continental Europe, took an unhealthily lively interest in the broader cultural scene. As Priscilla Johnson reported at the time: 'Arriving for the festival, several Italian film directors who are usually at odds in all but their left-wing views joined forces for once to badger Moscow officialdom with questions about their beleaguered [Soviet film] brethren Romm, Chukhrai, and, above all, the youthful Marlen Khutsiev.' Lombadori, editor of *Riniscita*, who knew Moscow well, arrived to defend Fellini's $8\frac{1}{2}$; Priscilla Johnson summed up the dilemma confronting the Russians:

> By naming Federico Fellini's introspective, somewhat surrealistic film $8\frac{1}{2}$, as the Italian entry, they were making a choice that could not fail to confound their hosts in the Kremlin. Predictably, the Italian entry outclassed all others in the two-week

competition. It made the Soviet entry, an exercise in socialist realism called *Meet Baluyev*, seem painfully banal by comparison. Thus, when the 15-man jury—nine from Communist countries, one each from France, India, Japan, the United States, Italy and the United Arab Republic—sat down to its deliberations, it faced a thorny dilemma: to award the prize to an inferior entry and damage the festival's reputation abroad, or give it to Fellini and outrage its sponsors in Moscow.[48]

One can understand the Russians' reservations. The 'hero' of Fellini's $8\frac{1}{2}$, Guido, is a charmingly passive Italian film director in his forties, an always elegant *homme couvert de femmes*, played by the glamorous box-office idol Marcello Mastroianni, the actor with three-and-a-half cosmopolitan expressions, each a variation on a coquettish pout. $8\frac{1}{2}$ explores the indolent but visually fertile imagination of a highly financed film director who is so readily distracted by women, actresses, memories of a Catholic childhood, fantasy encounters with cardinals, a space rocket erected on the set at great expense, and anything else that catches his eye, that he never progresses on location beyond screen tests. As usual Fellini capitalizes on the erotic make-believe and stardust of the sixties which he affectionately satirizes. Always witty in his choreography, a film-maker whose command of scenario enables him to offer effortless pastiches in the style of Pasolini, Buñuel, Visconti, and, of course, himself, Fellini mocks both indolence and energy, the 'Catholic conscience' and the futile quest of the thoroughly secularized Guido to recover it. The solemnly didactic scriptwriter whom Guido ludicrously calls in as a consultant advises that the screenplay lacks any central issue, any serious philosophical dimension, and is merely a series of arbitrary episodes, perhaps amusing in their ambiguous realism—but what is the aim? What is the film saying? Later Guido comments that he can no longer remember what he once had in mind. 'I've nothing to say, but I want to say it anyway.' Priscilla Johnson reported:

Sure enough, the jury was deadlocked. As late as July 21st, the day the [Moscow] festival was to end, no way out had been found. Liberals in the Soviet film world are said to have privately urged that the award go to $8\frac{1}{2}$. Stanley Kramer, the American judge, is reported to have felt that even Communist-bloc members of the jury wanted him to force the issue. The last morning, the six jurors from non-Communist countries [France, India, Japan, the USA, Italy, and the UAR] voted to give the prize to Fellini, with the nine from bloc countries casting their ballots against. At this point Sergio Amidei, the Italian judge and himself a Communist, stalked out, shouting angrily, 'What kind of festival is this, when the juror from Czechoslovakia tells me Fellini's film is best but he can't vote for it?' He was followed by Kramer and the other non-Communist judges.[49]

Yuri Zhukov launched an attack on Fellini's film in *Literaturnaia gazeta* (20 July), 'Eight and a Half Circles of Cinematographic Hell'. Zhukov quoted approvingly Alberto Moravia's view of $8\frac{1}{2}$ and its place in bourgeois culture: 'The principal characteristic of contemporary culture is the neurosis of impotence, the ruin of creative abilities, resulting from the absence of vital strength. However, realism is stronger than any feebleness. Even when the artist has nothing to say, he can still relate how and why he has nothing to say. This Fellini has done, having given wonderful proof of vital strength.' Zhukov commented: *Eto tak*—'Quite so'—but Fellini's film-director hero did not succeed in implementing his idea in concrete terms. Everything is scattered around at the whim of wind and rain. Zhukov ended by contrasting $8\frac{1}{2}$ to the 'unforgettable' *The Four Days of Naples* (1962) by the young Italian neo-realist director Nanni Loy.

Khrushchev was said to have asked for a private showing of $8\frac{1}{2}$. In a rage, he walked out after half an hour, calling upon Alexei Romanov, chairman of the newly formed State Cinematography Committee, to do something about it. The *New York Times* (26 and 30 July) speculated that a decision was reached to give the award to Fellini rather than compromise the Festival's standing abroad. But the conservative establishment, again dominant after Khrushchev's series of attacks on avant-garde art and literature, was in no mood to lie down. Even before the award to Fellini, A. V. Romanov, spokesman for the Soviet Ministry of Cinematography, gave a press conference: 'However, we in this country have to state that Soviet audiences, like other audiences including the Italians, do not accept this film—and not because they do not understand it. The ideo-philosophical conception of the film is contrary to our world outlook. Its resonance is pessimistic.' Romanov added: 'We reject any implication that the jury's verdict marks a retreat in our own ideological struggle—contrary to misleading comments in the foreign press.' 'Soviet Outcry Over Moscow Film Award', announced *The Times* (30 July). The Soviet press had launched a 'bitter attack' on the film; in *Sovetskaia kul'tura* the eminent director Grigorii Aleksandrov had contested the jury's verdict.

Foreign journalists wanted to know which films shown at the Festival would be purchased for distribution in the USSR. A. H. Davidov, of Soveksportfil'ma, explained that among those chosen were films from Yugoslavia, Poland, Hungary, the GDR, Italy, and elsewhere. Talks were in progress with Stanley Kramer (a member of the jury) concerning two of his films, including *Judgment at Nuremberg*. Fellini was not mentioned.[50] Declassified documents from the Central Committee archives (RGANI), including an intervention by the head of the KGB, shed further light on these manoeuvres and the cold-war pressures on Furtseva. Only three months before the Festival, in March, she was vigorously lobbying the Soviet ambassador to the United States, A. Dobrynin, and the Central Committee in her determination to thwart by all possible measures (*vse vozmozhnye mery*) the American producer L. Cohen's proposal for a joint American–Soviet film of Solzhenitsyn's ground-breaking gulag novel, *One Day in the Life of Ivan Denisovich*. Cohen seems to have come to his senses and dropped the plan by the time he spoke to A. Romanov, deputy minister of cinematography, during the Moscow Film Festival.[51] But other Soviet–American tensions had surfaced: the head of the KGB, Vladimir Semichastny, sent a 'Top Secret' (*Sovershenno sekretno*) letter to the Central Committee on 12 July,[52] the subject being the screening of *West Side Story* (directed by Robert Wise and Jerome Robbins, 1961) in Moscow. A Soviet newspaper had complained that a key song had not been translated into Russian in order to thwart the audience's understanding of white–Puerto Rican tensions in the United States. Apparently Stanley Kramer had signalled his intention of protesting the Soviet attack while in Moscow; Semichastny thought this should not be allowed and proposed 'to discontinue the practice of speechmaking (*prekratit' praktiku vystuplenii*) outside competition'. Kramer duly made his speech; the decision not to translate the song had been taken 'purely not to interrupt the flow'. He added: 'Evidently we have our problems, as you have yours, and we will just have to learn to love each other.'[53]

A further document in the Central Committee archive claims that the planned showing of Kramer's own film about two convicts, one black (Sidney Poitier) and one white (Tony Curtis), escaping detention while chained together, *The Defiant Ones* (1958)—called 'Chained Together' in Russia—had been dropped from the out-of-competition section of the Festival, along with Kramer's *Judgment at Nuremberg* (1961), under pressure from the American Embassy; the films would be shown only in closed session.[54]

Grigorii Chukhrai later stated that he had voted in favour of Fellini's $8\frac{1}{2}$ at the 1963 Moscow Film Festival. This emerged in the course of a public debate between Soviet and Italian *cinéastes* during the Italian Film Week held in Moscow in February 1966. The Soviet directors Gerasimov, Romm, Chukhrai, Donskoi, and Yutkevich discussed a broad range of cultural issues with Italian directors and critics. The director Nanni Loy asked why $8\frac{1}{2}$ had never been released to the Soviet public. Passing to the attack, the Soviet directors criticized Italian cinema for its 'alienation' and 'incommunicability', its eroticism and its gratuitousness. Michelangelo Antonioni (not present in Moscow) was singled out for portraying life as useless and man as powerless.[55] Challenged about the recent trial and imprisonment of the dissident writers Yuli Daniel and Andrei Sinyavsky, which had been condemned by Western Communist parties, Chukhrai remarked that Daniel and Sinyavsky were worthy of scorn, but it was 'an error to transform these cowards into heroes, yesterday known to hundreds of persons, today known to millions. We have gained a ruble but we have provoked a million rubles in damages.' This produced some applause in the hall but also hisses from the orthodox. Reporting from Moscow, Peter Grose, of the *New York Times* (28 February), linked Chukhrai's liberalism with market forces: 'He is heading an experimental film studio that aims to tie its production budget directly to box-office proceeds, a revolutionary idea under the Soviet system in which state funds are allotted to film studios in advance, regardless of their eventual earnings.'[56]

Mikhail Romm, present at the discussion, was a strange case. Former head of the Mosfilm Experimental Studio, himself responsible for several hard-line cold war films, among them the dramatically clumsy *The Russian Question* and the historically contemptible *Secret Mission*, Romm inspired awe and reverence among former pupils.[57] In late November 1962 he addressed a large audience at the Theatrical Society, complaining that the *Oktiabr'* issue of 10–11 October had poured 'pig's swill' on Soviet avant-garde cinema. Recalling that V. Kochetov, editor-in-chief of *Oktiabr'*, had been at the fore-front of the anti-cosmopolitan campaign, Romm likened him to a hooligan now operating outside the Party's guidelines. On 3 December Romm de-livered a passionate speech against conservative cultural officials to a meet-ing of the RSFSR Writers' Union. Kochetov wrote angrily to the Central Committee (7 December), the result being that Romm was so severely called to account that on 7 February 1963 he composed a long letter of repentance to Leonid Ilychev.[58] This was the time when Romm was making his impres-sive but fundamentally Stalinist documentary *Ordinary Fascism* (*Obyknoven-nyi Fashizm*, 1964), the product of two years' research in over twenty film archives. Shown throughout the USSR and the German Democratic Repub-lic, as well as in London, Brussels, Munich, and West Berlin, much of his footage was edited tendentiously or cynically used out of context. The anti-American shots crammed into the end of *Ordinary Fascism*—reminiscent of the Depression clips jammed into Romm's *The Russian Question*—confirm that it was inspired by the Berlin crisis. According to the official Soviet view, *Ordinary Fascism* waged an open battle against neo-fascists of every stripe'.[59] But not of the Stalinist stripe, who had banned the same 'degenerate art' as the Nazis did—a major episode carefully neglected by Romm. As for the 1939 Nazi–Soviet Pact, sixteen years after his Stalin-era film *Secret Mission*, Romm once again contrived to make no mention of it. *Ordinary Fascism* was seen by

40 million Soviet viewers; in other words, it was an official film. Visiting Germany at the time, Mark Zak observed the amazement of audiences, students, art clubs. 'Why haven't our own directors made such a film?' they asked him.[60]

The orthodox view (and tone of voice) of Soviet cinema as the Brezhnev era took hold was projected in 1968 by the first deputy chairman of the Committee on Cinematography under the Council of Ministers—a bureaucratic title worthy of the strong-jawed Vladimir Baskakov. A war veteran sharing the psychosis of his generation, he wrote about cinema in often military terms: 'a major victory of the Soviet cinema, a victory on the road to realism.' Standard phrases abound: 'lofty humanism', 'profoundly stirring', and (repeatedly) 'heroism.' He talks of 'Soviet man's unbending character', adding: 'Soviet art is alien to the trends of so-called deheroization, to assertions that there is nothing heroic in nature . . .' Soviet films 'extol faith in ideals and not faithlessness, humanism and not misanthropy, the truth of life, and not visionary projects'.[61]

Baskakov devotes special attention to *The Living and the Dead*, a film by Aleksandr Stolper, based on Simonov's novel about heroism in the darkest days of 1941—but accords only four lines to Andrei Tarkovsky's first film, *Ivan's Childhood*—despite its award at Venice. Heroism is an obsession with Baskakov, whether in *Ballad of a Soldier* or *The Cranes are Flying*: 'They lived a full life—worked, loved, suffered, and pondered. Their inner world was rich. They were strong in spirit. They were positive heroes.'[62]

Having noted the impact of Soviet cinematography in the 1920s and 1930s, the universal praise for Eisenstein's *Battleship Potemkin*—'Dissertations are now being written about it in Munich and Hamburg'—Baskakov displayed touching pride and pleasure whenever current Soviet films were lauded in the West as works of art: *Ballad of a Soldier* had triumphed at the 13th Cannes Festival in competition with Fellini's *La Dolce Vita*, Antonioni's *L'Avventura*, and Bergman's *Virgin Spring*—a fact celebrated in the *Istoriia sovetskogo kino*.[63] In the opinion of this Soviet spokesman, Antonioni and Bergman 'posed and illustrated in their films the idea of "incommunicability", "alienation among people", severance of ties and contacts among the men and women populating the world'. With *Ballad of a Soldier*, just the opposite!—'the simple but great truths of friendship, kindness, and love couched in beautiful cinematic imagery'. Moreover, the hero and heroine 'are so chaste and strong, and regard the world with such serene and candid eyes!' Later the film 'made its triumphal march over the screens of the world, and newspapers of many countries sang the praise of its heroes—those remarkable young people of the land of the Soviets'. It was 'a major victory on the front line of cinemart' (an ugly hybrid term constantly employed by Baskakov). *The Cranes are Flying* 'successfully developed the pictorial traditions of the twenties. The camera seems to participate in the narration, creating a definite pitch of emotions.'

The *Istoriia* too celebrated the award of the Palme d'or to *Ballad of a Soldier*, which stood for exactly the opposite of the 'primary Western motifs', 'non-communication' (*nekommunikabel'nost'*), 'rupture of the links and contacts between peoples', the 'tragic solitude of man', and finally the all-encompassing 'alienation' (*otchuzhdenie*). Instead of complexity, *Ballad* offered the simple knowledge of what is right and what is wrong. Instead of portraying the tragic solitude of man, the film showed brotherly love emerging even in the hell of war—because it was a natural need of man.[64]

⌗ ⌗ ⌗

Andrei Tarkovsky, the major dissident talent of post-1960 Soviet cinema, was by the early seventies thoroughly alienated from the official culture. In a diary entry dated 17 November 1970, after news of Solzhenitsyn's Nobel Prize, Tarkovsky commented: 'Noble and stoical. His existence lends a point to my life too.' As for the film industry, he noted in his diary, 16 February 1972, it was in 'the most abysmal state'. 'Just because it provides the money, the State is able to ride roughshod over new ideas and wallow in a slough of vapid, bootlicking muck'. Tarkovsky rivalled Meyerhold in his dislike of the Stanislavsky method, referring in his diary to 'the idiot, megalomaniac Stanislavsky [who] did great harm to future generations of the theatre'.[65] On 14 October 1973 his alienation was darkening: 'A bad thought: nobody needs you, you are utterly alien to your own culture, you have done nothing for it, you are a nonentity. But if anyone in Europe, or indeed anywhere, asks who is the best director in the USSR, the answer is—TARKOVSKY. But here—not a word, I don't exist . . .'[66]

His first feature film, *Ivan's Childhood* (*Ivanovo detstvo*, 1962), with its blend of realism, expressionism, and surrealism, was never popular within the USSR but enjoyed an international success for which the cameraman, Vadim Yusov, also deserved credit.[67] Based on Vladimir Bogomolov's story *Ivan* (1957), about a young scout in the Great Patriotic War, an orphan boy who serves the army by reconnoitering behind enemy lines in the Pripet marshes, this touching film ends with Lieutenant Galtsev coming across a record of Ivan's execution among a pile of documents inside the ruined Gestapo headquarters in Berlin. As Tarkovsky told his mentor Romm, he wanted young Ivan to dream of the life he has been robbed of, a normal childhood. Natasha Synessios writes: 'This simple solution became the pivotal point of the film; the pivotal point, moreover, of Tarkovsky's entire oeuvre.'[68]

It was a triumph for Soviet cinema when *Ivan's Childhood* won the Golden Lion at the 1962 Venice Film Festival and a host of international prizes.[69] When the film reached America, under the title *My Name is Ivan*, Bosley Crowther of the *New York Times* (28 June 1963) greeted it as 'A keening cry of sadness...for all youngsters lost in World War II, for the youths whose lives were exhausted in hatred, bloodshed and death.' Tarkovsky, he added, belonged to the 'new impressionistic school, which achieves its strongest cinematic statement in random pictorial images'.

Perhaps his greatest film, the sombre and Bergmanesque *Andrei Rublev* (1965), is based on the story of the early fifteenth-century monk who brought the Russian school of icon painting to its peak. The film describes the Christian passions of icon painters and bell casters in the Vladimir region of Russia ('Rus'), beset by marauding Tartars and the capriciousness of princes. In a world of famine and violence, Rublev stands for brotherly love, art, and beauty; for idealism and faith. Tarkovsky and his cameraman, Vadim Yusov, drew inspiration from Eisenstein while achieving a modern cinematic view of history as the real present.[70] Graced by brilliantly achieved scenes of devastation and heroic industrial improvisation—the Tartar raid on Vladimir, the casting of the bell—the film was not released for distribution in the USSR, where it passed directly from the studio to the 'stake' via a memorable showing for the Moscow elite in the Old Dom Kino. After Tarkovsky refused all editing demanded by the censors, the film was shelved for five years. The *New York Times*'s Moscow correspondent filed a very brief report on 24 October 1967, about the delay in releasing a film called 'Rublyov': according to those who had seen private screenings, 'Rublyov's struggle is open to interpretation with modern parallels'. According to Naum Kleiman, the Central Committee vetoed Mosfilm's plan to send *Andrei Rublev* to Cannes, but it was nevertheless shown out of competition in 1969 against the wishes of the Soviet authorities and won the FIPRESCI prize, followed by other international awards.[71] Yet it was not cleared for export by the Soviet Film Department until 1973. In the course of his rebellious open letter on the Solzhenitsyn affair, the cellist Mstislav Rostropovich cited the internal ban on Tarkovsky's film, which 'I had the good fortune to see among delighted Parisians', as a further example of absurd censorship.[72] A limited distribution of a mutilated version was now allowed within the Soviet Union. A document dated 4 January 1972, found by the author in the RGANI archive, signed by V. Shaurov, head of the Central Committee's culture department, and marked *Sekretno*, reported that only 277 copies had been printed compared with the normal 1,500 to 3,000; between 20 December 1971 and 2 January it had been seen in only five Moscow cinemas (194,000 viewers). 'The release has stopped the spread of rumours especially among the creative intelligentsia.' *Komsomol'skaia pravda* (25 December) published a hostile review. The actress Bibi Andersson told Tarkovsky that Ingmar Bergman regarded it as 'the best film he has ever seen'.[73] Indeed Bergman—director of the comparable *Seventh Seal*—called Tarkovsky 'one of the greatest of all time', shrewdly adding a reservation: 'But I also feel that Tarkovsky began to make Tarkovsky films and Fellini began to make Fellini films. Yet Kurosawa has never made a Kurosawa film.'[74]

Soviet state patronage clearly cushioned a chosen director like Tarkovsky against the cruel time-scales prevailing in Western studios, despite his frequent clashes with keepers of the seals, the bureaucrats of Goskino and Mosfilm. If the system set up a large number of hurdles and checkpoints to ensure ideological acceptability, it also allowed a freedom undreamed of in the West once a script was given the go-ahead. Yet the best art is often produced under commercial pressure. Shooting schedules were too long and relaxed; Tarkovsky was notorious for changing his scripts and adding voice-over during the post-dubbing.[75] In Sweden Bergman not only benefited from experience in the theatre—how to handle actors, how to meet a tight schedule—but also knew that he must entertain, must cut and edit to attract a large art-house audience across the world. Tarkovsky, meanwhile, was gloomily measuring himself against eternity, the 'great artist' both rejected and revered by the sullen bear.

His film *Mirror* (*Zerkalo*, 1974) was made after he had won further international awards for *Solaris* (1971),[76] a metaphor-laden science-fiction film. *Mirror* is a finely woven tapestry of childhood reminiscences with Tarkovsky's beloved mother the central figure.[77] In Fellini terms, this is Tarkovsky's *Amarcord*. Intercutting a series of fragmented autobiographical episodes, which have only the internal logic of dream and memory, with a startling documentary footage, Tarkovsky lovingly builds a world where the domestic expands into the political and criss-crosses back again. But the characters do not gain full autonomy. As fragments of the director's own world view they are primarily engaged in dialogue with him. In general Tarkovsky is at his best when his images are uncluttered by words; or—to borrow his description of Bach and Leonardo—when he sees the world as it is for the first time.[78]

Mirror confirms that Tarkovsky's freedom from commercial constraints encouraged a lack of discipline and outright self-indulgence. 'What is important here', he wrote, 'is not the *logic* of the flow of events, but the *form* of their flow, the form of their existence within the film material. These are different things. Time is already form.'[79] What this meant in practice is that shards of stories, of dialogue, of images, were picked up, developed, abandoned, reinvented, cut, reshuffled. Tarkovsky's diaries confirm this was a film which refused to cohere and fell apart along the way. To his credit he resisted half-baked notions from the 'new journalism': he had been tempted, for example, to use a hidden camera while a female psychiatrist put questions to his own mother, but the numbered questions in the script are often affected and phoney. What do you think about nuclear energy? Do you like animals? Which ones? Dogs, cats, horses? What do you think about flying saucers? One actress (the spellbinding Margarita Terekhova) plays both mother and wife to Aleksei, while one boy actor plays both the 12-year-old Aleksei and his own 12-year-old son Ignat. So peaceful and idyllic are most of the scenes of rural evacuation from Moscow during the war that the spectator is hard pressed to know who is who, where is where, and when is when— whether at any one moment we are in the 1930s, 1940s, or in the 'present'. Flashes of humour are rare; Tarkovsky is always a heavily solemn fellow. *Mirror* was completed in 1974 against strong bureaucratic resistance—it was judged to be incomprehensible—and reached Western Europe only later. Not until 1979 did it win two prizes in Italy.

And so to *Stalker* (1979). Arkady and Boris Strugatsky published their story 'Roadside Picnic' in 1972. Three years later Tarkovsky encouraged them to send a script proposal to Mosfilm. The film which eventually emerged begins in an outer world virtually as grey, cold, wet, and dilapidated as the inner 'Zone' itself. The Stalker (Aleksandr Kaidanovsky), an enslaved pagan of the Zone who ardently wants to believe that anyone can be granted his dearest wish in 'the Room' (which lies within the Zone) if only he sincerely believes. The Stalker meets his two clients in a café then drives them in an open vehicle through deserted alleyways, dodging helmeted soldiers and motor-cycle patrols guarding the perimeter of the Zone but unable to pursue anyone into it because of their fear. The Stalker could also be likened to a 'priest' of the Zone, possessed by superstitious fears—one must never go back by the same path, or retrace one's steps; the shortest route is the most dangerous; the person who is sent ahead is in the gravest danger. He embarks on his life-threatening safari with muttered prayers, his fine face often blank with imprecation. Could the Zone be construed as the post-Stalinist socialist state, derelict yet still darkly powerful, vengeful, subject to its own obscure laws and whims, offering the uncritical, the faithful, an elusive future happiness at the end of a blindfolded passage?

The Stalker leads the Writer and the Professor (Anatoly Solonitsin and Nikolai Grinko) across the bleak landscape of industrial detritus, a constantly mutating maze of traps and mirages, towards the Room, which can (perhaps) lay bare the devices and desires of your heart. Many others—scientists, opportunists, the unhappy, the curious—have made the pilgrimage. Obscure objects are found there, studied, even sold. The Zone and its contents continue to defy human logic: as one character puts it, 'humanity has been left to deal with the debris of a roadside picnic on some cosmic road'. Tarkovsky is a master of puddles, mud, filthy water, *objets trouvés* below the water, fear, superstition, skeletons, motionless shapes slowly observed which turn out to be something else. His sounds and sound-effects are unique, the specifics of metal on metal, wheels on rails, the 'technical' sound at a distance, the inhuman noise of the human industrial wasteland at its most grim and pollutant (i.e. Communist Europe). He typically moves a character but does not track after him, restraining the camera as if in self-denial. His camerawork is jewelled with revelations and reversals which add up to nothing except—as with Beckett—life as an impossible mission, an impasse. But this is not Tarkovsky's view: 'In *Stalker* I make a complete statement—namely, that human love is the miracle capable of withstanding any dry theorisation about the hopelessness of the world.' But, he added, 'we no longer know how to love ...'.[80] The verbal dimension, muted for long periods, bides its time and periodically overspills in flatulent dialogue which could have been written by Jean-Luc Godard. For example, having reached 'the Room', the Professor berates the Stalker:

PROFESSOR: None of the Stalkers knows what people come here with, or what they go away with, those that you bring ... But random crime is growing. Isn't that your doing? Military takeovers, animals in power, mafia in government—maybe they're clients of yours too! And lasers, monstrous bacteria, all that filthy underhand stuff, until now tucked away in safes ...

WRITER: Money, women, revenge—running your boss over in your car. That's all very well. But rule the world! A fair society! The kingdom of God on earth! Not desire but ideology. Action. Conceptions. Unfelt compassion is not ready to be realized. Like ordinary desire, born of instinct.[81]

Speaking to a national film conference in March 1980, and embittered about his own low box-office rating within the Soviet Union,[82] Tarkovsky took the opportunity to reject official demands that films should focus on topical themes such as agriculture. Like any art, cinema was about human beings, not topical themes. Quoting Engels—'The more concealed the author's views the better for a work of art'—Tarkovsky lamented how the high level and prestige of the Soviet cinema in the 1920s and 1930s had been lost. Like Andrei Konchalovsky, he finally left to work in the West, unable to survive in a climate where Filipp Ermash, head of Goskino from 1972 to 1986, pursued a policy of bland commercialism, the greatest success being Vladimir Menshov's romantic comedy *Moscow Does Not Believe in Tears* (*Moskva slezam ne verit*, 1980), which miraculously contrived to please Party ideologues, Soviet audiences (75 million viewers in its first year), and Hollywood Oscar prize-givers. In January 1981 Tarkovsky noted in his diary: 'I cannot support my family as a result of the way Goskino distributes my films.'[83] In March 1982 he flew from Moscow to Rome.

At Sheremetevo [airport] there was an awful incident with the customs. The official told me to open my suitcase, and he took one of my diaries out of it, and gave it to his assistant to examine. Apparently you have to have special permission to take out manuscripts, and I didn't have it. Then he went off somewhere, and at that moment his assistant found a photograph of Solzhenitsyn and his daughters in my diary. I had no idea it was there. He demanded an explanation . . . [84]

Tarkovsky's films were banned from Soviet screens from the moment of his enforced exile in 1982. His last film was a Franco-Swedish production, *The Sacrifice* (*Offret*), released in 1986. His death[85] in Paris on 29 December of that year, at the age of 54, coincided with the onset of Gorbachev's *perestroika*; his work returned to Soviet kinos, but the director himself was no longer available.

PART III

Stage and Screen Wars:
Europe

Germany Divided: Stage and Screen

The battle of the stages had also been gathering pace in Berlin, an occupied city divided into four sectors of rubble and hunger, but still allowing free passage between them—the audience for a play by Sartre or a concert by Menuhin would include the uniforms of all four Powers.

In the American zone New Deal culture remained in the ascendant immediately after the war. Anti-fascism still outweighed anti-Communism. For their part, the Russians were in a handshaking mood, anxious to embrace fellow-travellers or friends wherever they could be found. Radical American plays of the 1930s soon arrived on Berlin's surviving stages.[1] But there were early skirmishes: on 8 August 1945 the *Herald Tribune* reported that the Russians had closed the Deutsches Theater in East Berlin after a two-day run of Thornton Wilder's Pulitzer Prize-winning play *Our Town*, because of its 'defeatist' theme—and this despite the fact that the newly installed manager of the theatre, Gustav von Wangenheim, had fled Nazi Germany and become a Soviet citizen.[2] The official reason given was that the German actors had failed to obtain the proper licence from the Soviet Cultural Bureau, but no one believed this version. Set in the years 1899–1913, the epitome of magical realism, and first produced in the United States in 1938, Wilder's fictional town, Grover's Corner, is a humanistic democracy in microcosm, with a complacent, pastoral, and somewhat uncultured view of the world, and much inclined to folksy rhetoric. The play returned to the Berlin stage in a production by Max Kruger at the Schonberg Stadt Theater in March 1946. By 1948 295,000 Germans had seen it.

In September 1945 the Soviet Propaganda and Censorship Department took direct control of East Berlin's four leading theatres. At the Deutsches Theater the last act of a play by the Hungarian Communist Julius Hay was rewritten, with Soviet officers taking an active part in the final two rehearsals.

Soviet intentions are spelled out in a Decree of the Supreme Commander of Soviet Military Government (SMAD), No. 51, 4 September 1945, Berlin.[3]

On 6 November the eminent correspondent William L. Shirer, famous for his dispatches from Nazi Germany, accompanied 'Nicky Nabokoff' (Nicolas Nabokov, future general secretary of the Congress for Cultural Freedom), 'who is helping to guide our Military Government in its cultural endeavors', to see the première of Robert Ardrey's *Thunder Rock* (*Leuchtfeuer*) at the Hebbel Theater, with Ernst Busch in the lead. 'It is the first American play the Berliners have seen in more than ten years, and the audience liked it.' Despite the lack of heating, there was no shortage of fur coats. The play, which was due to start at 5 p.m., was delayed because of a rumpus with four Soviet officers who arrived with carbines over their shoulders 'and a little in their cups', demanding entry although the play was sold out. Placed in the balcony, they saw scores of American officers sitting below and made a row at the box office. Nabokov intervened as translator, kidded them, and finally induced them to depart. 'I was touched that Soviet officers should be so interested in seeing an American play: how many of our own would walk across town to see a Russian play?'[4]

Soviet cultural officers, meanwhile, many of whom had personal ties with Russian theatres, worked with German colleagues like Max Valentin, Wolfgang Langhoff, and Herbert Ihering to reassemble the personnel and rebuild the repertoires of German theatres. By April 1946 more than 100 playhouses were operational in the Soviet zone, most run directly by provincial or municipal authorities under the overall control of SMAD, which set the guidelines: German and European 'progressive' classics (Schiller, Molière, Offenbach's operettas); German anti-fascist plays; Russian classics; and contemporary Soviet plays.

The Allied occupation authorities, the Besatzungsbehörden, initially set themselves the aim of *Umerziehung*, anti-Nazi re-education. Americans and Russians shared a belief in the possibility of re-education through the theatre; the British were more sceptical, and the French lacked theatres in their zone.[5] However, historians differ about this. Wigand Lange[6] points out that theatre (like music) did not figure as politically relevant in the US *Manual for the Control of German Information Services* until, in April 1947, with the onset of the cold war, theatre and music were promoted.[7]

The Americans initially presented their own most esteemed modern playwrights as evidence that the Goebbels portait of a philistine transatlantic megalopolis (a perspective shared by the majority of Germans, including many on the left) was unfounded. Widely performed were Eugene O'Neill's *Mourning Becomes Electra* and *Anna Christie*,[8] as well as Tennessee Williams's plays of the steamy South, *The Glass Menagerie* and *A Streetcar Named Desire*.[9] O'Neill, America's pre-eminent playwright and four times a Pulitzer Prize-winner, was in effect the suspension bridge between Ibsen, Strindberg, and Nietzsche before him, and Tennessee Williams, Arthur Miller, and Edward Albee in his wake. Death, loss, mourning; alcohol, morphine addiction, and incapacity; guilt and the enduring bonds of family—these had been the enormously prolific O'Neill's great working themes for the past twenty-five years.[10] In 1936 he was awarded the Nobel Prize. Following the first night of O'Neill's *Anna Christie* at the Jürgen Fehling-Theater, Berlin, on 8 November 1945, the US Military Government put a series of his plays into translation.[11] *Ah, Wilderness* (*O Wildnis. Eine Kömodie der Erinnerung in drei Akten*), although criticized as too long, a *Buchdrama*, was praised in the Communist *Neues Deutschland* as well as papers of the Western zones,[12] critics noting the influence of Ibsen and Strindberg. O'Neill's *Marco Millions*, first produced in 1928, was, however, evidently considered too subversive by the American authorities.[13] Soviet hostility to O'Neill was to surface as an aspect of a wider disparagement of American theatre.

Theatrical coexistence between the Russians and the Western Powers continued into 1947, by which time the cold war had supplanted the shared anti-Nazi policy. Benno Frank, a Polish American who was in charge of theatre and music at Berlin HQ, later told the historian Wigand Lange that he got on well with his Soviet counterpart, the cultivated and dynamic Major Aleksandr Dymshits, chief of the cultural section of SMAD's[14] Information Administration, and a Jew, who consulted him about most appointments (*Ernennungen*) in the Ostzone, while Frank arranged for Wolfgang Langhoff to come through the American Zone from Zurich to take up his post as *Intendant* of the Deutsches Theater. Dymshits enjoyed good relations with his superior, Colonel Tiul'panov, and was able to pursue the recruitment of émigré German writers—not least Bertolt Brecht, although paradoxically, Benno Frank later claimed that he virtually had Brecht in the bag for the US zone when reactionaries intervened.[15] In general one should take Benno Frank's recall, as reported by Wigand Lange, with considerable reserve.

Following the Zhdanov decree on literature in February 1946, Dymshits informed the Brandenburg Information Administration that Mayakovsky's *The Bedbug* was no longer to be performed—Dymshits did not advertise the fact that he himself had been writing a dissertation on the poetry of Mayakovsky when the war broke out. In Thuringia a Soviet cultural officer by the name of Babenko boasted that he and his men took a direct part in the production of every Russian play, whether Soviet or classical. Chekhov, Pushkin, and Gogol had to be performed exactly as in the Soviet Union.[16]

One of several productions imposed on the Deutsches Theater by Soviet military administration officers during Gustav von Wagenheim's brief tenure (July 1945–August 1946) as director,[17] was *Stürmischer Lebensabend* (*The Stormy Evening of Life*), by the Soviet playwright Leonid Rakhmaninov, described by Wolfgang Schivelbusch as 'a schmaltzy revolutionary play fulfilling all the demands and criteria of high Stalinism'. The première at the end of May 1946 was a flop, with a disastrous performance by the actor playing the bourgeois-liberal professor converted to Communism by the October Revolution. Even the theatre critic of the Party's *Neues Deutschland* described the heroic professor as 'a ridiculous figure who would convince no one ... he killed the whole play ...'.[18] Radically different was a Soviet view of the same play and production. According to the critic I. Novodvorskaia, *Stürmischer Lebensabend* (*Bespokoinaia starost'*)[19] and other Soviet dramas afforded German actors, directors, and theatre companies a valuable opportunity to sharpen their artistic weapons (*oruzhie*). For example, the well-known actress Lucy Kheflich, previously accustomed to decadent bourgeois dramas, had discovered new dimensions for her remarkable talents in Rakhmaninov's play, where she played the wife of Professor Polezhaev. Khelflich was able to convey the nobility, the purity of spirit, and the steadfast truthfulness of a Russian woman, a faithful friend and spouse of the progressive scholar. Or so said I. Novodvorskaia.[20]

Governor of the Province,[21] by the brothers Tur and Sheinin, was retitled *Colonel Kuz'min* when performed in Germany in 1947 at the Schiffbauer-damm Theater (later celebrated as the home of Brecht's Berlin Ensemble). Directed by Fritz Wisten, the play made (according to Novodvorskaia) a huge impression. Reactionary critics and the corrupt press operating under Western licences strove to convince their readers that the figure of Colonel Kuz'min was idealized, and that such Soviet officers were not to be found in real life. Particularly effective was the scene in which Kuz'min and Professor Dietrich discuss the fundamental principles of Soviet policies in the Eastern zone; this 'invariably aroused stormy applause from the German audience'.[22]

Productions at the Hebbel Theater in the American sector of West Berlin came under frequent attack from the Soviet-sector press. (Designed by Oskar Kaufmann and built in 1907–8, the Hebbel displays a version of the Jugend-stil, with a brutalist exterior of rough-hewn stone contrasting with ultra-modern doors of glass and brass, and fine panelling in the foyer.) When performed at the Hebbel, Thornton Wilder's *By the Skin of Our Teeth*,[23] the most successful serious American play in Germany, was accused by the Soviet-licensed press of 'rotting in the destructive pessimism of a lethargic, sceptical, decrepit bourgeoisie'. Wolfgang Harich[24] offered a partial defence of Wilder in *Die Weltbühne*, but *Neues Deutschland* found nothing to redeem the play, which was also attacked by an officer of SMAD in the *Tägliche Rundschau* (31 December 1946). Other Wilder plays, *Our Town* and *The Happy Journey to Trenton and Camden*, were widely performed in West Germany but banned in the East. The East Berlin press also objected to Paul Osborn's *Stay of Execution* at the Hebbel Theater, and generally damned as decadent the 'contemporary significance' (*zeitgeschichtliche Bedeutung*) of plays by Sartre, Anouilh, and Giraudoux on show in the Western sectors.[25] Writing in *Neues Deutschland* (1 January and 27 April 1947), the hard-line Stalinist critic Fritz Erpenbeck lamented the 'flood' of 'surrealist' and 'existentialist' plays in Western-zone theatres; varieties of nihilism were served up like narcotics.[26] But even Erpenbeck had to admit that contemporary dramas (*Zeitstücke*) staged in the Soviet sector were not attracting audiences to compare with the foreign productions in West Berlin.

By late 1947 peaceful coexistence was in disintegration and the Berlin blockade was less than a year away. On 28 October 1947 the US Military Government, headed by General Lucius Clay, launched what it called 'an educational and informational program to explain to the German people the basic concepts of democracy as opposed to the communist system'.[27] On 16 February 1948 a Reuter report described the city as 'Europe's biggest and brassiest showcase for the contrasting ideologies and cultures of the opposing sides'. According to this report: 'In static exhibitions of "culture" the Soviet authorities have so far won the battle hands down.' The Haus der Kultur der Sowjetunion, housed since May 1947 in the former Prussian Ministry of Finance, offered regular lectures in the great marble hall, often delivered by Soviet officers, increasingly harsh in tone. Theatre performances, films, and scientific displays were supplemented by a library containing 22,000 volumes, both Russian and German. In July 1948 the director of the Deutsches Theater, Wilhelm Langhoff, returning from a visit to the USSR, addressed a conference of theatre personnel at the Haus der Kultur and sang the praises of Soviet culture, while Herbert Ihering, of the Max Reinhardt Theater, thanked the Russians for helping to rid the German repertoire of 'the contentless, idea-barren, escapist, banal, unambitious' productions of the past.[28]

In the American zone the playwrights Lillian Hellman and Clifford Odets were now deemed politically unacceptable and banned by directive from Washington.[29] It was a major retreat, not only in German eyes but for those Americans who yearned for cultural recognition. Gerard Willem van Loon, US theater officer for Bavaria, complained in a memo: 'These people have been brought up to believe that . . . Americans were all illiterate millionaires whose sole ambition was to live in a skyscraper on a diet of gin and jazz.' Both van Loon and Eugene Bahn in Berlin were firm believers in American drama as the solution for German audiences, 'for our spiritual wealth is second only to our material wealth', wrote van Loon. The classics 'had been done to death during the Third Reich' and should be shelved indefinitely. You couldn't perform *The Merchant of Venice* to a German audience, could you? As for modern German dramas, even when world-famous, like Gerhardt Haupt-mann's, or Frank Wedekind's *Frühlings Erwachen* (*Spring Awakening*)—who really needed that stuff? 'The Bavarian producers attempted to warm over some of the left-wing drama of the late Twenties and early Thirties', reported van Loon. 'But the public, in general, would have none of it. Not only did the stuff seem about as "corney" as a cloche hat but audiences were fed up with the misery of the working classes and misery in general.'[30] The solution was to provide the best of American drama.

But was 'the best'? John van Druten's successful comedy *The Voice of the Turtle* (*Das Lied der Taube*), first performed in America in 1943, achieved 1,085 performances in post-war Germany.[31] From 1947 onward Washington would allow nothing but varieties of turtle soup in the theatres of the American zone.[32] Highly popular were Emmet Lavery's Catholic drama about nuns, *First Legion*, and Karl Zuckmayer's *Der Teufels General* (*The Devil's General*). Written in exile in the United States, this play about a Luftwaffe pilot who fought and won battles out of pure joy of combat, but who fails to conceal his kindness under a mask of cynicism, was destined to become a huge success in Germany. At the end of the play the hero realizes his political mistake and dies a noble death. Initially banned by the Allies, who weren't so keen on Luftwaffe pilot heroes, the play was performed in Hamburg at the end of 1947 and became the most frequently staged drama of the next two years.[33]

Keenly observing the coming and going of American cultural officers, the Soviet zone's *Tägliche Rundschau* (30 May 1948) published an article 'Hexen-jäger als Theateroffizier'—'Witch-hunter as Theatre Officer', in which two of the CIA's key cultural agents of the 1950s, Michael Josselson and Melvin Lasky, enjoy the unloving attention of Soviet Intelligence:

A sudden change of personnel in the culture department of the American Military Administration is currently creating discussion: the position of Theater Officer for Berlin is to be reassigned. Until now Mr Benno Frank has filled this post to the best of his abilities, displaying prudence and knowledge. One is assured that his loyal service has earned him the objective esteem (*sachliche Schätzung*) and personal respect of the German artists and administrators who worked with him. The real reason for the surprising recall and imminent departure of Mr Frank from Berlin, about which one now learns, must lie in his democratic professions. However, in Berlin artistic circles it has long been known that his work has been hindered by the systematic troublemaking and frequent and varied, attempts at intimidation by the secret service officer (*Geheimdienstoffizier*) Josselson. The current recall of Mr Frank, it seems, can be put down to his initiative. The motives become clearer when one simultaneously learns that Frank's planned successor is to be none other than that strange Herr Melville [*sic.*: Melvin] Lasky, of all people, whose previous official capacity was that of Berlin correspondent of 'New Leader' and 'Partisan Review', two journals of evil repute financed by the American secret police. In his official capacity as agent provocateur for his paymaster, Lasky has not made himself a particularly glorious name. Add to this now the rumour that on similar grounds Mr Clark, Head of the Cultural Office for the American Zone of Occupation, and his Berlin departmental head, John Bitter, who as musician and conductor of numerous concerts has acquired so many friends in Germany, must give up their posts, so are the last doubts about the aim of this remarkable reshuffle removed. Progressive German society sees the entire episode, which culminates in the replacement of a man of honour by a shady police informer, as a new intensification of the increasingly apparent oppressive (*beherrschenden*) imperialist course of the American Military Administration in Germany. Much discussed is the downfall of the last adherents of Roosevelt's democratic thinking and their replacement by the witch-hunters of reaction.[34]

The attack on Lasky reflected Soviet hyper-sensitivity about a remarkable incident some seven months previously, in October 1947, when the first post-war German Writers' Congress convened in East Berlin, after some delays. SMAD sponsored the event, with funding from the Soviet-zone German Administration for Culture and Administration (Deutsche Verwaltung für Volkbildung), with overruns covered by the Russians. On 27 October, a few days after the opening of the Congress and twenty-four hours before General Clay's cultural offensive, a relatively obscure American intellectual, Melvin Lasky, stepped to the rostrum and split the Writers' Congress right down the middle, sending the Communist novelist Anna Seghers scurrying out of the hall to fetch Dymshits. Editor of the American-funded journal *Der Monat* (and ten years later of the CIA-funded London journal *Encounter*), Lasky boldly assailed the climate of censorship in the Soviet police state, in particular the recent sanctions imposed on the writer Mikhail Zoshchenko and the poet Anna Akhmatova. The historian David Pike later discovered the unpublished transcript of Lasky's remarks in the Friedrich-Wolf-Archiv: 'What must it be like, he asked, for a Russian writer to worry continually whether "the new party doctrine, the revised state form of social realism or formalism or objectivism, or whatever it might be, was not already superseded and they might not have been branded overnight as 'decadent counterrevolutionary tools of reaction'?" '

Despite angry shouts from Communists in the hall about what had happened to the composer Hanns Eisler in the United States—and indeed the House Un-American Activities Committee was grilling Brecht more or less as Lasky spoke—he went on to condemn 'the Russian apparatus of political concentration camps and forced labor'. Focusing his gaze on the Soviet writers in the hall, Lasky said: 'We all know how soul-crushing it is to work and write when behind us stands a political censor and behind him stands the police.' Lasky ended with a quotation from André Gide, to 'tumultuous applause' which lasted several minutes.[35]

Soviet-zone newspapers expressed indignation, challenging Lasky's credentials as a writer and independent journalist, while exposing his association with the anti-Communist American journals *New Leader* and *Partisan Review*. The most vehement abuse came when Dymshits, who had contemplated having Lasky ejected from the podium, referred to his 'repulsive external appearance' (he sported a goatee that reminded Dymshits of Trotsky) and damned him as a 'creature' of the group connected with Ruth Fischer, who had denounced her brothers Hanns and Gerhardt Eisler, both resident in the United States. Dymshits's 'Ein Provokateur ohne Maske' (A Provocateur without a Mask) duly appeared in the 11 October edition of the *Tägliche Rundschau*.[36] This—and Lasky's continuing provocations as editor of *Der Monat*—explains why 'Herr Melville Lasky' was still playing the role of Ahab's whale in Dymshits's imagination when the *Tägliche Rundschau* denounced the removal of Benno Frank as US theater and music officer in Berlin.

Refused a licence in the US zone of Germany was James Gowe and Arnaud d'Usseau's American success *Deep Are the Roots*, because of its 'unbalanced accent to the American racial problem'. An East German production promptly surfaced in Dresden. Lange quotes a protocol of a US Civil Affairs Division (CAD) Staff Conference:

The play has to do with the return of a negro war hero to his home in the South and with racial problems, consequently lending itself to anti-U.S. propaganda. Long ago we had disapproved the play from policy standpoint. The play was previously done without authorization in Moscow [at the Vakhtangov Theatre] in April '47. A Moscow radio broadcast at that time quoted *Pravda* as follows: 'Authors boldly expose the American slave owners who have retained their racial hatred of the negroes up to the present.'

On the basis of a signed statement obtained by CAD from Gowe and d'Usseau that they had not authorized any performance of *Deep Are the Roots* in the Soviet Union, Germany, or Austria, OMGUS intended to protest to the

Russians. But evidently without effect; the play did good business in Thuringia, garnering 39,000 spectators in 1948–9, the highest for any dramatic work.[37]

American censorship tightened further. John Evarts, chief of the Theater and Music Section of CAD, Bad Nauheim, wrote a memo on 4 May 1949 citing two categories of plays which 'are often prohibited from being released and distributed'. The first was 'Plays which tend to contain an element of criticism of life in America, or deal with major problems facing America'. The second was 'Plays, *regardless of content*, written by authors who are considered to be either communist, or communist-sympathizers'. Likening the 'ironic' situation to 'Nazi times when there were also many forbidden authors', Evarts candidly concluded: 'Practically, this results in the prohibition of a good proportion of the best serious plays written in America.'[38] Productions of the same banned plays in the Soviet zone or sector of Berlin merely turned them 'into downright anti-American vehicles'—as with *Deep Are the Roots* and Arthur Miller's *All My Sons*.[39] By the early 1950s American officials in Germany had embraced full-blown McCarthyism. A clear example is the 1951 report 'Theater and the German People', written by an official named Gilbert Hartke for the Office of the High Commissioner for Germany: 'American plays tend to criticise American life too strongly and lay heavy stress on negative aspects of American life . . . Exceptional cases are frequently taken as the rule by German audiences.' He too cited *Deep Are the Roots*, which gave an 'unbalanced accent to the racial problem'.[40]

⊞ ⊞ ⊞

In a notable article published in *Sovetskaia muzyka* (December 1948), Sergei Barskii began by noting that when Hitler's '1000 Year Reich' collapsed the German public was totally ignorant of everything concerning Russian culture. Not for fifty years did Rimsky-Korsakov's wonderful *opera-bylina* (traditional Russian heroic poem) *Sadko* arrive on the stage of Germany's leading opera theatre. Under Hitler false allegations about a supposed lack of independence (*nesamostoiatel'nost'*) of Russian music had been hammered into the consciousness of German audiences. Russian music was dismissed as dependent on the work of 'European' composers, above all the Germans themselves. Glazunov became the 'Russian Brahms', Rimsky-Korsakov the 'Russian Verdi', and Tchaikovsky was praised as 'the most Western of Russian composers'. According to Barskii, the pressing post-war task was to introduce the German public to Russian music, above all operas. The first such production was of *Eugene Onegin* at the State Opera in Berlin. The necessary transference of the directorial centre of gravity to the conductor's stand was complicated, not only because German opera directors usually did not possess experience of working with what Barskii called 'a musical text', but also because, as a rule, the conductor did not function as artistic director of the stage spectacle. The experiences of such maestros as Erich Kleiber and Otto Klemperer, who actively influenced the *mise-en-scène* of opera as a spectacle, was considered in Germany to be 'eccentric'. According to Barskii, all attempts to adapt well-worn production techniques and operatic vocal-orchestral conventions to *Eugene Onegin* at the Berlin Opera immediately broke down when confronted by Tchaikovsky's sincere and genuinely human intonation. The soprano who played Tatiana, an excellent opera singer with considerable stage experience, but brought up on Wagner, was in a state of complete confusion when faced with the truthful and natural monologue of suffering in the letter scene. The hero of the opera *Sadko* strives to bring glory to his native town of Novgorod. German tradition was not familiar with works in which the hero is so closely linked to the people. Only in the sixth scene did 'the heroic tenor' Ludwig Zuthaus feel his way into the living qualities and 'popular character' of Sadko.[41]

A totally new experience for the German actors of the young Berlin 'Comic Opera' (continued Barskii) was working on Mussorgsky's *Sorochinskaia iarmarka* (*Sarochintsy Fair*). This kind of Russian 'people's musical comedy' was 'imbued with great chastity and purity', and therefore strange to a German theatre-going public which associated popular musical comedy with burlesque, *double entendre*, and indecorous elements both in the text and in the actions of the characters.

Typically (Barskii went on), the bought-up press of the Western sectors, following the Goebbels line with necessary modifications, attempted to discredit great Russian musicians, but having discovered that the Berlin public flocked to Russian opera, the press reversed itself and began to attack the City Opera Theatre in the British zone for not staging Russian operas. This had no practical result because British cultural officers kept their only musical theatre in a beggarly financial condition, and Russian operas can be expensive to mount.[42] Even so, Russian opera was now firmly established, not only in the Soviet zone but in West Germany as well. Barskii listed fourteen such productions during the previous three years.[43] Even now, when visiting performances in the Soviet sector might be considered an unwise step, to be written down in one's personal file as an un-American activity, Western officials continued by hook or by crook to visit Russian operas. Although invitations sent to them by the theatre were normally returned with a proud refusal, these Western officials instructed the messenger to go straight to the box office and obtain tickets somewhere other than the front row.[44]

Walter Felsenstein, born in Vienna in 1901, a specialist in musical theatre, had produced operas under the Nazis, including Verdi's *Falstaff* in 1942. After the war he worked as a director at the Hebbel Theater but moved into the Russian sector to found the Komische Oper and become its *Intendant* in 1947. A succession of fine classical productions followed: *Falstaff, Carmen, Die Zauberflöte*. The resources put at his disposal were in the most generous German tradition: 387 rehearsals for *Falstaff*, 375 for *Carmen*, and he was free to recruit leading singers from Munich, Hamburg, or Zurich. Congratulating Felsenstein on his fiftieth birthday, Walter Ulbricht praised him for transcending the bad habits, false images, and comfortable illusions left over from the reactionary capitalist theatre.[45] The 'political elements' in Mozart's *The Marriage of Figaro* were accentuated, and likewise the allegory in Weber's early nineteenth-century opera *Der Freischütz* was 'psychologically deepened'. Meanwhile the most obvious classical operettas by Johann and Richard Strauss were squarely set in their 'social contexts'.[46]

But why, asked the defecting theatre critic Jürgen Rühle,[47] was the Komische Oper so orientated to old operas and operettas? This, he believed, threw light on 'the total poverty of musical life under Communist rule'. Originally Felsenstein was committed to producing contemporary work like *Die Kluge* (the title refers to a farmer's clever daughter) by Carl Orff, directed by Paul Schmitz and rewarded with a national prize for the 1948–9 season, when the campaign against formalism had not yet erupted. But, continued Rühle: 'Some time later this bold work with its refined, primitive, antique (*altertümelnden*) forms scarcely retained the approval of Party officials.'[48] The major change of line in 1950–1 resulted in condemnation of the Dresden Staatsoper's production of Orff's *Antigone*. *Neues Deutschland* accused the composer of turning Sophocles' 'humanistic-democratic content' back into unintelligibility and cultish archaic mysticism. The Greek dramatist, a 'fighter for social progress', had been buried by Orff under the dark origins of Attic culture. The opera was banned. Some years later, during the thaw of 1954, the Dresden Opera attempted to revive various works by Orff but, noted Rühle, despite success with the public, they were 'very quickly suppressed'.

Soon after the Dresdeners' bad luck with Orff's *Antigone*, the Komisches Oper suffered a similar fate. At Felsenstein's invitation, Oscar Fritz Schuh was invited as guest director to stage Puccini's *Gianni Schicchi* together with a more modernist piece, Darius Milhaud's *Der Arme Matrose*, with a libretto by the politically suspect Jean Cocteau (a *fascisant* collaborator with Stravinsky, etc.). *Neues Deutschland* came out against this 'pessimistic literati piece' (*Literatenstück*), accusing it of 'cold affectation' (*eine kalte Künstelei*). The offending stage designer, Caspar Neher, Brecht's distinguished collaborator in the time of the Weimar Republic, had set the murderous story in the desolate atmosphere of a Parisian suburban bar. *Neues Deutschland* demanded, and got, the immediate replacement of this decadent piece, and contemporary operas disappeared, according to Rühle, from the Soviet zone.[49]

Then in 1952 the Socialist Unity Party (SED) issued an appeal, or demand, 'Für eine deutsche Nationaloper', in what Rühle, writing for a Western audience some years later, called 'an astonishing document'. Setting out at length the historical reasons why no monumental 'German national opera' had been forthcoming, the Party pointed to Russian national opera as the 'model' (*Vorbild*) for deep and vital operas reflecting the power of the people within the national tradition. A German version, a most urgent task, could be achieved only by means of a planned, collective collaboration between composer, writer, and 'scientist'—the latter being particularly necessary 'in order to convey accurately to the artists the concrete historical situation'. The Academy of Art, the State Commission for the Arts, and the musicians' and writers' unions must create a committee (*Gremium*) to carry through the work. As for the most 'effective' (*zweckmässig*) subject, that could be decided here and now: the peasants' war of the sixteenth century under the rebel leader Thomas Münzer.[50]

Despite all these cogs, wheels, and pulleys, the commission simply went to National Prize-winner Hanns Eisler, who took on the libretto as well as the music with apparently no intervention from writer or 'scientist'—and came up with a thoroughly 'unscientific' script for an opera called 'Johann Faustus', about a humanistic intellectual who breaks with the Catholic Church, leagues up with Luther, then moves over to the radical Thomas Münzer, whom he in turn betrays when, corroded by restlessness and vain ambition, he makes a pact with the Devil not unlike the one made more recently by sections of the German intelligentsia with Hitler. Delighted, Felsenstein secured the rights to first production for the Komisches Oper, but then all hell broke loose. As a former pupil of the twelve-toner Arnold Schoenberg, and a former exile in the United States, Eisler was held in suspicion by what Rühle calls 'the Party pharisees', and was said to have been on a 'dissipated pub crawl' (*Zechtour*) in imperialist West Berlin. *Neues Deutschland* came up with a programmatic article regretting that Eisler, for all his gifts, had not overcome certain formalistic influences from the past. Chief ideologist Wilhelm Girnus laid down that Eisler's Faustus conception was 'pessimistic, alien to the people (*volksfremd*), hopeless, anti-national'. Citations from Marx/Engels/Goethe/Heine/Stalin/Malenkov were hurled against him. An episode in the second Act gave particular offence, reflecting Eisler's personal experience of exile in America. Faustus encounters a place called 'Atlanta'; returning home to Germany at the start of the third Act, he complains how grey, cold, and dirty the Heimat is, compared to the huge, illuminating sun of 'Atlanta': *Und doch—Atlanta, ungeheur leuchtet deine Sonne!* To address America in the informal and thus affectionate idiom of *deine* was absolutely *verboten* (said *Neues Deutschland*), when that America belonged to Dulles, Ridgway, the Korean War, and witch-hunters. Eisler was guilty of 'homeless cosmopolitanism'.[51]

⌗ ⌗ ⌗

Ufa (Universum-Film Aktiengesellschaft) had dominated film production under the Weimar Repubic and the Third Reich, latterly under the close supervision of Goebbels's propaganda ministry.[52] Ufa's studios in Neubabelsberg ended up in the Soviet zone—though most of Ufa's stars and its rhombus-shaped logo ended up in the West. In November 1945 the Russians set up DEFA (Deutsche Film Aktiengesellschaft)[53] under total Soviet control. Scripts had to be approved by the military administration, SMAD, and by Sovexportfilm, the distribution agency.

Hot on the heels of the Soviet tanks came Soviet films, with German subtitles. But Soviet film exports to the conquered nation soon ran into difficulties. In January 1946 the rampant patriotic militarism of Soviet cinema led the Socialist Unity Party's Anton Ackermann to petition the Soviet cultural boss in Berlin, Colonel Tiul'panov, an upright military figure with a round, close-cropped, head: 'We urgently request that the film *Suvorov* be removed as soon as possible from the repertoire . . . It makes our ideological work in the elimination of militarism harder.' *Parade of Victors*, which showed Soviet soldiers tossing German army insignia in a heap in front of the Lenin Mausoleum, left German audiences sobbing. Similar objections applied to *Admiral Nakhimov* and *The Cruiser Variag*—but Ackerman's petition was not granted, and the Soviet authorities merely instructed their German subordinates that audiences should be persuaded to understand the Soviet defence of the motherland.[54]

Soviet films were boring, as well as heavy-handed reminders of conquest. Major Dymshits found himself in the delicate position of suggesting to his superiors that films like *Traktorist* (*Tractor Driver*), a collective-farm saga, should not be shown in the Soviet zone. Even nineteenth-century Russian classics were too ponderous for the taste of most German audiences. A Soviet cultural officer from Brandenburg reported that romance and adventure were popular—but films about war, revolution, or poverty were not.[55]

The first feature film made in post-war Germany, Wolfgang Staudte's *The Murderers Are Among Us* (*Die Mörder sind unter uns*, 1946), released by Deutsche Film AG in East Berlin, achieved an international impact with its apparently non-partisan exploration of guilt and culpability. Director-writer of this chiaroscuro immersion in misery, angst, and degradation, Staudte was obviously influenced by the Weimaresque work of G. W. Pabst and Fritz Lang. The gods were here wallowing not only in their customary twilight, but in a first-class nervous breakdown. The setting is Berlin, 1945. The poster artist Susanna Wallner (Hildegard Knef) returns from a Nazi concentration camp to what is left of her native Berlin and finds an embittered, brooding (and hugely unshaven) man occupying her old apartment. This, it transpires, is Dr Hans Mertens, who, permanently inebriated, is next found moving through shadows and ruined cellars to one of those prototypical Berlin nightspots where swindlers are at work by candelight—for example, the elderly clairvoyant, Herr Timm, who will relieve the bereaved watchmaker Mondtschein of 10 marks in return for dispensing 'a little happiness'. But the implication is inescapable that these small-time charlatans represent the major industrialists of the Nazi era, still at large.

Visibly at large is the war criminal whose atrocities give our destroyed hero, Dr Mertens, his screaming nightmares. This is the dapper little bourgeois family man Bruckner, already owner of the Bruckner Reconstruction Company, who believes that 'some more pudding' will chase away life's silly doubts. We see Bruckner, a Himmler lookalike, gobbling his breakfast and some more breakfast while reading a headline, '2 Million People Gassed'; as Captain Bruckner this man had once ordered the brutal execution of 100 men, women, and children in occupied Poland. Dr Mertens, meanwhile, is groping his way back to a useful life; he volunteers to work at a hospital; he saves the life of a choking child with a sterilized kitchen-knife; he enjoys a white Christmas with Susanna as studio snow falls on studio ruins beyond studio windows. He has now shaved. Then he sets out to kill Bruckner during a Christmas service—they are singing *Heilige Nacht*—which reminds him of that other Christmas in 1942, when he had pleaded with Captain Bruckner not to massacre the helpless civilians. On that occasion Bruckner, unwrapping Christmas presents, had gone off to church, just as he does now, in 1945. The film's commentary on the hypocrisies of bourgeois morality are obvious and effective—this is not a film likely to have emerged from the Western zones of Germany. The film ends with a grim collage of crosses covered in snow, defeated soldiers, victims—echoes of Brecht and Käthe Kollwitz. Interestingly, there is not a sign or sound of the Allied military occupation forces throughout; German film-makers were not yet allowed to portray their conquerors.

The Murderers Are Among Us took two years to reach New York's Avenue Playhouse. Reviewing it in the *New York Times* (17 August 1948), Thomas Pryor (T.M.P.) noted with suspicion that it came from the DEFA studio in the Russian sector of Berlin; Pryor found the central character unconvincing, 'a doctor who strives to conceal through drink and cynicism the utter revulsion of his experiences with the Nazi Army'. The doctor's encounter with his former captain, a murderous Nazi now passing himself off as a 'good' German, struck Pryor as contrived 'for propagandist rather than dramatic effect'. The director was mainly interested in camera effects—'but his technique is stilted and old-fashioned'.[56]

East German films were soon pinning their ideology to their sleeves. DEFA's *Our Daily Bread* (*Unser Tägliche Brot*, 1949), written and directed by Slatan Dudow, reflected the sharpening of ideological conflicts.[57] In this frankly Zhdanovist film about post-war reconstruction, with music by Hanns Eisler, the positive members of the family are depicted as putting their faith in a socialist future. When the film reached America, H.H.T. of the *New York Times* (9 October 1950) described the plot in an accent somehow combining cold war hostility with baffled enthusiasm: 'The father, an unemployed, middle-class accountant, sits around the house brooding pompously about the good old days...and scorning [his eldest son] who is helping comrades in the herculean reconstruction of a bombed-out factory...With an eventual assist from the "government," the plant progresses and opens in a blaze of co-operative glory.' H.H.T. described *Our Daily Bread* as 'the most absorbing and level-headed piece of propaganda for socialism' to have reached America from DEFA. Acting, directing, and photography were 'above reproach', as was Eisler's score. But was it (he asked) a 'cunningly restrained account of post-war German family life that basically toes the party line every inch of the way', or merely 'a fine, smooth sample of movie-making'?[58]

For four or five years after the war East and West German film-makers alike avoided expressing overt antagonism towards any of the victorious Allied powers, not only because Allied censorship forbade it, but also because hope still persisted that, despite the Berlin blockade and currency reform, the split was not irretrievable. But with the founding of two German states and the failure of the London Foreign Ministers Conference in 1950, these hopes were at an end.[59] In 1950 Kurt Maetzig joined forces with Slatan Dudow as co-directors of *The Benthein Family* (*Die Familie Benthein*), which was duly praised in orthodox terms in East Germany's *Neue Filmwelt* (no. 10, 1950):

'We see faces whose interest lies in the destruction of West German youth by means of unemployment and the black market. There, it is not a matter of creating new, free people.'[60] The first DEFA film to embrace fully the ideological animosities of the cold war, and to make a firm link between fascism and capitalism, was Kurt Maetzig's *Der Rat der Götter* (*Council of the Gods*, 1950). Based on a script by Friedrich Wolf, this was a propaganda superproduction of the type being made by Mikhail Chiaureli in the Soviet Union. The Russians provided material from the Nuremberg trials. Costing 3 million marks, the film set out to prove that I.G. Farben collaborated with Standard Oil America throughout World War II and was now helping the United States to prepare a new war—a theme we have already encountered in Mikhail Romm's *Secret Mission*. According to *Iskusstvo kino* (February 1954), the three military commandants of West Berlin registered a complaint with their Soviet counterpart that Maetzig's film undermined the authority of the occupation forces and the Bonn government.[61]

Radically different in setting, but pointing even more intimately at cold war cultural conflict, Maetzig's *Story of a Young Couple* (*Roman einer jungen Ehe*, 1952) portrays a German actress, Agnes, in search of a part. Offered one in a play by Sartre, *Les Mains sales*, due to be staged in West Berlin, she refuses, contemptuously dismissing the play as 'green jelly'; she chooses instead a part in Konstantin Simonov's *The Russian Question* in East Berlin. Her misguided husband, meanwhile, performs in Sartre's play. Divorce seems inevitable until the husband realizes that truth and justice reside in the East; he enters the divorce court carrying a paper dove.

West Germany is again the centre of evil in Stefan Dudow's *Frauenschicksale*[62] (*Women's Fate*, 1952), the story of young girls who cross into West Berlin and fall victim to the decadent night-life. The film (shot by Robert Baberske in Agfacolor) not only captured typical Eastern-bloc attitudes of men towards women, it also carried a stark political message which was to become a running theme of East German films—insecurity and criminality in the West versus health and stability in East Berlin.[63] *Sovetskoe iskusstvo* (February 1954) noted that Maetzig and Dudow had been guests of honour at the closing ceremony of the Berlin Youth Festival; delegates from capitalist countries 'fought their way to Berlin like sailors seeking the lighthouse which beacons the way'. An American plane had circled overhead, dropping leaflets.[64]

Martin Hellberg's *Das verurteilte Dorf* (*The Condemned Village*, 1952),[65] a classic of manipulative socialist realism, offered a surprisingly ambivalent portrait of American forces and their German stooges (provincial politicians and policemen) as oppressors. As 'fascists' go, these ones were well short of graduation; not a gun, not a tank in sight. The main flaw, running from stem to stern of the scenario, was the attempt to say one thing (how cruel to destroy a peaceful, productive German village, with its worthy peasants, thriving church, fat white geese, and lovable carthorses, by turning it into a US military airfield) while meaning another (US airfields signal a new world war, regardless of where they are built).

What greater happiness can fate bestow on the village of Bärenweiler than the return from a prisoner-of-war camp in the East of Heinz Weimann? (In reality few POWs had been released by 1951, and fewer still told family and friends of a better life in the East.) It so happens that Heinz's old pre-war flame is now married, unhappily of course, to Vollmer, a smooth, chuckling, Schnapps-drinking warmonger who has lost vast estates in East Germany ('behind the Iron Curtain') to 300 'New Peasants'. He in turn is hand in glove with the German capitalists who will make fat profits out of building runways and aircraft hangers for the United States Air Force. 'Some of our imprisoned friends [i.e. Nazis] will be wanted soon', he confides. 'Things have gone much further than people realize.'

Vollmer calls Heinz a Communist, but Heinz denies it. 'I'm just interested in peace.' Heinz also denies that religion has been abolished in Russia. 'Religion *verboten*? Nonsense. I've seen people going to church.' Does Russia want war? 'I don't believe it. They're all cheerful people just like us. They're rebuilding their destroyed towns and villages just like we are.'

But Bärenweiler occupies just the kind of flat terrain that brings out the beast in the smooth US colonel, who wears dark glasses, sports untypically long hair, and calculatingly lights cigarettes as the women in the fields innocently work at the harvest. When the villagers get wind of the threat to their *Heimat*, the director, Martin Hellberg, puts his film into standard socialist realist choreography, a succession of carefully set-up mass scenes with the logic of children's stories: support arrives from Village A by *this* bridge into Bärenweiler just as support from Village B arrives by *that* bridge. Everything is synchronized as affirmative motion. The workers invariably arrive in the nick of time to express solidarity and call a strike in support of the villagers. The set resounds with inaudible megaphone instructions and stopwatches, marches and processions, floats and banners: *Stadt und Land Hand in Hand, Deutschland den Deutschen!*, and *Bärenweiler—ein deutsches Dorf*.[66] As the camera tracks from one concerned elderly peasant face to the next, the sense of contrivance is total.

At the forefront of the resistance, apart from the hero Heinz, are the staunch mayor and the staunch village priest, who naturally always see eye to eye. A smiling civilian of the Amerikanische Kontrollkommission, meanwhile, receives the anguished petition of the villagers of Bärenweiler, instructs his svelte secretary in Germanic English: 'Put that on the desk of the Boss', and then pinches her cheek, telling us all we need to know about Americans. The reply to the villagers is uncompromising. A little girl asks the village schoolmaster: 'Please, are we going to be thrown out?' 'Ich weiss nicht', he replies.

The police arrive in trucks with water cannon to clear a demonstration in the provincial capital. The German Wharf at Hamburg sends a message of solidarity; so, likewise, the soda factory at Baden, all hands raised; then Zeiss Jena; then the workers of the German Democratic Republic, seen from above, thousands of hands clapping in unison. One is reminded of the orchestrated letters to Soviet newspapers, and of Joris Ivens's documentary *Song of the Rivers*.

Enter a US general who, lighting an enormous cigar, snaps 'Out of the question!' when a distraught German minister requests a delay. Not only do the Americans not seem to give a damn for public relations, there is no mention of any offer of compensation to the villagers. The villains invariably perch on the edge of desks and tables, a sure sign. In short, Hellberg's *The Condemned Village* is socialist realism without the reality.

Heinz's mother prays. The camera cuts from the simple wooden cross on her breast to the bejewelled cross worn by a cynical bishop, in the process of being disrobed by an underling. 'Send some charity to the evicted villagers and find a new post for the village priest', drawls the bishop.

Truckloads of police storm the village but are met by effective passive resistance. 'I never thought I'd live to see Germans evicting Germans', says the mayor. 'We have our orders', comes the haunting answer. But then the police suddenly declare it to be a 'rotten business', and simply disappear.

Heinz is on trial for defying the state. He makes a speech from the dock which, it must be granted, is briefer than the legendary perorations of Dimitrov and Thälmann from the dock. 'These people will not easily be led to war. That's all that matters.' The fine old parish priest thunders in the pulpit: 'These fields of ours will never become battlefields.'

This time it's truckloads of US military police who move in, though they carry no arms. The church bells in neighbouring villages sound the alarm, one after another. A bored American soldier is spotted filching fruit from a tree as the crushed villagers load their belongings into carts. American military police in white helmets confront the people of Germany; the very success of the popular resistance, like the absence of American firearms, must surely remind the viewer that Americans are not 'fascists'. But the eviction of villagers from their *Heimat* is merely a pretext for opposing any American military presence in Germany. At one point Heinz rejects the proposal that the Americans be asked to build their airfield elsewhere, because, as he casuistically says: 'It will be somebody else's village.' The Peace Movement could not entertain the notion of an American military installation not built on the ruins of a village.

At an East German film conference held in September 1952, the strengths and weaknesses of DEFA's productions were spelled out in terms of a recent SED Politburo resolution. The number one weakness was said to be: 'An insufficient number of *Spielfilmen* (feature films) devoted to the struggle for German national unity and for peace.' East German cultural criticism, like its Soviet model, constantly castigated the dreary results of its own dogmas, the only available remedy being a double dose of tangled dogma. For example, the SED complained that: 'Many [East German] films whose content and form developed from the standpoint of "critical realism" exhausted themselves in social analysis and criticism but scarcely conveyed the task of achieving the ideal conditions and the education of the working masses in the spirit of socialism.'[67]

Films like *The Condemned Village* could not achieve general distribution in the Federal Republic. Censorship was severe. In 1949 the West German film industry had set up a Hollywood-style self-censorship body, the Freiwilligen Selbstkontrolle der Filmwirkschaft (FSK). In 1950 the interior minister decreed that DEFA films could be released in West Germany only with his consent. Four years later this censoring role was taken over by an Inter-Ministerial Examination Committee for East–West Film Matters (Prüfungs-ausschuss für Ost/West-Filmfragen). Its work as a Western frontier post checking films from all of Eastern Europe was politically motivated as well as unconstitutional.

A major West German contribution to cold war cinema was the pernicious *Der Arzt von Stalingrad* (*The Doctor from Stalingrad*, 1958), directed by Geza von Radvanyis, which begins in a fictitious German prisoner-of-war camp near Stalingrad in 1949. The moral leader of the prisoners is a brain surgeon, Böhler from Würzburg. It so happens that the child of the Soviet camp commander can be saved only by the skill of Böhler from Würzburg. He operates, a Russian doctor assists, and when it is all over the Russian sighs: 'No one watching this would know who won the war and who lost.' German superiority is comprehensive. As a result of this successful operation the first prisoners are released carrying a banner—'Never again war!' The film typifies Russians as either subjugated or subjugators—*unterjochten bzw. unterjochenden Russen*—as they are always described in the film, with the guards often picked out for their Asiatic, Mongol faces. Germans—men, women, and children—are seen as victims. The critic Irmgard Wilharm comments that: 'The spectator must assume that the USSR began the second world war.'

⊞ ⊞ ⊞

Highly tendentious documentary films poured out of Central Documentary Film Studios in Moscow and DEFA in East Berlin. Reviewing *We Are For Peace*, a colour documentary about the 1951 World Festival of Youth and Students held in East Berlin, Joseph L. Anderson commented that the film's director, Joris Ivens, 'like Soviet directors, has apparently forgotten his former ability'. The picture opens with peaceful landscapes. 'Suddenly there is a tremendous explosion and savage scenes of the Korean War appear. Overlooking the destruction is a wolf-like General MacArthur who gloats, "This is a good sight for my old eyes." ' The film ends with 100,000 young people shouting, 'Stalin, Stalin, Stalin, Stalin!'[68]

In 1954 the Communist World Federation of Trade Unions (WFTU) sponsored and released a DEFA film describing working conditions along the world's great rivers. The exiled Dutch director Joris Ivens[69] continued to 'lose his former ability' with this film, *Song of the Rivers* (*Lied der Ströme*), made with the participation of the Leipzig Radio Orchestra and Choir performing a continuous score taken from Shostakovich's music. The stiffening voice of Paul Robeson, 'ol' man river' himself, renders settings of Brecht's verses honouring the peoples of six great rivers of the world, the Volga, Mississippi, Amazon, Ganges, Yangtze, and Nile (only one of which, the Volga, can boast a truly human society, where man is the 'most precious thing'). We also gather that things are good in Poland, where the land has been 'returned to the people', East Germany (no mention of the recent uprising), China, and North Korea.

Some of the photography is under Ivens's direction, but much is taken from friendly sources. The screenplay, by Ivens and the Soviet writer Vladimir Pozner, is banal, one-dimensional, propagandistic. The enthusiastic Asians, Africans, and Caucasians, all deciding to resist exploitation by sending delegates to the 1953 Vienna Congress of the WFTU, seem to have been taken from a thousand Peace Movement posters. Everyone smiles, everyone agrees, everyone clasps hands, everyone claps in unison, everyone rises to their feet when leaders orate, again and again. There is no debate, no dissension, no discussion.

The film conveys the Stalinist obsession with machines and industrialization. On factories and farms the Communist world is mechanized and happy. Wheels turn, conveyor-belts convey, technicians in smart white coats supervise assembly lines—and everyone wears a soapy smile. In the imperialist lands haggard workers and their families suffer starvation while clawing the earth with bare fingers. Profits go to Wall Street and the City of London. F. Bowen Evans commented: 'The depiction of American working conditions is as usual distorted, showing only such things as slums, policemen clubbing workers on strike, the Ku Klux Klan . . . The pictures of Russia, however, show smiling workers and clean, modern shops.'[70]

The scenes at the WFTU Congress are interminable. Mankind resembles the animals of Noah's Ark. Utopia is evidently a boring place. The Communist Party is never mentioned in any context: 'Communists, Socialists and Catholics' merely join forces for peace (there are shots of Italian priests joining in). Quick clips of Ulbricht and Togliatti, plus the lesser known leaders of the Communist union federations, are not allowed to add up to the impression of Soviet control. The film concludes with shots of American atomic explosions and of John Foster Dulles rejoicing in them. The voice-over relentlessly tells us what to think—an inversion of the posh male narrator of the British Pathé–Gaumont newsreels. Eighteen different versions were finally produced, but the film ran into censorship in France and Britain. The British première had to be cancelled after the Board demanded cuts from the last two reels, dealing with German rearmament and the H-bomb, 'which would give serious offence'.[71]

Following the disastrous workers' uprising of 1953, and pushed by competition from West German television, DEFA turned from enlightening the masses to entertaining them, investing in musicals, light operettas, and revues.[72] The typical DEFA musical of the fifties was clean, healthy, and cheery, with constant borrowings from bouncy Hollywood production values—though not forgetting the work of Grigorii Aleksandrov in the 1930s.[73] A recent documentary film, *East Side Story*,[74] shows clips of these productions, with singing farmers, dancing factory girls, vacationing teenagers, and the usual Cinderellas. DEFA came up with some entertainment involving bikinis, scooters, and women singing under hair-dryers. A musical directed by Heinz Heinrich on the improbable theme of the heroic life of the KPD leader Ernst Thälmann (who had died in Buchenwald) survived Party objections and grossed 1 million roubles in four weeks in the USSR.

During the relative thaw after the 20th Congress of the Soviet Party, the Bitterfeld conference took place between Ministry of Culture officials and the DEFA Studio für Spielfilme in July 1958. DEFA's duty to follow the Party line was reaffirmed, the result being that during 1959–64 at least eight films with cold war themes were made in the DDR. One of them, Kurt Maetzig's *Septemberliebe* (1961), lauded the role of the notorious Stasi

(Staatssicherheitdienst)—much as American movies still celebrated the heroic patriotism of J. Edgar Hoover's FBI.[75]

In 1962 at a film festival in the Ruhr town of Oberhausen, young film-makers signed the Oberhausen Manifesto demanding a break with 'Papas Kino'. This was a preview of the generational turmoil that would sweep the Bundesrepublik in the late 1960s and 1970s, reflected in the work of Werner Herzog, Wim Wenders, Edgar Reitz, and above all Rainer Werner Fassbinder. The rigid assumptions of cold war culture in the Federal Republic, cultivated by the generation of the Nazi era, were yielding to self-scrutiny and the damning criticism of the young.[76] But no such development was allowed in the German Democratic Republic under Walter Ulbricht, Erich Honecker, and the Stasi. Ulbricht's clampdown followed the 11th ZK-Plenum of the SED in December 1965. Punitive measures resulted in the interruption of many directors' work. The arrival of Erich Honecker as general secretary of the SED in 1971 fostered false hopes of liberalization: 'If one comes from a firm socialist position,' he declared, 'there can, in my opinion, be no taboos in the realm of art and literature.' The problem, as could have been predicted, was coming from a 'firm socialist position'.[77]

Brecht and the
Berliner Ensemble

Last night I dreamed I saw fingers pointing at me
As at a leper. They were worn with toil and
They were broken.
'You don't know!' I cried
Guiltily.
(Bertolt Brecht, 'Nasty Morning')

I had to leave Germany in 1933, in February... Then I went to Denmark, but when war seemed imminent in '39 I had to leave for Sweden, Stockholm. I remained there for one year and then Hitler invaded Norway and Denmark. I had to leave Sweden and I went to Finland, there to await for my visa to the United States.
(Bertolt Brecht, Testimony to HUAC, 30 Oct. 1947)[1]

In his *Brecht in Context*, the late John Willett commented that whereas other artists have confined their political commitment to particular aspects of their work, 'Brecht systematically made it a part of everything he did. Far more than Picasso or Eluard, or George Grosz or André Malraux, he was all of a piece, fusing political and aesthetic considerations on a whole series of different levels. It is this that makes him special to admirers and critics alike...'[2] Certainly no twentieth-century dramatist and poet has excited such controversy, such adulation and furious condemnation, as Bertolt Brecht (1898–1956). No dramatist loomed larger in cold war cultural conflict than he.

He was a Marxist, yet his theory of theatre, of which a central pillar was *Verfremdung* (alienation), was anathema to orthodox socialist realism. The kind of radical theatre practised by Brecht and Erwin Piscator in Weimar

Germany, and by Mayakovsky in the USSR, was brutally closed down with the liquidation of Sergei Tretyakov (Brecht's translator) and Meyerhold in Stalin's purges. Henceforward only the 'Stanislavsky method', as practised by the Moscow Art Theatre, was permitted, a victory for everything that Brecht derided: total verisimilitude on the stage, total empathy between actor, character, and audience, total 'realism'. The curtain was simply the 'fourth wall' of the room of life; when it went up, the audience was gazing into life itself. According to Brecht, what the audience should encounter was a form of debate between itself and actors playing characters in a text. A play is a play, a performance a performance. Mother Courage is an actress simultaneously inside and outside the eponymous role. By contrast, Stanislavsky and his Soviet disciples insisted that an actor in rehearsal should 'become' and 'breathe' the character off-stage, round the clock. Stalinism preferred certainties to debates, carved stone to workshop arguments.

This theory of empathy, or 'immersion', is of course older than socialist realism, and variants of it can be found in modern Western dramatic practice—for example, the so-called 'method' school exemplified by Lee Strasberg's Actors Studio in post-war New York. It has also been pointed out that Brecht's own practice as a director was not always faithful to his theory; a shrewd showman, he assessed his audience and what he thought it could absorb. He admired aspects of Stanislavsky's practice. In the opinion of at least one authority, the great performances of the plays Brecht directed contradicted his theory of *Verfremdung*: with Helene Weigel as Courage, Ernst Busch as Galileo, Eckehard Schall as Arturo Ui, both actors and audience completely identified with the characters portrayed.[3] Either way, by the mid-1950s Brecht's plays had been performed virtually everywhere except in the Soviet Union—as Western commentators did not hesitate to point out, even when hostile to Brecht's politics. Walter Laqueur quoted an admission in *Inostrannaia literatura* (no. 12, 1956) that Brecht had been performed all over the world but never in the USSR—except for a not very successful showing of *Die Dreigroschenoper* (*The Threepenny Opera*) at the Kamerny Theatre in or about 1930.[4] A decade later the situation had changed radically: according to *Drama Review* (Fall 1967), nine Brecht productions had been playing in Moscow the previous season.

However, Brecht's life and personality continue to excite almost as much controversy as his plays and productions. To what extent were his plays his own—or did he borrow to the point of outright plagiarism? Did he financially exploit his gifted collaborators? Did his tongue carry him in one direction, his feet in another? Why did he take care to acquire an Austrian passport when settling in the German Democratic Republic? Did he deposit his Stalin Prize money in a Swiss bank? Was he callous and destructive in his relationships with the many women who adoringly worked with and for him? Most of these questions have been raised in recent biographies, long after Brecht's premature death at the age of 58, but most of them were lively cold war issues during his lifetime: is the great Communist writer an opportunist and a hypocrite—or merely a master of dialectical flexibilty?

His masterly play, *Life of Galileo*, is a case in point. Brecht wrote three versions over seventeen years, eventually taking its production into his own hands. First written in 1937–8, *Leben des Galilei* was performed in Zurich's Schauspielhaus in September 1943. Galileo Galilei discovers that Copernicus was correct: the Earth does revolve around the sun—whereas the Church insists that the Earth (and the Church) occupy a uniquely central position in God's universe. Determined that Galileo shall renounce his own theory, the Church finally shows him the instruments of torture when all other means of persuasion have failed. Galileo capitulates and is placed under a civilized 'house arrest', able to pursue his work—but to publish nothing.

Brecht seems to sympathize with Galileo's lack of personal heroism, and with his confidence that true science will prevail in the end, despite repression. 'Happy the land that needs no heroes.' But in the revised version of the play, written in American exile, Galileo is reviled for his betrayal; it's more a case of 'unhappy the land that has no heroes'. Fired up by the cold war and the 'treason' of the American atomic scientists, Brecht now wanted Galileo to condemn himself savagely in his final conversation with his disciple Andrea: 'Then welcome to the gutter, dear colleague in science and brother in treason.' Galileo adds: 'I surrendered my knowledge to those in power, to use, or not to use, or to misuse, just as suited their purposes.'

Charles Laughton, who played the lead in the American production, vigorously resisted this shift of meaning, largely because it undermined the subtlety and cunning of Galileo's personality. Some years later, in East Berlin, the actor Ernst Busch put up similar resistance (Brecht was directing rehearsals of the play when he died). Paradoxically, Brecht had inadvertently turned the moral point away from Marxism in a way entirely typical of the Soviet-led culture of the 1940s, the era of the Great Patriotic War, of Resistance heroes, of *les lendemains qui chantent*. History now depended on the courage, the heroism, of an individual (Galileo). The parallel between Galileo's 'betrayal' and that of the Manhattan Project scientists is hardly convincing. Brecht discovered his disgust about Hiroshima only some time after the bomb was dropped—and only when America's atomic arsenal could be viewed as a threat to the Soviet Union—not a murmur was heard from him in August 1945. Some years later, resident in East Germany, he was eager to press the case even further, rubbing salt into the wound of American liberalism after the persecution and downfall of the physicist J. Robert Oppenheimer. (Brecht's diary entry for 8 July 1954, responding to news from America of Oppenheimer's protracted loyalty-security interrogation, again showed his basic ignorance on this issue.)[5]

Joseph Losey, whom Brecht chose as director of *Galileo* after failing to obtain Orson Welles, spent the last three months of 1946 in New York working with him on pre-production: 'The Hegelian legend *Die Wahrheit ist konkrete*' [The truth is concrete] was tacked in bold letters to the bare wall above the draftsman's bench which constituted Brecht's desk...', Losey reported to Hella Wuolijoki (Finnish originator of Brecht's play *Herr Puntila und sein Knecht Matti*): 'It is such a great play, so clean and clear and architectural... So frighteningly above all of the little squirming talents in our commercial theatre.'[6] Losey later recalled that Brecht was always accompanied by two or three devoted women friends, and that 'he ate very little, drank very little, and fornicated a great deal'.[7] When rehearsals officially began in June, it soon became apparent to the cast and producers that Brecht, with assistance from Charles Laughton, was the effective director, with Losey fetching and carrying. Prowling the theatre in his habitual denims, reeking of cheap cigars, Brecht conducted himself in a style which the producer, John Houseman, described as 'consistently objectionable and outrageous... harsh, intolerant and, often, brutal and abusive. The words *scheiss* and *shit* were foremost in his vocabulary...'[8] Losey described Brecht as 'full of anger and sudden rages, utterly enthusiastic, but opinionated and intolerant...a man-eater, every person, every thing served his art'.

The first American performance of *Galileo* opened at the 260-seat Coronet Theatre, Hollywood, on 30 July 1947, shortly before HUAC launched its full-scale hearings in October.[9] Every performance was standing-room only: 'Turn out for the Theatah', mocked *Variety*. The main problem was the blistering heat. 'Ich muss ein 7-Up haben', declared a dehydrated Brecht, leaving the theatre. When the play closed on 17 August, 4,500 spectators had attended the seventeen performances; the friendly reviews confirmed that elements in the West Coast press could still display a politically 'progressive' (the current term) frame of mind. Lloyd L. Sloane, of the Hollywood *Citizen News*, applauded all concerned. Virginia Wright, drama editor of the Los Angeles *Daily News*, came up with a long and sympathetic article about Brecht's life and work. The *Los Angeles Times*—'An arresting footlight event' —was sympathetic. But there was no shortage of critical notices: Hearst's *Examiner* complained of a 'juvenile fussy harangue', adding: 'Mr Brecht's corn is red.' *Variety*'s complaint can be seen as indirectly ideological: 'Hardly a sigh of sympathy is inspired when Galileo's scientific determination cuts off his daughter's romance. His recantation comes out cut and dried.'

By the time the production opened in New York on 7 December, Brecht had been subpoenaed by HUAC, testified (as will be described later)—and fled from America. Losey received an undated letter from Gartenstrasse 38, Zurich:

Dear Joe, Now, from a distance, I feel even more satisfied with the Coronet perform-ance. L[aughton]'s creation of a dialectical (contradictory, changing) character on the stage, the first of this kind, I believe, is a case of sheer genius. I am sure, the basic content of the play, the *treason* of Galileo, will come out even clearer in N.Y., after our experience of the audience in Hollywood, which led us to the alterations of scene XIII. Of course, it will be necessary to lose nothing of the gay character of the first scenes when the end will be more sinister. On the other side, the more repugnant, criminal, destroy [destroyed?] Galileo (in XIII) will appear, the more positive the highest achievement of this great brain, his self-condemnation, will appear. . . .
Please send copies of the scripts!
greetings from helli![10]

Writing in the *New York Times* (8 December) after the production moved to New York, Brooks Atkinson was less than enthusiastic. The New York edition of *Variety* praised Laughton but not the play, finding it dull, 'too heavy to be digested easily by the majority of ticket buyers'. Lee Newton's review in the *Daily Worker* (10 December), which was duly clipped into Losey's file by the FBI, lost no time in linking HUAC and the Legion of Decency with the Catholic Church's suppression of Galileo's teachings in order to keep the peasantry in cowed ignorance. Taking note of the Epic Theatre technique associated with Brecht and Erwin Piscator, and of the fact that Robert Davison's sets were functional rather than realistic, using projected blow-ups of Michelangelo, Leonardo, and Galileo himself, Newton responded with enthusiasm: the effect of this minimalist decor, of Hanns Eisler's music and of Losey's direction was to concentrate on the essentials. Laugh-ton's studied lack of intensity, his casual intelligence, his insatiable curiosity, his power of concentration, were far removed from the gaudy, showy Laughton of his usual 'Hollywood stuff'.

❖ ❖ ❖

Brecht had been a resident of the United States since 21 July 1941, having been granted a visa by the American vice-consul in Helsinki. FBI surveillance shows his itinerary in detail during 1946–7, when he moved between the West Coast and New York, preparing the revised English version of *Galileo* with Laughton. Professor Alexander Stephan, who received more than 400 pages of Brecht's FBI file under the Freedom of Information Act, remarks that the Bureau, like HUAC, took an exceptional interest in his literary work as well as his contacts within the Free Germany movement. Special Agent in Charge R. B. Hood reported to J. Edgar Hoover on 16 April 1943 that: 'subject is a writer of Communist and revolutionary poetry and drama . . . looked upon by German Communists as their poet laureate.' The FBI concluded that the Free Germany movement 'has as its aim the establishment of a postwar German government favorable to Soviet Russia'. Such thoughts were not merely speculative; the practical purpose was to make a case for Brecht's internment as an enemy alien. He was alleged by undisclosed sources to have worked as 'Technical Advisor concerning the Underground' on Fritz Lang's anti-Nazi film *Hangmen Also Die* (1943). However Assistant Attorney-General Attilio di Girolamo, to whom the FBI recommended Brecht's internment, pointed out that the Soviet Union was an ally of the United States, not an enemy. Brecht was subject to wiretapping in 1945; visits he received from Soviet diplomats based in San Francisco and Los Angeles were duly reported. A 'trash cover' (search of household garbage) was applied to Ruth Berlau in New York in the hope of uncovering secrets about Brecht.[11]

His German colleague Hanns Eisler, who composed the incidental music for *Galileo*, appeared before HUAC under subpoena in May 1947 and again on 24 September. Professor of Music at the New School for Social Research, New York, with a grant from the Rockefeller Foundation, Eisler had supplemented his income by writing film scores. Like Brecht's, his movements and associations remained of keen interest for the FBI. Unrepentant about having composed 'The Comintern March', Eisler was described by HUAC's counsel, Robert Stripling, as 'the Karl Marx of Communism in the music field'. Eisler responded, 'I would be flattered'— adding: 'The Communist underground workers in every country have proven that they are heroes. I am not a hero. I am a composer.' But Stripling insisted that the International Music Bureau, which Eisler had 'organized and reorganized' in 1935, was a section of the Communist International and 'a major program of the Soviet Union in their effort to bring about a world revolution and establish a proletarian dictatorship'.[12] Stripling hammered away: had Eisler actually joined the Communist Party in Germany? The composer repeatedly took evasion behind a formula: he had 'applied' for membership but had 'dropped out'. Stripling wanted to know how one could 'drop out' unless one had first joined.

MR EISLER: I did not really join. I made an application, and I got an answer, but I neglected the whole affair.

THE CHAIRMAN: . . . Were you a member or were you not a member?

This line of inquiry went on and on, stopped, then later resumed—on and on. Eisler admitted he had joined the Party in January 1926, but since he had never paid his dues he had been suspended from membership 'automatically'. But when? After how long? He didn't know. Stripling produced *The Red Song Book*, published by the Workers' Music League, with the hammer and sickle on the front and Eisler's song 'Comintern' on the back. The words (though not Eisler's) were scarcely 'music' to the ears of HUAC, whose members included some of the most reactionary Congressmen from the Deep South:

> The Comintern calls you,
>   Raise high the Soviet banner,
> In steeled ranks to battle
>   Raise sickle and hammer.
> Our answer: Red Legions
>   We raise in our might
> Our answer: Red Storm Troops
>   We lunge to the fight.[13]

Stripling insisted that Hanns Eisler had perjured himself to the Immigration authorities in 1940:

MR STRIPLING: Do you hate Stalin?

MR EISLER: No.

MR STRIPLING: Why did you tell the immigration authorities that you hated Stalin . . . You said, 'I hate Stalin just as I hate Hitler' . . .

MR EISLER: I am surprised . . . I think Stalin is one of the greatest historical personalities of our time.

And why, asked Stripling, had *The Great Soviet Encyclopedia*, published in 1933, volume 63, columns 157–8, described Eisler as 'head of the proletarian movement in German music'? A member of the Committee, Rep. McDowell, engaged the composer in 'dialogue':

'Did you write "The Ballad of the Maimed"?'

'I wrote the music to it.'

'Did you write the words?'

'No. I never write words.'

'Did you write "Ballad of Nigger Jim"?'

'I wrote the music.'
'You didn't write the words?'
'No.'
'You read the words?'
'I read the words.'
'Did you write "Song of the Dry Bread"?'
'Yes. It was in a play.'
'Did you write the words?'
'No. I never write the words.' . . .
'Did you write "Song of Demand and Supply"?' . . .

McDowell asserted that the words of these songs 'couldn't be sent through the mails in the United States . . . such words as are in those sheets have no place in any sort of civilization'. Rep. John Rankin, the rabid racist from Mississippi, called them 'filth'. Eisler protested indignantly. The personal statement that the composer was not allowed to read to HUAC was printed in the *New Masses* on 14 October.[14] HUAC recommended that Eisler be prosecuted for perjury and illegal entry, then deported. Eisler left the United States on 20 March 1948, and settled in East Germany, where he was to become a National Prize-winner and once again a working colleague of Brecht's.

Brecht himself appeared before HUAC in Washington on 30 October 1947. Fearing that hotels were bugged and full of informers (recalled Losey), Brecht and he walked 'the empty streets of that mausoleum city' at night, discussing tactics. Brecht's performance before HUAC was an exercise in cunning—many would say duplicity. He later likened the experience to a zoologist being cross-examined by apes. Although his English was now good, he preferred German and requested an interpreter. David Baumgardt, of the Library of Congress, volunteered, but his English was so thick that the Committee chairman, J. Parnell Thomas, complained, 'I cannot understand the interpreter any more than I can the witness'. Losey advised Brecht to request permission to smoke cigars on the witness stand. Chairman Thomas smoked, they all smoked. Brecht, who was appearing as number eleven of the subpoenaed 'Hollywood Nineteen', charmed and baffled the 'apes' by turn. He denied membership of the Party at any time and explained his collaboration with Hanns Eisler on such songs as 'In Praise of Learning' in terms of the democratic Popular Front spirit of the 1930s. When Committee Counsel Robert Stripling read aloud one of his songs, 'Forward, We've Not Forgotten', then asked him whether he had written it, Brecht replied: 'No, I wrote a German poem, but that is very different from this.'[15]

The heart of Stripling's inquiry was Brecht's collaboration with Eisler on his agit-prop play *Die Massnahme* (*The Measures Taken*), which can be interpreted as endorsing what Auden called 'the necessary murder' for the good of the cause. When Stripling had asked Eisler whether 'Die Massnahme' could be translated as 'the disciplinary measures to be taken', Eisler had agreed. Confronted by the same question, Brecht took refuge in a discussion with his interpreter, who finally answered in the negative.[16] In fact, Brecht's *Lehr-stücke* typically took an idea then carried it, with perfect theatrical symmetry, to its unacceptable conclusion. In *The Measures Taken*, the Mukden Party leader reminds the Agitators: 'One and all of you are nameless and mother-less, blank pages on which the revolution writes its instructions.' But this was far from the Party line—the pious humanism, the quasi-religious memorials, the praise poems erected by the Soviet and German parties to their 'martyrs', who were never nameless and rarely motherless. The mothers of Communist heroes became the subjects of hagiography, like so many Marys experiencing Annunciation.

MR STRIPLING: Now, Mr Brecht, is it true that you have written articles which have appeared in publications in the Soviet zone of Germany within the past few months?

MR BRECHT: I do not remember to have written such articles. I have not seen any of them printed . . .

It turned out that what Stripling had in his hand was not an 'article' but a section from Brecht's play *Furcht und Elend des Dritten Reiches*,[17] published in Alfred Kantorowicz's East Berlin periodical *Ost und West* (July 1947). Stripling asked Brecht whether he knew Kantorowicz: yes, he did. And did he know him to be a member of the German Communist Party? Brecht did not know. Ignorance and amnesia were his best friends.

Brecht agreed that he had twice visited Moscow in the 1930s, and had known the director Sergei Tretyakov, but he claimed to have no memory of his interview with Tretyakov published in *International Literature* (no. 5, 1937). 'It must have been written twenty years ago or so', Brecht explained (in reality, ten years). Shown the interview, he remembered it—indeed Tretyakov had translated some of his plays and poems into Russian. Towards mid-afternoon the Committee congratulated Brecht on his willingness to answer its questions and, unlike the American Hollywood witnesses (the Ten), to avoid trading insults. J. Parnell Thomas sent him on his way (though Stripling had just begun a further question) with 'Thank you very much, Mr Brecht. You are a good example to the witnesses of Mr Kenny and Mr Crum' (the lawyers representing the Nineteen). As Brecht exited left, the Chairman adjourned these famous 'Hollywood' hearings *sine die*—in effect for four years.[18]

Brecht's (uncapitalized) work journal (30 October 1947) expresses no regret: 'it is to my advantage that i had practically nothing to do with hollywood, that i never mixed in american politics, that my predecessors on the witness stand had refused to reply to the congressmen. The 18 are very satisfied with my testimony, and also the lawyers'.[19] But he was not sanguine—as a non-citizen he could be held in custody before deportation, a point he made in a letter to Hanns Eisler; he was sufficiently frightened to forgo the pleasure of attending the imminent transfer of *Galileo* to New York. 'It's like a *Bauern* court in Austria under Dollfuss', he told Losey, and flew to England the following day, travelling on to Switzerland via Paris. His wife Helene Weigel followed.

One of his most hostile recent biographers, John Fuegi, alleges that Brecht 'weakened the case of his colleagues in the Hollywood script-writing community and anybody else who was under attack by this unscrupulous body [HUAC]. As at other moments in history when he could have stood up and been counted, Brecht chose public co-operation...' According to Fuegi, whose hostility toward Brecht is irrepressible, Brecht was 'among the millions whose tacit complicity helped turn the tide toward Hitler, Stalin and McCarthy'.[20] In September 1974 the screenwriter Lester Cole was interviewed by Bruce Cook: 'I was the tenth witness called up, and Brecht was the eleventh. I stayed through his testimony, and we drove back together [to the Shoreham hotel] in a cab... he was in tears because, as he said, he had wanted to take the same position as the rest of us and refuse to answer the Committee's questions... he felt he had betrayed us by taking a different position.'[21] Fuegi cites both Cook and the historian James K. Lyon on the hostility of John Howard Lawson and Albert Maltz to Brecht's decision to testify, yet Lyon actually cites Cook, whom he interviewed in 1976, as having got a different impression from Dalton Trumbo:

Dalton Trumbo is reported to have felt that, in contrast to the others, Brecht in his hearing struck the right balance between belligerence and passivity, while John Howard Lawson, who had not been present at the hearing, remembers how impressed he was when he heard the testimony. Brecht, he felt, was a born theoretician, who had the makings of a great legal mind by the way he led the investigators in circles.[22]

⌗ ⌗ ⌗

In August 1945 the Hebbel Theater, in the American sector of West Berlin, staged the most famous and popular of Brecht's dramatic works, the musical *Die Dreigroschenoper*. From the Soviet zone, *Deutsche Volkszeitung* (18 August) responded with an attack on the decision to stage a play which 'cynically celebrates' the motto, *Erst kommt das Fressen, dann die Moral* (food first, then morality), in front of German audiences in need of moral re-education. Although Brecht's motto had been aimed at the hypocrisy of the bourgeoisie in lecturing the hungry about morality, East Berlin critics like Fritz Erpenbeck argued that the twelve years of Nazism and of moral deformation had liquidated the moral standards which had still been understood in 1930.[23] One of those responsible for the production at the Hebbel Theater, Günther Weisenborn, responded in *Deutsche Volkszeitung* (23 August), arguing that the play was a means of re-establishing a link with pre-Nazi cultural life, and of clearing the minds of a younger generation ignorant of it. In the Soviet sector the Deutsches Theater, run by Gustav von Wangenheim, recently returned from the USSR, announced plans to stage *Leben des Galilei* in February 1946, but nothing came of it, and shortly thereafter the Russians dispensed with von Wangenheim. On 16 May there was a performance of Brecht's *Die Gewehre de Frau Carrer* (*Señora Carrar's Rifles*) and *Der Jasager* (*He Who Says Yes*), once again in the Hebbel Theater. At this juncture Brecht, still resident in America, may have seemed to belong to the West.

After his hasty exit from the United States Brecht remained a resident of Zurich for a year, reluctant to commit his personal security to either Germany. The cultural officer in the Soviet zone, Aleksandr Dymshits, eventually gave the Swiss author Max Frisch a sealed envelope for delivery to Brecht and his wife Helene Weigel (she a Party member, he not), inviting them to settle in Berlin and virtually promising them a theatre. In two articles published in 1947, Dymshits praised Brecht and offered flattering comparisons with Mayakovsky.[24] Brecht's fiftieth birthday in February 1948 was marked by a production of *Furcht und Elend des Dritten Reiches* at the Deutsches Theater under its new *Intendant* Wolfgang Langhoff. A month later Brecht wrote the following in his journal:

16 mar 48
the bourgeoisie is now staging a worldwide mobilisation of intellectuals for a crusade for 'western civilisation' . . . the intellectuals cast a veil over the dictatorial character of bourgeois democracy not least by presenting democracy as the absolute opposite of fascism . . . it is precisely the loss of individual freedom in capitalism that often turns the intellectuals into rabid defenders of a pure mock-up of freedom.[25]

On 22 October 1948 Brecht and Weigel boarded the train for the German frontier. They were allocated quarters in the surviving section of the Hotel Adlon. On 24 June the Russians had cut off all passenger and freight traffic from the Western zones to West Berlin.[26] Awaking before dawn, Brecht took a walk under the incessant roar of Western aircraft breaking the blockade, to smoke a cigar, as Churchill had done before him, in the ruins of Hitler's Chancellery.[27]

In one respect, as his diary records, Brecht's eyes were rapidly opened: still felt acutely among the workers was the impact of 'the raping and plundering after Berlin was overrun...in the working-class quarters they had been looking forward to the liberators with desperate joy, arms outstretched, but the meeting turned into an assault which spared neither the seventeen-year-olds nor the twelve-year-olds, and in public at that'. Red Army behaviour was gallant while the fighting lasted (letting women go for water and bread), but 'after the fighting hordes of drunken soldiers stormed through the houses, hauling out women and shooting men and women who resisted, raping women in front of their children, standing in queues in front of houses...'. Brecht blamed this barbaric behaviour on 'the psychological havoc that Hitler's marauding armies have wreaked on the czar's dehumanised "muschiks" who had only just been exposed to the process of civilisation...the regiments that run amok were mostly peasant regiments from beyond the Urals.' (Brecht had clearly been talking, on arrival, to Dymshits, who appears in the journal as d.)[28] His diary entry for 25 November 1948 reports eleven teeth pulled to make a tabula rasa for dentures, 'since i have been too much hampered in speaking lately'.[29] Then a poem on privilege, dated '7 May 1949', a poem about moving into 'a fine house' amid the ruins. The house was at 190 Berliner Allee in the Weisensee district, where the Brechts lived for the next four years.[30] But when and why did Brecht and Weigel decide to take up permanent residence in East Berlin? According to Hannah Arendt, his first preference was West Germany, preferably Munich, but the American military occupation authorities refused permission. In her opinion Martin Esslin, one of Brecht's biographers, was wrong to claim that Brecht could have gone back to West Germany whenever he wanted. As Benno Frank, the US theater officer in Berlin, later told it to Wigand Lange, he made an effort (*sich eingesetzt*) at the turn of the year 1948 to persuade Brecht to return to the American zone, encouraged by an invitation to the playwright from Erich Engel, *Intendant* of the Munich Kammerspiele. However, this narrative is suspect: Frank offered an improbable chronology in recalling the affair to Lange, and the historian appears not to have noticed the mistakes.[31]

Brecht arrived in East Berlin, according to Arendt, 'well provided against all hazards with a Czech passport soon to be exchanged for an Austrian one, a Swiss bank account, and a West German publisher'. Unfortunate for Brecht, she adds, and unfortunate for Germany.[32] In the words of Jürgen Rühle, he acquired 'all earthly privileges, honours and state prizes, but also—the Inquisition'.[33] The first Brecht production after his arrival, on 11 January 1949, was *Mutter Courage und ihre Kinder* (*Mother Courage*), with music by Paul Dessau, and Helene Weigel in the title role. It was a huge success; the audience wept when Courage's daughter Kattrin is shot; Weigel's silent scream as she is forced to view her son's body brought the Brechtian epic theatre and the starkest tragedy together—even if emotion and Brecht's theatrical instincts had prevailed over his theory of 'alienation'. The acting style remained cool but the impact was hot. At the end the audience stood and wept and clapped as the cast, and Brecht, took countless curtain calls. The following day *Neues Deutschland* ran a piece brimming with praise, hailing him as the most significant creative personality of the modern theatre. In letters to friends, Brecht stressed that cultural affairs officers from all the occupying powers had attended the opening night, and that the press notices in the Western sectors were also good—although this was the winter of the Russian blockade and of the allied airlift. 'Inside Berlin there's unrestricted freedom of movement and it's perfectly peaceful.'[34]

Fuegi reports that Dymshits and the Soviet zone commander, Vladimir Semyonov, were no less enthusiastic. Semyonov took Brecht aside: 'Comrade, Brecht, you must ask for anything you want. Obviously, you are very short of money.' The fact that Brecht had chosen the East over the West, and chosen freely, was arguably the greatest cultural coup achieved by the Communists throughout the entire span of the cold war.[35] But the critic Fritz Erpenbeck (who had spent ten years in the USSR), maintained his implacable hostility in *Die Weltbühne*, accusing Brecht of taking his considerable gifts along 'the path into decadence that is alien to the people'.[36] Wolfgang Harich replied in Brecht's defence, insisting that progressive content could be conveyed in innovative forms, yet Erpenbeck was far from alone in his discontents. The socialist realist dramatist Friedrich Wolf asked why Mother Courage learns nothing, why she is just the same at the end of the play as at the beginning. Why does she keep dragging her cart across the battlefield, losing child after child, never understanding the heartless mechanics of war, uttering the laments of a bereft creature?—this hardly fitted the purposeful enthusiasm for the peace campaign demanded by the Party. In a ritually comradely reply to Wolf, Brecht answered that the play had been written in 1938 when the playwright foresaw a great war and had not been convinced that men would learn the lesson. However, the theatre-going public could learn from Courage's failure to learn. Brecht concluded that the question was how the playwright could best activate the public to get things done (*in Schwung bringen*).[37]

The 'Party inquisition' was now focused on his adaptation of Gorky's celebrated novel of the 1905 Russian revolution, *Die Mütter*.[38] At the 5th Plenum of the Central Committee in March 1951 Fred Oelssner delivered the report on formalism. He praised the power of the mass scenes in Brecht's *Die Mütter* but asked: 'Is this really realism? Are typical characters (*Gestalten*) depicted in typical circumstances (*Umgebung*)?' Oelssner virtually charged the 'gifted' (*begabt*) Brecht with heresy when he declared that this was 'not theatre', this was 'a crossing or synthesis of Meyerhold and Proletkult'. And how could Brecht allow the scene, set in Russia in 1914, when the Mother falls into a panic and jabbers, 'The Party is dying'? Was that an accurate comment on the Bolsheviks? Another high functionary, described by Rühle as 'the intermediary agent (*Vertrauensmann*) of the Soviets in the Sector Theatre', added that Brecht was a brilliant dialectician, but one might ask whether his materialism did not contain 'vulgar elements'. Brecht needed 'more time' to reflect and 'set himself again on the right course' and write 'a play for our time'.[39]

Brecht made it clear that he wanted to acquire his own theatre and his own permanent company. In April 1949 a letter signed by Walter Ulbricht indicated that the politburo of the SED had approved the creation of the Berliner Ensemble company under Helene Weigel's direction. Located in the Deutsches Theater, it would play in Berlin four months a year and spend five touring the Soviet zone. Evidently it was the Russians who forced this through over Ulbricht's suspicions of Brecht. As Fuegi exhaustively documents, Brecht and Weigel were set to enjoy every kind of scarce material privilege available to the East German elite: a car, spacious accommodation, fine furniture, servants, hard currency, travel documents, freedom to negotiate contracts in West Germany and further afield. Brecht was in a position to negotiate joint publication of his work by the West German publisher Suhrkamp and the East Berlin Aufbau Verlag. On 28 August 1949 he travelled to Salzburg on an interzonal pass issued by the Russians, then went on for discussions in Munich and Augsburg—evidently the civil authorities in the West were more relaxed about BB than the US Military Government had been. At the Munich Oktoberfest he encountered a student song about the 'Saujud', the Jewish swine, and furiously declared to his companion, Eric Bentley: 'And they say these people have changed! Good liberals now, are they?'[40] A month later the Berlin Ensemble scored a triumph with its opening production, *Herr Puntila und sein Knecht Matti*, somewhat borrowed (without acknowledgement) from the Finnish writer Hella Wuolijoki, whom Brecht had visited while in exile.

13 Nov 49

the first night of puntila last night was greeted with laughter and many curtains. the russians left the centre box to the new government, who joined in the laughter and applause. The BERLINER ENSEMBLE—as a symbol of our theatre we had picasso's dove of peace sewn on the curtain at the deutsches theater... the mode of acting is wholly accepted by the press ('if that is epic theatre, fine'). it is of course only as epic as they can take (and we can offer) today.[41]

On 1 May 1950 he watched from the official stands as the Berliner Ensemble took part in the demo at the Lustgarten: 'the BE rolls by on its lorry, barbara [Brecht's daughter] sitting in courage's wagon and waving a red flag. helli is greeted in every street, women holding up their children. 'that's mother courage!'[42]

The eightieth anniversary of the Paris Commune came round in 1951, a sacred event in the Communist calendar. Of Brecht's *Die Tage der Kommune* (*The Days of the Commune*), written in Zurich in 1948–9, the Party critic Herbert Ihering commented that the play's fatal failing was typical of Brecht: he had not depicted a human conflict but a sociological and doctrinaire one, a tendency exacerbated by the years of exile. The Central Committee and the Karl Marx Party Institute (Parteihochschule) condemned the play as *objektivistisch* and *defaitistisch*. The play was banned.[43]

Matters got worse. In March 1951 Brecht's musical drama *Das Verhör des Lukullus* (*The Trial of Lucullus*), whose libretto dated from 1937, was closed after one performance following an attack by *Neues Deutschland*—mainly because of its blanket condemnation of war and the modern idiom of Paul Dessau's music.[44] Following his death and pompous burial as a war criminal (*Kriegsverbrecher*), the Roman general Lucullus appears before a Shadow Tribunal which has mustered for hideous display the slaughtered sacrifices of his much praised campaign.[45] According to Rühle, the first performance at the Staatsoper was packed with Party officials, Volkspolizei, and officials of Freie Deutsche Jugend, all there in support of 'the endangered Party line', but the first night brought applause from young spectators selected more for their interest in music than for their political standpoint.[46] The representatives of the regime, meanwhile, 'slunk out of their boxes'. The Party complained about the absence of violins, 'this most noble of all instruments', no oboes or clarinets, but nine percussion instruments, including large and small drums and metal discs struck with stones. Dessau was accused of underestimating the role of melody and harmony, indeed of ignoring it—one could only conclude that this was no accident but a conscious promotion (*bewussten Einstellung*) of formalism.[47] Further performances were banned.

Under pressure Brecht began to display the string-pulling sycophancy towards Communist potentates that his Western detractors made much of. On 12 March he wrote to Walter Ulbricht: 'The opera is a unique condemnation of wars of conquest, and given the shameless way in which West Germany is mustering former generals with a view to a new invasion, such a work . . . is worth producing in a city like Berlin, whence its influence will radiate powerfully to the West . . . May I ask you to help me?'[48] Brecht and his illustrious composer, Paul Dessau,[49] were hauled in on 14 March to meet the three most senior Communists, Ulbricht, Otto Grotewohl, and Wilhelm Pieck. After an eight-hour discussion with the authorities, Brecht emerged with the famous quip: 'Where else in the world is there a government which shows so much interest and care in their artists!'[50] On 19 March he wrote to Paul Wandel, Minister for People's Education: 'We are deeply grateful to you for [authorizing] the performance of *Lucullus* before an audience of the most progressive elements of our republic . . . Your generosity in putting the magnificent resources of the State Opera at our disposal and your engagement of a world-famous conductor . . .' On the same day he again wrote, humbly, to Ulbricht, suggesting that the qualities in Dessau's score 'which may make the music difficult for the new public are in the last analysis superficial, and that the composer with his great talent and his devotion to this public will undoubtedly be able to rid himself of these qualities. His aim is an intelligent, realistic people's opera, which will generate new socialist impulses.'[51] On 6 April Brecht wrote to Pieck enclosing reworked passages and thanking him for his criticisms. Again the East–West cold war tension was in evidence: Brecht assured Pieck that Dessau had rejected an offer from the Cologne Opera to perform the work.

The rewritten version surfaced as *Die Verurteilung des Lukullus* (*The Condemnation of Lucullus*)—but the Party was still not satisfied, and the enterprise ended with a couple of formal presentations at the Staatsoper. According to Rühle, Brecht was free to allow productions of 'the original pacifist version' in the West, with Dessau's musical score unaltered, including the liturgical arias and recitative which had to be altered in the East.[52]

For the August 1951 World Youth Festival, held in East Berlin, Egon Monk staged Brecht's agit-prop documentary drama *Herrnburger Bericht* (*Herrenburg Report*), based on an incident when Young Communists had been prevented by West German police from travelling to attend a demonstration in East Berlin. On the far side of the Iron Curtain, Peter Demetz, associate professor of German at Yale, writing in the USIA's magazine *Problems of Communism* after Brecht's death, described the piece as 'a trashy anti-Adenauer cantata which should be prescribed reading for uncritical American Brecht enthusiasts' and as 'a further humiliating price he had to pay for survival'.[53] Brecht wrote a 'Ballade für Chor' which got only five performances before, according to his diary, it was 'suppressed'.[54] He noted in his journal:

21 aug 51
they tell me the members of the government were satisfied with the HERRNBURG REPORT, though grotewohl is supposed to have made an interesting objection. he objected to 'something academic' about it ... the desire that artistic expression should merely be heightened expression, and should not turn into a different quality, namely that of art. they want people to write—or paint, or make music—from the heart.[55]

By the end of 1951 Brecht had been awarded the National Prize for Literature and 50,000 marks in cash. The grant of Austrian citizenship in April 1950 was kept hush-hush until the United States leaked the information in October 1951. Brecht bought a house on a lake at Buckow. The hostile Fuegi reports: 'The estate was and is surrounded on the landward side by a high fence and is prominently marked Private—No Entry.'[56]

A letter dated 18 January 1952 summarizes Brecht's political overview. The GDR had achieved 'expulsion of the Prussian junkers, distribution of the land, ending of the bourgeois monopoly on education, schooling of the proletarian youth'. But the weak point attracting critical attention in the West was 'the GDR's art and philosophy'. However: 'If only because of the economic and political upheavals, no one in his right mind can expect the new system to function without errors and slip-ups in the cultural field.'[57] Conspicuously absent from this is any principled objection to government and Party control of the arts. He never managed to write the Brechtian aphorism: 'Our mistakes were not the actions taken. We were the mistake.'

On 23 February 1953 the Stasi arrested one of Brecht's young colleagues, Martin Pohl, a homosexual in his early twenties who at the end of the war, when 15, had seen his mother and younger brother burned to death in a building by the SS. Brutally interrogated by the Stasi, Pohl was made to sign a confession that he was a US intelligence agent. According to Fuegi, it was not until July that Brecht wrote privately to the justice minister conveying 'great uneasiness' within the Ensemble as a result of Pohl's arrest. *Urfaustus*, directed by Egon Monk, on which Pohl had worked, was taken off after six performances. Ulbricht personally entered the arena on 27 May 1953: 'We will not allow that one of the most important works by our greatest German writer, Goethe, is formalistically raped...'[58] *Neues Deutschland* described the play as 'marionetteish' and lacking 'deep human feeling', and as guilty of 'garishness' (*Grelle*) and 'formlessness'. Brecht received a letter from the Academy of Arts cutting off his monthly stipend. On 4 March he noted in his journal: 'our performances in berlin have almost no resonance any more. the press notices appear months after the first night . . . the public is the petty-bourgeois public of the volksbühne, workers make up scarcely 7 per cent of it.'[59]

Then came the East Berlin uprising, the first worker-led insurrection against Soviet rule since the war, prompting from Brecht his famously con-tradictory response, a source of Western mockery for the three years remaining to him and for years beyond the grave. To understand this, we need briefly to point up both the reality and the general Western image of life in the Soviet zone. A junior minister in the Attlee government, Christopher Mayhew, told UNESCO that 200,000–300,000 prisoners were held in Soviet-zone camps; he claimed that since the war Stalin's MVD (Ministry of Internal Affairs) had imprisoned more people than Hitler did in the same territory during his twelve years in power. An editorial in the *Manchester Guardian* (23 February 1949) described the MVD's activities in the Soviet zone as similar to the Gestapo's, except 'in their scope and in their appallingly haphazard methods'. Ten years earlier the Nazi commandant of Buchenwald had known who his prisoners were and why they had been arrested, but the Russians displayed chaotic indifference to their own Buchenwald prisoners. On 7 January 1950 the *Yorkshire Post* estimated that the East German popula-tion of 18 million had declined by 3 per cent during 1949. Westward migra-tion was one factor, but deaths were exceeding births by 50,000 a year. Industrial output was at about 60 per cent of the 1936 level, compared with 98 per cent in the West, largely due to the Soviet policy of carting away industrial plant and skilled labour, but also to chaotic planning. 'Red Gestapo to rule the East,' announced the *Daily Express* (9 February 1950). The *New York Times* (5 November) reported the creation of a Ministry of State Security under Wilhelm Zaisser, a hero of the Spanish Civil War, with unlim-ited powers of arrest and imprisonment.

According to Louis Halle, between 1949 and 1961 over 2.6 million people departed East Germany (out of a 1949 population of 17.5 million). The Western Allies and the West German government actively encouraged the exodus, mainly through West Berlin. The brain-drain of doctors, dentists, pharmacists, and teachers was threatening a breakdown in essential services, while the flight of farmers was threatening a crisis in food production.[60] André Fontaine described the two Berlins:

In East Berlin, along streets empty of cars, ruins were only slowly being rebuilt. When night came, inadequate lighting gave them a sinister aspect which was reinforced by the long red and blue streamers which, with complete disregard of aesthetics, bore the heavy-handed slogans of a regime which had concentrated all its efforts on a gigantic plan of industrialization.[61]

West Berlin, by contrast, was 'a city of light, brightly glowing in the middle of the Red night'. The Soviet writer Ilya Ehrenburg, whose memories of Berlin reached back further than most, despised the Western glitter; serious theatregoers, he said, crossed into the Eastern sector, where he himself met Brecht, Anna Seghers, and Arnold Zweig: 'The West Berlin papers attacked them, saying they had "sold out to Moscow", were "careerists" and "trimmers". This was silly...'[62] For Brecht himself the Western sector, the 'city of light', was the city of revanchism. Brecht's old colleague and mentor from the Weimar Republic, the director Erwin Piscator,[63] reluctantly settled in West Germany in 1951 after some years in America. 'It stinks', he wrote to a friend. He found no evidence that West Germans were trying to learn the lesson of the Nazi era—as evidenced by their taste for Anouilh, Giraudoux, Fry, and Eliot, then later Beckett and Ionesco.[64] Such dovetailed composites—Germans refusing to acknowledge war guilt while sitting in a theatre 'waiting for Godot'; Americans protecting I. G. Farben while promoting T. S. Eliot on the Ku'damm—proved seductive to minds schooled in the Marxist doctrine of infrastructure and superstructure; everything is connected to, and the product of, everything else (one way or another, as Engels might have put it).

The immediate cause of the uprising which began on 17 June 1953 was neither Beckett nor Eliot; it was the Ulbricht government's inept squeeze on the working class: higher production norms, less pay. Worse, these norms had been hastily retracted only to be suddenly reimposed. 'When men fight under the banner of liberty they are fighting and dying for all of us', declared the *New York Times* on 18 June. On 21 June the London *Sunday Times* spoke of 'the intense hatred in the Russian zone for Russia and Russian rule and above all for the complaisant German puppets through whom the zone is administered'. By contrast, the official SED newspaper *Neues Deutschland* kept referring, day after day, to 'der faschistische Putschversuch am 17 Juni im demokratischen Sektor von Berlin'. The threat of 'fascism' had become the swollen alibi—or blackmail—of a regime whose own behaviour owed much to Hitler's legacy. In France *L'Humanité* (3 July) described the events in Berlin as a provocation perpetrated by 'the fascist mercenaries of the Western powers, using methods combined from Nazi assassins and American gangsters'. The London *Daily Worker* (23 June) and *L'Unità* ploughed the same furrow. According to *Soviet News* (23 June), the London *Economist* gave the game away when it declared: 'Here, surely, is the kind of climax towards which the propaganda of the BBC, the Voice of America and Radio Free Europe have been working for years...'

Brecht agreed. On 17 June, eager to view at first hand what was happening on the streets, he and his assistant Manfred Wekwerth watched the Russian tanks advance down the Stalinallee from the Brandenburg Gate, preceded by a jeep from which a high-ranking Soviet officer waved at the crowd. According to Wekwerth, Brecht waved back. Returning to the Ensemble, he called a meeting and discussed the situation. He then addressed identical letters to Walter Ulbricht, Otto Grotewohl, and the Soviet commandant, the (unpublished) text of which is believed to have run as follows:

History will pay due respect to the revolutionary impatience of the Socialist Unity Party. The great discussion with the masses about the tempo of socialist construction will lead to a sifting and securing of our socialist achievements. At the moment I feel the need to express my solidarity with the Socialist Unity Party.

Neues Deutchland (21 June) printed only the last sentence:

National Prize Laureate Bertolt Brecht has sent ... Walter Ulbricht a letter, in which he declared: 'At the moment I feel the need to express my solidarity with the Socialist Unity Party.'

Brecht followed up with a telegram to Ulbricht, in which he (famously) expressed the hope that

the provocateurs will be isolated, and their networks destroyed, but that the workers who had demonstrated with their justifiable grievances, will not be placed on the same footing as the provocateurs, so that the great discussion about errors committed on all sides may not break down at the start.[65]

However, this telegram was not published. In the West, Brecht's support for the regime caused indignation, uproar, and a boycott of his work. His West German publisher, Peter Suhrkamp, wrote anxiously asking him to clarify his attitude. Brecht replied on 1 July with an exceptionally long letter which offered a relatively balanced account, but once again evaded the central problem of the one-party state and the state-controlled press and radio. Evidently Brecht believed that the working class deserved better in the material sphere, but top-down; he always declined to question the democratic legitimacy of the SED's control of the state. Free elections never interested Brecht. Hadn't they brought Hitler to power?

The workers had reason to be embittered [he wrote to Suhrkamp]. The unfortunate, unintelligent measures taken by the government in an attempt to precipitate the development of heavy industry in the GDR outraged peasants, artisans, tradesmen, workers and intellectuals alike. [Brecht went on to detail these measures.] Yet even in the early hours of 17 June the streets displayed a grotesque mixture of workers not only with all sorts of déclassé youth, who poured through the Brandenburg Gate, across the Potsdamer Platz... but also with gross, brutish figures from the Nazi era. [Bookshops had been stormed and the works of Marx and Engels burned.] Fire is not the weapon of people who build. All day long RIAS suspended its regular programmes, broadcasting incendiary speeches, with refined voices mouthing the word 'freedom'. [Brecht had heard] *Deutschland über Alles* resounding from middle-class voices and the workers on the roadway drowning it out with the Internationale.

He would continue to support the SED against 'the proponents of fascism and war'.[66] Brecht's 'Buckow Elegies' contain a poem, 'The Solution', with its now-famous, ironic comment on the uprising:

> After the uprising of the 17 June
> The Secretary of the Writers' Union
> Had leaflets distributed in the Stalinallee
> Stating that the people
> Had forfeited the confidence of the government
> And could win it back only
> By redoubled efforts. Would it not be easier
> In that case for the government
> To dissolve the people
> And elect another?[67]

On the other hand, the hypocrites in the West must be exposed, with their 'deafening thunder of applause | From beyond the Sector boundary' in support of criticisms of Communist institutions. In Brecht's ear the Western cry of 'Freedom for the artists! Freedom all round!' was a 'Judas kiss' meaning 'Freedom for the exploiters! Freedom for the warmongers! Freedom for the Ruhr cartels! Freedom for Hitler's generals!' And thus:

> The Judas kiss for the artist follows
> Hard on the Judas kiss for the workers...[68]

Brecht had made his bed in the East and intended to lie in it. Vigorously opposed to West German rearmament, he signed appeals to theatre-people in the West urging them to resist. For this he was awarded a Stalin Peace Prize in 1954; he received it in Moscow in May of the following year, his first venture into the USSR for almost two decades. While in Moscow he saw Mayakovsky's recently revived *Bathhouse* at the Theatre of Satire, and was delighted to find 'alienation effects everywhere'. But the odour of stale Stalinist aesthetics still lingered:

in the art theatre [Moscow Art Theatre] the same evening, where mostly younger actors are performing MUCH ADO ABOUT NOTHING under a pupil of stanislavsky's. 'traditional' (within the bad tradition of the 80s), with hollow emotions, petty bourgeois inwardness, garden-gnome comedy and the usual coarse jibes at a major-domo who believes he has to love his mistress. of stanislavsky's sense of naturalness and truth, no trace.

[But on another occasion]: in the art theatre saw ostrovsky's THE PASSIONATE HEART WITH ENORMOUS PLEASURE. all stanislavsky's greatness made apparent.[69]

According to Martin Esslin, Brecht 'deposited a large proportion of his 160,000 rubles of [Stalin] prize money in his Swiss bank account, to the undisguised dismay and fury of the East German party stalwarts'.[70]

The Berliner Ensemble now enjoyed a budget of 3 million marks, five-sixths of it from a state subsidy, supporting a staff of 212 people including fifty-five actors. In March 1954 the company had taken over the riverside Schiffbauerdamm (the 'Schiff'), the 890-seat, nineteenth-century theatre where Brecht had enjoyed his great successes three decades earlier and on which he had long set his heart. It was only now that he could stage for the first time in Berlin *The Caucasian Chalk Circle* (*Der Kaukasische Kreidekreis*), the most complex of his unperformed plays. The production travelled to Paris in 1955 and to London the following year, days after Brecht's death.

One can scarcely exaggerate the international prestige of the Berliner Ensemble and the lustre it brought to the East German regime. The Ensemble took *Mère Courage* to the Paris International Festival of Dramatic Art, at the Théâtre des Nations, in the summer of 1954 and was rewarded with first prize for the best play. *Le Cercle de craie caucasien* followed in 1955.[71] Sartre went to see the productions:

In this sense, one could almost say that Brecht is too 'formalist'. Or, rather, that if he isn't for his own public, for the politicized crowds (*pour des foules politisées*), that's to say who already know, he would risk being so for us, for a public as invertebrate as ours... I recognize that Brecht has been the only one to pose the problems of the theatre in their true terms, the only one to have understood that all popular theatre could only be political theatre, the only one to have given thought (*réfléchi*) to a *technique* of popular theatre.[72]

The year after Brecht died, Sartre saluted his doctrine that: 'There is no such thing as individual salvation: society must change entirely; and the function of the dramatist remains the "purification" of which Aristotle spoke; it reveals us for what we are: victims and accomplices at the same time.'[73]

Brecht was now established as the genius of his generation. Every word he spoke during rehearsals was being written down for posterity. 'Visitors from all over Europe came to East Berlin to watch Brecht at work as he sat in his special director's chair in the front row of the auditorium.'[74] And yet he remained embittered. At the 4th Writers' Congress in 1956, shortly before his death, he declared: 'The theatres of the German Democratic Republic are—regrettably from my point of view—among the few theatres in Europe that do not perform my plays.' Before his arrest the philosopher and theatre critic Wolfgang Harich[75] recalled in the manifesto he wrote for young SED dissidents: 'In our frequent discussions with Bertolt Brecht we could see how bitterly he felt about the conditions around us.'

In the summer of 1956 the Berliner Ensemble arrived in London to perform three Brecht plays at the Palace Theatre. Brecht himself was too ill to travel: he died on 14 August, three days before the company reached London. Newly declassified documents reveal that the Foreign Office had been in-clined to ban the visit:

We do not recognize [East Germany] and the purpose of a visit by the Berliner Ensemble would be to build up that regime's prestige. Interesting though it would be for a sophisticated London audience to see *The Caucasian Chalk Circle*, it would be even better from HMG's[76] point of view if the BBC's Welsh listeners were allowed to listen to their wirelesses without interference from the DDR.

The Home Office argued (23 April 1956) against a ban, having already admitted a party of East German athletes: 'to refuse a visa now to the Berliner Ensemble would look reactionary.' The Foreign Office conceded that a ban would conflict with free movement of ideas, 'which has always been one of our most powerful arguments against the Soviet system'.[77]

A classic attack on Brecht, delivered at a high intellectual level, was launched in the pages of *Encounter* days (as it so chanced) before the death of the target. The bitterness aroused by Brecht within the Congress for Cultural Freedom was not unlike that excited by Sartre: their talent and prestige in Western Europe was regarded as far more subversive than any-thing the Russians could offer. Herbert Luthy's long article, ' "Of Poor Bert Brecht" ', displayed its naked grievance in an early paragraph:

The vogue of Bertolt Brecht, whose 'didactic plays' no longer bob up for a moment in little avant-garde theatres but who has become the playwright, and above all, the house-ideologist, of the Théâtre National Populaire in France, and who passes for a dramatic oracle in the world of the 'progressive' theatre in London and New York, is a product of this archaeological revolution.

What did he mean? According to Luthy, the self-destructive Weimar culture had been reborn after 1945, not only in Germany but also in France, 'where existentialism, Kafka, Marxian exegesis, and "the decline of the West" combined to produce a mixture of near Weimarian *Weltschmerz*'. Luthy pointed to the paradox whereby 'nowhere in the whole zone of Communist domination, with the single exception of the privileged "show-window" that is Berlin, is a single play of Brecht's ever presented'. From 'this Brecht's rank hypocrisy followed:

The subsidies for his work that he receives from the East German Government are paid into his Swiss bank account in dollars—as was the Stalin prize he won in 1954. Even the ideologically 'purified' versions of his works appear in editions authorised by a West German publishing firm and are paid for in Western currency into the same bank account. The way back has been kept open.

Beyond our immediate concerns are Luthy's sensitive exploration of Brecht's early work, of the 'smuggler's path' from the heritage of the medieval and baroque drama, with its verbal extravagance and proliferating metaphors, to the expressionism of the young Brecht and his play *Baal*; likewise Brecht's passion for blasphemously parodying German hymns. Excellent is Luthy's ear for Brecht's anarchist phase, the biting satire of the poem 'Legend of the Dead Soldier', and for the laughing, mocking, pre-Marxist social criticism of *Mann ist Mann*. Clearly it appealed to Luthy that: 'The dead soldier [of 1918] has no intention of shouldering his rifle again for some other cause—certainly not for the revolutionary Spartacus Bund.' But then came Brecht's fatal turning: the expressionist ballad singer became an ascetic pedant: 'All Brecht's lyric strength was abruptly buried under the weight of the revelation that the poet's task is to "change the world" and "teach the people".' This 'threadbare doctrine' provided Brecht during the ensuing twenty-nine years (1927–56) with no communicable vision of the future socialist society. Fatally for Brecht's art, the 'lostness and isolation of man' became 'the alienation of the worker from his product'. Thus Brecht's refusal to despair ontologically on behalf of Man caused despair in the ranks of the Congress for Cultural Freedom—how could art survive any weakening of a necessary lyrical pessimism?

What fascinated Brecht, according to Luthy's (not uncommon) view, was not the goal and ethos of Communism but 'its harsh, inhuman discipline as an end in itself'. Once again *Die Massnahme* is held up as the supreme example, ignoring the fact that Brecht's play, like his contemporary André Malraux's famous novel *La Condition humaine*, proved utterly unacceptable in orthodox Communist circles because far too lucid and coolly geometrical in its exploration of the conflict between personal sentiment and public duty. Stalinist aesthetics in every country distrusted this lucidity, preferring a romantic fusion of heroic behaviour (which Luthy himself rightly calls 'plush and flowers'). The full extent of Luthy's bias is discovered when he juxtaposes lines from *Die Massnahme* with transcripts from the Moscow trials of five years later. Yet what separated Brecht's fictional agitators from Stalin's very real prosecutors like Vyshinsky and policemen like Beria was the latters' banal insistence that the defendants had really done this or that wicked, blood-soaked, conspiratorial deed—rather than pursuing the idea of a para-doxical 'objective' guilt transcending the actual facts—a concept explored (with sharply varying conclusions) by a succession of Western intellectuals, including Brecht, Koestler, Sartre, and Merleau-Ponty. Luthy's claim that in *Die Massnahme* there is 'only one crime worthy of death: to obey one's own conscience, to maintain one's own will, to do the right thing without being ordered to by the Party', ignores the fact that Brecht stacks the cards in such a way that we the audience are bound to embrace the executed hero. Luthy admitted that no Communist country or organization has ever staged the play—'The Party itself does not like so much candour...'—but failed to notice that Brecht's 'candour' in exposing the ruthlessness of the Party line is incompatible with subscribing to it. The true believers invariably kept their knowledge to themselves.

Moving forward in time to Brecht's exile from Nazi Germany, Luthy drew attention to his reluctance to settle in the USSR in the 1930s; the 'small door' for escape he saw in one of his poems—*Sehe ich noch eine kleine Tür*—could not be Finland's long frontier with the Soviet Union. Skipping Brecht's American years and (rather conveniently) his encounter with HUAC, Luthy arrived at the 'shop window' of East Berlin, where Brecht was part of the display: 'And so he sits, surrounded by the secret odour of heresy, sedition, decadence, formalism, and objectivism, tolerated for his propaganda value and gently scolded for his wilfulness—and armed, moreover, with the Austrian citizen-ship he foresightedly acquired...on the very outermost limb of the free world—busily sawing it through.' Despite its political hostility, Luthy's long essay displayed an impressive sensitivity to Brecht's *oeuvre*, poetic as well as dramatic. A small pity, therefore, that the editors of *Encounter* chose to fill the space on the last page with a poem called 'Hubris', so crude as barely to qualify for a school magazine.[78]

⊞ ⊞ ⊞

Brecht never wrote a play about life in the GDR. One intended subject was the Stakhanovite industrial worker hero Hans Garbe, an employee of a Siemens–Plania factory who risked his life in 1949–50 to rebuild a broken kiln before it was fully cooled down, serving the Five Year Plan and saving the company a lot of money. To his worker colleagues, however, he was not a hero but a *Lohndrücker* (scab)—literally, one who depresses wages by working too hard and devaluing the labour of others. Brecht never finished the text, despite extensive research into the oven incident by his assistant Käthe Rülicke. The subject was taken up by an admiring writer thirty years his junior, Heiner Müller, in his provocatively titled play *Der Lohndrücker*, written in 1956 and first performed in Leipzig two years later, even though it raised such sensitive questions as incentives under socialism, and socialism blindly exploiting the German ethic of efficiency lauded by the Nazis.[79]

One of the last letters Brecht wrote (9 August 1956) was to the Iskusstvo Publishing House, in Moscow. Too exhausted to write a preface to the Soviet edition of his plays, he suggested they use his poem 'To the Actors' instead.[80] In July 1957, less than a year after his death, the Berliner Ensemble arrived in Moscow for the first time with productions of *Mother Courage*, *The Caucasian Chalk Circle*, and *Galileo*, all highly praised.[81] Having attended a production of *The Threepenny Opera* at the Lenin Komsomol Theatre in Leningrad, Harrison Salisbury of the *New York Times* adopted Brecht and held up the Tyrone Guthrie Theatre, Minneapolis, as the Mecca of Brecht presentation. 'As recently as five years ago hardly a single Brecht production was to be found in all of Russia . . .' This 'Brecht the artist belongs to us' motif was to become an odd, seemingly perverse, theme of Western critics otherwise hostile to Brecht's politics. He was 'East' in the German context but 'West' in the Soviet context. In Yuri Lyubimov's 1963 production of *The Good Woman of Setzuan*, the Chinese element was virtually eliminated; everything was recognizably Soviet. Brecht's songs were Russified: 'The sheep step into line, the drums beat out . . . And the sheep themselves supply the drumskins.' Lyubimov argued that the play was a parable about the impossibility of existing in an unjust class society, while Konstantin Simonov, writing in *Pravda* (8 December 1963), called it 'a frontal—yes, frontal—attack on capitalist ideology and morality', a 'gust of fresh air.'[82]

The CIA may have agreed; the Agency took Brecht's ghost seriously enough to set up a mail cover operations in the early sixties on 'Helen [*sic*] Weigel', who was suspected of teaching American slang to the East German police: 'Arrange for coverage of correspondence between persons in U.S. and Helen Brecht by Communications Intercept Service. This coverage should include correspondence to her son [Stefan] at Chausseestr. 125, Berlin.'[83]

Brecht's ambivalent response to the uprising of June 1953 refused to be buried with the playwright. Ten years after his death, Günter Grass published a play, *Die Plebejer proben den Aufstand* (*The Plebeians Rehearse the Uprising*), which imagined the fictitious convergence of two events:

—Brecht is directing his adaptation of Shakespeare's *Coriolanus*, including the revolt of the plebs;
—when a genuine uprising occurs in the socialist city beyond the doors of the theatre.

Brecht appears in *The Plebeians* not by name but as the Boss of the theatre. To obtain greater realism for his production of *Coriolanus*,[84] he has been encouraging his actors to listen to tape-recordings of contemporary plebs—for example, housewives grumbling outside a government store. When news of a real uprising reaches the Boss, he doubts its seriousness but seizes on the opportunity to encourage his actors to get outside and observe the faces of the marchers. 'We'll learn from those faces.' But the Boss remains, for all that, a prisoner of theatrical illusions—his world remains the stage. When real workers enter the theatre and demand his support, he is nonplussed. 'You stand for something', says the Mason. 'Can't get around it. Everybody listens to you.' The actress playing Volumnia encourages him: 'A few words from you will give their stammering meaning.' The Boss replies: 'Too much pointing crimps the fingers.'

Pressed by the workers, the Boss expresses contempt for their modest demands about work norms and wage levels. Real revolution is a serious business, history teaches us. Scornfully he asks the workers' delegation whether they have occupied the radio station, called a general strike, over-powered the Vopos, and sent reassuring messages to the Soviets. If not, back down quickly, go home.

Shakespeare's ancient Rome remains more vivid and important to him than his own city. He keeps translating real life, here and now, back into art, there and then. Meanwhile he is under pressure from the Party function-ary Kozanke, who likens the rising to the Kronstadt mutiny: 'The rats are coming up for air.' But Kozanka, modelled by Grass on Kuba, a prominent Stalinist member of the East German Academy of Arts, is in a panic: 'We need you. Only your name, your words can help us.'

The workers become enraged by the Boss's equivocations and threaten to hang him on the spot.

When the rising is suppressed, Kozanke's tone changes from wheedling to threats: display open support for the Party or lose your theatre. Finally the Boss composes a document: the first two sentences are critical of the Party, the third proclaims his solidarity. Volumnia predicts that only the third will be printed.

'No one will dare to censor me', he declares.

Speaking in West Berlin on 23 April 1964, to mark the 400th anniversary of Shakespeare's birth, Grass lamented that Brecht had by the end of his life become a 'kind of privileged court jester'.[85] Frederic Ewen attempted a defence of Brecht in the left-wing weekly *The Nation:* 'Alas, poor B.B.!...There are people who cannot forgive him for not having chosen the West, so they must paint a Brecht who sold out to the East—for a theatre!'[86] In his poorly informed *Bertolt Brecht: His Life, His Art and His Times* (1967), Ewen adopted a cold war-style rearguard polemical advocacy of Brecht by targeting the icons of the Western avant-garde and the theatre of the absurd, an oddly outdated procedure in the New York of the late sixties:

Can Brecht's advocacy of reason and intelligence counterpoise the liturgies of the brothel and the litanies of self-castration and illusion promulgated by Jean Genêt [*sic*: Genet]? Or Eugene Ionesco's 'existential vacuum' and his pyrotechnic and necrophilic world of absurdity? Or bring relief to the heartbreak of Samuel Beckett and his last sacraments administered to a crippled and blinded humanity? A humanity living in figurative dustbins and refuse heaps, hopeless relics of aborted civilization?[87]

⌗ ⌗ ⌗

It became increasingly clear, as the archives were opened, that the exiled Brecht of the Nazi emigration had been a tactical writer, whose most explicit criticisms of Stalinism and the purges were not intended for immediate publication. The incomplete *Me-Ti* (or Book of Changes) voiced his most private criticisms of the corrupting effect of Stalinism on foreign Communist parties, and of Stalin worship.

Among his sharpest political critics was Hannah Arendt, fellow of the American Academy of Arts and Sciences and of the Deutsche Akademie für Sprache und Dichtung. Although she speaks of 'this great poet and play-wright', endowed with poetic intelligence and the 'supreme gift of conden-sation which is the prerequisite of all poetry', she was scathing in her condemnation of Brecht's decision to live and work in East Germany.[88] While living in a totalitarian state, she pointed out, he wrote not a single original play or great poem. 'He had stumbled into a situation in which his very silence—let alone his occasional praise of the butchers—was a crime.' Her posthumous profile of Brecht in the *New Yorker* presented his cardinal sin as 'his ode to Stalin and his praise of Stalin's crimes, written and published while he was in East Berlin but mercifully omitted from the collection of his works'. Furthermore, immediately after Stalin's death, Brecht had described him as 'the incarnation of hope' for 'The oppressed of five continents, those who have already freed themselves and all who are fighting for world peace must have felt their heart stop beating when they heard that Stalin is dead. He was the embodiment of their hopes.'

Had not Brecht exposed his own guilt about this? Hannah Arendt offered her own English version of 'Nasty Morning': 'Last night in a dream I saw fingers pointing at me as though I were a leper. They were worn and they were broken. "You don't know!" I cried, conscious of guilt.'[89]

John Willett, who was by no means convinced of Brecht's guilt, entered into correspondence with Hannah Arendt on these highly charged issues. Willett poses the questions, Arendt answers:

Q: What have you in mind when you speak of an 'ode' or 'odes' to Stalin?
A: It is indeed difficult to find Brecht's odes to Stalin because they are not included in his Collected Works . . . If you look at *Sinn und Form* II 5 (1950), you will find an example of what I allude to in my essay.[90]
Q: Where does Brecht praise Stalin's crimes?
A: If you know Brecht's prose works, especially *Me-Ti* which was published posthumously, you will see that Brecht praises Stalin as 'the useful one', which refers to the well-known old Communist theory that Stalin's crimes were necessary and useful for the development of socialism in Russia as well as, by implication, the world revolution.

Then there was the question of Brecht's alleged attitude to the Moscow trials. 'As for the trials, it would be quite wrong when discussing them to adopt an attitude hostile to their organizers, the Soviet government . . .', he wrote. In 1929 the American philosopher Sidney Hook had met Brecht when attending Karl Korsch's lectures in Berlin. In 1935 Brecht visited Hook's house in Manhattan. When Hook raised the question of the recent arrest and imprisonment of Zinoviev, Kamenev, and thousands of others, Brecht is alleged by Hook to have replied calmly in German: 'The more innocent they are, the more they deserve to be shot.'[91] As Hook tells it, he then handed Brecht his hat and coat. Brecht left 'with a sickly smile'.

In 1976 Willett and Ralph Manheim edited Brecht's *Poems 1913–1956* in English translation. 'Die Erziehung der Hirse' (The Cultivation of the Millet, 1950), a ballad of praise for a nomad hero of Kazakhstan who turns to the cultivation of millet and manages to grow enough to support the Red Army against Hitler, was not included by the editors, who describe it as 'the major poem of 1950, with its fifty-two stanzas in praise of the generally discredited genetic theories of Trofin Lysenko and its one mildly flattering reference to Stalin ("our great harvest-leader")', but as 'hard to stomach for all its technical skill'.[92]

Prominent among Brecht-detestors, James Fenton (later professor of poetry at Oxford) agreed with Arendt that 'The Cultivation of the Millet' in effect 'praised Stalin's crimes', citing lines in praise of collectivization—'Und die Felder waren plötzlich gross—And the fields were suddenly big.' Calling this 'among the glibbest, stupidest, and most disgusting lines of twentieth-century verse', Fenton quoted an earlier Oxford professor of poetry, W. H. Auden's feeling of revulsion for Brecht: 'He was simply a crook. Never gave up either his Austrian nationality or his Swiss bank account.'[93] Auden's rapid transit from Britain to America in 1939, at the outbreak of war, was perhaps a poor podium from which to wave this kind of baton. In addition, Auden and Chester Kallman had translated the 'crook's' *The Rise and Fall of the City of Mahagonny*, though their version was never published. They also translated *The Seven Deadly Sins of the Petty Bourgeois*. Brecht's eight-line poem, 'Encounter with the Poet Auden', as translated by John Willett, begins by thanking Auden for giving him lunch: 'And kept harping with persistence | On the bare fact of existence | i.e. a theory built around it | Recently in France propounded.'

Fenton explained his own aversion to Brecht in terms not dissimilar to Auden's: 'To offer your art in vocal support of the Party is one thing. To do so and *still* keep a bolt-hole and nest-egg is quite another... From the moment of his espousal of Communism, Brecht stood on the sidelines, cheering on a party he most emphatically did not wish to join, recommending that others submit to a discipline which he himself refused.'[94] Yet no one who had to leave Germany and stay beyond the Nazi reach was 'on the sidelines'; and no one who wished to remain 'on the sidelines' took himself to live and work in East Germany at the time of the Berlin blockade and airlift—it simply was not a sideline-ish place to be. More to the point was the censure offered by Willett and Manheim of Brecht's failure to do better than the 'silent poets' described in his poem 'In Dark Times' ('In finsteren Zeiten'):

> However, they won't say: the times were dark
> Rather: why were their poets silent?[95]

So why was he himself silent whenever the dark places of the USSR and the international Communist movement were concerned? Clearly Brecht was not prepared to wash dirty linen in public in a world threatened by Hitler, but Willett and Manheim remained uneasy:

From today's perspective [1976] even this can be seen to have been a mistake, since it helped to create unrealistic assumptions, and nowhere more so than in Brecht's own camp. How much harder then must it be to justify the maintenance of the same attitude after Hitler's defeat. None the less Brecht did maintain it, so that his subsequent criticisms of East Germany too, though nothing like as powerful as the poems about the fates of Sergei Tretiakoff and Carola Neher in the USSR, were only very partially made public at the time.[96] Even now there are poems which have been withheld from publication and/or withdrawn from the material in the Brecht Archive: two of the 'Buckow Elegies' for a start, together with a well-authenticated poem attacking Stalin as 'honoured murderer of the people'...[97]

The central charge in all criticisms of Brecht is one of hypocrisy and posturing: he is held to have possessed a forked tongue, a forked pen, and forked bank accounts. Brecht-the-man is regarded by his detractors as a cynical and rapacious plagiarist, a heartless womanizer. How much of his work was his own? John Willett—among the more admiring of Brecht scholars—has noted that the original manuscripts of Brecht's short stories of the 1920s often show few or no marks of his hand; Willett believes that at least seven of the eleven 'Berlin' stories were by Elisabeth Hauptmann, a writer and translator whom Brecht met in 1924. At once they became lovers and literary collaborators. The famous 'Benares Song' is written in Brecht's hand, but underneath it Hauptmann wrote at the time: 'By Hauptmann. Brecht's handwriting.' Although she had written most of *Happy End*, he gave her nothing from the $15,000 film rights. He swindled her and Kurt Weill of royalties from a Paris production of *The Threepenny Opera*, staged as *L'Opéra de quat'sous* at the Théâtre Montparnasse in 1930, telling Weill that he himself had received nothing.[98]

And—further pursuing the indictment of Brecht's personal behaviour—what about Hella Wuolijoki's original version of the Puntila legend, as told to Brecht when he was her guest-in-exile in Finland? How much of his work derived from the pens and directorial talents of his collaborators, particularly Elisabeth Hauptmann and Ruth Berlau? How much of *The Threepenny Opera* and *The Threepenny Novel* was properly Hauptmann's work? How much of *The Good Woman of Setzuan*, *Days of the Commune*, and *Tales of the Calendar* was properly Berlau's? How much did he ever pay them? John Fuegi's massive indictment, *The Life and Lies of Bertolt Brecht*, likens Brecht's treatment of women to Mack the Knife's in *The Threepenny Opera* and Shui Ta's in *The Good Woman of Setzuan*.[99] Michael Meyer concluded that Fuegi sums Brecht up, 'not unfairly', as: 'a wealthy man who compulsively presents himself as poor; a Communist who mercilessly exploits those around him; a man who denigrates women and then proudly presents their work under his own name...he held others to promises and contracts while breaking them himself at will.'[100]

Michael Hofmann's review of Fuegi's book, sardonically entitled 'That Brecht was a nasty piece of work, and he didn't even write his own plays', steams with exasperated indignation about Fuegi's obsessive hostility to BB.[101] Four scholars sceptical of Fuegi's thesis, including John Willett, compiled a 130-page list of what Willett alleges to be Fuegi's 'mistakes, misquotes and malpractices'.[102] According to Willett, '[Fuegi's] aim was openly stated—Brecht was a 'socialist icon' that had to be demolished—and it was openly supported by a dozen or so reputed American foundations, receiving mysteriously generous coverage in the English-language press too: six pages in the [London] *Observer* for a start, whose critical review only appeared later.'[103] Fredric Jameson has more recently accorded Fuegi an elaborately sarcastic dismissal, its aloof, patrician tone reminiscent of the one adopted by Ivy League defenders of Alger Hiss against the vulgar allegations of Whittaker Chambers—or the one adopted by sections of the Parisian Left against the vulgar claims of Soviet defectors. Jameson concludes that Fuegi's book 'will remain a fundamental document for future students of the ideological confusions of Western intellectuals during the immediate post-cold war years'.[104]

⌗ ⌗ ⌗

Brecht became a hallowed figure in the GDR; the illustrious dead, who can say no more, settle down as the comfortable occupants of Poet's Corner. His disciple, the satirical balladeer Wolf Biermann, came to prominence in East Germany during the cultural thaw of 1962–5, somewhat resembling the ghost of the young Brecht, the author of *Baal*. Biermann's father, not only a Communist but a Jew from Hamburg, had perished in Auschwitz. In 1953, at the age of 17, Biermann had made the highly unusual move from West to East, studying philosophy at the Humboldt University, joining the Berliner Ensemble as an assistant director, and befriended by Hanns Eisler, whose style influenced songs like Biermann's 'Ein deutscher Kommunist'. He wrote poems and songs about village life, the setting up of collective farms, ballads about tractor drivers and lorry drivers, as well as songs for the CND movement and the emergent civil rights movement in America.

To 'Meister Brecht' he remained permanently indebted: 'The secret of his poetic art lies in its prosaic tone', he commented many years later, adding: 'We write his language today.'[105] The influence of Brechtian fable and 'Chinese' hermeneutics remained apparent in Biermann's ballads and poems: for example 'Drei Worte an die Partei' ('Three Words to the Party'), and 'Frage und Antwort und Frage' ('Question and Answer and Question'). The latter implies that the Party's answer is not enough and what the poem says, in prose paraphrase, is this: 'They say one cannot change horses in mid-stream. Good. But the old ones are already drowned. You say: the admission of our failings only serves the enemy. Good. But who do our lies serve—*aber wem nützt unsere Lüge?*' (a Brechtian question in content and form). Finally Biermann adds this: 'Many say that in the long run Socialism is completely unavoidable. Good. But who sets it up [or 'who gets it across']?[106]

Biermann was soon in trouble with the regime, as Margaret Vallance carefully charted in the London-based anti-Communist journal *Survey*:

In 1961 he was instrumental in the creation of a Students and Workers Theatre; he had written two plays, one of which, called *Berliner Brautgang*, reached dress-rehearsal stage, when it was banned and the theatre disbanded . . . The banned play's theme was that of the love between a worker and a doctor's daughter in the divided city of Berlin. Then came a ballad about a young drain-layer who dances the forbidden twist and ends up with twelve weeks in prison; this, together with the doubts Biermann had expressed about protective measures being taken at the frontier (i.e. the building of the wall), was enough to provoke the anger of a decisive proportion of the Central Committee, and he received the disciplinary measure of *Auftrittsverbot*—he was forbidden to perform anywhere in the DDR until June 1963.[107]

Biermann's work in the early sixties was characterized by terse lyrics, simple melodies, a sparse guitar accompaniment. Vallance associated Biermann with the German satirical tradition of Wedekind, Brecht, and Wolfgang Neuss, the West Berlin cabaret artist, alongside the *chansonnier* tradition of François Villon, the poet and clown who (as Biermann wrote in his 1964 ballad dedicated to 'Mein grosser Bruder Franz Villon') 'always hides when people come snooping . . . and waits till the air is clear. The air is never quite clear.'

On 11 December 1962 Biermann appeared at the Academy of Arts before party officials:

> Look at me, comrades
> With your tired eyes
> With your hardened eyes

Following this he was banned from performing in public. He suffered constant harassment. 'Every time before going out on stage, the lighting man would say to me: "Herr Biermann, you are aware of the fact: only those four songs, otherwise I will have to turn off the lights." '[108] He wrote sardonically about the rejectionist line adopted by Alfred Kurella and the East German delegation to the 1964 Kafka Conference in Prague, when Marxist revisionists sought to rehabilitate the author of *The Trial*. Allowed to perform again that year, he became a popular guest star at the satirical cabaret *Die Distel* (*The Thistle*) in East Berlin. In December he made a tour of West Germany, enjoying a success comparable to Yevtushenko's. Biermann's appearance—mop of dark hair and walrus moustache—uncannily resembled that of Günter Grass, whose play *The Plebeians Rehearse the Uprising* could well have encompassed the case of Biermann as well as Brecht. Disaster struck in May 1965, when Wolfgang Neuss indiscreetly published a private letter of Biermann's in the satirical *Neuss Deutschland*; as a result Biermann was again forbidden to perform or travel; a painful series of cancellations followed. Arriving to take part in a 'Jazz and Lyric' evening at the Congress Hall, he was intercepted by police and bluntly informed that he was banned. A record made by the East German company Eterna containing six of his songs was also banned. Despite divisions within the Writers' Union, he was attacked in a long polemic by Alfred Kurella in *Neues Deutschland*, the accusations including anarchism, irresponsibility, scepticism, and composing verses 'against the anti-fascist protective wall and our border guards'. In a socialist state someone like Biermann, a purveyor of 'toilet-stall poetry', enjoyed no 'justification for existence' (*Daseinsberechtigung*); he was banned from performing in public by a Plenum of the Central Committee. As he put it later: 'I was lucky, protected by the political bureaucrats' fear of publicity.'[109] Writing in *Die Zeit*, Marcel Reich-Ranicki commented that Biermann was feared by the SED partly because he was himself a product of the party's *Kulturpolitik*.[110]

Indeed, some of his output did follow the traditional Party line, praising 'peace' and condemning warmongers. When Rudi Dutschke, a leading New Left student militant at the Free University, West Berlin, was gravely wounded in an assassination attempt during the 1968 riots, Biermann's response—'Three Bullets For Rudi Dutschke'[111]—was unoriginal. Before describing the source of each of the three bullets, Biermann insisted that 'we have seen exactly who did the shooting'[112] So who was it that 'we' had 'exactly seen'—apart from the actual culprit, a lone-wolf admirer of Hitler called Josef Bachmann, who reportedly told the police, 'I read about Martin Luther King and I said to myself I must do this too'? Biermann's predictable ballad attributed the first bullet to the Axel Springer press, and the third to the head of the West German coalition government, 'Der Edel-Nazi-Kanzler' Kissinger.[113]

In 1966 the American Peace Movement singer Joan Baez appeared in the East German cabaret *Die Distel* and dedicated a song to Biermann while protesting the restrictions placed upon him.[114] For the next ten years the muzzled bard continued to perform for friends and for those Western record companies granted access to his apartment in Chausseestrasse. In West

Germany he (like his mentor Brecht) was big business. The West Berlin publisher Verlag Klaus Wagenbach issued anthologies and albums. CBS Records signed him as a recording artist after it became clear that technicians could be sent to his apartment. Out of this came the albums *Don't Wait For Better Times* (1973) and *Chaussee Street* (1975). In November 1976 he was allowed to perform in Cologne on condition that he refrain from several songs, including his 'Stasi-Lied'—his tribute to the East German secret police. The concert, before an audience of 7,000, was broadcast by West German TV—and he did sing his 'Stasi-Lied', the temptation was too great, whereupon his East German citizenship was furiously revoked. A cartoon of the time showed an East German soldier atop the wall with a machine-gun in hand. On one side of the wall could be seen a sea of East Germans clutching suitcases; on the other a lone Wolf Biermann clutching a guitar.

Twelve prominent East German authors, including Christa Wolf and Stefan Heym, criticized the revocation of Biermann's citizenship, but neither letters of protest nor a sharp rise in emigration applications moved the regime—indeed, exit visas, the *Ausreiseniträge*, were on the whole granted swiftly—good riddance.[115] Professor Mary Fulbrook, having gained access in the 1990s to archives of the FDGB trade union organization, examined File 3023, which reported widespread disgust among the intelligentsia, teachers, and young people about the treatment of Biermann. An official report dated 17 December 1976 complained of confused conceptions (*unklaren Auffassungen*) and people obstinately supporting 'mistaken views': '[A minority] express themselves openly, cynically, and provocatively against the decisions of the government and engage themselves in favour of Biermann in the worst possible way. Young people (*Jugendliche*) collected signatures, wrote open letters on wall newspapers, made and circulated tapes of Biermann's concerts in the West.'[116]

Biermann returned to live in Hamburg, for the tang of whose salt water he had never ceased to yearn. Reflecting on the collapse of the East German state in 1989–90, he declined to abandon his Marxist–Brechtian perspective:

Karl Marx has been overtaken but so also has Isaac Newton. Yet despite everything the apples continue to fall downwards. And freedom without enough to eat (*genügend Frass*) is only a beautifully sad word . . . The market economy descends on the five new Federal States [i.e. East Germany] like the severe malaria with which syphilis was driven out in earlier times.[117]

Dirty Hands:
The Political Theatre of
Sartre and Camus

'I don't take sides. A good play should pose problems, not resolve them.'[1]
(Jean-Paul Sartre, *Combat*, 31 March 1948).

This was an era when, despite cinema and radio, French people still cut the pages of books with keen anticipation. Few writers are pursued by photographers today; we know their appearance only from portrait poses (often out of date) and the occasional prize-giving (out of focus). Yet fifty years ago Jean-Paul Sartre, Albert Camus, and Simone de Beauvoir attracted the kind of attention normally reserved for film stars—though Camus later became reclusive. On every issue—the nature of individual consciousness, the meaning of 'freedom' and moral choice, the cold war—when Sartre or Camus took up a position it was news. Each had saluted the other's work before they met at the première of Sartre's play *Les Mouches* (*The Flies*) in 1943. The salad days of their friendship lasted until 1946; it was Camus who, as the 32-year-old editor of *Combat*, dispatched Sartre on his first trip to America early in 1945, before the guns had fallen silent in Europe. The relationship was not definitively broken until Sartre's outright condemnation of Camus's *L'Homme révolté* (*The Rebel*) in 1952.

Sartre's productive years as a dramatist extended from 1940 to 1965; as a novelist, from 1931 to 1949; as a biographer, from 1944 to 1972; as an essayist and journalist, from the late 1930s to his death in 1980.

⊞ ⊞ ⊞

The American impact on France, not least on Paris, was huge immediately after the war. Young Americans brashly knocked on Picasso's studio door—

there was no saying no to them. Sartre embarked on an extensive journalistic tour of the United States. During the summer of 1946 the large cinema-going public in France enthusiastically received a succession of American films, many minor masterpieces in the genre which came to be known as *film noir*. Fifteen years earlier Sartre and Simone de Beauvoir had been riveted by the films of the Soviet master directors Eisenstein and Pudovkin; now it was Orson Welles they went to see, with virtually nothing to excite from Stalin's Russia. French cinephiles and intellectuals, led by the critic André Bazin, embraced both the *film noir* and the Western, whose 'naive grandeur' (as he put it) was recognized by the simplest people of all countries (*de tous les climats*). The heroes of the Western were, he said, 'universal heroes': 'The March towards the West is our Odyssey.' The issues contested in these American movies, likewise, were universal: good and evil, light and dark, city and country, the stark encounters between human beings and nature.[2] The influential Bazin described a profound opposition between the American and Soviet models of film-making, extrapolating a moral authority based on the greater 'realism' of American cinema, its capacity 'to reveal the hidden meaning of beings and things', and its positioning of the viewer as an explorer of a liberated visual field. In many respects Sartre was far from anti-American; he was much impressed by Orson Welles's *Citizen Kane*, a *film noir* which reached France in 1946. The film, whose central character is based on the right-wing newspaper magnate Randolph Hearst, takes the form of a detective story in which pieces of a puzzle gradually fall into place by means of associations, flashes back and forwards, ellipses, discontinuities. Sartre saw it as a cinematic version of the multiple points-of-view technique of 'Anglo-Saxon' novelists, particularly Dos Passos and Faulkner, which had influenced his own fiction, notably *The Reprieve* (*Le Sursis*). In short, Sartre was writing plays, essays, journalism, and novels at a time when American art, the worst as well as the best, was sweeping all before it, the Communists alone lashing themselves to the masthead of Stalin–Zhdanov, where nothing was permitted and rigid devotion stood in for entertainment.

Sartre's play *La Putain respectueuse* (*The Respectful Prostitute*, 1946)[3] reflects the impact of contemporary American life and art shortly before the cultural cold war got fully into its stride. However, the title remains something of a mystery, since Sartre's white prostitute Lizzie MacKay, who has come South from New York, is surprisingly and untypically *un-respectful* towards white racism and lynch-mob law; her straightforward respect for the truth, when confronted by a white, upper-class lie, a false accusation against a Negro accused of molesting her on a train, is admirable—she stands by what she has seen, namely, a well-connected young white boarding the train dead drunk and shooting another Negro dead. Sartre may have based himself on the well-known case of the 'Scottsboro Boys' in 1931.

The characters are all stereotypes without possibility of internal development, the important exception being the prostitute Lizzie herself, who is on stage from start to finish in her seedy apartment in a southern town. It may be the case, as the *New Yorker*'s Paris correspondent Janet Flanner remarked, that Sartre had not met many Southern-gentlemen lynchers during his tours of America, and there are occasional anachronisms, as when the arrogant young Fred Clarke boasts to Lizzie that one of his ancestors 'tutoyait' George Washington (addressed him intimately as 'tu' rather than by the more formal 'vous'); we also hear that the young college boys had got drunk after winning a 'rugby match'.[4] Although this is not a 'cold war' play, because the issue of Communism is subordinate, it does mark the onset of Sartre's anger and contempt for American racial injustice, lynch law, and the hypocrisy of the ruling class. It was later performed in the Soviet Union after Sartre's first visit to that country in 1954, under the title *Lizzie Mackay*, starring Lyubov' Orlova (the spy-temptress in *Meeting on the Elbe*) in the title role. (It was also performed in Havana when Sartre and de Beauvoir paid their 'state' visit to Castro's Cuba.)[5]

Sartre keeps his structure 'tight'. Lizzie never refers to her own life, parents, upbringing, or how she came to be what she is. She takes the dramatic and dangerous situation in which she finds herself on its own terms. Her clarity of moral outlook is clouded by confusions: 'I've nothing against them [Negroes], but I wouldn't want them to touch me', she says. She is horrified when it is suggested she might be a Communist.[6] Though poor, she won't take bribes, but she proves susceptible to the prospect of a wealthy, high-born mother's personal gratitude if only she, Lizzie, will testify that the lady's drunken, Negro-murdering son had done nothing wrong. This is where the prostitute becomes 'respectful'. But all Lizzie gets from the lady in return for her perjury is a $100 bill and not a line of written gratitude. Lizzie is a finely drawn character, truculent, tender, brave, vulnerable, and—most important—a moral stranger to the codes of the Deep South, where she finds herself. She is not ashamed to share a certain fellow-feeling with the Negro, a common fear of the police, of 'them', almost a class solidarity—but not quite. Sartre possessed an ingrained French talent for conveying both sexual relationships and relationships between the sexes.

The play was written at the height of Sartre's enthusiasm for 'existentialism', and one therefore asks how 'free' is Lizzie to choose her course of action while contending with violent men, overbearing wealth, and lynch-mobs. The answer seems to be that Lizzie was bound to betray the innocent Negro because the only social system she knew from personal experience systematically relegated blacks to the margins of humanity. Sartre's awareness was reinforced by his recent friendship with the black writer Richard Wright, who was enduring an insidious racial segregation in the supposedly enlightened Greenwich Village.

Senator Clarke tells Lizzie that although his nephew Thomas did not do well to kill a Negro on the train, he was after all educated at Harvard, he's an officer, employs two thousand workers, he's a leader, a solid rampart against Communism, the labour unions, and the Jews: 'Do you believe a whole town can be wrong? A whole town, with its pastors and curates, with its doctors, its lawyers and its artists, with its mayor and his deputies and its benevolent associations?'[7] This all sounds too good (i.e. bad) to be true, and manipulative on Sartre's part, but both Sartre and Camus possessed an uncanny ability, reflected in high audience figures, for turning the obvious into something searching and painful. Both in Paris, at the Théâtre Saint-Antoine, and London, at the Lyric, Hammersmith, the play was staged as a double bill with *Morts sans sépultures* (*Men without Shadows*). After 100 performances the production was still playing to enthusiastic audiences in Paris.[8] Sartre recalled that he approved of the original Paris production of *La Putain* in comic mode (*en bouffe*), and again in London, 'thanks to Peter Brook'. Characters hide in bathrooms and behind doors, then jump out. 'But everywhere else, a drama was made of it, and this comic piece has become a ridiculous melodrama.'[9] These strictures applied to the New York production, adapted by Eva Wolas, which opened on 9 February 1948 and enjoyed a success—more than 350 performances. In a preface to the American translation Sartre denied accusations of anti-Americanism, pointing out that *Pravda* was simultaneously accusing him of being an agent of American propaganda.

Writing for an edition of his collected plays in 1947, Sartre insisted on the pure existentialist doctrine of freedom: 'In every circumstance, time and place, man is free to choose to become a traitor or hero, cowardly or brave. In choosing for himself slavery or liberty, he will choose by the same act (*du même coup*) a world where man is free or a slave—and drama will be born from his efforts to justify his choice.' Twenty-two years later he commented: 'It's incredible. I really believed it' (*je le pensais vraiment*).[10]

The Communists were not concerned whether he 'really believed it' or not. In their view he was not only an enemy but *the* enemy. In January 1948, two months before Sartre's profession of politically 'clean hands' regarding his new play, *Dirty Hands*, the East German SED functionary Anton Ackermann expressed indignation that the Hebbel Theater in West Berlin was currently performing Sartre's play *The Flies*. Writing in *Neues Deutschland* (4 January),

Ackermann demanded that it should be banned. What offended the Communists was less the play itself—far from 'formalist' in structure and first staged in occupied Paris as an allegory of revolt against oppression—than Sartre's recent journalism on behalf of a small 'Third Force' grouping known as the Rassemblement Démocratique Révolutionnaire, founded in February 1948, and his scathing comments in *What is Literature?* on the Communist Party's current literary line. Here he condemned 'Stalinist Communism' as 'incompatible with the honest practice of the literary craft', and called for a literature distanced both from propaganda and escapist diversion, a critical and constructive literature capable of revealing the roads to freedom.[11] As Sartre put it, the well-intentioned intellectual entering the Party immediately finds himself in a Kafkaesque situation, surrounded by unknown accusers yet bound to prove his innocence.

Among Communists, Sartre had rapidly achieved the status of *bête noire*. Ackermann denounced *The Flies* as 'wanton contra-humanism', while other Communist critics cynically tossed in such phrases as 'coffeehouse art' and 'foul justification of the capitalist system'. Major Aleksandr Dymshits added his own invective, contrasting Sartre, a mere scribbler, a *pasquillant*, with that noble French Communist writer Louis Aragon.[12] 'Every class', wrote the French Communist ideologue Roger Garaudy, 'has the literature it deserves. The big bourgeoisie in decay delights in the erotic obsessions of a Henry Miller or the intellectual fornications of a Jean-Paul Sartre.'[13] The rabid attack on Sartre in East Berlin pretty well confirmed his own characterization of the Communist style of argument, which he had learned closer to home from the hatchet-men of the French Party: 'The opponent is never answered; he is discredited; he belongs to the police, to the Intelligence Service; he's a fascist.'[14]

First performed in June 1943, at the Théâtre de la Cité in Nazi-occupied Paris, *The Flies* is a marvellously 'logical' and fluid play, inspired by *The Libation Bearers*, the second play in Aeschylus's trilogy, the *Oresteia*. The young Orestes returns from exile to avenge the murder of his father Agamemnon with the help of his rediscovered sister Electra, even unto the death of their guilty mother, Clytemnestra. Clearly Sartre was tilting at Marshal Pétain's Vichy regime in occupied France by depicting the almighty Zeus as both an ugly statue and an old man in disguise, who feeds off human guilt and remorse, keeping Argos in a condition of permanent morbidity and fear of the avenging dead.[15] Paradoxically, given the German Communist onslaught against the play in 1948, five years earlier it had been damned by the Parisian *collabo* press and praised in the clandestine *Les Lettres françaises*: 'Orestes has broken the vicious circle and paved the way that leads from the kingdom of necessity to that of freedom.'[16] Even so, the freedom which Sartre offers through Orestes is hyper-individualist. Orestes's final 'I am alone, alone' is both a lament and a proud affirmation.

Sartre travelled to Berlin for the production of *The Flies*, accompanied by Simone de Beauvoir. His play, however, was staged in the American rather than the French sector, which has been described as a somewhat stunted afterthought hived off from the British sector, a cultural wasteland spread across two districts, Reinickendorf and Wedding, and without a single theatre, opera house, museum, or university, merely a few public libraries.[17] Writing to her American lover Nelson Algren in her fast-improving English, de Beauvoir reported how appalled she was by the Berlin production:

> The producer purposely did a nihilist play with it; he had cut-off whole scenes, and made the actors play in such a way that it meant just the contrary of what Sartre had intended. Then all was so ugly, the faces, gestures, scenery, everything . . . The actors were always screaming, sweating, and lying on their backs . . . just as asylum [*sic*] of crazy people. All the French people thought it was a shame. But German people applaud for half an hour and it is a regular triumph.

After Sartre had been led on stage they were taken to what she called the Russian club: 'We had a long dinner, with bad food but much vodka. It was very interesting to speak with Russian and German communists; they were really friendly, made friendly speeches, while French communists, you know, tear us to pieces.'[18]

The effortless, 'classical' fluency of *The Flies* contrasts favourably with the artificial contrivances of Sartre's most political play, *Les Mains sales* (*Dirty Hands*), with its stage business and its busy doors, window curtains and locked drawers. (Perversely he insisted that 'it is not, to any degree, a political play'.)[19] Sartre constantly works the routine of boulevard drama, revolvers and silk stockings. If one compares the dramatic dialogues between Orestes and Electra (the desired sister) with the tedious bickering and play-acting between Hugo and Jessica (the undesired wife in *Les Mains sales*), one might be stretched to believe they belong to the same writer.

The setting is Illyria (an East European country, not unlike Hungary) in 1943. A right-wing dictatorship is in power, the Red Army has begun to turn the military tide but is still far away to the East, and the pro-Soviet 'Proletarian Party' is operating clandestinely. Hugo Barine, a very young intellectual so riddled with class-guilt that he is almost ashamed to possess a doctorate, is convinced by Louis, leader of the dissident faction of the PP leadership—to which Hugo's persuasive former mistress Olga also belongs—that the leader of a rival faction (Hoederer) must be assassinated. Hoederer, general secretary of the Party, has been given leave to negotiate. He is not a traitor but is pursuing the 'wrong' policy, a tactical accommodation with the Regent and the bourgeois party, the 'Pentagone'. 'Objectively he is a traitor. That's enough for me', Louis tells Hugo.[20]

Hoederer has requested a secretary who is married. Why married?—Louis does not know. A plot is hatched: Hugo will present himself to the unsuspecting Hoederer as his new secretary—though anyone less 'unsuspecting' than Hoederer would be hard to imagine. Sartre is here influenced by the murder of Trotsky in 1940 by a planted secretary, Ramon Mercader, secretly loyal to Stalin and the Party. De Beauvoir reports that Sartre was fascinated by Trotsky's assassination and by the intimacy of this *in camera*, 'huis clos' situation.[21] Hugo's role (Louis explains) will only be to keep an eye on Hoederer and then, on the appointed evening, to open the door to three comrades who will finish the job. Hugo bridles: 'Is that all you judge me capable of? I'll do what has to be done myself' (*Je ferai l'affaire moi-même*). Olga speaks up for Hugo: 'Have confidence in him. He's a young chap looking for his chance. He'll go all the way.'[22]

Louis's trust in this young 'anarchist' intellectual, a dreamer, is as improbable as the security-conscious Hoederer's failure to choose his own secretary. But this is boulevard stuff, the traditional *pièce bien faite*. Only 21 (yet precociously already editor of the Party's clandestine newspaper), Hugo arrives in a well-tailored suit at Hoederer's hideout, carrying slim volumes of Lorca and Eliot. Hoederer's bodyguards, Slick and Georges, are scornful of the pampered Hugo, though admiring of his pretty wife Jessica. Hugo will come to respect Hoederer and find in him a father figure, a substitute for his own bourgeois father, whom he naturally despises.

Les Mains sales means 'dirty hands', but what did Sartre mean? The title came to him while dwelling on the conflict between morality and praxis during the French Revolution. In November 1792 Saint-Just had purportedly argued for the execution of Louis XVI with the observation: 'No one governs innocently.'[23] In *Franc-Tireur* (25 March 1948) Sartre gave his interpretation: the pursuit of politics, whether for good causes or bad, invariably involves soiling the hands.[24] But this far from resolves what is meant: is the 'dirty' dimension a willingness to shed blood, or a willingness to compromise and engage in expedient short-term alliances (as Hoederer is doing)? Hoederer tells Hugo that purity is an idea for fakirs and monks. 'You intellectuals, you bourgeois anarchists, you take it as a pretext to do nothing.'[25]

Leaving aside the question of what 'dirty hands' means, did Sartre himself prefer Hugo's attitude to Hoederer's? As we have seen, he claimed neutrality when interviewed by *Combat*: 'A good stage play ought to pose problems, not resolve them.' Eight years later, in 1955, he came out for Hoederer: 'Hugo has never been a sympathetic character for me, and I have never thought that he was right against Hoederer... It's Hoederer's attitude alone which seemed to me sane.' Hugo had been a portrait of his own bourgeois-leftist students, whereas Hoederer was 'what I would have liked to have been if I'd been a revolutionary... '.[26]

Albert Camus (still on friendly terms) had come to one of the late rehearsals without having read the text. At the end he told Sartre that he would have reversed an exchange between Hugo and Hoederer. It should have been Hoederer who said: 'As for men, it's not what they are that interests me but what they will become',[27] while it should have been Hugo who replied: 'As for me, I love them for what they are' (*Et moi, je les aime pour ce qu'ils sont*).[28] Sartre told the story years later, conveying undiminished astonishment at Camus's lack of understanding. Yet Camus was perhaps right as well as wrong. It is, after all, Hoederer who embodies Sartre's naive futuristic Marxism when he blames necessary mendacity on class society: 'It's not in refusing to lie that we will abolish the lie; it's in using all means to suppress classes.'[29] Sartre later abandoned this simplistic determinism in *Critique de la raison dialectique*. Interviewing him in 1964, Paolo Caruso pointed out that the play is constructed in such a way that the public is bound to identify with Hugo, who is the protagonist, which is the internal reason why the play was seen as anti-Communist. Sartre insisted that the play had never been intended as anti-Communist, but the Communists and the wider public had regrettably taken it as such; these many years later he still regarded it as subjectively the work of a 'critical *compagnon de route*'— which was what he'd always wanted to be. Regrettably, Stalinism would tolerate no brotherly criticism, particularly from a 'brother' who had recently associated himself with the 'third force' RDR, founded at the turn of 1947–8, some four months before the play opened.[30]

Les Mains sales played in the Théâtre Antoine, where Simone Berriau was the powerful *directrice*, from 2 April 1948 until the autumn of 1949. With 625 performances in Paris and 300 in the provinces, this play was to remain his greatest success with the public.[31] Jean Cocteau served as adviser to the director, Pierre Valde. Asked why he chose boulevard rather than classical actors—notably André Luguet, who played Hoederer, François Périer, who was cast as Hugo, and Marie Olivier, as Jessica—Sartre explained that he wanted *l'école du naturel*. Yet this 'naturalism' is (as Brecht might have pointed out) framed in artificial strategies and tricks of the trade. 'Sartre was an instinctive and inveterate exploiter of all the *ficelles*, the tricks, of the boulevard and the well-made play', comments Ted Freeman.[32]

Particularly ridiculous is the contrivance of the fifth tableau. In the pre-ceding scene a bomb has been thrown from the garden, aimed at Hoederer, who is in negotiation behind locked doors with the Prince and the Pentago-ne's emissary Karsky. Hoederer's guards rush out to search the garden but find no one. When the fifth tableau opens, a drunken Hugo is fast asleep while Jessica sits nearby, stupidly serene or serenely stupid, as always. Olga is found hiding behind the window curtain, then reveals herself to Jessica and freely admits to having thrown the 'bomb' (earlier identified by Hoederer as a grenade or *petard*):

JESSICA: It was you who threw this bomb, Madame?
OLGA: Yes.[33]

Is this meant to be funny? A photograph of the original production shows Olga wearing a smart tweed dress, stockings, and high-heeled shoes in this scene. Are we to believe that, even if the Party entrusted this wall-climbing and bomb-throwing to a woman, she would set about it dressed in such chic attire? The unpolitical Jessica placidly enquires whether Olga is in love with Hugo. Olga, who defines herself as a *femme de tête*, Jessica as a *femme de coeur*, does not seem worried that Jessica might call Hoederer's guards and hand over the bomber—but she then says severely, 'I've no time to lose', ordering Jessica to wake Hugo up despite his hangover: 'Hugo, in a quarter of an hour a comrade will throw a rope over the wall and I will have to go.'[34]

After shooting Hoederer, Hugo spends two years in prison. By the time he is freed the USSR has instructed the Party to form an alliance with the pro-fascist Regent and the liberal-bourgeois Pentagone—precisely the late Hoederer's strategy. The Party leadership has adopted the very policy of compromise for which it condemned Hoederer to death.[35] His executioners need to expunge all traces of their involvement—Hugo can be allowed to live only if his assassination of Hoederer turns out to have been strictly a *crime passionel*. This absurdity obviously owes more to boulevard theatre than to life, but so does the entire play. Convention awkwardly compromises realism throughout: Hugo performs as a 'third-person' character in what spuriously claims to be his own 'first-person' narrative. There is even a scene between Hoederer and Jessica (VI/1) where Hugo is not on stage (or listening at the keyhole)—yet he can later tell Olga what transpired.

Why did Hugo kill Hoederer? Because he found Jessica in his arms? The promised 'secret' is never revealed and does not exist. 'It's not me who killed, it's chance.'[36] He tells Olga that the crime he committed seems 'light, hor-ribly light. It doesn't weigh.' Is this reminiscent of Camus's *L'Étranger*, when

Meursault kills the Arab, an act which he honestly cannot explain later? 'It was because of the sun.'[37]

Visiting Paris at the turn of 1948–9, the Soviet critic V. Poltoratskii had so little to say about *Les Mains sales* (*Griaznye ruki*) that he cannot have spent money on a theatre ticket. Finding Paris at first sight 'carefree, gay, and frivolous', with *The Count of Monte Cristo* playing in the cinemas alongside something called '13 Murdered in One Night' (very probably Agatha Christie), the Soviet critic ventured to the Place Pigalle where carousels whirled and the plate-glass doors of all-night cabarets banged until dawn. But beneath the surface he found sinister implants of the Marshall Plan, particularly calls to 'Enjoy yourself, dance to boogie-woogie (*bugi-vugi*)', and American songbooks going for, well, a song—only 50 francs. Sartre's play, evidently, was part of the Marshall Plan—'[Sartre] pours out a stream of slanders against the partisans who fought the Hitlerites.'[38]

'The play didn't seem to me to be anti-Communist', recalled the ever-loyal de Beauvoir, as if answering Poltoratskii's specific point: 'The Communists were presented as the only valid force against the Regent and the bourgeoisie; if a leader, in the interests of the Resistance, of socialism, of the masses, had another leader suppressed, it seemed to me as it did to Sartre that he was exempt from all judgement of a moral order.'[39] Thus the play seemed anti-Communist to Communists, and also to anti-Communists, but not to Sartre or de Beauvoir. Yet these good companions must have known that Stalinist culture was quite incapable of admitting that it was in the habit of liquidating its own cadres whenever the Party line reversed itself. Sartre and de Beauvoir must have known that the PCF could not identify itself with the outright elitism of all the characters in *Les Mains sales*; each faction claimed to think and speak on behalf of the masses, but without a hint of consulting them. Francis Jeanson tells us that this is the first play by Sartre in which a 'collectivity' (the working class) figures off-stage—but it does not figure, apart from the two clownish bodyguards, Georges and Slick. As Hazel Barnes puts it: 'So far as his constituents are concerned, [Hoederer] might as well be a dictator.'[40] Just as bad for Communist ears, Hoederer, while looking forward to the eventual arrival of the Red Army, adds candidly: 'Our peasants will detest the Russians, it's inevitable, how do you expect them to like us as the party imposed on them by the Russians?'[41]

Nor could the real PCF, which indeed took its orders and policy-reversals from Moscow, accept Sartre's portrait of the Illyrian Party—which took its orders and policy-reversals from Moscow. Admittedly Sartre's play spared the Communists any overt reference to the Nazi–Soviet Pact of August 1939, yet by drawing dramatic attention to the zig-zags of the Party line,

Sartre was implicitly reminding his audience of the most dramatic and odious reversal of all—the PCF's abrupt conversion to the 'imperialist war' line after the Pact. And not only that: Hoederer's strategy is precisely the one reluctantly adopted by the PCF in 1944–5, collaboration with Gaullism in a broad national front. Hugo is scathing: 'Perfect. I suppose the Soviets have also given you to understand that they don't wish to hand over power to the Proletarian Party alone; they would have problems with the Allies and, besides, you would be rapidly swept away (*balayés*) by an insurrection.'[42]

This is what anti-Communist spectators wanted to hear. During the play's run in Paris, the moment in the last tableau when Hoederer's rehabiliation is announced by the Party brought gasps of recognition from the anti-Communist audience. By contrast, Communist plays of the socialist realist school normally begin with the external political situation—a strike, a civil war, a foreign invasion—then rapidly establish that the Party alone has adopted a progressive stand. Communist fiction and theatre normally serves a short-term, propagandist task, as if an editorial from *Pravda* or *L'Humanité* had been fitted out with wigs and false eyelashes. Reviewing Sartre's play in *L'Humanité* (7 April), Guy Leclerc blasted him as a 'nauseous writer', a 'Third Force demagogue', and—supreme insult—an 'understudy for [Arthur] Koestler'. Visiting France in February 1949, Ilya Ehrenburg expressed contempt for the play. The tension was heightened by the opening of the Kravchenko trial in Paris, by the Berlin blockade, and by the 'fall' of China. A caricaturally inept New York adaptation called *Red Gloves* did not help. As de Beauvoir tells it: 'The production of *Red Gloves* in New York was a flop. The script had been sabotaged . . . They had stuck in a speech about the assassination of Lincoln and butchered the whole thing . . . Sartre tried to make them take it off and brought suit against [his French publisher] Nagel, who had authorized the whole thing without his permission.'

De Beauvoir quotes 'one Russian critic' who wrote: 'For 30 pieces of silver and a mess of American pottage, Jean-Paul Sartre has sold out what remained of his honour and probity.' *Les Lettres françaises* printed 'Le Génie de Six Heures', in which Magnane had sketched a heavily distorted and scarcely recognizable portrait of Sartre. De Beauvoir recalled: 'Elsa Triolet was writing a book and lecturing in an attempt to instigate a boycott of the filthy writings of Sartre, Camus and Breton; my sister heard her speak publicly against Sartre in Belgrade with the deepest hatred in her voice.'[43] The Soviet film director Sergei Gerasimov linked Sartre to 'corrosive surrealism' and the idea that man is the worst enemy of man, condemned to a solitude both terrible and unfathomable. (Sartre was in fact a severe critic of surrealism.)

As a printed text *Les Mains sales* became Sartre's most popular fiction in France; by the end of 1978 1,892,000 copies had been sold.[44] However, during the period of his reconciliation with the PCF, from 1952 to 1956, he exercised rigid control over permission to perform the play abroad. In December 1952, before he set out for the Vienna World Peace Council, as a gesture against the warmongers he cancelled a scheduled production of the play in Vienna. Henceforward foreign productions would be authorized only with the consent of the local Communist parties. Permission was refused in Vienna (1952 and 1954), in Spain, Greece, Indochina, and at Anvers in 1966. Only after 1962 did he authorize new productions in Yugoslavia, Italy, and Czechoslovakia (the latter in 1968).[45]

⌘ ⌘ ⌘

Whatever their chosen historical setting,[46] the plays of Albert Camus, like those of Sartre, impressed contemporary audiences as up-to-the-minute interventions in the great moral dilemmas of the cold war. Both writers were capable dramatists, but neither would have stood the test of time on the basis of his plays alone. It was what they said that counted—and by the late 1940s these two erstwhile friends had almost parted company.

The young Camus had been briefly a Communist, fired up by the revolt of the Asturian miners, the Spanish Civil War, the novels of Malraux, and the appalling poverty of the Arabs of Kabylia. Raised in Algiers, Camus had been the prime mover in the late thirties behind two local theatre companies, the Théâtre du travail and the Théâtre de l'équipe, taking an acting role in most of their productions. Later, in Paris, he insisted on involving himself in the casting and direction of the half-dozen original or adapted plays for which he is now remembered. Both he and Sartre slept with actresses, but Camus also preferred the company of actors, sportsmen, and journalists to that of university-trained intellectuals. He added that he always felt—or was made to feel—that he had something to apologize for in intellectual society.[47]

His preferred model was 'our classical drama and the Greek tragedians', involving 'human fate in all its simplicity and grandeur'. What he could do without was the bric-a-brac of modern theatre: 'Psychology, ingenious plot-devices, and spicy situations, though they may amuse me as a member of the audience, leave me indifferent as an author.'[48] He declared himself averse to ludic games and 'acrobatics de l'intelligence' in the theatre, more concerned with the lonely isolation of individuals dedicated to a noble cause.[49] As Henry Popkin has pointed out,

Camus's characters tear right into the issues, and they ignore small details. Just as Lear's 'Pray you, undo this button,' could not have occurred in Racine, so it would also be an unlikely line in Camus. Everyone in [his] plays is ready for action—or, more often, for argument. Nothing may intervene . . . to explain the characters or to provide contexts for the events.

In *L'État de siège* (*State of Siege*) and *Les Justes* (*The Just Assassins*) the play tends to become a formal exchange of weighty remarks framed in lofty, pure language, which clearly exposes the writer's demands on us. 'Hardly anyone else in the modern theatre lectures us so directly.' By contrast, in his fiction Camus's method of narration always prevents us from colliding too abruptly with his ideas. (Only in *Caligula*, perhaps, did he achieve a theatrical equivalent for his sophisticated fiction.)[50] Presented by the Compagnie Madeleine Renaud–Jean-Louis Barrault, *L'État de siège* opened at the Théâtre Marigny on 27 October 1948. Although Camus was anxious to deny that it was in any way a stage adaptation of his celebrated novel *La Peste*, published to great acclaim the previous year, at the centre of the play is the same metaphor of the plague, but now portrayed as something imposed by human beings, the curse of autocratic, indeed totalitarian, rule. Camus, who wanted 'to imagine a myth which could be intelligible for all the spectators of 1948', spoke of blending in this play all forms of dramatic expression, from the lyrical monologue and simple dialogue to collective theatre, mime, farce, a chorus (*choeur*).[51] The product suffers.

In October 1944 Camus had written that 'Anti-Communism is the beginning of dictatorship', but four years later he was already a firm anti-Communist.[52] *L'État de siège* is not an anti-Communist play by any means, but it was capable of that interpretation and it followed his complete break with the PCF. In December 1946, at a Paris party, he had accused Maurice Merleau-Ponty, co-editor with Sartre of *Les Temps modernes*, of trying to justify the Moscow trials as historically necessary though based on trumped-up charges; Sartre joined in the argument, supporting Merleau-Ponty; Camus walked out, slamming the door.[53] Increasingly estranged from the political follies and philosophical conceits of the post-war Left Bank, Camus held that individual morality is the key, the paradigm for political morality. While Sartre gradually absorbed Marxism as the one, totally rational explanation of an irrational world—and as a means of achieving a rational one by political action—Camus by contrast found only a permanent disjunction between man's reasonable expectations and the irrationality of the world. When Sartre spoke of the 'absurd' he meant the intrusion of contingency; Camus meant life itself. The Party ideologist Jean

Kanapa announced that Camus had taken his place among the *bourgeois fascisants*—a much-favoured word at that time, falling short of 'fascist', or even 'neo-fascist', but suggesting 'on the way to fascism'.[54]

The setting of *L'État de siège* is a Spanish fortified city, Cadiz. A comet rises in the sky and plague strikes. As in *La Peste*, Camus aims to prove that man can construct a noble humanism without the help of God or his secular counterpart, rationalism. Both Sartre and Camus continued to maintain this 'passionate unbelief' despite their deepening political divergences, but Camus, unlike Sartre, offered a godless universe in which Reason can never fill the hole left by God.[55] Despite decors and costumes by Balthus, and music by Arthur Honegger, the play was a failure. A false note of facetiousness, not unlike that later found in Václav Havel's satires, results in an unfortunate impression of an arid intellectual exercise on the theme of conceited bureau-cracy and bogus statistics, rather than a heartfelt *cri de coeur* again totalitar-ianism. The Catholic critic and playwright Gabriel Marcel expressed astonishment that *L'État de siège* was set in Spain rather than Eastern Europe. Camus replied that he had already denounced Soviet camps elsewhere, but Western democrats continued to treat Franco's regime with unjustified in-dulgence.[56]

Despite the critical and box-office failure of *L'État de siège*, Camus's next play, *Les Justes*, which opened at the Théâtre Hébertot in December 1949, was a long-running success. Directed by Paul Oettly, the cast was headed by Serge Reggiani and the beautiful Maria Casarès, Camus's former mistress, who played a 1905 Russian terrorist in a tight-fitting gown *circa* 1950 Paris.

Camus is little interested in naturalism, samovars, or snow-covered boots. The terrorists speak a correct, idiomatic, syntactically formal French, with little slang.[57] Set in Moscow at the time of the 1905 revolution, the play portrays a Socialist Revolutionary Party terrorist group dedicated to the assassination of the Grand Duke Sergei Alexandrovich, uncle of Tsar Nich-olas II and a man detested for his reactionary views. Camus seals the action off from the wider reality of mass revolt and strikes provoked by the Bloody Sunday massacre in St Petersburg a month earlier. The central theme of this five-act play—the standard structure of French drama at that time—corresponds to 'Les Meutriers délicats', a chapter in his contentious book *L'Homme révolté*, which was to be published in October 1951, two years after the première of *Les Justes*. There must be limits to morally permissible polit-ical violence: 'I merely wanted to show that action itself had limits . . . Our world of today seems loathsome to us for the very reason that it is made by men who grant themselves the right to go beyond these limits, and first of all to kill others without dying themselves.'[58] Camus's love and admiration (as he explained) is focused on the hero and heroine, the lovers Kaliayev and Dora, the bomb-thrower and the bomb-maker, who recognize these sacred limits in the most dramatic way when, as the Grand Duke's carriage approaches, Kaliayev (off-stage) catches sight of two children, as well as the Grand Duchess, inside the carriage—and cannot bring himself to throw the bomb.

In Act 2 Kaliayev's humane yet not wholly rational scruple is loyally supported by all the members of the cell except Stepan Fedorov, a hard-line revolutionary who has suffered imprisonment and torture by the Tsarist police and who finally admits in the heat of argument that he 'hates' the fellow-creatures on whose behalf he demands universal justice. It is thirst for this ruthless and undefined 'justice' which grips Stepan by the throat. Why show solicitude for two privileged children when Russia is groaning under the starving children of the poor?[59] When Dora insists that to have killed the Grand Duke's nephew and niece in the carriage would have incurred the hatred of the whole of humanity, Stepan replies that humanity has to be saved from itself. Camus has reached his destination: Stepan here represents the frosty elitism of omniscient revolutionaries from Robespierre to Lenin, the self-selected sons of History; for Stepan 'the Revolution' (as he keeps repeating) is a self-evident, all-wise, totally benevolent force whose triumph will eradicate every human evil:

STEPAN: When we resolve to forget about children, that's the day the revolution will triumph, and we will be masters of the world.
DORA: When that day comes, the revolution will be loathed by the whole human race.
STEPAN: What matter, if we love humanity enough to force our revolution on it; to rescue humanity from itself and its slavery?
DORA: And suppose mankind at large rejects that revolution? Suppose the masses for whom you are fighting won't stand for the killing of their children? Would you strike at the people, too?
STEPAN: Yes, if necessary, until they understand. I, too, love the people.
DORA: That's not how love looks (*l'amour n'a pas ce visage*)....
STEPAN: You're a woman, and your idea of love is unsound.[60]

Yet the sources of Stepan's rage, the 'hatred' he keeps polishing, are ambiguous: is he a man possessed in the Dostoyevskyan tradition, or is his fanaticism biographical, based on the pain and humiliation he has suffered? Or both—as with Lenin himself? And does he totally confuse 'the Revolution' with his own ego? Kaliayev finally expresses the view that the triumph of 'the Revolution' would be an unpleasant experience if synonymous with the triumph of Stepan who, still bearing the marks of the prison lash, comes out with a succession of chilling comments: 'The bomb alone is a revolutionary force . . . Everyone lies, be a good liar, that's what matters . . . Nothing is forbidden that advances the cause.'

Two days after the first botched attempt, another opportunity to assassinate the Grand Duke occurs. On this occasion he is travelling alone and Kaliayev (again off-stage) throws his bomb, blows the Grand Duke to pieces, and makes no attempt to escape.

In Act 4 the Chief of Police holds out prospects of clemency if Kaliayev will betray the identity of his colleagues. More dramatic is a visit by the distraught widow, the deeply religious Grand Duchess. Camus here achieves a masterly confrontation, as the Duchess imposes on Kaliayev some truths which he cannot bear to hear, describing the mutilation of her husband's body, the blood, the annihilation. She urges Kaliayev to repent within the bosom of the holy Church: 'God alone will justify you.' Camus is here on familiar territory:

KALIAYEV: What God? Yours or mine? . . . The Church has kept to itself the exercise of grace, and left to us the exercise of charity. . . .
THE GRAND DUCHESS: God reunites.
KALIAYEV: Not on this earth. And my meetings take place on this earth.
THE GRAND DUCHESS: It's the meeting place of dogs, their noses to the ground, sniffing here and there, always disappointed.[61]

At no point in the play do any of the revolutionaries mention the Russian peasants or the masses as agents of change—merely as beneficiaries.

ANNENKOV: All Russia will know that the Revolutionary Socialist Party has executed the Grand Duke Sergei by this bomb to hasten the liberation of the Russian people. And the Imperial Court will also learn that we are resolved to carry on the terror until the land is given back to the people.[62]

One is therefore puzzled as to how the death of one man, even a Grand Duke, could precipitate the overthrow of the system. Camus does not seem to question the utter futility of the anarchist secret cell hugging its own virtue and supposed destiny, although this of course was the main thrust of the Bolshevik–Menshevik case against anarchists of the Bakunin–Nechayev mould. Sartre's view was less sympathetic to anarchism. In *Les Mains sales* Hugo makes reference to an assassination in Tsarist Russia similar to the one portrayed (a year later) in *Les Justes*, but the date is given as 'the end of the last century'—not 1905—and the assassin is said to have died in the blast. When Hugo adds, 'I can do that', a veteran Communist retorts scornfully that he is an anarchist intellectual at heart, 'fifty years out of date'. Terrorism is finished. Sartre clearly agreed.[63]

Whereas Sartre's concern is with praxis and the practical, with what works effectively, Camus's main thrust is introverted: the individual conscience is what counts, in other words, a man's relationship with himself. He brings a 'religious' passion to his humanism—though the passion is masked by his appetite for Corneille-like oral fencing, for sculpting aphorisms out of human disaster:

STEPAN: Honour is a luxury reserved for people who have carriages-and-pairs—
KALIAYEV: No. It's the poor man's last penny (*la dernière richesse du pauvre*).

If Kaliayev comes out well from that exchange, one may nevertheless find his credo somewhat vaporous, even though Camus is clearly stacking the cards:

KALIAYEV: I joined the revolution because I love life.
STEPAN: I do not love life; I love justice, which is something higher than life.

But who in history has or would say such a thing? Certainly not Lenin. Worse, Kaliayev, the lover of life, appears to contradict himself and to embrace the very metaphysics that Camus found so dangerous, the deified Idea: 'Do you understand why I asked to throw the bomb? To die for an idea—that's the only way of proving oneself worthy of the idea. It's our justification.'

Equally dubious is Camus's insistence on atonement through self-sacrifice: his hero and heroine hold passionately that assassination is justifiable only if the assassin dies in the act or gives himself up to execution—only then is he not a 'murderer', a word which makes these sensitive assassins shudder; indeed, Kaliayev recoils when a real triple-murderer comes to mop out his cell floor in prison (he also doubles as prison executioner).

DORA: That's how it should be, Yanek. To kill, and to die. But to my mind, there's a still greater happiness. [KALIAYEV *gazes at her for a moment. She lowers her eyes.*] The scaffold![64]

But why should the just revolutionary carry this sackcloth and his own ashes in his knapsack—would Camus also apply it to the soldier in a just war, or to the Resistance he himself had joined against the Nazi occupation? In the final act the comrades await news of Kaliayev's execution and how he conducted himself. With noble dignity, it transpires; Dora, who loves Kaliayev passionately, is granted her request: she will throw the next bomb as well as make it.

Camus was undoubtedly a better novelist than playwright, and the reason is not hard to find. Whereas Malraux's heroes must breathe the oxygen of high historical crisis or fade back into the paper, Camus's forte was the implicit: Meursault's initial resistance to the claims of emotion in *L'Étranger*, the understated professional dedication of Dr Bernard Rieux in *La Peste*. But the dramatic medium—despite the eloquence of its silences—tends to be explicit, argumentative.

At the first night, 15 December 1949, Camus warmly greeted Sartre and de Beauvoir, who (she later wrote) found the play well acted but the text 'academic'. When a woman rushed up to Camus in the theatre foyer to enthuse, 'I like this better than *Les Mains sales*', without noticing Sartre standing nearby, Camus smiled and quipped to Sartre: 'Two birds with one stone.'[65] Although the socialist *Le Populaire* found *Les Justes* 'powerful and moving', the conservative *Le Figaro* and the Communist *L'Humanité* were in notable agreement: *Le Figaro*'s Jean-Jacques Gauiter complained of pessimism, negation, murder, execution, death, death, death without a saving tenderness. 'A play? No! An ideogram. Living creatures? No!...' *L'Humanité*'s verdict was 'worse than cold—icy. Fabricated characters. Banal dialogue... Unbelievable action.' Camus was pleased by praise from the *Manchester Guardian*, a paper he admired: 'But for the first time for a long time we hear again in this work, and in the theatre, the authentic voice of God, without the help of God, in the hearts of the same men.' Nicola Chiaromonte reported in *Partisan Review*: 'What made the Parisians applaud *Les Justes* and burst into tears at some of the scenes was not the debate about the Revolution which is present in only a few sketchy scenes, but the reminder of the Resistance which it obviously contains.'[66]

Camus's subject (but not his play) arrived in Moscow some twenty years later, when the Sovremennik Theatre staged a trilogy spanning the century from the abortive Decembrist revolution to the triumphant Bolshevik one: three 'generations' of Russian revolutionaries, beginning with Leonid Zorin's *The Decembrists*, then Aleksandr Svobodin's *The People's Will* (*Narodovol'tsy*), and finally Mikhail Shatrov's *The Bolsheviks*.

In *Narodovol'tsy*, directed by Oleg Efremov, one of the heroes of the People's Will Party, Zheliabov, and his comrades are hunting down Alexander II. Eight times their assassination attempts on the tsar-emancipator fail, but finally they run him to ground. Martyrs to their idea, the *narodovol'tsy* are portrayed as having expunged all personal feeling except hatred—the human in them is utterly consumed by the idea. Efremov explored the resources of the stage to convey the inherent tragedy of a population indifferent, even hostile, to the endeavours of revolutionary idealists who—unlike the Bolsheviks later—might have descended from Mars.[67]

First produced by Efremov in 1966, Shatrov's *The Bolsheviks* is set in the Kremlin, 30–1 August 1918, immediately after the near-fatal shooting of

Lenin by the Socialist Revolutionary Fanny Kaplan. Lenin lies wounded in the next room while the Commissars debate the use of Red terror, recalling the French Revolution, the Convention, the Committee of Public Safety, when terror had mutated into a bloodbath, a policy of annihilation. In Shatrov's *The Bolsheviks*, despite intimate knowledge of the self-destruction of the Jacobin movement in France, the Bolsheviks plunge into the same nightmare of unbridled violence:

KRESTINSKY: Well, you know, I think the French petty bourgeois can be excused for using the death penalty to try and get rid of profiteers.

LUNACHARSKY: Agreed, but I'm afraid that our provincial Robespierres and home-grown Dantons will also turn the bullet into the main means of solving all conflicts and problems.

SVERDLOV: Of course they will if we don't caution them! It's a lot easier to call on the Cheka for help than it is to work with the masses, explaining, publicising, persuading, organising.[68]

Shatrov's dialogue in *The Bolsheviks* is pure politics, pure history, despite routine 'human touches' and prefatory phrases such as 'That's true', 'And why?', 'Wait just a minute!', and 'You're absolutely right, Anatoly Vasilyevich'. The verbal texture is wooden. What dramatic power the play possesses springs not from the theatre but from the consequence of the decision these Bolshevik leaders made: class enemies to be put in concentration camps; all persons implicated as White Guards, or in plots and revolts, to be executed by a firing squad; the leading figures of the bourgeoisie, officer corps and Right Socialist Revolutionary Party to be held hostage. As for Fanny Kaplan, an heir to the heroes and heroines of Camus's *Les Justes*, who had just attempted to assassinate Lenin because she saw him as the new tsar, all the Bolsheviks present echo Anna Kollontai's recommendation: 'When the investigation is concluded, the firing squad [for her].'[69]

The playwright Shatrov certainly knew what he was writing about. Born Mikhail Marshak in 1932, he lost about thirty relatives in the Stalin purges.[70] His father was shot in 1937, his mother arrested in 1949: 'All my other relatives were victims of the Purges, too.' The central censorship banned *The Bolsheviks*, but Efremov[71] persuaded the minister of culture, Furtseva, to attend a run-through. She came out of the theatre calling it the 'best Party meeting' she had ever attended, assumed personal responsibility, and the production opened on 7 November 1967, the fiftieth anniversary of the Revolution.[72]

⌗ ⌗ ⌗

First performed on 7 June 1951, Sartre's *Le Diable et le bon dieu* (*Lucifer and the Lord*) ran at the Théâtre Antoine until March 1952. Jean-Louis Barrault had once told Sartre the story of Cervantes's *Il Rufio Dichoso*, in which a bandit decides to reform on a throw of the dice. Inspired by this, Sartre wrote *Le Diable*, though in his version the hero cheats in order to lose. 'I want to show a character as alien to the spirit of his age as Hugo, the young bourgeois in *Les Mains sales*, and equally torn by contradictions.' As de Beauvoir put it, in 1944 he had believed that any situation could be transcended by individual will-power; by 1951 he realized that individual salvation is impossible under force of circumstance—only collective struggle is viable.

But a play cannot dispense with differentiated individuals—Sartre hotly rejected the term 'characters' in both fiction and drama, because it suggested a fixed mould—and *Le Diable* was clearly influenced by his recent study of the scandalous life and work of Jean Genet. The medieval warlord Goetz in *Le Diable* is both Genet pushed to the extreme of evil in his quest for the absolute, as well as the incarnation of the growing dialogue between Sartre and Marxism. Goetz is a nobleman's bastard, the cruellest and most successful military leader of his time. Sartre himself was a semi-orphan who liked to claim affinity with bastards, 'bastardy being a symbol of the vital contradiction Sartre had experienced between his bourgeois birth and his intellectual choice'. Sartre held himself to be a 'false bastard', whereas Genet, Edmund Kean (the illegitimate English actor who became the subject of a Dumas play refurbished by Sartre), and Goetz are all genuine bastards. Goetz, like Genet, is a bastard who feels himself made of two halves which don't stick together.[73]

The project had been sustained from the outset by the dynamic *directrice* of the Théâtre Antoine, Simone Berriau, who (Sartre observed) moved around the theatre with her hands mechanically imitating the movement of a pair of scissors, so eager was she for cuts in his over-long text. Rehearsals began before Sartre had finished writing—he would never finish. Indeed, Pierre Brasseur's part as Goetz was too long for him to memorize.[74] The leading actors were all major figures: Jean Vilar took the role of Heinrich; Hilda was played by Maria Casarès, the revolutionary bomb-maker Dora in Camus's *Les Justes* and Death in Cocteau's film *Orphée*. The legendary Louis Jouvet produced—he died two months after the première.

The action takes place during the early years of the sixteenth century, the time of Luther's revolt against Rome, when the papal emissary Tetzel is touring Germany selling indulgences to the poor. This is an excellent vignette, lively and cynically comic; a flute sounds as each ecu drops into the alms-box, releasing a soul from purgatory like (as Tetzel himself puts it) 'beautiful white butterflies'.[75] In the first act we find the warlord Goetz strutting about doing evil for evil's sake. He is inclined to believe that God has given him carte blanche to violate women, impale children, decapitate men—'moi je fais le Mal pour le Mal'. It is his 'reason for living.' By the end of the act, however, he finds himself the lawful owner of his father's estates following the death of his legitimate half-brother. The bastard is no longer the bastard.

Heinrich, a shrewd but shifty priest, persuades Goetz that there is nothing wonderful in doing evil. A man could deserve Hell just by staying in bed, so impregnated is the world with evil. According to Heinrich, God's desire is to make *le Bien* impossible on earth. Goetz takes this as a challenge and vows to do Good, dropping his plans to seize and sack Worms, etc. Heinrich is a somewhat 'Brechtian' priest who plays double games when convenient—he calls the suffering of the poor a 'test' when speaking in Latin and an iniquity when using the vernacular German.

Like the Bible—and almost as long—*Le Diable* is an inexhaustible source of quotations, mainly *marxistantes*: 'When the rich make war, it's the poor who die.' (Yet equally valid might be, 'When the fathers make war, it's the sons who die.') Goetz's propensity to speak in aphorisms and abstractions about *le Bien* and *le Mal* may seem improbable in a warlord, but Sartre is a shameless ventriloquist. The priest Heinrich, wrestling with the conflict between his commitment to the poor of Worms and his ultimately greater duty to the Church, tells the insurgent leader Nasty: 'I am for you when you suffer, against you when you are set to spill the Church's blood.' Nasty replies: 'You're for us when we are murdered, against us when we dare to defend ourselves.' Anticipating Marx by 300 years, Nasty declares that there are two types of poor, those who are poor together and those who are poor alone. 'The former are the true ones, the others are the rich who haven't had any luck.'[76]

Nasty can be said to represent the Party in an era when there is none. Like Hoederer in *Les Mains sales*, he lies freely in a good cause—as when he cynically misinforms the starving people of Worms that the Bishop's granaries are full, though they are not. Nasty insists that this is a mere detail, because the Church is rich and yet allows people to starve.[77] He employs an anabaptist or Hussite idiom when he speaks of building the City of God where all men will be equal in brotherhood, and God will be in each as each is in God. Every man will be priest and prophet, entitled to baptize and marry, to announce good news and remit sins—'tous sont en Dieu et Dieu est en tous.'[78]

At the beginning of Act II Goetz accepts Nasty's proposition, an alliance with the poor. He now believes that one must suppress the conditions which prevent men from loving each other, most obviously inequality, servitude, and poverty. Goetz intends to hand over his land to the peasants and organize a truly Christian community of equals, but Nasty urges caution: if Goetz gives away his lands now, the peasants will inevitably rise against other landlords and be massacred. (These calculations remind us of Hoederer's when assessing the weakness of his forces in 1943.) Nasty therefore urges Goetz to hold on to the domains he has inherited by the accident of his legitimate brother's death, and offer them as a refuge for Nasty, whose orders will spread through 'Germany'.

Deferred gratification does not appeal for long to Goetz, who is not the man for doing Good (or anything else) on the instalment plan ('Je ne ferais pas le Bien à la petite semaine'). He wants to build the City of God here and now. Following a comic scene, a satire on the utopian impulse, in which Goetz tries to bully the old man leading a group of his own servile peasants into calling him 'brother' rather than 'seigneur', we now come to utopian socialism, the isolated community, the City of God built on Goetz's land, where the peasants have been schooled in pacifism.

Shortly afterwards Nasty brings news of what he had feared, premature peasant revolt. He urges Goetz, as the finest captain in Germany, to lead his men into just one victorious battle to inhibit the barons from massacring their peasants. But Goetz now lives only for Love; when he visits the peasants' camp to urge them to desist from war, they jeer at him and he curses them as swine. In a scene that may be a commentary on modern Communist Party tactics, a version of Brecht's *Die Massnahme*, Goetz and Nasty agree that to instil discipline one must create fear by hanging some peasants, the innocent as well as the guilty. 'Nasty, one must hang the poor. Hang them at random, the innocent with the guilty.'[79] Yet Goetz remains locked into his high-minded pacifism, and after the barons do indeed massacre Nasty's peasant army, leaving 25,000 dead, Nasty, who has escaped, reproaches Goetz: 'In a single day of virtue you have caused more deaths than in thirty-five years of malice.' Goetz now decides to resort to all-out war on the side of the peasants, leaving God out of it: 'I want to be a man among men. No more Heaven, no more Hell; nothing but Earth.' To prove the point, he stabs a subordinate commander who refuses to follow him.

The play's unmistakable message is that non-violence belongs to religion and quietism, the politics of the next world, not this one. This world is so deeply touched with evil (the consequence, in Sartre's view, of scarcity), that to master it one must ruthlessly soil oneself in mendacity and bloodshed— evidently the same message as in *Les Mains sales*. What the author of *La Nausée* found irresistible was everything opposed to viscosity: the hard, austere, metallic, mathematical, predictable, inflexible, unsentimental. Sartre was embracing his own existential version of Marxism—and shortly thereafter Frantz Fanon's—at a time when that ideology was poised to leave the stage, discredited precisely by Marx's failure to consider the psychologically damaging impact of violence on the rebel. Like Marx, Sartre failed to recognize in the oppressed tomorrow's oppressor.

The critics generally preferred the first Act of *Le Diable*, but 'the play's meaning escaped them', de Beauvoir reported:

They all made the enormous error of supposing that Goetz, by committing the murder at the end of the last scene, was returning to Evil. In fact, Sartre was once more confronting the vanity of morality with the efficacy of *praxis* ... *Le Diable et le bon dieu* is the mirror of Sartre's entire ideological evolution. The contrast between Orestes's departure at the end of *Les Mouches* and Goetz's final stance illustrates the distance Sartre had covered ... [80]

Yet Sartre, we can safely say, is never quite serious about man as a political animal. There is always that suspicion, absent in socialist realism, that the world is really a stage. Common to all of Sartre's heroes is the consciousness of acting out a succession of roles. Orestes (*Les Mouches*) yearns to tie down his freedom through a real act; Hugo (*Les Mains sales*) asks himself whether he is a revolutionary or merely playing at one; Goetz (*Le Diable*) says: 'So everything was merely lying and playacting? I have not acted; I have made gestures.' The eponymous Nekrassov of Sartre's farcical satire realizes that he is merely an 'instrument' and that others have 'manipulated him like a child'. Genet (in Sartre's *Saint Genet*) is 'an actor despite himself, his rejection of the world is only a gesture'. The actor Kean (as portrayed by Sartre) achieves the highest awareness of being merely a succession of roles; but, in trying to cast off all roles, he finds himself merely playing at being a man.[81]

In November 1947 Sartre had recommended a type of theatre in which a character is shown 'creating himself, the moment of choosing'; the dramatist should build situations which force the characters to make a choice involving death. But why death? Why must Sartre's stage heroes wrestle with their existential freedom through murderous violence? Orestes kills his own mother and her lover, Hugo kills Hoederer, Goetz kills as a way of life. In the cases of Orestes and Goetz, not to kill, not to go through with it, is tantamount to bondage. With Camus it is much the same: who will pluck up courage to assassinate Caligula? In *Le Malentendu* murder is a way of life for the mother and daughter; in *L'État de siège* Death is a character who struts about, chortling and reaping; in *Les Justes* everything focuses on a planned assassination. Was this because Sartre and Camus were in the grip of a murderous mid-century, or was it because they had absorbed the conventions of adventure fiction, the detective story and 'thriller', which must run with blood?

Camus's long essay *L'Homme révolté* (*The Rebel*) was published in October 1951, ahead of two other notable anti-Marxist polemics, Raymond Aron's *L'Opium des intellectuels* (1955) and Jean-François Revel's *La Tentation totalitaire* (1976). Camus's target was Utopia and the metaphysics which would stop at nothing to impose it. 'In this New Jerusalem, echoing with the roar of miraculous machinery, who will still remember the cry of the victims?'[82] Camus again argued the case for an ethic of political moderation (*mésure*) expressed in *Les Justes*—though assassination is an odd kind of moderation. His principal target was the Germanic philosophy of history, the obsession with ultimate ends and the justification of organized violence and repression in the name of those ends. The alternative to authoritarian revolution he recommended was 'rebellion', the act of individual refusal which, even when it assumes a violent form, does not lose sight of the values promoting it and protects its own purity by an emphasis on personal sacrifice rather than personal power. In short, Kaliayev and Dora, not Stepan. According to Sartre—this was a famous polemic—Camus had now made his 'Thermidor' (counter-revolution) by attempting to stand outside or above history; his fastidious emphasis on means would merely gratify the consciences of those who preferred to criticize the status quo rather than abolish it. 'To merit the right to influence men who are struggling, one must first participate in their struggle, and this first means accepting many things, if you hope to change a few of them.' Sartre was now (1952–3) dedicated to the Communist Peace Movement and applauded accordingly in the Soviet press. In a polemic published in Moscow in 1950, the Soviet critic V. Gorodinskii had written: 'Jean-Paul Sartre and his band (*Zhan-Pol' Sartr i ego banda*) . . . admire thieves, murderers, sexual neuropaths, traitors and liars'; however, when the Soviet critic's book appeared in East German translation three years later, by which time Sartre was an esteemed figure on Peace Movement platforms, the words 'Jean-Paul Sartre and his band' were deleted from the derogatory passage and replaced simply by *die Existentialisten*—the Existentialists'. Ehrenburg also expressed regret at having attacked Sartre as a 'caustic, coldly cerebral drawing-room writer'—though in fact this had been among his lesser insults.[83]

⊞ ⊞ ⊞

Sartre's astringent satire *Nekrassov* opened on 8 June 1955, directed by Jean Meyer at Simone Berriau's Théâtre Antoine, Paris. As usual rehearsals were marred by arguments about the exorbitant length of Sartre's script. Several of the actors withdrew. The date of the opening had to be postponed more than once.[84] Right-wing satire is always tolerated,' he told an interviewer; 'one will see if satire of the left is going to be...'[85]

The plot is entirely political yet improbable; we are told that a feverish by-election is taking place off-stage in Seine-et-Marne. The government candidate, Mme Bounoumi, supporting German rearmament, is facing a dangerous challenge, not only from the Communists but also from a Radical Party candidate, Perdrière, whose hostility to German rearmament outstrips his hostility to the USSR. He must be persuaded to step down in favour of Mme Bounoumi—but how? The president of the paper *Le Soir à Paris*, Mouton (which means 'sheep', singular), instructs the newspaper's director, Jules Palotin, to mount a campaign demonstrating that the material survival of France depends on the German army and American supremacy. Easier said than done! Palotin passes the buck by warning one of his reporters, poor old Sibilot, that if he doesn't come up with something for the regular Red scare page 5 ('le cinq') by tomorrow, he's out—'tu peux faire tes bagages'. In despair, Sibilot comes up with a solution—a propaganda campaign revealing how many Frenchmen have been listed by Moscow to be shot after a Communist takeover.

This solution emerges fortuitously after a confidence-trickster on the run from the police, Georges de Valera, happens to take refuge in old Sibilot's Parisian residence. Before reaching this point, however, Sartre, begins the play in a standard 'boulevard' idiom with a scene on the banks of the Seine, near to a bridge, under a full moon. A couple of nattering, Beckett-like elderly tramps, male and female (whom we shall not encounter again), see a man about to commit suicide by jumping into the river. When they fish Georges de Valera out, he is not grateful: 'Your supreme joy is to deprive of their death those who have been deprived of life.' (Evidently the tramps have fished out Sartre.) Later the droll Inspector Goblet, who has been hunting the conman Georges, turns up. All of this covers twenty-eight pages of text, and could have been discarded without disadvantage to the play, a point worth registering before we reach the critical attacks on *Nekrassov*.

The second tableau is set in the offices of *Le Soir à Paris*. Palotin produces two election posters for Seine-et-Marne: 'Fraternity Through Rearmament' and 'To Protect Peace, all Means are Good, Including War.' The paper also specializes in photographic montages: for example, Stalin on horseback entering Notre Dame in flames. Reports come through from Reuter and AFP that the Soviet minister of the interior, Nekrassov, was not seen at the

Moscow opera and has not been sighted since not being seen. Not a word from Tass—therefore he must have fled to freedom.

The farcical mode follows. The crook Georges de Valera, on the run from Inspector Goblet, takes refuge purely by chance in the apartment where Sibilot lives with his left-wing journalist daughter Veronique. Finding the stranger hiding, she is quickly reassured by Georges's personality and does not hand him over to Goblet. Georges claims to have been born in Moscow in 1917, 'un enfant bleu', son of 'un garde noir' father and a white Russian mother. The juxtaposition of 'blue,' 'black', and 'white' is about as close to humour as Sartre comes.

Arriving home, Sibilot lets his hair down to Veronique, listing all his page–5 anti-Communist campaigns and lamenting his editor's ingratitude. The fugitive Georges, overhearing Sibilot's laments, proposes a solution: he will present himself as the missing Soviet politician Nekrassov—Sartre's way of hinting that all Soviet defectors are fraudulent, one way or another. When Sibilot turns up at the office with his 'Nekrassov', Palotin shrugs—since the Kravchenko affair he has reported 122 Soviet officials defecting across the Iron Curtain, the *Rideau de Fer*, 'vrais ou faux'. Here Sartre gets in side-swipes against two real newspapers, *Le Figaro* and *France-Soir*, including the latter's proprietor Pierre Lazareff (although in an interview with *Combat* Sartre denied that Lazareff was his model, 'because I consider that the evening press is not systematically anti-Communist'). So why had he chosen an evening paper as the scene of the play?[86] Ironically, and no doubt unnoticed by Sartre, Pierre and Hélène Lazareff had signed the same letter as he had, protesting the Laniel government's cancellation of the Russian ballet performances at the Paris Opéra in May 1954. This followed the Lazareffs' own visit to Russia, when French journalists were granted visas to witness the warm welcome in Moscow for the Comédie française—which had done nothing to lessen their hostility to the regime.

The confidence-trickster Georges tells his slightly sceptical audience of right-wing journalists that his lack of identity papers merely confirms the authenticity of his claim to be the real Nekrassov, who 'has killed one hundred and eighteen people with his own hands and imposed a reign of terror for ten years'. 'Nekrassov' then unveils the infamous 'Soviet Plan C' for the occupation of France, as well as a list of 100,000 French people destined to be shot (*fusillés*), including all former ministers, which means one parliamentary deputy in four—a jest at chronic governmental instability under the Fourth Republic. Georges assures the journalists of *Le Soir à Paris* that he remains a Communist by conviction, but the Kremlin has betrayed the Revolution. He regrets that in giving them the means to overthrow the Soviet regime he risks prolonging bourgeois society by a century. Two hundred years hence the Revolution will arise, purified, from the ashes. The directors of the paper all shout Bravo!

As a result of these scare tactics, the evening newspaper doubles its sales and Sibilot more than doubles his salary as Nekrassov-Georges provides a steady stream of 'revelations':

GEORGES: Look, read this telegram; it's from MacCarthy [sic] who is proposing me for a permanent post as a witness. Here are the congratulations from Franco, and from United Fruit, a cordial word from Adenauer, a signed letter from Senator Borgeaud. In New York my revelations have sent Wall Street prices up; everywhere war industries are booming. Big interests are at stake; Nekrassov is no longer only me; it's a generic name for dividends from shares in armaments factories.[87]

To no one's astonishment, *L'Humanité* and *Les Lettres françaises* enthusiastically lauded the play. '*Nekrassov* makes decent people laugh, makes the riffraff pull faces, and gives everyone food for thought', declared Guy Leclerc, who, as may be recalled, had seven years earlier responded to *Les Mains sales* by describing Sartre as an 'understudy for Koestler'.[88] Interviewed by Bernard Dort, Sartre reflected that although *Nekrassov* had been upheld 'unconditionally' by the Communists, by their trade union confederation (CGT), and by their cultural association, Théâtre et Culture, which offered tickets at reduced prices, 'the workers arrived only slowly, little by little'. For the workers the theatre remained part of the bourgeois ceremony, far from home in the centre of Paris. According to Sartre: 'The whole tradition of the theatre was popular until the arrival of the bourgeoisie.' He described Shakespeare's theatre as 'the great example that exists of popular theatre: in this theatre the public refound, and still rediscovers, its own problems, and relives them.'[89] Under the *ancien régime*, despite fierce class struggle, 'everyone goes to the theatre and the theatre is for everyone. But from the nineteenth century the town belongs to the bourgeoisie. They put the theatres in the centre, in the heart of their citadel.'[90] The thesis is modified when he speaks of a strong, realist bourgeois theatre at the end of the nineteenth century, still possible 'when the bourgeoisie did not feel itself threatened directly'. But nowadays bourgeois theatre tolerated only light and satirical pieces which did not challenge anything (*qui ne mettent rien en cause*). To produce a play like *Nekrassov* in these conditions was (he noted) paradoxical.[91] Yet one must reiterate that Sartre's own theatrical instincts, like his relations with managements and actors, were in the traditional bourgeois-boulevard mould. He wanted the big theatres for his plays, and never did quite get around to writing for progressive theatre companies like Jean Vilar's Théâtre nationale populaire (TNP).[92]

The 'bourgeois' press responded with predictable hostility. A month before the opening performance, *Le Figaro* warned of a work 'inspired by pure "crypto" Communism', then damned the play 'as mortally boring and theatrically stultifying, but also as so mentally simplistic and politically inaccurate as to be an insult to the spectator's intelligence'.[93] Sartre had given hostages to fortune by explicitly ridiculing his critics in *Nekrassov*; for example, Thierry Maulnier is described in Tableau IV, scene 1, as 'an eminent thinker' whose anti-Communist newspaper articles amount to excellent recruitment propaganda for the PCF. Maulnier duly hit back in *Le Figaro* and (a year later) in 'Nekroutchov?', following Khrushchev's revelations about Stalin.[94]

Françoise Giroud wrote a scathing review in *L'Express*, and there were attacks in *France-Soir*, *Paris-Match*, and *L'Aurore*. 'A thick-ankled farce, repartees as heavy as boulders, the elegance of a rhinoceros: Jean-Paul Sartre's play tramples on the spectators for four solid hours', wrote Pierre Macabru in *Arts* (15–21 June 1955). Robert Kemp joined the onslaught in *Le Monde* (14 June 1955): Sartre had written 'a variety show for which even the least talented cabaret singer from Montmartre would hesitate to claim responsibility'.[95] The Catholic playwright and critic Gabriel Marcel called the play 'dangerous . . . since it tends towards classifying as hysterical publicity or mindless McCarthyism the very real anxieties that we might have regarding the future of the free world, we who now know where we stand on the Polish, Hungarian or Czech paradise'.[96] But Roland Barthes rallied to Sartre, likening the dazzling writing to Beaumarchais; he mocked the critics for vainly debating whether the play should be seen as a farce, comedy of manners, a satire, a revue, or a burlesque.

Nekrassov would have been saved and praised if it had been an ambiguous play (referred to as 'complex'), an inoffensive play (referred to as 'objective'), an uncommitted play (referred to as 'literary'). Unfortunately, *Nekrassov* is a resolutely political play, with a political viewpoint that is not appreciated; this is why it is being rejected.[97]

Yet Sartre had often insisted that (as he later put it to Kenneth Tynan): 'I do not think that theatre can emerge directly from political events. Theatre must take these issues and transform them into a *mythical* form.' Certainly *Nekrassov* broke his own rules, including 'the necessity of taking a certain distance from the object evoked, displacing it in time and space',[98] but he defended the play as the exception which aimed at a 'demystification' and, above all, at clarity: '...this play demonstrates my wish to confront social reality without myths',[99] he told Guy Leclerc of *l'Humanité*, adding that he wished to contribute 'to the struggle for peace'.[100]

In November 1955 Sartre returned to Moscow for performances of *The Respectful Prostitute* and *Nekrassov*. The second edition of the *Great Soviet Encyclopedia*, published in the same year, praised his work for the Peace Movement while describing his 'world outlook' as 'contradictory'. In his artistic work, whether plays like *The Flies* (*Mukhi*) and *No Exit* (*Za zakrytoi derv'iu*), or the novels, his striving for a truthful depiction of life and his opposition to repression collided with his pessimistic existentialist metaphysics. The *Encyclopedia* had no difficulty with the critique of American racism in *The Respectful Prostitute*,[101] or with the satire *Nekrassov*, but evidently had so much difficulty with *Les Mains sales* that the play's existence was not mentioned. Nor was *Le Diable et le bon dieu*.[102]

For his part, Sartre's comments on the Soviet productions he saw were somewhat solemn and laboured. In the main cities of the USSR the theatre public was 'petit bourgeois as with us', but the cultural centres close to the factories provided a form of workers' theatre in which leading actors took part. 'Soviet theatre is educative; it's not very good, it could be better. The essential thing, however, is that it has a public, that it truly speaks to the public of workers...'[103]

When the Soviet Union suppressed the Hungarian Revolution in 1956 by military force, this proved too much even for Sartre. The Red Army tanks swept aside the subtle paradoxes of *Les Mains sales* and left no one laughing at the farcical scenario of *Nekrassov*.

⊞ ⊞ ⊞

In stark contrast to the commercial successes of Sartre and Camus, Roger Vailland's *Le Colonel Foster plaidera coupable* (*Colonel Foster Will Plead Guilty*) fell victim to outright censorship, the virulent, state-controlled anti-Communism of the early 1950s. Directed by the Communist film director Louis Daquin, *Le Colonel Foster* had its fateful dress rehearsal at the Théâtre de l'Ambigu on 15 May 1952. The pro-American Pinay government, in office since 8 March, and the municipal authorities had been trying to block the production by bureaucratic methods—the prefect of police suddenly decided that the theatre's exits, doors, safety-rails, and electrical apparatus did not conform to safety requirements, and the projected first night on 9 May was aborted despite an unavailing appeal by the Communist lawyer Joe Nordmann to the Tribunal de la Seine. Interviewed in *Combat* (9 May), Vailland said: 'I am a Communist in spirit, but this is certainly not a propaganda play.

It shows that every foreign war inevitably turns even the most honest man into a war criminal.'[104] On the first night, 16 May, the play was broken up by well-organized gangs who invaded the stage, attacked the actors, and wrecked the set. Jacques Duclos, acting leader of the PCF during Maurice Thorez's convalescence in the Soviet Union, had to be protected by his bodyguards. No one was prosecuted. The decree banning the play was signed on behalf of the prefect of police by the infamous Nazi collaborator Maurice Papon.[105] *Colonel Foster* was never again performed in its entirety in France. Vailland joined the Party, and soon embarked on a four-month tour of the Soviet bloc which, with characteristic efficiency, duly turned out productions of the banned play in Prague, Budapest, Warsaw, Moscow, Leningrad, and the Deutsches Theater, East Berlin.

On 28 May, a few days after the play was banned in Paris, Communist riots occurred—and were violently repressed—when General Matthew Ridgway, successor to MacArthur in Korea, arrived in Paris as Supreme Commander, NATO. The Communist press accused him of responsibility for biological warfare in Korea—one crime somehow omitted from Vailland's play. The editor of *L'Humanité* and Duclos were arrested—the latter, a tubby gourmet, in the suspicious company of a pigeon—prompting Vailland to send a signed copy of his play, and his at last successful application to join the PCF, to Duclos's prison cell in the Santé.

Vailland, the epitome of radical chic, had written the play while staying in Curzio Malaparte's villa in Capri in July 1950. The action takes place in South Korea during that same month. Colonel Foster, the local American commander, is a humanitarian caught in the vices of his social system. 'We have come here', he says, 'to protect the peasants against Communism, and not to kill them.' But his racist lieutenant warns him: 'You think too much, Harry. You'll end up a Communist.'[106] As a counterfoil, Vailland uses the radio operator, Sergeant Paganel, to utter withering asides which puncture the pretensions of the main speakers with sarcastic references to racism, militarism, the *pax americana*, and the atom bomb.

All five acts are set in the house of the local mayor, a rich Korean businessman, grain-dealer, and cynical exploiter, Cho Aodi Yang, requisitioned as the command post of Colonel Foster. Admitting that most of the local peasants are Communists by conviction, Cho calls for brutal measures and reminds the shocked Colonel Foster that in South Korea a man is less valued than a mule. His American-educated daughter Lya, secretly a keen Marxist theorist with Communist convictions, fluent in French and ancient Greek, plays baseball, drinks whisky, shoots like an ace—and secretly works for the Revolution, betraying troop movements to the partisans. Not bad looking either—Vailland won't let us down on that—Lya is the Mata Hari whose sensuous beauty has beguiled Foster, despite his devotion to wife and children. At one point he kneels before her: 'I'd be prepared to re-read Karl Marx . . . at your side.' (Was his first reading of Marx at West Point?)[107]

France and the French figure with surprising prominence in the play, given that in reality French forces were deployed in Indochina, not Korea. As Ted Freeman comments: 'For no obvious reason Lieutenant MacAllen bursts into song, a French North African marching song taught to him by a tough old French army captain in Normandy. The French are gallant, sexy (Vailland had an obsession about that) and cultured.' They are also described by the American characters as 'all Commies'—*tous les cocos*, 'except for those we have bought'.

Professionally adept, the play ranks above average as propaganda. Throughout the action no mention is made of the North Korean army, only of 'partisans' defying the imperialist war machine and supporting the Stockholm Appeal. Although Foster himself is a decent and honest liberal, a Southern gentleman—despite ordering villages to be burned and prisoners shot—the mass of his fellow soldiers come across as crass, sex-crazed brutes treating Koreans as less than animals, as gooks or *sales gouques*.[108]

With American forces on the retreat, Foster receives an order to execute all political prisoners. Before his execution the partisan leader Masan holds a conversation with Cho's daughter about Spain, Greece, Indochina, the Stockholm Appeal, and McCarthyism—not forgetting France, 'the giants of 1793'—he certainly covers the ground. In the fifth and final act partisan forces capture Foster, who has carried out the executions and burned the village. He must now face a Popular Tribunal. On behalf of himself and American imperialism, he pleads guilty.[109]

Anti-Communist theatre critics were predictably severe after seeing the fatal dress rehearsal. In *Paris-Presse* (17 June) Max Favalelli dismissed it as 'une ennuyeuse image d'Epinalskoï', meaning a stereotyped, pious cardboard cut-out. Vailland broke with the Party four years later, after the suppression of the Hungarian Revolution.

Squaring the Circle:
Ionesco, Beckett,
Havel, Stoppard

The Theatre on the Balustrade (*Divadlo na zábraldí*) opened in 1958 in a derelict hall by the Vltava river not far from the Charles Bridge, Prague. On the basis of a promising script, Václav Havel was invited to join the company as a stage-hand in the summer of 1960, later as literary adviser. Acknowledging the influence of both Kafka and the Theatre of the Absurd on his plays, Havel adds the factor of his own bourgeois origins, the experience of 'being excluded through no fault of my own'. The Havels were of 'pampered bourgeois stock' (as he put it); in 1948 the family business had been removed from their control, and later the estate was confiscated.[1] When Havel and his brother finished elementary school at the age of 15 they were barred by their social origin from high school and university. The young Václav worked as a carpenter and laboratory assistant for five years.

The auditorium of the Balustrade Theatre was cramped and spectators could sit where they wished. Discussions between players and audiences often went on long into the night. Under the new director, Jan Grossman, the Balustrade quickly developed a European reputation as the groundbreaking (in East European terms) showpiece of the Theatre of the Absurd. Grossman offered Havel the space and scope to thrive. For the young writer the crucially eye-opening productions in the early sixties at the Balustrade were Ionesco's *The Bald Prima Donna*, Beckett's *Waiting for Godot*, Alfred Jarry's *Ubu Roi*, a dramatization of Kafka's *The Trial*, and Ladislav Fialka's *Pantomime*. The latter's quiet influence was enormous. As with other great exponents of mime—Chaplin, Marcel Marceau—Fialka had fashioned a form of dramatic expressionism which stood back from what it expressed and from itself. Having brought two productions to the World Theatre season in London in 1967, in the fateful spring which followed Fialka opened *Buttons* at the Theatre on the Balustrade, a show which (the present writer recalls) radiated a sly, Schweikian cunning, an oblique, between-the-lines style of bloodletting evolved during thirty years of authoritarian government. Václav Havel was part of this, a member of the family. Richard Coe has described the Theatre of the Absurd as 'quite clearly the product of the Frightened Fifties. Its pessimism, its sense of waste and futility... were as manifestly the echo of that long nightmare which stretched from the accession of Hitler to the catastrophe of Hiroshima as was the Existentialist philosophy which accompanied them and in many cases provided their *raison d'être*.'[2] To this we may add that the Theatre of the Absurd implied outright rejection of the politics and aesthetics of Stalinist Communism. Characteristic of this 'decadent' genre was minimalization of scenery and action, depersonalization, characters given little social identity and sometimes no names, plus elements adopted from the music hall or circus such as marionettes or clowns. Yet the obvious surrealist heritage from Jarry, Cocteau, and Artaud was in certain respects divided between Artaud's preference for non-verbal theatre, mime, painting, music, dance, gesture, lighting, on the one hand; and, on the other, the conservative emphasis of Beckett and Ionesco on the primacy of the sacred text—heaven help any director or actor who changes a word of *Waiting for Godot* or *Rhinoceros*![3]

The political innocence of the Theatre of the Absurd can be exaggerated. Samuel Beckett's *Waiting for Godot* is in one dimension a recognizable rejection of Bolshevik messianism—*Waiting for Lenin*—and Marxist worship at the altar of Progress. A powerful anti-Communist, anti-Soviet ideological current in mid-century Western culture scorned the vulgar optimism and 'lofty humanism' of Soviet message-theatre. In Kafka, Ionesco, and Beckett, Man is found to be solitary, alienated, and bewildered, trapped in a circular time-warp, a slave to language and always aspiring to be and have what is *sine die* out of reach. Images of ontological decay are presented with relish: Ionesco's *The Chairs*, first performed in Paris in April 1952, puts on display an old couple in their nineties ploughing through every available motion of senile dementia, vanity, snobbery, pretentiousness, geriatric infantilism, and self-deception. In Ionesco's *Amedée or How to Get Rid Of It* (1954), a respectable suburban couple have a corpse in their bedroom which swells at an alarming rate. As Richard Coe comments of Ionesco: 'From *La Cantatrice* to *Jeux de massacre*, every conceivable degree of thick-headedness is lovingly and caressingly analysed and lingered over. Nor is there any hope of cure: stupidity and self-deception are the very heritage of man, ingrained, ineradicable; humanity is born dumb, blinkered and doomed.'[4]

Yet Ionesco's personal heritage was an intensely political one. At their last, unhappy meal together in pre-war Bucharest, his father, a lawyer, called his son:

someone who sided with the Jews . . . we had a falling out because he was a rightist intellectual; today he would be a leftist intellectual . . . He believed in the State, no matter what it represented . . . This was how he came to be an Iron Guard, a Freemason democrat, and a Stalinist. As far as he was concerned, all opposition was wrong. As far as I was concerned, all opposition was right. (*Today, in 1967, I don't like the opposition either, for I know that it is a potential State, that is to say, tyranny.*)[5]

Ionesco emphasized his special debt to a Jew, Kafka, particularly his *Metamorphosis*—guilt without a cause.[6] Anyone could turn into a monster. The monster in us can get the upper hand in the way that crowds or whole nations can, resulting in pogroms, collective frenzies, tyrannies. Hence Ionesco's play *Rhinoceros* (1960), where an ordinary man, Berenger, is finally the only inhabitant of the town who has not succumbed to mass conformism and turned into a rhino. The mechanical element progressively takes over until there is only the machine, wild and out of control. In *The Chairs* it is mechanical chaos (*dérèglement mécanique*); in *The Lesson* it is language that leads the way into the cul-de-sac. Interviewed by *Figaro littéraire*, Ionesco made it clear that his fable in *Rhinoceros* applied to all fanaticism, right or left—although critics who saw Barrault's version at the Théâtre de France reported that it emphasized the Nazi parallel.[7]

Rhinoceros is more than a study of conformism and mass hysteria; it is also about the betrayal of man by his own intellect: excessive respect for the laws of cause and effect, willingness to justify anything that can be proved to be inevitable. Rationalism is disguised fatalism. After Botard becomes a rhinoceros, Dudard tells Bérenger: 'Everything is logical. To understand is to justify.' Bérenger alone resists and embraces the irrational. 'Well, in that case, I . . . *I refuse to think*!' For Ionesco, political revolution would always fail unless preceded by a radical change in modes of thought and language. This was the surrealist heritage. Accused of formalism, he replied that the most dangerous kind of formalism reduced the living texture of original thought and language to the dead formulae of slogans, politics, and propaganda. 'A committed theatre is dangerous—exceedingly dangerous. It leads directly to the concentration camp.' Ionesco's anarchism had seemed progressive in the 1950s, but since 1960 he described himself as a 'right-wing anarchist' for whom 'Every single belief for which we are prepared to go to war is worth neither more nor less than any other belief'.[8] Socialists, Communists, existentialists, intellectuals, Brecht and Sartre—they all got it in the neck from

Ionesco: 'Sartre is not alone, for example, in his pigheadness. He reflects the mentality of the petit bourgeois whose feelings have been corrupted and whose minds, of course, have been corrupted too.' Ionesco added: 'I have never known any poor Communists. I have known many rich Communists: artists, theatrical directors, rich producers...'[9] Like Camus, Ionesco associated totalitarianism with monopolistic and deterministic claims on 'History': 'In order to resist these currents, one must tell oneself that history is always wrong, whereas it is generally believed that history is always right.'[10] At the core of Marxism he identified nostalgia for a lost paradise; the ideology was a degradation of a mythical truth; Russian writers were stifled by academic realism and academic socialism; the young East European writers were yearning to break away from committed literature. A passionate Zionist, convinced that the Arabs were planning genocide, Ionesco supported the Vietnam War, detested Castro, and loathed Maoism—'dazed hordes who are ready for anything'.

Although written in 1948–9, Samuel Beckett's *Waiting for Godot* was not published until 1952 and not performed in Paris until the following year. These were hard times for Beckett, whose novels were little known and who lived off translation fees and his wife. World fame, however, was hiding behind the tree that is the most constant feature of the stage in *Godot*. Interpretations differed. That Beckett loved the films of Laurel and Hardy, and that his characters Vladimir and Estragon are sculpted from the music-hall tradition, is certain. Is Godot God? Was there a divine blueprint, of which the real world is an imperfect copy, or is existence the only available meaning?[11] A comparison with Brecht's play *Herr Puntila und sein Knecht Matti* comes to mind as soon as Pozzo appears with his slave Lucky haltered round the neck. But Beckett was not interested in class struggle; he wanted all four characters to wear bowler hats, *chapeaux melons*, and did not like the costumes chosen by the play's first director, Roger Blin, dressing Pozzo up as master and Lucky in rags as slave. This may be one reason why Brecht was rewriting *Godot* in a notebook when he died.[12]

The Babylone, which seated 230 spectators, possessed a minute stage 4 metres deep and 6 wide. Here *Godot* opened on 5 January 1953. Play and author became famous. The influential Jean Anouilh called it a masterpiece, as important an event as Pirandello's *Six Characters in Search of an Author*. The snobs arrived, often leaving after the first act, or at the start of the second, as soon as they saw that the curtain rose on the same old scene. Sometimes a full house became an empty one. Many were bored. Some came to be reassured that most avant-garde works were fakes. The most popular allegorical interpretation was that Godot was God and the play was about his disappearance from human affairs. Others saw a morality play, Vladimir and Estragon representing mankind, fallen, exiled, and awaiting its salvation. The tree and its blossom reinforced this view. Whereas Christians saw Vladimir and Estragon keeping faith to the end, the existentialist concluded that Vladimir and Estragon were guilty of bad faith, having put themselves in the hands of Another. But was Beckett guilty of perversely condemning the human condition as barren—'perversely', because he enjoyed writing plays applauded by other humans? Marxists pointed out that things get steadily worse during the course of the play: Pozzo returns deprived of sight, dragged on by Lucky deprived of speech. The climax of this disintegration comes when the four characters fall to the ground together, creating a formless mass from which Didi's voice emerges: 'We are men!' But Marxist charges that *Godot* fits the general 'anti-humanist' decadence of modernism are wide of the the mark. Passages of the second act are deeply affecting—for example, Pozzo's new blindness, and his periodic, almost mechanical, call of 'Au Secours!', culminating in one passionate cry of 'Pitié!'

Although Gogo's trousers fall down and the dangers of gravity are ever present, while Vladimir suffers from prostate trouble and frequently needs to piss, and Pozzo has a heart condition, *Godot* is strangely divorced from naturalism; no bottle, full or empty, appears throughout—here is a play about men who would normally be alcoholics, yet live without alcohol. Here are 'drunken' quarrels without inebriation. The tramps carry no food either, except the odd secreted carrot, and don't seem to notice hunger. Sex is out of sight and out of mind. There is a tree but no one stands against it to urinate. Yet this is not due to the decorousness so dear to the Moscow school of socialist realism. By relieving man of his normal demons of thirst, hunger, bladder, and sex, Beckett in effect emphasizes the frailty, the unreliability, of the 'higher' faculties which distinguish man from animal: speech, language, the ability to turn time into clocks—sociability. Pozzo rails against Vladimir's insistence on pinpointing events within time—'When? When?':

Pozzo: *C'est incensé! Quand! Quand! Un jour, ça ne vous suffit pas*—On a day like other days he became dumb, one day I became blind, one day we will become deaf, one day we were born, one day we will die, the same day, the same instant, that doesn't satisfy you?[13]

For Marxists, by contrast, a scientific philosophy must be historical and sequential. In 1956 Beckett told a Dublin acquaintance that both critics and public worldwide sought allegorical or symbolic meaning, whereas the intention was to avoid definition at all costs. 'The end is to give artistic expression to something hitherto almost ignored—the irrational state of unknowingness where we exist, this mental weightlessness which is beyond reason.'[14]

The play ran for a full year in Paris but was out of the question in Moscow. The Lord Chamberlain interfered when *Godot* reached London, directed by Peter Hall—not long out of university but already the director of Ionesco's *The Lesson*. On the first night of *Godot* at the Arts Theatre Club, 3 August 1955, there was derisive laughter at the line 'I have been better entertained elsewhere'; on the line 'Nothing happens, nobody comes, nobody goes. It's awful', a loud and very English voice said 'Hear! Hear!'[15] By the start of the second act there were few people in the theatre. Poised to close, but rescued by the critic Harold Hobson in the *Sunday Times*, six weeks later the play transferred to the Criterion in the West End and ran for eight months to fairly full houses. Before the New York production opened the producer, Michael Myerberg, placed an ad in the *New York Times* offering a limited engagement of only four weeks and warning away all those who went to the theatre 'for casual entertainment'. This proved to be a shrewd move—*Godot* rapidly became an event, and ran.

Beckett—as if carrying on from Ionesco's *The Chairs*—increasingly views senility as the metaphor for the human condition. His elderly characters have reached a point where they can no longer fool themselves—though they can try. In *Endgame* (1957) Hamm is tormented by his dead parents, who remain stuffed into dustbins but refuse to rot or get themselves collected. Critics contrasted the bleak anger of *Endgame*, its introversion and solitary despairs, to the good humour of *Godot*. Between Vladimir and Estragon there was warmth and mutual dependence, whereas the blind but evidently powerful Hamm is hostile to everyone. Only his slobbering old parents, Nag and Nell, fastened in their dustbins, have anything that could be described as tenderness and love for each other. Krapp, in the one-act *Krapp's Last Tape* (1958), replays memories of his youth to while away the time but is disgusted by his own optimism of yesteryear. Reviewing the play in the *Observer*, Kenneth Tynan wrote a humorous parody about the agonies of a bewildered critic, ending:

'*Is that all the review he is getting?*'
'That's all the play he's written.'
'*But a genius. Could you do as much?*'
'Not as much. But as little.'[16]

In the 1960s, when Kafka came back on the Marxist agenda, though not without fierce polemics, Georg Lukács, the Hungarian doyen of Marxist critics, continued to dismiss Beckett as plain negative. At a Prague literary conference in the spring of 1964 the heterodox Austrian Marxist Ernst Fischer came to the defence of Beckett, a moralist whose 'absolute negation' in, for example, *Endgame* was 'explosive'. Eugene Ionesco, by contrast, was a positive glorifier of the bourgeois world, 'its clown for the gallery'. We ought not (concluded Fischer) to abandon Proust, nor Joyce, nor Beckett, and even less Kafka to the bourgeois world. Although performed in the little theatres of Warsaw and Prague, for thirty years Beckett's plays were not produced in the USSR, except rarely in the Baltic republics.[17] Robert Dalglish, for many years a translator resident in Moscow, lamented: 'And yet, I have heard people say they would like to know what the Theatre of the Absurd really looks like properly staged. And would not the critics have a beneficial battle royal over, say, *The Rhinoceros*?'[18] Following travels abroad, the film director Andrei Tarkovsky noted in his diary on 4 February 1974: 'It is curious that performances of what is known as the "Theatre of the Absurd"—Beckett, Ionesco— should as a rule produce an impression of naturalism; or at any rate of total truth.'[19]

Aleksandr Anikst, a leading Soviet theatre critic and Shakespearean scholar, described a visit to a New York theatre where *Rhinoceros* was running. Given the relentless disparagement of Ionesco and the 'Theatre of the Absurd' in the USSR, Anikst's review was astonishingly favourable, although in a devious manner involving two American books he had read, both unlikely companions to Ionesco: *Rhinoceros* (said Anikst) was in the classical French tradition, a real play, not an anti-play, with the Logician character descended from Molière's pedants, no less. Ionesco had shown up 'the whole of bourgeois society as wallowing in the mire of vulgarity and provincialism'. Here Anikst's view was precisely the opposite of Ernst Fischer's: whereas Beckett 'maintains that one cannot overcome life's absurdity', Ionesco was said by the Soviet critic to be opposed to the loud-mouthed ideologists of the reactionary ruling elite in France, the USA, the German Federal Republic, and other countries of the 'free' West. In an interview Ionesco had said: 'In my opinion the ordinary man is superior to the semi-intellectual. Nazi slogans were thought up by semi-intellectuals—Nazi journalists, novelists, artists, ideologists.' Anikist brazenly evaded Ionesco's scathing view of Communist intellectuals, while chiding the playwright for omitting politics from his arguments and for wishing a plague on both camps; but—and was this a coded message to Soviet readers?—Ionesco was right in showing that 'the only people who remain human are those who do not join the horde of rhinoceroses, but try to remain true to themselves'. (Michael Glenny, who scorned 'the hidebound incomprehension and philistinism of the Soviet cultural bureaucrats', interpreted Anikst's long essay as 'mirror-writing', a technique well known in the Soviet

Union, whereby the evils of the capitalist world are described with straight-faced horror and indignation, while the reader understands that the real target lies closer to home.)[20]

The second edition of *The Great Soviet Encylopaedia*, published in the mid-fifties, had ignored Ionesco, but the third edition (1972) accorded him some worth for his early farces and allegories parodying linguistic automatism and stereotyped thinking. However, this provisional merit-award was soon withdrawn:

In his later parable plays, Ionesco tried to switch . . . to criticism of bureaucratic totalitarianism and fascist degradation of the bourgeois philistine . . . [but] In later plays, the reality that formerly had been satirized was supplanted by arbitary (*proizvol'nyi*) phantasmagoria. Ionesco's confusion and gloom intensified, reducing the dramatist to a repetition of decadent themes . . . [and] hysterical attacks against the socialist camp.[21]

⊞   ⊞   ⊞

The run-up to the Prague Spring was a hot season for the Czechoslovak theatre. Havel's *The Garden Party*[22] (*Zahradní slavnost*, 1963) was directed at the Balustrade by Otomar Krejca and drew a flurry of controversy. Written in the 'absurd' tradition, it focuses on a young good-for-nothing, Hugo Pludek, whose ambitious father sets him up in the Liquidation Office. Hugo curries favour with the officials and soon finds himself appointed liquidator of a rival Liquidation Office. The frequent use of the word 'liquidation', in circumstances that sometimes bordered on the lunatic, amused but also disconcerted the audience.

Havel's own reflections on *The Garden Party* may be paraphrased as follows: the main character, Hugo, goes into the world like Jack in the folk-tales, 'and he encounters the cliché as the central principle of that world'. The more he learns to identify with the cliché, the higher he rises, and when he is at the top it turns out that he has dissolved in clichés and lost himself. The play ends with Hugo going to visit someone he has heard is extremely important and who turns out to be himself. Not even his parents can recognize him any longer. There is virtually no story line in *The Garden Party* and nothing much happens. *Rudé Pravó* (Prague's *Pravda*) sighed heavily in its review, complaining about the wearisome glut of satire filling Prague's stages.

The bohemian New Left of the sixties was anathema to the authorities in Prague as well as Moscow. The American Beat poet Allen Ginsberg, anti-Vietnam War protester and author of *Howl*, having visited the Soviet Union the previous year, accepted an invitation from students at the Charles University. 'In clubs and inconspicuous public establishments throughout

Prague, thousands of Czech youths indulged in the euphoric rituals of *bigbit* music.' Ginsberg held poetry readings in the famous 'small theatres' of Prague and Bratislava. On 1 May 1965 Charles University students honoured him as King of the Majales. During his stay he was arrested three times: once for singing drunk on Narodni Street, 'once knocked down on the midnight pavement by a mustached agent who screamed out BOUZERANT'.[23] Early in May the police ransacked his room and found 'my notebooks of unusual sex politics dream opinions'. On 7 May Ginsberg was escorted to the airport, *Rudé Pravó* commenting that Czechoslovakia could not 'tolerate someone who brings habits that make a normal person shudder with disgust'—i.e. seducing young men and staging homosexual orgies.[24]

Václav Havel's *The Memorandum* (*Vyrozumeni*), directed by Grossman, opened at the Balustrade in July 1965. This—perhaps the best-known of Havel's plays, although not translated for many years—is a satire about the manipulation of language and the ultraconformity of the bureaucrat to whatever is the current Party line. A new bureaucratic language, Ptydepe, is imposed by fiat, dividing those who blindly adopt it, often in a careerist spirit, from the Director, Josef Gross, who hesitates, even resists, until he is blackmailed into conformity, relieved of his post, and relegated to the role of hidden 'staff watcher'. Gross is reprieved when the Ptydepe directive is abruptly reversed in favour of a new artificial language. The principle of Ptydepe, which scarcely anyone can understand apart from the instructors, is that no two words should be remotely similar. But, more fundamentally, natural languages are said to be vitiated by emotion, *double-entendre*, and various 'vibes' inimical to clear-cut scientific understanding. A number of scenes show the character Lear teaching Ptydepe, and some of the dialogue is spoken in the artificial language. Lear's exposition is lengthy and jargon-ridden: any Ptydepe word must differ from any other word of the same length by at least 60 per cent of its letters.

As usual with Havel, the female characters are pretty much the mid-sixties mini-skirted appendages favoured on the New Left, running to get the milk, the tea, and always combing their hair—creatures of superficial routine. When we first encounter Helena, who is said to be 'Chairman', her main concern is to have a snack-bar set up. She does not know what she is chairman of; her main preoccupation is what the grocer across the street has in stock on the day. Characterization is generally thin. Havel's concern is the schematic, geometrical pursuit of the Absurd, done in terms of a farcical coming and going, with heavy roles for the various stage doors. A standard Havel tactic is to have one character trying to say something important or ask a vital question, while the others are distracted by trivialities and thoughts of roast goose, vodka, or tinned peaches. Such motifs are repeated like musical phrases. Lear and the other acolytes of Ptydepe switch easily into total condemnation of it when the word comes down from Above. The newly installed synthetic language, Chorukor, is said to operate on the opposite principle to Ptydepe, that of maximum similarity between words, so that (for example) the words for the days of the week must differ only minimally. Lear explains that if a typist makes a mistake: 'The most that can happen is that the staff will meet on Tuesday, instead of on Friday, and the matter under consideration will thus even be expedited.'[25]

The London *Times* declared that *The Memorandum* should be compulsory viewing for white-collar workers everywhere; had it been written by a young English dramatist, *The Times* might have complained of fatigue, of 'a nice idea cooked too long'. In the mid-sixties Havel's target was not so much Leninism as reform Communism, that 'peculiar dialectical dance of truth and lies'. The Party had called for a special Writers' Union conference to mark the twentieth anniversary of the liberation. In what he later called 'an incendiary speech', Havel used the occasion to pillory the bureaucracy for blocking young creators.[26] He then referred to specific cases of blacklisting, both of magazines and individuals, including Jan Grossman, head of the Theatre on the Balustrade but 'blacklisted for eight years because he once said things about literature which it would be practically a *faux pas* today *not* to say'.[27]

In the spring of 1965 Havel was invited to join the editorial board of *Tvář* (*The Face*), a monthly magazine for young writers to which he contributed essays like 'Notes on Being Half-Educated'. Foreign authors in its pages included Heidegger, Eliot, Ionesco, Robbe-Grillet, plus previously banned Czech writers. In June the Writers Union moved to close it. Havel and other editors circulated a petition against closure, in the cause of which he travelled to Bratislava and climbed over a successful novelist's high wall in the vain hope of securing a signature. He was rewarded with a secret-police file and an open attack from the head of the Ideological Department of the Central Committee, as a 'bourgeois' writer whose wealthy family had owned various businesses, including the Barrandov Studios. Pavel Auersperg, the Party functionary in charge of ideology, took note of Havel as a danger. The tenth and final issue of *Tvář* appeared in December 1965.[28] Now a marked man, Havel was denied a passport even though his plays were being performed in Austria, Britain, Finland, Hungary, Sweden, Switzerland, the USA, West Germany, and Yugoslavia. No Czechoslovak playwright since Karel Čapek, writing nearly forty years before, had had such an impact. Together with Grossman, he was obliged to cancel plans to travel via London to New

York where they were to be guests of honour of PEN. At the time Grossman's rendering of Kafka's *The Trial* was playing to packed houses at the Balustrade.[29] Foreign journalists visiting Prague to interview Havel were not yet treated by the shy young playwright to the full-blown discourse on the necessity of modernism he would offer ten years later, when his plays could no longer be performed and he began to speak of Man and the Absurd:

> He waits, unable to understand that he is waiting in vain: *Waiting for Godot*. He is plagued by the need to communicate the main thing, but he has nothing to communicate: Ionesco's *The Chairs*. He seeks a firm point in recollection, not knowing that there is nothing to recollect: Beckett's *Happy Days*.[30] He lies to himself and those around him by saying he's going somewhere to find something that will give him back his identity: Pinter's *The Caretaker*. He thinks he knows those closest to him and himself, and it turns out that he doesn't know anyone: Pinter's *The Homecoming*... There is no philosophizing in these plays as there is in Sartre, for example. On the contrary, what is expressed tends to be banal. In their meaning, however, they are always philosophical... Absurd theatre does not offer us consolation or hope. It merely reminds us of how we are living without hope... it leaves the instructing to Brecht.[31]

In 'Politics and the Theatre', published in London by the *Times Literary Supplement* (28 September 1967), Havel wrote: 'The theatre can depict politics precisely because it has no political aim.' Later, emphasizing the 'non-ideological' nature of the Balustrade Theatre, he insisted: 'We didn't try to explain the world... The humour was described as... an example of *l'art pour l'art*, as dadaistic.' Yet, he reflected, it gave expression to what man really is, 'despair, empty hope, bad luck, fate, misfortune, groundless joy'. Modern man has lost something, a sense of certainty, 'but is unable to admit this to himself and therefore hides from it'.[32]

April 1968, during the Prague Spring, saw the première of *The Increased Difficulty of Concentration* (*Žtížená možnost souslředděnií*), directed at the Balustrade by Václav Hudecek, who had staged Ionesco's *The Lesson* and Beckett's *Waiting for Godot*. Havel deals with the question of identity through the device of a man apparently in the hands of a machine, albeit in a quasi-homely setting. The hero is defined as 'a condensed model of human individuality', and the manipulative machine is the system. The computer, named Puzuk, displays more emotion than any of the nominal human beings.[33] Here, as in other plays, Havel's robot-like dystopian organizations are purposeless despite the power they exercise, and 'everything is just the way it was planned'. Vacuous bureaucratic language is at the heart of the oppression. And there is invariably an Ordinary Individual, normally a man, a variant of Orwell's Winston Smith but less rooted in time, place, and soil, who finds himself struggling against the web of intrigue. Havel's fictional bureaucracies contain both the world of Kafka, 'choking on meta-physical anguish', and of Jaroslav Hašek, 'populated with low-life clowns'.[34] As in Pinter's universe, there is a tendency towards enclosure, a world sealed off, with a whiff of threatened violence.

With the approach of the Prague Spring, Havel joined KAN, the Club of Committed Nonpartisans, none of whose members was a Communist. In March 1968 he signed a declaration by twenty writers calling for an Inde-pendent Writers' Circle within the Writers' Union. In April he was elected chairman of the Circle. On 4 April *Literárni listy* (successor to *Literárni noviny*) published his article 'On the Subject of Opposition', in which the playwright ridiculed the puppet pluralism of the National Front. 'We are frequently told that because we now have freedom of speech (which is supposedly the basis of democracy), public opinion, assisted by the media, will carry out the natural restraining function of an opposition.' But, he continued, democracy 'is not a matter of faith, but of guarantees', and the real source of guarantees had to be 'a public, legal contest for power'.[35]

The Soviet reaction to Prague's challenge to the Communist Party's mon-opoly of power was one of deep anger: the tank-tracks were already being greased. In the meantime Havel was at last free to leave the country and visit Paris, New York, and London for the first time in his Iron-Curtained life. In New York *The Memorandum* was given an off-Broadway première at Joseph Papp's Shakespeare Festival Theater, winning rave reviews and an Obie Prize. He went along with the film director Milos Forman to join demonstrations of the young and rock gatherings. To mention Forman is to be reminded that Czechoslovakia had made its bright but short-lived leap into international cinema during the 1960s, when production groups gained relative auton-omy and previously suppressed talents surfaced, shouting for studio space. Forman remarked: '...the cruellest kind of helplessness, the kind that arouses deepest sympathy, is the individual's helplessness against the Establishment...And from then on, it is interpreted politically, I guess.' Czechoslovak films won a succession of international awards and were broadly hailed in the West as harbingers of liberalization.[36]

While in New York, Havel angered Soviet observers by visiting Ferdinand Peroutka, then in his seventies, once a friend of Havel's father and subse-quently involved with Radio Free Europe. Havel raised the temperature by looking up 'about thirty important personalities in the post-February 1948 wave of exiles', including Jirí Voskovec, with whom he stayed in New York for several weeks. During an interview Havel called for Czechoslovak legislation to remove censorship and guarantee freedom of speech and freedom of assembly. In London he was interviewed on BBC television's arts programme *Late Night Line-Up*.[37] He returned to Prague in the last week of June in time for the Fourth Czechoslovak Writers' Congress, during which he praised the 'supreme, self-reliant poise' of Solzhenitsyn. His report from the Western capitals was to have been serialized in *Literární listy*, but the Soviet occupation intervened and Havel later 'destroyed the entire file in a critical moment', although, as he was to discover, the Ministry of the Interior had already managed to photograph it.[38]

On 6 June 1968 the present writer attended a meeting of the Independent (non-party) Writers' Circle at the Union of Writers building in Narodni Street. Among those present were some who had not set foot in the building for years. The meeting discussed a manifesto prepared by Václav Havel. A strong consensus emerged challenging the 'ruling idea'—namely, that to be a Communist is necessarily to be morally or intellectually superior to other people. Havel argued that democracy must imply genuine plurality and free competition between groups for acceptance by the people on the basis of free elections. He challenged the built-in control of the Union of Writers by Communists; he refused to accept a liberty which was granted on sufferance and which might at any time be withdrawn.[39]

On 21 June *Trud*, the Soviet trade union paper, attacked Havel for advocating 'full freedom for any views, including anti-socialist ones, and no obligation on writers to defend proletarian ideology'.[40] Two months later the Red Army invaded. Havel, his wife Olga, and his friend the young actor Jan Tríska were in the northern Bohemian town of Liberec on 22 August. They watched as Soviet tanks tore into arcades on the square, burying people who had rushed there for shelter. A tank commander began shooting into the protesting crowd. In Liberec Havel wrote speeches for local Communist officials, prepared material for wall posters, and broadcast on clandestine radio: 'I wrote a commentary every day. Honza read them on the air, and we even appeared on television, in a studio that was rigged up on Jested [a hill where a TV station and transmitter were sited] . . . I even wrote lengthy declarations for the District Committee of the Communist Party.'[41]

One broadcast, resembling a message in a bottle tossed with a prayer into stormy seas, appealed for support to a long list of literary figures including Kingsley Amis, Beckett, Günter Grass, Ionesco, Arthur Miller, John Osborne, and Sartre. All the broadcasts called for the triumph of 'conscience' and 'humanity' over 'beastliness' and 'the pistol'. The Soviet press lashed out at Havel—why had *The Memorandum* and its author recently been so well received in New York? But he still had his passport in January 1969, when he attended performances of *The Increased Difficulty of Concentration* in Berlin

and Vienna, where he had been awarded the State Prize for European Literature, and where the Burgtheater was later to stage premières of his plays
when they could no longer be performed in Czechoslovakia. Havel also
had an offer from the Ford Foundation to undertake a study tour. One of
Literární listy's last issues before it was closed down reported how he had
invited the police to his flat to inspect a concealed microphone in the ceiling,
observed by a dozen Prague liberals.[42]

Under the incoming Party secretary Gustav Husák, a ruthless purge
followed Alexander Dubček's removal as Party leader and house-arrest. On
21 August 1969 Havel signed, with nine others, 'Ten Points' condemning the
post-Dubček clampdown euphemistically known as 'normalization'. A full
trial of all ten signatories was set for October 1970, but failed to materialize.
The director of the National Theatre was replaced, as were thirty out of thirty-
two theatre directors throughout the country. The entire management of
the film industry was sacked, and hundreds of actors, writers, cameramen,
and directors were out of work. Music-hall artists, scriptwriters, painters, and
sculptors were screened and re-screened and then forced on to a long-term
treadmill of persecution; 475 of the 590 members of the Czech Writers'
Union were removed. Havel, Kohout, Vaculík, and Klíma were among the
130 (later over 200) writers whose works bookshops and libraries were forbidden to stock. The entire management and senior editorial staff of television, radio, and the news agency were booted out. Out of forty influential
dailies and weeklies, thirty-seven editors were replaced. Many emigrated,
including Milan Kundera,[43] of whom Havel wrote some years later: 'For
years [he] was the darling of his readership [in Czechoslovakia], and to this
day everyone knows who he is. When he was young, he was decorated with
the highest state prize for literature, and if his books could be published here,
the sales figures would undoubtedly parallel those in the West.'[44]

It was a difficult time for writing plays, let alone getting them staged.
Despite encouragement from the West—in 1970 Havel received a second
Obie Prize following the off-Broadway success of *The Increased Difficulty of
Concentration*—his first post-1968 script was a disappointing one. Writing to
Kenneth Tynan, literary manager at the National Theatre, London, on 2
April 1971, Havel described *The Conspirators* (*Spiklenci*, 1970), for which he
had no hope of finding a theatre, director, or actors in his own country:

Five conspirators set out to protect a weak democratic government in a country newly
rid of a colonial legacy. The audience gradually learns that, paradoxically, the danger
comes from the plotters themselves who become, by the nature of their actions,
sympathetic to the former dictator. They want to seize power, in order to save

the country from the danger that they might take possession of the government themselves.

Two weeks earlier he had written to Tynan: 'Nothing that bears my name may be published at present in my country, and the monopoly-state-agency DILIA is forbidden to conclude any contracts for any play with partners abroad.' By the end of November Tynan had read the play in a rough translation and found it disappointing, vitiated by plots and counter-plots 'less brilliant and exciting than the original idea, which was at once fantastic and utterly logical, like all your best work'.[45] *The Conspirators*, which was not performed in England, had its première in Baden-Baden in February 1974. Havel later called it his weakest play, but German patronage of foreign playwrights was then highly altruistic and sometimes indiscriminate.

In 1974 Havel found himself working in a brewery in the town of Trutnov, stacking empty barrels—bringing a change of scene, wages, and contacts with ordinary people. One day an amateur listening device was found in the brewery cellars. The brewmaster had installed it himself, and the wires led to his flat. The man was trying to kill two birds with one stone: he wanted to know what the workers were saying about him, and at the same time he wanted to ingratiate himself with the authorities by offering to keep an eye on Havel. But who 'found' the device? Who reported it to whom? Did Havel really need this job, or was he setting up life to serve his art? The police pretended to know nothing. 'They were afraid I'd publish the story abroad . . .'[46] His absorbing one-act play *Audience* (1975), the first of three about a writer called Ferdinand Vanek, was followed by *Private View* and *Protest*. In *Audience*, the Maltster (brewmaster) character evokes the clumsy, back-slapping bonhomie of the self-deluding, increasingly drunk, Czech citizen of the Husák era. *Audience*, which proved popular in the West,[47] also circulated as a clandestine text at home, as performed by Pavel Landovsky and Havel 'on a tape that was later released as a record by Safrán in Sweden'.

The simple naturalism and humanism of *Audience* came as something of a relief after the head-splitting robots and lobotomized personalities in the earlier satires. The Absurd could be hard going in Havel's hands. *Audience* is a cleverly constructed play about power and those who wield it. Reduced to working in a brewery, Vanek is summoned to a meeting with the Head Malster. In the bizarre conversation which ensues, Vanek is offered the chance of a better job, as stock checker in the 'fulls' store of the brewery. 'You don't want to go on handling casks with the gypsies! You'll have a little office all to yourself. You'll keep warm . . . You might even have a little shut-eye in there.'[48] The catch is, however, that Vanek must inform—on himself. The drunken Maltster, a benign figure far gone into permanent, bottle-opening inebriation, has been instructed to inform on Vanek, but loathes this task because he is too lazy and does not know what to report. So Vanek himself must help out—Havel's ear for the absurd here finds a perfectly natural outlet. As is Havel's style, the dialogue follows a pattern of repetitions. The Maltster constantly exits to relieve himself, the lavatory flushes (off), he returns, opens another bottle, urges Vanek to drink, is irritated that he won't, constantly inquires after a particular actress, and announces that a man has rights and is entitled to any visitor he likes—but not this fellow Kohout who was in the habit of visiting Vanek.

The second Vanek play, *Private View*, written in 1975, depicts Ferdinand Vanek taking an evening off from the brewery to visit a prosperous couple, Michael and Vera, who are going along with the system, can travel, and have money. Their living-room is 'freshly decorated and over-stuffed with antiques, including a Turkish yataghan, a Baroque confessional, a Gothic Madonna and a musical Rococo clock on the mantelpiece'. Hearing that a disused church was to be scrapped, Michael had hurried down and grabbed the confessional from the sacristan for only 300 crowns. Periodically the mantelpiece clock breaks into a 'period tune'. As the play opens, the latest American pop hit blares out from the hi-fi set. Michael has been in the United States and brought back a special Bourbon as well as the pop hits. Here again Havel uses the technique of exact dialogue repetition to indicate an almost robotic dehumanization. Michael and Vera are programmed not so much by the state, or Big Brother, as by the kind of alienation described by Herbert Marcuse and Western critics of late capitalism. They are 'one-dimensional' (in Marcuse's phrase). The mild-mannered and (of course) stubbornly three-dimensional writer Vanek does his best to enthuse over such things as American groombles served with woodpeak, but is overwhelmed by the saccharine secretion of self-satisfaction which Michael and Vera wear like a cheap scent as they celebrate every aspect of their relationship, their little son, Michael's work (but what is it?), his skills in the house, her cooking, and their sex life—they offer to demonstrate to Vanek their sexual congress, 'what sophisticated things we do to one another'.

As Michael and Vera happily express the perfection of their marriage, their tone gradually develops into a personal attack on Vanek, their 'best friend' (as they insist), his home, his wife Eva, his sex life, his childlessness, and his work as a writer. As the abuse builds to a climax Vanek turns to leave, only to find Michael and Vera begging him to stay. As in *Audience*, Vanek then realizes he must do something to help the bullying yet insecure social climbers, who desperately need the appreciation of a real man. Many years later, when president of Czechoslovakia, Havel delivered a lecture in Washington, DC, recalling the time when he was avoided in the street by friends and acquaintances because he was an 'inconvenience' who was embarrassing as well as a contagion. The exiled Russian poet Joseph Brodsky responded by suggesting that Havel had been less an inconvenience than a source of moral comfort, 'the way the sick are for the healthy majority'. Havel replied that this logic may have applied better in Russia, where many professionals critical of the system continued working in laboratories, publishing houses, and research institutes—whereas no such compromise, known as the 'grey zone', was available after 1970 to the Czechoslovak dissident historians, writers, and poets who instead washed windows, worked as night watchmen and stokers, or measuring water-flow in remote areas. These people formed the core of those who signed Charter 77 and were a source of embarrassment, of discomfort, to the 'grey zone'.[49] This comment deepens our understanding of *Private View*; Havel was making a specific point about post-1968 Czechoslovakia—as was made clear in the playwright's April 1975 Open Letter to President Gustav Husák, which was circulated underground, published abroad, and broadcast on Western radio:

Seldom in recent times, it seems, has a social system offered scope so openly and brazenly to people willing to support anything so long as it brings them some advantage; to unprincipled and spineless men...to born lackeys...it is not surprising that so many public and influential positions are occupied, more than ever before, by notorious careerists, opportunists, charlatans...by typical collaborators...

The state, 'by fixing a person's whole attention on his mere consumer interests...hoped to render him incapable of realizing the increasing extent to which he has been spiritually, politically and morally violated'. Why (Havel asked) are people behaving as they do? Fear is the answer—though no longer fear of trials, deportations, or executions:

For fear of losing his job, the schoolteacher teaches things he does not believe; fearing for his future, the pupil repeats them after him; for fear of not being allowed to continue his studies, the young man joins the Youth League...fear that, under the monstrous system of political credits, his son or daughter will not acquire the necessary total of enrolments at a school leads the father to take on all manner of responsibilities and 'voluntarily' to do everything required. Fear of the consequences of refusal leads people to take part in elections...and to pretend that they regard such ceremonies as genuine elections...it is fear that carries them through humiliating acts of self-criticism and penance and the dishonest filling out of a mass of degrading questionnaires...[50]

The letter was returned to Havel by a member of the president's staff, 'with the explanation that I had made it available to hostile press agencies and thus revealed my hostility to my country.' (The letter was first published in English in *Encounter* in September 1975.)

It was in 1975 that a work by Havel was performed on Czech soil for the first time in seven years—and, as it was to turn out, for the last time for a further fifteen. This was his adaptation of Gay's *The Beggar's Opera*, performed clandestinely in a village restaurant on the eastern outskirts of Prague. Havel's *Zebrácká Opera* was of necessity without music or singing, and without happy endings. The notion of honour among thieves is exposed as romantic nonsense; everyone behaves selfishly, or 'realistically', which means lying, double-crossing, back-stabbing. Morality has vanished. Words and sentences are mere tools of manipulation. At the party after the performance, held in a restaurant around the corner from Prague's police headquarters, Havel told the troupe that the occasion had brought him more joy than any of the foreign premières of his plays. Then all hell broke loose. Havel was brought in for questioning.[51]

'Provocations' from beyond the frontier continued to inspire rage in the presidential fortress overlooking Prague, Hradčany Castle. *Audience* and *Private View* were the première productions at Vienna's Burgtheater in October 1976.[52] Havel was invited to attend by the Austrian minister of education, but the Czechoslovak Foreign Ministry refused him a passport because he 'is not representative of Czech culture'. Havel reflected that 'under totalitarian conditions' the written word acquires 'a kind of heightened radioactivity—otherwise they wouldn't lock us up for it'. Western colleagues may envy 'the degree of attention and social resonance that we enjoy. But it's a double-edged thing: it can bind one, tie one down, limit one.'[53]

Havel was far from alone in his challenges to the moral and cultural authority of the Castle. After an initial banning, a Czech band calling themselves the Plastic People of the Universe purged their repertoire of Western songs and obtained the all-important professional licence—which was promptly withdrawn. On 1 September 1974 the Plastic People sponsored the first Music Festival of the Second Culture in a small Bohemian village. The event attracted hundreds of fans and brought together the leading figures of the underground music scene. No police action was taken against either of the first two festivals, but on 17 March 1976 some twenty people were arrested, tape-recordings, films, and notebooks were confiscated, and charges brought. Despite international protests from Heinrich Böll,[54] Arthur Miller, and others, in September 1976 the trial began of Ivan Jirous and Vratislav Brabenec of the Plastic People, and members of the group

DG-307, charged with criminal acts of disturbing the peace. Havel, who managed to be one of the few non-participants allowed to observe the trial, signed a letter to Böll appealing for solidarity with the defendants. *Rudé Pravó* commented: 'But not even the most tolerant person could call what they did art. Modesty and law prevent us from publishing examples of the lyrics... They are filthy, obscene.' The defence argued in court that 'vulgarisms' occupied an honourable place in Czech culture, not excluding Comenius, the seventeenth-century theologian, and in the work of Lenin himself. The defendants received sentences of eighteen, twelve, and eight months.[55]

Charter 77 was the next challenge to the one-eyed regime, prominently reported in the Western media.[56] In the course of delivering Charter 77's 'Declaration' to the government, parliament, and the press agency, Havel was detained on 14 January along with Vaculík and the actor Pavel Landovsky. Repressive action against most of the signatories followed, *Rudé Pravó* announcing that the Charter was produced on orders from anti-Communist and Zionist 'centres' in the West. Workers were summoned to factory meetings. A packed gathering of famous artists declared their loyal support for socialism, with television cameras closing in on the actress Jiřina Švorcová as she declared her disgust at certain persons who acted as if they were 'the chosen' but who were in fact isolated traitors, worshippers of money, imperialist agents. After her speech actors, TV personalities, musicians, and entertainers queued up to sign a declaration in favour of 'New Creative Works in the Name of Socialism and Peace'. Perhaps they had chosen to forget Havel's memorable satires on abject conformism. *Rudé právo* accused Havel of being in the pay of the 'CIA agent' Pavel Tigrid, his friend and the editor of a Paris-based Czech-language magazine, and of receiving funds from the American and West German intelligence services. Czechoslovak Radio rushed out a programme, 'Who is Václav Havel?', describing him as 'extremely conceited' and holding everyone in contempt.[57]

Incarcerated for the first time, Havel was held for four months in Ruzyne Prison and systematically interrogated. Scope for reading, writing, and reflection were virtually nil. On many nights he barely slept. Visits were minimal and letters censored. More than 100 British MPs signed a Commons motion recognizing the courage of the Chartists. A letter from the playwright Tom Stoppard and other members of the theatrical profession appeared in *The Times* (7 February 1977), lamenting that Charter 77 had been suppressed and Havel with three others arrested, even though—as Western Communists acknowledged—no law had been broken.[58] In July, having recently visited Czechoslovakia, Stoppard held a press conference alongside Dr Zdenek Mlynar, a senior official of the Dubček government in 1968, who had recently emigrated after months of harassment. They presented a thick dossier on new violations of human rights.[59] Meanwhile the Orange Tree Theatre, Richmond, staged *Audience* and *Private View*.[60]

Havel was released on 20 May pending trial, but several times he was placed under house arrest, and his flat was broken into, his car vandalized. The trial took place in October in a small room of the Prague Municipal Court which had seating for only fourteen. He was sentenced to fourteen months, suspended for three years, for attempting to damage national interests abroad. Police were permanently posted outside his Prague apartment and his country home in Hrádecek. Visitors were harassed. Wherever he went, by car or on foot, a policeman with a walkie-talkie followed, trying to hear what he said, checking the identity papers of anyone he talked to. 'He would look over my shoulder when I sent off letters, listen at the telephone booth when I made calls.' Two policemen would walk behind him while a third crept along nearby in a Tatra 603. They set up a table on the landing outside his apartment and refused to let him leave, even to do the shopping. 'All this uncertainty about what mischief they would dream up next has not been good for my nerves, I have not been able to concentrate on writing, I fell into depressions, I suffered from insomnia, headaches, stomach trouble, and a strange bubbling in the blood.'[61]

Shortly before Havel's long imprisonment in 1979, Pentti Ruohonen, an editor of the Finnish Broadcasting Company, tried to visit the playwright. In a letter to PEN he described what happened. A meeting was arranged for the evening of 7 March:

Outside the building a black Tatra was parked, its lights switched off; in the car were three men in plain clothes, most probably from the secret police ... On the landing, three policemen—two in uniform and one in plain clothes—were sitting at a table. They stopped me, demanded to see my passport, and then made a record of it in a book. Meanwhile, Havel appeared at the door of his apartment, and we were able to talk to each other at a distance of some four or five metres ... He told me that he had been under house arrest and police surveillance for three months now without a break. His phone had been cut off, and the only mail he received were a few occasional postcards. He was prevented from going out to shop often enough to be left without food.[62]

The Committee for the Defence of the Unjustly Persecuted (VONS) was set up, with Havel among its eighteen members. The regime's diatribes against VONS intensified. After Havel wrote to the president of Austria, the playwright was again arrested and on 29 May 1979 (along with fourteen VONS committee members) charged with subversion. The October trial of VONS, again in the Prague Municipal Court, was held virtually *in camera*, with no notes allowed. All six defendants were found guilty under Article 98 of the Criminal Code, Havel's sentence of four-and-a-half years being the most severe because he was to be confined in a Category One prison. Speaking on his own behalf before sentence was passed, Havel challenged his purported 'hostility' to his country, claiming that he had turned down the chance of release if he had accepted an offer from Joseph Papp to work in the United States.[63]

The French and Italian Communist parties came out in support of the VONS defendants, as did President Carter, Prime Minsiter Thatcher, and the European Parliament. In Hermanice Prison Havel worked as a spot-welder on metal gratings, later with a big oxyacetylene welder, cutting flanges out of enormous, thick pieces of metal. After he was shifted to Bory he worked in the laundry, and finally he was assigned to a scrap-metal plant, stripping the insulation off wires and cables in 'cold and endless filth' (he recalled). In prison he was not allowed to write at all, apart from one letter a week to his wife, maximum four sides, and only about 'personal matters'. The commandant at Hermanice, who took a sadistic delight in enforcing these instructions, remembered his great days in the 1950s when he had more than a thousand political prisoners. He kept calling Havel in. 'Stop numbering your moods!' 'No foreign words!' 'No underlining!' 'No exclamation marks!'[64]

Between June 1979 and September 1982 Havel wrote *Letters to Olga* under conditions of severe prison censorship:

If I were a West German, for example, I would probably be involved at this time [February 1982] amongst many other things, in preventing the construction of the new runway at Frankfurt, in collecting signatures against the siting of Pershing II and Cruise missiles, and in voting for the 'Green Party'. I feel deep down inside that the long-haired people who do this and whom I am able to see almost every day on television are my brothers and sisters, which is a new experience for me, moreover: during my visit to the USA in 1968, I rarely felt so much at ease as in the company of the revolutionary youth.[65]

In 1983 Václav Havel was hastily transferred from prison to the intensive care unit of a hospital. Released, he thanked Amnesty and KOR (the Polish Workers Defence Committee), by then suppressed, for their support.

⊞ ⊞ ⊞

Among Havel's most gifted and influential admirers was the British playwright Tom Stoppard, born in Czechoslovakia in 1937, the year after Havel.

Stoppard's parents had chosen emigration, and he grew up in England with an English name and an acute ear for local speech patterns. In his Introduction to the English version of *The Memorandum*, Stoppard comments that it remains Havel's most widely performed play:

and the one which best shows off the hallmarks of his gift: the fascination with language; the invention of an absurd society raised only a notch or two above the normal world of state bureaucracy; the absurdities pushed to absurdity compounded by absurdity and yet saved from mere nonsense by their internal logic and, not least, the playfulness with which it is done, the almost gentle refusal to indulge a sense of grievance, the utter lack of righteousness or petulance or bile—the same quality, in fact, which was to distinguish the Vanek plays ten years later, by which time Havel might have been forgiven for writing with bitterness.[66]

Kenneth Tynan wrote to William Shawn, editor of the *New Yorker*, regarding a profile of Tom Stoppard:

The recent arrest of the Czech playwright Václav Havel has given me a new idea for the shape of the piece . . . Havel, like Stoppard, is a writer of the dandy type, and many of his plays—absurdist and full of fantastic wordplay—read as if Stoppard could have written them . . . You may have seen Stoppard's piece in the *New York Times* a few days ago, protesting against the arrest of Havel and other Czech dissidents.[67]

In reality, Havel's plays lack Stoppard's richness of observation, language, and invention. Havel is more remarkable for his life, courage, and spirit than for his art. A sense of the playful and of the comic-absurd may join the two writers, and needless to add a love of freedom, but whereas Havel's Absurd and Surreal tend to be laborious, laden with debt to Western culture,[68] Stoppard's surrealism (in for example *Jumpers* or *Travesties*) carries a light touch and a nose for history's masks and masques entirely his own. As a dramatist Stoppard seems to have been touched by cold war cruelties some time after he had established a reputation as a stage and radio playwright noticeably removed from the political preoccupations of dramatists like John Arden, Edward Bond, David Mercer, David Edgar, John McGrath, Howard Brenton, and David Hare—he was a figure apart, like Harold Pinter, and a master of laughter; but when the shadow of tyranny began to lie across Stoppard's pages,[69] it was the 'left' tyranny of Eastern Europe, whereas Pinter's bogeymen typically belonged to CIA-backed military juntas.

Every Good Boy Deserves Favour, a fifty-minute orchestral play for Actors and Orchestra, with music composed and conducted by André Previn, and directed by Trevor Nunn, was performed at the Royal Festival Hall in July 1977 by 80 musicians of the London Symphony Orchestra and five leading actors of the Royal Shakespeare Company.[70] Squeezed in among the music stands were three white platforms for the actors. Stoppard's target was polit-ical incarceration in Soviet psychiatric institutions; the work is dedicated to two Soviet dissidents who were expelled to the West, Victor Fainberg and Vladimir Bukovsky.[71]

The notion of a musical play about a lunatic triangle-player who thought he had an orchestra came to Stoppard after he met Victor Fainberg, who had been among those arrested in Red Square in August 1968, protesting against the invasion of Czechoslovakia. Stoppard was responding to the growing scandal of punitive medicine in the USSR. The playwright had stood outside the Eighth Department of the Third Civil Mental Hospital in Leningrad, bearing witness to the incarceration inside of Vladimir Borisov, arrested on Christmas Day 1976, 'The Face in the Window'.[72] In 1977 the World Psychi-atric Association's annual meeting condemned the 'systematic abuse of psychiatry for political purposes in the Soviet Union.'

Stoppard's fictional lunatic triangle-player who thinks he has an orchestra, Ivanov, is now sharing a cell with a political prisoner, Alexander, whose speech about his treatment in the Leningrad Psychiatric Hospital is taken from an article by Fainberg. The off-stage hero of the play, referred to as 'my friend C', is Vladimir Bukovsky. In December 1976 the international Bukovsky campaign had brought about his release and expulsion. At Stop-pard's invitation Bukovsky visited the RSC's rehearsal rooms in Covent Garden to watch *Every Good Boy* for an hour or two: 'He was diffident, friendly, and helpful on points of detail in the production, but his presence was disturbing. For people working on a piece of theatre, terra firma is a self-contained world even while it mimics the real one . . . One of the actors seized up in the middle of a speech touching on the experiences of our visitor, and found it impossible to continue.[73]

According to the initial stage directions for *Every Good Boy Deserves Favour* (a mnemonic familiar to any child suffering piano lessons), three separate acting areas are needed: a cell with two beds; an office with a table and two chairs; a schoolroom with a desk. The cell is occupied by two men, Ivanov (played by John Wood), a genuine mental patient, who carries a triangle and imagines himself in control of a symphony orchestra, and by Alexander (Ian McKellen), a political prisoner, who has survived KGB brutality and a near-fatal hunger strike. The riddle thickens when the state's doctor (Patrick Stuart) reveals himself as a keen violinist. He tells Ivanov that he must stop believing he has an orchestra, and then he will stop hearing it.

In a distant schoolroom we see Alexander's son Sasha with a female music teacher who tells him, in a succession of brief speeches, 'Your name is notorious . . . Your name goes round the world. By telegram. It is printed in the newspapers. It is spoken on the radio... The asylum is for malcontents who don't know what they're doing... They know what they're doing but they don't know it's anti-social... They know it's anti-social but they're fanatics... They're sick.'[74]

Alexander makes a long speech explaining to Ivanov how he had been arrested by chain reaction, each 'mad' dissident rallying to the support of others, the Czechoslovakia demonstration included, each sent to prison, labour camp, psychiatric hospital, internal exile. *'The children's percussion band enters as a discreet subtext.'* A moment later the percussion is sabotaged by a snare drum being violently beaten. We are back with Sasha and the Teacher. She fulminates against Sasha's father. *'Lies!* Bombarding *Pravda* with lies! What did he expect?'

Alexander recalls thirty months in the Leningrad Psychiatric Hospital on Arsenal'naya Street, including two on hunger strike. 'Russia is a civilized country, very good at *Swan Lake* and space technology, and it is confusing if people starve themselves to death.' The Doctor tells Alexander: 'Your opinions are your symptoms. Your disease is dissent.' He refers to the case of General Pyotr Grigorenko, whose well-adjusted behaviour, according to the Serbsky Institute psychiatrist, indicates a pathological development. Indeed Alexander's own file is stamped 'pathological development of the personality with paranoid delusions.' When Alexander says, 'No, there's nothing the matter with me', the Doctor closes the file: 'There you are, you see.' Later he adds: 'Taken as a whole, the sane are out there and the sick are in here. For example, *you* are here because you have delusions that sane people are put in mental hospitals.'

ALEXANDER: I was given injections of aminazin, sulfazin, triftazin, haloperidol and insulin, which caused swellings, cramps, headaches, trembling, fever and the loss of various abilities including the ability to read, write, sleep, sit, stand and button my trousers. When all this failed to improve my condition, I was stripped and bound head to foot with lengths of wet canvas, As the canvas dried it became tighter and tighter until I lost consciousness.[75]

The Teacher tells young Sasha: 'Things have changed since the bad old days. When I was a girl there were terrible excesses. A man accused like your father might well have been blameless. Now things are different...' Stoppard strikes an improbable, anachronistic note when the Teacher praises the Soviet constitution as guaranteeing 'freedom of conscience, freedom of the press, freedom of speech, of assembly, of worship and many other freedoms.' This was not how Soviet citizens thought or spoke. Nor would she be likely to mention Bukharin as the author of the constitution and how he was shot.

Finally the Colonel arrives and asks Ivanov the questions intended for Alexander, and vice-versa, with the result that each gives the desired answers and the Colonel orders their release. The absurd belongs not to the playwright but to the totalitarian mind.[76] Reviewing *Every Good Boy Deserves Favour* in *The Times* (2 July 1977), Irving Wardle wrote:

The orchestra occupies an integral place in the drama. It functions partly to show what is going on in Mr Wood's [Ivanov's] fantasy; partly to represent the safe anonymity of mass society (as where the doctor refuses to aid the plainly innocent hero, and scurries to his violin desk in evening dress). Finally, Mr Previn's score, with its muted, divided string intensities, tortured melodic jumps and passages of icily sparse scoring with a top line carried by a heavy, growling bass, serves to convey the frustrations and hysterically suppressed anger beyond the scope of dialogue.

Tom Stoppard had promised the BBC to come up with a television play by the end of 1976 to mark Amnesty International's 'Prisoner of Conscience' Year (1977). *Professional Foul*, which is dedicated to Havel, was first shown on BBC TV in September 1977, directed with masterly understanding by Michael Lindsay-Hogg. Stoppard reverts to his own lifelong interest in philosophy by describing a Prague international colloqium, or 'bunfight', designed to bolster the flagging prestige of an oppressive regime.

It soon emerges that the urbane Professor Anderson (Peter Barkworth) is smugly guarding a secret: his most prized possession is a ticket to a football match between Czechoslovakia and England, which he plans to attend by skipping an afternoon at the conference. While proud to hold a chair at one of the 'old universities', in contrast to other British delegates, some of whom have concocted pseudo-subjects mixing up philosophy with social science, Anderson is more passionately interested in the potential tactics of the Czech football team at set-piece free kicks than in hearing the predictably pretentious papers of colleagues. When a persecuted dissident philosopher, Pavel Hollar, who was once his own pupil but now works as a cleaner of lavatories, arrives at his Prague hotel begging him to smuggle out to England a 10,000-word essay on the moral basis of individual rights, Anderson is less than pleased—he even argues that to do so he would be breaking his 'contract' with the host government. But the pleasure principle is due to run out on Anderson fairly rapidly. Returning the essay to Hollar's apartment on his way to the match, he discovers that the young philosopher had been arrested on leaving his hotel; the apartment is being ransacked by police wearing seventies haircuts and clothes from the wrong end of Carnaby Street. Anderson also discovers that he is not free to leave or to attend the football match, which he is forced to listen to on the radio in a language he doesn't understand—England take a beating—while secret policemen cynically 'discover' illegal dollars under the floorboards and claim that the terrified Mrs Hollar (who speaks no English) is insisting on Anderson's presence as her legally entitled 'witness' during the search. Even the policemen register shock at some of the routine English fouls described by the Czech radio commentator. Asked to show what he carries in his briefcase, Anderson plucks out a philosophical paper which is not Hollar's, and gets away with it.

No doubt Stoppard had taken note of the brave resistance of the Prague philosopher Julius Tomin and his wife Zdena, friends of Havel, and how British philosophers from Balliol College and elsewhere made a point of visiting Tomin at home, with or without policemen on the landing and stairs. The scene describing the police raid on the Hollar apartment in Stoppard's play is clearly rooted in documentary accounts—though the wit and taste for paradox is all Stoppard's. It's an intensely comic play, not least when philosophers, footballers, and football journalists tangle at the Prague hotel, each mistaking the other's meaning when talking of Stoke, Newcastle, and Leicester—soccer clubs or universities? What makes the play so poignant is the alternation between the trivial arguments among the drunken English visitors in their bugged hotel rooms and the deadly game of oppression in process outside. The most touching scene occurs when Mrs Hollar furtively brings her son to the hotel garden to beg Anderson not to attempt to smuggle out her husband's essay through airport customs. It is the boy who has learned enough English to act as interpreter—one feels that the child's maturity is a tragic reflection of the oppression confronting him.

'England awakes' (in a sense) when Anderson, incensed at last, abandons decorum and abruptly changes the subject of his keynote lecture to the colloquium, baffling the interpreters and upsetting the Czech chairman, who hurries down to the basement to arrange for the fire alarm to be sounded, terminating Anderson's lecture on the inflammatory theme of individual human rights and social rules. This echoes Hollar's own essay: 'The collective ethic can only be the individual ethic writ big'—Anderson has changed 'big' to 'large'. High principle does not prevent him smuggling Hollar's pages out of the country by slipping them into the suitcase of an obnoxious British colleague (John Shrapnel), who has loudly argued that principles mean little. Anderson's justification is, of course, to hand: 'But they were very unlikely to search *you* . . . Ethics is a very complicated business. That's why they have these congresses.'[77] The 'professional foul' has taken place on both the football field and in the winged tent of the travelling philosophers. In the *Sunday Times* (25 September) Peter Dunn found the writing, direction, and acting 'stunningly effective', not least Lindsay-Hogg's avoidance of stereotyped images of the totalitarian state. Police officers searched rooms and baggage 'with the grave precision of Transylvanian valets'.

Three years later, when the issue of the United States-led boycott of the Moscow Olympics came up, Stoppard returned to the case of Vladimir Borisov, 'back behind the same window' of a Leningrad mental hospital 'in what is the heaviest crackdown since dissent began to organize itself in the Soviet Union fifteen years ago'. No one, he added, had been preparing for the XXnd Olympiad so strenuously as the KGB. A keen student of the samizdat 'Chronicle of Current Events', circulated by Amnesty International, Stoppard reported how the KGB was purging every Soviet Olympic venue, not only Moscow and Leningrad, but Minsk, Kiev, and Tallinn. Describing himself as 'someone who gets breathless when he kicks a plastic football around his garden,' he apologized to athletes who had spent years preparing for the Olympics, but he nevertheless urged a boycott. Why should athletes carry the can while scientific, cultural, and commercial traffic continue as normal? His answer: 'Firstly, the Olympics are a unique case. The ups and downs of ballet visits and biology seminars and trade agreements barely break the surface in a society where control over information aspires to the absolute and where reality can be overwritten. The Olympics are simply too big to hush up.' Secondly, one had to consider the USSR's pivotal position in the socialist camp where the 'indecent' way of governance prevailed, not in a relative but an absolute sense: the Russians must learn that 'there is some bread we will not break' with them.[78]

It was a fine polemic but its shifting axis reflected the State Department's: an Olympic boycott which President Carter began with a single demand—'Be out of Afghanistan by late February'—became also a protest against the political cleansing of dissidents, the Jewish question—and the one-party state. Stoppard mentioned the invasion of Afghanistan only fleetingly; he was more interested in punishing a regime which could tolerate no opposition, even a poem. But the broader the basis of the boycott, the clearer it became to the Soviet establishment that Afghanistan was merely a pretext in an American presidential election year.

Stoppard's television play, *Squaring the Circle*, first broadcast on Channel 4 TV in May 1984, encompassing events in Poland from the fall of Gierek, through the rise of Solidarity to the imposition of martial law, is discussed in the next chapter, alongside the 'Solidarity' films of Andrzej Wajda.

⊞   ⊞   ⊞

In November 1988 a group of foreign intellectuals were invited by Havel and others to a symposium to discuss 'all those eights' in Czech history, 1918, 1938, 1948, 1968. The Czech hosts were arrested and Havel was in hiding, though he had gone to the Prime Minister's office to explain the project. The bemused foreign guests were sitting in what Timothy Garton Ash called the 'faded Jugendstil splendour of the Hotel Pariz' when in burst Havel himself, sat down at the table and declared the meeting open. Within seconds three plainclothes policemen were behind him. 'Well, in this moment I am arrested', said Havel. But before they hurried him away he managed to repeat, with quiet emphasis, that he had declared the symposium open. Sally Laird of *Index on Censorship* photographed the scene. More secret police moved in to confiscate her film.[79]

In 1989 Havel was awarded the Peace Prize of the German Booksellers Association presented in his absence at the Frankfurt Book Fair. The new Civic Forum, which Havel announced on 19 November, was Charter 77 writ large, with posters demanding *'Havel na Hrad*—Havel to the Castle'. The dissident playwright was indeed soon to climb the hill above the Vltava river. 'New Year's Address' (January 1990) was his first major public statement as the first elected president of a democratic Czechoslovakia since 1948. He quoted his illustrious predecessor, Masaryk: 'Jesus, not Caesar.'[80]

Andrzej Wajda:
Ashes and Diamonds,
Marble and Iron

The film thaw in Poland, the rebellion against Stalinism, announced itself in September 1954 when criticism of socialist realism was boldly voiced at a conference of film workers. The outstanding talent of the younger generation emerged in the shape of Andrzej Wajda,[1] who had studied painting at the Cracow Academy of Fine Arts and, later, film-making at the Łódź High Film School, from which he graduated in 1953, having worked (and hidden) as a locksmith for his uncle during the Nazi occupation. 'I was scared even to go to the tram stop, because there was always some kind of control going on.'[2]

The Łódź Film School was the first of its kind: 'In the 1950s the Film School was an ideological school . . . it was meant to be a school for "janissaries" and intended to educate a film elite, so to speak, which would later become an ideological commando and play a decisive role in the political and social transformations of Poland.' Yet even post-war cultural life in Poland was resistant to outright Stalinism, as Wajda recalled:

But at the same time our Rector, Jerzy Toeplitz, brought from Paris a whole collection of French avant-garde movies . . . so I was able to see [Buñuel's] *L'Age d'or* and *Le Ballet mécanique* once again, all the films which opened my eyes to a completely different kind of cinema . . . The inconsistency was fantastic: on the one hand our professors at the school wanted us—perhaps in a way of justification—to make all these socrealist films, and, on the other, they brought us closer to real art.

Wajda created in *Generation* (1954) arguably the first genuine tragedy in East European cinema. Based on a novel by Bohdan Czeskzko, it tells of a Communist resistance group operating below the streets of Warsaw.

Youthful, ardent, undisciplined, these are flesh-and-blood characters rather than cardboard cut-out heroes. *Kanal* depicts the Warsaw uprising of 1944 as a resistance group moves through the sewers from the German-occupied section of the city towards the fighting. In historically significant scenes Wajda's camera reaches the far side of the Wisla River; the physical presence of the waiting Red Army is felt by any audience aware that the Russians deliberately halted there until the Germans had suppressed the Polish rising.

Ashes and Diamonds (*Popiol i diament*), based on a novel by Jerzy Andrze-jewski, is set in a provincial town immediately after the war's end on 7–8 May 1945. Maciek, a member of the Home Army (the non-Communist anti-fascist resistance) accepts the last order from his commander to kill a Communist functionary. Civil war is already rampant. Maciek and his two anti-Communist colleagues of the Home Army begin by making a tragic error: they ambush the wrong vehicle, killing a young worker, a 21-year-old 'just back from Germany'. Distressed workers, comrades of the dead man, discuss the matter with the CP secretary, Szczuka, the intended target of the assas-sination, who turns out to be an elderly man plagued by doubts. Maciek (played by the charismatic Zbigniew Cybulski, wearing trademark dark glasses) sets about his assigned task of eliminating Szczuka with fatigue and disgust rather than conviction. In the course of a few hours Maciek has a brief affair, commits murder without knowing why, and perishes alone. *Ashes and Diamonds* is a romantic and indeed 'decadent' film about a brave new, post-Nazi, world whose perspectives for liberty were aborted in the womb. For the first time since the Communists took power in Poland a film-maker was able to show the force and legitimacy of the anti-Communist Resistance.[3]

Maciek's colleague Andrzej, a cool, disciplined, laconic man who joined the Resistance in 1940, engages his colleague Waga in conversation soon after the abortive ambush:

WAGA: You must be aware, lieutenant, that in Poland as it is, the only chance for you and thousands like you is to fight on. Where can you go with your record? In this country everything is closed to you. Except prison.
ANDRZEJ: I know.[4]

Maciek enjoys a brief affair with the hotel's pretty barmaid between one killing and another. Krystyna's father had been arrested by the Germans and perished in Dachau; her mother was killed in the Warsaw rising. Maciek, who is without a family, tells her: 'I had a brother. He was killed in action, in forty-three. Father's in England. I expect he'll stay there.' After assassinating the Party boss Szczuka, who has been occupying the adjoining hotel room, Maciek is shot and dies in agony on a garbage heap—his last moments are intercut with the banquet in the hotel, where Krystyna is dancing the polonaise. Following the night's celebratory fireworks, a flock of crows is seen against the morning sky as Maciek dies.

Cybulski was the Marlon Brando and James Dean of Polish cinema—a restless, emotional sensualist, a heavy drinker in constant pursuit of women, highly patriotic and conscious of belonging to a tragic generation of Poles, and like Wajda himself, marked for life by experience of the Resistance. Compulsively theatrical, addicted to heroic action, the actor identified totally with Maciek. Wajda was fascinated by Elia Kazan's use of his 'method' actors, the gut feeling in his films, the sense of reality, in contrast to the formal, rhetorical, presentational acting still dominant in Poland. The Polish cultural scene—*Encounter* jubilantly reported in February 1958—was thoroughly Westernized: seventeen Western plays were in performance and not a single Soviet play had been seen for a year. *Kiss Me Kate* was a huge box-office success and theatre managers had duly come under attack from the Party organ, *Trybuna literacka*.[5] Visiting Warsaw later in the year, *Encounter*'s co-editor, Stephen Spender, admired *Ashes and Diamonds* (though his report did not mention Wajda by name):

The censor, and the producer's attempts to anticipate his objections, introduce new ambiguities. Apparently part of the banquet scene has been cut, where the satire seemed too pointedly anti-Russian; and at the last moment a scene has been inserted . . . in which the party secretary, looking sepulchrally benevolent, attired in a mackintosh, and photographed from below—in the manner of the Ascension-like appearances of political commissars in Russian films of the twenties—delivers a homily whose emphatic humanity and constructiveness are apparent without one having to know Polish.

Spender discerned a 'patchwork direction' by a director whose name eluded his rather patronizing report:

It opens in the early Russian style of lyrical ideological realism. The banquet scene, ending with a drunkard grotesquely dancing along the table and upsetting the guests, is pure René Clair. The love sequences and the barmaid recall glimmering shadowy whispered close-ups of *Sous les toits de Paris*. There is a good deal of documentary, and the scene in the ruined church, with a charred crucifix hanging upside down and swaying to and fro in the foreground, is Scandinavian symbolic. Yet in Warsaw this collage of ideologies and styles seems to reflect exactly the shape of life going on in Poland outside the cinema.[6]

Wajda's trilogy captivated art cinemas throughout Western Europe, where Polish culture was recognized as the first to have achieved a break with Stalinism. Yet *Kanal* (1957) and *Ashes and Diamonds* (1958) were not shown in other socialist countries until the 1960s—if at all—*Ashes and Diamonds* remaining banned in the USSR. Wajda views his aims as modest:

But what did we want? We only wanted to expand a little the limits of freedom, the limits of censorship, so films such as *Ashes and Diamonds* could be made. We never hoped to see the fall of the Soviet Union, to see Poland as a free country. I saw quite soon that it was better to remain independent . . . I didn't have to follow the party line. I was a filmmaker.[7]

After 1956 the Polish film industry enjoyed a form of self-management within Groups of Cinematic Creation, each group headed by a triumvirate of seasoned film-makers, a director, a writer or critic, and a production director. As Wajda recalled, throughout the years of Communist rule censors pounced on dialogue 'because for the censors the word is the privileged channel of ideology'. Fortunately, the essence of film lay in images and performance, harder to censor: no one could alter Zbyszek Cybulksi's performance in *Ashes and Diamonds*: 'It is precisely the way he is that contains that certain "something" representing political obscenity...'[8] Wajda provides 'a fragment from a confidential document relating to Polish censorship' and date-lined Warsaw (he deletes the date) concerning his film *Promised Lands*, written by 'the Department of Ideological and Educational Action of the Central Committee of the United Polish Workers' Party':

A. Wajda is one of four Polish film directors who have achieved worldwide recognition. He is one of the two (the other is [Krzysztof] Zanussi) who continues to work in Poland. His cinematic and theatrical creations, as well as the interviews he has granted, show that he is not politically involved in a pro-Marxist sense. Rather he has adopted a viewpoint that is not all that uncommon among artists—that of an 'objective judge' of both the past and the present . . . [9]

Wajda's *Man of Marble* (*Czlowiek z marmuru*, 1978), made in Poland with an all-Polish crew, is a beautifully conceived and devastatingly executed indictment of Polish Stalinism and post-Stalinism. Wajda had been seeking permission to make *Man of Marble* for fourteen years, ever since he read Aleksander Scibor-Rylski's screenplay, but the Ministry of Culture continued to veto the project until permission was suddenly granted early in 1976.

The film is set principally in two time-frames: 'now', the mid-1970s; and 'then', the post-war years. The ardent and fiercely tenacious young film student Agnieszka (Krystyna Janda), given twenty-one days to make her diploma film using TV studio facilities, is determined to disinter the buried truth of a real episode which the TV studio director supervising her—and everyone else—wants to leave undisturbed: the story of Mateusz Birkut, a Stakhanovite bricklayer of the late Stalin era, the subject of posters and a gigantic marble statue in the early 1950s, who had later fallen from favour and been airbrushed from the record. What had become of him?

Agnieszka comes across his statue in a museum basement and sets out to track down the story behind it. The story begins with a series of silent 'documentary' scenes at a shipyard in the Stalin era: Birkut (played by Jerzy Radziwilowicz) building a wall; Birkut smiling at a Party meeting; Birkut posing for his statue; Birkut at a workers' demo; and finally the façade of an apartment block surrounded by scaffolding and huge portraits of elite workers. The one of Birkut is being taken down: it descends slowly, touches the ground.

The studio archivist at first treats Agnieszka with outward cynicism—'I'm not paid to think', she says—but she and other members of the crew become increasingly helpful, as if the student director had awakened their dormant idealism. Agnieszka tracks down Jerszy Burski, an internationally renowned film-maker now enjoying the adulation and lifestyle of his Western counterparts (except for the giveaway little car he owns). As an ambitious young director in the 1950s he had discovered Mateusz Birkut, a friendly, peasant-born, and photogenic hero of labour; the young director had promptly snapped him up for his *Architects of our Happiness* propaganda documentary. Using an assembled support team, including Birkut's friend, the mason Wincenty Witek, to ensure the success of a highly publicized bricklaying challenge, a norm-breaking performance against the stopwatch, he had turned Birkut into a roving celebrity and done himself no harm either. But then a staged demonstration of Birkut's prowess turns to tragedy as the great worker is handed a scalding-hot brick before the rolling cameras. His hands are wrecked.

Who did it? The mason Witek comments: 'When one exceeds the norms, one makes enemies.' Fearful of admitting the truth, the authorities decide to accuse Birkut's closest colleagues of sabotage, notably Witek himself. The secret police move in; Witek disappears from a security office while Birkut waits in the reception room, his peasant bewilderment finally turning to fury and outright rebellion. Taking the train to Warsaw, he is given half a minute by a smoothly dressed official who promises to set things right 'in case a mistake has been made.' The loyal Birkut is making himself increasingly unpopular in his search for his friend and for justice.

Wajda uses a masterly simulation of an old documentary film to show Witek and three other workers on trial, accused of various acts of sabotage including the deliberate scalding of Birkut's hands. Called as a witness, the disillusioned Birkut sabotages the proceedings by declaring, straight-faced in his sarcasm, that he himself has taken part in terrorist activity. Both men go to prison. There are oblique suggestions that Birkut may later have been shot during the 1970 Gdansk riots. A cemetery scene confirming this was excised from *Man of Marble* but later included in *Man of Iron* (*Czlowiek z zelaza*, 1981).

Years later—'now', the late 1970s—the young film-maker Agnieszka, still fighting obstructionism, tracks Witek, now an industrial boss with a state-of-the art helicopter at his disposal, to the modern steel factory which is the pride of the regime. Agnieszka's supportive father, a simple postman, advises her that she should go in search of Birkut himself, even though she has been deprived of her camera and film stock by her young, careerist-conformist producer, whose haircut and flaired trousers reek of 'seventies'. (In disgust she finally asks him, 'How old are you?' 'Twenty-eight,' he replies coolly. Careerism is not a matter of generation.)

This quest takes her to the Lenin shipyard, Gdansk, where she finds Birkut's son—Birkut himself is dead. She leads the son to the TV film headquarters in something like triumph: youth and truth are about to have their day.

Reaching France in 1978, *L'Homme de marbre* ran for nine months in Paris and was hailed throughout the press—a reflection of the East–West divide in this late, but bitter, phase of the cold war. Even *L'Humanité*'s (31 May) critic, François Maurin, applauded its modern style, the film-within-a-film structure, its depiction of the criminal aberrations of the Stalin period, and the bad conscience of those who prolonged it to the present day. Michel Thierry commented in *Libération* (4 October) that Wajda had reconstituted that vital faculty, memory: 'Because, as in all the socialist countries, Poland has no history.' In *Le Monde* (7 October), Jacques Siclier spoke of 'a socialism with an inhuman face', and congratulated Wajda on his 'magisterially directed' film, 'a hymn to youth and the truth it promotes (*qu'elle fait surgir*)'. In *Le Quotidien de Paris* (31 May) Anne de Gasperi lauded Wajda's grasp of post-war Polish history and of 'l'embourgeoisement des notables communistes.' In *Jeune Cinéma* (July–August), Jean Delmas delivered a diatribe against 'the imposture of Stakhanovism, the imposture of the trials, the best plunged into the shadows while the worst made their place in the sun, saints sacrificed to Tartuffes . . .' In *Cahiers du Cinéma* (December), Jean-Paul Fargier celebrated the film as a triumph for fiction, for documentation, and for the rapport between the two.[10]

Man of Marble also proved to be exceedingly popular in Poland, but the ruling Party's reaction was hostile and punitive. Positive reviews were spiked, Wajda and his film unit were airbrushed out of the media, and the film was excluded from consideration for an award at the annual Gdansk Festival. When a new strike wave broke out at Gdansk in August 1980, Wajda was welcomed into the Lenin shipyard, conversed with Solidarity leader Lech

1. Vera Mukhina, 'Worker and Collective Farm Woman'. Exhibition of the Achievements of the People's Economy, Moscow. NOVOSTI (London)

2. Konstantin Stanislavsky (left) and Vladimir Nemirovich Danchenko, founders of the Moscow Art Theatre, later deans of theatrical style under Stalin. NOVOSTI (London)

3. Konstantin Simonov, author of *The Russian Question*, at Stalingrad, September 1942. NOVOSTI (London)

4. Mikhail Chiaureli's *The Fall of Berlin* (1949). The Red Army storms the Reichstag. bfi collections

. N. Cherkasov in the title role of Sergei Eisenstein's *Ivan the Terrible* (1945–6). NOVOSTI (London)

6. Grigorii Aleksandrov's *Meeting on the Elbe* (1949). The vulgar Americans make their mark. bfi collections

7. *Big Jim McLain* (1952). American Commies are brought to justice by John Wayne (on the ground) and Hawaii police. bfi collections

8. American producer-director Cecil B. DeMille displaying his 'archive' for *The Ten Commandments* (1956). bfi collections

9. American playwright Arthur Miller testifying before HUAC, 1956. Bettmann/CORBIS

10. American stage and screen director Elia Kazan on location. Hulton Archive Photos

11. Hero and heroine in Grigorii Chukhrai's *Ballad of a Soldier* (1959), warmly received in the West. NOVOSTI (London)

12. German playwright and poet Bertolt Brecht. Hulton Getty

13. French writer Jean-Paul Sartre at a rehearsal of *Les Mains Sales* (Paris, 1949) with impresario Simone Berriaut and Jean Cocteau (rear). New York Times Co./Hulton Archive Photos

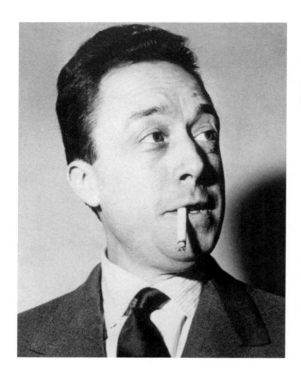

14. French playwright, novelist, and essayist Albert Camus. Hulton-Deutsch Collection/CORBIS

15. Playwright Václav Havel soon to be elected president of post-Communist Czechoslovakia. Peter Turnley/CORBIS

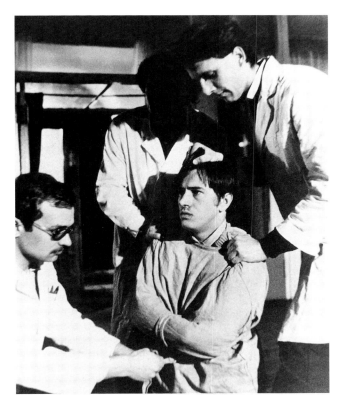

16. Andrzej Wajda's
Man of Iron (1981).
The dissident Polish
hero in a straitjacket.
bfi collections

17. Soviet premier Nikita Khrushchev congratulating Van Cliburn, American winner of
the International Tchaikovsky Piano Competition, Moscow, 1958. Bettmann/CORBIS

18. British composer Benjamin Britten with Soviet soprano Galina Vishnevskaya during a rehearsal of his 'War Requiem', 1963. Hulton Getty

19. Russian-born composer Igor Stravinsky (left) greets Soviet cellist and conductor Mstislav Rostropovich, London, 1964. Hulton Archive

20. Soviet composer Dmitri Shostakovich in 1974 with Solomon Volkov, compiler of the controversial *Testimony*. Solomon Volkov/ Lebrecht Music Collection

21. American singer, actor, and activist Paul Robeson at a Soviet Embassy party. Bettmann/CORBIS

22. The Kirov's star Rudolf Nureyev on the beach with his new dancing partner Dame Margot Fonteyn after his defection. Bettmann/CORBIS

23. Defecting dancers Mikhail Baryshnikov and Natalia Makarova in *Don Quixote*. Hulton-Deutsch Collection/CORBIS

24. America's leading choreographer, the Russian-born Georges Balanchine. Bettmann/CORBIS

25. Statue of Stalin, entrance to the Lenin Volga-Don Canal, 1952. NOVOSTI (London)

26. American
abstract-expressionist
Jackson Pollock at
work. CORBIS

27. Henry Moore – *Family
Group*, under fire from
Soviet critics. Christie's
Images/CORBIS

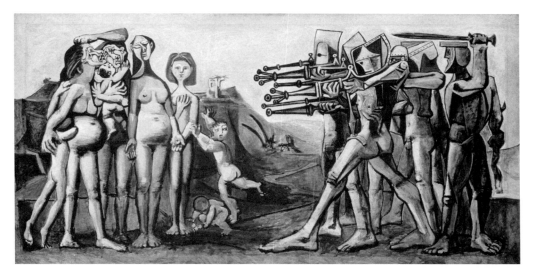

28. Pablo Picasso – *Le Massacre en Corée* (The Massacre in Korea), 1951. Musée Picasso, Paris/ Peter Willi/The Bridgeman Art Library. © Succession Picasso/DACS 2003

29. Three dissident Soviet artists soon after the 'bulldozer' exhibition, September 1974: Oskar Rabin (holding one of his paintings), his son Aleksandr, and Nadezhda Elskaya. Popperfoto

30. *Les Lettres françaises*, carrying Picasso's controversial portrait marking Stalin's death, March 1953.

Walesa (pronounced Vawensa), and was permitted to shoot a documentary, *Workers 80*. The metal hulls and cranes of the shipyards had suggested the title of the sequel, *Man of Iron*, for which Scibor-Rylski wrote a quick—but far from brief—script; the result is protracted and self-indulgent. By good fortune Jozef Tejchma, minister of culture when *Man of Marble* was made but later dismissed, had been reinstated during the liberal flare-up of 1980–1. During his brief tenure he was able to approve the script. Production started during the early spring of 1981.

Man of Iron spells out the fate of the disgraced worker-hero Mateusz Birkut during the protest strikes of 1970, whose martyrs are now celebrated by three crosses soaring ten storeys high near the shipyards, the Martyrs' Monument built in 100 days. Like the earlier film, *Man of Iron* takes the form of a reporter's investigation. To tie the elements together, the screenwriter created the somewhat one-dimensional character of an alcoholic journalist, Winkiel, a nervous time-server who is ordered by the network bosses and the secret police to defame the Gdansk strike leaders by getting inside the heavily guarded, security-tight Lenin shipyard, and by tape-recording incriminating conversations. (Wajda uses alcohol and alcoholism as metaphors for the uneasy moral lives of policemen, informers, and jailers. 'We are not in business to share power', growls a maddened, sweating official, one drink short of his heart attack, after Solidarity and the strikers turn Gdansk into a dry city and even the hotels obey.)

A prime target of the secret police is Maciek, son of Birkut, and now married to Agnieszka Hulewicz, the student documentary film-maker from *Man of Marble*. (Maciek carries the same name as the hero of *Ashes and Diamonds*.) Rapid ellipses indicate that they have married, had a child, and continued to practice their dissident politics. In *Man of Iron* Maciek is a positive hero in a highly articulate—and perhaps European—mould. He never gives up or lies down. He lives and acts by a declaration of human rights written in his head if nowhere else, sticking up street posters single-handed, hurling abuse when Edvard Gierek appears on television in 1970. Forced into a straitjacket, placed in a hospital jail, he is fortunate to be tended by a politically sympathetic woman psychiatrist. In a scene set further back in time, in the traumatic year 1968, Maciek quarrels bitterly with his father Birkut because neither Birkut nor the workers in general will support the student revolt. They will fight 'when the time comes'—but according to the furious Maciek it will never come. It does though, only two years later, and then the students turn down the workers' repentant appeals for solidarity.

Scibor-Rylski's scripts are modern in their splicing of various narratives and of different cinematic techniques (documentary footage, hidden cameras, and the *auteur*'s free re-creations), but they are traditional in so far as almost all the narratives confirm rather than subvert one another. In short, *Man of Iron* ultimately provides one story of Birkut and his son Maciek, one ultimate truth. In this respect the traditions of realism prevail over the generally preferred modernism of the era. *Man of Iron* offers an inversion of Gorky's *Mother*—an old working-class woman grieves for what the Communist police did to her children's generation, not merely the killing, but the indignity of the morgue where the bodies are laid out in rows, only the feet visible beneath the sheet. Although hero and heroine meet not on a tractor but in a television studio, within the emerging information technology, *Man of Marble* and *Man of Iron* firmly locate Birkut and his son Maciek within the old industrial working class, on building sites and shipyards—despite Maciek's higher education.

Pervading these two very modern films is the image of the journalist-investigator, the hidden tape-recorder, the microphone concealed behind flowers, the hand-held camera drawn like a revolver. Rare are the Joan of Arcs, the Agnieszka's, many are the collaborators of itching conscience, the Witiek's. The knowledge industry, not least in the West, has been self-admiring and self-romanticizing about fearless cameramen and women, and Wajda is no exception, but the power of his portrait gains from the nature of Communism, the jealous monopoly of information in the one-party state, the news blackouts, the government-driven distortions of strikes, the posters ripped down, the narrow limits of 'legality', constant police transgressions, the cynicism of policemen and personnel managers schooled in the blackmail of the personal dossier, experts in sneering persuasion. The crusading Agnieska, who ends up in jail—though in a remarkably comfortable cell with its own telephone—is the conscience of a nation which is reluctant to locate its conscience.

Wajda's genius is nowhere more apparent than in his depiction of the regime: the decorous party officials in their suits and ties seated across the negotiating table from Lech Walesa and the workers: the muted, correct, always reasonable voices of the officials who genuinely desire to avoid a repeat of the massacres of 1970 but who can only resort to platitudes about the government and the working class. In one scene Wajda perhaps overdoes it: we see a bloated Party chief occupying a hotel dining room alone, a napkin tucked into his collar, stuffing himself and slurping wine while threatening the timid, alcohol-starved journalist Winkiel, who has failed to convert the bribes offered to him—money, a car, hotels—into real information from inside the barricaded fortress of the Gdansk shipyard. Anyone familiar with cartoons of capitalist bosses in *Krokodil* may smile.

Enter here the Church. Being Poland, its role is immense, indeed unique. Religion serves even the undevout. Maciek plants a wooden cross on his father's makeshift grave and then, after the body is cruelly spirited away by the regime lest it become a point of pilgrimage, he thrusts a steel cross into the hard roadside ground where Birkut had fallen, shot, in 1970. Agnieszka (in white) and Maciek are married in church, with Lech Walesa (playing himself) as the one who gives the bride away. Even Maciek's thrusting of his own shoes onto his father's bare feet in the morgue carries religious symbolism.

Finally the shifty Winkiel, a human hamster in permanent need of vodka and tobacco, is so impressed by the integrity of the strike leaders (while worming his way inside the gate to witness the historic accords of 1980) that he cops out on his assignment. The alcoholic government official, who earlier turned a cello into a drinks cabinet, murmurs to him through a car window 'It's only a piece of paper', as he drives off.[11]

Man of Iron opened in Poland on 26 July 1981, after winning the Palme d'or at Cannes, and quickly became the most popular Polish film of all time. Frank Turaj writes: 'For effect it compares with Costa-Gavras's *"Z"* or *State of Siege*.' The 1981 Gdansk Film Festival was held only a few blocks from the Lenin Shipyard. Andrzej Wajda's docu-drama on the birth of Solidarity opened the schedule. Films sequestered by the censor over the past decade were screened. Film of the year was *Man of Iron*, though not entered for the festival competition.

Wajda was due to deliver a lecture to a Polish Cultural Congress in December 1981, but martial law descended, the doors were locked, and a number of participants arrested. *Man of Iron* was not seen again.[12] Under General Wojciech Jaruzelski's martial law Wajda was attacked by the official press, forced to resign as president of the Polish film union, and stripped of the directorship of his film unit, the vehicle not only for creating many of his own films but also for others by young directors. A photograph shows him with some twenty members of Cinematic Group X in February 1982 before it was forcibly dissolved. 'I think', said Wajda, 'that the political liquidation of Solidarity cannot change anything. It is of no consequence, because irrespective of the movement's fate . . . what occurred immortalized the movement by transporting it into the realms of the ideal.'[13] Broadly in agreement with Wajda's perspective was Tom Stoppard's *Squaring the Circle*, a filmed drama first broadcast on British television (Channel 4) in May 1984, encompassing events in Poland from the fall of Gierek through the rise of Solidarity to the imposition of martial law by General Jaruzelski, now first secretary of the party and prime minister. *Squaring the Circle* embodies a notable paradox of Western cold war culture: Stoppard's Polish workers are held to be right in their wage demands, right in their insistence on the release of imprisoned comrades, and right to strike. Ironically, *Squaring the Circle* appeared on television while Mrs Thatcher was crushing the miners' strike in Britain by massive use of police power, employing 'national interest' arguments not unlike those of Gierek and Jaruzelski in Poland.[14]

Both *Man of Marble* and *Man of Iron* were banned in the USSR, until the former received a public showing at the tail-end of the Soviet (Gorbachev) era. 'Wajda brought us his own copy of *Man of Iron* to show privately,' recalls Naum Kleiman, director of Moscow's Muzei Kino.[15]

⌗ ⌗ ⌗

Wajda's impressive Franco-Polish production *Danton*, with Gérard Depardieu in the title role, and based on Stanislawa Przybyszewska's play *The Danton Affair*, is an intellectual drama focused on the meaning of history, with human relationships of secondary importance. Whereas Robespierre repre-sents an adherence to principle capable of turning into dogmatic and de-structive absolutism, Danton incarnates compromise, man's defective nature. Przybyszewska—who had died young, in 1935—evidently sympa-thized with Robespierre, but Wajda's film predictably transfers the audience's allegiance to the imperfect man of compromise. Though faithful to the playwright's intentions when he had directed the stage play in 1975 at Warsaw's Popular Theatre (Teatr Powszechny), in the film, angered by the recent imposition of martial law in Poland, Wajda presented Danton as the more human face of Revolution, paradoxically infuriating the French Left, which had only recently lauded *Man of Marble*; President Mitterrand is said to have left the theatre before the end of a private viewing—this was when Communists were still members of his government and before his own sharp turn to the right.

Despite martial law the film was shown in Poland, even though, as could have been predicted, a Polish public schooled in reading between the lines saw it as a metaphor for their own situation, with ideology and reasons of state at variance with human needs and personal freedom. Many equated Lech Walesa with the character of Danton and General Wojciech Jaruzelski with the tense, tight-mouthed Robespierre. (The posture and carriage of the actor Wojciech Pszoniak, who played Robespierre, suggests he might be imitating Jaruzelski.) Interviewed on West German television in 1984, Wajda confirmed that many of his films had a political aim: 'I want the country to submit to certain changes and films can decidedly help... there will always be a conflict between summary law, as represented by authority, and the law the people wish to follow: that age-old law, laid down by religion, agreed upon by us all.'

After the war the Polish intelligentsia had tended to be opposed to the Church, but thirty years later Wajda found it to be the guarantor of Polish national existence. No longer able to make films in Poland, he turned once again to theatre[16]—with the same political aims in view. Whereas Tadeusz Kantor and Jerzy Grotowski had created their own companies,[17] Wajda did not, preferring to work with professionals in a variety of theatres and using the full panoply of dramatic forms and repertoire. His *Antigone* (1984) brought utterly differing responses from the government periodical *Polityka* and the Catholic paper *Tygodnik Powszechny*, the closest thing to an organ of legal opposition. The latter wrote: '*Antigone* in Wajda's interpretation is a play about the inner freedom of man, of the need to be true to oneself and to one's conscience, and of the infectious strength of good example—as regards truth, love and sacrifice.' By contrast, *Polityka* complained: 'The use of a journalistic rationalization showing the necessity of opposing unjustified tyranny, does not excuse a slapdash artistic presentation, the mixing up of different dramatic conventions, or the imprecise and rushed interpret-ation.'[18]

In 1985 Ernest Bryll, previously a poet and playwright in good odour with the Party, wrote *Easter Vigil*, a religious dramatic poem. The censor having disallowed a production at the Teatr Atheneum, the Catholic Church spon-sored an independent production by Wajda in the Church of the Lord's Mercy, Warsaw, where it could be staged without the censor's authorization. Based on the tradition of the Passion Plays, *Easter Vigil* was first performed on Good Friday. Set in the room where the Apostles had eaten the Last Supper with Christ, it shows them in hiding after the Crucifixion. They struggle to understand why the cause, until recently so near victory, has been defeated. Finally Mary Magdalene (played by Krystyna Janda, the heroine in *Man of Marble* and *Man of Iron*) brings news of the Resurrection. Some 6,000 people attended the twelve performances.[19]

PART IV

Music and Ballet Wars

Classical Music Wars

The innocent might have expected classical music to dwell, alongside 'pure' mathematics and chess theory, in a zone immune to invasion by ideological polemic. This was far from the case. The political argument between classicism (or realism) and modernism was as lively in music as in literature and art. Furthermore, musical performance standards, requiring no linguistic translation, offered a uniquely exacting trial of cultural strength.

To begin with, harmony prevailed. On 3 July 1945 a jointly sponsored concert of American music was performed in the Tchaikovsky Hall, Moscow, before political dignitaries and the US ambassador by the USSR Symphony Orchestra, conducted by Nikolai Anosov.[1] When Yehudi Menuhin, the American son of Russian Jews, and by nature a musical ambassador, was on his way to perform in Moscow that year, the young violinist had encountered the lesser hazards of a divided Berlin:

I was shown into the presence of the commandant . . . From behind her makeshift desk she surveyed me coolly and asked if I had heard of David Oistrakh. Not only had I heard of him, but I was looking forward to meeting him that very day. And did I know how great a musician he was? Yes, indeed, I admired him enormously, I said. But [she pressed] had I ever won any medals? . . . Oistrakh, it appeared, had won dozens of decorations: he was a Hero of the Soviet Union, the darling of the people, the holder of this, that and the next award, she knew them all by heart.[2]

Oistrakh, a Jew from Odessa, and Menuhin became firm friends and shared platforms 'in half the capitals of the developed world' (but never in Moscow). 'Commands to perform were a feature of Oistrakh's life, as of any Soviet artist's . . . I don't think they enjoyed being summoned to the Kremlin and ordered to impress visitors, but it was a way of life which Mozart and Haydn also submitted to . . . ' Menuhin felt glad to have been brought up an American, 'free of courtly obligations'.[3] Reaching Moscow, he was greeted by a warmth of affection outstripping his fondest hopes. As a gesture of good-will, he was allowed to meet two female relatives of his mother's. Assigned a room in the Metropole overlooking Theatre Square, he gave three concerts and was inundated by 'a joyous rabble of young musicians', but he soon discovered the underside of Stalin's Russia. Before leaving for the USSR he had offered to carry a message to the father of Grisha Piatigorsky, the émigré cellist, whose letters and parcels had gone unacknowledged by his father for years. Meeting the old man in Moscow, not without difficulty, Menuhin learned that he had never received his son's gifts. Hearing that his indignation against his heartless son was misplaced, Piatigorsky senior immediately and loudly cursed the regime.[4]

A year later the chords were more discordant. 'Against Formalism in Soviet Music', an editorial, presumably written by Vladimir Kemenov, editor of *VOKS Bulletin*, began cordially enough but soon began to bristle regarding Western criticism: 'The trouble is, however, that a section of the foreign intelligentsia, including some art workers and musicians, have not understood... Among these foreign intellectuals there are many who are quite loyal and friendly... who sincerely desire to understand.'[5] Kemenov did not include in this well-meaning category Bertrand Russell, who had offended Soviet ears on BBC radio by ruling out any obligation for the artist beyond individuality, and by insisting that the only question was whether the artist or musician should be subject to external control.

By 1947 the Western press had its ear cocked for discord in Russia's concert halls and conservatories. On 16 May 1947 the *New York Times* carried a report of *Pravda*'s attack on the production and sets of *Boris Godunov* at the Bolshoi Theatre: 'Ideological Failure Seen in Soviet Opera.' Those responsible for the production were castigated by *Pravda* for failure to depict 'the triumphant character of Russian greatness'. '*Pravda* Blasts New "Godunov". Even Arts Must Bow to Lenin', added the *Christian Science Monitor* (27 May).

The Soviet spine was now stiffening in music as in all other cultural fields. In June the talented young pianist Lev Oborin reported on a five-week concert tour of the Soviet zone of Germany, starting with a performance at the House of Soviet Culture on Unter den Linden. He found that young Germans suffered from ignorance about musical life in the USSR, its diversity, and the thorough grounding in Bach given to Soviet students, some of whom were trained to play all 48 preludes and fugues. After the concert he was approached by a woman reporter for *Telegraf*, a British-sector paper: 'Tell me, did you rehearse Bach and Beethoven specially for your German tour, or do you play that in Russia too?' The Soviet pianist was shocked. That the Americans were philistines Oborin could no longer doubt—after all, when they had occupied Weimar, before the Russians replaced them, the bomb-damaged Goethe Haus remained shut up! It was restored only after the Soviets arrived! (He did not ask why the Americans would embark on restoration work, knowing they would soon be leaving.) As for the Liszt Haus in the same town, it was visited mainly by Soviet troops![6]

The iron fist descended on 10 February 1948, when the Central Committee issued a decree (or 'resolution')[7] condemning V. Muradeli's opera *The Great Friendship*, produced at the Bolshoi Theatre to celebrate the thirtieth anniversary of the Revolution. Stalin's spokesman A. A. Zhdanov broadened the attack to castigate key figures in the Union of Composers, despite their numerous Stalin Prizes: 'The rewards you received were in the nature of a substantial advance payment', Zhdanov reminded them, but Soviet society had been poorly rewarded:

The question here concerns composers who follow a formalistic, anti-popular trend. This trend has found its fullest expression in the work of composers D. Shostakovich, S. Prokofiev, A. Khachaturian, V. Shebalin, G. Popov, N. Myaskovsky and others, whose work most strikingly illustrates the formalistic distortions and anti-democratic tendencies in music... It makes a cult of atonality, dissonance, and discord, which are supposed to represent 'progress' and 'novelty' in the development of musical form. It renounces vital principles of musical composition such as melody, and prefers confused, neuropathological combinations that turn music into cacophony, into a chaotic conglomeration of sounds. This music distinctly smacks of contemporary modernistic bourgeois music in Europe and America, which expresses the decay of bourgeois culture, the total negation of musical art, its impasse.

Many contemporary works from the West reminded Zhdanov of a dentist's drill or a musical murder.[8] Did this really apply to Sergei Prokofiev, a composer with several Stalin Prizes under his belt, the most recent in 1947? It did!

The work of many students of the conservatories amounts merely to blind imitation of the music of D. Shostakovich, S. Prokofiev, and others. The Central Committee of the CPSU(B) finds the state of Soviet musical criticism utterly intolerable... they glorify subjectivism, constructivism, extreme individualism, and technical complexity of idiom, in other words, the very qualities that merit criticism.

Educated under the tsars, Prokofiev had left Russia in 1918 and lived for almost two decades in America and Western Europe.[9] He and his Spanish-born wife Lina, a singer, visited the USSR for concerts before deciding to settle in Moscow in 1935 and make efforts to accommodate to the regime. Prokofiev's opera *Semyon Kotko*, based on Valentin Katayev's novel *I am the Son of Working People*, and set in the German-occupied Ukraine of 1918, glorifies the Red Army as it marches south to combat the Haydamaks, the Ukrainian nationalists. The soldier Semyon Kotko, returning home from the trenches, is caught up in the civil war. Lenin is constantly hallowed in the libretto, but the score belongs to modernism. Constructvist fury erupts in the orchestra and massive *ostinati* shred the nerves. Prokofiev originally planned a collaboration with Vsevolod Meyerhold, but the expressionist director was arrested when rehearsals had scarcely begun. The production was discreetly withdrawn after the Hitler–Stalin Pact because of its portrayal of barbaric German behaviour in 1918.

The year Hitler invaded the USSR, 1941, Prokofiev left his wife Lina (and their two sons) for another woman, Mira. Lina was arrested on 20 February 1948 immediately after Zhdanov's attack on Prokofiev and other 'formalists'. Her foreign relatives and connections now provided an obvious pretext for arrest; fluent in several languages, she did occasional interpreting for diplomats and was a regular guest at the US Embassy. Charged with passing information to foreigners, she spent eight years in Siberian labour camps, bravely refusing to sign a 'confession' as the price of release.

Pleading poor health, Prokofiev managed to evade the fateful January 1948 meeting which launched the Party's onslaught. Many resented his international past and connections, his Western manners, his privileges, his alleged arrogance. Serebryakov, director of the Leningrad Conservatory, berated Prokofiev for composing his *War and Peace* for 'a narrow circle of connoisseurs'.[10] Prokofiev sent a letter pleading that since his return to Russia he had striven to a create an accessible, yet artistically viable, style, for example in his *Alexander Nevsky, Romeo and Juliet*, and Fifth Symphony. He grovelled to the Party: 'The Resolution is valuable precisely in that it pointed out how alien the formalistic movement is to the Soviet people.' Describing his current work on *Story of a Real Man* (which was ill-destined), he promised that he was employing 'clear melodies and a harmonic language that is as simple as possible'.[11]

In 1949 he (like Shostakovich) received a letter identical to the ones sent to other blacklisted victims of the previous year's decree.

The Council of Ministers of the USSR. Order No. 3197 of 16 March 1949. Moscow, The Kremlin.
1. To recognize as illegal the Order No. 17, dated 14 February 1948 . . . and to rescind this illegal order. 2. To reprimand Glavrepertkom for publishing an illegal order.
Signed: Chairman of the Council of Ministers of the USSR, J. Stalin.

Attached by staple was the original decree, now rescinded:

Copied Extract from the Order No.17 of the Chief Direction of Representations and Repertoire of the Commission in Charge of the Arts under the Auspices of the Council of Ministers of the USSR. Moscow, 14 February 1948. To forbid the performance and to remove from the repertoire the following works by Soviet composers . . . [a list followed.] Signed, Head of the Chief Command in Control of Representations and Repertoire, M. Dobrynin.[12]

Until his death Prokofiev lived in a communal apartment of three small rooms with his second wife and stepfather. After 1948 he was seldom performed—until the Seventh Symphony (1948–50) was hailed as a masterpiece by Soviet critics, although criticized posthumously by Olin Downes in the *New York Times* (22 and 26 April 1953). The American musicologist Boris Schwarz was critical of Prokofiev's Festive Poem, *The Volga Meets the Don*, and of his oratorio *On Guard for Peace*, composed in collaboration with the notoriously hardline novelist Aleksandr Fadeyev.[13] Schwarz held that as a result of the 1948 decree the composer had simplified harmony and weakened both his satirical streak and his instinct for innovation. Schwarz likewise criticized Prokofiev's essay 'Music and Life' (1951), which takes as its point of departure a cold war incident in Salt Lake City when an anonymous call was made in an attempt to prevent a performance of his Fifth Symphony. Schwarz dismissed the essay as seemingly ghost-written, 'verbose, portentous, self-advertising', and full of such hollow phrases as the composer being 'duty bound to serve Man, the people'.[14] Prokofiev died on the same day as Stalin, 5 March 1953. It took a tremendous effort by family and friends to move his coffin from his apartment to the basement of the Composers' House on Myausskaya Street. Flowers were hard to obtain, police barriers were everywhere, and few came.

Writing on Prokofiev for a foreign audience in February 1956, the erstwhile Stalinist polemicist Israil Nestiev managed to avoid any mention of the 1948 decree, though Nestiev himself had been in the forefront of a howling pack at the time, attacking 'universal cosmopolitan phenomena', that is, 'the lifeless constructions of the atonalists and quarter-tonists . . .'.[15] But now Nestiev let drop not a word to suggest that Prokofiev's life from 1948 until his death in 1953 might have been anything but normal: 'In recognition of his achievements the Soviet Government awarded Prokofiev six Stalin Prizes . . . It was only after his death that the new versions of his cello concerto . . . and 5th piano sonata . . . were introduced to Soviet audiences.'[16]

During these fraught and dangerous years the two most famous Soviet composers, Prokofiev and Shostakovich—Prokofiev was by a large margin the senior—passed each other occasional letters of congratulation on their new compositions, but usually not without expressing reservations. Speaking privately, long after Prokofiev was gone, Shostakovich was relentlessly disparaging about the 'condescending' Prokofiev, who always had money and success and 'the personality of a spoiled *Wunderkind*'. He added: 'I don't think Prokofiev ever treated me seriously as a composer; he considered only Stravinsky a rival and never missed a chance to take a shot at him...' Shostakovich also gloated over Prokofiev's fear of Stalin—indeed, everyone else's pants-soiling fear of Stalin:

There was a period when Prokofiev was frightened out of his wits. He wrote a cantata with words by Lenin and Stalin—it was rejected. He wrote songs for solo, chorus, and orchestra, also praising Stalin—another failure... And then, to cap it all, Prokofiev ran over a girl in his Ford... Prokofiev had the soul of a goose... He was always afraid that he was being overlooked—cheated out of his prizes, orders and titles... [17]

⌗ ⌗ ⌗

Following the 1948 decree, *Pravda* promptly published a rush of supporting letters from workers, an engineer, and the foreman of a tractor plant, under the headline: 'The Soviet people warmly approve the Central Committee's decree.' A fourth-year music student added his own message of gratitude: 'When I read the decree I at once heaved a deep sigh. Can you believe it—I now walk about singing to myself, and the thoughts which I used to suppress pour out of me in melodies.'[18] The organ of the Composers' Union, *Sovetskaia muzyka* (January–February 1948) was equally quick off the mark in publishing several pages of cartoons satirizing R. M. Glier, D. D. Shostakovich, A. I. Khachaturian, Iu. A. Shaporin, and D. B. Kabalevsky, all depicted as Catholic seminarians. Another cartoon, 'Lyrical Duet from "The Great Friendship"', depicted a standard peasant woman covering her ears in horror as a cacophany of musical notes was generated by means of primitive machines and pulleys.

As general secretary of the Composers' Union, the young Tikhon Khrennikov was one of Zhdanov's most loyal sword-bearers. The Central Committee resolution, he declared, 'deals a crushing blow to modernist art as a whole.' Detailing the 'musical fiascos' of the last three decades, he went on to demolish the 'foreigners', including such Russians as Stravinsky and the Diaghilev circle. 'One can hardly name a single important composer of the West who is not infected.' Hindemith, Berg, Britten, Messiaen, Menotti, and Max Brandt all offered 'a conglomeration of wild harmonies, a reversion to primitive savage cultures... eroticism, sexual perversion, amorality and the shamelessness of the contemporary bourgeois theories of the twentieth century'. Commenting on this 'ludicrous speech', Boris Schwarz noted that within a dozen years every one of the insulted composers was performed in Soviet concerts. Schwarz pointed out that whereas the attack on Soviet composers aroused a storm in the West, the parallel action a year later against the musicologists of the Composers' Union went barely noticed. Yet the purge of critics, historians, and theorists was even more radical, beginning in February 1949, with Khrennikov leading the attack. Thirty-five were censured by name, many being accused of grovelling to Western formalism, Jews prominent among them. The harshest treatment was meted out to the 'rootless cosmopolite' Alex Ogolevetz, who had dared to envisage the expansion of the tonal system from twelve to seventeen and twenty-two tones, and who cited Stravinsky with approval.[19]

The utterly arid Prague Manifesto of the second International Congress of Composers and Musical Critics followed, bringing the blessings of Zhdanovism to all progressive musicians throughout the Soviet bloc.[20] There was no mention of the individual in the Manifesto, but repeated emphasis on national cultures and 'the musical inspiration of each people' (whom the composer must serve—the key term, always, was *zadachi*, 'tasks'). The Manifesto called for 'vocal music—operas, oratorios, cantatas, chorals', to which Jean-Paul Sartre responded derisively:

They want . . . to sing the praises of the Soviet world as Haydn sang those of divine Creation . . . to set an example to [the] public of submission to an established order . . . a means of enhancing the glory of the word . . . of Stalin, the Five Year Plan, the electrification of the Soviet Union. Set to other words, the same music could glorify Pétain, Truman, Churchill, the TVA. By changing the words, a hymn to the Russian dead of Stalingrad will become a funeral oration for Germans fallen before the same city. What do the sounds contribute? A great blast of sonorous heroism.[21]

Zhdanov's edict against modernist composers was frenetically taken up in the East German press. *Tägliche Rundschau* (17 January 1948) lashed out at four 'notorious' French composers whose music had nothing in common with the French people or the French nation. Igor Stravinsky's music was dismissed as 'pathetic clownery', and Benjamin Britten's as 'amoral, sexually pathological, and sick'. Even in the West, Zhdanovism had its fellow-travellers among non-Communists, although outright, unconditional subscription was on the whole confined to Party members. For example, early numbers of the new, Glasgow University-based journal *Soviet Studies* tended to give cultural Zhdanovism the benefit of the doubt in the name of 'academic method' and 'internalism', a form of 'objectivity' broadly defined as not judging a 'post-market society' like the USSR by Western criteria. Reviewing Alexander Werth's outspoken *Musical Uproar in Moscow* (1949), J. Miller, one of the co-editors, chided Werth for failing to understand that 'where a society is so constituted that the majority of its members must be careless of past human achievements, a specialist profession must equally take the task of trusteeship into its own hands'. He meant Russia and he meant Zhdanov.[22] (George Orwell, castigator of academic fellow-travelling, lay mortally ill in University College Hospital when Miller's article appeared.)

American music, like American everything, was by 1948 emerging as a prime target for Soviet critics. Under *Sovetskaia muzyka*'s rubric 'Abroad'—*za rubezhom*, Grigorii Shneerson published 'American Musical Engineers' (March–April 1948). According to Shneerson,[23] during the war years Soviet readers of the American press were frequently pained to encounter the 'haughty/proud' (*gordelivye*) claim that the centre of world music and culture was shifting from Europe to America. The emigration of musicians following the Nazi occupation may have encouraged such aspirations—yet neither Stravinsky, Schoenberg, Hindemith, nor Milhaud had brought glory to American music. Shneerson ran through the standard faults of American capitalism, the rule of the dollar, formalism, the cult of novelty.[24] Worse, Americans capitulated to the worst kind of charlatanism. Shneerson had clearly made a careful study of 'The Schillinger System of Musical Composition', published in twelve volumes in 1946 by the New York publisher Carl Fisher. Schillinger's central concept was the application of abstract mathematical logic to all elements of music: typical phrases used included 'pre-fabrication', 'assembly', and 'industrial music'. 'All very scientific and in the spirit of the time'—*Ochen' nauchno i v dukhe vremeni!*—commented the Soviet critic, dismissing Schillinger's 'ten systems' as a table-top book for American composers of cinema and radio music. As for America, the popularity of the heavily promoted Schillinger system confirmed it as 'this classical country of standardized and soulless technologism'.[25]

Two of the fiercest anti-American music critics of the late Stalin era were V. Gorodinskii and I. Nestiev. According to the scornful Gorodinskii, America, in pathetic contrast to the USSR, was struggling to import its music: 'The creation of a national music culture out of so-called "imported material" is quite impossible, just as it's impossible to create a national architectural style in which one buys old castles with ghosts in Europe.' Gorodinskii, music critic of *Komsomol'skaia pravda*, discovered a family photograph in a 1948 edition of *Musical America*: President Truman accompanied by his wife, his daughter—and the head of an émigré singing troupe Nikolai Kosturkov, a 'white guard'. It was symbolic that, at the highest level of indecency, the president entertained a pack of singing wolves howling 'the Don Cossacks' chorus of General Platov'. This 'inhuman ensemble', heard performing on American radio with their incessant wild pipes, sang Russian songs like they were not sung even in the darkest taverns of tsarist Russia.[26]

I. Nestiev, a keen student of the degradations of the American musical scene, scoffed that the Metropolitan Opera season in New York lasted only five months a year—with nothing to fill its place off-season! As for Gian-Carlo Menotti's opera *Medium*, it reportedly described the pathological love between the heroine, a drunken old epileptic, and her deaf-and-dumb lover. The music, even from the reports of sympathetic critics, was filled with various terrifying effects, resembling a sinister requiem service. Yet this 'delirious' (*bredovoi*—a word frequently used to describe Western culture) production had been hailed by American critics as 'an opera for Americans'.

Nestiev turned to the exploitation of amateur and would-be composers. Not long ago an American paper had exposed the widespread practice of the 'singing swindle'; swallowing the bait, large numbers of gullible authors rained down dollars on speculators in the hope of a quick production of their modest creations. The 'song sharks' were calculated to have extorted 10–12 million dollars a year from desperate amateurs. And further degrad-ations!—for example, during intervals in Beethoven's Fifth Symphony, per-formed by the New York Philarmonic, the radio announcer promotes the launch of the new model Ford. The tyre manufacturer Goodyear buys up radio concerts by J. Heifetz or V. Horowitz; the fashionable club singers, before performing new jazz on radio, promote the cigarette brand Chester-fields![27]

The State Department, meanwhile, was dispatching American musicians to Germany.[28] The 1948 consignment included Leonard Bernstein, the com-poser-ballad singer Tom Scott, and the harpsichordist Ralph Kirkpatrick, who gave a series of concerts in the Soviet zone, following Yehudi Menuhin's recitals in Leipzig and Dresden. The *New York Times* (26 July 1948) quoted the American military governor, General Lucius Clay, as approving 'any type of penetration into the Soviet zone'. It was an odd situation: the Berlin blockade and airlift were in full operation, yet the East German press felt bound to praise any American artist invited by their Soviet masters. Berlin was the showcase—citizens could still travel across the sector boundary.

The most sustained general onslaught on Western music arrived with V. Gorodinskii's *Muzyka dukhovnoi nishchety* (*The Music of Spiritual Poverty*, 1950). Gorodinskii began by noting that bourgeois culture was desperately striving to renew the musical aesthetics of Kant and Schopenhauer, with Pythagorian conceptions, Freudian mysticism, the abject amoralism of Gide and Aldous Huxley [Oldos Khaksli in the Cyrillic], both described by Gorodinskii as 'troubadors of filth and swinishness'.[29] (By contrast, any Western composer of pro-Soviet tendency—Arnold Bax, Alan Bush, Chris-tian Darnton—was awarded laurels by Gorodinskii.)

Gorodinskii was at pains to establish the Russian classical tradition as the stairway to the stars for Elgar, Grieg, and Puccini: page after page is devoted to Russian music and to the claims of the nation (not to be confused with chauvinism, which was synonymous with 'cosmopolitanism'). This obsessive patriotism was obligatory during the autumn of the patriarch. According to Gorodinskii:

From the time of Glinka, progressive West European music was linked one way or another to the rapid development of Russian musical realism. The tradition of patriotic civic responsibility (*grazhdanstvennost'*) arose and was precisely defined in Russian musical art, as was understood from an early time by the most perspicacious minds among Western musicians. Sufficient to mention Henri Merimée, who rightly assessed the signifance of Glinka's *Ivan Susanin* as the first Russian national opera, and who found no West European music artistically analogous to Glinka's great work.[30]

Gorodinskii attributed all that was best and most life-enhancing in Puccini and the *veristi* to Russian influences (*vliianiiami*). At this time the soprano Galina Vishnevskaya was beginning her career at the Bolshoi; her privately held view of current Soviet musical practice was rather different from Gorodinskii's: 'Even in classical operas, the directors would come up with some outlandish characterization or bit of stage business to correspond to the Soviet ideological line. In Puccini's *Madame Butterfly*, as produced during the cold war, for example, the American consul—a fine, kindhearted man— was transformed into a hard, cynical "Uncle Sam".'[31]

Without Russian guidance, insisted Gorodinskii, West European composers were bogged down in petty-bourgeois eclecticism, offering audiences shallow 'psychological' melodramas instead of the lofty dramaturgy and life-enhancing truths of Russian art. The French impressionist composers, Debussy and Ravel, had wanted to emulate the Russians as students and followers, but the mere wish was not enough; the creative method of Modest Mussorgsky and Nikolai Rimsky-Korsakov remained beyond their reach. As pure impressionists Debussy and Ravel limited themselves to technical points of contact and the 'crust phenomenon' (*'koroi iavlenii' ogranichivalis'*), without penetrating the essence (*sushchnost'*) of the Russian realists. Maurice Ravel 'wrote music in French but with a Russian pedal'.[32]

Gorodinskii worked his way along the modernist family tree, hacking and chopping. 'Wagner was the spiritual father of modernism, although he was also the last truly powerful creative personality produced by West European bourgeois culture on the borderline of the beginning of its decline.'[33] But even Wagner could not have anticipated the current crop of Western 'musical obscurantists' and 'atonalists' affecting 'formalistic radicalism', at whose peak stood Schoenberg's and Stravinsky's followers, for example Virgil Thomson's opera *Four Saints in Three Acts* (1934), 'frenzied jazz-lovers', 'musical speculators and adventurers', 'white guard scoundrels like the radio-liar Nicolas Nabokov'. Gorodinskii reserved an unkind paragraph for the 'concrete composer' John Cage, 'one of the most "famous" and "enigmatic" (*zagadochnyi*) of contemporary composers,' whose latest piece headed up the 'dada movement' and must be regarded as an advanced symptom of a deadly illness rather than the *jeu d'esprit* of a 'circus eccentric'.[34]

That many of Gorodinskii's illustrious targets were hostile to Soviet Communism is beyond doubt. Igor Stravinsky and Arnold Schoenberg, whom he called 'the father of ultramodernism' and 'leader of the decadents', are obvious examples. Schoenberg, like Stravinsky, declined to join the welcoming party for the Soviet delegation arriving for the Waldorf-Astoria Peace Conference in March 1949. A refugee from Nazi Germany, Schoenberg, replied to the invitation: 'Being scapegoat [*sic*] of Russian restrictions I cannot sign.' Stravinsky, who preferred exile to Soviet Russia, replied: 'Regret not to be able to join welcomers of Soviet artists coming this country. But all my ethic and esthetic convictions oppose such gesture.'[35] On 11 September Schoenberg was to deliver a bitter radio address accusing American conductors of suppressing his music and ideas, concluding: 'Even Stalin cannot succeed and Aaron Copland even less.' Schoenberg regarded the American composer as a fellow-traveller, but underlying the apparent confusion of his *cri de coeur* was his long experience of America as a country resistant to the twelve-tone idiom in practice, if not in theory. During his first decade as a resident in the USA he composed only four dodecaphonic (12-note) pieces, earning a living by composing and teaching in the tonal idiom. Mainstream American taste was not so different from Gorodinskii's; indeed, 'ultramodern' avant-garde musical innovation by no means reflected mainstream taste among audiences who frequented concert halls in Cologne, Boston, Edinburgh, or Lyons. After the première of Schoenberg's Violin Concerto at the Academy of Music, Philadelphia, in December 1940, Edwin Schloss of the *Philadelphia Record* damned it: 'Yesterday's piece combines the best sound effects of a hen yard at feeding time, a brisk morning in Chinatown, and practice horn at a busy music conservatory. The effect on the vast majority of hearers is that of a lecture on the fourth dimension delivered in Chinese.'[36]

From Gorodinskii's standpoint, the fact that Schoenberg and Hindemith were refugees from Nazism scarcely atoned for their triptych of sins: being German, being modernists, and being permanent residents of the United States by choice. The Soviet critic Nestiev, author of the celebrated '*Dollar-ovaia kakofoniia*' ('Dollar Cacophany', published in *Izvestiia* on 7 January

1951) scornfully quoted Schoenberg: 'He who writes music to please others and thinks of the hearer is no true artist.'[37] Hindemith had left Berlin in 1937 after the debate about his music, 'Der Fall Hindemith', went against him. He was granted a teaching post only after the dean of the Yale School of Music had assured the president of the university that he had lately 'softened his style considerably' and could now be 'trusted not to proselyte [sic] among students in favor of modernistic music'.[38] After the war Hindemith was invited to tour the American zone as conductor, lecturer (on American democracy and American music), and general cultural ambassador. His *Requiem*, based on a Civil War poem by Walt Whitman, and linking popular grief following the death of Lincoln to the mourning Hindemith observed after Roosevelt died, received its première in Vienna in 1948. If the composer's outright pro-Americanism was received coolly by some German students and musicians, it infuriated the Russians. Aleksandr Dymshits, head of SMAD's cultural division, launched a personal attack in September 1948, claiming that the composer's opposition to fascism was 'not revolutionary' and that the hero of his opera *Mathis der Maler*, the sixteenth-century artist Grünewald, was a progressive fatally flawed by 'pernicious' individualism.[39] By now Dymshits was insisting that there could be only two cultures in the contemporary world: an ideological or cultural 'third road' was inconceivable. In March 1949 *Tägliche Rundschau* and *Neues Deutschland* resumed the attack on Schoenberg and Hindemith, the latter being a *musikalischer Kosmopolit aus übersee* (a foreign musical cosmopolitan) whose spoken German was now embellished by fragments of American; indeed, there was no longer 'any such person as the *German* composer Paul Hindemith'.[40] Citing Hindemith's *Unterweisung im Tonsatz* (1937), later published in America as *The Craft of Musical Composition*, Gorodinskii accused him of 'denying' (*otritsaiushchii*) inspiration and poetry in art and promoting 'factual music' (*delovaia muzyka*).

The prime Soviet target, because a Russian, was Igor Stravinsky, who had left Russia for Paris in 1910, returning briefly in 1914; at the time of the Bolshevik Revolution he was again living in Paris, and although he never went back his works continued to be performed in Russia during the 1920s— *Petrushka* (in Leningrad) as late as 1935. But the fifth of Stravinsky's Charles Eliot Norton lectures at Harvard, 'The Avatars of Russian Music', contained biting criticisms of 'Bolshevik' music. Resident in the United States since 1939, and a naturalized American citizen since 1945, he now lived in Hollywood. Soviet vilification intensified in 1948; following Shostakovich's notorious attack on Stravinsky, delivered under duress at the Waldorf-Astoria Conference in New York against his own tastes and judgement, critics like Gorodinskii and Nestiev sustained a barrage of abuse and derision.[41]

The Stravinsky quotation most favoured by the Soviet avatars was: 'Music explains nothing and underlines nothing—and when it strives to do that, it absolutely inevitably becomes disagreeable and even harmful.'[42] Gorodinskii ridiculed what he called the most famous attempt in our time (1927) to create an opera-oratorio in a dead language (Latin), written in dead words by a morbid poet (*mertvetskim poetom*), Jean Cocteau: this was Gorodinskii's description of Stravinsky's *Oedipus Rex*, adapted from Sophocles, which 'scarcely lived through a few public performances and what's more did not live through them'. 'It was born a mummy [and] conveyed nothing except deadly boredom and yawning.'[43] Gorodinskii savaged what he called Stravinsky's 'unctuous, Christ-like mysticism', as well as the 'frivolous' *Circus Polka* (*Tsirkovaia pol'ka*) composed in the course of the war and dedicated to a young elephant of the New York circus. All this 'modernistic idiocy' attempted to mask terror at the unavoidable destruction of capitalism.

Benjamin Britten and Gian-Carlo Menotti are included in Gorodinskii's blacklist of 'ultra-modern' opera composers, along with the expressionist operas of Alban Berg, Ernst Krenek, and Paul Hindemith. Richard Strauss was the spiritual father of them all. As for Britten, how triumphantly English critics had announced in 1945 that the long period of operatic unfruitfulness in England, a drought lasting since Purcell in fact, had come to an end in the shape of a work, *Peter Grimes*, which would have a significance for British music equal to Glinka's *Ivan Susunin* for Russian:

Critical opinions of *Peter Grimes* have already appeared in our [Soviet] press, noting the complete arbitrariness of the high evaluation of this Benjamin Britten work. In reality, only the enduring 'lack of quality' (*bezryb'e*) of English music could attribute a significance equal to *Ivan Susunin* to such a work as *Peter Grimes*. One would have to assume that in Britten's opera great historical events were unfolding, a genuine national hero, seething with great suffering. But in point of fact the subject of the opera turns out to be extraordinarily petty, philistine 'events' going on in the small-time milieu of a small seaside fishing village. The hero of the opera, Peter Grimes, is a wretched neurasthenic (an almost obligatory figure for such decadent operas), sick and unsociable, and caring for no one . . . In this opera everything is petty (*melko*)—the people, the fears, the thoughts, the words, the music.[44]

Gorodinskii may have picked up the reference to Purcell from the Sadler's Wells handbook accompanying the opera, in which Britten himself explained: 'One of my chief aims is to try and restore to the musical setting of the English language a brilliance, freedom and vitality that have been curiously rare since the death of Purcell.'[45] Gorodinskii (a keen student of London music critics) may also have discovered Desmond Shawe-Taylor's view that '*Grimes* should acquire for us something of the significance which *A Life for the Czar* has for the Russians or *The Bartered Bride* for the Czechs: it should lay at last the foundation-stone of a national school of opera.' From the London newspapers came a chorus of affirmation, doubtless keenly observed in the Soviet Embassy. In *Time and Tide* (14 June 1945) Philip Hope-Wallace called the première 'the most important operatic event since Hindemith's *Mathis der Maler* at Zurich' (we have already encountered Soviet critical disparagement of *Mathis*).[46] Yet Gorodinskii's strictures touched upon a profound ambiguity in British responses to the opera. Members of the Sadler's Wells Opera Company had bitterly complained about the production on several grounds, two of which would have won Gorodinskii's wholehearted approval: first, the composer, the leading tenor (Peter Pears), and the producer (Tyrone Guthrie) were all conscientious objectors; and secondly, it was held to be a waste of time and money to stage 'a piece of cacophany' days after the war ended in Europe. Joan Cross, who sang Ellen Orford at Sadler's Wells, recalled how many members of the company found Britten's plot unattractive, his music 'very difficult and, indeed, unrecognizable in any way at all as operatic music as they understood it'.[47] Geoffrey Sharp, editor of *Music Review*, had damned *Peter Grimes* as 'opera virtually without melody', 'poverty-stricken' and 'devilish smart'—reminding us that journals like *Music Review* and *Sovetskaia muzyka* shared tastes in common.[48]

Soviet disparagement intensified after *Peter Grimes* triumphed in the West. Within three years Britten's opera had received nineteen stage productions worldwide, including at Covent Garden, La Scala, the Metropolitan, New York,[49] and Paris. On 22 March 1947 *Peter Grimes* received its first German performance at Hamburg, moving in May to the State Opera House, Berlin, as the lead item for a series of concerts of British chamber and symphonic music.[50] This was precisely the moment when the Russians had set off theatrical fireworks by presenting Simonov's *The Russian Question* at the Deutsches Theater (see Chapter 4). Privately the Russians took note of Britten's debt to the most unacceptable works by Shostakovich. When the suite from Shostakovich's *The Nose* was broadcast in January 1934 it had left Britten doubtful, but in March 1936 he attended a concert performance of *Lady Macbeth of Mtsensk* which he vowed to defend against charges of 'lack of style', adding: 'The eminent "English renaissance" composers sniggering in the stalls was typical'—no doubt a reference to the Vaughan Williams generation[51] and another reminder that no clear water divided Stalinists from mainstream Western taste.

⊞ ⊞ ⊞

The American composer Aaron Copland[52] had taken part in the Waldorf-Astoria Peace Conference and was thereafter marked down by the FBI and Congressional inquisitors. His reputation as a fellow-traveller was not exaggerated; when, for example, Shostakovich and Prokofiev were condemned by the February 1948 decree, Copland put the boot in: 'They were rebuked for failing to realize that their musical audience had expanded enormously in the last several years ... and that composers can no longer continue to write for only a few initiates.' During the Waldorf-Astoria Conference, of which he was a sponsor, Copland gave a talk to a fine arts panel on 'The Effect of the Cold War on the Artist in the US', attributing main blame to the United States, although he regretted that the Soviet Union was officially adopting 'a disapproving attitude toward much contemporary art, and especially in the field of music'. (This aspect of his address was omitted in the *Daily Worker* report.) In the autumn of 1949 he attended a National Council for American–Soviet Friendship dinner in honour of foreign minister Andrei Vyshinsky, prosecutor in the 1937 show trials. All of this earned him many laudatory mentions as a 'progressive' in Gorodinskii's *Music of Spiritual Poverty*—Copland was praised for recognizing the strength of the Russian 'classical realist' tradition since the time of Glinka.

By June 1950 Copland was having second thoughts and severing ties. In his Norton lectures (1951–2) he criticized the loss of freedom suffered by Soviet artists. In his Piano Quartet, first performed at the Library of Congress in October 1950, he created a stir by adopting Schoenberg's twelve-tone method of composition, even though he had previously expressed doubts about serial[53] techniques. In 1952 he wrote: 'The twelve-tone composer ... is no longer writing music to satisfy himself; whether he likes it or not, he is writing against a vocal and militant opposition.' Much as he had absorbed neoclassical, jazz, and folkloric resources, so Copland now came to terms with dodecophany.[54]

His reputation as a Red was not one which the witch-hunters were quick to abandon; this was the general pattern regarding artists and intellectuals who failed to hurry to Washington to name names. Copland was among the 151 artists included in *Red Channels: The Reports of Communist Influence in Radio and Television*. On 3 January 1953 Illinois Representative Fred Busbey protested on the floor of the House against a planned performance of Copland's *Lincoln Portrait* at the Eisenhower inaugural concert, listing the composer's alleged ties with the CPUSA and its fronts. The chairman of the arrangement committee immediately dropped *Lincoln Portrait*, 'because we don't want anything to bring criticism'. Paul Hume commented in the *Washington Post*: 'It was through such machinery as the Congressman advocates that the music of Mendelssohn and a dozen others was silenced in Germany.'[55] In May 1953 Copland was subpoenaed by McCarthy's Permanent Subcommittee on Investigations. It was a private hearing, with chief counsel Roy Cohn in attendance. Copland was a friendly but not a particularly co-operative witness, talking his way round questions and avoiding naming names. 'I have not been a Communist in the past and I am not now a Communist.' Asked repeatedly by Cohn whether Communists should be allowed to teach 'in our schools', Copland avoided a direct answer. Confronted with a host of affiliations, he answered: 'I don't remember', 'I don't know', 'I may have'. Requested by the Committee to furnish the names of Americans who had attended the Waldorf-Astoria Conference, he referred the Committee to the *New York Times* and a *House Report*, adding: 'I do not personally remember having seen anyone in the Conference who is not listed in those published sources.' But it was, not of course, the names that the Committee wanted, it was the act of personal abasement by the witness.[56] Because of an informant's sworn testimony to the FBI in 1952 that Copland had been a Party member, the FBI continued to investigate a possible charge of perjury until dropping the matter for want of evidence in 1955. Invitations to lecture at the University of Colorado and the University of Alabama were cancelled, but in general Copland's career did not suffer.[57]

⌗   ⌗   ⌗

An Arts Festival staged in West Berlin during 1951–2 by the State Department and the Office of the High Commissioner for Germany (HICOG) reflected the high priority now accorded by Washington to cultural cold warfare on the frontier of a divided Europe.[58] *Porgy and Bess* proved popular with Berlin audiences three years before its intrepid all-black cast set out to conquer the Russians. The Boston Symphony Orchestra, conducted by Charles Munch and Pierre Monteux, performed in West Berlin and Frankfurt—likewise the Paganini Quartet. HICOG reported that the Berlin Festival 'did more to elevate American prestige in one month than anything else attempted in Germany in the past seven years'.[59] At a meeting of the American Committee for Cultural Freedom in March 1952, the historian Bertram D. Wolfe castigated Soviet culture, describing how a Soviet composer's opera, *From the Depths of the Heart*, had received a Stalin Prize on 15 March 1951, and how on 13 May the Council of Ministers had revoked the prize. As a result, 'the composer was condemned and forced to confess his error, the director of the theatre was discharged, the head of the All-Union Arts Committee removed'.[60]

In April 1952 the general secretary of the Congress for Cultural Freedom, Nicolas Nabokov, set up a major cultural festival, Masterpieces of the

Twentieth Century[61] (*Oeuvre du vingtième siecle*), in Paris, after enlisting the support of Stravinsky and Charles Munch, artistic director of the Boston Symphony Orchestra (BSO).[62] Charles Douglas Jackson, known as 'C.D.', who had taken leave from *Time-Life* to work on Eisenhower's election campaign, was a trustee of the BSO as well as president of the Free Europe Committee. Together with Julius Fleischmann, president of the dummy Farfield Foundation, Jackson evidently arranged for $130,000 of CIA money to fund the orchestra's tour.[63] The CIA's senior culture officer, Thomas Braden, later revealed that the BSO's visit to Paris in 1952 had of necessity been secretly funded by the CIA, because official funding would have required loyalty clearance for every musician.[64]

Most of the festival events were housed in the Théâtres des Champs-Elysées, where the première of Stravinsky's *Rite of Spring* had taken place in 1913, provoking a raucuous response. Now Stravinsky was present, flanked by the president of France and Madame Vincent Auriol, to hear it conducted again by Pierre Monteux and the BSO. Stravinsky, who had fled Paris in 1939, returned to the Champs-Elysées to conduct his own work, *Oedipus Rex*, warmly received by René Dumesnil of *Le Monde* (21 May).

Nabokov laid on a series of concerts offering work by Prokofiev, Ravel, Copland, Rachmaninov, and Richard Strauss.[65] Benjamin Britten conducted two performances of *Billy Budd*, which *Le Monde* (28 May) found inferior to *Albert Herring* and *Peter Grimes*. 'Musicians are frankly disappointed', reported *The Times* (10 June 1952), which paid tribute to the work of Nabokov and the generosity of the sponsors, headed by Julius Fleischmann. Topping Nabokov's bill were composers proscribed by Hitler or Stalin (Berg, Schoenberg, and Hindemith), his intention being to parade anything condemned in *Sovetskaia muzyka*—for example, Georges Auric and Darius Milhaud, described as 'servile teasers of the snobbish bourgeois tastes of a capitalist city'. More than 100 symphonies, concertos, operas, and ballets were performed in thirty days.[66] The State Department paid for yet another of Gorodinskii's 'decadents', Virgil Thomson's *Four Saints in Three Acts*, first performed on Broadway in 1934, and now starring the black soprano Leontyne Price. 'Not a measure of music composed before 1900 was heard,' Denis de Rougement reported proudly, 'and every night the auditoriums were full.' Ticket sales were good, critical responses mixed up[67] with political uproar over the arrival of General Matthew B. Ridgway, accused of using bacteriological weapons in Korea, as C.-in-C., NATO; the arrest of a senior Communist, Jacques Duclos; and mass demonstrations.

In December 1952 six Soviet musicians—two singers, a violinist, and two pianists, under the leadership of the composer Dmitri

Kabalevsky—performed in a half-full Usher Hall, Edinburgh, on a cold Monday evening. An interesting commentary, written by 'C. G.' and published in the *Scotsman* (18 December), reflected the freeze on musical exchanges under Stalin. The Russians, said C. G., had been 'chary of introducing their artists into Western Europe', thus making it difficult to assess the state of Soviet composition following the fateful Conference of Musicians at the Central Committee in January 1948. 'To what extent has the party line been followed by Prokofieff, Shostakovich, or Kabalevsky in their music?'[68] C. G. found the standard of performance in the Usher Hall 'amazingly high. In happier times the main soloists would have been swept into the merry-go-round of world-wide engagements.' But the concert also gave a disturbing indication of the sort of modern music favoured in the USSR: 'I wonder for how long the clock can be put back. I can see that the "back to Tchaikovsky" movement represents a reaction against the "formalist" experiments of the '20s and '30s, and also that it is aimed to entertain everyone and all the rest of it, but can it be sustained indefinitely?' C. G. concluded that there were too many 'strings attached' to Russian music.

During the winter of 1953–4 Nicolas Nabokov, string-puller extraordinary, settled into a temporary residency as musical director of the American Academy in Rome, where he organized the International Conference of Twentieth Century Music sponsored by the CCF and Radio-Televisione Italiana in April 1954.[69] In evidence was a heavy concentration on atonal, dodecaphonic composition, with work by Berg, Elliott Carter, and Peter Racine Fricker alongside Hindemith, Webern, and Schoenberg. Hans Werner Henze's twelve-tone opera *Boulevard Solitude* was given its première in Rome—all presented 'to prove that art thrives on freedom'. William Glock assured readers of the CIA-funded *Encounter* that the twelve-tone method was not so much a denial of tonality as an enlargement of it.[70]

But twelve-tone compositions were conspicuous by their absence in September 1956, when the Boston Symphony Orchestra fulfilled its long-held ambition to become the first from the West to perform in Soviet Russia, Charles Munch and Pierre Monteux conducting. After the BSO's reported triumph in Leningrad, the orchestra took its repertoire before an audience of 2,000 in the Great Hall of the Moscow Conservatory, with Shostakovich, Khachaturian, and Emil Gilels in attendance to hear Beethoven's Third Symphony, the 'Eroica'. Harold Schonberg, music critic of the *New York Times*, claimed that 'the Russians heard a quality of playing previously unknown to them. They still shake their heads about it. "It was a blow to our pride," a Russian musician told me. "The difference between Boston and our orchestras was so great it was insulting." '[71] The year 1956 also saw the launch of the Metropolitan Opera in Europe—eight years before the Bolshoi Opera reached the West.[72]

By now Soviet instrumentalists—less contentious than composers—were increasingly on the move: 'Oistrakh Scores Recital Triumph. Carnegie Hall Full as Soviet Violinist Demonstrates Mastery of His Art.' By comparison to composition, performance was relatively free of ideology; there was no 'Soviet way' to play the violin (or conduct an orchestra). Performance reflected well (or not) on the entire educational system but within internationally agreed parameters, hence the Soviet obsession with competition, medals, laurels, international recognition: 'Great attention is devoted to the propaganda of genuine art.'[73] The word *pobeditelei* ('winners' or 'laureates') was frequently used. 'Soviet musicians are always among the winners and laureates. During 40 years they took part in 94 International Competitions, won 102 first prizes, 94 second and 64 third prizes...' What the Russians most wanted to prove was the superiority, and the broad social base, of their educational system. When Yehudi Menuhin first visited Moscow in 1945, junior music boarding schools, for children aged 5 to 16, were unique to the USSR, one in each major city. During his several visits to such schools over the years, Menuhin was never allowed to see the teaching, only the product. Menuhin took note of the Soviet model when he opened his own small school (initially eleven pupils) in London in 1963.[74] 'What I disagreed with in the Moscow school's approach (and found odd in a country which so honours the collective) was the tremendous stress on producing individual performers...Consequently chamber music did not flourish in Russia and the wonderful orchestras of Moscow and Leningrad consisted largely of disillusioned soloists.' One evening after a concert at the Bath Festival given by the Moscow Chamber Orchestra, Menuhin and the section leaders settled down for some informal music, including Schubert's Quintet in C Major: 'Astonishingly these young players who were drilled beyond belief, who played with a perfection that was fantastic, proved untrained to sight-read.'[75]

The pace of exchanges accelerated under the first Soviet–American cultural agreement of 1958. In April of that year the 23-year-old Texan pianist Van Cliburn won the International Tchaikovsky Piano Competition in Moscow. Khrushchev attended the ceremonial concert, which was marked by rave reviews, standing ovations, and shrieking followers. According to *Time*, which likened him to an 'American sputnik', Cliburn generated mass hysteria among women, who cried 'Vanya, Vanya', threw flowers, tugged at his clothes, and stood for hours in front of his hotel. State Department officials became worried in case his young head was turned and he made 'unwise' political statements, but Ambassador Llewelyn Thompson came away from a talk with the charming young pianist able to offer reassurance to the State Department.[76] Even so, the Russians were inclined to claim that they, and they alone, had 'discovered' Cliburn (who had reached Moscow with the aid of a grant from the Martha Baird Rockefeller Foundation). No less illustrious a composer than Shostakovich said as much: 'This outstanding young American artist earned his first wide and entirely deserved recognition among us here in Moscow.' Abram Chasins, who had chaired the 1954 Leventritt International Competition jury which had awarded its first prize to Cliburn, recalled how the award had been recorded 'by a few paragraphs in a few American papers without so much as a picture'... So Shostakovich was close enough to the mark 'to hurt'.[77]

Another prize-winning young pianist, Vladimir Ashkenazy, made the reverse journey. Born in 1937 of Jewish parents, he gained the second prize in the Warsaw Chopin Competition in 1955, finally achieving the summit when he won the Moscow Tchaikovsky Competition in 1962.[78] But under the Soviet system such international networking incurred brutal demands. In 1956–7 he was called to the office of the Personnel Supervisor (*Otdel kadrov*) of the Moscow Conservatoire and made to sign up as an informer for the KGB on foreign music students, taking the code name Dmitri. When he returned from his first American tour in 1958, his Ministry of Culture–KGB travelling companion, with whom he had shared second-class hotel rooms, accused him of buying and reading a Russian-language edition of Pasternak's *Doctor Zhivago*, purchased in New York—though according to Ashkenazy his minder also read it. Banned from further foreign tours, he was later discarded as a KGB informer after refusing to take part in compromising a homosexual French musician and even warning the foreigner of the danger.[79] Ashkenazy's troubles and discontents were compounded by his engagement to an Icelandic pianist brought up in London. When they married she became a Soviet citizen under pressure—after which it took five months to obtain an exit visa to visit her parents in London. (Central Committee files confirm that keeping the wife and family at home in the USSR while the artist travelled abroad was an established practice—although economic factors may have been almost as important.)[80] Reaching London, the couple obtained Home Office permission to prolong the visit: 'Russian Pianist Given Asylum', announced *The Times* (17 April 1963), but the following day Ashkenazy held a press conference to deny it: 'There is nothing political in it whatever. I know nothing about politics... I retain my Soviet passport and am perfectly free to return to Russia whenever I want.'[81] Khrushchev claimed that he told his colleagues: 'He's not an anti-Soviet, but we could turn him into one if we put him into the position of having to choose between staying with his wife and obeying his government.'[82] The couple settled in London without making a formal break, and the Soviet bureaucracy seemed keen to trade on an image of liberality.[83] Ashkenazy had meanwhile engaged an English manager, Jasper Parrott, the son of a former British ambassador to Moscow and Prague and—on the evidence of his biography of the pianist—sharply anti-Communist. Soviet man, for example, is said to be 'confronted by a labyrinth of lies', and so on. Elsewhere and more recently Ashkenazy has spoken of 'this totalitarian state, this huge Potemkin village'.[84]

⌗ ⌗ ⌗

Western critics continued to portray Soviet composers as suffering from crippling inhibitions as a result of the refusal of Stalin's heirs to disown in full the Zhdanov decrees of 1948 (although the trade in insults was far from one-way: writing in *Sovetskaia muzyka* (April 1954), Aram Khachaturian quoted Arthur Honneger on the sad plight of the composer in the West—like an uninvited guest who insists on sitting at a table where he is not wanted).[85] Stories in *Le Monde*, *The Times*, and the American press frequently carried headlines such as 'Soviet Composers Scored by *Pravda*' or '*Pravda* Chides Soviet Composers'. New York's leading cold war publisher, Frederick A. Praeger, published Andrey Olkhovsky's[86] *Music Under the Soviets* in its Research Program on the USSR series: 'Russian culture, particularly music, is undergoing the agony of a dark night in its history . . . the personal and creative lives of Soviet composers, even the greatest of them, depend completely and unreservedly on the overt and covert intrigues of the politburo and its apparatus of coercion.'[87]

The Glasgow-based academic journal *Soviet Studies* continued to diverge from the Western cold war consensus and to promote 'internalism' (jargon for academic fellow-travelling). According to Thomas Russell, a participant in the All-Union Peace Conference held in Moscow in 1949, Westerners should understand that in Russia 'Self-expression is only valid when the self is identified with the aims and desires of the people as a whole'—exactly the opposite view of his more famous namesake, Bertrand Russell. According to Thomas Russell, too many Soviet writers, artists, and musicians suffered from elitism, artistic inbreeding, and separation from the people.[88]

At the opposite end of the ideological spectrum stood *Soviet Survey*, edited by Walter Laqueur and Leopold Labedz, which welcomed an unsigned editorial in *Sovetskaia muzyka* (January 1956) criticizing 'recent' Soviet musicologists for insisting on a clear and total opposition between Russian and Western classical music. This had amounted in practice to a coarse condemnation of Italian nineteenth-century opera, and unfounded (*ogul'nyi*) negative treatment of Wagner, Brahms, and Meyerbeer. Only recently had articles appeared in the Soviet press showing the way towards a more correct understanding of Wagner, Brahms, Debussy, Saint-Saëns, Berlioz, Ravel, and other Western composers. But this version of the thaw was short-lived; conservatives rallied in every cultural sphere: at the Second All-Union Congress of Soviet Composers in March–April 1957, the Central Committee's message of greetings, conveyed by Shepilov, referred to the 'deep-going weakness of bourgeois-modernistic art' and 'its divorce (*otryv*) from the people, extreme individualism, departure from the classical heritage and the traditions of national music'. Tikhon Khrennikov, secretary of the Composers Union, dismissed the editor of *Sovetskaia muzyka* for 'revisionism'. Shostakovich later commented in disgust: 'Revisionism was the new insult, to replace formalism.'[89] *Encounter's* regular cold war column, 'From the Other Shore', edited by Leopold Labedz, reported in February 1958 that the liberal editorial board of *Sovetskaia muzyka* had been dropped for 'having defined the years 1948–1955 as a single chain of musical failures and mistakes'. Two months later the same column reported how the new, conservative editorial board of *Sovetskaia muzyka* had castigated its predecessor for having been corrupted by formalism and for praising Stravinsky, who 'carried out with equal readiness the orders of the Vatican and of the American "jazzmen" or circus companies'. The February 1958 issue of the Soviet journal published I. Nestiev's polemic 'The Sacred Cacophany', which blasted Stravinsky for using his seventy-fifth anniversary to issue numerous declarations and 'cheap philosophizing', such as his attack on Soviet music in *Encounter*.[90]

In 1958 the Party published its first post-Stalinist programmatic document on music, confirming that limits must be set on innovation. The Central Committee acknowledged that Zhdanov's criticisms of particular composers in 1948 had been unduly harsh, but insisted that the condemnation of Muradeli's opera *The Great Friendship* had been fundamentally correct. The 1958 decree upheld the importance of melody and renewed the condemnation of formalism, 'the cult of atonality, dissonance, and disharmony', and the 'neo-pathological combinations that transform music into cacophany, into a chaotic conglomeration of sounds'. An American visitor, the critic Faubion Bowers, believed that young Russians were bored by a non-stop diet of classical music: 'In the evenings and on holidays loudspeakers in parks and on the downtown streets blare out the classics—complete symphonies, full operas—in unmitigated continuation. Soviet Russia feeds off its musical past and reiterates its masterpieces the year round in a way we normally confine to the use of *The Messiah* at Christmastime.'[91]

The charismatic conductor and composer Leonard Bernstein managed to anger the Soviet musical establishment after he arrived in August 1959 with the New York Philarmonic. Huge applause greeted his rendering of Shostakovich's Fifth Symphony in the concert hall of the Tchaikovsky Conservatory—dozens of bows, bouquets. More of a departure was a performance of Stravinsky's Piano Concerto (played by Seymour Lipkin) and *The Rite of Spring*, composed in 1913 but hitherto proscribed in the USSR, but the Moscow audience greeted this performance, too, with acclaim.[92] What infuriated the Soviet elite was the fact that Bernstein felt it necessary to remark in public that the *The Rite* had not been performed in Russia in over thirty years. (In fact it had been performed in Tallinn the previous year.) Bernstein compounded the sin on another occasion by speaking from the conductor's podium about Charles Ives's 'Unanswered Question', a piece four minutes long. So enthusiastic was the reception that he played the piece again. Words like 'immodest' and 'conceited' were beginning to appear in the press. In *Sovetskaia kul'tura*, organ of the Ministry of Culture, Aleksandr Medvedev complained that Bernstein had violated tradition by presuming to instruct a Russian audience from the podium.[93] The American conductor officially protested this article as an 'unforgivable lie', freely expressing his anger to correspondents during a party given at Spaso House, the residence of the American ambassador. Speaking on colour television at the American National Exhibition, Bernstein said he regretted not having talked about other pieces, especially Aaron Copland's 'Billy the Kid' Suite, which had fallen flat at the previous night's concert.

But the deeper cause of Soviet anger resided in an unspoken subtext, namely the Bernsteins' provocative seeking-out of the disgraced poet and novelist Boris Pasternark, dining at his dacha at Peredilenko (a rather ugly, two-storey house built in the late 1930s), and inviting him to a Bernstein concert. This was Pasternak's first public appearance, resulting in prominent photographs in the American press, since he had won the Nobel Prize ten months earlier and been expelled from the Writers' Union. Bernstein had also gone on record that his meeting with Pasternak was 'the high point of the entire trip'; his extended remarks about the difficulty of making contact with the author of *Doctor Zhivago* were surely calculated to infuriate the Russians.[94]

Normal warfare was now resumed. In November 1959 five Soviet composers, including Tikhon Khrennikov and Dmitri Shostakovich, visited

America under the exchange agreement— and promptly renewed attacks on Leonard Bernstein. The music of three of the composers was performed at Philadelphia's Academy of Music, including a new cello concerto by Shostakovich played by Mstislav Rostropovich, with Eugene Ormandy conducting. 'This was a special occasion,' reported Howard Taubman in the *New York Times* (7 November), 'and the electricity took hold of the audience.' On 18 November the visiting Soviet composers attended a luncheon at the New York Harvard Club, hosted by the Music Critics Circle, and were confronted by provocative questions about changes in cultural life since Stalin. Khrennikov came up with the standard line: Soviet composers and critics often disagreed about every issue except one: 'Art cannot be separated from life, and art must serve the people.' As leader of the delegation, Khrennikov controlled every move, cancelling a scheduled radio appearance on Columbia's *Face the Nation* by Shostakovich and Kabalevsky after the network refused his demand that the entire delegation appear. The *New York Times* (5 November) commented that 'Khrennikov has been known to have prevented Soviet composers from talking freely with American music critics visiting the Soviet Union'.[95]

The next clash of cymbals occurred when the Russians were taken to Columbia University's electronic music studio to hear experimental tape-recordings and an electronic music synthesizer. The Soviet composers took issue with the practice of teaching twelve-tone music; the compositions they had heard in America were 'largely scholastic and without artistic merit'. Such music was destructive of melody and harmony, and 'spiritless'. Renewing the attack on Leonard Bernstein, Shostakovich accused him of unloosing 'a flood of fables and nonsense' about Soviet music, and dismissed Bernstein's claim that Soviet composers were officially restricted, forced to avoid experiments, and 'repeating the old melodies of Czarist times'. It was not, however, clear to Tom Lambert, reporting from Moscow in the *Herald Tribune*, where or when Bernstein had made these comments. 'Mr Bernstein is quoted here as having said...'[96] Boris Schwarz, who knew the Soviet musical scene as well as any, judged the Soviet composers' visit to the United States a 'near failure' from the musical point of view. 'No amount of hospitality, oratory, and good-will could disguise the fact that the music presented by the visitors was of little interest to American audiences, with the exception of Shostakovich.' Soviet music, concluded Schwarz, seemed to be caught in a cul-de-sac.[97] Isaiah Berlin's overall verdict on Soviet composers was less detailed than Schwarz's, and blunter: 'Even such moderately competent composers as Shebalin and Kabalevsky have taken this line of least resistance...monotonous and tirelessly productive purveyors of routine music of remorseless mediocrity.'[98]

On 30 November Minister of Culture Furtseva received a Central Committee internal report about the visit, signed by B. Yarustovsky, who listed the main 'negative tendencies' which had surfaced during the tour: the interpreter was a certain émigré called Volkonsky, 'obviously fulfilling other functions as well'. The visitors were not allowed to meet anyone outside the programme. All efforts to meet ordinary people were thwarted. When it visited a tobacco factory near Louisville, the delegation found itself cut off from the workers. Attempts were made to manipulate and create tensions within the Soviet delegation. The press presented Shostakovich and Kabalevsky as crushed in 1948 by the regime. A broadcast did not take place because Khrennikov, backed by the entire delegation, refused to allow Shostakovich and Kabalevsky to appear without the others. Attempts were made to depict the artistic life of the USSR as monotonous and uniform, in contrast to American artistic life. When received in private houses, black servants were invited in after lunch so that the host could ostentatiously thank them for cooking a delicious meal. When the delegation visited Howard University (a black college), one 'student' of advanced years kept talking about high-school scholarships for black students. At press conferences the delegation was asked why American music was not played in the USSR. The composer Dankewich was spontaneously invited to conduct, but did not have a starched shirt to go with his tails. Because none of his size could be bought, a tailor was called to measure him up; this was shown on television as if to indicate that Russians lacked shirts.[99]

From the late 1950s the tone and political direction of the Union of Soviet Composers was constantly affected by the need to clarify its reaction to avant-garde, dodecaphonic, and foreign tendencies in general. On the one hand the Composers' Union organized a series of closed performances by foreigners accessible' only to professionals. (The Union also printed a quarterly digest of foreign musical opinions in Russian translation.) During a concert tour of the USSR in 1957, the pianist Glenn Gould was offered an informal master class in the Small Hall of the Moscow Conservatoire, and took advantage of the invitation to discuss the twelve-note techniques of Schoenberg, as well as playing music by Berg, Webern, and Krenek. But the audience was confined to the elite; typically, the recording made at the time was not issued by Melodiia until 1984. Whatever the private concessions to the professionals, typical of Soviet internal cultural strategy, paranoia continued to prevail in the public arena, as reflected in Khrennikov's keynote speeches castigating the errors of the USSR's own 'modernistic' composers, most of them born in the era of the Five Year Plans: Arvo Pärt (b. 1935), Alfred Schnittke (b. 1934), and Edison Denisov (b. 1929), and those composers who 'hobnobbed with foreigners' in order to get their music performed outside the USSR.[100]

The Warsaw Autumn Festival, held every year since 1956, became a citadel of modern music and a permanent challenge to Soviet cultural hegemony. The festival played host to Soviet composers who could not easily get a hearing at home, like Andrei Volkonsky and Galina Ustvolskaya, and— almost as if to challenge Shostakovich—performed one of his early works still suppressed in Russia, the orchestral suite from the opera *The Nose*.[101] (Interviewed in the autumn of 1959, Shostakovich declared himself 'very much worried that certain Polish composers, particularly the younger ones, cling to the "revelation" of dodecophany... The Western avant-garde music played at the Warsaw Festival is contrary to human nature and to the lofty human art of music.')[102] But Warsaw was not Moscow, and not until October 1974 was Schnittke's First Symphony given its belated first performance in Gorky, a city closed to foreigners, after permission to perform it in Moscow had been refused by the Union on account of its outrageous modernism. (At the start the orchestra wanders on to the stage improvising until the conductor appears and imposes order.)

Major instrumentalists like Sviatoslav Richter became increasingly free of ideological confinements during tours abroad. Fascinated by the work of Boulez, Stockhausen, and Hindemith, Richter recalled: 'As for contemporary non-Russian music, I've essentially tackled Britten, Hindemith, Stravinsky, Berg (notably his opera *Wozzeck*, seen at Salzburg, twice), and Webern.' Richter himself had only with difficulty surmounted cold war barriers and the curse of a tragic family background. Richter's father, a musician, though born in the Ukraine, was German by family origins and upbringing: 'As far as my father is concerned, no one has ever dared to describe events exactly as they happened. People said nothing about his execution—he was shot by the Soviets in 1941, before the Germans arrived in Odessa. I didn't discover the truth until twenty years later... I myself was living in Moscow, cut off from all communication with my parents.'[103] Prior to Richter's American concert tour in 1960, Khrushchev recalled how 'the people around me started shaking their heads and saying it would be risky to send Comrade Richter abroad because of his German background. He had a mother living in West Germany...' Richter's willingness to play at Boris Pasternak's funeral in 1960 may have exacerbated suspicion, though Khrushchev does not say so. In the event the impresario Sol Hurok reached a deal with Khrushchev; Richter's

American début, at the age of 45, comprised eight recitals and orchestral concerts at Carnegie Hall.[104]

⊞ ⊞ ⊞

Most remarkable was the invitation to Igor Stravinsky to visit the USSR in 1962—and his acceptance. The thaw had brought no backing down in the attacks on the Russian composer; in a polemic entitled 'Cviashchenniia Kakophoniia' (Sacred Cacophany, 1958),[105] I. Nestiev began by taking note of Stravinsky's outspoken '35 Questions and 35 Answers' published in *Encounter*, and an interview in UNESCO's journal, *La Musique dans le monde*. Nestiev jibed that the role of self-consciously wise (*mudrstvuiushchii*) maestro occupying international platforms appealed to Stravinsky—hence his 'enigmatic and pretentious aphorisms'. For example:[106]

—Musical form is closer to mathematics than to literature.
—The foundations of disharmonic music is what attracts in the main the contemporary generation in an epoch when harmonic discoveries are exhausted.
—The tonal foundation of music is optional (*neobiazael'na*); it's possible without tonality to cultivate in oneself the sense of returning to the same place.[107]

(Nestiev inserts here a question-mark signalling his own incomprehension.) He mocked the supposed 'universality' of Stravinsky's creative powers: 'He can produce any music in any style for any aims. Catholic masses, circus polkas, up-to-date jazz, ballet on the most eccentric themes . . . How ravaged, how emasculated must have been the soul of the composer capable of creating such dreadful music.'[108]
Stravinsky duly hit back:

My music is unobtainable, all of it and in any form, disc or printed score, east of NATO; not only my music but Webern's, Schoenberg's, Berg's, as well.[109] Russia's musical isolation—she will call it our isolation—is at least thirty years old. We hear much about Russian virtuoso violinists, pianists, orchestras. The point is, of what are they virtuosi? Instruments are nothing in themselves; the literature they play creates them . . . The Soviet virtuoso has no literature beyond the nineteenth century. I am often asked if I would consent to conduct in the Soviet Union. For purely musical reasons I could not. Their orchestras do not perform the music of the three Viennese and myself, and they would be, I am sure, unable to cope with the simplest problems of rhythmic execution that we introduced to music fifty years ago . . . I discovered something of the same situation in Germany at the end of the war. After so many years of Hitler in which my *L'Histoire du soldat*, Schoenberg's *Pierrot lunaire*, Berg's and Webern's music was banned, the musicians were for a long time unable to play the new music.[110]

Following Bernstein's Moscow performances of the *Rite of Spring* and the Piano Concerto, the Royal Ballet first visited Russia in June 1961, bringing Stravinsky's *The Firebird*.[111] Simultaneously a delegation of Soviet musicians, headed by Khrennikov, invited Stravinsky to visit the USSR on the occasion of his eightieth birthday. Shortly before his departure he told *Newsweek* (21 May 1962): 'No artist's name has been more abused in the Soviet Union than mine, but one cannot achieve the future we must achieve with the Russians by nursing a grudge.'[112]

The programme of concerts included three early ballets, *The Rite of Spring* (1913), *The Firebird* (1910), and *Petrushka* (1911).[113] This music was more accessible than his recent serialism and the music for *Agon* (1957), written for Balanchine's New York City Ballet, where the old harmony based on the major and minor scales was being stretched by the new counterpoint of twelve-note patterns, with harmonic resolutions often jammed and frustrated.[114] After an absence of forty-eight years Stravinsky arrived to conduct two orchestras in Moscow and one in Leningrad. His concert programmes did not offer any of his later, serial, compositions. At Sheremetyevo airport the elderly composer, wearing dark glasses and leaning heavily on his cane, surveyed the smiling Russians about him and said (in Russian): 'I left Tsarist Russia and have returned to the Soviet Union, which I greet. It is a great joy for me to be in my native Russian land.' A motorcade swept him to his hotel where (gushed *Soviet News*), 'he partook with relish of caviar and vodka'.

Khrushchev and Minister of Culture Ekaterina Furtseva were in the audience when Stravinsky attended performances of *Orpheus*, *Petrushka*, and *The Firebird* in the Kremlin Palace of Congresses, where the 6,000 spectators rose and enthusiastically applauded him on cue. After meeting Khrushchev the composer commented, no doubt tongue in cheek: 'I knew he was a very wise man, but he is also most charming.'[115] Stravinsky's musical comments were more candid: 'I liked the staging and the dancing. I was less impressed by the orchestra which at times lacked accuracy. Besides, the tempo was sometimes arbitrary.' But he paid tribute to the Moscow State Symphony Orchestra, with whom he had been rehearsing his own first concert.

The Kennedy White House was alerted to the competition. Nicolas Nabokov recalled:

Then in 1962, when he reached his eightieth year, it was I again who took the initiative, through my friend Arthur Schlesinger, Jr., of proposing that the President and Mrs Kennedy give an anniversary dinner for Stravinsky. And in 1964, when he was already ill and deprived of the free use of one foot, I arranged a triumphal concert for him at the Festival of Berlin in the presence of Mayor Willy Brandt and in the beautiful new Philarmonic Hall. I followed Stravinsky everywhere, except, alas, to the Soviet Union [in 1962].[116]

After Stravinsky, Benjamin Britten. The spring of 1963 brought a festival of British music to the USSR. Britten—now promoted from the sneers of Gorodinskii to the acceptable face of modernism—was the centre of attraction, and the programmes were built around his works: *Sea Interludes* from *Peter Grimes*, the *Sinfonia de Requiem*, songs interpreted by Pears, and the new Cello Sonata played by Rostropovich.[117] On cue Nestiev described Britten as 'a major contemporary musician, an honourable and serious artist',[118] who spoke of his huge admiration for Soviet music and warned Soviet readers: 'Don't judge the English outlook by what sometimes is printed in our papers.' Britten apparently set himself into congenial positions against dodecophany, against the ivory tower and art for art's sake. Interviewed by *Pravda* during his visit, he was quoted as saying that 'the artist's social duty' was 'to form, educate, and develop [the] people's artistic tastes'. Martin Cooper of the *Daily Telegraph* inserted the square brackets round '[the]' and wondered whether Britten had said 'the people' or 'people'; the way it was printed, readers of *Pravda* would assume 'that he [Britten] was in fact subscribing to the full Communist doctrine of art as an instrument of ideological propaganda'. Britten himself, it turned out, was not happy. 'I was sickened by Pravda getting me all wrong', he wrote to William Plomer, adding, 'deliberately wrong'.[119]

In October 1964 the English Opera Group, led by the singers Peter Pears and Janet Baker, performed three Britten operas in Leningrad. A review by Leonid Entelis, critic and composer, in *Leningradskaia pravda* displayed a sophisticated grasp of the English settings and social context of *Peter Grimes*, *Albert Herring*, and *The Turn of the Screw*. Entelis's review of *Peter Grimes* was in spectacular contrast to Gorodinskii's demolition in 1950.[120] 'Britten shows deep-felt sympathy for a disillusioned man who no longer believes that there is good on the earth . . .' he wrote. But the ghost theme of *The Turn of the Screw* irritated him: 'the subject is strange and archaic in the extreme . . . It is a pity that Britten gave his talent to the embodying of such a trifling subject.'[121]

Britten did not mention in public his own recent difficulties with the Soviet government—he always held that difficulties were better treated in private. In 1961 he had given a garden party at his Red House, in Aldeburgh, dressed in one of his checked suits that he had worn (he told Galina Vishnevskaya) for twenty years. He was then working on his *War Requiem* and wanted to write a part for her, in Latin, to sing alongside Peter Pears and Dietrich Fischer-Dieskau. The première was scheduled for 30 May 1962, in the new Coventry Cathedral. Britten wrote to Vladimir Stepanov, head of the foreign department of the Ministry of Culture, requesting Vishnevskaya's participation on strictly artistic grounds—no mention of wanting a Russian to sing alongside an Englishman and a German as a gesture of historic reconciliation. Summoned by Ekaterina Furtseva, the soprano was told that she could not take part because of the West German contribution to the rebuilding of the cathedral.[122] Not until a January 1963 performance in the Albert Hall was she able to sing in the *Requiem* (with Pears and Fischer-Dieskau). The first Soviet performance followed in May 1966, by 350 members of the Leningrad Conservatory, with Britten in attendance. During this visit he also conducted the première of his Cello Concerto, dedicated to the soloist, Mstislav Rostropovich, in Moscow and Leningrad.

Vishnevskaya visited Aldeburgh annually; in 1965 she and Rostropovich invited Bitten and Pears to holiday with them in Armenia under the patronage of the Composers' Union, despite knowing little of each other's languages.[123] Pears noted in his diary: 'Slava and Galya with tremendously expensive gadgets, chandeliers from Venice, four or five American fridges, which don't work, cupboards full of hair-dryers and electric toasters.' At New Year 1966–7, Britten and Pears stayed in the Rostropoviches' Moscow flat and enjoyed an all-night feast, rotating between their apartment and those of Shostakovich and his neighbour, an eminent nuclear physicist.[124] But the feasting had to stop for Britten, Rostropovich, and Vishnevskaya when Soviet forces invaded Czechoslovakia on 22 August 1968. By coincidence a Festival of Soviet Art was taking place in London that month; by an even sharper coincidence, Rostropovich and the USSR State Symphony Orchestra were scheduled to perform the work of a Czech composer, Dvořák's Cello Concerto, at the opening concert in the Albert Hall. An angry demonstration against the military invasion was churning in the street outside. As Vishnevskaya recalled:

In the hall, six thousand people greeted the appearance of the Soviet symphony musicians with prolonged shouting, stamping of feet, whistling. They would not allow the concert to begin...Slava was pale, and stood as if on an executioner's block...I closed my eyes and...shrank into a far corner of the loge. Finally the audience quieted down. Dvořák's music poured forth like a requiem for the Czech people...

A British critic witnessed the event, broadcast on the BBC's '24 Hours' series. 'To see and hear Rostropovich's impassioned rendering of Dvorjak's Cello Concerto while foreign tanks crept through the streets of Prague...seemed to strike at the very heart of tragedy'...[125] Britten and Pears were reported to be 'stunned and bewildered' by the invasion, although inclined to equate it with the American 'occupation' of Bentwaters', the USAF airbase near Aldeburgh, whose planes regularly roared over the composer's Red House. Contacted by the Czech conductor Rafael Kubelik, Britten was asked to sign a telegram of protest, but apparently decided against it in order to keep cultural and intellectual contacts open. He told the *Guardian:* '...I prefer to do it privately, which I did do. I can't say exactly how I did, but I did.' Britten was back in Russia for the Days of British Music held in Moscow in April 1971.[126]

It was at this time that Mstislav Rostropovich, cellist and conductor, jeopardized his privileged status and supply of foreign fridges by offering firm friendship to the Soviet writer who posed the most acute threat to the entire Soviet cultural system. At the time of Aleksandr Solzhenitsyn's expulsion from the Union of Writers in November 1969, Rostropovich had incurred official anger by putting his country dacha in the village of Zhukovka, 17 miles west of Moscow, at the disgraced dissident's disposal.[127] In an open letter, dated 30 October 1970, to the editors-in-chief of *Pravda*, *Izvestiia*, *Literaturnaia gazeta*, and *Sovetskaia kul'tura*—which none of them published, but which became well known in the West, Rostropovich drew attention to the paradox of Soviet yearning for international cultural recognition. The award of the Nobel Prize to Pasternak and Solzhenitsyn had been denigrated as a 'dirty political game', but when Sholokhov received the award, that was taken to be 'a proper recognition of the leading global importance of our literature'. He broadened the attack:

I remember, and I would like to remind you of, our newspapers of 1948. How much claptrap they published about S. S. Prokofiev and D. D. Shostakovich. Now recognized as giants of our music!...Can it really be that the times we have lived through have not taught us to take a more cautious attitude toward crushing talented people?...I remember with pride that I did not come to the meeting of arts people at the Central House of Workers in the Arts, where B. Pasternak was smeared and I was supposed to speak...Why, for example, was G. Vishnevskaya not allowed to perform, at her concert in Moscow, Boris Chaikovsky's brilliant song cycle based on a text by Joseph Brodsky?...[128] Plainly OPINION has prevented my compatriots from seeing Tarkovsky's film *Andrei Rublev*...which I was lucky enough to see along with the enraptured Parisians. Obviously it was OPINION that stopped the publication of Solzhenitsyn's *Cancer Ward*, which had already been set in type by *Novy mir*.[129]

At 43, the cellist had everything to lose. The Ministry of Culture cancelled concert tours of Finland and France—involving not only a loss of foreign currency for the state but the payment of cancellation compensation. When the biologist Zhores Medvedev—a long-standing friend of Solzhenitsyn— visited Rostropovich after a concert at Obninsk, the cellist told him: 'I can divide my musical activity into two periods now, *before* my letter in defence of Solzhenitsyn and after.'[130]

The biennial Congress of the International Music Council was held in Moscow in October 1971. In the course of his presidential address Yehudi Menuhin committed the sin of naming Solzhenitsyn, along with Shostakovich and Yevtushenko, as exemplars of Russian profoundity. Not a word of the speech appeared in the Soviet media, but in the days following he experienced 'lightning encounters with anonymous Muscovites who knew all about it. In the street, in theatre cloakrooms after concerts, I would feel a hand touch me, or a gift slipped into my pocket, and hear a whispered congratulation.' He also attempted an appeal on behalf of two Soviet citizens, one imprisoned for his politics, the other a defector who wanted his family to join him. At Gosconcert he was received by the number three in the Ministry of Culture, Supagin, who told him: 'We cannot afford to let people do what they want, because we have great plans.' Supagin then asked why Menuhin had mentioned Solzhenitsyn in his presidential address: 'He does not deserve to be free. If the laws of our country were effective he would be in prison.' Menuhin got no joy for his two supplicants.[131]

On 14 April 1972 Rostropovich's name came up when the tormented Politburo met yet again to hear another report on the Solzhenitsyn case by the head of the KGB, Yuri Andropov:

Kosygin: Besides, we must somehow deal with Rostropovich. We should summon him and tell him to stop his tours abroad.

Brezhnev: Instead of touring Barnaul, for example, or other Soviet cities, he prefers to go to New York, Paris, and other cities abroad. We did tell them to stop Rostropovich from going abroad, but he continues to tour all over the world.[132]

From exile, Solzhenitsyn later described what happened to his friend: the loss of the post he loved best, conducting at the Bolshoi Theatre, the banning of his trips abroad, 'a long succession of naggling, needling attacks, hindrances and humiliations at every step of his daily life ... For some time they took him and Galina Vishnevskaya off radio and television ... Quite a number of his concerts in the Soviet Union were cancelled for no apparent reason, sometimes when he was on his way to the town where the concert was to be held.'[133] Early in 1974 the International Music Council's twenty-fifth anniversary was to be celebrated in Paris with a concert to which Rostropovich had been invited. At this time the cellist had been confined to the USSR for two years, and rarely allowed to perform in Moscow. Menuhin sent a telegram to the Ministry of Culture insisting on Rostropovich's presence in Paris; in reply he got an offer of Shostakovich and his new quartet played by the Borodin Quartet, all expenses to be borne by the Soviet government. Menuhin refused, then went over Furtseva's head to Brezhnev, 'and threatened to release to the press the whole story of Rostropovich's punishment and the exchange of cables, pointing out the harm this might do to détente'. Rostropovich got his visa.[134]

Galina Vishnevskaya's life had been as hard and dramatic as that of any Soviet international star. More or less abandoned by both parents, then pitched into the horror of the siege of Leningrad, twice married at an early age, she suffered the loss of her baby son in cruel conditions. Accepted after an audition at the Bolshoi in 1952, she had to fill in the usual form about her origins and relations, disguising the fact that her odious father had been convicted under Article 58 of the penal code. With her husband Mark she settled into a small communal apartment near the Bolshoi and worked on her roles, Leonore in *Fidelio*, Tatyana in *Eugene Onegin*, Kupava in *The Snow Maiden*, and Cio-Cio-San in *Madame Butterfly*. Summoned to the Metropole Hotel, she was recruited as an informer by the KGB—by her account, all soloists of the Bolshoi were thus approached. Later she was asked: 'You're on friendly terms with the ballet pianist Petunin. We have information that he often says things against the Soviet regime. Is that true?' Her father, released from prison after almost ten years but still set on regaining his Party membership, headed for the Bolshoi's personnel department to denounce Galina for withholding the fact that he had been arrested under Article 58.[135]

Whenever top Soviet delegations went abroad, as when Khrushchev visited Yugoslavia to rebuild bridges with Tito in 1955, they travelled like Renaissance princes, accompanied by a retinue of top performers—ballerinas, singers, and pianists were taken along. The young Vishnevskaya, handsome, talented, sexually attractive, was included.[136] Ivan Serov, successor to Beria as head of the secret police, slithered up behind her and whispered: 'Propose a toast to Tito's wife.'[137] It was evidently during the trip to Belgrade that the eye of the elderly Nikolai Bulganin, then at the height of his power, fell upon the soprano. She was summoned to a concert at his dacha to celebrate his birthday. Next day a debonair colonel carrying a huge bouquet arrived at her door. 'Three black ZIL limousines glided into our narrow street that night. There were bodyguards in the first and third, and our new master himself was in the middle one . . . People were peering out of the windows of every building.' It was through her influence with Bulganin that she got herself removed from the roster of KGB informers.[138]

In December 1959 Vishnevskaya accompanied the State Symphony Orchestra on a two-month tour of the United States—the first Soviet opera singer to do so; the Soviet government paid her $100 for each of her ten concerts.[139] On New Year's Eve the American impresario Sol Hurok laid on a reception for her at the Waldorf-Astoria. In 1961 she was invited to the Metropolitan Opera to sing in *Aida* with Jon Vickers. Clearly foreign tours were reinforcing her disdain for the Soviet way of life. 'When our Soviet airliner landed in a foreign country,' she later recalled from exile, 'we would pour out of it like a band of gypsies, carrying our sacks and bags overflowing with saucepans, hot plates, sugar, canned goods, and other groceries, including potatoes'... According to her account, when the Bolshoi performed in Paris in 1969 the company stayed in a hotel not far from the Opéra, and the smell of cabbage soup and onions wafted over the Boulevard Haussmann. Within days all the regular residents had fled—400 hot-plates plugged in simultaneously had plunged the hotel into darkness.[140]

On one occasion, a week before her scheduled departure for America, the singer was summoned by Dylatov, the Bolshoi's Party secretary, who wanted to know why she did not take part in the company's weekly political meetings. When she responded dismissively she was told that her tour was cancelled, because the Bolshoi was refusing to issue her statutory certificate of good behaviour signed by the Party secretary, the chairman of the local committee, and the director. Vishnevskaya concluded that Ekaterina Furtseva wanted to teach her a lesson. Furtseva was evidently keen on collecting diamonds, gold, and furs. Vishnevskaya alleges that during the Bolshoi Opera's forty-day tour of France in 1969, 'I gave her $400—my entire fee at $10 a day. Quite simply, I gave her a bribe so that she would let me go abroad on my own contracts.' Often drunk on vodka, this peasant woman, who had begun as a loom operator in a textile plant then risen to be Minister of Culture for fourteen years and the only female member of the Politburo, combined great charm with remarkable resilience.[141]

In 1976, by order of the Central Committee, Vishnevskaya's name was deleted and her photographs removed from the jubilee album celebrating the 200th anniversary of the Bolshoi, and in due course from all Soviet reference works. By the time she wrote her vivid autobiography *Galina* (marred by dialogue that could not possibly have been remembered), her hostility to any form of welfare socialism extended to low-price concerts, 'free' education, 'free' medical care, and cheap rents. It all came out of taxation. 'So that, whether you wanted to go to the concert or not, the money was taken from you long ago.' So free was 'free'.[142]

In 1977 Rostropovich was appointed director of the National Symphony Orchestra in Washington—a post he was to retain until his return to Russia seventeen years later. In 1978 he and Vishnevskaya were stripped of Soviet citizenship for 'systematic acts that bring harm to the prestige of the Soviet Union'. In February 1980 they staged a three-hour concert at the Salle Pleyel in Paris to honour their friend the physicist, social philosopher, and civil-rights campaigner Andrei Sakharov, sent into exile in Gorky, 'one of the greatest men in the world'. They also called for a boycott of the Moscow Olympics.[143] The time would come when Rostropovich would play Bach in Berlin to celebrate the collapse of the wall, and two years later, at the time of the abortive coup in the USSR, hurry to join Boris Yeltsin in the besieged White House. By 2002, when he was still going strong as a conductor at the age of 75, he had given 120 premières as a cellist, seventy as a conductor.[144]

⊞ ⊞ ⊞

During the mid-sixties Western critics were hunting down Soviet musical dissidents like an endangered species. American universities had begun to mount symposia and concerts of Soviet avant-garde music.[145] Harold C. Schonberg, chief music critic of the *New York Times*, was in the forefront of the safari; in the issue of 12 October 1967 he reported a visit to Kiev, where he sought out Ukrainian avant-garde composers in close contact with the Poles. His verdict on some taped performances by these autodidacts in serial technique was not particularly encouraging—'a mishmash'—yet Schonberg contrived to reach a hyperbolic conclusion:

The most astonishing esthetic phenomenon of the Soviet Union in the last few years ... is the existence of a musical avant-garde unmistakably derived from the West ... Using scores, studying records and tapes of such international avant-garde heroes as Pierre Boulez in France, Luciano Berio in Italy, Yannis Xenakis in Greece, John Cage and Lukas Foss in the United States, a handful of composers began to work on serial technique, aleatory and other devices that the West had enthusiastically adopted after World War II ended.

Yet the music produced by Schonberg's 'not more than a dozen or so avant-garde composers' in the USSR resulted, for 'conventional listeners', in what he himself called 'excruciating dissonance'. This music was, he freely conceded, 'as little liked and understood by the Russian public as it is in the West, being athematic, pointillistic, dissonant, and a complete break with the past'.[146] Most Soviet Establishment composers, according to Schonberg, were incapable of understanding 'the squeals, blips, glissandi, tonal ruptures, and wild clumps of jagged sound that the modernists are producing. They are intellectually aware that the new music has taken root all over the West, but emotionally they refuse to believe it. They *cannot* believe it.' One must sympathize with the unbelieving Russians: Schonberg's 'taken root all over the West' married ill with his 'little understood . . . in the West'.[147]

Shostakovich's *Testimony*

The most controversial Soviet composer to suffer Zhdanov's denunciation in 1948 and the ensuing public onslaught was Dmitri Shostakovich. This taut, nervy genius remained throughout his life a grid of high-voltage tensions: international in outlook yet fiercely protective of the Russian tradition; a Communist who publicly praised the Party's interventions in music yet feared and despised them; a modernist who frequently warned against the excesses of Western innovation. Shostakovich developed a kind of tidal motion in his compositions by which the dark depths contradicted the happy surge of the surface.

Born in St Petersburg in 1905, and educated at the Petrograd (Leningrad) Conservatory during the years following the Revolution, Shostakovich had shot to fame while in his twenties only to suffer all the fears—if not the worst fate—of the Stalin Terror. His contact with European music was intense in the late 1920s. Printed music arrived from abroad and there were frequent concerts of Western music in Moscow, even more in Leningrad. Even so, his Second Symphony was dedicated to the October Revolution, his Third was titled *May Day*. He was 'a real Soviet composer, and one the West took seriously'.[1] More radically modernist was his opera *The Nose* (from Gogol's rather tedious story *Nos*, which begins with the civil servant Kovalyov losing his nose while in the barber's chair), which had its première in Leningrad on 18 January 1930 but soon disappeared from the repertoire. The parade of dozens of people changing places kaleidoscopically and moving like mechanical dolls was attacked by Soviet critics as a malignant ridicule of operatic tradition; the musical idiom was intricate and tangled. 'To all this was added the most impossible tricks in orchestral onomatopoeia, a sort of cascade of musical witticisms.'[2]

His opera *Ledi Makbet Mtsenskogo uezda* (*Lady Macbeth of Mtsensk District*), first performed when the composer was only 29, enjoyed an enormous success—until Stalin struck it down. Although this happened a decade before the onset of the cold war, the brutal act of censorship was recalled in the Central Committee decree of February 1948 (translated into English in VOKS *Bulletin* (no. 54): 'As far back as 1936, in connection with the appearance of D. Shostakovich's opera *Lady Macbeth of Mtsensk Uyezd, Pravda*, the organ of the Central Committee of the CPSU(B), subjected to pointed criticism the antipopular, formalistic distortions in his music and exposed the harm and danger of this trend for the future development of Soviet music.'

Shostakovich had based the libretto on Nikolai Leskov's nineteenth-century tale of lust and murder (but by no means the same story as Shakespeare's *Macbeth*, and in vital respects the reverse). A poor girl, Katerina, is given in marriage to a rich merchant. Childless, she falls for a handsome scoundrel, Sergei, a clerk in her husband's warehouse. Having lost her virtue, she poisons her lecherous father-in-law then murders her husband. Now sole legatee of the Izmailov family capital, she lives openly with her lover Sergei until the corpses are discovered and the couple condemned to penal servitude. The bleak view of humanity is unredeemed. The Izmailovs, father and son, are monsters matched by the blackmailers and extortioners among the police, by the hypocrites and lickspittles who come as wedding guests, and the heartless convict women, one of whom puts Sergei up to robbing Katerina of her precious stockings. Shostakovich intended Katerina's crimes to be a protest against the dismal, stifling, hypocritical milieu of the nineteenth-century merchant class. His dramatic and passionate music is astonishing for its dark knowledge of evil and despair, for its relentless and even cacophonous shrieking and snarling, its heart-stopping climaxes: a score which abandons itself as shamelessly as the heroine does to the musical equivalent of original sin—the modernist murder of melody and harmony.

Two simultaneous premières took place in 1934, the more successful one by the Mali Opera Theatre in Leningrad, the other in Moscow under the title *Katerina Izmailova*. Performed thirty-six times in Leningrad during the five months after its première, with ninety-four performances in Moscow, the opera was presented almost immediately in Stockholm, Prague, London, Zurich, Copenhagen, and the United States. The American première under Arthur Rodzinsky aroused great interest; Virgil Thomson's review in *Modern Music* (1935) appeared under the title 'Socialism at the Metropolitan'. On 26 December 1935 a new production was launched in Moscow by the Bolshoi Theatre's Second Company. This was the one attended by Stalin and Molotov on 26 January 1936. Calamity followed when a devastating review, unsigned and therefore carrying the force of a Party editorial, 'Sumbur vmesto muzyki' (Muddle Instead of Music), reputedly written by Andrei Zhdanov, appeared in *Pravda* on 28 January.

Like Meyerhold's productions and other 'leftist' art, *Lady Macbeth* was casti-gated as a wanton repudiation of classical principles, 'simplicity, realism, comprehensibility of image, and the natural sound of the word'. It was damned as discordant, confused, and borrowed from jazz, a din of grinding noises and screams, nervy, convulsive, epileptic. The target of the editorial was clearly modernism itself:

Fragments of melody, embryos of musical phrases appear and disappear, once more in crashing, grinding, and screeching. To follow this 'music' is difficult, to remember it is impossible. The music quacks, grunts, pants and sighs, so as to convey the love scenes in the most naturalistic manner. And 'love' is smeared all over the opera in the most vulgar form. The merchant's double bed occupies the central place in the stage design.[3]

Also held against *Lady Macbeth*—with its vertiginous swings between brittle satire, dissonant expressionism, and luscious romanticism—was its warm reception by the foreign bourgeoisie with its 'perverted tastes', panting for novelty and sensation. Within ten days *Pravda* weighed in again with an attack on Shostakovich's collective-farm ballet staged at the Bolshoi, *Svetlyi ruchei* (*Limpid Stream*, 1934, op. 39), celebrating the harvest at a kolkhoz in the Kuban. Shostakovich was held guilty of failing to investigate the folk culture and songs of the area. Following the two savage attacks in *Pravda*, the composer and everyone around him were now certain that his arrest was inevitable. While friends kept their distance, Shostakovich kept a small suitcase packed and ready. He lay awake listening, waiting in the dark for the creatures of the night, the NKVD.

I was completely destroyed. It was a blow that wiped out my past. And my future. To whom could I turn for advice? To whom could I go? I went to Marshal Tukhachevsky. He had recently returned from his triumphant visit to London and Paris. *Pravda* wrote about him every day . . . We locked ourselves in his office. He turned off his phones. We sat in silence . . . Tukhachevsky spoke softly because he feared prying ears.[4]

Yet Stalin had decided that Shostakovich was to be spared arrest, despite his closeness to such 'enemies of the people' as Tukhachevsky and Meyerhold, both of whom perished in the pre-war purges.

Shostakovich's comments on the fellow-travelling Western intelligentsia of the 1930s are powerful if confusing:

For they're always right, the great Western humanists, lovers of truthful literature and art. It's we who are always at fault. I'm the one who gets asked, 'Why did you sign this and that?' But has anyone ever asked André Malraux why he glorified the construction of the White Sea Canal, where thousands upon thousands of people perished? No, no one has . . . And what about Lion Feuchtwanger, famous humanist? I read his little book *Moscow 1937* with revulsion.

This was said more than thirty years later—yet the composer himself had written music in praise of collectivization. Shostakovich also poured scorn on Bernard Shaw's comment after his visit to Stalin: 'You won't frighten me with the word "dictator".' Naturally Shaw wasn't frightened! England had not had a dictator since Cromwell! 'And what about Romain Rolland? It makes me sick to think about him.'[5] He was equally scathing about foreign delegations invited to Russia, 'defenders of this, fighters for that', of whom Yevgeni Yevtushenko wrote: 'Meal coupons in the hand bring friends from all the continents.' Flora Litvinova, daughter-in-law of the Jewish diplomat and ambassador to London Maxim Litvinov, reported hearing an outburst by Shostakovich against Picasso in 1956 at the time of his first exhibition in Moscow since the Revolution:

Suddenly Dmitri Dmitriyevich burst out, 'Don't speak to me of him, he's a bastard... Yes, Picasso, that bastard, hails Soviet power and our Communist system at a time when his followers here are persecuted, hounded and not allowed to work... Well, yes, I too am a bastard, coward and so on, but I'm living in a prison... I am frightened for my children and for myself. But he's living in a freedom, he doesn't have to tell lies... All those Hewlett Johnsons, Picassos and Joliot-Curies, they're all vermin... And Picasso's revolting dove of peace! How I hate it!'[6]

Still composing, despite the trauma of *Lady Macbeth*, he developed a coded style apparent in the Fifth Symphony (1937), which contains the most famous passages, the 'signature' chords, in Shostakovich's work. Rousing on the surface, an exultant cry of triumph and joy, a hailing of a dawn, a great blast of brass and horns pealing the bells of the heart, this work becomes increasingly forced and frenetic, the praise-poet offering his desperate eulogy under the tyrant's raised boot. This view is confirmed by the composer's own private reflections on the Seventh Symphony, written during the siege of Leningrad:

Actually, I have nothing against calling the Seventh the 'Leningrad' Symphony, but it's not about Leningrad under siege, it's about the Leningrad that Stalin destroyed and that Hitler merely finished off. The majority of my symphonies are tombstones. Too many of our people died and were buried in places unknown to anyone, not even their relatives.[7]

In London, 60,000 people heard the Seventh 1942 when it was performed under the baton of Sir Henry Wood at the Albert Hall and broadcast by the BBC. The composer later recalled: 'In the United States, leading conductors... vied for the right to present the première of the sensational symphony. They wrote letters and sent telegrams to the Soviet Embassy'. Arturo Toscanini entered the fray with the power of NBC behind him, and won. He received the first copy of the score, on film, brought to the United States by military ship. The radio première, broadcast from Radio City on 19 July 1942, was heard by millions. During its first season the symphony was performed sixty-two times in the USA. Shostakovich's face grew familiar in the magazines; he appeared on the cover of *Time* (20 July 1942)—'Fireman Shostakovich'—a profile in an ornate steel helmet, more than faintly absurd.

Stalin—according to Shostakovich—was incensed by his popularity in the West and his failure to present Stalin with a suitably triumphal and extended Choral symphony at the end of the war—the Ninth. The composer, who met the Soviet leader more than once, describes him as 'an ordinary, shabby little man, short, fat, with reddish hair. His face was covered with pockmarks and his right hand was noticeably thinner than his left. He kept hiding his right hand.'

Stalin was like a spider and everyone who approached his nets had to die... He was like a frog puffing himself up to the size of an ox... And they demanded that Shostakovich use quadruple winds, choir and soloists to hail their leader... When my Ninth was performed, Stalin was incensed. He was deeply offended because there was no chorus, no soloists. And no apotheosis. There wasn't even a paltry dedication.[8]

In January 1947 the Leningrad Composers Union elected Shostakovich as its chairman and simultaneously nominated him as a candidate for the Supreme Soviet of the Russian Federation (not to be confused with the USSR), and he was duly elected on 9 February 1948. Then came the bombshell resolution of the Central Committee a day later. By order of Glavrepertkom, the central censorship board, on 14 February, a long list of Shostakovich's 'formalist' works were proscribed for performance and removed from the repertory.[9] Suddenly the newspapers were full of letters of denunciation from indignant workers. Schoolchildren memorized texts about the great harm that Shostakovich had brought to art. The chief editor of *Sovetskaia muzyka*, the lean, balding M. Koval', a member of the secretariat of the Composers' Union, wrote a long article, 'The Creative Path of Shostakovich', which appeared in three consecutive issues, with copious notational illustrations, in which he found evidence of 'decadence' and 'cacophany' in almost all of the composer's works, dubbing them 'formalist vermin'.[10]

A cartoon by A. Kostomolotskii in the same journal shows a line of cloned boyish figures, each wearing a bow tie and short trousers, emerging from the Moscow and Leningrad Conservatories. The rhyming caption (here translated literally) comments: 'Every year from these glorious walls (*sten*) march a succession of inglorious replacements (*smen*). They march, they march like obedient guardsmen—these little Shostakoviches'. Vladimir Ashkenazy recalls being told by his piano teacher how she met Shostakovich outside the Leningrad apartment building where they both lived. It was shortly after the Zhdanov decree. He asked her whether her water supply, like his, had been cut off. She said no. Looking like a hunted animal, he muttered that he was sure he knew why.[11] When Zhdanov died on 31 August 1948, Shostakovich was quoted by *VOKS Bulletin* (no. 55): 'For us intellectuals, who, in our work, were in constant touch with our dear Andrei Alexandrovich, now departed from us, this is a grievous, bitter loss. This man of broad education, of remarkable erudition in every field of art . . . a genuine Bolshevik . . .'

How odd! They want to disgrace him but they want to quote him! Presumably this was an exercise in power and humiliation; a month later, in September 1948, Shostakovich was driven out of the Leningrad and Moscow conservatories, where he had been teaching composition. He never taught again. On 12 December he wrote to his friend Isaak Glikman: 'During the last week or so I have aged strikingly, and this ageing process is now proceeding with amazing speed.' His violet-coloured cheeks were puffy. Film music, he added, was keeping him alive, 'but exhausts me in the extreme'.[12] Western critics of the Soviet Union had a field day. Arthur Schlesinger, Jr. mockingly quoted Shostakovich: 'I know the Party is right, that the Party wishes me well and that I must search and find concrete creative roads which will lead me toward a realistic Soviet people's art.'[13]

Some of the remarks in *Testimony* attributed to the elderly Shostakovich by his controversial amanuensis Solomon Volkov, blending as they do megalomania with paranoia, defy logic (though doubtless authentic). For example, he says that following the historic resolution of February 1948 condemning the 'formalist' composers, 'Stalin was rather deflated by the reaction in the West. For some reason, he thought they'd be tossing their hats in the air as well, or at least be silent.' (Unlikely.) A few phrases later comes the apparent contradiction: 'Naturally, Stalin didn't give a damn about the West, and the Western intelligentsia in particular. He used to say, "Don't worry, they'll swallow it." ' Shostakovich tells a story, real or apocryphal, of how the secretary of the Composers' Union, Khrennikov (whom he loathed), while reading out to Stalin a list of candidates for the annual Stalin Prize, so panicked that he fouled his trousers.[14]

In March 1949 Stalin (famously) telephoned Shostakovich, urging him to make the journey to the imminent Cultural and Scientific Conference for World Peace in New York. Shostakovich objected that his music was widely performed in America but no longer performed in Russia and the Americans would ask him why. 'Over there all my symphonies are played. Whereas over here they are forbidden. How am I to behave in this situation?'

Stalin answered in his Georgian accent: 'How do you mean forbidden? Forbidden by whom?'

'By the State Commission for Repertoire (Glavrepertkom)', said the composer.[15]

By Stalin's personal instruction, Order No. 3197 of 16 March 1949, the Glavrepertkom order dated 16 February 1948, banning from performance and removing from the repertory the works of the 'formalists', was rescinded and declared 'illegal' by the Council of Ministers of the USSR. This happened four days before Shostakovich left for New York along with Fadeyev and the film directors Sergei Gerasimov and Mikhail Chiaureli.

Arriving at La Guardia on 24 March, the Soviet delegates were welcomed by Norman Mailer and Aaron Copland. Addressing an audience of 800 people two days later in the Perroquet Room of the Waldorf-Astoria Hotel, Shostakovich spoke briefly in Russian, thanking the conference for inviting him; his speech was then read by an interpreter while he looked on. *Time* (4 April) described him as: 'A shy, stiff-shouldered man with a pale, wide forehead. Shostakovich was painfully ill at ease . . . He cringed visibly from the photographers' flashbulbs, mopped his brow, twiddled his spectacles.'[16]

Clearly he had not written the 5,200-word speech he delivered, a bureaucrat's standard homily on the role of art in the political struggle, the 'bitter struggle' (*ozhestochennaia bor'ba*) between the two world-views of art, the need to devote art to the civic service (*grazhdanskomu sluzheniiu*) of the people and to combat formalism. Talk of 'pure art' or of 'autonomous art' (he said) has long been ridiculed by art itself. Art must be veracious and convey optimism, combating the pessimism of bourgeois cosmopolitanism. 'When abroad I feel myself to be a representative of the great Soviet people and of the world cultural centre—Moscow.' He then quoted Stravinsky: 'My music expresses nothing realistic in character, my music has no story to tell (*nechego rasskazyvat'*).' This was the Stravinsky who 'betrayed his native land and severed himself from his people by joining the camp of reactionary modern musicians'; Shostakovich accused him of open cynicism, of a bleakly destructive role, mindlessness, emptiness.[17]

And yet, after attending the Prague Spring Festival in 1947, Shostakovich had been quoted in *Vecherniaia Moskva* (11 June) as having heard Stravinsky's Symphony in Three Movements, (1945), 'in which his typically brilliant orchestration is accompanied by a simpler, pithier musical language and more profound emotions'. What did Shostakovich really think of Stravinsky? This emerged—though with the usual contradictions typical of this twisted and mordant soul, whose memoirs resemble a box with several false bottoms—thirty years later: 'Stravinsky is one of the greatest composers of

our time and I truly love many of his works . . . I not only studied and listened
to his music, but I played it and made my own transcriptions as well . . . He
was probably right not to return to Russia . . .'

On the other hand—and there was invariably another hand up Shostakovich's twisted sleeve—his sense of a 'national' music, of authentically Russian music, echoed that of the Soviet state: he could not help describing
Stravinsky and Prokofiev as

children, even though adoptive ones, of Western culture. Their love and taste for
publicity is, I feel, what keeps Prokofiev and Stravinsky from being thoroughly Russian
composers. There's some flaw in their personalities, a loss of some very important
moral principles . . . Stravinsky—always spoke only for himself, while Mussorgsky
spoke for himself and for his country.[18]

But why should a composer speak 'for his country'? Shostakovich's comments here go some way towards explaining the contradiction between the
artist who despised the Party and the artist who apparently felt the need to
defend it abroad, to the point of finally joining it. The view that Shostakovich mounted Party platforms, delivered Party speeches, and signed Party-
inspired letters condemning dissidents only in order to 'get them off his
back' and 'lead a quiet life' is untenable—although in his last years he made
apologies to friends along those lines.

Shostakovich's recall of Stravinsky's final, very grand, 'state visit' to Russia
in 1962 is startling for its embittered sarcasm and lack of self-scrutiny. Had
Shostakovich forgotten his own Party-fed diatribes against Stravinsky?

At the very top it was decided to make him the Number One national composer, but
this gambit didn't work. Stravinsky hadn't forgotten anything—that he had been
called a lackey of American imperialism and a flunkey of the Catholic Church—and
the very same people who had called him that were now greeting him with outspread
arms. Stravinsky offered his walking stick instead of his hand to one of those hypocrites, who was forced to shake it, proving that he was the real lackey . . . [Stravinsky]
didn't make the mistake of Prokofiev, who ended up like a chicken in the soup.[19]

The two composers were brought together at a reception on 1 October 1962,
seated on either side of Madame Furtseva. Shostakovich also attended the
farewell banquet for Stravinsky ten days later; Stravinsky's American amanuensis Robert Craft recalled that Shostakovich was cripplingly shy during both
meetings: 'He chews not merely his nails but his fingers, twitches his pouty
mouth and chin, chain smokes, wiggles his nose in constant adjustment of
his spectacles, looks querulous one moment and ready to cry the next . . .
There is no betrayal of the thoughts behind those frightened, very intelligent
eyes.'[20]

The same had been true in 1949, when he addressed the Waldorf-Astoria Conference. The *New York Times* (28 March) reported his speech on its front page, complaining that it rivalled in bitterness the diatribes of Soviet Foreign Minister Vishinsky. Shostakovich declared: 'Here I must stress that Party criticism of formalism in Soviet music is a life-giving source of musical creativeness. It helps all of us to paralyse alien influences and completely devote our art to the people and the motherland.' He regretted that in some of his post-war works he had lost contact with the people and thus failed as an artist. So abject was his abasement that he even attacked disgraced colleagues—Prokofiev, for example, was in danger of a 'relapse into formalism' if he, too, failed to heed Party directives.[21]

Nicolas Nabokov, a Russian émigré soon to become general secretary of the Congress for Cultural Freedom, had joined the anti-Soviet activists, led by the philsopher Sidney Hook, who also gathered in the Waldorf-Astoria. Nabokov offered two versions of his own involvement, published twenty-six years apart. In *Old Friends and New Music* (London, 1951), he described how Shostakovich reminded him of 'dirty laundry washed, ironed out, and sent to America to meet with the peace-makers, peace addicts and peace dupes of the Waldorf-Astoria conference'. As for the composer's speech, it was 'part of a punishment, part of a ritual of redemption he had to go through before he could be pardoned again . . . He told in effect that every time the Party found flaws in his art, the Party was right, and every time the Party put him on ice, he was grateful to the Party. Because it helped him to recognize his flaws and mistakes.'[22] In Nabokov's second version, *Bagázh*, published in 1975, he writes:

Shostakovich and his KGB nurse-interpreter took seats to the left of the chairman, Olin Downes. The session was long and verbose. When I was finally able to ask my question, it was: 'On such-and-such a date in No. X of *Pravda* appeared an unsigned article that had all the looks of an editorial. It concerned three Western composers: Paul Hindemith, Arnold Schoenberg, and Igor Stravinsky. In the article they were branded, all three of them, as "obscurantists," "decadent bourgeois formalists", and "lackeys of imperialism". The performance of their music should "therefore be prohibited in the USSR". Does Mr Shostakovich personally agree with this official view as printed in *Pravda*?' There was suddenly a bewildered expression on the faces of the Russians. One of them, near Mr Downes, muttered quite audibly, '*Provokatsya*'. The nurse-interpreter was whispering something in Shostakovich's ear. Shostakovich got up, was handed a microphone, and looking down at the floor, said in Russian: 'I fully agree with the statements made in *Pravda*.'[23]

The final session of the Waldorf-Astoria Conference took place in Madison Square Garden, attended by 18,000 people, while 2,000 counter-demonstrators assembled outside. He ended the session at 11.40 p.m. by playing on the piano the second movement (Scherzo) of his Fifth Symphony. By now cold war tensions were running high in the United States. Yale University refused the use of a hall for a concert and lecture by Shostakovich. The Soviet press accused the US government and the 'Black Hundreds' of repressing all who advocated peace.[24] *Time*, which had once elevated Shostakovich to its cover, now portrayed him fanatically screaming into a microphone. On 4 April the Soviet delegation left by plane for Stockholm. 'Shostakovich holds U.S. fears his music', announced the *New York Times* (27 May). The composer came away unimpressed by concert audiences slouching in their seats with their coats and hats on, by 'depressing' skyscrapers, and by 'disorder' at La Guardia airport.[25] He particularly detested the aggressiveness of American reporters. After his trip he published *Travel Notes*: 'We had scarcely landed on Berlin aerodrome when we were surrounded by a crowd of American reporters and photographers ... I must say that I simply cannot stand this familiarity—an unknown man comes up to me, slaps me on the shoulder, and shouts at me: "Hello, Shosty. What d'you like best, blondes or brunettes?"' Twenty years later his aversion remained sharp: 'It cost me a great deal, that trip. I had to answer stupid questions and avoid saying too much.' Stalin (he recalled) 'liked leading the Americans by the nose that way. He would show them a man—here he is, alive and well—and then kill him ...'[26] Stalin certainly kept him on the move: in July 1950 Shostakovich headed the Soviet delegation to the Bach bicentenary in Leipzig, then attended the second World Peace Congress in Warsaw in November. The paradox of cultural life under Stalin is further illustrated by an event which took place in May 1951 in the Small Hall of the Union of Composers; indeed, Soviet cultural practice had something of the 'Chinese' quality of 'struggle' later associated with Mao's Cultural Revolution. A form of free-speaking debate among the professionals was encouraged, provided the outcome was Party-line denunciation. On two successive evenings Shostakovich was invited to play his latest work, the Twenty-Four Preludes and Fugues for piano, and then to talk about it. One after another, the music officials (including the composer Kabalevsky) rose to voice disapproval: not typical of our Soviet reality, our life, formalistic, past sins revisited, morbid, unhealthy. The critic Israil Nestiev, a member of the Central Committee and virulently anti-Western, acted as principal rabble-rouser alongside Tikhon Khrennikov; only the ever-brave pianist Mariia Yudina rose to Shostakovich's defence: 'Your quibbling, negative judgements will wither away at the roots.'[27]

In March–April 1952 Shostakovich was in Berlin, Leipzig, and Dresden for the Beethoven Festival; December of that year took him to the Vienna Peace

Congress. Shostakovich was constantly walking into the jaws of bitter Western derision. Addressing a gathering of writers and artists under the auspices of the American Committee for Cultural Freedom on 29 March 1952, the historian Bertram D. Wolfe commented sarcastically: 'Shostakovich responded [to the February 1948 decree] by writing music to Stalin, to his great irrigation works, his power plants, his "transformation of nature". The composer became an accomplice to injustice by condoning the punishment of his colleagues and of the critics who had committed the crime of praising his work.'[28]

American commentators constantly goaded Shostakovich into an irritated self-defence: 'The typical Western journalist is an uneducated, obnoxious, and profoundly cynical person. He needs to make money and doesn't give a damn about the rest. Every one of these pushy fellows wants me to answer his stupid questions "daringly"... Why do I have to risk my life?... What right does he have to expect my frankness and trust?'[29] Interviewed by Harrison E. Salisbury in the *New York Times*'s Sunday supplement (27 November 1953), Shostakovich cited *Pravda* (11 November) on the creative freedom enjoyed by Soviet composers. 'And I go on writing and the Government goes on supporting me, and generously, too.' An accompanying piece by the Soviet-born composer-pianist Julie Whitby was headlined 'Music in a Cage'.[30] In 1954 Shostakovich received the World Peace Prize and the title of People's Artist of the USSR, further inflaming Western animosity. According to the American critic Boris Schwarz: 'The accumulation of sorrow that Shostakovich experienced during that time came out with elemental, explosive force in the Tenth Symphony, written in 1953—the great work that heralded the liberalization of the human spirit.'[31] The young pianist Vladimir Ashkenazy attended the première of the Tenth Symphony and was struck by 'the gloomy helplessness and desperation in it'. Even the happy ending 'we later understood' to be mocking. Shostakovich himself later commented: 'The second movement is inexorable, merciless, like an evil whirlwind—a "musical portrait" of Stalin.'[32]

On 9 March 1956 Shostakovich resumed his parrot-like repetition of the Party line in *Izvestiia*: 'Lenin's Party... the mind and conscience of our age. Its greatest achievement is the new spiritual make-up of the Soviet people... I am now composing my Eleventh Symphony, dedicated to the first Russian Revolution... I would like to express the soul of the people who first paved the way for socialism.' In *Novoe vremia* (no. 6, 1956) he replied to Howard Taubman's review in the *New York Times* (8 January 1956) of his Violin Concerto, played in New York by David Oistrakh. Shostakovich found it 'highly insulting' that Taubman should write that he was entitled to a 'little freedom'—as if to imply that the Party had damaged his music.[33] Addressing the second Congress of Composers, he dealt in platitudes about the 'interests of all the people'—*obshchenarodnykh interesov*, 'the struggle against scholasticism', and against 'swimming with the current'.[34] But he was a great composer, and foreign honours now found their proper season: Honorary Doctor of Music at Oxford, Commander of the Order of Arts and Letters in France (both 1958).

For Boris Schwarz, the Eleventh and Twelfth Symphonies were Shostakovich's 'true monuments to Socialist Realism', both 'gigantic frescoes depicting Russia's revolutionary past'. Sally Belfrage was living in Moscow in 1957: 'The day after Shostakovich's Eleventh Symphony was performed for the first time, hardly another subject was mentioned anywhere in Moscow...It was impossible to imagine such an event having such significance to the ordinary people of any other country.'[35] The Eleventh had its Western supporters, too; writing in the *Observer* (31 January 1960), Peter Heyworth ridiculed automatic Western condemnation, 'with Dulles-like promptitude', of anything hailed in Russia. He defended the composer's motives in writing a 'programmatic' symphony; to regard the Eleventh as a sacrificial offering to the regime 'seems to me as silly and unsubtle as to describe Elgar's Second Symphony as a salute to British imperialism'.

Since 1990 some Russian musicologists have joined Western colleagues in laying emphasis on double-meaning, masked sarcasm, and Aesopian language in the work of Shostakovich. The musicologist Lev Lebedinsky, who met Shostakovich in 1957 when the Eleventh Symphony ('1905') was being written, is convinced that the composer concealed its 'contemporary meaning', particularly in the second movement, called 'The Ninth of January', where he reproduces what Lebedinsky interprets as the roar of engines and the clatter of tank tracks, 'sounds strongly suggestive of the massacres during the 1956 uprising in Budapest'.[36]

The Twelfth Symphony (the 'Lenin') was given its Western première at the 1962 Edinburgh Festival.[37] Peter Heyworth lamented in the *New York Times* (6 September 1962) that the Twelfth could lay claim to be Shostakovich's worst. 'The majority of musicians and critics at Edinburgh were frankly aghast at its crudity and lack of interest.' Martin Cooper commented: 'To the Western ear its alternately drab and garish colours, and its obsessive repetition of commonplace musical ideas, are intolerable, while the naïve ideological programme suggests that perhaps the work's true home might be the cinema.'[38]

⌗ ⌗ ⌗

Shostakovich's private attitude towards the CPSU remained at variance with his public position—and the contradiction reverberated through his music. Came the 1958 Central Committee decree 'On Correcting Mistakes Made in Evaluating the Work of Leading Soviet Composers'. This was a partial retraction of Zhdanov's outburst ten years earlier. Galina Vishnevskaya recalls Shostakovich's great excitement: '[Dmitry Dmitriyevich] poured vodka into the tumblers and all but shouted, "Well, Slava and Galya, let's drink to the great historical decree 'on Abrogating the Great Historical Decree' ".'[39] This was the period (1957–8) when he composed in secret the satirical, anti-Stalin cantata *Rayok* (after Mussorgsky's work of the same name). Lev Lebedinsky has claimed authorship of the libretto, which he wrote at Shostakovich's behest, using old speeches by Stalin and Zhdanov. Shostakovich was particularly mocking of the Party official Shepilov, who mispronounced the name of Rimsky-Korsakov, wrongly placing the accent on the middle 'a'; he also instructed Lebedinsky that in *Rayok* Stalin should be called Edinitsyn, Zhdanov Dvoikin, and Shepilov Troikin—each a play on the Russian words for 'one,' 'two,' and 'three', but also (Elizabeth Wilson points out) referring to school grades, where Three is the lowest pass mark and One means abysmal failure. Shostakovich's wit revelled in numbers; he dubbed Minister of Culture Furtseva, 'Ekaterina the Third' (i.e. next after Catherine the Great). Kept under wraps for thirty years, *Rayok* was first publicly performed in Washington in January 1989 by Mstislav Rostropovich, and shortly afterwards in the USSR in a slightly different version.[40]

A clear indication of the line that the Party wished to spread abroad after the Central Committee decree 'On Correcting Mistakes' is found in D. Rabinovich's, *Dmitry Shostakovich*.[41] Here one discovers that the Party's mistakes in the field of music had been few. Shostakovich's early susceptibility to Western modernism, expressionism, and 'exaggeratedly grotesque eccentricity' is still regretted. But: 'To his good fortune, Shostakovich's Soviet environment and the strength of public opinion helped him to overcome the infantile disorders of modernism.'

Shostakovich's peculiar combination of international stature and personal vulnerability excited an almost sadistic interest in the West. 'I found a curious little musical playing in Moscow', recalled Harrison Salisbury at this time. 'It was written by Dmitri Shostakovich, and it was being performed by the Operetta Theatre, an organization devoted to cheap middle-European concoctions . . . [Shostakovich] took as his theme the new Cheremushki housing development.' Salisbury rated it 'trash' and a 'fairy story': 'Never have buildings been so beautiful . . . Never have neighbours been so happy (once the bad wolf of the corrupt manager has been put in his place).'[42] The 'curious little musical' Salisbury referred to was Shostakovich's *Moskva, Cheremushki* (*Paradise, Moscow*), libretto by V. Mass and M. Chervinsky, first performed by the Moscow Operetta Theatre on 24 January 1959.[43]

During his November 1959 visit to the United States with four other Soviet composers, Shostakovich was asked whether his opinion of America had changed since his visit as a delegate to the Waldorf-Astoria Conference ten years earlier. The situation, he replied, had changed and his earlier remarks 'cannot be related to the whole American people'.[44] 'Since 1948', lamented the *New York Times* (7 November), 'the music of Shostakovich has had nowhere near the daring and excitement it had in his earlier years. Many critics believe that the composer is playing it safe.' Howard Taubman was only partly impressed by the new Cello Concerto he heard in Philadelphia, performed by Rostropovich. 'The first movement reflects a habit of the latter-day Shostakovich. It takes commonplace material, and manipulates and reiterates it well beyond a point of no return.'

According to the Soviet Central Committee's cultural department internal report, Shostakovich refused to answer American questions whose persistence infuriated him (*privodila v razdrazhenie*)—for example, when was *Lady Macbeth of Mtsensk*, last seen in 1936, going to be granted a new production? Asked whether he felt pressure from the CPSU, he replied: 'I believe every artist has to reveal the front-line ideals of his time. In our time and country the leadership of the Communist Party is important and necessary for composers.' Asked whether he resented non-payment for performances of his work in the USA, he said he was not particularly upset, but this (according to the Central Committee memorandum) was edited out by the American press.[45]

Howard Taubman's insistent questions about *Lady Macbeth of Mtsensk* clearly aggravated the composer. In the words of a *New York Times* reporter (19 November), 'Mr Shostakovich said he was too tired to comment and that at an off-the-record meeting he had explained his revisions of *Lady Macbeth* to Mr Taubman when he invited the critic to attend the première of the revised version in Leningrad next March [1960]'. This proposed date makes little sense in terms of the desperate caution of the Soviet Party and musical establishment, as reflected in confidential correspondence lodged in the Soviet Central Committee archives. It was not until 31 January 1961 that D. Polikarpov, director of the cultural department, raised the subject in a memorandum to the Composers' Union. Recalling *Pravda*'s original criticisms of *Lady Macbeth*, Polikarpov commented that some Soviet musicians were now complaining in private that the original attack on the formalism of the music had been excessive. An 'unhealthy group atmosphere' (*nezdorovaia gruppovaia obstanovka*) regarding this opera had developed in the run-up to the Third Congress of Composers, reinforced by the fact that it was banned in the USSR but performed abroad. The solution was to ask the Composers' Union to consider a rewriting of the opera.

On 19 April 1961 Khrennikov, writing to the cultural department of the Central Committee, reported that Shostakovich had been at work on a new version. The secretariat of the Composers' Union agreed to a new production on certain conditions, notably a monitoring of rehearsals. As far as possible, everything was to be kept under wraps until the last minute. The tortuous language of the Central Committee mentioned 'a future public discussion of a private showing or closed viewing'. In his second letter on the subject (29 April), Polikarpov stressed the need for an elite evaluation after closed rehearsals (*posle . . . obsuzhdeniia zakrytogo spektaklia*). In June 1961 the secretariat of the Composers' Union, having read the new libretto and score, supported production.[46] On 24 December Khrennikov wrote to Ilychev, secretary of the Central Committee's ideological commission, giving his impressions of the new version of *Lady Macbeth* (*Katerina Izmailova*) after closed rehearsals at the Stanislavsky–Nemirovich–Danchenko Theatre. Praise had been unanimous for realistic characters showing the dark, ugly side of the old feudal-merchant Russia. Some naturalistic elements remained and were criticized. No mention was made of the musical score. In January 1963, after a further gap of twelve months, Ilychev wrote to Furtseva recommending production after 'objectionable elements are removed' from the opera (Shostakovich's agreement having already been obtained). In view of the complexity of the issues, Ilychev advised that production be confined to five or six opera theatres with the necessary creative resources.[47]

Shostakovich attended rehearsals of *Katerina Izmailova*, op. 114,[48] in Moscow, Riga, and London; in November 1963 he spent the best part of a month at Covent Garden, returning for the première on 2 December. He forbade La Scala to use the first version, *Lady Macbeth*.[49] Even so, the revised version was regarded sceptically in the West as the product of political pressure; more than thirty productions of the 1932 version were performed in America and Europe from 1980 to June 1994. A programme note, signed 'NJ', for the 2001 production by English National Opera at the London Coliseum, retains the cold war perspective:

In order to make the work more acceptable to the Soviet authorities, Shostakovich made a second version of the opera between 1956 and 1963, and officially retitled it as *Katerina Izmailova* . . . He strenuously opposed in print the desire of Western opera houses to revert to any earlier sources for the opera . . . In the case of all the revisions, it is not clear what official pressure and censorship there might have been to account for his 'second thoughts'. With the aim of performing his true original intentions, we are using the text and the score of the first Russian production.

As we have seen from the Central Committee archive (RGANI), it is indeed clear that Shostakovich experienced protracted official pressure and censorship in arriving at a revised version. On the other hand, the phrase 'true original intentions' rubs up against the fact that Shostakovich had freely altered the published score from 1933 to 1935, well before Stalin's intervention. Professor Laurel E. Fay, having studied the different versions held in RGALI,[50] concluded that Shostakovich had made genuine improvements and knew it.[51] The continued flouting of Shostakovich's expressed instructions is inconsistent with such Western codes as *droit d'auteur* and reflects a strictly commercial attitude fairly widespread at the turn of the millennium, not only in Western opera companies but also in post-Soviet Russia: anything banned by Stalin is good box office. The ENO production of 2001, for example, transposed the story of Katerina Izmailova from nineteenth-century Russia to a never-never land where serfdom continues and a meat-packing factory could be privately owned, yet the police appear in bright red, 1930s-style uniforms—Nazi and Communist uniforms being the stock-in-trade not only of Western theatre designers but of Russian directors keen for success in the West (hence, for example, the anachronistic arrival of a chorus of Red Guards waving Little Red Books at the climax of Yuri Alexandrov's Kirov Opera production of Prokofiev's *Semyon Kotko*, seen at the London Coliseum in 2000).

Soon after Shostakovich's return from the United States[52] in 1959, this tense man, who typically sat with clenched, trembling hands pushed up under his chin, thick, horn-rimmed glasses having replaced the round lenses of the 1930s, was appointed first secretary of the Russian Republic Composers' Union—and was therefore required to join the Party for the first time in his life. At the 14 September 1960 open meeting of the Union, he mumbled his prepared text without lifting his eyes from the paper, except for one moment when he suddenly raised his voice dramatically: 'For everything good in me I am indebted to my parents.' Along with the speech came an article in *Pravda*, 'The Artist of our Time', in which he challenged Western critics who claimed that: 'Socialist aesthetics are mere dogmas violating the artist's creative personality... The history of music knows of no more dogmatic and barren system than the so-called dodecaphonic music. Based on mathematical calculations, artificially constructed, it has killed the soul of music—melody...' Likewise with pointillism, and electronic and concrete music. On the surface Shostakovich now totally embraced not only the guiding role of the Party but censorship as well: 'We do not conceal that we reject the right to fruitless formal experimentation, to the advocacy—in our art—of pessimism, scepticism, man-hating ideas'.[53] Listing Western composers, he approved some[54] but condemned others, including Stravinsky. Yet, according to Laurel E. Fay, the archives show that Karlheinz Stockhausen, after being singled out in one of Shostakovich's speeches as 'the archrepresentative of decadent capitalist culture', received a private letter from the composer professing admiration and encouraging him to visit the USSR.[55]

In May 1962 Shostakovich was elected to the Supreme Soviet, but his new position was no guarantee of artistic acceptance in a rapidly deteriorating cultural climate. Overjoyed when he read the young Yevgeni Yevtushenko's poem, 'Babiy Yar', which broke new ground by confronting the mass shootings of Jews (as well as non-Jews) in Kiev during the Nazi occupation, 'a poem which astounded me', Shostakovich completed a cantata on 'Babiy Yar' and went on to extend it into a five-movement symphony, his Thirteenth, set to five Yevtushenko poems, scored for bass soloist, bass chorus, and full orchestra. Shostakovich had always been attracted by Jewish folk music and disgusted by his fellow-Russians' endemic anti-Semitism.

Jews became a symbol to me. All of man's defencelessness was concentrated in them. After the war I tried to convey that feeling in my music. It was a bad time for Jews then. In fact it is always a bad time for them...And if they saw a Jew with military decorations, they called after him, 'Kike, where did you buy the medals?' That's when I wrote the Violin Concerto, the Jewish Cycle [based on Jewish folk poetry], and the Fourth Quartet. None of these works could be performed then. They were heard only after Stalin's death.[56]

Yevtushenko recalled visiting Shostakovich's house on Nezhdanova Street, the composer very nervously playing the piano with a damaged hand and singing in a strange, tinkling voice, as if something was broken inside—yet singing wonderfully.[57] The first movement is a requiem for the Jews shot in Kiev in 1941; then comes 'Humour', followed by 'In the Shop', which tells how Russian women waste their lives queuing for food. The next poem, 'Fears,' evokes the Stalin terror, and the last, 'Career', affirms that careers are made by those who raise their voices and sacrifice themselves. Due to be performed by the Moscow State Symphony Orchestra, the event ran counter to Khrushchev's insistence that there was no Jewish question in the Soviet Union. Kirill Kondrashin bravely stepped in as conductor at a late hour after the conductor most familiar with Shostakovich's work, E. Mavrinsky, withdrew with cold feet.[58] One lead singer dropped out, intimidated, then attempts were made to sabotage the opening performance. Vishnevskaya and Ashkenazy recall that the Party pressured the bass soloist who appeared in all movements, Nechiplaylo, to declare himself ill. Kondrashin recalls how he was telephoned by Georgi Popov, Minister of Culture of the Russian Republic: 'Is there anything that might prevent you conducting tonight?' Then: 'Tell me your expert opinion, can the symphony be performed without the first movement?'[59]

Some of this was leaked to foreign correspondents, providing a new scandal in the Soviet arts exactly contemporaneous with Khrushchev's boorish blundering at the Manezh Gallery (see Chapter 21). Boris Schwarz offered an eye-witness description of the first night:

> The city was buzzing with rumours of a possible last-minute cancellation of the performance . . . the government box remained unoccupied, and a planned television transmission did not take place . . . the entire square [had been] cordoned off by the police. Inside, the hall was filled to overflowing . . . The tension was unbearable. The first movement, *Babiy Yar*, was greeted with a burst of spontaneous applause. At the end of the hour-long work, there was an ovation rarely witnessed. On the stage was Shostakovich, shy and awkward, bowing stiffly. He was joined by Yevtushenko, moving with the ease of a born actor.[60]

The following morning *Pravda* carried a report only one sentence long. 'Attack on Anti-Semitism in Shostakovich Symphony,' announced the *Herald Tribune* (17 December 1962). Schwarz rushed to the Composers' Union in search of a score or a piano reduction, but was met with 'evasive excuses'. After the second rendition on 20 December, all further performances were cancelled. No reviews appeared in the Moscow press. Shostakovich was angry and caustic in mocking the 'hypocrites' who attacked Yevtushenko's verses, muttering 'tut tut' (*gy gy*) about the young poet's deliberate misuse of the hallowed stock-phrase *da slavitsia*, meaning 'all glory to' [Lenin, Stalin, the motherland, etc.] when he applied it to humour: 'All glory to humour!'[61] But Shostakovich was taken aback and expressed dismay to Kondrashin when Yevtushenko published a revised version of 'Babiy Yar' in *Literaturnaia gazeta*, twice as long, with new lines about the role of the Russian people and the Party. 'What am I to do about it? If I set the new version to music, I will have to change the whole symphony.' According to Shostakovich's Soviet biographer, S. M. Khentova, these changes in Yevtushenko's text threatened the integrity of Shostakovich's composition and he felt able to change only a few lines. There were two performances of this version in Moscow in February 1963, then in Minsk with the old text, with further performances in Gorky, Novosibirsk, and Leningrad in 1965–6.[62]

Khentova comments that the mixture of opera, oratorio, and symphony in the Thirteenth was to influence composers of the younger generation keen to develop hybrid forms in opera, ballet, and chamber music. Unfortunately Khentova regularly buries her head in the political sand, resorting to euphemisms like 'in the difficult years'—*v trudnye gody*—although she does point up Shostakovich's desire 'to guard the world from the recidivists of fascism in whatever form they might appear'.[63] Khentova manages not to mention that Mavrinsky dropped out as conductor of the Thirteenth from sheer fear of the political consequences, or the intimidation of the singers, or Party pressure to cancel the entire production. Khentova describes the composer as actively helping with performances in the regions, in 'disseminating the symphony', but does not mention how few performances actually took place.

Given the rising agitation in the West on behalf of Soviet Jewry, the episode became a cold war gem. When Rostropovich went on tour he smuggled the score to Eugene Normandy, conductor of the Philadelphia Orchestra. But Shostakovich himself remained a 'good Communist' and first secretary of the Russian Republic Composers' Union; he was quoted in *Pravda* (23 March 1963) as describing Khrushchev's harsh attacks on Yevtushenko, Nekrasov, Ehrenburg, and other artists as 'exceptionally benevolent . . . helping all of us to find the necessary direction in creativity . . . the firm Leninist position'. Western observers rushed to their telex machines. Cold war cultural conflict had reached a new pitch of fury following the U-2 spy plane crisis, the collapse of the Paris summit, civil war in the Congo, the Berlin wall, and the Cuba missile crisis.

His amanuensis, Solomon Volkov, recalls that Shostakovich observed the dissident movement of the 1960s 'with interest and sympathy, but he could not join in . . . Shostakovich was a moralist . . . but he never had a political programme'. In 1966 the composer, along with Kornei Chukovsky, Konstantin Paustovsky, and Pyotr Kapitsa, signed a letter to the Central Committee demanding that Solzhenitsyn—unable to publish any of his novels after *One Day in the Life of Ivan Denisovich* (1962)—be accorded proper living conditions. Solzhenitsyn himself recalled that he could not hope to get the same names to sign his protest against Soviet armed intervention in Czechoslovakia two years later: 'The shackled genius Shostakovich would thrash about like a wounded thing, clasp himself with tightly folded arms so that his fingers could not hold a pen.'[64] According to Volkov, Shostakovich's attitude to Solzhenitsyn was 'ambivalent':

He thought highly of him as a writer, and felt that his life had been extraordinarily courageous. But he also felt that Solzhenitsyn was creating an image of 'luminary' for himself, aspiring to be a new Russian saint. This ambivalence was reflected in two of his compositions, which appeared one after the other following Solzhenitsyn's expulsion to the West in 1974. In the vocal suite on the poems of Michelangelo, Shostakovich uses the poet's angry lines about the expulsion of Dante from Florence to address Solzhenitsyn with poignant music. And then appears the satiric section called 'Luminary' written to the parodying words of Dostoievsky in *The Possessed*.[65]

On 21 August 1973, the fifth anniversary of the occupation of Czechoslovakia, another large thorn in the Kremlin's flesh, the nuclear physicist and civil libertarian Andrei Sakharov gave what Solzhenitsyn called 'a breathtakingly candid and hard-hitting press conference on international problems.' Sakharov described the USSR as 'one great concentration camp, one great restricted area'. In the *Pravda* edition of 3 September, Shostakovich signed a joint letter of eminent composers and musicians, including Khrennikov, Kabalevsky, and Khachaturian, wholly associating themselves with their colleagues in the USSR Academy of Sciences in condemning Sakharov under the title 'He disgraces the calling of a citizen'—*Pozorit zvanie grazhdanina*. Reactionary Western elements were exploiting these anti-Soviet so-called 'revelations' (*otkroveniia*); by publishing his allegations in the Western press, Sakharov was a disgrace to the honour and dignity of the Soviet intelligentsia. Lydia Chukovskaya issued an open letter in defence of the physicist in which she commented that Shostakovich's signature 'demonstrates irrefutably that the Pushkinian question has been resolved forever: genius and villainy are compatible.' When Rostropovich expressed hurt surprise that Shostakovich could have done such a thing, the composer responded, 'Look, Slava, I never read these things on principle.' He is said to have told the theatre director Yuri Lyubimov, 'I'd sign anything even if they hand it to me upside down. All I want is to be left alone.'[66] Writing in 1979, the writer Andrey Bitov concluded that Shostakovich was not the first man to have run from a danger after it was past: 'I too was puzzled. How could he? Join up, become a deputy… allow himself to be decorated like a Christmas tree with Brezhnev-era awards, make official speeches, even sign things of a dubious nature.'[67]

Shostakovich is certainly a difficult figure to 'read'. Given his conflicting utterances, the pressure to conform set against his almost iconic status with the Soviet public and leadership, one may be inclined to interpret his excuses to friends about the Party-dictated letters he should not have signed as simultaneously reflections of a timid soul and indications of genuine discomfort—he did not turn his back on his young devotee Rostropovich as he fell under a black cloud. But Shostakovich was ambivalent in his allegiances:

hating Stalinism, he nevertheless valued the state patronage of the arts (not just of himself) and the sense of 'belonging' which went with it. He was attached to creative freedom but, unlike Solzhenitsyn, accepted the Party or some such centralizing power as both inevitable in Russia and perhaps necessary. It was all too easy for the Western intellectuals to play the harlequin, surfing on every passing wave of fashion. The flamboyant Western cornucopia of 'freedom' he found vulgar and alien. He was never an émigré-in-waiting. The American ethos was not for him. While admiring the Vienna school of his youth and Stravinsky, he remained attached to his Russian heritage, desiring only a more intelligent and expanded version of it than Stalin, Zhdanov, and Khrennikov were willing to grant.

⊞ ⊞ ⊞

Shostakovich died in August 1975. His often mordant 'autobiography', *Testimony*, dictated to Solomon Volkov in a series of tape-recorded interviews, was to become the subject of a bitter cold war controversy before and after its publication in the West. It was Volkov[68] who brought order to the material:

> Gradually, I shaped this great array of reminiscence into arbitrary parts and had them typed. Shostakvich read and signed each part.

> It was clear to both of us that this final text could not be published in the USSR; several attempts I made in that direction ended in failure. I took measures to get the manuscript to the West.[69]

The manuscript had reached the West by 1974, a year before the composer's death and two years before Volkov was granted permission to leave for New York, where he became a research associate of the Russian Institute at Columbia University. Volkov deposited the signed pages in a Swiss Bank, as he tells it. Harper & Row undertook publication. But are these memoirs genuine? This question became a lively issue in the cultural cold war when the All-Union Agency for Authorial Rights (VAAP) brought legal pressure on Harper & Row to abandon publication. A partial dossier of exchanges was published in *Literaturnaia gazeta* (14 November 1979). Six Soviet composers (who paraded their academic credentials and state prizes, etc.) signed an indignant letter, in their capacity as former pupils and close devotees of the master. They had read with 'pain and indignation' (*s bol'iu i vozmushcheniem*) the book *Testimony*, purporting to be Shostakovich's memoirs, but in reality the work of the besmirched hands of a certain S. Volkov. This book, they insisted, had nothing in common with the authentic live memories of D. D. Shostakovich.[70] Yes, admittedly, the great composer had suffered; the attacks on the opera *Lady Macbeth* and the ballet *Limpid Stream*, followed by the criticisms of 1948, all this had amounted to a bitter experience for Shostakovich. 'However, we know that this delicate and easily wounded man possessed iron steadfastness. Again and again he sustained unfounded (*neobosnovannye*) accusations in a manly manner and maintained his integrity and grandeur.' What is more, the Central Committee in 1958 had withdrawn the accusations of formalism as unfounded and unjustified, so why should he nurse a grievance?

A long editorial article in the same edition of *Literaturnaia gazeta*, headlined with the single word 'Bedbug' (*Klop*), as in Mayakovsky's play, described Volkov as a 'deserter/turncoat' (*perebezhchik*) who impertinently claimed to have become Shostakovich's spiritual confessor and biographical confidant. Volkov was accused of depicting Shostakovich as an envious misanthropist, vilifying his colleagues with unconcealed malice: Prokofiev, Glière, Mayakovsky, Mravinsky, Stanislavky, Rolland, Shaw, Feuchtwanger. Volkov also portrayed him as anti-Soviet and a double-dealer (*dvurushnik*). 'Dmitri Shostakovich was never like that.' The editorial listed all of the composer's foreign awards and honorary degrees, as well as his Soviet ones, as if this pile of metal and parchment put the matter beyond doubt; how could this wholly artistic, Communist citizen be the 'evil petty spirit' (*melkii bes*) presented by Volkov?[71]

Turning to the Western reception for *Testimony*, *Literaturnaia gazeta* pointed out that even Harold Schonberg, music critic of the *New York Times*, had asked whether these were really the words of Shostakovich:[72] 'We have to take his [Volkov's] word on trust but this will not satisfy the majority of musicologists and historians and irritates many of us who require proof.' *Literaturnaia gazeta* also quoted the BBC (no specific programme was cited): 'At any given moment it is difficult to say how much belongs to Shostakovich and how much to Volkov.'

The editorial then focused on the question of copyright and the legality of Harper & Row's publication. Much was made of the American publishers' title-page formula, 'as related to Solomon Volkov and edited by him'.

The publishers have claimed that there are marks on the pages of the manuscript made by Shostakovich saying *chital'*—'I have read it'. What is easy to see on the pages are Volkov's dirty fingerprints, which are no doubt genuine. For a man who has distorted the whole life of the composer it would not be difficult to do something similar with his marks (*vizami*) as well.

Was *Literaturnaia gazeta* accusing the American publishers of deliberately promoting what they knew to be a forgery? The Soviet paper provided a summary of the legal exchanges leading up to publication, but the Central Committee archives now reveal significant lacunae in the Soviet account as published. Deliberately omitted was Shostakovich's young widow Irina's conversation on 22 November 1978 with two officials of VAAP, N. Kartsov and G. Krestova. The widow, an editor for a music publisher who became his second wife in 1962, explained to VAAP that not long before his death Shostakovich had told his life story to Solomon Volkov; they met for two hours at a time on four occasions. Several days after the work was finished, Volkov applied to emigrate. At her husband's request she personally telephoned Volkov and asked him to return the manuscript. He refused, claiming that his notes had already been sent abroad. She threatened to make his departure difficult. Now, in discussion with VAAP, Irina Shostakovich was asked why she had not requested help at that time (i.e. three or four years previously). Her replies, as reported in the Central Committee memorandum, were vague and contradictory: 'Everyone knew about it. I don't see any reason to worry. The book can contain only the authorized statements (*avtorizovannye vyskazyvaniia*) which Shostakovich signed. We only want to sue to make sure the American publisher doesn't add anything.'[73]

Volkov's version of how he and Shostakovich collaborated on the memoirs is incompatible with Irina Shostakovich's. Volkov claimed that the work began in the composer's cottage near Leningrad—this 'dragged out our work'—then things went more smoothly after Volkov moved to Moscow in 1972, with an office (he worked for *Sovetskaia muzyka*) located in the building where Shostakovich lived. 'And the exhausting hours of cautious exploration would begin.' This cannot be reconciled with Irina's too-neat 'four occasions for two hours'. While it seems to be agreed that Volkov applied to leave the USSR as soon as the manuscript was complete, he insisted that Shostakovich had consented to the manuscript being sent to the West— rather than demanding its return, as Irina claimed. According to Volkov, Shostakovich invited him home and repeated that nothing must be published until after his death: he then inscribed a photograph showing the bearded Volkov seated beside the composer and Irina: 'To dear Solomon Moiseyevich Volkov with affection, D. Shostakovich, 13.XI.74.' Then, as Volkov was about to leave, he added a few words: 'A reminder of our conversations about Glazunov, Zoshchenko, Meyerhold. D. S.' The photograph is reproduced in the book; it scarcely seems compatible with Irina's claim that Shostakovich demanded the return of the manuscript. Yet another picture shows Volkov, hugely bearded, close to the open coffin at the composer's funeral—can this be reconciled with Irina's claim that she had 'threatened to make his departure difficult'?

If Shostakovich had really demanded the return of the material; if Irina had threatened Volkov; if she was really alarmed, as wife and then as widow, why was Volkov granted his exit visa? The implication must be that she was not alarmed; that she shared her late husband's willingness to let Volkov go ahead after his death; and that she began to feel the heat only three years later, in 1978. What remains a puzzle is how and why the Party allowed Volkov to emigrate if, as he claimed rather cursorily in the preface to *Testimony*, he had already made 'several attempts'[74] while Shostakovich was still alive to find a publisher in the USSR. Surely the hounds would have been out to prevent this Jew from leaving the Soviet Union at the height of the international storm over the right to emigrate?

It seems clear that in December 1978 Shostakovich's widow and two children were pushed by the Soviet authorities to write to Robert Bench, of Harper & Row (13 December), demanding the full text, the proposed title, the length of the book, and an expert's report on the authenticity of the manuscript. The Central Committee issued a statement the following day, 14 December, 'On Measures for the Propagation and Protection of the Creative Inheritance of D. D. Shostakovich', alleging that the American publishers intended to give the book an anti-Soviet character. The Central Committee also announced publication of Shostakovich's collected work in 42 volumes, of which the first three were on their way.[75]

In their book *Shostakovich Reconsidered* (1998), a stout defence of *Testimony*, Allan B. Ho and D. Feofanov make much of a recent study, A. V. Bogdanova's *Muzyka i vlast'* (*Music and the Regime*, 1995),[76] which cites this Central Committee memorandum, 'On Measures...', to confirm that the Party knew perfectly well that *Testimony* was genuine. But the memorandum is inconclusive, even if the following threat could be construed as evidence of a cynical manoeuvre: '...it is suggested, through the Soviet and foreign organs of mass media, to describe the publication as an anti-Soviet forgery, discrediting the name of the great composer.' A reading of the memorandum suggests that the Party was already preparing a rather desperate defence, judging by the feeble quality of the 'proofs' (*dokazatel'stv*) of Shostakovich's 'real' opinions wheeled out by F. Shauro, an official of the Central Committee's culture department. These 'proofs' evidently amounted to two recorded statements, one referring to the patriotism of Soviet composers, the other discussing his trip to the Edinburgh Festival in 1962 and 'critical of the capitalist way of life'.[77] This may be a reference to his complaint that, while he quite liked Lady Rosebury, a powerful patron of the Edinburgh musical festival, who attended all his concerts, he was less than pleased when she insisted on showing him her vast estate with its maids, butlers, and gillies.[78]

Regrettably, Volkov's preface to *Testimony*, written in June 1979, makes no mention of the manuscript's contested authenticity, its copyright status, or the several written protests from the composer's family and VAAP.

In a speech to the Sixth Congress of Composers, published in *Sovetskaia kul'tura* (23 November 1979), Tikhon Khrennikov, so loathed, despised, and defamed by Shostakovich in *Testimony*, called the book a 'vile falsification'. The few remaining friends of the Soviet Union in the West—they no longer included Western Europe's Eurocommunists—rallied to the Moscow line. David Bonoksy responded to *Testimony* in the Communist West Coast *Daily World* (10 November 1979) under the title 'Defaming the Memory of a Russian Composer', claiming that Volkov's book was 'a lie from beginning to end'. The Soviet establishment in the Brezhnev and Gorbachev eras remained determined to prove Volkov a liar and the book a forgery.[79]

Testimony has been published in twenty languages and praised by many musical celebrities, including Yehudi Menuhin and André Previn, but Western academic opinion was soon bitterly divided regarding the book's authenticity. In 1980 Laurel E. Fay, when still a graduate student, published a challenge to Volkov's integrity provocatively titled 'Shostakovich versus Volkov: Whose *Testimony?*',[80] in which she claimed to identify eight pages in *Testimony* as 'plagiarized' from Shostakovich's previously published articles.[81] Laurel Fay has not been alone in her scepticism. Christopher Norris commented on Shostakovich's alleged memoirs: 'They supply the same kind of retrospective slant on Shostakovich's life and music as Western ideologists have long been anxious to provide . . . every suggestive ambiguity is worked up into a more or less conscious gesture of private defiance . . . the memoirs are just too good to be true from an anti-Soviet propaganda viewpoint.' Norris added that the composer's distinguished son, Maxim Shostakovich, had 'decisively rejected Volkov's claims to authenticity'.[82] But Maxim, who left Russia permanently for the West in 1981, has proved a dubious ally for the sceptics; both he and his sister Galina can now be counted among Volkov's supporters.[83]

Laurel Fay's recent life of Shostakovich is more oblique in its criticism of Volkov; even if (she writes) the authenticity of *Testimony* were to be accepted, the embittered, 'death-bed' disclosures of someone ravaged by illness, with 'festering psychological wounds and scores to settle would furnish a poor source for the serious biographer'. This is a long way from accusing Volkov of concocting a cold war forgery. But she adds: 'Unfortunately, Volkov was not forthright about the nature of the manuscript and its authenticity was never properly vetted. Whether *Testimony* faithfully reproduces Shostakovich's confidences, and his alone, in a form and context he would have recognized and approved for publication, remains doubtful.'[84]

Although Elizabeth Wilson's *Shostakovich: A Life Remembered* depends heavily on interview material and memoirs, no interview with Volkov appears in her pages. She quotes from *Testimony* frequently but never tackles head-on the issue of its authenticity.[85] The personalities she quotes (Rostropovich for example) do not so much doubt Volkov's integrity as Shostakovich's own erratic reliability when into his storytelling stride. The most exhaustive claim for the authenticity and transparency of *Testimony* can be found in Ho and Feofanov's book,[86] partly based on 'hundreds of hours of face-to-face and 'phone conversations in 1993–97' with Volkov himself. Volkov remains adamant that *Testimony* was the result of 'dozens of meetings with Shostakovich over the four-year period of 1971–74'.[87] Clearly the grave of the greatest of Soviet composers retains a full orchestra.

All That Jazz:
Iron Curtain Calls

Like the nuclear arms race, classical music was two-way traffic; the Russians arguably possessed classical composers able to inspire larger audiences than the major modernists of the West. This was not the case in the field of popular music and entertainment. The Russians regularly exported spectacular folk- dancing ensembles, the Red Army Choir, and circus acrobats, but the balalaika was no match for the 25-watt electric guitar, the synchronized stamping of a hundred boots no match for a 100-watt PA system. If Western youths wanted balalaikas they could have them—but they didn't. Jazz, swing, twist, rock, beat, and disco were simply what the people—above all the young people—wanted, East and West; the USSR did not lack fine popular musicians, but the Party scowled, growled, punished, and banned these 'foreign' sounds. In the 1930s and 1940s few political leaders regarded young adults and teenagers as a potentially powerful social force, but by the mid-fifties a generation revolution was occurring, and by the 1960s the Politburos and Komsomols of the Soviet constellation were attempting to erect new iron curtains against the sound waves from the Beatles and the Rolling Stones. It was one-way traffic; propelled by a huge demand, this 'sound of capitalism' deafened and defeated the elderly guardians of Soviet culture, the Stalingrad generation, as in no other field of performance art.

The first wave of jazz in the USSR ran from the 1920s to the assimilation of big-band swing music—with its analogous implication of sexual emancipation and individual expression—in the 1940s. The Soviet Union's first authentic experience of jazz (*dzhaz*) was probably the six-month-long tour by Sidney Bechet's sextet in 1925. Russian musicians began to imitate the Negro jazz idiom in some of their compositions, and its influence showed in the work of classical composers like the young Shostakovich. But hostility to jazz—as well as appreciation—had a history extending back to the early years of the Revolution. According to Lunacharsky, commissar for Public Enlightenment, jazz was a capitalist plot to make man live through his sexual organs and forget class struggle. Maxim Gorky's essay 'Music For the Gross' was hostile. In 1929 the Association of Proletarian Musicians succeeded in getting jazz banned as 'a product of bourgeois decadence'. However, in 1932 the APM was dissolved and jazz was allowed back, along with modern ballroom dancing. In 1938 a State Jazz Band of the USSR was created, bringing together the best instrumentalists, but it was more of a light concert orchestra in the Paul Whiteman mode than real jazz. Early in the war it was renamed the State Concert Ensemble.[1] 'Variously tolerated and ruthlessly condemned by Communist leaders, big-band jazz was a living alternative to collectivized puritanism and organized xenophobia',[2] writes S. Frederick Starr, who reports that when the Bessarabian city of Kishinev was liberated in 1943, and again after the capture of Bucharest in 1944, Shiko Aranov's jazz orchestra took part in the celebrations. When Cracow was liberated, a Soviet *dzhaz* band gave a concert during which Glenn Miller's 'Chattanooga Choo-Choo' was performed repeatedly.[3] A Red Army jazz orchestra marked the liberation of Prague in May 1945 by performing the Glenn Miller piece, as well as 'In the Mood' and other tunes from the film *Sun Valley Serenade*. The young Czech jazz enthusiast Josef Škvorecký was fascinated by this film, which the Red Army brought to Czechoslovakia, with Russian subtitles, the print 'badly mangled by frequent screenings at the battle front'. He naively believed that the age of jazz had arrived. During Moscow's VE celebrations, on 9 May, Leonid Utesov's State Jazz Orchestra of the USSR performed from the bandstand in Sverdlovsk Square.[4]

So far so good! Then came the anti-Western clamp-down. In November 1946 Eddie Rosner, a dapper German Jew, born Adolph Rosner in 1910 and a star of the Berlin jazz scene until forced to flee to Warsaw, then to the USSR, was arrested. A brilliant trumpeter (he could play two at a time), admired by Duke Ellington, widely considered second only to Louis Armstrong, and showered with gold while in favour, Rosner and his band had toured the Soviet Union during the war, on one occasion secretly observed and approved by Stalin himself. Attempting in 1946 to escape back to Poland without an exit visa, he was intercepted and incarcerated in the Lyubianka, where he was interrogated for months, persistent questions probing his American and 'cosmopolitan' connections. Accused of espionage (despite admirers in the Party and state security hierarchy), warned at the highest level that he must sign the required confession or risk death, he was shipped to the Kolyma gulag in 1947. Also arrested were A. G. Alekseev, prominent in the Moscow jazz scene, and the band-leader Leonid Piatigorsky, brother of the celebrated cellist, who served a ten-year sentence. Lidia Ruslanova, the most popular folk singer of the war years, was exiled on charges of illegal ties with America.[5] Josef Škvorecký commented acidly: 'During benign times [1935] a Soviet marshal [Voroshilov] swings to the call of the saxophones; during seasons of frost, a pioneer jazzman like Valentin Parnakh is arrested for exceeding the permitted percentage of syncopation, and perishes anonymously in the Gulag.' Eddie Rosner and his band arrived in the same gulag camp at the time Parnakh was dying there. It turned out that the camp commander used to listen to Rosner in the trenches and was a fan. He issued the band with instruments, which they played for five or six years, becoming a feudal court orchestra in the service of Alexander Derevenko, the grand duke of the entire camp system.[6]

The *New York Times* (2 February 1947) picked up an article in *Kul'tura i zhizn'*, organ of the Propaganda Commission of the Central Committee, reproving Soviet songwriters for slavish imitation of Tin Pan Alley and 'endless repetition of the vulgar themes of commercial beer-hall Bohemias'. The following day the *New York Times* latched on to the announcement in *Izvestiia* that a ban had been imposed on the tango, foxtrot, and blues dances in the clubs, factories, and parks of Vladivostock. The London *News Chronicle* (17 February) was intrigued by an article in the paper *Red Fleet* (*Krasnyi flot*), warning Soviet sailors to beware of vulgar Western music like 'Tipperary', 'There is a Tavern in the Town', and Lehar's 'Merry Widow'. (The first two had been taken up by the Red Army Choir towards the end of the war.) *Red Fleet* wanted to know why the Black Sea Choir had sung the music-hall ditty 'K-K-K-Katie', which was 'only capable of ruining the artistic taste of a Soviet audience'. In June 1947 Lev Oborin, pianist, reported on a five-week concert tour of the Soviet zone of Germany. 'They ask, "Is it true that jazz is banned in the Soviet Union? Is it true that dancing is not allowed in your country?" '[7] This was the time of the *Zhdanovshchina*; in line with Zhdanov's teaching, every choir song must be ideologically sound. But it was an uphill struggle: American songs, like American films, were simply winners. Harrison Salisbury reported that Russian officers were bringing American pop music records back from Berlin. 'They are sent back to Moscow and played over and over in young people's apartments and at young people's parties. Many times, walking the back streets of the Arbat and other old quarters in Moscow, I have heard American music coming from dingy rooms and flats.' Even very old records could fetch 23 roubles.[8]

Tikhon Khrennikov, secretary of the Union of Soviet Composers, organized a travelling inquisition, arriving in Prague and Budapest in 1949 to grade popular musicians. Soon after the Communists took power, a concert of 'model' jazz pieces took place in Prague. Beside Karel Vlach, 'greatest among Czech pioneers of swing', sat the Soviet visitors, Khachaturian and the 'gloomy, silent' Shostakovich. The Party proclaimed the creation of an official jazz band, the Youth Musical Ensemble, in which they tried to replace the saxophone (which can be learned rapidly) with the violoncello (which can take five years). As Škvorecký commented, jazz was no longer back again but 'back under again'.[9] Milan Kundera recalls the elimination of jazz in Communist Czechoslovakia:

No one had ever done a fraction as much for our folk art as the Communist government did. It devoted enormous funds to the setting up of ensembles. Folk music with violin and cymbalo resounded daily from the radio. The universities were inundated with Moravian and Slovak songs ... Not only did jazz disappear entirely from the face of the land but it became the symbol of Western capitalism and decadence. Young people stopped dancing the tango and boogie-woogie when they had a party or celebration. Instead they took each other round the shoulders and danced in a circle to the Slavonic chorovod.[10]

In the late forties music accounted for more than half of the broadcasting time of all Soviet internal radio stations, but central broadcasting allocated three times as much space to serious, or classical, music as to popular forms. The popular music broadcast consisted of choral songs, folk songs, operettas, and balalaika.[11] The State Jazz Orchestra became the State Variety Orchestra. Starr recalls that specific musical elements connoting *dzhaz* or jazziness also came under the ban: chords built on flattened fifths, vibrato by brass players, and the deliberate use of semitone 'blue notes' were all proscribed. The new piston-valve trumpets were banned; plucking a double-bass instead of bowing it could put the performer under suspicion. All saxophonists in the Radio Committee Orchestra were fired. On a particular day in 1949 every saxophonist in Moscow was required to bring his instrument to the State Variety Music Agency, where it was promptly confiscated. Identification papers were altered to remove any reference to the saxophone. The tenor saxophonist Yuri Rubanov emerged from the agency's office as a bassoonist, though he had never held a bassoon in his hand. The alto saxophonist Thomas Gervarkian became an oboist. At the Riga conservatory, Prokofiev's *Lieutenant Kizhe*, whose score called for a saxophone, was struck from the repertoire. Many jazz musicians were now in labour camps.[12] Jazz was designed to 'deafen the ears of the Marshallized world by means of epileptic loud-mouthed compositions'. In his excellent *Rock Around the Bloc*, Timothy Ryback reports how in East Germany the Communists played on the prejudice against 'Negermusik'; Professor Ernst Mayer, publisher of the journal *Musik und Gesellschaft*, equated American music with preparation for war.[13]

⊞ ⊞ ⊞

Eric Hobsbawm calls jazz 'the most serious musical contribution of the United States to world culture'. It had been 'discovered' as a serious art form by political radicals (notably John Hammond) committed to the joint cause of blacks and their music. Of all the plebeian city arts taken up by a secondary public, American black music had the greatest capacity to conquer far and wide.[14] Platoons of American jazzmen were touring Europe and Japan. Louis Armstrong received an enthusiastic reception in France during his 1948 tour. In 1949, by his own account, the band which took Miles Davis to Paris was the hit of the city's jazz festival: 'That's where I met Jean-Paul Sartre and Pablo Picasso and Juliette Greco.'[15] Armstrong's 1950 tour included a papal visit and earned him the formal thanks of the State Department. The US Armed Forces Network in Germany and Austria broadcast regular jazz and bebop programmes. By the late 1940s the US government and the Voice of America, which was beaming live broadcasts from 52nd Street, New York, had begun to equate the sound of jazz with the sound of freedom. A diatribe in the journal *Sovetskaia muzyka* (March–April 1948), by G. Shneerson, reflected Soviet hostility: 'Several times each evening propagandists from the Voice of America send us examples of American music, obviously in the full conviction that such musical additions to verbal propaganda on the idea of "Americanism" will attract a large number of listeners.' Highly popular was the programme 'Jazz Club USA', hosted by Leonard Feather; the title of his article for Hearst's *New York Journal American* (4 October 1952) was bound to further enrage the Russians: 'Let Hot Jazz Melt Joe's Iron Curtain.'

Victor Gorodinskii linked jazz to the American ruling class in his book *Music of Spiritual Poverty*; I. Nestiev's *Dollar Cacophany* adopted the same line (which Josef Škvorecký called 'fascistoid' and 'not very different from that of the Little Doctor [Goebbels] . . . '). Turning to jazz and 'convulsive boogie-woogie', Nestiev produced some anti-American quotes from the West, probably real, though no sources were given.[16] Taking up Commissar Lunacharsky's description of the 'erotic bye-bye' of modern dance music and jazz as a narcotic, a doping of the workers, a hypnotization of the will by machine rhythms, Gorodinskii called jazz 'Big Business Music'. The 'real' Negro musical culture (as Paul Robeson had recently explained in the pages of *Sovetskaia muzyka*)[17] was better represented by spirituals and blues, by Marian

Anderson, Roland Hayes, Robeson himself, and Ella Bella Davis. Commercial jazz was merely prostitution.[18] These words found their way into the *Great Soviet Encyclopaedia* (1952): 'Jazz is the product of the degeneration of the bourgeois culture of the USA.' Typical forms of jazz were said to be the foxtrot, one-step, Charleston, tango, blues, and rumba. Elements of a Negro musical tradition had been 'distorted and debased' (*iskazheny i oposhleny*) during the huge commercial expansion of jazz in America and Western Europe by radio and gramophone records, giving rise to mass-industrial standardized fashions in jazz dances and songs. The *Encyclopedia* quoted Gorky's essay 'Music For the Gross' (*Muzyka dlia tolstykh*), which had lamented 'the evolution from beautiful minuets and lively, passionate waltzes to the cynicism of the foxtrot and the convulsions of the Charleston, from Mozart and Beethoven to the Negro jazz bands, who are probably secretly laughing, because their white masters are evolving into the kind of barbarians that the Negroes have long left behind'.[19]

⌗ ⌗ ⌗

Paul Robeson was a man writ large, a demonic figure to Congressional committees and federal loyalty-security boards, a genuine Red on the Stalinist model as well as a genuine black radical. Born in 1898, the son of a Methodist minister who had once been a slave, the young Robeson emerged brilliantly from the segregated schools of Princeton, New Jersey, graduating Phi Beta Kappa from Rutgers (where he was also an All-American footballer). Columbia Law School granted him his LL.B in 1922, but his fine voice and charismatic stage presence lofted him into a theatrical career and the prime roles in *Othello* and Eugene O'Neill's *The Emperor Jones*. In Britain aristocrats competed to entertain him, Welsh miners invited him to sing at their galas, and he accompanied the Labour leader, Clement Attlee, to Spain where Robeson sang for Republican troops in his huge, gentle, cathedral-organ voice.

No evidence about Stalinism ever deflected him from his unqualified praise for the Soviet Union. A recipient of the Stalin Peace Prize, he was also honorary professor of the Moscow State Conservatory of Music. Although he informed HUAC in 1946 that he was not a Party member, he never deigned to answer that question again, insistently though it was repeated. Co-chairman of the Progressive Party, he supported the American Labor Party in New York, a large number of fronts, and a broad swathe of African decolonization movements. Vigilante groups began to agitate locally for the cancellation of his concerts by denying him civic venues. In April 1949 he was in Paris to attend the Congress of the World Partisans of Peace, alongside a galaxy of distinguished intellectuals including W. E. B. Du Bois, Louis Aragon, Pablo Picasso, Frédéric Joliot-Curie, J. D. Bernal, and Pietro Nenni. Robeson sang, then told the gathering that the wealth of America had been built

on the backs of the white workers from Europe . . . and on the backs of millions of blacks . . . And we shall not put up with any hysterical raving that urges us to make war on anyone . . . We shall not make war on the Soviet Union . . . It is unthinkable that American Negroes should go to war on behalf of those who have oppressed us for generations against a country which in one generation has raised our people to the full dignity of mankind.[20]

Amid the ensuing uproar in the American press, black leaders hastened to dissociate themselves from Robeson—who only three years earlier had been received by Truman in the White House. Whereas A. Philip Randolph was prepared to invite blacks to boycott the army so long as it practised segregation, Robeson's bold call to blacks not to fight the Soviet Union—and making the speech on foreign soil—was perceived as very different. Robeson travelled to Prague, where he was lavishly received, with extravagant receptions hosted by the country's highest dignitaries from President Gottwald down. The young jazz aficionado Josef Škvorecký reacted with disgust: . . . 'how we hated that black apostle who sang, of his own free will, at open-air concerts in Prague at a time when they were raising the Socialist leader Milada Horáková to the gallows,[21] the only woman ever to be executed for political reasons in Czechoslovakia by Czechs, and at a time when great Czech poets . . . were pining away in jails.'[22]

Robeson continued his Red Pilgrim's Progress to Warsaw, reaching Moscow on 4 June 1949, but without his accompanist Bruno Raikin, a white South African Jew to whom the Russians had refused a visa. The *New York Times* reported that Robeson was being received with 'greater acclaim than had been given in recent years to any United States visitor'. During a concert he dedicated the song 'Scandalize My Name' to the 'international bourgeois press'.

His biographer, Martin B. Duberman, reports that Robeson felt uneasiness about his inability to locate friends among Jewish performers and intellectuals. Solomon Mikhoels, the actor-director, film-star, and chairman of the Jewish Anti-Fascist Committee, whom Robeson had played host to when he visited New York in 1943 at the invitation of Albert Einstein, had been found brutally murdered on 13 January 1948, his body smashed (it later turned out) on Stalin's orders. It was officially put out that Mikhoels had been the victim of 'hooligans'.[23] The 'hooligans' promptly deleted his famous lullaby scene from the 1936 film *Circus*. They also closed the Yiddish Theatre. Many of the bandleaders, singers, and figures in the film industry arrested or demoted were Jews. And where was the Jewish poet Itsik Feffer? Unknown to Robeson, he had been arrested on 24 December 1948. As a result of Robeson's persistent inquiries, Feffer was produced at his hotel and, through mute gestures, signalled that the room was bugged. Writing notes while chatting harmlessly, Feffer indicated to Robeson that Mikhoels had been murdered by the secret police and other Jews were under arrest. Feffer drew a hand across his throat to indicate his own likely fate—three years later he was shot. How do we know these details? From whom?—it's not clear. Shostakovich, for example, offered a different version of this story:

Stalin pulled his usual base trick. Itsik Feffer invited Paul Robeson to dine with him in Moscow's most chic restaurant. Robeson arrived and was led to a private chamber... where the table was set with drinks and lavish *zakuski*. Feffer was sitting at the table, with several unknown men. Feffer was thin and pale and said little... Robeson went back to America, where he told everyone that the rumours about Feffer's arrest and death were nonsense and slander.[24]

To his credit, at his last Moscow concert Robeson stressed his respect for Mikhoels, Feffer, and the Jewish tradition. He then sang in Yiddish, to a hushed hall, 'Zog Nit Kaynmal', the Warsaw Ghetto resistance song, first reciting the words in Russian. When he finished, a moment's stunned silence was followed by a great burst of emotion, people with tears in their eyes coming up to the stage, calling out 'Pavel Vasil'evich!' and reaching out to touch him. Returning to the United States, he told a reporter from *Soviet Russia Today* that charges of anti-Semitism in the Western press failed to square with what he had encountered. To the end of his life he never criticized the USSR openly (and barely in private). 'Loves Soviet Best, Robeson Declares', ran a *New York Times* headline. 'An Undesirable Citizen', declared a Hearst newspapers editorial.[25] HUAC grabbed at such headlines in mid-July 1949, subpoening Robeson. In her nationally syndicated 'My Day' column, Eleanor Roosevelt condemned the singer for trying to line his people up 'on the Communist side of the political picture'.[26]

The most dramatic physical confrontation in post-war America took place shortly after the Moscow visit, at two Robeson concerts on 27 August and 4 September 1949, in the Lakeland area near Peekskill, a small town on the Hudson River some 40 miles from New York City. The inhabitants of Peekskill increasingly resented the annual summer influx of 30,000 New York Jews, and the regular arrival of Communists, many of them Jews or blacks, to hold conferences at Camp Beacon. Although Paul Robeson had held successful concerts at Peekskill for three years in succession, singing 'Ol' Man River' and 'Peat Bog Soldiers', cold war fever gripped the veterans when People's Artists Inc., a left-wing New York theatrical agency, announced a Robeson concert to raise funds for the Harlem chapter of the (Communist) Civil Rights Congress. Legionnaires surrounded the Lakeland area, barricaded the approach roads, threw stones, and burned chairs, platforms, and songbooks. The sponsors decided to hold the same concert a week later, with the aid of 3,000 security guards drawn from the ranks of the Red unions—fur workers, longshoremen, seamen armed with baseball-bats and tire irons. This time Governor Dewey ordered state troopers to guard the grounds. One thousand policemen were on hand, but the violence repeated itself. To shouts of 'niggers!' and 'kikes!', buses were attacked and cars stoned as far away as Yonkers. All accounts agree that while the state troopers did their best to curb the violence, the Westchester County police openly fraternized with the stone-throwing veterans.[27]

After the State Department withdrew his passport, Robeson went every year to Peace Arch Bridge, to sing to Canadian miners and lumber workers from one side of the border to the other. When HUAC again subpoenaed him in 1956, Robeson was sick, proud, stubborn, always willing to carry the leper's staff but hopelessly wedded to an obsolescent musical and discredited political culture. He told the Committee: 'In Russia I felt for the first time like a full human being. No color prejudice like in Washington.' When Representative Scherer asked him—perhaps forgetting that Robeson had been denied a passport—'Why do you not stay in Russia?', Robeson replied: 'Because... my people died to build this country, and I am going to stay here and have part of it just like you.' Asked about Soviet labour camps, he described them as places where 'only fascists' were held. Leaving a meeting, he told a reporter that the Hungarian revolution 'was brought about by the same sort of people who overthrew the Spanish Republican Government'.[28] To make HUAC smell good was a rare achievement.

In 1959, passport finally restored, Robeson carried his staff to England, although his old role of Othello was a tall order at the age of 61 after years away from the classical stage. The reviews were friendly but mixed; even Shakespeare had moved on. Robeson flew on to Moscow where he was mobbed by loving crowds, appeared live on television, and gave his first public concert in the USSR in nine years, with 18,000 people filling the Lenin Sports Stadium to hear him sing 'Moia shirokaia rodnaia strana' ('My Broad Native Land'), singing twice the refrain, 'I know no other land where people breathe so free', and opening his arms wide to the audience. There followed feasts the length and breadth of the USSR, including one with Khrushchev, Voroshilov, and Mikoyan in a hunting lodge in the hills above Yalta. The Hungarian leader Janos Kadar, a faithful servant of the Soviet suppression of the Hungarian revolution, shot the most birds. Four thousand people attended evensong in St Paul's Cathedral to hear Robeson's half-hour recital in aid of the South African defence fund—he was back with the broad British Left, which adored him but did not shoot birds.

⊞ ⊞ ⊞

According to Škvorecký, the Oratsov Puppet Theatre was thronged every night because the satire on Hollywood was accompanied by genuine American jazz records.[29] After the Great Helmsman's death, Charles E. Bohlen, American ambassador to the USSR, proposed a jazz programme specifically aimed at Soviet youth; in 1955 the Voice of America launched the landmark programme 'Music USA', hosted by Willis Conover, whose role is lauded by S. Frederick Starr: 'Over the next quarter-century this unassuming man from Buffalo, New York, was to be the single most influential ambassador of American jazz in the USSR and Eastern Europe.' By late 1955 'Music USA' was blaring out 'the staccato sounds of jazz piercing the shield of Soviet jamming far more successfully than a legato string section could have done'.[30]

What hesitantly emerged in the Soviet Union after Stalin was a jazz of spiritual resistance, with its own cults, rituals, and slang. American influences resurfaced: 'Gershwin Back in Soviet Favor.' 'Rhapsody in Blue', once condemned as musical claptrap, was performed by the Grand Symphony Radio Orchestra in Moscow's Hall of Columns. A week earlier (18 January 1955) *Le Monde* reported that the trumpeter Eddie Rosner, sent to the Kolyma gulag in 1947, was rehabilitated and had formed a new orchestra. 'Soviet Sweetens Tone On Some Types of Jazz', announced the *New York Times* (19 March), quoting *Komsomol'skaia pravda*. In fact Rosner's rehabilitation remained incomplete, although popularity and wealth once again flowed his way; the espionage accusation was withdrawn but not the charge of attempting to leave the country (in 1946) without a permit; as a Jew much admired in the West he remained suspect, and his attempts to go abroad were blocked despite invitations from the United States and a meeting with Benny Goodman in Moscow in 1962; not until 1973 did Rosner reach Berlin, where he died three years later.[31]

Successive correspondents of the *New York Times*, Harrison Salisbury and Clifford Daniel, admired a leading figure in the *estradnyi* (variety) theatre,

Leonid Utesov (regularly spelled 'Utyosov' by *NYT* writers), an Odessa Jew with an obvious, if cunningly disguised, love of American jazz. Salisbury, who was inclined to praise anything in which he detected American influence—these Russians desperately want to be like us if only they were allowed to be—claimed that Utesov reminded him of Eddie Cantor, George Jessel, and Al Jolson.[32] Clifton Daniel laid out 19 roubles of the paper's money and took himself to the Central House of Culture of the Railway Workers on Komsomol Square to attend a concert by 'the oldest and best-known popular music combination in the Soviet Union', Leonid Utesov's State Stage Orchestra. Here again one finds the American obsession with American models. This was the twenty-fifth anniversary of Utesov's orchestra—he was 'obviously as durable as Guy Lombardo':

His style of presentation is reminiscent of Fred Waring and His Pennsylvanians—with a touch of Kostelanetz...a man could think he was back in the Paramount on an evening in 1939, or standing around the bandstand of a Paul Whiteman jazz concert in the early Thirties. He even hears some of the same tunes. Although several American songs are played, only one is announced as being American: 'Brother, Can You Spare a Dime?' Utesov describes it as 'the song of the American unemployed'...and gives the title in English: 'Broder, Kan Yoo Spar e Daim?'[33]

The *Daily Telegraph* (21 May 1955) revealed that the Ministry of Culture was set to clamp down on 'illegal gramophone records' and home-made discs. This was to be done in 'a resolute and merciless manner, even if the offence is not specifically mentioned in the penal code'. People who made and sold such records were being denounced as morally unclean, dealers in 'spiv music, hooligan songs, pornographic verses and the abominable creations of White Russian émigrés'. The reporter claimed that the great majority of 'spiv songs' originated from the labour camps and were often directed against leading Government personalities and the régime in general.

Nevertheless liberalization continued. On 6 June 1955 the *New York Times* extensively reported, with obvious pleasure, an article in *Sovetskaia muzyka* by Isaak Dunaevskii, whom it introduced to American readers.[34] This Soviet artist had admitted that light music in the USSR was now twenty years behind the times—and clearly the 'times', though he could not say so, belonged to the United States of America. The thrust of Dunaevskii's polemic was against unnamed, zealous (*retivyi*) figures in the Union of Composers. The point of view long since holding sway declared that everything not derived from peasant songs was heretical and cosmopolitan.

At one time it seemed that jazz was forever banished (*izgnan*) from our music. The saxophone was anathematized, the accordion was stricken from the list of instruments which could be taught to the young in music schools, the foxtrot and tango vanished from everyday dances and were replaced by the dances of our great grandmothers. Is it really possible by banning measures to destroy the love of many people for good jazz music and jazz dances? And always, in such cases, jazz appears as a foreign dirty word (*pakost'*), an importation into our country... I cannot understand what harm to the Soviet situation may be caused by hearing good, beautiful, masterly executed jazz music.[35]

A report in the *Süddeutsche Zeitung* (20 June 1955) described how listeners in London could not believe their ears when Radio Moscow's 25m band suddenly came up with seven hours of American music, including dance music and jazz. Ralph Parker commented in the London *Daily Worker* (9 September) that, 'Russian taste in jazz seems to have settled down at the Benny Goodman level... The bands that play in about a dozen Moscow restaurants... are loud, brassy and energetic, belonging to the Paul White-man vintage.' The *Herald Tribune* (10 October) reported that the previous evening Moscow Radio had delivered its first all-American concert, including excerpts from Gershwin's *Porgy and Bess*.

⌗ ⌗ ⌗

Porgy and Bess[36] came, astonishingly, to Leningrad. In his ferocious attack on Western music, *Muzyka duchovnoi nishchety* (*Music of Spiritual Poverty*), V. Gorodinskii had little imagined that an American company would, only five years later, be bringing George Gershwin's popular opera to the USSR when he insisted that Negro elements in Gershwin's music were mere colouring, mere exoticism, and in no way expressing 'a living national idea' (a category which the Soviet critic mechanically transposed to the USA from the 'national' cultures of the USSR, and deemed essential). The opera *Porgy and Bess*, declared Gorodinskii, provided the clearest proof that Gershwin was using *négritude* (*negritianskoe*) as mere colouring. Gorodinskii admitted that this claim would astonish the many Soviet critics who had praised the opera. There was no point in denying Gershwin's abilities. Taken against the general background of modernism, and the anti-vocal, voice-destructive music of Hindemith or Krenek and their followers, Gershwin always created music for the human voice, music for singing; the dramatic transformation spiritualized in Clara's dying song was truly tragic. But, objected Gorodinskii, this was to ignore the 'Achilles heel' of the opera. 'The musical language of the American Negro and the musical language of American jazz are not only different, they are in principal hostile to one another, as must be the case when the clear and simple humanity of a national musical language is eccentrically distorted and absolutely deprived of realistic expression (*lishennaia realisticheskoi vyrazitel'nosti*) by salon-modernistic speech with its trivial artificiality.' Mixing the two modes had resulted in an eclectic work, lacking an organic interior unity. *Porgy and Bess* acquired a 'suite' quality, a vocal-orchestral pot-pourri—as with the sudden introduction of an operatic, long-since-worn-out 'Puccini-ism', which invariably appears as the composer endeavours to widen a little, with difficulty, the framework of the singing-dancing form. The underlying decadence of *Porgy and Bess* is seen in its harmonic structure, in the overflow of polytonal episodes, in dissonant combinations, artificial linearity in the choral episodes—and more![37]

When the Everyman Opera Company's production of *Porgy and Bess* reached Leningrad in December 1955, it was the first time since the Revolution that an American theatre troupe had performed in Russia. After touring the world for four years, the show had been sold out in West Berlin every night. The *New York Times* (22 December 1954) had reported from Belgrade: 'with charm and grace, members of the cast created a new perspective here for a communist-led people sensitive to reports of American race prejudice and exploitation.'[38] Happily, the writer Truman Capote accompanied the troupe to the USSR, and his book-length report, *The Muses are Heard* (1957), is rich in comic observation of the baffled mingling of good-will and mutual incomprehension.

The trip followed months of complicated negotiation between the Ministry of Culture and the producers, Robert Breen and Blevins Davis, of Everyman Opera. According to Capote, 'Everyman Opera had invited itself'. Breen had written to the Soviet premier, Marshal Bulganin, after the State Department refused to sponsor the visit despite its moral and financial support of *Porgy and Bess* over the years. 'The Russians stepped forward and offered to pick up the tab themselves.'[39]

Setting out from Berlin, the company of fifty-eight actors, seven backstage personnel, two conductors, 'assorted wives and office workers', six children and their schoolteacher, three dogs, and one psychiatrist, numbered ninety-four persons. Capote, whose travelling expenses were paid by the *New Yorker*, foresaw trouble at the end of the line. Compared with the Comédie française's Molière or Shakespeare from Stratford-upon-Avon, *Porgy and Bess* was dynamite, 'a test tube brimming with the kind of bacteria to which the present Russian regime is most allergic'. Two minuses: the show was extremely erotic; it was also God-fearing, stressing the necessity of faith in a world above the stars. It sang out loud that people could be happy with plenty of nothin'. On the positive side, 'despite its folkish accent on fun', the opera depicted the American Negro as an exploited race at the mercy of ruthless Southern whites, segregated and poverty-pinched in the ghetto of Catfish Row. This had to be a plus in the Union of Soviet Socialist Republics.

Two officials from the American Embassy in Moscow travelled to West Berlin to brief the players before their departure on 17 December 1955. One of them, Walter N. Walmsley, Jr., congratulated the company in advance: 'Since nothing happens in the Soviet Union that isn't planned, and since it is *planned* that you should have a success there, I feel perfectly safe in congratulating you now.' His colleague, Roy L. Lowry, added: 'Yes, there are some nice Russians. Very nice people. But they have a bad government. You must always bear in mind that their system of government is basically hostile to our own.' Whereupon a member of the cast, John McCurry, who played to perfection the villainous role of Crown, raised 'the big problem'. 'The big problem is, now what do we say when they ask us political stuff? I'm speaking of the Negro situation.' Mr Walmsley hesitated. 'You don't have to answer political questions . . . It's all dangerous ground. Treading on eggs.' Thus a free American actor was voluntarily delivering his right of free speech to his government, and being advised: say nothing. Jerry Laws, a legend in the company for his fighting quick temper, jumped to his feet, his body stiff with tension. 'Then how do we handle it? Should we answer the way it is? Tell the truth? Or do you want us to gloss it over?' Walmsley advised that the Russians didn't 'give a damn' about the Negro situation, except for propaganda purposes. He also warned that anything said by members of the company 'will be picked up by the American press and re-printed in your home-town newspapers'.[40] Willem Van Loon, a Russian-speaker handling publicity for Everyman Opera (and previously a theater officer for the American military occupation in post-war Bavaria, though Capote seemed unaware of it), interjected: 'The other day I had a couple of the cast taping an interview for the American Service stations here in Germany, and touching on this point, this racial question, I knew we had to be very, very careful, because of being so near to East Berlin and the possibility of our being monitored'. Mr Walmsley remarked drily that they were 'being monitored right now'. That terminated the discussion of the 'Negro question'.

At the Soviet border the astonished cast witnessed 'herds of women with shawl-wrapped heads . . . swinging picks, shovelling snow, pausing only to blow their noses into naked, raw-red hands'. Militia-men lounged about with hands stuffed into coat pockets. This didn't go down well with some ladies of the cast. One excited performer, Robin Joachim, promptly broke the rules by descending from the train with his camera. 'Now he was racing zigzag across the tracks, narrowly avoiding the wrathful swipe of a woman worker's shovel.'[41] An estimated one thousand Leningraders turned out to greet them at the station; the crowd stared at their exotic visitors 'with immense silence, an almost catatonic demeanour'.

Visiting the Maryinsky (Kirov) Theatre, the company found it chilly and some of the ladies began to shiver after being forced to leave their coats at the cloakroom—in Russia it was *nekul'turno* to enter a theatre, restaurant, or museum wearing a coat or wrap. The American ladies also felt overdressed: all eyes in the auditorium fixed on them. After the performance (Capote reported), even the ballerinas rolled their eyes and sighed as they gazed at the visitors' shoes, touched their dresses, rubbed silk and taffeta between their fingers.

The Ministry of Culture official delegated to look after the company—and to convey the outrage of hotel management and staff when they misbehaved—was a predictably dour fellow, Savchenko, whose favourite toast was: 'To the free exchange of culture between the artists of our countries. When the cannons are heard, the Muses are silent. When the cannons are silent, the Muses are heard.' On Sunday, Christmas Day, eleven members of the cast were bussed to Leningrad's Baptist Evangelical Church. Afterwards Capote found Miss Boggs sitting alone in the Astoria dining room, dabbing at her eyes, deeply moved by the experience. ' "I'm tore to pieces," she told me, her breasts heaving. "I've been going to church since I can walk, but I never felt Jesus like I felt Jesus today." ' The Russian pastor had invited the American visitors to render a spiritual. Afterwards the congregation, mainly elderly people, had stood up and waved white handkerchiefs in the air.[42]

The Russian orchestra in the pit had been contracted from Moscow's Stanislavsky Theatre, but the company brought its own conductor, Alexander Smallens, 'a Russian-born American who has made rather a life's work of *Porgy and Bess*, having maestroed its every incarnation, including the original 1935 production'. He described the Stanislavsky as the sixty-first orchestra under his command and the best of the lot: 'Superb musicians, a joy to work with. They love the score, and they have the tempo, the rhythm. All they need now is a little more the *mood*.'[43] A capacity audience of 2,300 gathered in the Leningrad Palace of Culture. Ambassador Charles E. Bohlen declined to wear a dinner jacket at the première, because 'No one wears them here'. Mrs Ira Gershwin and Mrs Sulzberger, consort to the publisher of the *New York Times*, were also talking clothes. The Greek-born Mrs C. L. Sulzberger felt that the Russians no longer had any excuse for dressing so drably. 'When we first came here, I felt sorry for them . . . I thought the way they dressed, the dreariness of it all, I imagined it was because they were terribly poor. But really, you know, that's not true. They look this way because they want to. They do it on purpose.' American journalists arrived in force.[44]

The two national anthems were played before the first performance, and the ballet master of the Leningrad Theatre spoke briefly in welcome. 'We know and cherish the works of such fine artists as Mark Twain, Walt Whitman, Harriet Beecher Stowe, Jack London and Paul Robeson. We appreciate the talents of George Gershwin, and that is why this meeting is so joyous.' According to Capote, Mrs Ira Gershwin later commented: 'I thought I'd faint when I heard the name Gershwin being lumped in with all those Communists.' It was soon clear to Capote that the audience did not fully understand the story line or where to applaud. Numbers which normally stirred acclaim were greeted by a puzzled silence. When a jazzy crap-game began on stage, the audience began whispering 'as though they were asking each other what it meant, those excited men tossing dice'. The whispering gathered momentum and turned into gasps, a tremor of shock, when Bess, making her initial appearance, hiked up her skirt to adjust her garter. Then 'Sportin' Life's witty, lascivious gyrations ignited fresh firecrackers of audible astonishment'. During the opening twenty minutes of Act 2 the audience was stunned by the sensuality. Crown attempts to rape Bess: 'He grips her to him, gropes her buttocks, her breasts; and ends with Bess raping him—she rips off his shirt, wraps her arms round and writhes, sizzles like bacon on a skillet: black-out. Areas of the audience suffered something of a blackout, too.'[45]

Reviews in the city's leading papers on 27 December were laudatory regarding the music and the performance, but *Vechernii Leningrad* made its political point: 'We, the Soviet spectators, realise the corrosive effect of the capitalistic system on the consciousness, the mentality and the moral outlook of a people oppressed by poverty.' Writing in *Smena* (*Change*), the critic U. Kovalyev found the 'astoundingly erotic colouring of some of the dancing scenes...unpleasant'. He suspected that this had less to do with Negro tradition than with one stemming from Broadway burlesques and revues. In the *New York Times* Welles Hangen reported that few in Leningrad understood the strange, 'happy dust' dispensed with such fiendish glee by Sportin' Life: 'Many actually thought that the little white packets were letters.' By the time the show ended its eleven-day run, 30,000 people had seen the fourteen performances. The troupe then left for the Moscow gala opening, where Khrushchev, Molotov, and Malenkov turned up to applaud.[46]

On one occasion, finding Leningrad's elite restaurant unduly subdued, and bored by the orchestra's respectable rhythms, five members of the *Porgy* company had commandeered the bandstand. The hotel musicians had no objection: 'They were all fans of American jazz, and one of them, a devotee of

Dizzy Gillespie, had accumulated a large record collection by listening to foreign broadcasts and recording the music on discs made from old X-ray plates.' As Junior Mignatt spat into a trumpet, banana-fingered Lorenzo Fuller struck piano chords, and Moses Lamar opened his sandpaper lungs, 'smiles broke out like an unfurling of flags, tables emptied on to the dance floor... couples rocked, swayed in each other's arms'.[47] The *New York Times* (3 February 1957) reported that American jazz, broadcast by the Voice of America, and relayed on Swedish and German short-wave stations, could be heard every night in the dormitories of Moscow University's thirty-seven-storey skyscraper. In 1956 the Polish Blue Jazz Band visited the Soviet Union. Some thirty jazz bands were invited to the World Youth Festival held in Moscow during July–August 1957. Scores of new jazz bands were surfacing throughout the USSR.[48] Sally Belfrage, who was living in Moscow, reckoned that the jazz wedge 'has long since passed the thin end. I found more fanatical jazz enthusiasm in Russia than anywhere else I've been. Almost everyone loved it, if only as an expression of resentment at the ban... They listened religiously every evening to the Voice of America jazz hour.'[49]

⌗　⌗　⌗

And not only jazz: 'I even had to learn rock 'n' roll in Moscow', Belfrage added, 'because I could hardly go to any young person's house without finding everyone doing it, or playing it, or at least discussing it.' Typical American headlines now pointed up 'Presley Records a Craze in Soviet. Soviet Youth Said to Show Hunger for Things Foreign, Especially American.' Recordings of Elvis cut on discarded hospital X-ray plates were selling in Leningrad for fifty roubles ($12.50) each.

This was the latest craze of the *stiliagi* ('style-hunters' or zoot-suiters), many of whom grew sideburns and sported long, combed-back, Presley-like pompadours—the curling irons often left burns on their necks. Soviet youngsters began bidding each other farewell with the words 'See ya later alligator' (from the Bill Haley song). 'Love Potion Number 9' and 'Tutti Frutti' were blasting out of apartments. The cult divided between *shtatniki* ('Americans', who adhered to the zoot suit and the big band) and *bitniki* (proto-hippies in jeans and sweaters, who preferred 'beat' or rock music).[50] Conservatives reacted with hostility: addressing the 1957 Congress of Soviet Composers, former *Pravda* editor Shepilov warned of 'wild cave-man orgies' and the 'explosion of basic instincts and sexual urges'.

Disregarding their own domestic anxieties about Mods and Rockers, the new generation of working-class 'rebels without a cause', Western newspapers carried numerous reports about zoot-suited youths loitering in the area of Gorky Street, wearing long jackets, broad shoulders, and narrow trousers, who disdained work, hung around foreigners, and loved imported music. These *stiliagi*, who were periodically rounded up as parasites and had their long hair shorn, spoke in slang about 'dudes', 'chicks', and 'groovy'. The true test was to crash a restaurant reserved for foreigners. This required the right clothes, a foreign language, and a lot of hard currency. Some gambled on billiards at the Moskva Hotel, while others gravitated to the black market operating near the National Hotel in Stoleshnikov Alley. The stretch of Gorky Street between Pushkin Square and the Hotel Moskva became known as 'Broadway'. On Saturdays and Sundays they hung about the Cocktail Hall, which remained open, astonishingly, to 5 a.m. Another hangout was the Dynamo ice-rink, where you could skate to jazz, moving against the flow and menacing the regular couples. This was the time when Bill Haley, a country-and-western singer turned rock'n'roller on the Decca label, was all the rage[51] ('Rock Around the Clock', 'See you later, Alligator'), while the crooners worshipped Robertino Loretti, an Italian teenager who sang sentimental pop songs in a piercing falsetto. Western commentators, meanwhile, had been eagerly speculating about the impact of foreign music and clothes on Soviet youth culture. Allen Kassof's 'Youth vs the Regime: Conflict in Values,' published in the USIA's *Problems of Communism*, and clearly intended to counter the impact of the 1957 Moscow Youth Festival, drew attention to the spread of *bezdel'nichestvo* (laziness) among the work-shy and the *stiliagi*. *Problems of Communism* reprinted a *Krokodil* cartoon in which the Enthusiast leads the class in the slogan *Vse, kak odin, poedem na tselinu!*—'All, as one, let us go to the virgin lands!' In the second frame he leads with the slogan, *Vse, kak odin, poedem na novostroiki!*—All, as one, let us go to the construction sites!' In the third frame everyone else has left and the Enthusiast cunningly remains behind, on his own: *Odin ne kak vse*—One is not like all.'[52]

Robert Conquest noted that an article published in *Sovetskaia iustitsiia* (*Soviet Justice*, September 1958) during the music-purification drive revealed that 'it is already a punishable offence to produce "home-made records of a criminally-hooligan trend" '. This trade in illicit records was also described in a long letter in *Komsomol'skaia pravda* (15 October 1958), headed 'Melodies in Short Supply', which described how X-ray plates were peddled for exorbitant sums in Kuibyshev market.[53]

Nothing so inflamed Soviet puritanism as tangos, foxtrots, and the more urgent modern versions of sensual dancing. In Kiev, Komsomol patrols were trained to distinguish between acceptable popular music and *bugi-vugi*. Infiltrating restaurants and clubs, the worthy young Communists boogied with the rest, then confronted the musicians with the awful evidence. *Sovetskaia kul'tura* (9 April 1961) introduced eleven ballroom dances approved by the All-Union Conference of Ballroom Dancing. The Eastern bloc was constantly searching for ersatz alternatives to the genuine article, for example the East German 'Lipsi', combining two waltz steps to create a dance in 6/4 beat that assured continuous body contact but evidently gave the dancer a sensation reminiscent of the jitterbug. Ulbricht praised it, the Young Communists adopted it. On 2 January 1958, the East German Ministry of Justice and the Ministry of Finance issued an 'Ordinance for the Programming of Entertainment and Dance Music'. Sixty per cent of music performed in public must henceforth originate in the USSR, the GDR, or other Popular Democracies. The GDR's 'Zhdanov', Alexander Abusch, spoke of a *Kampfziel* or military target, an offensive to eradicate the jitterbug and boogie-woogie. Signs were posted banning couples from 'dancing apart'. The balladeer Wolf Biermann recalled the physical abuse suffered by those found to have committed the indecency of 'dancing apart'. In the Soviet Union *Komsomol'skaia pravda* (6 April 1962) attacked the twist and rock, citing dozens of cases in the West where the dancers 'obsessed and infuriated, have demolished the building where they have gathered, have broken windows and chairs, and, out in the streets, have staged riots'.[54] In his arresting study, *Moscow Graffiti*, John Bushnell explains that the twist was judged repellent because of its 'sexuality, its deliberate intimacy, its isolation from everyone and everything and its demonstrative contempt for social principles'.[55] But nothing could prevent teenagers dancing the shake, the monkey, and the jerk.

Nadezhda Nadezhdina, Art Director of the Beryozka Dance Ensemble, attempted to resist the tide: 'The twist and rock'n'roll have not become popular with our teenagers . . . the general trend of aesthetic education, the attitude to women, the concept of beauty, do not create the soil on which these dances can become popular.'[56] The Ministry of Culture was still attempting to promote alternatives; the Institute of Physical Culture came up with dances too contrived, complicated, and athletic.[57] A sardonic letter in *Komsomol'skaia pravda* (29 April 1964), from a dance teacher in Moscow recalled how the first new Soviet dances surfaced in 1959, under the title 'Eleven Unknown Dances'. They were heard on the radio, gramophone records appeared in shops, and the dances were promoted in the magazine *Muzykal'naia zhizn'*. But they never caught on: 'Let us be straightforward: to come up with American rock'n'roll inoculated by Russian heel-thumping and then to consecrate it to the Donets miners and call it the "Terrikon", does not amount to a choreographical miracle.' Quite the contrary, she concluded: it could only lead to fakery and pseudo-dances.

⌗ ⌗ ⌗

'Russia Said "Nyet" to Jazz At Forthcoming U.S. Fair'. Under criticism about the absence of jazz at the impending 1959 United States Fair in Moscow, the State Department blamed the Soviet veto. Attempts had failed to convince the Russians 'that cool combos with hot licks are a "definite", "genuine", "representative" part of American culture—to quote a few of the selling terms unsuccessfully applied.' The Department went so far as to arrange a visit by Soviet officials in New York to hear Duke Ellington, *West Side Story*, and a jazz recording session laid on by the music critic Marshall Stearns. But Moscow's answer was still *'nyet'*. 'Not only that, the grounds for turning down the Jerome Robbins composition, *Ballets U.S.A.*, a hit at the Brussels World Fair, appeared to be that it was too jazzy or at least a departure from standard ballet.' But why did the Russians say no to jazz at the US Exhibition? Jazz, after all, was now officially OK. The Central Committee's internal memorandum on reasons for rejecting the American proposal (January 1959) feared 'unhealthy agitation and the moral corruption of certain elements'.[58] The Soviet publishers who had translated and published *Oklahama!* were severely rebuked and fined for the grave error of judgement in a classified Central Committee report.[59]

Despite these Soviet obstacles, Benny Goodman had developed something of an obsession about playing in Russia. In 1955 he wrote to US Ambassador Charles Bohlen in Moscow: 'I sent records and had a lot of correspondence with various Russian and American officials. I now have a sheaf of letters and cables two inches thick. But I kept being put off.' In March 1961 Goodman 'set up' two visiting Soviet musicologists by inviting them to his dressing room in an East Side night club, with the *New York Times*'s Arthur Gelb on hand to write it all down. The visitors were Konstantin K. Savka, editor-in-chief of the State Music Publishing House, and Israil V. Nestiev, author of the notorious Stalinist diatribe, *Dollar Cacophany*, deputy editor of *Sovetskaia muzyka* and a fierce anti-modernist. Goodman asked them why his records could be obtained in Russia only through the black market and were usually played in secrecy. 'They say', the State Department interpreter interpreted, 'that these things take time. They ask if you have been in touch with the right people, and if it is known in the official places that you requested to come to Russia.' At this Goodman 'laughed a mirthless laugh'.[60]

In May 1962 Benny Goodman's 19-piece orchestra finally arrived in the Soviet Union under the cultural exchange agreement. After two years of hesitation, the Ministry of Culture had given a green light—the Russians regarded Goodman as more acceptable than the modern jazz musicians. The band's four blacks included the 50-year-old piano player Teddy Wilson and the vocalist Joya Sherrill, who said she had turned down a role in a Broadway musical to come. On 30 May, Goodman's fifty-third birthday, Khrushchev and other Soviet leaders attended the first concert in the Sports Palace of the Soviet Army, which was besieged by fans—5,000 in the hall and overflowing despite a 6 ruble top price compared to the Bolshoi Theatre's top of 3.30 roubles. Leading Soviet popular music men, including Leonid Utesov and Oleg Lundstrem, were there. So was Theodore Shabad of the *New York Times*: 'With Teddy Wilson at the piano, the group shook the hall with "Avalon", "Body and Soul", "Rose Room", "Stompin' at the Savoy" and "China Boy"...[Joya Sherrill] charmed her audience by appearing in a white strapless gown somewhat daring by Soviet standards.'

Portraits of the best-known American orchestra leaders were displayed on the stage, reported Shabad, 'as Mr Goodman indulged in his musical reminiscences. Judging by the applause, the favorites among the Russians appeared to rank in this order: Louis Armstrong and Duke Ellington in the top positions, with Glenn Miller, Dave Brubeck and Count Basie close behind in popularity.' Khrushchev, who brought his family and chuckled amiably to the American ambassador and his wife in the government box, nevertheless left at the interval, a sign of less than wholehearted approval. He sent diplomatically polite messages of appreciation to the performers. 'I enjoyed it', he said as he left the hall. 'I don't dance myself, so I don't understand these things too well.' But *Sovetskaia kul'tura* was friendly, describing Goodman as a genuine poet of the clarinet, and his orchestra as an ensemble of master virtuosos.

'One-Man Session by Goodman Attracts a Crowd in Red Square', announced the *New York Times*. Close to the Kremlin the King of Swing played 'Yankee Doodle Dandy' and 'Midnight in Moscow' on the clarinet. During the second week of the tour there was trouble at the Black Sea resort, Sochi, when the police prevented the band from handing out Benny Goodman buttons to the audience. In Tiflis a Georgian audience of 8,000 whistled their resentment as Joya Sherrill sang 'Katiusha' in Russian—which she had imagined would be a friendly thing to do—the same song (popular in the 1930s and the one which gave its name to Red Army rocket-launchers) having been a hit in Moscow and Sochi. The Tiflis audience applauded her next two numbers to make clear their point. 'They must really hate the Russians', she said afterwards. Later Sherrill brought the house down in Leningrad's Winter Stadium with a jazz rendition of 'Katiusha' and a throaty, drawled '*spasibo bol'shoe*' ('huge thanks'). The tour ended in Moscow's Sports Palace. Goodman reckoned the Soviet authorities had harvested half a million dollars at the box office, incurring expenses of only $60,000–70,000. When the band reached New York, the trumpeter John Frosk publicly complained that they should have played 'more modernistic arrangements' and 'good modern music'—Goodman had been too cautious, believing Russian audiences would prefer his old Carnegie Hall stuff of the 1930s.[61] According to Škvorecký, two native-born American Communists, Charles E. Smith and Mike Gold, had come up with a radical distinction between Judeo-Negro proletarian 'hot' jazz, as with early Dixieland or Duke Ellington, and sweet decadent bourgeois jazz loaded with sex (presumably Benny Goodman was included in this category?).[62]

At the end of 1962 a sharp reaction, closely associated with Khrushchev's own tastes, hit all the arts. The Soviet press condemned in retrospect a series of jazz concerts which had taken place during the autumn as displaying 'a reckless taste for foreign jazz'. In December, while paying his notorious visit to an art exhibition at the Manezh Gallery in Moscow, Khrushchev told his retinue: 'I don't like jazz. When I hear jazz, it's as if I had gas on the stomach. I used to think it was static when I heard it on the radio.' His diatribe rolled on into the Dance War: 'Or take these new dances which are so fashionable now. Some of them are completely improper. You wiggle a certain section of the anatomy, if you'll pardon the expression . . . Jazz comes from the Negroes. They've had it for a long time and here it's treated as a novelty. I understand our own Russian dances a lot better—Georgian and Armenian ones too.'[63] In March 1963, addressing the Plenum, Khrushchev castigated 'infatuation with the outlandish yowlings of various foreign—and not only foreign—jazz bands'. The thaw was over for the time being. The Moscow Jazz Club was now closed, the Dream Café in Kiev no longer engaged jazz bands, and the manager of the Aelita in Moscow was fired for 'disseminating Western influences'. Writing in *Encounter*, H. T. Willetts predicted: 'While prohibiting everything fresh and original . . . the Soviet authorities will probably encourage the cheery, toe-tapping tea-room twiddling which passed for jazz in the Soviet Union before the war.'[64]

Josef Škvorecký, who celebrates jazz as a free and spontaneous form intolerable to 'slavers, czars, führers, first secretaries', draws mordant parallels between his experiences under Communism and, earlier, in Nazi-occupied Bohemia, where the Gauleiter issued an exceedingly complex and erudite ten-part set of regulations binding on all dance orchestras: 'Pieces in foxtrot rhythm (so-called swing) are not to exceed 20% of the repertoires of light orchestras and dance bands.' Musicians were commanded to avoid

'Jewishly gloomy lyrics' and 'Negroid excesses in tempo (so-called hot jazz)'. In 1958, ten years short of the Dubček era, Škvorecký[65] attempted to set down these anti-Nazi recollections within a story published in Communist Czechoslovakia's first jazz almanac. As he later reported, 'the censors of an entirely different dictatorship confiscated the entire edition'. He and Milos Forman worked on a film script of the story which was finally banned by Novotny himself.[66]

On rare occasions a Communist regime attempted to reverse the usual stack of cards by playing host to a defecting Western artist (almost invariably an American). Škvorecký tells of one, the bass player Herbert Ward, who had once performed alongside Louis Armstrong, then decided that political asylum in Czechoslovakia was the ticket, 'delivering [Škvorecký recalls] another serious blow to imperialism':

We immediately looked him up in his hotel in Prague . . . we used him ruthlessly. We quickly put together a jazz revue entitled *Really the Blues* . . . printed Herb's super-anti-American statement in the programme, provided the Prague Dixieland to accompany Herb's home-made blues about how it feels to be followed by American secret-police agents . . . dressed his sexy dancer-wife Jacqueline in original sack dresses . . . then settled down to enjoy her dancing of the eccentric, decadent Charleston.[67]

Herb and Jacquie went home in the end, as American 'defectors' usually did.

The Prague Spring of 1968 was now on the horizon. The Czech jazz tradition, which extends back to ragtime pre-World War I, was bound to play its part alongside satirical theatre and the film boom. By the mid-sixties the Czechoslovak Government was sponsoring international jazz festivals; rock was already heard on Czech radio when the first Czech beat festival took place in 1967. But the arrival of Soviet tanks in Prague was soon to put an end to liberalization.

Even so, the Brezhnev–Kosygin regime adopted a relatively liberal attitude towards jazz; although jazz became increasingly associated with anti-Soviet elements, Jews, and malcontents, the authorities treated it as a lesser evil to rock. Indeed, in a remarkable volte-face Communist youth organizations sponsored more than six-dozen regional jazz festivals, while Melodiia issued recordings. The Union of Composers also reversed itself and sponsored the teaching of jazz at some forty institutes. Duke Ellington came to Russia in 1971, the New York Jazz Repertory Company four years later. Little short of astonishing is the contrast between the entries on *dzhaz* to be found in the (brief) 1952 and (much longer) 1972 editions of *The Great Soviet Encyclopedia*. Learned, detailed, objective, the entry in the third edition, written by the musicologist L. B. Pereverzev, could have sat well in a Western publication.[68]

But there was no stemming the tide of emigration; according to Starr, more than sixty well-established jazz musicians left the USSR during the 1970s, many of them Jews, like the Leningrad saxophonist Roman Kunsman. Most headed for New York, but they found the competition was stiff and work elusive.[69] The time was to come, in the mid-eighties, when the Soviet state concert agency, Goskonsert, was pleased to send a new generation of avant-garde jazz musicians to the West to earn hard currency.[70]

Czechoslovakia was marginally a different case following the suppression of the reform movement in 1968–9. Škvorecký's 'slavers, czars, führers, first secretaries' were positioning themselves for a neo-Stalinist restoration. Even so, given current Soviet liberalization on the jazz front, the Husak regime could not entirely suppress jazz. In 1971 the Union of Czech Musicians was permitted to form a Jazz Section, although membership was limited to 3,000 by the Ministry of the Interior. When threatened by the authorities, the Jazz Section successfully sought the shelter of membership of UNESCO's International Jazz Federation. Its bulletin, *Jazz*, was reserved for members only and thus not subject to censorship. As 'supplements' to the bulletin a series of uncensored books were published under the name of Edition *Jazzpetit*, along with a line of art monographs called *Situace* (*Situations*). It was estimated that *Jazz* and *Jazzpetit* series each reached about 100,000 readers.[71]

Škvorecký quotes Paul Wilson's article, 'What it's like Making Rock'n'Roll in a Police State', (*Musician*, February 1983). Wilson describes the left gig scene in London, summer of 1977, with punk rock in full swing and the new Sex Pistols documentary, 'full of arrests, rage and *lèse majesté*.' Wilson approached someone in the Pistols' entourage: why not smuggle a copy into Czechoslovakia to give the Plastic People a lift? ' "The Plastic People?" he responded with a dead-eyed, cocky public school whine. "They're anti-socialist. I don't support fascist rock bands. I'd rather send the film to South Africa." '[72]

The Jazz Section sponsored yearly festivals, Prague Jazz Days, at first orthodox in jazz terms and therefore not attracting multitudes, but latterly playing to audiences of up to 15,000 who listened to what Škvorecký calls 'jazz rock, New Wave, rock-in-opposition and modern jazz.' After 1982 the Party media orchestrated a clamorous witch hunt, overtly against punk rock but covertly against the Jazz Section. The annual Jazz Days were banned at short notice leaving the Jazz Section to refund ticket sales and reimburse foreign bands already arrived. Karel Srp, chairman of the Jazz Section, was fired from his editorial job with a printing company; in 1985 Srp was informed that the Jazz Section had been abolished. His arrest followed in September 1986; seven defendants were given prison sentences despite protests from abroad. Srp spent sixteen months in jail.[73]

⊞   ⊞   ⊞

Rock music not only offended elderly Soviet ears, it was not only derisive of seniority, but, most important, it was an alien invasion threatening Party hegemony. From 1967 the Voice of America devoted a weekly programme to rock and soul music; Brezhnev, Suslov, Husák, and Honecker all set their steely chins against rock. Raymond Anderson, of the *New York Times* (13 August 1968), picked up a story from *Pravda Ukrainy*: a group of young people had written in to protest against the paper's expressed disgust that 'howling' Western songs had been performed at a Komsomol meeting: 'Please tells us why in Poland, Czechoslovakia and Yugoslavia and other non-Western countries no one reproaches young people for singing modern songs and dancing to pop music? . . . And what is the situation in our country? Here, people like the author of the article go almost into hysterics when they see a young man with hair à la Beatles, and with a guitar as well.'[74] *Pravda Ukrainy* did publish this riposte, but wheeled in a soloist from the Kiev Philharmonic to warn that popular music in the West was an insidious weapon used by the imperialists to dull the senses of young people and turn them into killers 'who could bloodily hurl napalm onto Vietnamese farms and villages'. When the Beatles craze hit Russia the bans were reinforced. The word *bitlz* entered the language as a generic term for local longhairs who imitated the Liverpool four. Beatlemania followed the group's phenomenally successful visit to the United States in 1964, although the Soviet press was mainly hostile, displaying its most sourly myopic tone in a *Krokodil* (20 March 1964) article which failed to mention the Beatles' musical gifts. Referring to them as 'Little Beetles' (*Zhuchki*), *Krokodil* reported fabulous commercial success—the sale of 2 million records in under four weeks of their American tour. On the radio day and night one heard 'I want to hold your hand'—*Ia khochu derzhat' tvoiu ruku* and 'Only me'—*Tol'ko menia*. Commented *Krokodil*: 'One cannot doubt that if Christ himself visited the United States, he would not receive a tenth of the publicity.' (Christ, in fact, was soon to make a semi-official visit to the Soviet Union in the guise of *Jesus Christ Superstar*.)[75] *Krokodil*'s readers were informed that Lennon and Harrison had exchanged their trousers while observed by pressmen; as their train left New York for Washington, Ringo had uttered a Tarzan cry and started jumping like a monkey across the seats. The Beatles failed to speak up on musical and cultural questions, and about their sense of life in general. ' "We're in no way musicians," admitted George

Harrison, who was lying sprawled in the luggage rack, "we can't sing and generally we can't do anything properly" ' (*ne umeem pet' i voobschche delat' chto-libo tolkom*). The Beatles 'know how to rouse the darkest and most primitive passions in their audience mainly among people aged 12 to 16 susceptible to the Beatles' "educational"[76] role'. Not for nothing were there fights and faintings in the audience. *Krokodil* predicted that their success would not last long. 'They are not the right calibre'—*ne tot kalibr*. Like the Republican presidential candidate Barry Goldwater, shown by the cartoonist Herblock desperately wearing a Beatles haircut and carrying a guitar, these 'beetles' (said *Krokodil*) relied principally on advertising and knew only how to wail (*vopit'*). The anonymous music critic of the London *Times* (27 December 1963), by contrast, praised the Beatles' 'chains of pandiatonic clusters', their 'autocratic but not by any means ungrammatical attitude to tonality', and their 'translation of African Blues or American Western idioms . . . into tough, sensitive Merseyside'. Further technicalities followed in *The Times* as the bourgeois West provocatively unbuttoned: 'Those submediant switches from C major into A flat major . . . are a trademark of Lennon–McCartney songs.'

The Russian passion for melody was one reason why the Rolling Stones never rivalled the Beatles craze in the USSR. The Beatles—'She Loves You'— offered joy, rhythm, beauty, spontaneity. When *A Hard Day's Night* opened in Warsaw, cinemas were besieged and absenteeism was rampant in schools. In 1965 the East German record company Amiga released an album of Beatles hits—although Walter Ulbricht told the Central Committee: 'The incessant monotony of this "yeah, yeah, yeah" is not only ridiculous, it is spiritually deadening.'[77] *Sovetskaia kul'tura* (3 December 1968) went further; the Beatles had been exploited by big business, and now sought refuge in drugs and Eastern religion. Beatlemania reflected the sickness of society. Meanwhile, Beatles-style bands proliferated across the Soviet Union.[78]

Soviet fears of disorder were not infrequently borne out. Major disturbances occurred in Poland when the British band The Hollies visited Krakow in March 1966. Thousands of rock fans parading along the Vistula clashed with students bearing signs, 'Long Live Chopin! Hollies Go Home!' Dozens were arrested in the ensuing fray. The Rolling Stones reached Warsaw on 13 April 1967, two months after Mick Jagger and Keith Richards had been arrested in England on drugs charges. Stones concerts in Copenhagen, Oslo, and Stockholm had resulted in predictable mayhem. Black market tickets (and forged ones) for the 3,000 seats at the Warsaw concert were commanding vastly inflated prices. Those who could not get in rioted and clashed with militia units, while inside the hall the Stones noticed that the best seats were occupied by the children of Party officials. Keith Richards recalled. 'About three numbers, and I say, "Fuckin' stop playing, Charlie. You fuckin' lot, get out and let those bahstads in the back down front." ' The first four rows reportedly left the hall. Jagger worked the audience up and militia units had to intervene. A Soviet observer specially dispatched on a recce by the minister of culture, Ekaterina Furtseva, returned with a grim report.[79] The Kremlin maintained a rearguard action, refusing in 1974 to accept a tour by The Fifth Dimension, proposed by the US government under the cultural exchange agreement.[80] Meanwhile the young regularly gathered outside the Melodiia shops on Kalinin Prospekt in Moscow and Nevsky Prospekt in Leningrad, to trade in Anglo-American albums. (Melodiia had not issued a single Beatles album.)[81]

By now penetration of Russian culture had achieved surprising proportions: bands mouthed English sounds (the *ryba* or 'fish' technique), and wrote their own lyrics mainly in English—now the language of rock just as Italian had once been the language of opera.[82] In 1978 the German-based disco-reggae group Boney M. were invited to Moscow on condition that they did not perform their song 'Rah! Rah! Rasputin. Russia's greatest love machine'—but 'Rasputin' became the rage. In December 1980, immediately after the fatal shooting of John Lennon in New York, a memorial was held in the Lenin Hills overlooking Moscow. Arrested, the devotees covered the walls of the police station with the pun on Lenin: 'Lennon lived, Lennon lives, Lennon will live.' And he did. Three decades of Soviet anti-rock policy ended when Mikhail Gorbachev and his wife Raisa received Yoko Ono and told her of their affection for John Lennon. But they stopped short of renaming the high ground the Lennon Hills.[83]

The Ballet Dancer Defects

The ballet dancer's defection was the most spectacular of all: ovations, flowers, embraces—then a flying 'leap to freedom'. Raised, protected, and tutored by ballet masters and mistresses second to none, the absconding Soviet dancer was taken to have betrayed his teachers, his colleagues, his native land (*rodina*). Yet defectors were the exception; Soviet dance companies regularly transported hundreds of performers across the world and brought them all home.

Was cold war cultural conflict to be found within the art, craft, and vision of ballet itself? What form did the almost inevitable clash between 'modernism' and 'realism', the abstract and the concrete, assume? The most abrasive issue, as it transpired, was not for or against the revolutionary heroics of modern Soviet ballets like *Spartacus* (*Spartak*, about a slave revolt in ancient Rome) or *The Red Poppy* (celebrating the role of the Red Army in the Chinese Revolution). It was less a question of political content than of dramatic and musical form which separated the Bolshoi's vision from that of Georges Balanchine, Frederick Ashton, Anthony Tudor, John Cranko, and other leading Western choreographers. Finally it came down to 'realism' once again, even though balletic realism as seen in *Giselle* or *Swan Lake* at the Bolshoi and Kirov theatres was about as unrealistic as could be imagined: a fairy-tale world of romance, chivalry, passionate colours, glorious costumes, richly coloured, three-dimensional sets, perfectly synchronized choruses— but all of it embodying the great battle between good and evil, all of it about 'man' and his 'lofty spirit'; about 'humanism'. By contrast, Western ballets increasingly avoided stories, dramas, heroes, heroines, villains, dénouements, dying swans. Dance was developed as an *en-soi*, a thing apart, a suggestive form of motion, mime, and gesticulation in which meaning remained ambiguous, and intentions ambivalent. The external referent, the story, essential to Soviet audiences, had been deliberately cauterized. Abstraction prevailed. This was the balletic equivalent of non-representational painting, and it aroused the same sort of bafflement and outrage among Soviet critics and spectators. Ballet, of course, reached a huge audience in theatres across the Soviet Union, whereas in the West it was largely confined, like grand opera, to metropolitan elites. Even so, a million Americans applied for tickets when the Bolshoi first visited the United States in 1959.

On no other performing art did Soviet Russia expend such lavish devotion as the ballet. A Soviet critic offered a short history of the Bolshoi to a British audience, explaining how the Bolsheviks and Commissar Lunacharsky had voted to keep the Bolshoi Theatre open:

Free tickets were distributed to factory and office workers, and the forces, so that in 1919–20, some 85 per cent of the audience was getting in free . . . people who in their wildest dreams never thought of sitting in the gilded boxes of the former imperial theatre discovered a new world of beauty. Far from clashing with socialist ideals, the ballet was found to enrich them, and mass support made possible a vast amount of exploration and experiment.[1]

Yet how unlikely an art form it is for cultivation by a proletarian revolution in a land of thumping peasant dances. Born in the Renaissance, ballet did not acquire its most salient characteristics—pointework for women, full (180-degree) turn-out of the legs for both sexes—until the end of the Romantic era.[2]

Ballet was the universal language requiring no translation, but in the post-war years a meeting of pointed feet—pirouettes, fouettes, pas de deux—proved as difficult to achieve between Russia and America as a meeting of minds. In 1949, the Berlin airlift notwithstanding, Blevins Davis, president of the Ballet Theater Foundation, which had enjoyed a successful season at New York's Metropolitan Opera House, announced that he had offered to take the company to the USSR at its own expense, if the Russians provided an orchestra. On 26 May S. Striganov, first secretary of the Soviet Embassy in Washington, responded frostily to this *grand jeté*: it might benefit American ballet dancers 'to acquaint themselves with the achievements of the ballet art in our country, which has stepped up to a new high level of perfection during the days of Soviet power'—but Soviet spectators were not used to seeing 'fragments of ballets', such as the American company was offering.[3] Soviet critics sneered at Western ballet, not least V. Gorodinskii, who claimed that in America there was no national opera theatre because no national opera:

For this reason there is also no national ballet in America. Up to the present time in England and America the so-called 'ballet' comes in the main from the remnants of earlier Russian ballet groups, from abandoned collectives, formed from the remains of the once famous Diaghilev ensemble and managed either by a certain White 'colonel' Basil or, in America, by the former Russian dancer Balanchine. And a Russian surname is not always proof of the Russian origins of the artists. The fame of the Russian ballet prompted English and American artists to pass themselves off as 'Russian'. For example the English dancer Alicia Markova is really Elisa Marx [sic: Alice Marks], and the artist who bears the sonorous name Anton Dolin, is really Patrick Key.[4]

In any case in no capitalist country is there a ballet theatre as a national art institution. In France, once the flower of ballet, there is none available. Not for nothing was the Paris Opéra recently an arena for the idiotic experiment of the white émigré Serge Lifar (who collaborated with the Hitlerites during the war years),[5] and who undertook the attempt to create a ballet performance without music, but achieved a still greater success by creating a ballet performance without dance.

Gorodinskii's polemic was shortly followed by the first defections of dancers through the iron curtain. A Soviet report on the 1952–3 Moscow theatre season praised the visit by the Budapest Opera House dancers Norá Kovács and István Ráb (Raab), both of whom had won prizes at the Third World Student and Youth Festival in Berlin, and both of whom had studied under the finest Soviet ballet masters.[6] Both dancers were young, pampered prodigies of the Communist system; both had received every official honour and privilege. Kovács and Raab bought a little villa on the Balaton, and a small car—which required a special permit. They were both awarded the Kossuth Prize and appeared in parliament to receive it. Ordered to attend the 1951 World Youth Festival in East Berlin, they were dressed up in the uniforms of DISZ, the Hungarian Komsomol, and required to listen to long speeches of welcome on the larger station platforms of Hungary, Czechoslovakia, and East Germany. The couple danced in the presence of Pieck, Grotewohl, and Ulbricht.

Under instructions, they returned to East Berlin in May 1953 and were accommodated in a luxury suite in Thälmann Platz. Before their gala performance Kovács and Raab slipped away into the U-Bahn, she carrying her jewels in her raincoat pocket, both determined but terrified of the short journey ahead. At Wittenberg Platz they alighted. As Kovács later described it to the Hungarian émigré George Mikes: 'We ran up the stairs...In the tenth of a second we realised that we were in a different world. Lights were blazing; well-dressed, cheerful, smiling people...bright shop windows...an almost incredible sight—a barrow was standing right in front of us, laden with oranges and bananas...I had not tasted a banana for more than eight or nine years.'[7]

Kovács, 21, and Raab, 22, wife and husband, prima ballerina and first dancer of the Hungarian Opera, had defected. Their noisy welcome in the West was classical choreography for the summer of the Berlin uprising. 'Communist Grip on the Ballet. Dancers' Flight from Hungary', reported the London *Times* (5 June 1953). Because of the 'danger of kidnap', journalists were asked not to file their stories until the plane carrying the precious pair reached Frankfurt. At the press conference Nora Kovács complained about Communist policy in the arts: Ravel had been condemned as too erotic, Richard Strauss and Stravinsky as too formalist. An American official took her on a shopping spree and begged her to choose frocks, hats, stockings, shoes, handbags, and cosmetics. A military plane flew the couple to Munich, where they were taken to the home of Mr and Mrs Alessandro, of Radio Free Europe. More shopping, more clothes, more press conferences, and a short documentary film, 'Dance to Freedom'. The impresario Sol Hurok arrived in Munich at 2 a.m. in a State Department car and accompanied by three colonels of the US Army. As soon as he saw Kovács and Raab dance he offered them a long-term contract and handed over their first dollar cheque. (The Russians must have known this when they later awarded him such lucrative contracts.) The two Hungarians danced in London and New York, they danced with Roland Petit, they performed in a Las Vegas night club when Marlene Dietrich was on the programme, then moved on to Spain, Paris, Brussels, and Anton Dolin's Festival Ballet in London. The workload appalled them: in Hungary they had performed four or five times a month; in the West, six nights a week plus matinées.[8]

⌗   ⌗   ⌗

Stalin died, a thaw followed, Odette, Odile, and Giselle began to stir from their long winter hibernation. The first visit to the West by a full Soviet ballet company occurred in 1954 and ended in disaster. Under a Franco-Russian agreement, a combined Bolshoi–Kirov company was to perform in France while the Comédie française displayed its theatrical brilliance in Moscow. When the Russian dancers[9] reached Paris in May 1954, all seats had been sold for a season of performances due to last from 8 May to the 30th. France was the particular target of a Soviet cultural embrace at a time of acute French resentment concerning the re-militarization of Germany, reinforced by the McCarthyite hysteria prevailing at the height of the Wisconsin senator's destructive powers. But France was also in the grip of anti-Communist crisis and political tension—the beleaguered French military outpost at Dienbienphu had just fallen to Ho Chi Minh's Vietminh forces. All French theatres were closed for two days of mourning for the overrrun garrison troops. However, on 10 May *L'Humanité* fully expected the first performance to take place that night. But Premier Joseph Laniel and Foreign Minister Maurice Schuman summoned Ambassador Vinogradov to explain that they feared hostile demonstrations if the performance went ahead. Although 10,000 tickets had been sold for the first five performances, the Soviet dancers remained confined to the Hotel Commodore on the Boulevard Haussmann. Angry scenes in the foyer of the Opéra and outside reflected general frustration. *L'Humanité* called Premier Laniel's decision 'scandalous' and announced that 'the heart of Paris is open to the Soviet artists'.[10] M. I. Chulaki, manager of the Soviet troupe, issued a statement clearly formulated in Moscow, avoiding any reference to the specific reasons (Dienbienphu) given by Laniel, and accusing the French government of having an 'ill-disposed attitude' (*neblagozhetal'noi pozitsiei*).[11] '*L'Humanité* printed a letter signed by fifty-two intellectuals' insisting that, regardless of political position, 'art ought not to be the victim of politics'.[12] According to the London *Daily Worker*, the cancellation revealed 'the hollowness of the claims that NATO powers are the guardians of European cultural values'.[13]

Two years later, in the autumn of 1956, the Bolshoi company reached London in exceptionally fraught circumstances, despite the generally successful visit of Khrushchev and Bulganin to the UK earlier in the year, preceded by the Moscow State Dance Company[14] and followed by the 160-strong Song and Dance Ensemble of the Soviet Army. But then a female discus-thrower took a fancy to some Oxford Street hats and Anglo-Soviet relations plunged back into mutual suspicion and recrimination. A letter appeared in *Izvestiia* (21 September) signed by M. Chulaki, G. Ulanova, Iu. Kontradtov, and other members of the Bolshoi Ballet referring to the recent, highly publicized arrest in London of the athlete Nina Ponomereva, accused of stealing hats from a department store:

We have worked hard to prepare for the production of four ballets at Covent Garden: *Swan Lake*; *Romeo and Juliet*; *Fountain of the Bakhchisarai*; and *Giselle*.[15] All the more completely incomprehensible (*neponiatnym*) to us in terms of the conditions for a successful tour is the act of provocation against Nina Ponomereva. By the same token, we ask where is the guarantee that one of us will not suffer a similar provocation in London. In such conditions the trip by the Bolshoi ballet troupe cannot be undertaken.

On 29 August, the day before a scheduled GB–USSR athletics match, arousing considerable public anticipation in the era of the 'heroic runner' (Zatopek, Kuts, Pirie, Chataway), 27-year-old Nina Ponomereva,[16] Olympic and European discus champion, herself the mother of a small boy and a teacher by profession, had gone shopping in Oxford Street along with other Soviet athletes, armed with pocket money in sterling. She had left the ground-floor hat department of C&A Modes Ltd and reached the street when she was apprehended by a female store detective. The police were summoned, followed by a Russian-speaking Special Branch officer and a Soviet consular official. The five hats she was charged with stealing were valued at a total of £1.12s.11d., at that time equivalent to $4.62. The Russians promptly cancelled the athletics match, even though all tickets had been sold for the meeting and the British team manager estimated the losses at £25,000 ($70,000). Reports in *Izvestiia* and *Pravda* (1 September), 'Dirty Provocation' (*Griaznaia Provokatsiia*), focused on the sinister mystery role of the C&A (*Si end Ei*) shop detective who appeared on the scene and mysteriously turned out (*obnaruzhilsia*) to speak Russian, which, he explained, he had learned at Oxford University, although he could not explain why he worked in a department store. This 'shop detective' turned out to be a bilingual officer of the Metropolitan Police called to the scene.

After the Soviet Embassy failed to produce Nina in court next day, as promised, a warrant was issued for her arrest. Two leading Oxford athletes, Chris Chataway and Chris Brasher, famous among other achievements for pacing Roger Bannister during the first-ever sub-four-minute mile in 1954, wrote to the London *Evening Standard*, describing the charge against Nina as an unbearable blow to the pride of all the Russian athletes. The story was spread across four columns in the *New York Times* (2 September); on the same day *Neues Deutschland* lumped together the Givras Diaries (Cyprus), British attempts to upset Suez Canal traffic, and the case of the missing frogman-spy Commander Crabb, all of them machinations of the British Secret Service, with the 'frame-up' of Nina Ponomereva.

Hearing that the Bolshoi Ballet was threatening to cancel its imminent visit, the august *Scotsman* (22 September) went into thunder mode: 'We can separate politics from the arts, and admire the sporting prowess of our political enemies. To the Communists everything is political, and is viewed in terms of propaganda.' The Russians had 'an Oriental regard for "face"', hence their reaction to the shoplifting charge. The law was the law and a visiting athlete had 'no claim to diplomatic immunity'. Time and again press comment stressed the fact that British justice was independent of the government—something the Russians could not understand—yet this was not the case: the attorney-general, Sir Reginald Manningham-Buller, a politician in the Eden Cabinet, could have dropped the proceedings at any time as 'not in the public interest'. The decision to pursue the charge was taken at Cabinet level.

Already 50,000 tickets had been sold in London for twenty-five scheduled performances by the Bolshoi Ballet. Eighty tons of stage props were frozen at the Surrey Commercial Docks by order of the Russians. On 28 September it was announced that the Bolshoi would after all come to London, presenting the Royal Opera House, Covent Garden, with a nightmare five days of preparation. No orchestra rehearsals had taken place and the scenery was still in storage. *Romeo and Juliet* alone involved fifteen complicated scene changes.[17] After flight delays due to bad weather, buses finally conveyed the company to Govent Garden where a throng of reporters was waiting. Prima ballerina Galina Ulanova, 'looking small and white with fatigue', was whisked away to her hotel in a taxi.[18] On 12 October, six weeks after her arrest, Nina Ponomereva (who was never going to look small) appeared in Marlborough Street Court, where she pleaded not guilty. The magistrate, finding the case proved, commented on the fallibility of human nature in the face of temptation. Ponomoreva was driven straight from the court to Greenland Dock, where she boarded the SS *Molotov* and departed (as *Pravda* reported) 'for the motherland' (*na Rodinu*).

The opening night of Prokofiev's *Romeo and Juliet* marked the Bolshoi's first performance outside Russia in 200 years.[19] Afterwards a champagne supper for 500 guests was held on stage. Moscow Radio reported the evening live. *The Times*'s special correspondent set out what was to be expected from the Bolshoi. First, 'dazzling virtuosity':

Soviet dancers excel precisely where our own are weakest: they jump splendidly, there seems to be no limit to the number or accuracy of the turns (pirouettes or fouettes) which they can execute, and their pas de deux are remarkable, above all, for their 'lifts' . . . On the other hand, in the matter of quick, delicate (terre à terre) movements, they have little to offer. Soviet choreography, the new as well as the old, is so remarkably unvaried . . . the Soviet Union has never known that revolution and that emancipation in choreography which began with Fokine at the Maryinsky, in St Petersburg fifty years ago and which Diaghilev's company brought to Western Europe.

One important characteristic of Soviet ballet—which makes a dismal impression on the Western observer—is its remarkable lack of taste and imagination in the matter of décor. The style tends to be out of date and shoddy.

Reviewing *Romeo and Juliet* in the following day's edition of the *Manchester Guardian*, 'J.H.M.' was negative in strikingly similar terms. He called it 'a considerable disappointment', and found the mime and crowd scenes disproportionate to the amount of dancing. The anonymous ballet critic of *The Times*, by contrast, delivered a eulogy from start to finish: the dramatic conviction of the dancers, the tension they generated, the 'electric fluid' of the choreography, was surpassed only by Ulanova's performance. She was quite simply a 'flame'. The *Daily Telegraph*—'Covent Garden Acclaims the Bolshoi'—also lauded Ulanova to the skies, but regretted that Soviet choreography 'has a smaller vocabulary than is in use here with mainly big, open steps and gestures; there are few of those subtle, refined head-hand-and-arm movements that make up most of the Western choreographer's apparatus.' The *Scotsman* commented: 'The least one can say is: better Ulanova than Elvis the Pelvis.'

Ulanova finally consented to meet the press.[20] Wearing a tailored brown woollen suit, she sat ramrod-straight, slightly smiling, very confident, every inch a queen, a living legend. At one point she opened her shiny black handbag and took out a packet of English cigarettes, but could not find her matches. So up came the two slim arms in a kind of forward, fluttering movement, culminating in the faintest of snaps. The director of the Bolshoi, the choreographer, and the deputy minister of culture each scrambled to offer her a lighted match. Ulanova[21] had not joined the Bolshoi until 1944, in her mid-thirties. A People's Artist of the USSR, she was an almost forbiddingly orthodox model of virtue and Soviet womanhood—every correct emotion, like every hair, was in place, fiercely sincere in her commitment to dramatic dancing and her reiterated admiration for Stanislavky and his underscoring of the words 'lofty aim': 'The very features that I sought for and found in the Swan, in Giselle, in Maria, in Juliet and Tao Hoa—poetry, chastity of spirit, courage, faith in man, in man's reason and will to do good—are inherent in the new person born of the Soviet age. A champion of peace and justice, the new Soviet citizen has a noble and big heart. He is modest and selflessly devoted to his Homeland.' She remembered dancing before an audience of wounded soldiers in Leningrad in 1944, recalled how most of the Bolshoi's spectators during the war were men in uniform, and noted (with approval) the 'almost reverential' attitude of Soviet audiences, a 'great impulse for poetry and high culture, the loftiness of the people's spirit'. Ulanova danced straight up and down the Party line. In 1949 she had attended a women's peace congress in Italy: 'I was horrified at the contrasts existing in that country of breath-taking scenery, at the destitution of the poor and the fabulous luxury of the hotels where the Americans stayed. I saw men and women strikers, who refused to unload guns, distributing the newspaper *Unità* despite the threat of severe reprisals.'[22]

Typical of Soviet eulogies to Ulanova is the critic Lvov-Anokhin's:

For all their precision and integrity, you never detect any muscular tension, any striving after effect in Ulanova's *pirouettes*. The lightness of her *fouetté* is impressive

...the thirty-two *fouettés* in *Swan Lake* seem, when performed by Ulanova, to be one single, flowing and vigorous expression of emotion.... Her *pas de bourrée* has the fluidity of a stream of water... Her *jeté*—transfers from one foot to another—create the impression of flight. [This was not to forget her *pointes*, her *arabesques*, her *port de bras* technique—and everything else.][23]

Now, in London, a British journalist asked her what she thought of London press criticisms describing Russian choreography as old-fashioned. Ulanova explained with the patience of a ballet mistress coping with a backward student: 'In the twenties we had this "modern" idea, these experimental pieces. Not only in ballet, but in painting, films, and all the arts. But we discarded it.[24] Now we try to find what is real life, real humanity, and re-create it in dancing. We think you will come around to this, too.' Modernism had been suppressed, not 'discarded', but her use of the word was a sincere reflection of the official mentality—despite her article published in *Sovetskaia muzyka* (April 1953) in which she asked why three years had passed since the Bolshoi had staged a new ballet—*The Bronze Horseman* in 1949, *The Red Poppy* in 1950. Taking issue with the Bolshoi's Committee for Art Affairs and several individuals by name, she (like Igor Moiseyev) had complained of 'timidity' and 'stagnation'.[25]

The Danish-born Hélène Bellew (who danced as 'Kirsova'), having visited the USSR in the spring of 1956, published *Ballet in Moscow Today*, an acutely observant book which, while praising the spectacular productions at the Bolshoi and the vast financial resources placed at its disposal, nevertheless reiterated the prevalent Western complaint:

to visit the Bolshoi is to step back into another epoch. It is a shock to discover that the whole vast field of ballet production has been almost completely untouched since the departure of Diaghilev. Sitting watching this company... one wonders how the spirit of twentieth century experimentation and invention could have passed by the many choreographers and producers of this huge organisation... All the ballets performed are like perfectly kept period pieces, jealously preserved within their heavy, lavishly ornamented, nineteenth-century frames.

She then raised the spectre of modernism in general:

A comparison not too far astray might be: Petipa, Fokine, Massine and Balanchine—Impressionism, Cézanne, Cubism and Abstract art. But this transition, in both choreography and painting, has passed, if not unnoticed, certainly unheeded in the USSR... Only three 'modern' composers have been utilised—Prokofiev, Shostakovich and Khachaturian. [And none of their ballets, she reported, were currently performed.][26]

Bellew criticized the Bolshoi's neo-classical décor for neglecting the painting of Malevich, Sonia Delaunay, Chagall, Kandinsky, Gontcharova, and Larionov, who embodied 'native tradition and true spirit of revolution'. These artists, she added, 'express the very spirit of the twentieth century'. As for *The Red Poppy*, which celebrated the Chinese Revolution, and in which Ulanova danced the role of Tao Hoa, it was 'an outstanding proof of how the inclusion of political propaganda in a work of art results in failure both aesthetically and politically'.[27]

Leaving theory aside, the Bolshoi company flew out of London, to Berlin, on 3 November 1956, broadly triumphant. But the harmony achieved was very rapidly to be soured by the cold war. Sadler's Wells Ballet Company (predecessor of the Royal Ballet) was scheduled to return the visit almost immediately, opening in Moscow on 15 November with a programme of thirteen ballets, many of them one-acters and ten of them by British choreographers. Although British ballet was the child and pupil of the Russian ballet through Diaghilev—Ninette de Valois, Marie Rambert, Alicia Markova, and Anton Dolin had all worked under the great Russian—the *Manchester Guardian*'s special correspondent had predicted that Sadler's Wells would have much to teach the Russians: 'a delicacy, artistry and inventiveness in genuinely neo-classical dancing and choreography (as distinct from the hide-bound classicism of Soviet choreographers) ... and a whole new world of décor.'[28] Sir William Hayter, the British ambassador to Moscow, was reported to have given the Sadler's Wells company a pep-talk in London, advising them to keep away from the GUM department store, perhaps anticipating retaliation for the affair of 'Nina's hats'. 'Don't tip your dressers. Do give them gifts like ties, or socks, or cigarettes, or chocolate. Don't discuss politics. Do be friendly. Do visit the Kremlin. Do go to the museums. And do, do admire what you see.'[29]

The visit was then cancelled. On 7 November David Webster, general administrator of the Royal Opera House, sent a cable to Chulaki explaining the cancellation 'in view of public opinion in this country, which strongly condemns the renewed suppression by Soviet forces of Hungarian liberty and independence'. Regretting this decision, Chulaki referred to the 'just position taken by the Soviet Government' over the 'aggression unleashed by Britain, France and Israel against the freedom and independence of the Egyptian people'. Chulaki claimed that this was the real reason for the cancellation. As for events in Hungary, Covent Garden was advised to study the 'documents published by the Hungarian revolutionary Government of Workers and Peasants'.[30]

Travelling solo, the British ballerina Beryl Grey made her first appearance at the Bolshoi in December 1957, and wrote an interesting account of her experiences, *Red Curtain Up* (1958), in which she expressed unbounded admiration for the Russian ballet, its leading ballerinas, its muscular male partners, its rehearsal techniques, and for the physical conditions in which Soviet ballet dancers worked. Russian travel conditions and clothes were another story: 'Looking down from a window on to a Moscow street, filled with crowds of people, mostly wearing black, all hurrying, reminded me of some Lancashire scene painted by Lowry.'[31] The American critic Faubion Bowers paid an extended visit to Moscow in 1958. Like many Western observers, he missed the restless experimentation he associated with Tudor, Ashton, Cranko, and Balanchine, although he was impressed by the genuine modernity of Igor Moiseyev's *Spartacus*, with music by Khachaturian and script by Plutarch: 'It is the first ballet since the Revolution to break entirely with classic movements and the toe slipper. In order to execute this new approach, none of the established stars except Plisetskaya were utilized, and all the leading roles were taken by junior members of the corps de ballet who presumably are less ingrained with the traditions.'[32]

During his long interview with Ulanova, Faubion Bowers gained an impression of severe conservatism, an insistence on classical forms and strict discipline. 'All dance depends on classical ballet', she told him. 'You can have deviations, but the classics have to be the foundation.' Ulanova kept using the phrase 'everything falls to pieces' to describe what happened if dancers became too individualistic or failed to follow the general pattern and the music. Towards the end of his interview Bowers made a big cold war mistake: he presented Ulanova with a pair of ballet tights which he had brought from New York; these tights were fine and thin and did not 'crawl'. But Ulanova bristled. 'I have plenty. If these are so precious, I'll put them in a museum.'[33]

⊞ ⊞ ⊞

The Russians are coming! In 1958 the Igor Moiseyev Dance Company paid its first visit to the United States, two years after the Ministry of Culture cancelled a scheduled tour by the ensemble because of the fingerprinting requirement. Born in 1906, Moiseyev had become a leading dancer and ballet master at the Bolshoi by the age of 30. In Stalin's time Moiseyev had published a sharp attack on Bolshoi choreography in *Literaturnaia gazeta* (24 April 1952). He traced the Bolshoi's fear of innovation to the 1936 *Pravda* attack on Shostakovich's ballet set on a collective farm, which followed the blistering assault on his opera *Lady Macbeth of Mtsensk*. 'A fear of the new is making itself more and more apparent in ballet; as an art form it has hardly any links with contemporary reality. . .' He spoke of 'the stagnation which frequently passes for loyalty to tradition', adding: 'The lack of competent ballet criticism is simply amazing.'[34]

A month after Eisenhower approved the idea of a cultural exchange agreement in June 1956, but eighteen months before the treaty was signed on 27 January 1958, the Ukrainian-born impresario Sol Hurok arrived in Moscow to sign up the talent, including the Moiseyev Dance Company (as the State Folk Dance Ensemble of the Soviet Union came to be known). Reporting from Moscow on Moiseyev's new genre, 'Modern Male Ballets', Faubion Bowers hailed them as really new forms of dance movement executed with 'precision and perfection'. In the popular show *Soccer*, one of Moiseyev's 'Modern Male Ballets', the choreographer parodied 'the sliding, tackling piles of human flesh that swarm over the hapless football. To enlarge this dance Moiseyev introduces an aggressive newspaper photographer who darts in and out among the struggling players. Of course, he adds the inescapable after-game riot, a mockery of the passions aroused by competitive sports.' Another piece which Moiseyev took to America was *Navy*, representing the officers and sailors of a ship going about their duties: 'One sailor is late; he is punished. Another smokes on duty; another punishment. Finally they weigh anchor and the ship breaks down. Repairs begin. The sailors turn into pieces of machinery; they need oiling, the row of human hands becomes a giant wrench, then an engine.'[35]

Paul O'Neill, Jr., a Foreign Service officer acting on behalf of the East–West Contacts Staff of the State Department, arranged the visas for the Moiseyev company but left most of everything else to Hurok, who paid the bills at the Hotel Claridge on Times Square. When the dancers (including forty-eight females) first arrived they displayed nervousness out on the streets and meekly obeyed their Soviet interpreters who, for example, forbade them being photographed in front of Times Square shop windows. Next door to the Claridge was a neon-and-chrome cafeteria which they quickly adopted, pointing to the food they wanted—omelettes, fried potatoes, toast, fruit, Danish pastry, orange juice. They would hold out a handful of bills with their checks and trust the cashier to pass the correct change. Don Hogan, who got these details into *The Reporter*, described Moiseyev as looking like a football coach, 'square-built with a rugged face and soft but aggressive voice'.[36] Hurok announced ticket sales of $300,000 for the tour. On 17 April 1958 the *Herald Tribune* reported an enthusiastic reception for Moiseyev from more than 3,000 spectators at the Metropolitan Opera House. Later, at the Shrine Auditorium in Los Angeles, movie stars formed a guard of honour for the Russian dancers after the performance. But Moiseyev, it turned out, liked America too much. On 12 December he addressed 600 actors, dancers, and musicians in Moscow's House of Actors on 'The Cultural Life of America', enchanting his audience for three-and-a-half hours. He was invited to repeat his talk at the House of Journalists but, fatally, on 19 January the *New York Times* published a summary of his comments—'Moiseyev Glows In Report on U.S.'—by Dana Adams Schmidt:

Mr Moiseyev seemed pleased to tell that there was a restaurant in New York of nearly every nationality. He noted the great variety of goods in stores at reasonable prices and made this comment about American drugstores: '. . . would you believe that you can eat whole meals there, that you could buy food, toys, household goods and things which have nothing to do with medicine?'

He had loved *West Side Story* and *My Fair Lady*. He spoke with particular enthusiasm of Jerome Robbins's choreography and Leonard Bernstein's music in *West Side Story*.

On the whole he did not care for American movies. *The Ten Commandments* bored his dance troupe, but *The Young Lions* pleased him. He called the latter 'anti-fascist' and the camera work and Marlon Brando's portrayal of a young German officer absolutely first class.

His most enthusiastic comments were on American musical life. Every sizeable city, he said, has a symphony orchestra. He said that superb musicianship and discipline of individual artists allowed different orchestras to accompany his dancers satisfactorily, although the musicians had received the unfamiliar scores only on the morning of the performance.

Harrison Salisbury's account of Moiseyev's remarks gives a more inflammatory impression. (According to Salisbury, envious remarks were being dropped in Moscow about Moiseyev's beautiful new Mercedes, a gift from Sol Hurok.)

Russia, [Moiseyev] said, must take a new look at American art. It must rid itself of the cliché that America was a land of immature culture. He clearly implied that the ponderous machinery of the Bolshoi company was not the last word. That the Russian dance could learn as well as teach, that it was time to listen to the driving rhythms of American music and look at the soaring dreams of American Ballet . . . [37]

The Kremlin was furious. Moiseyev was summoned by the minister of culture, Nikolai A. Mikhailov. The scheduled lecture at the House of Journalists was postponed indefinitely. In April the *New York Times* reported that the Soviet government had censured Moiseyev for his too favourable account of life and art in the United States. Harrison Salisbury again: 'Promptly the heavy batteries of Agitprop, of the dedicated bureaucrats of the Party, the panjandrums of ballet and of socialist realism had laid down a counterbarrage.' An acerbic article in *Znamia* by Igor Filatov, of the Moiseyev group, was obviously designed to offset Moiseyev's own glowing account of life in New York: 'All around the clock hundreds of police cars drive around the city ... On the next day the glassy eyes of corpses look out at readers from the front pages of newspapers that offer the most detailed descriptions of beastly crimes... We saw need, we saw Harlem and the queues of un-employed standing in line for aid.' Moiseyev took cover, cutting the Ameri-can numbers from his new programme and presenting in their place what Salisbury called 'a collection of banalities... The program was dull and dis-appointing'.[38]

The Bolshoi Ballet was due to begin an eight-week season in the United States,[39] headed by Galina Ulanova, now 'believed to be' 48,[40] accompanied by her husband Vadin Rindin, the chief stage designer. The Bolshoi's formid-able corps of ballerinas included Maya Plisetskaya, Marina Kondratieva, and Nina Timofeyeva. Ballet-lovers to a man, ILA local 824 unloaded the troupe's equipment at the docks despite a boycott of shipments from Communist nations. According to a jubilant Sol Hurok, there had been 1 million applica-tions for 165,000 tickets, with standees queuing for admission in the rain thirty-nine hours before the opening performance at the Metropolitan Opera House (whose stage proved to be sub-standard).[41] Every one of 3,616 tickets for the première had been sold (the top price was $50 but tickets were trading at $100 to $150 in the hands of 'scalpers'). As in London three years earlier, the Bolshoi began with Ulanova and Yuri Zhdanov in Prokofiev's *Romeo and Juliet*.[42] Thunderous applause and excited bravos greeted the performance. 'Seldom has such an international atmosphere of glamour and excitement been seen in New York in many years', wrote Harrison Salisbury.[43]

The Bolshoi dancers were taken on a visit to Wall Street and the Stock Exchange, where Ulanova was handed a tall glass of orange juice by Robert W. Dowling, president of the City Investing Company and self-styled 'capit-alist shark'. From the Exchange's balcony the Russians looked wonderingly down at the dark-suited traders who darted about and yelled and squinted up at the huge, mysterious moving sign that read YAT 35 1/2 ... MOL 26 7/8 ... GRA 46 3/8. Hundreds of Americans on their lunch-hour jammed the area around Exchange Place to get a close view of the Russians. 'Why,' exclaimed a blonde secretary, 'those Russians look just like Americans'. Indeed, many of the dancers carried cameras—the women wore low-heeled white shoes.[44]

Some 300,000 spectators witnessed fifty-two performances in New York, Washington, Los Angeles, and San Francisco. However, the critics were not unreserved in their praise. Walter Terry of the *Herald Tribune* asked himself whether *The Stone Flower*[45] was choreographically a good ballet as well as a spectacle:

The answer must be no... For although it is big, colorful (if you don't mind garishness), dramatic, melodramatic, romantic and peppered with bits of virtuosity, its choreographic invention, except for the folk-dance episodes, is very limited, its movement style is dated, and some of its tableaux would feel right at home on the stage of the Radio City Music Hall.

Harrison Salisbury expected that when the Bolshoi returned to Moscow, 'Exposure of these wonderful artists to the lean muscularity and bright imaginativeness of American ballet, to Balanchine, to the realism of *West Side Story* and the exhilaration of *My Fair Lady* would... set off a chain reaction leading beyond the bounds of imagination.' His hopes were disappointed in general,[46] and in particular by the Moscow première of *Path of Thunder*, a ballet staged by K. Sergeyev and based on Peter Abrahams's novel of racial discrimination in his native South Africa, a story about the love between a coloured youth and a white girl, the daughter of the master of the estate. The *New York Times* (28 June 1959) took this new ballet to task for its propagandist tone. (*Holiday on Ice*, meanwhile was a smash hit in Moscow, and its season was extended from March 1959 to 24 May, delighting a total audience of 400,000.)

Shortly before Khrushchev's 1959 visit to the United States 200 singers and dancers from all over Russia were dispatched there, including the celebrated Pyatnitsky Choir, a ballet group from Kiev, and principals of the Bolshoi Opera. Valery Panov,[47] then dancing with the Mali Company, at 21 the youngest member of the troupe, was partnered by Tatyana Borovikova, a Mali leading lady. Many years later, following his highly publicized defection, he recalled:

Rehearsals [in Moscow] were interspersed with *three* talks in a Central Committee building. The country's most experienced lecturers put us on to a dozen different forms of treacherous temptation that might confront us on America's street corners. 'The main thing is vigilance. They'll all be trying to disgrace you.' Sad incidents of previous Soviet performers and athletes were cited...[48]

The troupe departed on 2 July for New York (where they opened in Madison Square Garden), Chicago, Los Angeles, and San Francisco. The weather was sweltering. Panov, who fell instantly in love with America and its fantastic abundance, suffered stretched groin ligaments with a threat of hernia. The impresario Sol Hurok paid for a truss, but Panov's general attitude angered his Soviet minders. Like the soprano Galina Vishnevskaya, he was eager to depict Soviet artistes as travelling gypsies desperate to hoard material goods and overseas wages acquired while in the West. To save money, the performers took their basic, non-perishable food with them: 'All thoughts about pirouettes and grands jetés were buried under stockpiles of sugar, sausage, canned fish, condensed milk, tea...', wrote Panov. And Vishnevskaya: 'For many—in dance companies, choruses, orchestras—foreign trips are indeed the only way to survive.' Panov recalled the troupe's horror when all tins of meat were confiscated by New York customs. Later (he claimed) two ballerinas fainted from under-nourishment after three weeks of eating out of cans in order to save every American cent for purchases. Demeaning the dignity of Russian artistes in the face of Western prosperity was central to the cold war narratives of both Panov and Vishnevskaya.[49]

In Chicago the Russian performers experienced hostile demonstrations on behalf of enslaved peoples. When they reached San Francisco, Panov was ordered home. No clear reason (he says) was given. He and his distraught dancing partner were flown to New York, ringed by Soviet officials and by the FBI.[50] Fifteen years after he was sent home from America in disgrace Valery Panov was to become an international *cause célèbre*.[51]

American Ballet Theatre was the first American troupe to visit the USSR. The ABT—fifty-three dancers headed by Maria Tallchief—began a five-month European tour sponsored by the State Department in May 1960. Reaching Moscow in September, they performed at the Stanislavsky Theatre and the vast Sports Palace, before proceeding to Tiflis, Leningrad, and Kiev. Seymour Topping of the *New York Times* (14 September) described an audience of 1,000 in the Stanislavsky Theatre, including Ulanova and Mrs Khrushchev:

The Russians were alternately delighted and puzzled with the cowboy ballet *Rodeo*. The critics found the Americans generally did not perform with the authority or classicism of their own Bolshoi and Stanislavsky ballet companies. Only Erik Bruhn and Maria Tallchief [in the 'pas de deux' of *Swan Lake*] evoked the bravos and cadenced clapping the Russians award as their highest accolade.

⌗ ⌗ ⌗

No ballet scandal outstripped the Nureyev affair. The form it took reflected rising cold war tension: the U-2 spy plane, the consequent breakdown of the Paris summit, a crisis in the Congo, Khrushchev's desire to get the better of America's 'new boy' president, John F. Kennedy, and the mounting Berlin crisis, soon to result in the erection of the Wall. Much of this had probably escaped the attention of the Kirov's young star Rudolf Nureyev, but he, perhaps the first Soviet performing artist to defect, was destined to escape nobody's attention.[52]

Anarchic, hyper-individualistic, fascinated by the West, Nureyev was already so distrusted by the Kirov management and the Ministry of Culture that he had almost been excluded from the company's trip to France. According to Panov, cut-throat competition within the Kirov encouraged informing for the KGB: 'Even innately decent, upstanding dancers succumbed because there was no other route to the airport.' Shortly before Nureyev set out on his fateful trip to Paris with the Kirov, he visited the Mali Theatre and asked Panov what had happened to him in America, listening intently.[53] Nureyev gained a reprieve after the Paris impresario Georges Soria cabled that the Kirov's leading female and male dancers were too old to attract Parisian audiences: Nureyev was told that he would be going to Paris after all.

The Leningrad State Kirov Theatre of Opera and Ballet, Order of Lenin, to give it its full title, opened at the Palais Garnier on 16 May 1961 with *The Sleeping Beauty*. Nureyev's performance was a colossal success. He made his impact at the *répétition générale*, the dress rehearsal regularly attended by journalists and balletomanes, but the director, Konstantin Sergeyev, refused to grant him the opening performance, which went to Vladilen Semenov. Nureyev showed his feelings by forgoing a seat in the audience and taking himself to hear Yehudi Menuhin playing at the Salle Pleyel.[54]

In *La Bayadère*, the first production of this ballet staged in the West, Nureyev danced the warrior Solor and was permitted to insert his own bravura *Corsaire* solo, a show-stopper that had won him acclaim as a student in Leningrad. Olivier Merlin of *Le Monde* responded to Nureyev's eruption in *La Bayadère*: 'We will not quickly forget his arrival racing from the back of the stage . . . with his large, strange eyes and hollow cheeks beneath the plumed turban . . . this was already the Nijinsky of *L'Oiseau de feu*.'[55] Olivier Merlin also hailed 'the most marvellous interpretation of *Swan Lake* that I have ever seen. The names of Alla Osipenko and Nureyev are joined with those of Tamara Karsavina and Vaslav Nijinsky in the firmament of the sylphs.' Fifty-two years had passed since Nijinsky conquered Paris.[56] Janet Flanner informed her American readers that French balletomanes regarded Nureyev as 'the strangest, and uncontestably the most influential, personality—as well as the greatest technician—since Nijinsky, to whom he is the first ever to be so compared'.[57]

Nureyev's self-taught English enabled him to communicate with French dancers and balletomanes who showed him round Paris and introduced him to Clara Saint, Chilean fiancée of the late Vincent Malraux, son of the minister of culture André Malraux. Nureyev was warned by the director of the Kirov, Sergei Korkin, to end the liaison. It was the KGB's Embassy *rezidents*, notably Captain Strizhevski, who first proposed the exit-solution. On 1 June they sent word to Moscow that Nureyev's behaviour had become intolerable. The theatre and ballet critic Clive Barnes commented: 'In those first days of Soviet touring the dancers were herded together as a collective. They did everything together... All this hardly had to be imposed, for such behaviour comes absolutely naturally to most Soviets.'[58] But not to Rudolf Nureyev, who made lunchtime visits to the Louvre with Michael Wishart, an English painter with the kind of bohemian past—friendships with Jean Cocteau and the painter Francis Bacon—which appealed to the homosexual Nureyev. On 3 June the secretary of the Leningrad Regional Party Committee and deputy minister of culture Kuznetsov sent instructions to Paris that Nureyev be sent home immediately, 'taking all the necessary precautions'.[59] However, the situation on the ground now looked a little different: the Kirov had just transferred from the Palais Garnier into the larger Palais des Sports, and Nureyev had that week been awarded the Nijinsky Prize. Konstantin Sergeyev, Korkin, and the Soviet ambassador decided to stall. On 6 June a further message of recall arrived, but two days later the order was rescinded after Nureyev dutifully joined a Kirov contingent for photos and interviews at the offices of *L'Humanité*. A third order for his return was dispatched on 14 June, but Korkin refused to comply on the grounds that Nureyev's behaviour had improved—although in fact he was still coming back to the hotel at six in the morning.[60]

After this third summons it was finally decided to send him back to Moscow on 16 June, the day the company departed for London.[61] A blue bus ferried the company to Le Bourget airport. Each dancer was given his or her flight ticket. Korkin broke the news to Nureyev that he alone of the dancers must fly to Moscow because of his mother's poor health, and to take part in 'important concerts' there.[62] According to the account confidentially circulated to the Central Committee, Nureyev threatened to commit suicide. The Moscow plane was due to leave two hours after the London plane; Korkin went on to London, leaving Strizhevsky behind to get Nureyev on the Moscow flight. Alerted by a telephone message from Nureyev relayed through an intermediary, Clara Saint located the office of the airport police, informing them that a Russian dancer wanted to stay in France. They replied: 'We can't go looking for him. He must come to us.' When two French plain-clothes policemen descended the stairs and casually ordered coffee at the bar, Nureyev ran to them: 'I want to stay!' When one of the KGB men moved to grab the dancer, he was intercepted: 'On est en France ici.' Presently Mikhail Klemenov, a secretary at the Soviet Embassy, arrived and demanded that Nureyev be handed over, but to no avail. Nureyev kept repeating 'Nyet!'

The events at Le Bourget made the front pages in the evening papers, in London as well as Paris, alongside the Kennedy–Khrushchev summit in Vienna. 'Russians say romance caused Dancer's Flight', the *New York Times* (18 June) announced, quoting an interpreter travelling with the Kirov. The London *Daily Express* story—GIRL SEES RUSSIANS CHASE HER FRIEND—began: 'Ballet star Rudolf Nureyev skipped to freedom at a Paris airport today, to the fury of Red security men and the delight of a red-haired girl.' A photograph on the back page of *The Times* of Nureyev dancing was accompanied by a report in the classic cold war mould: 'At Le Bourget airport he ran through the barrier shouting, "I want to be free," and sought political asylum.' Perhaps to confuse Aleksandr Shelepin and the KGB, *Time* (23 June) ran the caption 'Defector Rudolf Nureyev' under a photo of a different Kirov dancer, Yuri Soloviev, with whom Nureyev had shared a room in Paris for five weeks.[63]

Clara Saint appeared on magazine covers across Europe, Garboesque in a scarf and sunglasses. *Le Monde* (18–19 June) noted her denial that she had influenced Nureyev but found her presence at the airport when he defected 'fort remarquée'. The paper also quoted Serge Lifar as describing Nureyev and Serge Golovin as the best dancers in the world; the defection of a dancer who had recently won the Nijinsky Prize, said Lifar, was a disaster for the Kirov. That it was a disaster for Soviet prestige no one, least of all the Russians, doubted. They were caught unawares; it had not happened before.

Life in Paris, with its powerful Communist Party, was less than secure for a renegade; Nureyev told *Paris Presse* that he was changing his address every two or three days. He said he had wanted to leave the USSR for a long time, and had 'nearly done so four times before'. 'Nureyev "Afraid of Reprisals." Russian Dancer's Dangers', announced the *Guardian* (23 June). The Soviet Central Committee archives also contain a report (18 June) by the KGB's boss, Aleksandr Shelepin, following an emergency meeting of the Committee of State Security: NUREYEV Rudolf Hametovich, born 1938, single, Tatar, non-party member, had 'betrayed his motherland in Paris'. He had consorted with homosexuals.[64] Was the CIA involved in Nureyev's defection? One biographer, Peter Watson, frequently refers to a 'KGB file', seen by him in translation after the end of the Soviet regime, which evidently claims that Clara Saint (transliterated as Clare Sene) was 'recruited' by a CIA agent, 'Mr Wilson', who covered as the London-based 'editor' of the *Baltimore Sun*. We can safely forget 'Mr Wilson' and this for-sale 'KGB file'.[65] 'My leaving Russia was purely artistic and not political', Nureyev told Clive Barnes on television. Male dancing in Russia he described as 'very rough' and anti-lyrical: 'they did not believe men could execute women's steps, and that's what I was doing. They could not believe it, they could not be emotional...'[66]

His first contract with a Western ballet company was signed within three days—he was to receive FF30,000 a month to appear with the Marquis de Cuevas Ballet in Paris. Nureyev opened in *Sleeping Beauty* on 22 June, only six days after he bolted at Le Bourget. For the first night the Théâtre des Champs-Elysées was surrounded by police and packed out by *le tout Paris*. Before his second performance, Nureyev recalled, a female journalist arrived with a photographer in his dressing room. The photographer brought three envelopes from the Soviet Embassy, three painful messages from the homeland. His father Hamet, a devoted Party member, could not bring himself to believe that his son would betray the motherland. Rudolf's mentor and friend Aleksandr Pushkin wrote to warn Nureyev that he would lose his technique and his moral integrity if he did not return home. Finally, a telegram from his mother begged him to return.

The Bluebird duet takes place in the third act of *Sleeping Beauty*. As Nureyev came on stage, hostile shouting and whistling almost drowned out Tchaikovsky: 'I was perfectly aware that some communists were trying to sabotage the performance. I could hardly hear the music and I saw pieces of what looked like glass thrown on to the stage at me but I kept dancing...That little group of excited men, paid to prevent me from dancing, made me wonder about the people the communist regime had attracted.'[67] This is cold war prose, not least the word 'paid'. According to the London *Sunday Times* (2 July), he had barely begun his variation when a group of Communists began shouting 'Traitor!' and 'Go Back to Moscow!' (though the latter, surely, is an epithet traditionally used by anti-Communists), while pelting the stage with tomatoes, banana-skins, and pepper bombs. These jeers and catcalls were countered with cheers of encouragement from other members of the audience, creating a cacophany.

On 11 August Polikarpov, head of the Central Committee's Commission for Foreign Journeys, privately blamed the Kirov management for ignoring Nureyev's character 'as a scandalous and morally unstable person' (*moral'no neustoichivyi chelovek*) when planning the trip. The Party committee of the theatre had not been properly involved in the selection process, which was undertaken by the director (Korkin) and ballet master (Sergeyev). Striz-hevsky, the deputy director, was also blamed. Nureyev was a *predatel'* (trai-tor).[68] Korkin was later sacked by decision of the Leningrad Party Committee. The Ministry of Culture was urged to bring administrative charges against Sergeyev.[69]

After their return to Leningrad the Kirov dancers were summoned to KGB headquarters for debriefing, notably Yuri Soloviev. Nureyev's *Corsair* solo was excised from *A Leap by the Soul*, a film about Russian ballet. Images of him in magazines arriving from abroad were cut out or pasted over. A closed trial of the dancer was held *in absentia* on 2 April 1962, at the Municipal Courts Building, Fontanka 16 (on the Neva embankment), Leningrad. The charge was state treason. Several witnesses from the Kirov testified that Nureyev had not intended to defect. Only his fellow-dancer and room-mate in Paris, Solo-viev, maintained the opposite. Nureyev's dancing partner, Alla Osipenko, a member of the Kirov since 1950, insisted that if Nureyev had been allowed to go on to London with the rest of the company, 'none of this would have happened'. The real source of this account is undoubtedly Osipenko.[70]

According to Solway, 'the day before' the trial a letter signed by all the leading ballerinas of the company assailing the director of the Kiev, Konstan-tin Sergeyev, then 51, and his wife Natalia Dudinskaya, 49, doyenne of Kirov teachers, for their high-handedness was published in *Izvestiia*. In Solway's opinion, publication of this letter in *Izvestiia* must have meant that highly placed Party officials wanted Sergeyev and Dudinskaya punished for Nur-eyev's defection. Although the letter did not mention Nureyev, his woman lawyer latched on to it, read it aloud in court, and accused the KGB of setting a trap for him in Paris. The major problem with this theory, however, is that no such letter can be found in *Izvestiia* on, before, or after 1 April.[71] Once again we are dealing with Alla Osipenko's memory—Solway quotes as her source not *Izvestiia* itself but the recall some thirty years later of two eyewit-nesses, Tamara Zakrzhevskaya and Osipenko herself. In a telephone conver-sation with the present writer, Alla Osipenko confirmed that the letter was indeed written, but she was no longer sure whether it was published in *Izvestiia* (clearly it was not) or read out in court. A tribute to Nureyev, published in St Petersburg in 1995, confirms the seven-year sentence but makes no mention of such a letter.[72]

In November 1961 Nureyev paid a secret visit to London at Margot Fon-teyn's invitation and made his first appearance at a Gala. On 21 February 1962 he opened his career with the Royal Ballet when he danced with Fonteyn—twenty years his senior—in *Giselle*. Tickets were over-subscribed by 70,000 applications and were selling on the black market for £25, four times their face value. Soon Nureyev and Fonteyn were to triumph in Frederick Ashton's *Marguerite and Armand* and to forge a partnership which endured until 1976, shortly before Fonteyn's retirement.

A year after his defection Nureyev published a ghosted and precocious autobiography:

Now and then in life one has to take a decision like lightning, almost quicker than one can think. I have known this in dancing when something on the stage goes wrong. That is how it felt that hot morning in June 1961 on Le Bourget airfield, outside Paris, as I stood in the shadow of the great Tupolev aircraft which was to fly me back to Moscow. Its huge wing loomed over me like the hand of the evil magician in *Swan Lake*...I was to be despatched to Moscow and there judged. For my 'irresponsible' way of life, as they had called it. For insubordination, non-assimilation, dangerous individualism...[73]

⌗ ⌗ ⌗

The Bolshoi's 1959 triumph in America was repeated in the autumn of 1962, when the company embarked on a three-month tour of New York, Washington, Philadelphia, Chicago, Montreal, and Toronto. The highly praised Maya Plisetskaya, the prima ballerina since Ulanova's retirement, received a half-hour ovation at the Met. The *Herald Tribune* (11 September) reported a party given for the dancers by Rebekah Harkness Twist. 'They sipped champagne, gorged on rich canapés, filled their plates with all manner of food piled on shining silver service, and then took an uninhibited go at the quaintly [*sic*] American Twist.' Jerome Robbins explained through an interpreter to Plisetskaya that ever since her last tour of America he had wanted to create a ballet especially for her. In his memoirs Khrushchev recalled that Plisetskaya, 'who was not only the best ballerina in the Soviet Union, but the best in the whole world, used to be excluded from the company whenever the Bolshoi Theatre went abroad. It was reported to me that she couldn't be trusted, that she might not come back...Her defection would have been useful for the West as anti-Soviet propaganda, and we would have been painfully stung.' As secretary of the Central Committee he received a letter from Plisetskaya, a long and forthright expression of her patriotism and her indignation that it should be doubted. The Presidium had read the letter and decided to let her go on the 1962 tour, despite misgivings.[74] But evidently she remained a wild card. Some years later, in December 1965, the Soviet government responded to a demonstration on behalf of the writers Daniel and Sinyavsky in Mayakovsky Square by proposing to amend the RSFSR criminal code. This touched off a wave of petitions, one of them signed by thirteen leading cultural figures, including the physicists Kapitsa and Sakharov, the film director Romm—and the ballerina Plisetskaya.[75] According to an anti-Soviet source, Plisetskaya is said to have later alleged that the KGB had tried to recruit her in 1966 to be 'friends' with Robert Kennedy.[76]

Following the Bolshoi's 1962 tour, Georges Balanchine returned to Russia with the New York City Ballet. This gifted choreographer, né Balanchivadze, born in St Petersburg in 1904,[77] came under the influence of Mikhail Fokine at an early age. Fokine had worked with Sergei Diaghilev in Western Europe but returned to stage ballets at the Maryinsky in 1914. In 1917 Bolshevik troops searched the Petrograd Ballet School and, in Cromwellian mood, closed it. Members of the Balanchivadze family disappeared or were persecuted. The 14-year-old Georgi survived as best he could. In 1918 Anatoly Lunacharsky, commissar for education, got the Ballet School reopened. In 1923, aged only 19, appointed ballet master of the Mikhialovsky Opera Theatre, Balanchine fell in with Vladimir Pavlovich Dmitriev, a croupier in a licensed gambling house, who obtained permission to take a troupe of artists abroad ostensibly to display Soviet culture. In the early 1920s a fair amount of private enterprise was still allowed. Off they went to Germany, London, and Paris—Balanchine never returned.

Balanchine's collaboration with Stravinsky was to become a vital dimension of the New York City Ballet's repertoire, notably his version of *The Firebird* (1950) and of the Stravinsky *Triple Bill* which included the world première of *Agon* (1957). Balanchine's decision to perform Stravinsky's *Apollo* and *Agon* in Russia followed a similar gesture the previous year, in June 1961, when the Royal Ballet on its first visit to the USSR brought *The Firebird*, based on Fokine's original choreography. But the stylistic leap from *The Firebird* (first performed in 1910) to *Agon* is even greater than the passage of years might suggest. *The Firebird* is a late Romantic *ballet d'action*, in which dance occurs only when the story will support it; *Agon* is a stripped-down, modern, all-dance ritual of contest and tension. 'The part atonal sound-world of Stravinsky's score suggests at one and the same time New York traffic horns and baroque fanfares, the prepared piano of John Cage and the plucking of a mandolin.'[78] How would this go down in Russia? The risk (or provocation) was not diminished by Stravinsky's own, loud and very recent disparagement of current Soviet ballet: 'The [Soviet] repertoire is a few nineteenth-century ballets. These and sentimental, realist, Technicolor *Kitsch* are all the Soviets do. Ballet in this century means the Diaghilev repertoire and the creations of the few very good choreographers since.'[79] In mentioning Diaghilev in these terms, Stravinsky knew exactly the contours of the Soviet wound. The *Ballets russes* remained so great an embarrassment to the regime that virtually nothing was published within the Soviet Union about Diaghilev or his company.[80]

Balanchine's modernism was manifest in his preparedness to reveal dance by stripping away the visual and theatrical accoutrements beloved of classical, and particularly Soviet, ballet. He simplified acting and the usual armoury of elaborate facial expressions; he dispensed with 'interpretation', aiming for precision, spontaneity, musicality, energy. His company learned how to dance to the complex rhythms of Gershwin, Stravinsky, and Ravel, with all of whom Balanchine had collaborated. His hostility to the Soviet system was not in doubt. On 26 September 1956, for example, he had given a news conference in Berlin: 'I don't ever want to see Russia again. But if President Eisenhower would tell me to go, then I would probably have to. Otherwise I would just send my dancers.'[81] The first full-length ballet by Balanchine to be seen at the Bolshoi Theatre, in June 1958, *Le Palais de cristal* (known also as *Symphony in C*), arrived with the first Western ballet company to penetrate the Soviet Union, the little-regarded Paris Opéra Ballet.[82] He had been a US citizen for twenty-two years when the ninety-strong New York City Ballet finally arrived in Moscow from a successful tour of Germany, Switzerland, and Austria in October 1962.[83] Balanchine was reunited with his brother Andrei at the airport after a separation of forty-four years.

The opening performance was given in the Bolshoi Theatre.[84] The recent German appreciation of Balanchine's *Episodes* (music by Webern) and Stravinsky's *Agon* was unlikely to be replicated by Soviet critics and audiences. A report by John Martin appeared in the next morning's *New York Times*: the Soviet public, he warned, was accustomed to larger-than-life, swashbuckling stuff punctuated by applaudable bursts of bravura:

The Russian audience is an altogether honest one. It applauds furiously when it is moved to do so, and it sits in absolute silence when it is not so moved. The evening opened in the latter mood. The first ballet was ... *Serenade*, beautifully danced ... But the response was a perplexed and fairly indifferent one. The atmosphere began to warm with the Robbins–Gould *Interplay* ... Then followed *Agon* ... which is not easy for an audience to take at first seeing. But the pas de deux by Miss [Allegra] Kent and Arthur Mitchell brought forth the first sign of genuine enthusiasm. When the curtain rose on ... *Western Symphony* and revealed a painted backdrop, there was a wave of heartfelt relief ... From then on the temperature was high ... At the final curtain Mr Balanchine was the center of the greatest ovation ...[85]

After one performance at the Bolshoi, the NYCB moved to the 6,000–seat Palace of Congresses within the walls of the Kremlin. John Martin described the difficulties encountered by Balanchine's minimalist style in the vast spaces of a stage one-third wider than the Bolshoi's. Ponderous openings and closings of curtains did not help. Returning to the Bolshoi Theatre, NYCB achieved a greater rapport. Bizet's *Symphony in C* brought repeated curtain calls and rhythmic cries of 'Bal-an-chine' until the choreographer was forced to come forward and bow his acknowledgement. Webern's *Episodes* was greeted with 'tumultuous favor'.[86] Even so, press and public complained about barren, skimpy scenery, a lack of themes, of stories, of dramatic plots—and of human emotion. The critic of the English-language *Moscow News* referred to *Agon* as a 'morbid tragedy'. Writing in *Nedelia*, Boris Lvov-Anokhin called Balanchine a fanatic prepared to sacrifice the classical virtues to his own slight and often frivolous vision. Aram Khachaturian, in a generally favourable review of the NYCB repertory in *Izvestiia*, failed to mention *Agon*. The Russian critics, rather like the English ones in 1950, complained that Balanchine and his company lacked 'soul'.

On 18 October, the day that Edward Villella's solo in *Donizetti Variations* was encored in the Palace of Congresses, Foreign Minister Andrei Gromyko, on a visit to Washington, denied the existence of Soviet missile sites in Cuba. It was in the bus, returning from an evening performance, that Balanchine's dancers heard that there was a risk of war. Lincoln Kirstein devised plan A and plan B in case of emergency, but the cultural attaché told him, '*You* don't have plans. You leave when they tell you to leave. The first thing that we will know at the Embassy is that the phone will be cut off.'[87] But the missile crisis only intensified displays of Russian good-will. Meanwhile Balanchine invited Soviet dancers and teachers to watch his ballet classes, and the Bolshoi reciprocated with a class of its own lasting two hours. Richard Buckle writes: 'But Balanchine had secretly told Suki Shorer, Gloria Govrin, Patricia Neary and Suzanne Farrell to bring their practice clothes, and it needed only a few minutes of their haphazard *tendues* and *battements* at the barre to make clear that Balanchine has given them a speed the Russians never acquired.'[88]

They moved on to his native Leningrad. As told by the dissident Kirov dancer Valery Panov, at Leningrad airport the Kirov's artistic director, Konstantin Sergeyev, greeted Balanchine: 'Welcome to the homeland of the classical ballet.' Balanchine reportedly replied: 'No, the homeland of the classical ballet is New York. Russia is the homeland of the romantic variety.' Panov was not there and the story is hearsay. The more sophisticated Leningrad audience at the old Maryinsky Theatre, renamed the Kirov, responded immediately: *Serenade* had five curtain calls, *Agon* 'carried the house along with it', a huge ovation greeted *Western Symphony*. After two performances the company moved on to the shabby old Lensoviet Palace of Culture, which held twice as many spectators. Balanchine flew home to New York, rejoining the company in Tbilisi, Georgia, where he met more members of the family. A mass was sung in the cathedral. Balanchine took a curtain-call alone in the old, Moorish-style opera house. On 26 October, when the company returned to the Bolshoi Theatre for their last four days in Moscow—the day when Khrushchev admitted to Kennedy that the missiles were already installed in Cuba—Balanchine was mobbed at the stage door by balletomanes. In 1964, in a happier installation, the NYCB was to become resident company at the Lincoln Center (New York State Theater.)

☷ ☷ ☷

Nureyev, meanwhile, remained a thorn in the Soviet flesh. *Marguerite and Armand*, a new ballet created for Fonteyn and Nureyev by Frederick Ashton, with a score for piano and orchestra by Franz Liszt, was destined to be as successful in America as it had been in London. The *Sunday Telegraph* (17 February 1963) assessed the dancer's current cold war status:

If Rudolf Nureyev, the Russian dancer who defected to the West, appears with the Royal Ballet on its forthcoming American tour, the impresario, Mr Sol Hurok, is in danger of losing his future contracts with other Russian artists who appear in the United States. This is the latest piece of blackmail in Russian tactics which three [*sic*: two] years ago made Nureyev the scapegoat over similar cultural exchanges between Russia and France. The French gave in and Nureyev will not now appear at the Paris Opéra.

In the spring of that year the Royal Ballet did indeed take 160 personnel and 500 tons of scenery on an American tour sponsored by Hurok, who had overcome his nervousness about Russian retaliation (he imported the Kirov, Bolshoi, and many Russian musicians). A teenage immigrant from the Ukraine who had achieved wealth by his tremendous drive, intelligence, and organizational ability, Hurok was already a legendary figure in the twenties and thirties, when he made and lost several fortunes as an impresario. He took the lead in arranging post-thaw tours of America. The soprano Galina Vishnevskaya, the USSR's leading vocalist abroad, adored Hurok—she relates how an interpreter from his office took her to Saks Fifth Avenue and bought her a $2,000 dress for Hurok's 1967 birthday party:

He was a generous man. Above all, he realized that Soviet artists earn a miserable pittance; that all their earnings go to the embassy. So one had to feed them, to pay for luxurious accommodations for the famous soloists, to take them to expensive restaurants; otherwise they simply wouldn't come ... With Hurok, you felt protected ... whenever you appeared with him in New York—be it a restaurant, an elegant store, or a splendid hotel lobby—you would be noticed and indulged . . . When he appeared in a concert hall, especially with a female artist, every detail was planned. Three minutes before the curtain . . . he would promenade her.[89]

Hurok was certainly a generous man to Soviet stars who did not make trouble for him in his dealings with the Moscow Ministry of Culture and Gosconcert. According to the pianist Vladimir Ashkenazy, Hurok, who had accommodated the 21-year-old pianist in third-class hotels for his first American tour in 1958, urged him to go home to Moscow after Ashkenazy decided to settle in London; when the pianist stayed in the West, Hurok turned his back on him for two years. Natalia Makarova, the Kirov ballerina, recalled that Hurok had often visited Leningrad and knew her dancing—but after she defected in 1970 he was careful not to be seen visiting her at the American Ballet Theatre. Finally he invited her to a secret dinner in Connecticut, and for five hours assured her that she was destined to dance with all the great companies.[90]

Returning to the Royal Ballet tour of 1963, Jacqueline Kennedy sent a private plane to New York to bring Fonteyn, Nureyev, and Ashton to the White House for tea. In the empty Cabinet room Nureyev made a dash for the president's chair; moments later Kennedy received them in the Oval Office. Goaded by this Western triumphalism, the Soviet press broke a two-year silence when *Izvestiia* (10 April 1963) published an interview with *Paris Jour* (2 April) by Serge Lifar, under the headline 'He Loves Nobody and Betrays Everyone.' *Izvestiia* described Lifar as the ballet director of the Paris Opéra, avoiding the usual Soviet description of him as a White Russian Nazi collaborator. Contrary to reports, it was not Lifar but the preamble by *Izvestiia* which described Nureyev (misspelled in the cyrillic) as a deserter/turncoat (*perebezhchik*) who had betrayed his art and his country and who was now decaying as a dancer (*degradiruet kak tantsovshchik*) while reaching 'the limits of moral debasement'. However, the sneering Lifar, describing the dancer as 'unstable, hysterical and vain', and clearly petulant that Nureyev had chosen to work with the Royal Ballet in London rather than with Lifar at the Paris Opéra, speculated that Nureyev 'dreamed absurdly of becoming a lord'. What he needed was the discipline of work, 'not whisky at five in the morning'. Two months later *Kommunist* (No. 8, 1963) denounced him as a 'contemptible traitor' serving a 'slanderous anti-Soviet campaign' in the West which depicted him as a '"fugitive from behind the iron curtain." Imperialism needs Nureyev only to blacken the Soviet Union.' Thereafter the Soviet press blanketed Nureyev in silence, although a book called *Sinister Spider's Web* (*Zloveshchaia pautina*), published in 1965, did report a press conference he gave in Rome the previous year, apparently praising the superiority of Soviet ballet, and 'hotly complaining about the "tactlessness" of bourgeois journalists, criticizing the rules and customs of the "free world"'. Meanwhile Nureyev's name was removed from the honour-board of graduates of the Leningrad Ballet School and from all ballet publications; a book about the Kirov Theatre containing an article on Nureyev was withdrawn; if magazines posted from abroad contained photographs of him, they would reach the subscriber pasted over.[91]

In July 1965 the Bolshoi arrived for a two-month tour of Britain. Ekaterina Furtseva, the minister of culture, attended the opening at the Royal Festival Hall as the guest of the new Labour government's arts minister, Jennie Lee, along with the tour's impresario, Victor Hochhauser.[92] Trouble arose when the Foreign Office intervened to veto a special Bolshoi performance scheduled for Wimbledon Town Hall—the Albert Hall had refused the booking—in aid of the Bertrand Russell Peace Foundation, which was strongly opposed to the Vietnam War. The Foreign Office explained that its policy was not to allow Soviet artists visiting Britain under the Anglo-Soviet cultural agreement to appear in support of political or controversial causes. Bertrand Russell himself appealed to the minister (widow of Aneurin Bevan), but to no avail; immediately following a series of damaging university teach-ins on the Vietnam War, Harold Wilson was determined to prove his reliability as America's ally.[93]

In 1970 the Kirov was performing at the Royal Festival Hall, presented by Victor Hochhauser, from 23 July to 5 September.[94] Nureyev had a chance street encounter in London with Natalia Makarova, who was heading for her hotel, the Strand Palace. She and Nureyev had worked together in Leningrad in 1959–60, when she was only 19; she had been in Paris and London with the Kirov in 1961 when Nureyev defected, one of three soloists in *La Bayadère*. Shortly after the street meeting Makarova, now 29 and on her third performing visit to London, herself defected. Her last performance was scheduled for the final night at the Festival Hall, 5 September. Dining with her friends Irina and Vladimir Rodzianko, she made her decision. It was far from her first opportunity; indeed, she had travelled abroad alone. After spending the night at the local police station they were driven to the Home Office. Interviewed on BBC radio, Makarova said her decision was not political and purely work-related: 'In the West I would be able to use my energies to the full.' Moving on to BBC television, she said she had been thinking about it for two years.[95] Immediately after her defection she was 'inundated with letters filled with persuasion, flattery, and promises to forget the whole incident if I would only reconsider and return'. An agitated Konstantin Sergeyev stayed on in London, writing to her via the Soviet Embassy and Scotland Yard. 'I am sure that much is being concealed from you and that your answers are being dictated to you...It is extremely suspicious and I am sure that it is not coming from you', he wrote. (Shortly afterwards Sergeyev lost his job as director of the Kirov.) Tatiana Vecheslova, 'my dear coach', who had supervised Makarova's first roles at the Kirov, wrote angrily: 'Your not returning home is monstrous. Do you really think any foreigner can respect you? And how would an Englishman look upon someone who had left his homeland?' The dancer Alla Osipenko wrote: 'Your soul is Russian. It will not survive what you are doing.' On reflection, Makarova became more definite about her motives: 'I remained in the West because I did not want to die an early death as a ballerina in the Kirov's routine...' That, at any rate, was her constant position during interviews—in twelve years as a leading dancer she had not been called upon to give a single interview in Russia.[96]

Makarova had hoped for an offer from the Royal Ballet, but none came, though she danced a pas de deux from *Swan Lake* with Nureyev on television soon after her defection: 'I only regret that I did not rise to the occasion and that the tape remains as a kind of eternal reproach.' Later they made their stage debut in *The Sleeping Beauty* and *Romeo and Juliet* at Covent Garden, but they were not a happy pairing. With Vladimir Rodzianko acting as her interpreter and manager, Makarova accepted an offer from American Ballet Theatre, working with Anthony Tudor in New York. Balanchine, she reflects, disliked star dancers: 'In Balanchine's ballets the dancers form an orchestra of musical instruments that he alone can play. He is the conductor, the choreographer, the creator, the demiruge.'[97] Brought up in the Soviet interpretative tradition, 'where I can partially express my own human experience', she was baffled by Balanchine's penchant for abstraction.[98]

Mikhail Baryshnikov, leading male dancer of the Kirov, defected while in Toronto, on 29 June 1974, at the age of 26.[99] Born in Riga, and ten years younger than Nureyev, Baryshnikov's defection was carefully planned while he and his fellow Kirov dancer Irina Kolpakova were on tour with a contingent from the Bolshoi. The company had encountered pro-Jewish demonstrations at the O'Keefe Centre, Toronto, where shouting broke out in the balcony during *The Nutcracker* Suite. Members of the company were walking to a chartered bus after a reception following their last performance in the city when Baryshnikov was seen fleeing, pursued by 'persons identified as belonging to the KGB', then assisted into an automobile by 'Canadian police'. The Soviet Embassy's counsellor for press and information claimed that the dancer had been 'abducted' by Christina Berlin, daughter of the

Hearst Corporation's president Richard Berlin, with a promise of money. 'Baryshnikov was a poor boy at home', the counsellor added proudly.[100]

The poor boy was rapidly issued with a one-year permit to stay in Canada. The Bolshoi continued its tour of Vancouver and British Columbia without him. Commenting on Baryshnikov's defection, Clive Barnes, ballet critic of the *New York Times*, described him as the finest classical male stylist ever produced by the USSR. 'Soviet dancers are chained to a balletic bureaucracy that is threatening to destroy their dance. Like all the Kirov dancers who have defected since 1961, Mikhail Baryshnikov seems to have been motivated by a simple desire for artistic growth.' (This was inaccurate; as we shall see, it did not apply to the Panovs.) Dressed in bleached jeans and a striped shirt, with his blond hair in a modified shag cut, Baryshnikov told the *New York Times* (23 July) that he wanted to dance in ballets by Robbins, Balanchine, Tudor, Kenneth MacMillan, and Petit, and to work with them if they so wished. Interviewed by Anna Kisselgolf in Russian, he explained that he would not have defected if allowed to spend periods abroad working as a guest artist. True, dancers were sent to appear in one-night galas, as with a recent tribute to the late Sol Hurok, but such appearances were merely commercial ventures to profit Gosconcert. Baryshnikov also complained of a lack of good choreographers at the Kirov, a refusal to invite Western choreographers on patriotic grounds, no freedom to choose his own repertory. 'I have no relationship to politics and I don't wish to have any.'

Baryshnkiov made his American debut for American Ballet Theatre with Makarova in the pas de deux from *Don Quixote*. 'One of the hottest things on two legs', commented Clive Barnes: 'The man is sculpturally pure—a Donatello in movement—in a way few dancers have ever been.' Nureyev was in the audience when he made his debut as Solor in Makarova's staging of the Shades scene from *La Bayadère*. Later, as Nureyev's house guest in London, Baryshnikov dined with Princess Margaret, Ashton, Fonteyn, and Robert Helpmann. Nureyev is said to have dragged Baryshnikov to 'weird cabaret shows' featuring transvestites and impersonators who, if they knew Nureyev was in the audience, would impersonate him.[101] Baryshnikov became artistic director of American Ballet Theatre in the fall of 1980.

Baryshnikov had been the Kirov's star performer while his older colleague, Valery Panov, suffered a protracted agony of disgrace and unemployment. Sent home from an American tour in 1959, as already described, Panov had resumed his dancing. In 1962, while performing Stravinsky's *Petrushka* for the Mali in Moscow, Panov caught sight of the eminent composer himself seated in the audience beside Khrushchev. According to Panov, Stravinsky praised his performance to his Ministry of Culture hosts, while damning the production as mediocre. 'I told our Party secretary that both Stravinsky and [Serge] Lifar had said they'd like to meet me', but his request was refused. When Georges Balanchine's New York City Ballet arrived in October 1962, Panov sat, so to speak, in the front row. 'I was in the vanguard of Balanchine's worshipers. Despite Soviet ballet's splendrous staging and execution, I recognised it as heavy, solemn and provincial.'[102]

Jewish on his father's side, Panov mentions the impact of the Six Day War of 1967 on Soviet Jews like himself. Zionism was particularly strong in his native Vilnius. 'Backs bent over for generations straightened before my eyes ... My years of protesting that I had nothing in common with Jewishness had been shown up for what they were.' He now regretted having changed his name. 'I began to think of myself as an exiled Israelite and to take pride in the few Jews allowed to emigrate.'[103] Inwardly he applauded Natalia Makarova's defection during the Kirov's visit to London in 1970, but the impact of her action on the company, following Nureyev's nine years earlier, was devastating. Dudinskaya was relieved of her *classe de perfection* and was virtually barred from the Kirov after forty years's service as ballerina and teacher—Makarova had been one of her star pupils. After Sergeyev pleaded on her behalf, Dudinskaya was allowed to keep the Academy class. Everything was tightened. Foreign ballet lovers could no longer approach the stage door without a pass from the Ministry of Culture. 'Soon half a dozen Kirov stars with the strongest individuality would be in the West.' Panov got to know John Cranko, South African director of the Stuttgart Ballet, which he brought to the USSR in 1972. For Panov, Cranko 'represented all that beckoned from the West'. In Tel Aviv Cranko had staged a ballet about the Holocaust. 'He did not hide his opinion of the military government when he was in Greece or of our regime when he was a Soviet guest.'[104]

Panov's young second wife, Galina (Galya) Ragozina, was not Jewish, and was now enjoying international success. In March 1972 the couple took the fateful step of applying to emigrate to Israel—the sky fell in. She was dismissed. 'Wide arcs were negotiated around me in the corridors [Panov recalled]. Members of the orchestra looked at me as if I were the first aborigine in Europe.' Following his scheduled performance as the devil in *The Creation of the World* on 27 March 1972, Panov was banished from the stage. On the Kirov's bulletin board he was publicly rebuked: 'A reprimand is hereby announced to V. M. Panov for having performed ... without a wig.' (Yet he had dispensed with it a year before.) He was also subjected to a confrontation worthy of Mao's Cultural Revolution (which Russians despised): 'A vanguard of Party activists rushed in, followed by the entire company, with administrators, accompanists, and coaching staff. Almost three hundred people spilled around the studio's perimeter, pushing me against the piano in the far corner. Then I heard voices trying to pry Galina loose from her warming up.' Yuri Maltsev, long Panov's friend, had the floor, referring to him as Shulman: 'Shulman, a Jew, has submitted an application to go to Israel. Having fattened himself like a swine on the art of the Soviet people, he now wants to sell it elsewhere. But that's not all. If he goes, foreign newspapers will carry the stink of his slander and lies.' Another dancer declared that he wanted to 'vomit up all the putrid leftovers Panov gave me'. Another pitched in: 'Panov and Ragozina have sold themselves to a foreign intelligence service. We must fix a punishment for them usually not provided for in humane Soviet law. We must exile them to Siberia for the rest of their lives.' A character dancer, Konstantin Rassadin, said: 'Panov wants to betray the greatest art in the world for the West's dirty degradation . . . If he wants to trade the best ballet in the world to rummage in moneymaking garbage, he is an animal, and we must treat him as such.' People's Artist Irina Kolpakova then spoke of Panov's 'loathsome betrayal . . . But what really hurt me was a young girl's surrender, a Russian girl agreeing to go to Israel with him. This disgusting scum befouling our theatre—I wanted to throw up. Now I want to spit in their direction. Out! I say. Out forever, you Zionist fascists.' Panov's old friend and frequent partner Gabriella Komleva demanded that he 'tell us once and for all what you did in America [in 1959]. Tell us what filth you're preparing to write about our art.' Meanwhile 'corps de ballet boys with eyes full of unrehearsed menace muttered, "Israel," "Shulman," "enemy". I looked at Galya and froze. Her face was a pool of shame and distress. Everyone else was staring at her and waiting.' When urged to disown him, Galya crossed the room in tears and silently laid her head on his chest.

The hatred (he reports) spread like fire. 'Everyone welcomed it for settling every kind of score: women who had liked me, men who sought my roles; Kirov patriots who had always despised my style.'[105] Nixon visited the USSR in the summer of 1972; Panov was not the first beleaguered Soviet Jew to fall into uncritical admiration for America and the Nixon administration, including 'the cultivated Dr Kissinger', who was scarcely capable of understanding 'Soviet ruthlessness': 'We simply couldn't understand the crusade of some Americans to cut off Radio Liberty's appropriation. Although not our favorite station, it always carried hard news that the others didn't about Soviet abuses . . . Liberty was jammed to death. Finding a place and angle where the receiver could catch wisps of speech was an art as delicate as positioning arms in a ballet.'[106]

In the person of Fedya Medina, a young cellist from Bogotà, studying at the Leningrad Conservatory, Panov found a brave friend who acted as his go-between with the foreign press in Moscow. 'Publicity in the West was our only protection.' Baroness Batsheva Rothschild, Tel Aviv's patron of modern dance, sent the unemployed Panov dollars to sustain himself and Galya. Panov needed regular exercise. 'Without the daily battle my body would turn thick.' Living-room exercises were not enough. 'The sickly slackness of my muscles was advancing toward incurable rot.' KGB agents followed him everywhere, pushing into his apartment whenever foreigners arrived and threatening to confiscate their film. He was constantly threatened under Article 70: slander of the homeland.

Balanchine came back to Russia with the New York City Ballet in the autumn of 1972. 'I told some of his dancers how I worshipped him and how much I wanted to meet him. They answered that he had suggested to his company that they avoid me, fearing great danger to me—and warning of serious company consequences to them—if they did see me.' But some of the dancers took that risk: 'They made Balanchine's unwillingness to listen to my despair even harder to accept.'[107] Senator Edward Kennedy visited the Soviet Union, determined, like New York's Mayor Lindsay before him, to put in a word for the beleaguered Jewish dancer. A Kennedy aide contacted Panov to request an outline of his story. Panov was hauled in and bullied in the Big House by Party activists, but crop failures had made the Kremlin ultra-sensitive to Western pressure for Human Rights.

By June 1974 Galina was three months pregnant and suffering complications in a Vilnius hospital, resulting in a miscarriage. Panov had to pay 2,000 roubles for exit visas and repairs to their Leningrad flat. The British prime minister, Harold Wilson, appealed to Kosygin to release the pair before the Bolshoi began its British tour. Grenville Janner MP, chairman of the All-Party Parliamentary Committee for the Release of Soviet Jewry, was promoting a planned demonstration when the Bolshoi reached London. On 8 June the Western press announced that the Panovs had been granted permits to emigrate to Israel. In Vienna the couple were met by Jewish Agency officials, then flew on to Tel Aviv, affirming their support for demonstrations against the Bolshoi in London. More than fifty banner-waving members of the Women's Campaign for Soviet Jewry had jeered outside the Royal Horse-guards Hotel when the Bolshoi company arrived. Noisy protests occurred outside the Coliseum, with a counter-demonstration by the Palestine Action Campaign.[108] Meanwhile, the ever-outspoken columnist Bernard Levin un-leashed a fierce polemic (*The Times*, 8 June) against his fellow-Jew, the increasingly beleaguered impresario Victor Hochhauser, 'a former refugee from persecution' who seemed remarkably insensitive to anti-Semitism in the USSR.[109]

A long-haired Panov and his wife were photographed with Laurence Olivier, who had led the Equity campaign, at a reception at the Israeli ambassador's residence. Ten days later the couple were outside the Soviet Embassy demonstrating for the release of Dr Victor Polsky, a Jewish physicist. The Panovs were reunited for the first time with other former Kirov stars, Nureyev,[110] Baryshnikov, Makarova, and Sasha Minz, at a party in New York. There was thunderous applause when they all embraced at the curtain-call.[111]

⌗ ⌗ ⌗

Were these defectors in constant danger of physical reprisal from the KGB? Did Moscow Centre plot stratagems to sabotage their careers? There has been a lively outpouring of books trading in exciting allegations, but these prove impossible to substantiate on closer inspection. Take the case of Nureyev: during the early months of 1977 press reports indicated that he had been trying for fourteen years to obtain an exit visa for his mother to visit him. A petition pleading for his family's release from the USSR was presented to the Soviet embassies in Washington and London, but it was rejected and Nureyev's sister was refused a passport.[112] Increasingly honoured in France, where Madame Jacques Chirac, wife of the Gaullist mayor of Paris, presented him with the city's Grande Médaille de Vermeil on 7 December 1978, Nureyev was appointed artistic director of the Opéra Ballet in 1983, supported by the Socialist minister of culture, Jack Lang, and remained in the post until November 1989.

According to Peter Watson's 'KGB file', the KGB 'devised two plans to get back at Rudolf. In one he was approached to see if he would work six months in the West and six months in Russia ... The other plan was for both his legs to be broken. The KGB file contains some amusing exchanges reflecting on the effect that would have on Russia's international image.' More follows: Nureyev's name was supposedly placed on the KGB's 'wet list' as a candidate for assassination: 'He had originally been targeted by none other than Nikita Khrushchev. The Soviet President [*sic*!] who had championed him to Ekaterina Furtseva after Rudolf had danced on the afternoon when Voroshilov had sung, had taken Rudolf's defection particularly personally... He had first authorized Nureyev's elimination in October/November 1962...' By this account Nureyev's name was 'un-wet listed' after Khrushchev's fall in 1964, but restored in the summer of 1967 after Yuri Andropov became head of the KGB.[113]

The corsair-like Nureyev has exercised an obvious attraction for authors peddling hocus-pocus about the KGB; for example, Professor Christopher

Andrew has written in *The Times* that the KGB—Moscow Centre—invested 'enormous time and effort' to devise ways 'to damage the careers of Rudolf Nureyev, Natalia Makarova, Mikhail Baryshnikov and other defectors from Soviet ballet'. Andrew is co-author, with the KGB defector Vasili Mitrokhin, of *The Mitrokhin Archive* (1999),[114] in which the same claim is found on several occasions although Baryshnikov is not put in the same category.[115] According to Andrew, 'Mitrokhin still recalls his sense of personal outrage on discovering in the FCD [First Chief Directorate] files an operation to maim the star defector, Rudolf Nureyev. Mercifully, the operation failed.'[116] *The Mitrokhin Archive* offers a fuller account:

The November 1962 plan for dealing with defectors also specified 'special action' against the world-famous ballet dancer Rudolf Nureyev...The KGB had begun a campaign of intimidation immediately after Nureyev's defection. On the night of his first major performance with a Western company, when he was due to dance the part of the Blue Bird in a Paris production of *Sleeping Beauty*, he received emotional letters from both his parents and his former ballet teacher, appealing to him not to betray the motherland. Having steeled himself to go ahead, Nureyev then found his performance interrupted.[117]

Professor Andrew produces no evidence that the KGB masterminded either the content or timing of these letters—unless one drifts with the general implication in this and other books of the genre that the KGB controlled the weather. Then follows a quotation from Nureyev's own description of Paris Communists trying to sabotage his performance in *Sleeping Beauty*.[118] Although Nureyev does not attribute responsibility to the KGB, Andrew comments on this passage: 'The KGB's early attempts at intimidation failed.' This in effect turns speculation about the long arm of the KGB in the Théâtre des Champs-Elysées into a fact.[119] Nine lines later an additional KGB plot arrives: 'Though the November 1962 plan of campaign against leading defectors did not specify the nature of the "special action" to be employed against him, it was clear from the context that it would henceforward involve a good deal more than sprinkling broken glass on the stage.'[120] Why was it 'clear'? The narrative technique here is disreputable: the so-called November 1962 'plan of campaign' remains undocumented and unproven.

Andrew and Mitrokhin then come to the alleged leg-breaking plot, which seems to echo Watson's: 'Subsequent FCD directives discussed schemes (which were never actually implemented) to break one or both of Nureyev's legs.'[121] The source reference given here is not Mitrokhin and his 'archive' of notes, but 'Victor Sheymov, *Tower of Secrets. A Real Spy Thriller*, Annapolis, Md., Naval Institute Press, 1993, 92–3.' Who is Sheymov? The index accords him only a single mention: 'a defector from the Eighth Chief Directorate' who spoke to the CIA in 1980. One might ask why, despite Nureyev's role as a thorn in the Soviet flesh for more than twenty years, there is no record of an attempted assault on him? Indeed, why is there not a single recorded instance of a physical assault on a Soviet dancer, musician, performer, writer, artist or sportsman following their defection in the West?

Concerning Natalia Makarova's later defection, Andrew and Mitrokhin offer more hocus-pocus:

A joint memorandum by the heads of the First and Second Chief Directorates proposed that, if a way could be found to injure Nureyev without the hand of the KGB being obvious, a similar 'special action' should be taken against Makarova. Depending on the results of special actions taken with respect to Nureyev, aimed at lessening his professional skills, [the KGB] should consider carrying out a special action with respect to Makarova, in order to localize the negative effect of her forthcoming performances in Britain and the United States. If the British propaganda organs are activated and information provided by her is used to slander Soviet life, additional measures will be devised.[122]

We may pause here—Makarova defected fully nine years after Nureyev! When was this infamous 'joint memorandum' (of whose existence there is no evidence beyond Mitrokhin's so-called 'notes') supposedly written? Are we to believe that nine or more years after Nureyev had been floating across the stages of London, Paris, and New York, the KGB was still puzzling out ways to slow him down? As regards the 'joint memorandum', Andrew–Mitrokhin tell us that: 'As usual, the reference in their memorandum to physical injury was expressed in euphemistic bureaucratic prose.' This would seem to suggest—and the lack of precision leaves no alternative to speculation—that the term 'injure', in the physical sense, has been invented by Andrew and Mitrokhin out of 'special action'. In the passage quoted below each sentence does not follow from its predecessor although there is a hazy implication that it does:

An approach was made by the Centre to the Bulgarian intelligence service to seek the possible assistance of one of their agents in a company where Makarova was due to dance. On one occasion Makarova was slightly hurt in an accident behind the stage caused by a beam falling from the set. The files seen by Mitrokhin, however, do not make clear whether this was the first nearly successful 'special action' by the KGB against a defecting ballerina or merely an act of clumsiness by a stagehand.[123]

In short: (1) The Bulgarians were asked to do what? We are not told. (2) Makarova is 'slightly hurt' by a falling beam. (3) We don't know what happened or why. Or when. The dance company is not named. The authors add in a reference note: 'Both Nureyev and Makarova were also the targets of numerous KGB active measures designed to discredit them.' But not a single example is given.

Of Mikhail Baryshnikov, who defected thirteen years after Nureyev and four years after Makarova, the authors write: 'What struck Mitrokhin, however, was the apparent lack of plans to maim Baryshnikov similar to those which had been devised, though not apparently implemented, against Nureyev and Makarova a few years earlier.'[124] The word 'maim' now joins 'injure' not in any demonstrated KGB document but in our authors' narrative. 'Plans to maim' Makarova have slipped into the category of fact—typical of the technique used in *The Mitrokhin Archive*. Injure—maim—cripple! What Mitrokhin actually did or did not see in the way of genuine KGB documents is the question throughout *The Mitrokhin Archive*, a question which neither of its authors nor the British Foreign Office is prepared to expose to normal scholarly scrutiny.[125] In short, the Mitrokhin archive remains closed.

⌗ ⌗ ⌗

In August 1979, Aleksandr Godunov, a 29-year-old soloist of godlike appearance, was dancing with the Bolshoi, then in its fourth and final week at Lincoln Center's NYS Theatre, when he was granted asylum, explaining that he wanted to broaden his art and dancing experience. His wife Lyudmilla Vlasova, also beautiful but 36 and apparently a lesser soloist, was withdrawn from the company and put aboard an Aeroflot airliner by Soviet embassy men, whereupon US officials surrounded the plane with vehicles to prevent its departure. More than that: although a foreign airliner is treated as 'foreign territory', the Americans boarded the plane, removed Vlassova's passport, and, in the interests of determining whether she was returning to Moscow of her own free will, insisted that she leave the plane and be interviewed in a 'non-coercive atmosphere'. She—or her minders—refused. The plane stayed on the runway for three days, filling weekend television, with all the Soviet passengers still on board and the non-Soviets disembarking. Moscow expressed outrage. Aleksandr Godunov, meanwhile, was saying that he thought his wife might wish to stay in America, though neither he nor the *New York Times* managed to explain why he had jumped ship alone if that was the case. Finally, Vlassova consented to step into a luxurious, air conditioned, 'mobile lounge' parked beside the airliner accompanied by an equal number of Soviet and American officials, and to be interviewed by Donald F. McHenry, deputy US representative at the UN, who was heading the Carter administration team's cynical exercise on the ground. After further delay because of a thunderstorm she flew to Moscow. Tass and other

Soviet news media managed to denounce the entire 'outrage' without once mentioning Godunov or his defection. The *New York Times* fully supported the Carter administration's actions: 'It is not greed or excessive ambition but the Soviet system that forces artists to turn career decisions into ideological gestures.'[126]

In the late Gorbachev era some Soviet dancers were granted leave to perform with New York City Ballet and other companies. For example, in October 1987 the legendary Bolshoi prima ballerina, Plisetskaya, the 'defector' who never defected, appeared on stage at a New York gala with Nureyev and Baryshnikov. That year Makarova and Baryshnikov were invited to dance at the Bolshoi. By contrast Nureyev's return to the USSR in 1987 was a strictly private visit to see his dying mother in Ufa after twenty-six years apart. Nureyev had caused more offence than any, not only because he was the first among leading Soviet ballet dancers to 'leap to freedom', but because he had rubbed Russian noses in it from the moment of his defection; he was not judicially rehabilitated until September 1998, five years after his death.

PART V

Art Wars

Stalinist Art:
Tractor Drivers' Supper

The years before the 1917 Revolution had been a time of brilliant artistic innovation. Chagall, Kandinsky, Malevich, Goncharova, Tatlin, Lissitsky, and Rodchenko were at work, and Russian art was hurtling out of isolation. The Bolshevik seizure of power gave grounds for hope that the long-awaited marriage of the political and artistic avant-gardes would be consummated. Agit-prop trains bearing modernist art set out for the provinces. Ilya Ehrenburg recalled that during the May Day celebrations of 1918 'Moscow was decorated all over with Futurist and Suprematist paintings. Demented squares battled with rhomboids on the peeling façades of colonnaded Empire villas. Faces with triangles for eyes popped up everywhere'...That year, the first of May coincided with Good Friday. Worshippers thronged outside Iverskaya Chapel. Staring petrified at a cubist picture with a huge fish-eye in it, an old woman wailed: 'They want us to worship the devil.' Ehrenburg laughed, 'but my laughter was not happy'.[1]

He had reason not to be happy. It soon became clear that Lenin and his colleagues were impatient with the new 'isms' and 'art for art's sake'. Lenin made his own sentiments famously clear to his German Communist biographer Clara Zetkin:

The beautiful must be preserved, taken as an example, as the point of departure, even if it is 'old'...Why worship the new as a god compelling submission merely because it is 'new'? Nonsense! Bosh and nonsense! Here much is pure hypocrisy and of course unconscious deference to the art fashions ruling in the West. We are good revolutionaries but somehow we feel obliged to prove that we are also 'up to the mark in modern culture'. I, however, make bold to declare myself a 'barbarian'. It is beyond me to consider the productions of expressionism, futurism, cubism and other 'isms' the highest manifestations of artistic genius. I do not understand them. They give me no joy.[2]

Despite a token acknowledgement of the individual artist's right to freedom of expression, Lenin was growling ominously: 'Nevertheless we are Communists, and must not quietly fold our hands and let chaos bubble on as it will . . . Art belongs to the people . . . It must be understood and loved by them and no others . . . On their behalf let us learn a prudent administration . . . in the sphere of art and culture.'

In that phrase, 'on their behalf', resides the oppressive paternalism of 'Ilych' and pedagogic Bolshevism. The adjoining phrase—'Art belongs to the people'—embodied the split mind without which the Communist Party could not have sustained itself.[3] As Alfred H. Barr was to comment in 'Is Modern Art Communistic?', Lenin's phrase 'and no others' signalled a 'dictatorship of the proletariat more absolute than any foreseen by Marx and Engels'.[4] The year 1922 saw the formation of the Association of Artists of the Revolution (RAPP) dedicated to 'revolutionary realism', genre and portrait painting, historical tableaux and battle scenes, Party meetings and scenes of class conflict—and portraits of Lenin and Red Army commanders. Style and technique reverted to those of the Salon in the late nineteenth century. After 1924 no further exhibitions of the avant-garde were possible. Between 1920 and 1925 Chagall, Kandinsky, Gabo, Pevsner, and many other artists chose to emigrate. The works of cubists, futurists, and constructivists were transferred to museum vaults closed to the public and open, if at all, only to selected art experts.

In April 1932 the Central Committee passed a resolution abolishing independent artistic groupings, establishing in their place a monolithic Union of Soviet Artists. The complete shut-down of Russian formalism was reflected in a sudden shift of emphasis in display policy: when the exhibition 'Artists of the RSFSR: 15 Years' opened in Leningrad on 17 November 1932, it was organized by groupings. By the time it opened in Moscow on 27 June 1933, 'left' (i.e. modernist) art was displayed as a negative example in a separate hall: the central subject was now the battle for a new thematic realism. In 1934 socialist realism became the only acceptable aesthetic for both literature and art. Early in 1936 *Pravda* launched a series of articles attacking formalism, fully ten years before the same campaign was renewed at the onset of the cold war. 'Chaos instead of music' (28 January), 'Cacophany in architecture' (20 February), 'On artist-daubers' (1 March).[5] All 'left' art was now taken from the halls of Moscow's Tretyakov Gallery and the Russian Museum, Leningrad, and put in reserves.[6]

This was happening as Hitler consolidated his power and *Kulturkampf* in Germany. The most destructive anti-Soviet weapon in the post-1945 Western critical arsenal was guilt by association; the prejudices, persecutions, and policies imposed by the Soviet and Nazi regimes were held to be variants of a single 'totalitarian art', a blend of 'realism' and 'neo-classicism' demanding a uniform and strictly disciplined dedication of the artist to the *Volk* or the Proletariat—but always to the State and its Leader. A painting depicting Young Pioneers saluting Comrade Kirov in the 1930s discovers a mass of girls with Nordic fair hair and no trace of the Slav cheekbone: leaving aside their red kerchiefs, they could equally be Nazi *Mädchen* saluting Hitler. Hellmut Lehmann-Haupt's *Art Under a Dictatorship* (New York, 1954)[7] stressed the parallels between Nazi and Soviet art and freely applied the term 'totalitarian' to both, but without venturing a definition. 'The function of art in the dictatorship', he wrote, 'is to serve in the complete absorption of the individual into totalitarian society.' Lehmann-Haupt drew attention to 'a seemingly insoluble paradox': 'The Nazis called modern art Bolshevistic, degenerate, Jewish. The Soviets call it capitalistic, bourgeois, degenerate.' Hitler and Stalin banned precisely the same species of painters. He concluded that 'modern art is a powerful symbol of anti-totalitarian belief . . . not the implementation of an ideology, but the inevitable result of a genuine belief in individual freedom'.[8]

Hitler's words, when opening the House of German Art, bore a remarkable similarity to Lenin's diatribe against the 'isms': 'Amateurs in an art that is contemporary today and forgotten tomorrow: Cubism, Dadaism, Futurism, Impressionism, Expressionism; none of this is of the least value to the German people.' 'And what do you manufacture?' Hitler had rhetorically asked the fugitive painters, whom he called 'dilettantes'—'Misformed cripples and cretins, women who could only inspire aversion, men who are more like beasts than men . . .' It was all *Kulturbolschewismus*.[9] Under the direction of the Nazi propaganda minister, Joseph Goebbels, the Reichskulturkammer (State Culture Chamber) was established in 1933: membership was an essential precondition for patronage. When the Exhibition of Degenerate Art opened in July 1937, the sculptures were displayed without pedestals and the pictures were hung at random, some of them without frames, from floor to ceiling, lit by a dim light and furnished with mocking explanatory labels.[10] During 1937–8 a State Commission toured Germany, removing 15,997 works of art from thirty-three museums. The modernist art collection in the Kronprinzen-Palais in Berlin was closed; the purged artists included Van Gogh, Gaugin, Matisse, Picasso, Kandinsky, Chagall, and Lissitsky.[11]

What was the contemporary Soviet response? In 1937, at the time when pictures by Kokoschka, Nolde, Kandinsky, Klee, Chagall, and Max Ernst hung unframed and accompanied by insulting notices in the Munich Exhibition of Degenerate Art, the official organ of the Soviet Union of Artists, *Iskusstvo*, published a deliberately misleading editorial on these artists: 'In the West these "jokers" have very quickly found their way to the hearts of people of "culture" in the fascist countries—Germany and Italy—because their pretended lack of ideology serves fascism very well and very "ideologically".'[12]

The allegation of 'totalitarian' convergence was rarely, if ever, contested by Soviet commentators, because too damaging to repeat even by way of denial. Igor Golomshtok, author of the definitive work on totalitarian art[13] after he left the Soviet Union, never used the term during his years as a seemingly orthodox Soviet art critic. Mikhail Romm's documentary film *Ordinary Fascism* (*Obyknovennyi fashizm*, 1965), contained a section deriding heroic Nazi sculptures in the monumental-heroic-Aryan mould associated with Thorak—yet Romm's extensive quotations from Hitler contrived not to include the words 'Cubism, Dadaism, Futurism, Impressionism, Expressionism; none of this is of the least value to the German people'. The distinguished Soviet director carefully ignored the Nazi exhibitions of Degenerate Art, the removal of thousands of works of art from museums. Convenient footage was not lacking—Nazi cameramen had recorded every step taken—Romm's silence was imposed by the enduring influence of Stalinism even into the 1960s.

Not all Western critics have fully embraced the theory of a single totalitarian art joining Soviet and Nazi aesthetics.[14] Christine Lindey, while acknowledging that Arthur Kamft's depictions of heroic workers and soldiers closely resemble Soviet paintings, warns against a facile theory of convergence. The idealized neo-classicism of German painting, with its fondness for nudes and its nostalgia for a golden past, for the union of blood and soil, clearly separated it from Soviet art. 'Nazi art,' she writes, 'dwelled upon mysticism, individualism and timelessness. Soviet art glorified materialism, collectivism and change.'[15] Yet the eye is struck time and again by the convergences. Igor Golomshtok has juxtaposed reproductions of Soviet and Nazi paintings and sculptural poses to convincing effect. History itself juxtaposed the German and Soviet pavilions at the Paris International Exhibition of Arts, Crafts, and Sciences in 1937. On either side of the avenue leading from the Eiffel Tower to the Tower of Peace, the massive Soviet and German pavilions[16] confronted each other. Both nations fronted their building with heroic, muscular sculptures of monumental proportions. The Russians raised up into the sky Vera Mukhina's *Worker and Collective Farm Woman*, hammer and sickle aloft, male and female thrusting joyfully towards the Communist future.[17] Mukhina's totalitarian image was to dominate Soviet public art for the next twenty years.

⌗ ⌗ ⌗

In 1947 the Academy of Arts, closed after the Revolution, was refounded, with Aleksandr Gerasimov as first director.[18] The Academy not only regulated all the important Soviet art institutes and schools, but also controlled new acquisitions by museums through the State Purchasing Commission.[19] With membership restricted to the elite of state-honoured artists, the new Academy of Arts of the USSR was a pillar of Stalinism. 'Greetings to the Soviet people and its art! Greetings to the Communist Party and the Soviet government! Long live Great Stalin!'—*Da zdravstvuet, Stalin*! In the 1930s painters had frequently showed Stalin meeting and mingling with the people, but the post-war Stalin was depicted as aloof, elevated, 'classical', monumental, and isolated even when smilingly going through his mail, as in Fedor P. Reshetnikov's painting *Dear Stalin* (1950). Fedor S. Shurpin's evocative *The Morning of Our Native Land* (1948) shows Stalin standing alone after dawn before a countryside vista of distant tractors and refineries. Gerasimov himself kept pace, with his ghastly painting *Stalin and Voroshilov in the Kremlin* (1938) and his *Stalin at a Meeting with the Commanders*, an enormous post-war canvas, with bright, harmonious lighting within a palatial, pillared room. Stalin's modest uniform, without medals or braid, stands out against the glittering uniforms of the generals surrounding him.[20] The dominant Soviet painter between 1932 and 1953, Aleksandr Gerasimov could paint well, as in his *Portrait of Eminent Artists* (1944), a richly three-dimensional view of four elderly artists seated at a table with drinks, fruit, and cigars; but the sheer servility of his canvases depicting Stalin compare poorly to Velasquez's sixteenth-century portraits of the King of Spain.

As president of the Academy, Gerasimov began the 1947 general session by emphasizing the tasks set by the Party and government for painters, sculptors, and graphic artists, together with 'scientific workers in the field of theory and history of fine art'—the word 'tasks' (*zadachi*) came up again and again. The Soviet people had shown themselves to be politically, ideologically, and morally the most advanced in the world; their socialist culture was prevailing over the rotting (*gniiushchii*) capitalism and its 'pseudodemocracy'. He quoted Zhdanov: 'Each day our whole people strives higher and higher.'[21] The first modern works to receive specific praise from Gerasimov included a high proportion of portraits of Lenin, Stalin, Kirov, and Gorky, plus such paintings as *Workers and Collective Farmers* and *Interrogation of the Communists*. 'Our Academy, uniting the best strengths of Soviet fine art, must be regarded as the most progressive Academy in the world.'[22]

Without alluding to Hitler's declared tastes, Gerasimov attacked decadent cubists, futurists, and proponents of art for art's sake, who painted for the elect (*dlia izbrannykh*). The salons and exhibitions of fine art in capitalist countries, he remonstrated, were attended by an extremely high proportion of bourgeois—no sign of workers and peasants. Such exhibitions considered themselves a success if they attracted a few thousand visitors, in comparison with packed-out Soviet exhibitions.[23] Capitalist art exhibitions were invariably concentrated in capital cities and almost never reached the provinces. 'Bourgeois ideologists love to talk of the "freedom" of art under capitalism. But as Lenin clearly pointed out, this freedom is a sham (*mnimaia*) because in reality it displays a crude dependence of art on the money bags (*ot denezhnogo meshka*).'[24]

Even now Gerasimov detected a relapse into formalism among Soviet art-school teachers, lacking respect for 'the rules of composition': 'Let us not forget that within the walls of the All Russian Academy of Art not long ago worked such enemies of Soviet realistic art as the not unknown N[ikolai] Punin and his followers . . . eulogizing Cézanne, Matisse, and other ancestors of contemporary decadent bourgeois art.'[25] Confirmation of this is available from the ranks of the delinquents themselves. The dissident artist Oskar Rabine recalled how, at the Riga Academy immediately after the war: 'We were not obliged to do thematic compositions . . . Some of us adopted the impressionist or cubist style. In the library there were some beautiful reproductions of paintings already banned in Moscow.'[26] Gerasimov's presidential peroration to the Academy resonated with authoritarianism: 'In educating young artists we must make it absolutely clear that penetration (*proniknovenie*) of the walls of Soviet art schools by this or that decadent influence from the capitalist West is absolutely out of the question.'[27] Yet Gerasimov's public position as head of the Academy and the *orgkomitet* by no means coincided with his private inclinations. During the brief period of relative liberalism in 1945 he had produced *A Russian Communal Bath*, a major composition of female nudes with an obvious debt to Degas and Renoir. Several other pillars of the Soviet art establishment were known to be admirers of impressionism, including Boris Ioganson, vice-president of the Academy, Igor Grabar, head of the visual arts section of the Stalin Prize committee, and Sergei Gerasimov, head of the Moscow Artists' Union. Ioganson declared, with the French impressionists clearly in view: 'There are artists for artists. They exist, legitimately, as stimuli, as seekers after new paths, as experimenters, opening up new possibilities.'[28] In April 1946 Nikolai Punin (Aleksandr Gerasimov's particular target) had delivered a lecture at the Leningrad artists' union, 'Impressionism and the Problem of the *kartina*', praising Manet for his creative transformation of the heritage of the old masters; lauding Monet's versions of Rouen Cathedral; and finding in the spatial and compositional techniques of Monet and Cézanne the prerequisites for the contemporary picture (*kartina*). Punin warned against returning to the Renaissance, the Baroque, or Rococo as sole models. This lecture caused a huge debate in a room hung with impressionist reproductions; the artist Petr Mazepov argued that impressionism led on to the formalism of cubism and fauvism, in which 'there is no social struggle, the class soul, the party soul, the great soul of the people is absent'.[29] Voices were raised for and against Pablo Picasso, most famous of contemporary heretics.

Then came the crackdown in practice as well as theory. A work like Arkadi A. Plastov's oil on canvas, *Haymaking* (1945) shows impressionist influences, and although awarded a Stalin Prize in 1946 was criticized in 1949 for its 'superfluous "dappled effect" that interferes with perception'. His *Threshing on the Collective Farm* (1949), among its other sins, was accused of 'impressionist "painterliness", which deprives the human face of expressiveness'.[30] Impressionism was now viewed as the foundation-stone of Western aesthetic subversion. Vladimir Kemenov faithfully conveyed the new Party line in its entirety:

The decline of bourgeois art became most rapid at the end of the 19th and the beginning of the 20th centuries, with the rise of the epoch of imperialism and the decay of bourgeois culture which it involved. Even in impressionism we have a suggestion of the artist's indifference to subject matter, reflecting an indifference to the message of art. The interests of the artists of this school became greatly limited; the impressionists painted mostly landscapes and portraits, but their landscapes were approached almost exclusively from the point of view of portraying light, while their portraits, strange as it may seem, reflect a 'landscape' approach to the portrayal of the human face. The interpretation of the sitter's character, his inner world and psychology are all subordinated to problems of *plein air* and the object of conveying the vibrations of light on the body and clothes of the sitter. But the impressionists still saw 'nature' whole, perceiving it directly through man's visual channels.

The post-impressionists, especially Cézanne, criticised the impressionists for making the portrayal of light the exclusive concern of their pictures, sometimes allowing light to diffuse, as it were, the forms of objects. Going to the opposite extreme in their zeal to confirm 'material substance,' they banned light from painting entirely, and in their portrayals of man and nature began to emphasise properties (volume, weight, form, structure) common to both animate and inanimate objects, gradually turning both landscapes and portraits into still-lifes. In Cézanne's still-lifes the objects become doubly lifeless: his fruits and flowers lack texture and aroma. Particularly lifeless are his portraits, which completely express the artist's profound and even demonstrative indifference to man. This paved the way for the ensuing anti-humanistic trends of bourgeois art. 'But in his compositions Cézanne could not yet dispense with natural objects as a foundation,' laments the suprematist K. Malevich. Cubism and futurism finally broke up objects into geometric lines and planes, dissected them into the elements composing their outer forms and attempted to bring some kind of order into the resulting chaos. Realism was done for, as Picasso openly proclaimed. . . .

The futurists, just as one-sidedly, developed problems of motion, making a fetish of that, and subordinating all else to it. The expressionists, again, one-sidedly emphasized the subjective factor and the element of exaggeration (factors which, as such and no more, may be said to be intrinsic to the creative process), hypertrophying them, for the purposes of greater 'expressiveness,' to the point of hideously deforming the objects and phenomena depicted. Lesser schools have contented themselves with making a fetish of such components of paintings as surface texture, geometric line, and so on (purism, tactilism).[31]

Kemenov's 'Aspects of Two Cultures' extended its onslaught to 'paranoic' surrealism—Salvador Dali, Kandinsky, Joan Miró, Paul Klee, André Breton, and 'the psychiatrist Lokan' (presumably Lacan). This led on to an attack on Alfred Barr, critic and curator of the New York Museum of Modern Art, whose explanation of Paul Klee's painting *Around the Fish* Kemenov cited as further illustration of bourgeois irrationality. *Art News* (June 1946) had announced an exhibition of 'Subconscious' ink-painting; 'Washington University' was said to be offering six-week courses on surrealist techniques, including photomontage and automatism. Kemenov, who thought that six weeks would be more than enough, quoted *Life* (17 February 1946): abstraction was sweeping American art; in exhibitions from New York to the Pacific north-west the day belonged to 'vague, unidentifiable forms and the scissors-and-pastepot look that are the earmarks of the confirmed abstractionist'. Kemenov eagerly picked up every detail from *Life*, including the modernist outlook of three art schools in Provincetown. Again and again he described contemporary Western art in what was emerging as a standard Soviet vocabulary: 'sick', 'pathological', 'diseased', 'social insanity', 'paranoia', 'hypertrophy of the Ego', 'infantilism', 'egocentricity', 'delirium', 'hallucinations', 'chicanery', 'daubs painted by the donkey's tail'. Yet too wide a vocabulary of damnation is self-defeating—hell loses its visible frontiers.

⊞ ⊞ ⊞

Most favoured by A. Gerasimov and late Stalinism was the populist realism of the last quarter of the nineteenth century, as exemplified by Russia's so-called Wanderers. Three genres were favoured: (1) the portrait, mainly of political and military leaders (e.g. Boris Iakovlev's lurid portrait of Marshal Zhukov on his white stallion before the flaming ruins of Berlin); (2) the history painting, a splendid example being Geli Korzhev's triptych *Communists* (1959–60), the middle section of which, *Raising the Banner*, shows with formidable detail and in intense close-up a worker bending to the tramlines in a cobbled street to take up his dead comrade's red flag;[32] (3) the so-called genre painting (workers on the production line, collective farmers bringing in the harvest, a peace parade).[33] *Youth of the World—For Peace* (1951), a canvas six metres wide and three metres high, was the work of four Georgian artists. Typically, this joyful procession, the picture of health, displays best clothes and gleaming teeth while descending, clapping, and smiling, a flight of very best steps.

Many genre pictures were the work of 'brigades' like the Kukryniksy, who shared the painstaking labour of painting scores of individualized figures, photographically accurate in the case of leading Party officials and generals. Such a work is Vadil P. Efanov's *Leading People of Moscow in the Kremlin* (1949), which might have been the work of the enemies of the Soviet Union intent on proving the rise of the new class. Here, in a great marble reception room, under vast chandeliers, observed by an elevated bust of Stalin, the 'leading people' have gathered beneath a podium to ritually applaud a ritual. Accorded a Stalin Prize, this work was widely reproduced and imitated.[34]

The 'still life' landscape was increasingly under attack. The key concepts were man's purposeful control of nature, telling a story, learning from Stanislavsky the need for the psychological depiction of all the minor figures on a canvas. Essential was *zhanr* or *bytovoi zhanr*, meaning the depiction of everyday, current reality which the artist himself has seen with his own eyes. Deeply suspect was an individual overwhelmed by nature or 'lost' in a panoramic landscape, as in Martiros S. Saryan's *The Ararat Valley* (1945–6), of which *Iskusstvo* complained: 'Man is alone in nature, lost in mighty, cosmic expanses. Such a depiction of man can hardly be judged correct in our landscape painting.'[35] Foreshortening or cropping could also offend, as could fragmentation of the sacred human body, as in Arkady A. Plastov's controversial *Threshing on the Collective Farm* (1949).

Ever greater praise was heaped on the 'Wanderers', especially the portrait and landscape painter Ivan Repin, after whom a Leningrad institute of painting, sculpture, and architecture was named: his masterpieces of *plein-air* painting were hailed as uniquely Russian. The Moscow publishing house Isskustvo issued, from 1946 to 1950, successive volumes of Repin's correspondence with friends and leading figures in the art world. In their introduction to Repin's correspondence with the painter V. V. Stasov, the editors highlighted his letters from Paris in 1874, critical of the new French painting. Yet Repin does not mention the impressionists or any 'school' by name, nor does he allude to such subsequently illustrious artists as Manet, Pissaro,

Monet, or Degas. Indeed, Ilya Ehrenburg later published an essay, when it was safe to do so, claiming that in the year 1874, when the term 'impressionism' was first heard in Paris and Repin was there, he wrote home: 'I adore all the impressionists, who are gaining more and more ground here.'[36] (If so, the editors of Repin's collected letters were guilty of fraudulent omission.) Indeed, Repin's portrait of Leo Tolstoy resting recumbent in a wood and reading a book is obviously impressionistic, and even more so is the idyllic meadow scene *Na Mezhe* (On the Land, 1879), which could be mistaken for a Monet.

In 1947 the Moscow State Museum of New Western Art, the country's major collection of works from impressionism to early cubism, was closed down and turned over to a permanent exhibition of gifts to Comrade Stalin. Alfred H. Barr, a director of the New York Museum of Modern Art, who had visited the Museum in 1927, described its collection, expropriated by the state from the businessmen Morozov and Shchukin in 1919:

It remains the greatest collection in the world of French painting of the post impressionist and twentieth century schools. During the Twenties and Thirties the museum served as a bait for foreign tourists. But apparently such formalistic canvases as Cézanne's still lifes, Gaugin's Tahitian scenes, and Van Gogh's 'Walk in Arles', not to mention a hundred Matisses and Picassos, seemed too powerfully subversive.

The decree of the USSR Council of Ministers authorizing the closure of the Museum of New Western Art, quoted below, was never published in the Soviet Union:

The formalist collections belonging to the State Museum of Western Art, bought in the countries of Western Europe by Moscow capitalists... were a breeding ground for formalist views and self-abasement before the decadent Western culture of the age of imperialism and caused great harm to the development of Russian and Soviet art. The display of the museum's collection to the broad masses of the people is politically harmful and enables the dissemination in Soviet art of alien, bourgeois, formalist views.[37]

Increasingly quoted in the Western press were Soviet polemics against Cézanne, Rouault, Matisse, Picasso, and Henry Moore. 'Pravda Attacks Art', announced the *New York Times* (12 August 1947). After Moscow Radio assailed the 'formalistic wriggling and posing of demoralized bourgeois art', Edward Crankshaw commented that Soviet artists were still painting in the style of Landseer. Henry Moore's *Family Group* was held to exemplify the ruin of bourgeois art, 'a decay and mockery of the image of man'. Vladimir Kemenov commented that Western art journals 'vie with one another in the publication of hideous incongruities, many of them of a pathological nature':

The March 1947 number of the *American Magazine of Art*, published by the American Federation of Arts . . . reproduces a sculpture called *Family Group* by Henry Moore. The same number quotes the sculptor as saying: 'Beauty, in the later Greek or Renaissance sense, is not the aim of my sculpture.' The explanation is superfluous. In *Family Group* Moore has turned a man, woman and child into hideous animals with reptilian heads. The appearance of these revolting creatures is an affront to man . . . In the 8th, 1947, number of *America*, a magazine put out by the United States information Bureau for dissemination in the USSR, we find a color print of a painting by the American artist Georgia O'Keeffe, here called *The Sky Seen Through a Hip Bone* . . . Why should Georgia O'Keeffe have wanted to look at the sky through the cavity of the pelvis? For the same reason, evidently, that Henry Moore felt impelled to give a distorted picture of the human family. Their artistic individuality demanded it.[38]

A flood of anti-modernist articles appeared from 1949 to 1952. The All-Union exhibitions of 1951 and 1952 were the culmination of *fotografii-nost'* in Soviet art.[39] Soviet history painting was derided in the West for its servility and unscrupulous erasures—although the full extent of Stalinist censorship of photography by cropping, airbrushing,[40] and photo-montage insertions was not fully appreciated until the archives were opened years later. David King, an expert collector of doctored photographs, writes: 'From the time of [Stalin's] birth in 1879 until he was appointed General Secretary in 1922, there probably exist fewer than a dozen photographs of him . . . A whole art industry painted Stalin into events and places where he had never been, glorifying him, mythologizing him.' Paintings were often withdrawn from museums and art galleries so that compromising faces could be blocked out of group portraits. Under Khrushchev, the practice of cropping and airbrushing was vigorously pursued, normally to exclude Stalin: in Vladimir Serov's *Lenin Proclaiming Soviet Power at the Second Congress of Soviets* (1947), which received a Stalin Prize, Stalin can be seen behind Lenin with Dzerzhinsky and Sverdlov. Under pressure from Khrushchev, Serov had to repaint the portrait in full in 1962; revolutionary workers now surrounded Lenin, replacing Stalin and the other two leaders.[41]

⌗ ⌗ ⌗

Membership of the Union of Soviet Artists was the legal prerequisite for any artist wishing to practice professionally. The rules stipulated adherence to socialist realism. The Union and the Ministry of Culture were the only bodies empowered to commission works of arts and to make payment. It was illegal for an artist to sell his own work. The Union, which included over 10,000 painters, graphic artists, sculptors, craftsmen, and designers, appointed adjudicators of works submitted for exhibition. It also published two of the three main art journals in the USSR, *Tvorchestvo* (*Creativity*) and the journal devoted to decorative art.

Under Stalin, comments Igor Golomshtok:

the Union of Soviet Artists, particularly in the provinces, was numerically dominated by a conservative grey mass of artists who had received the apt nickname of 'dry-brushmen'... Their pictures embellished all the towns, villages and hamlets of the Soviet Union at holiday time and, at any other time, the walls of every state establishment. In the execution of these very profitable commissions they expended the last grains of their professional expertise and talent.

Such a hack artist is Vladimir A. Pukhov (Volodya) in Ilya Ehrenburg's novel *The Thaw*. After finishing art school, Volodya paints a big picture called *The Feast at the Kolkhoz*, which is greatly praised. He is rewarded with a studio in Moscow: 'Volodya dreamed of fame, of money, he always knew which were the "shock" themes, what artists had been rewarded and who had been told off.'[42]

But consider the plight of the average artist in the West, deprived of all social support! In September 1955 Moscow Radio's domestic service serialized a witty, keenly observed feature, 'One Thousand Miles Across Britain', by Igor Kobzev and Georgi Ostroumov, who had been members of a visiting student delegation. They observed a pavement artist in Trafalgar Square, crouching on the ground, 'a not-too-young man, a workless artist. In a hat by his side you can see a few coppers. It is terrible to think that a few hours' rain will wash away his artistic work.' More fortunate artists (they reported) found employment in advertising. 'In this city advertising surrounds one like the air one breathes... motley and loud colourings on the walls, fences, and red buses somehow do not harmonize with the severe beauty of this ancient city.'[43] Geli Korzhev's *Artist* (1960–1), painted after a trip to London, shows an artist reduced to drawing on a pavement. The 'down and out in Paris and London' syndrome horrified Soviet visitors. The Soviet painter Aleksei Burak, known for his industrial landscapes, made a trip to France in the late 1950s. He too encountered a frightful spectacle: 'Under an open sky at a metro station near Montmartre I saw people sleeping on the steps and on the ground, wrapped up in paper and scraps of newspaper. I got out my notebook and quickly drew this terrible scene and afterwards, back at the hotel, I painted a big canvas, *Homeless People at the Metro Station*.'[44] It wasn't only the physical hardship, the exposure to the sky and apparent material poverty that upset the Soviet mind, but also, one can infer, the transitory, non-academic, non-institutionalized, unregulated, anarchic nature of street art, with its dependence on the instantaneous reactions of passers-by.

There were, of course, no slums in Russia.[45] Often reproduced mockingly in the West was Aleksandr Laktionov's painting *Moving to a New Apartment* (1952), a luminous, photographic picture in which a delighted Russian mother in a headscarf gazes, awed, at the splendid new apartment allocated to her family—parquet floors, high ceilings, spacious double doors with glass panels—watched by her Young Pioneer son, who is holding a portrait of Stalin. The 'linen bag' of possessions gleaming at the woman's feet gives a sense of the old society, while modern suitcases, piles of books, a radio, and a globe herald the new. The picture was hung in the Tretyakov Gallery, but Stalin-laureate Laktionov and his family lived in a cramped cellar until shortly before he undertook the painting.[46]

⌘ ⌘ ⌘

Barely had the artillery fallen silent across the defeated Third Reich when the victorious allies began firing at each other's canvases. In the American zone of Germany, *Die Neue Zeitung* pressed for freedom and tolerance in the arts as synonymous with democracy. Founded in the autumn of 1945 by OMGUS, with offices in Munich, *Die Neue Zeitung* rapidly became influential; by January 1946 circulation was at 1.6 million, with 8–10 million readers.[47] The ICD distributed the paper in all four zones, including the Soviet, as well as in Austria. Kenneth Clarke wrote on 'Art and Democracy', Franz Werfel on 'Bliss through art', Julian Huxley on 'World community of art', André Malraux on 'Man and the artistic culture'. But who in Germany was listening? The modernist works displayed at the exhibition 'Maler der Gegenwart'(Painter of the Future), held in Augsburg in December 1945, provoked violent outbursts among the viewers and some of the canvases were mutilated. Students yelled 'Filth!' and 'These artists should be done away with! Concentration camp!' and 'Shoot the painter who did this!'[48]

Partly under Hellmut Lehmann-Haupt's influence, OMGUS's Museums, Fine Arts and Archives department was transformed from an organization solely concerned with the restitution of art looted by the Nazis into a sponsor of exhibitions and art competitions, a patron of German artists with added linkage to American galleries and collectors.[49] Originally OMGUS had not regarded the fine arts as a suitable vehicle for positive re-education, although it pursued a negative policy of purging Nazi influence from museums and public spaces; in a programme run by Captain Gordon Gilkey, 8,000 works of art are said to have been shipped to military deposits. But until 1946 the Americans paid little attention to contemporary German artists.[50]

In November 1946 a small posse of OMGUS functionaries stationed in Berlin privately and somewhat covertly created the Prolog group, providing material help and friendship for selected German artists, none of them former concentration camp inmates or prominent anti-Nazis. The Blevins Davis Prize, described as the 'most prestigious art contest of the immediate postwar period in Germany', had an international jury and offered a first prize of $1,000 plus a trip to the United States, with ten cash prizes for runners-up. From 3,700 entries, 170 finalists had their work exhibited in Munich. The winner in 1948 was George Meistermann's *Der Neue Adam*, a figurative oil painting influenced by Picasso's *Guernica*.[51]

Soviet criticism of art exhibits in the Western sectors of Berlin echoed the standard vocabulary: Klee and Picasso, for example, were dismissed as 'formalists'. On 21 August 1945 SMAD's *Tägliche Rundschau* reported a visit to a show in one of the Western sectors—'a mixture of inexpressive naturalism, lifeless formalism, and crass expressionism'. The exhibit displayed not 'a trace of understanding for liberated Germany's awakening from Nazism to true humanity and democracy'.[52] By 4 September the Soviet supreme commander had issued Decree 51, calling for 'the mobilization of art as part of the struggle against Fascism and of the re-education of the German people in the spirit of true democracy'. This was followed by an article in *Deutsche Volkszeitung*, (11 October), ' "Ismus" oder Kunst?' assailing expressionism, surrealism, and every other kind of 'ism'. On the other hand the Soviet administration was anxious to extend *la main tendue* to all 'progressive' elements, fostering a new popular front tolerant of diverse artistic traditions. The Soviet zone's first major art exhibition, 'Allgemeine Deutsche Kunstaus-tellung', which opened in Dresden in May 1946, took care to embrace artists of all tendencies—this occurred immediately before the Soviet zone's first legislative elections and the shotgun marriage between the Soviet-zone Social Democrats (SPD) and the Communist SED. Stressing the value of 'diversity' and 'the rich possibilities available to German culture', the Party newspaper *Neues Deutschland* (22 May) emphasized that the exhibition answered to no 'programmatic demand'. Artists from every zone of Germany were invited to submit work to a jury headed by Karl Hofer and the expressionist painter Max Pechstein. Among the 500 works chosen for display were many which could never have been shown in the USSR, including expressionist canvases[53] which had been the glory of Weimar Germany.

Opening the show, the Soviet cultural boss in Germany, Aleksandr Dymshits, expressed the hope that it would serve as a form of 'intellectual and cultural bridge-building' spanning all zonal borders. Similar comments about 'German unity' were offered by SMAD's Major General Timofei

Dudorov. Questionnaires filled out by visitors to the Dresden exhibition exposed the convergence of Nazi, Soviet, and indeed popular prejudice: 65.7 per cent singled out the 'expressionist and abstract art' as particularly objectionable, many of the comments echoing the vocabulary of Hitler's famous 'Decadent Art' exhibition: *Kunstschund* (art-trash), 'manure', and 'mentally insane'. But no one writing in the Soviet zone could even hint at parallels between Nazi and Soviet attitudes towards modernist 'decadence'. Discussions held during the Saxon cultural congress which marked the close of the Dresden exhibition contained some of the sharpest rhetoric yet heard in Soviet-occupied Germany. SMAD's senior cultural officers, Tiul'panov and Dymshits, delivered belligerent addresses, Tiul'panov enjoining German artists to look to the Soviet Union for guidance and rejecting slanders in the reactionary press that 'there is supposedly no free creative activity in the Soviet Union'. His answer to that simply confirmed the 'slander': in the Soviet Union 'criticism of anti-artistic manifestations is not regarded as intrusion into the area of art but as protection of art from the attempt by these insipid, vile, pseudo-artistic manifestations to intrude themselves into this exalted sphere'. These remarks were duly published in SMAD's *Tägliche Rundschau* (29 October 1946).

Licensed by SMAD following the Dresden exhibition, the journal *Bildende Kunst*, which first appeared in April 1947, was intended to provide each group of artists with a forum, while allowing the party (SED) to mediate. But deep divisions among the editors became apparent from the first issue, which was confronted by the massive challenge of an exhibition in the Soviet sector sponsored by the French occupation administration.[54] Rousseau, Cézanne, Manet, Renoir, Gaugin, and Van Gogh found themselves on the far side of the Iron Curtain and in the firing-line. Responding in *Bildende Kunst*, Gustav Leuteritz dismissed the French exhibition as the swan-song of the wealthy, decaying bourgeoisie. Chagall's violin-playing Easter donkey (wrongly interpreted by Leuteritz as a rabbit) earned the critic's special scorn. But the argument was far from over in *Bildende Kunst*. The next issue featured a vividly coloured Matisse on the back cover, and the following number carried a Picasso portrait of a woman. In two major articles, 'Wege der Kunst', Karl Hofer cast doubt on the notion of a single linear 'progress' in art, while arguing the case for an inevitable pluralism. A certain element of 'abstraction', he added, had always been present in the history of art.[55]

In November 1947 the Haus der Kultur der Sowjetunion issued invitations to a lecture by Dymshits and two subordinates on 'Soviet Art and Its Relation to Bourgeois Art'. The House of Culture on the Unter den Linden, furnished with antiques, carpets, chandeliers, and a bar and smoking room, impressed more than one visiting officer from the West. Special seats in the front row of the crowded hall were reserved for Allied personnel and a few prominent Germans. The US officer Hellmut Lehmann-Haupt[56] recalled: 'One felt very conspicuous and had the uneasy sensation of being watched. The speakers seated on the platform coldly eyed their audience with a mixture of suspicion and arrogance.' Speaking in excellent German, Dymshits laid down the law: art must be realist in style and must contribute to the building of the new, anti-capitalist world order. Lehmann-Haupt saw a 'clear implication of a cultural world conquest'. German art experts in the audience registered dismay: ' "Exactly like the Nazis—from the ideas down to the very wording," was their verdict.'[57]

A year later, in November 1948, the Party was running out of patience with the deviations of *Bildende Kunst*. An offending sentence by Karl Hofer— 'Politicians use art like a whore'—was viewed as an attack on the SED and SMAD and therefore expunged, but Hofer was allowed to argue that political demands on art merely produced charlatans—and it made no difference whether these demands served good or evil causes. Dymshits struck back in *Tägliche Rundschau* (19 November 1948) with two Zhdanovist articles entitled 'The Formalist Direction in German Art', including an attack on Hofer's own work. Allowing Hofer some credit for his opposition to the 'countless new post-war varieties of fascist ideology', Dymshits took him to task for artistic indulgences and for ignoring the principle of realism. A kind of 'masked theatre' had replaced the vibrant depiction of life in Hofer's painting—and subjective practices constituted a direct threat to 'life and art'.[58]

This attack prompted Herbert Sandberg, a veteran Communist who had spent years in Buchenwald, and was now editor of the satirical Berlin weekly *Der Ulenspiegel*, to write a letter of dissent to *Tägliche Rundschau* (17 December 1948), defending Hofer and insisting that form must be dynamic, whether from Daumier to Kollwitz or from impressionism to Chagall. Formalism did not mean non-objective art, 'but merely superficial, purely arbitrary, and soulless formulations'. Further incensed, the authorities closed down *Bildende Kunst* in 1949. In Halle, where the Moritzburg had been reopened in October 1948 as a museum dedicated to modern art, including work by leading expressionists such as Schmidt-Rottluff, Heckel, Kirchner, Pechstein, Klee, and Dix, a series of attacks on the collection, probably officially inspired, culminated in the demand that the pictures be labelled as examples of bourgeois decadence or removed. Shades of Hitler! The director of the museum, Dr Händler, fled to the West.[59]

An exhibition opened in East Berlin on 10 September 1950. Some 1,500 works had been submitted, 670 of them from West Germany, mostly by artists who agreed to participate only if assured in advance that their work would be shown. Stefan Heymann, head of the Party's Department of Political Instruction, Culture and Education, (Parteischulung, Kultur und Erziehung), launched a bitter attack, calling the exhibition a 'show of formalism' and 'a screaming contradiction to democratic development in our zone'. Stalinism was now firmly in the ascendant; the show was dominated by busts of Marx, Wilhelm Pieck, and Ernst Thälmann, together with innumerable portraits of Volkspolizei, people's judges, SED politicians, workers in every pose, smiling Soviet soldiers, peaceful reconstruction, and plaster casts of female tractor drivers.[60] These were German female tractor drivers, but they could have been Soviet, Polish, Bulgarian; homogenity of style and content now extended throughout the People's Democracies, the sphere of the *Zhdanovshchina*. Hellmut Lehmann-Haupt described with acuity a March 1949 congress of Slovak artists and architects:

Here are the peasants at work and play, in picturesque costumes; here is the rhythm of labor; the portrait of the leader, including numerous busts and paintings of Lenin, Stalin, Gottwald; the village scene; the rustic landscape; and some current events. There is no personal, no private expression anywhere, no statement from the individual artist to the individual beholder... The costumes in these paintings are probably authentic in detail, but are rendered in exactly the same style, in precisely the same atmosphere found in Soviet Armenian or Soviet Siberian paintings.[61]

Writing in *Tägliche Rundschau* (21 and 23 January 1951), a commentator signing himself 'N. Orlov' delivered an even fiercer attack on artists, art magazines, and publishing houses in the Soviet zone who had failed to combat 'decadence and disintegration, mysticism and symbolism'. In American art, as in literature and films, 'the leading roles are played by gangsters, thieves, murderers, prostitutes, sadists, and even the insane, along with monsters, wandering skeletons, and corpses'. Lehmann-Haupt commented: 'The parallel with the Nazi doctrine is obvious. If we substitute "Aryan" for "Proletarian" the differences become negligible... Here is the same totalitarian demand that artists speak "in an art language comprehensible to the people."'[62] (At that time 'totalitarian' was becoming a mind-set term of Western commentary.) It would be a mistake, however, to assume that East German policy on the fine arts had become monolithic. Controversies continued to surface, particularly with regard to the uneasy inter-play between socialist realism and the best of the Weimar heritage. For example, work by

Ernst Barlach, an expressionist sculptor and playwright who had died in 1938, a year after the Nazis banned his work, went on display in the Academy of Art in 1952. Bertolt Brecht used his position in the Academy to support Barlach's art against criticisms by Wilhelm Girnus and other Stalinists in the party press.[63] An (uncapitalized) entry in Brecht's journals (1 February 1952) reads:

the Barlach exhibition in the akademie der künste was attacked so violently in the TÄGLICHE RUNDSCHAU and NEUES DEUTSCHLAND that the few surviving artists were cast into lethargy. i made notes, bringing out the positive values and the exemplary quality of the work, defending it against their completely abstract demolition using social-critical weapons.'[64]

It may also be to the credit of the East German establishment that it continued to display the often gloomy and introspective work of another artist of the Weimar era, Käthe Kollwitz—although her left-wing allegiances helped. But the contrary view is expressed by James Fenton, reviewing the Hayward Gallery exhibition, 'Art and Power' (1995):

After the first German room in the London exhibition, there is a corridor marked 'Crisis and Conscience'. It might have been better labelled 'Propaganda' since it features works by Käthe Kollwitz, Ernst Barlach and John Heartfield. They are three notorious manipulators of response—Kollwitz forever advertising her grief, Barlach with his pseudo-medievalism, the caricaturist of the folksy apocalypse, and Heartfield, the brilliant advertising man with the Party Line account.[65] The idea that these three represent the conscience of Germany under fascism is familiar—but familiar from East Germany under communism.[66]

The collection in the Deutsches Historiches Museum, Berlin, reflects the sad decline of Germany's outstanding expressionist heritage. Even outside that lineage, within the social-realist canon itself , there is a loss of vitality and poignant detail from the desolate winter confrontation in Robert Koehler's *Der Streik* (*The Strike*, 1886) to the poster-ish colours and static poses of Willy Colberg's *Thälmann in Hamburger Aufstand* (*Thälmann in the Hamburg Uprising*), painted thirty years after the event, in 1953—the year of the Berlin uprising against the Communist regime. The exhilarating fusion of expressionism and social realism found in Hugo Krayn's *Gross Stadt* (*Big Town*, 1915), or the compelling, full-frontal choral effect of Otto Griebel's neo-primitive *Die Internationale* (1929/30), is replaced by a different version of neo-primitivism, the grinning buffoonery of Johannes Grützke's *Walter Ulbricht*, in which the white-bearded Stalinist is seen clasping the hands of admiring and no doubt super-achieving peasant women at a harvest festival. Later work in the Deutsches Historiches Museum and other collections, running into the 1970s, includes ghastly fusions of a defunct expressionism—though with surviving elements of vitality in Wolfram Schubert's *Brot für alle* (*Bread for All*), in which the abundant countryside breaks into a riot of colour around a modern farm-worker rewarding himself with bread, wine, and cheese. Late Communist art—and not only in the GDR—settled for the collage-effect, tossing junk-piles of cold war symbols on to the canvas, as in Bernhard Heisig's *Ikarus* (1975) and Walter Womacks's *Wenn Kommunisten träumen* (*When Communists Dream*, also 1975). Here an openended scrapbook of topical themes, executed with incoherent coloration, replaces the discipline of composition and focus.

⊞ ⊞ ⊞

Why not rejoice? We're working for ourselves!
Beat the capitalists to the finishing line!

Whether agitational posters should be regarded as 'works of art' is a dead question: a poster artist is an artist, even when he works to order, manipulates, deceives; and even though the poster is designed for buildings, streets, places of work and institutions, and not for exhibition as an art form.[67] The prevailing image of the Stalin-era poster is of monumental style, posed and heroic, bas-reliefs of lantern-jawed heroes of labour. Images and icons soared above skylines, imposing a world-system already completed and architected beyond question. Statues to the Great Helmsman loomed over the cities of Russia and Eastern Europe. Posters often adopted neo-religious or kitsch iconography, as in the 1949 Soviet Latvian poster showing a full-length Stalin framed in a kind of red altar, with Lenin (God the Father) inscribed above. Some Stalin posters capture the gilt intricacy of fussily illustrated popular editions. Leonid Fedorovich Golovanov's *Forward to the Victory of Communism!* (1952) shows the genial genius in military uniform in the foreground, and behind him a long column of political pilgrims, bearing red flags, marching up from the estuary of a river below. Viktor Govorkov's *We beat the drought!* (1949) shows a wise, ruminative Stalin, pipe and pencil in hand, poring over a map of a vast afforestation scheme extending from Moscow to the Black Sea. This poster was printed in an edition of hundreds of thousands and was even paraded in a hand-made version in Wenceslas Square during the May Day celebrations of 1953, more than a month after Stalin's death. Time and again prototypical characters, whether Marx–Engels–Lenin–Stalin, soldier–sailor–worker–peasant, or members of the different national groups, are arranged by poster artists along a diagonal, shoulder to shoulder, all gazing ahead, with the key figure on the right—the viewer's left.

But more intimate, personal images were also part of the poster propagandist's art: a family comforted by the voice of Moscow Radio while surrounded by Siberian snows. A striking 'new woman' poster shows in close-up a handsome, severely dressed young Komsomol activist, with a medal pinned to her breast, watched by two admiring female colleagues as she addresses an unseen audience while behind her looms a large portrait of Stalin, warm and animated with hand gently outstretched, also addressing a meeting. Clearly her words and thoughts are his. The caption is a quote from Stalin: 'Such women did not and could not exist (*byt'*) in old times.' The repeated impression is that of a demand which the ruling ideology must constantly reiterate: the dedication and transformation of natural human energy, cheerful self-sacrifice for the great cause. In Viktor Koretsky's *Welcome, Work Victories 1917–1953*, a young welder who has lost a hand in battle or an industrial accident appears to be almost hysterically cheerful. Workers gaze sternly and steadily, steely-eyed, into the Soviet future. Every industrial or agricultural tool is gripped like a weapon; even when the class enemy is invisible, underdevelopment is the great foe.

Cold war themes figured almost as frequently in posters as in the cartoons of *Krokodil*. The handshake was a ritual theme in posters promoting the peace movement, as for example in Alexei Kokorekin's *Peace! Ties of Friendship and Solidarity with Campaigners for Peace in the World—Unshakeable!* In an East German poster, issued in the mid-1950s, *Illegal Border Crossing from the Republic* (artist unknown), we are shown a pattern of footprints degenerating from sole markings to skeletal bare feet to describe the likely fate of those emigrating to the capitalist West. Widely favoured also was the close-up of a raised boot, which might reveal studs in the shape of swastikas. In the mid-1950s the serpent was often employed to denote the capitalist saboteur (*Let's Watch Our Factories Carefully*) or the capitalist atom bomb attempting to wrap its snakeform round the globe but firmly thwarted by a worker's grasp, as in John Heartfield's *Demand an Atomic Weapons Ban* (1955). Snakes, scorpions, and hybrid creepy-crawlies served to represent Western bacteriological warfare in Korea. A long skeletal hand hanging over the potato crop protrudes from cuffs showing the stars and stripes in a Czech poster, Wolfgang A. Schlosser's *How We Struggle Against the American Beetle* (1951). A repellent green insect bearing General Matthew Ridgway's head injects poisons from a grey US plane in a poster put out in the GDR in 1952, based on a caricature by the Kukryniksy group, Moscow. The caption reads: *Pest-Ridgway in Westeuropa. Highest Vigilance and Battle Readiness Protects Our German Democratic Republic.*

⊞ ⊞ ⊞

Hidden from the Soviet public in the vaults, the forbidden paintings, both Western and Russian, were on the whole well preserved against damp and temperature. A philistine regime (Hermann Göring) would have sold the works by Matisse and Picasso for hard currency, correctly counting on flamboyant 'rescue' expenditure by the Museum of Modern Art, the Louvre, or the Tate—but the Soviet elite, not least its highly schooled art historians, lived within a double standard: private taste against public policy. In the USIA's *Problems of Communism*, Nina Juviler described how she was allowed a glimpse of the forbidden paintings: 'Certainly, nobody fortunate enough to have received a pass, having then slipped anxiously through the *"Vkhoda Niet* (No Entry)" door and presented the pass to the tired *"babushka"* seated just inside, will forget the first sight of dozens of closely packed, carelessly hung paintings of Chagall, Kandinsky, Malevich, Pevsner, Gabo, Tatlin and Goncharova.'[68]

By the end of 1954 *Iskusstvo* was reversing the line on impressionism, and in 1955 an exhibition of French art, including Renoir, Gaugin, Cézanne, and Matisse, opened at the Pushkin Museum, Moscow. Soviet critics fell back into the formula that while the impressionists' so-called 'anti-realistic theory' was wrong, the talents of individual painters transcended it. The painter A. Magaram was wheeled out to recall attending an exhibition in Zurich early in 1917 with Lenin, who admired and expressed personal pleasure on viewing a picture which turned out to be by Claude Monet.[69] The anti-Communist London journal *Soviet Survey* mocked wavering attempts to reconsider the impressionists: 'Manet is regarded as tolerable... Monet is judged more harshly... Something may be learned from Degas's gift of observation and Renoir's use of colour, but their general approach was all wrong. Cézanne is already beyond the pale...'[70]

Ilya Ehrenburg's long-suppressed and eloquent eulogy to the impressionists first appeared in 1958 in a collection he called *Frantsuzkie tetradi* (*French Exercise Books*). 'The paintings of Uccello, Michelangelo and Tintoretto', he reminded his readers, 'seemed shocking, even heretical, to many of their contemporaries'... When Manet's *Déjeuner sur l'herbe* was shown in 1863 it provoked a storm of indignation: 'A crowd of well-dressed hooligans surrounded the artist and hurled the coarsest abuse at him.' Manet, Pissarro, Cézanne, Monet, Renoir, Sisley, and Degas were constantly rejected because united by a common hostility to academic art—here Ehrenburg provided a devastating catalogue of rejections by official salons and art critics from the 1860s through the 1890s, from the Salon des refusés to the eventual decision in 1907 to put Manet's *Olympia* in the Louvre. Yet they 'are always being called decadent in our country'. By implication he likened Soviet critics to

Wolff, art critic of *Figaro*, who had vented his disgust about the 1894 impressionist exhibition: 'Try and tell Monsieur Degas that there is such a thing in the world as drawing, colour, technique. He'll burst out laughing and call you a reactionary.'[71]

⊞   ⊞   ⊞

In 1959 an Exhibition of Russian Art finally opened at the Royal Academy (Burlington House, Piccadilly). On display from 1 January to 9 March were 122 works of Russian art spanning the centuries. According to *Iskusstvo*, the exhibition drew in more than 78,000 visitors, including 'thousands of ordinary people'—*tysiachi prostykh liudei*. (The admission price was 2/6d.) 'The huge interest of the English public in the exhibition is explained by one particular fact: the great prestige of the Soviet Union in the eyes of the population, but in England almost no one has seen Soviet fine art. In English museums these works are missing. English criticism keeps silent (*zamalchivaetsia*) about the fine art of our native land.'[72]

It was not the first Russian exhibit to reach the Royal Academy.[73] With the war in Europe approaching its climax, an exhibition of Soviet Graphic Art had been shown there from January to March 1945 under the auspices of the Soviet Embassy, mainly of 'paintings and drawings done by their war artists at the front'.[74] On display were brilliant anti-Nazi-cartoons by the 'Kukryniksy' brigade (Kuprianov, Krylov, and Nikolai Sokolov). *The Times* commented that 'the artists are almost completely unaffected by modernist tendencies... a little touch of impressionism here and there... a nice-mannered tradition of the nineteenth century'. The anonymous reviewer found some 'extremely competent, often effective, things', including woodcuts from Mikhail Polyakov's series 'The Germans in Russia'. Hellmut Lehmann-Haupt got to see the exhibition: 'There was a high level of illustrative draftsmanship and considerable mastery of graphic technique.' The Soviet exhibits represented 'just about all that was going on in Soviet Russian art... This was the art officially demanded, the only kind of expression tolerated.'[75] The exhibition was accorded forty-three lines by *The Times*, only two more than an adjoining piece on 'The Course of Nature. Visits by Continental Robins'. No greater joy arrived a year later, in March 1946, when an exhibition of Soviet graphic art at the Whitechapel Art Gallery again focused on war artists. According to *The Times* (15 March 1946), most of the works on display 'have the air of being done for an illustrated newspaper which has been temporarily deprived of the benefits of photography'. The critic found them disappointingly 'utilitarian' in contrast to 'the highly individual styles of most of our own war artists'.

If this was mildly disparaging, it was not hostile. Attitudes within the British art establishment were strikingly different from those prevailing in America—whether the Dondero school of vigilantism or the MoMA school of ultra-modernism. Aesthetic conservatism in Britain was not on the whole linked to 'nativism' or fear of the Red Peril. Parliamentary diatribes against the 'isms' did not fill *Hansard*. Among the fellows of the Royal Academy, not a few regarded the challenge of Soviet socialist realism as of little account compared to the domestic subversion wrought by modernism in the major museums and collections of the West. One could discount the propaganda element in Soviet art, but the Russians hadn't forgotten 'how to paint'.

The Russian Art project[76] extended back to August 1955, when the Soviet Embassy suggested an exhibition to take place in London early in 1956 (presumably to precede the first state visit to London by Soviet leaders). The idea of reciprocal exhibitions was now afloat,[77] but the Hungarian Revolution intervened. Undeterred, Sir Alfred Munnings, the Tory painter of racehorses whom Soviet curators praised with a lopsided smile, wrote to *The Times* (2 January 1957) in effect urging the Academy and Arts Council to get on with it. Munnings's letter began with a typical expression of his own priorities: 'Many will welcome the Aga Khan's first-rate letter in *The Times* of December 27 on British racing.' This was followed by a crack at the Foreign Office (they kept saying 'Not Yet' to a Russian exhibition). *Komsol'skaia pravda* welcomed Munnings's intervention.[78]

A key figure was Professor V. Loewinson-Lessing, the English-speaking vice-director of the Hermitage Museum, Leningrad; he and Madame Kuznetsova, of the Pushkin Museum, attended a meeting at Burlington House on 20 November, when he undertook to provide a final list of the Russian paintings to be exhibited, plus photographs, by January. But he did not do so, and in February he fell ill. By June 1958 the Arts Council was expressing anxiety to the Soviet Embassy and to the British ambassador in Moscow. The problem was mainly bureaucratic on the British side: the Russians were insisting on a firm promise of a comparable exhibition of British paintings—but that was a province reserved to the British Council, which in turn was not involved in the Soviet exhibition heading for London.[79] Meanwhile the secretary of the RA wrote a hush-hush memo expressing 'misgivings' over the imminent display of the red flag outside Burlington House in Piccadilly. Two Soviet experts arrived in London to supervise the hanging and care of the art works[80] ahead of the private and press showing on the last day of 1958. The exhibition catalogue carried a brief introduction by G. Nedoshivin, deputy director of the State Tretyakov Gallery, who commented on the absence of 'works analogous to widespread tendencies in the West, such as tachism, surrealism, abstract painting, etc.' This, he explained, 'reflects the non-existence of such tendencies in Soviet art . . . we believe that these formalistic tendencies merely reflect the painful contradictions of present-day culture'. The missing word, of course, was 'bourgeois', no doubt omitted on diplomatic grounds.[81] The editors of *Iskusstvo* later blasted 'Representatives of reactionary circles and proponents of abstract art who maliciously complain that we don't display Chagall, Malevich, and Kandinsky. One even reads that our artists should learn from English abstractionists!'[82]

Although the works on display extended from the thirteenth century to the present day, only thirty-seven of the 122 exhibits were by artists of the Soviet period.[83] Of these only one was by a woman—and it did not turn up. Few of the London critics remarked on this extraordinary gender imbalance. *Iskusstvo* quoted every extractable favourable comment in the British press, citing a headline in the *News Chronicle*, 'This Russian art's an eye-opener', but ignoring the subheading: 'The modern stuff is 50 years out of date.' Eagerly quoted was the Tory *Daily Telegraph*: 'Russian art is realist: it is linked to the life and aspirations of the people, and on the whole it reflects the greatness and constancy of traditional values, but not fashionable experiments.' But *Iskusstvo* did not quote the *Telegraph*'s diarist, who lamented that the exhibition merely showed 'what happens when a country cuts itself off from the mainstream of European culture—and its leaders have the gall to dictate to its artists'. Much quoted in Moscow was the 'prominent English art critic Prof. Thomas Bodkin', writing in the *Birmingham Post*. Bodkin rambled on at length about 'the great Soviet People', the Fatherland, and the 'tradition of glorious classical painting'. He lauded Lenin's dictum that 'art belongs to the people', and gave thanks that Russian art 'was never revolutionary in its approach or its technique'—indeed, artists like Chagall and Marc Soutine were justifiably unrepresented, expatriates whose work was quite unknown 'in their Fatherland'. Sir Alfred Munnings sent the *Telegraph* (10 February) an eloquent lament over the 'sad lack of enthusiasm in our Press about the Russian pictures on view'. He praised the painting called *The End* (1948), depicting Hitler's last hour—a wild-eyed Führer clutching at his throat while three comatose Nazi officers reflect versions of despair, flight, or drunkeness beside a table covered with empty bottles. Singled out for amazement or derision by most London critics, *The End* was hailed by Munnings as 'a masterpiece', intense expressionism in the true meaning of the word (i.e. not the 'so-called School of Expressionism'). Munnings urged Britons who might be tempted to scoff at such a canvas to recall how 'this murderous maniac' Hitler and his myrmidons had filled London's skies with deadly Doodlebugs.

Whereas the 1945 exhibition had passed entirely unremarked in the haughty yet splendid *Burlington Magazine*, the return of the Soviet easels in the Khrushchev era earned a full-page editorial which conveyed, with icy aloofness, total contempt for the Soviet claim to realism:

... their art is not an art of realism at all. If there had been the slightest indication . . . of a development from the Russian realist movement of the nineteenth century, or from Géricault, Constable, Millet, Courbet, Daumier—the grand names the Russians evoke—the enlightened sections of the British public would have been the first to acclaim it . . . But their art . . . reverts to a stylistic fashion which flourished in the first decade of this century in reactionary circles in Western Europe and which was already by 1910 being condemned as unrealistic . . . There is only one work of real artistic merit; this is the *Defence of Petrograd* (No. 97), which could even hold its own in the company of Wyndham Lewis or even of Léger. The sinister fact emerges that this was painted in 1928 and that nineteen years later this remarkable artist had sunk to the banality of the *Relay Race* (No. 98).

The artist here was Deneika, but the *Burlington* did not deign to name him or any other Soviet artist in the exhibition, the editorialist tailing off into invective in his final onslaught on the 'debased, pseudo-academic impressionism now served up to us' by Moscow.[84] Critics from the British daily press were not, on the whole, more favourably impressed. Frederick Laws in the *Manchester Guardian* complained of 'the official twaddle of socialist realism'; the anonymous art critic of *The Times* likened Soviet painting to Western cinema: huge screens, eccentric colour, simplification of heroic virtues. In the *News Chronicle* Wilma Moy-Thomas derided the painting from which the present chapter borrows its title, Arkady Plastov's hyper-dramatically illuminated *Tractor Drivers' Supper* (*Uzhin traktoristov*), painted in 1952: 'The Soviet Union turns out to be fifty years behind this country in its taste in art.' Where, asked Denys Sutton in the *Financial Times*, were Kandinsky, Chagall, and the constructivists? Sutton was one of several critics to contrast Deneika's vibrant *The Defence of Petrograd* (1928) with his pallid *The Relay Race* (1947): the former carried the impact of an Eisenstein film, a fusion of passion and propaganda; whereas the *The Relay Race* resembled a mere poster, 'as if the Soviet State Railways were inviting us to come to the sunny Caspian Sea'.[85]

And the public? Comments in the Burlington House visitors' book (rarely a reflection of average opinion) included 'Dull and tedious', 'The biggest bore I have ever seen', 'Where have Russian painters been in post-war years, in Siberia?', 'Place a Degas, Bonnard, Bracque [*sic*] next to them', 'Art cannot be chained but you have chained it'. The *Punch* cartoonist Bernard Hollowood offered a series of imagined exchanges. Inside the exhibition two men stare at a blank space: 'It's been withdrawn—Pasternak must have praised it.' Leaving the exhibition, a woman exclaims to her husband: 'Well, it explains why they're so mad keen on science.'

The Russians, meanwhile, were plotting their summer display of painting and sculpture at the Soviet Exhibition in New York. On 3 March the Central Committee took note that Pimenov's painting *Planting Potatoes* gave the impression that simple spades were still used by Soviet farmers—but no recommendation for its removal from the list drawn up was attached.

⊞ ⊞ ⊞

'It was in architecture that totalitarianism recognized its elective medium', writes Roger Cardinal. 'The overriding rhetoric of collective triumph and the awesome physical scale of its buildings and avenues matched the ultimate totalitarian message'...[86] Isaiah Berlin's verdict on the Stalin-era architecture he witnessed in 1945 was the normal one: '... the erection of vast, dark, bleak buildings repulsive even by the worst Western standards.'[87] Soviet–American rivalry was intense on the architectural front, not least because Stalin and his architects opted for an alternative form of big-city gigantism. The 1935 'General Plan for the Reconstruction of the City of Moscow' had been blueprinted in quasi-visionary drawings of new Metro stations, with tiny human figures *à la* Piranesi. Alfred H. Barr, one of America's foremost exponents of modernism, recalled that during the 1920s a considerable number of Soviet buildings had been designed under the influence of Le Corbusier and Walter Gropius but, regrettably, during the 1930s

Russian architects were enjoined to look backward to the great public buildings, first of imperial Rome, then of imperial Russia. Iofan and Gel'freykh's revised design for the Palace of Soviets, of about 1935, marked the victory of academic reaction—a vast skyscraper dressed in the styles of the past. The celebrated Moscow subway stations confirmed it ... The new Government palaces and big apartment houses of Moscow, 1950, emulate the baroque or neo-classical American skyscrapers of 1920 at their worst—and in the name of Socialist Realism![88]

The former Soviet curator Igor Golomshtok confirmed the point: in 1936 it had still been possible for Le Corbusier to win a competition and design the Ministry of Light Industry on one of the main streets of Moscow. After the war this was out of the question. In the thirties purely functional constructions such as the Dnieper Hydroelectric Station were hailed as models of Soviet architecture; after the war the Volga–Don canal complex, constructed in record time, at huge expense, and on the backs of slave labour, turned into a monument to Stalin. Each of the thirteen sluices was constructed in the shape of a triumphal gate or arch, richly adorned with reliefs and crowned by large sculptural compositions. The approach to the complex was dominated by cyclopean sculptures of Stalin. The realms of architectural and industrial design, like those of genetics, cybernetics, and relativity theory, were declared under Stalin to be 'bourgeois pseudo-sciences' and were not rehabilitated until the early sixties.[89]

An exhibition of American prefabricated housing had been shown, in a climate still glowing with good-will, at the Moscow Architects Club, 15–30 March 1945. A Russian visitor reported keen appreciation among Soviet engineers: 'Particular interest was attracted by the use of steel and reinforced concrete in large-scale housing construction . . . [and] the application . . . of methods used in aircraft and automobile engineering.' With the onset of the cold war, Soviet commentators discarded sympathetic attitudes towards, for example, English town-planning,[90] and abruptly rediscovered that buildings and engineering projects display the taste and environmental priorities of the ruling class. Returning in August 1947 from an international architects' congress in Brussels, the vice-president of the USSR Academy of Architects claimed that West European architecture had lost its 'national' character. Edward Crankshaw responded sharply that Soviet cultural palaces resembled multi-tiered wedding cakes.[91] The battle between genuine modernism and Stalinist classicism resumed.

Conspicuous among post-war monumental 'wedding cakes' were Moscow State University (1953) and the Ukrainia Hotel (1956). Little anticipating Khrushchev's onslaught on high buildings following Stalin's death, the most influential of Stalinist architects, B. M. Iofan (designer of the Soviet pavilion at the pre-war Paris Exhibition), claimed in 1952 that 'Russian high buildings are always effectively situated'. The idea behind the tiering of high buildings was to have the lower levels of a height with the surrounding buildings, thus creating 'an impression of grandeur'. The sixteenth-century tower of Ivan the Great had the same aim, declared Iofan: 'In the one-storeyed Moscow of those days it represented an architectural and ideological focal point.' Years later this monarchical principle was mocked by the Soviet theatre critic Anatoly Smeliansky: the seven famous skyscrapers erected above Moscow after World War II, he said, when seen from the ground, suggested the watch-towers of the Gulag—from the Boss's vantage-point they were supposed to suggest that there was 'one above you all' who saw everything and knew everything.[92] But architect Iofan saw only 'socialist principles' in the first eight high buildings[93] erected in Moscow, five of which stood on the Sadovaya ring; architects had in mind their relationship to the future Palace of Soviets. Iofan predicted that the forthcoming Palace—which he himself had designed in 1935—'will tower above all other buildings, linking together the architecture of the entire city'.

Was this the spirit of socialism? It was! Socialist principles, insisted Iofan, determined the underlying principles and 'distinguish Soviet tall buildings from those built abroad'; for this, among other reasons, he was unrepentant that the drive to construct a grandiose Moscow had destroyed the famous Red Gates, the Sukharev Tower, and part of the Simonov Monastery. By pitiful contrast American architects (said Iofan), while erecting numerous skyscrapers, had been unable 'to develop towns along scientific and artistic lines'. 'Skyscrapers are built wherever their owners find it expedient.' Indeed, 'Wall Street, with all its skyscrapers, is one of the most dismal streets in the world'. Maxim Gorky had described the twenty-storey buildings along the Manhattan shoreline: 'Thick, heavy, square-faced, lacking all urge to beauty, they tower in grim unloveliness. And each of them seems to take a supercilious pride in its bulk and ugliness.' Iofan quoted Lewis Mumford's book *Sticks and Stones*: 'One need not dwell upon the way in which these obdurate overwhelming masses take away from the little people who walk in their shadows any semblance of dignity as human beings.'[94]

Four new glittering stations of the Moscow Metro were opened in 1952, notably Komsomol Circle, the work of the late Alexei Shchusev, its walls faced with dark red Salietti marble, lit by gilded chandeliers, and bearing a mosaic dedicated to Aleksandr Nevsky and the historical victory of Russian arms, with ancient and modern weapons as motifs. The Moscow Metro was described by the Soviet architect N. P. Bylinkin as an 'underground palace giving an impression of majesty', a symphony of veined marble, tinted granite, stained glass, and glittering mosaics. The Metro was grudgingly described by Ronald Hingley as 'part folly, part efficient public amenity'.[95]

The first issue of the journal *Arkhitektura SSSR* (*Architecture of the USSR*) to appear after Stalin's death criticized the prevailing policy, heralding Khrushchev's violent attacks on specific grandiose buildings and 'the campaign of struggle against architectural excesses'. Blaming Stalin and Kaganovich for Iofan's proposed Palace of Soviets, full of unfunctional space and visible as a five-pointed star only from an aeroplane, Khrushchev himself castigated the squandering of the people's money on 'over-indulgences' and the failure to adapt to modern housing requirements. He also dissolved the Soviet Academy of Architecture. Western observers rapidly picked up the confusion now prevailing among Soviet architects.[96]

Khrushchev's no-nonsense approach resulted in teams of Soviet architects and building constructors visiting the United States to absorb the latest techniques in low-cost housing. In 1955 a Western 'architectural provocation' took place in the shape of the Vlasov affair. Alexander V. Vlasov had been touring the United States with a delegation of ten architects studying American housing projects at the invitation of the National Association of Home Builders. Discovering that Vlasov had outspoken views of his own which often clashed with those of the leader of his delegation, I. K. Kozulia, the minister of urban construction, American newspapers ran a story that he had been dismissed as chief architect of Moscow—evidently on the ground that he had promoted expensive skyscrapers rather than more utilitarian buildings. Vlasov was said to be accused of designing metro stations resembling palaces, and advocating the construction of ornate, colonnaded skyscrapers at public expense. This turned out to be a misleading rehash of some remarks made by Khrushchev a year earlier (7 December 1954), which were both critical and admiring of Vlasov. In reality it had been Vlasov who, on 9 March 1955, had announced the cancellation of a project to build a forty-storey building not far from the Kremlin, in favour of a ten-storey utilitarian apartment building. It was equally Vlasov who had announced that Moscow would not proceed with further skyscrapers beyond the seven already built under Stalin.

Vlasov, who was also president of the Soviet Academy of Architecture dissolved by Khrushchev, was hastily put on board the *Queen Elizabeth*, bound for Cherbourg. Before leaving America he told reporters—while nervously chain-smoking—that his dismissal was a surprise, but he was sure he would have 'interesting work forever' in the USSR. On his arrival at the Gare St-Lazare in Paris he was hustled by Soviet Embassy employees through a throng of White Russians anxious to 'liberate' him, taken to a local police station, then driven to the Embassy. The French Ministry of the Interior adopted the view that he was returning home of his own free will, but the conservative *Le Figaro* (17 November) complained that Vlasov had looked more like a man being 'carried than accompanied' (*porté plus qu'accompagné*). Was he being punished for making an unauthorized visit to the great architect Frank Lloyd Wright, whom he had met in Moscow in 1937 during an international conference? Passing through Spring Green, in the state of Wisconsin, Vlasov had allegedly taken a taxi without informing his Soviet colleagues and driven to Wright's home.

Two weeks later Georges Andersen, of the left-wing paper *Combat* (30 November), reported that Vlasov had been well received on his return to Moscow and had taken part in an architects' congress held in the Kremlin. Andersen attributed 'l'incident romantico-diplomatique, sinon policier' to a deliberate campaign of disinformation provoked by political circles such as 'Americans for Liberation from Bolshevism', in an attempt to persuade

Vlasov to defect. Interviewed by *Pravda*, Vlasov himself blamed 'the American police' and 'the American press' for sabotaging the trip: AP and the *New York Times* had published reports 'grossly distorting' the decisions of the Central Committee of the CPSU and the Council of Ministers 'on extravagances in design and building'. These provocations had continued when the ship reached Cherbourg and at the Gare St-Lazare.[97]

The Khrushchev reforms undoubtedly released architects from the ponderous neo-classicism of the Stalin era while diverting funds into desperately needed domestic building—although one recent commentator argues that in both the short and long term the effect of Khrushchevism was to undermine the 'master architects' and bring about 'architecture's rapid subordination to the construction industry'.[98] Harrison Salisbury, of the *New York Times*, celebrated the arrival of Western architectural concepts. Visiting Moscow's House of Architecture to inspect the latest competition designs, he concluded that under Khrushchev Soviet architects had taken a giant stride into modernity: 'There was not a Kremlin tower in the lot, not an ornamental column, not a single hero-sized statue. Here were cool, clean, crisp, modern designs. Glass and metal and square planes. The architects had been studying the United Nations Buildings, the new glass palaces of Park Avenue, the light and graceful concepts erected in Caracas and Rio de Janeiro.'[99]

Passports for Paintings: Abstract Expressionism and the CIA

On 20 March 1957 B. J. Cutler, Moscow correspondent of the *Herald Tribune*, reported how a chimpanzee's finger painting had been 'seized as a weapon in the ideological cold war' and 'used by Communist art propagandists in an effort to discredit the entire field of modern art'. This Soviet campaign was touched off when the 6-year-old simian Betsy was given a 'one-chimp' show in Baltimore and local connoisseurs bought $125-worth of her work, including *Cabbage Worms* for $40 and *Hell* for $25. The story was widely picked up in the USSR. A cartoon showed a chimp at an easel wielding paint-brushes with its feet while three moronic modern-art lovers applauded. *Sovetskaia kul'tura* did grant to Betsy that her style was 'more restrained' than that of one unnamed artist recently exhibited at New York's Museum of Modern Art, 'financed by the Rockefeller family'. Cutler complained that the Soviet press campaign 'carefully omitted the information, available here [in Moscow], that money from her paintings is to go toward buying a male chimpanzee, since Betsy is lonely as well as artistic'.

So there you go: Monkey Business—or Russians Bury Human Angle on Chimp.

⌗ ⌗ ⌗

Recent studies of American cold war art require correction. For more than twenty-five years art historians and journalists have sought to prove that one particular American style, 'abstract expressionism' or 'action painting', known as 'tachisme' in France, was the cutting edge of the American cultural offensive against Soviet art. By the same theory, the CIA intervened, both rapidly and clandestinely, to support the private museums' export of abstract expressionism to Europe after Congressional opposition to all modernist movements made overt support by the State Department and the USIA/ USIS politically impossible. Proponents of this theory argue that it applied in practice from the late 1940s.

The attempt to impugn the independence and integrity of the New York Museum of Modern Art (MoMA), and to inject the CIA into the equation, was of course rooted in the 1967 public scandal concerning the CIA's revealed clandestine cultural role at home and abroad. Revisionism was all the rage— and the rage has scarcely diminished. Max Kozloff kicked off with 'American Painting During the Cold War', a fine example of New Left rhetoric which at the eleventh hour shrank back from the collusive conclusions it had promised—Kozloff limped away with the thought that abstract expressionism and the cold war had little connection beyond contemporaneity: 'Never for one moment did American art become a conscious mouthpiece for any agency... But it did lend itself to be treated as a form of benevolent propaganda for foreign intelligentsia.' The comment is unjustifiable: it was owners, not painters or paintings, which 'lent themselves'. Then, in only three pages of text, Eva Cockcroft achieved lasting damage with her 'Abstract Expressionism: Weapon of the Cold War' (*Artforum*, June 1974). Cockcroft accused Nelson Rockefeller,[1] MoMA, Alfred H. Barr, Jr, the Museum's International Council, and the CIA of using abstract expressionism for political ends, providing the well-funded arguments and exhibitions 'needed to sell the rest of the world the benefits of life and art under capitalism'.[2] In 1983 Serge Guilbaut's now-famous *How New York Stole the Idea of Modern Art* (a fine polemic which nevertheless confused itself by pointing the rifle of criticism in too many directions) claimed that the American avant-garde had been co-opted by cold war liberalism, 'which views the artist's individualism as an excellent weapon with which to combat Soviet authoritarianism'.[3] Twenty years after Eva Cockcroft's essay, a young English writer came down the same trail, with a television crew. Frances Stonor Saunders set out to nail CIA clandestine involvement in a range of cold war cultural activities and to establish its role as the mover and shaker responsible for promoting American abstract expressionist art abroad.

True or not? While this relatively young agency did certainly involve itself in clandestinely promoting literary magazines, music festivals, and orchestral tours, along with much else within the United States, the financing of American art exhibits abroad was largely the work of the Rockefellers, the Whitneys, and the Guggenheims—the package which the Russians used to call *Uoll Strit*. Western attention post-1967 has been so fixated by the machinations of the CIA, the FBI, and the KGB that no historical episode is now deemed worthy of attention unless some clandestine agency of the state can be shown to have been at the back of it. The 'secret state' has ousted Wall Street, the City of London, and *les deux cents familles* from the pantheon of ever-ready demons of patronage.

In practice, what the Museum of Modern Art and other sponsors exported throughout the 1950s was a mixed bag of styles and movements, the result not only of political nervousness, compromise, and continual vigilante howling, but also of a common-sensical appraisal of European taste and opinion. One reason for the exaggerated role attributed to abstract expressionism as an instrument of the *pax Americana* is the inclination of historians and journalists to be influenced by ink rather than paint; in this case the ink of Alfred Barr, Clement Greenberg, and Harold Rosenberg, the principal critics and curators, pundits and prophets of abstract expressionism between 1945 and 1960. Too much attention has been paid to manifestos, too little to what actually hung on the walls of America's itinerant exhibitions.

In reality, American art made little impact in the Soviet Union until the 1959 US exhibition in Sokol'niki Park, although 'abstraction' always figured in the Soviet critical vocabulary. Soviet attention post-war was mainly focused on the old, familiar European foes: impressionism, expressionism, surrealism, cubism.

⌗　⌗　⌗

One main difficulty in promoting Western avant-garde art resided in the fact that modernist painting and sculpture was almost as much disliked and distrusted by the Western public as by the Soviet. Churchill, Truman, and Eisenhower were no more inclined than Stalin and Khrushchev to admire the portrait of a woman whose eyes and ears had perversely—and pervertedly—disassembled themselves. Powerful academies and associations in the West were as loud in their warnings against the subversive advance of modernism as were their state-sanctioned counterparts in the USSR, and indeed the expletive 'decadent' was heard on both sides of the Iron Curtain. Naturally the language of denunciation varied according to ideology; the term 'bourgeois' cut no ice in the Royal Academy or in such London clubs as Brooks and the Athenaeum, where elaborately sardonic letters to *The Times* ridiculing Picasso were composed after large lunches. Admittedly, impressionism and post-impressionism had become absorbed into the Western academic canon, not only because the passage of time validates, but also because with Renoir, Degas, Manet, and Monet you knew, broadly, what you were looking at: human figures, landscapes, buildings—certainly no less than with Turner, who couldn't be despised. Stalinism, by contrast, refused to countenance even impressionism.

The realist-roman portraits of Lenin and Stalin which hung in Soviet schoolrooms and meeting halls were echoed by the same sort of thing devoted to monarchs and presidents which adorned public places in the West—although the latter were not subject to airbrushing at the command of new incumbents. Pietro Annigoni's *HM. Queen Elizabeth II* (1954) was commissioned by the Worshipful Company of Fishmongers rather than by the Central Committee of the Communist Party, but the artist's viewpoint is at knee-level, gazing up at the aloof young queen in her Garter robe in a manner that A. Gerasimov and V. Serov would have appreciated. The style is as translucently realist, with a strong hint of the photographic, as any official Soviet portrait. However, Annigoni allows no demeaning intrusion by the modern world: the aloof young queen's timeless inheritance is free of pylons, telegraph poles, roads, or smokestacks. A tiny, allusive figure in a boat at the bottom-left of the painting is the only concession to the existence of the queen's subjects. F. Shurpin's famous *Dawn Over Our Homeland* (1948), showing a serene, white-tuniced Stalin gazing at flat countryside with power pylons and combine harvesters, provides a Soviet counterpart to Annigoni's portrait. Soviet critics had no quarrel with monarchical deference; what infuriated them was modernist anarchy, the teasing dreams of Chagall, the Freudian fellatio of Dali. The neo-classicism and illusionism obligatory under Stalin were also prevalent styles in Western academies.[4] The influence of photography on mainstream painting was almost universal. Clement Greenberg's influential 'Avant Garde and Kitsch' (1939), a neo-Trotskyist manifesto, depicted kitsch as mass-produced style and facile conformity promoted by all governments, particularly totalitarian ones, but also by business—a prime example being Norman Rockwell's popular, illusionistic covers for the *Saturday Evening Post*. The avant-garde artists patronized by the cutting-edge galleries and art journals, by contrast, were suspected by mainstream Western opinion of fraudulence, pretentiousness, lack of basic skills, and opportunism. They were charlatans.

The first objective of State Department cultural policy after the war was not to associate American culture with ultra-modernism but to convince Europeans that America was more than Walt Disney and Mae West, corned beef, chewing-gum, and nylons. In June 1946, the king and queen attended a private view at the Tate Gallery, London, of an exhibition of 'American Painting from the Eighteenth Century to the Present Day', selected by John Walker, chief curator of the National Gallery of Art, Washington.[5] The anonymous art critic of *The Times* (14 June) barely mentioned twentieth-century American abstract artists in reviewing the exhibit, while an editorial in the same issue praised the Federal Arts Project, with its emphasis on social painting within the realist mould. The token examples of American abstraction, by Robert Motherwell and a few others, on display at the Tate escaped the attention of *The Times*.

That same year the State Department's brighter heads—notably J. LeRoy Davidson, 'a very modern young man' in charge of the art programme—and the progressive museum curators they consulted assembled an exhibit designed to display the nation's best in all its variousness, under the title 'Advancing American Art'. The target areas for the roadshow were to be Europe and Latin America. Seventy-nine works were assembled on a modest budget of $49,000. As soon as it went on display at the Metropolitan Museum, New York, the backlash was immediate. In a letter worthy of the Soviet Academy, the American Artists Professional League wrote to Secretary of State James F. Byrnes deploring the growing influence of 'revolutionaries' who were busily 'debauching' all that was 'noble in art'. The collection was tainted by radical European trends 'not indigenous to our soil'. Similar complaints were voiced by the National Academy of Design, Allied Artists, and the Society of Illustrators. ' "Modern" Painting Dominates in State Department and Pepsi-Cola Selections', reported the *New York Times*. The term 'Left', as used in the headline 'Eyes to the Left', apparently meant 'modern' rather than politically radical.[6] The Hearst press castigated this latest federal 'folly' and ran illustrations with abusive quotes, the New York *Journal American* directing its fire at the 'incomprehensible, ugly and absurd' work on display—a 'lunatic's delight'; *Look* magazine published a spread to show how the taxpayers' money had been misspent.

Almost invariably parallel political objections were voiced, *ad hominem*, as when the *Baltimore American* complained about the inclusion in the exhibition of works by 'left-wing painters who are members of Red Fascist organizations'. Here 'left' meant pro-Communist. Congressman Fred E. Busbey[7] (Illinois) made a fine art (if the phrase may be excused) of conflating artistic and political radicalism, modernism and Marxism—even though in practice, as every Soviet diatribe confirmed, they had become in the Stalin era deadly enemies. Busbey deplored the 'weird' and 'unnatural' depiction of human beings in the State Department exhibits: skins were a 'sullen, ashen grey', features were always 'depressed and melancholy'. And why? Because 'the Communists' wanted 'to tell the foreigners that the American people are despondent, broken down, or of hideous shape . . . and eager for a change of government'. Busbey also cited twenty-four of the forty-five artists selected by the State Department as listed in the files of the House Un-American

Activities Committee.[8] The ultra-conservative Congressman John Rankin (Mississippi) claimed that the exhibits were 'Communist caricatures... sent out to mislead the world as to what America is like'.

President Truman himself, a keen amateur artist, did not conflate modernism with the world Communist conspiracy, but he was less than impressed by the chosen paintings. Of a Yasuo Kuniyoshi semi-abstract, *Circus Rider*, he famously commented: 'The artist must have stood off from the canvas and thrown paint at it... if that's art, I'm a Hottentot.' A keen pre-breakfast visitor to the National Gallery, the president admired the Dutch masters, the Holbeins and Rembrandts who, he said, 'make our modern day daubers and frustrated ham and egg men look just what they are'. In 1962 Khrushchev was to express similar sentiments, including admiration for the Dutch school, though less decorously.[9] On the instructions of Secretary of State George Marshall, the State Department cancelled its own exhibition in the middle of a successful tour of Europe, when it had reached Prague, despite the protests of New York artists, dealers, and art journal editors. The collection was consigned for disposal as war surplus, the War Assets Administration selling off the lot for a mere $5,544. With the future of the Office of International Information and Culture Affairs in doubt, Marshall announced that there would be 'no more taxpayers' money for modern art'.

Art News might promote modernism but *American Artist* did not. An editorial by Ernest Watson in the May 1951 edition assailed 'the defeatist school' of artists, whose 'canvases drip with melancholy'. According to Watson, modernist art was an importation 'from countries brutalized by militarism and impoverished by economic disaster. It came primarily out of Germany and its name is Expressionism.' Meanwhile in Los Angeles the City Council purged the City's Greek Theater Annual Exhibition and brought the offending works into City Hall, where they were held up to scorn and ridicule at a meeting of citizens. A witness from Sanity-in-Art told the gathering that 'Modern Art' was actually a means of espionage; if you knew how to read them, the paintings would disclose the weak spots in US fortifications and such crucial constructions as Boulder Dam.[10]

Two separate criteria for censorship coexisted: the artist's political biography, and his or her aesthetic style. Although Reds tended to be traditionalists, realists, the trick was to see no clear water between one kind of 'left' and the other. Most outspoken and obsessive among the Congressional enemies of modernist art was Representative George A. Dondero (Michigan), defender of 'the high standards and priceless tradition of academic art', who revealed to the House of Representatives that modernism had been used against the Tsarist government when Trotsky's friend Wassily

Kandinsky had released on Russia 'the black knights of the isms': cubism, futurism, dadaism, expressionism, constructionism [constructivism], surrealism and abstractionism. 'The artists of the "isms" change their designations as often and as readily as the Communist front organizations. Léger and Duchamp are now in the United States to aid in the destruction of our standards and traditions. The former has been a contributor to the Communist cause in America; the latter is now fancied by the neurotics as a surrealist . . .'[11] Dondero explained how each 'ism' in the devil's larder carried its own deadly virus:

> Cubism aims to destroy by designed disorder.
> Futurism aims to destroy by the machine myth . . .
> Dadaism aims to destroy by ridicule.
> Expressionism aims to destroy by aping the primitive and insane . . .
> Abstractionism aims to destroy by the creation of brainstorms.
> Surrealism aims to destroy by the denial of reason.[12]

Dondero had to admit that the Soviet regime had suppressed the viruses at home, but he maintained that it covertly propagated them for the purpose of subversion abroad. A xenophobic nativist and a master of what Richard Hoftstadter called 'the paranoid style', Dondero delighted in such phrases as 'an effeminate elect' and a 'polyglot rabble'. Pointing to the 'pen-and-brush phalanx of the Communist conspiracy' which had spawned the American front organizations of the 1930s, Dondero jumped on such non-Communist power centres as MoMA and Harvard's Fogg Museum, as well as a 'horde of foreign art manglers' and subversive cosmopolitans, heirs to 'a sinister conspiracy conceived in the black heart of Russia', who now 'dominated' museum juries, art journals, and the art columns of the metropolitan press. The abstract expressionists Jackson Pollock, Robert Motherwell, and William Baziotes were exposed as practitioners of an 'abstractivism or non-objectivity . . . spawned as a simon pure, Russian Communist product'.[13]

Regionalist rhetoric shared much in common with its Soviet counterpart: both detested the Eastern capitalist elite, especially the Rockefellers. Writing in *Masses and Mainstream*, the Marxist critic Sidney Finkelstein also condemned MoMA for 'creating' abstract expressionism.[14] But opposition to the new wave of abstract art patronized by the major collectors was by no means confined to nativists and Marxists. The marvellous Edward Hopper was among the artists who in 1952 criticized MoMA's passion and partiality for abstraction. Even the sophisticated Lincoln Kirstein (founder of the New York City Ballet), a close friend and collaborator of MoMA's curator Alfred Barr, voiced opposition in *Harper's Magazine* (October 1948) to MoMA's new image as 'a modern abstract academy'. Kirstein complained about 'improvisation as a method, deformation as a formula, and painting (which is a serious matter) as an amusement manipulated by interior decorators and high pressure salesmen'...[15] Writing in the Atlantic Monthly, Francis Henry Taylor, director of the Metropolitan Museum of Art, New York, derided an art appreciated only by snobs, 'the fashionably initiated', and rejected by the broad public. Such was the climate of the time that, in 1948, Boston's Institute for Modern Art changed its name from 'Modern' to the less provocative 'Contemporary'. The Institute's director, James S. Plaut, commented that modernist artists had gradually withdrawn 'from a common meeting ground with the public...This cult of [bewilderment] rested on the hazardous foundations of obscurity and negation, and utilized a private, often secret, language.'[16] Picking up this story, Life magazine claimed that the Boston Institute had turned its back on modernism as a European-based 'silly and secretive faddism'.

The neo-Masonic modernist conspiracy bided its time, coming together in night covens and whispering-galleries. At a conference for abstract artists held at the Manhattan Art School in April 1950, Alfred Barr urged them to become the first group of artists ever to name themselves, suggesting not only 'abstract expressionist', but also 'abstract-symbolist' and even 'intra-subjectionist'—the latter a grim reflection on the semantic tyranny favoured by curators and critics. However, the painters themselves did not buy it. Willem de Kooning ended the discussion: 'It is disastrous to name ourselves.' There was never an aesthetic manifesto joining Jackson Pollock, Willem de Kooning, Robert Motherwell, Arshile Gorky, and Mark Rothko.[17] Did they regard themselves, even in the loosest sense, as a movement? Fifty years later, in 1998, the novelist John Updike discerned a clear unity: 'They worked on a heroic scale, and made heroic breakthroughs into sublime simplifications— Rothko's hovering rectangles of color, Kline's sweeping bars of black, De Kooning's infernos of flickering, flashing strokes, and above all Pollock's epic drips.'[18] There was certainly evidence of anti-Communism among some abstract expressionist artists, but here again the evidence was audible rather than visible.[19] Unsustainable is the opinion advanced by Frances Stonor Saunders: 'It is hard to sustain the argument that the Abstract Expressionists merely "happened to be painting in the cold war and not for the cold war." Their own statements and, in some cases, political allegiances, undermine claims of ideological disengagement.'[20] But here she confuses the painter with the painting; indeed, almost without exception the leading abstract expressionists had developed their characteristic painterly style by 1945, before the cold war began. It was the collectors, curators, and critics who sought to turn a certain kind of 'ideological disengagement' among contemporary artists to political advantage.

Abstract expressionism clearly celebrated 'individualism', loosely defined as subjective freedom, and represented extreme aesthetic detachment from ordinary human emotions and daily life. Jackson Pollock, who was by the 1950s its most famous practitioner, had been in the early 1930s the foremost pupil of the narrative painter Thomas Hart Benton, who typically portrayed an energetic, enterprising, working-man America striving to better itself. Equally remarkable, the Pollock who achieved fame as 'Jack the Dripper' had some time earlier been involved with Communist-sponsored artists' workshops in America and Mexico; having signed up for the new Federal Art Project of the WPA, by 1936 he was working in the West 14th Street experimental workshop run by David Alfaro Siqueiros, a hardline Stalinist Mexican painter of talent later imprisoned for an attempt on Trotsky's life, who was producing banners and floats for Communist demonstrations. Here Pollock learned new mural techniques, including the use of spray-guns and airbrushes; the floor of the Siqueiros workshop was covered with splatter and drip.[21] After entering psychotherapy in 1939 and reading Jung's *Psychology of the Unknown*, with its emphasis on the role of myth and the collective unconscious in artistic creation, Pollock's outlook changed radically as he defected towards a thick, gestural application of paint within ambivalent spatial relationships, passing through a loudly coloured phase, with obvious debts to cubism and expressionism, before emerging as an action painter working with household and metallic paints, mainly in muted colours, crouching over horizontal canvases like a whirling dervish, trailing black drips like barbed wire—and warmly supported by the patronage of Peggy Guggenheim. In 1945 Clement Greenberg hailed him as 'the strongest painter of his generation and perhaps the greatest one to appear since Miro'.[22]

In tracing the unfolding of a *pax Americana* in the field of art, it is the critic, not the painting, which commands attention. Although Greenberg in 1947 was still describing Pollock's work in terms of European derivations, the claim to American artistic supremacy was already audible:[23] 'Much to our own surprise, the main premises of Western art have at last migrated to the United States, along with the center of gravity of industrial production and political power.' Authentic art (wrote Greenberg) must not only avoid the kitsch *vulgarity* fostered by totalitarianism, it must also be 'uninflated by illegitimate content—no religion or mysticism or political certainties. And in its radical inadaptability to the uses of any interest, ideological or institutional, lies the most certain guarantee of the truth with which it expresses us.' The former Trotsykist from the editorial staff of *Partisan Review* now came to view private wealth, the 'golden umbilical cord', as the only possible source of funding for the avant-garde artist.[24] (The CIA in that role did not occur to him.) In short, Greenberg (like Daniel Bell) subscribed to that powerful current of cold war liberalism which mistook American ideology for the 'end of ideology'.

That Greenberg's *pax Americana* was as much directed against the traditional hegemony of the School of Paris as against Moscow's claims is common knowledge and need not detain us here.[25] The road to Moscow's Pushkin Museum and Leningrad's Hermitage lay through the Musée nationale d'art moderne. In *How New York Stole the Idea of Modern Art* Serge Guilbaut explained how the 'theft' had been engineered by critics such as Greenberg and Harold Rosenberg. According to Guilbaut, the promotion of American abstract expressionism amounted to the cultural counterpart of the Truman Doctrine and the Marshall Plan; it fitted 'the needs of the cold war'. This thesis seriously misdated American artistic dominion as effective from 1948 rather than, more realistically, from the late fifties. The distortion has, however, remained seductive to post-1967 revisionists.

Another priestly voice raised on behalf of abstract expressionism, second in influence only to Clement Greenberg's, belonged to Harold Rosenberg, who described how the vanguard of 'action painters' (his term) was currently developing its own procedures and possibilities, resisting any exterior reference, such as social and historical progress. Rosenberg compared this art with existential philosophy—committed to isolation, anguish, and struggle.[26] The only choice now open to American painters was 'to hang around in the space between art and political action', creating an art which stood as a symbol of freedom in an age of political conformities. Thus Rosenberg reached, by his own route, Clement Greenberg's 'art for art's sake':

The big moment came when it was decided to paint . . . just TO PAINT. The gesture on the canvas was a gesture of liberation from Value—political, esthetic, moral . . . The French artist thinks of himself as a battleground of history; here one hears only of private Dark Nights . . . At its center the movement was away from, rather than toward. The Great Works of the Past and the Good Life of the Future became equally nil . . . The lone artist did not want the world to be different, he wanted his canvas to be a world.[27]

In Rosenberg's essay Pollock was seen as a cowboy artist, a 'Coonskinner', a frontier sharpshooter taking aim at the best of European modernism and hitting his mark. By rolling out his canvas and walking on it as he painted, Pollock transcended European landscape painting by treating the canvas itself as part of the landscape.[28] In 1954 Greenberg (who held that advanced painting continued to create scandal when little that was new in literature or music managed to do so) again declared that

the best art of our day, tends, increasingly, to be abstract. And most attempts to reverse this tendency seem to result in second-hand, second-rate painting . . . In fact it seems as though, today, the image and object can be put back into art only by pastiche or parody.

Though it may have started towards modernism earlier than the other arts, painting has turned out to have a greater number of *expendable* conventions embedded in it, or at least a greater number of conventions that are [not?] difficult to isolate in order to expend . . . Painting continues, then, to work out its modernism with unchecked momentum because it still has a relatively long way to go before being reduced to its viable essence.[29]

⌗   ⌗   ⌗

If Clement Greenberg and Harold Rosenberg provided the creed and cult, the Museum of Modern Art provided the cathedral and the liturgy. Like the great European abbeys before it, the Rockefellers' MoMA confirmed the power and social authority of a patron class.[30] At the age of 27 Alfred H. Barr, Jr. had been appointed its first director, rapidly building up a permanent collection of post-impressionists, cubists, and surrealists, with special attention to Matisse and Picasso; his tenure as director lasted until 1943, but his influential role within MoMA continued through the 1950s. In his much-quoted article 'Is Modern Art Communistic?', published in the *New York Times Magazine* (14 December 1952), Barr maintained that: 'The modern artist's nonconformity and love of freedom cannot be tolerated within a monolithic tyranny and modern art is useless for the dictator's propaganda.'

MoMA assumed responsibility for organizing America's exhibits at the Venice Biennales from the late 1940s. From 1952 the Museum's promotion of modern art abroad was carried out through its International Circulating Exhibitions Program, begun in that year with a five-year grant of $625,000 from the Rockefeller Brothers Fund. The tie-in with the State Department and the Marshall Plan was close[31]—for example, the State Department regularly tape-recorded relevant lectures given by leading artists at the Museum. MoMA was stepping in where the US government no longer dared to display sponsorship—with the added ideological advantage of demonstrating the role and value of private sponsorship of the arts. But some of the State Department's bruised caution in the face of virulent conservative opposition—Busbey and Dondero—rubbed off on MoMA too. As Irving Sandler writes:

In actuality, art-conscious capitalists and the museums of which they were trustees were hesitant until well into the fifties to collect Abstract Expressionist paintings, even though prices were very low... It was only after 1952 that the Museum [of Modern Art] launched an international program of any scope and ambition... and not until 1958, a decade after the inception of the cold war, that a major show of Abstract Expressionist painting introduced it into Europe in numbers sufficient to make a strong impression.[32]

This is exactly correct. But as we noted earlier, in her 'Abstract Expressionism, Weapon of the Cold War', Eva Cockcroft contended that the link between Western values and abstract expressionism was consciously forged by influential figures who controlled MoMA and who advocated 'enlightened cold war tactics designed to woo European intellectuals'. Barr's role was pivotal: 'In terms of cultural propaganda, the functions of both the CIA's cultural apparatus and MoMA's international programs was similar and, in fact, mutually supportive.'[33] Cockcroft's thesis has recently received further elaboration in the work of Frances Stonor Saunders: 'Operating at a remove from the CIA, and therefore offering a plausible disguise for its interests, was the Museum of Modern Art.'[34] Here we have moved on from Cockcroft's 'mutually supportive' to 'offering a plausible disguise'—a sustained attempt to prove that the best brains of the newly created (1947) CIA, mainly liberals from elite East Coast schools, rapidly decided that they must assume the clandestine role of sponsoring American abstract art abroad, now that open State Department sponsorship was proven to be politically impossible in the reactionary climate imposed by Congressmen Busbey, Dondero, and the native-traditionalist pressure groups. The operation must therefore be conducted through 'dummy Foundations' and the great East Coat museums, both serving as fronts. The ever-available former CIA man Carl Braden, blowing the same whistle for over thirty years, is quoted: 'it had to be covert because it would have been turned down if it had been put to a vote in a democracy.'[35] Saunders's central thesis—that MoMA and the CIA were hand-in-glove to promote abstract expressionism from the earliest phase of the cold war—is extended to granting the newborn CIA senior partnership in the enterprise: 'Once again, the CIA turned to the private sector to advance its objectives.'

In rejecting this approach, there is no need to invoke the integrity of the Museum and its personnel; merely to understand that the CIA was less experienced and less well endowed than the major museums and the Rockefeller Brothers Fund, whose spending went beyond anything the CIA could contribute to the art *Kulturkampf*. Retrospective claims that the CIA from day one spotted that abstract expressionism could bring down the onion domes in the East belong to 'interview history' rather than history. Saunders, for example, quotes a certain 'Agency man Donald Jameson': 'We recognized that this was the kind of art that did not have anything to do with socialist realism, and made socialist realism look even more stylized and more rigid and confined than it was. And that relationship was exploited in some of the exhibits.'[36] How wide of the mark this simplistic dichotomy is and was may be seen below, when we discuss *Time* magazine's praise for Renato Guttuso and MoMA's Ben Shahn exhibit at the Venice Biennale. During the first decade of the cold war, abstract expressionism on the whole baffled or even alienated more West European viewers than it attracted; in Russia it bypassed the local cultural heritage which inspired dissident art.

The attempt to prove CIA–MoMA collusion has been supported by family trees showing interlocking personal connections[37] rather than by a close examination of patterns of art patronage and exhibition policy. A family tree of Ivy League conspirators (who worked for whom and when, or who knew Allen Dulles in person) generated a spider-web of largely imagined machination spinning a procession of fertile *ergo*'s. 'There is no *prima facie* evidence', Saunders writes, 'for any formal agreement between the CIA and the Museum of Modern Art. The fact is, it simply wasn't necessary.'[38] Her approach is almost exclusively *ad hominem*—the 'hidden hands' behind the galleries—and largely ignores the actual composition of American exhibits abroad, as well as the reaction of European opinion and how this affected selection policy. For the first seven or ten years of its existence, until the late fifties, the CIA ate at the table of the East Coast magnates rather than the other way round. After the big lunches and stiff martinis had been downed—the 'Art and the CIA' episode in Saunders's documentary film *Hidden Hands* (1994) is full of suspicious eating and drinking—it was the art-loving bankers who paid for shipping the canvases to Europe, as is precisely documented in MoMA's private correspondence with, for example, the British Arts Council and the Tate Gallery.

Interviewed for *Hidden Hands* forty years later, Waldo Rasmussen, assistant to Porter McCray, director of MoMA's international programme, dismissed allegations of MoMA's involvement with the CIA as 'categorically untrue'. Although former CIA men like William Colby, Donald Jameson, and, most important, Thomas Braden were interviewed at length in *Hidden Hands*, none specifically alluded to the purchase, shipment, or exhibiting of painting and sculpture by the CIA. Jameson's contribution was mainly generalized waffle. Neither he nor Braden—who was head of the CIA's International Organizations Division, and who in 1967 was to blow the whistle on the CIA's cultural operations—had any direct evidence to offer about the funding of fine arts exhibitions abroad. MoMA's defenders have consistently (and credibly) denied any connection to the secret state and have insisted that the Museum's exhibitions of abstract expressionism belonged to the late 1950s.[39] The CIA did things in secret, like the Count of Monte Cristo, but it could not afford to do much. The spymen's (probably exaggerated) passion for abstract expressionism as a cultural H-bomb was not consummated until the late 1950s, when Jackson Pollock was finally dropped on Russia but failed to cause widespread damage.

In April 1952, Nicolas Nabokov, general secretary of the Congress for Cultural Freedom (CCF), set up a major cultural festival, 'Masterpieces of the Twentieth Century' or 'Oeuvre du Vingtième Siècle' in Paris. The narrative of *Hidden Hands* claims that the CIA 'had a handle on several MoMA exhibitions in Europe', including 'Masterpieces of the Twentieth Century', but this last claim goes unsubstantiated. The Congress contracted as curator of the art and sculpture exhibition James Johnson Sweeney, a former director of MoMA[40] who envisaged the exhibition as a coup in the culture war: 'On display will be masterpieces that could not have been created nor whose exhibition would be allowed by such totalitarian regimes as Nazi Germany or present-day Soviet Russia and her satellites.'[41] Such sentiments were standard at the time. Sweeney did not represent the CIA; abstract expressionism, 'weapon of the cold war', was in any case barely visible at the 1952 Paris exhibition. The most prominent of the works Sweeney had shipped from America aboard the SS *Liberté* for display in the Musée nationale d'art moderne were by European masters, Gauguin, Rousseau, and Picasso from New York, Renoir from Chicago; they, along with Van Gogh, Bonnard, Matisse, Derain, Cézanne, Seurat, Chagall, and Kandinsky, dominated the 120 works of the exhibition. André Chastel's long review in *Le Monde* (7 May), which found difficulty in locating common denominators amid the inevitable discontinuity, did not mention a single American work of art or any political dimension. Indeed, Sweeney's role as curator brought an anti-American rebuke from Claude Roger-Marx in *Figaro littéraire* (10 May), whose review appeared under the somewhat perverse title '20th Century, American Taste'—given that the painters he listed were all Europeans. The essential thing, added the art critic of the conservative *Figaro*, was to make sure that 'America's preferences don't influence us'— *ne déteignent pas sur nous*.

The show 'Twelve Contemporary American Painters and Sculptors', which opened an extensive, two-year European tour at the Musée d'art moderne in the summer of 1953, following negotiations between the curator of the Musée, Jean Cassou, MoMA, and the US Embassy in Paris,[42] was—claims Frances Stonor Saunders—the first by MoMA dedicated exclusively to 'the

New York School'. But what was 'the New York School'? According to a leading authority on abstract expressionism, the term 'has no descriptive value whatsoever'. Furthermore, of the twelve contemporary American artists on display (nine painters, three sculptors), only half were undeniably abstract expressionists (Pollock, Arshile Gorky, David Smith, and Theodore Roszak among them); Edward Hopper and Ben Shahn were manifestly nothing of the kind, while John Marin (born 1870) and Stuart Davis (born 1894) were classified by MoMA as belonging to the 'Older Generation of Moderns'. The funding was provided openly by the Nelson Rockefeller Fund. On the whole, European commentaries were disappointing, and some critics ignored the show.[43] Attracting greater attention—and with a more direct cold war significance—was the 'Unknown Political Prisoner' competition organized by the Institute of Contemporary Art in London, shown at the Tate Gallery, and supported by MoMA, which dispatched several American entries. Reg Butler's winning maquette, enlarged into a working model, a highly abstract and aggressively asymmetrical design, contained allusions to the cage, scaffold, cross, guillotine, and the watch-tower of the concentration camp. The 300-feet-high monument that Butler had in mind never materialized.[44] Baffled or outraged mainstream opinion in Butler's native England was as relieved as the Russians must have been (though they were ever spoiling for a fight).

Abstract expressionism achieved real international impact only (and quite briefly) towards the end of the 1950s. This is vividly illustrated by an exhibition to which MoMA attached the greatest importance, describing it in private correspondence as 'the first major exhibition of modern art in Britain', and badgering the Tate Gallery for more and better space than originally offered. But by 'modern' MoMA's Porter McCray did not mean modernist; he meant contemporary and recent.[45] MoMA's exhibition, 'Modern Art in the United States', which toured Europe in 1956, was divided into five thematic sections, of which the largest was the first in time:

I. 'Older Generation of Moderns' (41 works, Marin, Davis);
II. 'Realist Tradition: Fact, Satire, Sentiment,' (19 works, including Hopper, Shahn, and Wyeth)
III. 'Romantic Painting' (11 works).
IV. 'Contemporary Abstract Art' (28 Abstract Expressionist paintings, the earliest dating from 1942, by 17 artists including Pollock, Gorky, Franz Kline, Rothko, de Kooning, Motherwell, Newman, Baziotes, and Hartigan.
V. 'Modern "Primitives" ' (8 works).

It may be that MoMA attached particular importance to the abstract expressionist section; the numbers displayed in each category do not necessarily tell the whole story; ten of the twenty-nine plates in the exhibition catalogue were given to abstract expressionists, and the catalogue carried an introduction by Alfred Barr describing the abstract expressionists as gripped by 'anxiety' and by their 'dreadful freedom'. While rejecting conventional social values, these artists (he explained) were not politically *engagé*; their work was to be taken as a symbolic demonstration of freedom.[46] But what clearly emerges is MoMA's desire, almost anxiety, to reveal the breadth and diversity of modern American painting. The information release for the press (November 1955) emphasized how Dorothy C. Miller's selection was designed 'to reveal four or five principal directions of American art over a period of approximately forty years'.[47] Although no attendance figures were taken by the Tate, because entrance was free, it was obvious that a 'broad church' approach was likely to attract a wider public, even if less intense excitement among artists and critics. According to MoMA's own private 'Press Analysis': 'Although abstract expressionism was certainly the most frequently discussed and controversial section of the exhibition, there was an overwhelming preference for the more realistic canvases.' The report also mentioned 'considerable response' to the social commentary in works by Shahn, Levine, and Hopper. Among critics and public alike the most popular single painting was Andrew Wyeth's *Christina's World*, a naturalistic rural idyll darkened only by the faintest hint of Christina's physical incapacity as she sits in a cornfield, caressed by a light summer breeze, gazing up the gentle slope at the eternal mystery of her own solitary homestead. MoMA had bought *Christina's World* in 1948, when it was supposedly obsessed by abstract expressionism, and when in fact it was acquiring more works by Lucien Freud than by Pollock. (From 1947 to 1952 MoMA acquired eleven works by abstract expressionists; the Whitney Museum purchased the same number between 1943 and 1953.) Wyeth had the possibly unique but significant distinction of winning the Presidential Freedom Award (1963), becoming the first American artist since Sargent to be elected to the Académie des beaux-arts (1977), and being elected an honorary member of the Soviet Academy of Arts (1978). Wyeth's work and universal popularity remind us, in short, why the cold war in the domain of painting could not be won by the rejection of human content.

In 1959 MoMA at long last cast aside all inhibition and released 'New American Painting, As Shown in Eight European Countries',[48] a massive display of abstract expressionism (eighty-one pictures by seventeen artists), which opened at the Tate Gallery on 24 February, sponsored once again by

MoMA's International Council,[49] and without overt co-sponsorship from the USIA or any other government department—although the files show minimal USIS involvement in fostering publicity.[50] A Jackson Pollock retrospective (thirty-one paintings plus twenty-nine drawings and watercolours) toured seven European cities more or less contemporaneously. In general the Pollock canvases were by far the most highly valued for insurance, typically $15,000, but $30,000 for his canvas *November 12, 1952*. Next in value was Arshile Gorky ($10,000–15,000), perhaps a reflection of the fact that he, like Pollock, would paint no more. Barnett Newman's vertical stripe-paintings, which irritated many members of the public, leading to derisive comments, along with Rothko's horizontal bands of smudged paint, were down in the $3,000–4,000 category, slightly below de Kooning at $5,000–6,000. USIS staff attached to the London Embassy were happy to announce their assistance in a bulletin issued on the eve of the exhibition, which conveyed the uniting characteristics of the exhibits: large-scale canvases (a breadth of eight feet was typical), and concern with the actual painting process as the artist's prime instrument of expression, coupled with the elimination of mimesis and a highly charged emotional content. The USIS also summarized Alfred Barr's introduction to the catalogue: 'in principle their individualism is as uncompromising as that of the religion of Kierke-gaard, whom they honour' (English spelling of this last word was tactfully used). What? Did all of these artists honour the dead Dane? Either way, 'Modern Art in the United States' greatly excited British artists: '[The paintings'] massive size, bold reductionism and physical impact instantly made much English painting seem domestic in scale, gutless and dilettante . . . Not since Roger Fry's two Post-impressionist exhibitions of 1910 and 1912 had the [British] art world been so divided. American Abstract Expressionism aroused violently opposed responses.'[51] The exhibition ran for four weeks and was seen by a record 14,718 visitors.[52] By complete accident it coincided with the first display of Soviet art at the Royal Academy, some 2 miles away, which ran for nine weeks and attracted five times as many visitors, despite an admission charge.

The anti-American Claude Roger-Marx, art critic of *Figaro littéraire* (17 January 1959), had attacked the exhibition when it invaded Paris a month earlier: 'GIGANTISME ET PETITESSES de la nouvelle peinture américaine'. As in 1952, he urged French artists not to allow themselves to be influenced by these 'contagious heresies'.[53] Only 7,000 Parisians turned up. André Chastel, of *Le Monde* (17 January), commented: 'It becomes apparent that the two arts in which the United States reveals itself most forcefully are architecture and photography, and after that, of course, film.' According to MoMA's private

'Press Analysis', the painting and sculpture on display were 'treated almost dismissively'.[54]

In Rome *Avanti!* called Pollock 'Il Presley della pittura'; in Berlin *Der Tur* spoke of 'Vom Chaos bis zu Pollock'. The Italian critic Leonard Borgese declared the exhibited work not new, not American, and not painting—and damned it as 'rubbish'—like contemporary Soviet art.[55]

A year later, in January 1960 the show 'Antagonismes' opened at the Musée des arts décoratifs, featuring, among others, Mark Rothko, Jackson Pollock, and Franz Kline. Many of the paintings were brought to Paris from Vienna, where the Congress for Cultural Freedom had exhibited them as part of the campaign to counter the city's 1959 Communist youth festival.[56] *Le Monde* (29 January) responded with French eyes, emphasizing the inclusion of provocative work by the Parisian avant-garde (Mathieu, Degotex, Burri, Appel, etc.) which would normally be on display in the rue de Seine and the rue Miromesnil. The only American painter mentioned in this review was de Kooning, without comment, and the whole show was put down with the phrase 'contemporary anti-painting' (*anti-peinture actuelle*). If this was a display of American abstract art as the big gun against Communism, *Le Monde* failed to notice.

⌗ ⌗ ⌗

The great American museums and collections by no means surrendered their funds, space, and patronage to abstraction. The jury remained out for many years on the value of abstract art as a weapon in the cultural cold war. Not only the thundering condemnation of nativists and conservatives inhibited the curatorial elite; so too did the guarded suspicion, and on occasion outright hostility, of the general public and the press both at home and abroad.

No clearer illustration of this can be found than the later career of the painter Ben Shahn, whose allegiances and affiliations during the 1930s had much in common with Pollock's; but Shahn was to remain loyal to them, much to the irritation of Clement Greenberg.[57] Although much assailed by red-hunters, Shahn did not forfeit the patronage of the East Coast art establishment responsible for selecting the nation's art armoury for foreign campaigns.

Associated during the New Deal era with such Communist-dominated bodies as the American Artists' Congress, he worked as Diego Rivera's assistant on his Rockefeller Center mural sponsored by the Federal Art Project—the Mexican mural style married clear narrative realism to the formal simplification and shallow space of modernism.[58] Shahn's work was acquired by major collections such as the Whitney Museum and MoMA, which accorded him a retrospective despite his open support for the Henry Wallace campaign. Writing in the *Nation* (1 November 1947), the emergent high priest of abstract art, Clement Greenberg, commented that although by no means photographically 'realist', and certainly not academic on the Soviet model, Shahn represented a style of American art, rooted in the 1920s and 1930s, which was now effectively blocking the avenues of major patronage to the new and innovative abstract expressionism. Greenberg dismissed Shahn as a mere comic-strip illustrator using 'that routine, quasi-expressionist, half-impressionist illustrative manner derived from Cézanne, Vlaminck, and other pre-Cubist French artists, examples of which year in and year out fill the halls of the Whitney, Carnegie and Pepsi-Cola annuals and the showrooms of the Associated American Artists'... Shahn's art, according to Greenberg, was 'essentially beside the point as far as ambitious present-day painting is concerned, and is much more derivative than it seems at first glance'.[59] But the major museums were not listening to Greenberg; in 1949 MoMA honoured Shahn with two medals for his graphic work; a year later his paintings appeared in group exhibitions at the Whitney, the Metropolitan, MoMA, and the Carnegie Institute, selling almost as soon as they were finished for sums ranging from $450 to $2,000. Sixty of his works were to be found in thirty American museums, and many others belonged to private collectors. In 1951 Shahn received a letter from James Laughlin, a consultant to the Ford Foundation, about a project to launch an international magazine, *Perspectives, USA*, whose purpose would be 'To promote peace by increasing respect for America's non-materialistic achievements among intellectuals abroad'. The Ford Foundation would fund the magazine for three years. The pilot issue appeared in January 1952; American art was represented by Shahn, with an accompanying article by Selden Rodman advancing the claims of an American figurative modern art which 'addressed the daily reality of individuals, contemporary political events, and spiritual concerns', fusing 'idea with matter', 'emotion with form'. In short, Ben Shahn! 'Creator of the most "American" of images, he is more critical of his country's "materialism", political backwardness and local prejudices than any Paris Existentialist on a six-months' shopping tour of native blight.'[60]

The Ford Foundation was in no hurry to accept either the conservative cold war culture propounded by Congressman Dondero or, at the opposite extreme, Clement Greenberg's passionate advocacy of abstract expressionism as America's ambassador abroad.[61] Even though the 25 July 1952 edition of the blacklisting newsletter *Counterattack* carried a lengthy denunciation of Shahn, prompted by a full-page advertisement executed by the artist for CBS

Television (which promptly blacklisted him),[62] Selden Rodman continued undeterred to promote him. By all conventional accounts of the 'McCarthy' period, Shahn (who had signed a petition requesting an amnesty for the CPUSA leaders imprisoned under the Smith Act) should by now have been working as an encyclopaedia salesman (likewise Rodman). An FBI report[63] noted that the painter had also called for an end to the Korean War, designing Christmas cards for the New Jersey Committee for Peaceful Alternatives. Only slightly less grave, he had 'a tendency to play up the lower class' in his paintings. Interviewed by two FBI agents on 27 February 1953, Shahn insisted that he had never been a member of the CPUSA, but the artist and his wife courteously refused to name anyone they considered to be a Communist—the acid test. This visit may have prompted Shahn to reconsider his position. Writing in *Art News* (September 1953), he complained about Communist manipulation of 'liberals' and offered disparaging comments about Soviet art: 'Neither the formulae of commissars, nor inducements of honor, nor pretentious awards have yet succeeded in breathing life into Soviet art. Its deadly procession of overdrawn generals and overidealized proletarians bears sharp testimony to the fact that there is no conviction in the artists' hearts.'[64]

A repudiation of Soviet socialist realism may have eased Shahn's passage to MoMA's pavilion at the 1954 Venice Bienniale (the first to display exhibits from several Iron Curtain countries). The fact that MoMA, which had purchased its pavilion the previous year with Rockefeller funding, and which was the only non-governmental sponsor of a national exhibit, chose to display two contrasting American artists, Shahn and de Kooning, the latter representing the ultra avant-garde, the former a more eclectic tradition sometimes called 'magic realism', is clear evidence that neither abstract expressionism nor the CIA was firing all the guns of the American cultural offensive.[65] MoMA anxiously analysed the reaction of European critics, press, and public. The message was clear; the America that Europeans wanted, and wanted to like, was not that of the violent, arrogant, and insulting 'splash school', whose imperviousness to content so excited Greenberg and Rosenberg. De Kooning's work shown at Venice was reproduced only in 'the more advanced [European] periodicals'. French critics found his work 'too boring' or 'lacking in freshness'. His *Woman* series was poorly received, Alain Jouffroy describing it as 'horrible' and 'violent' in *Beaux-Arts*, and G. Mario Marini as 'disproportionate, contorted, mutilated', in the Rome periodical *Notiziario d'Arte*. Ben Shahn, by contrast, was hugely applauded. Several European museums and galleries asked MoMA to arrange Shahn exhibits for them. The Italian minister of fine arts expressed interest in sponsoring a one-man show, an honour previously accorded only to Picasso, Matisse, and Rouault. Franco Catania wrote in *Corriere de Sicilia*: 'This Lithuanian-born Jew paints precisely the myth of America—the America of Washington, of Ford, of gangsters; of the America that grew so rapidly out of the courage, the simplicity and the struggles of the early pioneers.' . . . The Army–McCarthy hearings had ended only two days before the Bienniale opened: America's image was at its lowest.

If Shahn was to steal some of the thunder from the leading Italian Communist painters, Carlo Levi and Renato Guttuso, all well and good. Far from being obsessed by abstraction, American opinion-makers had taken careful note of striking differences in style between Italian and Soviet socialist realism: indeed, *Time* (30 November 1953) had praised Guttuso as 'one of Italy's most talented artists', lauding him for his unwillingness to fit his artistic conscience 'into the tight jacket of Red discipline'. Certainly his canvases were filled with 'miners, child laborers, peasants and decadent rich folks sunning at Capri', but he had rejected the academic style of Soviet art for a style less rigid, more flexible. Driving a wedge between the Russians and their European sympathizers was a high priority for *Time*. Yet MoMA's boldness of choice for the 1954 Venice Biennale did falter politically. Eight highly polemical Shahn posters arrived but were not put on display—they could be inspected on request. The titles are indicative: *We Demand the National Textile Act* (1935), *This is Nazi Brutality, We French Workers Warn You, For Full Employment After the War, Break Reaction's Grip: Register/Vote*. The Roman Communist weekly *Il Contemporaneo* pounced on MoMA's shyness with a front-page article headed 'Shahn in the Cellar'. To keep the posters in a back room was not only a 'grave insult' to both logic and culture, but probably reflected 'State Department censorship'.[66]

Shahn visited London in February 1956 to deliver a lecture, 'Realism Reconsidered', under the sponsorship of MoMA and the USIA. Yet, even as he was paraded by the establishment, he was embroiled in yet another vigilante protest as one of the artists whose work had been included in the USIA's 'Sport in Art' exhibition, scheduled to end up at the 1956 Melbourne Olympics. Curated by the American Federation of Arts, the exhibition had been on display at the Corcoran Gallery in Washington when orchestrated protests from the American Legion, the Daughters of the American Revolution, and the Dallas Country Patriotic Council, among others, demanding that Shahn, Kroll, Kuniyoshi, and the sculptor Zorach be removed, forced the USIA to abort the show.[67] Three years later HUAC subpoenaed Shahn after he had called for its abolition; Chairman Francis E. Walter invited him to justify the inclusion of his work—one painting!—in the American exhibition in

Moscow.[68] Deriding HUAC for turning America into 'an international laughing-stock', Shahn took the opportunity to display the May 1959 issue of *Amerika*, the glossy Russian-language magazine distributed in the USSR by the State Department, containing a lecture he had delivered at Harvard 'On Nonconformity', a blast at past and present attempts to censor art.[69]

⌗ ⌗ ⌗

The great American exhibition which opened in Moscow in July 1959 was the first occasion on which American art had actually penetrated the Soviet frontier. Would abstract expressionism and the CIA call the shots at this moment of supreme confrontation with the enemy? Not in the least; only one Jackson Pollock canvas, *Cathedral*, made the journey. A panel of four experts[70] nominated by the USIA selected seventy paintings and sculptures by sixty-seven American artists representing almost all schools—early modernists, the New York School, social realists, scene painters, and others. HUAC's chairman, Francis E. Walter, charged that thirty-four of the paintings and sculptures chosen were by artists 'with records of affiliation with Communist fronts and causes'.[71] The greatest uproar was raised by HUAC and the vigilantes over the inclusion of a picture permanently held in the Brooklyn Museum, Jack Levine's savagely satirical oil painting *Welcome Home* (1946), depicting a general salting his celery with infinite care at a victory dinner, while being served by an elderly waiter whose body is a masterpiece of obsequious grace.

Eisenhower himself, meanwhile, offered some homespun aesthetic comments at a news conference: 'We are not too certain exactly what art is but we know what we like, and what America likes—whatever America likes is after all some of the things that ought to be shown.' The president called Levine's contentious painting 'lampoon more than art', adding that his own favourite painter was Andrew Wyeth.[72] Under pressure, the USIA made a last-minute decision to add some traditional American paintings, some twenty-five to thirty works by nineteenth-century artists, to those already in transit, including Gilbert Stuart's portrait of George Washington and George P. A. Healy's beardless Abraham Lincoln.[73]

It was Alfred Barr who carried the assault to the Soviet capital by displaying 150 slides and film-clips showing the mobile sculptor Alexander Calder at work and Jackson Pollock's drip technique. At long last the atomic weapon of abstract expressionism was being dropped on the Kremlin. A group of Soviet artists, critics, museum directors, and students spent several hours inspecting Barr's slides. How would the Russians respond to Pollock—and who was Jackson Pollock really? A version of Elvis Presley, as the Italian critic suggested? A long-serving alcoholic, Pollock had been killed in 1956 at the age of 44, along with a female companion, in an automobile accident while drunk at the wheel, a year after James Dean's fatal and fabled crash—both victims, it could be said, of a peculiarly American flash-success and some degree of self-disgust. Discovered by Clement Greenberg and Peggy Guggenheim (Pollock had urinated in the fireplace of her mansion on the Grand Canal, Venice), he was made famous by *Life* in 1949, when the photographer Martha Holmes showed him crouched over a canvas spread across a studio floor, pouring sand or applying paint with a stick. *Life* used such terms as 'dribbles', 'drools', 'scrawls', and 'scoops' under the sceptical headline: 'Jackson Pollock Is He the Greatest American Living Painter?' America, or its media, was fascinated by the anarchic, introverted, pained, semi-coherent, mumbling, addicted, lone-wolf male genius: Brando, Dean, Kerouac, Pollock. Cigarettes dangled from their lips, causing them to screw up their eyes during the agony of creation. Their talent was real, compelling, captivating, very American—but Pollock could not captivate millions, as Brando and Dean did. He did not captivate Picasso either: the old man's reported verdict on Pollock *et al.* was: 'As far as these new painters are concerned, I think it is a mistake to let oneself go completely and lose oneself in the gesture. Giving oneself up entirely to the action of painting—there's something in that which displeases me enormously.' Speaking to Samuel Kootz, agent for many American artists, he compared Jackson Pollock's work to a used blotter without structure.[74]

Hans Namuth's intimate photographs of Pollock at work became an enduring part of the Pollock image, indeed of his art; they frequently appeared alongside the paintings on the walls of galleries. The action in action painting counted for as much as the painting. *Life*'s 1959 retrospective stressed the dead painter's bohemian image, searching eyes, stress-torn personality: his drinking and bar-fights received greater attention than his interest in the cubist treatment of line and space and the surrealist technique of automatic drawing.[75]

The Russians were not likely to show interest, still less enthusiasm; their constant tactic was never to mention America's favoured sons by name—unless, as with the pianist Van Cliburn, they embodied traditional virtues. The director of the Pushkin Museum, A. Zamoshkin, found the American exhibit of abstract art interesting 'because it shows sterility of technique. It has transcribed a full circle.' More than thirty years ago, he said, the Russian artist Malevich painted a famous black square.[76] Two generations later abstraction had not advanced beyond that point. To this Alfred Barr countered that 'each generation must paint its own black square'. Emotions were

running high. In Harrison Salisbury's typically patriotic report of this encounter, the director of the Pushkin was merely a nameless 'bureaucrat,' a
'Soviet official':

But as I looked at the faces of those who listened to Barr and looked at his
slides... those who exclaimed at Calder's 'Whale', cried with pleasure at Pollock's
compositions, and gasped at Richard Lippold's dazzling 'Sun', it seemed to me that
the younger [Soviet] artists were inclined to agree with Barr... Every day artists
came and copied or photographed the modern paintings. And in the closing hours
of the exhibition, even as the paintings were being taken down for crating, a crew of
photographers worked to copy each of the pictures in color.[77]

One would not have gathered from Salisbury's account that not a few
leading American art critics remained unconvinced by, or hostile to, abstract
expressionism, notably John Canaby and Howard Devree of the *New York
Times*, and Emily Genauer of the *Herald Tribune*. A quite different impression
is derived from another *New York Times* correspondent, Osgood Caruthers,
reporting from Moscow[78] as the US exhibition drew to its close. A knot of
more than fifty persons were clustered around three or four young Russians
who had appointed themselves advocates of the abstract art:

'What good is abstract art?'
'Did a monkey really win first prize in an American art contest?'
'But what good is this crazy painting? What does it mean? Who would buy it?'

asked a ruddy-faced, heavy-set and excited *rabotnik* (working man) in his
fifties. 'Loud guffaws and jeering gestures are hurled at paintings of Jackson
Pollock and Ben Shahn.' But, noted Caruthers, 'Many visitors study these
paintings carefully, and many flock around Richard B. K. McLanathan, a
museum director of Utica, N.Y., to ask questions.' Yet another *New York
Times* correspondent, Max Frankel, also offered a negative report: 'While
the abstract paintings were important to demonstrate freedom of expression,
especially when properly explained, nearly all the abstract sculpture encountered disinterest or hostility.' As Alexander Glezer explained thirty years
later: '[Russian] Artists felt the need to express so much, after the long
repressive Stalinist era, that abstraction could not fulfil their need to express
so many ideas. Secondly, there was no recent tradition of abstraction, and
their deep desire to reach their audience precluded the use of abstract language. Thirdly, they wanted to re-establish a tradition of Russian art.'

The Russians duly retaliated by lauding their own version of American art,
mainly the realistic art of the eighteenth and nineteenth centuries, which
was rapidly put on display at the Pushkin and the Hermitage (November–
December 1959), relying on small American collections held in Soviet

museums. Writing in *Iskusstvo* (no. 5, 1960), Igor Golomshtok[79] complained that in America serious studies of national art were confined to relatively modern times, and this despite the continuance throughout the present century of the realist, socially directed tradition (well illustrated in his article, with sharecroppers, rural hovels, etc.). Realism had experienced a new revival in the late 1920s and early 1930s, prompted by the Depression and the rise of fascism; progressive artists formed the John Reed Clubs. Golomshtok arrived at Rockwell Kent,[80] famous for his vigorously expressed pro-Soviet views, spirited defiance of Congressional committees, and passport contest with the State Department. The Soviet critic (later an illustrious defector) praised Kent's illustrations for *Moby Dick*, mentioned his Moscow exhibition in 1957, and described him—fatuously—as 'the most important (*krupneishii*) contemporary American artist'.

In October 1963 an American exhibition of the graphic arts opened in Alma-Ata, reaching Moscow early in December.[81] By routine reflex *Izvestiia* criticized the abstract prints, complaining that such alien 'ideological subversion' gave 'cultural exchange' a bad name.

⌗ ⌗ ⌗

Following the Russian Art exhibition at the Royal Academy in January 1959, the reciprocal exhibition of British art opened at the Pushkin Museum on 5 May 1960. On display were 141 oil paintings, from William Hogarth to the present day (watercolours were ruled out by the summer light problem). Valued at over £2 million, the most valuable collection of British art ever to be sent abroad, the exhibition had been transported by the Royal Navy. In Moscow 170,000 people visited the exhibition over thirty-two days, 200,000 in Leningrad, where it opened on 17 June, averaging 7,000 visitors per day.

Not everyone (as the archive confirms) was willing to send a valuable painting to the wilds of Russia: John Dewar & Sons, the Scotch whisky distillers, for example, declined to part company with a requested MacNab. By contrast, Lord and Lady Cholmondeley (pronounced 'Chomley'), owners of a prime collection at Houghton, had a high old time being well received in Leningrad and well receiving in their turn a Soviet woman curator, Dr Kroll, at Houghton in August 1959. In one of his letters (20 December 1960) to Mrs Lilian Somerville, director of the British Council's Fine Arts Department, and the key figure in organizing the show, from the time of her visit to Russia in 1958 (along with various British museum directors), Lord Cholmondeley opined: 'This goes to show that the Russian government are not against them seeing private houses or meeting private people.'[82] He meant the rich, but did not know he meant it.

The ad hoc selection committee chosen by the British Council amounted to an unrestrained parody of British establishmentarianism. Knighthoods abounded. Every major art institution in England, Scotland, and Wales was represented by its director. Not a single artist sat on it. The great and the good were all there: Sir Philip Hendy, Sir John Rothenstein, Sir Kenneth Clark (chairman of the Arts Council). The selection committee secretly declared its attachment to secrecy. Its minutes (written by the committee's secretary, the same Mrs Somerville), gave nothing away as to what anyone might have said about an individual artist or painting. (The *Burlington Magazine* complained that the list of works selected was not released to the British press until the day the show opened in Moscow.) Occasionally there is an oblique reference to grumbling or dissent—as when, for example, Sir Anthony Blunt, wearing two of his three hats, as Keeper of the Queen's Pictures and director of the Courtauld Institute, told the committee that he would 'recommend' (i.e. allow) only two paintings belonging to the queen to be sent to Russia, a Reynolds and a Wilkie. According to the minutes, the committee 'regretted that the Royal Collection would not be better represented'. The committee did not regret Blunt's third hat, as Soviet spy, because (perhaps) unaware of it.

The British Council's Fine Arts Advisory Committee, as well as this special selection committee, was chaired by Sir Philip Hendy, chairman of the National Gallery and chairman of everything in sight, who believed in a softly-softly approach to the Russians. 'There has been little or no preliminary publicity in this country', he reported in a confidential whisper, 'in order to minimize the chance that the Russians might bar abstract paintings.' Hendy's brief introduction to the exhibition's catalogue timidly mentioned 'the diversity of styles in use in Great Britain today'. What brought fire to Hendy's belly was not the suppression of artistic freedom in the Soviet Union but a noise from down the street in Piccadilly, a challenge from Sir Charles Wheeler, president of the RA, delivered at the Academy's annual banquet on 29 April 1959: Wheeler complained not only about the absence of artists on Hendy's selection committee, but let fly a dire insult: '. . . past experience goes to show that the British Council . . . is blindly and passionately devoted to leftish modern art'—in contrast to the Academy's good example of 'countenancing the left *and* the right'. (In using the terms 'left' or 'leftish' to describe the modernists, Wheeler was following the same semantic fashion we noted in reviews of the 1947 State Department exhibition.) Most probably Wheeler had got wind of yet another confidential memorandum written a month earlier (24 March) by Hendy to Christopher Mayhew, MP, chairman of the British Council's Soviet Relations Committee, in which he described two veteran RA's, Sir Alfred Munnings and Dame Laura Knight, as 'superficial and indeed incompetent artists', who would 'bring us discredit if their work was shown abroad [i.e. in Russia]'. Indeed, Hendy added, the Royal Academy had produced nothing of value in over a century, since Turner. Whether these comments hastened Munnings's death shortly afterwards, they surely contributed to Wheeler's venom. As it turned out, Hendy was unable to prevent one Munnings horse-painting, *Derby Day at Epsom Downs 1921*, reaching Moscow.

Mary Chamot, assistant keeper at the Tate Gallery, wrote the main introduction to British painting in the catalogue, of which the Soviet Ministry of Culture printed 25,000 copies, although Miss Chamot's comments on abstraction caused offence and called forth an attack from a certain Chegodaev in the Ministry's weekly *Sovetskaia kul'tura*, 'The Greatness and Decline of English Painting', in which he described the Tate (*Gallereia Teit*) as 'the main propaganda centre for abstract and surrealist art in Britain'. Yet Chamot had been courteously received when she was invited to lecture in Russian to the staff of the Pushkin Museum and other professionals; she was also invited to address Hermitage museum guides preparing to conduct visitors round the British Exhibition when it reached Leningrad. What had she written that caused offence? 'The younger generation in Britain, as elsewhere in the West, find non-objective art (*bespredmetnoe iskusstvo*) more suited to their aim, which is to treat painting, like music, as a vehicle for the direct communication of experience, emotions, and sensations through the purely pictorial means of form, colour, rhythm, and harmony.'[83] She went on to mention the influence of surrealism on Graham Sutherland and Francis Bacon, both exhibited, and to laud Ben Nicholson as an abstract artist who 'seeks perfection and purity of form and colour'... Among the non-figurative British artists on display whom she praised,[84] most were associated with the St Ives School, in Cornwall, and pursued a dialogue between abstraction and landscape or nature, developing a rapid, instinctive method, a meeting of solids and fluids.[85] Perhaps inadvertently, Mary Chamot went on to offer socialist realists further offence: 'The perfection of colour photography has made representation less stimulating to artists'... (This argument, surely, does not stand up against the work of, say, David Hockney, who had not yet 'arrived'.)[86]

The *Burlington Magazine* thought the selection committee had done not a bad job, with the 'great quintet' of Hogarth, Reynolds, Gainsborough, Constable, and Turner carrying the show, though Blake and Palmer were not up to so long a journey. Hogarth would teach the Russians what realism was all about—here the *Burlington*'s editor resorted to the tone of condescension which he'd perfected a year earlier, reviewing the exhibition of Russian art at

Burlington House: Russia, he wrote, was 'a country which...no longer knows the true meaning of realism, yet pretends to have a monopoly of it'... He sniffed at the decision to send a Josef Herman as smelling of pleasing the hosts (the *Burlington* did not mention the omission of other social painters), but fortunately there had been 'no compromise' when sending in such storm-troopers of modernism as Nicholson and Bacon.[87] In the *Daily Telegraph* (9 May), Terence Mullaly was impressed: 'Besides hanging all the pictures, the Russians have in all respects treated this fine exhibition most generously.' To achieve the right scale for the paintings, temporary walls had been installed in some rooms. The Russians issued a catalogue containing over thirty illustrations, while seven booklets written by members of the Pushkin's staff were devoted to Hogarth, Gainsborough, Reynolds, Turner, Constable, the Pre-Raphaelites, and Whistler. Contemporary artists on display included Jack Smith, Ben Nicholson, and Graham Sutherland.

Mullaly found three conducted parties of Soviet visitors in the eighteenth- and nineteenth-century galleries—Gainsborough appeared to be a particular favourite—but the greatest crowd was gathered in the small area devoted to modern abstracts, where Mullaly found himself drawn into intelligent and good-natured discussions through an interpreter. 'In particular I was asked searching questions as to how many people in England liked abstract painting and what proportion of artists painted abstracts.' Two stark paintings by Francis Bacon were drawing what Nora Beloff of the *Observer* called 'apologetic interest'. 'The majority of Russians who join the argument', she reported, 'jeer at the whole concept [of modernism], but there always seem to be enough impenitent intellectuals to take up the case for the defence, scoff at the lack of sensibility and artistic education of the critics, and avow that forty years hence they will know better.'

The paintings sent to Moscow by Sir Philip Hendy's selection committee excluded most of the 'kitchen sink' or 'socialist' painters exhibited at the Venice Biennale in 1956,[88] despite the inclusion of the realist artist Jack Smith, who had won first prize at the John Moores Exhibition in Liverpool (1956). The Soviet critic Valentin Brodskii asked why none of the eight progressive British artists who had set up a group called 'Looking at People'—*Gliadia na liudei*—in 1956, exhibiting in Moscow the following year, had been selected for the official British exhibition in 1960.[89] Brodskii's attack on Henry Moore was prefaced by a quotation from the Soviet art critics' favourite British critic, the *New Statesman*'s John Berger: 'A new academy arose: the academy of formalism...formalist art makes use of official patronage and takes over the teaching methods of all well known art schools in England.'[90] Brodskii commented that Moore's apologists, like a named Polish critic, extolled him on the ground that his sculpture was 'abstract and mysterious' (*tainstvenna*), while the aerodynamic, capricious (*kapriznye*) heads of Moore's figures awaken a sense of anxiety (*bespokoistvo*):

Indeed Moore does sense the general form and rhythm in large-scale, monumental mass. However, attentive consideration of his works reveals that they are a combination of abstractly treated masses (*abstraktno traktovannikh ob'emov*) with a deliberately surrealist, mindless combination of 'subconsciously' extracted lumps of real form and a snobbish, bogus imitation of the naivety of primitive sculpture of the neolithic era. From a distance it seems that Moore's statues portray human figures, but on closer inspection it becomes apparent that instead of a torso there is an 'aerodynamic' hole and instead of a head there is something similar to the section of an I-beam (*dvutavro-vaia balka*).

Noting that Lynn Chadwick's sculpture *Inner Eye* (1952) had won first prize at the 1956 Venice Biennale, Brodskii termed this sculpture a 'scandal-ous absurdity' (*vopiiushchaia nelepost'*).[91] His own absurdity arrived when he routinely inflated the talents of the old, conservative school of anti-modernists: 'Take the master painter, who has exercised a big influence on the younger generation, Alfred Munnings.' An illustration showed a detail from a typical Munnings 'jockeys and horses'.

Picasso and Communist Art in France

Pablo Picasso joined the French Communist Party (PCF) immediately after the Liberation of Paris, where he had been living throughout the war. Under the Nazi occupation he had continued to work but, classified as a 'degenerate' artist (like Matisse), was forbidden to exhibit. Periodically German officers would search his studio in the rue des Grands-Augustins. After the Liberation the invaders were admiring young Americans GIs.

On the front page of *L'Humanité* (5 October 1944) Picasso was styled 'the greatest of living painters' and shown, hat in hand, earnestly conferring with two elder statesmen of the Party, Marcel Cachin and Jacques Duclos. Describing itself as 'the Party of the French renaissance', the PCF welcomed Picasso into the 'Communist family'. The painter was equally effusive:

My adherence to the Communist Party is the logical outcome of my whole life... I have always been an exile, and now I am one no longer; until Spain can at last welcome me back, the French Communist Party has opened its arms to me. I have found there all those whom I esteem the most, the greatest scientists, the greatest poets and all those faces, so beautiful, of the Parisians in arms which I saw during those days in August. I am once more among my brothers.

By 'the greatest poets' he meant his friend Paul Eluard, the most important single influence on Picasso's decision to join, and Louis Aragon, the prince[1] of Communist intellectuals, poet, novelist, and reformed surrealist. As editor of *Les Lettres françaises*, Aragon set the tone for 'les lendemains qui chantent' (the tomorrows which sing), the Party's claim on a majority shareholding in the future. Warning those who 'wear the livery of the harlequin', Aragon sternly rebuked Roger Garaudy and other potential deviants: 'The Communist Party has an aesthetic and it is called realism.'[2] Was Pablo Picasso a 'realist'? The Russians certainly did not think so, and showed open hostility to his painting. The pressure to conform intensified with the breakdown of post-war good-will and the birth of the Cominform, successor to the defunct Comintern. Aragon greeted A. Zhdanov's notorious theses on literature, art, and music as 'far-sighted', 'plunging', and 'profound', likening them to a friendly hand held out to those hesitant spirits whose vacillations had hitherto prevented them from becoming true 'engineers of human souls' (to quote Stalin). Decadence, formalism, pessimism, and art for art's sake were constantly castigated in the French Communist press.[3] The Party's general secretary, Maurice Thorez, periodically denounced 'the formalism of the painters for whom art begins where the picture has no content'—but he did not breathe a word against Picasso, whose prestige counted for more than his contributions to Party funds. (During the August 1948 miners' strike, Picasso delivered 1 million francs to the offices of *L'Humanité*.)

As with Russian art, French socialist realist painting embraced national tradition, notably the historic-'epic' style of Jacques-Louis David and Eugène Delacroix and the 'realism' of Courbet.[4] The Party made every effort to introduce the work of its artists to working-class audiences in industrial suburbs and factories, and by subsidizing cheap bus excursions to the annual Salon d'Automne and Salon de Mai, which Party leaders invariably attended in force. Communist trade unions of the Confédération générale du travail (CGT) frequently commissioned the work of approved painters. Most heavily promoted was the work of André Fougeron, described by Aragon in his preface to *Dessins de Fougeron* (1947) as 'the carrier of the destiny of figurative art'. (Aragon was to change his mind about that, as about much else.)[5] Laurent Casanova (France's 'Zhdanov', but without the power to destroy lives) went so far as to equate current criticisms of André Fougeron, the Party's leading socialist realist painter, with a direct political attack on the Party.[6] In 1948 Fougeron exhibited *Parisiennes au marché*, depicting a group of expressionless women gazing at a fish on a stall while the fish glassily stared back; all but one figure seems drained of animate life and the picture shocked many observers and critics, including *Le Monde*'s. In the same frozen style, his *Hommage à André Houillier* commemorated the death of a young miner killed while pasting up posters based on Fougeron's design.[7] To be a good Communist was evidently to be permanently in mourning—the art of tears already achieved in Germany by Käthe Kollwitz. Party aesthetics worked by transference; it was as if the Resistance martyrs of the German occupation, the actual *fusillés*, were being killed all over again by the American 'occupiers'—though American troops had sacrificed their own lives to liberate France. French socialist realist painting focused on a limited number of tragic motifs, some permanent—a worker either dead, mutilated, or exhausted, lying prostrate while his wife wept on his breast, the children clinging to her skirts and his comrades standing in the rear in static, classical postures. Prominent among urgently topical themes were American atrocities in Korea, the brutality of the police (*les flics*) in suppressing street demonstrations, and the case of the sailor Henri Martin, jailed for his opposition to the Indo-China War—at the 1951 Salon d'Automne, Picasso exhibited a portrait of Martin.[8]

The year 1951 marked the high point of the new realism. At the Galerie Bernheim-Jeune, forty canvases and drawings by Fougeron went on display under the title *Le Pays des mines*, commissioned by the miners' federation of the Nord and the Pas-de-Calais. Wallowing in *misérabilisme*, one of Fougeron's intense, paint-dense, canvases presented a mining-accident victim laid out like Holbein's dead Christ; in another a group of industrially mutilated workers sit rigid with accusation, each locked in his or her individual anguish. Tazlitzky's *The Death of Danielle Casanova* depicted the death of a leading Communist in Auschwitz in what an English scholar calls 'conventional hagiographical terms based on Zurbaran and Géricault'.[9]

The subjects chosen by Party painters were becoming more contentious, more inflammatory: on the eve of President Vincent Auriol's visit to the 1951 Salon d'Automne, seven paintings by Communist artists were removed by the police at the request of the secretary of state for the fine arts, the minister of education, and the prefect of police. By no means all of these seized works could be accused of inviting violence,[10] but some were distinctly inflammatory: *Ripsote*, by Boris Taslitzky, showed strikers on the quays of Marseilles fighting off police-dogs; in *Le 14 février 1950 à Nice*, by Gérard Singer, a huge crate containing part of a V-2 rocket was being heaved over the dockside by angry workers. Ordavazt Berberian's *Manifestation* contained an extremely hostile portrayal of the Paris police, while *Les Dockers*, by Georges Bauquier, showed a docker addressing his comrades under the slogan 'No departures for Indo-China'.[11] Following protests, five of the offending seven paintings were returned to the Salon d'Automne, but three of these were again removed.[12]

The Stalinist cult of personality was echoed by numerous portraits of Maurice Thorez and other Party leaders. Fougeron painted the general secretary several times, not forgetting Thorez's good mother. The Lyons sculptor Georges Salendre produced a number of busts of Party leaders on display at the exhibition 'From Marx to Stalin', presented at the Maison des Métallurgistes in 1953; a canvas by Boris Taslitzky portrayed Thorez listening intently to a wise point made by Stalin. There were acute internal tensions; French Communists did not invariably admire the Soviet aesthetics they recommended. In 1952 Aragon published a series of articles praising such Soviet neo-classical enormities as Topuridze's *Victory* and the painting *Sitting of the Presidium of the Academy of Sciences of the USSR* by the 'Gritsai Brigade'. When Aragon's line ran into internal opposition, Casanova summoned a meeting of artists but, according to a hostile source, 'about two-thirds of France's 200 Communist painters and sculptors' stayed away, notably the two with the greatest international reputations, Picasso and Léger. *L'Humanité*'s report spoke discreetly of a fraternal discussion; the meeting finally substituted a condemnation of bacteriological warfare in Korea for any specific endorsement of Soviet art.[13]

Virtually every militant theme was tossed into the stew in Fougeron's *Civilisation atlantique* (1953), a montage which dominated the Salon d'Automne by its sheer size and which abandoned the conventions of perspective in its quest to draw attention to NATO headquarters in Paris, the Rosenbergs' electric chair (empty) on a pedestal at the top of the picture, the prison where Henri Martin was held, the coffins of soldiers killed in Indo-China, an American barracks in France, an American soldier reading a porn magazine, an SS officer in a huge Pontiac car (German rearmament), a fat capitalist ruling the roost—and more demonic iconography employing techniques used in surrealist paintings, collage, or photomontage. Aragon, who had eulogized Fougeron, now attacked him for producing a 'peinture hâtive, grossière, méprisante'—hasty, coarse, scornful.[14] Behind this attack were complex, even Byzantine, manoeuvres around the return of Maurice Thorez from his long convalescence in the USSR. Aragon knew that a feverish critical re-evaluation, involving even respectful references to Kafka, was imminent; impressionism would resurface in the pages of *La Nouvelle critique*; Van Gogh, Cézanne, and Renoir would once again be spoken of with affection; there was to be a less strident emphasis on the disarray of bourgeois painting and criticism.[15]

⊞ ⊞ ⊞

The Party never succeeded in extracting an endorsement of the official Soviet aesthetic from its three most illustrious painters, Pablo Picasso, Fernand Léger, or Edouard Pignon. Pignon's renderings of the miners of the north and of peasant life (as in *Les Paysans de Sanary*) remained highly personal in style, with the influence of Cézanne and of cubism in evidence, and not readily identifiable as Communist art. Although a good Stalinist, like his wife, the writer Hélène Parmelin, Pignon was a friend of Picasso's and known to oppose the official Gerasimov aesthetic and the attempts of Casanova and Aragon to impose it in France on middle-ranking Communist artists. (The great inhabited a stratosphere of immunity.) Pignon's *L'Ouvrier mort*, welcomed with reservations by *L'Humanité*, was warmly praised by the conservative *Figaro* (23 June 1952) and contrasted with the banal 'poster painting' of the socialist realist school.[16]

Profoundly influenced by his experiences in the trenches during World War I, the outstanding Norman painter Fernand Léger had brought workers and machines together in (often enormous) futurist-cubist canvases marked by bright, primary colours and by the epic quality of Mexican mural art. He believed passionately that the doors of education, galleries, and museums must be made accessible to workers; accordingly he regarded the Communists as the guardians of civilization, the only force in society determined to donate the great legacy of culture to the masses. Léger joined the Party during the Popular Front era. In 1953 he lectured on his epic painting *Les Constructeurs* at the Renault works under the auspices of the Communist CGT, but Léger, like Pignon, remained unmoved by the agitational and programmatic demands of socialist realism; although a delegate to the Wroclaw Peace Congress in 1948, his painting incurred, like Picasso, rigid Soviet resistance, despite the almost utopian harmony and happiness his compositions awarded to the day after tomorrow, when man and machine, picnickers and iron pincers, flesh and steel, would achieve what the painter called a religion of tangible human joys free of the dark, mystical religion of the past. John Berger mentioned the complaint that Léger's figures are as cold as robots, which he had heard both in the commercial galleries of Bond Street and in Moscow, where they wanted 'to judge Léger by the standards of Repin'.[17] However, in January 1963 the Pushkin Museum in Moscow finally opened an exhibition of 300 of his canvases which ran for three months.

⊞   ⊞   ⊞

Picasso's famous anti-fascist canvas *Guernica* had been commissioned for the Spanish pavilion at the 1937 Paris Exhibition, in rapid response to the bombing of the town of Guernica on 29 April by German planes of the Condor Legion. Regarded by the Russians as ultra-formalist and degrading despite its ardent dedication to the Spanish Republic, the painting had been acquired by New York's Museum of Modern Art. Its symbols echoed those the artist had been using for some years: the bull, representing darkness and violence; the horse, the epitome of innocence and goodness; the women witnesses, a chorus. The central motif is a head thrown back in agony, echoing the open mouths of Greek and Roman masks. At the onset of the cold war the Soviet art journal *Iskusstvo* attacked *Guernica* as 'monstrous' and 'pathological'; Picasso's work in general was 'morbid, repulsive', and designed 'to make an aesthetic apology for capitalism'. The painter's recent adherence to the French Communist Party went unmentioned.[18]

By contrast, the distinguished art historian (and Soviet spy) Sir Anthony Blunt pointed up derivations from Poussin, as well as Breughel and the German art of the Thirty Years War—the chaos of fear and straining limbs. Not least was Picasso's debt to Goya's depiction of massacre and rape in Spain under Napoleon. According to Blunt, Picasso's invention of cubism (with Georges Braque) changed the course of art throughout the world, not merely in painting but in the industrial arts as well. All new and worthwhile forms of painting during the past fifty years had been affected by cubism. This, of course, was far from the Soviet view; Blunt's clandestine loyalty to Moscow had nothing to do with the fine arts.[19]

Picasso's recent work was prominently displayed at the 1944 Salon d'Automne (styled Salon de la Liberté that year), with Party leaders in respectful attendance. Before the war Picasso had steered clear of official salons, but in future years he was also to become a regular exhibitor at the Salons de Mai, held in the Communist-sponsored Maison de la Pensée. Long lines formed outside the 1944 Salon d'Automne, for which Picasso had selected seventy-four of his paintings and five sculptures, predominantly from the war years. Once inside the spectators found themselves baffled or shocked by a style alien to their predominantly 'realist' and 'progressive' taste. While some of the canvases in the *Femme couchée* series were rhythmical portraits of the painter's former mistress Marie-Thérèse Walter, those from a later period depicted Walter's successor, the gifted photographer and painter Dora Maar, in tormented deformity—far from what was expected by admirers who had seen Picasso's work displayed in Daniel-Henry Kahnweiler's Paris gallery in the 1930s.[20] This looked like an assault on human physiognomy, and therefore on human dignity. Were not the horrors of a war still in progress enough without this gratuitous assault on human coherence? It is a numbing thought that even as Parisians formed queues to view these pictures, Jews were still forming queues at Auschwitz. There were angry altercations; photographs show young policemen called in to guard the Picassos. The Communist-dominated Comité national des écrivains blamed reactionaries, 'a vestige of the intimidation tactics experienced under the Nazi occupation'.

For a short time after the Liberation the Communists were members of a coalition government and given charge of the Department des Beaux Arts of the Ministry of Education. At the July 1945 exhibition staged in the Palais de Luxembourg, 'Art français contemporain', Picasso was presented as an exemplar of French art, but his 'monsters' and neo-cubist constructions brought cries of 'la France aux Français' from conservatives, who pointed out that Picasso was an outsider, not French, unlike Matisse, Braque, and Bonnard. His *pantins* (puppets) with both eyes on the same side of the face were assailed as oriental, barbaric, expressionistic, morbid, corrosive, Jewish, Spanish, even Slav, and alien to the French tradition of sublime harmony.[21]

In the Soviet Union, East Germany, and the Eastern bloc satellites Picasso was rarely mentioned, and then only in denigratory terms. On 11 August 1947 *Pravda* published a polemic, 'The Russian Painters and the School of Paris', by the leading socialist realist artist Aleksandr Gerasimov, who accused Picasso and Matisse of 'poisoning the pure air' of art. This was dutifully reproduced in *Les Lettres françaises*—though in painful contradiction of the PCF's own policy. The attack was continued in *VOKS Bulletin* and *Literaturnaia gazeta*, without mentioning Picasso's membership of the PCF.[22] Vladimir Kemenov's remarkably sophisticated onslaught was illustrated by two Picasso works, both titled *Portrait of a Woman*, from the years 1939–43:

Certain of Picasso's champions manage to find that his art is 'humane,' although every one of his pictures refutes this by tearing the body and face of man to pieces and by distorting him beyond recognition ... It is frequently said that in his pathological work Picasso has deliberately created an ugly and repellent image of contemporary capitalist reality in order to rouse the spectator's hatred for it—that Picasso is the artist of 'Spanish democracy.' This, obviously, is not true. Although Picasso's early works of his 'blue' period still retain some connections with Spanish painting, when he turned to cubism his art became absolutely abstract ... and followed the line of cosmopolitanism, of empty, ugly, geometric forms ... [Even in his *Guernica*] he showed us the same wretched, pathological and deformed types as in his other ... morbid, revolting pictures. His is an aesthetic apologetics for capitalism; he is convinced of the artistic value of the nightmares called into being by the disintegration of the social psyche of the capitalist class....

As for his pictures 'upsetting' the bourgeoisie, it is just the bourgeoisie who represent his principal admirers and supporters. American magazines are always prompt to report how many thousands of dollars Picasso's latest picture has been sold for.

But Kemenov was on fragile ground when he invented a social category previously unknown to Marxism, 'plain people', and claimed that:

It was just these plain people who were most incensed by Picasso's London [1945] exhibition. Even the magazine *Studio* wrote that the pictures in this exhibition were severely judged and were defined as degrading, demoralizing, decadent and degenerate. The [London] *Times* received more letters about this exhibition than it received when the atom bomb was invented, and the overwhelming majority of the letters expressed indignation.[23]

The Direction Générale des Relations Culturelles, working through the British Council, had sponsored a small Picasso–Matisse exhibition at the Victoria & Albert Museum in December 1945.[24] Even the director of the V&A, Leigh Ashton, had groaned when he unpacked the consignment and found 'three or four paintings by Picasso which I should normally have some hesitation in exhibiting'... However, 'the loan of the space was given with the express idea of propaganda' and any interference would offend the French.'[25] It is not clear how Kemenov knew how many letters *The Times* had received—and what sort of 'plain people' were in the habit of writing to it. In fact, two of the most prominent anti-Picasso letters (2 and 7 January 1946) were written from exclusive London clubs, the Athenaeum and Brooks, while others rumbled from the backwoods of the shires; most of them parodied the genre, the elaborate syntax of upper-crust, literate sarcasm.[26] At a Royal Academy dinner attended by Churchill and Field-Marshal Montgomery, the president of the Academy, Sir Alfred Munnings, gave a speech inveighing against modernism—Picasso and Matisse in particular, both incapable of drawing a tree that looked like a tree. During a walk Churchill had asked Munnings whether, if they happened to run into Picasso, he would join him in kicking the painter's backside. Picasso, when shown a newspaper cutting about this by Ilya Ehrenburg, laughed: 'A good thing I'm not in London. After all, there were two of them. And what if the Field-Marshal had joined in?'[27] Kemenov, editor of *VOKS Bulletin* was clearly not coming clean about the swinish company he was keeping!

The paradox of the PCF ardently championing the non-realist art of Comrade Picasso despite anathemas from Moscow caused Jean-Paul Sartre to comment sardonically on 'the nausea of the Communist boa constrictor, unable to keep down or vomit up the enormous Picasso'. Art was a permanent revolution, Sartre continued, but the social revolution demanded a conservative aesthetic while the aesthetic revolution tended towards social conservatism (under which he included 'art for art's sake'). Condemned by the Soviets, the avant-garde was purchased by rich Americans. André Malraux offered a comparable comment: 'It is not by chance that the Russian communists attack Picasso. His painting challenges the very system upon which they base everything: willy-nilly this painting represents the most acute presence of Europe.'[28] The right-wing press rejoiced over the Soviet attacks on Picasso: *Le Figaro* was pleased to report that *Pravda* had condemned Western art as *une pourriture*—'putrefaction'.

To please the comrades, in August 1948 Picasso took to the air for the first time and attended the World Congress of Leaders of Culture for the Defence of Peace, which opened in Wroclaw, Poland. Here he was exposed at close quarters to the full fury and scorn of the Soviet cultural offensive. Fadeyev, first secretary of the Soviet Writers' Union, delivered the harsh keynote address in words soon to be rendered notorious in the Western media: 'If jackals could learn to use the typewriter and hyenas could master the fountain pen, they no doubt would write just like Henry Miller, [T. S.] Eliot, [André] Malraux, and other Sartreans... Spiritual lechery is inspired by the "existentialist philosophy" of the type of Sartre which attempts to put man on all fours...' According to Ilya Ehrenburg, who had first met Picasso in Montparnasse in 1914, the great artist was taken aside and asked by Fadeyev why he chose to paint in forms which 'plain people' did not understand. Picasso in turn enquired whether Fadeyev had ever been taught to understand painting (Picasso was particularly contemptuous when Soviet critics conflated the different modernist schools, calling him an 'impressionist' or a 'surrealist'). But Picasso did not turn for home; he went on from Wroclaw to visit the Warsaw ghetto, Auschwitz, and Birkenau. This was his first venture in an airplane, at the age of 67.[29] Picasso's wife of the time, Françoise Gilot, gives another version of Wroclaw, as Picasso told it to her:

At the end of the dinner, when toasts were being proposed, one of the Russian delegation stood up and said he was pleased to see I had come to the Congress but he went right on to say that it was unfortunate that I continued to paint in such a decadent manner representative of the worst in the bourgeois culture of the West. He referred to my 'impressionist-surrealist style.' As soon as he sat down I stood up and told him that I didn't care to be talked to like that by some party hack and... if he wanted to insult me, at least he should get his terminology straight and damn me for being the inventor of Cubism. I told him that I had been reviled in Germany by the Nazis and in France during the German occupation as a Judaeo-Marxist painter... Then everybody began to get excited... The Poles tried to calm down the Russians by agreeing that perhaps *some* of my painting was decadent, but in any case, they said, the Russians couldn't be allowed to insult their guests.[30]

The US Embassy in Moscow reported an Ehrenburg lecture on his return from Wroclaw, one thousand seats filled and more outside begging for tickets. Someone in the audience asked Ehrenburg to describe Picasso's work. He replied: 'The best thing of course would be to show them to you'—and hastily turning to his notes he added half in an aside—'but that does not depend on me.'[31] Clearly Picasso did not forget what he had suffered at Wroclaw. As reported by Françoise Gilot, when asked (no date given) to sign a letter protesting the current right-wing pressures in America, by Congressman Dondero[32] in particular, on innovative art, Picasso refused on the ground that art is subversive and should not be free or accepted by the state:

Only the Russians are naïve enough to think that an artist can fit into society. That's because they don't know what an artist is...Even Mayakovsky committed suicide. There is absolute opposition between the creator and the state...People reach the status of artist only after crossing the maximum number of barriers. So the arts should be *dis*couraged not *en*couraged.[33]

Picasso talked a lot, and he talked his fair share of nonsense. Much depended on who he was talking to, where, and when. In an interview with Simone Téry for *Les Lettres françaises* (24 March 1945), he described the artist as: 'a political being, constantly alive to heart-rending, fiery, or happy events, to which he responds in every way...No, painting is not done to decorate apartments. It is an instrument of war for attack and defence against the enemy.' However, interviewed only two weeks earlier by Jerome Seckler in *New Masses* (13 March 1945), he had said pretty much the opposite: 'If I paint a hammer and sickle people may think it's a representation of Communism, but for me it's only a hammer and sickle. I just want to reproduce the objects for what they are and not for what they mean...I make a painting for the painting...It's in my subconscious...There is no deliberate sense of propaganda in my painting.' He then granted that *Guernica* was an exception: 'In that there is a deliberate appeal to people, a deliberate sense of propaganda'.

Many American Communists and progressives voiced objections to Picasso's art, resulting in a lively argument in *New Masses* running from April to June 1945. The artist Rockwell Kent, an ardent fellow-traveller, attacked 'such silly, ivory-tower self-expressionism as Picasso boasts'.[34] Picasso, unlike Kent, took care never to set foot in the Soviet Union. Ilya Ehrenburg, who lived there, loved to get away, and palpably enjoyed the 'radical chic' elegance of left-wing intellectual life in the 'old Europe' of France and Italy, dining with poets, painters, and theatre producers. During a sojourn in Italy with Picasso, Ehrenburg was entertained every night by Renato Guttuso: 'We dined in different good, very expensive restaurants.' Guttuso always paid the bill, but Ehrenburg noticed that they were invariably joined by a man whose profession Guttuso never mentioned. It turned out that he was footing the bills for the honour of sitting at the same table as Picasso. 'One night we were dining at a restaurant in what used to be the ghetto; we were eating *artichauts à la juive*...There was a beautiful girl from Calabria at another table. "I want to draw her," Picasso said suddenly.' Was this Ehrenburg's version of the classless society?[35] Ehrenburg spoke on occasion of the PCF as 'the party of Picasso', while claiming that Communists were the 'legitimate heirs of human civilization'.[36]

The talent of Renato Guttuso justifies a brief ultramontane excursion from France to Italy, where the Communist Party and Communist art flourished under the benign leadership of Palmiro Togliatti. Born in 1912 in Palermo, Guttuso had joined the Resistance in 1943, producing his savagely anti-fascist cycle of work, *Gott mit uns* (God with us), then entered his most politically committed phase of painting in the 1950s—for example his *Boogie-Woogie* (1952), showing the younger generation dancing in a mindless frenzy in a cellar. Praised in *Time* (30 November 1953) for refusing to fit his artistic conscience 'into the tight jacket of Red discipline', his case was taken up in 1955, from the opposite point on the political spectrum, by John Berger, art critic of the *New Statesman*. According to Berger, Guttuso's work proved that 'it is neither necessary for a West European artist to cut off his right hand and paint as though he were an old academician in Moscow, nor to cut off his left to feel at home in the Museum of Modern Art, New York'. But Moscow did not smile on the expressionist and non-utopian qualities in Guttuso's work until the general re-evaluation of the Khrushchev era, when a German translation of an essay by Berger was published in Dresden, signalling the painter's acceptability in the GDR. Guttuso's art straddled the Iron Curtain; his first one-man show in New York took place in 1958, nine years before the Pushkin Museum and the Hermitage accorded him the same honour.[37]

Despite the many good tables and good comrades, the cold war also brought Picasso painful fractures. The writer André Breton, *doyen* of surrealism, admirer of Trotsky, and fierce critic of Stalinism, returned from America where he had spent the war in June 1946. Spotting him in the street in Golfe-Juan, Picasso stretched out his hand but Breton declined the greeting on account of Picasso's joining the PCF and his Party-line stand on the post-war purges of French intellectuals accused of collaboration. On the street Picasso told Breton that he placed friendship above differences of political opinion. Breton replied that it was a pity that Picasso had allowed himself to be so influenced by Eluard. Breton then walked away and they did not meet again.[38] Picasso's work, wrote Breton shortly thereafter, was the passionate negation of socialist realism: 'In 1937 or 1938 Picasso told me that what disposed him favourably towards Stalinist leaders was that they reminded him of the Spanish Jesuits, whom he held in high esteem when he was young.'[39] Breton's 'Of "Socialist Realism" as a Means of Mental Extermination' included a sarcastic attack on Aragon's long articles in defence of Soviet painting and sculpture, including the Gritsai Brigade's *Sitting of the Presidium of the Academy of Sciences*, published in *Les Lettres françaises* in January and April 1952. Breton assailed it as cemetery art, trite and pompous;

and if some freedom was allowed as to technique, 'who will doubt that this modicum of freedom on the formal level is granted exclusively to those who apply themselves to spreading hatred—in this case of America?' Here Breton referred to Prorokov's illustrations for Mayakovsky's *Of America*, showing the Statue of Liberty deformed by eyes made up of policemen's ugly mugs.[40]

Breton's attack was prolonged and devastating: from the list of twenty 'subjects' prescribed to painters by the minister of culture of Hungary, he invited his readers to take note of the following:

> *The heroes of labor sit in their box at the theater;*
> *The first tractor arrives in the village;*
> *A policewoman helps a child cross the street;*
> *A view of the courtroom during the Rajk trial;*
> *The preparations for Stalin's birthday;*
> *The police arrest a foreign agent at the border.*

Breton derided the issues of *Les Lettres françaises*[41] which had reprinted an article from *Sovetskoe Isskustvo* praising such paintings as:

> *Dimitrov Accuses;*
> *The Stakhanovites are Keeping watch;*
> *The Innovators of the Kolkhozian Fields;*
> *V. I. Lenin and J. V. Stalin in Razliv;*
> *J. V. Stalin at V. I. Lenin's Tomb;*
> *Children Offering J. V. Stalin Their Best Wishes On His Seventieth Birthday.*

Breton had news of an entertaining peroration—almost too good to be true—by Zamuchekin, director of the Tretyakov Gallery, while opening the Budapest Salon on 24 May 1949:

> *Cézanne must be proscribed,*
> *Matisse does not know how to draw,*
> *Picasso will make your brains rot,*
> *Any artist who does not follow the example of Soviet art is an enemy of socalism.*

'All this bespeaks madness, all this exudes terror', wrote Breton. To flirt with this wolf, Picasso and Matisse 'need to be naïve to a degree that is unbelievable to me'.[42] Picasso's encounter with Breton may have excited the painter's suspicions about another former friend who had been living in the United States, the Russian émigré artist Marc Chagall, briefly a commissar of fine arts in Vitebsk in 1918. Picasso admired his mastery of light and colour but—Françoise Gilot recalled—when Chagall arrived back from America and came to lunch with Picasso, the latter started in on him sarcastically about not going to see what his own country was like after all these years. Chagall smiled broadly: 'My dear Pablo, after you ... According to all I hear, you are greatly beloved in Russia, but not your painting. But once you get there and try it awhile, perhaps I could follow along after.' At this Picasso got nasty: 'With you I suppose it's a question of business. There's no money to be made there.' Such was the insult that they never met again.[43]

⌗ ⌗ ⌗

Picasso's dove of peace, *la colombe de la paix*—in fact drawn from one of the Milanese pigeons given him by Matisse—adorned the banners of the Moscow-inspired Peace Movement after Louis Aragon had picked it out from a pile of Picasso lithographs. The delicate transparency of several shades of grey represented a technical feat, achieved by mixing lithographic ink with water and fuel. The dove made its first bid for peace in *Les Lettres françaises* and on the front page of the New York *Daily Worker*. The novelist François Mauriac commented in *Le Figaro Magazine*: 'Oh! Colombe de Paix, what a nice little beak you have.'[44] The Paris-based Paix et liberté organization launched posters showing a Stalin-figure skulking behind a street corner, his left hand holding a leash attached to a visible dove designed to lure innocents, his concealed hand gripping a spiked iron ball. The Picasso dove stretched its wings and flew as far afield as China; the UN delegates to the Korean peace negotiations at Panmunjon would refuse to enter the armistice building until the peace dove installed over the entrance by the North Koreans was taken down. 'I have seen them in Chinese villages, in India and Argentina ... helpless as a child and unconquerable as the conscience of peoples', wrote Ehrenburg, recalling walking with Picasso after a peace rally held in a working-class district of Rome. 'People crowded round him, embracing him, asking him to hold their babies, shaking his hand.'[45] Paul Eluard produced lines to accompany a series of Picasso drawings in which a woman's face merged with the dove:

> I know all the places where the dove lodges
> And the most natural is man's head.[46]

Picasso's *Massacre en Corée* (*Massacre in Korea*), oil on plywood, and indebted to Goya, showing a squad of robotic yet virtually medieval soldiers receiving the order to fire on naked women and children, was clearly directed against the American imperialists, and was duly exhibited at the annual Salon de Mai. According to Hélène Parmelin, Party activists objected to the mood of resignation instead of resistance in *Massacre en Corée*, which certainly evoked scenes from the Holocaust.[47] In April 1952 Picasso signed a declaration by French Communist artists denouncing bacteriological warfare in Korea. In a series of drawings executed in April–May, sketches for the murals entitled *La Guerre et la Paix*, he depicted a bird of prey sowing poisoned grains. Reaction in the *New York Times* and *Time* were hostile when the drawings went on display in Rome and Milan. The *New Yorker*'s Paris correspondent, Janet Flanner, otherwise Genêt, called Picasso 'the most illustrious propaganda feather in the cap of any Communist Party in Europe'. The Party, she added, used him like an 'exotic golden pheasant, displayed him on its scarlet-hung platforms at its workmen's meetings at the Vélodrome d'Hiver'.[48]

Flanner's irritation with Picasso reflected a growing hostility to the painter in the United States. It was mutual—his anti-Americanism probably dated back to the Spanish–American war of 1898, when he was 17. Fifty years later, in May 1948, Picasso sent a cable to a Madison Square Garden rally in support of Spanish Republicans: 'Fight today or you will have an American Guardia Civil tomorrow.' 'Picasso Urges US Fight Fascism, Greets Rally for Spanish Republicans at Garden May 17', announced the New York *Daily Worker* (5 May 1948)—this was duly clipped into the FBI's Picasso file. According to Gertje R. Utley's excellent study, *Picasso: The Communist Years*, the FBI's file had been opened in December 1944 (Subject Pablo Picasso: security matter C; file: 100–337396). The US Office of Cable and Radio Censorship reported to the FBI cables sent to and from Picasso. The painter supported the Hollywood Ten and a decade later, in 1957, was still signing petitions requesting the release of American Communists imprisoned under the Smith Act. As honorary president of the Joint Anti-Fascist Refugee Committee (listed as subversive by the US attorney-general), Picasso was fined $1.5 million *in absentia* by the State of New York for the Committee's alleged misuse of funds.

In 1950 he did apply for an American visa. From Paris Ambassador David Bruce cabled Secretary of State Dean Acheson that 'the disadvantages of refusing visas to Picasso and [Professor Eugène] Aubel outweigh advantage in so far as France is concerned'. 'France' presumably meant the French government, but the visas were refused: 'Picasso Barred from US with Red "Peace" Unit', announced the *New York Herald Tribune* (4 March 1950). Henry Luce, proprietor of *Life* and *Time*, contributed his own mockery in 'Captain Pablo's Voyages'.[49] Picasso was among numerous artists who produced portraits of Julius and Ethel Rosenberg, condemned to death in 1951 and executed under President Eisenhower: his ink-on-paper sketches appeared in *L'Humanité Dimanche* to commemorate the anniversary of their execution.

⊞ ⊞ ⊞

On 12 March 1953 Louis Aragon, the director of *Les Lettres françaises*, brought a storm of wrath down on his own head when he published a Picasso sketch to mark Stalin's death—a mere doodle depicting Stalin as a youthful dreamer, an almost naive figure; nothing so uncanonical had been done since the extraordinary *Portret I. V. Stalina* by Georgy Rublyov (1935), where a youthful Stalin is found wearing a brilliant white suit, lounging in a white wicker chair, his Georgian calculations undeflected by the copy of *Pravda* in his hand, a red dog at his feet (a mere smear of Rublyov's insolent brush against a blazing all-red background).

As Françoise Gilot tells the story, she was with Picasso in Villauris when a telegram arrived asking for the Stalin portrait. Pierre Daix, editor of *Les Lettres françaises*, later recalled sending the telegram to Picasso on Aragon's instructions: 'We are doing a number of LLF in homage to Stalin stop it's not possible to do it without you stop send what you wish text or drawing before Tuesday stop affectionately Aragon.' Gilot says she then telephoned Aragon, at whose insistence she interrupted Picasso in his studio. ' "How do you expect me to do a portrait of Stalin?" he said irritably. "In the first place I've never seen him and I don't remember at all how he looks, except that he wears a uniform with big buttons down the front, has a military cap, and a large moustache." ' Gilot found an old newspaper photograph. When Picasso had finished, 'it looked like my father' (whom Picasso had also never seen). 'We laughed until Picasso began to hiccough.'[50] But not for long.

It was a botched job from any perspective; on this occasion Picasso's talent for conjuring a remarkable likeness with a few strokes of the crayon deserted him; the wide, reflective, innocent eyes entirely missed the foxlike gleam in Stalin's slits, nor did the oval face and soft jawline belong to the Generalissimo. On either side of the portrait Aragon ('Staline et la France'), and the physicist Joliot-Curie ('Staline, le marxisme et la science') poured forth ritual tributes; page 2 carried a picture of Tomsky's bust of Stalin (1950), as if in stern correction of Picasso's whimsical effort. Pierre Daix, who was later to jump ship, contributed a vast eulogy to the dead dictator entitled *Il nous a appris à grandir*—He has taught us to grow (perhaps 'grow up', perhaps 'grow tall').

The editorial offices of *Les Lettres françaises* were flooded with calls and insults. The following issue (19–26 March) announced the Secretariat's profound regret that Comrade Aragon, a member of the Central Committee, had permitted publication of the portrait. The key word was *désapprobation*; Aragon was expected to publish the *passages essentiels* of letters received from readers. In the issue of 26 March–1 April Aragon did just that, affirming his 'accord sans réserve' with the Party's position. A key phrase from each of the eighteen letters was captioned in bold.[51] The extracts published sizzled with 'indignation', 'disapproval', 'profound sadness', 'stupefaction'. They did not 'recognize' Stalin in Picasso's drawing: where was his 'goodness, love of mankind, luminous intelligence, genius'—not to mention his honesty, kindness, strength, radiance, humanity, and fatherliness? Returning to the subject in the edition of 2–9 April, Aragon rejected the complaint that all this would play into the hands of the class enemy, 'those who claim to give us lessons from the depths of decadence and national treason'.

The bourgeois press at home and abroad monitored this blood-letting with evident enjoyment. 'Vacant-Stare Portrait of Stalin by Picasso Stirs French Reds', declared the *Herald Tribune*. 'Picasso Rebuked by Reds', reported the *New York Times*. 'Reds Score Editor on Picasso's Work'—a reference to Aragon. The socialist *Populaire* ran a sardonic piece, 'Lèse-Majesté', asking whether Aragon was now to be relieved of editorial control of *Les Lettres françaises* as previously of *Ce Soir*. *Le Monde* quoted the London *Daily Mail*, 'Portrait of a Woman with a Moustache', which found Stalin's smile in the portrait resonant of the Mona Lisa's.[52] On the same day *Le Monde* published a telephone interview with the painter. 'I did what I felt because I never saw Stalin myself. *J'ai forcé sur la resemblance*. It doesn't seem to have gone down well—*cela n'a pas l'air d'avoir plu*. Too bad!—*tant pis!*'[53]

Lucie Fougeron, daughter of the Party's leading socialist realist painter, has studied twenty-four of the angry letters, mainly handwritten, which remain in the Party archives. In her view, largely dependent on the recall of Pierre Daix, the letters of protest were selected and edited by top Party brass, François Billoux and Victor Joannès, with Daix merely servicing their selections: 'I functioned strictly as a technician.' Lucie Fougeron has discovered that a few of the letters in the archive expressed satisfaction; these were not published; she also doubts whether the archives are representative of what came in. In her analysis, the real target of the hard-line, *ouvriérist* operation by Auguste Lecoeur, acting head of the PCF during Thorez's convalescence in the USSR, was not Picasso but Aragon. Indeed, sneering letters carrying references to Picasso as a grand, avant-garde artist who disdained the working class, and so on, were deliberately not published. Nor (a rather sensational discovery by Lucie Fougeron) was a letter from Fernand Léger to Aragon, written the day after the portrait appeared and before the Secretariat's statement, in which Léger disdained to mention Picasso by name; it angrily suggested that the anti-Communist Paix et liberté could plaster walls with 'the drawing'. Daix has recalled a separate violent telegram from Léger referring to the portrait as 'La Picasse'.[54]

Selected for prominent publication in *Les Lettres françaises* (26 March) was a long letter of complaint from the most orthodox of Party artists, André

Fougeron: 'With other painter comrades, I know the difficulties we have in positioning ourselves on the firm Party line for literature and art as defined by our secretary-general Maurice Thorez.' How could Communist artists be expected to make 'the necessary effort' if drawings like Picasso's were permitted publication? Fougeron accused Picasso of 'the sterile tricks (*jeux*) of aesthetic formalism', and refused in advance to accept the Stalin sketch for the forthcoming Karl Marx exhibition to be held in Paris in May. But someone had got to work on Fougeron's letter as well; edited out of it were servile references to the reigning PCF bosses, Lecoeur, Billoux, and Joannès, for their recent guidance about 'certain of our weaknesses on the ideological front.' Oddly—and this carries us even deeper into the byzantine recesses of the *coulisses*—eleven years later Aragon claimed that it was he who had suppressed Fougeron's servile passages 'with a view to protecting his future'. Lucie Fougeron speculates that Aragon knew of Thorez's imminent return from Russia, bringing with him a new sympathy for intellectuals.[55] But if it was Aragon himself who cut passages from André Fougeron's diatribe, does it not undermine Pierre Daix's insistence that the letters were selected and edited by the Party functionaries Billoux and Joannès alone? And why did Aragon, if so solicitous on Fougeron's behalf, go on to savage his painting *Civilisation atlantique* as 'hasty, coarse, scornful'?

For his part, Picasso was stung by the attacks from fellow-Communists: 'Can you imagine if I had done the real Stalin, such as he has become, with his wrinkles, his pockets under the eyes, his warts . . . A portrait in the style of Cranach! Can you hear them scream?' Among friends he embarked on salacious ruminations about a nude Stalin, Stalin's phallus, big or small, erect or not, and so on.[56]

Thorez did send an angry telegram from Moscow, demanding an end to a campaign which could only damage the Party's relations with intellectuals. Later in the year, following the general secretary's return, the Party's Political Bureau went into abrupt retreat, regretting its 'error'; the Secretariat's manner of criticism had been 'inopportune'; on behalf of the Party, François Billoux wished to dispel any impression that it proceeded on the basis of commands, rather than free conviction. [57]

⊞   ⊞   ⊞

In May 1954 the Leningrad Hermitage signalled the passing of Stalin—and the coming of the Comédie française—by opening an exhibition of French paintings, including three by Van Gogh and works by Matisse, Gauguin, Cézanne, Matisse, and Picasso. The Russians agreed to lend works by Picasso in their possession for an exhibition at the Maison de la Pensée in Paris. Then valued at $500,000, the pictures had been the property of the wealthy Russian collector Sergei Shchukin until confiscated by a Bolshevik decree signed by Lenin in 1918.[58] The collection became a huge black hole in the history of modern art after it was locked out of sight under Stalin.[59] The Russians were schizophrenic about 'forbidden culture'. The banned works had been kept in good condition; there were no bonfires; teams of specialist curators and Soviet art historians had compiled unpublished *catalogues raisonées* on the forbidden fruit. Now, following Stalin's death, the Russians duly obliged Picasso and the PCF with thirty-seven paintings, twenty-eight of them never previously exhibited outside Russia, including the wonderful *Femme avec un eventail* (*Woman with a Fan*) and *Trois femmes*. Thorez and other PCF leaders ceremonially visited the exhibit at the Musée de la Pensée. Fourgeron and Taslitsky were also conscripted, along with the more sympathetic artists Léger and Pignon.[60] However, soon after the exhibition, 'Oeuvres des Musées de Leningrad et de Moscou 1900–1914', opened on 9 June it ran into unexpected trouble: Shchukin's daughter, Madame Irina Stchoukine de Keller, a French citizen, was now laying claim to the paintings, forcing the exhibition to close abruptly on 6 July, although it had been scheduled to run until the end of September. Faced with a court order that the paintings remain in place pending a full hearing, the Embassy sent a fleet of cars to remove them from the Maison de la Pensée, the PCF's anachronistically sumptuous villa on the rue St-Honoré, near the Elysée, and carted the paintings back to the Embassy. 'Russia Grabs its Picassos and Closes Paris Exhibition', announced the *Herald Tribune* (7 July 1954). The American paper saw this as the year's second major cultural setback in Paris for the Russians, following the disastrous visit of the Moscow ballet corps.[61]

Addressing the Tribunal de la Seine, Picasso's long-standing art dealer, now approaching 80, Daniel-Henry Kahnweiler (Kahn-Weiler in *Le Monde*), described as a 'gallery director', told how before 1914 he had sold 'nine-tenths' of the thirty-seven Picassos on display to Russian collectors, including Serge Stchoukine (Shchukin). It was absurd for Madame Stchoukine de Keller to claim all thirty-seven now on display since many of them had never belonged to her father. Ivan Morozov had bought '*un bon lot*' from him.[62] Refusing to sequester the pictures on Madame Keller's behalf, Judge Jean Drouillat ruled that international law banned suits against a sovereign state in the courts of another.[63] In October 1956 an exhibition devoted to Picasso's work alone at long last opened, to mark his seventy-fifth birthday, in the Pushkin Museum (later moving from Moscow to Leningrad's Hermitage). Picasso sent some forty paintings from the period 1917–56. On 25 October a reception was held at the House of Architecture to honour his seventy-fifth birthday, the day before the exhibition opened. When Ehrenburg entered the reception he received an ovation. For two weeks a gigantic queue stretched outside the Pushkin; the militia was compelled to admit visitors in small groups. 'Like most Muscovites,' Yevgeni Yevtushenko recalled, 'I had failed to get into the Picasso exhibition when it came to Moscow—it was harder to get a ticket than to win a car in a lottery.'[64] Organized discussions about Picasso and modern art were held at the University of Moscow, the Stroganov Art School, and the Institutes of Architecture and Cinematography. In the Moscow House of Architecture Vladimir Slepian managed to get in to a packed hall. 'For me and for many young Soviet artists, the Picasso exhibition . . . was the most important single event of our artistic lives', Slepian recalled after his defection: 'Before an enormous portrait of Picasso were placed a table for the chairman and a row of a dozen or more chairs on each side. The first person to appear on stage, possibly as a result of someone's diabolical planning, was none other than Aleksandr Gerasimov . . . As he took a handkerchief out of his pocket to wipe the sweat pouring down his forehead, the laughter in the hall rose to a universal roar.' No one chose to sit anywhere near him. Ehrenburg's friend, the Turkish poet Nazim Hikmet, visited the exhibition and wrote in the guest book: '[Picasso], like a genuine Communist and poet, is not a sectarian, not a fanatic.'[65] The Moscow triumph was repeated in Leningrad, but little mention was made of it in the Soviet press. The militia had to control the crush of people struggling for entry. 'Every day at the exhibition I met outstanding writers, musicians, scientists, actors, and painters. But the most numerous spectators were young people.' . . .[66]

According to Ehrenburg's biographer (who gives no evidence), 'Picasso himself was supposed to attend, but the turmoil in Hungary made it impossible for him to come to Moscow'. But this is unlikely; had Picasso planned to travel to Moscow, his arrangements would have involved leaving France several days before the 24 October reception—Russian tanks in fact first entered Budapest shortly after 2 a.m. on that day. According to Utley he sent a handwritten note, drafted by Parmelin, dated 17 October: 'I regret not to be with you at this time, and hope one day to undertake that beautiful fraternal voyage which at present I must empower my pictures to make for me.'[67] There was indeed already 'turmoil in Hungary' when he wrote the note, but there was no hint of a Soviet invasion.

A full month passed after the Picasso exhibition opened in Moscow before the artist himself offered a muted, essentially private protest against Soviet armed intervention in Hungary. A group of former students of the University of Budapest wrote to him on 14 November: 'Do for Budapest what you did for Guernica and Korea. Support us . . . Put your reserve behind you.'[68] In

Warsaw a reproduction of *Massacre en Corée* appeared in a street, pinned to a blackboard, while the émigré Polish writer Czeslaw Milosz castigated Picasso in an open letter: 'During the years when painting was systematically destroyed in the USSR and the people's democracies, you lent your name to statements glorifying Stalin's regime . . . Your weight counted in the balance, and took away hope from those in the East who wanted not to submit to the absurd.'[69] But Picasso had no intention of drawing such parallels. While friends such as Vercors, Claude Roy, Michel Leiris, and Jacques Prévert denounced Soviet aggression, and while the Peace Movement lost stars like Gérard Philippe, Yves Montand, and Simone Signoret, Picasso clung to the loyalty which he evidently regarded as the supreme value. *L'Humanité* (16 November) could proudly claim that the greatest scientist, painter, and poet, Joliot-Curie, Picasso, and Aragon, 'remain firm in their positions'. Finally, a rather tame internal plea signed by Picasso and nine other Party members was leaked to *Le Monde*, probably by the busily conspiring Hélène Parmelin. Calling for an extraordinary congress of the PCF to discuss events in Hungary, they complained that 'the veil of silence, the disconcerting ambiguities, the blows to revolutionary probity' had proved profoundly disconcerting, playing into the hands of the Party's opponents.[70] The Central Committee duly accused the signatories of 'proud individualism' and lack of *esprit de classe*.

In Picasso's case all this was rapidly forgotten, not least by the painter, and soon afterwards Party dignitaries were photographed at the ceremony granting him honorary citizenship of Antibes. The anti-Communist *Paris-Presse l'Intransigeant* commented sarcastically: 'Thorez and Cachin were not there to ask the painter of "Guernica" to paint a canvas entitled "Budapest".'[71] In 1959 Andrei Sinyavsky and Igor Golomshtok approached Ehrenburg to ask for help in preparing a small book on Picasso—none had yet appeared in the USSR. Ehrenburg agreed to write a preface in which he recalled the sharp exchange at Wroclaw in 1948 between Fadeyev and Picasso. But on the eve of publication the entire edition of 100,000 copies issued by Znanie publishing house was halted by the Central Committee. Ehrenburg appealed to Mikhail Suslov, the Politburo's perennial ideologist, in a letter dated 4 June 1961 in which he stressed the political impact in France and Italy: 'This year the French Communist Party and progressive individuals . . . will commemorate Picasso's eightieth birthday. It would be very unpleasant if news of the destruction of a large portion of books printed here were to seep out to the West.' . . .[72] The book, a modest effort of fifty pages of text and two-dozen black-and-white reproductions, was published. In October 1966 Ehrenburg had to intervene with Ekaterina Furtseva when she, as minister of culture, objected to a display of graphics to honour Picasso's eighty-fifth birthday. Ehrenburg had brought 142 engravings from Paris. Once again his intervention was successful.[73]

The change in the Soviet line on Picasso was also reflected in the *Great Soviet Encylopedia*. The 1955 edition dismissed cubism in a single line as a 'formalistic tendency', whereas the 1974 edition is much more admiring of *Demoiselles d'Avignon*, arguing that Picasso's 'one-sided interpretation of Cézanne's system, and his fascination with African sculpture' led to his cubist phase. For the first time Soviet criticism discussed cubism almost objectively; the 1974 edition describes 'The panel *Guernica* [as] . . . the artist's greatest achievement of the period'.[74]

The Other Russia:
Pictures by 'Jackasses'

The dream scenario for the Western media played itself out on 1 December 1962, when Khrushchev and his retinue paid a sudden call on an art exhibition at the Manezh Gallery, close to the Kremlin. Khrushchev did everything but pull the offending canvases from the walls; he fumed, raged, and fulminated against the West. This was, perhaps, cold war culture's finest hour.

It was an outburst which, with the benefit of hindsight, had been about to occur since the Sixth World Youth festival in 1957. The festival (entry was free) brought extraordinary cultural excitement (anarchy) to Moscow.[1] Three two-storey pavilions in Sokol'niki Park of Culture housed a huge exhibition of over 4,500 works by young artists from fifty-two countries. 'For the first time in three decades', Golomshtok recalled, 'Russian artists saw the living art of the twentieth century.' Because of the State Department's boycott of the Youth Festival, only one American artist made the journey, the abstract expressionist (splasher) Garry Coleman.

The interest in foreign exhibitions...at the end of the Fifties can only be compared with the excitement surrounding important football matches. Many thousands of people spent whole nights in long queues...The exchange of opinions around the pictures expanded into mass discussions...It was this audience that created the fertile ground in which the unofficial art of the Soviet Union soon sprouted...Western culture, formerly only glimpsed through chinks in the Iron Curtain, became for the wider Soviet intelligentsia a light in the darkness, a beacon of freedom and a model for imitation.[2]

Even so, the public was not allowed to see all the works which had been shown to the international prize jury and the press. The minister of culture, N. A. Mikhailov, visited the exhibition to order the removal of several paintings and sculptures, prize-winners among them, prompting numerous messages in support of the jury from abroad.[3] Neo-Stalinist critics lost no time in denouncing much of what they had seen. Aleksandr Revyakin, a professor at the Potemkin Pedagogical Institute, Moscow, complained that during the festival 'one saw pictures consisting of nothing but a jumble of daubs and called *Composition No. 1*... or paintings of various geometrical figures called *Fable, Eventide, Summer*, and so forth'. Writing for the conservative magazine *Soviet Literature* (aimed at foreign readers), Revyakin used stale, stereotypical language while singling out surrealism and abstractionism as currently the most prevalent of the pernicious Western influences: 'The spiritual sponsors of surrealism and abstractionism are unquestionably making some headway because they are so tremendously rich, have the press, the cinema, the theatre, music, exhibitions and museums at their service, and control a super-system of advertisement, which makes its way into the home of every American.'[4] Citing Salvador Dali's 'grotesque' portrait of Picasso, he lamented 'misshapen bodies, macabresque scenes, decomposed corpses... pathological perversions... paranoidal ravings'. Abstractionism was 'the culmination of all preceding modernistic decadent trends... touching rock bottom... the death knell of art'. The continuing *bête noire* role of surrealism, a movement which enjoyed its classic heyday in the late 1920s and the 1930s, may have reflected the ongoing popularity in the West of Salvador Dali. The Soviet novelist Viktor Nekrasov noted that in the *Great Soviet Encyclopedia*, volume 41, one could read that 'the well-known representative of surrealism, the painter Salvador Dali, paints pictures that glorify atomic war'.[5] This, added Nekrasov, 'bears no relation to the truth'—Dali did not glorify or condemn anything. After a visit to the United States in 1960, Nekrasov noticed that in museums there was always a crowd around anything by Dali.

During the months before Khrushchev blew up at the Manezh Gallery, the Western media had been increasingly attentive to the Soviet art scene, running prominent stories about the struggle between liberals and conservatives: 'Soviet Artists Union Is Accused of Restraining Taste and Talent', declared the *New York Times* on 8 July 1962. 'Russians Irked by Restraint on Art', announced the London *Times* eight days later. The editors of the USIA's *Problems of Communism* commented: 'Even now, nine years after Stalin's death and six years after the beginning of the "de-Stalinization" campaign, there is still an officially decreed genre to which Soviet artists must defer, and many paintings are still being not only denounced but even secreted by the authorities lest the Soviet public fall prey to their corrupting influence.'[6] The *New York Times* (8 July) took up the case of Ilya Glazunov, who patterned his style after Russian icon painters of the fourteenth and fifteenth centuries. His one-man show at the Central House of Art Workers in 1957 had drawn a hostile reaction from leaders of the Artists' Union, 'and since that time the artist had been unable to exhibit his work'.[7]

The occasion of Khrushchev's sustained outburst was an exhibition organized by the Moscow Artists' Union (MOSK), 'Thirty Years of Moscow Art'. The planning of this exhibition, according to Igor Golomshtok, was 'the most unfettered in thirty years', the first showing in decades of some of the more moderately innovative artists of the 1920s (but not daring to include the radical avant-garde like Malevich and Tatlin). Contemporary works by artists of the 'Belyutin group' were hung in three semi-private rooms upstairs.[8]

Khrushchev arrived at the Manezh Gallery accompanied by four members of the Party Secretariat, four members of the Party Presidium, the president of the USSR Academy of Arts, Vladimir (V. A.) Serov, and his notorious predecessor, Aleksandr Gerasimov.[9] It was Serov who had painted *Lenin Proclaiming Power* with Stalin in the background, but later painted him out and replaced him with a smudged nobody. Khrushchev paused in front of a painting, *Nude in an Armchair*, by the late, greatly gifted Robert Falk (1886–1958), who had lived in France for ten years after the suppression of the Jack of Diamonds (*Bubnovyi valet*), a group he had helped to found in Moscow in 1910. 'I would say that this is just a mess', declared Khrushchev,[10] who then rambled on about a friend whose daughter was given a portrait of a lemon when she got married: 'It consisted of some messy yellow lines which looked, if you will excuse me, as though some child had done his business on the canvas.' Khrushchev then told his retinue that he did not mind if he was 'behind the times': 'As long as I am Chairman of the Council of Ministers, we are going to support a genuine art. We aren't going to give a kopeck for pictures painted by jackasses. History can be our judge. For the time being history has put us at the head of this state, and we have to answer for everything that goes on in it. Therefore we are going to maintain a strict policy in art.'

Khrushchev mentioned that when he had visited England in 1956 he and Prime Minister Anthony Eden had agreed that they could understand neither contemporary abstract painting nor Picasso (later repeated in Khrushchev's memoirs).[11] V. A. Serov then drew the chairman's attention to other offending works. 'Some connoisseurs claim that these pictures are programmatic. We dispute that.' Khrushchev agreed, scowling at Pavel E. Nikinov's (marvellous) painting *The Geologists* (1962), in which the tilting landscape of barren hills threatens the equilibrium of four impassive, non-naturalistic figures who pause while one sits to replace a boot and who may, one feels, be travelling in a pilgrims' dream.

We are going to take these blotches with us into communism, are we? If government funds have been paid for this picture, the person who authorised it will have the sum deducted from his salary. Write out a certificate that this picture has not been acquired by the government... Pictures should arouse us to perform great deeds. They should inspire a person. But what kind of picture is this? One jackass is riding on another...

Khrushchev then further berated the offending artists: 'Just give me a list of those of you who want to go abroad, to the so-called "free world." We will give you foreign passports tomorrow, and you can get out.' He confronted the painter Zheltovsky:

You're a nice-looking lad, but how could you paint something like this? We should take your pants down and set you down in a clump of nettles until you understand your mistakes. You should be ashamed. Are you a pederast or a normal man?... Do you want to go abroad? Go then, we'll take you free as far as the border. Live out there in the 'free world'... But we aren't going to spend a kopeck on this dog shit. We have the right to send you to cut trees until you've paid back the money the state has spent on you... They say you like to associate with foreigners.

He came to a painting by Gribkov. 'What's this?'
'It's the year 1917', replied Gribkov.
'Phooey... My opinion is that you can all go to hell abroad. This is an art for donkeys. Comrade Ilyichev [party secretary for ideology], I am even more upset by the way your section is doing its work. And how about the Ministry of Culture?...'

Khrushchev then asked a succession of offending artists who their parents were and how they earned a living. Belyutin, described as 'one of the ideologists of the formalists', said he was a teacher. 'How can such a person teach?' asked Khrushchev. 'People like him should be cleared out of the teaching profession. They shouldn't be allowed to teach in the universities. Go abroad if you want; and if you don't want to, we'll send you anyway. I can't even talk about this without getting angry. I'm a patriot.'

Khrushchev then enthused about some Dutch masters he had seen in the Dresden Gallery (he need have looked no further than the Pushkin Museum). 'You can look at their pictures through a magnifying glass and still admire them. But your paintings just give a person constipation, if you'll excuse the expression.' With further comments about 'smells coming from latrines' Khrushchev departed, one of the era's master showmen. According to *Encounter*, the Soviet art establishment had set the occasion up in order to stamp on non-orthodox art. However, Paul Sjeklocha and Igor Mead, who toured the USSR a year later, were disinclined to believe it: 'That Khrushchev had no previous knowledge of the existence of the Belyutin-group show within the exhibition is supported by the fact that he was led to the upstairs rooms on the insistence of [the sculptor] Neizvestny'. Neizvestny, a war hero, infuriated Khrushchev when he referred to the artists' right of self-expression; nor did Neizvestny's own work on display, *Robots and Semi-Robots*, soften Khrushchev's rage.[12] Oskar Rabin lauded Neizvestny's courage, given the menacing retinue of ministers and the head of the KGB in attendance. As a result the Union of Artists rapidly convoked a commission, which demanded a full self-criticism from the sculptor.[13] Fashioned from a wide range of materials, including bronze, wood, granite, pig iron, and plaster, Neizvestny's sculptures loudly echoed the horror of war and the horror of prison; more recently he had become fascinated by the relationship of man and machine in an age of cybernetics. Henry Moore was an obvious influence.

Three days after Khrushchev's visit to the Manezh a general meeting of the Academy of Arts unanimously condemned the formalist canvases on display. On 4 December the works criticized by the Soviet leader and the paintings by the Belyutin group were removed from view—but by 7 December only the work of the Belyutin group had not been returned. The exhibition ran for a further month.[14]

The Western press was delighted. 'Mr K Declares War on the New Wave', reported Walter Laqueur.[15] 'Soviet Orders Disciplining For Cultural Avant-Garde', announced the *New York Times* (4 December), quoting a front-page editorial and two other articles in *Pravda* indicating a clamp-down following what the Party newspaper called 'the bravado shown recently by Soviet abstractionists, individualistic writers and the composers of 12-tone and similar music'... Khrushchev was portrayed in the Western media as a crude, paranoid, homespun bully, wanting greater freedom yet choking on it. The *Observer* quoted him: 'One isn't able to tell if they were drawn by the hand of a man or smeared by the tail of a donkey.' 'M. Khrushchev delivers a veto (*coup d'arrêt*) on modernism in painting and music', announced *Le Monde* (4 December). The paper's Moscow correspondent, Michel Tatu, termed the brutal attack on abstract art a 'clap of thunder in a calm sky'.[16]

On 17 December Leonid Ilyichev, chairman of the recently formed Ideological Commission, addressed a meeting of the Central Committee attended by 400 artists, writers, and composers, for a reported ten hours. Ilyichev ruled out peaceful coexistence in the fields of art and literature. Ultra-sensitivity to Western jibes surfaced as usual: 'And, of course, the foreign journalists were quick to put in an appearance. Their cameras clicked, their motion-picture cameras whirred'... Foreign so-called 'tourists on special assignments' were hunting around for malcontents. 'Our ideological adversaries are yelling their heads off about a "new wave", about "dissonant voices", about a "crisis in Soviet art".'[17]

However, in a show of respect for the new democratic norms, Ilyichev read out a letter of protest addressed to Khrushchev. Signed by the writers Simonov, Ehrenburg, and Chukovsky, by Konenkov (the dean of Russian sculptors), by the veteran graphic artist Favorsky, Shostakovich (bolder than usual on this occasion), the film director Romm, and two Nobel Prize-winning scientists, Igor Tamm and Nikolai Semyonov, the letter requested Khrushchev to end the persecution of formalism and to give assurances that Stalinist methods would not be restored. Democracy, however, did not extend to the publication of the letter in the Soviet press.[18]

On 7 March 1963, Ilyichev attacked Ehrenburg's[19] views on modernism (in his recently published memoirs) before a large audience:

He lauds formalist artists to the skies, as workers in the graphic arts have correctly pointed out in *Pravda*, but he finds nothing of value in the great realist artists . . . He describes the development of Soviet painting after the 1920s as a counterattack by naturalism, the school of the mundane, academic forms, decorousness, simplification and photographic conventionality, and he ironically hints at its adherence to the canons of the Bologna Academy School of the 16th and 17th centuries.[20]

The following day Khrushchev delivered the most sweeping and all-embracing speech on the arts since Zhdanov's notorious peroration of 21 August 1946. He complained that the dissident artists were obsessed by gloom, doom, sickness, madness, alienation, isolation, and decay. Khrushchev's remarks, like Zhdanov's, bristled with military metaphors. Evidently Mr K. wanted monuments to be monumental: Yevgeny Vuchetich, who had harvested five Stalin Prizes between 1946 and 1950, was praised for his Berlin monument to Soviet soldiers (though Khrushchev did not mention his enormous Stalin statue on the Volga–Don canal). Also praised was Lev Kerbel's monument to Marx in Moscow. Khrushchev recalled that on New Year's Eve, when returning to Moscow 'from the suburbs', he had spent a day in the woods—a winter's day such as one only found in Russia. 'And now the modernists, the abstractionists, want to paint these fir trees upside down, and claim it as the new and progressive in art.'[21]

Khrushchev took swipes at Ehrenburg and Yevtushenko for 'the gross ideological mistake' of defending formalists and abstractionists. Yevtushenko had indeed given offence when, three months after the scenes at the Manezh Gallery, the young poet published his *A Precocious Autobiography* in a Paris weekly, *L'Express*, and in other Western capitals. Here he had told

Western readers: 'The impressionists were the most modern paintings I had seen'—by which he meant 'allowed to see'—as a young man under Stalin. Yevtushenko went on to list the schools of painting hanging on the walls of his own flat: realists, expressionists, surrealists, abstractionists: 'They don't clash with each other and they don't infect me with bourgeois ideology.'[22]

Later, recalling in his memoirs the 7 March 1963 meeting with the intelligentsia, which Neizvestny attended, Khrushchev was in penitent mood: 'There was no excuse for someone who held a high state position, as I did, to say something which could be taken the wrong way.' . . . He regretted having remarked that Neizvestny had taken his name so he would remain unknown (*neizvestny* means 'unknown' in Russian).[23]

⊞ ⊞ ⊞

Sjeklocha and Mead recalled how, a year after Khrushchev's outburst at the Manezh, they were tapped on the back while walking down Gorky Street by a tall young man speaking English and wearing a worn GI parka and blue jeans. He led them through back streets and alleys to an old building, where they ascended several flights of stairs. The 18-year-old artist 'knew more about the New York artistic scene than either of us . . . [and] the numerous subtleties of abstract expressionism . . . pop art and op art'. He spoke of Oldenburg, Lichtenstein, and Rauschenberg[24] 'as if he knew them personally'. He regularly visited the Lenin Library where, upon knowledgeable request, it was possible to obtain *Art News*, *American Artist*, *Amerika*, *Artforum*, *Du*, *Gebrauchsgrafik*, *Réalités*, and other publications restricted to library use only. Readers would sometimes rip out a page carrying a painting by de Kooning or Motherwell and sell it on the black market.[25]

By the end of the Khrushchev era Western galleries were beginning to offer showings of Soviet unofficial art; Neizvestny's work was shown in 1964 at the Grosvenor Gallery, the Zentralbuchhandlung, Vienna, and in Prague. John Berger was granted air-time by the BBC to present a television series on Neizvestny—who in effect occupied a position halfway between the official and unofficial art, and who enjoyed powerful patrons among the scientific and bureaucratic elite. In November 1963, for example, even though expelled from the Union of Artists and therefore theoretically cut off from commissions, he was officially commissioned to execute a series of bas-reliefs for the Pioneer Palace and statues for the Ministry of Culture.[26] In his celebrated *Art and Revolution: Ernest Neizvestny and the Role of the Artist in the USSR*, Berger remarked that for Neizvestny the human body was the field of all possible metaphors. Berger lauded him as an epic, public artist with a heroic conception of the human will.[27] (Only fourteen years later, in 1976, did Neizvestny succeed in emigrating to the West.)

A young art critic and novelist of exceptional ability and influence with the educated lay public, Berger had been writing for the *New Statesman* in the 1950s when he came to Moscow's attention as a promisingly sympathetic Marxist. Visiting London for the 1959 Soviet exhibition at the Royal Academy, the editor of *Iskusstvo* had invited Berger to contribute an article on 'Problems of Socialist Art'. The article was never published, Berger recalled: 'And when a few months later I was in Moscow, the editor of *Iskusstvo* did his best publicly to disassociate himself from me and my opinions, whilst warning his colleagues in the Ministry of the Interior of my presence there.' In the article rejected by *Iskusstvo* Berger—though still deploying such phrases as 'the decadence of bourgeois culture' and 'a truly materialist art'—posed the question: 'Can we dismiss the work of the impressionists and those who followed them as little more than an expression of the decadence of bourgeois culture—which is roughly what Plekhanov did?' The answer was no—Berger's thoughts on the history of impressionism and its 'degenerate' offshoots (Gauguin, Van Gogh, Cézanne) were far from *Iskusstvo*'s. 'Vision itself became the new *content of art* ... Nature was no longer something laid out in front of the painter. It now included him and his vision. Consciousness was now seen to be subject to the same laws as Nature.' The new art offered the possibility of creating 'for the first time in history—a truly materialist art'. Berger's manipulation of sacred phrases, of course, could only anger the heirs of Lenin. Nor was the Soviet Academy likely to agree with him that 'The works of Raphael and Michelangelo contain distortions that are as radical as those in the best works of contemporary artists like Léger or Matisse'. Nor with his contention (widely shared in the West) that 'It is impossible for any painter in Western Europe now to paint as if Picasso had never existed. And that is not a prejudice: it is a fact.' His final 'My warmest wishes and fraternal greetings to all socialist artists everywhere' was not likely to win over the editor of *Iskusstvo*—or anyone else.[28]

By the mid-sixties the Party line was in retreat. As Henri Pierre reported in *Le Monde* (4 March 1966), the Moscow Union of Artists remained a focus of modernist agitation. Artists whose canvases had been stored in Moscow and Leningrad museum basements were initially granted merit in the field of applied art, although any version of 'abstract' painting remained suspect. Writing in *Sovetskaia kul'tura*, the critic V. Zimenko emphasized the value of pre-1917 artistic movements in Russia, including the Light Blue Rose and Jack of Diamonds groups, previously condemned in the *Great Soviet Encyclopedia*, and the work of Vasily Kandinsky, Kazimir Malevich, Marc Chagall, El

Lissitsky, and Vladimir Tatlin. The *New York Times* picked up the story.[29] The Ministry of Culture, anxious to keep pace and build bridges to the West if permitted, staged a one-man show by the veteran surrealist Aleksandr Tyshler, whose paintings were scheduled for an imminent showing in Paris under the Franco-Soviet cultural exchange agreement, along with the work of other notable 'outcasts', Pavel Kuznetsov, Pyotr Konchalovsky, and Martiros Saryan. In November 1966 Robert Falk's paintings were back on exhibition for the first time since Khrushchev called his *Nude in an Armchair* 'just a mess' at the Manezh. Now, reported the *Herald Tribune* (4 November), an exhibition of some hundred drawings and paintings executed by Falk between 1913 and 1958 could be seen in four rooms of the Moscow Union of Artists. A month later the even more eminent Chagall's symbolist paintings were due to greet the light of day after being buried in Soviet museum vaults since his emigration.[30] Recently France's minister of culture, André Malraux, had commissioned Chagall to decorate the Paris Opéra—but the promised Moscow showing aborted. 'Chagall works fail to appear', the *Guardian* (30 December 1966) reported. According to the *Daily Telegraph* on the following day, work by Chagall and Kandinsky had gone on public display at the Tretyakov Gallery, as promised: 'But within a few hours the six abstract watercolours were taken from the walls and returned to the basement.' The *New York Times*'s (30 December) Raymond Anderson jumped on the same story: 'Moscow Mystery Over Chagall: First He's in Show, Then out. The Long-Banned Symbolist Is Apparently Scheduled Only To Be Removed.' Tass had to retract its original report that Chagall was on display for the first time at the Tretyakov.[31] A trial-run display of the work of Aleksandr Tyshler, on the initiative of the Pushkin Museum's director Irina Antonova, also came under heavy criticism.[32]

As Leonid Brezhnev consolidated his hold on power, official attitudes hardened[33] while unofficial artists grew bolder. Western observers noted that the *nomenklatura*, masters of the black market, spiritual as well as material, were increasingly purchasing unofficial art, paying on average 150 new roubles ($165 at the official rate of exchange) for an oil painting, 25 roubles for prints and sketches, and up to 2,000 roubles for sculptures. Support and patronage for abstract art came from scientists of the Nuclear Research Institute at Dubna, near Moscow; indeed, such patronage was the best guarantee of the new art's existence: for example, Raymond H. Anderson reported that the eminent but nonconformist physicist Pyotr L. Kapitsa had discovered the work of Aleksei Anikeyenok during a visit to the city of Kazan, on the Volga. The artist had been expelled from a Kazan art school and was living in a small, crowded room with hundreds of his paintings, and playing the saxophone in a theatre to survive. Kapitsa, a keen collector of modern art, organized an exhibition for him at the Institute of Physical Problems in Moscow. Anderson was there: 'The scientists at the institute and invited visitors reacted with enthusiasm to Anikeyenok's impressionist style of depicting Volga landscapes in bright splashes of color, flouting rules of perspective and evoking feelings of intense sunlight through total omission of shadows.' Yet still the Union of Soviet Artists refused to admit Anikeyenok to membership—without which he lacked legal sponsorship to show his work, and could not obtain a studio, travel grants, and other privileges.

Even the work of 'official' artists belonging to the Union had since the late 1950s been departing from sacred norms of socialist realism, though such deviations did not escape criticism. The term 'severe style' (*surovyi stil'*) was coined retrospectively in 1969 by Aleksandr Kamenski to describe a style with clear affinities to the European expressionist tradition. Prominent examples were the work of Geli Korzhev and Pavel Nikinov. Cézanne, Van Gogh, and Munch were haunting the corridors of Soviet art alongside medieval traditions, folk art, and icon painting.[34] Facial expressions became stereotypical and emotionally neutral, often in the style of the old icon paintings; the masters of the universe were merging back into the landscape, like rocks, but sadder than rocks, as if exhausted by all that scaling of 'lofty heights'.[35]

As nonconformist artists gained confidence, so the Party apparatus became more menacing in its strictures. In June 1966 *Sovetskaia kul'tura* issued a feature article written by V. Olshevsky warning the dissident expressionist-symbolist painter Oskar Rabin not to exhibit his work in the West (again) without official authorization. Rabin had exhibited in June 1965 at London's Grosvenor Gallery. This, complained Olshevsky, had been arranged in order 'to raise the stock of bourgeois propaganda'. The London exhibition of Rabin's 'absurd rubbish' had been accompanied by 'a strident press... another of those exhibitions that blacken Soviet art and give employment to sundry specialists on our artistic gutters... an ideological arena known to the West as a "great experiment in Russian art"'.

The ironic phrase 'great experiment' was a loaded reference to a revelatory academic study, published in London, about Russian art before and immediately after the Revolution. Written by a young English scholar, Camilla Gray, *The Great Experiment: Russian Art, 1863–1922* was first published in 1962. An American art critic visiting the Soviet Union, Hilton Kramer, noted how possession of this banned book was coveted by Soviet artists, academics, and critics. 'There is even said to be a copy of this book in the library of the principal art academy in Leningrad . . . available only to the faculty, not to students.'[36] This was written shortly before Camilla Gray's marriage in 1969 to Oleg Prokofiev, son of the composer, despite Soviet efforts to prevent her returning to the USSR.[37] Taking up her central theme, and subscribing to the more or less standard Western view that the years immediately before and after 1917 had been a heyday for innovative modern art, Kramer described Anatoly Lunacharsky, Lenin's commissar of education, as having become well versed in modernism during his eleven-year exile in Western Europe; indeed, his new Department of Fine Arts allocated positions to Tatlin, Kandinsky and to Chagall: 'The revolution was indeed the first political event in modern history to accord modernist artists such comprehensive, officially sanctioned power. Within a decade, however, the avant-garde was shattered, its power was lost, and the values of modernism placed under an official ban.'[38]

Let us return to V. Olshevsky fulminating in *Sovetskaia kul'tura* against Oskar Rabin's[39] 'scribblings on canvas', inspired by paranoia or 'just a half-litre of vodka'. According to Rabin, it was clear that Olshevsky had never seen his paintings, apart from some black-and-white reproductions in the Grosvenor Gallery's catalogue. The Western press homed in on this story; Rabin's work had also been exhibited at the Arleigh Gallery, San Francisco, three months before the London show.[40] Even the Western Communist press was now displaying increasing exasperation with Soviet artistic policy; a report on the Rabin affair by the London *Morning Star*'s Moscow correspondent was headlined: 'A Soviet artist is told: "your work is rubbish".' This organ of a reformed Eurocommunism expressed dismay that the critic Olshevky should have written of Rabin: 'You are in the pocket of a speculator. You will have to be pulled out of that pocket.' The art critic Charles Morris lauded Rabin's art as 'good, imaginative and serious'. The *New York Times* (10 June) covered the same story: 'Symbolist Artist Scored in Soviet.'

The art section of the 1959 US Exhibition had by his own account made a big impression on Rabin. Entry was free but tickets were marked with date and time, allowing the visitor in theory only two hours. The notoriously two-faced Soviet journalist Victor Louis obtained two press tickets for Rabin; it was the first time he had seen paintings by Pollock, Rauschenberg, and Rothko. Another 'first' was meeting a wealthy American whose Polaroid camera produced prints developed on the spot—Rabin didn't know such a camera existed.[41] Although an admirer of forbidden fruit—Kandinsky, Malevich, Mondrian, Van Gogh, Chagall—Rabin was admitted to the Gorkom, a union for illustrators and engravers, on condition that he obtained the union's permission if he intended to exhibit his paintings at dissident shows. Sjeklocha and Mead visited his low wooden home in the village of Lianozovo, just beyond Moscow's city boundary:

His art strongly reflects...the sacred and profane aspects of Russian life...For example, he juxtaposes a Da Vinci madonna with the Moscow slums, or floats a sensuous Titian nude on the same background; or, again, contrasts onion-domed Moscow churches with the tall Stalinesque official buildings. There are other motifs such as torn 'Moskva' vodka labels through which one sees parts of the city, an empty vodka bottle floating by the Taj Mahal.

Rabin told Sjeklocha and Mead: 'I live a simple life. I go nowhere and I see nothing. My life is spent between the *elektrichka* [electric commuter train], the *kontora* [office] where I work as a commercial illustrator, and my easel.'[42] By 1965 Rabin was able to buy a three-room apartment in a Moscow co-operative at a price of 5,600 roubles. His work was perhaps more discussed by Western critics and journalists than any other Soviet artist's. Although barred from the Artists' Union, he now made a good living from sales of his work both at home and abroad. Igor Golomshtok contrasted Rabin's work with the 'carefully scrubbed and washed chocolate-box world of Socialist-Realist culture':

Rabin...fills his pictures with the *realia* of Soviet life: slogans, banknotes, identity cards, newspapers with typical headlines: 'Forward to the Dawn in the Name of the Happiness of the People'...and so on. These he reproduces...not for the sake of affirming the artistic worth of objects of mass culture, as Jasper Johns has done with the American flag or Andy Warhol with soup tins...[Rabin] juxtaposes the exclamatory aspects of official life with...saucepans, tins of preserve, vodka bottles, dried-up bits of herring...Here we are dealing with the unmasking of stock-phrases of official culture, the belittling of their stale enthusiasm...[43]

And now, in 1967, according to Hilton Kramer: 'A specter is haunting Soviet art—the specter of modernism.' But the modernism which interested Kramer was not Rabin's; modernity now belonged to the United States. Kramer was insistent on discovering specifically American influences on dissident Soviet art, even when the artist himself demurred. Visiting a Leningrad painter in his late thirties, Yevgeny Mechnov-Voitenko, who had never sold or exhibited a single painting, Kramer discovered that his first abstractions, dating from the late 1950s, clearly revealed the influence of Jackson Pollock and Mark Tobey:

The artist himself is evasive on this point, at once insisting that his only masters have been Mikhail Vrubel (1856–1910) and Valentin Serov (1865–1911)...yet admitting to having seen reproductions of Pollock and Tobey in the pages of the magazine *Art in America*...Like Pollock, Mechnov-Voitenko often uses enamel, which is dripped onto the picture surface at great speed, and, like Tobey, he sometimes favors an almost Oriental calligraphic touch.[44]

⊞ ⊞ ⊞

At this stage dissident art moved into a phase unparalleled in any other cultural sphere—the circumstances of its physical display, and its physical suppression, became a subject of ongoing international scandal, starting with an exhibition organized by Aleksandr Glezer, which opened on 22 January 1967 at the Druzhba workers' club in Moscow. On display was the work of twelve artists, including Rabin. Glezer recalled that that this was the first occasion on which it had been possible to get tickets printed, with attendant publicity. 'To a Westerner this says very little—tickets are never a problem. But in the USSR . . . printers accept only texts that have been approved in writing by the censorship [Glavlit].' Two thousand people turned up on the first morning, including foreign diplomats and correspondents: 'The foreigners, of course, were briskly followed in by their state security tails. I was soon called to the club manager's office, where I found a puce-faced KGB major ensconced in the manager's chair. "This exhibition is a put-up job by the CIA!" "I put it up myself," I objected. "Then you must be a blind tool in the hands of the CIA," he insisted.'

Various party officials arrived. Abakumov, arts inspector for the Culture Section of the Moscow Party Committee, shouted: 'A typical provocation! Before the day's out all the Western radio stations will be whooping about these underground artists, and how they're breaking through and organizing themselves despite all the obstacles!' The exhibition was immediately 'suspended'. On 24 January the Central Committee closed it. Rabin reports that Yevtushenko and the US ambassador's wife, Mrs Thompson, briefly attended, as well as foreign correspondents. Next day the club was surrounded by cordons of vigilantes, *druzhinniks*. A lorry drove up to the back entrance. Pictures and painters were embarked on it and disembarked at their homes under vigilante escort, to make sure they stayed put. The Druzhba club manager was dismissed and blacklisted. The Moscow Party issued instructions that in future all exhibitions were to be inspected and approved by the Artists' Union, including, unprecedentedly, those by 'non-artists' who could not belong to the union. This deprived the nonconformists of their last loophole for exhibiting their work; for the following five years, despite many exhibitions abroad, all efforts by the unofficial artists to communicate with the public at home proved fruitless. Oleg Tselkov's exhibition at the Architects' Centre in 1971 lasted fifteen minutes.[45]

The Czech critic Arsen Pohribny, who emigrated to the West following the Soviet invasion of 1968, had visited Moscow the previous year, making clandestine contact with underground artists like the young Ukrainian painter V. Polevoy: 'He had just spread out before us some of his small terracotta sculptures and his drawings. Suddenly he jumped up, ran to the door and threw it open. Standing there, huddled up close to the door, was a man with a telephone receiver in his hand... "He does this to me several times a day," Polevoy explained.' Of another painter, 'T', Pohribny reported: 'He knew the faces of those assigned to shadow him, but he had reached the point where almost everyone seemed to resemble his watchful "guardians".' T's works were so crammed into his small studio that he could do no more than move them slightly apart when he wanted to show them. 'Suddenly the door bell rings. T stiffens, clutching at me with his eyes.' One painter told Pohribny: 'Only those who have been punished or persecuted are just; the others are more or less guilty, and we must keep our distance from them.'[46]

⊞   ⊞   ⊞

In Czechoslovakia artists had regained their freedom somewhat ahead of writers. Although a 1962 exhibition of cubist and expressionist works was closed an hour after it began, from 1963–4 greater tolerance prevailed. Visiting an exhibit at the Galerie Vaclava Spaly in May 1968, during the 'Prague Spring', the present writer found that much of contemporary avant-garde art was furiously derivative—an apparently indiscriminate absorption of American anti-art: pop art, kinetic art, and updated, three-dimensional versions of surrealism were all in contention. Easel art on canvas was old hat and the boundaries between painting and sculpture had been eroded. The work of J. Vozniak, for example, bombarded the spectator with movie queens, Frankensteins, Charles Addams weirdos, open vaginas, and football helmets—all liberally spattered with 'blood', but not, one felt, 'Czech blood'.[47]

After the Soviet (and East German) military invasion in 1968 Prague was to become an extended poster: bulletins, slogans, broadcasts, posters answered the tanks. Witty cartoons of the occupying forces appeared on wrapping paper. Handbills, posters, and graffiti covered monuments, walls, and windows, even though the Warsaw Pact forces soon occupied the print shops and union premises, and it was hard to achieve the technical quality of the contemporary insurrectionary posters produced by the Paris Ecole des beaux–arts. The surreal, the comic, and gallows humour prevailed: for example, bleeding, defecating doves of peace. Emblems of anti-fascist propaganda were now identified with the invaders: for instance, two comically sketched idiot-soldier heads in helmets, one Nazi, the other Soviet, representing 1938 and 1968. The old Bolshevik poster by Dimitri Moor, *Have you enlisted with the Red Army?* (1920), was transformed with the caption: 'You too are guilty for occupying Czechoslovakia.' Power structures are made strange and grotesque through parody; the protector becomes the violator. Nothing is sacred; all symbols can be invaded, dismantled, turned against themselves. By the end of the 1970s in Poland and Hungary poster production had become part of a dissenting culture.

⌗   ⌗   ⌗

The Brezhnev regime's cultural oppression was approaching its peak; the temper of the KGB had been goaded into maddened thuggery by the brazen insolence of dissidents and by the brazen presence of Western cameras and journalists on Soviet soil—the more intimately the KGB invaded the private homes and private space of a Solzhenitsyn or a Sakharov, the more closely the Western media watched the KGB. Following the enormous optimism of the 'Sputnik years', the USSR was losing the cultural and ideological war. By 1974 a number of young artists were offering active support for Oskar Rabin's project of an open-air exhibition, first mooted in 1969. Three days after Solzhenitsyn was expelled from the USSR in February, Rabin commented: 'Now he's off their hands they're free to turn against us.' He was right. The Leningrad artist Yevgeni Rukhin twice suffered broken windows at home. The KGB told his wife: 'If your husband stayed at home instead of traipsing off to Moscow to see his disreputable friends, those windows would still be in one piece.' Artists were seized in the street. Aleksandr Rabin, son of Oskar, was interrogated for three hours on a charge of stealing someone's watch in a church, then received weeks of anonymous phone-calls from strangers inviting him to lend them Solzhenitsyn's *The Gulag Archipelago*.

In September 1974 the artists announced in advance to Moscow City Council their plan to hold an open-air exhibition on a patch of waste-land. They were summoned and advised not to go ahead, although no regulation against it could be found. The confrontation took place on Sunday 15 September in the Cheremushki suburb (scene of Shostakovich's operetta), on a bare patch of waste-land drenched in the grey autumn rain. The Moscow Party apparatus moved in. Police in mufti, disguised as workers doing voluntary Sunday work, pitched in to the artists, threw some to the ground, and snatched their pictures away, slinging them into dump trucks or burning them on a bonfire. A bulldozer ran over two pictures by Oskar Rabin and pursued the artist himself. Scattered by ice-cold jets of cold water, bystanders were detained and fined for disturbing public order. Several Western journalists, soaked to the skin, were assaulted.

In his memoirs, written in French exile, Oskar Rabin gives the 15 September 'Bulldozers' exhibition the title 'Chaussée des Enthousiastes'—Enthusiasts' Pavement'. It was bitterly cold, he recalls, 25 degrees below zero. It was a happening without precedent, because staged in the open air and therefore without regulations, but officials had already made juridical objections. At the local metro station Rabin was stopped by the police and interrogated on the pretext that he resembled the description of a thief who had stolen a watch (apparently the same sort of charge as the one levelled against his son). Walking the kilometre to the site, he saw a car driving back towards the centre of town carrying a couple of US diplomats he knew well: 'They appeared to be in full disarray and made signs to us we didn't understand.' At the site they found a desolate group of painters surrounded by police cars, plainclothesmen armed with 'large spades', trucks with trees ready for planting, municipal watering machines, and bulldozers. The police claimed that it was *subbotnik*, a day, usually Saturday, when citizens gave their voluntary labour to cleaning up the town—even though it was a Sunday. Surrounded by threatening, shouting 'volunteers', Rabin unwrapped his two paintings, displaying them in his hands; one of these paintings may have been his notorious picture of a herring lying on a copy of *Pravda*. The 'volunteers' tried to snatch them from him. Rabin and his son crouched down in front of an advancing bulldozer; an American correspondent jumped into the cabin and cut off the engine as the artist was about to be crushed. Recalling the event twenty-five years later, the art-collector Leonid Talochkin, one of the *shestidesiatniki* (the liberals and dissidents of the sixties), attributed the unexpected bulldozer attack to the sudden whim of low-grade officials (*nizshe chiny*). Only those artists were grabbed who had unwrapped (*razvernut'*) their pictures in the hope of showing them. The mathematician Viktor Tupitzin, one of the moving spirits of the exhibition, had been struck between the legs and was a in a bad condition. They were all arrested, subjected to rude exchanges by the KGB at the police station, thrown into cells, and brought before panels of judges—Rabin appeared in front of a woman judge who told him he deserved fifteen days in prison but merely fined him 20 roubles. His son did get fifteen days, for 'hooliganism'.[48]

Nevertheless, Western journalists had been eyewitnesses to the savagery and news of it was instantly flashed around the world, together with photographs. After stalling and offering unacceptable conditions, Moscow Council officials allowed a second exhibition on a green-meadow site in the Izmailovsky Forest Park. On 29 September artists exhibited their work, with Western radio stations advertising the show. Glezer estimated the spectators at between 10,000 and 15,000. 'They were obliged to walk several abreast, it was hard for them to get a good look, so from time to time the artists would raise their pictures above their heads—to rapturous applause.'

At least three of the artists who took part in the Izmailovsky Park exhibition were rapidly confined to mental hospitals. The police forced Aleksandr Kalugin[49] to give an undertaking to paint no more abstract pictures, threatened him with a psychiatric hospital, and forbade him to live in his wife's apartment since he was not registered to reside there. This left him without a permanent residence, a place to paint, or a venue to show his work to prospective buyers. As Kalugin put it later, only his reputation in the West stood between him and 'starving to death', since he refused to accept a job as a caretaker or night-watchman on principle. In the winter of 1974–5 he was placed for a time in a psychiatric hospital. Kalugin, one of the most outspoken of the 'Westerners', was released in the summer of 1976. Asked about the cultural influences on his work, he named Klee and Chagall, Bosch and the medieval icon-painter Dionysius, with Malevich as 'the first and most striking influence'. And music, too: 'I like nothing better than working to the sound of, say, Emerson, Lake and Palmer, Bob Dylan or Arlo Guthrie. But it is almost impossible to get hold of records like these in Russia.' As for his own work: 'I am grateful to fate that my work appeals to the Americans, the most culturally advanced people in the world, a nation with a subtle feeling for modern art.'[50] Aleksandr Glezer was taken by the KGB to the Lyubianka and warned in terms of a Supreme Soviet decree dated 25 December 1972: 'Stop organizing provocative exhibitions, stop telling foreign journalists about them, stop creating anti-Soviet situations [i.e. press conferences].'

The established artists among the 'unofficials' were able to make a decent living by selling their work privately to foreigners. Exhibitions took place in France, the United States, Germany, Switzerland, Italy, and Denmark. Arsen Pohribny's Moscow guide explained that transactions with foreign buyers were supposed to come under the control of the Office on the Exportation of Art Works. Leonid Talochkin mentions an unpublished decree drawn up in 1971 by the KGB chief Andropov, on 'Possibilities and conditions for the sale of (*realizatsiia*) modernistic products for foreign customers', which did not appear in print until it was eventually published in a 1998 catalogue of the Tretyakov Gallery. By the Andropov decree, sales to foreigners were not forbidden. Artists were nominally paid in roubles, but it was hard currency that the foreigners deposited in the Russian bank—and which the state grabbed.

In February 1975 ninety-nine painters from Moscow, Leningrad, and three other Soviet cities sent the minister of culture an open letter demanding a joint exhibition of all artists regardless of domicile and without any pre-selection committee, and with free access for the public. There was no answer, but *Vecherniaia Moskva* (10 March) published a venomous attack by the editor-in-chief of the journal *Tvorchestvo*, Iurii Nekhoroshev, 'Avant-Garde of Mediocrity' (*Avangard meshchanstva*). Three times these artists[51] have shown their work, he complained, attracting attention in the Western press, although incompetent, messy, jumbled like a crossword puzzle, like a rebus, primitive, mystical. He singled out Oskar Rabin's 'vulgarities', including *The Shirt*, an erotic depiction of a female body, and *Drunken Doll* (*Pianaia kukla*). Should one display all these personal whims (*prikhoti*)? The dissidents were eclectically scavenging surrealism, expressionism, medievalism, usually to disguise poor artistic skills. Nekhoroshev ended with a quotation from Maxim Gorky about those who slunk away from 'life's battle... hiding in murky corners of mysticism... the poky paths of religion cluttered with centuries of lies... hollow and funereal'.

A new storm blew up later that year when Oskar Rabin and colleagues staged an exhibition in eight private apartments. The local Party committee and the militia tried to close them down on grounds of inconvenience to neighbours, too many visitors, bad hygiene. Rabin was threatened with the loss of his flat and of the right to live in Moscow. Described by Glezer as 'the undisputed leader of the nonconformists and the only man capable of uniting the majority of them in times of crisis', Rabin was now expelled from the Amalgamated City Committee of Moscow Artists and Draughtsmen (Gorkom)—the union grouping book, magazine, and poster designers. Membership of this union entitled artists to pursue their own work once they had completed commissioned work, for example, illustrations for a book of poems. Rabin's expulsion meant that he could at any time be declared a parasite. His son Aleksandr, exempted from military service years earlier on medical grounds, was now pronounced fit for two years' service. Two KGB men arrived at breakfast-time to take Rabin away for yet another warning: the new cultural group he had formed with the poet Leonid Pinski and the painter Kiblitzki, calling for greater freedom of contact with the West, had already been publicized on Radio Liberty and could be 'considered criminal'.[52] In 1978 Rabin, his wife, and son were granted a two-way visa to visit the West and return, but on 23 June he was stripped of his citizenship by the Presidium of the Supreme Soviet.[53] Among the artists who now chose to emigrate were Neizvestny and Glezer, who managed to take out the work of a wide range of artists. When an exhibition containing the work of dissidents was held in Paris, the Soviet Embassy protested to the director of the Palais des congrès against the 'anti-Soviet provocation.' The protests were repeated in January 1977 when an exhibition of alternative art from the USSR opened at the London Institute of Contemporary Arts (ICA).[54] Henry Moore and Yehudi Menuhin attended the opening. Heinrich Böll commented that what was true of Soviet literature and poetry was probably true of art: 'Too much of what is being rejected and forced into embarrassing illegality would most certainly bring honour to the Soviet Union.'[55] On display was a photograph of the Moscow militia disguised as workers breaking up the Moscow exhibition of September 1974. William Shawcross of the *Sunday Times* (19 January 1977) commented: 'During the past five years pictures have been burnt on bonfires, slashed, crushed by bulldozers, had acid poured on them and been trampled to pieces. The artists themselves have been subject to harassment, including mugging by the KGB, and imprisonment.' Shawcross reached back fourteen years to the notoriously quotable Khrushchev: 'This "spicy" stuff will, like carrion, attract flies, huge fat flies, and all kinds of bourgeois scum will crawl from abroad.' The *Sunday Times*'s art critic, Marina Vaizey, was more politically sympathetic than artistically impressed: 'Except for its origins, most of it would, to be frank, hardly merit a second glance . . . it looks merely like the distorted reflection of Western idioms.' The graphic work, however, she found stunning: 'delicacy of touch combined with a savagery of subject matter.'[56]

⌗ ⌗ ⌗

In an attempt to steal back the thunder, the Soviet art establishment suddenly reversed its policy of fifty years, presenting to the West the avant-garde of the Malevich–Tatlin era as the true Soviet art. From May to November 1979 a great exhibition was staged in the Centre Georges Pompidou, 'Paris–Moscou 1900–1930', organized in full collaboration with the Soviet Ministry of Culture and the major Soviet museums and galleries, the Pushkin, the Tretyakov, and the Hermitage, as well as libraries and provincial museums.[57] The exhibition covered not only the plastic arts and architecture, but also poster art, industrial design, theatre, ballet, literature, music, cinema, and photography. The central theme, obviously, was the interaction of French and Russian culture during the first thirty years of the century. It was a mighty and stunning exhibition, reflective of Franco-Soviet cultural collaboration throughout the 1970s.[58]

Aleksandr Khalturin, head of the department of Fine Art and Conservation of Cultural Monuments at the Ministry of Culture,[59] led the Soviet team, but Irina Antonova, director of the Pushkin Museum of Western Art since 1961, was clearly an important influence in persuading the Ministry and the Central Committee to bring the exhibition from Paris to Moscow.[60] In

Paris, the Musée de l'art moderne provided the critical initiatives. The French delegation, led by Pontus Hulten, museum director of the Pompidou Centre, reached Moscow in December 1977. Hulten's original triangular concept (Paris–Moscow–Berlin) was foiled by the cold war.

Of particular interest were the contributions of Soviet scholars to the catalogue of 'Paris–Moscou'. Would there be expressions of regret about the suppression of so much talent for so many years? There was none— indeed, the innocent visitor to the Pompidou Centre might never have guessed that such art had been banned and banished. Painters like Kandinsky and Chagall, who had emigrated in despair, were said to have merely 'settled' in Western cities as they might have done before 1914. Aleksandr Khalturin mentioned in his Introduction 'the line of parting between art inspired by social problems, and art where elitism and subjectivity became more and more evident'. Such a formula was merely stale neo-Stalinism; in reality, the attack on 'formalism', on what Lenin called the 'isms', had been directed against many artists ardently committed to the Revolution—but not committed to easel painting, realist figurative painting, and the nineteenth-century academy. Professor V. M. Polevoy did concede that 'certain hastily produced opinions on style moulted into a systematic dogma transmitted over the years', but neither Polevoy nor Professor D. V. Sarabianov offered any hint that Lenin and the Party had ever intervened in the quarrels between factions. 'One can say that the painters of RAPP and their adversaries were both right, each in its own way.' Admitting that RAPP had moved towards iconographic art, Sarabianov did not mention the hundreds of hagiographical portraits of Lenin and Stalin.

Asked about this in the year 2002, Lydia Romachkova, deputy director of the Tretyakov Gallery, who was in charge of storage at the time of the Paris–Moscou exhibition, comments: 'There was no mention of the Party in the catalogue because it was to be published abroad. It was also going out of fashion to talk about the Government and Party, unless you were working on a dissertation, in which case it was obligatory. As for the banning of the avant-garde, it was such a delicate subject.' She herself was part of the system which allowed only curators, scholars, and selected students to view the stored holdings in the Tretyakov: 'In the early sixties I brought students into storage on request from the university.'[61] Svetlana Dzhaforova, a research assistant to the Paris–Moscou project, recalls her difficulties in persuading Romachkova to release some work held by the Tretyakov, including Kandinsky's *No. 7*, which Romachkova said needed restoring. 'She called me a gangster because I had first-hand knowledge of the storage, so they couldn't get away with saying things weren't there.'[62]

The French contributors to the catalogue, led by Hulten, while avoiding routine Soviet jargon were evidently too well aware of what an elaborate collaboration with the Soviet Ministry of Culture entailed—the terms of trade—to attempt to fill the yawning gaps. Exquisitely formulated phrases from the Ecole des beaux-arts flew past awkward truths like a TGV locomotive speeding between glaciers.[63]

Would the exhibition reach Moscow in 1981? Its supporters were apprehensive of the outcome when Khalturin and Antonova made a statement in support to the Soviet Academy of Arts. The expected opposition did not materialize; the 'official' artists decided to welcome the exhibition. Long queues formed outside the Pushkin Museum from 3 June to 4 October 1981.[64]

In Lydia Romachkova's opinion, the Paris–Moscou exhibition of 1979–81 was not a decisive turning-point. The internal ban on the avant-garde continued in the USSR—Dzhaforova recalls that when an exhibition was being prepared in 1985 for display in Germany, Deputy Minister of Culture Zaitsev crossed out all thirty of the proposed Russian avant-garde works. Only through the mediation of the Soviet ambassador to the Federal Republic, Vladimir Simenov, was the avant-garde restored. A real change of policy began in 1987; the following year a Malevich exhibition opened in Moscow and Leningrad; finally the exhibition 'The Great Utopia, 1915–32, (*Velikaia utopiia*), which opened in March 1992 in Frankfurt, moved to Amsterdam, the Guggenheim Museum, New York, then worldwide, displayed all of the forbidden fruit.

In the 1975 edition of *Bol'shaia sovetskaia entsiklopediia* Mikhail Lifshits[65] attempted to wrestle with the demon of modernism: 'An authentic cultural revolution has nothing in common with the destruction of the old culture and the creation of a modernist "anticulture" '—hence Lenin's hostility to the avant-garde modernists set on tossing the classics overboard from the steamboat of modern life:

The schism between modernism and the 'naive realism' of the majority of the people, the covert polemic of the artist against reality as reflected in the human eye,[66] grows relentlessly. In modernist theory the reflection of life is regarded as an outdated project. In modernist practice art loses its representational quality and becomes a system of signs expressing only the artist's viewpoint. These signs are supposed to resemble as little as possible the way the spectator sees them (*na zrit. illiuziiu*).[67]

⌗ ⌗ ⌗

In March 2000, about a year before President Putin's administration closed down the lively magazine *Itogi*, Fedor Romer reported in its pages on the opening of the Leonid Talochkin collection of 'alternative art' (*drugoe iskusstvo*), accommodated in three foyers and a stairwell at the Russian State Humanities University (RGGU), Moscow, the second such museum of recent contemporary art. It had been a long time arriving, and Talochkin[68] charted the steps, starting with a July 1970 display held in the domestic courtyard of an American journalist, Edmund Stevens; then an August 1971 exhibition of Moscow artists in Copenhagen; the September 1974 'Bulldozer' exhibition; the February 1975 VDNKh 'beekeeping pavilion' exhibition; and another at the same site in September. Perhaps the most surprising aspect of the RGGU project is the revelation of the legal status of the Talochkin collection, as from 1976. Talochkin himself turned up at 'Minikult' and was respectfully addressed by his patronymic: 'Greetings, Leonid Prokhorovich, I presume? What brings you to us?' Talochkin then opened a little briefcase and displayed photographs of his collection. The Ministry was about to pass a law on the preservation of cultural monuments. 'Let's get your collection registered', the official suggested helpfully. 'We need to show everyone that we are not against such art.' Subsequently Talochkin received a proposition from the Ministry, recognizing his collection, at that time numbering more than 500 items, as a 'Cultural Memorial of All-Union Significance' (*Pamiatnik kul'turny vsesoiuznogo znacheniia*). In February 1976 fifty-four artists registered 545 works with the Ministry of Culture as work of 'All-Union significance'. The Ministry also contacted the housing department and arranged a two-room flat for Talochkin and his mother, instead of the communal flat. 'A chap was appointed to look after me, a member of my family, who could let them know everything.' Shortly before the 1980 Olympiad the Ministry installed a telephone in the flat; with all the foreigners arriving, it was simpler to monitor his calls at home than to send KGB agents running after him whenever he made calls from pay-phones.[69]

From 1976 to 1987 Talochkin regularly offered his collection for exhibits at 28 Malaia Gruzinskaya Street. For the film *Is the Sighted Responsible for the Blind?* (1989) six works by Neizvestny were borrowed from the Talochkin collection. In 1996 the collection became 'official': Talochkin was appointed curator of an exhibition staged by the Tretyakov Gallery and the Russian Museum, St Petersburg: 'The Other Art, Moscow 1956–76.'

The RGGU did not assist Talochkin with the exhibit except to provide the premises. The collector chose 200 items from the 2,000 in his possession, but, hanging in the cold interiors of the RGGU, the collection unfortunately abdicates its underground aura, the enthusiasm of the post-bulldozer exhibitions, of those 'distant times' (*davnosti*) when the painter Kira Prozorovsky would turn up desperate to sell Talochkin a painting by Vyacheslav Kalinin for 13.70 roubles—the price he needed for a bottle of port wine—

though the artist himself had not given permission for the sale. 'He won't mind when he learns I've given it to you', Prozorovsky had pleaded. Taloch-kin concluded this story with a nostalgic sigh for worse times: 'We were all in it together' (*vse svoi liudi*).[70]

Judging by two permanent displays in Moscow of the alternative or 'un-official' art of the late Soviet era, much of it was crude, derivative, a thick and guttural application of paint or bronze in imitation of something else.[71] On occasion the sheer iconoclasm of dissident art overcomes the *faux naif* style, for example, a large canvas by Viktor Popkov, *North Song* (1968), showing the interior of a wooden dwelling in the far north. A group of four obviously modern young Russians, comfortably dressed, who may be geologists or engineers, sit waiting, absorbing their situation, while across the table five phantom barefoot females, dressed in pink and purple and belonging to recent history, sing and testify to their suffering. Although the paint applica-tion is crude, in the 1960s style, this is one of the most moving of dissident history paintings.

Conclusion

Culture wars, unlike games of football and chess, do not yield undisputed winners and losers; they tend more towards the judgemental system prevailing in gymnastics, diving, and ice-dancing, with the jurors as much on trial as the performers. In the opinion of this writer there was never a moment when the USSR gained a clear cultural ascendancy; even after Sputnik (1957), when American educators were pouring into Russia to study the educational system and the scientific institutes, the Soviet Party could be counted on to haemorrhage its advantage by its suppression of Pasternak's *Doctor Zhivago* and its dire persecution of the author. Gagarin had no sooner become the first man in space than Khrushchev crashed into the Manezh Gallery like a baited bear, crudely tried to stifle Shostakovich's Thirteenth Symphony, yelled at Yevtushenko and Ehrenburg, and allowed the Fellini affair at the 1963 Moscow Film Festival to damage the international gains made by *The Cranes are Flying, Ballad of a Soldier*, and *Ivan's Childhood*. Even so, Moiseyev, the Bolshoi, the Kirov, and the Moscow Art Theatre performed to huge applause in the Western capitals, as did many renowned Soviet soloists, a credit to the teaching methods which spawned them. The years 1954–63 undoubtedly marked the height of Soviet cultural prestige, before the long twilight of Brezhnevism extinguished the candles.

If the West won the cultural cold war it was more by default than by artistic achievement. The Congress for Cultural Freedom could not present a playwright better than Brecht, a composer as popular as Prokofiev or Shostakovich, a ballet company superior to the Bolshoi, instrumentalists more skilled than Richter, Oistrakh, or Rostropovich, ensemble acting more subtle than the Moscow Art Theatre's, or, with the single exception of Bobby Fischer, chess players to compare with the Soviet grandmasters. The dominant Western idiom in the elite arts—'modernism'—was not particularly popular with the broad Western public, which generally found it inaccessible if not downright perverse; yet it prevailed over Soviet 'realism' far more thoroughly than it would have done if the Communist Party of the Soviet Union had not sought to stifle the modernist avant-garde with every weapon at its disposal.

Soviet Communism and American pluralist capitalism both inherited their professed humanistic values from the Western Enlightenment. Even conservative American commentators agree on this point. Samuel Huntington describes the cold war as a conflict within Western civilization, while Jeane J. Kirkpatrick writes: 'The East/West designations of the Cold War made sense in a European context, but in a global context Slavic/Orthodox people are Europeans who share in Western culture. Orthodox theology and liturgy, Leninism and Tolstoy, are expressions of Western culture.'[1] Yet an obvious complication arises when Huntington describes a boundary or 'fault line' running down the heart of Europe, to the West of which resides a common experience of the Renaissance, Reformation, and Enlightenment, while to the East are to be found traditionally Orthodox and Muslim communities less likely to develop liberal, pluralistic democracies. It may be that the cultural cold war between the Soviet camp and the West took the form it did because the USSR extended both to east and west of that 'fault line', fostering the contradiction within Soviet culture which sought to embrace Beethoven, Heine, Herzen, Repin, Tchaikovsky, Mussorgsky, Tolstoy, Chekhov, Anatole France, and Bernard Shaw—yet found itself incapable of embracing the freedom and tolerance incarnated by such artists and their work. (However, Nazi Germany, Fascist Italy, and Falangist Iberia should warn us against a facile equation of the West with eternal liberalism.) Soviet culture set the gifted individual artist on a pedestal, yet feared and loathed individualism. It called for heroic spirit yet distrusted *esprit*. It championed liberty of expression against McCarthyism, yet refused to countenance 'subversion' or 'slander' at home. The seemingly unstoppable Soviet impulse to censorship, bullying, and Party-line dogma squandered an extraordinary richness of talent and heritage, supported by the patronage of an exceptionally wide and devoted *zriteli* (audience). If Pasternak's novel *Doctor Zhivago* had not been banned, how many Westerners would ever have heard of it, still less read it? The archaic ramblings of Brezhnev and Andropov about how to dispose of Solzhenitsyn can now be viewed as the final gut-rumblings of the vast creature likened by John Lewis Gaddis to a doomed triceratops, fearsome when viewed from the outside, with its bristling armament and aggressive posturing, until one day 'the creature was found with all four feet in the air, still awesome but now bloated, stiff and quite dead'.[2]

A final thought (or three) about the current condition of cold war cultural studies: America possesses a fine corps of Russian-language, Russian-history, and Soviet-studies specialists, often engaged in path-breaking work and stimulating debates about the nature of the Soviet state and civil society; but these Russia experts have tended to remain a proud species set apart.

Their faculties, institutes, journals, conferences, and debates have not on the whole been engaged in active intercourse with the newer departments of 'Cold War Studies' which have proliferated during the last quarter-century and which have become, frankly, centres of Americocentricity, with English often the only operative language tool. At the two major Cold War Culture conferences I have attended,[3] only one scheduled contribution about Soviet cultural policies or products was on offer; no scholar from, or of, Eastern Europe was on the platform. In the cultural field Soviet Studies and Cold War Studies do not inhabit the same planet.

Closely related to this Americocentricity, as it transpires, is another problem in current cold war cultural studies—the rise and rise of jargon. If patriotism is the last refuge of a scoundrel, jargon is the first refuge of a lively but insecure intellect. The English language has become the plasticine playground of those who know no other. Toss in here a progressive political perspective and a spectrum of hummingly correct positions; the maltster (as Havel calls him) is now primed to market a vile brew of esoteric jargon far removed from, and indeed hostile to, the ordinary language of ordinary people, the *raison d'être* of this jargonfest apparently being to 'deconstruct' reality as a prelude to reassembling it. We hear, for example, about 'the Lacanian over-view', 'surplus surveillance', 'modes of enframement', 'process of eventuation', 'the hegemonic gaze',[4] 'the single basket effect', and 'alternative orders of credulity' (presumably 'credibility' was meant). The pain in Orwell's ear can be imagined.

'Deconstructionists' (it turns out) are close cousins to psychoanalysts: they know what you mean and what you feel better than you do. They know what George Kennan meant by 'containment' far better than he did. As a result, Kennan's geopolitical, anti-Soviet doctrine, finalized in the Moscow Embassy and dispatched to the State Department, is discovered to have been reflective of one repressed man's sexual inhibition. The supposed sub-text supersedes the text; criticism is paramount chief; 'deconstruction' is burial.

In the United States a new generation of scholars has increasingly settled for a unilateral cold war—an essentially domestic quarrel between a citizens' America and the 'Amerika' of the national security state. The two halves of the psyche are depicted as locked in an eternal conflict which, although played out exclusively within the frontiers of the USA, is global in reach— like the ongoing brawls of Tom and Jerry. By this approach 'Amerika' not only subjugates the world but is the world. The USA is both Punch and Judy; so powerful, influential, innovative, rich, and inexhaustibly wicked as to fill all the roles in the passion play. And who, then, can spell *Pravda*? No interventions are required from faraway aliens who speak inconvenient languages. This is a cold war without even a walk-on part for Russians, Poles, Czechs, or East Germans. It's a cold war which features Arthur Miller and Ralph Ellison but not Sartre and Camus, not Simonov and Havel, not Brecht, Romm, and Wajda. Cold war culture is said to have surfaced if a sexually deviant novel ran into some local fascism in small-town Amerika—but the fate of Roger Vailland's French play about Americans in Korea lies beyond the pale.

Endemic to post-New Left social criticism during the past thirty years has been its posting of a constant innuendo that the cold war was a phoney war waged by America's Power Elite to conceal or justify real(er) wars at home. By this reading the power elites who were raising scares about a Soviet military threat to Western Europe were really set on keeping American women out of the workplace, keeping realist perspectives and figurative motifs out of the fine arts, keeping serious social content off the stage and screen. Amerika, in other words, feared Soviet Communism, the aspirations of American women, the positive hero in the novel, gays, lesbians, and Mexican-Marxist mural painting all in one breath because all of them threatened white American capitalist-male hegemony. It was a package now called 'containment'.[5] This 'America-Amerika' fixation amounts to an intellectual cataract.

The central revisionist project is to demonstrate a gravitational pull between the large planet moulded by the Truman Doctrine and the Marshall Plan and a constellation of specifically American cultural satellites: DeMille's *The Ten Commandments*, the tiny waists of women's fashions in the 1950s, plus 'Home and Garden' magazine brainwashing, American homophobia, Hitchcock's *Rear Window*—the bikini. 'Containment', once thought to be a strategy to check a territorially expansionist, autocratic Great Power, the USSR, becomes a metaphor of beguiling elasticity, a weapon for corralling American women by shackling them to babies, aprons, and silk stockings while the men grab the world; a dozen nefarious Tory schemes for stifling Shelley and blacklisting Byron. The term 'cold war' is now tagged on to anything, tossed like Thousand Island dressing over every leaf of the American salad—pleasuredome hedonism, male chauvinism, conspicuous consumption, homophobia, hyper-individualism, armaments, Hollywood. (The opium in the American salad would have been much the same had the Romanovs continued to rule Russia, with Rasputin in charge of ideology.)

This marks a regression in historical understanding. The parents and grandparents, surely, had a wider perspective. The old stalwarts of the CPUSA loved their country, perhaps, but they loved Uncle Joe's Russia as much or more; the American New Left of the 1960s was genuinely international in perspective and reach—as indeed were the 'cold war liberals' of the Truman and Kennedy administrations whom the New Left passionately fought. American radicals of the sixties were at ease with the work of Sartre and Wajda, Godard and Brecht. But their younger cousins, today's relentless critics of the national security state from Truman to Bush, know only one country, which they simultaneously adore and love to hate—and that country is 360 degrees in circumference. The intense introversion of the new scholarship, fixated by networking, websites, and electronically transmitted virtual realities, is remarkable; likewise the tendency to ignore the critical axes of art, intellect, and power running from Paris and Rome to Berlin, Prague, and Warsaw. The new criticism tends to view international power politics as supererogatory, as *their* bad game. Borrowing here and there from the vocabulary of political science and international relations, the new criticism occasionally expresses token acknowledgement that Stalinism had to be resisted (of course)—before resuming sticking needles into the eyes of those who did resist it. This ritual 'of course' is shallow; the main enemy is always at home; if Stalin's moustache was allowed to show up on every page there would be less *Lebensraum* for General Swastika Amerika, architect of the planet-sized mushroom, the Bikini/bikini. Too many cultural commissars with square shoulders block the view of uncountable CIA–FBI agents slithering by night into the sewers of liberal leverage.

This carries us to a third major sin of contemporary scholarship—the obsession with covert action and the secret state (the counterpart of the cold warriors' obsession with Hiss, Rosenberg, and the Cambridge Five). That fronts and dummy foundations were a major feature of US cultural policy is undeniable, and one cannot blame revisionist scholars for pursuing trails of leverage and covert funding from the CIA, the British IRD, and other secret outfits to the Congress for Cultural Freedom, magazines like *Encounter* and *Preuves*, art exhibitions and music festivals staged in Paris and Vienna. Unfortunately the relentless pursuit of exposure—who paid the piper? who pulled the strings? where was the hidden hand? who persuaded who(m) to say what?—has resulted in a lopsided view of cultural activity and what inspires it. Considerable are the charms of sitting in a large, hushed reading room (RGANI) in Moscow, five minutes walk from Red Square, which can be entered only by an elaborate system of internal telephone calls and passes, a room whose glass cabinets are lined with the works of 'Marks' under the blank gaze of two crude portraits of Marx and Lenin but which cannot be photographed, a room where everything has to be signed for several times; here one may browse through documents headed *apparat tsk KPSS* (apparat of the Central Committee of the CPSU), with its various *otdely*, or departments, its *Sektor muzykal'nogo iskusstva* to ensure that Big

Brother's musical whims are observed. But those who spend too long in such rooms, the declassified archives of East and West, peering into coded files, may emerge suffering from a species of blindness—the naive belief that the once-secret memoranda and correspondence of the power elite are by definition revelatory. To this append the concomitant fallacy that almost everything of cultural importance has been engineered by one power elite or another, by some 'hidden hand' bearing a hidden agenda. Hardly any of the players, it transpires, picked up a pen, a paintbrush, or a violin without some chromium lever being inserted into his or her soul by the 'secret state'. The emphasis among scholars (abetted by publishers and their promotion strategies) has thus swung from conviction to conspiracy, from the work of art itself to the hidden funding behind it. The message to scholars became clear: go find your archive and its grim story of covert dollar (or rouble) subsidies, epistolary whispers, and phantom foundations; or, in the East, of Big Brother's hissed instructions, of the Party's long arm reaching out into the night. Too often this 'investigative' approach leads to the false conclusion that he who paid the piper wrote the tune; that the promotion explains the product; that all we need to know is who paid for the ink, for the acryllic and the auditorium. This approach is far from confined to revisionists who regard Amerika as the great Satan; anti-Communist scholars have attempted to show, for example, how the Comintern subsidized and manipulated the left-wing intelligentsia during the 1930s. The activities of the devious Willi Münzenberg, master manipulator of Moscow gold, Moscow flattery, Moscow masques and shadows, are said to explain, and explain away, the popular fronts and entire anti-fascist movement.[6] Another cataract.

Despite Zhdanov and despite McCarthy, sincere conviction lay at the root of most cold war cultural production—as the widespread persistence of Stalinist beliefs among older Russians still alive in the twenty-first century confirms. The real foundations and dynamics of cultural conflict ensure that what the Germans call *Einfühlung* (empathy-plus-understanding) is worth a year in the archives: cold war culture can be properly explored and understood only from multiple viewpoints based largely on evidence which resides within the public domain, the extraordinarily copious cultural production of the twentieth century.

Abbreviations

ABT	American Ballet Theatre
AFL	American Federation of Labor
ACLU	American Civil Liberties Union
ACCF	American Congress for Cultural Freedom
AP	Associated Press
BBC	British Broadcasting Corporation
BFI	British Film Institute
BM	*Burlington Magazine* (London)
BSO	Boston Symphony Orchestra
CBS	Columbia Broadcasting System
CCF	Congress for Cultural Freedom
CDN	*Chicago Daily News*
CIA	Central Intelligence Agency (USA)
CIO	Congress of Industrial Organizations
CP	Communist Party
CPSU	Communist Party of the Soviet Union
CSM	*Christian Science Monitor*
CT	*Chicago Tribune*
DE	*Daily Express* (London)
DEFA	Deutsche Film Aktiengesellschaft
DH	*Daily Herald* (London)
DNZ	*Die Neue Zeitung* (West Germany)
DM	*Daily Mail* (London)
DT	*Daily Telegraph* (London)
DW	*Daily Worker* (London or New York)
ECLC	Emergency Civil Liberties Committee (NY)
FAZ	*Frankfurter Allgemeine Zeitung*
FBI	Federal Bureau of Investigation
HICOG	Office of High Commissioner for Germany
HUAC	House Committee on Un-American Activities
ICD	Information Control Division of OMGUS
KGB	State Security Committee (Komitet Gosudarstvennoy Bezopasnosti).
KP	*Komsomol'skaia pravda*
KZ	*Kul'tura i zhizn'*
LF	*Le Figaro* (Paris)

LM	*Le Monde* (Paris)
LLF	*Les Lettres françaises*
LNC	*La Nouvelle critique*
LG	*Literaturnaia gazeta*
LTM	*Les Temps Modernes*
MG	*Manchester Guardian* (UK)
MGM	Metro-Goldwyn-Meyer
MoMA	Museum of Modern Art, New York
ND	*Neues Deutschland*
NC	*News Chronicle* (London)
NCASF	National Council for Soviet–American Friendship
NR	*New Republic*
NS	*New Statesman & Nation* (London)
NYCB	New York City Ballet
NYHT	*New York Herald Tribune*
NYJA	*New York Journal American*
NYRB	*New York Review of Books*
NYT	*New York Times*
NYU	New York University
OMGUS	US Military Government in Germany
PCF	Parti communiste français
PR	*Partisan Review*
RFE	Radio Free Europe
RGALI	Rossiiskii gosudarstvennyi arkhiv literatury i iskusstva— Russian State Archive of Literature and Art
RGANI	Rossiiskii gosudarstvennyi arkhiv noveishei istorii—Russian State Archive of Recent History
RIAS	Radio in the American Sector of Berlin
RL	Radio Liberty
SD	*Sunday Dispatch* (London)
SE	*Sunday Express* (London)
SED	Sozialistische Einheits Partei
SI	*Sovetskoe iskusstvo*
SK	*Sovetskoe kino*
SL	*Soviet Literature* (Moscow)
SM	*Sovetskaia muzyka*
SMAD	Soviet Military Administration in Germany
SN	*Soviet News* (London)
SW	*Soviet Weekly* (London)
ST	*Sunday Times* (London)
TLS	*Times Literary Supplement*
TR	*Tägliche Rundschau*
USIA (USIS)	United States Information Agency (Service)

VAAP	Vsesoiuznoe agentstvo poavtorskim pravam
VB	*Voks Bulletin*
VDNKh	Vystavka dostizhenii narodnogo khoziaistva
VoA	Voice of America
VOKS	[Soviet] All-Union Society for Cultural Relations with Foreign Countries (Vsesoiuznoe obshchestvo kul'turnykh sviazei s zagranitsei)
WFTU	World Federation of Trade Unions

Notes and References

Introduction: The Culture War

1. *Pax* means not only 'peace' but 'pacification'—peace on our terms.
2. Samuel Huntington has suggested that neither the USA nor the USSR was 'a nation state in the classical European sense' because each 'defined its identity in terms of ideology' (Huntington, 23).
3. The USA was spending 7 % of its GDP on armaments, the Soviet Union perhaps 25 %, an unsustainable burden (Hobsbawm 1995, 247).
4. Keep, 7. Eric Hobsbawm stressed economic failures, inability to generate a hi-tech economy and sustain the role of superpower, uncompetitiveness, only mentioning in a murmur the desire for 'freedom of choice', although populations throughout Eastern Europe were calling for liberty, freedom of the press, freedom of assembly and association (Hobsbawm 1995, 117).
5. I am using the term 'culture' in its differing senses: as a quest for high achievement and perfection; as the corpus of ongoing intellectual and imaginative work; as a social way of life reflected in art, learning, institutions, and manners; and (closer to Matthew Arnold and the *Oxford English Dictionary*), 'the training, development, and refinement of mind, tastes and manners'.
6. Kelly and Shepherd, 9–12.
7. The Russians launched heavy bombardments of cultural statistics. *Moscow News* (30 Aug. 1947) announced that the Soviet capital possessed 2,253 libraries containing 64 million volumes. The previous year 1.2 million users of the Lenin Library had borrowed 5 million items. Moscow had 60 museums, 24 theatres (offering 8 million spectators 9,000 performances, and staffed by 7,000 actors, musicians, and painters). The Moscow Conservatory of Music, which had only 150 students before the Revolution, now boasted 2,000. There were 26 music schools in Moscow, with 9,000 students, and four symphony orchestras.
8. Riesman, 39.
9. A somewhat perverse thesis concerning Zhdanov's leading role has been advanced by Werner G. Hahn, who argues that Zhdanov, 'Stalin's top deputy' in 1946, was really a 'moderate' because of his resistance to the geneticist Lysensko and the dogmatists in the field of philosophy. The *Zhdanovshchina* is to be understood in the light of Zhdanov's rivalry with the comparatively non-ideological, pragmatic Georgiy Malenkov: 'In fact, in 1946 he cynically sought to beat his enemies by campaigning against ideological softness and by enunciating crude, doctrinaire attacks on culture' (Hahn, 9–12, 69). Either way, it was of no comfort to the victims.
10. *NYT* 19 Nov. 1968.
11. Leavis quoted in Banham and Bigsby, 7–22.

12. On the 'nothingists' (*nichevoki*), see Stites (1989), 69–70 and Fitzpatrick, 5, 9.
13. Kemenov (1947), 34.
14. Fitzpatrick, 248–9.
15. Berlin (2000), 61, 63.
16. Scott-Smith (2000), 132, 135.
17. Salisbury (1968), 148.
18. Fyvel, 79.
19. *Bol'shaia sovetskaia entsiklopediia*, 2nd edn., vol. 28 (1954), 41.
20. These alien and recent American-based terms are printed in cyrillic, the first two in the distinct italicized alphabet, as *'non-arm'*, *'on-apm'*.
21. *Bol'shaia sovetskaia entsiklopediia* (1975), 404.

Chapter 1. Propaganda Wars and Cultural Treaties

1. *MG* 3 July 1945.
2. Yuri Averbakh, international grandmaster and later chairman of the Soviet Chess Federation, recalled that this telegraphic code meant in terms of normal chess notation d2–d4 (P-Q4), etc.
3. e.g. M. M. Botvinnik, in *Pravda*, 5 Nov. 1945.
4. *VOKS Bulletin*, 11/12 (1945), 91. *Krasny sport* quoted in *USSR–USA*, 174.
5. On 30 September a Red Army team had beaten a British Services XI 2–0 in Berlin. A rematch was scheduled for 7 October, but the Russians asked for a postponement and the game never took place.
6. Rabinovich, 30.
7. Downing, 59, 165, 125–6.
8. Ibid. 176.
9. *DT* 23 Nov. 1945; Downing, 192.
10. Orwell, 61–4.
11. Including the *NYT, NYHT, CSM, CDN, NYJA*.
12. *SD* 9 Dec. 1945; *DE* 4 Mar. 1946.
13. *DH* 18 Apr. 1946; *NC* 16 Apr. 1946; *DM* 6 May 1946.
14. *USSR–USA*, 175.
15. One valiant last attempt at preserving the spirit of wartime comradeship was made when a Soviet chess team arrived in London in September 1947 (sweeping the board by 15 to 5). The ice-cap then descended.
16. Howard Hanson, head of the Eastman School of Music; Douglas Moore, chairman of Columbia University's Music Department; and the composer Aaron Copland among them wrote indignantly to Truman and Attorney-General Tom Clark (*NYT* 15 Oct. 1946; *CSM* 18 Oct. 1946).
17. Witnesses in favour of the bill included Secretary of State George C. Marshall, Secretary of Commerce Averell Harriman, Chief of Staff General Dwight D. Eisenhower, and the US ambassador to Moscow, Walter Bedell Smith.

18. Hixson, 11. The United States Information Service (USIS) was established by the Act as 'an information service to disseminate abroad information about the United States, its people, and policies promulgated by the Congress, the President, the Secretary of State and other responsible officials of Government having to do with matters affecting foreign affairs'. The bulk of the foreign cultural programme, however, fell outside the ambit of the USIS and the USIA, set up on 1 August 1953 as an independent agency reporting to the president through the National Security Council. Its remit excluded educational exchanges and the 'overseas cultural presentations programs', which remained the responsibility of the State Department, whose Division of Cultural Relations had been established in 1938.

19. The USIS's budget for fiscal 1951 was increased by 250 % for fiscal 1950, and by 400 % for the first full year of the Smith–Mundt Act.

20. Wagnleitner, 291.

21. Marshall Plan agencies contributed a mass-circulation, glossy monthly entitled *Rapports France–États-Unis*, which carried stories on such topics as 'American Painters at Giverny'. Some 10,000 targeted French citizens received publications such as *Ce qui dit la presse américaine*, while 500 Fulbright awards per year facilitated Franco-American scholarly exchange. Prominent among American-subsidized publications were *Franc-tireur* and *Preuves*.

22. Kuisel, 25–6.

23. Lazar (2001).

24. These authors included John Dewey, Arthur Schlesinger, Jr., Henry Steele Commager, Zechariah Chafee, Sherwood Anderson, W. H. Auden, Theodore Dreiser, Archibald McLeish, and Edmund Wilson.

25. Walt Disney's *Bambi* was a hit with the 6–10-year-olds. Amerika Haus's library stocked 400 journals, of which the most popular were *Life, Esquire, Time, Reader's Digest*, and *Good Housekeeping*. Agencies located in Graz, Linz, and Salzburg used bookmobiles to convey books, records, and film equipment to remoter areas (Wagnleitner, 291).

26. 'Book Burning', 26 June 1953, 38–9.

27. McIver, 37. It has been estimated that between 1953 and 1955 the Department purged some 300 titles by some 40 authors, and that many more—perhaps 250 authors—were taken out of commission by overseas librarians playing safe.

28. *Rights* (ECLC), 2/3 (Nov. 1954), 7–8.

29. By June 1955 74 members of the USIA's 10,000 staff had resigned under political pressure; morale was so low that it became difficult to recruit qualified staff for the Voice of America and other USIA operations (Brown, 30 n.).

30. *NYT* 31 July 1954, cited by Mitchell, 57. See also Cushman, 47.

31. The phrase occurred in Churchill's speech delivered on 5 March 1946 in Fulton, Missouri, home state of President Truman, who was in attendance. The Truman Doctrine was most clearly articulated in the president's speech to Congress on 12 March 1947. Asking for $400 million in aid to Greece and Turkey, Truman warned that totalitarianism was already being inflicted on Poland, Romania, Bulgaria, and

'a number of other countries'. The United States would support 'free peoples who are resisting attempted subjugation by armed minorities or by outside pressures'. The means would be primarily economic and financial. Three months later, on 5 June, Secretary of State George Marshall delivered a speech at Harvard calling for a vast, co-operative effort, supported by US aid, to rebuild the economy of all Europe, East and West, the Soviet Union included. Stalin rejected the plan and none of the Soviet satellites was permitted to share in its benefits.

32. *NYHT* 25 Oct. 1953.
33. It was mainly one-way traffic. A variety of American oddballs, including Lee Harvey Oswald, turned up in Moscow in the late 1950s to request Soviet citizenship. None of them carried a major talent and most of them soon asked to go home.
34. For this and similar comments see Brezhneva, 148, 159, 162, 184–5.
35. *Vsesoiuznoe obshchestvo kul'turnikh sviazei s zagranitsei.*
36. Evans, 16–17, basing his account on Louis Nemzer in the *Public Opinion Quarterly* (Summer 1949), 271–5.
37. By 1960–1 the US government had 176 information libraries located in over 80 countries, and more than 28 million visitors. The USIA budget rose from $84.2 million in 1954 to $146.82 million in 1964. Even so, these sums were less than General Motors spent on automobile ads, or Proctor & Gamble on promoting soaps (Rubin, 59).
38. During the first two years of the agreement, 1,674 Americans travelling in 107 delegations visited the USSR, while 1,637 Soviet citizens, in 100 delegations, visited America. The symmetry was no coincidence (Hixson, 158).
39. *SN, The Times*, 19 June 1958; *MG* 28 June 1958.
40. *The Times*, 30 Mar. 1959.
41. *NYT* 23 Apr. 1959.
42. An agreement was signed on 20 February 1964, after seven weeks of stubborn bargaining between teams led by Ambassador Foy D. Kohler and Sergei K. Romanovsky, chairman of VOKS.
43. In July 1968 the USA and the USSR signed a new agreement curtailing cultural and educational exchanges while broadening scientific and technical ones. In March 1969 the sixth Soviet–British cultural agreement was signed, similar to its predecessors.
44. Gaddis, 284.
45. Reddaway (1985), 6.

Chapter 2. The Gladiatorial Exhibition

1. *Art News Bulletin* (USIS) (American Embassy, London, Nov.–Dec. 1957), 5. The structure was designed by Edward Stone, born in 1902 and architect of MoMA and of the US Embassy, Delhi (1954).

2. The Paris Exposition universelle of 1899 had 50 million visitors. The colonial or imperial motif in exhibitions was often apparent, not least in the 1883 Amsterdam colonial exhibition and the popular Exposition coloniale internationale, held in Paris in 1934.
3. See Rydell and Gwinn, *passim*.
4. On VDNKh (Vystavka dostizhenii narodnogo khoziaistva), see Gambrell, 30–7.
5. David Ellwood has called this the greatest mass propaganda campaign ever conducted in peacetime (Ellwood, *passim*).
6. In Austria the Information Services Branch began full-scale operations on 15 May 1945, its staff growing rapidly from 140 to 730 two years later. The US radio station Rot-Weiss-Rot became the most popular in Austria until it was closed in 1955. The formula was five minutes of propaganda wrapped in two hours of sugar-coating, mainly jazz and bebop.
7. Hixson, 47.
8. A half-century later, Prime Minister Tony Blair told the 1997 Labour Party conference (in his verb-less style): 'Most of the great inventions of modern times with Britain stamped on them; the telephone; the television; the computer; penicillin; the hovercraft; radar.' His speech writer left out the jet engine (*The Times*, 1 Oct. 1997).
9. Ignotus, 50.
10. Frederick Barghoorn, a strongly anti-Soviet professor at Yale, sardonically commented that the movie *Edison*, starring Spencer Tracey, was popular with the Soviet public—until it was 'discovered' that the electric light-bulb, like every other major invention, was the work of Yablochkov (Barghoorn 1950, 80).
11. 'Wer hat das elektrische Licht erfunden? Etwa Edison? Weitgefehlt: Jablochkow heisst der Mann.' 'Sowjetrussland will sich nunmehr also gegenüber westlichen Einflüssen immun machen' (*Die Welt*, 30 Sept. 1947).
12. In Margaret Mead's *Soviet Attitudes Toward Authority* (1955), a classic of cold war sociology, the problem of falsification is extensively discussed—for example, reports of overfulfilment of a production target, as when 'the readiness of the machines within a Machine Tractor Station is of such a nature that half of the tractors may break down within a week' (Mead, 45).
13. The day before their departure they hosted five American correspondents at Moscow's House of Journalists (Dom Zhournalista) and toasted the 'end of the cold war'. The cold war, however, was far from over, and the group were arbitrarily barred from the Detroit area by the State Department on a tit-for-tat basis. On 24 October they cancelled their visit to Chicago after hostile jostling from Slavic demonstrators in Cleveland. Soviet dispatches complained about 'drunken hooligans' in Cleveland, Phoenix, and Los Angeles picketing their hotels (*NYT* 30 Sept., 6, 12, 20, 25 Oct., 8, 20 Nov. 1955; *CSM* 16 Nov. 1955).
14. *NYT* 26 Dec. 1955. Polevoy and his colleagues made much of American 'lust for money', citing the case of John Gilbert Graham, accused of blowing up an airliner to collect his mother's insurance.

15. Bowers, 171.
16. This claim was described by Robert Conquest as 'quite unjustified' (Conquest 1960, 167).
17. Harrison Salisbury reporting in the *NYT* 21 May 1959.
18. *NYT* 23 Apr. 1959.
19. On 3 March the Central Committee reacted to the Ministry's revised proposals, adding a new stipulation: 'reactionary' writers like Dos Passos and Jules Romain should be excluded from the book section devoted to foreign works translated in the USSR (RGANI, Fond 5, op. 36, ed.kh. 88).
20. Ibid.
21. Perhaps best known for his regular, weekly 'Letter From America' for BBC radio, still running after 50 years.
22. *MG* 1 July 1959.
23. As an adjunct to the Coliseum exhibition, the Russians invited the American public to inspect the TU-114, the world's largest, turbine-propeller driven commercial plane, at Idlewild Airport. The *NYT* (30 June) commented that the interior was less Victorian and heavy-handed than that of the TU-104.
24. Five female and one male model displayed the work of Russian fashion designers from the GUM department store, the House of Fashion, and from a Moscow custom design house. Klara Pobedinskaya, a staff designer at GUM, explained that a new collection was shown at the Moscow store every month. Soviet customers (she said) jotted down the styles they preferred and the most popular ones were put into production.
25. Salisbury (1960), 56.
26. RGANI Fond 5, op. 36, ed.kh. 88.
27. Including American Express, General Foods, General Mills, and Grand Union.
28. Hixson, 168–9, 175, 189.
29. Notably in *Krokodil*, three weeks before the opening. See *NYT* 18 Apr. 1959; London *Observer*, 5 July 1959.
30. *NYT* 18 June 1959.
31. These documents carry titles like: 'On Countermeasures in Connection with the Forthcoming United States National Exhibition in Moscow'; 'On the Completion of Measures on Agitation and Propaganda Work Among the Population for the Duration of the National United States exhibition in Moscow'; 'Information of a Group of Party Activists of the Glavlit [Office of Censorship]'.
32. Hixson, 186–9.
33. Aged 20 to 35, the unsalaried guides received free transportation and $16 p.d.
34. Hixson, 171, 147, 198. The Little Rock, Arkansas, situation had precipitated a crisis in the fall of 1957, when Eisenhower sent in 1,000 paratroopers after Governor Orville Faubus called out the National Guard to prevent nine black children enrolling in the high school. The pictures of visceral hatred in the streets proved to be a worldwide disaster—though not for the Kremlin. Grasping the nettle, the organizers of the US exhibition at the 1958 Brussels World Fair had

settled for candour: a section called 'Unfinished Business' frankly informed visitors that 'these 17 million Negroes have yet to win all of the equal rights promised them by American democratic theory'. This caused a storm of protest from Southerners like Senator Olin Johnston (SC). Eisenhower and his secretary of state, Christian Herter, were far from happy with 'Unfinished Business'. Photos of mixed groups of schoolchildren and a photo of a black boy dancing with a white girl were hastily removed; a guard was posted in front of the exhibit to prevent the press from witnessing the removal.

35. Walter Hixson blames Soviet CP agitators for the aggressive challenges on the race issue to the American guides, including the four blacks (Hixson, 198).

36. Nixon, 255–6, 260.

37. Stephen J. Whitfield has commented in this connection that the push-buttons designed to make housework easier came from the same laboratories as the push-buttons for guided missiles. General Motors, Chrysler, GE, Goodyear, and Westinghouse were all major Pentagon contractors. Enlarging the defence budget, Goodyear ads claimed, would also result in safer, more durable tyres for the family car (Whitfield, 73–5). Z. Brzezinski turned this point against the Soviet system when he noted that compartmentalization of secret military research from the rest of the economy had meant that many skills were lost to the economy as a whole (cited by Conquest 1980, 113).

38. *NYHT* 27 July 1959.

39. 'U.S. Fair Derided by Soviet Press' was the headline of Max Frankel's report on 29 July. Although some Soviet commentators spoke kindly of 'The Family of Man' photographic exhibition, *Pravda* devoted half a page to expressions of disbelief that the average American family earned $90 a week. Accusing the electronic question-answering machine of glossing over the real facts about American unemployment, *Izvestiia* published a long article on the plight of evicted tenants and of debt-ridden, jobless, starving people roaming the USA (*NYT* 29 July 1959). Soviet reporters, visiting southern Italy, discovered that during the past year 1,200 children had been sold for transportation to the USA at prices ranging from $1,000 to $1,500. *Komsomol'skaia pravda* reported that robbery and rape was common in American high-school corridors. In December 1958 90 pupils and teachers had lost their lives in a Chicago school fire; the Soviet paper reported that on average 2,100 American schools were burnt down each year.

40. On 2 August Max Frankel reported that 7 out of 10 Russians rated the exhibition good or excellent; 5 out of every 100 rated it poor or very poor. But only 1,500 out of 500,000 visitors during the first week had the opportunity to use the voting machines.

41. *NYT* 5 Aug. 1959.

42. *NYT* 14 Sept. 1959. The next day NASA announced that it possessed no such information about Soviet moon-rocket failures. Khrushchev—now in the USA—declared that he would 'swear on the Bible' that there had been none—and challenged Nixon to do the same. After Khrushchev presented Eisenhower with

a model of the Soviet moon pennants, Ike told a news conference that he suspected the metal sphere carrying the pennants had 'probably vaporized' on impact (*NYHT* and *NYT* 18 Sept. 1959).

43. Casson, cited by Fyvel, 79.

44. O. G. Baiar and P. N. Blashkevich, *Kvartira i ee ubranstvo* (Moscow, 1962).

45. The new design journal *Dekorativnoe iskusstvo SSSR* informed readers about international modernism and 'The Organization of Interior Space', displaying interiors by Frank Lloyd Wright, Mies van der Rohe, and Le Corbusier. The first major exhibition of Soviet prototypes for mass production was held in 1961 under the title 'Art and Life', a constructivist slogan of the 1920s. Susan E. Reid associates this exhibition with attempts to rehabilitate the productivist theories of the Left Front of the Arts (Lef), and other Western-influenced modernist tendencies in disgrace since the early thirties. She notes that in 1962 the first secretary of the USSR Artists Union, Sergei Gerasimov, identified 'philistine bad taste', vulgarity, and sentimentality with the Stalinist legacy and personality cult (Reid, 'Destalinization', 198, n. 47, citing V. Gerasimov, 'Idei i resheniia XXII s'ezda KPSS—v zhizn! (Ideas and decisions of the 22nd Congress of CPSU—in life!)', *Iskusstvo*, 2 (1962), 2–7).

46. Alain Besançon, *Soviet Survey* (Jan. 1963), quoted by Priscilla Johnson (1965), 172. A parallel development was occurring in the GDR, which originally prioritized housing, architecture, and city planning but by the late 1950s was shifting the emphasis towards commodities and domestic spaces, a development signalled by the founding of the flagship journal *Form und Zweck* and the magazine *Kultur im Heim* as well as the Institüt für Innengestaltung. The fifties crusade against what was called the 'decadent formalism of cold functionalism' yielded in the 1960s to a moving away from the German arts-and-crafts tradition towards modern styling. The 5th German Art Exposition in 1962 incorporated designers to provide new sources of effective identification with the state, alongside writers and artists. In 1963 the Zentralinstitut (after 1972 Amt) für industrielle Formgestaltung was founded to promote East German design at home and abroad (see Betts, *passim*).

47. However, suppressed iconographies from the 1920s were beginning to surface: one display recalled El Lissitsky's work, a radical-modernist free-standing sculpture made from rusted metal twisted like snakes, combined with bricks, images of fascist destruction, and an expressive, wide-mouthed, staring-eyed face, but lacking any referent in human anguish or desire.

Chapter 3. Broadway Dead, Says Soviet Critic

1. Smelianksky, p. xx.

2. Alliluyeva (1967), 207

3. See *Soviet Studies*, IV/1 (July 1952), 205–9; Counts, 119.

4. 'Za vysokoe kachestvo repertaura dramaticheskikh teatrov' (For a high quality of repertory drama theatre), *Kul'tura i zhizn'*, 11 Mar. 1948 (quoted by Swayze, 54–5).

5. Swayze, 58.
6. A Chicago lawyer is desperately searching for the Russian heir to a fortune of many millions following the death of an American heiress. Heavily targeted is a cynically ruthless attaché at the US Embassy.
7. Parks, 121. A Soviet critic writing in 1952, and cited by H. Lazareff, listed some Soviet plays exposing 'the Anglo-American imperialist warmongers'. Titles mentioned included *Golos Ameriki* (*Voice of America*) by B. Lavrenev, in which a senior American army officer, Walter Kidd, joins the 'forces of peace and justice'; in *Liudi dobroi voli* (*People of Good Will*) by G. Mdivani, a people reunited in a single democratic government foils the machinations of the imperialists masquerading under the UN flag (Lazareff, 114–16).
8. Segel, 328.
9. *Court of Honour* is remembered by Milan Kundera in his novel *The Joke*. It is discussed in Ch. 5 below, 'Soviet Cinema Under Stalin'. In K. Simonov's *Alien Shadow*, Trubnikov, director of a Soviet bacteriological institute, makes an important medical discovery, but before he can publish his findings an old friend from Moscow appears with cunning talk of 'universal science' and 'humanism', and persuades him to turn over the results of his research to a visiting American delegation. The friend turns out to be an American spy; the Americans are interested because the discovery can hurt as well as heal. A colleague tells the naively trusting discoverer: 'You see how good and evil clashed, two worlds, theirs and ours, over this discovery' (Parks, 122).
10. Salisbury (1955), 74.
11. *CSM* 9 Feb. 1955.
12. Kulikova looked back to progressive theatres of the thirties, like Harold Clurman's Group Theatre and Eve Le Gallienne's Civic Repertory Theatre. But owing to unequal competition with the commercial theatre, they had either closed down or, as with the Theatre Guild, degenerated (Kulikova 1947, 56).
13. Including *Born Yesterday*, whose heroine is the stupid but beautiful lover of a millionaire. Driven by business instincts, the millionaire employs a journalist to introduce the curly-haired object of his love to culture. As in Shaw's *Pygmalion*, the young heroine is rapidly educated under the eye of her tutor, but in *Born Yesterday* she then sets out with him, leaving behind the millionaire. American 'Pygmalion' characters, Kulikova sighed, are not constrained as regards the means for achieving their ends.
14. The Soviet title was *Prodavets l'da griadet* (*The Salesman of Ice Cometh*).
15. Kulikova (1947), 57.
16. O'Neill, 32.
17. Morozov 64.
18. Ibid. 60, 64. Original titles: *Russkie liudi*; *Nashestvie*.
19. Ibid. 61; Jean Genet, *The Thief's Journal*, trans. Bernard Frechtman (New York, 1965; Paris, 1949).

20. Starring Laurette Taylor in the pivotal part of the mother, Amanda, the play opened in Chicago on 26 December 1944 and was saved from oblivion by the enthusiasm of two local critics. It opened in New York on 31 March 1945, won the Drama Critics Circle Award as best play of 1945, and two road companies were created to perform the play across the country. Tom Wingfield, a would-be writer held down by a menial job in a shoe factory, is both narrator and character. His withdrawn sister Laura, a cripple, suffers from a paralysing inferiority complex. Their mother Amanda, long since deserted by her husband, struggles against poverty while fantasizing not only about her own past but her daughter's future as someone's bride.

21. Morozov, 62.

22. Tennessee Williams (1956), 2.

23. A strong influence on the symbol-haunted Williams was D. H. Lawrence, the intertwining of the sensual and the spiritual, with Chekhov off-stage as a *beau idéal*. Williams is said to have carried Hart Crane's poems with him everywhere. See Lyle Laverick, *Tom: The Unknown Tennessee Williams* (London, 1995), and Tennessee Williams, *Memoirs* (London, 1976).

24. Kulikova (1949), 86.

25. Ibid. 87

26. State Senator Jack B. Tenney chaired California's Fact-Finding Committee on Un-American Activities from 1941 to 1949. The Actors' Laboratory Theatre was one of his targets. In his report for 1948 he listed several thousand individuals (Kulikova 1949, 91).

27. T. S. Eliot's verse tragedy about the murder in Canterbury Cathedral of Archbishop Thomas Becket (Kulikova 1949, 89). Kulikova uses the Russian title *Ubiistvo v khrame. Khram* can mean 'cathedral' or 'temple'.

28. According to whom, during a 12-month period, 50 % of actors worked for only 6 weeks, 25 % did not work at all, and a lucky 25 % for up to 16 weeks; 50 % of actors earned less than $760 a year, while 25 % were on an average of $305, compared to the official average family wage of $4,000 (Lapitsky, 100, 104). See also Fisunov, another report on 'the decline of the American theatre', citing sad cases of unemployed theatre artists, including the New York tenor William White working as a lift operator; the New York singer Olga Khotkovskaia working as a cashier in a cafeteria; and the Hollywood actress Coleen Townsend, star of *Willy Returns Home*, who, not wishing to be found to be out of work, 'heroically' enrolled in the choir of a Presbyterian church in a town in Pennsylvania (Fisunov, 106).

29. Eliot's earnings from *The Cocktail Party* worldwide finally amounted to £29,000 (worth at least half a million pounds today), but the British taxman took back £25,000 (Robert Sencourt, *T. S. Eliot: A Memoir* (London, 1971), 153).

30. Quoted in Werth (1949), 9. Eliot was hardly a 'Sartrist', quite apart from the discrepancy of age. Sartre's 'hell is other people'—*l'enfer, c'est les autres*, contrasts with Eliot's 'What is hell? Hell is oneself, | Hell is alone, the other figures | Merely projections'.

31. ALEX: There are also foreign agitators | Stirring up trouble (Eliot, 163).
32. Lapistky, 100–2.
33. Eliot, 163.
34. 'You may be sure that if Eliot had joined the British Union of Fascists, we would never hear the last of it', writes Hermoine Lee, reviewing a biography of Vivienne Eliot (*TLS* 5148 (30 Nov. 2001), 4).
35. Ackroyd, 243, 171, 247.
36. Early the following year he solicited public support from fellow-poets, visited Pound in St Elizabeth's asylum, and—what caused the public outcry—served on the jury of Fellows of the Library of Congress in February 1949 which awarded Pound the annual Bollingen Prize for *The Pisan Cantos*.
37. The Communist evening paper, but Lapitsky did not say so.
38. Lapitsky, 102.
39. *Sovetskoe iskusstvo* (29 Mar. 1952), 2, cited by Swayze, 77–9.
40. Swayze, 79. Rühle (1960), 43. Pravda's startling editorial (7 Apr. 1952) had been preceded by preparatory articles, including one by the dramatist Nikolai Pogodin in *Teatr* no. 8 (1951) and no. 4 (1952), who drily commented that he could find on the Soviet stage 'only good, very good, and exceedingly good persons'. Full documentation of the debate was published in 1953 in *Sowjetische dramatik 1946–1952*, by the publisher A. Kukhoff, Verlag Kultur und Fortschritt.
41. Rühle cited as an example *Sons of Moscow* by N. Roshkov, which 'derived its entire plot from an argument between two Stakhanovite workers about the technological details involved in further rationalization of high-speed forging. Another play dealt with the quarrels of two progressive lovers who were unable to agree on the best method of hilling potatoes' (Rühle 1960, 43).
42. Rühle (1959), 11.
43. Sergei Mikhailov came up with *Raki* (*The Crabs*, 1953), a modernization of Gogol's satire *The Inspector-General*. The plot centred around an intelligent young man who hoodwinks a high-ranking plant manager (a Party member) and his conceited wife into believing that he intends to marry their daughter. On the wedding day he absconds, taking the plant's funds with him. A whole swarm of corrupt and dull-witted Soviet bureaucrats, functionaries, and police are led by the nose and exposed to ridicule. *The Crabs* had been extremely popular, said Harrison Salisbury, 'because this sort of thing is happening all the time in the rural USSR—except that usually no one gets caught'.
44. Swayze, 98–9; Segel, 335–6.
45. Mehnert, 114–15.
46. 'V kollegii ministerstva kul'tury SSR. O p'ese L. Zorina "Gosti" ', *Sovetskaia kul'tura*, 5 Jun. 1954. Lazareff, 141–2.
47. Shteyn's target in *A Personal Matter* was the lack of democracy within the Party and the use of Party position to settle personal scores. A jealous Party official attempts to oust a talented engineer from the Party and to deprive him of an important professional position. The play ends with justice being done (Segel, 337).

48. A common theme of Thaw plays was corruption in high places, misuse of authority, privilege, and bourgeois materialism on the part of Party officials. Other examples are Viktor Rozov's *V dobryi chas!* (*Good Luck*) and Aleksei Arbuzov's *Gody stranstviia* (*Years of Wandering*), described as 'controversial' by Komissarzhevsky.

49. Rühle (1960), 46.

50. Conquest (1967), 129.

51. Reeve, 110–14, 124, 126.

52. Swayze, 177–9; Segel, 344–8.

53. Komissarzhevsky (1959), 162. A photograph shows A. Moskalyova as the wife Xenia, overdressed and wearing a double row of pearls, her expression mean and angry, while the handsome Yevgeny Samoilov, as construction chief Sukhodolov, gazes forthrightly into his own heart.

54. *Encounter*, X/2 (Feb. 1958), 58.

55. Spender (1958), 76.

56. In 1957 the Soviet critic Komissarshevsky emphasized the wide variety of foreign plays currently on Soviet stages: *Lady Windermere's Fan* (Wilde), *Pygmalion* and *Mrs Warren's Profession* (Shaw), Eduardo de Filippo's *My Family* and his 'democratic comedy' *Filumena Marturano*, 'which depicts the fight of an ordinary Italian woman for her family and human dignity', Sartre's *Lizzie MacKay* (the Soviet title for *The Respectful Prostitute*), Molière, Thackeray's *Vanity Fair*, Ibsen's *Ghosts*, Gerhardt Hauptmann's *Before Sundown*, and Lope de Vega's *Dancing Master*, which enjoyed a run of 800 performances.

57. Later the Royal Shakespeare Company (RSC).

58. *Observer*, 11 Jan. 1959. The film *Circus Festival*, which reached America in the spring of 1958, showed performers from eleven countries under the big top during the World Youth Festival. Writing in the *NYT* (17 Mar. 1958), H.H.T. found the acts 'astounding', whether acrobats from Bulgaria, Hungary, and Czechoslovakia, or Russian bears on motorbicycles, or remarkable Chinese jugglers. H.H.T. concluded that 'big-top audiences in Moscow behave exactly like the crowds at Madison Square Garden'.

59. *ST* 16 Jan. 1959. Some of Hall's comments were ill-informed or worse: e.g. his allegation that in the USSR there was 'very little dramatic criticism, and none in the newspapers which, in any case, were owned by the "same firm" as the theatres'.

60. e.g. 'The Literary Scene in Autumn 1956', unsigned, *Soviet Survey*, 9 (1956), in Laqueur, 23.

61. Shostakovich (1979), 60.

62. See Caute (1994), 46.

63. *Moscow News*, no. 14, 10–16 Apr. 2002, 6.

64. RGANI Fond 5, op. 36, ed.kh. 21.

65. Wekwerth, 20. By 1956 attacks on the monopoly of the Stanislavsky system were heard from Meyerhold's disciple Nikolai Okhlopkov and by disciples of

Vakhtangov. This found its way into *Teatr*, 8 (1958), V. Prokofiev and G. Dristi, 'K sporam o sisteme Stanislavskogo' (The Debate about the Stanislavsky System).

66. Komissarzhevsky (1959), 38–41.

67. Rühle (1960), 40, quoting J. Jelagin, *Taming of the Arts* (New York, 1951), 172–3. No original Russian source given.

68. Harrison E. Salisbury added: 'A dozen dramatists, among them Isaac Babel, Artem Vesely, Vladimir Kirshon, and Sergei Tretyakov, vanished into the concentration camps.' Tairov's Kamerny Theatre had carried on until closed during the anticosmopolitan campaign (Salisbury 1968, 150).

69. The knife between his teeth.

70. Directed by N. Petrov, V. Pluchek, and S. Yutkevich.

71. Brecht (1993), 460.

72. M. A. Rostotsky (1955), 31–4.

73. Malnick, 250.

74. e.g. N. Okhlopkov, 'Under the Name of Mayakovsky', *Sovetskaia kul'tura*, 13 Feb. 1954, 3; Laufer, 19.

75. Alexandrova, 76–7; Smeliansky, 6. Born in Russia, Alexandrova was in 1952 editor-in-chief of the Chekhov Publishing House, New York. She wrote regularly for *Novoe russkoe slovo*, *New Leader*, and *Saturday Review*. Alexandrova contributed 'Soviet Literature: 35 Years of Purge' to *Problems of Communism*, 1/2 (1952), and 'Soviet Literature Since Stalin' in issues 4/3 (1954) which, paradoxically, also contained a description by Leo Laufer of the Moscow Satirical Theatre production of *The Bathhouse* in December 1953. Her study, 'Control of Soviet Literature in the Post-Stalin Period (1953–1956)', was sponsored by Columbia University's project on the history of the Soviet Party.

76. Petrov, 524.

77. Mayakovsky had demanded a quality of 'spectacle' (*zrelishchnost'*), from the theatre just as the founder of the Moscow Art Theatre, Nemirovich-Danchenko, had called for the 'theatrical' dimension—very much the same thing. The other two qualities or 'waves' required by Nemirovich-Danchenko for a 'full-value' theatrical product were the 'social' and the 'lifelike'—precisely what Mayakovsky called (variously) 'agitational', 'propagandist', and 'tendentious'. As for Nemirovich-Danchenko's demand for the 'lifelike' (*zhiznennyi*), that must be the same as Mayakovsky's 'full of life' (*zhivoi*)—and so Petrov rambled on (Petrov, 521–2).

78. *zerkal'no-mertvym otrazheniem deistvitel'nosti*.

79. Petrov, 523.

80. The company was headed by doyen Jean Yonnel and doyenne Béatrice Bretty, plus Berthe Bovy, Germaine Rouer, Maurice Escande, and Jean Meyer among others. The Comédie française put on *Tartuffe* and *Le Cid* at the Mali Theatre, *Le Bourgeois Gentilhomme* at the Vakhtangov and the Leningrad Small Opera House. *Combat* struck a sour note when it linked Molotov's visit to the theatre to the Soviet campaign to keep France out of the European Defence Community, and to break up the Western bloc (*LM* and *Combat*, 23 Apr. 1954).

81. For an extended eulogy, see *L'Humanité*, 5, 9, 14, 15, 23 Apr. 1954; *LM* 23 Apr. 1954.
82. Zubov, 67–8.
83. Iosif Iuzovsky, 'Gamlet i drugie', *Teatr* 2 (1956), 145, cited by Smeliansky, 218. But Soviet critics could not accept Brook's stated position, in his programme note, that it was Hamlet's tragedy that he mistakenly believed he could commit a murder without being changed by it; the true Hamlet will not be able to go on living once he has been stained (Smeliansky, 7). In 1946, the year in which Stalin disparaged Eisenstein's film portrait of Ivan the Terrible as a weak-willed Hamlet, the editor in chief of *VOKS Bulletin*, Vladimir Kemenov, had cited Goethe's verdict that the fault lay not in Hamlet's weakness of character but, as Hamlet himself explained, ' . . . the native hue of resolution | Is sickled o'er with the pale cast of thought' (Kemenov 1946, 46). For an examination of Hamlet and Soviet culture, see Maya Turovskaya, 'Gamlet i my', in her *Pamiati tekushchego mgnoveniia* (Moscow, Sovetskii pisatel', 1987), 8–32.
84. Berlin (1980), 186–7.
85. Shostakovich (1979), 65.
86. The cast on this occasion was headed by Michael Redgrave, Dorothy Tutin, Richard Johnson, Geraldine McEwan, and Angela Baddeley. Eleven performances were given in Leningrad, fifteen in Moscow.
87. *ST* 14 Dec. 1958.
88. Bowers, 102–3.
89. Yevgeny Samoilov played Hamlet in N. Okhlopkov's controversial production, with its modernistic stage set (by the designer Ryndin), a huge grid of bolted iron squares, framing open rooms on two levels. An English visitor, Bertha Malnick, found the Moscow audience fiercely divided. Okhlopkov was by the late 1950s senior stage director of the Mayakovsky Theatre. Bertha Malnick mentions the perplexed reaction of Moscow audiences to Theatre Workshop's modern-dress version of *Macbeth*, seen in Moscow in the summer of 1957 (Malnick, 250; Komissarzhevsky 1959, 160).
90. Komissarzhevsky (1959), 148, 168–70.
91. Nine years after their first visit to Russia, Paul Scofield and Peter Brook returned with what was now the Royal Shakespeare Company, this time bringing *Lear* rather than *Hamlet*. The drama correspondent of Tass praised Brook's production for avoiding the fashionable habit of modernizing the classics, and for 'preserving the style and feeling of the original period' (*DW* (London), 3 Apr. 1964; *SN* 8 Apr. 1964). The visit was timed to coincide with the 400th anniversary of Shakespeare's birth, with massive celebrations, conferences, and performances in every Soviet language, plus huge printed editions and a documentary film by the Moscow Newsreel Studio. Meanwhile Lenfilm Studios was releasing Grigory Kozintsev's two-part film of *Hamlet*, with music by Shostakovitch and Innokenty Smoktunovsky in the title role. Also in the cinemas was Laurence Olivier's *Richard III*. In September 1965 President Mikoyan led ten minutes of applause at the Kremlin Theatre for Olivier's *Othello* (Elsom, 73).

92. Peter Daubeny was the impresario. Solodovnikov settled for the Sadler's Wells, which seated 1,700 spectators, after complaining that most London theatres were too small for his actors—a common Russian obsession.

93. In May 1964 the Moscow Art Theatre arrived at the Aldwych Theatre, London, with a repertoire including the inevitable Chekhov (*The Cherry Orchard*), Pogodin's *Kremlin Chimes*, and Gogol's *Dead Souls*. In February 1965, 67 members of the Moscow Art Theatre arrived for the company's first visit to New York since 1924.

94. First published in Russian by an émigré press, then in Columbia University's Slavic Studies series, the book conspicuously lacked an epilogue treating the subsequent Thaw and revitalization of Soviet theatre, an omission which reflected no credit on the American and British publishers, Columbia and Oxford.

95. Malnick, 286, reviewing Gorchakov. What Malnick failed to recognize is that Party-directed liberalizations, such as the one celebrated in *Spektakli etikh let*, were not and could not be genuine liberalizations. Her naivety on the question of power is fully conveyed by her admiration for the new theatrical emphasis on portraying Lenin 'in the ordinary way', e.g. Boris Smirnov's performance in Pogodin's *Kremlin Chimes*: 'The greatness of Lenin is revealed not by increasing the distance between him and his surroundings but, paradoxically, by shortening it.' Malnick naively welcomed this as 'a revision of political thinking which excludes the cult of personality' (ibid. 292).

96. Rühle (1960), 49.

97. Smeliansky, 2.

98. Viktor Rozov, introd. to Reeve, p. ix.

99. Successor to the London *Daily Worker*.

100. Lyubimov was born in 1917 of unpromising paternity: his grandfather was later dispossessed as a kulak, while his father was imprisoned as a 'nepman' after the New Economic Policy was abandoned. As a young man Lyubimov himself worked for seven years in the theatre ensemble of the NKVD, was moulded in the Vakhtangov Theatre, played in Fadeyev's *The Young Guard*, in Arthur Miller's *All My Sons*, and (like Oleg Yefremov) joined the Party after Stalin's death, having won a Stalin Prize.

101. Lyubimov included Brecht's *The Life of Galileo* in his repertoire.

102. Beumers, 102–3.

103. In the play a party meeting is called to criticize Mayakovsky: ' "Why don't you make everything beautiful the way they do at the Bolshoi Theater?" a woman party member demands' (Salisbury, 'Theater' (1968), 154).

104. Salisbury, 'Theater' (1968), 155. Smeliansky uncharitably describes the Taganka as recognized by the regime as the place where criticism was OK, chic; Lyubimov was in danger of becoming a tamed dissident (Smeliansky, 101).

105. Voznesensky's *Protect Your Faces* (*Beregite vashi litsa*) was banned from the repertoire of theatre in 1971 because of a reference to the moon taken as an allusion to American manned-landing triumphs.

106. Elsom's quoted source on Furtseva's behaviour at the Taganka is Valerie Zolotu-chin, *Teatr*, 6 (1989), title of article not given (Elsom, 83–4, 77; Smeliansky, 43–4).
107. Smeliansky, p. xvi.
108. *Dix jours qui ébranlèrent le monde*.
109. *The Times*, 3, 5, 13–15, 17 Sept. 1983; 25 Jan.; 7, 8 Mar.; 8 May; 27 July 1984.

Chapter 4. *The Russian Question*: A Russian Play

1. Berlin (2000), 59.
2. *NYT* 20 Apr. 1946.
3. Truman put before Congress legislation to take over industries he deemed vital to the national economy, including powers to draft strikers back to work under imposed wage settlements. The president's proposals were rejected.
4. 'News and Views of Three Visiting Russian Writers', *NYT* 19 May 1946, sec. VII, 3.
5. Corliss Lamont, chairman of the NCASF, Joseph E. Davies, former ambassador to Moscow, Senator Elbert D. Thomas, of Utah.
6. Simonov (1946), 33, 35.
7. Act I, Scene 1, MacPherson's office; Scene 2, The Press Bar. Act II, Scene 1, Smith's home four months later; Scene 2, The same ten days later. Act III, Scene 1, MacPherson's office; Scene 2, The Press Bar; Scene 3, Smith's home ten days later.
8. Gould (called Field in Simonov's original script) engaged in over-heated sexual banter with Jessie which had to be cut: 'Jessie: There is no reason why I should flirt with someone who has undressed me five hundred times' (RGALI, Fond 1814, op. 1, ed.kh 257).
9. Simonov, *Russkii* (1949), 14, 15.
10. Ibid. 15, 16.
11. Ibid. 25.
12. Ibid. 25, 40, 41.
13. Ibid. 29.
14. Ibid. 38.
15. Ibid. 38–9.
16. Ibid. 24.
17. Ibid. 41.
18. *Dovol'no predostavliat' monopoliiu na chestnost' kommunistam*.
19. Simonov, *Russkii* (1949), 49.
20. Ibid. 58.
21. Simonov, *Russkii* (1949), 60.
22. Ibid. 63–4.
23. If MacPherson had originally acquired *all rights* from Smith in return for the $30,000, then he would have assigned (sub-contracted) specific publishing rights to Kessler and would have a clause by which he retained control over the content of the book.

24. Simonov, *Russkii* (1949), 66.
25. Williams was originally called Jefferson in Simonov's script.
26. Simonov, *P'esy* (1949), 67.
27. Simonov, *Russkii* (1949), 74.
28. Ibid. 80.
29. RGALI, Fond 1814, op. 1, ed.kh 257.
30. *ne nado sverkh amerikanskogo tempa*. Ibid. See also S. Dreiden, 'Nezauriadnoe schast'e Garri Smita' (The Exceptional Happiness of Harry Smith), in *Teatral'nyi al'manakh* (Leningrad, 1947). Dreiden's article cited K. Simonov's author's notes in a collection of materials on the play, 'Neskol'ko avtorskikh zamechanii', in *Russkii vopros. Sbornik, materialy k postanovke pesy K. Simonova* (Moscow, 1947).
31. 'Une pièce vivante, pleine de scènes dramatiques, qui constitue un réquisitoire contre les magnats de la presse aux États-Unis.'
32. V. Aleksandrov, 3; Surkov, 17.
33. V. Aleksandrov, 3, 5.
34. Ibid. 8.
35. Ibid. 10.
36. Not 'like a top' (*volchok*), as in the English translation. The Simonov text (*Russkii*, 1949) says, *Ia ne globus*—'I'm not a globe', 46.
37. V. Aleksandrov, 15.
38. Ibid.
39. RGALI, Fond 1814, op.1, ed.kh 258.
40. Ibid., ed.kh 257.
41. The famous Lyubov' Orlova appeared as Jessie in another Moscow production in May, at the Mossoviet Theatre (ibid. ed.kh 258).
42. Surkov had not seen Simonov's previous play, *Pod kashtanami Pragi* (*Under the Chestnut Trees of Prague*, 1945), which had not succeeded. The most severe critic of it, Surkov recalled, turned out to be Simonov himself. In his speech to the All-Union Congress of theatrical personnel and dramatists, he came down on (*obrushilsia*) the production; the cast had concentrated too much on everyday life and sacrificed the political themes. The American critic Segel later described *Under the Chestnut Trees of Prague* as a vehicle for the 'smoke screen' masking Russia's true intentions.
43. Surkov, 16.
44. Ibid. 17.
45. Ibid. 18–20; Segel, 327.
46. Originally DIAS, Drahtfunk im Amerikanischen Sektor.
47. This German-language station was not to be confused with the English-language American Forces Network. See also *MG* 7 Feb. 1946.
48. *SE* 14 Apr. 1946.
49. Edited by Hans Habe, *DNZ* was mainly run by European, mostly Jewish, émigrés with US citizenship and backgrounds in Psychological Warfare Division of the US Army.

50. Gienow-Hecht, *Transmission* (1999), 58, 95, 103, 132–3, 179–80, 182.
51. *NC* 25 Apr. 1947; *Die Welt*, 26 Apr. 1947, organ of the British military government.
52. *TR* 25 Apr. 1947.
53. 'Das Thema ist nämlich kein spezifische amerikanisches, sondern in erster Linie ein internationales.' See also *NYT* 23 Apr. 1947.
54. Pike, 235.
55. Naimark, 427, 566, n.98.
56. Lange, 522.
57. Novodvorskaia (1949), 108.
58. Echoing Simonov's theme, Borisova complained that 'Clifford of the *Daily Mail*, among others, tried to convince his readers that the USSR wants war' (*SN* 16 May 1947). There were attacks on prejudiced reporting by 'Denny of the Scripps-Howard newspaper trust, Davis of the *Daily News*, the *Chicago Tribune* correspondent Fulton, and Ward of the *Baltimore Sun*'—and all this despite Generalissimo Stalin's well-publicized complaint about American correspondents when he received Harold Stassen. By contrast, Sulzberger of the *NYT* and Hightower of AP stressed the Soviet people's desire for peace, though Sulzberger 'contradicted himself' by claiming the Russians were storing grain in case of war (*SN* 23 May 1947). Borisova found a 'Harry Smith' figure in 'Griffith, who for several years was the Moscow correspondent of the *Observer* and *Manchester Guardian*', and who 'offered one of the big London papers a series of articles about Russia. He got them back six weeks later. . . with the curt advice that they presented the Soviet Union in too favourable a light' (*SN* 28 May 1947). The Rothermeres and Kemsleys, added Borisova, were in this regard no different from the Hearsts and Pattersons, likewise the Australian magnate Sir Keith Murdoch, whose *Melbourne Herald* had sent to Moscow a different 'Smith', not Simonov's good-hearted Harry, but a wicked Trevor Smith, who enraged the Russians by writing: 'Waitresses at the hotels in which we lived, and to whom we gave the sugar that was left over from tea, shed tears and went down on their knees when they took the sugar.' *Soviet News* (6 June) retaliated by publishing a letter from four named waitresses at the Hotel Moskva protesting Smith's lies and slanders: 'It insults our national and professional dignity, and our dignity as women.'
59. Glukhareva, 103–5. Quoting the Communist novelist Jack Lindsay—'Unity is opposed to the whole of English bourgeois theatre art'—Glukhareva noted that during his last visit to London in February 1949, Paul Robeson had appeared at the Unity Theatre (the equivalent of a papal blessing?).
60. *Illustrated* (London), 8 Nov. 1947; Victoria & Albert Theatre Museum, Unity Theatre Archive THM/9/6/5. Production Dates 1947–48.
61. The word 'produced' was normal for 'directed' in the English theatre at that time. However, Colin Chambers gives the director as Bill Owen (Chambers, 299).
62. The play was published in Iran in Farsi; by November 1948 it had been running for three months at a Polish theatre; it came on at the Scala Theatre, Vienna, and by 1954 it was running in Finland, Latvia, Japan, Albania, and Mongolia.

63. Salisbury (1955), 20.

64. Simonov, 'Tasks' (1949), 183–8.

65. Cited by Hahn, 120.

66. Romm (1962). The cast included Ve. Aksenov as Smith.

67. Zak, 165.

68. Simonov's rehearsal notes for the stage play contain the instruction that New York was a city where car horns were banned: 'You hear the rustle of tyres at traffic lights' (RGALI, Fond 1814, op. 1, ed.kh 257).

69. *Istoria*, vol. 3, 134.

70. A sharp attack on the film was delivered by Babitsky and Rimberg (1955) in a book published by the Austrian-born Frederick A. Praeger, the leading anti-Communist publisher in New York. On the evidence (p. 203), Babitsky and Rimberg had not managed to obtain a viewing copy of the film, their quoted source being S. Rozen, 'Sovetskoe kino v bor'be za mir', *Iskusstvo kino*, I, 1950, 2.

71. Deputy-director of the Scientific Research Institute of Cinema Art (Nauchno-Issledovatel'skii Institut Kinoiskusstva).

Chapter 5. Soviet Cinema Under Stalin

1. Alliluyeva (1969), 155–6.

2. 'In this way Greta Garbo and Shirley Temple, Bette Davis and Deanna Durbin, Katharine Hepburn and Spencer Tracey, Myrna Loy and Clark Gable, Barbara Stanwyck and Robert Taylor, were all familiar to me even before the war. Later Ingrid Bergman became my favourite movie actress for a long time' (ibid. 112).

3. Shostakovich (1979), 193.

4. Parks, 98.

5. *Die Frau meiner Träume—Devushka moikh mechtei.*

6. Rökk—who was so closely linked with the Nazi regime that she had trouble resuming a film career after the war—celebrated her 80th birthday in 1993 on German television, with a show called 'Marika Rökk: The Living Legend. A Star Turns 80' (see Kenez, 214; Graffy, 181). A Politburo meeting on 31 August 1948 gave permission for the release of 50 mostly German 'trophy' films. 35 German films are listed with their release dates in A. Demenok and E. Khokhlova, *Kino totalitarnoi epokhi (1933–1945)* (Moscow, 1989), 45–6.

7. Salisbury (1955), 268.

8. RGANI, Fond 5, op., 17, ed.kh. 501.

9. *A Great Life* (*Bol'shaia zhizn'*), originally released in 1939, written by Pavel Nilin and directed by Leonid Lukov, and now revived in an updated version, seemed tailor-made for socialist realism: the reconstruction of the Donets Basin's coal-mines and industry. The sequel dealt with the impact of the war and the difficulties of post-war reconstruction. This 'depraved' film, known as Part 2, offended the Central Committee by showing primitive mining technology, miners living in

filthy, dilapidated barracks, and Soviet citizens collaborating with the German invaders. Even though it had been approved for release with high praise by the Art Council of the Ministry of Cinematography, the Central Committee finally (Sept. 1946) banned distribution on the ground that that the film—which displayed drunken and 'depraved' workers, miserable housing, and callous bosses—was 'extremely weak artistically and ideologically and politically perverted... Songs... saturated with saloon blues and alien to Soviet people, are introduced' (Inkeles, 312–13; Counts, 127). The screenwriter Pavel Nilin duly set about correcting his mistakes. Writing in *Literaturnaia gazeta* (10 Nov. 1948), he described his own efforts to emulate 'the new Soviet man' and make himself 'worthy of our great Stalinist epoch'. This too was reported in ironic tones by American commentators. The revised film remained suppressed until twelve years later, in 1958 (Counts, 144; Leyda, 393). The *Istoriia sovetskogo kino* of the Brezhnev era conceded that the Central Committee's complaint about 'backward and uncultured (*otstalimi i malo kul'turnimi*) people of very low moral quality' in *A Great Life* had encouraged 'idealized, fabricated' film heroes as well as 'various unjust harsh evaluations of the creative work of talented artistic figures' (*Istoriia*, vol. 3, 116).

10. Berlin (1980), 164–5.
11. Bollag, 261–2.
12. Smeliansky, 3.
13. The film (*Bezhin lug*) was apparently destroyed, prints and negatives, during the war when bombs hit the studios, but some clips survive.
14. Kozlov, 112
15. Ibid. 121. Leonid Kozlov obtained this letter from Bolshakov's personal archive.
16. Kuznetsov, interviewed by Kozlov, 123.
17. Uhlenbruch, 278.
18. Kozlov, 126, quoting Mikhail Romm, *Besedy o kino* (Moscow, 1965), 91.
19. Kozlov, 127.
20. *Kul'tura i zhizn'*, a four-page publication, carried on its masthead 'Proletarians of all countries, unite!' and described itself as the Central Committee's organ of propaganda and agitation—*Gazeta upravleniia propagandy i agitatsii tsentral'nogo komiteta VKP(b)*.
21. RGALI, Fond 1923, op. 1, ed.kh. 1370.
22. Eisenstein's 'The Mistakes of *Bezhin Meadow*' had appeared in *Sovetskoe iskusstvo*, no. 18, 17 Apr. 1937, a month after the filming was halted. 'In recent years I have become self-absorbed', he wrote. 'I have retreated into my shell [while] the country fulfilled its Five-Year Plans.'
23. This translation is found in Seton, 460–3. See also Counts, 147.
24. RGALI, Fond 1923, op. 1, ed.kh. 1375.
25. Comment made by Naum Kleiman, interview, Moscow, 5 Apr. 2002. According to Kleiman, it was Cherkasov who set up the meeting. The translation of the conversation is by Richard Taylor and William Powell, who write: 'This account of the meeting on the night of 25 February 1947 was taken down by E[isenstein] and

Nikolai K. Cherkasov... and first published under the general heading "Groznye teni 1947 goda" (The Terrible Shadows of 1947) in *Moskovskie novosti*, 7 August 1988, pp. 8–9, from which this translation has been made' (Taylor 1988, 205, n.1).

26. See Christie, 165; Kenez, 219.

27. RGALI, Fond 1923, op. 1, ed.kh. 1370.

28. Schlesinger (1970), 77 n.

29. Wolfe (1969), 332. See also Barghoorn (1959), 227–8.

30. Macdonald made much of the drastic reduction in production, and films actually released, following the 1946 decree. In 1949 13 feature films were completed but only 6 released; in 1950, 11; in 1951, 9; in 1952, 9. By comparison, in 1951 432 films were produced in the USA, 260 in India, and 96 in Egypt (Macdonald, 31–2).

31. Dickinson, *Soviet Studies*, V/1 (Oct. 1953), 176; Sadoul, *LLF* 12–19 Mar. 1953.

32. *Bol'shaia sovetskaia entsiklopediia* (2nd edn.), vol. 48 (1957), 334.

33. Ibid. (3rd edn.), vol. 29 (1978), 573.

34. *Istoriia*, vol. 3, 91–2. The *Istoriia* does offer some plausible comments as to why Part 1 was less than a popular success when first released early in 1945, while the war against Germany still raged. This elegant film seemed too cold, its stylistic conventions and expressionistic acting alienating audiences, as did excessively introverted (*vnutrennei*) episodes, for example 'Wedding' or the almost balletic 'Ivan's Illness'.

35. The documentary was shown again at the National Film Theatre, London, on 13 March 2001, with an accompanying printed programme note sublimely innocent (one must hope) of this corruption.

36. The Central Committee resolution of 4 September 1946 had condemned V. Pudovkin's *Admiral Nakhimov*. Pudovkin's films included *The End of St Petersburg* (*Konets Sankt-Peterburga*, 1927), *Mother* (*Mat'*, 1926), *Storm Over Asia* (originally *The Heir of Genghis Khan—Potomok Chingis Khana*, 1928), and *General Suvorov* (1941). Pudovkin was accused in the 1946 Central Committee decree of having directed a film 'not about Nakhimov, but about balls and dances with episodes from the life of Nakhimov'. The director had unforgivably left out the important fact that 'in the battle of Sinop a whole group of Turkish admirals, including the commanding officer, were captured'. Pudovkin responded with a 'radical revision of the entire scenario conception of the film'. Cast as the villains of the story, the English double-cross their French and Turkish allies, whose last drop of blood they are, most callously, happy to shed. George S. Counts remarked sardonically: 'Pudovkin demonstrated that he can change history, even as Michurin and Lysenko can change nature' (Counts, 145). Antonín J. Liehm adds: 'Pudovkin, who had, in the last years of his life, became a mere decoration for peace assemblies and congresses, had identified completely with the [Stalinist] style of the epoch.' He died in June 1953, shortly after Stalin (Mira and Antonín Liehm 1977, 69).

37. Six years later another Soviet 'admiral' film, Mikhail Romm's *Admiral Ushakov*, surfaced in New York, this one set in the era of Catherine the Great and Potemkin, but the geopolitical similarities were striking, with Britain and France ganging up

on Russia and wielding the bewildered Turks as a buffer—the British and French ambassadors continually skulk about the St Petersburg waterfront (*NYT* 18 Jan. 1954).

38. *NYT* 27 Dec. 1948.
39. Kenez, 228–32.
40. *Iskusstvo kino*, I/8 (1947), cited by Kenez, 230–1.
41. *Izbrannye* vol. 5, 24.
42. Mira and Antonín Liehm (1977), 70.
43. Hugh Lunghi argued that we should, however, be cautious about celebrating an earlier golden age of tolerance, even before 1930. 'Eisenstein's first picture, *Strike*, was a failure in Russia but won a prize in Paris; even his *Battleship Potemkin* was accepted in Russia only after an initial success in Berlin.' Dovzhenko, Eisenstein's great contemporary, had suffered in Russia because of his films' 'unorthodox and non-naturalist style' (Hugh Lunghi, *Encounter* pamphlet, no. 9, 14–15).
44. As Kenez comments, great artistic talent did not save Soviet directors from less than admirable servility. Vsevelod Pudovkin played a lamentable part in the anti-cosmopolitan campaign. Kenez maintains that '[Fridrich] Ermler, [Ivan] Pyr'ev, [Sergei] Eisenstein, and [Aleksandr] Dovzhenko, among others, made films that justified the terror and encouraged people to denounce each other and be suspicious of those who were closest to them' (Kenez, 252).
45. Pudowkin, Romm und Andere, 92, 94, 101.
46. *LLF* 12–19 Mar. 1953.
47. Said to originate in 1938 in the Limehouse district of East London, the 'Lambeth Walk' was a walking dance done in a jaunty, swaggering, knee-slapping style. Bonnet, it must be said, keeps raising his hand and snapping his fingers in the Lambeth Walk style.
48. *Izbrannye*, vol. 5, 47–51.
49. Kenez, 241. According to Julian Graffy, the fashion for filming the lives of leading composers like Mussorgsky, Rimsky-Korsakov, and two lives of Glinka can be attributed to 'Stalin's inordinate love of *The Great Waltz*, Julien Duvivier's 1938 Hollywood life of Johann Strauss, and to the relative ideological safety of music rather than words' (Graffy, 181). In the 22 December 1947 issue of the *NYT* A. H. Weiler (A.W.) had reviewed *The Great Glinka*, written and directed by Lev Arnshtam for Mosfilm, and found most of its characters one-dimensional, but enjoyed the highlights from the opera *Ivan Susanin* as sung by the Bolshoi Theatre Choir.
50. Kenev cites 'Against Schematisation and Stock Phrases in Biographical Scenarios' by A. Solov'ev, in *Iskusstvo kino*, 5/84 (1952).
51. Anderson, Part I, 8–10. Stalin's impersonator and fellow Georgian, M. Gelovani, was the busiest actor in the industry.
52. Kenez, 242.
53. Pudowkin, Romm und Andere, 91.
54. Irene Nove offered this skilful English version of Yuri Blagov's verses, faithful to the spirit of rhyme in the original and, as a result, fairly free in choice of words. In

fact Blagov merely hinted at a general dozing off in the auditorium rather than 'all asleep': 'a v zale dremliut mezhdu tem . . .'

55. Blagov, 14; Nove, 445.

56. The Research Program on the USSR, published in New York by Praeger, produced a statistical breakdown of heroes and villains in Soviet films. For example, in the years 1945–50 the number of American villains appearing each year was said to have been 0, 0, 0, 1, 5, 4, with the corresponding figures for British villains at 0, 1, 1, 0, 2, 3; Germans at 1, 1, 0, 4, 4, 2; and Russian villains at 0, 2, 2, 0, 0, 2. As regards heroes, only 1 American is given, in 1948, presumably Simonov's Harry Smith in *The Russian Question* (Babitsky and Rimberg, 223–4).

57. *NYT* 18 Mar. 1949; *CSM* 21 Apr. 1949.

58. 'Kak menia predavali sudu chesti . . .' While Romm was shooting *The Russian Question* in 1947, the film industry minister, Ivan Bolshakov, raised a letter written by Romm two years earlier, on the instructions of VOKS, to persuade the émigré actor Mikhail Chekhov to return to the motherland. Versions of the letter that were never sent were now presented as 'grovelling to the West'. Romm threatened to implicate Pudovkin, who in 1945 had asked him to write the letter, and who was now to be one of the judges of the Court of Honour. Pudovkin prevailed on the minister to drop the case (Kenez, 225).

59. 'O gruppe estetvuiushchikh kosmopolitov v kino'.

60. Including the director Leonid Trauberg, the scenarist Mikhail Bleiman, the critics Vladimir Sutryin, Nikolai Otten, and N. Kovarski.

61. Babitsky and Rimberg, 191, citing *Iskusstvo kino*, 1 (1949), 14–15.

62. *Kul'tura i zhizn'*, 10 Mar. 1949, cited by Kenez, 222–3.

63. G. Aleksandrov's hit musicals included *The Circus*, *Volga-Volga* (1938), and *Radiant Path* (*Svetlyi put'*, 1940).

64. On the stage production, see Severin, 52–6.

65. Cited by Kuby, 47.

66. Shostakovich composed several songs for the film, including 'Mir pobedit voinu' (Peace Will Conquer War), which was to become the hymn of the peace movement and was many times heard, according to Aleksandrov's memoirs, in the UN building on New York's East River (G. Aleksandrov, 253).

67. I owe confirmation of this to a resident of Moscow, Vera Adian.

68. 'chelovek kristal'noi chestnosti i chistoty'.

69. The reptilian American officer who chalks the degrading white cross on the young woman's back closely resembles one in Martin Hellberg's East German film *The Condemned Village*.

70. *Istoriia*, vol. 3, 135.

71. Gribachev, 3. Despite occasional mentions of 'cinema art', this long review is entirely given over to political content, and to the script, with no comments on the cinematic form or cinematography. It is simply a 'new victory for Soviet cinema'.

72. Ian Christie describes Aleksandrov and Orlova as the royal family of Soviet cinema. Both had been decorated with the Order of Lenin (Christie, 155–6).

73. G. B. Aleksandrov 255.
74. Ibid. 252.
75. Severin, 55, 56.
76. Stites, 120.
77. Including, among those discussed in this chapter, *The Russian Question*, *Conspiracy of the Doomed*, *They Have a Native Land*, *Secret Mission*, *Michurin*, and *Court of Honour*.
78. G. B. Aleksandrov, 256.
79. Part 1, *The First Front (Pervaia frontovaia vesna)*.
80. *MG* 5 Apr. 1950.
81. According to Artkino, the distributors, some 1.2 million people had already seen the film before it reached the USA.
82. '... vosproizvodiashchikh spokoinuiu, solnechnuiu prirodu strany'.
83. *Voprosy masterstva*, 78.
84. Chiaureli wrote: 'We hold that Alesha Ivanov, the chief protagonist—a Stakhanovite iron and steel worker, is a representative Soviet man'—so representative that he happened to be born on the very day of the revolution, 7 November 1917. 'Life to him is inconceivable without labour, without emulation, without his factory collective' (Chiaureli, 75–8).
85. Chiaureli added: 'Just as a gardener lovingly rears every plant, so Stalin rears the Soviet people and educates the generation of October.'
86. *Voprosy masterstva*, 75.
87. Chiaureli, 81.
88. *Voprosy masterstva*, 75.
89. Alliluyeva (1967), 175.
90. Babitsky and Rimberg, 195.
91. Lawson, 85.
92. *Istoriia*, vol. 3, 138–9.
93. The Soviet Union produced 15 feature films in 1949, 10 in 1950, 9 in 1951, 5 in 1952. These figures do not, however, take account of the filmed plays which occupied an important role in Soviet production: during 1952–3 25 plays were filmed in the most important theatres of Moscow, Leningrad, and Kiev, including Ostrovsky's plays from the Mali Theatre, plus Gorky's *Lower Depths*, Sheridan's *School for Scandal*, and a dramatization of *Anna Karenina* from the Moscow Art Theatre. Each film was released uncondensed in two parts and proved popular, competing on an equal footing with original films (Leyda, 400).
94. Shostakovich (1979), 195.
95. The stage play received the same kind of official promotion as Simonov's *The Russian Question*; by April 1949, according to *Teatr*, it was running in 20 theatres, including the Vakhtangov, the Central Transport Theatre, and the Moscow Art Theatre, and was to be produced in 100 of the country's theatres (*Teatr*, no. 4, Apr. 1949).

96. Joseph L. Anderson claimed that the resemblance of the film's heroine to the Romanian Jewish Communist leader Anna Pauker caused *Conspiracy of the Doomed* to be withdrawn.

97. '*. . . duiushchie v saksofon, lupiashchie v baraban, orushchie dzhazisti*' (*Istoriia*, vol. 3, 134).

98. Turovskaya, 134.

99. Anderson, Part I, 7; Babitsky and Rimberg, 207–8, citing B. Galanov, 'Ekran izoblichaet podzhigatelei voiny' (The Screen Exposes the Warmongers), *Iskusstvo kino*, 3 (1950), 31.

100. I owe this observation to Elena Smolina.

101. Babitsky and Rimberg, 202, citing the screenplay by Yu. Baltushis and Ye. Gabrilovich, 'Nad Nemanon—Rassvet', *Iskusstvo kino*, 3 (1952), 34–5.

102. Co-directed by Vladimir Legoshin, and written by Sergei Mikhailov, author of the original stage play, *I Want to go Home* (*La khochu domoi*, 1949), with music by Khachaturian. Andersen attributes the film to V. Legoshin under the title *They Have a Motherland*.

103. The indignant ripsote to *They Have a Native Land* by the American critics Babitsky and Rimberg was not entirely accurate: the head of the children's shelter, Captain Scott, does not, as they alleged, belong to the intelligence branch of the US Army—he is British (Babitsky and Rimberg, 207, citing Irina Kokareva, 'V zashchitu spravedlivosti', *Iskusstvo kino*, 3 (1950), 30).

104. According to Joseph L. Anderson, of the 9 Soviet features released during the first half of 1952, 3 had anti-American themes: A. Dovzhenko's *Farewell, America*; A. Romm's *Conscience of the World*; and L. Arnshtam's *The Big Warmongers*. 'A. Romm' might be A. Room.

105. *NYT* 12 May 1947.

106. Anderson, Part I, 8–9.

107. '. . . ty poimesh' chto u nas est' tol'ko odni vragi—krasnye! Eto nashi vragi na vsui zhizn''.

108. At the end of the film, driving through the streets of New York in a large limousine, Senator Heywood comments bitterly that the Russians have swept all before them. 'We must prepare for a new war, to the finish. Even if half the human race perishes'—*Dazhe esli ona budet stoit' zhizn' polovine chelovechestva* (Isaev, 129–31, 143, 145, 153, 194).

109. *Istoriia*, vol. 3, 132–3.

110. Romm (1950), 95, 99.

111. Ibid. 97. See also Babitsky and Rimberg, 204, citing Isaev's screenplay.

112. Fifty years after the fall of the Third Reich, the Soviet military HQ in the Karlshorst suburb of Berlin was turned into a museum under scholarly joint German–Russian, post-Communist management. The lengthy narratives in the museum's catalogue, which admit the reality of the Hitler–Stalin Pact, contain no allegation of Anglo-American malfeasance or attempts to negotiate a separate peace. On the contrary, the Western powers are said to have rejected repeated

German proposals for a separate peace from 1944 to April 1945: '... als ihnen von deutscher Seite mehrfach eine Teilkapitulation nur gegenüber dem Westen angeboten wurde/... kogda s nemetskoi storony im neodnokratno byla predlozhena chastichnaia kapituliatsiia tol'ko pered Zapadom' (Museum Berlin Karlshorst catalogue, 50).

113. Produced by Abram Room, directed by P. Armand, and based on the play *Shakaly* (*Jackals*) by the Estonian dramatist Avgust Yanobson, performed at the Mali Theatre. Yanobson and A. Filimonov wrote the screenplay.

114. *NYT* 31 Oct. 1953.

115. See also Marshall MacDuffie, 'Russia Uncensored', *Collier's*, 133/5, 5 Mar. 1954, 92; 'Reds'-Eye View of US', *Life*, 37/15, 11 Oct. 1954, 83–8.

116. Zoom lenses, however, have been utilized with great skill in some dramatic productions, although their chief use was in documentary work. Anderson was also impressed by Soviet film-cartoon technique; a Russian cartoon *The Magic Horse* had won praise in the *NYT* (24 June 1949): 'Despite occasional overdoses of saccharin, and deficiencies in humor, Soviet cartoons are probably the Soviet film industry's finest artistic achievements today... They are pleasantly free of the sickening violence of many American cartoons... The animation techniques are second to none' (Anderson, Part II, 65).

117. No. 3/6 (Nov.–Dec. 1954) and no. 4/1 (Jan.–Feb. 1955).

118. Macdonald, 34.

119. *DW* (London), 8 Jan. 1952. F. Bowen Evans commented in 1954 that: 'Even in countries such as England where Soviet films are shown regularly, the commercial showings are restricted generally to the large cities and even there usually do not attract any great attention.' Meanwhile, the Soviet press attaché invited scores of journalists to the Embassy in Kensington to view an animal cartoon in colour and a documentary about coal-mining mechanization in the Donbas. Those who survived this double bill were treated to a lavish buffet (*ST* 27 Jan. 1952). On 1 Nov. 1952 the British–Soviet Friendship Society took out a spread of ads for British–Soviet Friendship Month, advertising the kind of Soviet films that the wider British public could do without. On display at Battersea Town Hall were *Baltic Deputy* and *Yellow Stork*. Visitors to the Old Council Chambers, Beckenham, could see *Moscow Constructions*. Showing at Bromley Public Library was *Distant Bride*. The Scala Cinema, Charlotte Street, screened *Broken Fetters*, a 'superb colour film about Taras Shevchenko, the Ukrainian national poet', plus *Soviet Latvia*. At Islington Town Hall it was *Donetz Miners*; at the Morden Assembly Rooms, *Ukraine in Bloom*. Wishaw, Scotland, offered an opportunity to see *Moscow Dynamo Stadium*, *Soviet Turkmenistan*, *Soviet Armenia*, and a children's show, *Day at Moscow Zoo*. *New World Review*, a Communist-front organ published in New York, carried in its October 1954 edition an advertisement of Artkino Pictures, Inc., announcing the availability of such new Soviet films—'All in Spectacular Sovcolor'—as *Stars of the Russian Ballet*, *Bride With a Dowry*, *Adventure in Odessa*, *The Mistress*, and *The Inspector-General*.

120. *Istoriia*, vol. 3, 10–11.
121. Ibid. vol. 3, 134.

Chapter 6. Hollywood: The Red Menace

1. HUAC later blasted these films as Communist propaganda. Jack Warner insisted he had made *Mission to Moscow* only at the express personal behest of President Roosevelt.
2. Sayre, 59.
3. Collins was one of the Hollywood Nineteen in 1947. He later named names to HUAC and told the Committee that he and Paul Jarrico had been instructed by MGM to sanitize the script of *Song of Russia*.
4. Leyda, 388.
5. *CSM* 26 Oct. 1948. To what extent the Eric Johnston agreement of October 1948 was implemented is not clear. According to Harrison Salisbury, Soviet cinema managers were so frantic for pictures that three times negotiations were opened up to buy American films. 'But each time Stalin himself had killed the deal. So they bought "proletarian" Italian pictures; "arty French pictures"; an occasional solid British film; and the incredibly mediocre film output of Poland, of Czechoslovakia and China' (Salisbury 1955, 267–8).
6. By 1974 American movies occupied more than 50% of world screen time—no doubt losing money to service the flag (Guilbaut, 136; Bigsby, 4).
7. Guilbaut, 137–8.
8. Pells (1955).
9. See Ceplair and Englund; Ciment (1973); Kazan; Navasky; Suber; Caute (1978).
10. *Soviet Weekly* gave Gerasimov's initial as 'A', surely mistaking him for the leading portrait artist.
11. *Kul'tura i zhizn'*, 30 July 1946.
12. *SW* 29 May 1947, reporting Gerasimov's article in *Izvestiia*, n.d.
13. Bentley, 137–8.
14. Ibid. 302–7.
15. Krims had co-scripted *Confessions of a Nazi Spy* (1939), which (Nora Sayre notes) became a model for the cold war films.
16. *NYT* 11 Apr. 1948.
17. Directed by Felix Feist for the independent producers Jack Wrather and Robert Golden, script by Emmett Lavery from *As We See Russia*, by 'members of the Overseas Press Club of America'.
18. Pryor described it as a plodding film with stereotypical characters about an American reporter who develops a friendship with a Hungarian girl who in turn is in love with a young Soviet colonel. The characters had 'little substance' (*NYT* 11 Apr. 1950).
19. Pudowkin, Romm und Andere, 59, 60.

20. Sayre, 84–5.
21. The print viewed here, and held in the British National Film Archive, carries the latter title. Screenplay by Charles Grayson and Robert Hardy Andrews. See also Philip Roth's novel, *I Married a Communist* (1998), where a woman publishes her account of marriage to a secret and alleged Communist.
22. The conviction was set aside by the Supreme Court in 1954.
23. Sayre, 83.
24. In court Cvetic justified the inclusion of this incident in the film by claiming that Nelson had once confided to him that 'there would be a liquidation of one third of the United States population'. Cross-examined by Nelson, Cvetic revealed that he had been paid $18,000 for serial and motion-picture rights (it was also a successful radio serial), of which he himself retained 40%, the rest being shared by his ghost-writer and his agent-manager Harry Sherman, local vice-president of Americans Battling Communism. This case is discussed in Caute (1978), 216–23.
25. McCarey had been a friendly witness at the HUAC hearings in 1947; three years later he urged members of the Screen Directors Guild to take a loyalty oath. The film was nominated for an Oscar, 'not necessarily because of its virtues, which very few reviewers detected', but as 'a cue to HUAC that Hollywood was vigilant' (Whitfield, 136).
26. Sayre, 96, 98; Whitfield, 136–9; Lawson, 78.
27. Rogin, 251–9.
28. Lawson, 77.
29. These included *The Red Menace* (1949), *I Was a Communist for the FBI* (1951), *My Son John* (1952), *Walk East on Beacon* (1952), and *The FBI Story* (1959).
30. In 1977 Sayre was told that the CIA was leasing some 10 prints a year from Columbia Pictures, including 5 copies dubbed in foreign languages (Sayre, 91; Theoharis and Cox, 207).
31. Sayre, 80–1.
32. Ibid. 81.
33. Three scriptwriters are credited for *Big Jim McLain*: Richard English, Eric Taylor, and James Edward Grant. The original story was by Stephen Vincent Benet.
34. See also *Invasion U.S.A.* (1953), *Night People* (1954), *Special Delivery* (1954), *Trial* (1955), *Red Planet Mars* (1952), *Invaders from Mars* (1953), and *Invasion of the Body Snatchers* (1956).
35. Nadel, 92. In April 1953 Cecil B. DeMille was appointed special consultant to the government's Motion Picture Service (MPS) and promptly advised C. D. Jackson (president of the National Committee for a Free Europe and Eisenhower's special adviser on psychological warfare) how films worked best as propaganda—to make sure that the right line, the right aside, the right inflection, is introduced into normal themes (Saunders 1999, 287–9, 292, citing C. D. Jackson to Henry Luce, 19 May 1953, Psychological Strategy Board Records, Dwight D. Eisenhower Library, Abilene, Kansas). The MPS worked through 135 USIS

posts in 87 countries and deployed all the facilities of a production company. In June 1954 it listed 37 films as suitable for showing behind the Iron Curtain. It also regulated American participation in foreign film festivals. In January 1954 C. D. Jackson listed powerful Hollywood friends of the government, including DeMille, Spyros P. Skouras, Darryl Zanuck, Nicholas Schenk, Dore Schary, Barney Balaban, Harry and Jack Warner, James R. Grainger, Harry Cohn, Walt and Roy Disney, and Eric Johnston—in short, the great moguls of Fox, MGM, Warner, RKO, Columbia, Disney, and the American Picture Association— most of them determined to suppress the harsher side of American life as portrayed by such major novelists as Steinbeck, Caldwell, Faulkner, and Richard Wright.

36. Robert Wuthnow, *The Restructuring of American Religion: Society and Faith Since World War Two* (Princeton, 1988), 66.
37. Sayre, 207.
38. DeMille's mother was Jewish but abandoned the faith to marry Charles DeMille.
39. Nadel, 113–14.
40. DeMille, 393.
41. Nadel, 110.
42. Ibid. 115.
43. DeMille, 386–7.
44. Nadel, 100.
45. Sayre, 207.
46. DeMille, 400.
47. Ibid. 385–6.
48. Corber, cited by Nadel, 28.
49. The son of socialist-Zionist Russian immigrants, Paul Jarrico had been involved in radical student politics at UCLA in the early 1930s. By 1939 he had joined the Party, and belonged to the faction which believed that scriptwriters should, and sometimes could, influence films (Ceplair and Englund, 301–2).
50. Ibid. 417.
51. Kael, 331–2, 336–7, 339, 345.
52. Ceplair and Englund, 413–14.
53. Another heroic gentleman was Werner von Braun, German rocket scientist, architect of the V1 and V2 rocket attacks on London, now working for the USA, and hero of the film *I Aim at the Stars* (1950). The comedian Mort Sahl is reported to have quipped: 'I aimed at the stars and hit London.'
54. Lawson, 89, 83–4.
55. Ibid. 86.
56. Neve, 186. See also Sayre, 176–7.
57. Ranchal, 43.
58. Elaine Tyler May in Lary May, 165.
59. According to Stephen J. Whitfield, Sinatra blocked commercial re-release of the film for a quarter-century after Kennedy's assassination (Whitfield, 213).

60. Written by James Lee Barrett, based on a novel by Robin Moore (later known for his literary celebrations of white Rhodesian counter-insurgency), and directed by John Wayne and Ray Kellogg.
61. Writing in the *NYT* (20 June 1968), Renata Adler described *The Green Berets* as 'a film so unspeakable, so stupid, so rotten and false in every detail . . . It is vile and insane. On top of that, it is dull.' Fred Inglis comments that at a time of anti-war demonstrations and draft-card burnings, *The Green Berets* 'is really a hate-filled message (though gruff and clipped in delivery) to middle America about its disobedient children' (Inglis, 296).
62. In 1980 the US Writers' Guild set up a committee to restore credits to blacklisted writers, resulting in a final list of 94 lost credits drawn up in 1997. But the list will never be comprehensive.
63. Apart from the director Martin Ritt and the screenwriter Walter Bernstein, Zero Mostel, Lloyd Gough, and a percentage of cast and crew had themselves suffered blacklisting.
64. *The Front* thus diverged from the strictly libertarian position of an earlier production, *Fear on Trial*, a teleplay loosely based on a memoir by the broadcaster John Henry Faulk.
65. Written by Arnie Reisman and directed by David Helpern.
66. Kramer (1999), 75–9.
67. Ceplair and Englund, 416.
68. Ibid. 426.
69. Written and directed by Irwin Winkler.
70. Except for some gerrymandering about the date of the execution of the Rosenbergs.

Chapter 7. Witch Hunts: Losey, Kazan, Miller

1. 1909–84, Wisconsin-born director of 31 films.
2. The FBI file consists of 750 pages, of which 518 pages have been released; of these large sections have been blacked out to protect third parties, informants, and certain surveillance methods.
3. He had not been in contact with Brecht since 1936–7, despite his fruitless request, through Brecht's collaborator H. R. Hays, to broadcast *Trial of Lucullus* on NBC's 'Words at War' radio series. He was not destined to direct any other work by Brecht on the stage or screen after 1947 until his film adaptation of *Galileo* (starring Chaim Topol as Galileo) in 1974.
4. Adapted (heavily) from an original magazine short story by Betsy Beaton.
5. *Ebony*, Dec. 1948; Ciment (1985), 84.
6. BFI, Losey Archive, Item 1.
7. Also recorded by the FBI were favourable reviews of his film *The Lawless* in the New York *DW* (23 June 1950) and in the West Coast Communist paper, *Daily People's World* (22 June).

8. Years later, in 1966, when six directors challenged the oath successfully in the New York State Court, Losey wrote from London to the president of the Directors' Guild of America: 'Don't you and your fellow members of the board think it's high time that the ridiculous and shameful loyalty oath is discontinued as a requirement of membership?'
9. Ciment (1985), 38–9, 320–1.
10. The same general mistake, confusing McCarthy with HUAC, occurs in Saunders (1999), 191–2, 283, 286.
11. Ciment (1973), 45, 48.
12. Of Armenian stock, the son of George Kazan, Oriental Rugs and Carpets, Elia Kazan knew how to sell a project.
13. Gussow, 152.
14. Including *Gentleman's Agreement, Pinky, A Streetcar Named Desire*.
15. Ciment (1973), 90; Kazan, 400.
16. Kazan, 457.
17. Ibid. 458.
18. Ciment (1973), 90.
19. Kazan, 419–20.
20. Ciment (1973), 91, 89. The last three lines have been transposed from an earlier page.
21. Ibid. 91.
22. Directed by Gillo Pontecorvo, 1966.
23. Ciment (1973), 95, 94.
24. Members of the Group Theatre actors' company named by Kazan as having been Communists included Clifford Odets, Paula Miller (later Mrs Lee Strasberg), Morris Carnovsky, Phoebe Brand (later Mrs Morris Carnovsky), and the late J. Edward Bromberg. Kazan continued to name names.
25. Kazan, 387.
26. Ibid. 393, 460–1.
27. A. Miller, 'The Crucible in History' (2000), 2–4.
28. *The Times*, 22 Mar. 1999. One upshot was an exhibition about the blacklist years mounted by the Academy in 2002.
29. Bentley, 492.
30. Kazan had written two letters to the *Saturday Review*, the first of which appeared on 5 April 1952, five days prior to his testimony before HUAC.
31. Bentley, 494.
32. Kazan, 468–70.
33. During the 1950s Kazan went on to direct *On the Waterfront, East of Eden, Wild River*, and *Baby Doll*.
34. Lawson, 42–3.
35. On 23 August Zapata wrote a long open letter to President Wilson denouncing the head of the Constitutionalists now in control of the capital, Venustiano Carranza.

State Department papers show Washington hoping to bring Carranza and Zapata together (Womack, 184–205).

36. The slip of the tongue occurs when Mother says truthfully, 'He hasn't been laid up in fifteen years', undermining the alibi which kept Joe Keller out of jail and put an innocent colleague inside (A. Miller 1963, 152–3).

37. Kazan, 319.

38. A. Miller (1987), 237–8.

39. A. Miller (1963), 156–8; A. Miller (1965), 157; Raymond Williams, 74.

40. Lange, 524. OMGUS established an Information Control Division (ICD) in December 1945, with control of cultural affairs and the media. It issued licenses and monitored the press. The successor to OMGUS was HICOG, the Office of the High Commissioner for Germany.

41. On *All My Sons* see also Nelson, *passim*, and Lange, 374.

42. Clearly Lyubimov was the star of the show at the Vakhtangov, as Lyubimov himself confirms in his memoirs. He recalls how, while touring in Sochi before opening in Moscow, the Vakhtangov received a visit from the sardonic Nikolai Mekhlis, described by Lyubimov as minister of Goskontrol. Lyubimov claims to have been rebuked, as a candidate member of the Party, for 'falling so low as to portray our enemy [Chris] into a hero'. Beyond this rather incoherent passage, Lyubimov says nothing about the production or its fate (Lyubimov, 190).

43. Miller (1963), 167; Russian translation quoted by V. Zhdanov in *Trud*, 27 Nov. 1948.

44. *All My Sons* does not appear to have been published in Britain until 1958. The 1961 Penguin edition made no mention of a British production or cast list, while providing such information for a much later play, *A View from the Bridge*.

45. Information about the closure of *All My Sons* has not been found in *Izvestiia* or *Teatr*, while inquiries to the current Vakhtangov management also drew a blank. The play does not appear under *Izvestiia*'s Wednesday theatre listings during the first months of 1949.

46. A. Miller (1965), 36–7.

47. Ibid. 41.

48. Ibid. 42; A. Miller, 'The Crucible in History' (2000), 2–4.

49. A. Miller (1965), 293–5, 326.

50. Ibid. 277, 281. Pressed by the Revd Hale, Proctor does go so far as to say: 'I have wondered if there be witches in the world—although I cannot believe they come among us now.' But then he adds: 'the Bible speaks of witches and I will not deny them.'

51. Ibid. 249.

52. Abigail echoes the informants who regularly appeared before Congressional committees: 'I danced for the devil; I saw him; I wrote in his book . . . I saw Sarah Good with the Devil! I saw Goody Osburn with the Devil!' (ibid. 259).

53. Warshow, 111–21.

54. A. Miller (1967), 17; McAuliffe, 108.

55. Sartre (1973), 85–6.

56. Montand and his wife Signoret were two of the Communist Party's most loyal and popular players, although probably not members (Hayman 1986, 297; Cohen-Solal, 354).

57. See Mottram, 36–7. *Les Sorcières de Salem* was warmly praised in *Positif* by Marcel Ranchal, 41–2. Confessing his ignorance of Miller's play and therefore of Sartre's fidelity to it, Ranchal insisted that the syndrome portrayed—you confess, you live; you deny the charges, you die—applied to the executed Rosenbergs: evidently a microphone was situated within voice-range right up to the electric chair to catch a confession.

58. Sayre, 163; Kazan, 460.

59. Whitfield, 108, 112.

60. According to Miller, HUAC's chairman, Francis Walter, offered to call off the hearing if Miller would permit a photograph of Walter standing beside Miller and his famous fiancée, Marilyn Monroe.

61. Merle Miller, 119–20; Kanfer, 250–2; McCarthy, 25; Bentley, 820, 823.

62. Berkovsky, 184–7; *NYHT* 8 Sept. 1959. In September 1959 Miller's American producer, Kermit Blumgarten, complained of Soviet piracy of his shows, including Miller's *The Crucible*.

63. A. Miller (1964), 28, 40.

64. A. Miller (1987), 529.

65. A. Miller, 'The Crucible in History' (2000), 2–4. Miller notes the awful revelation of anti-Semitism in Russia, 'leaving people like me filled not so much with surprise as a kind of wonder at the incredible amount of hope there once was . . . '. Yet Miller had remained silent during the anti-cosmopolitan campaign, the executions of the Yiddish writers, and the so-called Doctors' Plot.

66. Kazan, 758.

Chapter 8. Soviet Cinema: The New Wave

1. In a memorandum dated 19 July 1954, the Soviet Central Committee's Department of Science and Culture noted the 'dangers' of over-enthusiastic Soviet ideological endorsements of 'progressive' Western films, citing a backlash after *Sovetskoe iskusstvo* (29 Dec. 1951) praised Jean-Paul Le Chanois's film 'Address Unknown' (presumably his *La Belle que voilà*, 1951). According to Grigorii Aleksandrov, Le Chanois had not made a film since the Soviet endorsement was reported in the bourgeois press (RGANI, Fond 5, op. 17, ed.kh 501).

2. *Marty* won the 1955 Palme d'or at Cannes and the US Academy Award for best picture, best director, best actor (Ernest Borgnine), and best screenplay (by Paddy Chayevsky).

3. *NYT* 3 May 1955.

4. *NYT* 11, 13 Nov. 1959.
5. Grigori Chukhrai (1921–2001), born in the Ukraine, studied at the All Union State Institute of Cinematography (VGIK) under Mikhail Romm. This was interrupted by the war, when he served as paratrooper and was twice wounded and decorated. After the war he resumed as Romm's assistant before graduating from VGIK in 1953. *The Forty-First* was a remake of a film with the same title shot in 1927, when Iakov Protazanov adapted Boris Lavrenev's story of Mariutka, a Red Army sharp-shooter. *The Forty-First* almost foundered when Mosfilm's artistic council met to discuss the script, even though Grigorii Koltunov, the experienced scenarist assigned to Chukhrai, had taken the precaution to include a few scenes in which the film explicitly condemned the heroine's love for a class enemy. But Chukhrai did not want that solution. He was advised by Ivan Pyrev, the man behind the film from start to finish, to ignore what he didn't want in the script as soon as he began shooting. Chukhrai later told an interviewer from the Belgian *Le Soir* (7 June 1957) that he had no ideology in mind, only to create a work of art with his brilliant cameraman Sergei Urusevskii (Woll, 37–9).
6. Ibid. 39.
7. In B. Lavrenev's original story the lieutenant simply feels gratitude to Mariutka for saving his life, at best a sympathetic protectiveness. But in the film he hotly and sincerely loves her (*Istoriia sovetskogo kino*, vol. 4, 57).
8. The film's generous approach to the Civil War was not without precedent in Soviet film history. The celebrated film *Chapeyev* (1934) was notable for the subtlety of its characterization of both sides in the Civil War (Richard Taylor, 'Ideology', in Taylor and Christie, 211–13).
9. '...c toi gruboi, ognennoi, zelenoglavoi proletarkoi'.
10. Stanislav Rostotsky, n.p.
11. Based on Viktor Rostov's play *Alive Forever* (*Vechno zhivye*). (See Segel, 350–4.) Kalatozov's films included *Conspiracy of the Doomed* (1950) and *The First Troop Train* (*Pervyi eshelon*).
12. In Viktor Rozov's original stage play, Veronika's parents are not portrayed, likewise the destruction of their home by bombing; there is no tempestuous rape or seduction scene. By 1967 *Alive Forever* had been in repertory at the Sovremennik Theatre for ten years.
13. Rozov, 58.
14. RGALI, Fond 2453, op. 3, ed.kh. 617.
15. Reshenie khudozhestvennogo soveta kinostudii Mosfil'm.
16. Woll, 78–9, 236; RGALI Fond 2453, op. 3, ed.kh. 619, 621.
17. Mira and Antonin J. Liehm (1977), 199–200.
18. *Soviet Film*, a glossy colour magazine launched in 1957 and published in Russian, English, French, German, Spanish, and Arabic, was generally restricted in circulation to foreigners and the Soviet elite.
19. Soon afterwards Samoilova accepted a role in a Franco-Soviet production under a French director.

20. *NYT* 11 Nov. 1959.
21. Kalatozov's *The Letter That Was Never Sent*, a story about four geologists and their losing battle with the raging elements in Siberia—the sacrifice of human lives to science—won extreme praise from Howard Thompson in the *NYT* (19 Nov. 1962): 'an extraordinary blend of awesome backgrounds and dramatic perspective . . .'
22. *Istoriia*, vol. 4, 1943.
23. Ibid., vols 4, 5. See also Vitalii Troianovskii, '*Letiat zhuravli* tret' veka spustia' (*The Cranes are Flying* a Third of a Century Later), *Kinovedcheskie zapiski* 17 (1993), 49–56. On *Cranes*, see also Stites (1992), 141. On the actress Samoilova, see her 'My Roles in the Cinema', *Soviet Film*, 7 July 60. See also Maya Turovskaya in *Aktery sovetskogo kino* (Moscow, 1966). On Soviet sixties films in general, see Lev Anninskii, *Shestidesiatniki i my* (*People of the* Sixties and Us), (Moscow, 1991).
24. The young principals, Vladimir Ivashov and Zhanna Prokhorenko, who captivated audiences across the world, were students from the Institute of Cinematography.
25. *Mastera sovetskogo kino*, 47.
26. Six named contributors collaborated on the chapter on Russian Art Cinema in the fourth volume of the *Istoriia*. The volume was collectively edited by eleven critics. The volumes were published by the All Union Scientific Research Institute of Art Studies (Iskusstvoznaniia) of the Ministry of Culture of the USSR and by the Goskino Scientific Research Institute of the Theory and History of the Cinema. The prose style was wordy, sometimes cloudy, rarely concrete and specific. For example: 'It would be tempting to ascribe to the union with the camera operator in *Cranes* the rare purposefulness of the quest'—*redkostnuiu tseleustremlennost' poiskov* (*Istoriia*, vol. 4, 41)
27. 'ego zloi tupost'iu i kulatskoi zhadnost'iu' (ibid. 59).
28. For Chukhrai's later career, see Golovskoy, 29.
29. The story was not published until 1959 due to its alleged lack of Party spirit and the episode in which the hero is welcomed home even though a prisoner of the Germans (Woll, 91).
30. Reviewing this film in the *NYT* (11 July 1961), Bosley Crowther found it to be 'a hideous and uncompromising account of the brutalities and indignities that are endlessly heaped upon the hero and his fellow Russian prisoners as they are herded as slave laborers into Germany'. Sergei Bondarchuk's 'heavy and gaunt-eyed theatrical style' served him well in the most gruesome scenes, 'but it becomes provokingly stilted in the sentimental scenes'. Even so, it was 'largely a one-man tour de force'. Penelope Houston (125–32) was less well impressed. Bondarchuk, who also directed, was awarded a Lenin Prize. The critical and commercial success enabled him to go ahead with *War and Peace*, the most expensive production in Soviet film history.
31. Salisbury (1955), 269.
32. Romm, 1962.
33. Houston, 125–32.

34. After a visit to America in 1960, Nekrasov—one of sixteen citizens chosen to spend two weeks in the USA—returned impressed by the new cine-journalism, Jean Rouch's *The Chronicle of a Summer*, Shirley Clark's *The Connection*, and Lionel Rogosin's films *On the Bowery* and *Come Back, Africa*. 'Why don't we [Russians] take a camera and a tape-recorder and go out into the street?' (Nekrasov, 59–61, 73).

35. Hixson, 155.

36. *Observer* (London), 29 Jan. 1961.

37. There were early warnings from the Gorky Studio's script department that the script was guilty of 'social passivity' and isolation of the young people from their work, their lack of certainty about the future. The script was published in *Iskusstvo kino* (July 1961).

38. Nekrasov, 125.

39. Screenwriter also of *Ia shagaiu po Moskve* (*I Walk Through Moscow*).

40. Quoted by Woll, 148.

41. *Guardian*, 16 Mar. 1963.

42. Woll, 144–5.

43. Ibid. 149.

44. Ibid. 150, citing Tat'iana Khlopliankina, *Zastava Il'icha: Sud'ba fil'ma* (Moscow, 1990), 31.

45. Mira and Antonín J. Liehm (1977), 216.

46. Woll, 203, 204.

47. The first Moscow International Film Festival took place in 1935, but without a sequel, and the new series began in 1959, following the Soviet–American cultural agreement. In the Stalin era the Americans had boycotted the Karlovy Vary Film Festivals in Communist Czechoslovakia. The Moscow International Festival alternated with Karlovy Vary.

48. Priscilla Johnson, 62–3; Naum Kleiman, interview, Moscow, 5 Apr. 2002.

49. Priscilla Johnson, 63.

50. *Pravda*, 30 July 1963.

51. RGANI Fond 5, op. 55, ed.kh 52.

52. V. Snastin, deputy head of the Central Committee's ideological department, and Romanov in his capacity as deputy head of the film department, responded on 16 July.

53. RGANI, Fond 5, op. 55, ed.kh. 52.

54. Ibid.

55. *LM* 1 Mar. 1966.

56. *NYT* 28 Feb. 1966.

57. Naum Kleiman, director of the Muzei Kino in Moscow, showed the present writer a black table and chairs built by Romm during a period of retreat and regret following Stalin's death.

58. RGANI, Fond 5, op. 51, ed.kh. 51.

59. Baskakov, 22.

60. Mark Zak, interview, Moscow, 11 Apr. 2002.

61. Baskakov, 6, 13, 14.

62. Ibid. 16–17.

63. *Istoriia*, vol. 4, 61.

64. '. . . estestvennaia potrebnost' cheloveka' (ibid.).

65. Tarkovsky (1994), 29, 41, 53, 78, 91–2.

66. 'The best director in the USSR'?—his own appraisal. Born in 1932, the son of a writer and an actress, in 1954 he entered VGIK, the All-Union State Institute of Cinematography, and studied under Mikhail Ilych Romm. The young Tarkovsky was fortunate to belong to the generation of the *shestidesiatniki* (the people of the sixties) who were allowed exposure to Western art. At the State Film Archive, Belye Stolby (White Pillars), he could immerse himself in the work of Kurosawa, Buñuel, Bergman, Bresson, and other giant *auteurs*. Tarkovsky himself was to become supremely an *auteur* director (see Tarkovsky 1986).

67. Mira and Antonín Liehm (1977), 210.

68. Tarkovsky (1999), 57.

69. San Francisco, Golden Gate Prize for best director, 1962; Acapulco, Nalence's Head; Warsaw, Polish Film Critics Club Prize for best film of 1963; Lublin, Czarcia-Zapa Prize for best foreign film; New York, D. Selznick Silber Laurel (critics's prize); Delhi, National Exhibition Prize.

70. Mira and Antonín Liehm (1977), 208 ff.

71. Paris, Film Critics' Association Prize, 1968; Cannes, FIPRESCI Prize, 1969; Paris, Crystal Star of French Academy for best female role, 1972; Filtre Prize for best foreign film, 1973; Helsinki, best film of year, 1973; Stratford International Film Festival, Diploma, 1973; Azolo, Italy, Grand Prize, 1973; Belgrade, best film of Festival, 2nd prize of Audience Jury, 1973.

72. Scammell, 112.

73. Tarkovsky (1994), 77.

74. Bergman, 334.

75. Tarkovsky (1999), p. xiii.

76. *Solaris* (1972): London Film Festival, best film of year, 1972; Cannes, Grand Jury Prize (2nd prize), 1972; Stratford International Festival, Diploma of Honour.

77. Tarkovsky was the son of the renowned poet and translator Arseny Tarkovsky, and Marina Vishniakova, who went to work as a proof-reader to support her two children after her husband left the family home in 1937. (In *Mirror* the mother is seen worrying that she has let slip an obscene word in the proofs of Stalin's collected works which are going to press.)

78. Tarkovsky (1999), p. xx.

79. Ibid., p. xxii

80. Ibid. 379

81. Ibid. 410

82. *Stalker* sold only 4 million tickets within the USSR, compared with 2.9 million tickets for *Andrei Rublev*, 10.5 million for *Solaris*, 2.2 million for *Mirror*. Tarkovsky was invariably a box-office failure in a massive market where 4–5 billion

cinema tickets were sold each year (Stites 1992, 126–7, 173; Golovskoy, 61; Graffy, 185).

83. Tarkovsky (1994), 269. Goskino (Gosfilm until 1963), the State Committee on Cinema, beholden to the film sector of the Central Committee's cultural apparatus, functioned through four bureaucratic committees dealing with scenarios, production, distribution, and foreign sales and purchases. Beneath these came the studios, notably Mosfilm, and then production units.

84. Tarkovsky (1994), 303.

85. Tarkovsky was buried in a graveyard for Russian émigrés in the French town of Saint-Geneviève-du-Bois.

Chapter 9. Germany Divided: Stage and Screen

1. Lillian Hellman's anti-fascist *Watch on the Rhine* (*Auf der anderen Seite*) was performed at the Hebbel Theater and in Hamburg, while Clifford Odets's *Awake and Sing* (*Die das Leben ehren*) was seen in Bremen, Darmstadt, Heidelberg, Wiesbaden, and Stuttgart in the US zone, as well as Berlin, Weimar, and Leipzig in the Soviet zone.

2. According to Erich Kuby, on 15 June 1945, Gustav von Wangenheim, a major theatre figure, was flown in from Moscow and installed in the Schiffbauerdamm. The Russians provided him with a car and chauffeur (Kuby, 327).

3. The head of the Education Department of SMAD, Comrade Zolotukhin, was to be responsible for implementation of the decree. Town and area commandants were to make sure it was locally adhered to. The decree was signed by G. Zhukov, supreme commander, and two other officers. The administrative structure it set up established parallel departments (e.g. Education), the one belonging to the German Central Administration (CGA) subordinate to the other—that of the Soviet Military Administration (SMAD). The appointment of theatre directors and producers must be approved by the Education Department of the CGA and confirmed by SMAD. Section 5 required registration not only of theatres and concert and exhibitions halls, but also 'all actors, singers, musicians, dancers'.

4. Shirer, 184.

5. Of French writers, Sartre's *La Putain respectueuse* received the most performances, with Anouilh, Giraudoux, and Claudel also favoured. Among the British, Christopher Fry, and J. B. Priestley's *An Inspector Calls*, a play whose detective mode does not conceal a massive indictment of capitalism, headed the list (Fries, 215).

6. Among several in-depth studies of the politics of theatre in post-war Germany, and the intrusion of the cold war under the proscenium arch, Wigand Lange's study of the American zone, *Theater in Deutschland nach 1945*, deserves pride of place, despite some errors of fact and a naive view of the USA as solely responsible for the cold war. For example, Lange quotes *The Limits of Power* by J. and G. Kolko: 'The so-called Cold War, in brief, was far less the confrontation of the United

States with Russia than America's expansion into the entire world—a world the Soviet Union neither controlled nor created.' Born in 1946, Lange presumably absorbed the New Left *Zeitgeist*, including historical revisionism, while a student in Munich and Regensburg, and in the 1970s as a teaching assistant at the University of Wisconsin. In 1978 he was appointed Assistant Professor of German Literature and Language at Marquette University, Milwaukee, Wisconsin. His book contains numerous attacks on the politics and scholarship of Hansjörg Gehring, author of *Amerikanischen Literaturpolitik in Deutschland 1945–1953* (Stuttgart, 1976). (Lange, 588.)

David Pike's estimable *The Politics of Culture in Soviet Occupied Germany, 1945–1949* (Stanford, 1992), published twelve years after Lange's book, does not list it in its bibliography or index many of Lange's 'characters', US theater officers like Benno Frank, Willem van Loon, and Eugene Bahn.

7. Lange, 278, citing a memo of Benno Frank to Col. Hills.
8. Anna Christie had been Greta Garbo's first talking role in a movie in 1930.
9. Lange, 398–9.
10. After the war his reputation was to be explosively revived in America with plays written in 1939–40 but not yet produced: *The Iceman Cometh*, *Long Day's Journey Into Night*, and the more recent *A Moon for the Misbegotten*.
11. Including *Mourning Becomes Electra* (*Trauer muss elektra tragen*), *The Iceman Cometh* (*Der Eismann kommt*), and *Strange Interlude* (*Seltsames Zwischenspiel*).
12. *Berlin am Mittag, Der Morgen*, and *Die Weltbühne*.
13. Lange, 365.
14. SMAD is SVAG in Russian. Dymshits is Alexander Dymschiz in German.
15. Ibid. 549.
16. Naimark, 425–6.
17. Gustav von Wangenheim was abruptly sacked without public explanation in August 1946. A member of the Weimar theatrical avant-garde and a dandy, Wangenheim had spent the Nazi period exiled in the USSR, where his survival seems to have involved giving evidence against the doomed actress Carola Neher. Returning to Berlin, he abandoned his avant-garde and Brechtian past in order to implement the Soviet policy of reviving the classical and 'humanist' tradition. Ten productions during his directorship of the Deutsches Theater included Lessing, Molière and Shakespeare, Chekhov, Hauptmann and Sternheim, and four plays by contemporary writers (Schivelbusch, 62–7).
18. Ibid. 67.
19. According to *Teatr*, the same playwright's *Velikaia sila* (*The Great Force*) was successful in East German theatres in 1948–9, along with such plays as *Gubernator provintsii* (*Governor of the Province*), *Ostrov mira* (*Island of Peace*), and Ilya Ehrenburg's *Lev na ploshchadi* (*Lion in the Square*), which was performed in Berlin, Chemnitz, Jena, and other towns, as well as N. Virta's *Zagovor obrechennykh* (*Conspiracy of the Doomed*) and Korneichuk's *Makar Dubrava* (Novodvorskaia, 106, 108).

20. Ibid. 108.
21. See pp. 134–42 on the film version, *Meeting on the Elbe*.
22. Novodvorskaia, 107.
23. *The Skin of Our Teeth* (*Wir sind noch einmal davon gekommen*), gained in translation the meaning 'we managed to pull through again—whatever the hardships of the past, all will be well'. Some 400,000 Germans went to see it and be well.
24. Wolfgang Harich, 22 years old in 1945, was theatre critic for the French-licensed *Der Kurier* and an *enfant terriblement intelligent*. Some years later, in 1956, he was famously arrested and imprisoned after he delivered to the Soviet ambassador to the GDR a report critical of the Ulbricht government.
25. Pike, 232–3.
26. Ibid. 235.
27. Gehring, 74.
28. Naimark, 408.
29. *NYT* 2 Nov. 1947; Fries, 53–7.
30. Lange, 279–80. In the mid-1950s van Loon was still in Berlin, acting as local PR man for *Porgy and Bess*.
31. Lange, 290.
32. The US zone prided itself on avoiding direct censorship, but Lange has found blacklists in the archive. Plays now reckoned to be too 'progressive' included Robert Ardrey's *Thunder Rock*, Sidney Kingsley's *The Patriots*, Robert Sherwood's *Abe Lincoln in Illinois*, John Steinbeck's *Of Mice and Men*, and William Saroyan's *The Time of the Your Life*. The change of line inevitably resulted in changes of personnel, the purge of officials still devoted to the progressive ideals of the New Deal.
33. Fries, 216.
34. Lange, 538–9. Benno Frank was succeeded in 1948 by Eugene H. Bahn as theater officer and music officer for the whole US zone—not by the notorious 'Herr Melville' Lasky.
35. Naimark, 473.
36. Ibid. 382–3.
37. The season of 1948–9 brought 81, and the season of 1949–50 158 performances in the 71 theatres of the Soviet zone (Lange, 584).
38. As examples he cited Arthur Miller's prize-winning *All My Sons*, which fell under both forbidden categories; *Deep Are the Roots* by Arnaud d'Usseau and James Gowe; and anything by Lillian Hellman or Clifford Odets. Gowe's play was among several dealing with racial discrimination in the USA listed in the Soviet Ministry of Culture's journal *Teatr* (Nov. 1947), 59–60. Others included Lillian Smith's *Strange Fruit*, set in a small Southern town, and Robert Arden's play *Jeb*, the story of a Negro veteran unable to find work after the war because of his race (Lange, 516; Ralph Willett, 71).
39. Ralph Willett, 71–2.
40. Lange, 310.
41. Barskii, 94.

42. Ibid. 95.

43. Including *Eugene Onegin*, The *Queen of Spades*, and *Iolanthe* (Tchaikovsky), *Sadko* (Rimsky-Korsakov), and *Boris Godunov* (Mussorgsky). For the 1948–9 season productions of *Ruslan and Ludmila* (Glinka), *The Tsar's Bride*, and *The Golden Cockerel* (Rimsky-Korsakov) were in preparation (Barskii, 96).

44. Ibid. 96.

45. Bizet's *Carmen* was revived with the original dialogue, Offenbach's *Orpheus in the Underworld* with an improved translation from the original French, while the direction of Smetana's *The Bartered Bride* (*Die verkaufte Braut*) won a national prize.

46. Impressive were Felsenstein's productions of Verdi's *Falstaff*, with its accurately stylized Elizabethan setting (the merry wives of Windsor come to East Berlin), god-blessed by the 'serene joyfulness' (*Heiterkeit)* of the 80-year-old Italian maestro, Verdi (Rühle 1957, 268–9).

47. Jürgen Rühle, a prominent theatre critic in the GDR from 1949 to 1955, broke with the SED, fled to the West, published articles on cultural affairs in *Der Monat*, and became editor of the magazine *SBZ-Archiv*, Cologne. His major work, *Das Gefesselte Theater* (*The Fettered Theatre*, 1957), carried an interesting section on the trials and tribulations of East German opera.

48. Rühle (1957), 273.

49. Ibid. 274–5.

50. Ibid. 277. Münzer became an iconic figure in East German culture, like the KPD leader Ernst Thälmann, who died in Buchenwald, a prisoner of the Nazis. Viewed at the Film Museum, Potsdam, the same choreography and the same social realist dramatic conventions are apparent in two feature films, *Thälmann* and *Thomas Münzer*, with the emphasis on the principal as Leader—bright-eyed, friendly, determined, often photographed at a level above the adoring, trusting people, who gather as a chorus below the necessary hero—somewhat in the idiom of Otto Griebel's painting *Die Internationale* (1929/30). In Willy Colberg's oil painting, *Thälmann in Hamburger Aufstand*, he is seen on a street corner talking to armed workers, at the same level as they, but his face alone is fully lighted.

51. In vain Felsenstein paraded support for Eisler's script from Arnold Zweig, the Austrian critic Ernst Fischer, and Brecht himself. Brecht is said to have come up with a quote from the *Great Soviet Encyclopaedia* confirming that German humanists of the Reformation had sided with reaction out of fear of the peasants' revolt, persecuting materialism and natural science with as narrow a hatred as that of the Catholic priests (Rühle 1957, 278–80).

52. During the war Germans, like Americans and Britons, went to the cinemas in record numbers. Even after 'total war' was declared in 1943 and concert halls, museums, and arenas were shut down, cinemas stayed open and, when destroyed in air raids, makeshift outdoor cinemas were improvised (Marcus, 41).

53. The six Germans who formed the nucleus of the directorate under Colonel Sergei Tiul'panov included the playwright Friedrich Wolf, the writer Hans Fallada, and the directors Kurt Maetzig, Wolfgang Staudte, and George C. Klaren.

54. In 1995, 50 years after the Russians reached Berlin, a new historical museum was set up under joint German and Russian sponsorship, in the Berlin suburb of Karlshorst. Its verdict on post-1945 cultural links, printed in both languages, was cool: 'To a significant extent cultural relations developed by command from above—*durch die Obrigkeit verordnet*—and without effecting the population—*i ne zatragivali naseleniia*' (Museum Berlin Karlshorst, 54).

55. At the beginning of the occupation cinemas typically showed 60 to 70% Soviet films and 30 to 40% German films; by 1947–8 it was about 50–50, with German productions accounting for slightly above half the showings and the public tending to stay away from the Russian ones (Naimark, 421–3).

56. A second early DEFA film, Kurt Maetzig's *Marriage in the Shadows*, reached the Little Met Theater, New York, in September 1948. Starring Paul Klinger, the film was inspired by the life of Joachim Gottschalk, who took a Jewish actress as his wife and defied the Nazis by committing suicide. Spanning a ten-year period from 1933, the screenplay explores the mounting terror of Jews and the lassitude of the German population. *The Affair Blum* (1948), directed by Erich Engel for DEFA, was reviewed in the *NYT* (18 Oct. 1949) in friendly fashion by Bosley Crowther, who lauded this 'trenchant dramatic exposition of the way in which an innocent German Jew is almost destroyed by nascent Nazis—back in 1926'.

57. Bulgarian by birth, and a friend of Brecht, Dudow was a product of Berlin radicalism during the Weimar era. Having worked for Fritz Lang and G. W. Pabst, he had directed Brecht's notorious *The Measures Taken* in 1930 and his contentious adaptation of Gorky's *The Mother*. Brecht also wrote the script for Dudow's film *Kühle Wampe* (later regarded as a classic), the story of a Berlin labourer's family. In 1934 Dudow had fled to Paris. Interned in 1939, he escaped and spent the war in Switzerland, returning to Berlin in 1945.

58. Mira and Antonín Liehm (1977), 89.

59. Wilharm, 11.

60. Mira and Antonín Liehm (1977), 89.

61. RGANI, Fond 5, op. 17, ed.kh. 501.

62. Also entitled *Frauensache*.

63. In 1956 Dudow directed for DEFA his satirical *Der Hauptmann von Köln* (*The Captain from Cologne*), the story of an unemployed headwaiter who exchanges names with a returning war criminal and makes a business career in Cologne.

64. RGANI, Fond 5, op. 17, ed.kh. 501.

65. The production company is given on the print as Progress Film-Vertrieb GMBH.

66. 'Town and country hand in hand!' 'Germany for the Germans!' 'Bärenweiler—a German village.'

67. Wilharm, 14.

68. Anderson, Part II, IV/2 (Feb. 1953), 64.

69. Ivens (1898–1989), director of *The Spanish Earth* (1937), and of *The Four Hundred Million* (1939), about the Japanese occupation of China, had been deprived of his Dutch passport after making *Indonesia Calling*. He recovered it two years later, took

up residence in Paris, and became increasingly devoted to Maoist China and the Communist cause in Vietnam (*The Threatening Sky*, 1966).

70. Evans, 81–3.
71. According to the WFTU this amounted to 30 minutes, or one-third of the film. An uncut version was shown at the Unity Theatre (National Film Theatre (London) Programme, May 2000, 38).
72. An increasing number of West German films were shown in the East: only 2 in 1951, 14 in 1954. The number of Soviet films shown fell from 23 in 1950 to 11 in 1955.
73. Aleksandrov directed *Jazz Comedy, Circus, Volga-Volga* (made at Stalin's behest and featuring smiling canal workers who break into song at the drop of a shovel), and *Bright Road*. Alexandrov could turn a blonde factory girl in dungarees into a universal sweetheart who danced for love of her work, for her country, and for Stalin—'We love you and we name our children after you' (Fitzpatrick, 209).
74. Produced by Andrew Horn, directed by Dana Ranga, and released by Downtown Pictures in 1999.
75. In Janos Veiczi's *For Eyes Only* (1962–3), an agent of the Stasi disguised as a Western agent flees with secret military information to East Berlin, bringing with him a comrade full of hope for a socialist future, fleeing from the decadent West.
76. Marcus, 41.
77. Leonhard, 52.

Chapter 10. Brecht and the Berliner Ensemble

1. The translation of 'Nasty Morning' is my own preferred hybrid version of several in print. The HUAC testimony is from Bentley, 208.
2. John Willett (1998), 194–5.
3. Meyer, 4.
4. Laqueur and Lichtheim, 61.
5. Brecht (1993), 458. Brecht's diary claimed that Oppenheimer and his colleagues had been 'appalled to find that it [the bomb] had been dropped on japan'. Oppenheimer, in fact, had rejoiced at the terrible proof that the Manhattan Project had succeeded. His subsequent difficulties with his government in the McCarthy era, leading to a witch-hunting of his youth as a Party member, were precipitated by his opposition to the immediate production of an H-Bomb.
6. Milne, 42, 90–1; Losey Files (private collection), Losey to Wuolijoki, 7 Jan. 1947.
7. Losey, draft typescript for 'L'Oeil du maître' (1960), BFI Losey archive. Losey's FBI file shows that on 17 January the Bureau's agents monitored Brecht and his wife Helene Weigel lunching with Losey at the Gotham Restaurant, Los Angeles.
8. Houseman, quoted by Callow, 186.
9. The film capital's most distinguished progressives (the 'radical glamour set') turned out for the première: Charles Chaplin, Charles Boyer, Ingrid Bergman,

Anthony Quinn, Van Heflin, John Garfield, Gene Kelly, Billy Wilder, Richard Conte, Howard da Silva, Sam Wanamaker, Lewis Milestone, Marlon Brando, and Burt Lancaster among them.

10. BFI Losey archive.
11. Stephan, 111, 113, 118, 121.
12. Bentley, 96, 86.
13. Ibid. 91.
14. *LLF* (27 Nov. 1947) reported that Chaplin had requested Picasso to form a committee in Eisler's defence; this committee duly sent a strongly worded protest to the US Embassy in Paris, signed by Picasso, Matisse, Cocteau, Jean-Louis Barrault, Aragon, Eluard, and Louis Jouvet (Bentley, 108–9).
15. Bentley, 220.
16. Lyon, 333.
17. Literally 'Fear and Misery of the Third Reich', but translated by Eric Bentley in 1945 and produced in Berkeley and New York as *Private Life of the Master Race*.
18. Cook, 196.
19. Brecht (1973), 491, cited by Cook, 198–9. Reaching Zurich in November 1947, he joined with Max Frisch and other writers to denounce the cold war and Western war propaganda. It was not until 20 November 1947 that the New York office of the FBI informed J. Edgar Hoover that Brecht had left the country on 31 October. Hoover wrote a memo to the CIA asking them to keep an eye on Brecht in Europe.
20. Fuegi, 483–4; Bentley, 220.
21. Cook, 197–8.
22. Lyon, 335, 384.
23. John Willett describes Fritz Erpenbeck as 'the former Piscator actor' and editor of *Theater der Zeit* since its foundation in July 1946. He was appointed in January 1949 to the new 'Bureau for Theatre Questions', which in November 1950 became a 'Repertory Commission' controlling choice of plays throughout East Germany. A constant critic of Brecht, he raised the question whether Brecht was moving towards *Volkstümlichkeit* (populism) or *volksfremde Decadenz* (alien decadence) (Brecht 1993, 519).
24. Pike, 620, citing Werner Mittenzwei, *Das Leben des Bertolt Brecht* (Berlin, 1988), 236; Fuegi, 498, citing *Dramaturgische Blätter*, nos. 1, 2 (1947).
25. Brecht (1993), 387.
26. This followed a decision to establish a joint currency in the three Western zones, clearly the foundation of a future West German state and acutely alarming to the USSR. The blockade was not lifted until May 1949.
27. Fuegi, 501.
28. Brecht (1993), 401.
29. Ibid. 403.
30. Ibid. 520.
31. Lange (1980), 549. Edward Stettinius is wrongly given as US secretary of state (Aussenminister) and Benno Frank, Lange's source, is said to have recalled to him

in 1975 that Senator McCarthy had intervened to scotch the proposal. Frank is said to have told Lange that he retracted his proposal to invite Brecht on 1 May 1948, as a result of the anti-Communism of the 'McCarthy-Zeit'. But Stettinius had in fact ceased to be secretary of state in 1945, shortly after Truman succeeded Roosevelt, and McCarthy did not rise to prominence until 1950.

32. Arendt, 216.
33. Rühle (1957), 236.
34. Brecht to Erwin Piscator, Mar. 1949 (Brecht 1990, 464).
35. Fuegi, 506.
36. *Weltbühne*, Feb. 1949, 101, cited by Fuegi, 507; Pike, 625.
37. Rühle (1957), 237.
38. Rühle speaks of 'a series of inquisitorial articles' which appeared under the pseudonym N. Orlow (Orlov) in the Soviet occupation newspaper *Tägliche Rundschau*.
39. Rühle (1957), 239.
40. Fuegi, 526.
41. Brecht (1993), 424.
42. Ibid. 427.
43. Rühle (1957), 240.
44. Brecht (1990), 436.
45. The direction was by Wolf Völker, sets by Caspar Neher, and the conductor, Hermann Scherchen, had been brought from Switzerland; the investment was exceptional.
46. A few provocative whistles when the curtain fell brought friendly spectators leaping from their seats and an answering storm of applause (*Beinfallssturm*) never before heard in the theatre.
47. Rühle (1957), 242–3.
48. Brecht (1990), 498.
49. Paul Dessau had emigrated to New York in 1934, joined Brecht in California in 1937, and returned to New York in May 1941 for a festival performance of his *Les Voix de Paul Verlaine et Anatole France*, an intricate work for two pianos, percussion, and voice. He returned to East Germany in 1947.
50. 'Wo sonst in der Welt gibt es eine Regierung, die so viel Interesse und Fürsorge für ihre Künstler zeigt!' (Rühle 1957, 243).
51. Brecht (1990), 500.
52. Rühle (1957), 244.
53. Demetz, 17.
54. Brecht (1990), 436.
55. Brecht (1993), 439.
56. Fuegi, 534.
57. Brecht (1990), 506–7.
58. Fuegi, 541.
59. Brecht (1993), 454.

60. Gaddis (1997), 138; Halle, 163, 355.
61. Fontaine, 419.
62. Ehrenburg (vol. 6, 1966), 206.
63. After five years in the Soviet Union, where his chief theatrical advocate, Sergei Tretyakov, was shot as a spy in 1937, Erwin Piscator, the innovative master of the new Marxist political theatre, a theatre of mobile architecture and scenic innovation, had moved to Paris and then, like Brecht, to the New School for Social Research, New York, where he was director of the Drama Workshop (John Willett 1978, 168–75).
64. Piscator's own productions in Hamburg, Marburg, Zurich, the Hague, and Mannheim included Arthur Miller's *The Crucible* (*Hexenjagd*). Not until 1955 did he undertake a production at the Schiller Theater, East Berlin. The following year, the year of Brecht's death, Piscator returned to the Schiller Theater to direct the seminal classic of epic theatre, Georg Büchner's *Dantons Tod*, with designs by Caspar Neher. The Deutsche Akademie der Künste zu Berlin elected Piscator a corresponding member, honouring him for his founding work in the epic theatre, but the liberties of the West continued to tempt him back—he directed Faulkner's *Requiem für eine Nonne* at the Schlossparkthaeter, West Berlin, and a production of O'Neill's *Mourning Becomes Elektra*. From 1962 to his death in 1966 Piscator was director of the Freie Volksbühne at the Theater am Kurfürstendamm, revived by the Social Democrat administration in West Berlin.
65. Ewan, 214; Fuegi, 544.
66. Brecht (1990), 517–18.
67. Brecht (1975), 440.
68. Brecht (1975), trans. Frank Jellinek, 437–8.
69. Brecht (1993), 460.
70. Esslin (1961), 187–8.
71. The Théâtre nationale populaire had staged *Mère Courage* in 1951. In 1947 *L'Exception et la règle* had been seen at the Noctambules.
72. Sartre (1973; 1992), 88.
73. Ibid. 91.
74. Esslin (1961), 92. A major study of his early work appeared in East Berlin in 1955, Ernst Schumacher's *Die dramatischen Versuche Bertolt Brechts 1918–1933*.
75. Martin Esslin likened Harich's group to the Petöfi Circle in Hungary and the *Po Postu* group in Poland.
76. Her Majesty's Government.
77. *Observer*, 28 Oct. 2001.
78. Luthy, 33–53. Originally published as 'Vom armen Bert Brecht', *Der Monat*, 44 (West Berlin, 1952).
79. Müller's play was written in an episodic, 15–scene structure, a harbinger of his habitual collage technique in later years, with a Brechtian emphasis on a process rather than a person. As described by Jonathan Kalb in his study of Müller, a character in the play, a young man, glancing round to see if anyone is watching,

rips down a poster that reads 'SED—Party of Reconstruction', after which tired workers trample it. Is the trampling accidental or malicious? Actors and directors may decide but the author does not. This epic technique had been condemned as 'didactic teaching theatre' by Ulbricht and the GDR's leading theatre critic Fritz Erpenbeck. Müller was destined for a tempestuous career between East and West. Although he and his wife had won the Heinrich Mann Prize in 1959, two years later his play *Die Umsiedlerin* (*The Woman Resettler*) was closed after the dress rehearsal because the play spoke too frankly about the land reforms of the post-1945 period. Müller was expelled from the Writers' Union and thus banned from production and publication for years (Kalb, 60–1 and *passim*).

80. Brecht (1990), 563.
81. *Encounter*, IX/4 (Oct. 1957), 21. Rühle (1959), 48, quotes two Soviet appreciations of Brecht: Yu. Iuzovskii, 'Na spektakliakh "Berlinskogo ansamblia" ' and A. Anikst, 'Zametki po povodu teatra Brekhta', *Teatr*, 8 (1957).
82. Smeliansky, 37.
83. Stephan, 133.
84. In reality Brecht and the Berliner Ensemble had been rehearsing not *Coriolanus* but Erwin Strittmatter's *Katzgraben* when the Berlin rising occurred.
85. Grass, *passim*. An English adapation of the same theme was David Caute, *The Demonstration*, a play performed at the Nottingham Playhouse, Unity Theatre, and Junges Theater, Hamburg, 1969–71 (London, 1970).
86. *The Nation*, 13 Feb. 1967, 214.
87. Ewen, *Brecht* (1967), 492, 443, 452. The building of socialism is seen by Ewen as a soul-struggle against 'the Kurfürstendamm garishly rebuilt, neon lights and all, and the coffee houses ostentatiously displaying whipped cream to crowding clienteles'. Ewen's remarks uncannily resemble those of Ilya Ehrenburg's late memoirs: 'In the Kurfürstendamm people danced the samba, drank hock and ogled shrill half-naked singers. But serious theatregoers went to East Berlin to see a Brecht play . . .' (Ehrenburg 1966, vol. 6, 206).
88. Arendt, 208, 226.
89. Arendt quoting Brecht's *Gesammelte Werke: Schriften zur Politik und Gesellschaft*, 325. Willett commented that 'their' hopes were 'not necessarily Brecht's'—a defence surely ruled out by the phrase 'and all who are fighting for world peace', which inevitably embraced himself (John Willett, writing in the *TLS*, 26 Mar. 1970, 335). See also Arendt, 245–7 and 210, quoting Brecht in *Sinn und Form* (II, 1953, 10), the organ of the East German Academy.
90. Willett did not agree that Brecht's one reference to Stalin as 'the Soviet people's great harvest-leader' (*Ernteleiter*) amounted to an 'ode'.
91. 'Je mehr unschuldig, desto mehr verdienen sie erschossen zu werden' (Hook, 493). Professor Henry Pachter, of City University, wrote to the *New Leader* (28 Apr. 1969) confirming that he had heard Brecht make remarks in the same vein. According to Pachter, Brecht admitted in conversation that Stalin's terror was 'terrible' but added: 'Fifty years hence the Communists will have forgotten Stalin,

but I want to be sure that they will read Brecht. Therefore I cannot separate myself from the Party.'

92. Brecht (1975), introd. by the editors, p. xx.

93. Ibid. 418–19.

94. Fenton (1984), 25–7.

95. Brecht (1975), 274.

96. Brecht was aware of the arrests of Carola Neher and Sergei Tretyakov by late November 1938. Béla Kun, leader of the Hungarian soviet in 1919, and one of Brecht's contacts in the Comintern, was shot (Brecht 1993, 465).

97. Brecht (1975), introd. by the editors, p. xxii.

98. Meyer, 4–5, citing *Brecht* (1993), n.p. given.

99. Fuegi, 621.

100. Meyer, 5.

101. Hofmann's claim that 'The real drama, the only drama, is the palace revolution in John Fuegi's mind some time in the last thirty years' fails to convince. According to Hofmann: 'Brecht's meanness [about money] is a primary quality and not interesting per se: some people just are mean . . . Secondly, though the case for these sexually and literarily exploited women as the originators of much of Brecht's dramatic work in particular is very strong—and again, not new— Fuegi makes it badly.' But Hofmann fails to fault the detail in Fuegi's indictment (Hofmann, 40).

102. Published in the *Brecht Yearbook*, no. 20 (1995).

103. John Willett (1998), 194. Willett maintains that E. Hauptmann was not, as Fuegi asserts, the principal author of *The Threepenny Opera*. He cites a new study by Sabine Kebir of Hauptmann's work with BB which (he holds) leaves Fuegi's thesis 'in tatters'. However, he concedes that 'the largest unsolved question in Brecht's life and works' remains 'the exact division of responsibility for the collective's output when Hauptmann was central to it' (ibid. 68).

104. An example of language apparently designed to intimidate and exclude all but a small elite familiar with the jargon is found in the first three sections of the contents page of Fredric Jameson's *Brecht and Method*, published by Verso in 1998. Brecht, a socialist in search of a mass audience, is carried off by Jameson and interred in a virtually impenetrable grove of academe. Jameson (31, n. 9) writes: 'But even today collaborative work arouses scandal: what about the private property of the signature, and did not Brecht exploit the people working with him (now called "Brecht")?' According to Jameson: 'This is in reality a political issue (masked by moralisms of various kinds); it first seeks to play off identity-political themes against class ones, and then, on another level, to depreciate politics altogether—as the action of collectives—in the name of the personal and of individual ownership.' He adds: 'So it is that the properly utopian features of Brecht's collective work, and of collective or collaborative work of all kinds, are occulted and repudiated . . . ' (Jameson, 10). BB is here the hog being washed.

105. 'Wer setzt ihn durch?' (Biermann, *Über*, 1991, 11).

106. Biermann (1968), 18.
107. Vallance, 178–9, 180.
108. Ryback, 42.
109. 'Ich hatte ja Glück, mich schütze die Furcht der Politbürokraten vor der Offentichkeit' (Biermann, *Preussischer*, 1991, 116).
110. West German writers who came to Biermann's defence included Peter Weiss and Heinrich Böll (*Die Zeit*, 17 Dec. 1965; Vallance, 184–5).
111. Biermann: 'Drei Kugeln auf Rudi Dutschke'.
112. 'Wir haben genau gesehen | Wer da geschossen hat.'
113. Biermann (1968), 73.
114. Ryback, 90.
115. Leonhard, 53. Biermann was not alone. Dissident balladeers became popular figures in the Soviet Union, for example: the melancholic, pacifistic songs of Bulat Okudzhava (expelled from the CP in 1964); the humorous songs of Vladimir Vysotsky, an actor at the Taganka Theatre; the satirical ballads of Aleksandr Galich (expelled from the USSR in 1974), recorded privately on tape and circulated by *magnitizdat* (Segel, 444).
116. The full title of this report is 'Information Concerning the Ideological Situation Among the Trade Union Rank and File on the Revocation of the GDR Citizenship of Biermann' (Information über die ideologische Situation in den gewerkschaftlichen Grundorganisationen zur Aberkennung der DDR Staatsbürgerschaft Biermanns) (Fulbrook, 83–4).
117. Biermann, *Über* (1991), 11–12.

Chapter 11. Dirty Hands: The Political Theatre of Sartre and Camus

1. 'Je ne prends pas parti. Une bonne pièce de théâtre doit poser les problèmes et non les résoudre.'
2. Jill Forbes argues that *film noir* 'combines the cosmography typical of the Cold War, the division of the world into a light and dark side, a heaven and hell, with the simplicity of a medieval morality play'. However, most *films noirs* were produced during the years of friendship with the USSR, and many of the directors involved—Huston, Dmytryk, Wilder—were later to be either victims or conspicuous opponents of the Hollywood witch hunt. Forbes, 34, cites André Bazin, *Qu'est ce que le cinéma?* (Paris, 1975), 226–7, and Raymond Borde et Étienne Chaumeton, *Panorama du film noir américain* (Paris, 1953), p. xi.
3. The title does not mean 'The Respectable Prostitute', a serious confusion, as in a majority of English-language versions, including Peter Brook's first London production, which Sartre admired.
4. Sartre, *Putain* (1946), 162. On the other hand it is inevitable in the original French text that the fugitive Negro addresses Lizzie as 'vous' and 'Madame', while she uses the familiar 'tu' to him.

5. Cohen-Solal, 397.

6. Sartre, *Putain* (1946), 62, 102.

7. Ibid. 107

8. Hayman (1986), 238.

9. Sartre (1992 (1973)), 352.

10. Ibid. 287–9.

11. 'L'homme n'est rien d'autre que ce qu'il se fait.' The quotation occurs in Sartre, *L'Existentialisme* (1961 (1946)), 22. *Qu'est-ce que c'est que la littérature?* was published in *Situations II* (1948). 'Roads of freedom' is a more accurate rendering of *chemins de la liberté*, not only literally but in terms of Sartre's meaning. Freedom for Sartre is not a destination (as in breaking through the Iron Curtain) but a human condition that the individual may embrace or evade.

12. Pike, 463.

13. Garaudy (1948), 61.

14. Pike, 464, quoting Sartre (1949), 257.

15. Sartre (1962), *passim*.

16. *LLF clandestines*, no. 12, quoted by Cohen-Solal, 183.

17. The French Mission Culturelle was set up by the Foreign Ministry late in 1946. Its leader, Félix Lusset, enjoyed cordial relations with Dymshits—evidently Lusset dreamed of a revived Paris–Berlin–Leningrad cultural axis (Schivelbusch, 31).

18. Beauvoir, (1998), 163. Lukács's attack on Sartre, *Existentialisme ou Marxisme*, published in 1947, had set the critical guidelines in the Soviet zone of Germany.

19. Sartre (1992 (1973)), 290.

20. Sartre (1948), 48.

21. Beauvoir (1963), 166.

22. Sartre (1948), 51.

23. 'Nul ne gouverne innocement'—although it has been argued that what Saint-Just really said was 'One cannot reign innocently' ('On ne peut pas régner innocement'), pointing the finger at the crimes of the monarchy (Sartre, 1992 (1973), 290.

24. 'Autrement dit, on ne fait pas de politique (quelle qu'elle soit) sans se salir les mains, sans être contraint à des compromis entre l'idéal et le réel.'

25. Sartre (1948), 203.

26. Sartre (1992 (1973)), 293, 304. Jeanson (1955), 49.

27. 'Quant aux hommes, ce n'est pas ce qu'ils sont qui m'intéresse, mais ce qu'ils pourront devenir.'

28. Sartre (1992 (1973)), 307 and 312, n. 7.

29. Sartre (1948), 202.

30. Sartre (1992 (1973)), 296–9.

31. A film adaptation (1951), with Pierre Brasseur as Hoederer and Daniel Gélin as Hugo, gave rise to a vociferous Communist campaign against the film. Sartre dissociated himself from the production (Sartre 1992 (1973), 312, n. 10).

32. Ted Freeman, 136.

33. Sartre (1948), 166–7.
34. Ibid. 171–2.
35. In November 1933 Jacques Doriot had called for a united front with the Socialists, had been expelled from the PCF, and a year later the United Front had been negotiated but Doriot remained excluded (Sartre 1992 (1973), 304, 311).
36. 'Ce n'est pas moi qui ai tué, c'est le hasard.'
37. Sartre (1948), 240, 242. The analogy with Camus is made by Hazel E. Barnes, 82.
38. Poltoratskii, 4.
39. Beauvoir (1965), 150. De Beauvoir has little to say about the conventions and possibilities of theatre; she is not concerned with opening and closing doors or the fact that *Les Mains sales* is composed in seven tableaux, with five in flashback: her focus is always on *what Sartre was saying now and had been saying previously*. In *Sartre par lui-même* (Paris 1960, (1955)), another uncritical disciple, Francis Jeanson, threads a passage from one Sartre play to another, one existential situation and moral dilemma to the next, from Orestes to Henri to Hugo to Goetz. This is done in a strictly philosophical-political vein without a glance at theatrics or, indeed, the use of language.
40. Hazel E. Barnes, 85.
41. Sartre (1948), 196.
42. Ibid. 249
43. Beauvoir (1965), 151.
44. Ibid. 169; Hayman (1986), 249.
45. Sartre (1992 (1973)), 180–2, 294.
46. Camus tended to distance his plays from contemporary France in time and space, whereas his novels—*L'Étranger* (1942), *La Peste* (1947), and *La Chute* (1956)—were all set in contemporary France or Algeria. Of the plays, *Révolte dans les Asturies* (1936) is set in Spain, *Le Malentendu* (1944) in Czechoslovakia, *Caligula* (1945) in imperial Rome, *L'État de siège* (1948) in Spain, *Les Justes* (1949) in Tsarist Russia. His stage adaptations included Faulkner's *Requiem for a Nun* and Dostoyevsky's *The Devils* (*Les Possédés*).
47. Speaking on television in 1959, shortly before his death in a car accident, he explained: 'Je préfère la compagnie des gens de théâtre, vertueux ou pas, à celle des intellectuels, mes frères.' (Todd, 659).
48. Camus (1962), p. x.
49. 'La solitude des grands sentiments, c'est la thème dramatique par exellence' (Ted Freeman, citing Camus (1965), 1406, 1407). Freeman remarks that Camus's drama made nothing of his gift for observing the minutiae and idiosyncracies of body language, inflections of speech, and relationships with physical objects which are a feature of his prose fiction, notably in *L'Étranger* (ibid. 132).
50. Popkin, 499–503. One might accord the same tribute to the classically constructed play *Le Malentendu*, set in Bohemia.
51. Todd, 474.
52. *Combat*, 7 Oct. 1944.

53. Beauvoir (1963), 125–6. Camus was referring to Merleau-Ponty's *Humanisme et Terreur* (Paris, 1947).

54. Kanapa, 105.

55. Camus (1948); Camus (1962), 167; Todd, 475. In 'Portrait d'un élu' (1943), Camus had written: 'Contemporary un-belief does not rest on science as it did toward the close of the last century. It denies both science and religion. It is no longer the skepticism of reason in the presence of a miracle. It is a passionate unbelief' (Peyre, 20–5). Camus's anticlericalism makes its entrance in *L'État de siège* when a priest urges the crowd to church and prayer, explaining the pestilence as God's ancient penalty for corrupt cities.

56. Camus, *Actuelles* (1950), 202. In December 1957 he recalled that the play had been 'played constantly for years in Germany' but never 'in Spain or behind the Iron Curtain' (Yugoslavia apart).

57. See Ted Freeman, 112, for a closer examination of the language Camus uses.

58. Camus (1962), p. x.

59. Camus (1950), 73.

60. Ibid. 69–71.

61. Ibid. 147, 150.

62. Ibid. 18.

63. Sartre (1948), 44.

64. Camus (1950), 78, 36, 43.

65. Lottman (1979), 475.

66. Ibid. 475–6.

67. Smeliansky, 26, 27. See also Ingrid Wassenaar, 'Can the Ideals of 1905 Be Made To Live in 2001?', *TLS*, 23 Feb. 2001, p. 19.

68. See Shatrov, *Bolsheviks* (1990), p. xii, and id. *Dramas* (1990), 79.

69. Shatrov, *Dramas*, (1990), 83–4.

70. Alexei Rykov, Lenin's successor as chairman of Sovnarkom, the Council of People's Commissars, executed after a show trial in 1938, married Shatrov's aunt (his father's sister).

71. Oleg Efremov was appointed artistic director of the Moscow Art Theatre in 1970.

72. Smeliansky, 28.

73. Beauvoir (1965), 240–3; Cohen-Solal, 317–18; Sartre (1961), 55.

74. Beauvoir (1965), 240.

75. Sartre (1961), 130.

76. 'Les premiers sont les vrais, les autres sont des riches qui n'ont pas eu de chance.'

77. 'Que n'importe! Il y a de l'or et des pierreries dans ses églises. Tous ceux qui sont morts de faim au pied de ses Christs de marbre et de ses Vierges d'ivoire, je dis qu'il les a fait mourir' (Sartre 1961, 36).

78. Ibid. 88–9.

79. 'Il faut pendre les pauvres. Les pendre au hasard, pour l'exemple: l'innocent avec le coupable' (ibid. 185).

80. Beauvoir (1965), 242.

81. Jeanson (1980), 250.
82. Camus (1952), 178.
83. Gorodinskii (1950; 1953); Ehrenburg, vol. 6 (1966), 217.
84. Hayman (1986), 293.
85. Sartre (1992 (1973)), 339.
86. Sartre (1955), 96–8; id. (1992 (1973)), 337–8.
87. Sartre (1955), 130.
88. Guy Leclerc, 'Au Théâtre Antoine: *Nekrassov* de Jean-Paul Sartre,' *Humanité*, 13 Jun. 55; *Humanité*, 7 Apr. 48. For Pierre Daix the issue was not the self-evidently theatrical quality of *Nekrassov* but 'whether a play in opposition to the government and its press can survive the initial political intrigue to which it is subjected' (P. Daix, '*Nekrassov* ou le défi de la critique au public', *LLF*, 23 June 1955, p. 2, cited by Scriven, 98, 171).
89. Sartre (1992 (1973)), 360.
90. Ibid. 77–8.
91. *Humanité*, 8 June 1955, in Sartre (1992 (1973)), 342, 340.
92. Vilar wrote to *L'Express* (24 Nov. 1955) that he had been asking Sartre for a play for four years.
93. Anon, 'Explosions au Théâtre à propos de la pièce "crypto" de Jean-Paul Sartre,', *LF*, 10 May 1955. Jean-Jacques Gautier, 'Au Théâtre Antoine *Nekrassov* de Jean-Paul Sartre,' *LF*, 13 June 1955. Both cited by Scriven, 97, 171.
94. Sartre (1955), 92; T. Maulnier, 'L'Opium du peuple', *LF*, 4 July 1955; *LF*, 18 July 1956. Thierry Maulnier, a contributor to *Action française*, had published *La Pensée marxiste* (1948) and *La Face de méduse du communisme* (1952). Produced at the Théâtre Hébertot in October 1953, his play *La Maison de la nuit* ran for 160 performances. The focal point is the smuggling of refugees across the border between 'two Central European Republics', one under the dictatorship of the Party, the other 'liberal'. The East is depicted as an unrelieved nightmare of fear, labour camps, and collectivized farms, and the exodus is so great that the Western transit camps cannot cope. Maulnier next adapted Malraux's *La Condition humaine* in co-operation with the author (Ted Freeman, 142, 155).
95. Kemp, '*Nekrassov* au Théâtre Antoine, cited by Scriven, 98, 171.
96. Gabriel Marcel, '*Nekrassov* par Jean-Paul Sartre', *Les Nouvelles littéraires*, 16 June 1955, p. 6, cited by Scriven, 109, 173. Staged at the Théâtre Hébertot, Gabriel Marcel's *Rome n'est plus dans Rome* (*Rome is No Longer in Rome*) had only a short run of 30 performances, beginning 18 April 1951. Inspired by fears of a Red Army invasion of Western Europe parallel to North Korea's invasion of the South, and by the dilemma of precautionary exile, the play has been described as 'one of the most comprehensive examples one could wish to find of a French play of this period being used as a directly aimed weapon in the cold war'. A Catholic dramatist and critic, Marcel was duly attacked by Guy Leclerc in *l'Humanité-Dimanche* (22 Apr. 1951) and by Elsa Triolet in *LLF* (26 Apr. 1951). Cited by Freeman 169, 158.

97. Roland Barthes, '*Nekrassov* juge de sa critique', *Théâtre populaire*, no. 14 (July–Aug. 1955), cited by Scriven, 99, 172.

98. Sartre (1992 (1973)), 349.

99. '. . . cette pièce marque ma volonté d'aborder la réalité sociale sans mythes.'

100. Sartre (1992 (1973)), 340.

101. Here given one of its two Soviet titles, *Pochtitel'naia prostitutka*, although performed in Moscow that year, 1955, as *Lizzie MacKay*.

102. *Bol'shaia sovetskaia entsiklopediia*, 2nd. edn., vol. 38 (1955), 122–3.

103. Sartre (1992 (1973)), 77.

104. Ted Freeman, 172.

105. A similar fate to Vailland's play almost befell André Cayette's feature film *Avant le déluge* (1954), which evokes the great fear in France of a third world war during the summer of 1950. Presented at a plenary session of the highest state censorship board, the Commission de Contrôle, on 7 January 1954, the film obtained its certificate by 10 votes (members of the film profession) to 9 (representatives of the administration, one of whom was missing on the day). The minister of defence, René Pleven, urged the Commission to reconvene, but in vain (Lindeperg, 76).

106. Vailland, 19.

107. Ibid. 176; Ted Freeman, 183.

108. Ted Freeman, 180.

109. Vailland, 53.

Chapter 12. *Squaring the Circle*: Ionesco, Beckett, Havel, and Stoppard

1. In the mid-fifties Havel's applications to various arts and film faculties were unsuccessful; paradoxically he was able to become involved with the theatre while serving in the army (sappers) from 1957 to 1959 (Simmons, 58, 63; Havel 1990, 22–3, 28–9).

2. The leading Absurd dramatists post-war were predominantly foreigners who had settled in France and were writing in French. In the case of Samuel Beckett (Ireland), Eugene Ionesco (Romania), Artur Adamov (Russia), Fernando Arrabal (Spain), and Armand Gatti (Italy), they were no longer working in their native language (Coe, 95, 59). *La Cantatrice chauve*, which made the name of Ionesco, resident in France since 1938, was staged in 1952 at the Théâtre de Noctambules, the 'delivery bed' of the Theatre of the Absurd.

3. Even twenty years later, directing *Godot* for the Schiller Theater, Berlin, Beckett was still making changes in the text. According to his biographer, he did not welcome public association of his plays with those of Ionesco or the 'theatre of the absurd' (Cronin, *passim*).

4. Coe, 91.

5. Ionesco, 18.

6. Another, more technical, influence was Feydeau's *A Flea in Her Ear*.

7. Elsom, 54, quoting Richard Stark, 'Ionesco's Art of Derision', *Plays and Players* (June 1960).

8. Coe, 103, 106.

9. Ionesco, 75–6.

10. Ibid. 19.

11. Did the name 'Godot' come from *godillot*, slang for a boot? Almost certainly not. For further speculation, see Cronin, 457.

12. Ronald Hayman's Berlin diary, dated 12 May 1982, records his discovery in the Brecht archives (Hayman 1982, 41). There is no reference to Beckett in Brecht's *Letters 1913–1956* or his *Journals 1934–1955*, but Martin Esslin remarks that at the time of his death Brecht was 'reported to have been planning a counterplay to Beckett's *Waiting for Godot*' (Esslin 1961, 96, 116).

13. Beckett, 126.

14. Cronin, 457.

15. Http://samuel-beckett. net/PeterHallGodot.html.

16. Cronin, 484. In *Not I* (1972) Beckett places a disembodied mouth in a tight spotlight high on a darkened stage. For 20 minutes words pour out of the mouth, heard, or not heard, by a large shadowy figure cowled like a monk. Winnie in *Happy Days* (1961) cheers herself by keeping track of her possessions, including her husband, while the sands pile high round her neck. In *Play* (1963), two women and a man transfixed in separate urns quarrel over who possesses whom. Time passes but why should it lead anywhere? The circle is complete and padlocked.

17. 'Entretien', 61–6, 73–84.

18. Dalglish, 19. See also Smeliansky, 47, 49, 59.

19. Tarkovsky (1994), 91–2.

20. Anikst, 307, 314, 326, 333.

21. *Bol'shaia sovetskaia entsiklopediia*, 3rd edn., vol. 10 (1972), 370.

22. *The Garden Party*, translated into English 1969, German 1970, French 1969.

23. *Bouzerant* was a derogatory term for homosexual.

24. Ryback, 69.

25. Havel (1981), 83.

26. 'On Evasive Thinking', a speech to the Union in June 1965, reprinted in *Literární noviny* (*Literary News*).

27. Havel (1991), 22–3.

28. Keane, 171–4; Simmons, 72–3; Havel (1990), 81.

29. Simmons, 74, 73.

30. John Keane writes: 'And Havel's characters—unlike Beckett's, for whom there are questions without answers—provide answers without being asked any questions' (Keane, 149).

31. Havel (1990), 53–4.

32. Ibid. 52. Further work by Havel: a short radio play, *Guardian Angel*, broadcast in 1968; a television play, *A Butterfly on the Antennae*, cancelled because of the Soviet

invasion, later broadcast in West Germany. *The Beggar's Opera* (1972), *Largo Desolato* (1984), and *Temptation* (1985)—all unproduced in Husák's Czechoslovakia.

33. Simmons, 67–8; Keane, 147.
34. Esslin (1970), 16.
35. Havel (1991), 26.
36. After he left Czechoslovakia Milos Forman was more reluctant to interpret *The Firemen's Ball* politically than some of his admirers, like the critic Vratislav Effenberger, who wrote: 'He has struck into the marrow of spiritual wretchedness out of which, essentially, springs various kinds of fascism and Stalinism' (Hames 1985, 141–2, quoting Antonín J. Liehm, *The Milos Forman Stories* (1975)). Czech films won a succession of awards at international festivals, then Hollywood Oscars, in 1967 for *The Shop on Main Street* and *Closely Watched Trains*. Forman's *Loves of a Blonde* ran for 25 weeks in Paris, 27 weeks in New York, 17 weeks on Sunset Boulevard (Antonín J. Liehm 1974, 222). The Czechs adopted a variety of forms and influences, neo-realism, *cinéma vérité*, the *nouveau roman*, the Theatre of the Absurd, Kafka, a return to the lyrical and surreal traditions of the inter-war years. The Czech new wave frequently met scornful criticism from the New Left in the West; for example, Godard dismissed it as bourgeois, escapist, fantasist (Hames, 8). Later, after the Soviet invasion and Husák's clampdown, a number of sixties films were suppressed, including Forman's *The Firemen's Ball* (1967). The years 1969–70 saw the banning or stopping of some ten new Czech features, a third of annual output. The blacklist now extended back to cover the entire 1960s (Hames 1985, 2; id. 1989, 108).
37. Stephen Klaidman, 'Czech Writer Here, Sees Opportunity for Liberals', *NYT* 5 May 1968, cited by Keane, 186.
38. Havel (1990), 19.
39. Caute (1974), 99.
40. Keane, 172.
41. Havel (1990), 107.
42. Havel's close allies then and later were the writers Ivan Klima, Ludvík Vaculík, and Pavel Kohout. In the autumn of 1969 he became chairman of the editorial staff of the revived monthly *Tvář* (finally closed down in June 1969), and a member of the Writers' Association Central Committee (dissolved in 1970) (Simmons, 96–7). It was in *Tvář* that Havel published 'The Czech Destiny [or Lot]?' in reply to Kundera's 'The Czech Destiny [or Lot]', which appeared in *Listy* on 19 December 1968.
43. Kundera, professor at the École des Hautes Études en Sciences Sociales, Paris, has lived in France since 1975. He was deprived of Czechoslovak citizenship in 1979.
44. Havel (1990), 172.
45. Tynan, 487, 502.
46. Havel (1991), 91.
47. The London edition of *Audience* (1978) indicates: 'First broadcast with *Private View* on Radio 3 in 1977, the two plays were later shown on BBC TV.'
48. Havel, *Audience* (1978), 12.

49. Brodsky and Havel, 28–30.

50. Havel (1991), 52–3, 55, 59, 88.

51. Simmons, 114–15; Keane, 237, 242.

52. The BBC television production of *Private View* starred Michael Crawford, Ian Richardson, and Zena Walker.

53. Havel (1990), 72.

54. Heinrich Böll (1917–85), German novelist, awarded Nobel Prize 1972.

55. Ryback, 147. In 1978 Invisible Records in Paris issued the Plastic People's first album, *Egon Bondy's Happy Hearts Club Banned*, along with Havel's report, 'The Trial'. This essay was strikingly non-informative, saying nothing about the group's activities, the charges, the sentences. Havel waffled on about 'spiritual manipulation, opportunism, emotional sterility, banality and moral prudery' (Havel 1991, 103). Havel had developed the habit of using ten words or images too many.

56. *LM*, *FAZ*, and *The Times* all reported on 7 Jan. 1977; 'Dirty Linen in Prague', *NYT* 11 Feb. 1977. A letter of protest was also published in the *NYT* on 17 Jan. and in the London *Times* on 7 February, with Stoppard among the signatories.

57. Keane, 248–50.

58. The four British members of the International Committee for the Support of the Principles of Charter 77 were Stoppard, Graham Greene, Iris Murdoch, and Stephen Spender.

59. *The Times*, 1 July 1977.

60. This little 'Balustrade'-like theatre under the direction of Sam Walters has staged more Havel plays than almost any other (Simmons, 127).

61. Havel (1991), 215–16, 228.

62. *Index on Censorship*, 8/5 (Sept./Oct. 1979), 41. An abridged version of 'Reports on My House Arrest', 6 Jan. and 23 Mar. 1979, appeared in the September issue of *Encounter*. In Britain a secretly televised interview showed pictures of his police shadows a few yards behind him wherever he walked and of the lunar-vehicle-like observation post erected within sight of his front door in Hradecek.

63. Simmons, 141.

64. Vladislav, 219. His reading in prison included Brod's life of Kafka, Camus's *The Stranger*, Bellow's *Herzog*, Werfel's *The Forty Days of Musa Dagh* ('wonderful'), and Harper Lee's *To Kill a Mockingbird* (Simmons, 146–7).

65. Vladislav, 211–12. Western spotlights continued to shine on the now invisible, chain-smoking playwright. Havel's trial was reconstructed and performed by the Cartoucherie Théâtre in Paris, later in Munich and New York, on television in Austria and Switzerland. Shortly before martial law was imposed in Poland in 1981, all three Vanek plays were performed in Warsaw. In the summer of 1982 the Avignon festival staged a 'Night for Václav Havel', including two short plays written for the occasion, Beckett's *Catastrophe* and Miller's *I Think About You a Great Deal*. In London the Writers' Guild staged a benefit at the Institute for Contemporary Arts, also in 1982.

66. Stoppard, introduction to Havel (1981), p. v.

67. Tynan to Shawn, 23 Feb. 1977 (Tynan, 589).
68. In a remarkably self-aware description of his own imagination and working method as a playwright, Havel puts his finger on what is theatrically so unsatisfactory in the pre-Vanek plays:

> Again and again I find myself tending toward the analogical construction of dialogue, repeating them, interchanging them, putting words spoken by one character in the mouth of another and then back again . . . my plays are consciously, deliberately, and obviously constructed, schematic, almost machinelike . . . I am interested in clichés and their meaning in a world where . . . 'real reality' often derives from clichés . . . The cliché organises life; it expropriates people's identity . . . (Stephen Klaidman, 'Czech Writer Here, Sees Opportunity for Liberals', *NYT* 5 May 1968, cited by Keane, 186).

Havel likened his plays to op art or geometrical abstraction where 'there may be only a series of concentric circles or colored squares . . . a computer might have painted it . . . the secret lies somewhere in the subtext, in what is not in the picture . . .' (Havel 1990, 196–7). The problem was not confined to the pre-Vanek plays but extended to the 1980s. *Temptation* opens in a scientific institute, with white coats in evidence. The dialogue is dry and Shavian. The Director reminds the assembled staff that the Institute, which is under criticism, aims to 'implement a programme of extensive educational, popular-scientific and individually therapeutic activity . . .' and to counter 'a whole range of mystic prejudices, superstitions . . . spread by certain charlatans, psychopaths and members of the intelligentsia . . .' The dialogue is banal and clogged by phrases like 'so kindly don't try to change the subject'. Scenes on the theme of sexual jealousy are talky and tedious and everything is overstated: 'You seem to be in the grip of a pathological jealousy' (Havel 1988, 196–7). The play was first performed in Britain at The Other Place, Stratford-upon-Avon, on 22 April 1987.

Havel's *Largo Desolato* was first produced in England (adapted by Tom Stoppard) at the Bristol Old Vic in October 1986. The exhaustion of 'Kafkaesque' themes is much in evidence in this schematic comedy of persecution, in which repetition of motif, scene, action, and dialogue figures prominently and characters are paper-thin concoctions with minimal differentiation beyond repeated—sometimes to excess—behaviour patterns (*Largo Desolato*, Havel 1987).

69. *Every Good Boy Deserves Favour* and *Professional Foul* were first published in 1978, *Squaring the Circle* in 1984.
70. Including Ian McKellen, John Wood, Patrick Stewart, Philip Locke, Barbara Leigh-Hunt.
71. *The Times*, 28 June 1977. Fainberg had been pronounced insane, spent five years in the prison-hospital system, and went into exile in 1974, describing his experiences in *Index on Censorship* (4/2), a journal admired by Stoppard. His main concern was to secure the release of Vladimir Bukovsky, whose exposures of Soviet psychiatry had earned him terms of imprisonment, labour camp, and internal exile amounting to twelve years.

72. Soon after Stoppard wrote an article with that title, Borisov was released, but three years later he was back inside. The case of Major General Petro G. Grigorenko commanded international attention. In May 1970, he was incarcerated in a special psychiatric hospital at Chernyakhovsk, where he was 'treated' for 40 months, before being sent to an ordinary insane asylum for a further nine. Sane political prisoners were deliberately scattered among genuinely insane patients— this is a point taken up by Stoppard's play.

73. Ibid. 20–1.

74. Ibid. 105–6.

75. Ibid. 109–12, 115.

76. Ibid. 115–16, 123.

77. Ibid. 179.

78. 'Tom Stoppard on the KGB's Olympic trials', *ST* 6 Apr. 1980.

79. 'As we argued with them,' Timothy Garton Ash recalled, 'we noticed a large, muscular woman in a tight-fitting leather jacket sitting in the foyer, with not just one flower but a whole bouquet. She moved towards us and theatrically distributed unmarked envelopes.' Typed and photocopied, in English, German, French, and Italian, the text informed them: '*Advertisement.* I am warning you that the action called CZECHOSLOVAKIA 88 is illegal and its performance would be contrary to the interests of Czechoslovak working people and consequently illegal. In this connection your efforts to take part in this action would be considered as a manifestation of hostility to Czechoslovakia and in virtue of this we would have to draw relevant consequences against your person.' (Ash 1998, 36–7).

80. Havel (1991), 394. On Havel's years as president, first of Czechoslovakia, then of the Czech Republic, see Ash (1999).

Chapter 13. Andrzej Wajda: *Ashes and Diamonds*, Marble and Iron

1. Born in 1926. Wajda's many films include: *A Generation* (*Pokolenie*), 1955; *Canal* (*Kanal*), 1956; *Ashes and Diamonds* (*Popiol i diament*), 1958; *Lotna*, 1959; *Innocent Sorcerers* (*Niewinni czarodzieje*), 1960; *Everything for Sale* (*Wszystko na sprzedaz*), 1968; *Man of Marble* (*Czlowiek z marmuru*), 1976; *Man of Iron* (*Czlowiek z zelaza*), 1981; *Danton*, 1982

2. Wajda's father, Jakub Wajda, was an army officer who went to war in 1939 and never came back. He died at the age of 40 in the notorious, and historically contentious, Katyn forest massacre of Polish officers by Stalin's orders. When the Germans occupied the whole of Poland in June 1941 they unearthed the graves: 'But until 1989 we were not allowed to make an inscription on the family tomb, saying where he was killed.' The copy of the Polish newspaper in which the Germans published the names of the victims—correctly alleging that the Russians were responsible—had been removed from the Polish archives.

3. The AK, the Home Army, headed by an émigré government in London, was pro-Western, while the AL, the People's Army, was sponsored by Moscow.

4. Wajda (1973), 184.

5. *Encounter*, X/2 (Feb. 1958), 58.

6. Spender (1958), 75.

7. Documentary Film, 'The Debit and the Credit', Wajda website (www.wajda.pl). Working with the screenwriter Jerzy Skolimowski, the prolific Wajda directed *Innocent Sorcerers* in 1960, a film about young people, unfulfilled yearnings, and disillusion. The Polish press response was negative—indeed, in 1963 the Party leader, Gomulka, named it as one of the films for which there was no room in the Polish cinema. The same fate befell Roman Polánski's *Knife in the Water* (1962), which attacks two generations and their common code of honour—the comfortable red bourgeoisie and the young who crave integration. A year later Polánski left Poland.

8. Wajda (1989), 122.

9. Ibid. 120

10. The film was also praised in *Le Figaro, Le Point, La Croix, France Catholique*, and *Les Nouvelles littéraires*.

11. See Koszarski, 286–7.

12. Turaj, 147 and *passim*.

13. Karpinski, 13.

14. Soon after martial law was imposed, a producer had proposed to Stoppard a television film about Solidarity. Stoppard worried that: 'Documentary fiction, by definition, is always in danger of seeming to claim to know more than a film maker *can* know. Accurate detail mingles with arty detail, without distinguishing marks, and history mingles with good and bad guesses.' This led him to the idea of a narrator 'with acknowledged fallibility', a play conveying a 'qualified reality'. The Polish designer, Voytek, working at Pinewood, built a structure of steel gantries squaring off a huge red circular carpet on a steel floor. To this was added background flats and a few large movable pieces, such as a Polish eagle and a huge bust of Lenin. This space served as an airport, a street, a dockyard, the Polish parliament, the meeting rooms of the Politburo and Solidarity, 'and anywhere else we needed'. As a framing motif Stoppard devised scenes in which successive first secretaries of the Polish United Workers' Party are found enjoying a Black Sea vacation with Leonid Brezhnev, who sees them come and sees them go (Stoppard, 89–91).

15. Naum Kleiman, interview, Moscow, 5 Apr. 2002.

16. Best known abroad are Wajda's adaptations of Dostoyevsky, *The Possessed* (seen at the World Theatre Season in London in 1972 and 1973), *Crime and Punishment*, and *Nastasya Filippovna*, based on *The Idiot*, performed in more than a dozen countries.

17. Tadeusz Kantor, a painter and scenographer, began his career as a director in the underground theatre during the German occupation. In 1956 he formed his own

company, Cricot-2, in Cracow. He created the first 'happening' in Poland. His best-known productions include *The Dead Class* (1975) and *Wielopole, Wielopole* (1980), presenting a fantasical world of memories, dreams, and hallucinations in which the main motif is the mystery of death. Cricot-2 and Jerzy Grotowski's Teatr Laboratorium were Poland's best-known experimental theatres.
18. Karpinski, 106.
19. Ibid. 110.

Chapter 14. Classical Music Wars

1. *VOKS Bulletin*, 9/10 (1945), 66–7.
2. Menuhin, 189–90.
3. Ibid. 195–6.
4. Ibid. 193–4.
5. *VOKS Bulletin*, 50 (1946), 9.
6. *SN* 6 June 1947.
7. 'On the Opera *The Great Friendship* by V. Muradeli. The Decision of the Central Committee of the Communist Party of the Soviet Union (Bolsheviks) of February 10, 1948', *VOKS Bulletin*, 54 (1948), 5–7.
8. Zhdanov, 53–73.
9. Prokofiev's comic opera *The Love of Three Oranges* was first staged in Chicago in December 1921. The music is ultra-modern, the action magical-absurd, with a debt to Meyerhold, and could never be performed in the Soviet Union.
10. According to Josef Škvorecký, Prokfiev's *Lieutenant Kijé* was struck from the repertoire because its score called for a saxophone (Škvorecký 1989, 196).
11. Robinson, 472–4.
12. Elizabeth Wilson, 213–14.
13. Prokofiev was awarded a Stalin Prize second class for *On Guard for Peace* and the suite *Winter Bonfire*.
14. Schwarz, 242, 237.
15. Nestiev, 'The Problem' (1951), 41.
16. Nestiev [given as Nestyev] (1956), *passim*.
17. Shostakovich (1979), 26.
18. Roxburgh, 39.
19. Schwarz, 225, 252.
20. Khrennikov headed the Soviet delegation and Hanns Eisler represented, for the moment, Austria.
21. Sartre (1965), 208–14.
22. *Soviet Studies*, I/2 (Oct. 1949), 159, 162. Even more sympathetic to Zhdanov was another of *Soviet Studies*'s academic contributors, Kupava E. Birkett, who described trends like atonality as 'a threat to the character of Russian music' and called jazz in Western Europe 'a replacement of the national tradition by an alien one'.

23. Grigorii Shneerson also coined the title *O muzyke zhivoi i mertvoi* (*On Music Alive and Dead*).

24. Shneerson quoted the composer Roy Harris, whose Fourth Symphony, dedicated to the heroic Soviet people, had been performed in Moscow in 1945, writing in *Musical Courier*.

25. Shneerson, 161–3.

26. Gorodinskii, 29, 18, 28 n.

27. Nestiev, *Dollarovaia* (1951), *passim*.

28. Under the Visiting Artists Program of the Military Government's Information Control Division, which paid for transport, accommodation, and interpreters on the basis of private donations, although the artists themselves went unpaid.

29. 'trubadura griazi i svinstva', rather tamely translated by the East Germans as 'Troubadors des Schmutzes und der Niedrigkeit'. The book was published in Halle, East Germany, in 1953 as *Geistige Armut der Musik*.

30. Gorodinskii, 8. Gorodinskii did not mention that Glinka's opera was called *Ivan Susanin* only during the Soviet period; when first performed in 1836 it bore the title *A Life for the Tsar*; the text was changed after the Revolution to play down the glorification of the monarchy.

31. Vishnevskaya, 91.

32. Gorodinskii, 7. The Soviet composer Edison Denisov later recalled that at the time he entered the Moscow Conservatoire in 1951 people were expelled just for mentioning the names of Debussy, Ravel, or Stravinsky (Denisov, interviewed by Gerald McBurney on BBC TV (1990), in McBurney, 128).

33. Gorodinskii, 63.

34. Ibid. 28, 22.

35. Fay (2391), 323, n. 31.

36. Babbitt, 38.

37. Nestiev, *Dollarovaia* (1951), 34.

38. Josephson, 102; Babbitt, 49.

39. A Degenerate Music exhibition was staged in Düsseldorf in May 1938. Here Hindemith was lumped together with Schoenberg as a 'theorist of atonality'.

40. Pike, 468, 628–9. See also Hinton, 267–8.

41. Nestiev's 'Dollar Cacophany' was published in *Izvestiia* (7 Jan. 1951). Israil Vladimirovich Nestiev's name is more strictly transcribed as Nest'ev but was invariably rendered Nestiev or Nestyev in the Western press.

42. Gorodinskii, 28. Stravinsky: 'Muzyka nichego ne ob'iasniaet i nichego ne podcherkivaet—i kogda silitsia eto delat', to vpolne posledovatel'no stanovitsia nepriiatnoi i dazhe vrednoi' (quoted by Gorodinskii, 23).

43. Gorodinskii had a point—Stravinsky himself was critical of the affectations in Jean Cocteau's linking French commentary for this exceptionally stylized opera-oratorio, in which the singers are masked and occupy fixed positions (English National Opera, *The Rake's Progress*, unsigned programme note on Stravinsky's oeuvre, 2001, n.p.).

44. Gorodinskii, 70. Gorodinskii's typically late-Stalinist demand for 'great historical events unfolding, a genuine national hero, seething (*kipiat*) with great suffering', and his contempt for Britten's 'wretched neurasthenic' fisherman do raise the question of how Britten and his original, but increasingly discarded, librettist Montagu Slater managed a portrait in flat contradiction of Crabbe's original poem, but this is a question beyond our scope here, apart from the fact that the Britten–Pears brand of sentimental, pacifist leftism, which rendered Crabbe's villain unrecognizable in the opera, was utterly foreign to Soviet cultural norms. It could not even be identified, let alone discussed.

45. Carpenter, 229.

46. Kennedy, 157, 165, 159.

47. Britten, 64. Britten later withdrew it from the Sadler's Wells repertory (Brett, 90).

48. *Music Review*, VI (1945), 187–90, cited by Brett, 92.

49. Britten appeared on the cover of *Time* magazine against a background of fishing nets, with the caption 'Britain's Britten'. Virgil Thomson, whom Gorodinskii included among his dangerous decadents, warmly reviewed the Met production in the *New York Herald Tribune* (12 Feb. 1948).

50. *The Times*, 26 May 1947.

51. Carpenter, 73.

52. In the 1930s Copland had read the Marxist classics, supported the Workers Music League (later American Music League), and in 1936 voted for the Browder–Ford presidential ticket. He became closely involved in the National Council of American–Soviet Friendship. In 1946 the American–Soviet Music Society was set up, with Serge Koussevitsky as chairman (he resigned in 1947) and Copland a vice-chair, alongside Leonard Bernstein, but it folded by the end of 1947. Copland supported the Henry Wallace campaign in 1948 (Pollack, 280–1).

53. Serial: using transformations of a fixed series of notes. An arrangement of the 12 notes of the chromatic scale as a basis for serial music.

54. Pollack 284, 446.

55. Copland was, of course, not the only musical figure to run afoul of the inquisition. Wishing to display the photographs of leading American composers in a roving cultural exhibition, the USIA was stalled when the State Department questioned the ideological acceptability of 23 of the selected composers, including the late Walter Damrosch. The exhibition was cancelled. In the spring of 1953 the Voice of America promised the Veterans of Foreign Wars that it would not broadcast the music of Roy Harris, who had dedicated his Fourth Symphony to the Soviet Union during the war, and who was thereafter accorded a status by Soviet critics equal to that of Rockwell Kent in painting. In March 1956 the State Department cancelled a tour of the Near East by the Symphony of the Air after some of its members publicly accused others of having spread Red propaganda during a tour of eight Asian countries in 1955 (*NYT* 24 Mar. 1956; ACLU 1956, 17).

56. Pollack 452, 457–8.

57. In 1956 he was awarded the Gold Medal of the American Academy of Arts and Letters, followed by the Presidential Medal of Freedom in 1964 and the Congressional Gold Medal in 1986.

58. Kellermann, 127. Not only the New York City Ballet arrived in Berlin, but also the conductor Eugene Ormandy, the sopranos Astrid Varnay and Polyna Stoska, a production of *Medea* starring Judith Anderson, the Juilliard String Quartet, a production of *Oklahoma!* starring Celeste Holm, the Hall–Johnson Choir, and more.

59. Ibid.

60. Wolfe, 329–30.

61. Presidents of the CCF included Benedetto Croce, Salvador de Madriaga, and Bertrand Russell. Prominent supporters of the Festival, apart from Stravinsky, were Georges Balanchine, Bruno Walter, and Arnold Schoenberg.

62. The Boston Symphony Orchestra, regarded by some as America's finest, was at the centre of the Festival strategy. Henry Cabot was president of the orchestra's Board of Trustees and was able to call on the support of other trustees such as J. P. Sprang, Jr., president of Gillette, and George N. Jeppson, president of Norton Co. The cost of the tour was put at $171,602.21 (Scott-Smith 2000, 134).

63. Saunders (1999), 117, gives no sources for this.

64. Braden, 1967.

65. Works by 62 modern composers were performed by, among others, the Vienna Philharmonic and State Opera, the NYC Ballet, the Suisse Romande, Radiodiffusion Française, RIAS Berlin, Santa Cecilia of Rome, and the Boston Symphony Orchestra.

66. The nine participating orchestras included the Vienna Philharmonic, the West Berlin RIAS Orchestra (funded by Marshall Plan counterpart funds), and National Rediffusion Française.

67. *Franc-Tireur, Le Figaro, L'Observateur,* and *Le Monde* were friendly.

68. Attempts to obtain gramophone records from Supraphon in Prague, through Collets Holdings in London, 'has not been encouraging', because little of their 'very exciting catalogue' was actually available on request.

69. Stravinsky was again involved, and the advisory board included Darius Milhaud, Britten, and Arthur Honegger. See also Rougemont, 51.

70. Glock, 62.

71. Schonberg, 1968. Boris Schwarz concluded that the teaching of the piano, violin, and cello in the USSR was superb but the standards of wind instruments was inferior to the West's. 'When the Moscow State Orchestra visited New York, the oboes and French horns were found particularly wanting in quality' (Schwarz, 395).

72. According to Saunders, the US Psychological Strategy Board spent $750,000 on the project. It was in 1956 that the Philharmonica Hungarica was assembled, according to Saunders with CIA initial funding of $70,000, after the conductor Zoltan Rozsnyay escaped to Vienna along with a hundred members of the Budapest Philharmonic (Saunders 1999, 225, 305).

73. From an unidentified Soviet booklet (1967).

74. Boris Schwarz admired the Soviet system of catching talent young, the gigantic national network of music schools. 'The figures are staggering'—2,219 elementary music schools with more than 400,000 pupils—and so on up the age pyramid to 24 college-level conservatories (Schwarz, 395).

75. Menuhin, 379.

76. Hixman, 156, quoting *Time*, 21, 28 Apr. 1958; *The Reporter*, 29 May 1958.

77. Chasins, 24–6.

78. According to *The Times*, Ashkenazy shared first prize with the British pianist John Ogdon (*The Times*, 17 Apr. 1963).

79. Parrott, 82.

80. For example, on 8 May 1959 Dmitri Polikarpov, head of the Central Committee's Department of Culture, reported that three senior Soviet musicians bound for England wanted their wives to accompany them, including the conductor K. Ivanov and the pianist Emil Gilels—the decision was negative, no reason given. Three months later Polikarpov advised that Khachaturian should spend two weeks in Czechoslovakia without his wife— *bez zheny*—but the composer was allowed to take his wife to Mexico (RGANI, Fond 5, op. 36, ed.kh. 102).

81. See *The Times*, 14 May, 1 July 1963; *Guardian*, 8 Oct. 1963.

82. Khrushchev (1971), 520–1.

83. When in July 1969 the Soviet press attaché in London issued a statement that the defecting writer Anatoly Kuznetsov could have applied for the same privileges afforded to Ashkenazy, the pianist told the *Guardian* that it was a gross distortion to say that he could move freely between London and Moscow.

84. Parrott 13; Ashkenazy in Ho and Feofanov, 11. The pianist Valery Afanasiev, 26, was granted refugee status in Belgium during a concert tour in July 1974, complaining of restrictions on his career.

85. Schwarz, 284. See 'Shostakovich Writes of the Artist's Independence', *Current Digest of the Soviet Press* (10 Feb. 1954), published by the Joint Committee on Slavic Studies (ACLS and Social Science Research Council).

86. Olkhovsky was an émigré, born in 1900, who had received his musical education in Kharkov, Leningrad, and the Kiev Conservatory before leaving the USSR in 1942. Resident in the USA since 1949, he was a member of the American Association of Musicologists.

87. Olkhovsky, 272–3.

88. Thomas Russell, untitled book review, *Soviet Studies*, VII/3 (Jan. 1956), 299–301.

89. 'Razvivat' (1956), 8–9; ' "Modernists" ' (1956 (1958)), 14–15; Shostakovich (1979), 115.

90. *Encounter*, X/2 (Feb. 1958), 57; X/4 (Apr. 1958), 53.

91. Bowers, 209.

92. *NYT* 23 Aug. 1959; *NYHT* 30 Aug. 1959.

93. Schwarz, 314.

94. *NYHT* 20 Sept. 1959.

95. Astonishingly durable, Tikhon Khrennikov was to remain secretary of the Composers' Union from 1948 to 1991. Interviewed at the age of 87, he conceded nothing and regretted nothing, pointing out that no composer had been shot and claiming that he refused to provide the damning written reports which Stalin's prosecutors demanded. Long a member of the Central Committee, he remains proud of Communist support for the arts: 'We built houses for them, dachas, holiday homes. Our union had a budget of 20 million roubles and our own publishing house' (Michael Binyon, 'Making Music Dance to the Party's Tunes', *The Times*, 4 Apr. 2000, p. 25). At best a song writer of genuine theatrical verve, Khrennikov claims that he is 'by temperament an artist, completely an artist', who had never wanted an administrative role but, as a member of the Party, could not refuse the grim burden when the summons arrived. As for the February 1948 Central Committee resolution against Shostakovich and Prokofiev, it was again his onerous duty to read out what had been written by others—'People forget how things were in those days'—but he hated to do it and takes credit for securing Stalin Prizes for Shostakovich and Prokofiev despite their condemnation. And (he again stresses) no composer, no member of 'his' union, was shot. Khrennikov certainly took pleasure in securing benefits and privileges for his members—a new apartment, a telephone, a trip abroad; there can equally be no doubt that his firmest convictions as a musician were conservative and 'anti-formalist'; even in the late 1970s he was raising fire against avant-garde composers whose 'unrepresentative' work was being performed in Austria without official authorization. They styled themselves the 'Khrennikov Seven', but it was not entirely a laughing matter: avenues of patronage and income, including broadcasting, were suddenly closed to them (Khrennikov, interviewed and profiled by Gerard McBurney on BBC Radio 3, 'Twenty Minutes', 7 Mar. 2002).

96. *NYT* 10 Nov. 1959, 18 Dec. 1959; *NYHT* 15 Dec. 1959.

97. Schwarz, who visited the USSR in 1960 under the exchange programme, returned in 1962 and was assigned to the Institute of Arts History, a research centre, where he found no interest in American musical life and research, and an 'enormous preponderance of projects on Russian and Soviet music' (Schwarz, 320–1, 375). Schwarz's views—as set out in 'Soviet Music Since Stalin' (*Saturday Review*, NY, 30 Mar. 1963)—did not pass unnoticed within the Soviet musical establishment. Following his April 1963 onslaught, 'The Critics and Apologists of the Polish Avant-Garde', Israil Nestiev published 'S Pozitsii "kholodnoi voiny"' ('From the Position of the "Cold War"') in *SM* (Oct. 1963). Nestiev granted that Schwarz had much to say of a positive nature about the successful première of Shostakovich's *Katerina Izmailova*, and a number of talented works 'undeservedly condemned (*osuzhdennyi*) in the years of the cult' (as Nestiev himself put it). However, Schwarz gave offence by complaining that Soviet music still 'required' many years for Soviet composers to catch up with the techniques of Western modernism. What most probably caused the deepest wound was Schwarz's first-hand report and musical detective-work concerning the disaster which

befell the Shostakovich–Yevtushenko Thirteenth Symphony, whose first (and, for some months, only) night he attended in December 1962 (Schwarz, 72, 425).

98. Berlin (2000), 62.

99. RGANI, Fond 5, op. 36, ed.kh. 102.

100. McBurney, 124.

101. At least two major Polish composers, Witold Lutoslawski and Krzystov Penderecki, emerged in this climate of freedom. Russian avant-gardists kept in close contact with the experimental group headed by Penderecki (Schonberg, 179).

102. Schwarz, 323.

103. Richter, 90–2.

104. Khrushchev (1974), 84–5; *Guardian*, 2 Aug. 1997; Kimmelman, 24; Richter, 94. Menuhin attended a concert in 'the early 1970s' by David Oistrakh and Sviatoslav Richter in Carnegie Hall, interrupted by a young man who leapt on to the stage, shouting 'Soviet Russia is no better than Nazi Germany!' Richter apparently found this offensive, not least to Oistrakh, as a Jew. According to Bruno Monsaingeon, editor of Richter's diaries: 'After four tours of the United States, he turned down all further invitations to appear in a country he loathed, with the exception, he said, of its museums, orchestras and cocktails.' Richter continued to perform in Europe, often with David Oistrakh and Mstislav Rostropovich, all of whom became regular visitors to Benjamin Britten's Aldeburgh Festival (Menuhin 298–9; Richter (Monsaingeon), p. xxvii).

105. Nestiev borrowed the title of his article 'Sacred Cacophany' from Stravinsky's *Canticum sacrum*, published in 1956 by Boosey & Hawkes in London, and here subjected to Nestiev's analysis, including notational illustrations.

106. The Stravinsky quotations are translated back from Nestiev, who gives no source for the originals.

107. '. . . .vospitat' v sebe chuvstvo vozvrashcheniia na to zhe samoe mesto.'

108. Nestiev (1958), 132.

109. Two works by the most important of Schoenberg's disciples were recorded in the USSR during 1968—the Symphony Op 21 by Anton Webern, performed by the Leningrad Philarmonic, and the Violin Concerto by Alan Berg, with Leonid Kogan as the soloist (Schwarz, 427).

110. Stravinsky, 126–7.

111. A year after the Royal Ballet's tour, *The Firebird* was one of the ballets performed by the Mali Opera House company in honour of Stravinsky's visit to Russia.

112. *Newsweek* quoted Khachaturian's dislike of Stravinsky's most recent work—'It isn't music'—and pointed out that this view was widely shared in the West. The critic Clarendon (Bernard Gavoty), of *Le Figaro*, regarded Stravinsky's last 25 years as 'nothing but sham'; Giuseppe Pugliese, of *Il Gazzettino* (Venice), regretted 'the squalid and sad panorama of his inexorable decadence . . . the aridity, the dry senility of Stravinsky' (*Newsweek*, 21 May 1962, p. 55).

113. Also the *Symphony in Three Movements* (1945), *Orpheus* (1947), *Ode* (1943), *Capriccio* (1929), *Le Baiser de la fée* (1928), and *Fireworks* (1908).
114. Like Schoenberg's pupil Anton Webern, Stravinsky was attracted to mosaic-like structures of interlocking motifs, variously coloured splinters of sound held in equipoise. When he started *Agon* in 1953 he had just made his first moves towards twelve-note serialism in his Septet (1952–3) and *Shakespeare Songs* (1953), culminating in the thoroughly serial cantata *Threni* (1957–8). (Iain Fenlon, 'Stravinsky and Les Noces' and Paul Griffiths, 'Agon', Royal Ballet Covent Garden programme (2001), n.p.).
115. *SN* 27 Sept. 1962, 12 Oct. 1962.
116. Nabokov (1975), 178. Stravinsky's visit to the Soviet Union evidently did nothing to soften his anti-Communism. See Spender (1978), 218.
117. Also performed were works by William Walton, Michael Tippett, Gustav Holst, and the old masters Purcell, Gibbons, Farnaby, and Byrd.
118. Nestiev (1963), 127. '...bol'shoi muzykant sovremennosti, chestnyi i ser'eznyi khudozhnik.'
119. Carpenter, 418–19.
120. *Peter Grimes* was given a Soviet production in 1965, with Ludmila Ravina and Petor Matves Garilkin.
121. *Guardian*, 6 Oct. 1964. See also Britten, 32; Brett, 100.
122. Vishnevskaya, 366.
123. Britten's lingua franca with Rostropovich was his fluent German.
124. Elizabeth Wilson, 402, 404.
125. Vishnevskaya, 386. Trevor Taylor, *Anglo-Soviet Journal*, 29/1 (Sept. 1968), 41.
126. Carpenter, 485–6; Elizabeth Wilson, 406.
127. The previous year, returning from the West, Rostropovich had bought Solzhenitsyn a fiftieth birthday present, which he got through customs: a duplicating machine that could turn out multiple copies from a single typed stencil (Solzhenitsyn 1997, 109).
128. A dissident young poet from Leningrad, and later Nobel Prize-winner, who was allowed to leave the Soviet Union.
129. Scammell (1995), 111; Vishnevskaya, 398–491.
130. Medvedev, 146–7.
131. Two years earlier Menuhin had been unanimously elected president of the IMC, an autonomous offshoot of UNESCO. Furtseva had told the Swiss ambassador that she would not allow David Oistrakh to play with Menuhin at the Gstaad Festival in August 1971 or anywhere else, but she relented and sent his son Igor Oistrakh after Menuhin made it known that he might not come to Moscow for the IMC meeting (Menuhin, 291–4).
132. Scammell, 221–2.
133. Solzhenitsyn (1980), 518.
134. Menuhin, 297.
135. Vishnevskaya, 136, 185.

136. In March 1956 her husband Rostropovich was performing in London ahead of Khrushchev's visit.
137. Vishnevskaya, 147.
138. Ibid. 171.
139. In 1978 in the Soviet Union the highest pay for instrumentalists was 180 roubles a performance, for singers 200 roubles for a solo concert. Abroad it would be $200 for instrumentalists, $240 for singers. But this was only when a soloist toured alone.
140. Vishnevskaya, 297.
141. 'Even in the last "dacha" scandal, when she was caught red-handed stealing rugs from the Palace of Congresses, she managed, like a cat thrown out of a window, to land on her feet.... She used the rugs to carpet her daughter's dacha; later it was revealed that the entire dacha had been built at government expense' (Vishnevskaya, 263–5).
142. Ibid. 110.
143. *The Times*, 20 Feb. 1980. The defection of Rostropovich and Vishnevskaya, and of Maxim Shostakovich, helped to create a model seductive to young musicians like Viktoria Mullova, a 23–year-old violinist, who defected in 1983 with the Georgian conductor Vartan Zhordania. Immediately after their meticulously planned defection they gave a press conference in Stockholm. Mullova complained that she had not been given the flat she was promised after winning the Tchaikovsky competition; she had been sent off to play in the provinces; and none of the promised recordings had been made of her work. As grounds for political asylum such complaints did not impress the Swedes. That evening Rostropovich telephoned Mullova and Zhordania to say that he had hastily intervened with the Reagan White House requesting letters of parole allowing them to fly to the USA (Krausova, 380–90).
144. Richard Morrison, 'I've forgiven everybody', *The Times*, 27 Mar. 2002, part 2, pp. 2–3. Rostropovich's medical charity had vaccinated more than a million Russian children against hepatitis.
145. Rodion Shchedrin, sometimes described as the official modernist of Soviet music in the 1960s, received a commission from the New York Philarmonic. 'Typical of his recent work is his Piano Concerto No. 2, a score with strong Bartókian dissonances, a touch of Hindemithian baroque, a leaping melodic line, a pointed avoidance of nationalism, and, here and there, some avant-garde devices' (Schonberg, 190).
146. Schonberg described serial technique as 'a sequel to the twelve-tone system worked out by Arnold Schoenberg around 1923...by Boulez and by Milton Babbitt...Not only were the notes "ordered", but also timbre, rests, silences, articulation, and duration of notes. In the process tonality was destroyed... pieces were no longer in C major or D minor. Indeed, there was no key at all' (Schonberg, 178–9).
147. Ibid. 179.

Chapter 15. Shostakovich's *Testimony*

1. Fitzpatrick, 184.
2. Rabinovich, 27. Andrew Porter comments of *The Nose*: 'Berg's opera *Wozzeck* (a big influence on the young composer) meets Charlie Chaplin. In matter, manner, moods, and modes, in tessitura and tonality, in fracture, forms and forces, the opera is exuberantly extravagant.' There are 82 singing or speaking roles (Porter, 21).
3. *Pravda*, 28 Jan. 1936, cited by Fitzpatrick, 188. Twenty years later the official Soviet view remained: whereas grotesquerie and crude caricature in *The Nose* were veiled by the pseudo-comical and by farce, in *Lady Macbeth* they are 'naked and unashamed' (Rabinovich, 32).
4. Shostakovich (1979), (Volkov's preface), pp. xxiii–xxiv, 74.
5. Ibid. 153.
6. Elizabeth Wilson, 271–2.
7. Shostakovich (1979), 118.
8. Ibid. 107.
9. The roster included Symphonies nos. 6, 8, and 9, the Piano Concerto, Two Pieces for String Octet, the Second Piano Sonata, Six Romances on Texts by W. Raleigh, R. Burns, and W. Shakespeare, and *Aphorisms*.
10. Koval', *passim*. See also Elizabeth Wilson, 214 n.
11. Ashkenazy, in Ho and Feofanov (1998), 9.
12. Isaac Glikman, a professor at Leningrad Conservatory, had acted as Shostakovich's unofficial secretary in the 1930s. The composer's letters to Glikman were published in Russia in 1993. The lines quoted here are translated by Harlow Robinson, 'The Noise of Time', Barbican Theatre programme (July 2001, n.p.). Shostakovich wrote film music for the *Young Guards* (1948), *Meeting on the Elbe* (1949), *Michurin* (1949), *Unforgettable 1919* and *The Fall of Berlin* (1950), for which he was awarded a Stalin Prize. Between 1947 and 1953 he wrote music for seven films, while Vissarion Shebalin wrote scores for five and Aram Khachaturian for four (see Egorova, 122–3). He received Stalin Prizes for the oratorio *Song of the Forests* (1949) and Ten Choral Poems by Revolutionary Poets (1951). Mstislav Rostropovich's recall that in 1949–50 Shostakovich had 'no money for food' may be taken with a pinch of salt (*The Times*, 27 Mar. 2002, part 2, p. 3).
13. *NYHT* 27 Apr. 1948.
14. As regards Shostakovich's scorn for him, Khrennikov denies it and insists that the Volkov book was concocted to create an 'anti-Soviet' sensation (Michael Binyon, 'Making Music Dance to the Party's Tunes', *The Times*, 4 Apr. 2000, p. 25).
15. Shostakovich (1979), 107, 111.
16. Fay (2000), 172.
17. Shostakovich (1949), *passim*.
18. Shostakovich (1979), 24.
19. Ibid.

20. Fay (2000), 232; Igor Stravinsky and Robert Craft, *Dialogues and Diary* (London, 1968), 291–2, quoted by Elizabeth Wilson, 376.

21. Shostakovich, quoted in *Novy mir*, 26 May 1949.

22. Nabokov (1951), 203–5.

23. Nabokov (1975), 237–8. Stravinsky's disparaging opinion of *Lady Macbeth of Mtsensk* was probably unknown to Shostakovich. In a letter to Ernest Ansermet, April 1935, Stravinsky was dismissive: 'The work is lamentably provincial, the music plays a miserable role as illustrator, in a very embarrassing realistic style . . . I regret being so hard on Shostakovich but he has deeply disappointed me, intellectually and musically.' Gerard McBurney adds that 'Stravinsky's attitude to Shostakovich did not grow warmer in later years' (McBurney, 122).

24. *NYT* 24, 27 Mar., 1 Apr. 1949.

25. *NYT* 28 May 1949. All quotations cited by Schwarz, 247.

26. Rabinovich, 145–6; Shostakovich (1979), 112, 152.

27. Elizabeth Wilson, 252–4.

28. Wolfe, 329–30.

29. Shostakovich (1979), 72, 151.

30. Schwarz, 284.

31. Ibid. 246.

32. Shostakovich (1979), (Volkov's preface), p. xxxi.

33. Shostakovich (1986), 169, 172.

34. *Sovetskaia kul'tura*, 2 Apr. 1957, reported in 'A Note on the Congress of Artists', *Soviet Studies*, IX/1 (July 1957), 110.

35. Belfrage, 83.

36. Lebedinsky, 475, first published in *Novy mir* (1990), no. 3.

37. The 1962 Edinburgh Music Festival was largely devoted to his work.

38. Cooper, quoted by Schwarz, 337.

39. Vishnevskaya, 244.

40. Elizabeth Wilson, 299, 375.

41. Translated by George Hanna, printed in the USSR, and published in London by the CPGB's publishers, Lawrence & Wishart, in 1959.

42. Salisbury (1960), 39. The villains in *Cheremushki* are comic: Drebednev, the big Party boss; Barabashkin, his servile sidekick in charge of allocating the virgin flats in the new housing estate (a key becomes increasingly a symbol of power and yearning). Drebednev's ruthless fixing of a flat for his girlfriend arouses the ire not only of the prospective tenants, but also of the stout lady leading the building-workers, Lusya. She finally goes to the top with her complaints, Drebednev is sacked, everyone is happy.

43. Shostakovich had a long involvement in lighter forms of music; indeed, in *Cheremushki*, where each main character is accorded his or her individual melody, he quotes from a song in the film *Vstrechnyi*. The new work, Andrew Porter notes, was 'lit at times by the composer's relish for Offenbach and Kurt Weill' (Khentova, 124; Mikheeva, 290–3; Porter, 21).

44. Schwarz, 318.
45. RGANI, Fond 5, op. 36, ed.kh. 102.
46. Ibid., ed.kh. 135.
47. Ibid., ed.kh. 144.
48. After *Lady Macbeth* he had completed no more operas until *Katerina Ismailova*. *The Nose* was revived in Moscow in 1974, following productions by the BBC in 1972 and the New Opera Company at Sadler's Wells in 1973 (Porter, 21).
49. Elizabeth Wilson, 350.
50. RGALI, Fond 2048, op. 2, ed.kh. 32–5.
51. Fay (1995), 161.
52. On Shostakovich's contentious and fraught trip to America in 1959, immediately following *Cheremushki*, L. Mikheeva, although writing in post-Communist Russia, can bring herself to say absolutely nothing of substance beyond reporting his membership of the American Academy of Sciences, except for Shostakovich's visit to Disneyland and his pleasure in riding the big dipper, which took him back to the days of his youthful friendship with Sollertinsky in St Petersburg (Mikheeva, 290–3).
53. Schwarz, 334–5.
54. Including Bartók, Britten, Honegger, Milhaud, Auric, Poulenc, and Barber.
55. Fay (2000), 215.
56. Shostakovich (1979), 119.
57. Khentova, 166.
58. Kirill Kondrashin (1914–81), artistic director of the Moscow Philharmonic from 1960 to 1975, and a close colleague of Shostakovich, whom he first met in 1937, applied for political asylum in Holland in 1978. The gaunt and formidable Y. Mavrinsky had conducted Shostakovich's triumphant Fifth Symphony in 1937.
59. Elizabeth Wilson, 361.
60. Schwarz, 367.
61. Khentova, 167.
62. Yevtushenko and Shostakovich collaborated again in the 1964 symphonic cantata *The Execution of Stepan Razin*, set for bass soloist, mixed choir, and orchestra, and first performed on 28 December 1964. According to Schwarz, Yevtushenko transforms the Cossack leader of a peasant uprising into a revolutionary hero. According to Khentova, the poem addresses the role of the leader (*vozhd'*) in relationship to the people; Shostakovich's music, she says, peeled away the laqueur from the historical figure, bringing criticism when it was first performed, though *Pravda* nominated it for a state prize in 1966 (Schwarz, 429; Khentova, 171).
63. '...predosterech' mir retsidivov fashisma, v kakom by oblich'e ni proiavlialis'. (Khentova, 161–72).
64. Solzhenitsyn, 221.
65. Shostakovich (1979) (Volkov's preface), pp. xxxiii–iv.
66. Ho and Feofanov, 65.

67. Bitov, 524.
68. Volkov had known the composer for fifteen years, starting in 1960 when he was the first to review the Eighth Symphony in a Leningrad paper.
69. Shostakovich (1979), 214.
70. 'Eta kniga ne imeet nichego obshchego s deistvitel'nymi vospominaniiami D. D. Shostakovicha.'
71. 'Melkii bes' are not of course Volkov's words, but may refer to the title of a story by Fedor Sologub.
72. Schonberg (no date given for *NYT*), as retranslated from the Russian. See Ho and Feofanov, 35.
73. RGANI, Fond 5, op. 75, ed.kh. 412. She added that it would be more appropriate to name Volkov as author—Volkov telling Shostakovich's story, 'Shostakovich Talking About Himself'. She suggested that VAAP could ask Harper & Row for the text and warn the publishers not to present it as an autobiography.
74. Shostakovich (1979) (Volkov's preface), p. xiv.
75. RGANI, Fond 5, op. 75, ed.kh. 412.
76. Bogdanova, 374–6; Ho and Feofanov, 43, 81, 79.
77. RGANI, Fond 5, op. 75, ed.kh. 412.
78. Shostakovich (1986), 233–4.
79. The original Russian version of Dmitri and Ludmilla Sollertinsky's *Pages from the Life of Dmitri Shostakovich*, which was copyrighted in 1979 by the official Novosti Press Agency, is a case in point. The book drew on Shostakovich's letters to the polymathic scholar Ivan Sollertinsky (whom he met in the late 1920s and who died in 1944), to Sollertinsky's wife Olga, and to Dmitri Sollertinsky. There are indications that this book was hastily promoted as part of the anti-Volkov campaign. Shostakovich and others are said to have been 'subjected to severe criticism in the Soviet press' in 1948—but there is no mention of the Party, Zhdanov, or Stalin. And no mention of Volkov (Sollertinsky, 126). In 1986 Progress Publishers, Moscow, put out a whitewash (or redwash) volume, *Shostakovich About Himself and His Times*, clearly in response to Volkov, although *Testimony* was not dignified with a mention.
80. Fay (1980), 484–93.
81. Ho and Feofanov, 117.
82. Norris, 8–9, cites *ST* 17 May 1981.
83. According to Ho and Feofanov, Maxim told the music critic Boris Schwarz that *Testimony* 'revealed for the first time the tragedy of the mask of loyalty that my father had to wear all his life'. On 27 Sept. 1986 BBC 2 broadcast Michael Berkeley's interview with Maxim Shostakovich, who confirmed, 'It's true. It's accurate' (Ho and Feofanov, 111). Shostakovich's daughter Galina, born the year her father packed a suitcase after Stalin took against *Lady Macbeth of Mtsensk*, and who now lived in Paris, told Ho and Feofanov on 15 Oct. 1995: 'This book is an outpouring of the soul. It represents, fairly and accurately, Shostakovich's political views'. Maxim shared an American platform in 1992 with Volkov alongside Yevtushenko.

On 23 Nov. 1992 Shostakovich's son appeared on Radio Liberty with Volkov, thanked him for the book and 'for your description of the political atmosphere of suffering of this giant artist'. On 19 Apr. 1997 Maxim confirmed this attitude to Ho and Feofanov (83, 113–14).

84. Fay (2000), 4.

85. See letter from Dmitry H. Feofanov (*TLS* 9 Apr. 1999).

86. Ho and Feofanov claim to 'raise grave questions concerning the scholarly integrity of Volkov's most prominent critics'—alleging selective scholarship, suppression of data, and quotes out of context. The tone adopted by Ho and Feofanov reeks of *post hoc* cold war belligerence: 'Soviet contentions were parroted by Western fellow-travellers' (who are duly listed). Targeted are Laurel Fay, Richard Taruskin, Christopher Norris, and Malcolm H. Brown, most of whom have been more concerned with 'mud instead of music' wherever *Testimony* is involved. Of Laurel E. Fay they write: 'Fay has feasted off the Soviet platter, without question or qualification' (Ho and Feofanov, 16, 237, n. 444, 129). See also correspondence in the *TLS* between Robin Milner-Gulland (12 Feb. and 23 Apr. 1999), Dmitry H. Feofanov (9 Apr. 1999), and Volkov (18 June 1999), writing from 2166 Broadway, Apt 23A, NY 10024. Milner-Gulland holds that *Testimony* fails to meet necessary standards of transparency. Volkov, more recently the author of *Conversations with Joseph Brodsky*, claims that the authenticity of *Testimony* was 'thoroughly explored' and validated in the book by Ho and Feofanov.

87. The present writer sent this chapter in draft to Volkov for comment but, despite a friendly reply, he offered no substantive comment. Attempts to reach Irina Shostakovich in Moscow failed. Evidently she still believes that Volkov added material and attributed it to Shostakovich—a claim that she is reported to have reiterated at California State University, Long Beach, on 16 February 1996.

Chapter 16. All That Jazz: Iron Curtain Calls

1. Utesov hailed from Odessa, a rich pool of Jewish entertainment life.

2. Starr (1985), 5. S. Frederick Starr was co-founder of the Louisiana Repertory Jazz Ensemble and former secretary of the Kennan Institute for Advanced Russian Studies at the Wilson Center, Washington. In 1982 he was appointed president of Oberlin College, Ohio.

3. Glenn Miller's plane vanished in December 1944 when the famous band-leader was on his way from Britain to Paris. At the time he was playing 35 troops concerts and doing 40 radio broadcasts a month.

4. Starr, (1983), 205.

5. Škvorecký lists other musicians sent to the gulag. (Škvorecký, 1989, 107).

6. Ibid. 101.

7. *SW* 5 June 1947.

8. Salisbury (1955), 116.

9. Škvorecký (1977), 21.

10. Kundera, 141.

11. Inkeles, 258.

12. Starr (1983), 216.

13. Ryback, 11–12.

14. Hobsbawm (1998), 247, 266.

15. Davis, 116.

16. Nestiev (1951).

17. P. Robeson, 'Songs of my People' (*Pesni moego naroda*), *SM*, no. 7, 1949.

18. Gorodinskii did not fail to mention the humiliation suffered by Anderson in Washington, DC, and the tragic death of the Negro singer Bessie Smith, whom no white hospital would admit following a car crash (Gorodinskii, 78).

19. *Bol'shaia sovetskaia entsiklopediia*, 2nd edn., vol. 14 (1952), 200.

20. Duberman, 342.

21. In fact the trial of Horáková began later, in June 1950.

22. Škvorecký (1977), 23.

23. Vasily Grossman's novel *Life and Fate* (completed in 1960 but not published during the Soviet period) has Stalin ordering Mikhoels's 'car crash' over the telephone.

24. Shostakovich (1979), 152.

25. Duberman, 353–4.

26. Ibid. 361.

27. ACLU 1950; Rorty and Raushenbush, *passim*. Robeson testified on behalf of the CP leaders at the Foley Square trial, but Judge Medina sustained so many objections to the questions put to Robeson by defence counsel that the result was a virtual gagging.

28. Duberman, 444; Bentley, 784, 777, 773; Robeson, 72, 73, 57, and *passim*.

29. Barban, 15; Škvorecký (1989), 101.

30. Radio Free Europe's pop music programme, 'Altogether', taped in English, was broadcast to the station's five target countries. In the Polish section Jan Tyszkiewicz developed a rock programme, 'Rendez-Vous', a 50-minute show which went out at 6.10 p.m. Monday through Saturday. 'Rendez-Vous' interviewed the Beatles during the filming of the immensely popular *A Hard Day's Night*, as well as the Rolling Stones. Jazz and bebop arrived in Austria via the American Armed Forces Network radio stations. The favourite show was 'Music USA'—the twanging voice of Willis Conover was widely emulated. With the rise of rock'n'roll in the fifties, German records began to sound like a crash course in pidgin English: 'I love you, Baby', 'Sugar Baby', 'Crazy Boy'. Crowds of fans turned out when Elvis—preceded by T-shirts, Coca-Cola, chewing gum, comics, movie stars, nylons, kitchens, cars, automatic washing-machines, and supermarkets—arrived in Germany as a national serviceman (Starr 1983, 243–4; Ryback, 86; Wagnleitner, *passim*).

31. On Rosner, see the documentary film re–creation, 'Storyville: The Jazzman from the Gulag', directed by Pierre-Henry Salfati (BBC 2, 4 June 2002).
32. Salisbury (1955), 263–4.
33. *NYT* 17 Apr. 1955.
34. 'His music, if not his name, is known to every Soviet radio listener. A few bars from one of his songs is the identifying tune of the Soviet radio network. He is otherwise known as a composer of operettas and motion picture music.'
35. Dunaevskii (19–23) mentioned that at a meeting of Moscow composers in February, Khrennikov, general secretary of the union, had declared an 'amnesty' for the saxophone and other not particularly grave jazz crimes.
36. First produced in 1935, with lyrics by Ira Gershwin and a score by his brother George.
37. Gorodinskii, 101–2.
38. Hixson, 137.
39. The contract drawn up in Moscow as late as 3 December stipulated not only that the USSR would supply 'one domesticated she-goat', but also weekly payments of $16,000, half in US dollars payable in New York, half in cash roubles at the official rate, 4 roubles to the dollar.
40. Capote, 7–10.
41. Ibid. 54–5.
42. Ibid. 144–5.
43. Ibid. 150–1.
44. Among them: Leonard Lyons, of the *New York Post*; Charles R. Thayer, of the *Saturday Evening Post*; C. L. Sulzberger, of the *NYT*, had arrived with Ambassador Charles E. Bohlen's party. The *Saturday Review* was sending Horace Sutton, *Time* and *Life* already had a photographer-reporting team on hand, and Mrs Richard O'Malley, of AP's Moscow bureau, was coming in on the Red Arrow Express, following CBS's Dan Schorr (ibid. 144–7, 150–1, 158).
45. Ibid. 161, 165–71.
46. *NYHT* 20 Dec. 1955; *NYT* 27 Dec. 1955; 6, 12, 15 Jan. 1956.
47. Capote, 138–9.
48. Starr (1983), 249.
49. Belfrage, 81.
50. Stites (1992), 132.
51. The film *Blackboard Jungle* featured Bill Haley and the Comets. Clashes between teenagers and police had followed screenings in several West European cities.
52. Utechin, 21.
53. Conquest (1960), 143.
54. Ryback, 28–9, 52.
55. Bushnell, 70.
56. *British–Soviet Friendship* (Jan. 1965), 5. Nadezhdina agreed that the old dances had lost popularity, and mentioned such new ones as 'Russian Lyrical', 'Gay Minute',

'Heels', 'Twilight Rhythm', and 'Swings', plus the 'Lipsi' and 'Perutti' from the GDR and a Cuban dance, 'Friendship'.

57. Ryback, 86.
58. RGANI, Fond 5, op. 36, ed.kh. 88.
59. '...*uderzhat' stoimost's lits, otvetstvennykh za vypusk'* (Letter dated 31 Jan. 1961, RGANI, Fond 5, op. 36, ed.kh. 135).
60. *NYT* 18 Mar. 1961.
61. *NYT* 29, 31 May; 2, 3, 5, 10, 22 June; 9, 11 July 1962; *SN* 1 June 1962.
62. Škvorecký (1977), 104–5. According to the *Guardian* (7 Aug. 1964), the previous day's issue of *Izvestiia* claimed that four members of the Benny Goodman band on the 1962 tour had been spies planted by the CIA. However, the cited report has not been found in *Izvestiia*.
63. *LM* 4 Dec. 1962; *NYT* 11 Dec. 1962; *Encounter*, 20/4 (Apr. 1963), 102.
64. *Encounter* pamphlet, no. 9 (1963), 39.
65. Škvorecký was fired from the staff of 'World Literature' after the banning of his first novel, *The Cowards*, in 1958. Soon after the Russian invasion of 1968, he emigrated to Canada. By 1977 he was Professor of English at the University of Toronto.
66. Škvorecký (1977), 13–15.
67. Škvorecký (1977), 26–7.
68. Contemporary jazz was said to be divided between commercial jazz, 'an integral part of the bourgeois entertainment industry', and the 'creative jazz' of, for example, Duke Ellington, Miles Davis, John Coltrane, and other named American artists (*Bol'shaia sovetskaia entsiklopediia*, 3rd edn., vol. 8 (1972), 184).
69. The first Soviet jazzmen to emigrate, in 1964, were the saxophonist Boris Midney and the bassist Igor Berukshtis. Valery Ponomarev sold pots and pans at Altman's before Art Blakey took him up. Vladimir Sermakashev, who had won virtually every available Soviet jazz prize, failed to find regular musical work for some years. Paradoxically, jazz was simultaneously falling into deep trouble in America, despite the talents of Charlie Parker, Miles Davis, and John Coltrane. Eric Hobsbawm comments: 'Some time in the 1950s American popular music committed parricide. Rock murdered jazz' (Starr 1983, 291; Hobsbawm 1998, 246).
70. For example, Vyacheslav Ganelin and the Ganelin Trio from Vilnius in the Lithuanian SSR, conservatory-trained musicians of high technical ability breaking with the old rules of composition and tonality; their style was elitist, avant-garde, Dadaist (Starr 1985, 8–9). On Ganelin, see also Annette Morreau, organizer of the Arts Council of Great Britain Contemporary Music Network, writing in *Britain–USSR*, organ of the GB–USSR Association, no. 68 (Sept. 1984), 10–11.
71. Škvorecký gives examples of articles in *Jazzpetit*: on New York's Living Theatre; an anthology called *Minimal + Earth + Concept Art*; a monograph on a pre-war surrealist painter; a study of E. F. Burian, a pre-war Communist jazzman and stage director; a study of the musical life of the Jews in Theresienstadt concentration camp; a book on John Lennon with photographs of Prague's John Lennon Wall, the spontaneous creation of youngsters covered with graffiti of grief which

the police regularly smeared with whitewash; an essay on Czech Rock'n'Roll, including photographs of performers who had left the country without permission (Škvorecký 1989, 115–17).

72. Ibid. 128–9.

73. Ibid. 117–18, 126; Jařab (1993), 214.

74. Although electric guitars from Czechoslovakia, Poland, and East Germany could be found in a few select Soviet stores since 1960, costing 300–400 roubles, and the first bass guitars appeared in 1967, amplifiers costing 1,000 roubles remained in short supply—engineering students at the technical schools built them for the 'second economy' and the black market.

75. In the early seventies *Jesus Christ Superstar* became a cult film in the USSR. Every variant recording was collected. In 1971 students at Vilnius staged the complete English-language version. *Inostrannaia literatura* compared Tim Rice's treatment of the Bible to the work of Bulgakov and Dostoyevsky (Ryback, 149).

76. Heavily ironic quotation marks round the word '*vospitatel'nuiu*'.

77. Ryback, 4. By contrast, the Kadar regime refused to curb Hungary's rampant rock culture. In 1970 Gyorgy Aczel, spokesman on cultural affairs, declared: 'As regards ideology and culture, Marxism is not in a monopoly position in Hungary.' Lajor Mehes, first secretary of the youth organization, announced: 'Beat music is per se not a political phenomenon.' The rock band Illes blatantly imitated the Beatles, appearing in psychedelic uniforms identical to those on the Sgt Pepper album cover (ibid. 99).

78. Alexander Gradsky was learning to sing Bach and Schubert at the age of 14 when he first heard the Beatles. He, with the grandson of Mikhail Sholokhov and two others, formed the Slavs, which became Moscow's premier Beatles band of the sixties (three 25-watt electric guitars, one 100-watt PA system, and a set of drums) (ibid. 62–3).

79. Ibid. 94, 104

80. It took three years of negotiations to win approval for a month-long tour by the Nitty Gritty Dirt Band in 1977. Then in quick succession came Boney M, a Jamaican reggae group based in West Germany, Elton John, and the king of rhythm and blues, B. B. King.

81. Even so, the entry on rock'n'roll ('big beat') in the 1975 edition of the *Great Soviet Encyclopedia* was surprisingly friendly. This 'pop music', described as a fusion of jazz, blues, and the country folk style, had succeeded—despite commercial exploitation—in creating 'works of genuine artistic value' from such ensembles as the Beatles and Chicago (*Bol'shaia sovietskaia entsiklopediia*, 3rd edn., vol. 8 (1975), 184). According to Ryback, a Deep Purple, Led Zeppelin, or Pink Floyd album could cost 100 roubles, over two weeks' wages. Komsomol patrols reported and apprehended 101 buyers and speculators in a two-month period (Ryback, 159).

82. Bushnell, 71.

83. Ibid. 120.

Chapter 17. The Ballet Dancer Defects

1. Alexander Avdeyenko, *SN* 5 July 1985, 15.
2. Macaulay (1999), 20.
3. *NYT* 2 June 1949.
4. V. Gorodinsky (Gorodinskii) (1953), 57.
5. 'sotrudnichavshego s gitlerovtsami' (Gorodinskii 1950, 59).
6. *VOKS Bulletin* 4(81) (July–Aug. 1953), 56.
7. Mikes, 203.
8. Ibid. *passim*.
9. The Soviet Ballet Group visiting Paris included G. Ulanova, N. Dudinskaya, K. Sergeyev, N. Anisimova, Y. Kondratov, Y. Zhdanov, and A. Shelest. Their planned, three-week schedule at the Opéra de Paris amounted to extracts from 13 major ballets (*SN* 4 May 1954).
10. *LM* editorialized gravely on 'L'Art et la politique': a time of national dismay and sadness could not justify the adjournment of all performances *sine die*. Non-Communist papers of the left such as *Franc-Tireur*, *Combat*, and *Le Populaire* complained of the government's 'discourtesy' and 'stupidity'. But *LF* discreetly supported Laniel and Schumann.
11. *Izvestiia* reported that the Soviet dancers were seen off at Le Bourget by members of the Association France–URSS, trade unionists, public figures, and representatives of the 'broad public' (*shirokaia obshchestvennost'*).
12. The signatories included not only fellow-travellers like Sartre but non-Communists such as François Mauriac, Roland Barthes, Jacques Prévert, Raymond Queneau, Jean-Claude Servan-Schreiber, the extremely anti-Communist André Breton, Claude Bourdet, J.-M. Domenach, Daniel Guérin, the CF actor Jean Meyer, recently returned from Russia, and Robert Kemp (*L'Humanité*, 17 May 1954). Perhaps most surprising were the signatures of Pierre and Héléne Lazareff.
13. *NYT* 11, 16 May 1954; *L'Humanité*, 12 May 1954; *DW* (London), 17 May 1954.
14. Giving their final performance at the Empress Hall, London, on 3 December 1955, the 80 artistes of the Moscow State Dance Company were pelted with flowers by an enthusiastic audience of 7,000.
15. *Lebedinoe ozero*; *Romeo i Dzhul'etta*; *Bakhchisaraiskii fontan*; *Zhizel'*.
16. A 210-pound discus-thrower who had won the gold medal at the Helsinki Olympics in 1952 (the first Soviet athlete to do so), and again at the European Games in 1954, and who was destined to set an Olympic record for the discus in 1960 with a throw of 180 ft $8\frac{1}{4}$ inches.
17. *NYHT* 28 Aug. 1956.
18. *The Times*, *DW* (London), 2 Oct. 1956.
19. But not Ulanova's: by the time she came to London she had danced in Italy, China, France, the GDR, Hungary, Austria, and Czechoslovakia.
20. To coincide with the first visit of the Bolshoi to London, the Foreign Languages Publishing House issued in English translation a wide range of ballet publications,

many devoted to Ulanova; for example: Y. Bocharnikova, M. Gabovich, *Ballet School of the Bolshoi Theatre* (*Baletnaia Shkola Bol'shogo Teatra*) (Moscow, n.d); B. Lvov-Anokhin, *Galina Ulanova* (Moscow, 1956); Galina Ulanova, *The Making of a Ballerina* (Moscow, n.d.); Galina Ulanova, *Autobiographical Notes and Commentary on Soviet Ballet* (*Soviet News*, London, 1956), all of them printed on cheap paper with inferior illustrations.

21. Born in St Petersburg in 1910, the daughter of a ballet-master and a ballet dancer, Ulanova had entered the Leningrad School of Choreography at the age of 9, graduating in 1928 and joining the ballet troupe of the Leningrad Theatre of Opera and Ballet.

22. Ulanova, *The Making*, 29–31.

23. Lvov-Anokhin, 14–18.

24. Mikhail Chulaki, the Bolshoi's director, intervened to support Ulanova but in terms indicating some affection for the 'discarded' modernism. 'Your modern ballet—I have seen it here at Sadler's Wells—compared to what we had in Moscow in the twenties, it is like a little kitten to a big cat.'

25. Brinson, 29.

26. Not Prokofiev's *Romeo and Juliet*, *Cinderella*, or *The Stone Flower*. And not Shostakovich's *The Golden Age* or *The Bright Stream*. Not Khachaturian's *The Prisoner* (Bellew, 8).

27. Ibid. 9, 11–12. A shift in the Soviet position became apparent in Natalia Roslavleva's, *Era of the Russian Ballet, 1770–1965*. Elaborate dramatic plots were no longer considered necessary; Roslavleva cited the work of the influential Bolshoi choreographer Professor Leonid Lavrovsky, a practitioner of 'abstraction' in so far as he sought choreographic inspiration in music itself, as with his evocation of Sergei Rachmaninov's *Rhapsody on a Theme of Paganini*, premièred under the title *Paganini* at the Bolshoi on 7 April 1960 (Roslavleva, 274–9).

28. *MG* 3 Oct. 1956.

29. *DE* 6 Oct. 1956.

30. *The Times*, 8 Nov. 1956; *Observer*, 18 Nov. 1956.

31. Grey, 76–7.

32. Bowers, 33–6.

33. Ibid. 47–8, 52.

34. Brinson, 12–13, 19.

35. Bowers, 187.

36. Hogan, 28–9.

37. *NYT* 19 Jan. 1959; Salisbury (1960), 103.

38. *NYT* 16, 18 Apr. 1959; Salisbury (1960), 103. Filatov was reported in *NYT*, 21 June 1959.

39. Sol Hurok complained that the State Department would not allow the company to visit San Francisco, off-limits to Soviet citizens. By 10 April the State Department had rescinded the ban (*NYT* 10 Apr. 1959).

40. Ulanova had been little seen in the United States, except in imported films like *Stars of the Russian Ballet*—a compendium extracted from *Swan Lake*, *The Fountain of Bakhchisarai*, and *The Flames of Paris*—which was screened in New York in September 1954, with Ulanova, Dudinskaya, N. M. Sergeyev, and Plisetskaya.

41. The dancers complained of rehearsal conditions; sections of the stage floor were then replaced.

42. Present in the first-night audience at the Met were Marlene Dietrich, Greta Garbo, Agnes de Mille, Lillian Gish, Noël Coward, Martha Graham, Georges Balanchine, Douglas Fairbanks, Jr., Van Cliburn, and Cole Porter. The repertoire for the tour embraced *Swan Lake*, *Giselle*, and Prokofiev's *Stone Flower*.

43. The only comparable event appeared to be the December 1910 première of Puccini's *The Girl of the Golden West*, with Enrico Caruso singing and Arturo Toscanini conducting.

44. *NYT* 13 May 1959.

45. *The Tale of the Stone Flower*, completed by Prokofiev a few days before his death, is set among Russian peasants of the last century who excelled as stone-carvers in the Urals.

46. Salisbury (1960), 102–3.

47. Valery Panov, born into the Jewish family Shulman, in Vitebsk, later changed his name although his brother did not.

48. A member of the Beryozka Folk Dancing Company, Gennady Petrovitch Lvov, had been accused of stealing $42.41-worth of merchandise from Macy's. 'Detectives said he had such items as a brassière, a handbag, 23 neckties and five pairs of socks under his coat when arrested. He was released on $500 bail, the merchandise was returned and the charges were dropped' (*NYHT* 7 Feb. 1959—spellings of the Russian names as given).

49. Panov, 120–7; Vishnevskaya, 206.

50. *NYT* 3 July 1959; *The Times*, 15 June 1974; Panov, 127.

51. Panov, 130, 137.

52. See Solway, 158.

53. Clive Barnes (1981), 23; Panov (1978), 119, 120, 186. Four years later Panov, now with the Kirov under the direction of Sergeyev, took over the role of Prince Albrecht in *Giselle*, previously danced by Nureyev (Solway, 114).

54. Solway, 137.

55. Ibid. 173.

56. In *Le Figaro* Claude Baignères hailed 'l'aérien Rudolf Nureyev', while *L'Aurore* declared 'Les Ballets de Leningrad ont leur "l'homme de l'espace" '—The Leningrad Ballet has its own 'man in space'—a reference to the first cosmonaut, Yuri Gagarin, launched into orbit two months earlier.

57. *New Yorker*, 3 Feb. 1962; Solway 138–9.

58. Clive Barnes (1981), 33.

59. 's sobliudeniem vsekh mer predostorozhnosti' (RGANI, Fond 5, op. 36, ed.kh. 135).

60. Ibid.
61. Solway, 146–8.
62. 'dlia uchastiia v otvetstvennykh kontsertakh v Moskve' (RGANI, Fond 5, op. 36, ed.kh. 135).
63. Solway, 169.
64. Ibid. 163, 553.
65. Watson himself found the file thin and 'self-serving', as if the KGB's successors are still trying 'to spread disinformation'. He urges 'the utmost caution'—but himself uses the suspect 'KGB file' freely (Watson, 174–6).
66. Clive Barnes (1981), 42.
67. Nureyev, 97.
68. The word 'defector' (*perebezhchik*) was not commonly used. Elena Smolina cites *otstupit'sia* (to defect from a party) and *otstupnichestvo* (defection).
69. RGANI, Fond 5, op. 36, ed.kh. 135.
70. But here accounts differ. According to Watson, 'the KGB file' records a trial in Leningrad between 19 September and 3 November. Watson writes: 'more than 90 pages of the testimony were made available to the author'. The bench consisted of a professional judge and two lay jurors. At least ten witnesses were called to testify about Nureyev's behaviour before and during his defection in Paris, including Strizhevsky, a KGB officer. The trial was closed to the public and the female judge handed down a lenient sentence on Nureyev of 6–7 years. This was never revoked in the dancer's lifetime (Watson, 216–17). Solway's account of the witnesses called overlaps with Watson's, but the trial is said to have lasted two hours not six weeks.
71. Solway, 234–6, 570. An enquiry to Diane Solway by the present writer went unanswered. In the event Sergeyev stayed on as artistic director and Dudinskaya, People's Artist of the USSR (1957), four times a Stalin Prize-winner, and ballet mistress of the Vaganova School, remained as principal ballet mistress, while Pyotr Rachinsky took over as director of the Kirov.
72. The court's sentence read: '*k 7-mi godam lisheniia svobody s konfiskatsiei imushchestva*' (Zakrzhevskaia, 14–15).
73. Nureyev (1962), 13–14.
74. Khrushchev (1971), 523–4.
75. Keep, 176.
76. Ho and Feofanov, 57, n. 39.
77. The family came from Georgia; Balanchine himself was half Georgian (his father), one-quarter Russian, and one-quarter German. Following the Revolution all the other members of his family, first his father, then his brother, and finally his mother, moved to Georgia. Balanchine never saw his parents again.
78. Goodwin, n.p. See also Macaulay (2001), 18.
79. Stravinsky (1962), 127.
80. This is confirmed by the bibliography of the catalogue of the exhibition *Paris–Moscou* (1979). Between 1921 and 1978 there are 16 Western entries on the subject of the *Ballets russes*, but not one from within the Soviet Union.

81. *NYHT* 27 Sept. 1956.
82. Clive Barnes, in Salisbury (1968), 209.
83. Leading the company was Lincoln Kirkstein, general administrator, with whom Balanchine had founded NYCB in 1933.
84. American Ballet Theatre, during its 1960 Russian tour, had danced at the Stanislavsky Theatre and the Lenin Palace of Sports.
85. Buckle, 233–4.
86. Ibid. 234. The NYCB performed Stravinsky's *Apollo* and *Agon*, Britten's *Fanfare*, and *The Prodigal Son* to Prokofiev's score. 'Ballets to Bach, Mozart, Weber and Morton Gould were new enchantments', adds Panov (Panov, 154, 156).
87. Buckle, 236.
88. Ibid. 238.
89. Vishnevskaya, 279, 299–300.
90. Parrott, 122–3; Makarova, 117.
91. These Soviet articles and the book extract have been reprinted in Zakrzhevskaia, 247–51. On Censorship of Nureyev's name, ibid. 14–15.
92. The following Soviet artists appeared under the Management of Victor Hochhauser, of 81 Kensington Church St., London, W8. Soloists: Sviatoslav Richter, David Oistrakh, Mstislav Rostropovich, Galina Vishnevskaya, Vladimir Ashkenazy. Orchestras and chamber ensembles: the Moscow Philharmonic, Leningrad Symphony, Moscow Chamber, Borodin String Quartet. Dance companies and ensembles: Bolshoi, Kirov, Moiseyev Dance Company, Red Army Ensemble.
93. *ST* 15 Aug. 1965.
94. Konstantin Sergeyev remained artistic director and had just been awarded the Order of Lenin on his sixtieth birthday; Dudinskaya remained ballet mistress; Oleg Zhuravkov *regisseur*. Mikhail Baryshnikov figured among the ten leading male dancers.
95. Makarova, 88; *The Times*, 14 Sept. 1970.
96. Makarova, 91.
97. Ibid. 110.
98. For two years she moved about the world—South Africa, Milan, Stockholm, Munich, Paris, Zurich, Berlin—until she found a haven with the Royal Ballet in 1974. On 30 June her former Kirov colleague Mikhail Baryshnikov, then 28, and five years her junior, telephoned from Toronto to say he had asked for political asylum. On 27 July they danced together in *Giselle* in New York (Solway, 392). Makarova's staging of *La Bayadère* for ABT was taken up by other companies, including the Royal Ballet. In February 1989 she was the first artistic exile to be invited back to perform in Russia.
99. Like Nureyev, Baryshnikov was a former pupil of the late revered Aleksandr Pushkin, and had taken over some of Panov's lead roles at the Kirov, notably in *Hamlet* and *The Creation of the World*. A year previously, in 1973, Aleksandr Minz, a former Kirov soloist, had emigrated to America and now taught at ABT's school. Aleksandr Filipov, a classmate of Mikhail Baryshnikov at the Kirov school, had

defected from the Moiseyev Young Classical Ballet in 1970 and was now a principal with the San Francisco Ballet.

100. *NYT* 1 July 1974.

101. *The Times*, 21 Aug. 1974; Solway, 395.

102. Panov, 156–7.

103. Ibid. 239, 288.

104. Ibid. 254, 258–9, 293–4.

105. Ibid. 302, 306–10.

106. Ibid. 320, 346.

107. Ibid. 339, 341.

108. *The Times*, 8, 9, 11, 13 June 1974.

109. Hochhauser, according to Levin, had repeatedly lied to him by denying any connection with, or financial stake in, the imminent visit by the Bolshoi to the London Coliseum. In 1972 the Russians had cancelled a ballet season sponsored by the Sadler's Wells Trust after the British government expelled 105 Soviet diplomatic personnel; the chairman of the Trust, Kenneth Robinson, had enlisted Hochhauser's expertise in arranging the current Bolshoi visit—but refused to comment when Levin telephoned to enquire about the Jewish impresario's financial involvement.

110. *The Times*, 3, 13 Aug. 1974. Six years later, in 1980, Nureyev was dancing at the Met with the Berlin Ballet as Prince Myshkin in *The Idiot*, choreography by Valery Panov.

111. Solway, 398 n., 449.

112. *The Times*, 2 Feb., 14 May, 9, 11, 19 Nov. 1977.

113. Watson, 252, 298.

114. In 1992 the British Government brought ('exfiltrated' in the jargon) Vasili Mitrokhin, an officer of the Soviet Foreign Intelligence Service (1948–84) to the UK. Born in 1922, Mitrokhin had been transferred to the KGB archive in 1956. We are told that from 1972 to 1984 he supervised the transfer of the First Chief Directorate's archive from Lubyanka to the new KGB headquarters at Yasenevo, a Moscow suburb. As described by Professor Andrew:

> Mitrokhin was alone responsible for checking and sealing the approximately 300,000 files in the FCD archive prior to their transfer to the new headquarters. While supervising the checking of files, the compilation of inventories and the writing of index cards, Mitrokhin was able to inspect what files he wished in one or other of his offices. (Andrew and Mitrokhin, 10)

> ... he began to take notes in minuscule handwriting on scraps of paper which he crumpled up and threw into his wastepaper basket. Each evening, he retrieved his notes from the wastepaper and smuggled them out of Yasenevo concealed in his shoes... After a few months he started taking notes on ordinary sheets of office paper which he took out of his office in his jacket and trouser pockets. Not once in the twelve years which Mitrokhin spent noting the FCD archives was he stopped and searched... (Ibid. 12)

115. Andrew (16 Sept. 1999), 39; Andrew and Mitrokhin (2000), 480–2, 727, and 855 refs. 69, 71–3, 76, 76.
116. Andrew (13 Sept. 1999), 41.
117. Andrew and Mitrokhin (2000), 480.
118. *Nureyev*, 96–7.
119. The source reference given here (p. 481, ref. 71) is to Mitrokhin's notes: 'vol. 2, app. 3'. We are told that the Mitrokhin Archive has been arranged in four sections, of which the third is called the 'vol.-series', consisting of typed volumes containing material drawn from numerous KGB files, mostly arranged by country, sometimes with commentary by Mitrokhin.
120. Andrew and Mitrokhin (2000), 481.
121. Ibid. 481, ref. 72.
122. Ibid. 481. The source reference is 'vol. 6, ch. 5, part 5' of the Mitrokhin Archive.
123. Ibid. 481. The source reference is 'vol. 2, app. 3'.
124. Ibid. 501, 857, ref. 49. The source reference is 'vol. 6, ch. 1, part 1; vol. 6, ch. 5, part 5' of the Mitrokhin Archive.
125. In a letter (25 June 2002) to the present writer, the minister of state at the Foreign Office, Denis MacShane, insisted that the 'Mitrokhin archive' remains the property of Mr Mitrokhin personally, and the Government is not at liberty to release any part of it without his permission. In a subsequent (1 August 2002) letter to the author, Gill Bennett, chief historian of the Foreign Office, reported that Mitrokhin had refused to allow the present writer to see even the few files (relevant to this chapter) requested.
126. Two more principals subsequently defected during the tour, Leonid Kozlov and his wife Valentina. Godunov signed up with ABT for the 1979–80 season. (*NYT* 24, 26, 28 Aug.; 23 Sept. 1979). In 1985 Sergei Mikaelyan directed a tedious, two-part docu-drama, *Flight 222* (*Reis 222*), based on these events. In the film the heroine-wife, Irina Panina, is an ice dancer with a Soviet company performing at Madison Square Garden; her husband, the defecting Gennadi Shiralov, is a famous sportsman. The Soviet Embassy staff refuse Irina's request to try and set up a meeting with Gennadi: 'No, they will try to brainwash you as well; given half a chance they will put drugs in your luggage.'

Chapter 18. Stalinist Art: *Tractor Drivers' Supper*

1. Ehrenburg, *Chekhov* (1962), 55.
2. Revyakin, 167–8.
3. Barr (1986), 214–15.
4. *NYT Magazine*, 14 Dec. 1952, in Barr (1986), 215.
5. Cited by Golomshtok (1990), 107.
6. The 'left' artists themselves, however, did not generally perish in the purges: Rodchenko and Malevich were not arrested, while Tatlin was even honoured with a Stalin Prize for stage designs in 1943 (Rakitin, 178–82).

7. The London magazine *Encounter* accorded his *Art Under a Dictatorship* a long and enthusiastic review by T. R. Fyvel, who began with an attack on the *bête noire* of *Encounter*'s editors and sponsors, the *New Statesman*, whose fault, evidently, was to have steered clear of 'really serious discussion of art or literature in the Soviet Union' (Fyvel, 1955).
8. Lehmann-Haupt, 236, 243–5.
9. Golomshtok (1990), 104–5.
10. Among the German modernists on display were Ernest Barlach, Max Beckmann, Paul Klee, Otto Dix, Ernst Ludwig Kirchner, Emil Nolde, and George Grosz. Beckmann and Oskar Kokoschka chose exile; others, like Emil Nolde, remained and were able to paint in secret (Golomshtok 1990, 104).
11. On 31 May 1938 a law was passed confiscating all works of 'degenerate' art. A majority of them were sold abroad, Hermann Göring having appropriated works by Van Gogh, Gauguin, Marc, and Munch for his private collection; the remainder, about 5,000 paintings, watercolours, and drawings, were burned in the spring of 1939 by the Berlin fire brigade.
12. Golomshtok and Glezer (1977), 85.
13. Golomshtok, 1990.
14. Matthew Cullerne Bown dispenses with the totalitarian model: 'The effect of concentrating on the totalitarian aspect of socialist realism has been, among other things, to play down the national roots of art' . . . Yet Cullerne Bown says that Igor Golomshtok's *Totalitarian Art* (1990) 'convincingly' advances the model (Cullerne Bown, p. xvii).
15. Lindey, 25.
16. Designed respectively by Boris Iofan and Albert Speer.
17. The convergences of 'totalitarian art' were convincingly reaffirmed by the show 'Art and Power: Europe Under the Dictators, 1933–1945', at the Hayward Gallery, London, in 1995.
18. Aleksandr Gerasimov, once a leading light of the Association of Artists of Revolutionary Russia, and president of the Moscow Union of Artists, became in 1938 first president of the Organizational Committee of the Union of Soviet Artists.
19. Together with the Ministry of Culture, it supervised artistic scholarship, museum work, exhibitions, and publishing. The Union, the Academy, and the Ministry were all subordinate in the final analysis to the Cultural Section of the Central Committee of the Communist Party (Golomshtok and Glezer 1977, 91–2).
20. Kelly and Milner-Gulland, 145–7, 151–2.
21. Gerasimov routinely established the most immediate antecedents of Soviet socialist realism, the Russian realists of the late nineteenth century, I. N. Kramskim, I. E. Repin, V. I. Surikov, I. Levitan, I. I. Shishkin, F. A. Vasil'ev: further back, Rembrandt and Velasquez were mentioned in a gesture to internationalism.
22. Akademiia, 19, 24.

23. 800,000 spectators attended the 1946 All-Union Art Exhibition. The exhibition at the Tretyakov Gallery to celebrate the 30th anniversary of the Revolution brought 14,000 visitors in the first two days alone.

24. Akademiia, 15.

25. 'Instead of a strict system and a definite consistency of teaching, students to this day are still sometimes taught to portray the world as emerging from a conventional "colour-spot" (*uslovnogo tsvetovogo piatna*). Students are instilled (*vnushaetsia*) with fear and loathing of precise, clear-cut, detailed representation of the objective world. Clarity and precision are rejected as "naturalism". By this strange bogey (*strannym zhupelom*) inability to portray the material world is often justified. Mannerism (*manernost'*), sketchism (*eskiznost'*), approximation (*priblizitel'nost'*), which cover up an absence of elementary capability, pass themselves off as genuine artistry.' Such theories were harmful (Akademiia, 60).

26. Rabine, 48. See also Slepian (1962), 54. Lydia Romachkova, now deputy director of the Tretyakov, and a student at Moscow State University Art History Department in the early 1950s, remembers the lectures on impressionism given by Valery Prokofiev (no relation to the composer) despite the general ban on the subject (Lydia Romachkova, interview, Moscow, 4 Apr. 2002).

27. Akademiia, 27.

28. *SI* 46, 6 Nov. 1945, 3 cited by Cullerne Bown, 283, 223. For Sergei Gerasimov's own impressionist work, see his *Winter Evening, Samarkand* (1941) and *Spring Trees in Blossom in Samarkand* (1942). Gerasimov's attempts at broad-canvas socialist realism suffer from lack of conviction and even from poor draughtsmanship, for example his *Collective Farm Celebration* (1937).

29. Cullerne Bown, 223.

30. *SI* vol. 6 (1949), 77; vol. 7 (1950), 34. Both cited by Cullerne Bown, 283.

31. Kemenov (1947), 24–7. For an anti-Communist overview published by the USIA, see Slepian, 54.

32. Korzhev's mastery of the grim close-up also led him in later years to paintings which offended Soviet romanticism: for example his *Lovers* (1959), showing an ageing, sunburnt, tired couple resting beside a motorbike; his almost photographic *On the Road* (1962), in which a poor woman holds a child swaddled against the cold while the legs of her man protrude from beneath a stalled truck.

33. For example, *A Song of Peace* (1950), showing Paul Robeson singing in the Peekskills, defended by fine-looking veterans; Fedor P. Reshetnikov's *For Peace* (1950), showing a group of Parisian urchins painting 'PAIX!' on a wall while gendarmes confront demonstrators further up the street; and Petr P. Belousov's 'classical' style *A Greek Patriot in a Fascist Jail* (1954)—here the woman is unnaturally illuminated in a dark cell, her child asleep on her lap, as her jailers peer through the door.

34. Cullerne Bown, 269

35. *SI* 1/12 (1947), cited by Cullerne Bown, 259.

36. I. E. Repin (1948), 10, 84–6; Repin (1946), 29; Ehrenburg, *Chekhov* (1962), 188.

37. Cullerne Bown, 283. Cullerne Bown gives as his source *RGALI* 2305/1/128 (presumably Fond 2305, op. 1, ed.kh. 128, p. 44).

38. Dismissing a defence of Moore by Kenneth Clark in *Art News* (Feb. 1947), 29, Kemenov wrote: 'Thus along with animal impulses, sculpture has undertaken the portrayal of people degraded to reptilian forms. The sculptures of [Jacques] Lipchitz, Henry Moore, and others are reactionary, for they aim to destroy that which is human in man and to rouse in him the beast... to whom the very word "humanism" is incomprehensible' (Kemenov 1947, 20, 23).

39. Guldberg, 165, 167. See also Groys.

40. An 'airbrush' is an ink-jet gun powered by a cylinder of compressed air.

41. King, 188–9. Sergei A. Grigoriev's *Admission to the Komsomol* (1949) was later repainted to exclude a bust of Stalin. Vyacheslav M. Mariupolski's *A Leader in the Pioneers* (*Her First Report*) (1949) was later repainted to exclude the mounted photograph of Stalin pinned to the wall behind the head of the rather unpleasant-looking female Pioneer, whose hard, very blue eyes and robotic expression seem to be hunting down someone in her unseen audience who may have nodded off (Cullerne Bown, 306).

42. Ehrenburg, *Thaw*, (1961 (1955)), 41.

43. *MG* 13 Sept. 1955.

44. Cullerne Bown, 337.

45. Harrison Salisbury, of the *New York Times*, described the living conditions of his translator Nina: an interior courtyard filled with toilet and cooking smells in summer and eternally dark in winter; her room was one of seven in a communal flat, sharing a tiny kitchen equipped only with electric hot-plates and in which the water tap had long since ceased to function (Salisbury 1955, 77).

46. As he recalled in a speech, 'Zhizn—istochnik vdokhnoveniia khudozhnika' (Life is the source of inspiration of an artist), to the Academy of Arts, Leningrad, on 14 April 1960. Extremely popular was his radiant *Letter From the Front* (1947), in which very strong, contrasting light illuminates a happy family grouped at an open front door and veranda, while a boy Pioneer reads aloud the letter from the front.

47. *DNZ* was mainly run by European, mostly Jewish, émigrés with US citizenship and background in the Psychological Warfare Division of the US Army, quartered in Luxembourg, 1944–5. Hans Habe led the team. Articles and editorials by Hans Habe, Erich Kästner, Franz Roh, Hellmut Lehmann-Haupt, and Conrad Westphal carried such titles as 'Offended Artists', 'Cleansing of German Art Culture', 'On Educational Snobbery, Particularly in Front of Works of Art', 'Thoughts About Degenerated Art', 'Education For the New Art', and 'The Awakening Art'.

48. *DNZ*, Jan. 1946, cited by Gienow-Hecht, 'Art is Democracy' (1999), 31–2.

49. See Hellmut Lehmann-Haupt Papers, MoMA archives, New York, cited by Goldstein.

50. Goldstein, 2–3, citing Gordon Gilkey, *German War Art* (Office of the Chief Historian Headquarters, European Command), 25 Apr. 1947.

51. Goldstein, 10–11.
52. Pike, 188.
53. By Erich Heckel, Karl Schmidt-Rottluf, Ernst Ludwig Kirchner, Max Beckmann, Oskar Kokoschka, Max Pechstein, Otto Dix, Paul Klee, Lyonel Feininger, and Käthe Kollwitz.
54. Of the three Western occupying powers, only the French rapidly implemented an active art programme. From the start 'Officiers des Beaux-Arts' worked closely with German museum curators and art scholars to bring exhibitions to Berlin and other bombed-out cities. By contrast, the American Monuments, Fine Arts, and Archives Section, which formed part of the Restitution Branch of the Economics Division, focused on art as property—primarily the restitution of Nazi loot to its rightful owners (Lehmann-Haupt, 197–9).
55. Pike, 309.
56. German by birth and education but an American citizen, Hellmut Lehmann-Haupt was now an intelligence liaison officer with the Monuments, Fine Arts, and Archives Section of OMGUS.
57. Lehmann-Haupt, 201. But Lehmann-Haupt's version should be accepted with caution. Soon after attending Dymshits's lecture, and many years before he published this account of it (in 1954), he made notes paraphrasing the Russian's remarks: 'All art that does not fit the specifications is . . . decadent, individualistic, capitalistic.' The term 'specifications' is clearly Lehmann-Haupt's own, and not a term Dymshits would have used to describe socialist realism. (Goldstein cites Lehmann-Haupt, 'German Art Today', undated essay, Lehmann-Haupt Papers, Box 4, Folder 16, MoMA archives.)
58. Pike, 535. Dymshits himself, a Jew, was called back to Moscow in March of that year as the 'anti-cosomopolitan' campaign picked up steam.
59. Lehmann-Haupt, 207.
60. Pike, 532.
61. As recorded in a profusely illustrated volume, *L'Art Slovaque sur sa voie du Réalisme socialiste*, published in Bratislava (Lehmann-Haupt, 234).
62. Ibid. 208–9.
63. Brecht (1993), 525 (note by John Willett (ed.)).
64. Ibid. 441.
65. In 1958 posters were included for the first time in the fourth German Art Exhibition in Dresden, largely as a result of the activities of Klaus Wittkugel and John Heartfield, both photo-montageists and arguably the most talented poster designers in the GDR; as examples one might cite Heartfield's grey-green poster celebrating 40 years since the 1917 Revolution, a fist gripping a rifle in the foreground; and Wittkugel's similar use of grey-green to celebrate the first 10 years of the GDR, emphasizing factory chimneys, a new refinery, and children playing happily in a foreground field.
66. Fenton (1996), 52.

67. The author is much indebted to the plates, reproductions, and perceptive commentary in the magisterial work by James Aulich and Marta Sylvestrová, *Political Posters in Central and Eastern Europe 1945–1995* (Manchester, 1999).
68. Juviler, 41–2.
69. *SI* vol. 4, (1960), 34, cited by Cullerne Bown, 384.
70. *Soviet Survey*, no. 6. (1956), 17–20.
71. Ehrenburg, *Chekhov* (1962), 179, 191–5, 203–4. A striking change of emphasis occurred between the second and third editions of the *Bol'shaia sovetskaia entsiklopediia*. In the 1952 entry the impressionists denied any connection between art and social struggle, they evaded (*obkhodili*) sharp social contradictions and took refuge in refined sensibilities and intimate experiences. The 1972 edition (written by O. V. Mamontova), by contrast, began on an utterly positive note. Monet, Renoir, and their colleagues 'had united in the struggle to renew... the process of liberating art from the conventions of classicism, romanticism, and academicism begun by the realists between the 1840s and 1860s; affirmed the beauty of daily reality and simple, democratic motifs.' In an important tribute from a Soviet source, the impressionists were credited with 'rebuilding the unity between man and the environment surrounding him' (*Bol'shaia sovetskaia entsiklopediia*, 2nd edn., vol. 17 (1952), 594–5; 3rd edn., vol. 10 (1972), 162–3).
72. Vystavki, 40. Three years later Vladimir Serov announced that more than 12 million people had visited 96 Soviet art exhibitions in 42 countries during the previous five years. This, he said, dispelled the 'mythical backwardness' of Soviet art. *The Times*, 28 Dec. 1962.
73. The first discovered exhibition of Soviet art in the USA, held at the Pennsylvania Museum of Art in 1934, had followed hard on the heels of diplomatic recognition and was sponsored by the fellow-travelling American Russian Institute.
74. More accurately, the exhibition consisted of drawings, watercolours, gouaches, etchings, lithographs, woodcuts, and book illustrations; it was open to the public from 26 January to 18 March. For some reason the exhibition went unrecorded in any of the *VOKS Bulletins* of 1945.
75. Lehmann-Haupt, 226.
76. Victoria & Albert Theatre Museum. Arts Council of Great Britain/121/906–7. RA 1947–57. Russian Exhibition 1958.
77. Philip James, art director of the Arts Council, and Sir William Coldstream visited Russia in August 1956, accompanied by Mrs Lilian Somerville, director of the British Council's Fine Arts Department.
78. *The Times*, 3, 7 Jan. 1957.
79. Christopher Mayhew, chairman of the Soviet Relations Committee of the British Council, had actually sent to the Russians, on 26 April 1958, the names of the selection committee and of the principal British artists likely to be put on display in the USSR (Victoria & Albert Theatre Museum. Britain/121/906–7. RA 1947–57. Russian Exhibition 1958).

80. V. M. Zimenko, editor of *Iskusstvo* (*Iskusstva* in the RA catalogue) and S. S. Chur-akov, of the Central Restoration Workshop.
81. 'An Exhibition of Works by Russian and Soviet Artists', Royal Academy catalogue, 17.
82. '...koe-kto schital, chto nashim khudozhnikam sledovalo by pouchit'sia u angliiskikh abstraktsionistov!'
83. Including works by Sergei Gerasimov, Vladimir Serov, Konstantin Youn, and Arkady Plastov.
84. *Burlington Magazine*, C1/671 (Feb. 1959), 43.
85. In the *Observer* Edward Crankshaw dismissed paintings like *The Relay Race* and *The Collective Farm* as mechanical reflections of the Party line. 'Today there are [Soviet] painters whose rooms are stacked with products of their imagination...their preoccupation with Western developments of the past hundred years'—but no sign of them at this Soviet exhibition. Sir Julian Huxley (briefly considered after the war as friendly to the USSR) agreed about the two Deneika pictures, pointing to *The Relay Race* as 'the most damning indictment of the official control of art in the USSR. Nineteen years of enforced Socialist Realism have driven a fine artist to produce a picture of almost incredible badness.' The exception was John Berger, who argued that critics had been unduly delighted by the Eisenstein-like expressionism of Deneika's *Defence of Petrograd*, which also betrayed poor technique (said Berger. It doesn't.).
86. Cardinal, 10.
87. Berlin (2000), 62.
88. Barr (1986), 217–18, reprinted from the *NYT Magazine* (14 Dec. 1952).
89. Golomshtok (1990), 284.
90. The American material was sent by the Architects' Committee of the National Council of American–Soviet Friendship, and the exhibits were prepared by the New York Museum of Modern Art (*VOKS Bulletin*, 3/4 (1945), 76). On English town-planning, see Bourov, *passim*.
91. *Observer*, 24 Aug. 1947.
92. Smeliansky, 1.
93. Iofan gives the dates of the eight buildings as 1947–9, presumably referring to design rather than completion, yet monumental edifices had already been realized in the 1930s, for example the Moskva Hotel (1938), the Council of Ministers (1933–6), and the Gorky Street complex (1941).
94. B. M. Iofan [given as Yofan], 47–8. See also John Bowlt in Auty and Obolensky, 169.
95. Bylinkin, *passim*; Hingley, 38. More recently Catherine Cooke has criticized American and British publications of the 1990s which continue the cold war tradition of denigrating Stalin-era architecture.
96. For example, a fold-out cartoon and text published in *Arkhitektura SSSR*, 11 (1955), entitled 'K novomu beregu (To a new shore)', highlighted the uncertainties of the profession following Khrushchev's speech in 1954 to the Congress of Soviet Builders, during which he attacked Dmitry Chechulin and Leonid Poliakov as

architects of high-rise buildings in Central Moscow, as well as Alexei Dushkin, star designer of Moscow's Metro stations.

97. *Pravda* interview, reported in *SN* 9 Dec. 1955.
98. Cooke, 138.
99. Salisbury (1960), 113.

Chapter 19. Passports for Paintings: Abstract Expressionism and the CIA

1. A liberal Republican, always close to the CIA, Nelson Rockefeller was to become governor of New York (1958–73), and vice-president (1974–6).
2. Stacy Tenebaum, who conducted extensive interviews with MoMA staff 30 years later, found them extremely bitter, particularly Porter McCray, about Cockcroft's attack ('a pack of lies'), to which the Museum itself had not then published a reply, although replies had been drafted (see Tenenbaum, 62, n. 138). Following Cockcroft, see also John Tagg, 'American Power and American Painting: The Development of Vanguard Painting in the United States Since 1945', *Praxis*, 1–2 (Winter 1976); David and Cecile Shapiro, 'Abstract Expressionism: The Politics of Apolitical Painting', *Prospects* (1977), reprinted in Frascina.
3. Guilbaut (1983), 141. Guilbaut blasted 'the imperialist machine of the Museum of Modern Art' in an article published in 1980.
4. Christine Lindey, 123–4 and 47, comments that Montague Dawson's *Racing Wings* could have come from the same studio as Eduard Kalinin's *The Seventh Baltic Regatta* (1954). 'I. Toidze's *Stalin at the Hydro-Electric Station* (n.d.) is not far removed in purpose or function from Terence Cuneo's *Visit of H. M. Queen Elizabeth with H. R. H. Duke of Edinburgh to lay the foundation stone of Lloyd's* (1953).'
5. The exhibition was in part financially sponsored by the State Department and the Office of War Information.
6. Quite misleading is Jane de Hart Matthews's claim that Edward Alden Jewell's article linked modernist art to the political left (Matthews, 777). Jewell, who neglected to mention a single painting or artist on display, was more interested in the Department's bold decision to buy the works, thus becoming a collector (Edward Alden Jewell, *NYT* 6 Oct. 1946, sec. 2, 8).
7. Noting that Busbey's views about modern art coincided with those of the *VOKS Bulletin* published in Moscow, Hellmut Lehmann-Haupt listed Busbey's conservative voting record on wider issues: 'He voted against rural electrification and soil conservation, against UNRRA and the Soldier Vote. He voted for the Dies Committee, the Taft–Hartley Bill, and for the Rees Loyalty Bill' (Lehmann-Haupt, 240).
8. Barr (1986), 222.
9. After viewing an abstract mural in the United Nations building, Eisenhower commented, 'To be modern you don't have to be nuts' (Barr 1986, 214; Sandler, introd. to ibid. 37).

10. Quoted by Lehmann-Haupt, 241.
11. George A. Dondero, 'Modern Art Shackled to Communism', speech to the House of Representatives, 16 Aug. 1949, reprinted in Chipp, 496–7.
12. Quoted by Pohl, 75.
13. Ibid. 76. Dondero addressed Congress on four separate occasions during 1949, calling on traditionalists within the National Academy of Design, the American Artists Professional League, Allied Artists of America, the Illustrators' Society, the American Watercolor Society, and the National Sculpture Society to purge their ranks and fight back before it was too late. The American Artists Professional League responded with a 'War Cry' against 'decadent isms' and the 'sensational-ists' who had 'infiltrated *our* large exhibitions, *our* art societies, and *our* museums' (Matthews, 776). Dondero's point of view was heartily endorsed by Wheeler Williams, president of the National Sculpture Society and a frequent 'friendly' witness before Congressional committees hunting down subversion. Traditional-ist and regionalist American artists like Thomas Craven did indeed feel acute resentment about the preference of elite museums and collectors for the for-eign-born 'isms'. Describing Alfred H. Barr, Jr., as 'master of a style that is one part mock-erudition and nine parts pure drivel', Craven called Picasso 'the Red idol deified by the Parisian Bohemia'.
14. Sandler, 14, 17.
15. Saunders (1999), 265, 455, n. 33.
16. Quoted by Sandler, 32.
17. Greenberg (1961), 208–9.
18. Cox (1982), 1; Updike, 11; Sylvester (1999), 8.
19. Greenberg joined the American Committee for Cultural Freedom (ACCF), as did Robert Motherwell, William Baziotes, Alexander Calder, and Jackson Pollock. Mark Rothko and Adolph Gottlieb both became committed anti-Communists as members of the Federation of Modern Painters and Sculptors.
20. Saunders (1999), 277, 457, n. 75. Saunders takes the quote she disagrees with from Giles Scott-Smith (1998).
21. O'Connor, 14, 20, 25.
22. In 'Towards a Newer Laocoon' (1940), Greenberg insisted on the cubist rather than the surrealist or Freudian-unconscious sources of Pollock's work and of abstract expressionism generally. Late cubism had been the first movement to come to terms fully with the flat surface of the canvas, which had resisted three-dimensionality and perspective for centuries. 'The history of avant-garde painting is that of a progressive surrender to the resistance of its medium' (Herbert, 7, quoting 'Towards a Newer Laocoon', *PR* 7/4 (July 1940), 305).
23. Greenberg (1947), 28–9.
24. Herbert, 10, quoting 'Art Chronicle: Our Period Style', *PR* 16/11 (Nov. 1949), 1138. Greenberg was ideologically at home on the staff of *Commentary*, from 1945 under senior editor Elliot Cohen, a leading anti-Communist. He was drawn deeper into cold war polemics when he, a former art correspondent for the *Nation*, accused the

journal and its foreign editor, Julio Alvarez del Vayo, of putting its pages at the service of Communist propaganda (Cox, 149; McAuliffe, 115).

25. According to Greenberg, American painters had been exposed to 'German, Russian or Jewish expressionism when they became restive with cubism and with Frenchness in general, but it remains that every one of them started from French art, and got his instinct for style from it' . . . (Greenberg 1961, 152–3, 210–11).

26. Harold Rosenberg and the painter Robert Motherwell produced a short anti-political manifesto as an opening statement for *Possibilities*, 'An Occasional Review', the first issue of which appeared in New York in the winter of 1947/8. The stress is on individual experience, the innocent conversion of energy, open-endedness, distrust of group formulas. 'Once the political choice has been made, art and literature ought of course [?to?] be given up' (reprinted in Chipp, 489–90).

27. Harold Rosenberg, *Art News* (Dec. 1952), reprinted in Rosenberg, 30; Herbert, 28–30.

28. Cox, 129–30, 140, 162.

29. Greenberg (1954), quoted in Sandler, 95–6.

30. In 1929 three immensely wealthy ladies, Mrs John D. Rockefeller, Miss Lillie P. Bliss, and Mrs Cornelius J. Sullivan, had decided to organize a new gallery or museum of modern art in New York.

31. Porter McCray, head of this programme, was a model case of the Ivy League curator who worked both for government and private museums. Born in 1908, he took a degree in architecture from Yale Graduate School, then served in Nelson Rockefeller's Office of the Coordinator of Inter-American Affairs during the war. In 1951 he took a year away from MoMA to work for the Marshall Plan's exhibitions section in Paris. McCray was responsible for organizing MoMA's overseas exhibitions throughout the 1950s.

32. Sandler, 45.

33. Cockcroft, *passim*.

34. Saunders (1999), 260.

35. Ibid. 257. An uncritical acceptance of Saunders's general thesis—one of many—is found in Laurence Zuckerman, 'How the CIA Played Dirty Tricks With Culture', *NYT* 18 Mar. 2000.

36. Saunders (1999), 260.

37. Nelson Rockefeller and his close friend John 'Jock' Hay Whitney were rich, cultivated, and highly connected cavaliers of successive wars against Nazism and Communism, as well as patrons of art on the scale of the Medicis. The innermost doors of intelligence organizations were open to them. The trustees and senior staff of MoMA were often found working for OSS and its successor, the CIA. Tom Braden served as executive secretary of MoMA from 1947 to 1949 before joining the CIA. René d'Harncourt, Viennese-born, emigrated to the USA in 1932 and worked in the arts section of Nelson Rockefeller's Office of the Coordinator of Inter-American Affairs (CIAA), the wartime intelligence operation in Latin America. By 1949 d'Harncourt was director of MoMA. William Burden, who had

likewise worked for CIAA during the war, became president of the CIA conduit, the Farfield Foundation, before assuming the presidency of MoMA in 1956. Joseph Verner Reed, Gardner Cowles, Julius Fleischmann, and Cass Canfield were trustees of both MoMA and the Farfield Foundation (Saunders 1999, 260–1 and *passim*).

38. Ibid. 262–4.

39. Frances Stonor Saunders, citing Michael Kimmelman's recent essay of denial (1994), called the case 'disingenuous', citing MoMA's steady acquisition of abstract expressionists 'from the time of their earliest appearance', i.e. from 1941. But there was no cold war in 1941 (Saunders 1999, 264).

40. Sweeney was a member of the CCF's American 'subsidiary', the ACCF.

41. Saunders (1999), 119, citing CCF/NYU archive, and 268.

42. The exhibit moved on from Paris to Zurich, Düsseldorf, Stockholm, Oslo, and Helsinki.

43. Anfam, 13, on the 'New York School'. The other artists exhibited were John Kane, Alexander Calder, Morris Graves, and Ivan Albright. On European critical reaction, see Tenenbaum, 30, n. 58.

44. Frances Spalding (1996), 166. The ICA, founded after the war and dedicated to the fostering of modern art, announced in June 1951 an International Sculpture Competition on the theme of 'The Unknown Political Prisoner', with a first prize of £4,500. Some 3,500 entries from 57 countries were received, and over 30,000 people attended the exhibition at the Tate Gallery, which opened in March 1953. The idea and set-up evidently came from two former members of the American OSS. John Hay Whitney anonymously provided the required £16,000, unknown to the ICA. The planned monument was to be erected, predictably, in West Berlin. For this information I am indebted to Scott-Smith (1998), who also quotes Robert Burstow, 'The Limits to Modernist Art as a "Weapon of the Cold War": Reassessing the Unknown Patron of the Monument to the Unknown Political Prisoner', *Oxford Art Journal*, 20/1 (1997), 76; and 'Unknown Political Prisoner', Folder 1, Box 26, ICA papers, Tate Gallery.

45. In a private 1956 memorandum to his director at MoMA, d'Harncourt, one of many American museum directors committed to the cultural war against Communism, McCray did emphasize that 'avant-garde' artists should be promoted abroad in view of the USIA's 'increasingly conservative orientation' (Kimmelman 1994, 49).

46. Matthews, 780; Doss, 195–216.

47. This material on the 1956 exhibition is found in the Victoria & Albert Theatre Museum, ACGB/121/662 (2 folders).

48. 'New American Painting' was also shown in Basel, Milan, Madrid, Berlin, Amsterdam, Brussels, and Paris.

49. The key movers and shakers, on this as on previous travelling exhibitions, were MoMA's senior staff, Porter McCray and Dorothy C. Miller. When the 1959 MoMA exhibition reached London, the US ambassador was John Hay Whitney, former

chairman of the board of trustees of MoMA and currently a member of its International Council.

50. The US government contributed only £165 to the £1,227 cost of printing 3,500 copies of the lavish, 92-page catalogue. The exhibits were valued at $415,569 for the purposes of insurance.

51. Frances Spalding (1996), 185. For the next two decades British avant-garde art followed American—for example, Anthony Caro's steel sculptures of the sixties, the work of Richard Hamilton, and the Pop Art movement (Frances Spalding 1999, 30–1).

52. The exhibition, like the 1956 show before it, was arranged by the Arts Council of GB and the International Programme of MoMA at the invitation of the trustees of the Tate Gallery. The attendance figure is in Hugh Shaw, of the Arts Council, to Dorothy Miller, of MoMA, 24 Apr. 1959. This, the valuations, and much other material is in the Victoria & Albert Theatre Museum, ACGB/121/747, 'The New American Painting'.

53. More favourable were Bernard Dorivel in *Arts* (22 Feb. 1959) and Georges Boudaille in the Communist *Lettres françaises*, who asked: 'What is the meaning of these disquieting outbursts?', then concluded that the American painters had given the school of Paris cause to be less self-congratulatory than usual.

54. Kimmelman (1994), 48.

55. I owe the Italian and Berlin press quotes to Tenenbaum.

56. According to Saunders, a CIA subsidy was involved. 'This show had cost the CIA $15,365, but for its expanded version in Paris they had to dig deeper. A further $10,000 was laundered through the Hoblitzelle Foundation, to which was added $10,000 from the Association française d'action artistique' (Saunders 1999, 274).

57. Ben Shahn (1898–1969) was born in Lithuania, the son of a Jewish socialist. Arriving in America in 1908, the family settled in Brooklyn. The narrative that follows owes much to Frances K. Pohl's outstanding study, *Ben Shahn: New Deal Artist in a Cold War Climate, 1947–1954*.

58. Lindey, 29–30

59. Cox, 145; Greenberg, 'Art' (1947), 481–2; Shapiro (1973), 296–7.

60. Pohl, 145.

61. For a vigorous defence in 1988 of the by-then much neglected Greenberg, see Frank, 246–63. According to Frank, '[Greenberg] has been the last and perhaps sternest schoolmaster in a line including Henry James and T. S. Eliot to insist that in order to compete with three thousand years of Western culture, we must understand history, and tradition and form' (Frank, 263).

62. Shahn had provided graphic work for *Masses and Mainstream*, *Morning Freiheit*, and another Communist publication, *Jewish Life*. He had designed a poster for the Wallace campaign; he had supported the Waldorf-Astoria Peace Conference, and had been a member of the Communist-front National Council of the Arts, Sciences and Professions. He had illustrated the cover of the *Nation's* recent special issue on civil liberties (Pohl, 118–19).

63. The painter George Biddle, a member of the Commission of Fine Arts, wrote to the *NYT* (17 Nov. 1954), revealing that the FBI regularly investigated artists before they were commissioned to decorate Federal buildings; he cited cases where artists approved by the Commission had later been rejected on the basis of an FBI report.

64. Quoted by Barr (1986), 223–4.

65. Indeed the prime mover in selecting Shahn, and the catalogue author for the Biennale, was Alfred H. Barr, Jr., an ardent proponent of modernism and a consistently outspoken defender of civil liberty for radical artists.

66. Pohl, 164–5.

67. Barr (1986), 225. Sandler, intro. to ibid. 37.

68. Both Shahn and Philip Evergood refused to answer questions about their affiliations, invoking the first, fifth, ninth, and tenth amendments to the Bill of Rights—a procedure which normally resulted in a citation for Contempt of Congress.

69. Pohl, 176–7.

70. The jury was headed by Franklin C. Watkins, of the Pennsylvania Academy of Fine Art, Lloyd Goodrich, director of the Whitney Museum of Art, Henry Radford Hope, chairman of the Fine Art Department of Indiana University, and Theodore Roszak, a sculptor often grouped with the abstract expressionists and a faculty member at Sarah Lawrence College, later to achieve international fame as the author of *The Making of a Counter Culture* (1968).

71. He cited Jack Levine, Ben Shahn, Max Weber, and Philip Evergood (Matthews, 778; Cong. Rec., 86th Cong., 1st Sess. (1959), 899–963).

72. *NYT* 2 July 1959. Saunders (1999), 271–2 and 456, n. 54, cites Eisenhower's address, 'Freedom in the Arts', to MoMA, 19 Oct. 1954, as evidence that he, unlike Truman, 'recognized the value of modern art as "a pillar of liberty"'. But it was not an 'address' that he gave, merely a very brief message sent on request to mark MoMA's twenty-fifth anniversary. What Eisenhower had to say was the standard endorsement of individual inspiration and freedom from state interference: 'When artists are made the slaves and tools of the state; when artists become chief propagandists of a cause, progress is arrested and creation and genius are destroyed.' The president said nothing about modern art.

73. Matthews, 779; *NYT* 8 July 1959; *NYHT* 9 July 1959.

74. Gilot, 251–3; Utley 105, 232–3.

75. Dorothy Seiberling, 'Baffling U.S. Art: What It Is About', *Life*, 9 Nov. 1959, pp. 68–80, cited by Cox, 89–90, 117.

76. A reference to Malevich's black square on a white ground, *Chernyi kvadrat*, painted in 1915—although the square, on close inspection in the Tretyakov, turns out to be intricately relieved with whiteish specks.

77. *NYT* 11 June 1959; Salisbury (1960), 108–9.

78. *NYT* 4 Sept. 1959.

79. Golomshtok, 'Realisty S Sh A' (1960). Like other Soviet critics, Golomshtok rigorously avoided mentioning by name any of the abstract artists shown at the US national exhibition.

80. In July 1953 the trustees of the William A. Farnsworth Gallery, Rockland, Maine, had cancelled a Rockwell Kent exhibition scheduled for the summer of 1954. A painter, lithographer, wood engraver, and illustrator, but a vigorous supporter of Communist fronts and later to be honoured by a Lenin Prize, Kent had been subpoenaed as an executive of the International Workers Order. After he took the Fifth Amendment the State Department persistently refused him a passport—*Kent v. Dulles* became a milestone case before the Supreme Court.

81. According to Paul Sjeklocha and Igor Mead, members of the exhibition's American staff, 1.6 million people visited the exhibition in 105 showing days. The *NYT* (20 Oct. 1963) reported that books kept disappearing from the art library, were replaced, and disappeared again. A volume containing the Russian text of Gabo's 'Realistic Manifesto' of 1920 was particularly popular.

82. PRO, British Council Archives, BW2 667

83. Ibid., BW2 665. Typescript in Russian.

84. Victor Pasmore, William Scott, Terry Frost, Roger Hilton, Bryan Wynter, Peter Lanyon, and Alan Davie.

85. Frances Spalding (1996), 172.

86. PRO, British Council Archives, BW2 665.

87. 'British Painting' (1960), 233. Herman was a Polish refugee notable for his moving devotion to Welsh miners, often depicted in static states of exhaustion.

88. Shown in Venice were Joseph Herman's Welsh miners, Joan Eardley's Glasgow tenement scenes, and Peter de Francia's political paintings—in a sense the counterparts to the new Royal Court plays and Angry Young Men novelists.

89. Brodskii, 52.

90. Brodskii gives the quotation as from Berger's study of Paul Hogarth, 8–9, published in Prague. This work has not been found.

91. Ibid. 51.

Chapter 20. Picasso and Communist Art in France

1. Françoise Gilot recalled that Aragon conducted himself like a cardinal or a prince, but he was also primarily an actor. He regarded himself as a *grand seigneur* of literature and demanded his due place at first nights or gatherings of *le Tout Paris* (Gilot, 259).

2. For the exchange between Aragon and Roger Garaudy, see Garaudy (1945), id. (1946), and Aragon (1946).

3. Aragon, *LLF* 9 Sept. 1948.

4. Modern socialist art was held to confront bourgeois values just as 'the battle for classicism during the Revolution, led by David, had clashed with aristocratic court

art'—a dubious proposition. Aragon's *L'Exemple de Courbet* (1952) described the struggle for realism in art as an aspect of the struggle for peace.

5. Fougeron had been a founding member of the Front National des Arts in 1941, and also a member of the purge committee for artists at the Liberation.

6. Casanova, 29.

7. See *LLF* 23 Sept. 1948 and 29 Sept. 1949.

8. Boris Taslitsky, painting under the pseudonym Julien Sorel, executed a notable portrait of Henri Martin.

9. Sarah Wilson, 30.

10. For example, *Le Défilé au premier mai*, by Marie-Anne Lansiaux; *Maurice Thorez va bien*, by Jean Milhau, showing happy readers of *L'Humanité dimanche* grouped around a vendor, with Thorez, at that time convalescing in the USSR, portrayed on the front page.

11. Dockers were as popular a theme among Party painters as miners: *Les Dockers de La Pallice*; *Les Dockers d'Alger*; *Les Dockers d'Oran*; *Le Refus des dockers*, to cite a few canvases.

12. *L'Humanité*, 7 Nov. 1951; *LM* 8 Nov. 1951.

13. *LLF* Jan.–Feb. 1951, *passim*; *DT* 25 Apr. 1962; *LM* 26 Apr. 1952.

14. Aragon, *LLF* 12–19 Nov. 1953, quoted by Verdès-Leroux, 301; Aragon (1954); Debra Kelly, 64.

15. Verdès-Leroux, 302, 318.

16. Lefebvre, *passim*; Pignon, *passim*.

17. Berger, 'Léger' (1972), 109, 107–21.

18. *SI* 7/8 (1947), 43, quoted by Golomshtok (1990), 145–6.

19. Author's notes on lecture by Anthony Blunt, as below. See also Blunt, 2. On 11 May 1965 Blunt, by then known to British security forces as a former Soviet spy, 'the fourth man', but still 14 years short of public exposure, lectured at Oxford on 'Picasso and the Spanish Civil War'. Blunt commented that he did not think much of Picasso's few political paintings: one on the theme of concentration camps, the mural on war and peace, and his *Massacre in Korea*.

20. D.-H. Kahnweiler, a German born in 1877, Picasso's dealer for years, had been obliged to flee France during World War I; as a Jew he again fled, this time to the so-called Free Zone, in 1940.

21. Utley, 92–4.

22. *LLF* had published a piece, 'Atomic Picasso' by Madelaine Rousseau, which Vladimir Kemenov quoted derisively (Kemenov 1947, 29–30). The Soviet critic also launched an attack on a series of articles published in 1946 in the PCF journal *Arts de France*, whose critic Anatole Jakovski had declared: 'Nothing human is alien to Picasso. He sees all that is human just as it is, with all its evils and ugliness, and only as a worthy contemporary of Buchenwald and Ravensbruck must often see it.'

23. Kemenov (1947), 29, 30.

24. The Victoria & Albert accepted the exhibition only because the Tate Gallery was war-damaged and the British Council urged acceptance on political grounds.

Most of the canvases were obtained from the two painters' own collections through the energetic personal visits to them of F. J. McEwen, fine arts officer of the British Council in Paris. It was for this reason (availability in conditions of immediate post-war difficulty) that all the Picassos dated from the 1940s, although Matisse provided work dating back to 1896.

25. Ashton's disparaging comments about three or four Picassos were in a memorandum, 30 Nov. 1945, to 'the Minister' (unnamed). He expected vociferous protests (Victoria & Albert Theatre Museum, RP/1945/576, 1945–6. VX. 1945.003. This file also contains a complete list of works exhibited.)

26. The veteran critic D. S. MacColl, senior enough to have dustbinned Cézanne before World War I, accused Picasso of 'what Catholic theologians call *accidia*, a wilful indulgence in dreary doldrums'. Cyril Asquith asked whether, in Dr Johnson's phrase, Picasso had 'done more than be dull in a new way'. What was to be gained by placing a woman's eyes in her scalp, one above the other? The art critic Douglas Cooper, a friend and collector of Picasso, suggested (9 Jan.) that the exhibition was guilty of presenting only paintings done under the German occupation, too 'raw a slice of work in progress'. (Predominant was Picasso's *'Femme'* series, including *Femme à la mandoline, Femme nue*, and *Femme assise*.)

27. Ehrenburg (1966), vol. 6, 143–4.

28. Sartre, préface à Leibowitz (1950), 11; Malraux, 181–2.

29. Utley, 107. See Futrell, 829.

30. Gilot, 207–8.

31. Rubenstein, 251, citing 'Public Lecture on the Warsaw Congress by Ilya Ehrenburg', 15 Jan. 1951, Dept. of State, National Archives, 700.001/1–1551, 1–2.

32. Dondero, addressing the House of Representatives on 16 August 1949, had described Picasso as 'also a dadaist, an abstractionist, or a surrealist, as unstable fancy dictates, the hero of all the crackpots in so-called modern art' . . .

33. Gilot, 186–7.

34. Kent, in *New Masses*, 55/1, 3 Apr. 1945, reprinted in Chipp, 487–9.

35. Ehrenburg (1966), vol. 6, 171. Françoise Gilot (p. 262) recalled that Picasso's guests among French Communists were always great eaters—the veteran Marcel Cachin would consume dish after dish, salad, cheeses, a good wine, a fancy dessert.

36. *France nouvelle*, 2 Sept. 1948, cited by Verdès-Leroux, 327.

37. In 1972 he was awarded the Lenin Prize for Peace. Four years later he was elected a senator of the Italian Republic (catalogue intro. to Renato Guttuso, *Recent Paintings, Watercolours and Drawings*, Marlborough Fine Art, 1–24 Mar. 1979).

38. Gilot, 132–3.

39. Breton, 277.

40. Ibid. 274–5.

41. *LLF* 27 Dec. 1951; 3 Jan. 1952.

42. Breton, 260–4.

43. Gilot, 265.

44. *LF* 30 Apr.–6 May 1949, quoted by Utley, 118.
45. Ehrenburg, 'Pablo Picasso', in *Chekhov* (1962), 219. Blown up to monumental proportions, the dove soared above 'Weapons on the Scrap Heap'; it later folded its wings round Picasso's portrait of Yuri Gagarin; etched into a vase of Bohemian glass, it became the trophy for a Prague–Berlin–Warsaw bicycle race in May 1963; it can be found on a 1981 50–kopek Soviet postage stamp celebrating Picasso's life, 1881–1973: *pochta CCCP, k.50*. Picasso was awarded the Prix International de la paix alongside Renato Guttuso, Paul Robeson, etc.
46. 'Je connais tous les lieux où la colombe loge | Et le plus naturel est la tête de l'homme' (Paul Eluard, 'Le Vrai Visage de la paix', *Défense de la paix* (Nov. 1951), 74.
47. Verdès-Leroux, 314.
48. Utley, 53.
49. H. Luce, in *Time*, 26 June 1950. Gertje Utley tells a story of former-President Truman visiting the Picasso Museum in Antibes (despite his professed contempt for modern art), requesting to meet the painter himself—and then asking Picasso why he had never visited America! (Utley, 113).
50. Fougeron, 128–9; Gilot, 259–61
51. 'Une telle erreur ne doit pas se renouveler; Comment un tel dessin a-t-il pu paraître?; Il est grave . . . Douloureuse surprise; Ce portrait n'exprime rien!; Un tel portrait n'est pas aux dimensions du génie immortel de Staline; Toute oeuvre, pour être durable, doit être impregnée des luttes, des espoirs, des certitudes en la victoire de la class ouvrière.'
52. All papers quoted 18, 19 Mar. 1953.
53. Fougeron, 123.
54. Ibid. 130–4.
55. Ibid. 136.
56. Utley, 189.
57. Billoux, 4–5. But it was to be some years yet before the Central Committee, meeting at Argenteuil in 1966, formally abandoned its claims to lay down the law in matters of art and culture.
58. *LM* 6 May 1954; *NYHT* 11 June 1954.
59. Shchukin's young son can be seen in a photograph, perched on the knee of Henri Matisse during the painter's visit to Moscow in 1911. Like Ivan Morozov, Shchukin had grown immensely rich on the proceeds of Russia's first industrial revolution. He began collecting art about 1908 and turned his gaze on the French avant-garde, acquiring 221 pictures, including 54 by Picasso, 37 by Matisse, 26 by Cézanne, 29 by Gauguin, 20 by Derain, 14 by Monet, and 13 by Renoir. The collections attracted considerable interest in tsarist Russia and in the years immediately following the Revolution.
60. *L'Humanité*, 30 June 1954.
61. See also 'L'Affaire des toiles de Picasso', *LF* 12 July 1954; 'L'Affaire de l'Exposition Picasso', *LM* 8 July 1954.

62. For example, the picture numbered 10, *La Jeune fille à la boule*, carried an inscription in cyrillic characters but it belonged to a Paris collection; Kahnweiler claimed that he had sold it to the American writer Gertrude Stein 40 years ago, and swore that it had never left her Paris apartment (*LM* 8 July 1954). So how had it got into the Soviet exhibition?

63. *NYHT* 7 July 1954.

64. Yevtushenko (1963), 120.

65. Slepian, 55, 56; Rubenstein, 297, 436, n. 40. Paradoxically, 30 years later, in August 1986, when the New York Metropolitan Museum showed 40 impressionist and early modern paintings loaned from the USSR, two cubist works by Picasso were described by the Soviet curators as 'two of the finest portraits of the 20th century' (Kempton, 65).

66. The Picasso exhibition and 'the mood of Leningrad young people' was the subject of an internal report by the Central Committee's culture department (RGANI, Fond 5, op. 36, ed.kh. 27).

67. Rubinstein, 297; Utley, 199, 245, n. 78.

68. 'Sortez de votre réserve' (Utley, 244, n. 56).

69. Quoted in ibid. 199.

70. *LM* 21, 23 Nov. 1956.

71. Utley, 201.

72. Rubenstein, 298–300, 436, n. 44, citing the archive of Ehrenburg's daughter Irina Ehrenburg.

73. According to Rubenstein, Picasso was so incensed by Soviet attitudes that in 1965 he refused a Lenin Peace Prize until Ehrenburg persuaded him the following year. However, Utley gives the date of the Lenin Peace Prize as April 1962 and does not mention any refusal (Rubenstein, 300; Utley, 46).

74. The Russian word *panno* is translated 'mural' in the American edition (1978), 525, but *Guernica* is not a mural (*Bol'shaia sovetskaia entsiklopediia*, 2nd edn., vol. 33 (1955), 28; 3rd edn., vol. 19 (1974), 527).

Chapter 21. The Other Russia: Pictures by 'Jackasses'

1. Some 'official' Soviet artists exploited the unprecedented freedom as a chance to unbutton—for example, Yuri Vassiliev, a well-known artist and a member of the Party, yet a private collector of abstract and tachiste canvases, sculptures in the manner of Arp, and mobiles in the manner of Calder, exhibited a portrait in the style of the forbidden Van Gogh. The artist Vaznetzov produced one *à la* Derain, and yet others on display were inspired by the neo-realism seen in Italian films (Rabin, 234).

2. Golomshtok and Glezer (1977), 89.

3. Sjeklocha and Mead, 75.

4. Revyakin, 164–8.

5. Nekrasov's criticism was perfectly accurate: the word used by the encyclopedia, *voskhvaliaiushchie*, means 'eulogizing', and Dali's paintings cited in support of this perverse claim were *Three Sphinxes of Bikini* and *Melancholic Atomic Idyll* (*Bol'shaia sovetskaia entsiklopediia*, 2nd edn., vol. 41 (1956), 432; Nekrassov, 153). The third edition of the encyclopedia is silent on Dali's supposed love of atomic war, merely charging him, along with other surrealists who had emigrated to America— Breton, Duchamp, and Tanguy—with 'distorted fantasy, persistently pathological images, cheap posturing . . . and pretentious mysticism' (*Great Soviet Encylopedia*, 3rd edn., vol. 25 (1980), 250).

6. Juviler, 41.

7. Following the young Soviet artist Vladimir Slepian's defection to the West (Paris) in 1958, his testimony was published by the US Information Agency's *Problems of Communism*. The editors described Slepian as an abstract painter: 'He has recently developed a theory of art which he calls *transfinitism*, and which holds that "the sole purpose of the creative act is the attainment by the artist of inner freedom which is possible only within this act"' (Slepian, 52).

8. Particularly influential among non-official artists was the studio of Eli Belyutin, who by day taught in the Moscow Polygraphic Institute and shared with his wife, N. Moleva, the authorship of orthodox works on the history of art education in Russia. By night (so to speak) he was opening eyes (Golomshtok and Glezer 1977, 102).

9. In 1957 Aleksandr Gerasimov lost his posts, including president of the Academy of Arts. But the Central Committee created a new union, the Union of Artists of the RSFSR, in which discharged Stalin Prize-winners obtained leading posts.

10. The London magazine *Encounter* published a transcript of the ensuing conversation in its April 1963 issue: 'The following document, of whose authenticity we are convinced, is translated from a hitherto unpublished stenographic account of some of [Khrushchev's] remarks.'

11. Khrushchev (1974), 82.

12. Sjeklocha and Mead, 94–6. At one point Khrushchev's son-in-law, Aleksei Adzhubei, who was editor-in-chief of *Izvestiia* and who knew Neizvestny, tried to break in to mediate: ' "Be quiet, young man", was Khrushchev's curt reaction.'

13. Born in the Urals in 1926, badly wounded during the war and a holder of the Red Star, Neizvestny later spent time in a Soviet prison camp. After his release he graduated from the Surikov Art Institute in Moscow. Arsen Pohribny, a Czech art critic, visited his studio in 1959: 'From childhood on, he had experienced only the most brutal and degrading aspects of Soviet life . . . In the small cellar he inhabited under a new apartment house on Leningrad Chaussée, I saw the horrible Baroque designs of his "War Cycle".'

14. *Encounter*, 20/4 (Apr. 1963), 102–3.

15. The newspaper magazine containing this article was found in a private collection without cover, title, or date: the date is certainly 1963 and the newspaper probably the *Observer*.

16. A few days later the *NYT* (9 Dec.) reported that the campaign was spreading to the provinces; for example, a meeting was scheduled to discuss the holdings of Alma-Ata's art gallery in Kazakhstan. See also *Observer*, 2 Dec. 1962; *DT* and *NYT* 6 Dec. 1962; *The Times*, 7 Dec. 1962.

17. Priscilla Johnson, 108.

18. Sjeklocha and Mead, 99.

19. Ehrenburg's private collection of modern art was legendary, although not on the scale of that of George D. Costakis, whose father, a Greek plantation owner, had lost his large holdings in the Tashkent region after the Revolution. Costakis himself had lived in Russia for 50 years, retained his Greek citizenship, and worked for the Canadian Embassy in Moscow, affording him direct access to the outside world. He had acquired a valuable collection of modern Russian art, including works by Kandinsky, Malevich, Lissitsky, and Popova from earlier times to Rabin and other contemporaries still at work. Costakis also negotiated sales agreements with Western dealers on behalf of official Soviet agencies selling oils, prints, and even icons to the West (Sjeklocha and Mead, 108–12).

20. Priscilla Johnson, 144.

21. Ibid. 172.

22. Yevtushenko (1963), 122.

23. Khrushchev (1974), 80.

24. In 1964 Robert Rauschenberg was awarded the Venice Biennale painting prize.

25. *NYT* 28 Dec. 1963.

26. Rabine, 111; Pohribny, 32.

27. Berger (1969), 63–85.

28. Berger (1972), 210–18. The discussion in *Iskusstvo* of an article by Berger on the state of contemporary Western art was the subject of a report by the Central Committee's cultural department (RGANI, Fond 5, op. 36, ed.kh.111).

29. *The Times*, 10 Mar. 1966; *NYT* 23 Mar. 1966.

30. Like Kandinsky, Chagall had actually returned to Russia on hearing news of the Revolution, anxious to play his part. Briefly 'commissar of art' in Vitebsk, his home town, he worked for the Jewish Theatre in Moscow before leaving the Soviet Union for good.

31. The gallery's holdings of Kandinsky were displayed only in foreign venues, Paris (1962), Japan (1975), and Munich (1976), although according to Lydia Romach-kova, deputy director of the Tretyakov, two works by Kandinsky and two by Malevich were on open display in the gallery 'in the late 1960s'.

32. Interview with Vitaly Mishin, deputy director of the Pushkin Museum, 4 April 2002, when the Pushkin's department of 'Private Collections' was staging a Tyshler retrospective. Symbolist, allegorist, sculptor, scene designer, and illustra-tor, Tyshler's 'Lyric Cycle' of the 1920s showed a Chagall-like dream quality—for example, two donkeys in a wicker cage, plus girl, plus bike, plus parasol.

33. Vladimir Serov, whose work included *Reception for Beet Workers in the Kremlin*, was re-elected president of the Academy of Arts in March 1966, a post he combined

with that of first secretary of the Russian Federation Artists' Union. Yet only the previous week *Komsomol'skaia pravda* had complained that Serov and his officials were responsible for maintaining the complex system of exhibition committees which prevented young artists showing their work (*NYHT* 3 Mar. 1966).

34. *Tvorchestvo*, vol. 1 (1963), 17, cited by Cullerne Bown, 409.

35. Ibid. 437, 444.

36. Kramer (1968), 160.

37. The couple had first met nine years earlier, when Miss Gray, daughter of Sir Basil Gray, keeper of Oriental Antiquities at the British Museum, was in Moscow researching the first volume. Camilla Gray's sympathetic treatment of Kandinsky, Malevich, and other modernists had angered the authorities, who repeatedly refused her re-entry. Now she planned to settle in Russia. In 1971, when the British Arts Council staged a major exhibit at the Hayward Gallery, London, 'Soviet Art and Design Since 1917', the introduction to the catalogue was written by Camilla Gray-Prokofieva. On this and other cases of Anglo-Russian marital engagements overcoming Soviet resistance, see *The Times*, 5 Feb., 30 Oct., 2 and 4 Nov. 1969; *Sunday Telegraph*, 26 Oct. 1969; *ST* 2 Nov. 1969; *DE* 3 Dec. 1969.

38. Kramer (1968), 162–3, 158.

39. Rabin was born in 1928. The story he told of his troubled childhood was an unusual one: not the purges but illness claimed his parents when he was young, the result being that at the age of 13 he found himself orphaned, alone, frozen, and hungry in an evacuated Moscow. The crucial influence during his youth was his future father-in-law Evgeny Leonidovich Kropivnitzki, who introduced him to French painting and read the work of banned Soviet poets to the boy. After various wartime adventures, including a period at the Riga Academy of Art, the young Rabin presented himself at the Surikov Institute, Moscow, directed by Sergei Gerasimov, but, confronted by the canons of socialist realism, he returned to Riga. Conscripted in 1950, Rabin later worked for the railways until he found employment as a book illustrator in the publishing house 'The Soviet Writer', illustrating volumes of poetry. He was also commissioned as a decorator at VDNKh.

40. Sjeklocha and Mead, 108–9; Rabin, 137.

41. Rabin, 105.

42. Sjeklocha and Mead, 138–43.

43. Golomshtok and Glezer (1977), 95.

44. Kramer (1968), 169.

45. Golomshtok and Glezer (1977), 110–11.

46. But the profile of oppression was far from uniform. For example, the kinetic artists known as *Dvizhenie* (The Movement) had been commissioned, with official subsidy, to contribute to Leningrad's festivities celebrating the 50th anniversary of the Revolution, working in the House of Engineers and provided with radio-electronics, projectors, and reflectors (Pohribny, 26–34).

47. Caute (1974), 102.

48. Rabin, 190–3. For Talochkin, see Romer, 60–2.
49. Born in 1949 and still in his twenties, Kalugin exhibited at a one-man show at the University of New Mexico, Albuquerque, USA, in 1972, and at the Russian museum of contemporary art, Montgeron, France, in 1976.
50. Golomshtok and Glezer (1977), 119–22.
51. His named targets included Dm. Plavinsky, E. Shteinbern, A. Masterkova, V. Yakovlev, V. Nemukhin, O. Rabin, and O. Kandaurov.
52. Rabin, 163–5. One therefore has to disagree with Leonid Talochkin's recall, 25 years later, that 'Straight persecution (*priamoe predsledovanie*) of artists did not happen', although he himself cites the case of an artist named Mukhametshin, 'insolent to the extreme limit', who was put away (Romer, 62).
53. The same technique was applied to the dissident General Piotr Grigorievitch Grigorenko, whom Rabin had met after attending, with his friend Andrei Amalrik, the trial of Pavel Litvinov and others who had dared to gather in Red Square to protest the 1968 invasion of Czechoslovakia. On a later occasion Grigorenko came to view Rabin's paintings (Rabin, 338).
54. The ICA exhibition, sponsored by the Writers and Scholars Educational Trust, was organized by Roland Penrose from Western collections and from the Musée d'art russe contemporain created by Aleksandr Glezer at Montgeron, near Paris. Among the artists represented were Neizvestny, Nussberg, Zelemin, and Mikhail Shemia-kin, now an exile but formerly a member of Leningrad's 'Saint-Petersburg Group' dedicated to what Rabin called 'synthetic mysticism'. Secker & Warburg published the massive and authoritative volume *Unofficial Art In the Soviet Union*, by Igor Golomshtok and Aleksandr Glezer.
55. Golomshtok and Glezer (1977), pp. xv, 81.
56. In particular 'Sveshnikov's drawings of labour camps; Yenkilevsky's ferociously witty drawings which fling recognisable elements of city life into irrational, telling juxtapositions... Kalugin's elaborate, mesmerising *Freedom with a clear conscience*' (*ST* 23 Jan. 1977).
57. In terms of Russian art holdings lent to the exhibition, the Tretyakov was the most important. But according to Svetlana Dzhaforova, the exhibition organizers en-countered difficulties in extracting some holdings from the Tretyakov Gallery and the Russian Museum, Leningrad, and had to turn to some 30 provincial museums which held Russian avant-garde collections—but largely uncatalogued. One in-ducement offered was the restoration of pieces in poor condition. 'But some of them refused to talk to us even when I was calling on behalf of the Ministry of Culture' (Svetlana Dzhaforova, interview, Moscow, 5 Apr. 2002).
58. In 1971 Picasso's work had been more extensively displayed in Soviet galleries than in 1956; in 1974 'L'URSS et la France, les grands moments d'une tradition' had opened in Paris, followed by '60 ans de peinture soviétique' in 1977, and indeed two further exhibitions of Russian painting. A Malevich retrospective was sent to Düsseldorf in 1980, even though the centenary of his birth (1978) had gone entirely unremarked within the USSR (Rakitin, 188).

59. Reporting to Khalturin was Natalia Morozova, the Ministry's inspector on Foreign Exhibitions, who brought in Svetlana Dzhaforova, who worked for the exhibition department of the E. Vucheticha All Union Artistic Production Combine (*Vsesoiuznyi proizvodstvenno khudokhestvennyi kombinat im. E. Vucheticha*).The Ministry's storage rooms were located in the Combine's building (interview with Dzhaforova). Other key members of the Soviet team included the art historian Vadim Polevoy, who had previously worked for the art department of the Central Committee, and Alla Butrova, head of the division of relations with capitalist countries of the foreign relations department of the Ministry.

60. Likewise Marina Bessanova, a Pushkin Museum specialist in French art and the Russian avant-garde.

61. Lydia Romachkova, interview with the author, Moscow, 4 Apr. 2002. In conversation Romachkova, who has worked at the Tretyakov since 1956, refers frequently to the 'post-Stalin thaw' but is reticent about the conservatism of the Brezhnev years and was probably part of it.

62. Svetlana Dzhaforova, interview.

63. *Paris–Moscou, passim.*

64. Recall of Lydia Romachkova, Vitaly Mishin, deputy director of the Pushkin Museum, Elena Smolina, and other Muscovites.

65. The veteran critic Mikhail Lifshits remained throughout the 1970s a powerful opponent of modernism within the Academy of Arts. He blamed the distorters of humanism and the Renaissance tradition (Picasso, the Bauhaus, and the expressionists among them) for the triumph of National Socialism. Lifshits's aesthetic philosophy closely echoed that of the Hungarian critic George Lukács (Rakitin, 181).

66. 'protiv otobrazheniia deistvitel'nosti nashim glazom.'

67. *Bol'shaia sovetskaia entsiklopediia*, 3rd edn. (1975), 403–4. The veteran Soviet critic and keeper of the seals ended by dismissing Roger Garaudy's revisionist *réalisme sans rivages*—realism without boundaries', and called for artists to rally 'under the banner of socialist realism'.

68. A colourful figure from Moscow's Bohemia, formerly an engineer, then a lift operator, janitor, and watchman, as a penniless collector Talochkin was not in a position to obtain a work from every artist of national museum standard.

69. Romer, 60–2.

70. Visiting the Talochkin collection at RGGU in 2002—a sleepy but willing curator had to be aroused to unlock the doors—the present writer found it of greater historical than aesthetic interest. Most arresting to this eye are two works by Oskar Rabin, *Optimistic Landscape* (1959) and *Drunken Doll* (1972); Lydia Masterova's *Composition* (1968), Anatoly Slepyshev's *Man with a Ladder* (1980), an undated, untitled Neizvestny lithograph, and three works of Vladimir Yakovlev painted in the 1970s. In general, however, Soviet dissident art is a disappointment. Russian artists were employing religious symbols without attaching to them any orthodox

meaning, or merely a wider, pantheistic spiritual yearning—for example, Valentina Kropivnitskaia's 'magical symbolic' Golden Age painting *Memories* (1968).

71. In this category can be placed some works on display in the new Tretyakov Gallery, by Marlen Shpindler, Yuri Zlotnikov, Yvgeny Rukhin, Alexei Tyapushkin, Natalia Yegorshina, Alexei Kamensky, Mikhail Shvartsmann, Vladimir Veisberg, Vladimir Sterligov, Boris Sveshnikov, Anatoly Brusilovsky, Sergei Bordachov, Oleg Yakovlev, and Mikhail Chernyshev.

Conclusion

1. Kirkpatrick, 23.
2. Gaddis, 284.
3. Toledo, Ohio, in 1996; Middleburg, the Netherlands, in 2001.
4. The term 'gaze' is popular, whether a 'centralizing and assimilative gaze' or 'the unerring gaze of the Puritan exegetical eye'.
5. Morris Dickstein is right to take issue with 'the school of Cold War critique which . . . tried to connect not only the visual arts but the most disparate cultural phenomena of the post-war years to the "national security state", the domestic witch hunt, and the containment policy towards the Soviet Union. In this variant of the hermeneutics of suspicion, even the most innocent-looking work could be explained in terms of Cold War ideology' (Dickstein, 14).
6. For a vivid example, see Koch, *passim*.

Acknowledgements (Archives)

My thanks are due to the librarians and staff of the following research institutions:

In the UK:
  British Library
  British Newspaper Library
  British Film Institute & BFI Library
  Courtauld Institute of Art Library
  London Library
  National Art Library, London
  Public Record Office
  Royal Academy of Art Library
  Royal Institute for International Affairs Library
  School of Slavonic & East European Studies Library, University College London
  University of Sussex Library
  Victoria & Albert Museum Archive of Art and Design, London
  Victoria & Albert Theatre Museum, London

In Paris:
  Bibliothèque nationale

In Berlin:
  Deutscheshistoriches Museum, Berlin
  Film Museum, Potsdam
  Museum Berlin Karlshorst

In the USA:
  American Civil Liberties Union Library, Los Angeles and New York
  Detroit Public Library, Burton Historical Collection
  Emergency Civil Liberties Committee, New York
  Harvard Law School Library
  New York Public Library Theater Collection, Lincoln Center
  Morris Library, Southern Illinois University—Carbondale Special Collections
  Museum of Modern Art, New York
  National Lawyers Guild, New York
  Princeton University Library
  United Electrical, Radio and Machine Workers of America, New York
  University of California, Irvine, Library
  Widener Library, Harvard

In Moscow:

Museum of Private Collections (Muzei lichnykh kollektsii)

Pushkin State Museum of Fine Art (Gosudarstvennyi muzei izobrazitel'nykh iskusstv imeni A. S. Pushkina)

Russian State Archive of Literature and Art (Rossiiskii gosudarstvennyi arkhiv literatury i iskusstva—RGALI) Here, as with RGANI (below), the documentation filing system reflected in this book's Notes and References is Fond (archive), Opis' (op.— list or schedule), edinitsa khraneniia (ed.kh.—item of storage).

Russian State Archive of Recent History (Rossiiskii gosudarstvennyi arkhiv noveishei istorii—RGANI)—until 1999 known as the Center for the Storage of Contemporary Documents (Tsentr khraneniia sovremennoi dokumentatsii—TsKhSD). RGANI holds the archive of the Central Committee of the Communist Party (TsK KPSS, Soviet era), which was taken over in 1991 by the Presidential administration of the Russian Federation, whose special commission has marked 'declassified' (*rassekrecheno*) about 30 per cent of the material (Spring 2002). Some documents are 'partially declassified' with 'limited access' (*ogranichennoe ispol'zovanie*). Each user is required to state in writing the reason for use: '*Dlia kakoi tseli ispol'zovan dokument.*' The most frequent response is the non-committal 'browsing—*prosmotr*'.

Russian State Film Archive, Belye Stolby (Gosfil'mofond Rossii)

Russian State Library (Rossiiskaia gosudarstvennaia biblioteka)

State Art Library (Gosudarstvennaia biblioteka po iskusstvu)

State Central Museum of Contemporary Russian History (Gosudarstvennyi tsentral'nyi muzei sovremennoi istorii Rossii)

State Public Historical Library of Russia (Gosudarstvennaia publichnaia istoricheskaia biblioteka Rossii)

State University of the Humanities Museum Centre (Muzeinyi tsentr rossiiskogo gosudarstvennogo gumanitarnogo universiteta)

Filmography

Soviet Films

Andrei Rublev, 1966 (released in the USSR in 1971), dir. Andrei Tarkovsky.
Ballad of a Soldier (*Ballada o soldate*), 1959, dir. Grigorii Chukhrai.
Battle of Stalingrad, The (*Bitva Stalingradskaia*), 1949, dir. Vladimir Petrov.
Bezhin Meadow (*Bezhin Lug*, fragments), 1934, dir. Sergei Eisenstein.
Chess Fever (*Shakhmatnaia goriachka*), 1926, dir. V. Pudovkin.
Conspiracy of the Doomed, The (*Zagovor obrechennykh*), 1950, dir. Mikhail Kalatozov.
Court of Honor (*Sud chesti*), 1949, dir. Abram Room.
Cranes are Flying, The (*Letiat zhuravli*), 1957, dir. Mikhail Kalatozov.
Dawn Over the Neman (*Rassvet nad Rooiyei*), 1952, dir. A. Faintsimmer.
Destiny of a Man, The (*Sud'ba cheloveka*), 1959, dir. Sergei Bondarchuk.
Fall of Berlin, The (*Padenie Berlina*), 1949, dir. Mikhail Chiaureli.
Flight 222 (*Reis 222*), 1985, dir. Sergei Mikaelyan.
Forty-First, The (*Sorok-pervyi*), 1956, dir. Grigorii Chukhrai.
Ilich's Watchpost (*Zastava Il'icha*), 1963, dir. Marlen Khutsiev. Released in 1965 as *I am Twenty* (*Mne dvadstat' let*).
Ivan's Childhood (*Ivanovo detstvo*), 1962, dir. Andrei Tarkovsky. In USA: *My Name is Ivan*.
Ivan the Terrible (*Ivan Grozny*), Part 1, 1945; Part 2, 1946, not released until 1959, dir. Sergei Eisenstein.
Lady with the Little Dog, The, 1959, dir. Josef Heifits.
Meeting on the Elbe (*Vstrecha na Elba*), 1949, dir. Grigorii Aleksandrov.
Michurin, 1949, dir. A. Dovzhenko.
Mirror (*Zerkalo*), 1974, dir. Andrei Tarkovsky.
Stalker, 1979, dir. Andrei Tarkovsky.
Ordinary Fascism (*Obyknovennyi fashizm*), 1965, dir. Mikhail Romm.
Russian Question, The (*Russkii Vopros*), 1948, dir. Mikhail Romm.
Secret Mission (*Sekretnaia missiia*), 1950, dir. Mikhail Romm.
Silvery Dust (*Serebryannaia pyl'*), 1953, dir. Abram Room.
They Have a Native Land (*U nikh est' rodina*), 1950, dir. A. Faintsimmer.
Vow, The, or *Oath, The*, (*Kliatva*), 1947, dir. Mikhail Chiarueli.
Zhukovski, 1950, dir. V. Pudovkin.

American Films

Big Jim McLain, 1952, dir. Edward Ludwig.
Boy with Green Hair, The, 1949, dir. Joseph Losey.
Dr Strangelove, 1963, dir. Stanley Kubrick.

Front, The, 1976, dir. Martin Ritt.
Green Berets, The, 1968, dir. John Wayne and Ray Kellogg.
Guilty by Suspicion, 1991, dir. Irwin Winkler.
Guilty of Treason, 1949, dir. Felix Feist.
I Married a Communist (Woman on Pier 13), 1949, dir. Robert Stevenson.
Iron Curtain, The, 1948, dir. William A. Wellman.
I Was a Communist For the FBI, 1951, dir. Gordon Douglas.
Manchurian Candidate, The, 1963, dir. John Frankenheimer.
Marty, 1955, dir. Delbert Mann.
Mission to Moscow, 1943, dir. Michael Curtiz.
My Son John, 1952, dir. Leo McCarey.
Ninotchka, 1939, dir. Ernest Lubitsch.
North Star, The, 1943, dir. Lewis Milestone.
On the Waterfront, 1954, dir. Elia Kazan.
Red Danube, The, 1949, dir. George Sidney.
Red Menace, The, 1949, dir. R. G. Springsteen.
Salt of the Earth, 1954, dir. Paul Jarrico.
Song of Russia, 1944, dir. Gregory Ratoff.
Storm Center, 1956, dir. Daniel Taradash.
Ten Commandments, The, 1956, dir. Cecil B. DeMille.
Walk East on Beacon, 1952, dir. Alfred Werker.
Viva Zapata!, 1952, dir. Elia Kazan.

European Films

Ashes and Diamonds (Popiol i diament), 1958, dir. Andrzej Wajda.
Bentheim Family, The (Die Familie Bentheim), 1950, dir. Slatan Dudow.
Canal (Kanal), 1956, dir. Andrzej Wajda.
Condemned Village, The (Das verurteilte Dorf), 1952, dir. Martin Hellberg.
Danton, 1982, dir. Andrzej Wajda.
East Side Story, 1999, dir. Dana Ranga.
8½, 1963, dir. Federico Fellini.
Four Men in a Jeep (Vier im Jeep), 1951, dir. Leopold Lindtberg.
Generation (Pokolenie), 1954, dir. Andrzej Wajda.
Man of Iron (Czlowiek z zelata), 1981, dir. Andrzej Wajda.
Man of Marble (Czlowiek z marmaru), 1976, dir. Andrzej Wajda.
Murderers Are Among Us, The (Die Mörder sind Unter Uns), 1946, dir. Wolfgang Staudte.
Our Daily Bread (Unser Tägliche Brot), 1949, dir. Slatan Dudow.
Song of the Rivers (Lied der Strome), 1954, dir. Joris Ivens.
Story of a Young Couple, The (Roman einen jungen Ehe), 1952, dir. Kurt Maetzig.
Witches of Salem, The (Les Sorcières de Salem), 1957, dir. Raymond Rouleau.
Women's Fate (Frauenshicksale), 1952, dir. Stefan Dudow.

Bibliography

ACKROYD, PETER, *T. S. Eliot* (London, 1984).

'Against Formalism in Soviet Music', editorial, *VOKS Bulletin*, 50 (1947).

Akademiia Khudozhestov SSSR, *Doklady, premiia, i postanovleniia*. Pervaia i vtoraia sessii, 22–4 Nov. 1947, 20–7 Mar. 1948 (Moscow, 1949).

ALEKSANDROV, GRIGORII V., *Epokha i kino* (Moscow, 1976).

ALEKSANDROV, V., 'Amerikanskoe Schast'e', *Teatr*, 5 (May 1947).

ALEXANDROVA, VERA, 'Soviet Literature Since Stalin', *Problems of Communism*, 4/3 (July–Aug. 1954).

ALLILUYEVA, SVETLANA, *Twenty Letters to a Friend*, trans. Priscilla Johnson (London, 1967).

—— *Only One Year*, trans. Paul Chavchavadze (London, 1969).

American Civil Liberties Union (ACLU), *Violence in Peekskill* (New York, 1950).

—— *Liberty Is Always Unfinished Business*, 36th annual report of the ACLU, 1 July 1955–30 June 1956 (New York, 1956).

ANDERSON, JOSEPH L., 'Soviet Films Since 1945', *Films in Review*, Part I, 4/1 (Jan. 1953); Part II, 4/2 (Feb. 1953).

ANDREW, CHRISTOPHER, 'The Mitrokhin KGB Archive', *The Times*, 13 Sept. 1999.

—— 'Waging War Against the Dissidents', *The Times*, 16 Sept. 1999.

—— and MITROKHIN, VASILY, *The Mitrokhin Archive: The KGB in Europe and the West* (London, 2000 (1999)).

ANFAM, DAVID, *Abstract Expressionism* (London, 1994 (1990)).

ANIKST, ALEKSANDR, 'Rhinoceroses in New York', *Novy mir*, 8 (1965), in Glenny (1972).

ARAGON, LOUIS, 'Art, zone libre?', *Les Lettres françaises*, 13 Dec. 1946.

—— 'L'Art de parti en France', *La Nouvelle critique* (July–Aug. 1954).

ARENDT, HANNAH, 'Bertolt Brecht: 1898–1956', in Hannah Arendt, *Men in Dark Times* (London, 1970).

ARVIDSSON, CLAES and BLOMQUIST, LARS ERIK (eds.), *Symbols of Power: The Esthetics of Political Legitimation in the Soviet Union and Eastern Europe* (Stockholm, 1987).

ASH, TIMOTHY GARTON, 'The Prague Advertisement', *New York Review of Books*, 35/20, 22 Dec. 1998.

—— *History of the Present: Essays, Sketches and Despatches from Europe in the 1990s* (London, 1999).

ATTWOOD, LYNNE (ed.), *Red Women on the Silver Screen: Soviet Women and the Cinema from the Beginning to the End of the Communist Era* (London, 1993).

AULICH, JAMES and SYLVESTROVÁ, MARTA, *Political Posters in Central and Eastern Europe 1945–1995* (Manchester, 1999).

AUTY, ROBERT and OBOLENSKY, DIMITRI (ed.), *An Introduction to Russian Art and Architecture*, Companion to Russian Studies, 3 (Cambridge, 1980).

BABBITT, MILTON, 'My Vienna Triangle at Washington Square Revisited and Dilated', in Brinkmann and Wolff (1999).

BABITSKY, PAUL and RIMBERG, JOHN, *The Soviet Film Industry* (New York, 1955).

BARBAN, EFIM, 'Soviet Jazz: New Identity', in Feigin (1985).

BARGHOORN, FREDERICK C., *The Soviet Image of the United States* (New York, 1959 (1950)).

—— *The Soviet Cultural Offensive* (Princeton, 1960).

BARNES, CLIVE, 'Fifty Years of Soviet Ballet', in Salisbury, *Anatomy* (1968).

—— *Nureyev* (New York, 1981).

BARNES, HAZEL E., *Sartre* (London, 1974).

BARR, ALFRED H., Jr., 'Is Modern Art Communistic?', *New York Times Magazine*, 14 Dec. 1952.

—— *What Is Modern Painting?* (New York, 1968).

—— *Defining Modern Art: Selected Writings*, ed. Irving Sandler and Amy Newman (New York, 1986).

BARRETT, WILLIAM, 'Cultural Conference at the Waldorf', *Commentary*, 7/5 (May 1949).

BARSKII, SERGEI, 'Russkaia opera v poslevoennoi Germanii 1945–1948 gg', *Sovetskaia muzyka*, no. 10 (Dec. 1948).

BARZMAN, BEN, 'Pour Joe', *Positif*, 293/294 (July–Aug. 1985).

BASKAKOV, VLADIMIR, *Soviet Cinema: A Brief Essay* (Moscow, 1968).

BEAUVOIR, SIMONE DE, *America Day by Day*, trans. Patrick Dudley (London, 1952).

—— *La Force de l'age* (Paris, 1960).

—— *La Force des choses* (Paris, 1963); *Force of Circumstance*, trans. Richard Howard (London, 1965).

—— *Beloved Chicago Man: Letters to Nelson Algren, 1947–1964* (London, 1998).

BECKETT, SAMUEL, *Waiting for Godot* (London, 1959).

BELFRAGE, SALLY, *A Room in Moscow* (London, 1958).

BELL, DANIEL, *The End of Ideology* (New York, 1960).

—— 'The "End of Ideology" in the Soviet Union', in Milorad M. Drachkovitch (ed.), *Marxist Ideology in the Contemporary World* (New York, 1966).

BELLEW, HÉLÈNE, *Ballet in Moscow Today* (London, 1956).

BENNETT, ALAN, *Single Spies* (contains *An Englishman Abroad* and *A Question of Attribution*) (London, 1989).

BENTLEY, ERIC, *Thirty Years of Treason: Excerpts from the Hearings before the House Committee on Un-American Activities 1938–1968* (New York, 1971).

BERGER, JOHN, 'A Socialist Realist Painting at the Biennale', *Burlington Magazine*, 94/595 (Oct. 1952).

—— 'The Missing Example', *New Statesman*, 49/1248, 5 Feb. 1955.

—— *Art and Revolution: Ernest Neizvestny and the Role of the Artist in the USSR* (London, 1969).

——'Problems of Socialist Art', in Lee Baxandall (ed.), *Radical Perspectives in the Arts* (London, 1972).

——'Fernand Léger', in *Selected Essays and Articles: The Look of Things* (London, 1972).

BERGMAN, INGMAR, *Images: My Life in Film* (London, 1994).

BERKOVSKY, NAUM, 'In Defence of Life', *Soviet Literature*, 12 (1959).

BERLIN, ISAIAH, *Personal Impressions* (London, 1980).

——'The Arts in Russia Under Stalin', *New York Review of Books*, 47/16, 19 Oct. 2000. Original title, 'A Note on Literature and Arts in the Russian Soviet Federated Socialist Republic in the Closing Months of 1945'.

BERNSTEIN, WALTER, *Inside Out* (New York, 1996).

BESSE, GUY, 'L'Expansionisme idéologique des Yankees', *La Démocratie nouvelle*, 2 Feb. 1948.

BETTS, PAUL, 'The Twilight of the Idols: East German Memory and Material Culture', *Journal of Modern History*, 72/3 (Sept. 2000).

BEUMERS, BIRGIT, 'Performing Culture: Theatre', in Kelly and Shepherd (1998).

BIERMANN, WOLF, *Mit Marx- und Engelszungen Gedichte. Balladen Lieder* (Berlin, 1968).

——*Preussischer Ikarus* (Cologne, 1991).

——*Über das Geld und andere Herzendinge* (Cologne, 1991).

BIGSBY, CHRISTOPHER and BANHAM, REYNOR, *Superculture: American Popular Culture and Europe* (London, 1975).

BILLOUX, FRANÇOIS, 'Sur les intellectuels', *La Nouvelle critique* (Dec. 1953).

BITOV, ANDREY, 'The Gulag and Shostakovich's Memorial', in Ho and Feofanov (1998).

BLAGOV, IVAN, 'Neobkhodimoe preduprezhdenie', *Krokodil*, 30 Sept. 1953.

BLUNT, ANTHONY, *Picasso's 'Guernica'*, The Whidden Lectures for 1966 (London, 1969).

BOGDANOVA, ALLA VLADIMIROVNA, *Muzyka i vlast' (poststalinsky period)* (Moscow, 1995).

BOLLAG, BRENDA, 'From the Avant-Garde to Socialist Realism: Some Reflections on the Signifying Procedures in Eisenstein's *Stachka* and Donskoi's *Raduga*', in Günther (1990).

Bol'shaia sovetskaia entsiklopediia, 2nd edn. (Moscow, date according to volume); 3rd edn. (Moscow, date according to volume); 3rd edn. trans. as *Great Soviet Encyclopedia* (New York, date according to volume).

BONNEFOY, CLAUDE, *Conversations with Eugene Ionesco*, trans. Jan Dawson (London, 1970).

'"Book Burning", Where U.S. Officials Stand', *U.S. News & World Report*, 34/26, 26 June 1953.

BOUROV, ANDREW K., 'The War and Architecture', *VOKS Bulletin*, 1/2 (1946).

BOWERS, FAUBION, *Entertainment in Russia* (Edinburgh and New York, 1959).

BRADEN, THOMAS W., 'I'm Glad the CIA is Immoral', *Saturday Evening Post*, 20 May 1967.

BRECHT, BERTOLT, *Brecht on Theatre: The Development of an Aesthetic*, trans. and notes by John Willett (London, 1964).

——*Arbeitsjournal 1938 bis 1955* (Frankfurt, 1973).

——*Poems*, ed. John Willett and Ralph Manheim with the co-operation of Erich Fried (London, 1975).

——*Letters 1913–1956*, ed. John Willett (London, 1990).

——*Journals 1934–1955*, trans. Hugh Rorrison, ed. John Willett (London, 1993).

BRETON, ANDRÉ, *Free Rein (La Clé des champs)*, trans. Michel Parmentier and Jacqueline d'Amboise (Lincoln, Nebr., 1995).

BRETT, PHILIP (ed.), *Benjamin Britten: Peter Grimes* (Cambridge, 1983).

BREZHNEVA, LUBA, *The World I Left Behind* (New York, 1995).

BRIGGS, ASA, *History of Broadcasting in the UK*, 4 vols. (London 1961–79). Vol. 3, *The War of Words* (London, 1970); Vol. 4, *Sound and Vision* (London, 1979).

BRINKMANN, REINHOLD and WOLFF, CHRISTOPH (eds.), *Driven into Paradise: The Musical Migration from Nazi Germany to the United States* (Berkeley and London, 1999).

BRINSON, PETER (ed.), *Ulanova on Soviet Ballet* (London, 1954).

'British Painting in the USSR', *Burlington Magazine*, 102/687 (June 1960).

BRITTEN, BENJAMIN, *Peter Grimes, Gloriana* (London, 1983).

BRODSKII, VALENTIN, 'Sovremennoe izobrazitel'noe iskusstvo anglii', *Iskusstvo*, no. 2 (1960).

BRODSKY, J. and HAVEL, V., ' "The Post-Communist Nightmare": An Exchange', *New York Review of Books*, 41/4, 17 Feb. 1994.

BROWN, RALPH S., Jr., *Loyalty and Security: Employment Tests in the United States* (New Haven, 1958).

BUCKLE, RICHARD, *George Balanchine Ballet Master: A Biography* (London, 1988).

BUSHNELL, JOHN, *Moscow Graffiti: Language and Subculture* (Boston, 1990).

BYLINKIN, N. P., 'New Achievements of Soviet Architecture', *VOKS Bulletin*, 76 (1952).

CALLOW, SIMON, *Charles Laughton* (London, 1987).

CAMUS, ALBERT, *L'etat de siège* (Paris, 1948).

——*Les Justes* (Paris, 1950).

——*Actuelles, I* (Paris, 1950).

——*L'Homme révolté* (Paris, 1952); *The Rebel* (London, 1953).

——*Caligula and Three Other Plays*, trans. Stuart Gilbert (New York, 1962).

——*Essais* (Paris, 1965).

CAPOTE, TRUMAN, *The Muses are Heard: Porgy and Bess Visit Leningrad* (London, 1957).

CARDINAL, ROGER, 'Creators Under the Dictators', *Times Literary Supplement*, 4832, 10 Nov. 1995.

CAROW, HEINER, 'Der Kalte Krieg der Unterhaltung', *Deutscheshistoriches Museum*, Heft 5, 2. Jahrgang (Summer 1992).

CARPENTER, HUMPHREY, *Benjamin Britten: A Biography* (London, 1992).

CASANOVA, LAURENT, *Résponsabilités de l'intellectuel communiste* (Paris, 1949).

CAUTE, DAVID, *Communism and the French Intellectuals 1914–1960* (London, 1964), *Le Communisme et les intellectuels français 1914–1966* (Paris, 1967).

—— *The Illusion: An Essay on Politics, Theatre and the Novel* (London, 1971).

—— *The Fellow-Travellers: A Postscript to the Enlightenment* (London, 1973); revised as *The Fellow-Travellers: Intellectual Friends of Communism* (London, 1988).

—— *Collisions: Essays and Reviews* (London, 1974).

—— *The Great Fear: The Anti-Communist Purge Under Truman and Eisenhower* (New York and London, 1978).

—— *Joseph Losey: A Revenge on Life* (London and New York, 1994).

CEPLAIR, LARRY and ENGLUND, STEVEN, *The Inquisition in Hollywood: Politics in the Film Community* (New York, 1980).

CHAMBERS, COLIN, *The Story of Unity Theatre* (London, 1989).

CHASINS, ABRAM, 'Van Cliburn in the USSR', *The Reporter*, 18/11, 29 May 1958.

CHIAURELI, MIKHAIL, 'The Fall of Berlin', *VOKS Bulletin*, 64 (1950).

CHIPP, HERSCHEL B. (ed.), *Theories of Modern Art: A Source Book by Artists and Critics* (Berkeley and Los Angeles, 1968).

CHRISTIE, IAN, 'Canons and Careers: The Director in Soviet Cinema', in Taylor and Spring (1993).

CHURAK, GALINA, *Il'ia Repin* (Moscow, 2000).

CIMENT, MICHEL, *Kazan on Kazan* (London, 1973).

—— *Conversations with Losey* (London, 1985).

CLARKE, GERALD, *Capote: A Biography* (London, 1988).

COCKBURN, ALEXANDER, *Idle Passion: Chess and the Dance of Death* (London, 1975).

COCKCROFT, EVA, 'Abstract Expression: Weapon of the Cold War', *Artforum*, 12/10 (June 1974); repr. in Frascina (1985).

COE, RICHARD, *Ionesco: A Study of His Plays* (London, 1971).

COGLEY, JOHN, *Report on Blacklisting*, 2 vols. (New York, 1956).

COHEN-SOLAL, ANNIE, *Sartre: A Life* (London, 1987).

COLEMAN, PETER, *The Liberal Conspiracy: The Congress for Cultural Freedom and the Struggle for the Mind of Postwar Europe* (London, 1989).

CONDON, RICHARD, *The Manchurian Candidate* (New York, 1959).

CONQUEST, ROBERT, *Common Sense About Russia* (London, 1960).

—— *The Politics of Ideas in the USSR* (London, 1967).

—— *We and They* (London, 1980).

COOK, BRUCE, *Brecht in Exile* (New York, 1982).

COOKE, CATHERINE, 'Beauty as a Route to "the Radiant Future": Responses of Soviet Architecture', in Reid, 'Design' (1997).

CORBER, ROBERT, *In the Name of National Security: Hitchcock, Homophobia, and the Political Construction of Gender in Postwar America* (Durham, NC, 1993).

CORRIGAN, ROBERT W. (ed.), *Arthur Miller: A Collection of Critical Essays* (Englewood Cliffs, NJ, 1969).

COUNTS, GEORGE S. and LODGE, NUCIA P., *The Country of the Blind: The Soviet System of Mind Control* (Boston, 1949).

Cox, Annette, *Art-as-Politics: The Abstract-Expressionist Avant-Garde and Society* (Ann Arbor, Mich., 1982).

Crankshaw, Edward, *Putting Up with the Russians 1947–1984* (London, 1984).

Cronin, Anthony, *Samuel Beckett: The Last Modernist* (London, 1996).

Cullerne Bown, Matthew, *Socialist Realist Painting* (New Haven and London, 1998).

Cushman, Robert E., *Civil Liberties in the United States* (Ithaca, NY, 1956).

Daglish, Robert, 'A Moscow Diary: Stage and Screen', *Anglo-Soviet Journal*, 29/2 (Jan. 1969).

Davis, Miles, *Miles: The Autobiography* (London, 1990).

Demetz, Peter, 'Literature in Ulbricht's Germany', *Problems of Communism*, 11/4 (July–Aug. 1962).

Demille, Cecil B., *Autobiography* (London, 1960).

Deutschland im Kalten Krieg 1945–1963, Eine Ausstellung des Deutschen Historischen Museums 28 August bis 24 November 1992 im Zeughaus Berlin (Argon, Berlin, 1992).

Dickstein, Morris, 'The Fifties Were Radical Too', *Times Literary Supplement*, 5123, 8 June 2001.

Doss, Erika, 'The Art of Cultural Politics: From Regionalism to Abstract Expressionism', in Lary May (1989).

Dovchenko, A., 'Michurin', *Izbrannye stsenarii*, vol. 5.

Downing, David, *Passovotchka: Moscow Dynamo in Britain 1945* (London, 2000 (1999)).

Drobny, Jaroslav, *Champion in Exile* (London, 1955).

Duberman, Martin B., *Paul Robeson* (London, 1989).

Dunaevskii, Isaak, 'Nazrevshie voprosy legkoi muzyki', *Sovetskaia muzyka*, no. 6 (June 1955).

Dymschiz, Alexander (Dymshits, Aleksandr), *Wandlungen und Verwandlungen des Antikommunismus. Essays zu Literatur und Äesthetik* (Berlin, 1977).

Eales, Richard, *Chess: The History of the Game* (London, 1985).

Egbert, Donald Drew, *Social Radicalism and the Arts: Western Europe* (New York, 1970).

Egorova, Tatiana, *Soviet Film Music: An Historical Survey*, trans. Tatiana A. Ganf and Natalia A. Egunova (Amsterdam, 1997).

Ehrenburg [Erenburg], Il'ya, *The Thaw*, trans. Manya Harari (London, 1961 (1955)).

——*Men, Years, Life*. Vol. 2: *First Years of Revolution, 1918–1921*, trans. Anna Bostock and Yvonne Kapp (London, 1962); Vol. 3: *Truce, 1921–33* (London, 1963); Vol. 4: *Eve of War, 1933–41* (London, 1963); Vol. 5: *The War, 1941–45* (London, 1964); Vol. 6: *Post-War Years, 1945–54* (London, 1966). (Vols. 5 and 6 trans. Tatiana Shebunina in collaboration with Yvonne Kapp.).

——*Chekhov, Stendhal and other Essays*, trans. Anna Bostock in collaboration with Yvonne Kapp (London, 1962).

Eliot, T. S. *The Cocktail Party*, (New York, 1950).

Ellwood, D. W., 'The Propaganda of the Marshall Plan in Italy in a Cold War Context', *Boundaries to Freedom*, Conference at the Roosevelt Study Center, Middleburg, the Netherlands (18–19 Oct. 2001).

ELSOM, JOHN, *Cold War Theatre* (London and New York, 1992).

'Entretien à Prague sur la notion de "décadence" ', *La Nouvelle critique* (June–July 1964).

ESSLIN, MARTIN, 'Bert Brecht's Difficulties', *Encounter*, 11/6 (Dec. 1958).

—— *Brecht: The Man and his Work* (New York, 1961).

—— 'Brecht at Seventy', *Tulane Drama Review* (Fall, 1967).

—— *Three European Plays* (London, 1970).

EVANS, F. BOWEN (ed.), *Worldwide Communist Propaganda Activities* (New York, 1955).

EWEN, FREDERICK, review of Günter Grass's *The Plebeians Rehearse the Uprising*, *The Nation*, 13 Feb. 1967.

—— *Bertolt Brecht: His Life, His Art and His Times* (New York, 1967).

FAY, LAUREL E., 'Shostakovich versus Volkov: Whose Testimony?', *Russian Review*, 39/4 (Oct. 1980).

—— 'From *Lady Macbeth* to *Katerina*: Shostakovich's Versions and Revisions', in David Fanning (ed.), *Shostakovich Studies* (Cambridge, 1995).

—— *Shostakovich: A Life* (Oxford, 2000).

FEIGIN, LEO (ed.), *Russian Jazz: New Identity* (London, 1985).

FENTON, JAMES, 'Aimez-vous Brecht?', *New York Review of Books*, 31/4, 15 Mar. 1984.

—— 'Subversives', *New York Review of Books*, 43/1, 11 Jan. 1996.

FISUNOV, P., 'Upadok amerikanskogo teatra. Pis'mo iz N'iu-Iorka', *Teatr* (Aug. 1950).

FITZPATRICK, SHEILA, *The Cultural Front: Power and Culture in Revolutionary Russia* (Ithaca and London, 1992).

FLANNER, JANET, *Paris Journal 1944–65* (New York, 1965).

FONTAINE, ANDRÉ, *History of the Cold War* (London, 1970).

FONTEYN, MARGOT, *Autobiography* (London, 1975).

FORBES, JILL, 'Winning Hearts and Minds: The American Cinema in France, 1945–49', *French Cultural Studies*, 8, part 1, no. 22 (Feb. 1997).

FORGACS, DAVID, 'The Making and Unmaking of Neorealism in Postwar Italy', in Hewitt (1999).

FOUGERON, LUCIE, 'Une "Affaire" politique: le portrait de Staline par Picasso', *Communisme*, nos. 53–4 (1998).

FRANK, ELIZABETH, 'Farewell to Athene: The Collected Greenberg', *Salmagundi*, 80 (Fall, 1988).

FRASCINA, FRANCIS (ed.), *Pollock and After: The Critical Debate* (London, 1985).

FREEMAN, SIMON, *Behind the Scenes of Soviet Sport* (London, 1980).

—— *Sport Behind the Iron Curtain* (London and New York, 1980).

FREEMAN, TED, *Theatres of War: French Committed Theatre from the Second World War to the Cold War* (Exeter, 1998).

French Cultural Studies, vol. 8, part 1, no. 22. Special number ed. Ted Freeman, 'France and the Cold War' (Feb. 1997).

FRIES, URSULA, 'West German Theatre in the Period of Reconstruction', in Hewitt (1999).

FUEGI, JOHN, *Brecht and Company: Sex, Politics and the Making of Modern Drama* (US title) (New York, 1994); *The Life and Lies of Bertolt Brecht* (UK title) (London, 1994).

FULBROOK, MARY, *Anatomy of a Dictatorship: Inside the GDR 1949–1989* (Oxford, 1995).

FUTRELL, MICHAEL, 'Banned Books in the Lenin Library', *Soviet Studies*, 10/3 (Jan. 1959).

FYVEL, T. R., 'The Past in Totalitarian Art', *Encounter* 5/7 (July 1955).

GADDIS, JOHN L., *We Know Now: Re-thinking Cold War History* (London, 1997).

GALICHENKO, NICHOLAS, *Glasnost—Soviet Cinema Responds*, ed. Robert Allington (Austin, Tex., 1991).

GAMBRELL, JAMEY, 'The Wonder of the Soviet World', *New York Review of Books*, 41/21, 22 Dec. 1994.

GARAUDY, ROGER, *Les Intellectuels et la renaissance français* (Paris, 1945).

—— 'Artistes sans uniformes', *Art de France*, 9 (Nov. 1946).

—— *Literature of the Graveyard*, trans. Joseph M. Bernstein (New York, 1948).

—— *D'un réalisme sans rivages* (Paris, 1963).

GEHRING, HANSJÖRG, *Amerikanische Literaturpolitik in Deutschland 1945–1953. Ein Aspekt des Re-Education Programms* (Stuttgart, 1976).

GIENOW-HECHT, JESSICA C. E., 'Art is Democracy and Democracy is Art: Culture, Propaganda, and the *Neue Zeitung* in Germany 1944–1947', *Diplomatic History*, 23/1 (Winter 1999).

—— *Transmission Impossible: American Journalism in Cultural Diplomacy in Postwar Germany, 1945–1955* (Baton Rouge, La., 1999).

GILOT, FRANÇOISE, with CARLETON LAKE, *Life With Picasso* (London, 1965).

GIMBEL, JOHN, *The American Occupation of Germany, 1945–1949* (Stanford, 1968).

GINZBURG, RALPH, 'Portrait of a Genius as a Young Chess Master', *Harper's*, 224 (Jan. 1962).

GLASER, HERMAN, *Kulturgeschichte des Bundesrepublik Deutschland. Zwischen Kapitulation und Währungsreform 1945–1948* (Munich, 1985).

GLENNY, MICHAEL (ed.), *Novy Mir: A Selection 1955–1967* (London, 1972).

GLOCK, WILLIAM, 'Musical Festival in Rome', *Encounter*, 2/6 (June 1954).

GLUKHAREVA, E., 'Angliiskii demokraticheskii teatr "Iuniti (Unity)"', *Teatr*, 7 (July 1950).

GOLDSTEIN, CORA SOL, 'The Control of Visual Representation: American Art Policy in Occupied Germany 1945–1949', *Boundaries to Freedom* Conference at the Roosevelt Study Center, Middleburg, the Netherlands, 18–19 Oct. 2001.

GOLOMSHTOK, IGOR, 'Realisty S Sh A', *Iskusstvo*, no. 5 (1960).

—— *Totalitarian Art: In the Soviet Union, the Third Reich, Fascist Italy and the People's Republic of China*, trans. Robert Chandler (London, 1990).

—— and GLEZER, ALEKSANDR, *Unofficial Art in the Soviet Union* (London, 1977).

GOLOVSKOY, VAL. S., with JOHN RIMBERG, *Behind the Soviet Screen: The Motion-Picture Industry in the USSR 1972–1982*, trans. Steven Hill (Ann Arbor, Mich., 1986).

GOODWIN, NOËL, 'George Balanchine', Royal Ballet Covent Garden programme (2001).

GORCHAKOV, N. A., *The Theater in Soviet Russia* (London and New York, 1958).

GORODINSKII, V., *Muzyka duchovnoi nishchety* (Moscow–Leningrad, 1950).

GORODINSKY [GORODINSKII], V., *Geistige Armut der Musik* (Halle, 1953).

GOULDING, DANIEL J. (ed.), *Post New Wave Cinema in the Soviet Union and Eastern Europe* (Bloomington, Ind., 1989).

GRAFFY, JULIAN, 'Cinema', in Kelly and Shepherd (1998).

GRASS, GÜNTER, *The Plebeians Rehearse the Uprising*, trans. Ralph Manheim (New York, 1966).

GRAY, CAMILLA, *The Great Experiment: Russian Art, 1863–1922* (London, 1962).

Great Soviet Encyclopedia, see *Bol'shaia sovetskaia entsiklopediia*.

GREENBERG, CLEMENT, 'The Present Prospects of American Painting and Sculpture', *Horizon*, nos. 93–4 (Oct. 1947).

—— 'Art', *Nation*, 1 Nov. 1947.

—— 'The Decline of Cubism', *Partisan Review*, 15/3 (Mar. 1948).

—— 'Irrelevance versus Irresponsibility', *Partisan Review*, 15/5 (May 1948).

—— 'Abstract and Representational', *Art Digest*, no. 1 (Nov. 1954).

—— *Art and Culture: Critical Essays* (Boston, 1961).

GREY, BERYL, *Red Curtain Up* (London, 1958).

GRIBACHEV, N., 'Vstrecha na El'be', *Kul'tura i zhizn'*, 10 Mar. 1947.

GROYS, BORIS, 'Socialist Realism and the Russian Avant-Garde', in Günther (1990).

GUGGENHEIM, PEGGY, *Out of this Century: Confessions of an Art Addict* (London, 1983).

GUILBAUT, SERGE, *How New York Stole the Idea of Modern Art: Abstract Expressionism, Freedom and the Cold War*, trans. Arthur Goldhammer (Chicago, 1983).

GULDBERG, JØRN, 'Socialist Realism as Institutional Practice', in Günther (1990).

GÜNTHER, HANS (ed.), *The Culture of the Stalin Period* (London, 1990).

GUSSOW, MEL, *Zanuck: Don't Say Yes Until I Finish Talking* (London, 1971).

GUTTUSO, RENATO, *Recent Paintings, Watercolours and Drawings*, Marlborough Fine Art catalogue, 1–24 Mar. 1979 (London, 1979).

HAHN, WERNER G., *Postwar Soviet Politics: The Fall of Zhdanov and the Defeat of Moderation, 1946–1953* (Ithaca and London, 1982).

HALLE, LOUIS, *The Cold War as History* (London, 1967).

HAMES, PETER, *The Czechoslovak New Wave* (Berkeley, 1985).

—— 'Czechoslovakia: After the Spring', in Goulding (1989).

HAUPTMAN, WILLIAM, 'Suppression of Art in the McCarthy Decade', *Artforum* (Oct. 1973).

HAVEL, VÁCLAV, *The Increased Difficulty of Concentration*, trans. Vera Blackwell (London and New York, 1976).

—— *Private View: A Play*, trans. Vera Blackwell (London, 1978).

—— *Audience: A Play*, trans. Vera Blackwell (London, 1978).

—— *The Memorandum*, trans. Vera Blackwell, introd. Tom Stoppard (London, 1981).

—— *Largo Desolato*, English version by Tom Stoppard (London, 1987).

—— *Temptation*, trans. George Theiner (London, 1988).

—— *Disturbing the Peace*, trans. Paul Wilson, (London, 1990).

——*Open Letters: Selected Prose, 1965–1990*, selected and ed. Paul Wilson (London, 1991).

HAYMAN, RONALD, 'In Search of Biography: Bertolt Brecht', *Literary Review* (July 1982).

——*Writing Against: A Biography of Sartre* (London, 1986).

HERBERT, JAMES D., *The Political Origins of Abstract-Expressionist Art Criticism: The Early Theoretical and Critical Writings of Clement Greenberg and Harold Rosenberg* (Stanford, 1985).

HEWITT, NICHOLAS (ed.), *The Culture of Reconstruction* (London, 1999).

HINGLEY, RONALD, *The Russian Mind* (London, 1978).

HINTON, STEPHEN, 'Hindemith and Weill', in Brinkmann and Wolff (1999).

HIXSON, WALTER L., *Parting the Curtain: Propaganda, Culture and the Cold War* (London, 1997).

HO, ALAN B., and FEOFANOV, DMITRY (eds.), *Shostakovich Reconsidered* (Toccata Press [n.p., UK], 1998).

HOBSBAWM, ERIC, *Age of Extremes: The Short Twentieth Century, 1914–1991* (London, 1995).

——*Uncommon People: Resistance, Rebellion and Jazz* (London, 1998).

HOFMANN, MICHAEL, 'That Brecht was a nasty piece of work, and he didn't even write his own plays', *London Review of Books*, 16/220, 20 Oct. 1994.

HOGAN, DAN, 'The Moiseyev Dancers in the USA', *The Reporter*, 8/11, 29 May 1958.

HOOK, SIDNEY, *Out of Step: An Unquiet Life in the 20th Century* (New York, 1987).

HOOPER, DAVID and WHYLD, KENNETH, *The Oxford Companion to Chess* (Oxford, 1984).

HOUSTON, PENELOPE, *The Contemporary Cinema* (London, 1966).

HUNTINGDON, SAMUEL P., 'The Clash of Civilizations?', *Foreign Affairs*, 72/3 (Summer 1993).

IGNATIEFF, MICHAEL, 'Isaiah Berlin (1909–1997)', *New York Review of Books*, 44/0, 18 Dec. 1997.

——*Isaiah Berlin: A Life* (London, 1998).

IGNOTUS, PAUL, *Political Prisoner* (London, 1959).

INGLIS, FRED, *The Cruel Peace* (London, 1992).

INKELES, ALEX, *Public Opinion in Soviet Russia* (Cambridge, Mass., 1950).

IOFAN (YOFAN), B. M., 'The Architecture of Moscow's High Buildings', *VOKS Bulletin*, 75 (1952).

IONESCO, EUGENE, *Present Past, Past Present: A Personal Memoir*, trans. Helen R. Lane (London, 1972).

ISAEV, K., 'Sekretnaia missiia', *Izbrannye stsenarii*, vol. 6.

Istoriia sovetskogo kino 1917–1967, vols. 3,4 (Moscow, 1975, 1978).

Izbrannye stsenarii sovetskogo kino. Redaktsionnaia kollegia: V. Kozhevnikov, G. Mdivani, M. Smirnova, M. Chiaureli, A. Shtein, vols. 5, 6 (Moscow, 1951).

JACOBS, DIANE, *The Magic of Woody Allen* (London, 1982).

JAMESON, FREDRIC, *Brecht and Method* (London, 1998).

JAŘAB, JOSEF, 'The Story of the Jazz Section in Czechoslovakia', in Robert Kroes and others (1993).

JEANSON, FRANCIS, *Sartre par lui-même* (Paris, 1960 (1955)).

——*Le Problème morale et la pensée de Sartre* (Paris, 1965); *Sartre and the Problem of Morality*, trans. Robert V. Stone (Bloomington, Ind., 1980).

JOHNSON, PRISCILLA, *Khrushchev and the Arts: The Politics of Soviet Culture 1962–1964* (Cambridge, Mass., 1965).

JOHNSON, VIDA T., 'The Films of Andrei Konchalovsky', in Graham Petrie and Ruth Dwyer (eds.), *Before the Wall Came Down: Soviet and East European Filmmakers Working in the West* (London and New York, 1990).

JOSEPHSON, DAVID, 'The Exile of European Music: Documentation of Upheaval and Immigration in the *New York Times*', in Brinkmann and Wolff (1999).

JUVILER, NINA, 'Art and Artists in the USSR', *Problems of Communism*, 11/3 (May–June 1962).

KAEL, PAULINE, *I Lost It At the Movies* (Boston, 1965).

KALB, JONATHAN, *The Theatre of Heiner Müller* (Cambridge, 1998).

'Kalte Krieg der Unterhaltung, Der', *Deutsches Historiches Museum Magazin*, Heft 5, 2 Jahrgang (Summer 1992).

KANAPA, JEAN, *L'Existentialisme n'est pas un humanisme* (Paris, 1947).

KANFER, STEFAN, *A Journal of the Plague Years* (New York, 1973).

KARPINSKI, MARCIEJ, *The Theatre of Andrzej Wajda*, trans. Christina Paul (Cambridge, 1989).

KARPOV, ANATOLII and ROSHAL, ALEKSANDR, *Deviataia vertikal'* (Moscow, 1978); trans. by Kenneth P. Neat as *Chess is my Life* (Oxford and New York, 1980).

KASSOF, ALLEN, 'Youth vs the Regime: Conflict in Values', *Problems of Communism*, 6/3 (May–June 1957).

——'Afflictions of the Youth League', *Problems of Communism*, 7/5 (Sept.–Oct. 1958).

KAZAN, ELIA, *A Life* (London, 1988).

KEANE, JOHN, *Václav Havel: A Political Tragedy in Six Acts* (London, 1999).

KEEP, JOHN L. H., *The Last of the Empires: History of the Soviet Union, 1945–1991* (London, 1995).

KELLERMANN, HENRY, *Cultural Relations as an Instrument of US Foreign Policy* (Washington, DC, 1978).

KELLY, CATRIONA and SHEPHERD, DAVID (eds.), *Soviet Cultural Studies* (Oxford, 1998).

——and MILNER-GULLAND, ROBIN, 'Building a new Reality: The Visual Arts, 1921–1953', in Kelly and Shepherd (1998).

KELLY, DEBRA, 'Loss and Recuperation, Order and Subversion: Post-war Painting in France, 1945–51', *French Cultural Studies*, 8/22, part 1 (Feb. 1997).

KEMENOV, VLADIMIR, 'Shakespeare. On the Occasion of the 330th anniversary of his death', *VOKS Bulletin*, 50 (1946).

——'Aspects of Two Cultures', *VOKS Bulletin*, 52 (1947).

KEMPTON, MURRAY, 'Thanks, Shchukin & Morozov', *New York Review of Books*, 33/14, 25 Sept. 1986.

KENEZ, PETER, *Cinema and Soviet Society, 1917–1953* (Cambridge, 1992).

KENNEDY, MICHAEL, *Britten* (London, 1993).

KHENTOVA, S. M., *Shostakovich v Moskve* (Moscow, 1986).

KHRUSHCHEV, NIKITA, *Khrushchev on Culture*, Encounter pamphlet, no. 9 (London, 1963).

——'Khrushchev on Modern Art', *Encounter* (Apr. 1963).

——*Khrushchev Remembers: Memoirs*, vol. 1, trans. and ed. Strobe Talbott (London, 1971).

——*Khrushchev Remembers: The Last Testament. Memoirs*, vol. 2, trans. and ed. Strobe Talbott (London, 1974).

KIMMELMAN, MICHAEL, 'Revisiting the Revisionists: The Modern, its Critics, and the Cold War', in *The Museum of Modern Art at Mid-Century*, Studies in Modern Art, 4 (1994).

——'Wandering Minstrel', *New York Review of Books*, 48/17, 1 Nov. 2001.

KING, DAVID, *The Commissar Vanishes: The Falsification of Photographs and Art in Stalin's Russia* (Edinburgh, 1997).

KIRKPATRICK, JEANE J., 'The Modernizing Imperative', *Foreign Affairs*, 72/4 (Sept.–Oct. 1993).

KOCH, STEPHEN, *Double Lives: Spies and Writers in the Secret Soviet War of Ideas Against the West* (New York, 1994).

KOESTLER, ARTHUR, intro. to Harry Golombek, *Fischer v. Spassky: The World Chess Championship 1972* (London, 1972).

KOMISSARZHEVSKY, VIKTOR, *Teatry Moskvy—Moscow Theatres* (Moscow, 1959).

——(ed.), *Nine Modern Soviet Plays* (Moscow, 1977).

KORCHNOI, VIKTOR, *Antishakhmaty* (London, 1981).

KOSZARSKI, DIANE KAISER, 'Gdansk Macabre', in David W. Paul (ed.), *Politics, Art and Commitment in the East European Cinema* (London, 1983).

KOTEK, JÖEL, *Students and the Cold War*, trans. Ralph Blumenau (London, 1996).

KOVAL', M., 'Tvorcheskii Put'', *Sovetskaia muzyka*, nos. 2, 3, 4 (Mar.–Apr., May, June, 1948).

KOZLOFF, MAX, 'American Painting During the Cold War', *Artforum* (May 1973), repr. in Frascina (1985).

KOZLOV, LEONID, 'The Artist and the Shadow of Ivan', in Taylor and Spring (1993).

KRAMER, HILTON, 'Art: A Return to Modernism', in Salisbury, *Anatomy* (1968).

——*The Twilight of the Intellectuals: Culture and Politics in the Era of the Cold War* (Chicago, 1999).

KRAUSOVA, KATJA, 'Defectors', in Norman Stone and Michael Glenny (eds.), *The Other Russia* (London, 1990).

KROES, ROBERT, RYDELL, ROBERT W., and BOSSCHE DOEKO, F. J., (eds.), *Cultural Transmissions and Receptions: American Mass Culture in Europe* (Amsterdam, 1993).

KUBY, ERICH, *The Russians and Berlin*, trans. Arnold J. Pomerans (London, 1968 (Munich, 1965)).

KUISEL, RICHARD F., *Seducing the French: The Dilemma of Americanization* (Berkeley, 1993).

KULIKOVA, I., 'Teatral'nyi Brodvei', *Teatr*, 10 (Oct. 1947).

KULIKOVA, I., 'Amerikanskii Teatr na sluzhbe Uoll Strit', *Teatr,* 4 (Apr. 1949).

KUNDERA, MILAN, *The Joke*, trans. David Hamblyn and Oliver Stallybrass (London, 1970).

LANGE, WIGAND, *Theater in Deutschland nach 1945. Zur Theaterpolitik der amerikanischen Besatzungsbehörden* (Frankfurt am Main, 1980).

LAPITSKY, I., 'Krizis amerikanskogo burzhuaznogo teatra', *Teatr,* 4 (Apr. 1950).

LAQUEUR, WALTER and LICHTHEIM, GEORGE (eds.), *The Soviet Cultural Scene, 1956–1957* (London, 1958).

LAUFER, LEO, 'Vladimir Mayakovsky and the "New Look" in Soviet Literature', *Problems of Communism*, 4/3 (July–Aug. 1954).

LAWSON, JOHN HOWARD, *Film in the Battle of Ideas* (New York, 1953).

LAWTON, ANNA (ed.), intro. to *The Red Screen: Politics, Society, Art in Soviet Cinema* (London and New York, 1992).

LAZAR, MARC, 'The Culture of Cold War of the French and Italian Communist Parties', *Boundaries to Freedom*, Conference at the Roosevelt Study Center, Middleburg, the Netherland, 18–19 Oct. 2001.

LAZAREFF, HELENE and LAZAREFF, PIERRE, *L'URSS à l'heure Malenkov* (Paris, 1954); trans. as *The Soviet Union after Stalin* (London, 1955).

LAZAREV, A., 'Dramaturgiia K. Simonova' (Moscow, 1952).

LEAB, DANIEL, 'Good Germans/Bad Nazis. Amerikanische Bilder aus dem Kalten Krieg und ihre Ursprünge', in 'Kalte Krieg' (1992).

LEBEDINSKY, LEV, 'Some Musical Allusions in the Works of Dmitry Shostakovich', trans. M. Marovic and Ian MacDonald, in Ho and Feofanov (1998).

LEFEBVRE, HENRI, *Pignon* (Paris, 1956).

LÉGER, FERNAND, 'Couleur dans le monde', *Europe*, 15 Mar. 1938.

LEHMANN-HAUPT, HELLMUT, *Art Under a Dictatorship* (New York, 1954).

LEONHARD, SIGRUN D., 'Testing the Borders: East German Film Between Individualism and Social Commitment', in Goulding (1989).

LEYDA, JAY, *Kino: A History of the Russian and Soviet Film*, 3rd edn. (London, 1983).

LIEHM, ANTONÍN J., *Closely Watched Films: The Czechoslovak Experience* (White Plains, NY, 1974).

LIEHM, MIRA and LIEHM, ANTONÍN J., *The Most Important Art: East European Films After 1945* (Berkeley, 1977).

LINDEPERG, SYLVIE, '"The Children of the Absurd": André Cayette and the Film-Making of the Cold War', *French Cultural Studies*, 8/22, part 1 (Feb. 1997).

LINDEY, CHRISTINE, *Art in the Cold War* (London, 1990).

LOSEY, JOSEPH, 'L'Oeil du maître', *Cahiers du cinéma* (Dec. 1960).

LOTTMAN, HERBERT R., *Albert Camus: A Biography* (London, 1979).

LUTHY, HERBERT, ' "Of Poor Bert Brecht" ', *Encounter*, 6/1 (July 1956).

LVOV-ANOKHIN, B., *Galina Ulanova* (Moscow, 1956).

LYON, JAMES K., *Brecht in America* (Princeton, 1980).

LYUBIMOV, IURII, *Rasskazy starogo trepacha* (Moscow, 2000).

MACAULAY, ALASTAIR, 'Castles in the Air', *Times Literary Supplement*, no. 5014, 7 May 1999.

—— 'Over the Brink of Tradition', *Times Literary Supplement*, no. 5122, 1 June 2001.

MCAULIFFE, MARY, *Crisis on the Left: The Cold War and American Liberals* (Amherst, 1978).

MCBURNEY, GERARD, 'Soviet Music after the Death of Stalin: The Legacy of Shostakovich', in Kelly and Shepherd (1998).

MCCARTHY, MARY, 'Naming Names', *Encounter*, 8/5 (May 1957).

MACDONALD, DWIGHT, 'Soviet Cinema: A History and an Elegy', *Problems of Communism*, 4/1 (Jan.–Feb. 1955).

MCIVER, ROBERT M., *Academic Freedom in Our Time* (New York, 1955).

MACKINNON, LACHLAN, *The Lives of Elsa Triolet* (London, 1992).

MAKAROVA, NATALIA, *A Dance Autobiography* (London, 1980).

MALNICK, BERTHA, 'The Soviet Theatre, 1957', *Soviet Studies*, 9/3 (Jan. 1958).

MALRAUX, ANDRÉ, pref. to id., *The Conquerors*, trans. J. Le Clerq (Boston, 1956).

MARCUS, J. S., 'Screentime for Hitler', *New York Review of Books*, 46/4, 4 Mar. 1999.

Mastera sovetskogo kino. Evgenii Urbanskii (Moscow, 1968).

MATTHEWS, JANE DE HART, 'Art and Politics in Cold War America', *American Historical Review*, 81 (Oct. 1976).

MAY, ELAINE TYLER, *Homeward Bound: American Families in the Cold War Era* (New York, 1988).

MAY, LARY, *Recasting America: Culture and Politics in the Age of the Cold War* (Chicago, 1989).

MEAD, MARGARET (ed.), *Soviet Attitudes Toward Authority* (London, 1955).

MEDVEDEV, ZHORES, *Ten Years After Ivan Denisovich*, trans. Hilary Sternberg (London, 1974).

MEHNERT, KLAUS, *The Anatomy of Soviet Man*, trans. Maurice Rosenbaum (London, 1961).

MENUHIN, YEHUDI, *Unfinished Journey* (London, 1996).

MEYER, MICHAEL, 'Giving the Devil his Due', *New York Review of Books*, 41/20, 1 Dec. 1994.

MIKES, GEORGE, *Leap Through the Curtain* (London, 1955).

MIKHEEVA, L., *Zhizn' Dmitriia Shostakovicha* (Moscow, 1997).

MILLER, ARTHUR, *A View from the Bridge, All My Sons* (London, 1963).

—— *After the Fall* (New York, 1964).

—— intro. to *Collected Plays* (London, 1965).

—— *The Crucible* (London, 1966).

—— 'It Could Happen Here—and Did', *New York Times*, part 2, 30 Apr. 1967.

—— *Timebends* (London, 1987).

—— *Echoes Down the Corridor: Collected Essays 1944–2000*, ed. Steven R. Centola (London, 2000).

—— 'The Crucible in History', *Guardian*, Review section, 17 June 2000.

MILLER, MERLE, *The Judges and the Judged* (New York, 1952).

MILNE, TOM, *Losey on Losey* (London, 1967).

MITCHELL, JOHN M., *International Cultural Relations* (London, 1986).

'"Modernists" v. "Socialist Realists" in Music', *Soviet Survey*, 6 (1956), repr. in Laqueur and Lichtheim (1958).

MONEY, KEITH, *Fonteyn & Nureyev: The Great Years* (London, 1994).

MOROZOV, M., 'Dve Kul'turi', *Teatr* (Nov. 1947).

MORTON, HENRY W., 'The Case of Soviet Sports', *Problems of Communism*, 9/6 (Nov.–Dec. 1960).

—— *Soviet Sport: Mirror of Soviet Society* (New York, 1964).

MOTTRAM, ERIC, 'Arthur Miller: Development of a Political Dramatist in America', in Corrigan (1969).

Museum Berlin Karlshorst/Muzei Berlin Karlskhorst, *Ein Ort der Erinnerung und Begegnung/Mesto pamiati i vstrechi*, catalogue of the joint German–Russian Museum est. May 1995.

NABOKOV, NICOLAS, *Old Friends and New Music* (London, 1951).

—— *Bagázh* (London, 1975).

NADEL, ALAN, *Containment Culture: American Narratives, Postmodernism and the Atomic Age* (Durham and London, 1995).

NAIMARK, NORMAN N., *The Russians in Germany: A History of the Soviet Zone of Occupation, 1945–1949* (Cambridge, Mass., 1995).

NAVASKY, VICTOR, *Naming Names* (New York, 1980).

NEKRASOV, VIKTOR, *On Both Sides of the Ocean: A Russian Writer's Travels in Italy and the United States*, trans. Elias Kulukundis (London, 1964).

NELSON, BENJAMIN, *Arthur Miller: Portrait of a Playwright* (London, 1970).

NESTIEV (NEST'EV), I., 'The Problem of Social Realism in Music', *VOKS Bulletin*, 67 (1951).

—— 'Dollarovaia kakofoniia', *Izvestiia*, 7 Jan. 1951.

—— 'Sergei Prokofiev and his Opera *War and Peace*', *VOKS Bulletin*, 2(97) (Feb. 1956).

—— 'Cviashchennia kakophoniia', *Sovetskaia muzyka*, no. 2 (1958).

—— 'S Pozitsii "kholodnoi voiny" ', *Sovetskaia muzyka*, no. 10 (Oct. 1963).

NEVE, BRIAN, *Film and Politics in America: A Social Tradition* (London, 1992).

NINKOVICH, FRANK, *The Diplomacy of Ideas: US Foreign Policy and Cultural Relations* (Cambridge, 1981).

NIXON, RICHARD M., *Six Crises* (London, 1962).

NORRIS, CHRISTOPHER (ed.), *Shostakovich, the Man and his Music* (London, 1982).

NOVE, IRENE, 'A Timely Warning', *Soviet Studies*, 5/4 (Apr. 1954).

NOVODVORSKAIA, I., 'Sovetskaia p'esa na germanskoi stsene', *Teatr*, 12 (Dec. 1949).

NUREYEV, RUDOLF, *Nureyev: An Autobiography with Pictures*, ed. Alexander Bland (London, 1962).

O'CONNOR, FRANCIS V., *Jackson Pollock* (New York, 1967).

OLKHOVSKY, ANDREY, *Music Under the Soviets* (New York, 1955).

'On the Opera *The Great Friendship* by V. Muradeli. The Decision of the Central Committee of the CPSU (Bolsheviks), 10 February 1948', *VOKS Bulletin* (1948).

O'NEILL, EUGENE, *The Iceman Cometh* (London, 1966 (1947)).

ORWELL, GEORGE, 'The Sporting Spirit', *Tribune*, 14 Dec. 1945, in *Collected Essays, Journalism and Letters*, vol. 4 (London, 1968).

PANOV, VALERY (with GEORGE FEIFER), *To Dance* (London, 1978).

Paris–Moscou 1900–1930, Catalogue de l'exposition, Centre Georges Pompidou (Paris, 1979).

PARKS, J. D., *Culture, Conflict and Co-Existence: American and Soviet Cultural Relations, 1917–1958* (Jefferson, NC, 1983).

PARROTT, JASPER, with VLADIMIR ASHKENAZY, *Beyond Frontiers* (London, 1984).

PAVLENKO, P. and CHIARUELI, M., 'Kliatva', *Izbrannye stsenarii*, vol. 5.

——— 'Padenie Berlina', *Izbrannye stsenarii*, vol. 6.

PELLS, RICHARD, *Not Like Us: How Europeans Have Loved, Hated and Transformed American Culture Since World War II* (New York, 1997).

PENROSE, ROLAND, *Picasso: His Life and Work* (London, 1958).

PETROV, N. V., *50 i 500* (Moscow, 1960).

PEYRE, HENRI, 'Camus the Pagan', *Yale French Studies*, 25 (Spring 1960).

PIGNON, EDUARD, *Documents* (Geneva, 1955).

PIKE, DAVID, *The Politics of Culture in Soviet-Occupied Germany 1945–1953* (Stanford, 1992).

POGODIN, NIKOLAI, 'A Petrarchan Sonnet', in *Contemporary Russian Drama*, ed. and trans. Franklin D. Reeve (New York, 1958).

POHL, FRANCES K., *Ben Shahn: New Deal Artist in a Cold War Climate, 1947–1954* (Austin, Tex., 1989).

POHRIBNY, ARSEN, 'Art and Artists of the "Underground"', *Problems of Communism*, 19/2 (Mar.–Apr. 1970).

POLLACK, HOWARD, *Aaron Copland, the Life of an Uncommon Man* (London, 2000).

POLONSKY, V., 'Lenin's View of Art and Culture', in Max Eastman (ed.), *Artists in Uniform* (London, 1934).

POLTORATSKII, V., 'Parizhskie zametki', *Kul'tura i zhizn'*, 11 Jan. 1949.

POPKIN, HENRY, 'Camus as Dramatist', *Partisan Review* (Summer 1959).

PORTER, ANDREW, 'Serious Swagger', *Times Literary Supplement*, no. 5126, 29 June 2001.

PUDOWKIN, ROMM und Andere, *Der sowjetische Film, eine Vortragsreihe*, trans. Erich Salewski (Berlin, 1953).

RABINE (RABIN), OSKAR, *L'Artiste et les bulldozers. Être peintre en URSS* (Paris, 1981).

RABINOVICH, D., *Dmitry Shostakovich*, trans. George Hanna (London, 1959).

RAKITIN, VASSILY, 'The Avant-Garde and Art of the Stalinist Era', in Günther (1990).

RANCHAL, MARCEL, 'Les Sorcières de Salem', *Positif*, 3/24 (May 1957).

' "Razvivat" i sovershenstvovat' muzykal'nuiu nauku', *Sovetskaia muzyka*, no. 1 (Jan. 1956).

REDDAWAY, PETER (ed.), *Uncensored Russia: The Human Rights Movement in the Soviet Union* (London, 1972).

—— 'KGB Psychiatry', *New York Review of Books*, 25/15, 12 Oct. 1978.

—— 'Waiting for Gorbachev', *New York Review of Books*, 32/15, 10 Oct. 1985.

REID, SUSAN E. (ed.), 'Design, Stalin and the Thaw', *Journal of Design History*, Special Issue, 10/2 (1997).

—— 'Destalinization and Taste, 1953–1963', in Reid (1997).

REEVE, FRANKLIN D. (ed. and trans.), *Contemporary Russian Drama* (New York, 1958).

REPIN, I. E., *Pis'ma I. E. Repin. Perepiska s P. M. Tret'iakovym 1873–1898* (Moscow–Leningrad, 1946).

—— and STASOV, V. V., *Perepiska, I, 1871–1876* (Moscow, 1948).

REVYAKIN, ALEXANDER, 'Decadence of Modern Art', *Soviet Literature*, 11 (1959).

RICHARDS, D. J., *Soviet Chess* (Oxford, 1965).

RICHTER, SVIATOSLAV, *Notebooks and Conversations*, ed. Bruno Monsaingeon (London, 2001).

RIESMAN, DAVID, 'The Nylon War', in *Abundance For What? And Other Essays* (London, 1964).

RIORDAN, JAMES, *Soviet Sport* (Oxford, 1980).

ROBESON, PAUL, *Here I Stand* (London, 1958).

ROBINSON, HARLOW, *Sergei Prokofiev: A Biography* (London, 1987).

ROGIN, MICHAEL, *Ronald Reagan, The Movie, and Other Episodes in Political Demonology* (Berkeley and Los Angeles, 1988).

ROMER, FEDOR, 'Dissidenty vsesoiuznogo znacheniia. Sobranie Leonida Talochkina', *Itogi*, 7 Mar. 2000.

ROMM, MIKHAIL, 'A Film in Support of Peace', *VOKS Bulletin*, 65 (1950).

—— 'Dramaturgiia kino i voprosy kompozitsii i fil'ma', in *Trudy vsesoiuznogo gosudarstvennogo instituta kinematografii*, Vypusk 1 (Moscow, 1962).

RORTY, JAMES and RAUSHENBUSH, WINIFRED, 'The Lessons of the Peekskill Riots', *Commentary*, 10/4 (Oct. 1950).

ROSENBERG, HAROLD, 'The American Action Painters', in id., *The Tradition of the New* (New York, 1959).

ROSLAVLEVA, NATALIA, *Era of the Russian Ballet, 1770–1965* (London, 1966).

ROSTOTSKY, M. A., 'Mayakovsky on the Stage', *VOKS Bulletin*, 2(91) (Mar.–Apr. 1955).

ROSTOTSKY, STANISLAV, 'Grigori Chukhrai and the "Ballad of a Soldier" ', *Soviet Film*, 7 (July 1960).

ROUGEMONT, DENIS DE, 'There is no "Modern Music" ', *Encounter*, 3/11 (Aug. 1955).

ROXBURGH, ANGUS, *Pravda: Inside the Soviet News Machine* (London, 1987).

Royal Academy, London: *An Exhibition of Works by Russian and Soviet Artists*, catalogue, n.d. (Dec. 1958).

ROZOV, VIKTOR, 'Alive Forever!', in *Contemporary Russian Drama*, ed. and trans. Franklin D. Reeve (New York, 1958).

RUBENSTEIN, JOSHUA, *Tangled Loyalties: The Life and Times of Ilya Ehrenburg* (London and New York, 1996).

RUBIN, RONALD I., *The United States Information Agency* (New York, 1966).

RÜHLE, JÜRGEN, *Das gefesselte Theater. Vom Revolutionstheater zum sozialistischen Realismus* (Cologne, 1957).

—— 'The Soviet Theatre', *Problems of Communism*, Part I (Nov.–Dec. 1959); Part II (Jan.–Feb. 1960).

RUSSELL, JOHN, 'Comrade Picasso', *New York Review of Books*, 48/6, 12 Apr. 2001.

RYBACK, TIMOTHY W., *Rock Around the Bloc: A History of Rock Music in Eastern Europe and the Soviet Union* (Oxford, 1990).

RYDELL, ROBERT W. and GWINN, NANCY (eds.), *Fair Representations: World's Fairs and the Modern World* (Amsterdam, 1994).

SALISBURY, HARRISON E., *An American in Russia* (New York, 1955); UK edn., *Stalin's Russia and After* (London, 1955).

—— *To Moscow and Beyond: A Reporter's Narrative* (London, 1960).

—— (ed.), *Anatomy of the Soviet Union* (London, 1968).

—— 'Theater: the Naked Truth', in Salisbury, *Anatomy* (1968).

—— *Without Fear or Favor* (New York, 1980).

SAMOILOVNA, TATYANA, 'My Roles in the Cinema', *Soviet Film*, 7 (July 1960).

SANDLER, IRVING, *The New York School: The Painters and Sculptors of the Fifties* (New York, 1978).

SARRIS, ANDREW, *Politics and Cinema* (New York, 1978).

SARTRE, JEAN-PAUL, *La Putain respectueuse* (Paris, 1946).

—— *L'Existentialisme est un humanisme*, (Paris, 1961 (1946)).

—— *Les Mains sales* (Paris, 1948).

—— *What is Literature?* (1947), trans. Bernard Frechtman (New York, 1949; London, 1950).

—— préface à René Leibowitz, *L'Artiste et sa conscience* (Paris, 1950).

—— *Le Diable et le bon dieu* (Edition Livre de Poche, Paris, 1961 (1951)).

—— *Nekrassov* (Paris, 1955).

—— *Altona, Men without Shadows, The Flies* (*The Flies* trans. Stuart Gilbert) (London, 1962).

—— 'The Artist and his Conscience', in *Situations*, trans. Benita Eisler (London, 1965).

—— *Un Théâtre de situations*, ed. Michel Contat and Michel Rybalka (Paris, 1973, new edn. 1992).

SAUNDERS, FRANCES STONOR, 'Hidden Hands. A Different History of Modernism', documentary film, Channel 4 TV (1995).

—— *Who Paid the Piper? The CIA and the Cultural Cold War* (London, 1999); US edn., *The Cultural Cold War: The CIA and the World of Arts and Letters* (New York, 2000).

SAYRE, NORMA, *Running Time: Films of the Cold War* (New York, 1982).

SCAMMELL, MICHAEL, *Solzhenitsyn* (New York, 1984).

—— (ed.), *The Solzhenitsyn Files: Secret Soviet Documents Reveal One Man's Fight Against the Monolith* (Chicago, 1995).

SCHILLER, HERBERT I., *Communications and Cultural Domination* (White Plains, NY, 1976).

SCHIVELBUSCH, WOLFGANG, *In a Cold Climate: Cultural and Intellectual Life in Berlin, 1945–1948*, trans. Kelly Barry (Berkeley, 1998).

SCHLESINGER, ARTHUR M., Jr., *The Vital Center: The Politics of Freedom* (London, 1970).

SCHONBERG, HAROLD C., 'The World of Music', in Salisbury, *Anatomy* (1968).

SCHMOLINSKY, GERHARDT, *Track and Field* (East Berlin, 1978).

SCHWARZ, BORIS, *Music and Musical Life in Soviet Russia, 1917–1970* (London, 1972, 1976).

SCOTT-SMITH, GILES, 'The Politics of Apolitical Culture: The United States, Western Europe, and the Post-War "Culture of Hegemony"', Ph.D. thesis, University of Lancaster (1998).

——'The "Masterpieces of the Twentieth Century" Festival and the Congress for Cultural Freedom: Origins and Consolidation 1947–1952', *Intelligence and National Security*, 15/1 (Spring 2000).

SCRIVEN, MICHAEL, *Jean-Paul Sartre, Politics and Culture in Post-War France* (London, 1999).

SEGEL, HAROLD B., *Twentieth-Century Russian Drama* (New York, 1987).

SETON, MARIE, *Sergei M. Eisenstein: A Life* (London, 1952).

SEVERIN, E., 'V poslevoennoi Germanii', *Teatr*, 12 (Dec. 1947).

SHAPIRO, DAVID (ed.), *Socialist Realism: Art as a Weapon* (New York, 1973).

——and SHAPIRO, CECILE, 'Abstract Expressionism: The Politics of Apolitical Painting', in Frascina (1985).

SHATROV, MIKHAIL, *The Bolsheviks and other Plays*, trans. and intro. Michael Glenny (London, 1990).

——*Dramas of the Revolution*, trans. Cynthia Carlile and Sharon McKee (Moscow, 1990).

SHIRER, WILLIAM L., *End of a Berlin Diary* (London, 1947).

SHNEERSON, G., 'Amerikanskaia muzykal'naia inzheneriia', *Sovetskaia muzyka*, no. 2 (Mar.–Apr. 1948).

SHNEIDMAN, N. NORMAN, *The Soviet Road to Olympus: Theory and Practice of Soviet Physical Culture and Sport* (London, 1979).

SHOSTAKOVICH, DMITRII, 'Velikaia bitva za mir', *Novyi mir*, 25/5 (May 1949).

——*Testimony: Memoirs as Related to Solomon Volkov* (London, 1979).

——*About Himself and his Times* (Moscow, 1986).

SHTEIN, A., 'Sud chesti', *Izbrannye stsenarii*, vol. 5.

SIMMONS, MICHAEL, *The Reluctant President: A Political Life of Václav Havel* (London, 1991).

SIMONOV, KONSTANTIN, 'Plays, the Theatre, and Life', *VOKS Bulletin*, 50 (1946).

——*Russkii vopros. P'esa v trekh deistviiakh semi kartinakh*, in *Za mir, za demokratiiu, P'esy* (Moscow, 1949).

——*P'esy. Russkii Vopros. Chuzhaia Ten'* (Moscow, 1949).

——'The Tasks Before Soviet Drama and Dramatic Criticism', *Soviet Studies*, 1/2 (Oct. 1949).

SJEKLOCHA, PAUL and MEAD, IGOR, *Unofficial Art in the Soviet Union* (Berkeley, 1967).

ŠKVORECKÝ, JOSEF, *The Bass Saxophone*, trans. Kaca Polackova-Henley (Toronto, 1977).

——*Talkin' Moscow Blues* (London, 1989).

SLEPIAN, VLADIMIR, 'The Young vs. The Old', *Problems of Communism*, 11/3 (May–June 1962).

SMELIANSKY, ANATOLY, *The Russian Theatre After Stalin*, trans. Patrick Miles (Cambridge, 1999).

SOLLERTINSKY, DMITRI and SOLLERTINSKY, LUDMILLA, *Pages from the Life of Dmitri Shostakovich* (Moscow, 1979).

SOLWAY, DIANE, *Nureyev: His Life* (London, 1998).

SOLZHENITSYN, ALEKSANDR, *The Oak and the Calf: Sketches of Literary Life in the Soviet Union*, trans. Harry Willetts (London, 1980).

—— *Invisible Allies*, trans. Alexis Klimoff and Michael Nicholson (London, 1997).

SORLIN, PIERRE, 'Tradition and Social Change in the French and Italian Cinemas of the Reconstruction', in Hewitt (1999).

'Soviet Painting at the Royal Academy', *Burlington Magazine*, 101/671 (Feb. 1959).

SPALDING, FRANCES, *British Art Since 1900* (London, 1996).

—— 'Political Purposes', *London Review of Books*, 21/8, 15 Apr. 1999.

SPALDING, ROBERT, 'Shostakovich and the Soviet System, 1925–1975', in Norris (1982).

SPENDER, STEPHEN, 'From a Diary', *Encounter*, 11/6 (Dec. 1958).

—— *The Thirties and After: Poetry, Politics, People (1933–1975)* (London, 1978).

STARR, S. FREDERICK, *Red and Hot: The Fate of Jazz in the USSR, 1917–1980* (Oxford, 1983).

—— 'Soviet Jazz: The Third Wave', in Feigin (1985).

STEINER, GEORGE, *The Sporting Scene: White Knights of Reykjavik* (London, 1973).

STEINER, WENDY, 'Scholarship and its Affiliations', *London Review of Books*, 11/7, 30 Mar. 1989.

STEPHAN, ALEXANDER, '*Communazis*'. FBI Surveillance of German Emigré Writers, trans. Jan van Heurck (New Haven and London, 2000); original *Im Visier des FBI: Deutsche Exilschriftseller in den Akten amerikanischer Geheimdienste* (Stuttgart, 1995).

STITES, RICHARD, *Revolutionary Dreams: Utopian Vision and Experimental Life in the Russian Revolution* (Oxford and New York, 1989).

—— *Russian Popular Culture: Entertainment and Society Since 1900* (Cambridge, 1992).

STOPPARD, TOM, *Squaring the Circle*. With *Every Good Boy Deserves Favour* and *Professional Foul* (London, 1984).

STRAVINSKY, IGOR, *In Conversation with Robert Craft* (London, 1962).

SUBER, HOWARD, 'The Anti-Communist Blacklist in the Hollywood Motion Picture Industry', Ph.D. thesis, University of California, Los Angeles (1968).

SURKOV, E., 'Sud'ba Garri Smita', *Teatr*, 5 (May 1947).

SWANN, BRENDA and APRAHAMIAN, FRANCIS (eds.), *J. D. Bernal: A Life in Science and Politics* (London, 2000).

SWAYZE, HAROLD, *Political Control of Literature in the USSR, 1946–1959* (Cambridge, Mass., 1962).

SYLVESTER, DAVID, 'The Venice Biennale', *Encounter*, 3/12 (Sept. 1954).

—— 'Jackson Pollock at the Tate', *London Review of Books*, 21/7, 1 Apr. 1999.

TARKOVSKY, ANDREI, *Sculpting in Time: Reflections on the Cinema* (London, 1986).

—— *Time Within Time: The Diaries 1970–1986*, trans. Kitty Hunter-Blair (London, 1994)

—— *Collected Screenplays*, trans. William Powell and Natasha Synessios (London, 1999).

TAYLOR, RICHARD (ed.), *The Eisenstein Reader*: 'Groznye teni 1947 goda', trans. Richard Taylor and William Powell (London, 1988).

—— 'Ideology as Mass Entertainment: Boris Shumyatsky and Soviet Cinema in the 1930s', in Taylor and Christie (1991).

—— and CHRISTIE, IAN (eds.), *Inside the Film Factory: New Approaches to Russian and Soviet Cinema* (London and New York, 1991).

—— and SPRING, DEREK (eds.), *Stalinism and Soviet Cinema* (London and New York, 1993).

TENENBAUM, STACY, 'A "Dialectical Pretzel". The New American Painting, the Museum of Modern Art and American Cultural Diplomacy, 1952–1959: Revisionism Revised', M. A. report, Courtauld Institute of Art, University of London (1992).

THEOHARIS, ATHAN G. and COX, JOHN STUART, *The Boss: J. Edgar Hoover and the Great American Inquisition* (London, 1989).

THOMPSON, TERRY L. and SHELDON, RICHARD, 'Soviet Society and Culture: Essays in Honor of Vera S. Dunham' (Boulder, Col., 1988).

THOMSON, CHARLES A. and LAVES, Walter H. C., *Cultural Relations and US Foreign Policy* (Bloomington, Ind., 1963).

TODD, OLIVIER, *Albert Camus: une vie* (Paris, 1996).

TROITSKY, ARTEMY, *Back in the USSR: The True Story of Rock in Russia* (London, 1987).

TUNSTALL, JEREMY, *The Media are American: Anglo-American Media and the World* (London, 1977).

TUR br. (Tur Brothers), 'Vstrecha na El'be', *Izbrannye stsenarii*, vol. 6.

TURAJ, FRANK, 'Poland: The Cinema of Moral Concern', in Goulding (1989).

TUROVSKAYA, MAYA, 'Soviet Films of the Cold War', in Taylor and Spring (1993).

TYNAN, KENNETH, *Letters*, ed. Kathleen Tynan (London, 1994).

UHLENBRUCH, BERND, 'The Annexation of History: Eisenstein and the Ivan Grozny Cult of the 1940s', in Günther (1990).

ULANOVA, GALINA, *The Making of a Ballerina* (Moscow, n.d.).

—— *Autobiographical Notes and Commentary on Soviet Ballet* (London, 1956).

UPDIKE, JOHN, 'Jackson Whole', *New York Review of Books*, 45/19, 3 Dec. 1998.

USSR–USA Sports Encounters (Moscow, 1977).

UTECHIN, S. V. and UTECHIN, P., 'Patterns of Nonconformity', *Problems of Communism*, 6/3 (May–June 1957); 7/5 (Sept.–Oct. 1958).

UTLEY, GERTJE R., *Picasso: The Communist Years* (New Haven and London, 2000).

VAILLAND, ROGER, *Le Colonel Foster plaidera coupable* (Paris, 1951).

VALLANCE, MARGARET, 'Wolf Biermann: The Enfant Terrible as Scapegoat', *Survey*, 61 (Oct. 1966).

VERDÈS-LEROUX, JEANINE, *Au service du parti. Le Parti communiste, les intellectuels, et la culture 1944–1956* (Paris, 1983).

VISHNEVSKAYA, GALINA, *Galina: A Russian Story*, trans. Guy Daniels (London, 1985).

VLADISLAV, JAN (ed.), *Václav Havel or Living in Truth* (London, 1987).

Voprosy masterstva v sovetskom kinoiskusstve. Cbornik stat'ei (Moscow, 1952).

'Vystavki sovetskogo izobrazitel'nogo iskusstva za rubezhom', *Iskusstvo*, 2 (1960).

WAGNLEITNER, REINHOLD, 'The Irony of American Culture Abroad: Austria and the Cold War', in Lary May (1989).

WAJDA, ANDRZEJ, *The Wajda Trilogy: Ashes and Diamonds, Kanal, A Generation*, intro. Boleslaw Sulik (New York, 1973).

—— 'Special Wajda. L'Homme de marbre', *L'Avant-Scène*, 1/15 (Jan. 1980).

—— *Double Vision: My Life in Film*, trans. Rose Medina (London, 1989).

WARSHOW, ROBERT, 'The Liberal Conscience in *The Crucible*', in Corrigan (1969).

WATSON, PETER, *Nureyev: A Biography* (London, 1994).

WEKWERTH, MANFRED, 'Anblick, Einblick, Ausblick. Bemerkungen zum Sowjet-Theater', *Theater der Zeit*, 19 (East Berlin, 1957).

WERTH, ALEXANDER, *Musical Uproar in Moscow* (London, 1949).

WHITFIELD, STEPHEN J., *The Culture of the Cold War* (Baltimore, 1990).

WILHARM, IRMGARD, 'Die verdreckten Spuren des Kalten Krieges im deutschen Unter-haltungsfilm', in 'Kalte Krieg' (1992).

WILLETT, JOHN, *The Theatre of Erwin Piscator* (London, 1978).

—— *Brecht in Context*, rev. edn. (London, 1998).

WILLETT, RALPH, *The Americanization of Germany, 1945–1949* (London and New York, 1989).

WILLIAMS, RAYMOND, 'The Realism of Arthur Miller', in Corrigan (1969).

WILLIAMS, TENNESSEE, *Four Plays* (London, 1956).

WILSON, ELIZABETH, *Shostakovich: A Life Remembered* (London, 1994).

WILSON, SARAH, 'Paris Post War: In Search of the Absolute', in Frances Morris, *Paris Post War: Art and Existentialism 1945–1955* (London, 1993).

WOLFE, BERTRAM, D. *An Ideology in Power: Reflections on the Russian Revolution* (London, 1969).

WOLL, JOSEPHINE, *Real Images: Soviet Cinema and the Thaw* (London and New York, 2000).

WOMACK, JOHN, *Zapata and the Mexican Revolution* (London, 1969).

WORTON, MICHAEL, '*Waiting for Godot* and *Endgame*', in John Pilling (ed.), *The Cambridge Companion to Beckett* (Cambridge, 1994).

YEVTUSHENKO, YEVGENI, *A Precocious Autobiography* (London, 1963).

—— 'Babiy Yar', in *The Poetry of Yevgeni Yevtushenko*, trans. George Reavey (New York, 1965).

ZAK, M., *Mikhail Romm i ego fil 'my* (Moscow, 1988).

ZAKRZHEVSKAIA, T. I., MYASNIKOVA, L. P., and STOROZHUK, A. G. (eds.), *Rudolf Nureev: tri goda na Kirovskoi stsene* (St Petersburg, 1995).

ZENCK, CLAUDIA MAURER, 'Challenges and Opportunities of Acculturation. Schoenberg, Krenek and Stravinsky in Exile', in Brinkmann and Wolff (1999).

ZETKIN, CLARA, 'Reminiscences of Lenin', *VOKS Bulletin*, 1/2 (1946).

'Zhalkaia poddelka', *Literaturnaia gazeta*, 46, 14 Nov. 1979.

ZHDANOV, A. A., *On Literature, Music and Philosophy* (London, 1950).

ZHUKOV, YURII, 'Vosem' s polovinoi krugov kinematografischeskogo ada', *Literaturnaia gazeta*, 20 July 1963.

ZUBOV, K. A., 'The Great French Theatre in Moscow', *VOKS Bulletin*, 4(87) (July–Aug. 1954).

Index

Boulez, Pierre 404, 413

Bowers, Faubion 39, 69, 80, 224, 400–1, 478, 479

Brabenec, Vratislav 354

Braden, Carl 550

Braden, Thomas 395, 551–2, 714 n 37

Brando, Marlon 192, 200, 201, 205, 213–15

Brandt, Willy 180, 406

Braque, Georges 573, 574

Brasseur, Pierre 325

Braun, Werner von 649 n 53

Brecht, Bertolt 73–4, 76, 124, 194, 251, 526, 612, 615, 616, 661 n 51, 675 n 12; appears before HUAC 275, 278–80; atomic bomb 74, 663 n 5; Austrian citizenship 287; Berlin uprising 288–91, 296–8; centrality of politics 271; character 274, 285, 301; controversies surrounding 272–3; creation of Berliner Ensemble 284–5; death 293; FBI surveillance 275–6, 664 n 19; Hannah Arendt's criticism of 298–9, 300; Joseph Losey 274, 275, 278; Moscow trials 299; moves to East Berlin 281–3; on Berlin 282; on East Germany 287; on Soviet theatre 291–2; on Stalin and Stalinism 298–9, 300, 667 n 89, 667 n 90, 667 n 91; 'Party inquisition' 283–4; plagiarism 301, 668 n 101, 668 n 103; privileges 284; receives Stalin Peace Prize 291; Soviet productions 296; support for Socialist Unity Party 290, 291; Swiss bank account 292; theory of theatre 271–2; Western critics 296; works banned 285, 287; *Baal* 294; 'Benares Song' 301; *Days of the Commune* 301; *Die Mütter* 284; 'Encounter with the Poet Auden' 300; *Furcht und Elend des Dritten Reiches* 281; *Galileo* 273–5, 296; *Happy End* 301; *He Who Says Yes* 281; *Herr Puntilla und sein Knecht Matti* 340; *Herrenburg Report* 286–7; 'In Dark Times' 300; 'Legend of the Dead Soldier' 294; *Mann ist Mann* 294; *Me-Ti* (Book of Changes) 298, 299; *Mother Courage* 283, 296; 'Nasty Morning' 299; *Poems* 1913–1956 299; *Senora Carrar's Rifles* 281; *Tales of the Calendar* 301; *The*

Caucasian Chalk Circle 292, 296; *The Condemnation of Lucullus* 286; 'The Cultivation of the Millet' 299–300; *The Days of the Commune* 285; *The Good Person (Woman) of Setzuan* 84, 296, 301; *The Measures Taken* 278–9, 294–5; *The Rise and Fall of the City of Mahagonny* 300; *The Seven Deadly Sins of the Petty Bourgeois* 300; 'The Solution' 291; *The Threepenny Novel* 301; *The Threepenny Opera* 280–1, 296, 301; *The Trial of Lucullus* 285; 'To the Actors' 296; *Urfaustus* 287

Breen, Robert 453

Brenton, Howard 358

Breton, André 516, 578–9, 699 n 12; 'Of "Socialist Realism" as a Means of Mental Extermination' 578–9

Brewer, Roy 182, 183, 213

Brezhnev, Leonid 29, 410, 411, 463, 465, 597, 603, 613

Brezhneva, Luba 29

Bridges, Harry 171, 172

Britten, Benjamin 385, 391, 395, 404, 407–409, 683 n 49, 687 n 104, 688 n 123; *Albert Herring* 395, 407; *Billy Budd* 395; Cello Concerto 408; Cello Sonata 407; *Peter Grimes* 391–2, 395, 407, 683 n 44, 688 n 120; *Sea Interludes* 407; *Sinfonia de Requiem* 407; *The Turn of the Screw* 407; *War Requiem* 407–8

Brodskii, Valentin 566–7

Brodsky, Joseph 353, 409

Brook, Peter 79, 309, 634 n 83, 634 n 91

Bruce, David 581

Bruhn, Erik 483

Brussels World Fair 33, 128, 460

Bryll, Ernest: *Easter Vigil* 375

Buchman, Sidney 193

Buckle, Richard 492

Bukovsky, Vladimir 359, 678 n 71

Bulgakov, Mikhail: *The Escape* 72

Bulganin, Nikolai 411

Burak, Aleksei 520; *Homeless People at the Metro Station* 520

Burden, William 714 n 37

Burdette, Franklin L 27

Burgess, Guy 81

Burnham, James 11–12